To MARJORIE
Christmas 1953
from Mom

# THESAURUS

## OF WORDS AND PHRASES

# THESAURUS
## OF WORDS AND PHRASES

BY

PETER MARK ROGET, M.D., F.R.S.

ENLARGED BY

JOHN LEWIS ROGET, M.A.

NEW EDITION REVISED AND ENLARGED BY

SAMUEL ROMILLY ROGET, M.A.

REVISED AND AUTHORIZED AMERICAN EDITION

Grosset & Dunlap
PUBLISHERS
NEW YORK

# WHAT ROGET CAN DO FOR YOU

As Mark Twain said: "The difference between the right word and the almost right word is the difference between lightning and the lightning bug." To find precisely the correct word is the problem of every writer and speaker—and that is where ROGET'S THESAURUS is invaluable.

Suppose you are an advertising copywriter seeking a new substitute for the much over-used "fascination." How to go about finding a fresh eye-catching simile? It's quite simple. First look in the alphabetical index which occupies the last third of the book.

There on page 486 you find "fascinate: *influence* 615." Turn back in the body of the book to section 615, which you will easily find from the numbers on the upper corner of each page.

And here is a vast store of welcome variants for "fascination": *temptation, enticement, allurement, cajolery, blandishment, magnetism*—and any number of additional choices—including that dashing word *bewitchery*. Surely one of these will fit your needs better than the weary and outworn "fascination."

Perhaps you're a minister wrestling with the knotty problem of how to strengthen next Sunday's sermon on "sin." What to do about it? Look up "sin" in ROGET. You find in the index "sin: 945, 947." Back again to the body of the book (sections 945 & 947), and there is a magnificent collection of all the virtues and most of the vices arrayed in parallel columns: *Immorality, infamy, depravity, knavery, lust,* and *pollution* vie for space with *morality, integrity, nobleness,* and *self-control.* You find that sinners may range in degree from *naughty* and *undutiful* to *base, sinister, satanic, depraved,* and even *irreclaimable.*

But then you may be neither a preacher nor a copywriter. The problem may be that of a student confronted with an assignment to write a composition about the evolution of the modern dance. You know, of course, all about *jitterbugging,* the *Shag,* and the *Big Apple.* But, after all, these represent only the last ten years of popular dancing. What of the centuries before? What were the names of the dances your grandparents enjoyed? Before the dictionary or encyclopedia can be used, at least their names must be known.

So look again in the index of ROGET under "dance" and find on page 453 "dance: *sport* 840." Turning to section 840 you discover an all-inclusive list of dance-names. The *morris dance* of medieval England is here; the *fandango, pavan,* and the *polka.* The *bolero* and *tango* from Spain; the *Charleston,* the *cakewalk, jazz,* and the *blues.* The *gavotte, mazurka, quadrille,* and *lancers* are found in the merry company of the *turkeytrot, shimmy,* and *rhumba.* Here truly is a stimulating introduction to the dance in all its manifold varieties from the *polonaise* to the *cancan!*

When you run through this list, not only will the right word automatically catch your eye but the rich array of colorful names will suggest fresh ideas that are sure to help you in your thinking and writing.

Briefly, the simplest and best way to use ROGET is this:

1. Look up in the index at the back of the book the word for which you want a substitute.

2. Note the category number of the group which seems to fit your needs best.

3. Turn back to this number which you will find at the top of a page in the main part of the book. And there you will find the right word, the exact word for your purpose.

This, then, is *your* ROGET, a book you will want to keep always in reach when writing or preparing a speech. You will be amazed at how easily you get the knack of its use—and how enormously valuable and profitable it will prove.

# FOREWORD

## TO THE

## AUTHORIZED AMERICAN EDITION

It is fitting that a new American edition of Roget's Thesaurus, issued by the American Company of its original London publishers, should have some account of its origin and progress.

Early in the nineteenth century the idea of the utility of a list of words classified according to the ideas that they express occurred to Dr. Peter Mark Roget, and his first draft was completed in 1805. It was added to from time to time, but it was not until Dr. Roget was over seventy years of age and had retired from the active secretaryship of the Royal Society that he was able to devote three or four years to the work of expansion.

It was first published in London by Longman, Brown, Green and Longmans in 1852, and went into a second edition in 1853. Two years later the "third and cheaper edition enlarged and improved" appeared, and was followed by the fourth edition in the same year. The fifth edition was issued in 1857, and since then edition has followed edition almost every year, and occasionally two or three times in one year, until seventy-seven printings have been called for, totalling more than two hundred thousand books.

The merits of the Thesaurus, its scholarship and erudition, were appreciated from the first, and successive improvements and enlargements by the author, the author's son and grandson, have caused it to maintain its great reputation.

In the course of years there have been several competing editions printed in America, all based on the London editions, but from none of these did the author or his representatives derive any pecuniary advantage.

The present edition, edited and revised by Willard Jerome Heggen, is the first one to be issued in America with the sanction and approval of Samuel Romilly Roget, the author's grandson, and holder of the existing British copyright.

It is worthy of note that it took three generations of the Roget family to compile and perfect this Thesaurus, and that after eighty years it is still published in London by the same firm, and from the same address in Paternoster Row, as when issued originally.

# PREFACE

SINCE the preface of March 17, 1879, was written, Mr. John L. Roget continued to revise periodical reprints of the Thesaurus until his death in 1908. It then devolved upon the undersigned, his son, to carry on this task, and it has been his endeavour to follow the same lines in making such additions that have seemed suitable from time to time. The opportunity has now, however, presented itself for a rather more complete revision, owing to the necessity of resetting the entire work, and in the edition that is now presented not only have a few hitherto unnoticed errors been corrected but some hundreds of new words and phrases have been added throughout the book, some of which have only recently become a part of the language as the result of progress in the various arts of peace and the unfortunate necessities of war. Many additional entries of words already represented have also been made, where the meanings have widened out or where for other reasons it has been thought advisable, but in practically no case has a word been removed, as archaic and even obsolete words are often sought for by authors. A few examples of alternative and obsolete spelling have been removed, but no alteration whatever has been made with the general arrangement and classification of the categories.

The editor would at all times welcome practical suggestions from users of the Thesaurus, and would take this opportunity of expressing his thanks for much kind help already afforded in this direction.

S. R. ROGET

July 1925

# PREFACE

TO

## THE FIRST EDITION

(1852)

It is now nearly fifty years since I first projected a system or verbal classification similar to that on which the present Work is founded. Conceiving that such a compilation might help to supply my own deficiencies, I had, in the year 1805, completed a classed catalogue of words on a small scale, but on the same principle, and nearly in the same form, as the Thesaurus now published.* I had often during that long interval found this little collection, scanty and imperfect as it was, of much use to me in literary composition, and often contemplated its extension and improvement; but a sense of the magnitude of the task, amidst a multitude of other avocations, deterred me from the attempt. Since my retirement from the duties of Secretary of the Royal Society, however, finding myself possessed of more leisure, and believing that a repertory of which I had myself experienced the advantage might, when amplified, prove useful to others, I resolved to embark in an undertaking which, for the last three or four years, has given me incessant occupation, and has, indeed, imposed upon me an amount of labour very much greater than I had anticipated. Notwithstanding all the pains I have bestowed on its execution, I am fully aware of its numerous deficiencies and imperfections, and of its falling far short of the degree of excellence that might be attained. But, in a Work of this nature, where perfection is placed at so great a distance, I have thought it best to limit my ambition to that moderate share of merit which it may claim in its present form; trusting to the indulgence of those for whose benefit it is intended, and to the candour of critics who, while they find it easy to detect faults, can at the same time duly appreciate difficulties.

P. M. Roget

April 29th, 1852

---

* A facsimile of the first page of this little manuscript book which is the original form of the Thesaurus is given in the frontispiece.

# EDITOR'S PREFACE
## (1879)
### (*Slightly Abridged*)

THE FIRST EDITION of Dr. Roget's Thesaurus was published in the year 1852, and a second in the ensuing spring. On the issue of the third, in 1855, the volume was stereotyped. Since that time until now, the work has been reprinted in the same form and with little alteration, in rapidly succeeding editions, the printing of which has worn out the original plates.

During the last years of the author's life, which closed, at a very advanced age, in the month of September, 1869, he was engaged in the task of collecting additional words and phrases, for an enlarged edition which he had long projected. This he did not live to complete, and it became my duty, as his son, to attempt to carry the design into execution.

The result of the author's labours was embodied in a copy of the Thesaurus, in which the margins and spaces about the letterpress were closely covered with written words and phrases, without any very precise indication of the places in the text where additions or alterations were intended to be made. On a careful examination of these *addenda*, I came to the conclusion that, in order to introduce them with advantage, it would be necessary to make some slight changes; without, however, interfering at all with the framework of the book, and but little with the details of its system. In this proceeding my course has been mainly determined by the following considerations.

Any attempt at a philosophical arrangement under categories of the words of our language must reveal the fact that it is impossible to separate and circumscribe the several groups by absolutely distinct boundary lines. Many words, originally employed to express simple conceptions, are found to be capable, with perhaps a very slight modification of meaning, of being applied in many varied associations. Connecting links, thus formed, induce an approach between the categories; and a danger arises that the outlines of our classification may, by their means, become confused and eventually merged. Were we to disengage these interwoven ramifications, and seek to confine every word to its main or original import, we should find some secondary meaning has become so firmly associated with many words and phrases, that to sever the alliance would be to deprive our language of the richness due to an infinity of natural adaptations.

Were we, on the other hand, to attempt to include, in each category of the Thesaurus, every word and phrase which could by any possibility be appropriately used in relation to the leading idea for which that category was designed, we should impair, if not destroy, the whole use and value of the book. For, in the endeavour to enrich our treasury of expression, we might easily allow ourselves to be led imperceptibly onward by the natural association of one word with another, and to add word after word, until group after group would successively be absorbed under some single heading, and the fundamental divisions of the system be effaced. The small cluster of nearly synonymous words, which had formed the nucleus of a category, would be lost in a sea of phrases, and it would become difficult to recognize those which were peculiarly adapted to express the leading ideas.

These considerations were material in dealing with the new and multitudinous store of words and phrases which the author had accumulated. Many of these were altogether new to the Thesaurus. Many were merely repetitions in new places of words already included in its pages. With reference to cases similar to the latter, the author had declared it to have been a general rule with him 'to place words and phrases which appertain more especially to one head, also under other heads to which they have a relation,' whenever it appeared to him 'that this repetition would suit the convenience of the inquirer and spare him the trouble of turning to other parts of the work.' But, with the now increased mass of words, it became a question, in many cases, whether such repetition would still prove convenient. Where categories might by that course be unduly swollen, or where they might, by reason of their being separated from each other by subtile distinctions or faint lines of demarcation, be thereby too nearly assimilated, I thought it would often be better to confine words of the kind referred to to their primary headings. The necessity of keeping the book within reasonable dimensions had also to be borne in mind.

Under these circumstances, the best method of ensuring the ready accessibility of the multitude of words now to be dealt with, and at the same time preserving unimpaired the unity of the several categories, appeared to me to lie in the copious use of references from one place in the book to another. Relying on this contrivance as a means of opening more widely the resources of the collection, by making the groups of words mutually suggestive, and thereby leading not only to more varied forms of expression, but to kindred ideas, I have added largely to the references already inserted by the author. I have also ventured occasionally to substitute a reference for a group of words, when the identical group existed in another place, and could thus be made immediately available.

In order, at the same time, to make the value of the references more appreciable, I have (whenever it has appeared to me to be necessary) inserted, in a parenthesis, a word indicating the nature of the group or category referred to. Any one using the book will thereby be enabled to judge whether it will be worth his while to turn to the place in question.

The cross references may also be looked upon as indicating in some degree the natural points of connection between the categories, and the ramification of the ideas which they embody. As would be the case under any classification of language, a large proportion of the expressions, to find which recourse is had to the Thesaurus, lie on an ill-defined border land between one category and another; and it is not always easy, even with the aid of a carefully compiled index, to determine under which of several allied headings they should be sought. In the present edition, when the inquirer has once started on his voyage of discovery, the references enable him to pass freely from one division to another without recurring to the Index.

Many new words have also been inserted which were not contained in the author's manuscript.

Except in a very few cases, where distinct ideas were obviously united under one head, I have not had the presumption to meddle with the author's division into categories; but, within each category, I have endeavoured to carry somewhat further the sorting of words according to the ideas which they convey.

With these objects in view, I have supplied the work with a new and elaborate Index, much more complete than that which was appended to the previous editions. Although, in the original design of his work, the author appears to have conceived the process of search for a required expression as one in which the system of classification would be first consulted, and the Index afterwards called in aid if necessary, I believe that almost everyone who uses the book finds it more convenient to have recourse to the Index first.

From the peculiar nature and use of the Thesaurus, its Index will be found to differ, in some of its essential functions, from an alphabetical table of contents. The present Index does not merely afford an indication of the place where every given word or topic occurs or is dealt with in the text; but it is intended as a guide to other expressions which may be found there. The word we look out in this Index is not that which we require, but that which we wish to avoid. It is, therefore, not necessary that every word there given should be a repetition of one in the text. It may even happen that the word selected as a guide, though suggestive of the group wanted, is wholly unfit to be comprised within it.

The new Index contains not only all the *words* in the book (without needless repetition of conjugate forms), but likewise the *phrases*, all of which had been excluded from the Index to the previous editions. It is hoped that these additions, although they increase the bulk of the book, will have the effect of extending its usefulness in at least a corresponding degree.

Some changes of detail have also been made, where the form of the work seemed susceptible of improvement, and there was no reason to suppose that the author would have disapproved of the alteration. In the previous editions, the *phrases* were in general placed in separate paragraphs, under the heading **Phr.**, in each of the subdivisions assigned to the different grammatical parts of speech. In the present edition, *words* and *phrases* are placed together, and the heading **Phr.** is only employed in the case of phrases which have no convenient place in such an arrangement. Much space has been saved, and many repetitions have been avoided, by the use of lines and hyphens, where words or phrases in the same group have syllables or parts in common, and by references from one part of speech to another. These abbreviations may be best explained by examples, of which the following are a few:—

'with -relation, – reference, – respect, – regard- to'; is meant to include the phrases 'with relation to,' 'with reference to,' 'with respect to,' 'with regard to.'

'root –, weed –, grub –, rake- -up, – out;' includes 'root up,' 'root out,' 'weed up,' 'weed out,' 'grub up,' 'grub out,' 'rake up,' 'rake out.'

'away from –, foreign to –, beside- the -purpose, – question, – transaction, – point;' includes 'away from the purpose,' 'foreign to the purpose,' 'beside the purpose,' 'away from the question,' 'foreign to the question,' 'foreign to the transaction,' 'beside the question,' 'away from the point,' 'beside the transaction,' 'foreign to the point,' 'away from the transaction,' 'beside the point.'

'raze – to the ground'; includes 'raze,' and 'raze to the ground.'

'campan-iform, -ulate, -iliform;' includes 'campaniform,' 'campanulate,' and 'campaniliform.'

'goodness &c. *adj.*'; 'badly &c. *adj.*'; 'hindred &c. *v.*'; include all words similarly formed from synonyms of 'good,' 'bad,' and 'hinder,' respectively, given under the headings **Adj.** and **V.** in the same categories where the abbreviations occur.

The participle 'to' before a verb has in all cases been rejected, the heading **V.** being thought sufficiently distinctive; the use of capitals for the initial letters of the first words of paragraphs has been abandoned, as giving those words undue importance; and the title of each category has been kept distinct from the collection of words under its heading.

I should be ungrateful were I not to acknowledge the assistance derived, both by my father and myself, from various suggestions made by well-wishers to the work, some of whom have been personally unknown to either of us; and also to record my thanks to several kind friends, and to Messrs. Spottiswoode and Co.'s careful reader, for valuable aid during the passage of the sheets through the press.

JOHN L. ROGET

March 17th, 1879.

# PLAN OF CLASSIFICATION

TABULAR SYNOPSIS OF CATEGORIES

# TABULAR SYNOPSIS OF CATEGORIES

## CLASS I. ABSTRACT RELATIONS

### I. EXISTENCE

| | | |
|---|---|---|
| 1°. ABSTRACT.......... | 1. Existence. | 2. Inexistence. |
| 2°. CONCRETE......... | 3. Substantiality. | 4. Unsubstantiality. |
| 3°. FORMAL........... | *Internal.* | *External.* |
| | 5. Intrinsicality. | 6. Extrinsicality. |
| 4°. MODAL............ | *Absolute.* | *Relative.* |
| | 7. State. | 8. Circumstance. |

### II. RELATION

| | | |
|---|---|---|
| 1°. ABSOLUTE......... | 9. Relation. | 10. Irrelation. |
| | 11. Consanguinity. | |
| | 12. Correlation. | |
| | 13. Identity. | 14. Contrariety. |
| | 15. Difference. | |
| 2°. CONTINUOUS....... | 16. Uniformity. | 16a. Non-uniformity. |
| 3°. PARTIAL.......... | 17. Similarity. | 18. Dissimilarity. |
| | 19. Imitation. | 20. Non-imitation. |
| | 20a. Variation. | |
| | 21. Copy. | 22. Prototype. |
| 4°. GENERAL.......... | 23. Agreement. | 24. Disagreement. |

### III. QUANTITY

| | | |
|---|---|---|
| 1°. SIMPLE........... | *Absolute.* | *Relative.* |
| | 25. Quantity. | 26. Degree. |
| | 27. Equality. | 28. Inequality. |
| 2°. COMPARATIVE...... | 29. Mean. | |
| | 30. Compensation. | |
| | *By Comparison with a Standard.* | |
| | 31. Greatness. | 32. Smallness. |
| | *By Comparison with a similar Object.* | |
| | 33. Superiority. | 34. Inferiority. |
| | *Changes in Quantity.* | |
| | 35. Increase. | 36. Decrease. |
| | 37. Addition. | 38. {Non-addition. / Subduction. |
| | 39. Adjunct. | 40. Remainder. |
| | | 40a. Decrement. |
| 3°. CONJUNCTIVE...... | 41. Mixture. | 42. Simpleness. |
| | 43. Junction. | 44. Disjunction. |
| | 45. Vinculum. | |
| | 46. Coherence. | 47. Incoherence. |
| | 48. Combination. | 49. Decomposition. |

4°: WITH REFERENCE TO DIRECTION—cont...

| | |
|---|---|
| 305. Ascent. | 306. Descent. |
| 307. Elevation. | 308. Depression: |
| 309. Leap. | 310. Plunge. |
| 311. Circuition. | |
| 312. Rotation. | 313. Evolution: |
| 314. Oscillation. | |
| 315. Agitation. | |

---

## Class III.  MATTER

**I. MATTER IN GENERAL.......**

| | |
|---|---|
| 316. Materiality. | 317. Immateriality: |
| 318. World. | |
| 319. Gravity. | 320. Levity. |

**II. INORGANIC MATTER**

**1°. SOLIDS.............**

| | |
|---|---|
| 321. Density. | 322. Rarity. |
| 323. Hardness. | 324. Softness. |
| 325. Elasticity. | 326. Inelasticity. |
| 327. Tenacity. | 328. Brittleness. |
| 329. Texture. | |
| 330. Pulverulence. | |
| 331. Friction. | 332. Lubrication. |

**2°. FLUIDS**

*1. In General*

| | |
|---|---|
| 333. Fluidity. | 334. Gaseity. |
| 335. Liquefaction. | 336. Vaporization. |
| 337. Water. | 338. Air. |
| 339. Moisture. | 340. Dryness. |

*2. Specific...*

| | |
|---|---|
| 341. Ocean. | 342. Land. |
| 343. { Gulf. / Lake. | 344. Plain. |
| 345. Marsh. | 346. Island. |
| 347. Stream. | |
| 348. River. | 349. Wind. |

*3. In motion*

| | |
|---|---|
| 350. Conduit. | 351. Air-pipe. |

**3°. IMPERFECT FLUIDS...**

| | |
|---|---|
| 352. Semiliquidity. | 353. Bubble. |
| 354. Pulpiness. | 355. Unctuousness. |
| | 356. Oil. |
| | 356a. Resin. |

**III: ORGANIC MATTER**

**1°. VITALITY**

*1. In General....*

| | |
|---|---|
| 357. Organization. | 358. Inorganization: |
| 359. Life. | 360. Death. |
| | 361. Killing. |
| | 362. Corpse. |
| | 363. Interment. |

*2. Special*

| | |
|---|---|
| 364. Animality. | 365. Vegetability. |
| 366. Animal. | 367. Vegetable. |
| 368. Zoology. | 369. Botany. |
| 370. Cicuration. | 371. Agriculture. |
| 372. Mankind. | |
| 373. Man. | 374. Woman. |

## Class IV. INTELLECT

### Division (I.). FORMATION OF IDEAS

## Division (II.).  COMMUNICATION OF IDEAS

**I. NATURE OF IDEAS COMMUNICATED**
516. Meaning.  517. Unmeaningness.
518. Intelligibility.  519. Unintelligibility.
520. Equivocalness.
521. Metaphor.
522. Interpretation.  523. Misinterpretation.
524. Interpreter.
525. Manifestation.  526. Latency.
527. Information.  528. Concealment.
529. Disclosure.  530. Ambush.
531. Publication.
532. News.  533. Secret.
534. Messenger.
535. Affirmation.  536. Negation.

**II. MODES OF COMMUNICATION**
537. Teaching.  {538. Misteaching. / 539. Learning.}
540. Teacher.  541. Learner.
542. School.
543. Veracity.  544. Falsehood.
545. Deception.
546. Untruth.
547. Dupe.  548. Deceiver.
549. Exaggeration.

## III. MEANS OF COMMUNICATION

**1°: Natural Means**
550. Indication.
551. Record.  552. Obliteration.
553. Recorder.
554. Representation.  555. Misrepresentation.
556. Painting.
557. Sculpture.
558. Engraving.
559. Artist.

**2°: Conventional Means**

**1. Language generally**
560. Language.
561. Letter.
562. Word.  563. Neology.
564. Nomenclature.  565. Misnomer.
566. Phrase.
567. Grammar.  568. Solecism.
569. Style.

*Qualities of Style.*
570. Perspicuity.  571. Obscurity.
572. Conciseness.  573. Diffuseness.
574. Vigour.  575. Feebleness.
576. Plainness.  577. Ornament.
578. Elegance.  579. Inelegance.

**2. Spoken Language**
580. Voice.  581. Aphony.
582. Speech.  583. Stammering.
584. Loquacity.  585. Taciturnity.
586. Allocution.  587. Response.
588. Interlocution.  589. Soliloquy.

**3. Written Language**
590. Writing.  591. Printing.
592. Correspondence.  593. Book.
594. Description.
595. Dissertation.
596. Compendium.
597. Poetry.  598. Prose.
599. The Drama.

Class V.  VOLITION

Division (I.).  INDIVIDUAL VOLITION

**I. VOLITION IN GENERAL**

1°. *Acts....*

| | |
|---|---|
| 600. Will. | 601. Necessity. |
| 602. Willingness. | 603. Unwillingness. |
| 604. Resolution. | 605. Irresolution. |
| 604a. Perseverance. } | 607. Tergiversation. |
| 606. Obstinacy. } | |
| | 608. Caprice. |
| 609. Choice. | 609a. Absence of Choice. |
| | 610. Rejection. |
| 611. Predetermination. | 612. Impulse. |
| 613. Habit. | 614. Desuetude. |

2°. *Causes..*

| | |
|---|---|
| 615. Motive. | 615a. Absence of Motive. |
| | 616. Dissuasion. |
| 617. Plea. | |

3°. *Objects..*

| | |
|---|---|
| 618. Good. | 619. Evil. |
| 620. Intention. | 621. Chance. |
| 622. Pursuit. | 623. Avoidance. |
| | 624. Relinquishment. |

**II. PROSPECTIVE VOLITION........**

1°. *Conceptional..*

625. Business.
626. Plan.
627. Method.
628. Mid-Course.    629. Circuit.
630. Requirement.

2°. *Subservience to Ends...*

1. *Actual Subservience.*
631. Instrumentality.
632. Means.
633. Instrument.
634. Substitute.
635. Materials.
636. Store.
637. Provision.    638. Waste.
639. Sufficiency.
641. Redundance.    640. Insufficiency.

2. *Degree of Subservience.*

| | |
|---|---|
| 642. Importance. | 643. Unimportance. |
| 644. Utility. | 645. Inutility. |
| 646. Expedience. | 647. Inexpedience. |
| 648. Goodness. | 649. Badness. |
| 650. Perfection. | 651. Imperfection. |
| 652. Cleanness. | 653. Uncleanness. |
| 654. Health. | 655. Disease. |
| 656. Salubrity. | 657. Insalubrity. |
| 658. Improvement. | 659. Deterioration. |
| 660. Restoration. | 661. Relapse. |
| 662. Remedy. | 663. Bane. |

3. *Contingent Subservience.*

| | |
|---|---|
| 664. Safety. | 665. Danger. |
| 666. Refuge. | 667. Pitfall. |
| 668. Warning. | |
| 669. Alarm. | |
| 670. Preservation. | |
| 671. Escape. | |
| 672. Deliverance. | |

### Division (II.). INTERSOCIAL VOLITION

## Class VI. AFFECTIONS

## II: PERSONAL

### 1°. PASSIVE

| | |
|---|---|
| 827. Pleasure. | 828. Pain. |
| 829. Pleasureableness. | 830. Painfulness. |
| 831. Content. | 832. Discontent. |
| | 833. Regret. |
| 834. Relief. | 835. Aggravation. |
| 836. Cheerfulness. | 837. Dejection. |
| 838. Rejoicing. | 839. Lamentation. |
| 840. Amusement. | 841. Weariness. |
| 842. Wit. | 843. Dulness. |
| 844. Humorist. | |

### 2°. DISCRIMINATIVE

| | |
|---|---|
| 845. Beauty. | 846. Ugliness. |
| 847. Ornament. | 848. Blemish. |
| | 849. Simplicity. |
| 850. Taste. | 851. Vulgarity. |
| 852. Fashion. | |
| | 853. Ridiculousness. |
| | 854. Fop. |
| | 855. Affectation. |
| | 856. Ridicule. |
| | 857. Laughing-stock. |

### 3°. PROSPECTIVE

| | |
|---|---|
| 858. Hope. | 859. Hopelessness. |
| | 860. Fear. |
| 861. Courage. | 862. Cowardice. |
| 863. Rashness. | 864. Caution. |
| 865. Desire. | 866. Indifference. |
| | 867. Dislike. |
| | 868. Fastidiousness. |
| | 869. Satiety. |

### 4°. CONTEMPLATIVE

| | |
|---|---|
| 870. Wonder. | 871. Expectance. |
| 872. Prodigy. | |

### 5°. EXTRINSIC

| | |
|---|---|
| 873. Repute. | 874. Disrepute. |
| 875. Nobility. | 876. Commonalty. |
| 877. Title. | |
| 878. Pride. | 879. Humility. |
| 880. Vanity. | 881. Modesty. |
| 882. Ostentation. | |
| 883. Celebration. | |
| 884. Boasting. | |
| 885. Insolence. | 886. Servility. |
| 887. Blusterer. | |

## III: SYMPATHETIC

### 1°. SOCIAL

| | |
|---|---|
| 888. Friendship. | 889. Enmity. |
| 890. Friend. | 891. Enemy. |
| 892. Sociality. | 893. Seclusion. |
| 894. Courtesy. | 895. Discourtesy. |
| 896. Congratulation. | |
| 897. Love. | 898. Hate. |
| 899. Favourite. | |
| | 900. Resentment. |
| | 901. Irascibility. |
| | 901a. Sullenness. |
| 902. Endearment. | |
| 903. Marriage. | 904. Celibacy. |
| | 905. Divorce. |

|  | | |
|---|---|---|
| | 906. Benevolence. | 907. Malevolence. |
| | | 908. Malediction. |
| 2°. DIFFUSIVE......... | | 909. Threat. |
| | 910. Philanthropy. | 911. Misanthropy. |
| | 912. Benefactor. | 913. Evil doer. |
| 3°. SPECIAL.......... | 914. Pity. | 914a. Pitilessness. |
| | 915. Condolence. | |
| | 916. Gratitude. | 917. Ingratitude. |
| 4°. RETROSPECTIVE.... | 918. Forgiveness. | 919. Revenge. |
| | | 920. Jealousy. |
| | | 921. Envy. |

# IV. MORAL

|  | | |
|---|---|---|
| | 922. Right. | 923. Wrong. |
| 1°. OBLIGATIONS....... | 924. Dueness. | 925. Undueness. |
| | 926. Duty. | 927. Dereliction. |
| | | 927a. Exemption. |
| | 928. Respect. | 929. Disrespect. |
| | | 930. Contempt. |
| 2°. SENTIMENTS........ | 931. Approbation. | 932. Disapprobation. |
| | 933. Flattery. | 934. Detraction. |
| | 935. Flatterer. | 936. Detractor. |
| | 937. Vindication. | 938. Accusation. |
| | 939. Probity. | 940. Improbity. |
| | | 941. Knave. |
| | 942. Disinterestedness. | 943. Selfishness. |
| 3°. CONDITIONS........ | 944. Virtue. | 945. Vice. |
| | 946. Innocence. | 947. Guilt. |
| | 948. Good Man. | 949. Bad Man. |
| | 950. Penitence. | 951. Impenitence. |
| | 952. Atonement. | |
| | 953. Temperance. | 954. Intemperance. |
| | | 954a. Sensualist. |
| | 955. Asceticism. | |
| 4°. PRACTICE.......... | 956. Fasting. | 957. Gluttony. |
| | 958. Sobriety. | 959. Drunkenness. |
| | 960. Purity. | 961. Impurity. |
| | | 962. Libertine. |
| | 963. Legality. | 964. Illegality. |
| | 965. Jurisprudence. | |
| | 966. Tribunal. | |
| | 967. Judge. | |
| 5°. INSTITUTIONS...... | 968. Lawyer. | |
| | 969. Lawsuit. | |
| | 970. Acquittal. | 971. Condemnation. |
| | 973. Reward. | 972. Punishment. |
| | | 974. Penalty. |
| | | 975. Scourge. |

# V. RELIGIOUS

|  | | |
|---|---|---|
| | 976. Deity. | |
| 1°. SUPERHUMAN BE- | 977. Angel. | 978. Satan. |
| INGS AND REGIONS.. | 979. Jupiter. | 980. Demon. |
| | 981. Heaven. | 982. Hell. |
| | 983. Theology. | |
| 2°. DOCTRINES........ | 983a. Orthodoxy. | 984. Heterodoxy. |
| | 985. Revelation. | 986. Pseudo-revelation. |
| 3°. SENTIMENTS........ | 987. Piety. | 988. Impiety. |
| | | 989. Irreligion. |

4°. ACTS.............

- 990. Worship.
- 991. Idolatry
- 992. Sorcery.
- 993. Spell.
- 994. Sorcerer.

5°. INSTITUTIONS......

- 995. Churchdom.
- 996. Clergy.
- 997. Laity.
- 998. Rite.
- 999. Canonicals.
- 1000. Temple.

## ABBREVIATIONS, &c.

| | | |
|---|---|---|
| **Adj.** | *adj.* | Adjectives, Participles, and Words having the power of Adjectives. |
| **Adv.** | *adv.* | Adverbs and Adverbial Expressions. |
| **Int.** | *int.* | Interjections. |
| **Phr.** | *phr.* | Phrases. |
| **V.** | *v.* | Verbs. |

The numbers are those of the headings, or Categories.

Words in italics within parentheses are not intended to explain the meanings of the words which precede them, but to indicate the nature of allied group of words under the numbers which follow them.

See also the Editor's Preface, p. xi.

# THESAURUS

OF

# WORDS AND PHRASES

## CLASS I

### WORDS EXPRESSING ABSTRACT RELATIONS

#### SECTION I. EXISTENCE

##### 1°. BEING, IN THE ABSTRACT

**1. Existence.—N.** existence, being, entity, *ens, esse,* subsistence, quiddity.

reality, realness, actuality; positiveness &c. *adj.*; fact, matter of fact, sober reality; truth &c. 494; actual existence.

presence &c. (*existence in space*) 186; coexistence &c. 120.

stubborn fact; not a -dream &c. 515; no joke.

substance, essence, prime constituent, hypostatis.

[Science of existence], ontology.

**V.** exist, be; have -being &c. *n.*; subsist, live, breathe, stand, obtain, be the case; occur &c. (*event*) 151; have place, rank, prevail; find oneself, pass the time, vegetate.

consist in, lie in, reside in, inhere in.

come into -existence &c. *n.*; arise &c. (*begin*) 66; come forth &c. (*appear*) 446.

become &c. (*be converted*) 144; bring into existence &c. 161; coexist, preexist, endure &c. 141.

**Adj.** existing &c. *v.*; existent, subsistent, under the sun; in -existence &c. *n.*; extant; afloat, on foot, current, prevalent, rife, in force, -vogue; undestroyed.

real, actual, positive, absolute; true &c. 494; substan-tial, -tive; self-existing, -ent;

**2. Inexistence.—N.** inexistence; non-existence, -subsistence; nonentity, *nil;* negativeness &c. *adj.*; nullity; nihil-ity, -ism; *tabula rasa,* blank; abeyance; absence &c. 187; no such thing &c. 4; nothingness, oblivion, *non esse.*

annihilation; extinction &c. (*destruction*) 162.

**V.** not -exist &c. 1; have no -existence &c. 1; be null and void; cease to -exist &c. 1; pass away, perish; be –, become-extinct &c. *adj.*; die out; disappear &c. 449; melt away, dissolve, leave not a rack behind, leave no trace; go, be no more; die &c. 360.

annihilate, render null, nullify; abrogate &c. 756; destroy &c. 162; take away; remove &c. (*displace*) 185.

**Adj.** inexistent, non-existent &c. 1; negative, blank, null and void; missing, omitted; absent &c. 187; visionary &c. 515.

unreal, potential, virtual; baseless, *in nubibus*; unsubstantial &c. 4; vain;

un-born, -created, -begotten, -conceived, -produced, -made.

perished, annihilated &c. *v.*; extinct, exhausted, gone, lost, departed; defunct &c. (*dead*) 360; *spurlos versenkt.*

fabulous, ideal &c. (*imaginary*) 515; supposititious &c. 514.

**Adv.** negatively, virtually, &c. *adj.*

[ 1 ]

well-founded, -grounded; un-ideal, -imagined; not -potential &c. 2.
**Adv.** actually &c. *adj.*; in -fact, – point of fact, – reality; indeed; *de* –, *ipso-facto.*

## 2°. BEING, IN THE CONCRETE

**3. Substantiality.—N.** substantiality, *hypostasis*; person, thing, object, article; something, a being, an existence; creature, body, substance, flesh and blood, stuff, *substratum*; matter &c. 316; physical nature.
[Totality of existences], world &c. 318; *plenum.*
**Adj.** substan-tive, -tial, concrete; hypostatic; personal, bodily; tangible &c. (*material*) 316; real, corporeal, evident.
**Adv.** substantially &c. *adj.*; bodily, essentially.

**4. Unsubstantiality.—N.** un-, in-substantiality; nothingness, nihility.
nothing, naught, *nil,* nullity, zero, cipher, no one, nobody; never –, ne'er -a one; no such thing, none in the world; nothing -whatever, – at all, – on earth; not a -particle &c. (*smallness*) 32; all -talk, – moonshine, – stuff and nonsense, matter of no import.
thing of naught, man of straw, John Doe and Richard Roe; *nominis umbra,* nonentity, figurehead, lay figure; flash in the pan, *vox et præterea nihil.*
shadow; phantasm, phantom &c. (*fallacy of vision*) 443; dream &c. (*imagination*) 515; *ignis fatuus* &c.

(luminary) 423; 'such stuff as dreams are made on'; air, thin air; bubble &c. 353; 'baseless fabric of a vision'; mockery.
hollowness, blank; vacuity, void &c. (*absence*) 187.
inanity, fool's paradise, fatuity, stupidity, emptiness of mind.
**V.** vanish, evaporate, fade, sink, fly –, die –, melt- away, dissolve, disappear &c. 449, become extinct, become invisible.
**Adj.** unsubstantial; fleeting; base-, ground-less; ungrounded; without –, having no- foundation.
visionary &c. (*imaginary*) 515; immaterial &c. 317; spectral &c. 980; dreamy; shadowy; ethereal, airy, imponderable, tenuous, vague.
vacant, vacuous; empty &c. 187; eviscerated; blank, hollow; nominal; null; inane.
**Phr.** there's nothing in it.

## 3°. FORMAL EXISTENCE

*Internal conditions*

**5. Intrinsicality.—N.** intrinsicality, unbeing, inherence, inhesion, immanence; subjectiveness; *ego*; essence; essentialness &c. *adj.*; essential part, essential stuff, substance, quintessence, incarnation, quiddity, gist, pith, core, kernel, marrow, sap, life-blood, backbone, heart, soul, life, flower; important part &c. (*importance*) 642.
principle, nature, constitution, character, ethos, type, quality, crasis, *diathesis.*
habit; temper, -ament; spirit, humour, grain, disposition, streak, tendency &c. 176.

*External conditions*

**6. Extrinsicality.—N.** extrinsicality, objectiveness, *non ego*; extraneousness &c. 57; accident; letter of the law.
**Adj.** derived from without; objective; extrin-sic, -sical; extraneous &c. (*foreign*) 57; modal, adventitious, additional, supervenient, fortuitous; a-, ad-scititious; incidental, casual, accidental, unessential, non-essential, accessory.
implanted, ingrafted, instilled, inculcated.
outward &c. (*external*) 220.
**Adv.** extrinsically &c. *adj.*

endowment, capacity; capability &c. (*power*) 157; moods, declensions, features, aspects; peculiarities &c. (*specialty*) 79; idiosyncrasy; idiocrasy; diagnostics.

**V.** be –, run- in the blood; be born so; be -intrinsic &c. *adj.*

**Adj.** derived from within, subjective; idiocratic, idiosyncratic, intrin-sic, -sical; fundamental, cardinal, normal; inherent, essential, natural; in-nate, -born, -bred, -dwelling, -grained, -wrought; radical, incarnate, thoroughbred, hereditary, inherited, immanent; congen-ital, -ite; connate, running in the blood; coeval with birth, genetic, ingenerate, -genite; indigenous; in the -grain &c. *n.*; bred in the bone, instinctive; inward, internal &c. 221; to the manner born ; virtual.

characteristic &c. (*special*) 79, (*indicative*) 550; invariable, incurable, ineradicable, fixed, settled, constant, unchanging.

**Adv.** intrinsically &c. *adj.*; at bottom, in the main, in effect, essentially, practically, virtually, substantially, *au fond*; fairly.

## 4°. MODAL EXISTENCE

### Absolute

**7. State.—N.** state, condition, category, estate, lot, case, trim, mood, pickle, plight &c. 735; temper; aspect &c. (*appearance*) 448.

constitution, habitude, *diathesis*; frame, fabric &c. 329; stamp, set, fit, mould.

mode, modality, schesis; fettle; form &c. (*shape*) 240.

tone, tenor, turn; trim, guise, fashion, light, complexion, style, character.

**V.** be in –, possess –, enjoy –, labour under- a -state &c. *n.*; be on a footing, do, fare; come to pass.

**Adj.** conditional, modal, formal; structural, organic.

**Adv.** conditionally &c. *adj.*; as -the matter stands, – things are; such being the case &c. 8.

### Relative

**8. Circumstance.—N.** circumstance, situation, phase, position, posture, attitude, place, point; terms; *régime*: footing, standing, status.

occasion, juncture, conjuncture; contingency &c. (*event*) 151.

predicament; emergen-ce, -cy; exigency, crisis, pinch, pass, push; turning point; crossroads.

bearings, how the land lies.

**Adj.** circumstantial; given, conditional, provisional; critical; modal; contingent, incidental; adventitious &c. (*extrinsic*) 6.

**Adv.** in the circumstances &c. *n.*, under the conditions &c. 7; thus, in such wise.

accordingly; that –, such- being the case; that being so, since, seeing that. as matters stand; as -things, – times-go.

conditionally, provided, if, in case; if -so, – so be, – it be so; if it so -happen, – turn out; in the event of; in such a -contingency, – case, – event; provisionally, unless, without.

according to -circumstances, – the occasion; as it may -happen, – turn out, – be; as the -case may be, – wind blows; *pro re natâ*.

## SECTION II.  RELATION

### 1°. ABSOLUTE RELATION

**9. Relation.—N.** relation, bearing, reference, connection, apposition, interconnection, concern, cognation; applicability, appositeness; correlation

**10.** [Want, or absence of relation.] **Irrelation.—N.** irrelation, dissociation; inapplicability; inconnection; multifariousness; disconnection &c. (*dis-*

&c. 12; analogy; similarity &c. 17; affinity, intimacy, friendship; homology, alliance, homogeneity, association, rapport; approximation &c. (*nearness*) 197; filiation &c. (*consanguinity*) 11; interest; relevancy &c. 23; relationship, relative position; relativity; interrelation &c. 12.

comparison &c. 464; ratio, proportion.

link, tie, bond, bond of union.

**V.** be-related &c. *adj.*; have a relation &c. *n.*; relate –, refer- to; bear upon, regard, concern, touch, affect, have to do with; pertain –, belong –, appertain- to; have respect to; answer to; interest.

bring -into relation with, – to bear upon; connect, associate, draw a parallel; link &c. 43.

**Adj.** relative; correlative &c. 12; cognate; relating to &c. *v.*; relative to, in relation with, referable *or* referrible to; belonging to &c. *v.*; appurtenant to, in common with.

related, connected; implicated, associated, affiliated, akin, allied to; collateral, cognate, congenial, kindred, affinitive, *en rapport*, in touch with.

approxima-tive, -ting; approaching; proportion-al, -ate, -able; allusive, comparable.

in the same -category &c. 75; like &c. 17; relevant &c. (*apt*) 23.

**Adv.** relatively &c. *adj.*; pertinently &c. 23.

thereof; as -to, – for, – respects, – regards; about; concerning &c. *v.*; anent; relating –, as relates- to; with -relation, – reference, – respect, – regard- to; in respect of; while speaking –, *à propos-* of; in connection with; by the -way, – by; whereas; for –, in -as much as; in point of, as far as; on the -part, – score- of; *quoad hoc*; *pro re natâ*; under the -head &c. (*class*) 75- of; in the matter of, *in re*.

**Phr.** 'thereby hangs a tale.'

*junction*) 44; inconsequence, independence; incommensurability; irreconcilableness &c. (*disagreement*) 24; heterogeneity; unconformity &c. 83; irrelevancy, impertinence, *nihil ad rem*; intrusion &c. 24.

**V.** have no -relation &c. 9 to, – bearing upon, – concern &c. 9 with, – business with; not -concern &c. 9; have -nothing to do with, – no business there; intrude, &c. 24.

bring –, drag –, haul –, lug- in head and shoulders.

**Adj.** irrelative, irrespective, unrelated, irrelated; arbitrary; independent, unallied; un-, dis-connected; adrift, isolated, insular; extraneous, strange, alien, foreign, outlandish, exotic.

not comparable, incommensurable, heterogeneous; unconformable &c. 83.

irrelevant; rambling &c. 279; inapplicable; not -pertinent, – to the purpose; impertinent, inapposite, beside the mark, *à propos de bottes*; away from –, foreign to –, beside- the -purpose, – question, – transaction, – point; misplaced &c. (*intrusive*) 24.

remote, far fetched, out of the way, forced, neither here nor there, quite another thing; detached, segregated, segregate.

multifarious; discordant &c. 24.

incidental, parenthetical, *obiter dictum*, episodic.

**Adv.** parenthetically &c. *adj.*; by the -way, – by; *en passant*, incidentally; irrespectively &c. *adj.*; without reference, – regard- to; in the abstract &c. 87; *a se.*

---

**11.** [Relations of kindred.] **Consanguinity.**—**N.** consanguinity, relationship, kindred, blood; parentage &c. (*paternity*) 166; filiation, affiliation; lineage, agnation, connection, cognation, alliance; family -connection, – tie; ties of blood; blood relationship; nepotism.

kins-man, -folk; people; kith and kin; rela-tion, -tive; connection; sib; next of kin; uncle, aunt, nephew, niece; cousin, -german; first –, second- cousin; cousin -once, – twice &c.- removed; near –, distant-relation; brother, sister, one's own flesh and blood.

family, patriarch, matriarch; fraternity; brother-, sister-, cousin-hood. race, stock, generation; sept &c. 166; stirps, side; strain; breed, clan, tribe.

**V.** be -related &c. *adj.* – to; claim -relationship &c. *n.*- with.

**Adj.** related, akin, consanguineous, matrilinear, patrilineal, of the blood, family, allied, collateral; cog-, ag-, con-nate; kindred; affiliated, affine; fraternal, avuncular.

intimately –, nearly –, closely –, remotely –, distantly- related, – allied; german.

**12.** [Double or reciprocal relation.] **Correlation.—N.** reciprocalness &c. *adj.*; recipro-city, -cality, -cation; mutuality, correlation, correspondence, interdependence; interchange &c. 148; exchange, barter; interrelation, interconnection; alternation, see-saw.

**V.** reciprocate, alternate; interchange &c. 148; exchange; counterchange; interact, correspond, mutualize, give and take.

**Adj.** reciprocal, mutual, commutual, correlative; alternate; interchangeable; international; correspondent, complementary, analogous.

**Adv.** *mutatis mutandis; vice versâ;* each other; by turns &c. 148; reciprocally &c. *adj.*; to and fro &c. 314.

**13. Identity.—N.** identity, sameness, oneness, ditto, homogeneity; unity, coincidence, coalescence; convertibility; equality &c. 27; selfness, self, oneself; identification.

monotony, tautology &c. (*repetition*) 104.

synonym.

fac-simile &c. (*copy*) 21; *alter ego* &c. (*similar*) 17; *ipsissima verba* &c. (*exactness*) 494; same; self –, very –, one and the- same; very –, actual- thing; no other.

**V.** be -identical &c. *adj.*; match, coincide, coalesce.

treat as –, render- -the same, –identical; identify; recognize the identity of.

**Adj.** identical; self, ilk; the -same &c. *n.*; self same; synonymous; one and the same.

coincid-, coalesc-ent, -ing; indistinguishable; one; equivalent &c. (*equal*) 27; much -the same, – of a muchness; unaltered.

**Adv.** identically &c. *adj.*; on all fours; *ibid-,* -em.

**14.** [Non-coincidence.] **Contrariety. —N.** contrariety, contrast, foil, antithesis, oppositeness; counterpole; contradiction; antagonism &c. (*opposition*) 708; counteraction &c. 179.

inversion &c. 218; the -opposite, – reverse, – inverse, – converse, – antipodes, – other extreme &c. 237.

antonym.

**V.** be -contrary &c. *adj.*; contrast with, oppose; differ *toto cœlo.*

invert, reverse, turn the tables &c. 218.

contra-dict, -vene; antagonize &c. 708.

**Adj.** contrar-y, -ious, -iant; opposite, counter, dead against; ad-, con-, reverse; opposed, antithetical, contrasted, antipodean, antagonistic, opposing; conflicting, inconsistent, contradictory, at cross purposes; negative; hostile &c. 708.

differing *toto cœlo;* diametrically opposite; as opposite as -black and white, – light and darkness, – fire and water, – the poles, as different as chalk from cheese; 'Hyperion to a satyr'; quite the -contrary, – reverse; no such thing, just the other way, *tout au contraire.*

**Adv.** contrarily &c. *adj.*; *contra,* contrariwise, *per contra,* on the contrary, nay rather; topsy-turvy; *vice versâ*; on the other hand &c. (*in compensation*) 30.

**15. Difference.—N.** difference, unlikeness; heterogeneity; vari-ance, -ation, -ety; diversity, dissimilarity &c. 18; disagreement &c. 24; disparity &c. (*inequality*) 28; distinction, contradistinction; distinctness; discrepancy, divergence, contrast &c. 18; nonconformity, incompatibility, antithesis.

discord &c. 713.

modification, moods and tenses.

nice –, fine –, delicate –, subtle- distinction; shade of difference, *nuance;* discrimination &c. 465; *differentia.*

different thing, something else, variant, apple off another tree, horse of another colour, another pair of shoes; this that or the other.

**V.** be -different &c. *adj.*; differ, vary, ablude, mismatch, contrast; diverge –, depart –, deviate- -from; divaricate; differ -*toto cœlo,* – *longo intervallo.*

disagree &c. 713.

vary, modify &c. (*change*) 140.

discriminate &c. 465.

**Adj.** differing &c. *v.*; different, diverse, divided, heterogeneous; distinguishable; varied, modified; divergent, incongruous, diversified, various; discrepant, dissentient, differential; divers, all manner of; variform &c. 81; discordant &c. 713.

other, another, not the same; unequal &c. 28; unmatched; widely apart.

distinctive, characteristic; discriminative; distinguishing.

**Adv.** differently &c. *adj.*

**Phr.** *il y a fagots et fagots; quot homines tot sententiæ;* one man's meat is another man's poison.

## 2°. Continuous Relation

**16. Uniformity. — N.** uniformity; homogene-ity, -ousness; continuity, stability, consistency; connatural-ity, -ness; homology; accordance; conformity &c. 82; agreement &c. 23.

regularity, constancy, even tenor, routine; monotony, evenness, sameness, dead level; steadiness, equability, unity.

**V.** be -uniform &c. *adj.*; accord with &c. 23; run through.

become -uniform &c. *adj.*; conform to &c. 82.

render uniform &c. *adj.*; assimilate, level, smooth, dress.

**Adj.** uniform; homo-geneous, -logous; of a piece, consistent, steady; connatural; monotonous, changeless, dreary, even, invariable, equable, level, regular, stereotyped, unchanged, unvarying; methodical &c. 60; habitual &c. 613.

**Adv.** uniformly &c. *adj.*; uniformly with &c. (*conformably*) 82; in harmony with &c. (*agreeing*) 23; in a -rut, – groove.

always, ever &c. 112; invariably, without exception, never otherwise; by clock-work; endlessly &c. 112.

**Phr.** *ab uno disce omnes.*

**16a.** [Absence or want of uniformity.] **Non-uniformity. — N.** diversity irregularity, unevenness; multiformity &c. 81; unconformity &c. 83; roughness &c. 256; heterogeneity, heteromorphism.

**Adj.** diversified, varied, irregular, uneven, rough &c. 256; multifarious; multiform &c. 81; of various kinds; all -manner, – sorts, – kinds- of.

**Adv.** in all manner of ways, here there and everywhere.

_____

## 3°. Partial Relation

**17. Similarity.—N.** similarity, resemblance, likeness, similitude, sem-

**18. Dissimilarity.—N.** dissimil-arity, -itude; unlikeness, diversity, disparity.

blance; affinity, approximation, parallelism; parity; agreement &c. 23; ana-logy, -logicalness; correspondence, equality &c.

connatural-ness, -ity; brotherhood, family likeness.

alliteration, rhyme, pun.

repetition &c. 104; sameness &c. (*identity*) 13; uniformity &c. 16.

analogue; the like; match, *pendant*, fellow, companion, pair, mate, twin, double, counterpart, brother, sister; one's second self, *alter ego*, chip of the old block, *par nobile fratrum*, *Arcades ambo*, birds of a feather, *et hoc genus omne*.

parallel; simile; type &c. (*metaphor*) 521; image &c. (*representation*) 554; photograph; close –, striking –, speaking –, faithful &c. *adj.* – likeness, – resemblance.

V. be -similar &c. *adj.*; look like, resemble, bear resemblance, favour; savour –, smack- of; approximate; parallel, match, rhyme with; take after; imitate &c. 19; run in pairs.

render -similar &c. *adj.*; assimilate, approximate, bring near; connaturalize, make alike; rhyme, pun.

Adj. similar; resembling &c. *v.*; like, alike; twin.

analog-ous, -ical; parallel, of a piece; such as, so.

connatural, congeneric, allied to; corresponding, cognate; akin to &c. (*consanguineous*) 11.

approximate, much the same, near, close, something like, such like; a show of; mock, *pseudo*, simulating, representing.

exact &c. (*true*) 494; lifelike, faithful, realistic; true to -nature, – the life; the -very image – picture- of; for all the world like, *comme deux gouttes d'eau*; as like as -two peas, – it can stare; *instar omnium*, cast in the same mould, ridiculously like.

Adv. as if, so to speak; as –, as if- it were; *quasi*, just as, *veluti in speculum*.

dissemblance; divergence, inequality, difference &c. 15; novelty; variation, variety, originality, disguise.

V. be -unlike &c. *adj.*; vary &c. (*differ*) 15; bear no resemblance to, differ *toto cælo*.

render -unlike &c. *adj.*; vary &c. (*diversify*) 140.

Adj. dissimilar, unlike, disparate; of a different kind &c. (*class*) 75; unmatched, unique; new, novel; unprecedented &c. 83; original.

nothing of the kind; no such –, quite another- thing; far from it, other than, cast in a different mould, *tertium quid*, as like a dock as a daisy, 'very like a whale'; as different as -chalk from cheese, – Macedon and Monmouth; *lucus a non lucendo*.

diversified &c. 16*a*.

Adv. otherwise, *alias*.

---

19. Imitation.—N. imitation; copying &c. *v.*; transcription; repetition, mimeograph, mimeotype, duplication, reduplication; quotation; reproduction.

mockery, mimicry, mime, simulation, impersonation; representation &c. 554; semblance, simulacrum; pretence; copy &c. 21; assimilation.

paraphrase, parody &c. 21.

plagiarism; forgery &c. (*falsehood*) 544.

imitator, echo, cuckoo, parrot, ape, monkey, mocking-bird, mimic, impersonator; copyist.

V. imitate, copy, mirror, reflect, reproduce, repeat, borrow; do like, echo, re-echo, catch; transcribe; match, parallel.

20. Non-Imitation.—N. no imitation, genuineness, originality; creativeness.

Adj. unimitated, uncopied; unmatched, unparalleled; inimitable &c. 33; *unique*, original, primordial, primary, pristine, underived, first-hand, archetypal, prototypal.

---

mock, take off, mimic, ape, simulate, personate, impersonate; forge; act &c. (*drama*) 599; represent &c. 554; counterfeit, duplicate; portray, parody, travesty, caricature, burlesque.

follow –, tread- in the- -steps, – footsteps, – wake- of; pattern after, take pattern by; follow -suit, – the example of; walk in the shoes of, take a leaf out of another's book, strike in with; take –, model -after; emulate.

**Adj.** imitated &c. *v.*; mock, mimic; counterfeit, false, pseudo; modelled after, moulded on, paraphrastic; literal; imitative, apish; second-hand; imitable; sham &c. 545.

**Adv.** literally, to the letter, strictly, precisely, *verbatim, literatim, sic, totidem verbis,* word for word, *mot à mot.*

**Phr.** like master like man.

20a. **Variation.—N.** variation; alteration &c. (*change*) 140.

modification, moods and tenses; modulation.

divergency &c. 291; deviation &c. 279; aberration; innovation.

**V.** vary &c. (*change*) 140; deviate &c. 279; diverge &c. 291.

**Adj.** varied &c. *v.*; modified; dissimilar &c. 18; diversified &c. 16*a.*

**21.** [Result of imitation.] **Copy.—N.** copy, fac-simile, counterpart, *effigies,* effigy, symbol, image, form, likeness, similitude, semblance, resemblance, cast, electrotype, stereotype, tracing, ectype; imitation &c. 19; model, representation, adumbration, study; counterfeit presentment, portrait &c. (*representment*) 554.

duplicate; transcript, -ion; reflex, -ion; shadow, echo; chip of the old block; reprint, reproduction, casting, engraving, replica; transfer; second edition &c. (*repetition*) 104; *réchauffé;* apograph, fair copy, revise.

**22.** [Thing copied.] **Prototype.—N.** prototype, original, model, pattern, founding, precedent, standard, scantling, type, arche-, anti-type; protoplast, copy-book, module, exemplar, example, ensample, specimen; paradigm; guide; templet; lay-figure.

text, copy, manuscript, MS., design; fugleman, keynote.

die, mould; matrix, engraving, last, plasm; pro-, proto-plasm; mint; seal, punch, *intaglio,* negative, stamp.

**V.** be –, set- an example; set a copy; standardize.

parody, caricature, cartoon, burlesque, travesty, paraphrase.

servile -copy, – imitation; counterfeit &c. (*deception*) 545; *pasticcio.*

**Adj.** faithful; lifelike &c. (*similar*) 17.

#### 4°. GENERAL RELATION

**23. Agreement. — N.** agreement; ac-cord, -cordance; unison, harmony, syntony; concord &c. 714; concordance, concert, understanding, convention, *entente -cordiale, consortium,* consensus of opinion, pact, mutual understanding, unanimity.

conformity &c. 82; conformance; uniformity &c. 16; consonance, consentaneousness, consistency; congruity, -ence; keeping; congeniality; correspondence, concinnity, parallelism, apposition, union.

fitness, aptness &c. *adj.*; relevancy;

**24. Disagreement. — N.** disagreement; dis-cord, -cordance; disunion, dissonance, dissidence, discrepancy; unconformity &c. 83; incongru-ity, -ence; discongruity, *mésalliance, oxymoron*; jarring &c. *v.*; clash, collision, dissension &c. 713; conflict &c. (*opposition*) 708; controversy &c. 720; falling out, wrangle, argument.

disparity, mismatch, misfit, disproportion; disproportionateness &c. *adj.*; variance, divergence, repugnance.

unfitness &c. *adj.*; inaptitude, impropriety; inapplicability &c. *adj.*; in-

pertinen-ce, -cy; sortance; case in point; aptitude, coaptation, propriety, applicability, admissibility, commensurability, compatibility, suitability; cognation &c. (*relation*) 9.

adaptation, adjustment, arrangement, graduation, accommodation; reconcil-iation -ement; assimilation; attunement.

consent &c. (*assent*) 488; concurrence &c. 178; co-operation &c. 709.

right man in the right place, very thing; quite -, just- the thing.

**V.** be -accordant &c. *adj.*; agree, accord, harmonize; correspond, tally, respond; meet, suit, fit, befit, do, adapt itself to; fall in -, chime in -, square -, quadrate -, consort -, comport- with; dovetail, assimilate; fit like a glove; fit to a -tittle, - T; match &c. 17; become one.

consent &c. (*assent*) 488.

render -accordant &c. *adj.*; fit, suit, adapt, accommodate; graduate; adjust &c. (*render equal*) 27; dress, regulate, readjust; accord, harmonize, reconcile; fadge, dovetail, square.

**Adj.** agreeing, suiting &c. *v.*; in accord, accordant, concordant, consonant, congruous, consentaneous, correspondent, corresponding, homologous, congenial; becoming; harmonious, reconcilable, conformable; in -accordance, - harmony, - keeping, - unison, &c. *n.*- with; at one with, of one mind, of a piece; consistent, compatible, proportionate, answerable; commensurate; on all fours.

apt, apposite, pertinent, pat; to the -point, - purpose; happy, felicitous, germane, *ad rem*, in point, bearing upon, applicable, relevant, admissible.

fit, adapted, *in loco*, *à propos*, appropriate, seasonable, sortable, suitable, idoneous, deft; meet &c. (*expedient*) 646.

at home, in one's proper element.

**Adv.** *à propos of*; pertinently &c. *adj.*; *pro rata.*

**Phr.** *rem acu tetigisti*, the cap fits.

consistency, inconcinnity; irrelevancy &c. (*irrelation*) 10.

misjoin-ing, -der; syncretism, intrusion, interference; *concordia discors.*

fish out of water.

**V.** disagree; clash, quarrel, jar &c. (*discord*) 713; interfere, intrude, come amiss; not concern &c. 10; mismatch; *humano capiti cervicem jungere equinam.*

**Adj.** disagreeing &c. *v.*; discordant, discrepant; at -variance, - war; hostile, antagonistic, repugnant, factious, contradictory, dissentious, incompatible, irreconcilable, inconsistent with; unconformable, exceptional &c. 83; intrusive, incongruous; disproportionate, -ed; unharmonious; unconsonant; divergent, repugnant to.

inapt, unapt, inappropriate, inept, infelicitous, improper; unsuit-ed, -able; inapplicable; un-fit, -fitting, -befitting; unbecoming; ill-timed, ill-adapted, unseasonable, *mal à propos*, inadmissible; inapposite &c. (*irrelevant*) 10.

uncongenial; ill-assorted, -sorted, -matched; mis-matched, -mated, -joined, -placed; unaccommodating, irreducible, uncommensurable, unsympathetic.

out of -character, - keeping, - proportion, - joint, - tune, - place, - season, - its element; at -odds, - variance with.

**Adv.** in -defiance, - contempt, - spite-of; discordantly &c. *adj.*; *à tort et à travers.*

---

# Section III. QUANTITY

## 1°. Simple Quantity

**25.** [Absolute quantity.] **Quantity.—**
**N.** quantity, magnitude; size &c. (*dimensions*) 192; amplitude, mass,

**26.** [Relative quantity.] **Degree.—**
**N.** degree, grade, extent, measure, proportion, amount, ratio, stint, standard

amount, *quantum*, measure, measurement, substance, strength.

[Science of quantity.] Mathematics, Mathesis.

[Definite or finite quantity] arm-, hand-, mouth-, spoon-, thimble-, capful; stock, batch, lot, dose, ration, quotum, quota, pittance, driblet, part, portion &c. 51.

**Adj.** quantitative, some, any, more or less.

**Adv.** to the tune of.

height, pitch; reach, amplitude, range, scope, size, calibre; gradation, shade; tenor, compass; sphere, station, rank, standing; rate, way, sort.

point, mark, step, stage &c. (*term*) 71; intensity, strength &c. (*greatness*) 31.

**V.** compare, graduate, calibrate, measure.

**Adj.** comparative; gradual, shading off, gradational; within the bounds &c. (*limit*), 233.

**Adv.** by degrees, gradually, inasmuch, *pro tanto*; how-ever, -soever; step by step, bit by bit, little by little, inch by inch, drop by drop, gradatim; by -inches, - slow degrees, - little and little; in some -degree, - measure; to some extent; just a bit.

## 2°. COMPARATIVE QUANTITY

**27.** [Sameness of quantity or degree.] **Equality.—N.** equality, parity, co-extension, symmetry, balance, poise; evenness, monotony, level.

equivalence; equi-pollence, -poise, -librium, -ponderance; par, quits; not a pin to choose; distinction without a difference, six of one and half a dozen of the other; identity &c. 13; similarity &c. 17; isotropism; coequality.

equalization, equation; equilibration, co-ordination, adjustment, readjustment.

drawn -game, -battle, draw, stalemate; neck and neck race; tie, dead heat.

match, peer, compeer, equal, mate, fellow, brother; equivalent.

**V.** be -equal &c. *adj.*; equal, match, reach, keep pace with, run abreast; come -, amount -, come up-to; bo -, lie on a level with; balance; cope with; come to the same thing; level off.

render -equal &c. *adj.*; equalize, level, dress, balance, equate, handicap, give points, trim, adjust, poise; fit, accommodate; adapt &c. (*render accordant*) 23; strike a balance; establish -, restore-equality, - equilibrium; readjust; stretch on the bed of Procrustes.

**Adj.** equal, even, level, monotonous, coequal, symmetrical, co-ordinate; on a -par, - level, - footing- with; up to the mark; equi parent.

equivalent, tantamount; quits; homologous; synonymous &c. 522; resolvable into, convertible, much at one, as broad as long, neither more nor less; much the same -, the same thing -, as good-as; all -one, - the same; equi-pollent, -ponderant, -ponderous, -balanced; equalized &c. *v.*; drawn; half and half; isochronous; isoperimetrical.

**28.** [Difference of quantity or degree.] **Inequality.—N.** inequality; dis-, im-parity; odds; difference &c. 15; ill-balanced; unevenness; inclination of the balance, partiality; shortcoming; casting - make- weight; superiority &c. 33; inferiority &c. 34.

**V.** be -unequal &c. *adj.*; countervail; have -, give the advantage; turn the scale; kick the beam; topple, -over; over-match &c. 33; not come up to &c. 34.

**Adj.** unequal, uneven, disparate, partial; un-, over-balanced; top-heavy, lop-sided.

**Adv.** *haud passibus æquis.*

**Adv.** equally &c. *adj.*; *pari passu, ad eundem, cæteris paribus*; *in equilibrio*; to all intents and purposes.

**Phr.** it -comes, -adds up, – amounts- to the same thing.

**29. Mean.—N.** mean, medium, intermedium, average, run of the mill, normal, balance; mediocrity, generality, rule, ordinary -run, -ruck; golden mean &c. (*mid-course*) 628; middle &c. 68; compromise &c. 774; neutrality; middle point, middle course.

**V.** split the difference; take the -average &c. *n.*; reduce to a -mean &c. *n.*; strike a balance, pair off.

**Adj.** mean, intermediate; medial; middle &c. 68; average, normal, standard; neutral; middling, moderate.

mediocre, middle-class; *bourgeois*, commonplace &c. (*unimportant*) 643.

**Adv.** on an average, in the long run; taking -one with another, – all things together, – it for all in all; *communibus annis*, in round numbers.

**30. Compensation.—N.** compensation, equation; commutation; indemnification; compromise &c. 774; neutralization, nullification; counteraction &c. 179; reaction; measure for measure; retaliation &c. 718; equalization &c. 27; redemption, recoupment, recompense.

set-off, offset; make- casting-weight; counterpoise, equipoise, ballast; indemnity, reparation &c. 790; equivalent, *quid pro quo*; bribe, hush-money, tribute &c. 784; amends &c. (*atonement*) 952; counterclaim, counterbalance, equiponderance, countervail, cross demand.

**V.** make -amends, – compensation; com-pensate, -pense; indemnify; counter-act, -vail, -poise; equiponderate; balance; out-, over-, counter-balance; set off, offset, cancel; hedge, square, give and take; make up -for, – lee way; cover, fill up, neutralize, nullify; equalize &c. 27; make good; redeem &c. (*atone*) 952; recoup, pay &c. 973.

**Adj.** compensat-ing, -ory; amendatory, reparative, countervailing &c. *v.*; in the opposite scale; equivalent &c. (*equal*) 27.

**Adv.** in -return, – consideration; but, however, yet, still, notwithstanding; neverthe-, nath-less; although, though; al-, how-beit; in spite of, despite; maugre; at -all events, – any rate; be that as it may, for all that, even so, on the other hand, at the same time, *quoad minus*, *quand même*, however that may be; after all, – is said and done; taking one thing with another &c. (*average*) 29.

## QUANTITY BY COMPARISON WITH A STANDARD

**31. Greatness.—N.** greatness &c. *adj.*; magnitude; size &c. (*dimensions*) 192; multitude &c. (*number*) 102; immensity, enormity; infinity &c. 105; might, strength, intensity, fulness; importance &c. 642; fame &c. 873.

great quantity, quantity, deal, power, sight, pot, volume, world; mass, heap &c. (*assemblage*) 72; stock &c. (*store*) 636; peck, bushel, load, cargo; cart -, wagon -, car -, truck -, ship- load; flood, spring tide; abundance &c. (*sufficiency*) 639.

principal -, chief -, main -, greater -,

**32. Smallness.—N.** smallness &c. *adj.*; littleness &c. (*small size*) 193; tenuity; paucity; fewness &c. (*small number*) 103; meanness, insignificance &c. (*unimportance*) 643; mediocrity, moderation.

small quantity, *modicum, minimum*; vanishing point; material point, electron, atom, particle, molecule, corpuscle, point, dab, fleck, speck, dot, mote, jot, iota, ace; *minutiæ*, details; look, thought, idea, *soupçon*, whit, tittle, shade, shadow; spark, *scintilla*, gleam; touch, cast; grain, scruple,

major –, best –, essential- part; bulk, mass &c. (*whole*) 50.

V. be -great &c. *adj.*; run high, soar, loom up, tower, bulk large, transcend; rise –, carry- to a great height; know no bounds; scale, overtop, ascend.

enlarge &c. (*increase*) 35, (*expand*) 194.

Adj. great; greater &c. 33; large, considerable, fair, above par; big, massive, huge &c. (*large in size*) 192; ample; abundant &c. (*enough*) 639; Herculean &c. 159; full, intense, strong, sound, passing, heavy, plenary, deep, high; signal, at its height, in the zenith.

world-wide, wide-spread, extensive; wholesale; many &c. 102.

goodly, noble, precious, mighty; sad, grave, serious; far gone, arrant, downright; utter, -most; crass, gross, arch, profound, intense, consummate; rank, unmitigated, red-hot, desperate; glaring, flagrant, stark staring; thorough-paced, -going; roaring, thumping, thundering, strapping, whacking; extraordinary; important &c. 642; unsurpassed &c. (*supreme*) 33; complete &c. 52.

vast, immense, enormous, extreme; inordinate, excessive, extravagant, exorbitant, outrageous, preposterous, unconscionable, swingeing, monstrous, over-grown; towering, stupendous, prodigious, astonishing, incredible; terrific, frightful; marvellous &c. (*wonder*) 870; grand.

unlimited &c. (*infinite*) 105; unapproachable, unutterable, indescribable, ineffable, unspeakable, inexpressible, beyond expression, fabulous.

un-diminished, -abated, -reduced, -restricted.

absolute, positive, stark, decided, unequivocal, essential, perfect, finished.

remarkable, of mark, marked, pointed, veriest; noticeable, uncommon, noteworthy, eminent &c. 873.

Adv. [in a positive degree] truly &c. (*truth*) 494; decidedly, unequivocally, purely, absolutely, seriously, essentially, fundamentally, radically, downright, in all conscience; for the most part, in the main.

[in a complete degree] entirely &c. (*completely*) 52; abundantly, &c. (*suf-*

granule, globule, minim, sup, sip, sop, spice, drop, droplet, sprinkling, dash, smack, tinge, tincture; inch, patch, scantling, dole; scrap, shred, tag, splinter, rag, tatter, cantlet, flitter, gobbet, mite, bit, morsel, crumb, seed, fritter, shive; snip, -pet; snick, snack, snatch, slip, scrag; chip, -ping; shiver, sliver, driblet, clipping, paring, shaving, hair.

nutshell; thimble-, spoon-, hand-, cap-, mouth-ful; fragment; fraction &c. (*part*) 51; drop in the ocean, drop in the bucket.

animalcule &c. 193.

trifle &c. (*unimportant thing*) 643; mere –, next to- nothing; hardly anything; just enough to swear by; the shadow of a shade.

finiteness, finite quantity.

V. be -shall &c. *adj.*; lie in a nutshell.

diminish &c. (*decrease*) 36, (*contract*) 195.

Adj. small, little, tiny, weeny; diminutive &c. (*small in size*) 193; minute; minikin, fine, inconsiderable, dribbling, paltry &c. (*unimportant*) 643; faint &c. (*weak*) 160; slender, light, slight, scanty, scant, limited; meagre &c. (*insufficient*) 640; sparing; few &c. 103; low, so-so, middling, tolerable, no great shakes; below –, under-, -par, – the mark; at a low ebb; half-way; moderate, modest; tender, subtle; petty, shallow, skin-deep.

inappreciable, evanescent, infinitesimal, homœopathic, very small, atomic, molecular, ultra-, -microscopic.

petty, shallow &c. 499.

mere, simple, sheer, stark, bare; near run.

Adv. [in a small degree] to a small extent, on a small scale; a -little, – wee, – tiny bit; slightly &c. *adj.*; imperceptibly; miserably, wretchedly; insufficiently &c. 640; imperfectly; faintly &c. 160; passably, pretty well, well enough.

[in a certain or limited degree] partially, in part; in –, to a certain degree; to a certain extent; comparatively; some, rather; in some -degree, -measure; some-thing, -what; simply, only, purely, merely; at –, at the- -least,

*ficiently*) 639; widely, far and wide.

[in a great or high degree] greatly &c. *adj.*; much, muckle, well, indeed, very, very much, a deal, no end of, most, not a little; pretty, – well; enough, in a great measure, passing richly; to a -large, – great, – gigantic-extent; on a large scale; so; never –, ever- so; ever so much; by wholesale; mightily, mighty, powerfully; with a witness, *ultra*, in the extreme, extremely, exceedingly, intensely, exquisitely, acutely, indefinitely, immeasurably; beyond -compare, – comparison, – measure, – all bounds; incalculably, infinitely.

[in a supreme degree] pre-eminently, superlatively &c. (*superiority*) 33.

[in a too great degree] immoderately, unduly, monstrously, grossly, preposterously, inordinately, exorbitantly, excessively, enormously, out of all proportion, with a vengeance.

[in a marked degree] particularly, remarkably, singularly, curiously, uncommonly, unusually, peculiarly, notably, signally, strikingly, pointedly, mainly, chiefly; famously, egregiously, prominently, glaringly, emphatically, strangely, wonderfully, amazingly, surprisingly, astonishingly, incredibly, marvellously, awfully, stupendously.

[in an exceptional degree] peculiarly &c. (*unconformity*) 83.

[in a violent degree] furiously &c. (*violence*) 173; severely, desperately, tremendously, extravagantly, confoundedly, deucedly, devilishly, with a vengeance; *à –, à toute- outrance*.

[in a painful degree] painfully, sadly, grossly, sorely, bitterly, piteously, grievously, miserably, cruelly, woefully, lamentably, shockingly, frightfully, dreadfully, fearfully, terribly, horribly, distressingly, balefully.

– most; ever so little, as little as may be, *tant soit peu*, in ever so small a degree; thus far, *pro tanto*, within bounds, in a manner, after a fashion.

almost, nearly, well nigh, short of, not quite, all but; near –, close- upon; *peu s'en faut*, near the mark; within an ·ace, – inch- of; on the brink of; scarcely, hardly, barely, only just, no more than.

[in an uncertain degree] about, thereabouts, somewhere about, nearly, say; be the same -more, – little more- or less.

[in no degree] no- ways, – wise; not -at all, – in the least, – a bit, – a bit of it, – a whit, – a jot, – a shadow; in no -wise, – respect; by no -means, – manner of means; on no account, at no hand.

---

## QUANTITY BY COMPARISON WITH A SIMILAR OBJECT

**33. Superiority.—N.** supremacy, superiority, majority; greatness &c. 31; advantage, odds, pull; preponderance, -ation; predominance, vantage ground, coign of vantage, prevalence, partiality; personal superiority; sovereignty &c. 737; nobility &c. (*rank*) 875; Triton among the minnows, *primus inter pares, nulli secundus*, superman; captain &c. 745.

supremacy, pre-eminence; primacy, lead, *maximum*; record; climax, crest, top; culmination &c. (*summit*) 210; transcendence; *ne plus ultra*; lion's share, Benjamin's mess; excess; bisque,

**34. Inferiority.—N.** inferiority, minority, subordinancy; shortcoming, deficiency; handicap; *minimum*; smallness &c. 32; imperfection, shabbiness.

[personal inferiority] commonalty &c. 876; subordinate, substitute, sub.

**V.** be -inferior &c. *adj.*; fall –, come- short of; not -pass, – come up to; want.

become –, render- smaller &c. (*decrease*) 36, (*contract*) 195; hide its diminished head, retire into the shade, yield the palm, play second fiddle, take a back seat; bow.

**Adj.** inferior, smaller; small &c. 32;

surplus &c. (*remainder*) 40, (*redundance*) 641.

**V.** be -superior &c. *adj.*; exceed, excel, transcend; out-do, -balance, -weigh, -rival, -Herod, outrank, pass, surpass, surmount, get ahead of; over-top, -ride, -pass, -balance, -weigh, -match; top, o'er-top, cap, beat, win out, cut out; beat hollow; outstrip &c. 303; eclipse, throw into the shade, take the shine out of, put one's nose out of joint; have the -upper hand, – whip hand of, – advantage; turn the scale, play first fiddle &c. (*importance*) 642; preponderate, predominate, prevail; precede, take precedence, come first; come to a head, culminate; beat &c. all others, bear the palm; break the record, take the cake.

become –, render- -larger, &c. (*increase*) 35, (*expand*) 194.

**Adj.** superior, greater, major, higher; exceeding &c. *v.*; great &c. 31; distinguished, *ultra*; vaulting; more than a match for.

supreme, greatest, maximal, maximum, utmost, paramount, pre-eminent, foremost, crowning; first-rate &c. (*important*) 642, (*excellent*) 648; unrivalled; peer-, match-less; none such, second to none, *sans pareil*; un-paragoned, -paralleled, -equalled, -approached, -surpassed; superlative, inimitable, *facile princeps*, incomparable, sovereign, without parallel, *nulli secundus, ne plus ultra*; beyond -compare, – comparison; culminating &c. (*topmost*) 210; transcendent, -ental; *plus royaliste que le Roi*.

increased &c. (*added to*) 35; enlarged &c. (*expanded*) 194.

**Adv.** beyond, more, over; over –, above- the mark; above par; upwards –, in advance- of; over and above; at the top of the scale, on the crest, at its height.

[in a superior or supreme degree] eminently, egregiously, pre-eminently, surpassing, prominently, superlatively, supremely, above all, of all things, the most, to crown all, *par excellence*, principally, especially, particularly, peculiarly, *a fortiori*, even, yea, still more.

**Phr.** 'we shall not look upon his like again.'

minor, less, lesser, deficient, minus, lower, subordinate, secondary; second-rate &c. (*imperfect*) 651; sub, subaltern; thrown into the shade; weighed in the balance and found wanting; not fit to hold a candle to.

least, smallest &c. (*see little, small* &c. 193); lowest.

diminished &c. (*decreased*) 36; reduced &c. (*contracted*) 195; unimportant &c. 643.

**Adv.** less; under –, below- -the mark, – par; at -the bottom of the scale, – a low ebb, – a disadvantage; short of, under.

---

## CHANGES IN QUANTITY

**35. Increase—N.** increase, augmentation, addition, enlargement, extension; dilatation &c. (*expansion*) 194; multiplication; increment, accretion; accession &c. 37; production &c. 161; development, growth; aggrandizement, aggravation, intensification; rise; ascent &c. 305; anabasis; ex-aggeration, -acerbation; spread &c. (*dispersion*) 73; flood-, spring-, -tide; gain, produce, profit &c. 618; booty, plunder &c. 793.

**V.** increase, augment, add to, en-large; dilate &c. (*expand*) 194; grow,

**36. Non-Increase, Decrease.—N.** decrease, diminution; lessening &c. *v.*; subtraction &c. 38; reduction, abatement, declension; shrinkage &c. (*contraction*) 195; coarctation; abridgment &c. (*shortening*) 201; extenuation.

subsidence, catabasis, wane, ebb, neap-tide, decline; descent &c. 306; decrement, reflux, depreciation; erosion, wear and tear, deterioration &c. 659; anticlimax; mitigation &c. (*moderation*) 174.

**V.** decrease, diminish, lessen; abridge

wax, mount, swell, get ahead, gain strength; advance; run –, shoot- up; rise; ascend &c. 305; sprout &c. 194.

aggrandize; raise, exalt; deepen, heighten; lengthen; thicken; strengthen; intensify, enhance, inflate, magnify, double, redouble; multiply; aggravate, exaggerate; ex-asperate, -acerbate; add fuel to the flame, *oleum addere camino*, superadd &c. (*add*) 37; spread &c. (*disperse*) 73.

Adj. increased &c. *v.*; on the increase, undiminished; additional &c. (*added*) 37; increasing &c. *v.*; growing, crescent, intensive, cumulative.

Adv. *crescendo*, increasingly.

Phr. *vires acquirit eundo.*

&c. (*shorten*) 201; shrink &c. (*contract*) 195; drop –, fall –, tail- off; fall away, waste, wear, erode; wane, ebb, decline; descend &c. 306; subside; deliquesce, melt –, die -away; retire into the shade, hide its diminished head, fall to a low ebb, run low, languish, decay, crumble, consume away.

bate, abate, dequantitate; discount; depreciate; extenuate, lower, weaken, attenuate, fritter away; mitigate &c. (*moderate*) 174; belittle, minimize; dwarf, throw into the shade; keep down, reduce &c. 195; shorten &c. 201; subtract &c. 38.

Adj. unincreased &c. (*see* increase &c. 35); decreased &c. *v.*; decreasing &c. *v.*; on the -wane &c. *n.*; deliquescent.

Adv. *diminuendo, decrescendo*, decreasingly.

## 3°. Conjunctive Quantity

**37. Addition.—N.** addition, annexation, adjection; junction &c. 43; super-position, -addition, -junction, -fetation; accession, reinforcement; increase &c. 35; increment, supplement; accompaniment &c. 88; interposition &c. 228; insertion &c. 300; summation &c. 85; adjunct &c. 39.

V. add, annex, adject, affix, attach, superadd, subjoin, superpose; clap –, saddle- on, tack to, postfix, append, tag; ingraft; saddle with; sprinkle; introduce &c. (*interpose*) 228; insert &c. 300.

become added, accrue; ad-, supervene; add up &c. 85.

reinforce, strengthen, swell the ranks of; augment &c. 35.

Adj. added &c. *v.*; additional; supplement, -al, -ary; suppletory, subjunctive; adjec-, adsci-, asci-titious; additive, extra, spare, further, fresh, more, new, ulterior, other, auxiliary, supernumerary, accessory.

Adv. in addition, more, plus, extra; and, also, likewise, too, furthermore, further, Item; and -also, – eke; else, besides, to boot, *et cætera*; &c.; and so -on, – forth; into the bargain, *cum multis aliis*, over and above, moreover.

with, withal; including, inclusive, as well as, not to mention, let

**38. Non-Addition. Subduction.—N.** sub-traction, -duction; deduction, retrenchment; removal; ab-, sub-lation; abstraction &c. (*taking*) 789; garbling &c. *v.*; mutilation, detruncation; amputation, severance; abs-, ex-, re-cision; curtailment &c. 201; minuend, subtrahend; decrease &c. 36; abrasion.

V. sub-tract, -duct; rebate, de-duct, -duce; bate, retrench; remove, withdraw; take -from, – away; detract.

garble, mutilate, amputate, sever, detruncate; cut -off, – away, – out; expurgate; abscind, excise; pare, thin, prune, decimate; abrade, scrape, file; geld, castrate, emasculate, unman, spay, caponize; eliminate.

diminish &c. 36; curtail &c. (*shorten*) 201; deprive of &c. (*take*) 789; weaken.

Adj. subtracted &c. *v.*; subtractive-tailless, acaudal.

Adv. in -deduction &c. *n.*; less, short of; minus, without, except, excepting, with the exception of, barring, bar, save, exclusive of, save and except, with a reservation.

alone; together –, along –, coupled –, in conjunction- with; conjointly; jointly &c. 43.

**39.** [Thing added.] **Adjunct.—N.** adjunct; addit-ion, -ament; *additum*, affix, appendage, annex; augment, -ation; increment, reinforcement, supernumerary, accessory, item; garnish, sauce; accompaniment &c. 88; adjective, *addendum*, accession, complement, supplement; continuation; extension, subscript, tag, appendix, postscript, interlineation, interpolation, insertion.

rider, codicil, off-shoot, episode, side issue, corollary; piece; flap, lapel, label, tab, strip, fold, lappet, apron, skirt, embroidery, trappings, *cortège*; tail, suffix &c. (*sequel*) 65; wing.

**Adj.** additional &c. 37.

**Adv.** in addition &c. 37.

**40.** [Thing remaining.] **Remainder·** **—N.** remainder, residue; remains, *remanet*, remnant, rest, relic, relict; leavings, heel-tap, odds and ends, cheese-parings, candle ends, orts; *residuum*; dottle, dregs &c. (*dirt*) 653; refuse &c. (*useless*) 645; stubble, result, educt; fag-end, stub; ruins, wreck, skeleton, stump; *alluvium*.

surplus, overplus, excess; balance, complement; superfluity &c. (*redundance*) 641; surviv-al, -ance; afterglow.

**V.** remain; be -left &c. *adj.*; exceed, survive; leave.

**Adj.** remaining, left; left -behind, – over; residu-al, -ary; over, odd; unconsumed, sedimentary; surviving; net; exceeding, over and above; outlying, -standing; cast off &c. 782; superfluous &c. (*redundant*) 641.

**40a.** [Thing deducted.] **Decrement.—N.** decrement, discount, rebate, defect, loss, deduction, eduction, tare; drawback; waste, wastage; reprise.

**41.** [Forming a whole without coherence.] **Mixture.—N.** mix-, admix-, commix-ture, -tion, mingling; commixion, immixture, interfusion, intermixture, alloyage, matrimony; junction &c. 43; combination &c. 48; entanglement, interlacing; miscegenation, interbreeding.

impregnation; in-, dif-, suf-, trans fusion: infiltration; seasoning, sprinkling, interlarding; interpolation &c. 228; adulteration, sophistication.

[Thing mixed] tinge, tincture, touch, dash, smack, sprinkling, spice, seasoning, infusion, *soupçon*.

[Compound resulting from mixture] alloy, brass, bronze, pewter &c.; amalgam, *magma*, blend, half-and-half, *mélange, tertium quid*, miscellany, *ambigu*, medley, mess, hash, hotchpotch, hodgepodge, *pasticcio*, patchwork, odds and ends, all sorts; jumble &c. (*disorder*) 59; salad, sauce, mash, *omnium gatherum*, gallimaufry, ragout, *olla podrida, olio*, salmagundi, *potpourri*, Noah's ark; texture, mingled yarn; mosaic &c. (*variegation*) 440.

half-blood, -caste, -breed, Eurasian; mulatto; terc-, quart-, quinteron &c.; quad-, octo-roon; *griffo, zambo*; cross, hybrid, mongrel &c. 83.

**42.** [Freedom from mixture.] **Simpleness.—N.** simpleness &c. *adj.*; purity, homogeneity.

elimination; sifting &c. *v.*; purification &c. (*cleanness*) 652.

**V.** render -simple &c. *adj.*; simplify.

sift, winnow, bolt, eliminate; narrow down; get rid of, exclude &c. 55; clear; purify &c. (*clean*) 652; disentangle &c. (*disjoin*) 44.

**Adj.** simple, uniform, of a piece, homogeneous, single, pure, clear, sheer, neat; Attic.

un-mixed, -mingled, -blended, -combined, -compounded; elementary, undecomposed; un-adulterated, -sophisticated, -alloyed, -tinged, -fortified; pure and simple.

free –, exempt- from; exclusive.

**Adv.** simply &c. *adj.*; only.

V. mix; join &c. 43; combine &c. 48; com-, im-, inter-mix; mix up with, mingle; com-, inter-, be-mingle; shuffle &c. (*derange*) 61; pound together; hash -, stir- up; knead, brew; impregnate with; interlard &c. (*interpolate*) 228; inter-twine, -weave &c. 219; associate with, miscegenate, interbreed.

be mixed &c.; get among, be entangled with.

instil, imbue; in-, suf-, trans-fuse; infiltrate, dash, tinge, tincture, season, sprinkle, besprinkle, attemper, medicate, blend, cross; alloy, amalgamate, compound, adulterate, sophisticate, infect.

Adj. mixed &c. *v.*; implex, composite, half-and-half, linsey-wolsey, hybrid, mongrel, heterogeneous; motley &c. (*variegated*) 440; miscellaneous, promiscuous, indiscriminate; miscible.

Adv. among, amongst, amid, amidst, with; in the midst of, in the crowd.

**43. Junction.**—N. junction; joining &c. *v.*; joinder, union; con-nection, -junction, -jugation, compendency, annex-ion, -ation, -ment; coalition; astriction, attachment, compagination, vincture, ligation, alligation; accouplement; marriage &c. (*wedlock*) 903; infibulation, inosculation, symphysis, anastomosis, confluence, communication, concatenation; concurrence, meeting, reunion; assemblage &c. 72.

copulation, coition, intercourse.

joint, joining, juncture, chiasma, pivot, hinge, articulation, commissure, seam, suture, gusset, stitch, splice; link &c. 45; mitre, mortise.

closeness, tightness &c. *adj.*; coherence &c. 46; combination &c. 48.

V. join, unite; con-join, -nect; associate; put -, lay -, clap -, hang -, lump -, hold -, piece -, tack -, fix -, bind up- together; embody, re-embody; roll into one.

attach, fix, affix, saddle on, fasten, bind, paste, secure, clinch, twist, make -fast &c. *adj.*; tie, pinion, string, strap, sew, lace, stitch, tack, baste, knit, button, buckle, hitch, lash, truss, bandage, braid, splice, swathe, gird, tether, moor, picket, harness, chain; fetter &c. (*restrain*) 751; lock, latch, belay, brace, hook, grapple, leash, couple, accouple, link, yoke, bracket; marry &c. (*wed*) 903; bridge over, span.

pin, nail, bolt, hasp, clasp, clamp, screw, rivet; impact, solder, braze, cement, set; weld -, fuse- together; wedge, rabbet, mortise, mitre, jam, dovetail, enchase; graft, ingraft, inosculate; en-, in-twine; inter-link, -lace,

**44. Disjunction.**—N. dis-junction, -connection, -unity, -union, -association, -engagement, -sociation; discontinuity &c. 70; inconnection; abstraction, -edness; isolation; insul-arity, -ation; oasis; separateness &c. *adj.*; severalty; *disjecta membra*; dispersion &c. 73; apportionment &c. 786.

separation; parting &c. *v.*; detachment, segregation; divorce, sejunction, seposition, diduction, diremption, discerption; elision; *cæsura*, division, subdivision, break, fracture, rupture; compartition; dis-memberment, -integration, -location; luxation; sever-, dis-sever-ance; scission; re-, ab-scission; circumcision; lacer-, dilacer-ation; dis-, ab-ruption; avulsion, divulsion; section, resection, cleavage; fission; separability; separatism.

fissure, breach, rent, split, rift, crack, slit, slot, incision.

dissection, anatomy; decomposition &c. 49; cutting instrument &c. (*sharpness*) 253; saw.

V. be -disjoined &c.; come -, fall- -off, - to pieces; peel off; get loose.

dis-join, -connect, -engage, -unite, -sociate, -pair; divorce, part, dispart, detach, uncouple, separate, cut off, rescind, segregate; set -, keep- apart; insulate, isolate; throw out of gear; cut adrift; loose; un-loose, -do, -bind, -tie, -hitch, -chain, -lock &c. (*fix*) 43, -pack, -ravel; disentangle; set free &c. (*liberate*) 750.

sunder, divide, subdivide, sectionalize, sever, dissever, abscind; cut; segment; in-cide, -cise; circumcise; saw, snip, nib, nip, cleave, rive, rend, slit,

-twine, -twist, -weave; entangle; twine round, belay; tighten; trice -, screw-up.

be -joined &c.; hang -, hold- together; cohere &c. 46.

**Adj.** joined &c. *v.*; joint; con-joint, -junct; corporate, compact; hand in hand.

firm, fast, close, tight, taut, taught, tense, secure, set, intervolved; in-separable, -dissoluble, -secable, -severable.

**Adv.** jointly &c. *adj.*; in conjunction with &c. (*in addition to*) 37; fast, firmly &c. *adj.*; intimately.

split, splinter, chip, crack, snap, break, tear, burst; rend &c. -asunder, - in twain; wrench, rupture, shatter, shiver, cranch, crunch, craunch, chop; rip up; hack, hew, slash; whittle; haggle, hackle, discind, lacerate, scamble, mangle, gash, hash, slice, shave.

cut up, carve, quarter, dissect, anatomize; take -, pull -, pick -, tear- to pieces; tear to tatters, - piecemeal; divellicate; skin &c. 226; dis-integrate, -member, -branch, -band; disperse &c. 73; dis-locate, -joint; break up; mince; comminute &c. (*pulverize*) 330; distribute, apportion &c. 786.

part, - company; separate, leave; alienate, estrange.

**Adj.** disjoined &c. *v.*; discontinuous &c. 70; bipartite, multipartite, abstract; digitate; disjunctive; isolated &c. *v.*; insular, separate, disparate, discrete, apart, asunder, far between, loose, free; unattached, -annexed, -associated, -connected; distinct; adrift; straggling; rift, reft, cleft, split.

[capable of being divided] scissile, partible, divisible, separable, severable, detachable.

**Adv.** separately &c. *adj.*; one by one, severally, apart; **adrift,** asunder, in twain; in the abstract, abstractedly.

**45.** [Connecting medium.] **Vinculum.—N.** vinculum, link, *nexus*; connec-tive, -tion; junction &c. 43; bond of union, copula, intermedium, hyphen; bracket; bridge, stepping-stone, isthmus.

bond, tendon, tendril; fibre; cord, -age; riband, ribbon, rope, guy, cable, line, halser, hawser, painter, moorings, wire, chain; string &c. (*filament*) 205.

fastening, tie; liga-ment, -ture; strap; bowline, halliard, tackle, lanyard, rigging, shrouds; standing -, running- rigging; traces, harness; yoke; band, -age; brace, roller, fillet; inkle; with, withe, withy; thong, braid; girder, tie-beam; girt, cinch, girth, girdle, cestus, garter, braces, suspenders, halter, noose, lasso, lariat, surcingle, knot, hitch, running knot, frog.

pin, corking pin, nail, brad, tack, skewer, staple, cleat, clamp; cramp, screw, button, buckle, clasp, hasp, hinge, hank, catch, latch, bolt, ring, latchet, pawl, tag; tooth; stud; hook, - and eye; morse, lock, holdfast, padlock, rivet; anchor, grappling-iron, drawbar, coupler, drawhead, coupling, treenail, trennel, stake, pale, pile, post, bollard.

cement, glue, gum, paste, size, wafer, solder, lute, putty, bird-lime, mortar, stucco, plaster, grout.

shackle, rein &c. (*means of restraint*) 752; suspender &c. 214; prop &c. (*support*) 215.

**V.** bridge over, span; connect &c. 43; hang &c. 214.

**46. Coherence.—N.** co-, ad-herence, -hesion, -hesiveness; concretion, accretion; con-, ag-glutination, -glomeration; aggregation; consolidation, set, cementation; sticking, soldering &c. *v.*; connection.

**47.** [Want of adhesion, non-adhesion, immiscibility.] **Incoherence.—N.** non-adhesion; immiscibility; incoherence; looseness &c. *adj.*; laxity; relaxation; loosening &c. *v.*; freedom; disjunction &c. 44; rope of sand.

tenacity, toughness; stickiness &c. 352; insepara-bility, -bleness; bur, remora.

conglomerate, concrete &c. (*density*) 321.

**V.** cohere, adhere, stick, cling, cleave, hold, take hold of, hold fast, close with, embrace, clasp, hug; grow -, hang-together; twine round &c. (*join*) 43.

stick like -a leech, – wax; stick close; cling like -ivy, – a bur; adhere like -a remora, – Dejanira's shirt.

glue; ag-, con-glutinate; cement, lute, paste, gum; solder, weld; cake, coagulate, consolidate &c. (*solidify*) 321; agglomerate.

**Adj.** co-, ad-hesive, -hering &c. *v.*; tenacious, tough; sticky &c. 352.

united, unseparated, sessile, inseparable, inextricable, infrangible; compact &c. (*dense*) 321.

**V.** make -loose &c. *adj.*; loosen slacken, relax; un-glue &c. 46; detach &c. (*disjoin*) 44.

**Adj.** non-adhesive, immiscible; incoherent, detached, loose, slack, baggy, lax, relaxed, flapping, streaming; dishevelled; segregated, like grains of sand; un-consolidated &c. 321, -combined &c. 48; non-cohesive.

---

**48. Combination.—N.** combination; mixture &c. 41; alloy; junction &c. 43; union, unification, synthesis, incorporation, amalgamation, embodiment, coalescence, crasis, fusion, blend, blending, absorption, centralization, federation.

compound, amalgam, composition, *tertium quid*; resultant, impregnation.

**V.** combine, unite, incorporate, alloy, intertwine &c. 41; amalgamate, embody, absorb, re-embody, blend, merge, fuse, melt into one, consolidate, coalesce, centralize, impregnate; put -, lump- together; federate, associate; fraternize; cement a union, marry, wed, couple, pair, ally.

**Adj.** combined &c. *v.*; conjunctive, conjugate, conjoint, allied, confederate; impregnated with, ingrained, inoculated.

**49. Decomposition.—N.** decomposition, analysis, diæresis, dissection, resolution, catalysis, electrolysis, hydrolysis, photolysis, dissolution; dispersion &c. 73; disjunction &c. 44; disintegration, decay, rot, putrefaction, putrescence, caries, necrosis, corruption &c. (*uncleanness*) 653.

**V.** decom-pose, -pound; analyze, disembody, dissolve; resolve -, separate into its elements; electrolyze; dissect, decentralize, break up; disintegrate; disperse &c. 73; unravel &c. (*unroll*) 313; crumble into dust; decay &c. *n.*; deteriorate &c. 659.

**Adj.** decomposed &c. *v.*; catalytic, analytical.

---

### 4°. Concrete Quantity

**50. Whole. [Principal part.]—N.** whole, totality, integrity; totalness &c. *adj.*; entirety, *ensemble*, collectiveness; unity &c. 87; completeness &c. 52; indivisibility, indiscerptibility; integration, embodiment; integer, integral.

all, the whole, total, aggregate, one and all, gross amount, sum, sum-total, *tout ensemble*, length and breadth of, Alpha and Omega, 'bo all and end all,' lock, stock and barrel.

bulk, mass, lump, tissue, staple, body, torso, *compages*; trunk, bole, hull, hulk, skeleton; greater -, major

**51. Part.—N.** part, portion; dose; item, particular; aught, any; division, ward; subdivision, section; chapter, verse; article, clause, count, paragraph, passage; phrase; number, volume, book, fascicule; sector, segment; fraction, fragment; cantle, -t; frustum; detachment, parcel, unit, class &c. 75.

piece, lump, bit; cut, -ting; chip, chunk, collop, slice, scale, shard; lamina &c. 204; moiety; small part; morsel, scrap, crumb; particle &c. (*smallness*) 32; instalment, dividend; share &c. (*allotment*) 786.

-, best -, principal -, main- part; essential part &c. (*importance*) 642; lion's share, Benjamin's mess; the long and the short; nearly -, almost- all.

V. form -, constitute- a whole; integrate, embody, amass; aggregate &c. (*assemble*) 72; amount to, come to.

Adj. whole, total, integral, entire; complete &c. 52; one, individual.

un-broken, -cut, -divided, -severed, -clipped, -cropped, -shorn; seamless; undiminished; un-demolished, -dissolved, -destroyed, -bruised.

in-divisible, -dissoluble, -dissolvable, -discerptible.

wholesale, sweeping, comprehensive.

Adv. wholly, altogether; totally &c. (*completely*) 52; entirely, all, all in all, considering all things, in a body, collectively, all put together; in the -aggregate, - lump, - mass, - gross, - main, - long run; *en masse*, on the whole, *in extenso*, throughout, every inch; substantially.

*débris*, odds and ends, oddments, *detritus*; *excerpta*; member, limb, lobe, lobule, arm, wing, scion, branch, bough, joint, link, offshoot, ramification, twig, stipule, tendril, bush, spray, sprig; runner; leaf, -let; stump; constituent, ingredient, component part &c. 56.

compartment; department &c. (*class*) 75; county &c. (*region*) 181.

V. part, divide, break &c. (*disjoin*) 44; partition &c. (*apportion*) 786.

Adj. fractional, fragmentary; sectional, aliquot; divided &c. *v.*; in compartments, multifid, incomplete, partial, divided &c. 44.

Adv. partly, in part, partially; piecemeal, part by part; by -instalments, - snatches, - inches, - driblets; bit by bit, inch by inch, foot by foot, drop by drop; in -detail, - lots.

as a whole, bodily, *en bloc*,

---

## 52. Completeness.—N. completeness &c. *adj.*; completion &c. 729; integration; integrality.

entirety; universality; totality; perfection &c. 650; solid-ity, -arity; unity; all; *ne plus ultra*, ideal, limit.

complement, supplement, make-weight; filling up &c. *v.*

impletion; satur-ation, -ity; high water; high -, flood -, spring- tide; fill, load, bumper, bellyful; brimmer; sufficiency &c. 639.

V. be -complete &c. *adj.*; come to a head.

render -complete &c. *adj.*; complete &c. (*accomplish*) 729; fill, charge, load, replenish; make-up, - good; piece -, eke- out; supply deficiencies; fill -up, - in, - to the brim, - the measure of; saturate &c. 869.

go the whole -hog, - length, go all lengths.

Adj. complete, entire; whole &c. 50; perfect &c. 650; full, good, absolute, thorough, plenary; solid, undivided; with all its parts.

exhaustive, radical, sweeping, thorough-going; dead.

regular, consummate, unmitigated, sheer, unqualified, unconditional, free; abundant &c. (*sufficient*) 639.

## 53. Incompleteness.—N. incompleteness &c. *adj.*; deficiency, short -measure, - weight; shortcoming &c. 304; insufficiency &c. 640; imperfection &c. 651; immaturity &c. (*non-preparation*) 674; half measures.

[part wanting] defect, deficit, shortage, ullage, defalcation, omission, *caret*; interval &c. 198; break &c. (*discontinuity*) 70; non-completion &c. 730; missing link.

V. be -incomplete &c. *adj.*; fall short of &c. 304; lack &c. (*be insufficient*) 640; neglect &c. 460.

Adj. incomplete; imperfect &c. 651; unfinished; uncompleted &c. (*see* complete &c. 729); defective, deficient, wanting; failing; in -default, - arrear; short, - of; hollow, meagre, lame, half-and-half, perfunctory, sketchy; crude &c. (*unprepared*) 674.

mutilated, garbled, mangled, docked, lopped, truncated; bobtailed, cropped, bobbed, shingled.

in -progress, - hand; going on, proceeding.

Adv. incompletely &c. *adj.*; by halves.

Phr. *cætera desunt*; *caret*.

---

brimming; brim-, top-ful; chock –, choke- full; as full as -an egg is of meat, – a vetch, – a tick; saturated, crammed; replete &c. (*redundant*) 641; fraught, laden; full-laden, -fraught, -charged; heavy laden.

completing &c. *v.*; supplement-al, -ary; ascititious.

Adv. completely &c. *adj.*; altogether, outright, wholly, totally, *in toto,* quite; over head and ears; effectually, for good and all, nicely, fully, through thick and thin, head and shoulders; neck and -heel, – crop; all out; in -all respects, – every respect; at all points, out and out, to all intents and purposes; *toto cælo;* utterly, clean, – as a whistle; to the -full, – utmost, – backbone; hollow, stark; heart and soul, root and branch; down to the ground.

to the top of one's bent, as far as possible, *à outrance.*

throughout; from -first to last, – beginning to end, – end to end, – one end to the other, – Dan to Beersheba, – head to foot, – head to heels, – top to toe, – top to bottom; *de fond en comble; à fond, a capite ad calcem, ab ovo usque ad mala,* fore and aft; every -whit, – inch; *cap-à-pie,* to the end of the chapter; up to the -brim, – ears, – eyes; as . . . as can be.

on all accounts; *sous tous les rapports;* with a -vengeance, – witness.

**54. Composition.**—N. composition, constitution, crasis, synthesis; make-up; combination &c. 48; inclusion, admission, comprehension, reception; embodiment, formation, conformation, production.

compilation &c. 72; (*musical*) composition &c. 415; painting &c. 556; writing &c. 590; typography &c. 591.

V. be -composed, – made, – formed, – made up- of; consist of, be resolved into.

include &c. (*in a class*) 76; subsume; synthesize; contain, hold, comprehend, take in, admit, embrace, embody; involve; implicate, drag into.

compose, constitute, form, make; make –, fill –, build- up; weave, construct, fabricate; compile; write, draw; set up (*printing*); enter into the composition of &c. (*be a component*) 56.

Adj. containing, constituting &c. *v.*

**56. Component.**—N. component; component –, integral –, integrant-part; element, constituent, ingredient, leaven, part and parcel; contents; appurtenance; feature; member &c. (*part*) 51; personnel.

V. enter into, – the composition of; be a -component &c. *n.*; be –, form-part of; merge –, be merged- in; be

**55. Exclusion.**—N. exclusion, non admission, omission, exception, rejection, repudiation; exile &c. (*seclusion*) 893; preclusion, lock out, ostracism, prohibition; disbarment, expulsion, ban.

separation, segregation, seposition, elimination, coffer-dam.

V. be excluded from &c.

exclude, bar, ban; leave –, shut –, thrust –, bar- out; reject, repudiate, spurn, blackball; ostracize, boycott; lay –, put –, set -apart, – aside; relegate, segregate; throw overboard; strike -off, – out; neglect &c. 460; banish &c. (*seclude*) 893; separate &c. (*disjoin*) 44.

pass over, omit; garble; eliminate, weed, winnow.

Adj. excluding &c. *v.*; exclusive.

excluded &c. *v.*; unrecounted, not included in; inadmissible; preventive, interdictive.

Adv. exclusive of, barring; except; with the exception of; save, bating.

**57. Extraneousness.**—N. extraneousness &c. *adj.*; extrinsicality &c. 6; exteriority &c. 220; alienism.

foreign -body, – substance, – element; alien, stranger, intruder, interloper, foreigner, tramontane, *novus homo,* new comer, immi-, emi-grant; creole, Afrikander; outsider, outlander, tenderfoot.

[ 21 ]

implicated in; share in &c. (*participate*)
778; belong -, appertain- to.

form, make, constitute, compose.
**Adj.** forming &c. *v.*; inclusive; inherent &c. 5.

---

**Adj.** extraneous, foreign, alien, ulterior; exterior, external, outside, outlandish; oversea; tra-, ultra-montane; excluded &c. 55; inadmissible; exceptional.

**Adv.** in foreign -parts, - lands; abroad, beyond seas, overseas.

## Section IV. ORDER

### 1°. Order in General

**58. Order.—N.** order, regularity &c. 80; uniformity, symmetry, *lucidus ordo*; harmony, music of the spheres.

gradation, progression; series &c. (*continuity*) 69.

subordination; course, even tenor, routine; method, disposition, arrangement, array, system, economy, disci pline; orderliness &c. *adj.*

rank, place, &c. (*term*) 71.

**V.** be -, become- in order &c. *adj.*; form, fall in, draw up; arrange -, range -, place- itself; adjust; fall into -, take- -one's place, - rank; rally round; arrange &c. 60.

**Adj.** orderly, regular; in -order, - trim, - apple-pie order, according to Cocker, - its proper place, neat, neat as a pin, tidy, *en règle*, well regulated, correct, methodical, uniform, symmetrical, ship-shape, business-like, systematic; habitual; unconfused &c. (*see* confuse &c. 61) arranged &c. 60.

**Adv.** in order; methodically &c. *adj.*; in -turn, - its turn; step by step; by regular -steps, - gradations, - stages, - intervals; *seriatim*, systematically, by clockwork, *gradatim*; at stated periods &c. (*periodically*) 138; O.K.

---

**59. [Absence, or want of Order, &c.]** Disorder.—N. disorder; derangement &c. 61; irregularity; anomaly &c. (*unconformity*) 83; anar-chy, -chism; want of method; dishevelment, untidiness &c. *adj.*; disunion; discord &c. 24.

confusion; confusedness &c. *adj.*; disarray, jumble, mix-up, huddle, litter, lumber; *cahotage*; farrago; mess, muss, mash, muddle, hash; hotchpotch; *imbroglio*, chaos, *omnium gatherum*, medley; mere -mixture &c. 41; fortuitous concourse of atoms, *disjecta membra*, *rudis indigestaque moles*.

complexity; complexness &c. *adj.*; com-, im-plication; intri-cacy, -cation; perplexity; network, maze, labyrinth; wilderness, jungle; involution, ravelling, entanglement; coil &c. (*convolution*) 248; sleave, tangled skein, knot, Gordian knot, kink, web; wheels within wheels.

turmoil; ferment, &c. (*agitation*) 315; to do, trouble, pudder, pother, row, disturbance, convulsion, tumult, pandemonium, uproar, riot, rumpus, stour, scramble, *fracas*, embroilment, *mêlée*, spill and pelt, rough and tumble; whirlwind &c. 349; bear garden, Babel, Saturnalia, Donnybrook Fair, confusion worse confounded, most admired disorder, *concordia discors*; Bedlam -,

hell- broke loose; bull in a china shop; all the fat in the fire, *diable à quatre*, Devil to pay; pretty kettle of fish; pretty piece of -work, - business.

slattern, slut, sloven, draggle-tail.

**V.** be -disorderly &c. *adj.*; ferment, play at cross purposes.

put out of order; derange &c. 61; ravel &c. 219; ruffle, rumple; bungle, botch.

**Adj.** disorderly, orderless; out of -order, - place, - gear, - whack; irregular, desultory; anomalous &c. (*unconformable*) 83; acephalous, disorganized, straggling; un-, im-methodical; unsymmetric; unsystematic; untidy, slovenly, bedraggled, messy; dislocated; out of sorts; promiscuous, indiscriminate; chaotic, anarchical, lawless; unarranged &c. 60; confused, tumultuous, turbulent, tempestuous; deranged &c. 61; topsy turvy &c. (*inverted*) 218; shapeless &c. 241; disjointed, out of joint.

com-plex, -plexed; intricate, complicated, perplexed, involved, ravelled, entangled, knotted, tangled, inextricable; irreducible.

troublous; riotous &c. (*violent*) 173.

Adv. irregularly &c. *adj.*; by fits and -snatches, – starts; pell-mell; higgledy-piggledy; helter-skelter, harum-scarum; in a ferment; at -sixes and sevens, – cross purposes; upside down &c. 218.

Phr. the cart before the horse, chaos is come again.

---

**60. [Reduction to Order.] Arrangement.—N.** arrangement; plan &c. 626; preparation &c. 673; dispos-al, -ition; col-, al-location; distribution; sorting &c. *v.*; assortment, allotment; grouping; apportionment, *taxis*, taxonomy, *syn-taxis*, graduation, organization, grading; re-organization, rationalization.

analysis, classification, division, digestion; systematism.

[Result of arrangement] order, orderliness, form, array; digest, synopsis &c. (*compendium*) 596; *syntagma*, table, atlas; register &c. (*record*) 551; score &c. 415; cosmos, organism, architecture.

[Instrument for sorting] sieve &c. 260; file, card index.

**V.** reduce to –, bring into- order; introduce order into; rally.

arrange, dispose, place, form; put –, set –, place- in order; straighten up, lay up; set out, collocate, allocate, pack, marshal, range, size, rank, array, group, parcel out, allot, space, distribute, deal; cast –, assign- the parts; dispose of, assign places to; assort, sort; sift, riddle; put –, set- -to rights, – into shape, – in trim, – in array.

class, -ify; divide; file, string together, thread; register &c. (*record*) 551; list, catalogue, tabulate, index, alphabeticize, graduate, digest, grade, codify; orchestrate, score.

methodize, regulate, systematize, standardize, co-ordinate, organize, settle, fix, apportion.

unravel, disentangle, ravel, card; disembroil.

**Adj.** arranged &c. *v.*; embattled, in battle array; cut and dried; methodical, orderly, regular, systematic, tabular.

**61. [Subversion of Order; bringing into disorder.] Derangement.—N.** derangement &c. *v.*; disorder &c. 59; evection, discomposure, disturbance; dis-, de-organization; involvement; dislocation; perturbation, interruption; shuffling &c. *v.*; inversion &c. 218; corrugation &c. (*fold*) 258; insanity &c. 503.

**V.** derange; dis-, mis-arrange; dis-, mis-place; mislay, discompose, disorder, de-, dis-organize; embroil, unsettle, disturb, confuse, trouble, perturb, jumble, tumble; huddle, shuffle, muddle, toss, hustle, fumble, riot; bring –, put –, throw- into -disorder &c. 59; break the ranks, disconcert, convulse; break in upon.

unhinge, dislocate, put out of joint, throw out of gear.

turn topsy-turvy &c. (*invert*) 218; bedevil; complicate, involve, perplex, confound; im-, em-brangle; tangle, en-tangle, ravel, tousle, dishevel, ruffle, rumple &c. (*fold*) 258; dement.

litter, scatter; mix &c. 41.

**Adj.** deranged &c. *v.*; syncre-tic, -tistic.

## 2°. CONSECUTIVE ORDER

**62. Precedence.—N.** precedence; coming before &c. *v.*; the lead, *le pas*; superiority &c. 33; importance &c. 642; anteced-ence, -ency; anteriority &c. (*front*) 234; precursor &c. 64; priority &c. 116; precession &c. 280; anteposition, preference.

**V.** precede; come -before, – first; forerun, head, lead, take the lead; lead the -way, – dance; introduce, usher in; have the *pas*; set the fashion &c. (*influence*) 175; lead off, kick off, open the ball; take –, have- precedence; outrank; have the start &c. (*get before*) 280.

place before; prefix; premise, prelude, preface.

**Adj.** preceding &c. *v.*; pre-, antecedent; anterior; prior &c. 116; before; former, foregoing; before-, above-mentioned; aforesaid, said; precurs-ory, -ive; prevenient, preliminary, prefatory, introductory; prelus-ive, -ory; proemial, preparatory.

**Adv.** before; in advance &c. (*precession*) 280.

**Phr.** *seniores priores*.

**63. Sequence.—N.** sequence, coming after; going after &c. (*following*) 281; consecution, succession; posteriority &c. 117.

continuation; prolongation, order of succession; successiveness; Elijah's mantle.

secondariness; subordinacy &c. (*inferiority*) 34.

**V.** succeed; come -after, – on, – next; follow, ensue, step into the shoes of; alternate.

place after, suffix, append.

**Adj.** succeeding &c. *v.*; sequent; sub-, con-sequent; sequacious, proximate, next; consecutive &c. (*continuity*) 69; alternate, amœbæan.

latter; posterior &c. 117.

**Adv.** after, subsequently; behind &c. (*rear*) 235.

---

**64. Precursor.—N.** precursor, antecedent, precedent, predecessor; forerunner, van-courier, *avant-coureur*, pioneer, prodrome, *prodromos*, outrider; leader, bell-wether; herald, harbinger; dawn.

prelude, preamble, preface, prologue, foreword, *avant-propos*, *protasis*, prolusion, proem, *prolepsis*, *prolegomena*, prefix, introduction; lead, heading, frontispiece, groundwork; preparation &c. 673; overture, voluntary, *exordium*, symphony, *ritornello*; premises.

prefigurement &c. 511; omen &c. 512.

**Adj.** precursory; prelu-sive, -sory, -dious; proemial, introductory, prefatory, prodromous, inaugural, preliminary; precedent &c. (*prior*) 116.

**65. Sequel.—N.** sequel, suffix, successor; tail, queue, train, wake, trail, rear; retinue, suite; appendix, postscript, subscript; epilogue; conclusion; peroration; codicil; continuation, *sequela*; appendage &c. 39; tail –, heelpiece; tag, more last words; colophon, *feliciter explicit*.

follower, after-glow, -growth, -crop, -taste, -math.

after-part, -piece, -course, -thought, -game; *arrière pensée*, second thoughts.

---

**66. Beginning.—N.** beginning, commencement, opening, outset, incipience, inception, inchoation; introduction &c. (*precursor*) 64; *alpha*; initial; foundation; inauguration, *début*, *le premier pas*, embarcation, rising of the curtain; zero hour; exordium, curtain raiser; maiden speech; prelude; outbreak, onset, brunt; initiative, move. first move; gambit, narrow –, thin-

**67. End.—N.** end, close, termination; desinence, conclusion, *finis*, *finale*, period, term, *terminus*, last, *omega*; extreme, -tremity; gable –, butt –, fagend; tip, nib, point; tail &c. (*rear*) 235; verge &c. (*edge*) 231; tag, epilogue, peroration; *bonne bouche*; bitter end, tail end; terminal; *apodosis*; appendix.

consummation, *dénouement*; finish &c. (*completion*) 729; fate; doom, -sday;

end of the wedge; fresh start, new departure; forefront.

origin &c. (*cause*) 153; source, rise; bud, germ &c. 153; egg, rudiment; genesis, birth, nativity, cradle, infancy, incunabula; start, starting-point &c. 293; dawn &c. (*morning*) 125.

title-page; head, -ing, caption; van &c. (*front*) 234, *feliciter incipit*.

en-trance, -try; inlet, orifice, mouth, chops, lips, porch, portal, portico, *propylon*, door; gate, -way; postern, wicket, threshold, vestibule; skirts, border &c. (*edge*) 231; tee.

first -stage, – blush, – glance, – impression, – sight.

rudiments, elements, outlines, *principia*, grammar, *protasis*; alphabet, ABC.

V. begin, commence, inchoate, rise, arise, originate, institute, conceive, initiate, open, dawn, set in, take its rise, enter upon, start; enter; set out &c. (*depart*) 293; embark in.

usher in; lead -off, – the way; take the -lead, – initiative; inaugurate, head; stand -at the head, – first, – for; lay the foundations &c. (*prepare*) 673; found &c. (*cause*) 153; set -up, – on foot, – agoing, – abroach, – the ball in motion; apply the match to a train; launch, broach; open -up, – the door to; set -about, – to work; make a -beginning, – start; handsel; take the first step, lay the first stone, cut the first turf; break -ground, – the ice, – cover; pass –, cross- the Rubicon; open -fire, – the ball; ventilate, air; undertake &c. 676.

come into -existence, – the world; make one's *début*, take birth; burst forth, break out; spring –, crop- up.

begin -at the beginning, – *ab ovo*, – again, – *de novo*; start afresh, make a fresh start, shuffle the cards, resume, recommence.

Adj. beginning &c. *v.*; initi-al, -atory, -ative; inceptive, introductory, incipient, inaugural; incho-ate, -ative; embryonic, rudimental; primogenial; primeval &c. (*old*) 124; rudimentary, aboriginal; natal, nascent.

first, foremost, front, leading, head; maiden.

begun &c. *v.*; just -begun &c. *v.*

Adv. at –, in- the beginning &c. *n.*; first, in the first place, *imprimis*, first and foremost; *in limine*; in -the bud, – embryo, – its infancy; from -the beginning, – its birth; *ab -initio, – ovo, – incunabulis*, primarily, originally.

crack of doom, day of Judgement, fall of the curtain, wind-up; goal, destination; limit, stoppage, end all, determination; expiration, expiry; death &c. 360; end of all things; finality; eschatology.

break up, *commencement de la fin*, last stage, turning point; *coup de grâce*, death-blow; knock-out.

V. end, close, finish, terminate, conclude, be all over; expire; die &c. 360; come –, draw- to a -close &c. *n.*; have run its course; run out, pass away.

bring to an -end &c. *n.*; put an end to, make an end of; determine; get through; achieve &c. (*complete*) 729; stop &c. (*make to cease*) 142; shut up shop.

Adj. ending &c. *v.*; final, terminal, definitive, conclusive; crowning &c. (*completing*) 729; last, ultimate; hindermost; rear &c. 235; caudal.

contermin-ate, -ous, -able.

ended &c. *v.*; at an end; settled, decided, over, played out, set at rest.

penultimate; last but -one, – two, &c.

unbegun, uncommenced; fresh.

Adv. finally &c. *adj.*; in fine; at the last; once for all.

---

first step, lay the first stone, cut the first turf; break -ground, – the ice, – cover; pass –, cross- the Rubicon; open -fire, – the ball; ventilate, air; undertake &c. 676.

come into -existence, – the world; make one's *début*, take birth; burst forth, break out; spring –, crop- up.

begin -at the beginning, – *ab ovo*, – again, – *de novo*; start afresh, make a fresh start, shuffle the cards, resume, recommence.

Adj. beginning &c. *v.*; initi-al, -atory, -ative; inceptive, introductory, incipient, inaugural; incho-ate, -ative; embryonic, rudimental; primogenial; primeval &c. (*old*) 124; rudimentary, aboriginal; natal, nascent.

first, foremost, front, leading, head; maiden.

begun &c. *v.*; just -begun &c. *v.*

Adv. at –, in- the beginning &c. *n.*; first, in the first place, *imprimis*, first and foremost; *in limine*; in -the bud, – embryo, – its infancy; from -the beginning, – its birth; *ab -initio, – ovo, – incunabulis*, primarily, originally.

**68. Middle.—N.** middle, midst, mediety; mean &c. 29; medium, middle term; centre &c. 222, mid-course &c. 628; *mezzo termine*; *juste milieu* &c. 628; half-way house, nave, navel, omphalos; nucle-us, -olus.

equidistance, bisection, half-distance; middle-distance, equator, diaphragm, midriff; interjacence &c. 228.

**Adj.** middle, medial, mesial, mean, mid; middle-, mid-most; middling; mediate; intermediate &c. (*interjacent*) 228; equidistant; central &c. 222; mediterranean, equatorial.

**Adv.** in the middle; in the thick; mid-, half-way; midships, *in medias res*.

**69. [Uninterrupted sequence.] Continuity.—N.** continuity; consecu-tion, -tiveness &c. *adj.*; succession, round, suite, progression, series, train, chain; cat-, concat-enation; catena; scale; gradation, course, constant flow, perpetuity.

procession, column; retinue, *cortège*, cavalcade, rank and file, line of battle, array.

pedigree, genealogy, lineage, race &c. 166.

rank, file, line, row, range, tier, string, thread, team; suit; colonnade.

**V.** follow in -, form- a series &c. *n.*; fall in.

arrange in a -series &c. *n.*; string together, catenate, file, thread, graduate, tabulate.

**Adj.** continu-ous, -ed; consecutive; progressive, gradual; serial, successive; immediate, unbroken, entire; linear; in a -line, - row &c. *n.*; uninter-rupted, -mitting; unremitting; perennial, evergreen; constant.

**Adv.** continuously &c. *adj.*; *seriatim*; in a -line &c. *n.*; in -succession, - turn; running, gradually, step by step, *gradatim*, at a stretch; in -file, - column, - single file, - Indian file.

**70. [Interrupted sequence.] Discontinuity.—N.** discontinuity; disjunction &c. 44; anacoluthon, *non sequitur*; interruption, break, fracture, flaw, fault, split, crack, cut; gap &c. (*interval*) 198; solution of continuity, *cæsura*; broken thread; parenthesis, episode; rhapsody, patchwork; intermission; alternation &c. (*periodicity*) 138; dropping fire.

**V.** be -discontinuous &c. *adj.*; alternate, intermit.

discontinue, pause, interrupt; intervene; break, - in upon; interpose &c. 228; break -, snap- the thread; disconnect &c. (*disjoin*) 44.

**Adj.** discontinuous, unsuccessive, broken, interrupted, *décousu*; dis-, un-connected, discrete, disjunctive; fitful &c. (*irregular*) 139; spasmodic, desultory, intermit-ting &c. *v.*, -tent; alternate; recurrent &c. (*periodic*) 138; few and far between.

**Adv.** at intervals; by -snatches, - jerks, - skips, - catches, - fits and starts; skippingly, *per saltum*; *longo intervallo*.

---

**71. Term.—N.** term, rank, station, stage, step; degree &c. 26; scale, remove, grade, link, peg, round -, rung- of the ladder, *status*, position, place, point, mark, *pas*, period, pitch; stand, -ing; footing, range.

**V.** hold -, occupy -, fall into- a place &c. *n.*

### 3°. COLLECTIVE ORDER

**72. Assemblage.—N.** assemblage; col-lection, -location, -ligation; compilation, levy, gathering, ingathering, mobilization, meet, foregathering, muster, *attroupement*; con-course, -flux, -gregation, -tesseration, -vergence &c. 290; meeting, *levée*, *réunion*, drawing room, at home; conversazione &c. (*social gathering*) 892; assembly, congress, eisteddfod; conven-tion, -ticle;

**73. Non-assemblage. Dispersion.—N.** dispersion; disjunction &c. 44; divergence &c. 291; scattering &c. *v.*; dissemination, broadcasting, diffusion; dissipation, distribution; apportionment &c. 786; spread, respersion, circumfusion, interspersion, spargefaction.

waifs and estrays, flotsam and jetsam, *disjecta membra*.

**V.** disperse, scatter, sow, dissemi-

gemote; conclave, &c. (*council*) 696; posse, *posse comitatûs*; Noah's ark.

miscellany, *collectanea*, symposium; museum, menagerie, &c. (*store*) 636.

crowd, throng, multitude; flood, rush, deluge; rout, rabble, mob, press, crush, *cohue*, jam, horde, body, tribe; crew, gang, knot, squad, band, party; swarm, shoal, school, covey, flock, herd, drove, kennel; array, bevy, galaxy; *corps*, company, troop, *troupe*; army, force, regiment, &c. (*combatants*) 726; host &c. (*multitude*) 102; populousness.

clan, brotherhood, association &c. (*party*) 712.

volley, shower, storm, cloud.

group, cluster, Pleiades, clump, pencil; set, batch, lot, pack; budget, *dossier*, assortment, bunch; parcel; pack-et, -age; bundle, *fasciculus*, fascine, bale; ser-on, -oon; faggot, wisp, truss, tuft; shock, rick, fardel, stack, sheaf, swath, gavel, haycock, stook.

accumulation &c. (*store*) 636; congeries, heap, lump, pile, *rouleau*, tissue, mass, pyramid; drift; snow-ball, -drift; acervation, cumulation, amassment, glom-, agglom-eration; conglobation; conglomeration, -ate; coacervation, coagmentation, aggregation, concentration, congestion, *omnium gatherum*, *spicilegium*, black hole of Calcutta; quantity &c. (*greatness*) 31.

collector, gatherer; whip, -per in.

**V.** [be or come together] assemble, collect, muster; meet, unite, join, rejoin; cluster, flock, swarm, surge, stream, herd, crowd, throng, associate; con-gregate, -glomerate, -centrate; centre round, *rendezvous*, resort; come -, flock -, get -, pig- together; forgather; huddle; reassemble.

[get or bring together] assemble, muster, mobilize; bring -, get -, put -, draw -, scrape -, lump- together; col-lect, -locate, -ligate; get -, whip- in; gather; hold a meeting; con-vene, -voke, -vocate; rake up, dredge; heap, mass, pile; pack, put up, truss, cram; acervate; ag-glomerate, -gregate; compile; group, aggroup, concentrate, unite; collect -, bring- into a focus; amass, accumulate &c. (*store*) 636; collect in a drag-net; heap Ossa upon Pelion.

**Adj.** assembled &c. *v.*; closely packed, dense, serried, crowded to suffocation, teeming, swarming, populous; as thick as hops; all of a heap, fasciculated; cumulative.

**Phr.** the plot thickens.

nate, radiate, diffuse, shed, spread, ted, bestrew, overspread, dispense, disband, disembody, demobilize, dismember, distribute; apportion &c. 786; blow off, let out, dispel, cast forth, draught off; strew, straw, strow; spirtle, cast, sprinkle, spatter; issue, deal out, retail, utter; re-, inter-sperse; set abroach, circumfuse.

turn -, cast- adrift; scatter to the winds; sow broadcast.

spread like wildfire, disperse themselves.

**Adj.** unassembled &c. (*see* assemble &c. 72); dispersed &c. *v.*; sparse, dispread, broadcast, sporadic, widespread; far-flung; epidemic &c. (*general*) 78; adrift, stray; dishevelled, streaming.

**Adv.** *sparsim*, here and there, *passim*.

**74.** [Place of meeting.] **Focus.**—**N.** focus; point of- convergence &c. 290; corradiation; centre &c. 222; gathering-place, resort; haunt; retreat; *venue, rendezvous*; rallying point, headquarters, home, club; *dépôt* &c. (*store*) 636; tryst, trysting-place; place of -meeting, - resort, - assignation; *point de -, lieu de- réunion*; issue.

**V.** bring to- a point, - a focus, - an issue; focus.

### 4°. DISTRIBUTIVE ORDER

**75. Class.**—**N.** class, category, *categorema*, head, order, section; division, subdivision; department, province, domain, sphere.

kind, sort, genus, species, variety, branch, family, race, tribe, caste, sept, clan, breed; *clique, coterie*; type, kit, sect, set; assortment; feather, kidney; suit; range; gender, sex, kin.

manner, description, denomination, persuasion, connection, designation, character, stamp; predicament; conviction &c. 484.

similarity &c. 17.

**76. Inclusion.** [Comprehension under, or reference to a class.]—**N.** inclusion, admission, incorporation, comprehension, reception.

composition &c. (*inclusion in a compound*) 54.

**V.** be -included in &c.; come –, fall –, range- under; belong –, pertain- to; range with; merge in.

include, compromise, comprehend, contain, admit, embrace, receive; enclose &c. (*circumscribe*) 229; incorporate, cover, embody, encircle.

reckon –, enumerate –, number- among; refer to; place –, arrange-under; – with; take into account.

**Adj.** includ-ed, -ing &c. *v.*; inclusive; comprehensive, all-embracing; congen-er, -erous: of the same -class &c. 75.

**Phr.** *et hoc genus omne*, &c.; *et cætera*.

**77. Exclusion.\*—N.** exclusion &c. 55.

---

**78. Generality.** — **N.** general-ity, -ization; universality; catholic-ity, -ism; miscel-lany, -laneousness; dragnet.

every-one, -body; all hands, all the world and his wife; any body, N or M, all sorts; *tout le monde*.

prevalence, run.

**V.** be -general &c. *adj.*; prevail, obtain, be going about, stalk abroad.

render -general &c. *adj.*; generalize; spread, broadcast.

**Adj.** general, usual, current, generic, collective; broad, comprehensive, sweeping; encyclopedical, panoramic, widespread &c. (*dispersed*) 73.

universal; catho-lic, -lical; common, world-wide; œc-, e-cumenical; transcendental; prevalent, prevailing, rife, epidemic, besetting; all over, covered with.

every, all; indeterminate, indefinite. unspecified, impersonal.

customary &c. (*habitual*) 613.

**Adv.** what-ever, -soever; to a man, one and all, without exception.

generally &c. *adj.*; always, for better

**79. Speciality.—N.** speciality, *spécialité*; individ-uality, -uity; particularity, peculiarity; idiocrasy &c. (*tendency*) 176; personality, characteristic, mannerism, idiosyncrasy, attribute, specificness &c. *adj.*; singularity &c. (*unconformity*) 83; reading, version, lection; state; *trait*; distinctive feature; technicality; *differentia*.

particulars, details, minutiæ, items, counts.

I, self, I myself, *ego*; my-, him-, her-, it-self.

**V.** specify, particularize, individualize, realize, specialize, designate, differentiate, determine, define, denote, indicate, itemize, detail.

descend to particulars, enter into detail, come to the point.

**Adj.** special, particular, individual, specific, proper, personal, intimate, original, private, respective, definite, concrete, determinate, especial, certain, esoteric, endemic, partial, party, peculiar, marked, appropriate, several, characteristic, diagnostic, exact, exclusive; singular &c. (*exceptional*) 83;

---

\* The same set of words is used to express *Exclusion from a class* and *Exclusion from a compound*. Reference is therefore made to the former at 55. This identity does not occur with regard to *Inclusion*, which therefore constitutes a separate category.

for worse; in general, generally speaking; speaking generally; for the most part; in the long run &c. (*on an average*) 29.

———

respectively, each to each; *seriatim*, in detail, bit by bit; *pro hac vice, – re natâ*.

namely, that is to say, *videlicet*, viz.; to wit; i.e., e.g.

idiomatic; typical, representative, distinctive.

this, that; yon, -der.

Adv. specially &c. *adj.*; in particular, *in propriâ personâ*; *ad hominem*; for my part.

each, apiece, one by one; severally,

## 5°. Order as regards Categories

**80. Rule.**—N. regularity, uniformity &c. 16; clock-work precision; punctuality &c. (*exactness*) 494; routine &c. (*custom*) 613; formula; system; rut; canon, convention, maxim; rule &c. (*form, regulation*) 697; key-note, standard, model; precedent &c. (*prototype*) 22; conformity &c. 82.

nature, principle; law; order of things; normal –, natural –, ordinary –, model- -state, – condition; standing -dish, – order; normality; Procrustean law; law of the Medes and Persians; hard and fast rule.

Adj. regular, uniform, symmetrical, constant, steady; according to rule &c. (*conformable*) 82; customary &c. 613; orderly &c. 58.

**82. Conformity.**—N. conform-ity, -ance; observance.

naturalization; conventionality &c. (*custom*) 613; agreement &c. 23.

example, instance, specimen, sample, quotation; exemplification, illustration, case in point; object lesson.

conventionalist, formalist, Philistine. pattern &c. (*prototype*) 22.

V. conform to, – rule; accommodate –, adapt- oneself to; rub off corners.

be -regular &c. *adj.*; move in a groove; follow –, observe –, go by –, bend to –, obey- -rules, – precedents; comply –, tally –, chime in –, fall in-with; be -guided, – regulated- by; fall into a -custom, – usage; follow the -fashion, – multitude; pass muster, do as others do, *hurler avec les loups*; do at Rome as the Romans do; go –, swim- with the stream, current, – tide; tread the beaten track &c. (*habit*) 613; rubber-stamp; keep one in countenance.

exemplify, illustrate, cite, quote, put

**81. Multiformity.**—N. multi-, omniformity; variety, diversity; multifariousness &c. *adj.*

Adj. multi-form, -fold, -farious, -generous; multiplex, variform, manifold, many-sided, multiplicate; omni-form, -genous, -farious; polymorphic; protean; heterogeneous, motley, mosaic; epicene, indiscriminate, desultory, irregular, diversified, different, divers; all manner of; of -every description, – all sorts and kinds; *et hoc genus omne*; and what not? *de omnibus rebus et quibusdam aliis.*

———

**83. Unconformity.**—N. non-conformity &c. 82; un-, dis-conformity; unconventionality, informality, abnormity, anomaly; anomalousness &c. *adj.*; exception, peculiarity, &c. 79; infraction –, breach –, violation –, infringement- of -law, – custom, – usage; eccentricity, *bizarrerie*, oddity, *je ne sais quoi*, monstrosity, rarity; freak of Nature.

individuality, idiosyncrasy, singularity, originality, mannerism.

aberration; irregularity; variety; singularity; exemption; *salvo* &c. (*qualification*) 469.

nonconformist; nondescript, character, original, nonsuch, monster, prodigy, wonder, miracle, curiosity, missing link, flying fish, black swan, *lusus naturæ*, *rara avis*, queer fish; mongrel; half-caste, -blood, -breed; *métis*, cross breed, hybrid, mule, mulatto, sacatra, marabou; *tertium quid*, hermaphrodite, gynander, androgyn.

phœnix, chimera, hydra, sphinx, minotaur; griff-in, -on; centaur; hippo-

a case; produce an- instance &c. *n.*

**Adj.** conformable to rule, adaptable, compliant, consistent, agreeable; regular &c. 80; according to -regulation, - rule, - Cocker; *en règle, selon les règles,* well regulated, orderly; symmetric &c. 242.

conventional, commonplace &c. (*customary*) 613; of -daily, - every day-occurrence; in the natural order of things; ordinary, common, - or garden, prosaic, habitual, usual.

in the order of the day; naturalized.

typical, normal, formal; canonical, orthodox, sound, strict, rigid, positive, uncompromising, Procrustean; point device.

*secundum artem,* ship-shape, technical. exemplary, illustrative, in point.

**Adv.** conformably &c. *adj.*; by rule; agreeably to; in -conformity, - accordance, - keeping- with; according to; consistently with; as usual, *ad instar, instar omnium; more -solito, - majorum.*

for the sake of conformity; of -, as a matter of- course; *pro formâ,* for form's sake, by the card; according to plan.

invariably &c. (*uniformly*) 16.

for -example, - instance; *exempli gratiâ; e.g.; inter alia.*

**Phr.** *cela va sans dire; ex pede Herculem, noscitur a sociis.*

griff, -centaur; sagittary; kraken, cockatrice, wyvern, roc, liver, dragon, sea-serpent; mermaid; unicorn; Cyclops, 'men whose heads do grow beneath their shoulders'; Teratology.

fish out of water; neither -one thing nor another, - fish flesh nor fowl nor good red herring; one in a -way, - thousand; out-cast, -law; Ishmael, pariah; oasis.

**V.** be -unconformable &c. *adj.*; leave the beaten -track, - path; infringe -, break -, violate- a -law, - habit, - usage, - custom; drive a coach and six through; stretch a point; have no business there; baffle -, beggar- all description.

**Adj.** unconformable, exceptional; abnorm-al, -ous; anomal-ous, -istic; out of -order, - place, - keeping, - tune, - one's element; irregular, arbitrary; lawless, informal, aberrant, stray, wandering, wanton; peculiar, exclusive, unnatural, eccentric, crotchety, egregious; out of the -beaten track, - common, - common run, - pale of; misplaced; funny.

un-usual, -accustomed, -customary, -wonted, -common; rare, singular, unique, curious, odd, extraordinary, strange, monstrous; wonderful &c. 870; unexpected, unaccountable; *outré,* out of the way, remarkable, noteworthy; queer, quaint, nondescript, none such, *sui generis;* original, unconventional, Bohemian, unfashionable; un-described, -precedented, -paralleled, -exampled, -heard of, -familiar; fantastic, new-fangled, grotesque, *bizarre;* outlandish, exotic, *tombé des nues,* preternatural; denaturalized.

heterogeneous, heteroclite, amorphous, mongrel, amphibious, epicene, half-blood, hybrid; androgyn-ous, -al; unsymmetric &c. 243. qualified &c. 469.

**Adv.** unconformably &c. *adj.*; except, unless, save, barring, beside, without, save and except, let alone.

however, yet, but.

**Int.** what -on earth! - in the world!

**Phr.** never was -seen, - heard, - known- the like.

## Section V. NUMBER

### 1°. Number, in the Abstract

**84. Number.—N.** number, symbol, numeral, figure, cipher, digit, integer; counter; round number; formula; function; series.

sum, total, aggregate, difference, complement, subtrahend; product; multipli-cand, -er, -cator; coefficient, multiple; dividend, divisor, factor, quotient, sub-multiple, fraction; mixed number; numerator, denominator; decimal, circulating decimal, repetend; common measure, aliquot part; reciprocal; prime number; totitive, totient.

permutation, combination, variation; election.

ratio, proportion; progression; arithmetical –, geometrical –, harmonical- progression; percentage.

figurate –, pyramidal –, polygonal- numbers.

power, root, exponent, index, logarithm, antilogarithm; modulus; differential, integral, fluxion, fluent.

**Adj.** numeral, complementary, divisible, aliquot, reciprocal, prime, fractional, decimal, figurate, incommensurable.

proportional, exponential, logarithmic, logometric, differential, fluxional, integral.

positive, negative; rational, irrational; surd, radical, real, imaginary, impossible.

**85. Numeration.—N.** numeration; numbering &c. *v.*; pagination; tale, tally, recension, enumeration, summation, reckoning, computation, supputation; calcu-lation, -lus; algorithm, rhabdology, dactylonomy; measurement &c. 466; statistics.

arithmetic, analysis, algebra, fluxions; differential –, integral –, infinitesimal- calculus; calculus of differences.

[Statistics] dead reckoning, muster, poll, census, capitation, roll-call, recapitulation; account &c. (*list*) 86.

[Operations] notation, addition, subtraction, multiplication, division, proportion, rule of three, practice, equations, extraction of roots, reduction, involution, evolution, approximation, interpolation, differentiation, integration.

[Instruments] abacus, swan-pan, logometer, sliding –, slide- rule, tallies, Napier's bones, calculating –, adding- machine, difference engine; cash register.

arithmetician, calculator, abacist; mathematician, actuary, statistician, surveyor, geodesist.

**V.** number, count, tell; call –, run- over, take an account of, enumerate, call the roll, muster, poll, recite, recapitulate; sum; sum –, cast- up; tell off, score, cipher, compute, calculate, set a price, reckon, – up, estimate; suppute, add, subtract, multiply, divide, extract roots.

check, prove, demonstrate, balance, audit, overhaul, take stock; affix numbers to, page, foliate, paginate.

amount –, come- to.

**Adj.** numer-al, -ical; arithmetical, analytic, algebraic, statistical, numerable, computable, calculable; commensur-able, -ate; incommensur-able, -ate.

**86. List.—N.** list, catalogue, enumeration, inventory, schedule; register &c. (*record*) 551; account; bill, – of costs; syllabus; terrier, tally, file; almanac, calendar, index, table, atlas, contents, card index; rota, ticket; book, ledger; synopsis, *catalogue raisonné*; *tableau*; scroll, manifest, invoice, bill of lading; prospectus, *programme*; bill of fare, *menu*, *carto*; *score*, census, statistics, returns, Red –, Blue –, Domesday- book; *cadastre*; directory, gazetteer, dictionary, glossary, lexicon, thesaurus, gradus.

roll; check –, chequer –, bead- roll, – of honour; muster -roll, – book; roster, panel; cartulary, diptych.

V. list, enrol, schedule, register &c. *n.*; indent, post, docket; matriculate.

Adj. cadastral, listed &c. *v.*

## 2°. DETERMINATE NUMBER

**87. Unity.**—**N.** unity; oneness &c. *adj.*; individuality; solitude &c. (*seclusion*) 893; isolation &c. (*disjunction*) 44; unification &c. 48.

one, unit, ace; item; individual; solo, none else, no other, naught beside.

**V.** be -one, – alone &c. *adj.*; dine with Duke Humphrey.

isolate &c. (*disjoin*) 44.

render one; unite &c. (*join*) 43, (*combine*) 48.

**Adj.** one, sole, single, solitary, only-begotten; individual, apart, alone; kithless.

un-accompanied, -attended; *solus*, single-handed; singular, odd, unique, unrepeated, azygous, first and last; isolated &c. (*disjoined*) 44; insular; unitary.

lone; lone-ly, -some; desolate, dreary.

in-secable, -severable, -discerptible; compact, irresolvable.

**Adv.** singly &c. *adj.*; alone, by itself, *per se*, only, apart, in the singular number, in the abstract; one -by one, – at a time; simply; one and a half, *sesqui-.*

**Phr.** *natura il fece, e poi roppe la stampa.*

**88. Accompaniment.**—**N.** accompaniment; appurtenance, adjunct &c. 39; context.

coexistence, concomitance, company, association, companionship; part-, co-part-nership; coefficiency.

concomitant, accessory, coefficient; companion, attendant, fellow, associate, consort, spouse, colleague, *fidus Achates*; part-, co-part-ner; satellite, hanger on, shadow; escort, *entourage*, suite, *cortège*; convoy, follower &c. 65; attribute.

**V.** accompany, coexist, attend, convoy, chaperon; hang –, wait- on; go hand in hand with; synchronize &c. 120; bear –, keep- company; row in the same boat; bring in its train, associate –, couple- with.

**Adj.** accompanying &c. *v.*; concomitant, fellow, twin, joint; associated –, coupled- with; accessory, attendant, *obbligato.*

**Adv.** with, withal; together –, along –, in company- with; hand in hand, side by side; cheek by -jowl, – jole; arm in arm; there-, here-with; and &c. (*addition*) 37.

together, in a body, collectively.

---

**89. Duality.**—**N.** dual-ity, -ism; duplicity; bi-plicity, -formity; span, polarity.

two, deuce, couple, couplet, doublet, brace, pair, cheeks, twins, Castor and Pollux, *gemini*, Siamese twins; fellows; yoke, conjugation, dyad, distich.

**V.** [unite in pairs] pair, couple, bracket, yoke; conduplicate, mate.

**Adj.** two, twain; dual, -istic; binary, binomial; twin, biparous; dyadic; conduplicate; duplex &c. 90; *tête-à-tête*; paired; dihedral.

coupled &c. *v.*; conjugate.

both, – the one and the other.

**90. Duplication.**—**N.** duplication; doubling &c. *v.*; gemi-, ingemi-nation; reduplication; iteration &c. (*repetition*) 104; renewal.

**V.** double; re-double, -duplicate; geminate; repeat &c. 104; renew &c. 660; duplicate, copy &c. 21.

**Adj.** double; doubled &c. *v.*; bicam-eral, bicapital, bi-fold, -form, -lateral,

**91.** [Division into two parts.] **Bisection.**—**N.** bi-section, -partition; di-, subdi-chotomy; halving &c. *v.*; dimidiation; *hendiadys.*

bifurcation, forking, branching, furcation, ramification, divarication; fork; prong; fold.

half, moiety.

**V.** bisect, halve, divide, split, cut in

-farious, -facial; two-fold, -sided, -headed, -edged &c.; duplex; double-faced; twin, duplicate, ingeminate; second; dual &c. 89.

Adv. twice, once more; over again &c. (*repeatedly*) 104; as much again, twofold.

secondly, in the second place, again.

two, cleave, dimidiate, dichotomize, divaricate.

go halves, divide with.

separate, fork, bifurcate; branch -off, ~ out; ramify.

Adj. bisected &c. *v.*; cloven, cleft; bipartite, biconjugate, bicuspid, bifid; bifur-cous, -cate, -cated; semi-, demi-hemi-.

**92. Triality.**—**N.** triality, trinity,* triplicity.

three, triad, triplet, trey, trio, ternion, trinomial, leash; tierce; tri-ennium; trefoil, triangle, trident, tripod, triumvirate, *troika*.

third power, cube.

Adj. three; tri-form, -nal, -nomial; tertiary; triune.

**93. Triplication.**—**N.** tripli-cation, -city; trebleness, trine, trilogy.

**V.** treble, triple, triplicate, cube.

Adj. treble, triple; tern, -ary; triplex, triplicate, threefold, trilogistic; third; trinal; trihedral.

Adv. three -times, - fold; thrice, in the third place, thirdly; trebly &c. *adj.*

**94. [Division into three parts.] Tri-section.** — **N.** tri-section, -partition, -chotomy; third, - part.

**V.** trisect, divide into three parts, trifurcate.

Adj. trifid; trisected &c. *v.*; tri partite, -chotomous, -sulcate.

**95. Quaternity.**—**N.** quaternity, four, tetrad, quartet, quaternion, square, quadrature, quarter, quadruplet; quadrilateral, quadrangle, quatrefoil; *quadriga*.

**V.** reduce to a square, square.

Adj. four; quat-ernary, -ernal; quadratic; quartile, quartic, tetractic. tetrad, tetrahedral; quadrennial; quadrivalent.

**96. Quadruplication.**—**N.** quadrupli-cation.

**V.** multiply by four, quadruplicate, biquadrate.

Adj. fourfold; quad-ruple, -ruplicate, -rible; quadruplex; fourth.

Adv. four times; in the fourth place, fourthly.

**97. [Division into four parts.] Quad-risection.**—**N.** quadri-section, -parti-tion; quartering &c. *v.*; fourth; quart, -er, -ern; farthing (*i.e.* fourthing); quarto.

**V.** quarter, divide into four parts, quadrisect.

Adj. quartered &c. *v.*; quadri-fid, -partite.

**98. Five, &c.**—**N.** five, cinque, quint, quincunx, quintuplet, quintet, penta-gon, pentameter, Pentateuch; six, half-a-dozen, sextet, hexagon, hexameter; seven, Heptarchy; eight, octet, octa-gon, octave; nine, three times three; ten, decade; eleven; twelve, dozen; thirteen; long -, baker's- dozen.

twenty, score; twenty-four, four and twenty, two dozen; twenty-five, five

**99. Quinquesection, &c.**—**N.** divi-sion by -five &c. 98; quinquesection &c.; fifth &c.; decimation.

**V.** decimate, quinquesect.

Adj. quinque-fid, -partite; quinquar-ticular; octifid; decimal, tenth, tithe, teind; duodecimal, twelfth; sexa-gesi-mal, -genary; hundredth, centesimal, millesimal &c.

and twenty, quarter of a hundred; forty, two score; fifty, half a hundred; sixty, three score, sexagenarian; seventy, three score and ten, septuagenarian; eighty, four score, octogenarian; ninety, four score and ten, nonagenarian.

* *Trinity* is hardly ever used except in a theological sense; *see* Deity 976.

hundred, centenary, hecatomb, century; hundredweight, cwt.; one hundred and forty-four, gross; bicentenary, tercentenary &c.

thousand, chiliad; myriad, millennium, ten thousand; lac, lakh, one hundred thousand, plum; million; thousand million, *milliard*. billion, trillion &c.

**V.** centuriate.

**Adj.** five, quinary, quintuple; fifth; senary, sextuple; sixth; seventh; octuple; eighth; ninefold, ninth; tenfold, decimal, denary, decuple, tenth; eleventh; duo-denary, -denal; twelfth; in one's 'teens, thirteenth.

vices-, viges-imal; twentieth; twenty-fourth &c. *n.*

cent-uple, -uplicate, -ennial, -enary, -urial; secular, hundredth; thousandth; millenary &c.

### 3°. Indeterminate Number

**100.** [More than one.] **Plurality.—N.** plurality; a -number, – certain number; one or ⁺wo, two or three &c.; a few, several; multitude &c. 102.

**Adj.** plural, more than one, upwards of, some, certain; not -alone &c. 87.

**Adv.** *et cætera,* &c., etc.

**Phr.** *non deficit alter.*

**100a.** [Less than one.] **Fraction.—N.** fraction, fractional part, fragment; part &c. 51.

**Adj.** fractional, fragmentary, partial.

**101. Zero.—N.** zero, nothing naught, nought, duck's egg, goose egg; cipher, none, nobody; not a soul; *âme qui vive;* absence &c. 187; unsubstantiality &c. 4.

**Adj.** not -one, – any.

**102. Multitude.—N.** multitude; numerousness &c. *adj.*; numer-osity, -ality; multiplicity; profusion &c. (*plenty*) 639; legion, host; great –, large –, round –, enormous- number; a quantity, numbers, array, sight, army, sea, galaxy; scores, peck, bushel, school, shoal, swarm, draft, bevy, cloud, flock. herd, drove, flight, covey, hive, brood, litter, farrow, fry, nest; mob, crowd &c. (*assemblage*) 72; lots, loads, heaps; all the world and his wife.

[Increase of number] greater number, majority; multiplication, multiple.

**V.** be -numerous &c. *adj.*; swarm –. teem –, crawl –, creep -with; crowd, swarm, come thick upon; outnumber, multiply; people; swarm like -locusts, – bees; be alive with.

**Adj.** many, several, sundry, divers, various, not a few; a -hundred, – thousand, – myriad, – million, – thousand and one; some -ten or a dozen, – forty or fifty &c.; half a -dozen, – hundred &c.; very –, full –, ever so- many; numer-ous, -ose; profuse, in profusion; manifold, multiplied, multitudinous, multiferous, multiple, multinomial, teeming, crawling, populous, peopled, crowded, thick, studded; galore.

thick coming, many more, more than one can tell, a world of; no end -of, – to; *cum multis aliis;* thick as -hops, – hail; plenty as blackberries; numerous as the -stars in the firmament, – sands on

**103. Fewness.—N.** fewness &c. *adj.*; paucity, small number; small quantity &c. 32; scarcity, sparsity; rarity; infrequency &c. 137; handful; maniple; minority, exiguity.

[Diminution of number] reduction; weeding &c. *v.*; elimination, sarculation, decimation.

**V.** be -few &c. *adj.*

render -few &c. *adj.*; reduce, diminish the number, weed, eliminate, thin decimate.

**Adj.** few; scarce; scant, -y; thin, rare, thinly scattered, few and far between; exiguous; infrequent &c. 137; *rari nantes;* hardly –, scarcely- any; to be counted on one's fingers; reduced &c. *v.*; unrepeated.

**Adv.** here and there.

...e sea-shore, – hairs on the head; and -what not, – heaven knows
what; endless &c. (*infinite*) 105.

Phr. their name is 'Legion.'

**104. Repetition.—N.** repetition, iteration, reiteration, duplication,
ding-dong, alliteration; *epistrophe*; harping, recurrence, succession, run;
batto-, tauto-logy; monotony, tautophony; rhythm &c. 138; pleonasm,
redundancy, diffuseness.

chimes, repetend, echo, *ritornello*, burden of a song, *refrain*; rehearsal;
encore; *réchauffé*, *rifacimento*, recapitulation.

cuckoo &c. (*imitation*) 19; reverberation &c. 408; drumming &c.
(*roll*) 407; renewal &c. (*restoration*) 660.

twice-told tale; old -story, – song, chestnut; second –, new- edition;
reprint, new impression; return game, return match, reappearance,
reproduction; periodicity &c. 138.

**V.** repeat, iterate, reiterate, reproduce, parrot, echo, re-echo, drum,
harp upon, battologize, hammer, redouble.

recur, revert, return, reappear; renew &c. (*restore*) 660.

rehearse; do –, say- over again; ring the changes on; harp on the
same string; din –, drum- in the ear; conjugate in all its moods, tenses
and inflexions, begin again, go over the same ground, go the same round,
never hear the last of; resume, return to, recapitulate, reword.

**Adj.** repeated &c. *v.*; repetition-al, -ary; recur-rent, -ring; ever
recurring, thick coming; frequent, incessant, redundant, pleonastic,
tautological.

monotonous, harping, iterative; mocking, chiming; retold; aforesaid,
-named; above-mentioned, said; habitual &c. 613; another.

**Adv.** repeatedly, often, again, afresh, anew, over again, once more;
ditto, *encore, de novo, bis, da capo.*

again and again; over and over, – again; many times over; time-
and again, – after time; year after year; day by day &c.; many –,
several –, a number of- times; many –, full many- a time; times out of
number, year in and year out, morning, noon and night; frequently
&c. 136.

**Phr.** *ecce iterum Crispinus, toujours perdrix*, cut and come again;
'tomorrow and tomorrow.'

**105. Infinity.—N.** infini-ty, -tude, -teness &c. *adj.*; perpetuity &c. 112.

**V.** be -infinite &c. *adj.*; know –, have- no -limits, – bounds; go on
for ever.

**Adj.** infinite; immense; number-, count-, sum-, measure-less; in
numer-, immeasur-, incalcul-, illimit-, intermin-, unfathom-, unap-
proach-able; exhaustless, inexhaustible, indefinite; without -number,
– measure, – limit, – end; incomprehensible; limit-, end-, bound-, term-
less; un-told, -numbered, -measured, -bounded, -limited; illimited;
perpetual &c. 112.

**Adv.** infinitely &c. *adj.*; *ad infinitum.*

## Section VI. TIME

### 1°. Absolute Time

**106. Time.—N.** time, duration;
period, term, stage, space, span, spell,
season; the whole -time, – period;
course &c. 109.

**107. Neverness.*—N.** 'neverness';
absence of time, no time; *dies non*,
Tib's eve; Greek Kalends.

**Adv.** never; at no -time, – period;

\* A term introduced by Bishop Wilkins.

intermediate time, while, *interim*, interval, bit, pendency; inter-vention, -mission, -mittence, -regnum, -lude; respite.

era, epoch, æon, cycle; time of life, age, year, date; decade &c. (*period*) 108; moment, &c. (*instant*) 113; reign &c. 737.

glass –, ravages –, whirligig –, noiseless foot- of time; scythe.

**V.** continue, last, endure, go on, hold out, remain, stay, persist, abide, run; intervene; elapse &c. 109.

take –, take up –, fill –, occupy- time.

pass –, pass away –, spend –, while away –, consume –, talk against –, kill- time; tide over; use –, employ- time; tarry &c. 110; seize an opportunity &c. 134; waste time &c. (*be inactive*) 683.

**Adj.** continuing &c. *v.*; on foot; permanent &c. (*durable*) 110.

**Adv.** while, whilst, during, pending; during the -time, – interval; in the course of; for the time being, day by day; in the time of, when; mean-time, -while; in the -meantime, – *interim*; *ad interim*, *pendente lite*; *de die in diem*; from -day to day, – hour to hour &c.; hourly, always; for a -time, – season; till, until, up to, yet; the whole –, all the- time; all along; throughout &c. (*completely*) 52; for good &c. (*diuturnity*) 110.

here-, there-, where-upon; then; *anno*, – *Domini*; A.D.; *ante Christum*; A.C.; before Christ; B.C.; *anno urbis conditæ*; A.U.C.; *anno regni*; A.R.; once upon a time, one fine morning.

**Phr.** time -runs, – runs against; *tempus fugit*.

on no occasion, never in all one's born days, nevermore, *sine die*.

---

**108.** [Definite duration, or portion of time.] **Period.**—**N.** period; second, minute, hour, day, week, sennight, octave, month, moon, quarter, semester, year, *lustrum*, *quinquennium*, decade, *decennium*, indiction, lifetime, generation, epoch, era, cycle.

century, age, *millennium*; *annus magnus*.

**Adj.** horary; hourly, annual &c. (*periodical*) 138.

**108a. Contingent Duration.**—**Adv.** during -pleasure, – good behaviour; *quamdiu se bene gesserit*.

---

**109.** [Indefinite duration.] **Course.**—**N.** course –, progress –, process –, succession –, lapse –, flow –, flux –, effluxion, stream –, tract –, current –, sweep –, tide –, march –, step –, flight- of time; duration &c. 106.

[Indefinite time] aorist.

**V.** elapse, lapse, flow, run, proceed, advance, pass; roll –, wear –, press –, drag- on; flit, fly, slip, slide, glide, crawl; run -its course.

out; expire; go –, pass- by; be -past &c. 122.

**Adj.** elapsing &c. *v.*; aoristic; progressive, transient &c. 111.

**Adv.** in due -time, – season; in -course, – process, – the fulness- of time; in time.

**Phr.** *labitur et labetur*; *truditur dies die*; *fugaces labuntur anni*; 'tomorrow and tomorrow and tomorrow creeps in this petty pace from day to day.'

---

**110.** [Long duration.] **Diuturnity.**—**N.** diuturnity; a -long –, length of- time; an age, a century, an eternity,

**111.** [Short duration.] **Transientness.**—**N.** transientness &c. *adj.*; evanescence, impermanence, fugacity, transi-

æons; slowness &c. 275; perpetuity &c. 112; blue moon.

dura-bleness, -bility; persistence, lastingness &c. *adj.*; continuance, assiduity, endurance, standing; permanence &c. (*stability*) 150; survi-val, -vance; longevity &c. (*age*) 128; distance of time.

protraction –, prolongation –, extension- of time; delay &c. (*lateness*) 133.

**V.** last, endure, stand, remain, abide, continue, brave a thousand years.

tarry &c. (*be late*) 133; drag -on, – its slow length along, – a lengthening chain; protract, prolong; spin –, eke –, draw –, lengthen- out; temporize; gain –, make –, talk against- time.

out-last, -live; survive; live to fight again.

**Adj.** durable; perdurable; lasting &c. *v.*; of long -duration, – standing; permanent, chronic, long-standing; intransi-ent, -tive; intransmutable, persistent; life-, live-long; longeval, long-lived, macrobiotic, diuturnal, sempervirent, evergreen, perennial; unin-, ter-, unre-mitting; perpetual &c. 112.

lingering, protracted, prolonged, spun out &c. *v.*; long-pending, -winded; slow &c. 275.

**Adv.** long; for -a long time, – an age, – ages, – ever so long, – many a long day; long ago &c. (*in a past time*) 122; *longo intervallo.*

all the -day long, – year round; the livelong day, as the day is long, morning, noon and night; hour after hour, day after day, &c.; for good; permanently &c. *adj.*

**112.** [Endless duration.] **Perpetuity.**
—**N.** perpetuity, eternity, timelessness; everness,* aye, sempiternity, immortality, athanasia; everlastingness &c. *adj.*; perpetuation; infinite duration.

**V.** last –, endure –, go on- for ever; have no end.

eternize, eternify, perpetuate, immortalize.

**Adj.** perpetual, eternal, eterne; everlasting, -living, -flowing; continual, constant, sempiternal, co-eternal; endless, unending; ceaseless, incessant, uninterrupted, indesinent, unceasing; interminable, having no end; unfad-

toriness, volatility, caducity, mortality, span; flash in the pan, nine days' wonder, bubble, May-fly; spurt; temporary arrangement, interregnum.

velocity &c. 274; suddenness &c. 113; changeableness &c. 149.

**V.** be -transient &c. *adj.*; flit, pass away, fly, gallop, vanish, fade, fleet, melt away, evaporate; pass away like a -cloud, – summer cloud, – shadow, – dream.

**Adj.** transi-ent, -tory, -tive; passing, evanescent, fleeting; flying &c. *v.*; fug-acious, -itive; shifting, slippery; spasmodic.

tempor-al, -ary; provis-ional, -ory; cursory, short-lived, ephemeral, deciduous; perishable, mortal, precarious; impermanent.

brief, quick, brisk; cometary, meteoric, extemporaneous, summary; pressed for time &c. (*haste*) 684; sudden, momentary &c. (*instantaneous*) 113.

**Adv.** temporarily &c. *adj.*; *pro tempore*; for -the moment, – a time; awhile, *en passant, in transitu*; in a short time; soon &c. (*early*) 132; briefly &c. *adj.*; at short notice; on the -point, – eve -of; *in articulo*; between cup and lip.

**Phr.** one's days are numbered; the time is up; here to-day and gone to-morrow; *non semper erit æstas; eheu! fugaces labuntur anni; sic transit gloria mundi.*

---

**113.** [Point of time.] **Instantaneity.**
—**N.** instantane-ity, -ousness; sudden-, abrupt-ness.

moment, instant, second, minute; twinkling, trice, flash, breath, crack, jiffy, *coup*, burst, flash of lightning, stroke of time.

epoch, time; time of -day, – night; hour, minute; very -minute &c., – time, – hour; present -, right -, true -, exact -, correct- time.

**V.** be -instantaneous &c. *adj.*; twinkle, flash.

**Adj.** instantaneous, momentary, extempore, sudden, instant, abrupt;

ing, evergreen, amaranthine; never-ending, -dying, -fading; deathless, immortal, undying, imperishable.

**Adv.** perpetually &c. *adj.*; always, ever, evermore, aye; for -ever, – aye, – evermore, – ever and a day, – ever and ever; in all ages, from age to age; without end; world –, time- without end; *in sæcula sæculorum*; to the -end of time, – crack of doom, – 'last syllable of recorded time'; till doomsday; constantly &c. (*very frequently*) 136.

**Phr.** *esto perpetua!; labitur et labetur in omne volubilis ævum.*

subitaneous, hasty; quick as -thought,* – lightning, – a flash; rapid as electricity.

**Adv.** instantaneously &c. *adj.*; in –, in less than- no time; *presto, subito, instanter*, suddenly, at a stroke, like- a shot, – greased lightning; in a trice, in a moment &c. *n.*; eftsoons, in the twinkling of -an eye, – a bed post; at one jump, in the same breath, *per saltum, uno saltu;* at –, all at- once; in one's tracks; plump, slap; 'at one fell swoop'; at the same -instant &c. | *n.*; immediately &c. (*early*) 132; | extempore, on the -spot, – spur of the | moment, – dot; just then; slap- dash &c. (*haste*) 684; before you could -turn round, – say -knife, – Jack Robinson.
**Phr.** touch and go; no sooner said than done.

---

**114.** [Estimation, measurement, and record of time.] **Chronometry.**—N. chrono-, horo-metry, -logy; date, epoch; style, era, age.

almanac, calendar, ephemeris; register, -try; chronicle, annals, journal, diary, chronogram.

[Instruments for the measurement of time] clock, watch; chrono-meter, -scope, -graph; repeater, alarum; time-keeper, -piece; dial, sun-dial, *gnomon, pendule*, horologe, pendulum, hour-glass, water clock, clepsydra.

mean –, Greenwich –, solar –, sidereal –, local –, summer- time; daylight saving.

chrono-grapher, -loger, -logist; annalist.

**V.** fix –, mark- the time; date, register, chronicle; measure –, beat –, mark- time; bear date.

**Adj.** chrono-logical, -metrical, -grammatical; isochronal.

**Adv.** o'clock; *a.m., p.m.*

**115.** [False estimate of time.] **Anachronism.**—N. ana-, meta-, para-, pro-chronism; *prolepsis*, misdate; anticipation, antichronism.

disregard –, neglect –, oblivion- of time.

intempestivity &c. 135.

**V.** mis-, ante-, post-, over-date; anticipate; take no note of time.

**Adj.** misdated &c. *v.*; undated; overdue; out of date; anachronous &c. *n.*

---

## 2°. RELATIVE TIME

### 1. *Time with reference to Succession*

**116. Priority.**—N. priority, antecedence, anteriority, pre-existence, precedence &c. 62; precession &c. 280; precursor &c. 64; the past &c. 122; premises.

**V.** precede, come before; forerun; antecede, go before &c. (*lead*) 280; pre-exist; dawn; premise, presage &c. 511.

be -beforehand &c. (*be early*) 132;

**117. Posteriority.**—N. posteriority; succession, sequence; following &c. 281; subsequence, supervention; futurity &c. 121; successor; sequel &c. 65; remainder, reversion.

**V.** follow &c. 281 –, come –, go-after; ensue, result; succeed, supervene; step into the shoes of.

**Adj.** subsequent, posterior, following, after, later, succeeding, postliminious,

* See note on 264.

steal a march upon, anticipate, fore-
stall; have –, gain- the start.

**Adj.** prior, previous; preced-ing, -ent;
anterior, antecedent; pre-existing, -ex-
istent; foresighted; former, foregoing;
afore –, before-, above-mentioned;
aforesaid, said; introductory &c. (*pre-
cursory*) 64; pre-war.

**Adv.** before, prior to; earlier; pre-
viously &c. *adj.*; afore, ere, thereto-
fore, erewhile; ere –, before- -then, –
now; erewhile, already, yet, before-
hand; aforetime, on the eve of, in
anticipation.

**118. The Present Time.—N.** the
present -time, – day, – moment, –
juncture, – occasion; the times, existing
time, time being; twentieth century;
nonce, crisis, epoch, day, hour.

age, time of life.

**Adj.** present, actual, instant, current,
latest, existing, that is.

**Adv.** at this -time, – moment &c.
113; at the -present time &c. *n.*; now,
at present.

at this time of day, to-day, now-a-
days; already; even –, but –, just-now;
on the present occasion; for the -time
being, – nonce; *pro hâc vice*; on the
-nail, – spot; on the spur of the -mo-
ment, – occasion.

until now; to -this, – the present day.

**119.** [Time different from the pres-
ent.] **Different Time.—N.** different –,
other- time.

[Indefinite time] aorist.

**Adj.** aoristic.

**Adv.** at that –, at which- -time, –
moment, – instant; then, on that
occasion, upon.

when; when-ever, -soever; upon
which, on which occasion; at -another,
– a different, – some other, – any- time;
at various times; some –, one- -of these
days, – fine morning, – day; sooner or
later; some time or other; once upon
a time, once.

postnate; successive &c. 63; postdiluvi-
al, -an; *puisné*; posthumous; post-war,
future &c. 121.

**Adv.** subsequently, after, afterwards,
since, later; at a -subsequent, – later-
period; next, in the sequel, close upon,
thereafter, thereupon, upon which,
eftsoons; from that -time, – moment;
after a -while, – time; in process of
time.

postcenal, postcibal, postprandial,
after-dinner.

**120. Synchronism.—N.** synchronism; coexistence, coincidence; simul-
taneousness &c. *adj.*; concurrence, concomitance, unity of time, interim.

[Having equal times] isochronism, syntony.

contemporary, coetanian.

**V.** coexist, concur, accompany, go hand in hand, keep pace with;
synchronize, isochronize.

**Adj.** synchron-ous, -al, -ical, -istical; simultaneous, coexisting, coin-
cident, concomitant, concurrent; coev-al, -ous; contempora-ry, -neous;
coetaneous; coterminous, coeternal; isochronous.

**Adv.** at the same time; simultaneously &c. *adj.*; together, in concert,
during the same time; in the same breath; *pari passu*; in the interim.

at the -very moment &c. 113; just as, as soon as; meanwhile &c.
(*while*) 106.

**121.** [Prospective time.] **Futurity.
—N.** futur-ity, -ition; future, here-
after, time to come; approaching –,
coming –, after- -time, – age, – days,
– hours, – years, – ages, – life; morrow,
to-morrow, by and by; millennium,
doomsday, day of judgment, crack of
doom, remote future.

**122.** [Retrospective time.] **Preteri-
tion.—N.** preterition; priority &c. 116;
the past, past time; days –, times- -of
yore, – of old, – past, – gone by;
bygone days, good old days; old –,
ancient –, former -times; fore time;
yesterdays; the olden –, good old-
time; auld lang syne; eld.

approach of time, advent, time drawing on, womb of time; destiny &c. 152; eventuality.

heritage, heirs, posterity, descendants.

prospect &c. (*expectation*) 507; foresight &c. 510.

**V.** look forwards; anticipate &c. (*expect*) 507, (*foresee*) 510; forestall &c. (*be early*) 132.

come -, draw- on; draw near; approach, await, threaten; impend &c. (*be destined*) 152.

**Adj.** future, to come; coming &c. (*impending*) 152; next, near; near -, close- at hand; eventual, ulterior; expectant, prospective, in prospect &c. (*expectation*) 507.

**Adv.** prospectively, hereafter, on the knees of the gods, in future; to-morrow, the day after to-morrow; in -course, - process, - the fulness- of time; eventually, ultimately, sooner or later; *proximo*; *paulo post futurum*; in after time; one of these days; after a -time, - while.

from this time; hence-forth, -forwards; thence; thence-forth, -forward; whereupon, upon which.

soon &c. (*early*) 132; on the -eve, - point, - brink- of; about to; close upon.

antiquity, antiqueness, *status quo*; time immemorial; distance of time; remote -age, - time; ancient history; remote past; rust of antiquity; ancientness.

pale-ontology, -ography, -ology; palætiology,* archæology; archaism, antiquarianism, mediævalism, pre-Raphaelitism; retrospection, looking back, memory &c. 505.

*laudator temporis acti*; mediævalist, pre-Raphaelite; antiqu-ary, -arian; archæologist &c.; Oldbuck, Dryasdust.

ancestry &c. (*paternity*) 166.

**V.** be -past &c. *adj.*; have -expired &c. *adj.*, - run its course, - had its day; pass; pass -, go- -by, - away, - off; lapse, blow over.

look -, trace -, cast the eyes- back; exhume.

**Adj.** past, gone, gone by, over, passed away, bygone, foregone; elapsed, lapsed, preterlapsed, expired, no more, run out, blown over, that has been, whilom, extinct, never to return, exploded, forgotten, irrecoverable; obsolete &c. (*old*) 124; extinct as the dodo.

former, pristine, *quondam*, *ci-devant*, late; ancestral.

foregoing; last, latter; recent, overnight; past, preterite, preter-perfect, -pluperfect, past perfect.

looking back &c. *v.*; retro-spective, -active; archæological &c. *n.*

**Adv.** formerly; of -old, - yore; erst, whilom, erewhile, time was, ago, over; in -the olden time &c. *n.*; anciently, long -ago, - since; a long -while, - time- ago; years -, ages- ago; some time -ago, - since, - back.

yesterday, the day before yesterday; last -year, - season, - month &c.; *ultimo*; lately &c. (*newly*) 123.

retrospectively, ere -, before -, till- now; hitherto, heretofore; no longer; once, - upon a time; from time immemorial; in the memory of man; time out of mind; already, yet, up to this time; *ex post facto*.

**Phr.** time was; the time -has, - hath- been.

## 2. *Time with reference to a particular Period*

**123. Newness.—N.** newness &c. *adj.*; neologism, neoterism; novelty, recency; immaturity; youth &c. 127; gloss of novelty.

**124. Oldness.—N.** oldness &c. *adj.*; age, antiquity; cobwebs of antiquity.

maturity, ripeness; decline, decay; senility &c. 128.

* Whewell.

innovation; renovation &c. (*restoration*) 660.

modernist, neologist, neoteric.

modernism, modernity; mushroom; latest fashion, *dernier cri.*

upstart, *parvenu, nouveau riche.*

**V.** renew &c. (*restore*) 660; modernize.

**Adj.** new, novel, recent, fresh, green; young &c. 127; evergreen; raw, immature; virgin; un-tried, -handseled, -used, -trodden, -beaten; fledgling.

late, modern, neoteric; new-born, -fashioned, -fangled, -fledged; of yesterday; just out, brand –, span-new, up to date, topical; vernal, renovated; innovatory.

fresh as -a rose, – a daisy, – paint; spick and span.

**Adv.** newly &c. *adj.*; afresh, anew, lately, just now, only yesterday, the other day; latterly, of late.

not long –, a short time- ago.

---

seniority, eldership, primogeniture.

archaism &c. (*the past*) 122; thing –, relic- of the past; megatherium.

tradition, prescription, custom, folklore, immemorial usage, common law.

**V.** be -old &c. *adj.*; have -had, – seen- its day; become -old &c. *adj.*; age, fade.

**Adj.** old, olden, ancient, antique; of long standing, time-honoured, venerable; eld-er, -est; first-born.

prime; prim-itive, -eval, -igenous; primordi-al, -nate; aboriginal &c. (*beginning*) 66; diluvian, antediluvian; pre-historic; patriarchal, preadamite; palæocrystic; fossil, paleozoic, preglacial, ante-mundane; archaic, classic, mediæval, pre-Raphaelite, ancestral, black-letter.

immemorial, traditional, prescriptive, customary, whereof the memory of man runneth not to the contrary; inveterate, rooted.

antiquated, of other times, rococo, of the old school, after-age, obsolete; fusty, moth-eaten; out of -date, – fashion; stale, old-fashioned, behind the -age, – times; exploded; gone out, – by; *passé*, outworn, run out; disused; senile &c. 128; time-worn; crumbling &c. (*deteriorated*) 659; second-hand.

old as -the hills, – Methuselah, – Adam, – history; Anno Domini.

**Adv.** since the -world was made, – year one, – days of Methuselah.

---

**125. Morning.** [Noon.]—**N.** morning, morn, matins, forenoon, *a.m.*, prime, dawn, daybreak, daylight, sun-up, peep –, break- of day; aurora, Eos; first blush –, prime- of the morning; twilight, crepuscule, sunrise, cockcrow.

spring; vernal equinox.

noon; mid-, noon-day; noontide, meridian, prime.

summer, midsummer; summer solstice.

**Adj.** matin, matutinal, vernal, æstival.

**Adv.** at -sunrise &c. *n.*; with the lark, when the morning dawns.

**127. Youth.**—**N.** youth; juven- -ility, -escence; juniority; infancy; baby-, child-, boy-, girl-, youth-hood; *incunabula*; minority, immaturity, nonage, teens, tender age, bloom.

cradle, nursery, leading-strings, pupilage, puberty, *pucelage.*

---

**126. Evening.** [Midnight.]—**N.** evening, eve; decline –, fall –, close- of day; eventide, evensong, vespers; candlelight; nightfall, curfew, dusk, twilight, blind man's holiday; eleventh hour; sun-set, -down; going down of the sun, cock-shut, dewy eve, gloaming, bed-time.

afternoon, *post meridiem, p.m.*

autumn; fall, – of the leaf; autumnal equinox, Indian summer, harvest-time.

midnight; dead –, witching time- of night; winter, – solstice.

**Adj.** vespertine, autumnal, nocturnal, wintry, brumal, hiemal.

**128. Age.**—**N.** age; oldness &c. *adj.*; old –, advanced- age; sen-ility, -escence; years, anility, grey hairs, climacteric, grand climacteric, declining years, decrepitude, hoary age, caducity, superannuation; second childhood, -ishness; dotage; vale of years,

prime –, flower –, spring-tide –, seed-time –, golden season- of life; heyday of youth, school days; rising generation, younger generation.

**Adj.** young, youthful, juvenile, green, callow, budding, sappy, *puisné*, beardless, unfledged, unripe, under age, in one's teens; *in statu pupillari*; younger, junior.

decline of life, 'sear and yellow leaf'; three-score years and ten; green old age, ripe old age; longevity; time of life.

seniority, eldership; elders &c. (*veteran*) 130; firstling; *doyen*, dean, father; primogeniture; nostology.

**V.** be -aged &c. *a²j.*; grow –, get-old &c. *adj.*; age; decline, wane.

**Adj.** aged; old &c. 124; elderly, senile; matronly, anile; in years; ripe, mellow, run to seed, declining, waning, past one's prime; grey, -headed; hoar, -y; venerable, time-worn, antiquated, *passé*, effete, doddering, decrepit, superannuated; advanced in -life, – years; stricken in years; wrinkled, marked with the crow's foot; having one foot in the grave; doting &c. (*imbecile*) 499.

old-, eld-er, -est; senior; first-born.

turned of, years old; of a certain age, no chicken, old as Methuselah; gerontic; ancestral; patriarchal &c. (*ancient*) 124.

**129. Infant.—N.** infant, babe, baby; nurse-, suck-, year-, wean-ling; *papoose*, *bambino*.

child, bairn, little- one, – tot, – mite, chick, brat, chit, pickaninny, kid, urchin; bant-, brat-ling; elf.

youth, boy, lad, slip, sprig, stripling, youngster, cub, unlicked cub, younker, callant, whipster, whipper-snapper, schoolboy, hobbledehoy, hopeful, cadet, minor, master.

scion; sap-, seed-ling; tendril, olive-branch, nestling, chicken, duckling; larva, caterpillar, chrysalis, cocoon; tadpole, whelp, cub, pullet, fry, callow; codlin, -g; *fœtus*, calf, colt, pup, foal, kitten; lamb, -kin.

girl; lass, -ie; wench, miss, damsel, *demoiselle*, damozel; maid, -en; virgin; nymph; colleen; minx, baggage, school-girl; tomboy, flapper, hoyden.

**Adj.** infant-ine, -ile; puerile; boy-, girl-, child-, baby-, kitten-ish; baby; new-born, unfledged, new-fledged, callow.

in -the cradle, – swaddling clothes, – long clothes, – arms, – leading strings; at the breast; in one's teens; young &c. 127.

**130. Veteran.—N.** veteran, old man, seer, patriarch, greybeard, dugout, grand-father, -sire; grandam, beldam; gaffer, gammer; hag, crone; pantaloon; sexage-, octoge-, nonage-, cente-narian; old stager; dotard &c. 501.

preadamite, Methuselah, Nestor, Rip van Winkle, old Parr; elders; forefathers &c. (*paternity*) 166.

**131. Adolescence.—N.** adolescence, pubescence, majority; adultness &c. *adj.*; manhood, virility, maturity; flower of age; prime –, meridian- of life.

man &c. 373; woman &c. 374; adult, no chicken.

**V.** come -of age, – to man's estate, – to years of discretion; attain majority, assume the *toga virilis*; have -cut one's eye-teeth, – sown one's wild oats, settle down.

**Adj.** adolescent, pubescent, of age; of -full, – ripe- age; out of one's teens, grown up, mature, full- blown, – grown, in one's prime, in full bloom, manly, virile, adult; womanly, matronly; marriageable, nubile.

### 3. *Time with reference to an Effect or Purpose*

**132. Earliness.—N.** earliness &c. *adj.*; morning &c. 125.

punctuality; promptitude &c. (*activity*) 682; haste &c. (*velocity*) 274; suddenness &c. (*instantaneity*) 113.

prematurity, precocity, precipitation, anticipation; prevenience, a stitch in time.

**V.** be -early &c. *adj.*, – beforehand &c. *adv.*; keep time, take time by the forelock, anticipate, forestall; have –, gain- the start; steal a march upon; gain time, draw on futurity; bespeak, secure, engage, pre-engage.

accelerate; expedite &c. (*quicken*) 274; make haste &c. (*hurry*) 684.

**Adj.** early, prime, timely, in time, punctual, forward; prompt &c. (*active*) 682; summary.

premature, precipitate, precocious; prevenient, anticipatory; rathe.

sudden &c. (*instantaneous*) 113; unexpected &c. 508; impending, imminent; near, – at hand; immediate.

**Adv.** early, soon, anon, betimes, rathe; eft, -soons; ere –, before- long; punctually &c. *adj.*; to the minute; in time; in -good, – military, – pudding, – due- time; time enough.

beforehand; prematurely &c. *adj.*; precipitately &c. (*hastily*) 684; too soon; before -its, – one's- time; in anticipation; unexpectedly &c. 508.

suddenly &c. (*instantaneously*) 113; before one can say 'Jack Robinson,' at short notice, extempore; on the spur of the -moment, – occasion; at once; on the -spot, – instant; at sight; off –, out of- hand; à vue d'œil; straight, -way, -forth; forthwith, incontinently, summarily, instanter, immediately, briefly, shortly, quickly, speedily, apace, before the ink is dry, almost immediately, presently, at the first opportunity, in no long time, by and by, in a while, directly.

**Phr.** touch and go, no sooner said than done.

**134. Occasion.—N.** occasion, opportunity, opening, room, scope, field; suitable –, proper- -time, – season; high time; opportuneness &c. *adj.*; tempestivity.

**133. Lateness.—N.** lateness &c. *adj.*; tardiness &c. (*slowness*) 275.

de-lay, -lation; punctation, procrastination; detention; deferring &c. *v.*; filibuster, postponement, adjournment, prorogation, retardation, respite, reprieve, stay; protraction, prolongation, moratorium; contango; demurrage; remand; Fabian policy, *médecine expectante*, chancery suit; leeway; high time.

**V.** be -late &c. *adj.*; tarry, wait, stay, bide, take time; dawdle &c. (*be inactive*) 683; linger, loiter, saunter, lag behind; bide –, take- one's time; hang -about, – around, – back, – in the balance; gain time; hang fire; stand –, lie-over.

put off, defer, delay, lay over, suspend; shift –, stave- off; waive, retard, remand, postpone, adjourn; procrastinate; dally; prolong, protract; spin –, draw –, lengthen- out; prorogue; keep back; tide over; push –, drive- to the last; let the matter stand over; reserve &c. (*store*) 636; temporize; consult one's pillow, sleep upon it.

shelve, table, lay on the table.

lose an opportunity &c. 135; be kept waiting, dance attendance; kick –, cool- one's heels; *faire antichambre*; wait impatiently; await &c. (*expect*) 507; sit up, – at night.

**Adj.** late, tardy, slow, behindhand, belated, postliminious, posthumous, backward, unpunctual; dilatory &c. (*slow*), overdue 275; delayed &c. *v.*; in abeyance.

**Adv.** late; late-, back-ward; late in the day; at -sunset, – the eleventh hour, – length, – last, – long; ultimately; after –, behind- time; too late; too late for &c. 135.

slowly, leisurely, deliberately, at one's leisure; *ex post facto*; *sine die*.

**Phr.** *nonum prematur in annum*.

_____

**135. Intempestivity.—N.** intempestivity; unseasonableness; unsuitable –, improper-time; unreasonableness &c. *adj.*; evil hour; *contretemps*; intrusion; anachronism &c. 115.

crisis, turn, juncture, emergency, conjuncture; turning point, given time.

nick of time; golden –, well-timed –, fine –, favourable- opportunity; clear stage, fair field; *mollia tempora*; *fata Morgana*; spare time &c. (*leisure*) 685.

V. seize &c. (*take*) 789 –, use &c. 677 –, give &c. 784- an -opportunity, – occasion; improve the occasion.

suit the occasion &c. (*be expedient*) 646.

strike the iron while it is hot, *battre le fer sur l'enclume*, make hay while the sun shines, take time by the forelock, *prendre la balle au bond*.

Adj. opportune, timely, well-timed, timeous, timeful, seasonable.

providential, lucky, fortunate, happy, favourable, propitious, auspicious, critical; suitable &c. 23; *obiter dicta*.

Adv. opportunely &c. *adj.*; in ·proper, – due- -time, – course, – season; for the nonce; in the -nick, – fulness- of time; all in good time; just in time, at the eleventh hour, now or never.

by the -way, – by; *en passant, à propos*; *pro -re natâ, – hac vice*; *par parenthèse*, parenthetically, by way of parenthesis; while -speaking of, – on this subject; extempore; on the spur of the -moment, – occasion; on the spot &c. (*early*) 132.

Phr. *carpe diem*; *occasionem cognosce*; one's hour is come, the time is up; that reminds me.

V. be -ill timed &c. *adj.*; mistime, intrude, come amiss, break in upon; have other fish to fry; be -busy, – engaged, – tied up, – occupied.

lose –, throw away –, waste –, neglect &c. 460- an opportunity; allow –, suffer- the -opportunity, – occasion- to -pass, – slip, – go by, – escape, – lapse; waste time &c. (*be inactive*) 683; let slip through the fingers, lock the stable door when the steed is stolen.

Adj. ill-, mis-timed; untimely, intrusive, unseasonable; out of -date, – season; inopportune, timeless, untoward, *mal à propos*, unlucky, inauspicious, unpropitious, unfortunate, unfavourable; unsuited &c. 24; inexpedient &c. 647.

unpunctual &c. (*late*) 133; too late for; premature &c. (*early*) 132; too soon for; wise after the event.

Adv. inopportunely &c. *adj.*; as ill luck would have it, in an evil hour, the time having gone by, a day after the fair.

Phr. after meat mustard, after death the doctor.

---

## 3°. RECURRENT TIME

**136. Frequency.**—N. frequency, oftness; repetition, &c. 104.

V. recur &c. 104; do nothing but; keep, – on.

Adj. frequent, many times, not rare, thickcoming, incessant, perpetual, continual, constant, recurrent, repeated &c. 104; habitual &c. 613; hourly, &c. 138.

Adv. often, often to be met with, oft; oft-, often-times; frequently; repeatedly &c. 104; unseldom, not unfrequently; in -quick, – rapid- succession; many a time and oft; daily, hourly &c.; every -day, – hour, – moment &c.

perpetually, continually, constantly, incessantly, without ceasing, at all times, daily and hourly, night and day,

**137. Infrequency.**—N. infrequency, infrequence, rareness, rarity; fewness &c. 103; seldomness, uncommonness.

V. be -rare &c. *adj.*

Adj. un-, in-frequent; uncommon, sporadic, rare, – as a blue diamond; few &c. 103; scarce; almost unheard of, unprecedented, which has not occurred within the memory of the oldest inhabitant, not within one's previous experience.

Adv. seldom, rarely, scarcely, hardly; not often, unfrequently, infrequently, unoften; scarcely –, hardly- ever; once in a blue moon.

once; once -for all, – in a way; *pro hac vice*; like angels' visits, few and far between.

day and night, day after day, morning noon and night, ever and anon.

most often; commonly &c. (*habitually*) 613.

sometimes, occasionally, at times, now and then, from time to time, there being times when, *toties quoties*, often enough, again and again &c. 104.

**138. Regularity of recurrence. Periodicity.—N.** periodicity, intermittence; beat; oscillation &c. 314; pulse, pulsation; rhythm; alter-nation, -nateness, -nativeness, -nity.

bout, round, revolution, rotation, turn.

anniversary, birthday, jubilee, centenary, bi-, ter-centenary.

[Regularity of return] rota, cycle, period, stated time, routine; days of the week; Sunday, Monday &c.; months of the year; January &c.; feast, fast, saint's day &c.; Christmas, Easter, New Year's Day &c. 998; quarter-, Lady-, Midsummer-, Michaelmas-day; May Day, the King's Birthday; leap year; seasons.

punctuality, regularity, steadiness.

**V.** recur in regular -order, – succession; return, revolve, rotate; come -again, – in its turn; come round, – again; beat, pulsate; alternate; intermit.

**Adj.** periodic, -al; serial, recurrent, cyclic-, -al, rhythmic-, -al, even; recurring &c. *v.*; inter-, re-mittent; alternate, every other.

hourly; diurnal, daily; quotidian, tertian, weekly; hebdomad-al, -ary; bi-weekly, fortnightly; monthly, menstrual, catamenial; yearly, annual; biennial, triennial, &c.; bissextile; centennial, secular; paschal, lenten, &c.

regular, steady, punctual, constant, methodical, regular as clockwork.

**Adv.** periodically &c. *adj.*; at -regular intervals, – stated times; at -fixed, – established- periods; punctually &c. *adj.*; *de die in diem*; from day to day, day by day.

by turns; in -turn, – rotation; alternately, every other day, off and on, ride and tie, round and round.

**139. Irregularity of recurrence.—N.** irregularity, uncertainty, unpunctuality; fitfulness &c. *adj.*

**Adj.** irregular, uneven, uncertain, unpunctual, capricious, erratic, desultory, fitful, flickering; rambling, rhapsodical; spasmodic, unsystematic, unequal, variable, halting.

**Adv.** irregularly &c. *adj.*; by fits and starts &c. (*discontinuously*) 70.

## Section VII.　Change

### 1°.　Simple Change

**140. [Difference at different times.] Change.—N.** change, alteration, mutation, permutation, variation, modification, modulation, inflexion, mood, qualification, innovation, *metastasis*, deviation, shift, turn; diversion; break.

transformation, transfiguration; metamorphosis; metabolism; transmutation; transubstantiation; metagenesis, transanimation, transmigration, me-

**141. [Absence of change.] Permanence.—N.** stability &c. 150; quiescence &c. 265; obstinacy &c. 606.

permanence, -cy, persistence, fixity, fixity of purpose, endurance, durability; standing, *status quo*; maintenance, preservation, conservation; conservatism; *laissez-faire*; law of the Medes and Persians; standing dish.

**V.** let -alone, – be; persist, remain,

tempsychosis; version; metathesis; transmogrification; catalysis; *avatar*; alterative.

conversion &c. (*gradual change*) 144; revolution &c. (*sudden or radical change*) 146; inversion &c. (*reversal*) 218; displacement &c. 185; transference &c. 270.

changeableness &c. 149; tergiversation &c. (*change of mind*) 607.

**V.** change, alter, vary, wax and wane; modulate, diversify, qualify, tamper with; turn, shift, veer, jibe, tack, chop, shuffle, swerve, dodge, warp, deviate, turn aside, evert, intervert; pass to, take a turn, turn the corner, resume.

work a change, modify, vamp, revamp, superinduce; trans-form, –mute, -ume, -figure &c. *n.*; metamorphose, ring the changes; convert, resolve; revolutionize; chop and change; patch, re-shape.

innovate, introduce new blood, shuffle the cards, spin the wheel; give a -turn, – colour- to; influence, turn the scale; shift the scene, turn over a new leaf.

recast &c. 146; reverse &c. 218; disturb &c. 61; convert into &c. 144.

**Adj.** changed &c. *v.*; new-fangled; changeable &c. 149; transitional; modifiable; alterative.

**Adv.** *mutatis mutandis.*

**Int.** *quantum mutatus!*

**Phr.** 'a change came o'er the spirit of my dream'; *nous avons changé tout cela*; *tempora mutantur et nos mutamur in illis*; *non sum qualis eram.*

stay, tarry, rest; hold, – on; last, endure, bide, abide, aby, dwell, maintain, keep; stand, – still, – fast; subsist, live, outlive, survive; hold –, keepone's -ground, – footing; hold good.

**Adj.** stable &c. 150; persisting &c. *v.*; permanent; established, fixed; durable; unchanged &c. (change &c. 140); unrenewed; intact, inviolate; persistent; monotonous, uncheckered; unfailing.

un-destroyed, -repealed, -suppressed; conservative, *qualis ab incepto*; prescriptive &c. (*old*) 124; stationary &c. 265.

**Adv.** *in statu quo*; for good, finally; at a stand, -still; *uti possidetis*; without a shadow of turning.

**Phr.** as you were!; *j'y suis j'y reste*; *esto perpetua*; *nolumus leges Angliæ mutari*; let sleeping dogs lie.

---

**142.** [Change from action to rest.] **Cessation.—N.** cessation, discontinuance, desistance, desinence.

inter-, re-mission; sus-pense, -pension; interruption, hitch; hartal; stop; stopping &c. *v.*; closure, stoppage, halt; arrival &c. 292.

pause, rest, lull, respite, truce, armistice, drop; interregnum, abeyance. closure &c. 261.

dead -stop, – stand, – lock; checkmate; comma, colon, semicolon, period, full stop; end &c. 67; death &c. 360; *cæsura.*

**V.** cease, discontinue, desist, stay; break –, leave- off; hold, stop, pull up, stall, stop short, check; stick, deadlock, hang fire; halt; pause, rest.

have done with, give over, surcease,

**143. Continuance** in action.—**N.** continu-ance, -ation; run; extension, prolongation; maintenance, perpetuation; persistence &c. (*perseverance*) 604a; repetition &c. 104.

**V.** continue, persist; go –, jog –, keep –, carry –, run – hold- on; abide, keep, pursue, stick to; endure; take –, maintain- its course; keep up.

sustain, uphold, hold up, keep on foot; follow up, perpetuate, prolong; maintain; preserve &c. 604a; harp upon &c. (*repeat*) 104.

keep -going, – alive, – at it, – the pot boiling, – the ball rolling, – up the ball; plod-, plug- along; slog on; die in harness; hold on –, pursue- the even tenor of one's way.

let be; *stare super antiquas vias;*

shut up shop; give up &c. (*relinquish*) 624.

hold –, stay- one's hand; rest on one's oars, repose on one's laurels.

come to a -stand, – standstill, – dead lock, – full stop; arrive &c. 292; go out, die away, peter out; wear -away, – off; pass away &c. (*be past*) 122; be at an end.

intromit, interrupt, suspend, interpel; inter-, re-mit; put -an end, – a stop, – a period- to; bring to a stand, -still; stop, cut out, cut short, arrest, avast; stem the -tide, – torrent; pull the check string; switch off.

**Int.** halt! hold! stop! enough! avast! have done! a truce to! soft! leave off! shut up! give over! chuck it!

*quieta non movere*; let things take their course.

**Adj.** continuing &c. *v.*; uninterrupted, unintermitting, unremitting, unvarying, unshifting; unreversed, unstopped, unrevoked, unvaried; sustained; undying &c. (*perpetual*) 112; inconvertible.

follow-up.

**Int.** carry on! right away!

**Phr.** *vestigia nulla retrorsum*; *labitur et labetur.*

144. [Gradual change to something different.] **Conversion.—N.** conversion, reduction, transmutation, transformation, development, resolution, assimilation; assumption; naturalization.

chemistry, alchemy; progress, growth, lapse, flux.

passage; transit, -ion; transmigration, shifting &c. *v.*; conjugation; convertibility.

crucible, alembic, caldron, retort, test tube &c.

convert, neophyte, proselyte, pervert, renegade, deserter, apostate, turncoat.

**V.** be converted into; become, get, wax; come –, turn- -to, – into; turn out, lapse, shift; run –, fall –, pass –, slide –, glide –, grow –, ripen –, open –, resolve itself –, settle –, merge- into; melt, grow, come round to, mature, mellow; assume the -form, – shape, – state, – nature, – character- of; illapse; assume a new phase, undergo a change.

convert –, resolve- into; make, render; mould, form &c. 240; remodel, new model, refound, reform, reorganize; assimilate –, bring –, reduce- to; transform.

**Adj.** converted into &c. *v.*; convertible, resolvable into; transitional; naturalized.

**Adv.** gradually &c. (*slowly*) 275; *in transitu* &c. (*transference*) 270.

145. **Reversion.—N.** reversion, return; revulsion; reaction.

turning point, turn of the tide; *status quo ante bellum*; calm before a storm.

alternation &c. (*periodicity*) 138; inversion &c. 218; recoil &c. 277; regression &c. 283; restoration &c. 660; relapse &c. 661; vicinism, atavism, throwback.

**V.** revert, turn back, return; relapse &c. 661; recoil &c. 277; retreat &c. 283; restore &c. 660; undo, unmake; turn the -tide, – scale; escheat.

**Adj.** reverting &c. *v.*; revulsive, reactionary.

**Adv.** *à rebours*, wrong side out.

146. [Sudden or violent change.] **Revolution.—N.** revolution, *bouleversement*, subversion, break up; destruction &c. 162; sudden –, radical –, sweeping –, organic- change; clean sweep, *coup d'état*, overthrow, *débâcle*; counter-revolution, rebellion &c. 742.

transilience, jump, leap, plunge, jerk, start; explosion; spasm, convulsion, throe, revulsion; storm, earthquake, eruption, upheaval, cataclysm; legerdemain &c. (*trick*) 545.

V. revolutionize; new model, remodel, recast; strike out something new, break with the past; change the face of, unsex; revert &c. 742.

Adj. unrecognizable.

Revolutionary, Bolshevik &c. 742.

**147.** [Change of one thing for another.] **Substitution.—N.** substitution, subrogation, commutation; supplanting &c. *v.*, supersession, metonymy &c. (*figure of speech*) 521.

[Thing substituted] substitute, *succedaneum*, make-shift, temporary expedient, shift, *pis aller*, stop-gap, jury-mast, *locum tenens*, warming-pan, dummy, goat, scape-goat; double; changeling; *quid pro quo*, alternative; remount; representative &c. (*deputy*) 759; palimpsest.

price, purchase-money, consideration, equivalent.

V. substitute, put in the place of, change for; make way for, give place to; supply –, take- the place of; supplant, supersede, replace, cut out, serve as a substitute; step into –, stand in- the shoes of; make a shift –, put up- with; borrow of Peter to pay Paul; commute, redeem, compound for.

**Adj.** substituted &c. *v.*; vicarious, subdititious; substitutional.

**Adv.** instead; in -place, – lieu, – the stead, – the room- of; *faute de mieux*.

**148.** [Double or mutual change.] **Interchange.—N.** inter-, ex-change; com-, per-, inter-mutation; reciprocation, transposal, transposition, shuffling; reciprocity, castling [at chess]; hocus-pocus.

interchange-ableness, -ability.

barter &c. 794; tit for tat &c. (*retaliation*) 718; cross fire, battledore and shuttlecock; *quid pro quo*.

V. inter-, ex-, counter-change; bandy, transpose, shuffle, change hands, swap, trade, permute, reciprocate, commute; give and take, return the compliment; play at -puss in the corner, – battledore and shuttlecock; retaliate &c. 718; barter &c. 794.

**Adj.** interchanged &c. *v.*; reciprocal, mutual, commutative, interchanged &c. *v.*; interchangeable, intercurrent.

**Adv.** in exchange, *vice versâ, mutatis mutandis*, backwards and forwards, by turns, turn and turn about, turn about; each –, every one- in his turn.

---

## 2°. Complex Change

**149. Changeableness.—N.** changeableness &c. *adj.*; mutability, inconstancy; versatility, mobility; instability, unstable equilibrium; vacillation &c. (*irresolution*) 605; fluctuation, vicissitude; alternation &c. (*oscillation*) 314.

restlessness &c. *adj.*; fidgets, disquiet; dis-, in-quietude; unrest; agitation &c. 315.

moon, Proteus, chameleon, kaleidoscope, quicksilver, shifting sands, weathercock, harlequin, Cynthia of the minute, April showers; wheel of Fortune; transientness &c. 111.

V. fluctuate, vary, waver, flounder, flicker, flitter, flit, flutter, shift, shuffle, shake, totter, tremble, vacillate, wamble, turn and turn about, ring the changes; sway –, shift- to and fro; change and change about; oscillate

**150. Stability.—N.** stability; immutability &c. *adj.*; unchangeableness &c. *adj.*; constancy; stable equilibrium, immobility, soundness, vitality, stabiliment, stabilization, stiffness, ankylosis, solidity, *aplomb*.

establishment, fixture; rock, pillar, tower, foundation, leopard's spots, Ethiopian's skin, law of the Medes and Persians.

stabilimeter, stabilizator.

permanence &c. 141; obstinacy &c. 606.

V. be -firm &c. *adj.*; stick fast; stand –, keep –, remain- firm; weather the storm.

settle, establish, stablish, ascertain, fix, set, stabilitate, stabilize; retain, stet, keep hold; make -good, – sure; fasten &c. (*join*) 43; set on its legs, float; perpetuate.

&c. 314; vibrate –, oscillate- between two extremes; alternate; have as many phases as the moon.

Adj. change-able, -ful; changing &c. 140; mutable, variable, checkered, ever changing, kaleidoscopic, prote-an, -iform; versatile.

unstaid, inconstant; un-steady, -stable, -fixed, -settled; fluctuating &c. v.; restless; mercurial; agitated &c. 315; erratic, fickle; irresolute &c. 605; capricious &c. 608; touch-and-go; inconso¹ant, fitful, spasmodic; vibratory; vagrant, wayward, wavering; desultory; afloat; alternating; alterable, plastic, mobile; fleeting, transient &c. 111.

Adv. see-saw &c. (oscillation) 314; off and on.

settle down; strike –, take- root; take up one's abode &c. 184; build one's house on a rock.

Adj. unchangeable, immutable; un-alter-ed, -able; not to be changed, constant; permanent &c. 141; invariable, undeviating; stable, durable; perennial &c. (diuturnal) 110.

fixed, steadfast, firm, fast, steady, balanced; confirmed, valid, fiducial, immovable, irremovable, riveted, rooted; settled, established &c. v.; vested; incontrovertible, stereotyped, indeclinable.

tethered, anchored, moored, at anchor, on a rock, firm as a rock; firmly -seated, – established &c. v.; deeprooted, ineradicable; inveterate; obstinate &c. 606.

transfixed, stuck fast, aground, high and dry, stranded.

indefeasible, irretrievable, intransmutable, incommutable, irresoluble, irrevocable, irreversible, reverseless, inextinguishable, irreducible; indissol-uble, -vable; indestructible, undying, imperishable, indelible, indeciduous; insusceptible, – of change.

Int. stet.

---

### Present Events

**151. Eventuality.—N.** eventuality, event, occurrence, incident, affair, transaction, proceeding, fact; matter of –, naked- fact; phenomenon; advent.

business, concern; circumstance, particular, casualty, happening, accident, adventure, passage, crisis, pass, emergency, contingency, consequence &c. 154.

the world, life, things, doings, affairs, matters; things –, affairs- in general; the times, state of affairs, order of the day; course –, tide –, stream –, current –, run –, march- of -things, – events; ups and downs of life; chapter of accidents &c. (chance) 156; situation &c. (circumstances) 8.

**V.** happen, occur; take -place, – effect; come, become of; come -off, – about, – round, – into existence, – forth, – to pass, – on; pass, present itself; fall; fall –, turn- out; run, be on foot, fall in; be-fall, -tide, -chance; prove, eventuate, draw on; turn –, crop –, spring –, cast- up; super-, sur-vene; issue, emanate, arrive, ensue,

### Future Events

**152. Destiny.—N.** destiny &c. (necessity) 601; hereafter, future –, post existence; future state, next world, world to come, after life; futurity &c. 121; everlasting -life, – death; prospect &c. (expectation) 507.

**V.** impend; hang –, lie –, hover-over; threaten, loom, await, come on, approach, stare one in the face; fore-, pre-ordain; predestine, doom, foredoom, foreshadow, have in store for.

**Adj.** impending &c. v.; destined; about to -be, – happen; coming, in store, to come, going to happen, instant, at hand, near; near –, close- at hand; overhanging, hanging over one's head, imminent; brewing, preparing, forthcoming; in the wind, on the cards, in reserve; that -will, – is to- be; in prospect &c. (expected) 507; looming in the -distance, – horizon, – future; unborn, in embryo; in the womb of -time; – futurity; on the knees of the gods; pregnant &c. (producing) 161.

**Adv.** in -time, – the long run; all in good time; eventually &c. 151; what-

arise, start, hold, take its course; pass off &c. (*be past*) 122.

meet with; experience; fall to the lot of; be one's -chance, – fortune, – lot; find; encounter, undergo; pass –, go-through; endure &c. (*feel*) 821.

Adj. happening &c. *v.*; going on, doing, current; in the wind, afloat; on -foot, – the *tapis*; at issue, in question; incidental.

eventful, momentous, signal; stirring, bustling, full of incident.

Adv. eventually, ultimately, in -the event of, – case; in the course of things; in the -natural, – ordinary- course of things; as -things, – times- go; as the world -goes, – wags; as the -tree falls, – cat jumps; as it may -turn out, – happen.

Phr. the plot thickens.

ever may happen &c. (*certainly*) 474; as -chance &c. 156- would have it.

---

# Section VIII.   CAUSATION

## 1°. Constancy of Sequence in Events

153. [Constant antecedent.] **Cause.** —N. cause, origin, source, principle, element; occasioner, prime mover, engine, turbine, motor, *primum mobile*; *vera causa*; author &c. (*producer*) 164; main-spring, agent; dynamo, generator, battery (electric); leaven; groundwork, foundation &c. (*support*) 215.

spring, fountain, well, font; fountain –, spring- head; *fons et origo*, genesis; descent &c. (*paternity*) 166; remote cause; influence.

pivot, hinge, turning-point, lever; key; kernel, core; proximate cause, *causa causans*; last straw that breaks the camel's back.

ground; reason, – why; why and wherefore, rationale, occasion, derivation; final cause &c. (*intention*) 620; *le dessous des cartes*; undercurrents.

rudiment, egg, germ, embryo, fœtus bud, root, *radix*, radical, etymon, nucleus, seed, stem, stalk, stock, *stirps*, trunk, tap-root; latent organism.

nest, cradle, nursery, womb, *nidus*, birth-, breeding-place, hot-bed.

caus-ality, -ation; origination; production &c. 161.

V. be the -cause &c. *n.*- of; originate; give -origin, – rise, – occasion- to; cause, occasion, sow the seeds of, kindle, suscitate; bring -on, – to pass, – about; produce; create &c. 161; set -up, – afloat, – on foot; found, broach,

154. [Constant sequent.] **Effect.—N.** effect, consequence, sequela; derivative, -tion; result; result-ant, -ance; upshot, issue, *dénouement*; outcome; termination, end &c. 67; development, outgrowth, fruit, crop, harvest, product, bud, blossom, florescence, ear.

production, produce, product, finished product, work, handiwork, fabric, performance; creature, creation; offspring, -shoot; first-fruits, -lings; *prémices*.

V. be the -effect &c. *n.*- of; be -due, – owing- to; originate -in, – from; rise –, arise –, take its rise –, spring –, proceed –, emanate –, come –, grow –, bud –, sprout –, germinate –, issue –, flow –, result –, follow –, derive its origin –, accrue- from; come -to, – of, – out of; depend –, hang –, hinge –, turn- upon.

take the consequences, sow the wind and reap the whirlwind.

Adj. owing to; resulting from &c. *v.*; resultant; derivable from; due to; caused &c. by, 153; dependent upon; derived –, evolved- from; derivative; hereditary.

Adv. of course, it follows that, naturally, consequently; as a –, in- consequence; through all, all along of, necessarily, eventually.

Phr. *cela va sans dire*, thereby hangs a tale.

institute, lay the foundation of, inaugurate; lie at the root of.

procure, induce, draw down, open the door to, superinduce, evoke, entail, operate; elicit, provoke.

conduce to &c. (*tend to*) 176; contribute; promote; have a -hand in, – finger in- the pie; determine, decide, turn the scale, give the casting vote; have a common origin; derive its origin &c. (*effect*) 154.

Adj. caused &c. *v.*; causal, original; prim-ary, -itive, -ordial; aboriginal; radical; inceptive, embry-onic, -otic; *in -embryo, – ovo*; seminal, germinal; formative, productive &c. 168; at the bottom of; connate, having a common origin.

Adv. because &c. 155; behind the scenes.

**155.** [Assignment of cause.] **Attribution.**—**N.** attribution, theory, etiology, ascription, reference to, rationale; accounting for &c. *v.*; palaetiology,* imputation, derivation from.

fil-, affil-iation; pedigree &c. (*paternity*) 166.

explanation &c. (*interpretation*) 522; reason why &c. (*cause*) 153.

**V.** attribute –, ascribe –, impute –, refer –, lay –, point –, trace –, bring home- to; put –, set- down- to; charge –, ground- on; invest with, assign as cause, charge with, blame, lay at the door of, father upon; saddle with; affiliate; account for, derive from, point out the -reason &c. 153; theorize; tell how it comes; put the saddle on the right horse.

**Adj.** attributed &c. *v.*; attributable &c. *v.*; refer-able, -rible; due to, derivable from; owing to &c. (*effect*) 154; putative.

**Adv.** hence, thence, therefore, for, since, on account of, because, owing to; on that account; from -this, – that- cause; thanks to, forasmuch as; whence, *propter hoc.*

why? wherefore? whence? how -comes, – is, – happens- it? how does it happen?

in -some, – some such- way; somehow, – or other.

**Phr.** that is why; *hinc illæ lachrymæ; cherchez la femme.*

**156.** [Absence of assignable cause.] **Chance.**†—**N.** chance, indetermination, accident, fortune, hazard, hap, haphazard, chance-medley, random, luck, raccroc, casualty, fortuity, contingence, coincidence, adventure, hit; fate &c. (*necessity*) 601; equal chance; lottery, raffle, tombola, sweepstake; toss up &c. 621; turn of the -table, – cards; hazard of the die, chapter of accidents; cast –, throw- of the dice; heads or tails, wheel of Fortune, whirligig of chance; *sortes, – Virgilianæ, -biblicæ.*

probability, possibility, contingency, odds, long odds, run of luck; main-chance.

theory of -probabilities, – chances; book-making; assurance; speculation, gamble, gaming &c. 621.

**V.** chance, hap, turn up; fall to one's lot; be one's -fate &c. 601; stumble on, light –, blunder –, hit- upon; take one's chance &c. 621.

**Adj.** casual, fortuitous, accidental, haphazard, random, stray, adventitious, adventive, causeless, incidental. contingent, uncaused, undetermined, indeterminate; possible &c. 470; unintentional &c. 621.

**Adv.** by -chance, – accident; casually; perchance &c. (*possibly*) 470; for aught one knows; as -good, – bad, – ill-luck &c. *n.*- would have it; as it may -be, – chance, – turn up, – happen; as the case may be.

### 2°. CONNECTION BETWEEN CAUSE AND EFFECT

**157. Power.**—**N.** power; poten-cy, -tiality; puissance, might, force; energy &c. 171; dint; right -hand, – arm;

**158. Impotence.**—**N.** impotence; in-, dis-ability; disablement, impuissance, imbecility, caducity; incapa-city,

---

* Whewell, 'History of the Inductive Sciences,' book xviii, vol. iii., p. 397 (3rd edit.).

† The word *Chance* has two distinct meanings: the first, the absence of assignable *cause*, as above; and the second, the absence of *design*—for the latter see 621.

ascendency, sway, control; pre-potency, -pollence; almightiness, omnipotence; authority &c. 737; strength &c. 159.

ability; ableness &c. *adj.*; competency; effi-ciency, -cacy; validity, cogency; enablement; vantage ground; influence &c. 175; horse power; dynamometer.

pressure; elasticity; gravity, electricity, magnetism, galvanism, voltaic electricity, voltaism, electro-magnetism, electrostatics, electrification, electric current &c.; attraction, repulsion; *vis -inertiæ*, − *mortua*, − *viva*; potential −, dynamic −, kinetic −, electrical −, chemical −, atomic- energy; friction, suction.

capability, capacity; *quid valeant humeri quid ferre recusent*; faculty, quality, attribute, endowment, virtue, gift, property, qualification, susceptibility.

**V.** be -powerful &c. *adj.*; gain -power &c. *n.*

belong −, pertain- to; lie −, be- in one's power; can.

give −, confer −, exercise- power &c. *n.*; empower, enable, invest; in-, en-due; endow, arm; strengthen &c. 159; compel &c. 744.

**Adj.** powerful, puissant; potent, -ial; capable, able; equal −, up- to; cogent, valid; effect-ive, -ual; efficient, efficacious, adequate, competent; multi-, pleni-, omni-, armi- potent; mighty, ascendent; almighty.

electric, electrical &c.

forcible &c. *adj.* (*energetic*) 171; influential &c. 175; productive &c. 168.

**Adv.** powerfully &c. *adj.*; by -virtue, − dint- of.

-bility; inapt-, inept-itude; indocility; invalidity, inefficiency, incompetence, disqualification.

*telum imbelle, brutum fulmen,* blank cartridge, flash in the pan, *vox et præterea nihil,* dead letter, bit of waste paper, dummy; scrap of paper.

inefficacy &c. (*inutility*) 645; failure &c. 732.

helplessness &c. *adj.*; prostration, paralysis, palsy, ataxia, apoplexy, syncope, sideration, *deliquium*, collapse, exhaustion, softening of the brain, emasculation, inanition, senility &c. 128; castrato, eunuch.

cripple, old woman, muff, mollycoddle, milksop.

**V.** be -impotent &c. *adj.*; not have a leg to stand on.

*vouloir -rompre l'anguille au genou,* − *prendre la lune avec les dents.*

collapse, faint, swoon, fall into a swoon, drop; go by the board; end in smoke &c. (*fail*) 732.

render -powerless &c. *adj.*; deprive of power; decontrol; dis-able, -enable; disarm, incapacitate, disqualify, unfit, invalidate, undermine, deaden, cramp, tie the hands; double up, prostrate, paralyze, muzzle, cripple, becripple, maim, lame, hamstring, draw the teeth of; throttle, strangle, *garrotte;* ratten, silence, sprain, clip the wings of, render *hors de combat,* spike the guns; take the wind out of one's sails, scotch the snake, put a spoke in one's wheel; break the -neck, − back; un-hinge, -fit; put out of gear.

unman, unnerve, devitalize, attenuate, enervate; emasculate, spay, caponize, castrate, geld; effeminize.

shatter, exhaust; weaken &c. 160.

**Adj.** powerless, impotent, unable, incapable, incompetent; ineff-icient, -ective; inept; un-fit, -fitted; un-, dis-qualified; unendowed; in-, un-apt; crippled, decrepit, disabled &c. *v.*; armless.

harmless, unarmed, weaponless, defenceless, *sine ictu,* unfortified, indefensible, vincible, pregnable, untenable.

para-lytic, -lyzed; palsied, imbecile; nerve-, sinew-, marrow-, pith-, lust-less; emasculate, disjointed; out of -joint, − gear; un--nerved, -hinged; water-logged, on one's beam ends, rudderless; laid on one's back; done up, dead beat, exhausted, shattered, demoralized; gravelled &c. (*in difficulty*) 704; helpless, unfriended, fatherless; without a leg to stand on, *hors de combat,* laid on the shelf.

null and void, nugatory, inoperative, good for nothing; dud; invertebrate; ineffectual &c. (*failing*) 732; inadequate &c. 640; inefficacious &c. (*useless*) 645.

**159.** [Degree of power.] **Strength.**

—N. strength; power &c. 157; energy &c. 171; vigour, force; main -, physical -, brute- force; spring, elasticity, tone; tension, tonicity.

stoutness &c. *adj*; lustihood, stamina, nerve, muscle, sinew, thews and sinews, *physique*; pith, -iness; virility, vitality.

athlet-ics, -icism; gymnastics, feats of strength.

adamant, steel, iron, oak, heart of oak; iron grip; grit, bone.

athlete, gymnast, tumbler, acrobat; Atlas, Hercules, Antæus, Samson, Cyclops, Goliath, Titan; tower of strength; giant refreshed.

strengthening &c. *v.*; invigoration, refreshment, refocillation.

[Science of forces] dynamics, statics.

V. be -strong &c. *adj.*, - stronger; overmatch.

render -strong &c. *adj.*; give -strength &c. *n.*; strengthen, invigorate, brace, nerve, fortify, buttress, sustain, harden, case-harden, steel; gird; screw -, wind -, set- up; gird -, brace- up one's loins; recruit, set on one's legs; vivify; refresh &c. 689; refect; reinforce &c. (*restore*) 660.

**Adj.** strong, mighty, vigorous, forcible, hard, adamantine, stout, robust, sturdy, hardy, powerful, potent, puissant, valid.

resistless, irresistible, invincible, proof against, impregnable, unconquerable, indomitable, inextinguishable, unquenchable; incontestable; more than a match for; over-powering, -whelming; all-powerful; sovereign.

able-bodied; athletic, gymnastic; Herculean, Cyclopean, Atlantean; muscular, husky, brawny, wiry, well-knit, broad-shouldered, sinewy, strapping, stalwart, gigantic.

man-ly, -like, -ful; masculine, male, virile, in the prime of manhood.

un-weakened, -allayed, -withered, -shaken, -worn, -exhausted; in full -force, - swing; in the plenitude of power.

**160. Weakness.**—N. weakness &c. *adj.*; debility, atony, relaxation, languor, enervation; impotence &c. 158 infirmity; effeminacy, feminality; fragility, flaccidity; inactivity &c. 683.

declension -, loss -, failure- of strength; delicacy, invalidation, decrepitude, asthenia, adynamy, cachexy, *cachexia*, anæmia, bloodlessness, sprain, strain.

reed, thread, rope of sand, broken reed, house -of cards, - built on sand.

soft-, weak-ling; infant &c. 129; youth &c. 127.

V. be -weak &c. *adj.*; drop, crumble, give way, totter, tremble, shake, halt, limp, fade, languish, decline, flag, fail, have one foot in the grave.

render -weak &c. *adj.*; weaken, enfeeble, debilitate, shake, deprive of strength, relax, enervate; un-brace, -nerve; cripple, unman, &c. (*render powerless*) 158; cramp, reduce, sprain, strain, blunt the edge of; dilute, impoverish; decimate; extenuate; reduce -in strength, - the strength of; invalidate; *mettre de l'eau dans son vin.*

Adj. weak, feeble, debile; impotent &c. 158; relaxed, unnerved &c. *v.*; sap-, strength-, power-less; weakly, unstrung, flaccid, adynamic, asthenic; nervous.

soft, effeminate, feminate, womanish.

frail, fragile, shattery, frangible, brittle &c. 328; flimsy, unsubstantial, gimcrack, gingerbread; rickety, cranky; creachy; drooping, tottering &c. *v.*; broken, lame, halt, game, withered, shattered, shaken, crazy, shaky, tumble-down; palsied &c. 158; decrepit; C3.

languid, poor, poorly, infirm; faint, -ish; sickly &c. (*disease*) 655; dull, slack, evanid, spent, short-winded, effete; weatherbeaten; decayed, rotten, worn, seedy, languishing, wasted, washy, wishy-washy, laid low, pulled down, the worse for wear.

un-strengthened &c. 159, -supported, -aided, -assisted; aidless, defenceless &c. 158.

stubborn, thick-ribbed, made of iron, deep-rooted; strong as -a lion, – a horse, – brandy; sound as a roach; in -fine, – high- feather; in fine fettle; like a giant refreshed.

**Adv.** strongly &c. *adj.*; by -force &c. *n.*; by main force &c. (*by compulsion*) 744.

**Phr.** 'our withers are unwrung.'

on its last legs; weak as a -child, – baby, – chicken, – cat, – rat; weak as -water, – water gruel, – gingerbread, – milk and water; colourless &c. 429.

**Phr.** *non sum qualis eram.*

## 3°. POWER IN OPERATION

**161. Production.—N.** production, creation, construction, formation, fabrication, manufacture; building, architecture, erection, edification; coinage; organization; *nisus formativus*; putting together &c. *v.*; establishment; workmanship, performance; achievement &c. (*completion*) 729; effect &c. 154.

flowering, fructification, fruition.

bringing forth &c. *v.*; parturition, birth, birth-throe, child-birth, delivery, confinement, *accouchement*, travail, labour, midwifery, obstetrics; geniture; gestation &c. (*maturation*) 673; evolution, development, growth; genesis, fertilization, breeding, conception, germination, generation, *epigenesis*, pro-creation, -generation, -pagation; fecundation, impregnation; spontaneous generation; *arche-genesis*, *-biosis*; bio-, abio-, homo-, xeno-genesis.*

authorship, publication; works, *œuvre, opus.*

edifice, building, structure, fabric, erection, pile, tower, flower, fruit.

**V.** produce, perform, operate, do, make, gar, form, construct, fabricate, frame, contrive, manufacture; weave, forge, coin, carve, chisel; build, raise, edify, rear, erect, put together; set –, run- up; establish, constitute, compose, organize, institute, get up; achieve, accomplish &c. (*complete*) 729.

flower, sprout, blossom, burgeon, bear fruit, fructify, spawn, teem, ean, yean, farrow, drop, calf, pup, whelp, kitten, kindle; bear, lay, bring forth, give birth to, lie in, be brought to bed of, evolve, pullulate, usher into the world.

make productive &c. 168; create; beget, conceive, get, generate, fecun-

**162. [Non-production.] Destruction. —N.** destruction; waste, dissolution, breaking up; di-, dis-ruption; consumption; disorganization.

fall, downfall, ruin, perdition, crash, smash, havoc, *délabrement, débâcle*; break -down, – up; prostration; desolation, *bouleversement*, wreck, crack-up, crash, wrack, shipwreck, cataclysm; Caudine Forks, Sedan.

extinction, annihilation; destruction of life &c. 361; knock-out, knock-down blow; doom, crack of doom.

destroying &c. *v.*; demo-lition, -lishment; biblioclasm; overthrow, subversion, suppression; abolition &c. (*abrogation*) 756; sacrifice; ravage, devastation, *sabotage, razzia*; incendiarism; revolution &c. 146; extirpation &c. (*extraction*) 301; *commencement de la fin*, road to ruin; dilapidation &c. (*deterioration*) 659.

**V.** be -destroyed &c.; perish; fall, – to the ground; tumble, topple; go –, fall- to pieces; break up; crumble, – to dust; go to -the dogs, – the wall, – smash, – shivers, – wreck, – pot, – wrack and ruin; go -by the board, – all to smash, – to pieces, – under; be all -over, – up- with; totter to its fall.

destroy; do –, make- away with; nullify; annul &c. 756; sacrifice, demolish; tear up; over-turn, -throw, -whelm; upset, subvert, put an end to; seal the doom of, do for, dish, undo; break –, cut- up; break –, cut –, pull –, mow –, blow –, beat- down; suppress, quash, put down; cut short, take off, blot out; dispel, dissipate, dissolve; consume; abolish.

smash, – to smithereens, quell, squash, squelch, crumple up, shatter,

*Huxley.*

date, impregnate; pro-create, -generate, -pagate; engender; bring –, call- into -being, – existence; breed, hatch, develop, bring up.

induce, superinduce; suscitate; cause &c. 153; acquire &c. 775.

**Adj.** produc-ed, -ing &c. *v.*; productive of; prolific &c. 168; creative; formative; gen-etic, -ial, -ital; fertile, pregnant; *enceinte*, big –, fraught-with; with child, in the family way; teeming, parturient, in the straw, brought to bed of; puerper-al, -ous.

architectonic; constructive.

shiver; batter; tear –, crush –, cut –, shake –, pull –, pick- to pieces; nip; tear to -rags, – tatters; crush –, knock-to atoms; pulverize; ruin; strike out; throw –, knock- -down, – over; lay by the heels; fell, sink, swamp, scuttle, wreck, crash, shipwreck, engulf, submerge; lay in -ashes, – ruins; sweep away, erase, expunge, strike out, delete, efface, raze; level, – with the -ground, – dust.

deal destruction, lay waste, ravage, gut; disorganize; dismantle &c. (*render useless*) 645; devour, swallow up, desolate, devastate, sap, mine, blast, confound; exterminate, extinguish, quench, annihilate; snuff –, put –, stamp –, trample- out; lay –, trample- in the dust; prostrate; tread –, crush –, trample- under foot; lay the axe to the root of; make -short work, – a clean sweep, – mincemeat- of; cut up root and branch; fling –, scatter- to the winds; throw overboard; strike at the root of, sap the foundations of, spring a mine, blow up; ravage with fire and sword; cast to the dogs; eradicate &c. 301.

**Adj.** destroyed &c. *v.*; perishing &c. *v.*; trembling –, nodding –, tottering- to its fall; in course of -destruction &c. *n.*; extinct.

destructive, subversive, ruinous, incendiary, deletory; destroying &c. *v.*; suicidal; deadly &c. (*killing*) 361.

**Adv.** with -crushing effect, – a sledge-hammer.

**Phr.** *delenda est Carthago.*

**163. Reproduction.**—**N.** reproduction, renovation; restoration &c. 660; renewal; new edition, reprint &c. 21; revival, regeneration, palingenesia, revivification; apotheosis; resuscitation, reanimation, resurrection, resurgence, reappearance, atavism; Phœnix; reincarnation.

generation &c. (*production*) 161; multiplication.

**V.** reproduce; restore &c. 660; revive, renovate, renew, regenerate, revivify, resuscitate, reanimate, refashion, stir the embers, put into the crucible; multiply, repeat, resurge.

crop up, spring up like mushrooms.

**Adj.** reproduced &c. *v.*; renascent, reappearing; reproductive; resurgent; progenitive; Hydra-headed.

**164. Producer.**—**N.** producer, creator, deviser, designer, originator, inventor, author, founder, generator, mover, architect; grower, constructor, maker &c. (*agent*) 690.

**166. Paternity.**—**N.** paternity; parentage; fatherhood; consanguinity &c. 11.

parent, father, sire, dad, daddy, papa, governor, *pater*, *paterfamilias*, *abba*; genitor, progenitor, procreator, begetter; ancestor; grand-sire, -father; great-grandfather.

**165. Destroyer.**—**N.** destroyer &c. (destroy &c. 162); cankerworm &c. (*bane*) 663; iconoclast; assassin &c. (*killer*) 361; executioner &c. (*punish*) 975; Hun, Vandal, nihilist, anarchist.

**167. Posterity.**—**N.** posterity, progeny, breed, issue, offspring, brood, litter, seed, farrow, spawn, spat; family, children, grandchildren, heirs; great-grandchild.

child, son, daughter; kid; infant &c. 129; bantling, scion; shoot, sprout, olive branch, sprit, branch; off-shoot,

house, stem, trunk, tree, stock, *stirps*, pedigree, lineage, line, family, tribe, sept, race, clan; genealogy, descent, extraction, birth, ancestry; forefathers, forbears, patriarchs.

motherhood, maternity; mother, dam, mamma, *materfamilias*; grandmother; matriarch.

**Adj.** paternal, parental; maternal; matrilinear, patrilineal, patriarchal.

**168. Productiveness.**—N. productiveness &c. *adj.*; fecundity, fertility, luxuriance, uberty.

pregnancy, pullulation, fructification, multiplication, propagation, procreation; superfetation.

milch cow, rabbit, hydra, warren, seed-plot, land flowing with milk and honey; second crop, after-crop, -growth, -math; fertilization.

**V.** make -productive &c. *adj.*; fructify; procreate, generate, fertilize, spermatize, impregnate; fecund-ate, -ify; teem, pullulate, multiply; produce &c. 161; conceive.

**Adj.** productive, prolific; teem-ing, -ful; fertile, fruitful, frugiferous, fruit-bearing; fructiferous; fecund, luxuriant; pregnant, uberous.

procre-ant, -ative; generative, life-giving, spermatic; originative; multiparous; omnific; propagable.

parturient &c. (*producing*) 161; profitable &c. (*useful*) 644.

-set; ramification; descendant; heir, -ess; heir -apparent, – presumptive; chip of the old block; heredity; rising generation.

straight descent, sonship, line, lineage, filiation, primogeniture.

**Adj.** filial.

family, ancestral, linear,

**169. Unproductiveness.**—N. unproductiveness &c. *adj.*; infertility, sterility, infecundity; impotence &c. 158-unprofitableness &c. (*inutility*) 645.

waste, desert, Sahara, wild, wilderness, howling wilderness.

**V.** be -unproductive &c. *adj.*; hang fire, flash in the pan, come to nothing.

**Adj.** unproductive, inoperative, barren, addle, unfertile, unprolific, arid, sterile, unfruitful, acarpous, infecund; *sine prole*; fallow; teem-, issue-, fruitless; unprofitable &c. (*useless*) 645; null and void, of no effect.

**170. Agency.**—N. agency, operation, force, working, strain, function, office, maintenance, exercise, work, swing, play; inter-working, -action, procuration, procurement.

causation &c. 153; instrumentality &c. 631; influence &c. 175; action &c. (*voluntary*) 680; *modus operandi* &c. 627.

quickening –, maintaining- power; home stroke.

**V.** be -in action &c. *adj.*; operate, work; act, – upon; perform, play, support, sustain, strain, maintain, take effect, quicken, strike.

come –, bring- into -operation, – play; have -play, – free play; bring to bear upon.

**Adj.** operative, efficient, efficacious, practical, effectual.

at work, on foot; acting &c. (*doing*) 680; in -operation, – force, – action, – play, – exercise; acted –, wrought- upon.

**Adv.** by the -agency &c. *n.*- of; through &c. (*instrumentality*) 631; by means of &c. 632.

**171. Physical Energy.**—N. energy, physical energy, force; keenness &c. *adj.*; intensity, vigour, strength, elasticity; go; pep, live wire, high pressure; backbone, mettle, fire, vim.

acri-mony, -tude, -dity; causticity,

**172. Physical Inertness.**—N. inertness, dulness &c. *adj.*; inertia, *vis inertiæ*, inertion, inactivity, torpor, languor; dormancy, quiescence &c. 265; latency, inaction, passivity.

mental inertness; sloth &c. (*inac-*

virulence, poignancy; harshness &c.
*adj.*; severity, edge, point; pungency
&c. 392.

cantharides; Spanish fly; seasoning
&c. (*condiment*) 393, stimulant, excitant.

activity, agitation, effervescence;
ferment, -ation; ebullition, splutter,
perturbation, stir, bustle; voluntary
energy &c. 682; quicksilver.

resolution &c. (*mental energy*) 604;
exertion &c. (*effort*) 686; excitation &c.
(*mental*) 824.

**V.** give -energy &c. *n.*; energize,
stimulate, kindle, excite, activate,
exert; sharpen, pep up, intensify;
inflame &c. (*render violent*) 173; wind up &c. (*strengthen*) 159.

strike, – into, – hard, – home; make an impression.

**Adj.** strong, energetic, forcible, active; strenuous, forceful,
mettlesome, enterprising, go ahead; intense, deep-dyed, severe,
keen, vivid, sharp, acute, incisive, trenchant, brisk, vigorous, live.

rousing, irritating; poignant; virulent, caustic, corrosive, mordant,
harsh, stringent; double-edged, – shotted, – distilled; drastic,
escharotic; racy &c. (*pungent*) 392; sarcastic &c. 932; irenic.

potent &c. (*powerful*) 157; radio-active.

**Adv.** strongly &c. *adj.*; *fortiter in re*; with telling effect.

**Phr.** the steam is up; *vires acquirit eundo.*

*tivity*) 683; inexcitability &c. 826;
irresolution &c. 605; obstinacy &c.
606; permanence &c. 141.

**V.** be -inert &c. *adj.*; hang fire,
smoulder.

**Adj.** inert, inactive, passive, pacific;
torpid &c. 683; sluggish, stagnant, dull,
heavy, flat, slack, tame, slow, blunt;
lifeless, dead, uninfluential.

latent, dormant, smouldering, unexerted.

**Adv.** inactively &c. *adj.*; in -suspense,
-abeyance.

---

**173. Violence.—N.** violence, inclemency, vehemence, might, impetuosity;
boisterousness &c. *adj.*; effervescence,
ebullition; turbulence, bluster; uproar,
riot, row, rumpus, *le diable à quatre*,
devil to pay, all the fat in the fire.

severity &c. 739; ferocity, rage,
berserk, fury; exacerbation, exasperation, malignity; fit, paroxysm, orgasm;
force, brute force; outrage; *coup de
main*; strain, shock, shog; spasm, convulsion, throe; hysterics, passion &c.
(*state of excitability*) 825.

out-break, -burst; burst, bounce,
dissilience, discharge, volley, explosion,
blow up, blast, detonation, rush, eruption, displosion, torrent.

turmoil &c. (*disorder*) 59; ferment
&c. (*agitation*) 315; storm, tempest,
rough weather; squall &c. (*wind*) 349;
earthquake, volcano, thunderstorm.

fury, dragon, demon, tiger, beldame,
Tisiphone, Megæra, Alecto, madcap,
wild beast; fire-eater &c. (*blusterer*) 887.

**V.** be -violent &c. *adj.*; run high;
ferment, effervesce; romp, rampage;
run -wild, – riot; break the peace;

**174. Moderation.—N.** moderation,
lenity &c. 740; temperance, temperateness, gentleness &c. *adj.*; sobriety;
quiet; mental calmness &c. (*inexcitability*) 826.

moderating &c. *v.*; relaxation, remission, mitigation &c. 834; tranquillization, alleviation, assuagement, appeasement, contemporation, pacification.

measure, *juste milieu*, golden mean
&c. 29.

moderator; lullaby, sedative, lenitive, demulcent, rose-water, balm,
soothing syrup, poppy, opiate, anodyne, milk, opium, laudanum, 'poppy
or mandragora'; wet blanket; palliative, calmative.

**V.** be -moderate &c. *adj.*; keep within -bounds, – compass; sober –, settle-
down; keep the peace, remit, relent;
shorten sail.

moderate, soften, mitigate, temper,
accoy; at-, con-temper; mollify, lenify,
dull, take off the edge, blunt, obtund,
sheathe, subdue, chasten; sober –,
tone –, smooth- down; censor, blue-

rush, tear; rush head-long, -foremost; run amuck, raise a storm, make a riot; make –, kick up- a row, – a fuss; bluster, rage, roar, riot, storm; boil, – over; fume, foam, come in like a lion, wreak, bear down, ride rough-shod, out-Herod Herod; spread like wildfire.

break –, fly –, burst- out; bounce, shock, strain; break-, pry-, force-, prize- open.

render -violent &c. *adj.*; sharpen, stir up, quicken, excite, incite, urge, lash, stimulate; irritate, inflame, ex-acerbate, kindle, suscitate, foment; accelerate, aggravate, exasperate, con-vulse, infuriate, madden, lash into fury; fan –, add fuel to- the flame; *oleum addere camino.*

explode, go off, displode, fly, de-tonate, thunder, blow up, flash, flare, erupt, burst; let -off, – fly; discharge, detonize, fulminate.

**Adj.** violent, vehement, forcible; warm; acute, sharp; rough, rude, un-gentle, bluff, boisterous, wild, vicious; brusque, abrupt, waspish; impetuous; rampant.

turbulent; disorderly; blustering, raging &c. *v.*; troublous, riotous; tumultu-ary, -ous; obstreperous, up-roarious; extravagant, unmitigated; ravening, tameless; frenzied &c. (*insane*) 503; desperate &c. (*rash*) 863; infuriate, towering, furious, outrageous, frantic, hysteric, in hysterics.

fiery, flaming, scorching, hot, red-hot, ebullient.

savage, fierce, ferocious, fierce as a tiger.

excited &c. *v.*; un-quelled, -quenched, -extinguished, -repressed, -bridled, -ruly; headstrong; un-governable, -appeasable, -mitigable; un-, in-controllable; insup-, irre-pressible.

spasmodic, convulsive, explosive; detonating &c. *v.*; volcanic, meteoric; stormy &c. (*wind*) 349.

**Adv.** violently &c. *adj.*; amain; by -storm, – force, – main force; with might and main; tooth and nail, *vi et armis*, at the point of the -sword, – bayonet; at one fell swoop; with a high hand, through thick and thin; in desperation, with a vengeance; *à* –, *à toute-outrance*; head-long, -foremost, -first; like a bull at a gate.

pencil, weaken &c. 160; lessen &c. (*decrease*) 36; check; palliate.

tranquillize, assuage, appease, dul-cify, swage, lull, soothe, compose, still, calm, cool, quiet, hush, quell, sober, pacify, tame, damp, lay, allay, rebate, slacken, smooth, alleviate, rock to sleep, deaden, smother; throw -cold water on, – a wet blanket over; slake; curb &c. (*restrain*) 751; tame &c. (*subjugate*) 749; smooth over; pour oil on the -waves, – troubled waters; pour balm into, *mettre de l'eau dans son vin.*

go out like a lamb, 'roar you as gently as any sucking dove.'

**Adj.** moderate; lenient &c. 740; gentle, mild; cool, sober, temperate, reasonable, measured; tempered &c. *v.*; calm, unruffled, quiet, tranquil, still; slow, smooth, untroubled; tame; peace-ful, -able; pacific, halcyon.

un-exciting, -irritating; soft, bland, oily, demulcent, lenitive, anodyne; hyp-notic &c. 683; sedative; assuaging.

mild as mother's milk; milk and water; gentle as a lamb.

**Adv.** moderately &c. *adj.*; gingerly; *piano*; under easy sail, at half speed; within -bounds, – compass; in reason.

**Phr.** *est modus in rebus.*

___

### 4°. INDIRECT POWER

**175. Influence.—N.** influence; im-portance &c. 642; weight, pressure, preponderance, prevalence, sway, pull; predomi-nance, -nancy; ascendency; control, dominance, reign; authority

**175a. Absence of Influence.—N.** impotence &c. 158; inertness &c. 172; irrelevancy &c. 10.

**V.** have no -influence &c. 175.

**Adj.** uninfluential; unconduc-ing,

&c. 737; capability &c. (*power*) 157; interest; spell, magic, magnetism.

footing; purchase &c. (*support*) 215; play, leverage, vantage ground.

tower of strength, host in himself; protection, patronage, auspices.

**V.** have -influence &c. *n.*; be -influential &c. *adj.*; carry weight, actuate, sway, bias, weigh, tell; have a hold upon, magnetize, bear upon, gain a footing, work upon; take -root, – hold; strike root in.

run through, pervade; prevail, dominate, predominate, subject; out-, over-weigh; over-ride, -bear, – come; gain head; rage; be -rife &c. *adj.*; spread like wildfire; have –, get –, gain- -the upper hand, – full play.

be -recognized, – listened to; make one's voice heard, gain a hearing; play a -part, – leading part- in; lead, control, rule, master; get the mastery over; make one's influence felt, cut ice with; take the lead, pull the strings; turn –, throw one's weight into- the scale; set the fashion, lead the dance.

**Adj.** influential; important &c. 642; weighty; prevailing &c. *v.*; prevalent, rife, rampant, dominant, regnant, predominant, in the ascendant, hegemonical; authoritative, recognized, telling, with authority.

**Adv.** with telling effect.

**176. Tendency.—N.** tendency; apt-ness, -itude; proneness, proclivity, bent, turn, tone, bias, set, warp, leaning to, predisposition, inclination, conat-us, propensity, susceptibility; liability &c. 177; quality, nature, temperament; characteristic, idio-crasy, -syncrasy; cast, vein, grain; humour, mood; drift &c. (*direction*) 278; con-duciveness, -ducement; applicability &c. (*utility*) 644; subservience &c. (*instrumentality*) 631.

**V.** tend, contribute, conduce, lead, dispose, incline, verge, bend to, warp, turn, trend, affect, carry, redound to, bid fair to, gravitate towards; promote &c. (*aid*) 707.

**Adj.** tending &c. *v.*; conducive, working towards, in a fair way to, calculated to; liable &c. 177; subservient &c. (*instrumental*) 631; useful &c. 644; subsidiary &c. (*helping*) 707.

**Adv.** for, whither.

**177. Liability.—N.** lia-bility, -bleness; possibility, contingency; suscepti-vity, -bility.

**V.** be -liable &c. *adj.*; incur, lay oneself open to; run the –, stand a- chance; lie under, expose oneself to, open a door to.

**Adj.** liable, subject; in danger &c. 665; open –, exposed –, obnoxious- to; answerable, responsible, accountable, amenable; unexempt from; apt to; dependent on; incident to.

contingent, incidental, possible, on the cards, within range of, at the mercy of.

-ive, -ting to; powerless &c. 158; irrelevant &c. 10.

---

## 5°. Combinations of Causes

**178. Concurrence.—N.** concurrence, co-operation, coagency; coincidence, consilience; union; agreement &c. 23; consent &c. (*assent*) 488; alliance; concert &c. 709; partnership &c. 712; collaboration, conformity.

**V.** con-cur, -duce, -spire, -tribute;

**179. Counteraction.—N.** counteraction, opposition; contrariety &c. 14; antagonism, polarity; clashing &c. *v.*; collision, interference, resistance, renitency, friction; reaction; retroaction; repercussion &c. (*recoil*) 277; counterblast; neutralization &c. (*compensa-*

agree, unite, harmonize; hang –, pull-together &c. (*co-operate*) 709; help to &c. (*aid*) 707.

keep pace with, run parallel to; go –, go along –, go hand in hand- with.

**Adj.** concurring &c. *v.*; concurrent, conformable, joint, co-operative, concordant, coincident, concomitant, harmonious; in alliance with, banded together, of one mind, at one with; parallel.

**Adv.** with one consent.

tion) 30; *vis inertiæ*; check &c. (*hindrance*) 706.

voluntary -opposition &c. 708, – resistance &c. 719; repression &c. (*restraint*) 751.

**V.** counteract; run counter, clash, cross; interfere –, conflict- with; jostle; go –, run –, beat –, militate- against; stultify; antagonize, frustrate, oppose &c. 708; withstand &c. (*resist*) 719; hinder &c. 706; repress &c. (*restrain*) 751; react &c. (*recoil*) 277.

undo, neutralize, cancel; counterpoise &c. (*compensate*) 30; overpoise.

**Adj.** counteracting &c. *v.*; antagonistic, conflicting, retroactive, renitent, reactionary; contrary &c. 14.

**Adv.** although &c. 30; in spite of &c. 708; *malgré*; against.

# CLASS II

## Words Relating to SPACE

### Section I.  SPACE IN GENERAL

#### 1°. Abstract Space

**180.** [Indefinite space.] **Space.—N.**
space, extension, extent, superficial
extent, expanse, stretch; capacity,
room, accommodation, scope, range,
latitude, field, way, expansion, com-
pass, sweep, play, swing, spread.

spare -, elbow -, house- room; stow-
age, roomage, margin; opening, sphere,
arena; lee-, sea-, head-way.

open -, free- space; wide open
spaces; void &c. (*absence*) 187; waste;
wild-, wilder-ness; up-, bottom-,
moor -land; *campagna, veld*, prairie,
steppe.

abyss &c. (*interval*) 198; unlimited
space; infinity &c. 105; world, wide
world; ubiquity &c. (*presence*) 186;
length and breadth of the land.

proportions, acreage; acres, - roods
and perches; square -inches, - yards
&c.

**Adj.** spacious, roomy, extensive, ex-
pansive, capacious, ample; wide-spread,
vast, world-wide, uncircumscribed;
boundless &c. (*infinite*) 105; shore-,
track-, path-less; large &c. 192.

**Adv.** extensively &c. *adj.*; wherever;
everywhere; far and -near, - wide;
right and left, all over, all the world
over; throughout the -world, - length
and breadth of the land; under the
sun, in every quarter; in all -quarters,
- lands; here, there and everywhere;
from -pole to pole, - China to Peru,
- Indus to the pole, - Dan to Beer-
sheba, - end to end; on the face of
the earth, in the wide world, from all
points of the compass; to the -four
winds, - uttermost parts of the earth.

**180a.** **Inextension.—N.** in-, non-
extension; point; atom &c. (*smallness*)
32; pinprick; limitation &c. 229.

**181.** [Definite space.] **Region.—N.**
region, sphere, sphere of influence, cor-
ridor, ground, soil, area, realm, hemi-
sphere, quarter, district, beat, orb,
circuit, circle; pale &c. (*limit*) 233;
com-, de-partment; domain, tract,
territory, terrain, country, canton,
county, shire, province, *arrondissement*,
diocese, parish, township, borough,
constituency, *commune*, ward, wapen-
take, hundred, riding, lathe, garth,
soke, tithing, bailiwick; empire, king-
dom, principality, duchy, grand -,
arch- duchy, palatinate; republic, com-
monwealth, dominion, colony, state,
island.

arena, precincts, *enceinte*, walk,
march; patch, plot, enclosure, &c. 232;
close, *enclave*, field, court; street &c.
(*abode*) 189.

clime, climate, zone, meridian, lati-
tude.

**Adj.** territorial, local, parochial, pro-
vincial, insular.

**182.** [Limited space.] **Place.—N.**
place, lieu, spot, point, dot; niche,
nook, &c. (*corner*) 244; hole; pigeon-
hole &c. (*receptacle*) 191; compartment;
premises, precinct, station, confine;
area, court, yard, court-yard, quad-
rangle, square, compound; abode &c.
189; locality &c. (*situation*) 183.

ins and outs; every hole and corner.

**Adv.** somewhere, in some place,
wherever it may be, here and there, in
various places, *passim*.

## 2°. RELATIVE SPACE

**183. Situation.**—N. situation, position, locality, *locale*, *status*, latitude and longitude; footing, standing, standpoint, post; stage; aspect, attitude, posture, *pose*.

place, site, base, station, seat, *venue*, whereabouts, environment, neighbourhood; bearings &c. (*direction*) 278; spot &c. (*limited space*) 182.

top-, ge-, chor-ography; map &c. 554.

V. be -situated, – situate; lie; have its seat in.

Adj. situ-ate, -ated; local, topical, topographical &c. *n.*

Adv. in -*situ*, – *loco*; here and there, *passim*; here-, there-, whereabouts; in place, here, there.

in –, amidst- such and such- -surroundings, – *environs*, – *entourage*.

**184. Location.**—N. loca-tion, -lization; lodgment; de-, re-position; stow-, pack-age; collocation; packing, lading; establishment, settlement, installation; fixation; insertion &c. 300.

anchorage, roadstead, mooring, mooring mast, encampment, camp, bivouac.

plantation, colony, settlement, cantonment, encampment, reservation; colonization, domestication, situation; habitation &c. (*abode*) 189; cohabitation; 'a local habitation and a name'; indenization, naturalization.

V. place, situate, locate, localize, make a place for, put, lay, set, seat, station, lodge, quarter, post, install; store, house, stow; establish, fix, pin, root; graft; plant &c. (*insert*) 300; shelve, pitch, camp, lay down, deposit, reposit; cradle; moor, tether, picket; pack, tuck in; embed; vest, invest in.

billet on, quarter upon, saddle with; load, lade, freight; pocket, put up, bag.

inhabit &c. (*be present*) 186; domesticate, colonize, populate, people; take –, strike- root; anchor; cast –, come to an- anchor; sit –, settle-down; settle; take up one's -abode, – quarters; plant –, establish –, locate- oneself; squat, perch, hive, *se nicher*, bivouac, burrow, get a footing; encamp, pitch one's tent; put up -at, – one's horses at; keep house.

indenizen, naturalize, adopt.

put back, replace &c. (*restore*) 660.

Adj. placed &c. *v.*; situate, posited, ensconced, embedded, embosomed, rooted; domesticated; vested in, unremoved.

moored &c. *v.*; at anchor.

**185. Displacement.**—N. displacement, elocation, transposition.

ejectment &c. 297; exile &c. (*banishment*) 893; removal &c. (*transference*) 270; unshipment.

misplacement, dislocation &c. 61; fish out of water.

V. dis-place, -plant, -lodge, -nest, -establish; misplace, unseat, disturb; exile &c. (*seclude*) 893; ablegate, set aside, remove; take –, cart- away; take –, draft- off; lade &c. 184, unship.

unload, empty &c. (*eject*) 297; transfer &c. 270; dispel.

vacate; depart &c. 293.

Adj. displaced &c. *v.*; un-placed, -housed, -harboured, -established, -settled; house-, home-less; out of -place, – a situation.

misplaced, out of its element.

## 3°. EXISTENCE IN SPACE

**186. Presence.**—N. presence; occupancy, -ation; attendance; whereness.

permeation, pervasion; diffusion &c. (*dispersion*) 73.

**187. [Nullibiety.\*]** **Absence.** — N. absence; inexistence &c. 2; non-residence, absenteeism; non-attendance, *alibi*.

\* Bishop Wilkins.

ubi-ety, -quity, -quitariness; omni-presence.

bystander &c. (*spectator*) 444.

**V.** exist in space, be -present &c. *adj.*; assist at; make one -of, – at; look on, attend, remain; find –, present- one-self; show one's face; fall in the way of, occur in a place; lie, stand; occupy.

people; inhabit, dwell, reside, stay, sojourn, live, room, abide, bunk, lodge, nestle, roost, perch; take up one's abode &c. (*be located*) 184; tenant, occupy.

resort to, frequent, haunt; revisit.

fill, pervade, permeate; be -diffused, – disseminated- through; over-spread, -run; run through; meet one at every turn.

**Adj.** present; occupying, inhabiting &c. *v.*; moored &c. 184; residential, resi-ant, -dent, -dentiary; domiciled.

ubiquit-ous, -ary; omnipresent.

peopled, populous, full of people, in-habited.

**Adv.** here, there, where, everywhere, aboard, on board, at home, afield; on the spot; here, there and everywhere &c. (*space*) 180; in presence of, before; under the -eyes, – nose- of; in the face of; *in propriâ personâ*.

**188. Inhabitant. — N.** inhabitant; habitant, resident, -iary; dweller, in-dweller; occup-ier, -ant, farmer, planter; householder, lodger, boarder, paying guest; inmate, tenant, renter, incum-bent, sojourner, *locum tenens*, com-morant; settler, squatter, backwoods-man, colonist; islander; denizen, citizen; burgher, oppidan, cockney, cit, towns-man, burgess; villager; cot-tager, -tier, -ter; compatriot.

native, indigene, aboriginal, aborig-ines, autochthones; Briton, English-man, John Bull; new comer &c. (*stranger*) 57.

garrison, crew; population; people &c. (*mankind*) 372; colony, settlement; household.

**V.** inhabit &c. (*be present*) 186; in-denizen &c. (*locate oneself*) 184.

**Adj.** indigenous; enchorial; national, nat-ive, -al; autochthonous; British, English; colonial; domestic; domicil-

emptiness &c. *adj.*; void, *vacuum*; vac-uity, -ancy; *tabula rasa*; exemp-tion; *hiatus* &c. (*interval*) 198; no man's land.

truant, absentee.

nobody; nobody -present, – on earth; no one; not a soul; *âme qui vive.*

**V.** be -absent &c. *adj.*; keep -away, – out of the way; play truant, absent oneself, stay away.

withdraw, make oneself scarce, va-cate; go away, slip out, slip away, retreat &c. 293.

**Adj.** absent, not present, away, non-resident, gone, from home; missing; lost; wanted, wanting; omitted; no-where to be found; inexistent &c. 2.

empty, void; blank, vac-ant, -uous; untenanted, -occupied, -inhabited; ten-antless; desert, -ed; devoid; un-, unin-habitable.

exempt from, not having.

**Adv.** without, *minus*, nowhere; else-where; neither here nor there; in de-fault of; *sans*; behind one's back.

**Phr.** the bird has flown, *non est inventus.*

———

**189. [Place of habitation, or resort.] Abode.—N.** abode, dwelling, lodging, -s; diggings, domicile, residence, ad-dress, habitation, where one's lot is cast, local habitation, berth, seat, lap, sojourn, housing, quarters, headquar-ters, resiance, tabernacle, throne, ark.

home, fatherland, mother country, country &c. 181; home-stead, -stall; fireside, chimney corner; hearth, – stone; household gods, *lares et penates*, roof, household, housing, *dulce domum*; paternal domicile; native -soil, – land, blighty.

nest, *nidus*, snuggery; arbour, bower &c. 191; lair, den, cave, hole, hiding-place, cache, cell, *sanctum sanctorum*, aerie, eyry, rookery, hive; *habitat*, haunt, covert, resort, retreat, perch, roost; nidification.

bivouac, camp, encampment, can-tonment, castrametation; barrack, casemate, casern.

lated, -ed; naturalized, vernacular, domesticated; domiciliary.

in the occupation of; garrisoned –, occupied- by.
_____

tent &c. (covering) 223; building &c. (construction) 161; chamber &c. (receptacle) 191.

tenement, messuage, farm, farm-house, grange, hacienda.

cot, cabin, log cabin, shack, hut, châlet, croft, shed, booth, stall, hovel, bothy, shanty, igloo, tepee, wigwam; pen &c. (inclosure) 232; barn, bawn; kennel, sty, dog-hole, cote, coop, hutch, byre; cow-house, -shed; stable, dove-cote, shippen.

house, mansion, place, villa, cottage, box, lodge, hermitage, rus in urbe, folly, rotunda, tower, château, castle, pavilion, hotel, court, manor-house, capital messuage, hall, palace, alcazar; country seat; kiosk, bungalow; temple &c. 1000; home of rest, alms-, poor-, work-house, asylum; boarding-, lodging-house; flat, maisonette, duplex, penthouse, suite of rooms, apartments, rooms, room, building &c. 161; Mansion House, town hall, Capitol.

assembly-room, auditorium, coliseum, meeting-house, pump-room, spa, health resort, watering-place; club; theatre &c. 840; drill hall, gymnasium, church &c. 1000; Houses of Parliament &c. 696; school &c. 542; inn; hostel, -ry; hotel, tavern, caravansary, khan, hospice; public-, ale-, pot-, mug-house; gin-palace, gin-mill; coffee-, eating-house; canteen, restaurant, rôtisserie, cafeteria, grill-room, buffet, café, estaminet, posada, bodega; bar; saloon, speakeasy, shebeen.

hamlet, village, thorp, dorp, ham, kraal; borough, burgh, town, county-seat, – town, city, capital, metropolis; suburb, quarter. parish &c. 181; ghetto; province, country.

street, place, terrace, parade, esplanade, promenade, pier, em-bankment, road, villas, row, walk, lane, alley, court, quadrangle, quad, wynd, close, yard, passage, rents, mansions, buildings, mews.

square, polygon, circus, crescent, mall, piazza, arcade, colonnade, peristyle, cloister; gardens, grove, residences; block of buildings, market-place, place.

anchorage, roadstead, roads; dock, basin, wharf, quay, port. harbour; dry-, graving-, floating-dock.

garden, park, pleasure-ground, pleasance, demesne.

V. take up one's abode &c. (locate oneself) 184; inhabit &c. (be present) 186.

Adj. urban, oppidan, metropolitan; suburban; provincial, rural, rustic; countrified; regional, parochial, domestic; cosmopolitan; palatial.

**190.** [Things contained.] **Contents.—N.** contents; cargo, lading, freight, shipment, load, bale, burden; cart-, ship-load; cup –, basket –, &c. (receptacle) 191- of; inside &c. 221; stuffing, ullage.

**V.** load, lade, ship, charge, fill, stuff.

**191. Receptacle.—N.** receptacle, container; inclosure &c. 232; recipient, receiver, reservatory.

compartment; cell, -ule; follicle; hole, corner, niche, recess, nook; crypt, stall, pigeon-hole, cove, oriel; cave &c. (concavity) 252.

capsule, vesicle, cyst, pod, calyx, cancelli, utricle, bladder, udder. stomach, paunch, venter, abdomen, ventricle, crop, craw, ingluvies, maw, gizzard, bread-basket, belly, little Mary; mouth.

pocket, pouch, fob, sheath, scabbard, socket, bag, vanity bag, compact, sac, sack, saccule, despatch –, attaché-, tachy- case, wallet, scrip, card-, note- case, billfold, poke, kit, knap-, haver-, ruck-sack, sachel, satchel, reticule, budget, net; ditty-, -box, -bag, kitbag; portfolio; saddlebags, holster; quiver &c. (*magazine*) 636.

chest, box, coffer, caddy, case, casket, pyx, pix, *caisson*, desk, *bureau*, reliquary, shrine; trunk, portmanteau, band-box, *valise*, suitcase, hand-, traveling-, overnight-, Gladstone-, carpet-bag, brief case; boot, imperial; *vache*; cage, manger, rack.

vessel, vase, bushel, barrel; canister, jar; pottle, basket, punnet, pannier, buck-basket, hopper, maund, creel, cran, crate, cradle, bassinet, wisket, whisket, *jardinière, corbeille*, hamper, wastepaper basket, dosser, dorser, tray, hod, scuttle, utensil, spittoon, cuspidor.

[For liquids] cistern &c. (*store*) 636; vat, caldron, barrel, cask, puncheon, keg, rundlet, tun, butt, firkin, hogshead, kilderkin, carboy, amphora, ampulla, bottle, jar, leather bottle, decanter, ewer, cruse, carafe, crock, kit, canteen, flagon; demijohn; flask, -et; stoup, noggin, vial, phial, *ampoule*, cruet, caster; gourd; urn, *épergne*, salver, *patella, tazza, patera*; pig-, big-gin; tea-, coffee-pot, percolator, *samovar*; tyg, nipperkin, pocket-pistol; tub, bucket, pail, skeel, pot, tankard, jug, pitcher, toby, mug, pipkin; gal-, gall-ipot, pannikin; matrass, receiver, retort, alembic, bolthead, can, kettle; bowl, basin, jorum, punch-bowl, cup, goblet, chalice, tumbler, glass, wineglass, rummer, beaker, tass, horn, saucepan, skillet, posnet, tureen, terrine, *casserole*, sauce-, gravy-boat.

plate, platter, paten, dish, vegetable –, *entrée-* dish, trencher, calabash, porringer, potager, saucer, pan, crucible.

shovel, trowel, spoon; table-, dessert-, tea-, egg-, salt-spoon; spatula, ladle; dipper; baler; watch-glass, thimble.

closet, commode, cupboard, cellaret, *chiffonnière*, locker, bin, bunker, *buffet*, press, safe, sideboard, drawer, chest of drawers, till, *scrutoire, secrétaire, éscritoire*, davenport, book-case, cabinet, canterbury; corner cupboard, wardrobe.

chamber, apartment, room, cabin; office, court, hall, atrium; suite of rooms, flat, story; saloon, *salon*, parlour; presence-chamber; sitting-, drawing-, reception-, state-, living-, work-room; gallery, cabinet, closet, cubicle; pew, box; *boudoir*; *adytum, sanctum*; bed-room, dormitory, dressing-room; refectory, dining-room, *salle-à-manger*; nursery, school-room; library, study; studio; billiard-, bath-, smoking-room; den, canteen, mess, officers' mess; gun-, ward-, mess-room.

attic, loft, garret, cockloft, clerestory; cellar, vault, hold, cockpit; *entresol*; mezzanine floor; ground-floor, *rez-de-chaussée*; basement, kitchen, cook-house, galley, pantry, scullery, offices; store-room &c. (*depository*) 636; lumber-room; dust-hole, -bin; dairy, laundry, coach-house; *garage; hangar*; out-, pent-house; lean-to.

portico, porch, piazza, verandah, lobby, court, hall, vestibule, corridor, passage; ante-room, -chamber; lounge; *foyer, loggia*.

conservatory, green-house, glass-house, vinery, bower, arbour, summer-house, alcove, grotto, hermitage, pergola.

lodging &c. (*abode*) 189; bed &c. (*support*) 215; carriage &c. (*vehicle*) 272.

Adj. capsular; saccular, -lated; recipient; ventricular, cystic, vascular, vesicular, cellular, camerated, locular, multilocular, poly-gastric; marsupial; siliqu-ose, -ous.

# Section II. DIMENSIONS

## 1°. General Dimensions

**192. Size.**—N. size, magnitude, dimension, bulk, volume; largeness &c. *adj.*; greatness &c. (*of quantity*) 31; expanse &c. (*space*) 180; amplitude, mass; proportions.

capacity; ton-, tun-nage; calibre, scantling.

turgidity &c. (*expansion*) 194; corpulence, obesity; plumpness, &c. *adj.*; *embonpoint*, corporation, flesh and blood, lustihood.

hugeness &c. *adj.*; enormity, immensity, monstrosity.

giant, Brobdingnagian, Antæus, Goliath, Gog and Magog, Gargantua, monster, mammoth, Cyclops; whale, porpoise, behemoth, leviathan, elephant, hippopotamus; colossus; tun, lump, bulk, block, loaf, mass, clod, nugget, bushel, thumper, whopper, spanker, strapper; Triton among the minnows.

mountain, mound; heap &c. (*assemblage*) 72.

largest portion &c. 50; full-, life-size.

V. be- large &c. *adj.*; become -large &c. (*expand*) 194.

**Adj.** large, big; great &c. (*in quantity*) 31; considerable, bulky, voluminous, ample, massive, massy; capacious, comprehensive; spacious &c. 180; mighty, towering, fine, magnificent.

corpulent, stout, fat, plump, squab, full, lusty, strapping, bouncing; portly, burly, well-fed, full-grown; stalwart, brawny, fleshy; goodly; in good -case, - condition; in condition; chopping, jolly; chub-, chubby-faced.

lubberly, hulky, unwieldy, lumpish, gaunt, spanking, whacking, whopping, thumping, thundering, hulking; overgrown; puffy &c. (*swollen*) 194.

huge, immense, enormous, mighty; vast, -y; amplitudinous, stupendous; monst-er, -rous; gigantic, elephantine;

**193. Littleness.**—N. littleness &c. *adj.*; smallness &c. (*of quantity*) 32; exiguity, inextension; parvi-tude, -ty; duodecimo; Elzevir edition, epitome, microcosm; rudiment; vanishing point; thinness &c. 203.

dwarf, pigmy, atomy, Liliputian, midget, chit, pigwidgeon, urchin, elf; doll, puppet; Tom Thumb, Hop-o'-my thumb, Humpty-dumpty; man-, mannikin; *homunculus*, dapperling, fingerling, dandiprat, cock-sparrow, scalawag.

animalcule, monad, mite, insect, emmet, fly, midge, gnat, shrimp, minnow, worm, maggot, entozoon; *bacillus*, microbe, micro-organism, *bacteria*; *infusoria*; microbe; grub; tit, tomtit, runt, mouse, small fry; millet-, mustard-seed; barley-corn; pebble, grain of sand; mole-hill, button, bubble.

point; atom &c. (*small quantity*) 32; fragment &c. (*small part*) 51; powder &c. 330; point of a pin, mathematical point; *minutiæ* &c. (*unimportance*) 643.

micro-graphy, -meter, -scope; vernier; scale.

V. be -little &c. *adj.*; lie in a nutshell; become small &c. (*decrease*) 36, (*contract*) 195.

**Adj.** little; small &c. (*in quantity*) 32; minute, diminutive, microscopic; inconsiderable &c. (*unimportant*) 643; exiguous, puny, tiny, wee, petty, minikin, miniature, pigmy, elfin; undersized; dwarf, -ed, -ish; spare, stunted, limited; cramp, -ed; pollard, Liliputian, dapper, pocket; port-ative, -able; duodecimo; dumpy, squat; compact, handy; short &c. 201.

impalpable, intangible, evanescent, imperceptible, invisible, inappreciable, infinitesimal, homœopathic; atomic, corpuscular, molecular; rudiment-ary, -al; embryonic.

weazen, scant, scraggy, scrubby;

giant, -like; colossal, Cyclopean, Brob-
dingnagian, Gargantuan, Titanic; in-
finite &c. 105.

large as life; plump as a -dumpling,
– partridge; fat as -a pig, – a quail,
– butter, – brawn, – bacon.

**194. Expansion. — N.** expansion;
increase &c. 35 -of size; enlargement,
extension, augmentation; ampli-fica-
tion, -ation; aggrandizement, spread,
increment, growth, development, pullu-
lation, swell, dilation, dilatation, rare-
faction; turg-escence, -idness, -idity;
obesity &c. (*size*) 192; dropsy, tume-
faction, intumescence, swelling, tu-
mour, *diastole*, distension; puff-ing,
-iness; inflation; pandiculation.

dilatability, expansibility.

germination, growth, upgrowth; ac-
cretion &c. 35.

over-growth, -distension; hyper-
trophy, tympany.

bulb &c. (*convexity*) 250; plumper;
superiority of size.

**V.** become -larger &c. (large &c. 192);
expand, widen, enlarge, extend, grow,
increase, incrassate, swell, gather; fill
out; deploy, take open order, dilate,
stretch, spread; mantle, wax; grow –,
spring- up; bud, bourgeon, shoot,
sprout, germinate, put forth, vegetate,
pullulate, open, burst forth, flower,
blow &c. 734; gain –, gather- flesh;
outgrow; spread like wildfire, overrun.

be larger than; surpass &c. (*be supe-
rior*) 33.

render -larger &c. (large &c. 192);
expand, spread, extend, aggrandize,
distend, develop, amplify, spread out,
widen, magnify, rarefy, inflate, puff,
puff out, blow up, stuff, pad, cram;
exaggerate; fatten; bloat, augment.

**Adj.** expanded &c. *v.*; larger &c.
(large &c. 192); swollen; expansive;
wide-open, -spread; fan-shaped; fla-
belliform; overgrown, exaggerated,
bloated, fat, turgid, tumid, hyper-
trophied, dropsical; pot-, swag-bellied;
œdematous, obese, puffy, pursy,
blowy, distended; patulous; bulbous &c. (*convex*) 250; full-blown,
-grown, -formed; big &c. 192.

thin &c. (*narrow*) 203; granular &c.
(*powdery*) 330; shrunk &c. 195.

**Adv.** in a -small compass, – nutshell;
on a small scale.

---

**195. Contraction.—N.** contraction,
reduction, diminution; decrease &c. 36-
of size; defalcation, decrement; lessen-
ing, shrinkage; collapse, emaciation,
attenuation, tabefaction, consumption,
marasmus, atrophy; systole, neck,
hour-glass.

condensation, compression, con-
straint, compactness; compendium &c.
596; squeezing &c. *v.*; strangulation;
corrugation; astringency, constrin-
gency; astringents, sclerotics; contrac-
tility, compressibility; coarctation.

inferiority in size.

**V.** become -small, – smaller; lessen,
decrease &c. 36; grow less, dwindle,
shrink, contract, narrow, shrivel, col-
lapse, wither, lose flesh, wizen, fall
away, waste, wane, ebb; decay &c.
(*deteriorate*) 659.

be smaller than, fall short of; not
come up to &c. (*be inferior*) 34.

render smaller, lessen, diminish, con-
tract, draw in, narrow, coarctate; con-
strict, constringe; condense, compress,
boil down, deflate, exhaust, empty;
squeeze, corrugate, crush, crumple up;
warp, purse up, pack, stow; pinch,
tighten, strangle; cramp; dwarf, be-
dwarf; shorten &c. 201; circumscribe
&c. 229; restrain &c. 751; fold &c. 258.

pare, reduce, attenuate, rub down,
scrape, file, grind, chip, shave, shear.

**Adj.** contracting &c. *v.*; astringent;
shrunk, contracted &c. *v.*; strangulated,
tabid, wizened, stunted; tabescent;
marasmic; waning &c. *v.*; neap; com-
pact.

unexpanded &c. (expand &c. 194);
inswept; contractile; compressible;
smaller &c. (small &c. 193).

---

**196. Distance.—N.** distance; space
&c. 180; remoteness, farness; far- cry

**197. Nearness.—N.** nearness &c.
*adj.*; proximity, propinquity; vicinity,

to; longinquity, elongation; offing, background; removedness; parallax; reach, span, stride; drift.

out-post, -skirt; horizon, sky-line; aphelion; foreign parts, *ultima Thule*, *ne plus ultra*, antipodes; long range, giant's stride.

dispersion &c. 73.

V. be -distant &c. *adj*.; extend -, stretch -, reach -, spread -, go -, get -, stretch away- to; range, outrange, outreach.

remain at a distance; keep -, stand- -away, - off, - aloof, - clear of.

Adj. distant; far -off, - away; remote, telescopic, distal, wide of; stretching to &c. *v*.; yon, -der; ulterior; trans-marine, -pontine, -atlantic, -alpine; tramontane; ultra-montane, -mundane; hyperborean, antipodean; inaccessible, out of the way; unapproach-ed, -able; incontiguous.

Adv. far -off, - away; afar, -off; off; away; a -long, - great, - good- way off; wide away, aloof; wide -, clear- of; out of -the way, - reach; abroad, yonder, farther, further, beyond; *outre mer*, over the border, far and wide, over the hills and far away; from pole to pole &c. (*over great space*) 180; to the -uttermost parts, - ends- of the earth; out of -hearing, - range, nobody knows where, *à perte de vue*, out of the sphere of, wide of the mark; a far cry to.

apart, asunder; wide -apart, - asunder; *longo intervallo*; at arm's length.

-age; neighbourhood, adjacency; contiguity &c. 199.

short -distance, - step, - cut; earshot, close quarters, stone's throw; bow -, gun -, pistol- shot; hair's breadth, span; close-up.

purlieus, neighbourhood, vicinage, *environs*, *alentours*, suburbs, confines, *banlieue*, borderland; whereabouts.

bystander: neighbour, borderer.

approach &c. 286; convergence &c. 290; perihelion.

V. be -near &c. *adj*.; adjoin, hang about, trench on; border -, verge upon; stand by, approximate, tread on the heels of, cling to, clasp, hug; cuddle, huddle; hang upon the skirts of, hov over; burn; abut.

bring -, draw- -near &c. 286; converge &c. 290; crowd &c. 72; place -side by side &c. *adv*.

Adj. near, nigh; close -, near- at hand; close, neighbouring, propinquent, bordering upon; adjacent, adjoining, limitrophe; proxim-ate, -al; at hand, handy; near the mark, near run; home, intimate.

Adv. near, nigh; hard -, fast- by; close -to, - upon, - up; at the point of; next door to; within -reach, - call, - hearing, - earshot, - range; within an ace of; but a step, not far from, at no great distance; on the -verge, - brink, - skirts- of; in the -environs &c. *n*.; at one's -door, - feet, - elbow, - finger's end, - side; on the tip of one's tongue; under one's nose; within a -stone's throw &c. *n*.; in -sight, - presence- of; at close quarters; cheek by -jole, - jowl; beside, alongside, side by side, *tête-à-tête*; in juxtaposition &c. (*touching*) 199; yard-arm to yard-arm; at the heels of; on the confines of, at the threshold, bordering upon, verging to; in the way.

about; here-, there-abouts; roughly, in round numbers; approxim--ately, -atively; as good as, well nigh.

**198. Interval.—N.** interval, inter-space; separation &c. 44; break, gap, opening; hole &c. 260; chasm, *hiatus*, cæsura; inter-ruption, -regnum; interstice, *lacuna*, cleft, mesh, crevice, chink, rime, creek, cranny, crack, chap, slit, slot, fissure, scissure, rift, flaw, breach, fracture, rent, gash, cut, leak, dike, ha-ha.

**199. Contiguity.—N.** contiguity, contact, proximity, apposition, juxtaposition, touching &c. *v*.; abutment, osculation; meeting, appulse, appulsion, *rencontre*, rencounter, syzygy, coincidence, conjunction, coexistence; adhesion &c. 46.

border-land; frontier &c. (*limit*) 233; tangent.

gorge, defile, ravine, cañon, *crevasse*, abyss, abysm; gulf; inlet, frith, strait, gully, gulch, nullah; pass; notch; furrow &c. 259; yawning gulf; *hiatus -maxime, – valde- deflendus*; parenthesis &c. (*interjacence*) 228; void &c. (*absence*) 187; incompleteness &c. 530.

**V.** gape &c. (*open*) 260.

**Adj.** with an interval, far between.

**Adv.** at intervals &c. (*discontinuously*) 70; *longo intervallo*.

**V.** be -contiguous &c. *adj.*; join, adjoin, abut on, march with, border; tick, graze, touch, meet, osculate, kiss, come in contact, coincide; coexist; adhere &c. 46.

**Adj.** contiguous; touching &c. *v.*; in -contact &c. *n.*; conterminous, end to end, osculatory; pertingent; tangential.

hand to hand; close to &c. (*near*) 197; with no -interval &c. 198.

## 2°. LINEAR DIMENSIONS

**200. Length.**—**N.** length, longitude, span, extent, mileage.

line, bar, rule, stripe, streak, spoke, radius.

lengthening &c. *v.*; pro-longation, -duction, -traction; ten-sion, -sure; extension.

[Measures of length] line, nail, inch, hand, palm, foot, cubit, yard, ell, fathom, rod, pole, perch, furlong, mile, league; chain, metre, kilo-, centi-, milli- &c. -metre.

pedometer, perambulator, odometer, odograph, speedometer, cyclometer, log, telemeter, range finder; scale &c. (*measurement*) 466.

**V.** be -long &c. *adj.*; stretch out, sprawl; extend –, reach –, stretch- to; make a long arm, 'drag its slow length along.'

render -long &c. *adj.*; lengthen, extend, elongate; stretch; pro-long, -duce, -tract; let –, pay –, draw –, spin- out; drawl.

enfilade, look along, view in perspective.

**Adj.** long, -some; lengthy, lank, wiredrawn, outstretched; lengthened &c. *v.*; sesquipedalian &c. (*words*) 577; interminable, no end of.

line-ar, -al; longitudinal, oblong.

as long as -my arm, – to-day and to-morrow; unshortened &c. (shorten &c. 201).

**Adv.** lengthwise, at length, longitudinally, endlong, along; *tandem*, in a line &c. (*continuously*) 69; in perspective.

from -end to end, – stem to stern, – head to foot, – the crown of the head to the sole of the foot. – top to toe, – head to heels; fore and aft.

**201. Shortness.**—**N.** shortness &c. *adj.*; brevity; littleness &c. 193; a span; shortening &c. *v.*; abbrevia-tion, -ture; abridgment, concision, retrenchment, curtailment, decurtation; reduction &c. (*contraction*) 195; epitome &c. (*compendium*) 596.

abridger, abstractor, epitomiser.

elision, ellipsis; conciseness &c. (*in style*) 572.

**V.** be -short &c. *adj.*; render -short &c. *adj.*; shorten, curtail, abridge, abbreviate, take in, reduce; compress &c. (*contract*) 195; epitomize &c. 596.

retrench, cut short, obtruncate; scrimp, cut, chop up, hack, hew; cut –, pare- down; clip, snip, dock, lop, prune; shear, shave, mow, reap, crop; snub; truncate, pollard, stunt, nip, nip in the bud, check the growth of; [in drawing] foreshorten.

**Adj.** short, brief, curt; compendious, compact; stubby, scrimp; shorn, stubbed; stumpy, thickset, podgy, stocky, pug; squab, -by; squat, dumpy; little &c. 193; curtailed of its fair proportions; short by; oblate; concise &c. 572; summary.

**Adv.** shortly &c. *adj.*; in short &c. (*concisely*) 572.

**202. Breadth. Thickness.—N.**
breadth, width, latitude, amplitude;
diameter, bore, calibre, radius; super-
ficial extent &c. (*space*) 180.

thickness, crassitude; corpulence &c.
(*size*) 192; dilatation &c. (*expansion*)
194.

**V.** be -broad &c. *adj.*; become –,
render- -broad &c. *adj.*; expand &c.
194; thicken, widen.

**Adj.** broad, wide, ample, extended;
discous;fan-like;out-spread,-stretched;
wide as a church-door.

thick, dumpy, squab, squat, thick-
set, tubby; thick as a rope, stubby &c.
201.

**203. Narrowness. Thinness. —N.**
narrowness &c. *adj.*; closeness, exility;
exiguity &c. (*little*) 193.

line; hair's -, finger's -breadth; strip,
streak, vein.

thinness &c. *adj.*; tenuity; emacia-
tion, macilency, *marcor*.

shaving, slip &c. (*filament*) 205;
threadpaper, skeleton, shadow, scrag,
anatomy, spindle-shanks, barebones,
lantern jaws, mere skin and bone.

middle constriction, stricture, neck,
waist, isthmus, wasp, hour-glass; ridge,
*ghaut*, pass; ravine &c. 198.

narrowing, coarctation, angustation,
tapering; contraction &c. 195.

**V.** be -narrow &c. *adj.*; narrow, taper,
contract &c. 195; render -narrow &c.
*adj.*

**Adj.** narrow, close; slender, thin, fine; *svelte*; thread-like &c.
(*filament*) 205; finespun, taper, slim, gracile, slight, slight-made;
scant, -y; spare, delicate, incapacious; contracted &c. 195; unex-
panded &c. (expand &c. 194); slender as a thread, capillary.

emaciated, lean, meagre, gaunt, macilent; lank, -y; weedy, skinny,
scrawny, scraggy; starv-ed, -eling; attenuated, shrivelled, wizened,
pinched, peaky, skeletal, spindling, spindle- -legged, -shanked;
extenuated, tabid, marcid, bare-bone, raw-boned; herring-gutted;
worn to a shadow, lean as a rake; thin as a -lath, – whipping post,
– wafer; hatchet-faced; lantern-jawed.

**204. Layer.—N.** layer, stratum,
course, bed, zone, *substratum*, floor,
flag, stage, story, tier, slab, escarpment,
table, tablet, panel, plaque; board,
plank; trencher, platter.

plate; lam-ina, -ella; sheet, flake,
foil, wafer, scale, coat, peel, pellicle,
ply, thickness, membrane, film, leaf,
slice, shive, cut, rasher, shaving, in-
tegument &c. (*covering*) 223.

stratification, lamination, scaliness,
nest of boxes, coats of an onion.

**V.** slice, shave, pare, peel; plate,
coat, veneer; cover &c. 223.

**Adj.** lamell-ar, -ated, -iform; lamin-
ated, -iferous; micaceous; schist-ose,
-ous; scaly, filmy, membranous, flaky,
squamous; folia-ted, -ceous; strati-
fied, -form; tabular, discoid, spathic.

**205. Filament.—N.** filament, line;
fibre, fibril; funicle, vein, hair, capilla-
ment, *cilium*, tendril, gossamer; hair-
stroke; harl.

wire, string, thread, packthread,
cotton, sewing-silk, twine, twist, whip-
cord, cord, rope, cable, yarn, hemp,
oakum, jute, wool, worsted.

strip, shred, slip, spill, list, band,
fillet, *fascia*, ribbon, riband, tape, roll,
lath, slat, strake, splinter, shiver,
shaving.

beard &c. (*roughness*) 256; ramifica-
tion; strand.

**Adj.** fil-amentous, -aceous, -iform;
fibr-ous, -illous; thread-like, wiry,
stringy, ropy; capill-ary, -iform; funicu-
lar, wire-drawn; anguilliform; flagelli-
form; hairy &c. (*rough*) 256; ligulate.

**206. Height.—N.** height, altitude,
elevation, ceiling; eminence. pitch;
loftiness &c. *adj.*; sublimity.

tallness &c. *adj.*; stature, procerity;
prominence &c. 250.

**207. Lowness.—N.** lowness &c. *adj.*;
debasement, depression; prostration
&c. (*horizontal*) 213; depression &c.
(*concave*) 252.

molehill; lowlands; bottomlands;

colossus &c. (*size*) 192; giant, grenadier, giraffe.

mount, -ain; hill, butte, monticle, fell, knap; cape; head-, fore-land; promontory; ridge, hog's back, dune; rising -, vantage- ground; down; moor, -land; Alp; up-, high-lands; heights &c. (*summit*) 210; knoll, hummock, hillock, barrow, mound, mole, *kopje*; steeps, bluff, cliff, craig, tor, peak, pike, clough; escarpment, edge, ledge, brae; dizzy height.

tower, pillar, column, pylon, obelisk, monument, steeple, spire, minaret, *campanile*, belfry, turret, roof, dome, cupola, pagoda, pyramid; sky scraper; Eiffel tower.

pole, pikestaff, maypole, flagstaff; mast, top -, topgallant- mast.

ceiling &c. (*covering*) 223.

high water; high -, flood -, spring- tide.

altimetry &c. (*angle*) 244; altimeter, height-finder, hypsometer, barograph.

**V.** be -high &c. *adj.*; tower, soar. command; hover; cap, culminate; overhang, hang over, impend, beetle; bestride, ride, mount; perch, surmount; cover &c. 223; overtop &c. (*be superior*) 33; stand on tiptoe.

become -high &c. *adj.*; grow, - higher, - taller; upgrow; rise &c. (*ascend*) 305.

render -high &c. *adj.*; heighten &c. (*elevate*) 307.

**Adj.** high, elevated, eminent, exalted, lofty, supernal; tall; gigantic &c. (*big*) 192; Patagonian; towering, beetling, soaring, hanging [gardens]; elevated &c. 307; upper; highest &c. (*topmost*) 210; monticolous, perching, hill-dwelling.

up-, moor-land; hilly, mountainous, alpine, sub-alpine, heaven-kissing; cloud-topt, -capt, -touching; aerial.

overhanging &c. *v.*; incumbent, overlying; super-incumbent, -natant, -imposed; prominent &c. 250.

tall as a -maypole, - poplar, - steeple; lanky &c. (*thin*) 203.

**Adv.** on high, high up, aloft, up, above, aloof, overhead; up -, above- stairs; in the clouds; on -tiptoe, - stilts, - the shoulders of; over head and ears; breast high.

over, upwards; from top to bottom &c. (*completely*) 52.

basement, ground-floor; *rez-de-chaussée* &c. 211; hold; feet, heels.

low water; low -, ebb -, neap -, spring- tide.

**V.** be -low &c. *adj.*; lie -low, - flat; underlie; crouch, slouch, wallow, grovel; lower &c. (*depress*) 308.

**Adj.** low, neap, debased; nether, -most; flat, level with the ground; lying low &c. *v.*; crouched, subjacent, squat, prostrate &c. (*horizontal*) 213.

**Adv.** under; be-, under-neath; below; down, -wards; adown, at the foot of; under-foot, -ground; down -, below-stairs; at a low ebb; below par.

---

**208. Depth.**—**N.** depth; deepness &c. *adj.*; profundity, depression &c. (*concavity*) 252.

hollow, pit, shaft, well, crater, abyss; gulf &c. 198; bowels of the earth, bottomless pit, hell.

soundings, depth of water, water, draught, submersion; plummet, sound, probe; sounding -rod, - line, - machine; lead; submarine, diving bell, bathysphere; diver.

**V.** be -deep &c. *adj.*; render -deep &c. *adj.*; deepen.

plunge &c. 310; sound. heave the lead, take soundings; dig &c. (*excavate*) 252.

**209. Shallowness.**—**N.** shallowness &c. *adj.*; shoals; mere scratch.

**Adj.** shallow, superficial; skin -, ankle -, knee- deep; just enough to wet one's feet; shoal, -y

Adj. deep, -seated; profound, sunk, buried; submerged &c. 310; sub-aqueous, -marine, -terranean, -terrene; underground.

bottom-, sound-, fathom-less; unfathom-ed, -able; abysmal; deep as a well, deep-sea.

knee-, ankle-deep.

Adv. beyond –, out of- one's depth; over head and ears, over one's head.

**210. Summit.—N.** summit, -y; top, vertex, apex, zenith, pinnacle, acme, acropolis, culmination, meridian, utmost height, *ne plus ultra*, height, pitch, maximum, climax, apogee; culminating –, crowning –, turning- point; turn of the tide, fountain head; water-shed, -parting; sky, pole.

tip, -top; crest, crow's nest, cap, truck, peak, nib; end &c. 67; crown, brow; head, nob, noddle, pate.

high places, heights.

top-, top-gallant mast, sky scraper; quarter –, hurricane- deck.

architrave, frieze, cornice, coping, coping-stone, zoophorus, capital, headpiece, capstone, epistyle, sconce, pediment, entablature; tympanum; ceiling &c. (*covering*) 223.

attic, loft, garret, house-top, upper story, roof.

V. culminate, cap, crown, top; overtop &c. (*be superior to*) 33.

Adj. highest, &c. (high &c. 206); top; top-, upper-most; tip-top; culminating &c. *v.*; meridi-an, -onal; capital, head, polar, supreme, supernal, top-gallant.

Adv. a-top, at the top of – the tree, – the heap.

**211. Base.—N.** base, -ment; plinth, dado, wainscot, baseboard; foundation &c. (*support*) 215; substructure, *sub·stratum*, sump, ground, earth, pavement, floor, paving, flag, carpet, ground-floor, deck; footing, groundwork, basis; hold, bilge, orlop deck.

bottom, nadir, foot, sole, toe, hoof, keel, kelson, root.

Adj. bottom; under-, nether-most; fundamental; founded –, based –, grounded –, built- on.

---

**212. Verticality. — N.** verticality; erectness &c. *adj.*; perpendicularity; right angle, normal; azimuth circle.

wall, palisade, precipice, cliff, steep, bluff.

elevation, erection; square, plumbline, plummet.

V. be -vertical &c. *adj.*; stand -up, – on end, – erect, – upright; stick –, cock-up.

render -vertical &c. *adj.*; set –, stick –, raise –, cock- up; erect, rear, raise, pitch, raise on its legs.

Adj. vertical, upright, erect, perpendicular, normal, plumb, straight, bolt upright; rampant; straight –, standing-up &c. *v.*; rectangular, orthogonal.

Adv. vertically &c. *adj.*; up, on end; up –, right- on end; *à plomb*, endwise; on one's legs; at right angles.

---

**213. Horizontality.—N.** horizontality; flatness; level, plane; stratum &c. 204; dead -level, – flat; level plane.

recumbency; lying down &c. *v.*; reclination, decumbence; de-, discumbency; proneness &c. *adj.*; accubation, supination, resupination, prostration; azimuth.

plain, floor, platform, bowling-green; cricket-ground; court; gridiron; baseball diamond; hockey rink; tennis-, croquet-ground, – lawn; billiard table; terrace, estrade, esplanade, *parterre*, table-land, *plateau*, ledge.

spirit-, level; T-square.

V. be -horizontal &c. *adj.*; lie, recline, couch; lie -down, – flat, – prostrate; sprawl, loll; sit down.

render -horizontal &c. *adj.*; lay, – down, – out; level, flatten, even, raze, equalize, smooth, align; prostrate, knock down, floor, fell, ground.

Adj. horizontal, level, even, plane;

flat &c. 251; flat as a -billiard table, – bowling green; alluvial; calm, – as a mill-pond; smooth, – as glass.

re-, de-, pro-, ac-cumbent; lying &c. *v.*; prone, supine, couchant, jacent, prostrate.

Adv. horizontally &c. *adj.*; on -one's back. – all fours, – its beam ends.

**214. Pendency.—N.** pend-, dependency; suspension, hanging &c. *v.*

pendant, drop, tippet, tassel, lobe, tail, train, flap, lappet, skirt, pig-tail, queue, pendulum.

peg, knob, button, hook, nail, stud, ring, staple, tenterhook; davit; fastening &c. 45; spar, horse.

chande-, gase-, electro-lier.

**V.** be -pendent &c. *adj.*; hang, depend, swing, dangle, droop, sag; swag; daggle, flap, trail, flow.

suspend, hang, sling, hook up, hitch, fasten to, append.

**Adj.** pend-ent, -ulous; pensile; hanging &c. *v.*; dependent; suspended &c. *v.*; lowering, overhanging, beetling, decumbent; loose, flowing.

having a -peduncle &c. *n.*; pedunculate, tailed, caudate.

**215. Support.—N.** support, ground, foundation, base, basis; *terra firma*; bearing, fulcrum, *point d'appui*, caudex, purchase, footing, hold, *-locus standi*; landing, – stage, – place; stage, platform; block; rest, resting-place; groundwork, *substratum*, sustentation, subvention; floor &c. (*basement*) 211.

supporter; aid &c. 707; prop, stand, anvil, fulciment; hod, stay, shore, skid, rib, sprag, truss, bandage; sleeper; stirrup, stilts, shoe, sole, heel, splint, lap; bar, rod, boom, sprit, outrigger.

staff, stick, crutch, alpenstock, bourdon; *bâton*, maulstick, colstaff, cowlstaff, staddle; stalk, ped-icel, -icle, – uncle.

post, pillar, shaft, column, pilaster; pediment, pedestal; plinth, shank, leg, socle, zocle; buttress, jamb, mullion, abutment; pile, baluster, banister, stanchion, king post; balustrade.

frame, -work, body, *chassis*, *fuselage*; scaffold, skeleton, beam, rafter, girder, lintel, joist, cantilever, travis, trave, corner-stone. summer, transom; rung, round, step, sill.

columella, back-bone; key-stone; axle, -tree; axis; arch, ogive, mainstay.

trunnion, pivot, rowlock; peg &c. (*pendency*) 214; tie-beam &c: (*fastening*) 45; thole pin.

board, ledge, shelf, hob, bracket, trevet, trivet, arbor, rack, hatrack; mantel, -piece, -shelf; slab, console; counter, dresser; flange, corbel; table, trestle, teapoy; shoulder; perch; horse; easel, desk; retable, predella.

seat, throne, dais; divan, musnud; chair, bench, form, stool, camp-stool, sofa, settee, davenport, stall, miserere, arm –, easy –, elbow –, rocking- chair; couch, day bed, *fauteuil*, woolsack, ottoman, settle, squab, bench, box, dicky; saddle, pannel, pillion; side –, pack- saddle; pommel.

bed, berth, pallet, tester, crib, cot, bassinet, hammock, shakedown, camp bed, bunk, truckle-bed, cradle, litter, stretcher, bedstead; four-poster, French bed; bedding, mattress, *paillasse*; pillow, bolster; mat, rug, cushion.

stool, footstool, hassock, faldstool, *prie-dieu*; tabouret; tripod: Atlas, Persides, Atlantos, Caryatides, Hercules.

**V.** be -supported &c.; lie –, sit –, recline –, lean –, loll –, rest –; stand –, step –, repose –, abut –, bear –, be based &c.- on; have at one's back; be-stride, -straddle.

support, bear, carry, hold, sustain, shoulder; hold –, back –,

[ 73 ]

bolster –, shore- up; up-hold, -bear; prop; under-prop, -pin, -set; bandage, &c. 43; brace, truss; cradle, pillow.

give –, furnish –, afford –, supply –, lend- -support, – foundations; bottom, found, base, ground, embed.

maintain, keep on foot; aid &c. 707.

**Adj.** support-ing, -ed, &c. *v.*; atlantean, columellar; sustentative, fundamental, basal.

**Adv.** astride on, astraddle; pick-a-back.

**216. Parallelism.—N.** parallelism; coextension, concentricity, collimation.

**V.** be –, lie- parallel to; collimate.

**Adj.** parallel; coextensive, collateral, concentric, concurrent.

**Adv.** alongside, abreast &c. (*laterally*) 236.

_____

**217. Obliquity.—N.** obliquity, inclination, skew, slope, slant; crookedness &c. *adj.*; slopeness; leaning &c. *v.*; bevel, bezel, ramp, tilt; bias, list, twist, swag, cant, lurch; distortion &c. 243; bend &c. (*curve*) 245; tower of Pisa.

acclivity, rise, ascent, grade. gradient, *glacis*, rising ground, hill, bank, declivity, downhill, dip, fall, devexity; gentle –, rapid- slope; easy -ascent, – descent; shelving beach; *talus*; *montagne Russe*; *facilis descensus Averni*.

steepness &c. *adj.*; cliff, precipice &c. (*vertical*) 212; escarpment. scarp.

[Measure of inclination] clinometer, theodolite, level, sextant. quadrant, protractor; angle, sine, cosine, tangent &c. hypothenuse. diagonal; zigzag, chevron.

**V.** be -oblique &c. *adj.*; slope, slant, lean, incline, shelve, stoop, decline, descend, bend, heel, careen, sag, swag, seel, slouch, cant. sidle.

render -oblique &c. *adj.*; sway, bias; slope, slant; incline, bend, crook; cant, tilt; distort &c. 243.

**Adj.** oblique, inclined; sloping &c. *v.*; tilted &c. *v.*; recumbent, clinal, skew, askew, slant, aslant, bias, plagiedral, indirect, wry, awry, ajee, crooked; knock-kneed &c. (*distorted*) 243; bevel, out of the perpendicular.

uphill, rising, ascending, acclivous; downhill, falling, descending; declining, declivous, devex, anticlinal; steep, abrupt, precipitous, break-neck.

diagonal; trans-verse, -versal; athwart, antiparallel; curved &c. 245.

**Adv.** obliquely &c. *adj.*; on –, all on- one side; askew, askant, askance, aslope, asquint, edgewise, at an angle; side-long, -ways; slope-, slant-wise; by a side wind.

**218. Inversion.—N.** in-, e-, sub-, re-, retro-, intro-version; contraposition &c. 237; contrariety &c. 14; reversal; turn of the tide.

overturn; somer-sault, -set; summerset; *culbute*; revulsion; *pirouette*. transposition, transposal, anastrophy, *metastasis*, *hyperbaton*, *anastrophe*, *hysteron-proteron*, hypallage, *synchysis*, *tmesis*, parenthesis; *metathesis*; palindrome; Spoonerism.

pronation and supination.

**V.** be -inverted &c.; turn –, go –, wheel- -round, – about, – to the right about; turn –, go –, tilt –, topple-over; capsize, turn turtle.

in-, sub-, retro-, intro-vert; reverse; up-, over-turn, -set; turn -topsy turvy &c. *adj.*; *culbuter*; transpose, put the cart before the horse, turn the tables.

**Adj.** inverted &c. *v.*; wrong side -out, – up; inside out, upside down; bottom –, keel- upwards; supine, on one's head, topsy turvy, *sens dessus sens dessous.*

inverse; reverse &c. (*contrary*) 14; opposite &c. 237. topheavy, unstable.

**Adv.** inversely &c. *adj.*; hirdie-girdie; heels over head, head over heels.

**219. Crossing.—N.** crossing &c. *v.*; inter-section, – lacement, – twinement, -digitation; decussation, transversion; convolution &c. 248.

reticulation, meshwork, network; inosculation, anastomosis, intertexture, mortise.

net, *plexus*, web, mesh, twill, skein, sleeve, felt, lace; wicker; mat, -ting; plait, trellis, wattle, lattice, grating, *grille*, gridiron, tracery, fretwork, filigree, reticle; tissue, netting, mokes.

cross, crucifix, rood, crisscross, crux; chain, wreath, braid, cat's cradle, knot; entanglement &c. (*disorder*) 59.

[woven fabrics] cloth, linen, muslin, cambric, drill, homespun, tweed, broadcloth &c.

**V.** cross, decussate; inter-sect, -lace, -twine, -twist, -weave, -digitate, -link.

twine, entwine, weave, inweave, twist, wreathe; anastomose, inosculate, dovetail, splice, link.

mat, plait, plat, braid, felt, twill; tangle, entangle, ravel; net, knot; dishevel, raddle.

**Adj.** crossing &c. *v.*; crossed, matted &c. *v.*; transverse.

cross, cruciform, crucial; reti-form, -cular, -culated; areolar, cancellated, mullioned, latticed, grated, barred, streaked; textile, secant, plexal; interfretted.

**Adv.** across, thwart, athwart, transversely, crosswise.

### 3°. Centrical Dimensions*

#### 1. *General*

**220. Exteriority. — N.** exteriority; outside, exterior; surface, superficies; skin &c. (*covering*) 223; *superstratum*; disk, disc; face, facet.

excentricity; circumjacence &c. 227. **V.** be -exterior &c. *adj.*; lie around &c. 227.

place -exteriorly, – outwardly, – outside; put –, turn- out.

**Adj.** exter-ior, -nal; extraneous, outer, -most; out-ward, -lying, -side, -door; round about &c. 227; extramural.

superficial, skin-deep; frontal, discoid.

extraregarding; eccentric; outstanding; extrinsic &c. 6.

**Adv.** externally &c. *adj.*; out, without, over, outwards, *ab extra*, out of doors; *extra muros.*

**221. Interiority.—N.** interiority; in, side, interior, endocrine; interspace, subsoil, *substratum.*

contents &c. 190; substance, pith, marrow; backbone &c. (*centre*) 222; heart, bosom, breast, abdomen; vitals, viscera, entrails, bowels, belly, intestines, guts, chitterlings, womb, lap; gland, cell; internal organs, *penetralia*, recesses, innermost recesses; cave &c. (*concavity*) 252.

inhabitant &c. 188.

**V.** be -inside &c. *adj.*, – within &c. *adv.*

place –, keep- within; enclose &c. (*circumscribe*) 229; intern; embed &c. (*insert*) 300.

**Adj.** inter-ior, -nal; inner, inside, intimate, inward, intraregarding: in-, inner-most; deep-seated; visceral, intes-

* That is, Dimensions having reference to a centre.

in the open air; *sub -Jove, – dio; à la belle étoile, al fresco.*

tine, -tinal; inland; subcutaneous; interstitial &c. (*interjacent*) 228; inwrought &c. (*intrinsic*) 5; enclosed &c. *v.*

home, domestic, indoor, intramural, vernacular; endemic.

Adv. internally &c. *adj.*; inwards, within, in, inly; here-, there-, where-in; *ab intra*, withinside; in –, within- doors; at home, in the bosom of one's family.

**222. Centrality.—N.** centrality, centricalness, centre; middle &c. 68; focus &c. 74.

core, kernel; nucleus, nucleolus; heart, pole, axis, pivot, fulcrum, bull's eye; hub, nave, navel; *umbilicus*, spine, backbone, marrow, pith; hot-bed; concentration &c. (*convergence*) 290; centralization; symmetry.

centre of -gravity, – pressure, – percussion, – oscillation, – buoyancy &c. metacentre.

**V.** be -central &c. *adj.*; converge &c. 290.

render central, centralize, concentrate; bring to a focus.

**Adj.** centr-al, -ical; middle &c. 68; axial, pivotal, focal, umbilical, concentric; middlemost, nuclear, centric, centraidal; spinal, vertebral.

**Adv.** middle; midst; centrally &c. *adj.*

**223. Covering.—N.** covering, cover; canopy, tilt, awning, baldachin, tent, marquee, *tente d'abri*, umbrella, parasol, sunshade; veil (*shade*) 424; shield &c. (*defence*) 717; pall.

roof, dome, cupola, mansard roof; ceiling; thatch, tile; pan-, pen-tile; tiling, shingles, slates, slating, leads; shed &c. (*abode*) 189.

**224. Lining.—N.** lining, inner coating; coating &c. (*covering*) 223; stalactite, -agmite.

filling, stuffing, wadding, padding, bushing.

wainscot, *parietes*, wall, brattice.

**V.** line, stuff, incrust, wad, pad, fill.

**Adj.** lined &c. *v.*

top, lid, covercle, door, *operculum*, eyelid, blind, curtain.

bandage, plaster, lint, wrapping, dossil, finger stall.

coverlet, counterpane, sheet, quilt, comforter, eiderdown; tarpaulin, blanket, rug, drugget, linoleum, oilcloth; housing.

in-, tegument; skin, pellicle, fleece, fell, fur, ermine, miniver, sable, sealskin &c.; leather, morocco, calf, pigskin, elk, kid, cowhide &c.; shagreen, hide; pelt, -ry; cuticle, *dermis*, scarf-skin, *epidermis.*

clothing &c. 225; mask &c. (*concealment*) 530.

peel, crust, bark, rind, *cortex*, husk, shell, coat.

capsule; ferrule; sheath, -ing; pod, cod; casing, case, theca, *elytron; involucrum*; wrapp-ing, -er, envelope, vesicle; dermatology, conchology.

armour, -plate, armouring; veneer, facing; pavement; scale &c. (*layer*) 204; coating, paint, stain; varnish &c. (*resin*) 356a; anointing &c. *v.*; inunction; incrustation, superposition, obduction, ground, enamel, whitewash, plaster, stucco, rough cast, pebble dash, compo; rendering; cerement; ointment &c. (*grease*) 356.

**V.** cover; super-pose, -impose; over-lay, -spread; wrap &c. 225; incase; face, case, veneer, pave, paper; tip, cap, bind, revet.

coat, paint, varnish, pay, incrust, stucco, cement, dab, plaster, tar; wash; be-, smear; be-, daub; anoint, do over; gild, plate, electroplate, japan, lacquer, lacker, enamel, whitewash; lay it on thick.

over-lie, -arch; conceal &c. 528.

Adj. covering &c. *v.*; cutaneous, dermal, cortical, cuticular, tegumentary, skinny, scaly, squamous; covered &c. *v.*; imbricated, loricated, armour-plated, iron-clad; under cover, hooded, cloaked, cowled.

**225. Investment.—N.** investment; covering &c. 223; dress, clothing, raiment, drapery, costume, attire, guise, toilet, *toilette*, trim; habiliment; vesture, -ment; garment, garb, palliament, apparel, wardrobe, wearing apparel, clothes, things.

array; tailoring, millinery; best bib and tucker; finery &c. (*ornament*) 847; full dress &c. (*show*) 882; garniture; theatrical properties.

outfit, equipment, *trousseau*; uniform, khaki, regimentals; academicals, canonicals &c. 999; livery, gear, harness, turn out, accoutrement, caparison, suit, rigging, trappings, traps, slops, togs, toggery; masquerade.

dishabille, morning dress, lounge suit, tea-gown, *kimono*, *négligé*, dressing-gown, *peignoir*, wrapper, undress; shooting-coat; smoking-jacket, mufti; rags, tatters, old clothes; mourning, weeds; duds; slippers.

robe, tunic, dolman, *paletot*, habit, gown, coat, coatee, frock, blouse, middy, sagum, *toga*, smock-frock; frock-, dress-, morning-, tail-coat; dress-suit, – clothes, swallow-tail coat, dinner-, Eton-jacket.

cloak, pall; mantle, mantlet, mantua, shawl, *pelisse*, veil, yashmak; cape, tippet, kirtle, plaid, muffler, comforter, Balaclava helmet, haik, huke, chlamys, mantilla, tabard, housing, horse-cloth, burnous, *roquelaure*; *houppelande*; sur-, top, over-, great-coat; *surtout*, spencer, cardigan, sweater, blazer; mackintosh, waterproof, slicker, raincoat, oilskin, trench coat, ulster, monkey-, pea-, pilot-jacket, redingote; wraprascal, poncho, cardinal, pelerine, talma.

jacket, jumper, vest, jerkin, waistcoat, doublet, *camisole*, gabardine; stays, *corsage*, corset, corselet, bodice; stomacher; skirt, petticoat, slip, farthingale, kilt, jupe, crinoline, bustle, hobble skirt, *panier*, apron, pinafore; loin cloth.

trousers; breeches, trews, pantaloons, unmentionables, inexpressibles, overalls, pyjamas, smalls, small-clothes; tights, pants, shorts, drawers; knickerbockers, knickers, plus fours, bloomers, divided skirt; phil-, fill-ibeg.

**226. Divestment.—N.** divestment; taking off &c. *v.*

nudity; bareness &c. *adj.*; undress; dishabille &c. 225, altogether; nu-, denu-dation; decortication, depilation, excoriation, desquamation; moulting; exfoliation.

baldness, alopecia, acomia.

**V.** divest; uncover &c. (*cover &c.* 223); denude, bare, strip; undress, unclothe, disrobe &c. (dress, enrobe, &c. 225); uncoif; dismantle; uncase; put –, take –, cast- off; shed, doff; husk, peel, pare, decorticate, desquamate, excoriate, skin, scalp, flay, bark, expose, lay open; exfoliate, moult, mew; cast the skin.

**Adj.** divested &c. *v.*; bare, naked, nude; un-dressed, -draped, -clad, -clothed, -appareled; exposed; in dishabille; *décolleté*; bald, threadbare, ragged, callow, roofless.

in -a state of nature, – nature's garb, – buff, – native buff, – birthday suit; *in puris naturalibus*; with nothing on, stark naked; bald as a coot, bare as the back of one's hand; out at elbows; barefoot; bareback; leaf-, nap-, hairless, shaved, clean shaven, tonsured, beardless, bald-headed, acomous.

head-dress, -gear; cap, *béret*, tam o' shanter, glengarry, topee, ßombrero; hat; cocked –, high –, tall –, top –, silk –, opera –, crush -hat, *gibus*, beaver, castor, bonnet, tile, wideawake, billy-cock; bowler; soft felt –, straw –, leghorn -hat, panama; toque; wimple; night-, mob-, skull-cap, biretta; hood, cowl, coif; capote, calach; scull-cap; kerchief, snood; head, *coiffure*; crown &c. (*circle*) 247; *chignon*, pelt, wig, front, peruke, periwig; caftan, turban, fez, *tarboosh*, taj, shako, csako, busby; *képi*, forage cap, bearskin; helmet &c. 717; mask, domino.

body clothes; linen; shirt, sark, smock, shift, *chemise, lingerie*; night-gown, -shirt; bed-gown, *sac de nuit*; jersey, guernsey; underwear, undies, underclothing, -waistcoat.

neck-erchief, -cloth; tie, ruff, collar, cravat, stock, handkerchief, bandana, scarf; bib, tucker; dicky; boa; girdle &c. (*circle*) 247; cummerbund.

shoe, pump, brogue, boot, slipper, sandal, galoche, goloshes, arctics, rubber boots, overshoes, patten, clog, sabot; high-low; Blücher –, Wellington –, Hessian –, jack –, top- boot; Balmoral; legging, puttee, buskin, greave, galligaskin, moccasin, *gamache*, gambado, gaiter, spatter-dash, spat, antigropelos; stocking, hose, gaskins, trunk-hose, sock, hosiery.

glove, gauntlet, mitten, cuff, muffettee, wristband, sleeve.

swaddling cloth, baby-linen, *layette*; pocket-handkerchief.

shroud &c. 363.

clothier, tailor, milliner, *costumier*, sempstress, seamstress, snip; dress-, habit-, breeches-, shoe-maker; cordwainer, cobbler, Crispin, hosier, hatter; draper, linendraper, haberdasher, mercer.

**V.** invest; cover &c. 223; envelop, lap, involve; in-, en-wrap; wrap; fold –, wrap –, lap –, muffle- up; overlap; sheathe, swathe, swaddle, roll up in, shroud, circumvest.

vest, clothe, array, dress, dight, drape, robe, enrobe, attire, tire, garb, habilitate, apparel, accoutre, rig, fit out; bedizen, deck &c. (*ornament*) 847; perk; equip, harness, caparison; dress up.

wear; don; put –, huddle –, slip- on; mantle.

**Adj.** invested &c. *v.*; habited; dight, -ed; clad, *costumé*, shod, *chaussé; en grande tenue* &c. (*show*) 882.

sartorial.

---

**227. Circumjacence.—N.** circum-jacence, -ambience; environment, encompassment; atmosphere, medium; surroundings, *entourage.*

outpost; border &c. (*edge*) 231; girdle &c. (*circumference*) 230; outskirts, *boulevards*, suburbs, purlieus, precincts, *faubourgs, environs, banlieue*, neighbourhood, vicinity.

**V.** lie -around &c. *adv.*; surround, beset, compass, encompass, environ, inclose, enclose, encircle, circle, embrace, circumvent, lap, gird; begird, girdle, engird; skirt, twine round; hem in &c. (*circumscribe*) 229; besiege, invest, blockade.

**Adj.** circum-jacent, -ambient, -fluent;

**228. Interjacence.—N.** inter-jacence, -currence, -venience, -location, -digitation, -penetration; permeation.

inter-jection, -polation, -lineation, -spersion, -calation; embolism.

inter-vention, -ference, -position; in-, ob-trusion; insinuation; insertion &c. 300; dovetailing; infiltration; intromission.

intermedi-um, -ary; go-between, agent, middleman, medium, bodkin, intruder, interloper; parenthesis, episode; fly-leaf.

partition, *septum*, diaphragm, mid-riff; party-wall, panel, vail, bulkhead, brattice, *cloison*; half-way house.

**V.** lie –, come –, get- between; inter-

ambient; surrounding &c. *v.*; circumferential, surburban.

Adv. around, about; without; on -every side, – all sides; right and left, all round, round about; in the neighbourhood.

vene, slide in, interpenetrate, permeate.

put between, introduce, intromit, import; throw –, wedge –, edge –, jam –, worm –, foist –, run –, plough –, work- in; inter-pose, -ject, -calate, -polate, -line, -leave, -sperse, -weave, -lard, -digitate; let in, dovetail, splice, mortise; insinuate, smuggle; infiltrate, ingrain.

interfere, put in an oar, thrust one's nose in; intrude, obtrude; have a finger in the pie; introduce the thin end of the wedge; thrust in &c. (*insert*) 300.

Adj. inter-jacent, -current, -venient, -vening &c. *v.*, -mediate, -mediary, -calary, -stitial, -costal, -mural, -planetary, -stellar; embolismal.

parenthetical, episodic; mediterranean; intrusive; embosomed; merged, mean, middle, medium, median.

Adv. between, betwixt; 'twixt; among, -st; amid, -st; 'mid, -st; in the thick of; betwixt and between; sandwich-wise; parenthetically, *obiter dictum*.

**229. Circumscription.—N.** circumscription, limitation, inclosure; confinement &c. (*restraint*) 751; circumvallation, encincture; envelope &c. 232.

**V.** circumscribe, limit, bound, confine, enclose; surround &c. 227; compass about; imprison &c. (*restrain*) 751; hedge –, wall –, rail- in; fence –, hedge- round; embar; picket, corral.

enfold, bury, incase, pack up, enshrine, inclasp; wrap up &c. (*invest*) 225; embosom.

Adj. circumscribed &c. *v.*; begirt, lapt; circumambient; buried –, immersed- in; embosomed, in the bosom of, imbedded, encysted, mewed up; imprisoned &c. 751; land-locked, in a ring fence.

**230. Outline.—N.** outline, circumference; peri-meter, -phery; ambit, circuit, lines, *tournure*, *contour*, profile, *silhouette*, lineaments; bounds, coastline.

zone, belt, girth, band, baldric, zodiac, girdle, tire, cingle, clasp, girt; *cordon* &c. (*inclosure*) 232; circlet &c. 247.

**V.** outline, delineate, *silhouette*, circumscribe &c. 229; profile, block out.

Adj. outlined &c. *v.*; circumferential, perimetric, peripheral.

**231. Edge.—N.** edge, verge, brink, brow, brim, margin, border, confines, skirt, rim, felloe, felly, flange, side, mouth; jaws, chops, chaps, *fauces*; lip, muzzle.

threshold, door, porch; portal &c. (*opening*) 260; coast, shore, strand, beach, bank, wharf, quay, dock.

frame, fringe, flounce, frill, list, trimming, edging, skirting, hem, selvedge, welt; furbelow, valance, exergue.

Adj. border, marginal, skirting; labial, labiated, marginated.

**232. Inclosure.—N.** inclosure, enclosure, envelope; case &c. (*receptacle*) 191; wrapper; girdle &c. 230.

pen, fold, croft, sty; pen-, in-, sheep-fold; paddock, pound, corral, kraal; yard, compound; net, seine net.

wall; hedge, -row; *espalier*; fence &c. (*defence*) 717; pale, paling, balustrade, rail, railing, gunwale; quickset hedge, park paling, circum-vallation, *enceinte*, ring fence.

barrier, barricade; gate, -way; door, hatch, *cordon*; prison &c. 752.
dike, dyke, ditch, fosse, moat, trench.
**V.** inclose; circumscribe &c. 229.

**233. Limit.—N.** limit, boundary, bounds, confine, *enclave*, term, bourn, verge, kerb-stone, curbstone, but, pale; termin-ation, -us; stint, frontier, precinct, marches.

boundary line, landmark, benchmark; line of -demarcation, – cir-cumvallation; pillars of Hercules; Rubicon, turning-point; *ne plus ultra*; sluice, flood-gate.
**V.** limit, bound, confine, define, circumscribe, demarcate, delimit, encompass.
**Adj.** definite; contermin-ate, -able, terminable, limitable; terminal, frontier, border, bordering, boundary.
**Adv.** thus far, – and no further.

## 2. *Special*

**234. Front.—N.** front; fore, – part; foreground; forefront, face, disk, disc, frontage, *façade*, *proscenium*, facia, frontispiece; priority, anteriority; ob-verse [of a medal].

fore –, front- rank, first line; van, -guard; advanced guard; outpost, scout.

brow, forehead, visage, physiognomy, phiz, features, countenance, map, mug; rostrum, beak, bow, stem, prow, prore, jib, bowsprit; forecastle.

pioneer &c. (*precursor*) 64; metopo-scopy.
**V.** be –, stand- in front &c. *adj.*; front, face, confront, breast, brave; bend forwards; come to the -front, – fore.
**Adj.** fore, forward, anterior, front, frontal.
**Adv.** before; in -front, – the van, – advance; ahead, right ahead; fore-, head-most; in the foreground; before one's -face, – eyes; face to face, *vis-à-vis*.

**235. Rear.—N.** rear, back, posterior-ity; rear -rank, – guard; background, *hinterland*.

occiput, nape, scruff, chine; heels; tail, rump, croup, buttock, posteriors, bottom, seat, backside, scut, breech, *dorsum*, loin; dorsal –, lumbar- region; hind quarters.

stern, poop, after-part, counter; postern, heel-, tail-piece, crupper.
wake; train &c. (*sequence*) 281.
reverse; other side of the shield.
**V.** be -behind &c. *adv.*; fall astern; bend backwards; bring up the rear; follow &c. 622; tail, shadow.
**Adj.** back, rear; hind, -er, -most, -ermost; post-ern, -erior; dorsal, after; caudal, lumbar; mizzen.
**Adv.** behind; in the -rear, – ruck, – back-ground; behind one's back; at the -heels, – tail, – back- of; back to back. after, -most, aft, abaft, astern, stern-most, aback, rear-, hind-, back-ward.

---

**236. Laterality.—N.** laterality; side, flank, beam, quarter, lee; hand; cheek, jowl, jole, wing; profile; temple, *parietes*, loin, haunch, hip.

gable, -end; broadside; lee side.
points of the compass; East, Orient, Levant; West, occident; orientation.
**V.** be -on one side &c. *adv.*; flank, outflank; sidle; skirt, border.
**Adj.** lateral, sidelong; collateral;

**237. Contraposition.—N.** contraposi-tion, opposition; polarity; inversion &c. 218; opposite side; antithesis; reverse, inverse; counterpart; antipodes; oppo-site poles, North and South.
**V.** be -opposite &c. *adj.*; subtend.
**Adj.** opposite; reverse, inverse; an-tipodal, subcontrary; fronting, facing, diametrically opposite.
Northern, Septentrional, Boreal, are

parietal, flanking, skirting; flanked; sideling.

many-sided; multi-, bi-, tri-, quadrilateral.

East-ern, -ward, -erly; orient, -al, auroral, Levantine; West-ern, -ward, -erly; occidental, Hesperian; equatorial.

Adv. side-ways, -long; broadside on; on one side, abreast, abeam, alongside, beside, aside; by, – the side of; side by side; cheek by jowl &c. (near) 197; to -windward, – leeward; laterally &c. adj.; right and left; on her beam ends.

tic; Southern, Austral, antarctic, polar.

Adv. over, – the way, – against; against; face to face, vis-à-vis; as poles asunder.

---

**238. Dextrality. — N.** dextrality; right, – hand; dexter, offside, starboard.

**Adj.** dextral, right-handed; ambidextral, dexterous, dextrorsal &c.

**239. Sinistrality.—N.** sinistrality; left, – hand; sinister, nearside, larboard, port.

**Adj.** sinistral, sinister, sinistrorsal &c., left-handed, sinistromanual, sinistrous.

## Section III.  FORM

### 1°. General Form

**240. Form.—N.** form, figure, shape; con-formation, -figuration; make, formation, frame, construction, design, cut, set, build, trim, cut of one's jib; stamp, type, cast, mould; fashion; contour &c. (outline) 230; structure &c. 329.

feature, lineament, outline, turn; phase &c. (aspect) 448; posture, attitude, pose.

[Science of form] morphology.

[Similarity of form] isomorphism.

forming &c. v.; form-, figur-, efformation; sculpture.

**V.** form, shape, figure, fashion, efform, carve, cut, chisel, hew, cast; rough-hew, -cast; sketch; block –, hammer- out; trim; lick –, put- into shape; model, knead, work up into, set, mould, sculpture; cast, stamp; build &c. (construct) 161.

**Adj.** formed &c. v.

[Receiving form] plastic, fictile, full-fashioned &c.

[Giving form] plasmic &c.

[Similar in form] isomorphous &c.

**241. [Absence of form.] Amorphism.** —**N.** amorphism, informity, uncouthness; unlicked cub, rough diamond; rudis indigestaque moles; disorder &c. 59; deformity &c. 243.

disfigure-, deface-ment, deformation; mutilation.

**V.** [Destroy form] deface, disfigure, deform, mutilate, truncate; derange &c. 61.

**Adj.** shapeless, amorphous, malformed, formless; un-formed, -hewn, -fashioned, -shapen; rough, rude, Gothic, barbarous, rugged, in the rough; misshapen &c. 243.

**242. [Regularity of form.] Symmetry.** —**N.** symmetry, shapeliness, finish; beauty &c. 845; proportion, eurythmy, eurythmic, uniformity, parallelism; bi-, tri-, multi-lateral symmetry; centrality &c. 222.

**243. [Irregularity of form.] Distortion.—N.** dis-, de-, con-tortion; knot, mop, warp, buckle, screw, twist; crookedness &c. (obliquity) 217; grimace; deformity; mal-, malcon-formation; monstrosity, misproportion, want

arborescence, branching, ramification.

Adj. symmetrical, shapely, well set, finished; beautiful &c. 845; classic, chaste, severe.

regular, uniform, balanced; equal &c. 27; parallel, coextensive.

arbor-escent, -iform; dendr-iform, ꭓid; branching; ramous, ramose.

of symmetry, *anamorphosis*; ugliness &c. 846; teratology.

V. distort, contort, twist, warp &c. *n.*; wrest, writhe, make faces, deform, misshape.

Adj. distorted &c. *v.*; out of shape, irregular, unsymmetric, awry, wry, askew, crooked, sinuous; anamorphous; not -true, – straight; on one side, crump, deformed; mis-shapen, -begotten; mis-, ill-proportioned; ill-made; grotesque, crooked as a ram's horn; hump-, hunch-, bunch-, crook-backed; bandy; bandy-, bow-legged; bow-, knock-kneed; splay-, club-footed; taliped; round-shouldered; snub-nosed; curtailed of one's fair proportions; scalene, stumpy &c. (*short*) 201; gaunt &c. (*thin*) 203; bloated &c. 194.

Adv. all manner of ways.

## 2°. SPECIAL FORM

**244. Angularity.**—N. angular-ity, -ness; aduncity; angle, cusp, bend; fold &c. 258; notch &c. 257; fork, bifurcation.

elbow, knee, knuckle, ankle, groin, crotch, crutch, crane, fluke, scythe, sickle, zigzag, kimbo.

corner, nook, recess, niche, oriel.

right angle &c. (*perpendicular*) 212; obliquity &c. 217; angle of 45°, mitre; acute –, obtuse –, salient –, re-entrant –, spherical –, solid –, dihedral- angle.

angular -measurement, – elevation, – distance, – velocity; trigon-, goni-ometry; altimetry; clin-, graph-, goni-ometer; theodolite; transit circle; sextant, quadrant; dichotomy.

triangle, trigon, wedge; rectangle, square, lozenge, diamond; rhomb, -us; quadr-angle, -ilateral; parallelogram; quadrature; poly-, penta-, hexa-, hepta-, octa-, deca-gon.

Platonic bodies; cube, rhomboid; tetra-, penta-, hexa-, octa-, dodeca-, icosa-hedron; prism, pyramid; parallelopiped.

V. bend, fork, bifurcate, crinkle, divaricate, branch, ramify.

Adj. angular, bent, crooked, aduncous, uncinated, aquiline, jagged, serrated; falc-iform, -ated; furcular, furcated, forked, bifurcate, crotched; zigzag; dovetailed; knock-kneed, crinkled, akimbo, kimbo, geniculated; oblique &c. 217.

fusiform, wedge-shaped, cuneiform; tri-angular, -gonal, -lateral; quadr-angular, -ilateral; rectangular, square, foursquare, multilateral; polygonal &c. *n.*; cubical, rhomboidal, pyramidal.

**245. Curvature.**—N. curv-ature, -ity, -ation; incurv-ity, -ation; bend; flexure, -ion; conflexure; crook, hook, bought, bending; de-, inflexion; arcuation, devexity, turn; deviation, *détour*, sweep; curl, -ing; bough; recurv-ity, -ation; sinuosity &c. 248; aduncity.

curve, arc, arch, arcade, vault, dome, bow, crescent, *meniscus*, half-moon, lunule, horse-shoe, loop, crane-neck;

**246. Straightness.**—N. straightness, rectilinearity, directness; inflexibility &c. (*stiffness*) 323; straight –, right –, direct-, bee- line; short cut.

V. be -straight &c. *adj.*; have no turning; not -incline, – bend, – turn, – deviate- to either side; go straight; steer for &c. (*direction*) 278.

render straight, straighten, rectify; set –, put- straight; un-bend, -fold,

para-, hyper-bola; catenary, festoon; conch-, cardi-oid; caustic, instep; tracery.

V. be -curved &c. *adj.*; sweep, swag, sag; deviate &c. 279; turn; re-enter.

render -curved &c. *adj.*; bend, curve, incurvate; de-, in-flect; crook; turn, round, arch, arcuate, arch over, loop the loop, concamerate; bow, coil, curl, recurve, frizzle.

-curl &c. 248, -ravel &c. 219, -wrap.

Adj. straight; rectiline-ar, -al; direct, even, right, true, in a line; unbent &c. *v.*; un-deviating, -turned, -distorted, -swerving; straight as an arrow &c. (*direct*) 278; inflexible &c. 323.

Adj. curved &c. *v.*; curvi-form, -lineal, -linear; devex, devious; recurv-ed, -ous; *retroussé*; crump; bowed &c. *v.*; vaulted; hooked; falc-iform, -ated; semicircular, crescentic; lun-iform, -ular; semi-lunar, meniscal; conchoidal; cord-iform, -ated; cardioid; heart-, bell-, pear-, fig-shaped; reniform; lenti-form, -cular; bow-legged &c. (*distorted*) 243; oblique &c. 217; circular &c. 247.

**247. [Simple circularity.] Circularity.** —N. circularity, roundness; rotundity &c. 249.

circle, circlet, clasp, ring, washer, areola, hoop, roundlet, *annulus*, am-ulet, bracelet, armlet, armilla; ringlet; eye, loop, wheel; cycle, orb, orbit, rundle, zone, belt, *cordon*, band; sash, girdle, cestus, cincture, baldric, fillet, *fascia*, wreath, garland; crown, corona, coronet, chaplet, snood, necklace, collar; noose, lasso, lariat.

ellipse, oval, ovule; ellipsoid, cycloid; epi-cycloid, -cycle; semi-circle; quad-rant, sextant, sector.

V. make -round &c. *adj.*; round. go round; encircle &c. 227; describe -a circle &c. 311.

Adj. round, rounded, circular, annu-lar, orbicular; oval, ovate; elliptic, -al; ovoid, egg-shaped; pear-shaped &c. 245; cycloidal &c. *n.*; spherical &c. 249.

**248. [Complex circularity.] Convolu-tion.**—N. winding &c. *v.*; con-, in-, circum-volution; wave, undulation, tortuosity, anfractuosity; sinu-osity, -ation, sinuousness; meandering, cir-cuit, circumbendibus, twist, twirl, windings and turnings, *ambages*; tor-sion; inosculation; reticulation &c. (*crossing*) 219.

coil, roll, curl, buckle, spire, spiral, helix, corkscrew, worm, volute, whorl, rundle; tendril; scollop, scallop, es-calop; kink.

serpent, snake, eel, maze, labyrinth

V. be -convoluted &c. *adj.*; wind, twine, turn and twist, twirl; wave, undulate, meander; inosculate; en-twine, intwine; twist, coil, roll; wrinkle, curl, crisp, twill; frizz, -le; crimp, crape, indent, scollop, scallop; wring, intort; contort; wreathe &c. (*cross*) 219.

Adj. convoluted; winding, twisted &c. *v.*; tortile, tortive; wavy; und-ated, -ulatory; circling, snaky, snake-like, serpentine; serpent-, anguill-, verm-iform; vermicular; mazy, tortu-ous, anfractuous, sinuous, flexuous, wavy, sigmoidal.

involved, intricate, complicated, perplexed; labyrinth-ic, -ian, -ine; circuitous; peristaltic; dædalian, curly.

wreathy, frizzly, crapy, buckled; ravelled &c. (*in disorder*) 59, spiral, coiled, helical, turbinated.

Adv. in and out, round and round.

**249. Rotundity.**—N. rotundity; roundness &c. *adj.*; cylindricity; spher-icity, -oidity; globosity.

cylin-der, -droid; barrel, drum; roll, -er; *rouleau*, column, rolling-pin, rundle; chimney-pot, drain-pipe.

cone, conoid; pear-, egg-, bell-shape.

sphere, globe, ball, boulder, bowlder; spher-, ellips , ge-, glob-oid, oblong -, oblate- spheroid; drop, spherule, globule, vesicle, bulb, bullet, pellet, *pelote*, clew, pill, marble, pea, knob, pommel, knot.

**V.** render -spherical &c. *adj.*; form into a sphere, sphere, roll into a ball; give -rotundity &c. *n.*; round.

**Adj.** rotund; round &c. (*circular*) 247; cylindr-ic, -ical, -oid; columnar, lumbriciform; conic, -al; spher-ical, -oidal; glob-ular, -ated, -ous, -ose; egg-, bell-, pear-shaped; ov-oid, -iform; gibbous; campaniform, -ulate, -iliform; fungiform, bead-like, moniliform, pyriform, bulbous; *teres atque rotundus*; round as -an orange, - an apple, - a ball, - a billiard ball, - a cannon ball.

### 3°. SUPERFICIAL FORM

**250. Convexity. — N.** convexity, prominence, projection, swelling, gibbosity, bilge, bulge, protuberance, protrusion; excrescency, camber.

intumescence; tumour, tumor; tubercle, -osity; excrescence; hump, hunch, bunch, gnarl, lump.

tooth, knob, elbow, process, *apophysis*, condyle, bulb, node, nodule, nodosity, tongue, *dorsum*, boss, embossment, bump, clump; sugar-loaf &c. (*sharpness*) 253; bow; mamelon.

pimple, wen, wheal, *papula*, postule, pock, proud flesh, growth, goitre, *sarcoma*, carbuncle, corn, bunion, wart, furnuncle, polypus, adenoid, fungus, fungosity, *exostosis*, bleb, blister, blain; boil &c. (*disease*) 655; bubble, blob.

papilla, nipple, teat, pap, breast, dug, mammilla; proboscis, nose, neb, beak, snout, nozzle, snozzle; Adam's apple; belly, paunch, corporation; withers, back, shoulder, lip, flange.

peg, button, stud, ridge, rib, jutty, trunnion, snag.

cupola, dome, bee-hive; arch, balcony, eaves; pilaster.

relief, relievo, *cameo*; *basso-, mezzo-, alto-rilievo*; low-, bas-, high-relief.

hill &c. (*height*) 206; cape, promontory, mull; fore-, head-land; point of land, naze, ness, mole, jetty, hummock, ledge, spur.

**V.** be -prominent &c. *adj.*; project, bulge, protrude, bag, belly, pout, bouge, bunch; jut -, stand -, stick -, poke- out; stick -, bristle -, start -, cock -, shoot- up; swell -, hang -, bend- over; beetle.

render -prominent &c. *adj.*; raise 307; emboss, chase.

**251. Flatness.—N.** flatness &c. *adj.*; smoothness &c. 255.

plane; level &c. 213; plate, platter, table, tablet, slab.

**V.** render flat, flatten, squash; level &c. 213.

**Adj.** flat, plane, even, flush, scutiform, discoid; level &c. (*horizontal*) 213; smooth; flat as -a pancake, - a fluke, - a flounder, - a board, - my hand.

**252. Concavity.—N.** concavity, depression, dip; hollow, -ness; indentation, *intaglio*, cavity, antrum, dent, dint, dimple, follicle, pit, *sinus, alveolus, lacuna*; excavation, trench, sap, mine, tunnel, burrow; trough &c. (*furrow*) 259; honeycomb.

cup, basin, crater, punch-bowl; cell &c. (*receptacle*) 191; socket, faucet.

valley, vale, dale, dell, gap, dingle, combe, bottom, slade, strath, glade, grove, glen, cave, cavern, cove; grot, -to; alcove, *cul-de-sac*, blind alley; gully &c. 198; arch &c. (*curve*) 245; bay &c. (*of the sea*) 343.

excavator, sapper, miner.

**V.** be -concave &c. *adj.*; retire, cave in.

render -concave &c. *adj.*; depress, hollow; scoop, - out; gouge, dig, delve, excavate, dent, dint, mine, sap, undermine, burrow, tunnel, stave in.

**Adj.** depressed &c. *v.*; concave, hollow, stove in; dished; spoon-like; retiring; retreating; cavernous; porous &c. (*with holes*) 260; cellular, spongy, spongious; honeycombed, alveolar; infundibul-ar, -iform; funnel-, bell-shaped; campaniform, capsular; vaulted, arched. —————

**Adj.** convex, prominent, protuberant, underhung, undershot; projecting &c. *v.*; bossed, bossy, nodular, bunchy; clav-ate, -ated; hummocky, *moutonné*, mammiform; papul-ous, -ose; hemispheric, bulbous; bowed, arched; bold; bellied; tuber-ous, -culous; tumorous; cornute, knobby, odontoid; lenti-form, -cular; gibbous.

salient, in relief, raised, *repoussé*; bloated &c. (*expanded*) 194.

**253. Sharpness.—N.** sharpness &c. *adj.*; acuity, acumination; spinosity.

point, spike, spine, *spiculum*, tine; needle, pin; tack, nail; prick, -le; spur, rowel, barb; spit, cusp; horn, antler; snag; tag; thorn, bristle.

nib, tooth, incisor, tusk; spoke, cog, ratchet.

crag, crest, *arête*, cone, peak, sugar-loaf, pike, *aiguille*; spire, pyramid, steeple.

beard, *chevaux de frise*, porcupine, hedgehog, brier, bramble, thistle; comb, awn, bur.

wedge; knife-, cutting- edge; blade, edge-tool, cutlery, knife, penknife, whittle, razor; scalpel, bistoury, lancet; chisel; ploughshare, coulter; hatchet, axe, pick-axe, mattock, pick, adze, bill; bill-hook, cleaver, cutter; skiver; scythe, sickle, scissors, shears; sword &c. (*arms*) 727; bodkin &c. (*perforator*) 262.

sharpener, hone, strop; grind-, whet-stone; steel, emery.

**V.** be -sharp &c. *adj.*; taper to a point; bristle with.

render -sharp &c. *adj.*; sharpen, point, aculeate, acuminate, whet, barb, spiculate, set, strop, grind.

cut &c. (*sunder*) 44.

**Adj.** sharp, keen; acute; aci-cular, -form; acu-leated. -minated; pointed; tapering; conical, pyramidal; mucron-ate, -ated; spindle-, needle-shaped; spiked, spiky, ensiform, peaked, salient, cusp-ed; -idate, -idated; corn-ute, -uted, -iculate; prickly; spiny, spinous; thorny, bristling, muricated, pectinated, studded, thistly, briery; craggy &c. (*rough*) 256; snaggy; digitated, two-edged, fusiform; denti-form, -culated; toothed; odontoid; star-like; stell-ated, -iform; arrow-headed; arrowy, barbed, spurred, sagittal; spear-shaped, hastate; horned; conical.

cutting; sharp-, knife-edged; sharp -, keen- as a razor; sharp as a needle; sharpened &c. *v.*; set.

**254. Bluntness.—N.** bluntness &c. *adj.*

**V.** be -, render- blunt &c. *adj.*; obtund, dull; take off the -point, - edge; turn.

**Adj.** blunt, obtuse, dull, bluff.

---

**255. Smoothness.—N.** smoothness &c. *adj.*; polish, gloss; lubric-ity, -ation.

down, velvet, silk, satin; slide; bowling green &c. (*level*) 213; glass, ice; asphalt, pavement, flags.

roller, steam-roller; iron, flat-iron, tailor's goose; sand-, emery-paper; burnisher, turpentine and bees-wax.

**V.** smooth, -en; plane; file; mow, shave; level, roll; macadamize; polish, burnish, planish, levigate, calender, glaze; iron, hot-press, mangle; lubricate &c. (*oil*) 332.

**256. Roughness.—N.** roughness &c. *adj.*; tooth, grain, texture, ripple; asperity, rugosity, salebrosity, corrugation, nodosity; arborescence &c. 242.

brush, hair, beard, shag, mane, whisker, mutton-chops, *moustache*, *mustachio*, imperial, Van Dyke, tress, lock, curl, ringlet, *fimbriæ*, *cilia*, *villi*; eyelashes, eye-brows, love-lock.

plum-age, -osity; plume, *panache*, crest; feather, tuft, tussock, fringe, toupee.

wool, velvet, plush, nap, pile, floss,

**Adj.** smooth; polished &c. *v.*; even; level &c. 213; plane &c. (*flat*) 251; sleek, glossy; silken, silky; lanate, downy, velvety; glabrous, slippery, glassy, lubricous, oily, soft; unwrinkled; smooth as -glass, – ice, – velvet, – oil; slippery as an eel; woolly &c. (*feathery*) **256.**

fluff, fur, down; byssus, moss, bur.
**V.** be -rough &c. *adj.*; go against the grain.

render -rough &c. *adj.*; roughen, rough cast, knurl; ruffle, crisp, crumple, crinkle, corrugate, engrail; set on edge, stroke –, rub- the wrong way, rumple.

**Adj.** rough, uneven; scabrous, knotted; nodular; rug-ged, -ose, -ous; asperous, crisp, salebrous, gnarled, unpolished, unsmooth, rough-hewn; knurled, cross-grained, crag-gy, -ged; crackling, scraggy, jagged, unkempt, prickly &c. (*sharp*) 253; arborescent &c. 242; leafy, well-wooded; feathery; plum-ose, -igerous; tufted, fimbriated, hairy, bristly, ciliated, filamentous, hirsute; crin-ose, -ite; bushy, hispid, villous, pappous, bearded, pilous, shaggy, shagged; fringed, befringed; set-ous, -ose, -aceous; 'like quills upon the fretful porcupine'; rough as a -nutmeg grater, – bear.

downy, velvety, flocculent, woolly; lan-ate, -ated; lanugin-ous. -ose; tomentous.

**Adv.** against the grain, in the rough, on edge.

**257. Notch.—N.** notch, dent, nick, cut; indent, -ation; serration; dimple.

embrasure, battlement, machicolation; saw, tooth, crenelle, scallop, scollop, vandyke.

**V.** notch, nick, cut, pink, mill, score, dent, indent, jag, scarify, scotch, crimp, scollop, crenulate, vandyke.

**Adj.** notched &c. *v.*; crenate, -d; dentate, -d; denticulate, -d; toothed, palmated, serrated.

**258. Fold.—N.** fold, plicature, pleat, plait, ply, crease; tuck, gather; flexion, flexure, joint, elbow, doubling, duplicature, wrinkle, rimple, crinkle, crankle, crumple, rumple, rivel, ruck, ruffle, dog's ear, corrugation, frounce, flounce, lapel; pucker, crow's feet.

**V.** fold, double, plicate, pleat, plait, crease, wrinkle, crinkle, crankle, curl, smock, cockle up, crocker, rimple, rumple, frizzle, frounce, rivel, twill, corrugate, ruffle, crimple, crumple, pucker; turn –, double- -down, – under; tuck, ruck, hem, gather.

**Adj.** folded &c. *v.*

**259. Furrow.—N.** furrow, groove, rut, *sulcus*, scratch, streak, *striæ*, crack, score, incision, slit; chamfer, fluting.

channel, gutter, trench, ditch, dike, dyke, moat, fosse, trough, kennel; ravine &c. (*interval*) 198.

**V.** furrow &c. *n.*; flute, groove, carve, corrugate, plough; incise, chase, enchase, grave, engrave, etch, bite in, cross-hatch.

**Adj.** furrowed &c. *v.*; ribbed, striated, sulcated, fluted, canaliculated; bisulc-ous, -ate; trisulcate; corduroy.

**260. Opening.—N.** hole, foramen; puncture, blow-out, perforation; pin-, key-, loop-, port-, peep-, mouse-, pigeon-hole; eye, – of a needle; eyelet; slot.

opening; apert-ure, -ness; hiation,

**261. Closure.—N.** closure, occlusion, blockade; shutting up &c. *v.*; obstruction &c. (*hindrance*) 706; gag; embolism; contraction &c. 195; infarction; con-, ob-stipation; blind -alley, – corner; *cul-de-sac*, *cæcum*; imper-foration,

yawning, oscitancy, dehiscence, patefaction, pandiculation; gap, chasm &c; (*interval*) 198.

embrasure, window, casement, light; sky-, fan-light; lattice; bay-, bow-window; oriel; dormer, lantern, *abatjour.*

out-, in-let; vent, vomitory; *embouchure*; orifice, mouth, sucker, muzzle, throat, gullet, placket, weasand, wizen, nozzle, *œsophagus.*

portal, porch, gate, ostiary, postern, wicket, trap-door, hatch, door; arcade; gate-, door-, hatch-, gang-way; lichgate.

way, path &c. 627; thoroughfare; channel, passage, tube, pipe; water-pipe &c. 350; air-pipe &c. 351; vessel, tubule, canal, gut, fistula; adjutage, ajutage; chimney, smoke stack, flue, tap, funnel, gully, tunnel, main; mine, pit, adit, shaft; gallery.

alley, aisle, glade, lane, vista.

bore, calibre; pore; blind orifice.

por-ousness, -osity; sieve, cullender, colander; grater, shredder; cribble, riddle, screen; honeycomb.

apertion, perforation; piercing &c. *v.*; terebration, empalement, pertusion, puncture, acupuncture, penetration.

opener, key, master-key, *passe-partout.*

V. open, ope, gape, dehisce, yawn, bilge; fly open.

perforate, pierce, empierce, tap, bore, drill; mine &c. (*scoop out*) 252; tunnel; trans-pierce, -fix; enfilade, impale, spike, spear, gore, spit, stab, pink, puncture, lance, trepan, trephine, stick, prick, riddle, punch; stave in.

cut a passage through; make -way, — room- for.

un-cover, -close, -rip; lay –, cut –, rip –, throw- open.

Adj. open; perforated &c. *v.*; perforate; wide open, agape, ajar; un-closed, -stopped; oscitant, gaping, yawning; patent.

tubular, cannular, fistulous; per-vious, -meable; foraminous; vesi-, vas-cular; porous, follicular, cribriform, honeycombed, infundibular, riddled; tubul-ous, -ated, piped.

opening &c. *v.*; aperient.

Int. *open sesame!*

**262. Perforator.** — **N.** perforator, piercer, borer, auger, gimlet, stylet, drill, wimble, awl, bradawl, scoop, terrier, corkscrew, dibble, trocar, trepan, trephine, probe, bodkin, needle, stiletto, broach, reamer, rimer, warder, lancet; punch, -eon; spikebit, gouge; spear &c. (*weapon*) 727.

-viousness &c. *adj.*, -meability; stopper &c. 263; *operculum.*

V. close, occlude, plug; block –, stop –, fill –, bung –, cork –, button –, stuff –, shut –, dam- up, obturate; blockade; obstruct &c. (*hinder*) 706; bar, bolt, stop, seal, plumb; choke, throttle; ram down, tamp, dam, cram; trap, clinch; put to –, shut- the door; batten down the hatches.

Adj. closed &c. *v.*; shut, operculated; unopened.

unpierced, imporous, cæcal; imperforate, -vious, -meable; impenetrable; un-, im-passable; invious; path-, way-less; untrodden.

unventilated; air-, water-tight; hermetically sealed; tight, snug.

---

**263. Stopper.**—**N.** stopper, stopple, plug, cork, bung, spike, spill, stop-cock, tap; rammer; ram, -rod; piston; stop-gap; wadding, stuffing, padding, stopping, dossil, pledget, tompion, tourni-quet. obturator; wad.

cover &c. 223; valve, slide valve; vent peg, spigot.

janitor, door –; gate- keeper, porter, commissionaire, *concierge,* warder, beadle, Cerberus, usher, guard, sentry, sentinel; ostiary.

## Section IV. MOTION

### 1°. Motion in General

**264. [Successive change of place.*]**
**Motion.**—**N.** motion, movement, move; motivity, motility, going &c. *v.*; unrest.

stream, current, flow, flux, run, course, stir; conduction, evolution; kinematics.

step, rate, pace, tread, stride, gait, clip, port, footfall, cadence, carriage, velocity, angular velocity; progress, locomotion; journey &c. 266; voyage &c. 267; transit &c. 270.

restlessness &c. (*changeableness*) 149; mobility; movableness, motive power; laws of motion; mobilization.

**V.** be -in motion &c. *adj.*; move, go, hie, gang, budge, stir, pass, flit; hover -round, – about; shift, slide, slither, glide; roll, – on; flow, stream, run, drift, sweep along; wander &c. (*deviate*) 279; walk &c. 266; change –, shift-one's -place, – quarters; dodge; keep -going, – moving.

put –, set- in motion; move; impel &c. 276; propel &c. 284; render movable, mobilize.

**Adj.** moving &c. *v.*; in motion; motile, transitional; motory, motive; shifting, movable, mobile, mercurial, unquiet; restless &c. (*changeable*) 149; nomadic &c. 266; erratic &c. 279.

**Adv.** under way; on the -move, – wing, – tramp, – march.

**265. Quiescence.**—**N.** rest; stillness &c. *adj.*; quiescence; stag-nation, -nancy; fixity, immobility, catalepsy; indisturbance; quietism.

quiet, tranquillity, calm; repose &c. 687; peace; dead calm, anticyclone; statue-like repose; silence &c. 403; not a -breath of air, – mouse stirring; sleep &c. (*inactivity*) 683.

pause, lull &c. (*cessation*) 142; stand, – still; standing still &c. *v.*; lock; dead -lock, – stop, – stand; full stop; fix; embargo.

resting-place; bivouac; home &c. (*abode*) 189; pillow &c. (*support*) 215; haven &c. (*refuge*) 666; goal &c. (*arrival*) 292.

**V.** be -quiescent &c. *adj.*; stand –, lie- still; keep quiet, repose, hold the breath.

remain, stay; stand, lie to, ride at anchor, remain *in situ*, mark time, tarry; bring –, heave –, lay- to; pull –, draw- up; hold, halt; stop, – short; rest, pause, anchor; cast –, come to an- anchor; rest on one's oars; repose on one's laurels, take breath; stop &c. (*discontinue*) 142.

stagnate, vegetate; *quieta non movere*; let -alone, – well alone; abide, rest and be thankful; keep within doors, stay at home, go to bed.

dwell &c. (*be present*) 186; settle &c. (*be located*) 184; alight &c. (*arrive*) 292.

stick, – fast; stand, – like a post; not stir a -peg, – step; be at a -stand &c. *n.*

quell, becalm, hush, stay, lull to sleep, lay an embargo on; put the brake on.

**Adj.** quiescent, still; motion-, move-less; fixed; stationary; at -rest, – a stand, – a stand-still, – anchor; stock-still; immotile; standing still &c. *v.*; sedentary, untravelled, stay-at-home; becalmed, stagnant, quiet; un-moved, -disturbed, -ruffled; calm, restful; cataleptic; immovable &c. (*stable*) 150; sleeping &c. (*inactive*) 683; silent &c. 403; still as -a statue, – a post, – a mouse, – death.

**Adv.** at a stand &c. *adj.*; *tout court*; at the halt.

**Int.** stop! stay! avast! halt! hold, – hard! whoa!

**Phr.** *requiescat in pace.*

*\** A thing cannot be said to *move* from one place to another, unless it passes in succession through every intermediate place; hence motion is only such a change of place as is *successive*. 'Rapid, swift, &c., as thought' are therefore incorrect expressions.

**266.** [Locomotion by land.] **Journey.**
—**N.** travel; travelling &c. *v.*; wayfaring, campaigning.

journey, excursion, expedition, tour, trip, grand tour, circuit, peregrination, discursion, ramble, pilgrimage, *trek*, course, ambulation, march, walk, hike, promenade, constitutional, stroll, saunter, tramp, jog-trot, turn, stalk, perambulation; noctambulation; somnambulism, sleep walking; outing, ride, drive, airing, jaunt.

equitation, horsemanship, riding, *manège*, ride and tie.

roving, vagrancy, pererration; marching and countermarching; nomadism; vagabond-ism, -age; gadding; flit, -ting; migration; e-, im-, de-, inter-migration.

plan, itinerary, guide; hand-, roadbook; Baedeker, Murray, Bradshaw, time table.

procession, parade, cavalcade, caravan, file, *cortège*, column.

[Organs and instruments of locomotion] vehicle &c. 272; locomotive &c. 271; legs, feet, pegs, pins, trotters.

traveller &c. 268.

**V.** travel, journey, course; tour; take –, go- a journey; take –, go out for- -a walk &c. *n.*; have a run; take the air.

flit, take wing; migrate, emigrate, *trek*; rove, prowl, roam, range, patrol, pace up and down, traverse; scour –, traverse- the country; peragrate; per-circum-ambulate; nomadize, wander, ramble, stroll, saunter, hover, go one's rounds, straggle; gad, – about; expatiate.

walk, march, step, tread, pace, plod, wend; promenade; trudge, tramp; stalk, stride, straddle, strut, foot it, stump, bundle, bowl along, toddle; paddle; tread –, follow –, pursue- a path.

**267.** [Locomotion by water, or air.] **Navigation.**—**N.** navigation; aquatics; boating, cruising, yachting; ship &c. 273; oar, scull, sweep, punt-pole, paddle, – wheel, screw, propeller, stern wheel, sail, canvas.

natation, swimming; fin, flipper-fish's tail.

aerial navigation, air service, airways, airmanship, aero-donetics, -dynamics, -mechanics, -station, -statics, -nautics; ballooning, balloonry; balloon &c. 273; flying, flight, aviation, volitation; wing, pinion, *aileron*.

voyage, sail, cruise, passage, circumnavigation, *periplus*; head-, stern-, lee-way.

mariner, aeronaut &c. 269.

**V.** sail; put to sea &c. (*depart*) 293; take ship, get under way; spread -sail, – canvas; gather way, have way on; make –, carry- sail; plough the -waves, – deep, – main, – ocean; walk the waters.

navigate, warp, luff, scud, boom, kedge; drift, course, cruise, coast; hug the -shore, – land; circumnavigate.

ply the oar, row, paddle, pull, scull, punt, steam.

swim, float; buffet the waves, ride the storm, skim, *effleurer*, dive, wade.

fly, aviate, be wafted, hover, soar, drift, glide, plane, sideslip, *volplane*, pique, dive, spin, roll, loop, flutter; take -wing, – a flight; wing one's -flight, – way.

**Adj.** sailing &c. *v.*; seafaring, nautical, maritime, naval; sea-going, coasting; afloat; navigable, aquatic, natatory.

volitant, volant, aerostatic, aerial, aeronautic; alar, alate, pennate.

**Adv.** under -way, – sail, – canvas, – steam; on the wing.

_____

take horse, ride, drive, trot, amble, canter, prance, fisk, frisk, *caracoler*; gallop &c. (*move quickly*) 274; motor, cycle, taxi; go by -car, – train, – tram, – bus, – plane.

peg –, jog –, wag –, shuffle- on; stir one's stumps; bend one's -steps, – course; make –, find –, wend –, pick –, thread –, plough-one's way; coast, slide, glide, skim, skate, ski; march in procession, file off, defile.

go –, repair –, resort –, hie –, betake oneself- to.

**Adj.** travelling &c. *v.*; ambulatory, itinerant, peripatetic, perambulatory, roving, rambling, gadding, discursive, vagrant, migratory, nomadic; circumforane-an, -ous; somnambular, nocti-, mundi-vagant; locomotive, automotive, self-moving.

way-faring, -worn; travel-stained.

Adv. on -foot, – horseback, – Shanks's mare; by the Marrowbone stage; *in transitu* &c. 270; *en route* &c. 282.

Int. come along!

**268. Traveller.—N.** traveller, wayfarer, voyager, itinerant, passenger.

tourist, excursionist, globe-trotter; explorer, adventurer, mountaineer, Alpine Club; peregrinator, wanderer, rover, straggler, rambler; bird of passage; gad-about, -ling; vagrant, scatterling, landloper, waifs and estrays, wastrel, stray; loafer; tramp, -er, hobo, beachcomber, vagabond, nomad, Bohemian, gipsy, Arab, Wandering Jew, Hadji, pilgrim, palmer; peripatetic; somnambulist, sleep walker, noctambulist; emigrant, fugitive, refugee, *émigré.*

runner, courier, King's messenger; Mercury, Iris, Ariel, comet.

**269. Mariner.—N.** sailor, mariner, navigator, argonaut; sea-man, -farer, -faring man; yachtsman; tar, jack tar, salt, gob, sea-dog, shellback, able seaman, A.B.; man-of-war's man, blue-jacket, marine, jolly; midshipman, middy, reefer; captain, commander, master mariner, skipper, mate; ship-, boat-, ferry-, water-, lighter-, barge-, longshore- man, hoveller; bargee, gondolier; oar-, -sman; rower; boat-, cock-swain; coxswain; steersman, helmsman, pilot; crew; lascar.

aerial navigator, aeronaut, balloonist, Icarus, aviator, pilot, observer, flyer, airman.

pedestrian, walker, foot-passenger; cyclist; wheelman.

rider, horseman, equestrian, cavalier, jockey, rough rider, trainer, breaker, huntsman.

driver, coachman, whip, Jehu, charioteer, postilion, post-boy, carter, wagoner, drayman, truckman; cab-man, -driver; *voiturier, vetturino, condottiere*; engine-driver; stoker, fireman, guard, brakeman, conductor; chauffeur, automobilist, motorist, motor –, truck –, taxi- driver.

**270. Transference.—N.** transfer, -ence; trans-, e-location; displacement; *meta-stasis, -thesis*; removal; re-, a-motion; relegation; de-, as-portation; extradition, conveyance, draft; carrying, carriage; con-vection, -duction, -tagion, infection; transfusion; transfer &c. (*of property*) 783.

transit, transition; passage, ferry, gestation; portage, porterage, carting, cartage; shovelling &c. *v.*; vect-ion, -ure, -itation; shipment, freight, wafture; trans-mission, -port, -portation, -umption, -plantation, -lation; shift-, dodg-ing; dispersion &c. 73; transposition &c. (*interchange*) 148; traction &c. 285.

[Thing transferred] drift, alluvium, detritus, *moraine*; gift, legacy, bequest, lease; freight, mails, cargo, luggage, baggage, goods.

**V.** trans-fer, -mit, -port, -place, -plant; convey, assign, carry, bear, fetch and carry; carry –, ferry- over; hand, pass, forward; shift; con-duct, convoy, bring, fetch, reach.

send, delegate, consign, mail, post, relegate, turn over to, pass the buck, deliver; ship, embark; waft; switch, shunt; transpose &c. (*interchange*) 148; displace &c. 185; throw &c. 284; drag &c. 285.

shovel, lade, dip, ladle, bale, decant, draft off, transfuse.

**Adj.** transferred &c. *v.*; drifted; movable; port-able, -ative; conductive; contagious, infectious.

transferable, assignable, conveyable, devisable, negotiable, transmissible.

**Adv.** from -hand to hand, – pillar to post.

on –, by- the way; on the -road, – wing; as one goes; *in transitu, en route, chemin faisant, en passant,* in mid-progress.

**271. Carrier.—N.** carrier, porter, red cap, bearer, messenger, postman, tranter, conveyer; stevedore; coolie; conductor, locomotive, tractor, caterpillar tractor, motor.

beast of burden, cattle, horse, steed, nag, palfrey, Arab, blood horse, thorough-bred, galloway, charger, courser, racer, hunter, jument, pony, filly, colt, foal, barb, roan, jade, hack, *bidet,* pad, cob, tit, punch, roadster, goer; race-, pack-, draft-, cart-, dray-, post-horse, mount; Shetland pony, sheltie; garran; jennet, genet, bayard, mare, stallion, gelding; stud.

Pegasus, Bucephalus, Rozinante.

ass, donkey, jackass, mule, hinny; sumpter -horse, – mule; reindeer; camel, dromedary, mehari, llama, elephant; carrier pigeon.

carriage &c. (*vehicle*) 272; ship &c. 273.

**Adj.** equine, asinine.

**272. Vehicle.—N.** vehicle, conveyance, carriage, car, caravan, van, furniture van, pantechnicon; wagon, wain, dray, cart, lorry.

carriole; sledge, sled, sleigh, bobsleigh, toboggan, *luge,* truck, tram; limber, tumbrel, pontoon; barrow; wheel-, hand- -barrow, – cart, trolley; perambulator; Bath -, wheel –, sedanchair, jinriksha, rickshaw; ekka; chaise; palan-keen, -quin; litter, horse-litter, brancard, crate, hurdle, stretcher, ambulance; velocipede, hobby-horse, coaster, scooter, go-cart; cycle; bi-, tri-, quadri cycle; tandem, safety; skate, roller skate; ski, snow-shoe.

equipage, turn-out; coach, chariot, *quadriga,* chaise, phaëton, break, brake, mail-phaëton, wagonette, drag, curricle, tilbury, whisky, landau, *barouche,* victoria, brougham, clarence, calash, *calèche,* britzska, *araba,* kibitka; berlin; sulky, *désobligeant,* sociable, *vis-à-vis, dormeuse;* jaunting –, outside- car; *tarantass;* runabout; shay.

post-chaise; diligence, stage; stage –, mail –, hackney –, glass- coach; stage-wagon; car, omnibus, bus, fly, *cabriolet,* cab, hansom, shofle, fourwheeler, growler, *droshki,* drosky.

dog-cart, trap, gig, whitechapel, buggy, four-in-hand, unicorn, random, tandem; shandredhan, *char-à-banc.*

automobile, motor-, auto-, touring-, racing-, cycle-, side-, steam-, electric-

**273. Ship.—N.** ship, vessel, sail; craft, bottom.

navy, marine, fleet, flotilla, squadron; shipping.

man of war &c. (*combatant*) 726; transport, tender, store-ship; merchant ship, merchantman; packet, liner; whaler, slaver, collier, coaster, tanker, freighter, freight steamer, cargo boat, lighter; fishing-, pilot- boat; trawler, drifter; cable ship; hulk; yacht; floating palace, ocean greyhound.

ship, bark, barque, brig, snow, hermaphrodite brig; brigantine, barquentine; schooner; topsail -, fore and aft –, three masted- schooner; *chasse-marée;* sloop, cutter, corvette, clipper, foist, yawl, dandy, ketch, smack, lugger, barge, hoy, cat-, -boat, buss; sail-er, -ing vessel, wind-jammer; steam-er, -boat, -ship; mail –, paddle –, screw –, sternwheel- steamer; tug; train-ferry; line of steamers &c.

boat, pinnace, launch, motor-boat, picket-boat; hydroplane; life-, long-, jolly-, bum-, fly-, cock-, ferry-, canal-boat, dory, dugout, galliot; shallop, gig, funny, skiff, dingy, scow, cockleshell, wherry, coble, punt, cog, lerret; eight-, four-, pair- oar; randan; outrigger; float, raft, pontoon; prame, ice-yacht.

state barge, bucentaur.

catamaran, coracle, gondola, carvel, caravel; felucca, caique, canoe; trireme;

car; motor-, -omnibus, – bus, – cab, – cycle; limousine, landaulette, cabriolet, *coupé*, *voiturette*, runabout, electromobile, taxi, -cab.

train; passenger –, express –, freight –, subway –, special –, corridor –, parliamentary –, luggage –, goods-train, *train de luxe*; 1st-, 2nd-, 3rd-class- -train, – carriage, – compartment; Pullman –, sleeping-, club-, observation-, dining-, restaurant-car; mail-, luggage-, brake-van, coach, car, carriage; rolling stock; horse-box, cattle-truck.

tramcar, trolley-omnibus, trackless trolley.

shovel, spoon, spatula, ladle, hod, hoe; spade, spaddle, loy; spud; pitch-fork.

**Adj.** vehicular.

galley, – foist; bilander, dogger, hooker, howker; argosy, carack; galliass, galleon; galliot, polacca, polacre, corsair, tartane, junk, lorcha, praam, proa, prahu, saick, sampan, xebec, dhow; dahabeah; nuggar, cayak, pirogue: submarine, submersible.

aircraft (*combatant*) &c. 726; flying machine, air mail, aero-, air-, mono-, bi-, tri-, hydroplane, plane, cabin plane, transport plane, *avion*, flying boat, glider, *aviette*, helicopter; balloon, air-, fire-, gas-, Mongolfier-, pilot-, captive-, free-, kite-, dirigible- balloon, air-ship, *Zeppelin*, blimp; kite, parachute.

nacelle, car, gondola, aileron; hangar, airport, landing field, airdrome; catwalk, controls, rudder, tail.

**Adj.** marine, maritime, naval, nautical, seafaring, sea-, ocean going, seaworthy.

aerial, aeronautical, air-worthy, flying &c. *n.*

**Adv.** afloat, aboard; on -board, – ship board, – board ship.

## 2°. Degrees of Motion

**274. Velocity.—N.** velocity, speed, celerity; swiftness &c. *adj.*; rapidity, eagle speed; expedition &c. (*activity*) 682; pernicity; acceleration; haste &c. 684.

spurt, rush, dash, race, steeplechase; smart –, lively –, swift &c. *adj.* –, rattling –, spanking –, strapping- -rate, – pace; round pace; flying, flight.

gallop, canter, trot, round trot, run, scamper; hand –, full- gallop; swoop.

lightning, light, electricity, wind; cannon-ball, rocket, arrow, dart, quick-silver; telegraph, express train; torrent; swallow flight.

eagle, antelope, courser, race-horse, gazelle, greyhound, hare, doe, squirrel.

Mercury, Ariel, Camilla, Harlequin. [Measurement of velocity] speed-ometer, log, -line, tachometer.

**V.** move quickly, trip, fisk; speed, hie, hasten, sprint, spurt, post, spank, scuttle; scud, -dle, scurry; scour, – the plain; scamper; run, – like mad; fly, race, run a race, cut away, cut and run, shoot, tear, whisk, whiz, sweep, skim, brush; cut –, bowl- along; rush

**275. Slowness.—N.** slowness &c. *adj.*; languor &c. (*inactivity*) 683; drawl; creeping &c. *v.*, lentor.

retardation; slackening &c. *v.*; delay &c. (*lateness*) 133; claudication.

jog-, dog-trot, walk; mincing steps; slow -march, – time.

slow -goer, – coach, – back; lingerer, loiterer, sluggard, tortoise, snail; dawdle &c. (*inactive*) 683.

**V.** move -slowly, &c. *adv.*; creep, crawl, lag, slug, walk, drawl, linger, loiter, saunter; plod, trudge, stump along, lumber; trail; drag; dawdle &c. (*be inactive*) 683; grovel, worm one's way, steal along; jog –, rub –, bundle-on; toddle, waddle, wabble, slug; traipse, slouch, shuffle, halt, hobble, limp, claudicate, shamble; flag, falter, totter, stagger; mince, step short; march in -slow time, – funeral procession; take one's time; hang fire &c. (*be late*) 133.

retard, relax; slacken, check, moderate, rein in, curb; reef; strike –, shorten –, take in- sail; put on the drag, apply the brake; clip the wings; reduce the

&c. (*be violent*) 173; dash -on, – off, – forward; bolt; trot, gallop, bound, flit, spring, dart, boom; march in double-time; ride hard, get over the ground, scorch.

hurry &c. (*hasten*) 684; accelerate, put on; quicken; quicken –, mend-one's pace; clap spurs to one's horse; make -haste, – rapid strides, – forced marches, – the best of one's way; put one's best leg foremost, stir one's stumps, wing one's way, set off at a score; carry –, crowd- sail; go off like a shot, go ahead, gain ground; outstrip the wind, fly on the wings of the wind.

keep -up, – pace- with; outstrip &c. 303.

**Adj.** fast, speedy, swift, rapid, quick, fleet; nimble, agile, expeditious; express; active &c. 682; flying, galloping &c. *v.*; light-, nimble-footed; winged, eagle-winged, mercurial, electric, telegraphic; light-legged, light of heel; swift as -an arrow &c. *n.*; quick as -lightning &c. *n.*, – thought.*

**Adv.** swiftly &c. *adj.*; with -speed &c. *n.*; apace; at -a great rate, – full speed, – railway speed; full -drive, – gallop; post-haste, in full sail, tantivy; trippingly; instantaneously &c. 113; like a shot.

under press of -sail, – canvas, – sail and steam; *velis et remis*, on eagle's wing, in double quick time; with -rapid, – giant- strides; *à pas de géant*; in seven league boots; whip and spur; *ventre à terre*; as fast as one's -legs, – heels- will carry one; as fast as one can lay feet to the ground, at the top of one's speed; by leaps and bounds; with haste &c. 684; in- high – gear, – speed.

**Phr.** *vires acquirit eundo.*

speed, decelerate; slacken -speed, – one's pace, lose ground; back -water, – pedal, put the engines astern, throttle down.

**Adj.** slow, slack; tardy; dilatory &c. (*inactive*) 683; gentle, easy; leisurely; deliberate, gradual; insensible, imperceptible; languid, sluggish, apathetic, phlegmatic, slow-paced, tardigrade, snail-like; creeping &c. *v.*

**Adv.** slowly &c. *adj.*; leisurely; *piano*, *adagio*; *largo*, *larghetto*; at half speed, under easy sail; at a -foot's, – snail's, – funeral- pace; slower than molasses in January; in slow time; with -mincing steps, – clipped wings; *haud passibus æquis*; in- low –, gear, – speed.

gradually &c. *adj.*; *gradatim*; by -degrees, – slow degrees, – inches, – little and little; step by step; inch by inch, bit by bit, little by little, *seriatim*; consecutively.

---

### 3°. MOTION CONJOINED WITH FORCE

**276. Impulse.**—**N.** impulse, impulsion, impetus; momentum; push, pulsion, thrust, shove, jog, jolt, brunt, booming, boost, throw; explosion &c. (*violence*) 173; propulsion &c. 284.

percussion, concussion, collision, occursion, clash, encounter, cannon, *carambole*, appulse, shock, crash, bump; impact; *élan*; charge &c. (*attack*) 716; beating &c. (*punishment*) 972.

blow, dint, stroke, knock, tap, rap, slap, smack, pat, dab; fillip; slam, bang; hit, whack, thwack, clout; cuff &c. 972; squash, dowse, whap, swap, punch, thump, swipe, jab, pelt, kick, punce, calcitration; *ruade*; arietation; cut, thrust, lunge, yerk.

**277. Recoil.**—**N.** recoil; re-, retro-action; revulsion; rebound, *ricochet*; re-percussion, -calcitration; kick, *contre-coup*; springing back &c. *v.*; elasticity &c. 325; reflection, reflex, reflux; reverberation &c. (*resonance*) 408; rebuff, repulse; return.

ducks and drakes; boomerang; spring; reactionist, reactionary.

**V.** recoil, resile, react; spring –, fly –, bound- back; rebound, reverberate, repercuss, recalcitrate, echo, *ricochet*.

**Adj.** recoiling &c. *v.*; re-fluent, -percussive, -calcitrant, -actionary; retroactive.

**Adv.** on the -recoil &c. *n.*

---

* See note on 264.

hammer, sledge-hammer, mall, maul, mallet, flail; ram, -mer; bat-tering-ram, monkey, pile-driver, punch, bat, tamper, tamping iron; cudgel &c. (*weapon*) 727; axe &c. (*sharp*) 253.

[Science of mechanical forces] mechanics, dynamics &c.

**V.** give an -impetus &c. *n.*; impel, push; start, give a start to, set going; drive, urge, boom; thrust, prod, foin; cant; elbow, shoulder, jostle, justle, hustle, hurtle, shove, jog, jolt, bean, encounter; run -, bump -, butt- against; knock -, run- one's head against; impinge.

strike, knock, hit, bash, tap, rap, bat, slap, flap, dab, pat, thump, beat, bang, slam, dash; punch, thwack, whack; hit -, strike- hard; swap, batter, dowse, baste; pelt, patter, skelter, buffet, belabour, tamp; fetch one a blow, swat; poke at, pink, lunge, yerk; kick, calcitrate; butt; strike at &c. (*attack*) 716; whip &c. (*punish*) 972; propel &c. 284.

come -, enter- into collision; collide; foul; fall -, run- foul of. throw &c. (*propel*) 284.

**Adj.** impelling &c. *v.*; im-pulsive, -pellent; booming; dynamic, -al; impelled &c. *v.*

### 4°. MOTION WITH REFERENCE TO DIRECTION

**278. Direction.**—**N.** direction, bearing, course, set, drift, tenor; tendency &c. 176; incidence; bending, trending &c. *v.*; dip, tack, aim, collimation; steer-ing, -age.

point of the compass, cardinal -, half -, quarter- points; North, East, South, West; N by E, ENE, NE by N, NE &c.; rhumb, azimuth, line of collimation.

line, path, road, range, quarter, line of march; alignment; straight shot, bee-line.

**V.** tend -, bend -, point- towards; conduct -, go- to; point -to, - at; bend, trend, verge, incline, dip, determine.

steer -, make- -for, - towards; aim -, level- at; take aim; keep -, hold- a course; be bound for; bend one's steps towards; direct -, steer -, bend -, shape- one's course; align -, one's march; go straight, - to the point; march -on, - on a point.

ascertain one's -direction &c. *n.*; s'*orienter*, see which way the wind blows; box the compass.

**Adj.** directed &c. *v.*, - towards; pointing towards &c. *v.*; bound for; aligned -, alligned- with; direct, straight; un-deviating, -swerving; straightforward; North, -ern, -erly, &c. *n.*

directable &c. *v.*

**Adv.** towards; on the -road, - high

**279. Deviation.** — **N.** deviation; swerving &c. *v.*; obliquation, warp, refraction; flection, flexion; sweep; de-flection, -flexure; declination.

diversion, digression, departure from, aberration, drift, sheer; divergence &c. 291; zigzag; *détour* &c. (*circuit*) 629.

[Desultory motion] wandering &c. *v.*. vagrancy, evagation; by-paths and crooked ways.

[Motion sideways, oblique motion] sidling &c. *v.*; *échelon*, leeway; knight's move (at chess).

**V.** alter one's course, deviate, depart from, turn, trend; bend, curve &c. 245; swerve, heel, bear off.

intervert; deflect; divert, - from its course; put on a new scent, shift, shunt, switch, wear, draw aside, crook, warp short circuit.

stray, straggle; sidle, edge; diverge &c. 291; tralineate, digress, divagate, wander; wind, twist, meander, meander around Robin Hood's barn; veer, tack, sheer; turn -aside, - a corner, - away from; wheel, steer clear of; ramble, rove, drift; go -astray, - adrift; yaw, dodge; step aside, ease off, make way for, shy.

fly off at a tangent; glance off; turn, wheel -, face- about; turn -, face- to the right about; wabble &c. (*oscillate*) 314; go out of one's way &c. (*perform a circuit*) 629: lose one's way.

road- to; *versus*, to; hither, thither, whither; directly; straight, – forwards, – as an arrow; point blank; in a -direct, – straight- line -to, – for, – with; in a line with; full tilt at, as the crow flies.

before –, near –, close to –, against- the wind; windwards, in the wind's eye.

through, *via*, by way of; in all -directions, – manner of ways; *quaquaversum*, from the four winds.

**280.** [Going before.] **Precession.—N.** precession, leading, heading; precedence &c. 62; priority &c. 116; the lead, *le pas*; van &c. (*front*) 234; precursor &c. 64.

**V.** go -before, – ahead, – in the van, – in advance; precede, forerun; usher in, introduce, herald, head, take the lead; lead, – the way, – the dance; get –, have- the start; steal a march; get -before, – ahead, – in front of; outstrip &c. 303; take precedence &c. (*first in order*) 62.

**Adj.** foremost, first, leading &c. *v.*

**Adv.** in advance, before, ahead, in the van; fore-, head-most; in front.

**Phr.** *seniores priores*.

**282.** [Motion forwards; progressive motion.] **Progression.—N.** progress, -ion, -iveness; advancing &c. *v.*; advance, -ment; ongoing; flood-tide, headway; march &c. 266; rise; improvement &c. 658.

**V.** advance; proceed, progress; get -on, – along, – over the ground; gain ground; jog –, rub –, wag- on; go with the stream; keep –, hold on- one's course; go –, move –, come –, get –, pass –, push –, press- -on, – forward, – forwards, – ahead; press onwards, step forward; make –, work –, carve –, push –, force –, edge –, elbow- one's way; make -progress, – head, – way, – headway, – advance, – strides, – rapid strides &c. (*velocity*) 274; go –, shoot- ahead; distance; make up leeway.

**Adj.** advancing &c. *v.*; pro-gressive, -fluent; advanced.

**Adj.** deviating &c. *v.*; aberrant, errant; ex-, dis-cursive; devious, desultory, loose; rambling; stray, erratic, vagrant, undirected; circuitous, indirect, zigzag; crab-like.

**Adv.** astray from, round about, wide of the mark; to the right about; all manner of ways; circuitously &c. 629.

obliquely, sideling, like the move of the knight on a chessboard.

**281.** [Going after.] **Sequence.—N.** sequence, run; coming after &c. (*order*) 63; (*time*) 117; following; pursuit &c. 622.

follower, attendant, satellite, shadow, dangler, train.

**V.** follow; pursue &c. 622; go –, fly- after.

attend, beset, dance attendance on, dog, be-dog; tread -in the steps of, – close upon; be –, go –, follow- in the -wake, – trail. – rear- of; trail, follow as a shadow, hang on the skirts of; tread –, follow- on the heels of, tag after.

lag, get behind.

**Adj.** following &c. *v.*

**Adv.** behind; in the -rear &c. 235, – train of; wake of; after &c. (*order*) 63, (*time*) 117.

**283.** [Motion backwards.] **Regression.—N.** regress, -ion; retro-cession, -gression, -gradation, -action; *reculade*; retreat, withdrawal, retirement, remigration; recession &c. (*motion from*) 287; recess; crab-like motion.

re-fluence, -flux; backwater, regurgitation, ebb, return; resilience; reflexion (*recoil*) 277; *volte-face*.

counter -motion, – movement, – march; veering, tergiversation, recidivation, backsliding, fall, relapse; deterioration &c. 659.

turning-point &c. (*reversion*) 145.

**V.** re-cede, -grade, -turn, -vert, -treat, -tire; retro-grade, -cede; back, – down, – out, crawl; withdraw; rebound &c. 277; go –, come –, turn –, hark –, draw –, fall –, get –, put –, run- back; lose ground; fall –, drop- astern; back water, put about; veer, – round; double,

**Adv.** forward, onward; forth, on ahead, under way, *en route* for, on -one's way, – the way, – the road, – the high road- to; in -progress, – mid progress; *in transitu* &c. 270.

**Int.** Forward, march!

**Phr.** *vestigia nulla retrorsum.*

-cidivous, -silient; crab-like; reactionary &c. 277; counter-clockwise.

**Adv.** back, -wards; reflexively, to the right about; *à reculons,* *à rebours.*

**Phr.** *revenons à nos moutons,* as you were.

**284.** [Motion given to an object situated in front.] **Propulsion.—N.** pro-pulsion, -jection; *vis a tergo;* push &c. (*impulse*) 276; e-, jaculation; ejection &c. 297; throw, fling, toss, shot, discharge, shy.

[Science of propulsion] gunnery, ballistics, archery.

missile, projectile, ball, *discus*, javelin, hammer, quoit, brickbat, shot, bullet; arrow, shaft; gun &c. (*arms*) 727.

shooter, shot; gunner, gun-layer; archer, toxophilite; bow-, rifle-, marksman; good -, crack- shot; sharpshooter &c. (*combatant*) 726.

**V.** propel, project, throw, fling, cast, pitch, chuck, toss, jerk, heave, shy, hurl; flirt, fillip.

dart, lance, tilt; e-, jaculate; fulminate, bolt, drive, sling, pitchfork.

send; send -, let -, fire- off; discharge, shoot; launch, send forth, let fly; dash.

put -, set- in motion; set agoing, start; give -a start, – an impulseto; push, impel &c. 276; trundle &c. (*set in rotation*) 312; expel &c. 297.

carry one off one's legs; put to flight.

**Adj.** propelled &c. *v.*; propelling &c. *v.*; pro-pulsive, -jectile.

**286.** [Motion towards.] **Approach.— N.** approach, approximation, appropinquation; access; appulse; afflux, -ion; advent &c. (*approach of time*) 121; pursuit &c. 622; convergence &c. 290.

**V.** approach, approximate; near; get -, go -, draw- near; come -, near, – to close quarters; move -, set intowards; drift; make up to; gain upon; pursue &c. 622; tread on the heels of; bear up; make the land; hug the -shore, -coast, – land.

**Adj.** approaching &c. *v.*; approximative; convergent; affluent; impending, imminent &c. (*destined*) 152.

wheel, counter-march; ebb, regurgitate; jib, shrink, shy.

turn -tail, – round, – upon one's heel, – one's back upon; retrace one's steps, dance the back step; sound -, beat- a retreat; go home.

**Adj.** receding &c. *v.*; retro-grade, -gressive; re-gressive, -fluent, -flex, reactionary &c. 277; counter-clockwise.

**285.** [Motion given to an object situated behind.] **Traction.—N.** traction; drawing &c. *v.*; draught, pull, haul; rake; 'a long pull, a strong pull and a pull all together'; towage, haulage.

**V.** draw, pull, haul, lug, rake, drag, draggle, tug, tow, trail, trawl, train; take in tow.

wrench, jerk, twitch.

**Adj.** drawing &c. *v.*; **tractive, tractile;** ductile.

**287.** [Motion from.] **Recession.—N.** recession, retirement, withdrawal; retreat; retrocession &c. 283; departure &c. 293; recoil &c. 277; flight &c. (*avoidance*) 623.

**V.** recede, go, move from, retire, ebb, withdraw, shrink; come -, move -, go -, get -, drift- away; depart &c. 293; retreat &c. 283; move -, stand -, sheer- off; swerve from; fall back, stand aside; run away &c. (*avoid*) 623.

remove, shunt, side track, switch off

**Adj.** receding &c. *v.*

Adv. on the road.
Int. come hither! approach! here! come! come near!

**288.** [Motion towards, actively.] **Attraction.**—N. attract-ion, -iveness; pull; drawing to, pulling towards, adduction, magnetism, gravity, attraction of gravitation; lure, bait, decoy.

loadstone, -star; magnet, siderite, magnetite.

V. attract; draw -, pull -, drag towards; adduce.

lure, bait, decoy.

Adj. attracting &c. v.; attrahent, attractive, adducent, adductive.

**290.** [Motion nearer to.] **Convergence.** —N. con-vergence, -fluence, -course, -flux, -gress, -currence, -centration; appulse, meeting; corradiation.

assemblage &c. 72; resort &c. (focus) 74; asymptote.

V. converge, concur; come together, unite, meet, fall in with; close -with, - in upon; centre -round, - in; enter in; pour in.

gather together, unite, concentrate, bring into a focus.

Adj. converging &c. v.; con-vergent, -fluent, -current; centripetal; asymptotical.

**292.** [Terminal motion at.] **Arrival.** —N. arrival, advent; landing; de-, disem-barkation; reception, welcome, vin d'honneur.

home, goal, bourn; landing-place, -stage; resting -, stopping -place; destination, harbour, haven, port; terminal, terminus, railway station, depot, airport; halt, halting -place, - ground; anchorage &c. (refuge) 666.

return, recursion, remigration; meeting; ren-, en-counter.

completion &c. 729.

V. arrive; get to, come to; come; reach, attain; come up, - with, - to; overtake; make, fetch; complete &c. 729; join, rejoin.

light, alight, dismount; land, go ashore; debark, disembark; put -in, - into; visit, cast anchor, pitch one's tent; sit down &c. (be located) 184; get to one's journey's end; make the

**289.** [Motion from, actively.] **Repulsion.**—N. repulsion; driving from &c. v.; repulse; abduction.

V. repel; push -, drive - &c. 276. from; chase, dispel; retrude; abduce, abduct; send away, repulse, dismiss.

keep at arm's length, turn one's back upon, give the cold shoulder; send packing; send -off, - away- with a flea in one's ear, - about one's business.

Adj. repelling &c. v.; repellant, repulsive; abducent, abductive.

**291.** [Motion further off.] **Divergence** —N. diverg-ence, -ency; divarication, ramification, radiation; separation &c. (disjunction) 44; dispersion &c. 73; deviation &c. 279; aberration, declination.

V. diverge, divaricate, radiate; ramify; branch -, glance -, file- off; fly off, - at a tangent; spread, scatter, disperse &c. 73; deviate &c. 279; part &c. (separate) 44; splay apart.

Adj. diverging &c. v.; divergent, radiant, centrifugal; aberrant.

**293.** [Initial motion from.] **Departure.**—N. departure, decession, decampment; embarkation; take-off; outset, start; removal; exit &c. (egress) 295; exodus, Hejira, flight.

leave-taking, congé, valediction, valedictory, adieu, farewell, good-bye, stirrup-cup.

starting -point, - post; point -, place- of -departure, - embarkation; port of embarkation.

V. depart; go, - away; take one's departure, set out; set -, march -, put -, start -, be -, move -, get -, whip -, pack -, go -, take oneself- off; start, issue, march out, debouch; go -, sally-forth; sally, set forward; be gone.

leave a place, quit, vacate, evacuate, abandon; go off the stage, make one's exit; retire, withdraw, remove; go -one's way, - along, - from home; take -flight, - wing; spring, fly, flit, wing

land; be in at the death; come –, get- -back, – home; return; come in &c. (*ingress*) 294; make one's appearance &c. (*appear*) 446; drop in; detrain; outspan.

come to hand; come -at, – across; hit; come –, light –, pop –, bounce –, plump –, burst –, pitch- upon; meet; en- ren-counter; come in contact.

**Adj.** arriving &c. *v.*; homeward-bound; terminal.

**Adv.** here, hither.

**Int.** welcome! hail! all hail! good-day, – morrow; greetings! hullo! well!

one's flight; fly –, whip- away; take off, hop off; embark; go -on board, – aboard; set sail; put –, go- to sea; sail, take ship; hoist blue Peter; get under way, weigh anchor; strike tents, break camp, decamp; walk one's chalks, make tracks, cut one's stick; cut and run; take leave; say –, bid- -good-bye &c. *n.*; disappear &c. 449; abscond &c. (*avoid*) 623; entrain, saddle –, harness –, hitch- up; inspan.

**Adj.** departing &c. *v.*; valedictory; outward bound.

**Adv.** whence, hence, thence; with a foot in the stirrup; on the -wing, – move.

**Int.** begone! &c. (*ejection*) 297; to horse! all aboard! farewell! adieu! good-bye, – day! *au revoir! auf Wiedersehen!* fare you well! so long! God -bless you, – speed! *bon voyage!*

---

**294.** [Motion into.] **Ingress.—N.**

ingress; entrance, entry; introgression; influx; intrusion, inroad, incursion, invasion, irruption; pene-, interpenetration; illapse, import, importation, infiltration; immigration; admission &c. (*reception*) 296; insinuation &c. (*interjacence*) 228; insertion &c. 300.

inlet; way in; mouth, door &c. (*opening*) 260; path &c. (*way*) 627; conduit &c. 350; immigrant, visitor, incomer, newcomer, colonist.

**V.** have the *entrée*; enter; go –, come –, pour –, flow –, creep –, slip –, pop –, break –, burst- -into, – in; set foot on; burst –, break- in upon; invade, intrude, butt in, horn in, crash; insinuate itself; inter-, penetrate; infiltrate; find one's way –, wriggle –, worm oneself- into.

give entrance to &c. (*receive*) 296; insert &c. 300.

**Adj.** incoming, ingressive &c. *n.*; inward bound.

**Adv.** inward.

**295.** [Motion out of.] **Egress.—N.**

egress, exit, issue; emer-sion, -gence; disemboguement; out-break, -burst; e-, pro-ruption; emanation; evacuation; ex-, trans-udation; extravasation, perspiration, sweating, leakage, percolation, distillation, oozing; gush &c. (*water in motion*) 348; outpour, -ing; effluence, effusion; efflux, -ion; drain; dribbling &c. *v.*; defluxion; drainage; out-come, -put; discharge &c. (*excretion*) 299.

export; expatriation; e-, re-migration; *débouche*; exodus &c. (*departure*) 293; emigrant, migrant, *émigré*, colonist.

outlet, vent, spout, tap, sluice, floodgate; pore; vomitory, out-gate, sally-port; way out; mouth, door &c. (*opening*) 260; path &c. (*way*) 627; conduit &c. 350; air-pipe &c. 351.

**V.** emerge, emanate, issue; go –, come –, move –, pass –, pour –, flow-out of; pass off, evacuate; migrate.

ex-, trans-ude; leak; run, – out, – through; per-, trans-colate; seep; strain, distil; perspire, sweat, drain, ooze; filter, filtrate; dribble, gush, spout, flow out; well, – out; pour, trickle &c. (*water in motion*) 348; effuse, extravasate, disembogue, discharge itself, debouch; come –, break- forth; burst- out, – through; find vent, escape &c. 671.

**Adj.** effused &c. *v.*; outgoing, outward bound.

**Adv.** outward.

**296.** [Motion into, actively.] **Reception.—N.** reception; admission, admittance, *entrée*, importation; initiation; intro-duction, -mission, -ception; im-mission, ingestion, imbibition, absorption, ingurgitation, inhalation; suction, sucking; eating, drinking &c. (*food*) 298; insertion &c. 300; interjection &c. 228.

**V.** give -entrance to, – admittance to, – the *entrée*; intro-duce, -mit; usher, admit, receive, import, initiate, bring in, open the door to, throw open, ingest, absorb, imbibe, inhale, infiltrate; let –, take –, suck- in; re-admit, -sorb, -absorb; snuff up; swallow, ingurgitate; engulf, engorge; gulp; eat, drink &c. (*food*) 298.

**Adj.** admit-ting &c. *v.*, -ted &c. *v.*; admissible; absorbent; introductory, introceptive, intromittent, initiatory.

**297.** [Motion out of, actively.] **Ejection.—N.** ejection, emission, effusion, rejection, expulsion, eviction, extrusion, trajection; discharge.

egestion, evacuation, vomition, disgorgement, voidance, eruption, eruptiveness; ruc-, eruc-tation, blood-letting, venesection, phlebotomy, paracentesis; tapping, drainage; clear-ance, -age, voidance; vomiting, excretion &c. 299.

deportation; banishment &c. (*punishment*) 972; rogue's march; relegation, extradition; dislodgment.

**V.** give -exit, – vent- to; let –, give –, pour –, send- out; des-, dis-patch; exhale, excern, excrete, disembogue, secrete, secern; extravasate, shed, void, evacuate, egest, emit; open the -sluices, – floodgates; turn on the tap; extrude, detrude; effuse, spend, expend; pour forth; squirt, spirt, spill, slop; perspire &c. (*exude*) 295; breathe, blow &c. (*wind*) 349.

tap, draw off; bale –, lade- out; let blood, broach.

eject, reject; expel, discard; cut, send to Coventry, boycott, ostracize; *chasser*; banish &c. (*punish*) 972; throw &c. 284 -out, – up, – off, – away, – aside; push &c. 276 -out, – off, – away, – aside; shovel –, sweep- -out, – away; brush –, whisk –, turn –, send- -off, – away; discharge; send –, turn –, cast- adrift; turn –, bundle- out; throw overboard; give the sack to; send -packing, – about one's business, – to the right about; strike off the roll &c. (*abrogate*) 756; turn out- neck and heels, – head and shoulders, – neck and crop; pack off; send away with a flea in the ear; send to Jericho; bow out, show the door to, dismiss, fire, sack.

turn out of -doors, – house and home; evict, oust; exorcise, un-house, -kennel; dislodge; un-, dis-people; depopulate; relegate, deport.

empty; drain, – to the dregs; sweep off; clear, – off, – out, – away; suck, draw off, extract; clean out, make a clean sweep of, clear decks, purge.

em-, dis-, disem-bowel; eviscerate, gut; unearth, root -out, – up; averruncate; weed –, get out; eliminate, get rid of, do away with, shake off; exenterate.

vomit, spew, puke, keck, retch; belch, – out, eract, eructate; cast –, bring- up; disgorge; expectorate, salivate, clear the throat, hawk, spit, sputter, splutter, slobber, drool, drivel, slaver, slabber.

unpack, unlade, unload, unship; break bulk.

be let out; ooze &c. (*emerge*) 295.

**Adj.** emitt-ing, -ed &c. *v.*

**Int.** begone! get you gone! get –, go- -away, – along, – along with you! go your way! away, – with! off with you! go, – about your business! be off! avaunt! aroynt! get out! beat it!

**298. [Eating.] Food.—N.** eating &c. *v.*; deglutition, gulp, epulation, mastication, manducation, rumination, gastronomy, gastrology; panto-, hippo-, ichthyo-phagy &c.; gluttony &c. 957; carnivorousness, vegetarianism.

mouth, jaws, mandible, mazard, chops.

drinking &c. *v.*; potation, draught, libation; carousal &c. (*amusement*) 840; drunkenness &c. 959.

food, *pabulum*; aliment, nourishment, nutriment; susten-ance, -tation; nurture, subsistence, provender, feed, fodder, provision, ration, keep, commons, board; commissariat &c. (*provision*) 637; prey, forage, pasture, pasturage; fare, cheer; diet, -ary; regimen; belly timber, staff of life; bread, -and cheese; proteins, carbohydrates, vitamines.

comestibles, eatables, victuals, edibles, *ingesta*; grub, prog, tack, hard tack, meat; bread, -stuffs; cereals; viands, cates, delicacy, dainty, creature comforts, contents of the larder, flesh-pots; festal board; ambrosia; good -cheer, – living.

*hors-d'œuvre*; soup, pottage, *potage*, broth, *bouillon, consommé, purée, borsch*, stock, skilly, gumbo; fish, – cakes, – pie; joint, *rôti, pièce de résistance, relevé*, hash, *réchauffé*, stew, *ragoût*, fricassee, mince, *salmi, goulash, bouillabaisse*, remove, *entrée, croquette, rissole*, sausage, curry, bubble and squeak; haggis, collops, giblets; poultry, game &c.; biscuit, bun, scone, rusk, pancake, pie, pastry, pasty, patty, *patisserie*, tart, turnover, *vol-au-vent, soufflé*, dumpling, pudding, duff, *compote*, fritters, cake, napoleon, *blancmange*, custard, jelly, jam, sweets &c. 396; *entremet*; oatmeal, porridge, hasty pudding, gruel; eggs, omelet, cheese, matzoon, savoury; vegetable, salad, *mayonnaise*, fruit; sauce, condiment &c. 393; kickshaws.

table, *cuisine*, bill of fare, *menu, prix fixe*, ordinary, *à la carte*; cover.

meal, repast, feed, spread; mess; dish, plate, course, side dish; regale; regale-, refresh-, entertain-ment; refection, collation, picnic, feast, banquet, junket; breakfast; lunch, -eon; *déjeuner*, bever, tiffin, tea, dinner, supper, snack, whet, bait, dessert; pot-luck, *table d'hôte, déjeuner à la fourchette*; hearty -, square -, substantial -, full- -meal; blow out; light refreshment; pemmican.

mouthful, bolus, gobbet, tit-bit, morsel, sop, sippet.

drink, beverage, liquor, broth, soup; potion, dram, draught, drench, swill; nip, peg, sip, sup, gulp.

wine, champagne, spirits, *liqueur*, beer, porter, stout, ale, malt liquor, julep, Sir John Barleycorn, stingo, heavy wet, bitter, lager-beer, cider; grog, toddy, flip, purl, punch, negus, cup, bishop, posset, wassail; bitters, *apéritif*, high-ball, cocktail; whisky, rum, absinthe; gin &c. (*intoxicating liquor*) 959; coffee, chocolate, cocoa, tea, *maté*, the cup that cheers but not inebriates.

eating-house &c. 189.

**299. Excretion.—N.** excretion, discharge, emanation; ejection &c. 297; exhalation, extrusion, secretion, effusion, extravasation, *ecchymosis*, evacuation, cacation, defecation, dysentery, dejection, *fæces*, excrement; perspiration, sweat; sud-, exud-ation; *diaphoresis*; sewage.

saliva, spittle, rheum; ptyalism, salivation, catarrh, diarrhœa; *ejecta, egesta, sputum, sputa; excreta*; lava; *exuviæ* &c. (*uncleanness*) 653.

hemorrhage, bleeding; catamenia, menses; outpouring &c. (*egress*) 295; leucorrhea.

**V.** excrete &c. (*eject*) 297; emanate &c. (*come out*) 295.

**Adj.** excretory, fæcal, secretory; ejective, eliminant.

V. eat, feed, fare, devour, swallow, take; gulp, bolt, snap; fall
to; despatch, dispatch; discuss; take -, get -, gulp-down; lay -,
tuck- in; lick, pick, peck; gormandize &c. 957; bite, champ, munch,
cranch, craunch, crunch, chew, masticate, nibble, gnaw, mumble.
live on; feed -, batten -, fatten -, feast- upon; browse, graze,
crop, regale; carouse &c. (*make merry*) 840; eat heartily, do justice
to, play a good knife and fork, banquet.
    break -bread, - one's fast; breakfast, lunch, dine, take tea, sup.
    drink, - in, - up, - one's fill; quaff, sip, sup; suck, - up; lap;
swig; swill, tipple &c. (*be drunken*) 959; empty one's glass, drain
the cup; toss -off, - one's glass; wash down, crack a bottle, wet
one's whistle.
    cater, purvey &c. 637.
    **Adj.** eatable, edible, esculent, comestible, alimentary; cereal,
cibarious; dietetic; culinary; nutri-tive, -tious; succulent; drinkable,
pot-able, -ulent; bibulous.
    omn-, carn-, herb-, frug-, gran-, gramin-, phyt-ivorous; ichthyoph-
agous.
    prandial.

**300.** [Forcible ingress.] **Insertion.—**
**N.** insertion, implantation, intercala-
tion, embolism, introduction; interpo-
lation, insinuation &c. (*intervention*)
228; planting &c. *v.*; injection, inocu-
lation, importation, infusion; forcible
-ingress &c. 294; immersion; submer-
sion, -gence; dip, plunge; bath &c.
(*water*) 337; interment &c. 363.
    **V.** insert; intro-duce, -mit; put -,
run- into; import; inject; interject &c.
228; infuse, instil, inoculate, impreg-
nate, imbue, imbrue.
    graft, ingraft, bud, plant, implant;
dovetail.
    obtrude; thrust -, stick -, ram -,
stuff -, tuck -, press -, drive -, pop -,
whip -, drop -, put- in; impact;
empierce &c. (*make a hole*) 260.
    embed; immerse, immerge, merge;
bathe, soak &c. (*water*) 337; dip,
plunge &c. 310.
    bury &c. (*inter*) 363.
    insert &c.- itself; plunge *in medias res.*
    **Adj.** inserted &c. *v.*

**301.** [Forcible egress.] **Extraction.—**
**N.** extraction; extracting &c. *v.*; re-
moval, elimination, extrication, eradi-
cation, evolution.
    evulsion, avulsion; wrench; expres-
sion, squeezing; extirpation, extermi-
nation; ejection &c. 297; export &c.
(*egress*) 295; distillation.
    extractor, corkscrew, forceps, pliers.
    **V.** extract, draw, pit; take -, draw -,
pull -, tear -, pluck -, pick -, get- out;
wring from, wrench; extort; root -,
weed -, grub -, rake- up, - out; eradi-
cate; pull -, pluck- up by the roots;
averruncate; unroot; uproot, pull up,
extirpate, dredge.
    remove; educe, elicit; evolve, extri-
cate; eliminate &c. (*eject*) 297; eviscer-
ate &c. 297.
    express, squeeze -, press- out; distil.
    **Adj.** extracted &c. *v.*

**302.** [Motion through.] **Passage.—N.** passage, transmission; per-
meation; pene-, interpene-tration; transudation, infiltration; *osmosis,*
osmose, endos-, exos-mose; intercurrence; ingress &c. 294; egress &c.
295; path &c. 627; conduit &c. 350; opening &c. 260; journey &c.
266; voyage &c. 267.
    **V.** pass, - through; perforate &c. (*hole*) 260; penetrate, permeate,
thread, thrid, enfilade; go -through, - across; go -, pass- over; cut
across; ford, cross; pass and repass, work; make -, thread -. worm -,
force- one's way; make -, force- a passage; cut one's way through;

find its -way, – vent; transmit. make way, clear the course; traverse, go over the ground.

**Adj.** passing &c. *v.*; intercurrent; osmotic &c. *n.*

**Adv.** *en passant* &c. (*transit*) 270.

**303.** [Motion beyond.] **Overstep.—**
**N.** trans-cursion, -ilience, -gression; infraction, intrusion; trespass; encroach-, infringe-ment; extravagation, transcendence; redundance &c. 641; ingress &c. 294.

**V.** transgress, surpass, pass; go- beyond, – by; show in –, come to the-front; shoot ahead of; steal a march –, gain- upon.

over-step, -pass, -reach, -go, -ride, -leap, -jump, -skip, -lap, -shoot the mark; out-strip, -leap, -jump, -go, -step, -run, -ride, -rival, -do; beat, – hollow; distance; leave in the -lurch, – rear; go one better, throw into the shade; exceed, transcend, surmount; soar &c. (*rise*) 305.

encroach, intrude, trespass, infringe, invade, trench upon, intrench on; strain; stretch –, strain- a point; pass the Rubicon.

**Adj.** surpassing &c. *v.*

**Adv.** beyond the mark, ahead.

**304.** [Motion short of.] **Shortcoming.**
**—N.** shortcoming, failure; delinquency; falling short &c. *v.*; de-fault, -falcation; leeway; labour in vain, no go.

incompleteness &c. 53; imperfection &c. 651; insufficiency &c. 640; non-completion &c. 730; failure &c. 732.

**V.** come –, fall –, stop- -short, – short of; not reach; want; keep within -bounds, – the mark, – compass.

break down, stick in the mud, collapse, come to nothing; fall -through, – to the ground, – down; cave in, end in smoke, fizzle out, miss the mark, fail; lose ground; miss stays, slump.

**Adj.** unreached; deficient; short, – of; *minus*; out of depth; perfunctory &c. (*neglect*) 460.

**Adv.** within -the mark, – compass, – bounds; behindhand; *re infectâ*; to no purpose; far from it.

**Phr.** the bubble burst.

**305.** [Motion upwards.] **Ascent.—N.** ascent, ascension; rising &c. *v.*; rise, upgrowth; leap &c. 309; acclivity, hill &c. 217; stair, stairs, stair-case, -way, flight of -steps, – stairs; ladder, companion, – way; lift, elevator &c. 307.

rocket, lark; sky-rocket, -lark; Alpine Club.

**V.** ascend, rise, mount, arise, uprise; go –, get –, work one's way –, start –, spring –, shoot- up; zoom; aspire.

climb, clamber, ramp, scramble, swarm, *escalade*, surmount; scale, – the heights.

tower, soar, hover, spire, plane, swim, float, surge; leap &c. 309.

**Adj.** rising &c. *v.*; scandent, buoyant; super-natant, -fluitant; excelsior.

**Adv.** uphill.

**306.** [Motion downwards.] **Descent.**
**—N.** descent, descension, declension, declination; fall; falling &c. *v.*; drop, cadence; subsidence, lapse; come-down, downfall, tumble, slip, tilt, trip, lurch; cropper, *culbute*; titubation, stumble;. fate of Icarus; dive, nose-dive, *volplane.*

*avalanche*, *débâcle*, land-slip, -slide. declivity, dip, hill; decline, drop.

**V.** descend; go –, drop –, come-down; fall, gravitate, drop, slip, slide, glissade, dive, plunge, settle; decline, slump, set, sink, droop, come down *ι* peg.

dismount, alight, light, get down; swoop; stoop &c. 308; fall prostrate, precipitate oneself; let fall &c. 308.

tumble, trip, stumble, titubate, lurch, pitch, swag, topple; topple –, tumble- -down, – over; tilt, sprawl, plump down, come a cropper.

**Adj.** descending &c. *v.*; descendent, declivitous; downcast; decur-rent, -sive; labent, deciduous; nodding to its fall.

**Adv.** down, -hill, -wards.

**307. Elevation.—N.** elevation; raising &c. *v.*; erection, lift; sublevation, upheaval; sublimation, exaltation; prominence &c. (*convexity*) 250.

lever &c. 633; crane, derrick, windlass, capstan, winch, dredger, lift, elevator, escalator, dumb waiter.

**V.** heighten, elevate, raise, lift, erect; set –, stick –, perch –, perk –, tilt- up; rear, hoist, heave; up-lift, -raise, -rear, -bear, -cast, -hoist, -heave; buoy, weigh, mount, give a lift; exalt, sublimate; place –, set- on a pedestal.

take –, drag –, fish- up; dredge.

stand –, rise –, get –, jump- up; spring to one's feet; hold -oneself, – one's head- up; draw oneself up to his full height.

**Adj.** elevated &c. *v.*; standing up; stilted, attollent, rampant.

**Adv.** on -stilts, – the shoulders of, – one's legs, – one's hind legs.

---

**308. Depression.—N.** lowering &c. *v.*; depression; dip &c. (*concavity*) 252; abasement; detrusion; reduction.

over-throw, -set, -turn; upset; prostration, subversion, precipitation.

bow; courtesy, curtsy; genuflexion, *kowtow*, obeisance, *salaam*.

**V.** depress, lower; let –, take- -down, – down a peg; cast; let -drop, – fall; sink, debase, bring low, abase, slash, reduce, detrude, pitch, precipitate.

over-throw, -turn, -set; upset, subvert, prostrate, level, fell; cast –, take –, throw –, fling –, dash –, pull –, cut –, knock –, hew- down; raze, – to the ground; humiliate, trample in the dust, pull about one's ears.

sit, – down; couch, squat, crouch, stoop, bend, bow, courtsey, curtsey; bob, duck, dip, genuflect, kneel; *kowtow*, *salaam*, make obeisance, prostrate oneself; bend, bow- the -head, – knee; incline the head; bow down; cower; recline &c. (*be horizontal*) 213.

**Adj.** depressed &c. *v.*; at a low ebb; prostrate &c. (*horizontal*) 213; detrusive.

**309. Leap.—N.** leap, jump, hop, spring, bound, vault, saltation.

dance, caper, gambol; curvet, caracole; *gam-bade*, *-bado*; capriole, demivolt; buck, – jump; hop, skip and jump.

kangaroo, jerboa, chamois, goat, frog, grasshopper, flea.

**V.** leap; jump -up, – over the moon; hop, spring, bound, vault, ramp, cut capers, gambol, trip, skip, dance, caper; curvet, *caracole*; foot it, bob, bounce, flounce, start, frisk &c. (*amusement*) 840; jump about &c. (*agitation*) 315; trip it on the light fantastic toe, dance oneself off one's legs.

**Adj.** leaping &c. *v.*; saltatory, frisky.

**Adv.** on the light fantastic toe.

---

**310. Plunge.—N.** plunge, dip, dive, header; ducking &c. *v.*; submergence, immersion, diver.

**V.** plunge, dip, souse, duck; dive, plump; take a -plunge, – header, make a plunge; bathe &c. (*water*) 337.

sub-merge, -merse; immerse, douse, sink, engulf, send to -the bottom, – Davy Jones' locker.

get out of one's depth; go -to the bottom, – down like a stone; founder, welter, wallow.

---

**311.** [Curvilinear motion.] **Circuition.—N.** circuition, circulation; turn, curvet; excursion; circum-vention, -navigation, -ambulation; north-west passage; ambit, gyre, lap, circuit &c. 629.

turning &c. *v.*; wrench; evolution; coil, helix, spiral; corkscrew.

**V.** turn, bend, wheel; go –, put- about; heel; go –, turn -round, – to the right about; turn on one's heel; make –, describe- a -circle, – complete circle; encircle; go –, pass- through -180°, – 360°.

circum-navigate, -aviate, -ambulate, -vent; put a girdle round the earth, go the round, make the round of.

turn –, round- a corner; double a point.

wind, circulate, meander; whisk, twirl; twist &c. (*convolution*) 248; make a *détour* &c. (*circuit*) 629.

Adj. turning &c. *v.*; circuitous; circum-foraneous, -fluent; devious, roundabout, circum-ambient, -flex, -navigable.

Adv. round about.

**312.** [Motion in a continued circle.] **Rotation.—N.** rotation, revolution, gyration, circulation, roll; circum-rotation, -volution, -gyration; volutation, circination, turbination, *pirouette*, convolution.

verticity; whir, whirl, swirl, eddy, vortex, whirlpool, gurge; cyclone, tornado; surge; *vertigo*, dizzy round; Maelstrom, Charybdis; Ixion; wheel of Fortune.

**313.** [Motion in a reverse circle.] **Evolution.—N.** evolution, unfolding, development; eversion &c. (*inversion*) 218.

V. evolve; un-fold, -roll, -wind, -coil, -twist, -furl, -twine, -ravel; disentangle; develop.

Adj. evolving &c. *v.*; evolved &c. *v.*

wheel, screw, propeller, whirligig, rolling stone, windmill; top, teetotum, merry-go-round; roller; cog-, fly-wheel, spit; jack; caster.

axis, axle, spindle, spool, pivot, pin, hinge, pole, swivel, gimbals, arbor, bobbin, mandrel, shaft.

[Science of rotatory motion] trochilics, gyrostatics.

V. rotate; roll, – along; revolve, spin; turn, – round; circumvolve; circulate, gyre, gyrate, wheel, whirl, swirl, twirl, trundle, troll, bowl; slew round.

roll up, furl; wallow, welter; box the compass; spin like a -top, – teetotum.

Adj. rotating &c. *v.*; rota-tory, -ry; circumrotatory, trochilic, vertiginous, gyratory; vortic-al, -ose.

Adv. head over heels, round and round, like a horse in a mill.

**314.** [Reciprocating motion, motion to and fro.] **Oscillation.—N.** oscillation; vibration, libration; motion of a pendulum; nutation; undulation; pulsation; pulse; throb; seismic disturbance.

alternation; coming and going &c. *v.*; ebb and flow, flux and reflux, ups and downs; wave, vibratiuncle, swing, beat, shake, wag, see-saw, dance, lurch, dodge; fluctuation; vacillation &c. (*irresolution*) 605.

seismometer, vibroscope, seismograph.

V. oscillate; vi-, li-brate; alternate, undulate, wave; sway, rock, swing; pulsate, beat; wag, -gle; nod, bob, courtesy, curtsy; tick; play; chatter, wamble, wabble; teeter, dangle, swag.

fluctuate, dance, curvet, reel, quake; quiver, quaver, shake, flicker; wriggle; roll, toss, pitch; flounder, stagger, totter, waddle; move –, bob- up and down &c. *adv.*; pass and repass, ebb and flow, come and go, shuttle; vacillate &c. 605.

brandish, shake, flourish.

Adj. oscillating &c. *v.*; oscill-, undul-, puls-, libr-atory; vibrat-ory, -ile; pendulous, shutterwise, seismic.

Adv. to and fro, up and down, backwards and forwards, see-saw, zig-zag, wibble-wabble, in and out, from side to side, like buckets in a well.

**315.** [Irregular motion.] **Agitation.—N.** agitation, stir, tremor, shake, ripple, jog, jolt, jar, jerk, shock, succussion, trepidation, quiver, quaver, dance; jactit-ation, -ance; shuffling &c. *v.*; twitter, flicker, flutter.

disquiet, perturbation, commotion, turmoil, turbulence; tumult, -uation; hubbub, rout, bustle, fuss, racket, *subsultus*, staggers, megrims, epilepsy, fits, twitching, vellication, St. Vitus' dance.

spasm, throe, throb, palpitation, convulsion, paroxysm; tetanus.

disturbance &c. (*disorder*) 59; restlessness &c. (*changeableness*) 149.

ferment, -ation; ebullition, effervescence, hurly-burly, *cahotage*: tempest, storm, ground swell, heavy sea, whirlpool, vortex &c. 312; whirlwind &c. (*wind*) 349.

**V.** be -agitated &c.; shake; tremble, – like an aspen leaf; quiver, quaver, quake, shiver, twitter, twire, dither, dodder; twitch, writhe, toss, shuffle, tumble, stagger, bob, reel, sway; wag, -gle, wiggle; wriggle, – like an eel; squirm; dance, stumble, shamble, flounder, totter, flounce, flop, curvet, prance.

throb, pulsate, beat, palpitate, go pit-a-pat; flutter, flitter, flicker, bicker; bustle.

ferment, effervesce, foam; boil, – over; bubble, – up; simmer.

toss –, jump- about; jump like a parched pea; shake to its -centre, – foundations; be the sport of the winds and waves; reel to and fro like a drunken man; move –, drive- from post to pillar and from pillar to post; keep between hawk and buzzard.

agitate, shake, convulse, toss, tumble, bandy, wield, brandish, flap, flourish, whisk, jerk, hitch, jolt; jog, -gle; jostle, buffet, hustle, disturb, stir, shake up, churn, jounce, wallop, whip, vellicate.

**Adj.** shaking &c. *v.*; agitated, tremulous; de-, sub-sultory; shambling; giddy-paced, saltatory, convulsive, jerky, unquiet, restless, all of a twitter.

**Adv.** by fits and starts; subsultorily &c. *adj.*; *per saltum*; hop, skip and jump; in -convulsions, – fits, pit-a-pat.

# CLASS III

## Words relating to MATTER

### Section I.  MATTER IN GENERAL

**316. Materiality.—N.** material-ity, -ness; materialization; corpor-eity, -ality; substantiality, material existence, incarnation, flesh and blood, *plenum*; physical condition.

matter, body, substance, brute matter, stuff, element, principle, protoplasm, plasma, *parenchyma*, material, *substratum*, hyle, *corpus*, *pabulum*; frame.

object, article, thing, something; still life; stocks and stones; materials &c. 635.

[Science of matter] physics; somatology, -ics; natural –, experimental-philosophy; physical science, *philosophie positive*, materialism, hylism; materialist, physicist.

**317. Immateriality.—N.** immateriality, -ness; incorporeity, dematerialization, unsubstantiality, spirituality; in, extension; astral plane.

personality; I, myself, me; *ego*, spirit &c. (*soul*) 450; astral body; immaterialism; spiritual-ism, -ist; subliminal –, subconscious- self.

**V.** disembody, spiritualize, dematerialize.

**Adj.** immateri-al, -ate; incorpor-eal, -al; asomatous, unextended; un-, disembodied; extramundane, supersensible, unearthly; pneumatoscopic; spiritual &c. (*psychical*) 450; aery.

personal, subjective.

___

**V.** materialize, incorporate, incarnate, substantiate, embody.

**Adj.** material, bodily; corpor-eal, -al; physical; somat-ic, -oscopic; sensible, tangible, ponderable, palpable, substantial; fleshly incarnate.

objective, impersonal, neuter, unspiritual, materialistic.

**318. World.—N.** world, creation, nature, universe; earth, globe, wide world; *cosmos*; terraqueous globe, sphere; macro-, mega-cosm; music of the spheres.

heavens, sky, welkin, empyrean; starry -heaven, – host; firmament; vault –, canopy- of heaven; celestial spaces.

heavenly bodies, stars, luminaries, nebulæ; galaxy, milky way, galactic circle, *via lactea*.

sun, orb of day, Apollo, Phœbus; photo-, chromo-sphere; solar system; planet, -oid, asteroid; comet; satellite; moon, orb of night, Diana, Luna; aerolite, meteor; falling –, shooting- star; meteorite.

constellation. zodiac, signs of the zodiac, Charles's wain, Great Bear Southern Cross, Orion's belt, Cassiopeia's chair, Pleiades &c.

colures, equator, ecliptic, orbit.

[Science of heavenly bodies] astronomy; urano-graphy, -logy; cosmo-logy, -graphy, -gony; *eidouranion*, orrery; geography; geodesy

&c. (*measurement*) 466; star-gazing, -gazer; astronomer; cosmogonist, geodesist, geographer; observatory.

**Adj.** cosmic, cosmical, mundane; terr-estrial, -estrious, -aqueous, -ene, -eous; telluric, earthly, geotic, geodetic, cosmogonal, under the sun; sub-lunary, -astral.

solar, heliacal; lunar; celestial, heavenly, empyreal, sphery; starry, stellar; sider-eal, -al; astral; nebular.

**Adv.** in all creation, on the face of the globe, here below, under the sun.

**319. Gravity.—N.** gravi-ty, -tation; weight; heaviness &c. *adj.*; specific gravity; ponderosity, pressure, load; bur-den, -then; ballast, counterpoise; lump –, mass –, weight- of.

lead, millstone, mountain, Ossa on Pelion.

weighing, ponderation, trutination; weights; avoirdupois –, troy –, apothecaries'- weight; grain, scruple, drachm, ounce, pound, lb., load, stone, hundredweight, cwt., ton, quintal, carat, pennyweight, tod, gramme, kilogramme &c.

[Weighing instrument] balance, scales, steelyard, beam, weighbridge, spring balance, weighing machine.

[Science of gravity] statics.

**V.** be -heavy &c. *adj.*; gravitate, weigh, press, cumber, load.

[Measure the weight of] weigh, poise.

**Adj.** weighty; weighing &c. *v.*; heavy, – as lead; ponder-ous, -able; lump-ish, -y; cumber-, burden-some; cumbrous, unwieldy, massive. in-, superin-cumbent.

**320. Levity.—N.** levity; lightness &c; *adj.*; imponderability, imponderableness, buoyancy, volatility.

feather, dust, mote, down, thistledown, flue, cobweb, gossamer, straw, cork, bubble; float, buoy; ether, air.

leaven, ferment, barm, yeast, enzyme.

**V.** be -light &c. *adj.*; float, swim, be buoyed up.

render -light &c. *adj.*; lighten, levitate; leaven.

**Adj.** light, subtile, subtle, airy; imponder-ous, -able; astatic, weightless, ethereal, sublimated; uncompressed, volatile; buoyant, floating &c. *v.*; barmy, frothy; portable.

light as -a feather, – thistle down, – air.

fermenting &c. *n.*

---

## Section II.  INORGANIC MATTER

### 1°. Solid Matter

**321. Density.—N.** density, solidity; solidness &c. *adj.*; impenetra-, impermea-bility; incompressibility; imporosity; cohesion &c. 46; constipation, consistence, spissitude.

specific gravity; hydro-, areo-meter.

condensation; solid-ation, -ification; consolidation; concretion, caseation, coagulation; petrifaction &c. (*hardening*) 323; crystallization, precipitation; deposit, precipitate, silt; inspissation; thickening &c. *v.*

indivisibility, indiscerptibility, indissolvableness.

solid body, mass, block, knot, lump; con-cretion, -crete, -glomerate; cake.

**322. Rarity.—N.** rarity; tenuity; absence of -solidity &c. 321; subtility; sponginess, compressibility.

rarefaction, expansion, dilatation, inflation, subtilization.

ether &c. (*gas*) 334.

**V.** rarefy, expand, dilate, subtilize, attenuate, thin.

**Adj.** rare, subtile, thin, fine, tenuous, compressible, flimsy, slight; light &c. 320; cavernous, spongy &c. (*hollow*) 252.

rarefied &c. *v.*; unsubstantial; uncom-pact, -pressed.

clot, stone, curd, coagulum, grume; bone, gristle, cartilage.
V. be -dense &c. *adj.*; become –, render- solid &c. *adj.*; solid-ify,
-ate; concrete, set, take a set, consolidate, congeal, coagulate; curd,
-le; fix, clot, cake, candy, precipitate, deposit, cohere, crystallize;
petrify &c. (*harden*) 323.

condense, thicken, inspissate, incrassate; compress, squeeze, ram
down, constipate.

Adj. dense, solid; solidified &c. *v.*; cohe-rent, -sive &c. 46; compact,
close, serried, thickset; substantial, massive, lumpish; impenetrable,
impermeable, imporous; incompressible; constipated; concrete &c.
(*hard*) 323; knot-ted, -ty; gnarled; crystal-line, -lizable; thick,
grumous, stuffy.

un-dissolved, -melted, -liquefied, -thawed.

in-divisible, -discerptible, -frangible, -dissolvable, -dissoluble,
-soluble, -fusible.

**323. Hardness.—N.** hardness &c.
*adj.*; rigidity, renitence, inflexibility,
temper, callosity, durity.

induration, petrifaction; lapid-ifica-
tion, -escence; vitri-, ossi-, corni-fica-
tion; crystallization.

stone, pebble, flint, marble, rock,
fossil, crag, crystal, quartz, granite,
adamant; bone, cartilage; heart of oak,
block, board, deal board; iron, steel;
cast –, wrought- iron; nail; brick, con-
crete; cement.

V. render -hard &c. *adj.*; harden,
stiffen, indurate, petrify, temper, ossify,
vitrify.

Adj. hard, rigid, stubborn, stiff, firm;
starch, -ed; stark, unbending, unlimb-
er, unyielding; inflexible, tense; in-
durate, -d; gritty, proof.

adamant-ine, -ean; concrete, stony,
rocky, lithic, granitic, vitreous; crys-
talline; horny, corneous; bony;oss-eous,
-ific; cartilaginous; hard as a -stone
&c. *n.*; stiff as -buckram, – a poker.

**324. Softness.—N.** softness, pliable-
ness &c. *adj.*; flexibility; pli-ancy,
-ability; sequacity, malleability; flabbi-
ness; duct-, tract-ility; extend-, extens-
ibility; plasticity; inelasticity, flaccid-
ity, laxity.

clay, wax, butter, dough, pudding;
cushion, pillow, feather-bed, pad, down,
padding, wadding.

mollification; softening &c. *v.*

V. render -soft &c. *adj.*; soften, mol-
lify, mellow, relax, temper; mash,
knead, squash, *massage.*

bend, yield, relent, relax, give.

Adj. soft, tender, supple; pli-ant,
-able; flex-ible, -ile; lithe, -some; lis-
som, limber, plastic; ductile; tract-ile,
-able; malleable, extensile, sequacious,
inelastic, mollient.

yielding &c. *v.*; flabby, limp, flimsy.

flaccid, flocculent, downy; spongy,
œdematous, medullary, doughy, argil-
laceous, mellow.

soft as -butter, – down, – silk; yield-
ing as wax; tender as a chicken.

**325. Elasticity. — N.** elasticity,
springiness, spring, resilience, reni-
tency, buoyancy.

india-rubber, caoutchouc, gutta-
percha, whalebone, gum elastic.

V. be -elastic &c. *adj.*; spring back
&c. (*recoil*) 277.

Adj. elastic, tensile, springy, ductile, resilient, renitent, buoyant.

**326. Inelasticity.—N.** want of –,
absence of- elasticity &c. 325; inelas-
ticity &c. (*softness*) 324.

Adj. inelastic &c. (*soft*) 324.

**327. Tenacity.—N.** tenacity, tough-
ness, strength; cohesion &c. 46; se-
quacity; stubbornness &c. (*obstinacy*)
606; viscidity &c. 352.

leather; gristle, cartilage.

**328. Brittleness.—N.** brittleness &c.
*adj.*; frag-, friab-, frangib-, fiss-ility;
frailty; house of -cards, – glass.

V. be -brittle &c. *adj.*; live in a glass
house.

**V. be -tenacious &c.** *adj.*; resist fracture.

**Adj.** tenacious, tough, cohesive, adhesive, strong, resisting, sequacious, stringy, gristly, cartilaginous, leathery, coriaceous, tough as whit-leather; stubborn &c. (*obstinate*) 606.

break, crack, snap, split, shiver, splinter, crumble, break short, burst, fly, give way; fall to pieces; crumble -to, – into- dust.

**Adj.** breakable, brittle, frangible, fragile, frail, friable, delicate, gimcrack, shivery, fissile; splitting &c. *v.*; lacerable, splintery, crisp, crimp, short, brittle as glass.

**329.** [Structure.] **Texture.—N.** structure, organization, anatomy, frame, mould, fabric, construction; frame-work, carcass, architecture; stratification, cleavage.

substance, stuff, *compages, parenchyma*; constitution, staple, organism: [Science of structures] organ-, oste-, my-, splanchn-, neur , angi-, aden-ology; angi-, aden-ography.

texture; inter-, con-texture; tissue, grain, web, surface; warp and -woof, – weft; tooth, nap &c. (*roughness*) 256; fineness –, coarseness-of grain.

[Science of tissues] histology.

**Adj.** structural, organic; anatomic, -al.

text-ural, -ile; fine-, coarse-grained; fine, delicate, subtile, gossamery, filmy; coarse; home-spun; linsey-woolsey.

**330. Pulverulence.—N.** [State of powder.] pulverulence; sandiness &c. *adj.*; efflorescence; friability.

powder, dust, sand, shingle; sawdust; grit; attrition; meal, bran, flour, *farina*, spore, sporule; crumb, seed, grain; particle &c. (*smallness*) 32; thermion; limature, filings, *débris, detritus*, scobs, magistery, fine powder; *flocculi*.

smoke; cloud of -dust, – sand, – smoke; puff –, volume -of smoke; sand –, dust- storm.

[Reduction to powder] pulverization, comminution, attenuation, granulation, disintegration, subaction, contusion, trituration, levigation, abrasion, detrition, multure; limation; filing &c. *v.*

[Instruments for pulverization] mill, millstone, grater, rasp, file, pestle and mortar, nutmeg-grater, teeth, molar, grinder, chopper, grindstone, kern, quern, muller.

**V.** come to dust; be -disintegrated, – reduced to powder &c.

reduce –, grind- to powder; pulverize, comminute, granulate, triturate, levigate; scrape, file, abrade, rub down, grind, grate, rasp, pound, bray, bruise; con-tuse, -tund; beat, crush, cranch, craunch, crunch, muller, scranch, crumble, disintegrate; attenuate &c. 195.

**Adj.** powdery, pulverulent, granular, mealy, floury, farinaceous, branny, furfuraceous, flocculent, dusty, sandy, sabulous; aren-ose, -arious, -aceous; gritty; efflorescent, impalpable.

pulverizable; friable, crumbly, shivery; pulverized &c. *v.*; attrite; in pieces.

**331. Friction.—N.** friction, attrition; rubbing &c. *v.*; erasure; con frication, -trition; affriction, abrasion, arrosion, limature, frication, rub; elbow-grease; rosin; massage.

**V. rub,** scratch, abrade, scrape, scrub,

**332.** [Absence of friction. Prevention of friction.] **Lubrication.—N.** smoothness &c. 255; unctuousness &c. 355.

lubri-cation, -fication; anointment; oiling &c. *v.*

fray, rasp, graze, curry. scour, polish, rub out, erase, gnaw; file, grind &c. (*reduce to powder*) 330; *massage.*
set one's teeth on edge; rosin.
Adj. anatriptic, abrasive.

synovia; lubricant, graphite, glycerine, oil &c. 356; saliva; lather.
V. lubri-cate, -citate; oil, grease lather, soap; wax.
Adj. lubricated &c. *v.*

## 2°. FLUID MATTER

### 1. *Fluids in General*

**333. Fluidity.—N.** fluidity, liquidity; liquidness &c. *adj.*; gaseity &c. 334; liquefaction &c. 334.

fluid, inelastic fluid; liquid, liquor; lymph, humour, juice, sap, serum, blood, serosity, gravy, rheum, ichor, sanies.

solu-bility, -bleness.

[Science of liquids] hydro-logy, -statics, -dynamics, hydraulics &c.

V. be -fluid &c. *adj.*; flow &c. (*water in motion*) 348; liquefy &c. 335.

Adj. liquid, fluid, serous, juicy, succulent, sappy; fluent &c. (*flowing*) 348.

liquefied &c. 335; uncongealed; soluble, hydrostatic &c. *n.*

**334. Gaseity.—N.** gaseity, gaseousness; vapourousness &c. *adj.*; flatulence, -lency; volatility, aeration, gasification.

elastic fluid, gas, air, vapour, ether, steam, fume, reek, *effluvium, flatus*; cloud &c. 353.

[Science of elastic fluids] pneumat-ics, -ostatics; aero-statics, -dynamics &c.

gas-, gaso-meter.

V. gassify, aerate, aerify; emit vapour &c. 336.

Adj. gaseous, aeriform, ethereal, aerial, airy, vaporous, volatile, evaporable; flatulent; aerostatic &c. *n.*

**335. Liquefaction.—N.** liquefaction; liquescen-ce, -cy, deliquescence; melting &c. (*heat*) 384; colliqu-ation, -efaction; thaw; de-, liquation; lixiviation, dissolution.

solution, apozem, lixivium, infusion, decoction, flux.

solvent, diluent, menstruum, alkahest, *aqua fortis.*

V. render -liquid &c. 333; liquefy, run, deliquesce; melt &c. (*heat*) 384; solve; dissolve, resolve; liquate; hold in solution; leach, lixiviate.

Adj. lique-fied &c. *v.*, -scent, -fiable; deliquescent, soluble, colliquative; solvent.

**336. Vaporization. — N.** vapor-, volatil-ization; gasification; e-, vaporation; distillation, cohobation, sublimation, exhalation; volatility.

vaporizer, still, retort, spray, atomizer; fumigation, steaming.

V. render -gaseous &c. 334; vaporize, volatilize; distil, sublime; evaporate, exhale, smoke, transpire, emit vapour, fume, reek, steam, fumigate.

Adj. volatilized &c. *v.*; reeking &cᵢ *v.*; volatile; evaporable, vaporizableᵢ

---

## 2. *Specific Fluids*

**337. Water.—N.** water; serum, serosity; lymph; rheum; diluent.

dilution, maceration, lotion; washing &c. *v.*; im-, mersion; humectation, infiltration, spargefaction, affusion, irrigation, *douche,* balneation, bath.

deluge &c. (*water in motion*) 348; high water, flood-, spring-tide.

**338. Air.—N.** air &c. (*gas*) 334; common –, atmospheric- air; atmosphere, stratosphere, isothermal layer, troposphere, Heaviside layer.

open, – air; sky, welkin; blue, – sky; cloud &c. 353.

weather, climate, rise and fall of the barometer, isobar.

V. be -watery &c. *adj.*; reek.

add water, water, wet; moisten &c.
339; dilute, dip, immerse; merge; im-,
sub-merge; plunge, souse, duck, drown;
soak, steep, macerate, pickle, wash,
sprinkle, sparge, lave, bathe, affuse,
splash, swash, douse, slosh, drench;
dabble, slop, slobber, irrigate, inundate,
deluge; syringe, inject, gargle; infil-
trate, percolate.

Adj. watery, aqueous, aquatic, lym-
phatic; balneal, diluent; drenching &c.
*v.*; diluted &c. *v.*; weak; wet &c. (*moist*)
339.

Phr. the waters are out.

**339. Moisture.—N.** moisture; moist-
ness &c. *adj.*; hum-idity, -ectation;
madefaction, dew; *serein*; marsh &c.
345; Hygromet-ry, -er.

V. moisten, wet; humect, -ate;
sponge, damp, dampen, bedew; imbue,
imbrue, infiltrate, saturate; seethe,
sop; soak, drench &c. (*water*) 337.

be -moist &c. *adj.*; not have a dry
thread; perspire &c. (*exude*) 295.

Adj. moist, damp; watery &c. 337;
undried, humid, wet, dank, muggy,
dewy; roric; roscid; juicy.

wringing wet; wet -through, – to the
skin; saturated &c. *v.*

swashy, soggy, dabbled; reeking,
seething, dripping, soaking, soft, sod-
den, sloppy, muddy; swampy &c.
(*marshy*) 345; irriguous.

**341. Ocean.—N.** sea, ocean, main,
deep, brine, salt water, waters, waves,
billows, high seas, offing, great waters,
watery waste, 'vasty deep,' briny
ocean, herring pond, steamer track,
the seven seas; wave, tide &c. (*water
in motion*) 348.

hydrograph-y, -er, oceanography;
Neptune, Thetis, Triton, Naiad, Ne-
reid; sea-nymph, Siren, mer-maid,
-man; trident, dolphin.

Adj. oceanic; mar-ine, -itime; pelagic,
-ian; sea-going, -worthy; hydrographic.

Adv. at –, on- sea; afloat, on the
high seas.

[Science of air] pneumatics, aero-logy ,
-scopy, -graphy; meteorology, climatol-
ogy; eudio-, baro-, aero-meter; aneroid,
baro-graph, -scope; weather-gauge,
-glass, -cock.

exposure to the -air, – weather; ven-
tilation; aero-station, -nautics, -naut
&c. 267 and 269.

V. air, ventilate; fan &c. (*wind*) 349.

Adj. containing air, flatulent, efferve-
scent; windy &c. 349.

atmospheric, airy; aeri-al, -form;
pneumatic; meteorological; weather-
wise.

Adv. in the open air, out of doors,
*à la belle étoile, al fresco; sub -Jove, – dio.*

**340. Dryness.—N.** dryness &c. *adj.*;
siccity, aridity, drought, ebb-, neap-
tide, low water.

drying, ex-, de-siccation; evapora-
tion; dehydration; arefaction, dephleg-
mation, drainage.

drier, desiccator.

V. be -dry &c. *adj.*; render -dry &c.
*adj.*; dry; dry –, soak- up; sponge,
swab, wipe; ex-, de-siccate, dehydrate,
anhydrate; drain, parch.

be fine, hold up.

Adj. dry, anhydrous, arid, waterless;
dried &c. *v.*; undamped; juice-, sap-
less; sear; husky; rainless; without
rain, fine; dry as -a bone, – dust, – a
stick, – a mummy, – a biscuit; desic-
cated; dehydrated; water-proof, -tight.

**342. Land.—N.** land, earth, ground,
dry land, *terra firma.*

continent, mainland, peninsula,
delta; tongue –, neck- of land; isthmus,
oasis; promontory &c. (*projection*) 250;
highland &c. (*height*) 206.

coast, shore, scar, strand, beach;
bank, lea; sea- board, -side, -shore,
-bank, -coast, -beach; rock-, iron-
bound coast; loom of the land; derelict;
innings; *alluvium*, alluvion.

soil, glebe, clay, loam, marl, cledge,
chalk, gravel, mould, subsoil, clod,
clot; rock, crag, cliff.

acres; real estate &c. (*property*) 780;
landsman, land-lubber, farmer.

geography &c. 318; agriculture &c.
371.

V. land, come to land; set foot on -the soil, – dry land; come –, go- ashore.

Adj. earthy; continental, midland; littoral, riparian, ripuarian; alluvial; terrene &c. (*world*) 318; landed, predial, territorial.

Adv. ashore; on -shore, – land.

**343. Gulf. Lake.—N.** land covered with water, gulf, gulph, bay, inlet, bight, estuary, arm of the sea, fiord, armlet; frith, firth, ostiary, mouth; lagune, lagoon; indraught; cove, creek; natural harbour; roads; strait, narrows; Euripus; sound, belt, gut, kyles.

lake, loch, lough, mere, tarn, plash, broad, pond, pool, lin, puddle, well, artesian well, tank, sump; standing –, dead –, sheet of- water; fish –, mill-pond; race; ditch, dike, dyke, dam; reservoir &c. (*store*) 636.

Adj. lacustrine; land locked.

**344. Plain.—N.** plain, table land, mesa, face of the country; open –, country; basin, downs, waste, weary waste, desert, tundra, wild, steppe, pampas, savanna, prairie, champaign, heath, common, wold, veld; moor, -land, uplands, fell; bush; plateau &c. (*level*) 213; *campagna*.

meadow, mead, haugh, pasturage, park, field, lawn, green, plat, plot, grass-plat, greensward, sward, grass, turf, sod, heather; lea, ley, lay; grounds.

Adj. campestrian, champaign, alluvial.

**345. Marsh.—N.** marsh, swamp, morass, marish, moss, fen, bog, quag-mire, slough, sump, wash; mud, squash, slush.

Adj. marsh, -y; swampy, boggy, plashy, poachy, quaggy, soft; muddy, sloppy, squashy, spongy; paludal; moor-ish, -y; fenny.

**346. Island.—N.** island, isle, islet, eyot, ait, holm, reef, atoll, breaker; archipelago; islander.

Adj. insular, sea-girt.

——————

### 3. *Fluids in Motion*

**347.** [Fluid in motion.] **Stream.—N.** stream &c. (*of water*) 348, (*of air*) 349.

V. flow &c. 348; blow &c. 349.

**348.** [Water in motion.] **River.—N.** running water.

jet, spirt, squirt, spout, splash, swash, rush, gush, *jet d'eau*; sluice, chute.

water-spout, -fall; fall, cascade, force, foss; lin, -n; ghyll, Niagara; cata-ract, -dupe, -clysm; *débâcle*, in-undation, deluge.

rain, -fall; *serein*; shower, scud; downpour, cloud burst; driving –, pouring –, drenching- rain; hyeto-logy, -graphy; rainy season, monsoon; pre-dominance of Aquarius, reign of St. Swithin; mizzle, drizzle, *stillicidium*, plash; dropping &c. *v.*

stream, course, flux, flow, profluence; effluence &c. (*egress*) 295; defluxion; flowing &c. *v.*; current, tide, race.

spring; fount, -ain; rill, rivulet, gill,

**349.** [Air in motion.] **Wind.—N.** wind, draught, *flatus*, *afflatus*, air; breath, – of air; puff, whiff, zephyr; blow, drift; *aura*; stream, current; under-current.

gust, blast, breeze, squall, gale, half a gale, storm, tempest, hurricane, whirlwind, tornado, samiel, cyclone, typhoon; simoon; harmattan, monsoon, trade wind, sirocco, *mistral*, *bise*, *föhn*, tramontane, levanter; capful of wind; fresh –, stiff- breeze; keen blast; blizzard.

windiness &c. *adj.*; ventosity; rough –, dirty –, ugly –, stress of- weather; dirty-, windy-, mackerel- sky; mare's tail; thick –, black –, white- squall.

anemography, aerodynamics; wind-gauge, anemometer, weather-cock, vane.

gullet, rillet; stream-, brook-let; runnel, sike, burn, beck, brook, stream, river; reach; tributary.

body of water, torrent, rapids, flush, flood, swash, spate; spring –, high –, full-tide; bore; eagre, *hygre*; fresh, -et; undertow, indraught, reflux, under-current, eddy, vortex, gurge, whirlpool, Maelstrom, regurgitation, overflow; confluence, corrivation.

wave, billow, surge, swell, ripple; roller, ground swell, surf, breaker, white horses; comber, beach-comber; rough –, heavy –, cross –, long –, short –, chopping –, choppy- sea, choppiness; tidal wave.

[Science of fluids in motion] Hydro-dynamics; Hydraul-ics &c.; rain-gauge &c.

water-bearer, – carrier, Aquarius.

irrigation &c. (*water*) 337; pump; watering-pot, – cart; hydrant, stand-pipe, hose, sprinkler, drencher; fire-engine, squirt, syringe.

**V.** flow, run; meander; gush, pour, spout, roll, jet, well, issue; drop, drip, dribble, plash, squirt, spurt, spirtle, trill, trickle, distil, percolate; stream, overflow, inundate, deluge, flow over, splash, swash; guggle, murmur, babble, bubble, purl, gurgle, sputter, regurgitate; ooze, flow out &c. (*egress*) 295.

rain, – hard, – in torrents, – cats and dogs, – pitchforks; come down in sheets; pour with rain, drizzle, mizzle, spit, sprinkle, set in.

flow –, fall –, open –, drain- into; discharge itself, disembogue.

[Cause a flow] pour; pour out &c. (*discharge*) 297; shower down; irrigate, drench &c. (*wet*) 337; spill, splash.

[Stop a flow] stanch; dam, -up &c. (*close*) 261; obstruct &c. 706.

**Adj.** fluent; dif-, pro-, af-fluent; tidal; flowing &c. *v.*; meand-ering, -ry, -rous; fluvi-al, -atile; streamy, showery, rainy. drizzly, drizzling, pluvial, pluviose, stillicidous.

suf-, insuf-, per-, in-, af-flation; blowing, fanning &c. *v.*; ventilation.

sneezing &c. *v.*; sternutation; hic-cup, -cough; catching of the breath; breathing &c.

Eolus, Eurus, Boreas, Zephyr, cave of Eolus.

air-pump, lungs, bellows, blow-pipe, fan, blower; pulmotor, ventilator, punkah, aspirator, exhauster, ejector.

**V.** blow, waft; blow -hard, – great guns, – a hurricane &c. *n.*; whistle, roar, howl, ring in the shrouds; stream, issue.

respire, breathe, in-, ex-hale, puff; whif, -fle; gasp, wheeze; snuff, -le; sniff, -le; sneeze, cough, belch.

fan, ventilate; in-, per-flate; blow –, pump- up.

**Adj.** blowing &c. *v.*; windy, airy, æolian, flatulent; breezy, gusty, squally; stormy, tempestuous, blustering; bois-terous &c. (*violent*) 173.

pulmon-ic, -ary.

---

**350.** [Channel for the passage of water.] **Conduit.**—**N.** conduit, channel, duct, watercourse, race; head –, tail-race; adit, aqueduct, canal, trough, flume, gutter, pantile; dike, canyon, ravine, gorge, hollow, main, gully, moat, ditch, drain, sewer, culvert, *cloaca*, sough, kennel, siphon, *piscina*; pipe &c. (*tube*) 260; funnel; tunnel &c. (*passage*) 627; water –, waste- pipe; emunctory, gully-hole, artery, aorta, vein, blood vessel; lymphatic; throat, alimentary canal, intestine; pore, spout, scupper; ad-, a-jutage;

**351.** [Channel for the passage of air.] **Air-pipe.**—**N.** air-pipe, – shaft, – way, – passage, – tube; shaft, flue, chimney, funnel, vent, blow-hole, nostril, nozzle, throat, weasand, *trachea*; bronch-us, -ia; larynx, tonsils, wind-pipe, spiracle; venti-duct, -lator; louvre, blow-pipe &c. (*wind*) 349; pipe &c. (*tube*) 260.

---

hose; gar-, gur-goyle; penstock, weir; flood-, water-gate; sluice,
lock, valve; rose; waterworks.
**Adj.** vascular &c. (*with holes*) 260.

### 3°. IMPERFECT FLUIDS

**352. Semiliquidity.—N.** semiliquid-
ity; stickiness &c. *adj.*; visc-idity,
-osity; gumm-, glutin-, muc-osity;
spiss-, crass-itude; lentor; adhesive-
ness &c. (*cohesion*) 46.

inspiss-, incrass-ation; thickening,
coagulation.

jelly, aspic, mucilage, gelatin, isin-
glass; colloid, mucus, phlegm; pituite,
lava; glair, starch, gluten, albumen,
milk, cream, protein; syrup, treacle;
gum, size, glue, paste; wax, bee's-wax;
emulsoid, emulsion, soup; squash, mud,
slush, slime, ooze; moisture &c. 339;
marsh &c. 345.

**V.** inspiss-, incrass-ate; coagulate,
gelatinize, gelatinify, gel, jell, emulsify,
thicken; mash, squash, churn, beat up.

**Adj.** semi-fluid, -liquid; half-melted,
-frozen; milky, muddy &c. *n.*; lact-eal,
-ean, -eous, -escent, -iferous; emulsive,
curdled, thick, succulent, uliginous.

gelat-, album-, mucilag-, glut-inous;
gelatine, mastic, amylaceous, ropy,
clammy, clotted; vis-cid, -cous; sticky,
tacky; slab, -by; lentous, pituitous;
mu-cid, -culent, -cous.

**353. [Mixture of air and water.]**
**Bubble. [Cloud.]—N.** bubble; foam,
froth, head, fume, spume, lather, suds,
spray, surf, yeast, barm, spindrift.

cloud, vapour, fog, mist, haze,
steam; scud, rack, *nimbus*; *cumulus*,
woolpack, *cirrus*, *stratus*; *cirro-*, *cumulo-
stratus*; *cirro-cumulus*; mackerel sky,
mare's tail, dirty sky.

[Science of clouds] nephelognosy,
nephology.

effervescence, fermentation; bub-
bling &c. *v.*

nebula; cloudiness &c. (*opacity*) 426;
nebulosity &c. (*dimness*) 422.

**V.** bubble, boil, foam, froth, spume,
mantle, sparkle, guggle, gurgle; effer-
vesce, ferment, fizzle; aerate; cloud,
overcast, befog.

**Adj.** bubbling &c. *v.*; frothy, nappy,
effervescent, sparkling, *mousseux*, up,
fizzy, with a head on.

cloudy &c. *n.*; vaporous, nebulous,
overcast; nubiferous, nephological;
foggy, brumous.

---

**354. Pulpiness.—N.** pulpiness &c.
*adj.*; pulp, paste, dough, sponge, curd,
pap, rob, jam, pudding, mush, fool,
poultice, grume, *papier mâché*..
**Adj.** pulpy &c. *n.*; pultaceous,
grumous.
**V.** pulp, pulpify, mash.

**355. Unctuousness.—N.** unctuous-
ness &c. *adj.*; unctuosity, lubricity;
ointment &c. (*oil*) 356; anointment;
lubrication &c. 332.
**V.** oil &c. (*lubricate*) 332.
**Adj.** unctuous, oily, oleaginous, adi-
pose, sebaceous; fat, -ty; greasy; waxy,
butyraceous, soapy, saponaceous, pin-
guid, lardaceous; slippery.

---

**356. Oil.—N.** oil, fat, butter, cream, grease, tallow, suet, lard,
dripping, margarine, oleomargarine, exunge, blubber; glycerine, stearine,
elaine, oleagine; soap; soft soap, wax, cerement; paraffin, spermaceti,
adipocere; petroleum, mineral -, rock -, crystal- oil, kerosene, vege-
table -, colza -, olive -, linseed -, cotton seed -, rape -, nut -, fusel- oil;
animal -, neat's foot -, signal -, train- oil; ointment, unguent, liniment,
salve, pomade, pomatum, brilliantine, spike -, nard.

**356a. Resin.—N.** resin, rosin, colophony; gum; lac, shellac, sealing-
wax; amber, -gris; bitumen, pitch, tar, asphalt, -e, -um; varnish, copal,
mastic, magilp, lacquer, japan.

**V.** varnish &c. (*overlay*) 223.

**Adj.** resinous, bituminous, pitchy, tarry.

# Section III. ORGANIC MATTER

## 1°: Vitality

### 1. Vitality in general

**357. Organization.**—N. organized
-world, – nature; living –, animated-
nature; living beings; organic remains,
organism; fossils; animal and vegetable
kingdom, *fauna* and *flora*, biota.
prot-oplasm, -ein; albumen; struc-
ture &c. 329; organ-ization, -ism.
[Science of living beings] biology;
natural history,* organic –, bio-chemis-
try, anatomy, physiology, embryology,
morphology, evolution, Darwinism,
Lamarkism, zoology &c. 368; botany
&c. 369; naturalist, biologist &c.
Adj. organ-ic, -ized.

**358. Inorganization.** — N. mineral
-world, – kingdom; unorganized –,
inorganic –, brute –, inanimate- matter.
[Science of the mineral kingdom]
mineralogy; geo-logy, -gnosy, -scopy;
metall-urgy, -ography; lithology;
orycto-logy, -graphy.
V. turn to dust, pulverize.
Adj. in-organic, -animate; unorgan-
ized; azoic; mineral.

**359. Life.**—N. life; vi-tality, -ability;
animation; vital -spark, – flame, –
force.
respiration, wind; breath -of life, –
of one's nostrils; life-blood; Archeus;
existence &c. 1.
vivification, vitalization; revivifica-
tion &c. 163; Prometheus; life to come
&c. (*destiny*) 152.
[Science of life] physiology, etiology,
embryology, biology; animal economy.
nourishment, staff of life &c. (*food*)
298.
V. be -alive &c. *adj.*; live, breathe,
respire; subsist &c. (*exist*) 1; walk the
earth; strut and fret one's hour upon
a stage; be spared.
see the light, be born, come into the
world; fetch –, draw- -breath, – the
breath of life; quicken; revive; come
to, – life.
give birth to &c. (*produce*) 161;
bring to life, put life into, vitalize;
vivi-fy, -ficate; reanimate &c. (*restore*)
660; keep -alive, – body and soul
together, – the wolf from the door;
support life.
have nine lives like a cat.

**360. Death.**—N. death, dying &c. *v.*;
de-cease, -mise; dissolution, departure,
*obit*, release, rest, *quietus*, fall; loss,
bereavement.
end &c. 67 –, cessation &c. 142 –, loss
–, extinction –, ebb- of -life &c. 359.
death-warrant, -watch, -rattle, -bed;
stroke –, agonies –, shades –, valley of
the shadow –, jaws –, hand- of death;
last -breath, – gasp, – agonies; dying
-day, – breath, – agonies; swan song,
*chant du cygne*; *rigor mortis*; Stygian
shore; crossing the bar, the great
adventure.
King -of terrors, – Death; Death,
Angel of Death; mortality; doom &c.
(*necessity*) 601.
*euthanasia*; happy release; break up
of the system; natural -death, – decay;
sudden –, violent- death; untimely end,
watery grave; suffocation, *asphyxia*;
heart failure; fatal disease &c. (*disease*)
655; death-blow &c. (*killing*) 361.
necrology, bills of mortality, obitu-
ary; death-song &c. (*lamentation*) 839.
V. die, expire, perish; meet one's
-death, – end; pass away, be taken;
yield –, resign- one's breath; resign

* The term *Natural History* is also used as relating to all the objects in Nature
whether organic or inorganic, and including therefore *Mineralogy*, *Geology*
*Meteorology*, &c.

**Adj.** living, alive; in -life, – the flesh, – the land of the living; on this side of the grave, above ground, breathing, quick, animated, viable; lively &c. (*active*) 682; alive and kicking; tenacious of life.

vital; vivi-fying, -fied &c. *v.*; Promethean.

**Adv.** *vivendi causâ.*

one's -being, – life; end one's -days, – life, – earthly career; breathe one's last; cease to -live, – breathe; depart this life; be -no more &c. *adj.*; go –, drop –, pop -off; lose –, lay down –, relinquish –, surrender- one's life; drop -, sink- into the grave; close one's eyes; fall –, drop- dead, – down dead; break one's neck; give –, yield- up the ghost; be all over with one.

pay the debt to nature, shuffle off this mortal coil, take one's last sleep; go the way of all flesh; join the -greater number, – majority, – choir invisible; awake to life immortal; come –, turn- to dust; cross the Stygian ferry; go to -one's long account, – one's last home, – Davy Jones's locker, – the wall; receive one's death warrant, make one's will, die a natural death, go out like the snuff of a candle; come to an untimely end; catch one's death; go off the hooks, kick the bucket, peg out; go West; hop the twig, turn up one's toes; die a violent death &c. (*be killed*) 361; make the supreme sacrifice.

**Adj.** dead, lifeless; deceased, demised, departed, defunct; late, gone, no more; ex-, in-animate; out of the world, taken off, released; departed this life &c. *v.*; dead and gone; bereft of life, stone dead, dead as -a door nail, – a door post, – mutton, – a herring, – nits; launched into eternity, gathered to one's fathers, numbered with the dead, gone to a better land, behind the veil, beyond the grave, – mortal ken.

dying &c. *v.*; mori-bund, -ent, Acherontic; hippocratic; *in -articulo,* – *extremis*; in the -jaws, – agony- of death; going, – off; *aux abois*; on one's -last legs, – death bed; at -the point of death, – death's door, – the last gasp; near one's end, given over, booked, fey; with one foot in –, tottering on the brink of- the grave.

still-born; mortuary; deadly &c. (*killing*) 361.

**Adv.** *post -obit, – mortem.*

**Phr.** life -ebbs, – fails, – hangs by a thread; one's -days are numbered, – hour is come, – race is run, – doom is sealed; Death -knocks at the door, – stares one in the face; the breath is out of the body; the grave closes over one; *sic itur ad astra.*

**361.** [Destruction of life; violent death.] **Killing.**—**N.** killing &c. *v.*; homicide, manslaughter, murder, assassination, trucidation, occision; lynching, effusion of blood; blood, -shed; gore, slaughter, carnage, butchery; *battue*, gladiatorial combat;

massacre; *fusillade, noyade, pogrom*; Thuggee, thuggism.

death blow, finishing stroke, *coup de grâce, quietus*; execution &c: (*capital punishment*) 972; judicial murder; martyrdom.

butcher, slayer, murderer, Cain, assassin, cut-throat, garrotter, *bravo,* thug, racketeer, gunman, mobster, gangster, Moloch, *matador, sabreur*; *guet-à-pens*; gallows, executioner &c. (*punishment*) 975; man-eater.

regicide, parricide, fratricide, infanticide, aborticide &c.

suicide, *felo-de-se, suttee, hara-kiri*, Juggernaut; immolation, holocaust.

suffocation, strangulation, garrotte; hanging &c. *v.*

deadly weapon &c. (*arms*) 727; Aceldama; the potter's field, the field of blood.

fatal accident, violent death, casualty.

[Destruction of animals] slaughtering; phthiozoics;* sport, -ing; the chase, venery; hunting, coursing, shooting, fishing; pig-sticking; sports-, hunts-, fisher-man; hunter, Nimrod; slaughterer, knacker, slaughter-house, shambles, *abattoir*.

**V.** kill, put to death, slay, shed blood; murder, assassinate, butcher, slaughter; victimize, immolate; massacre; take away –, deprive of-life; make away with, put an end to; despatch, decimate; burke, settle do, – to death, – for.

strangle, garrotte, hang, lynch, throttle, choke, stifle, suffocate, stop the breath, smother, asphyxiate, drown.

sabre; cut -down, – to pieces, – the throat; jugulate; stab, run through the body, bayonet; put to the -sword, – edge of the sword.

shoot, – dead; blow one's brains out; brain, knock on the head; stone, lapidate; give –, deal- a death blow; give a -*quietus*, – *coup de grâce*.

behead, bowstring &c. (*execute*) 972.

hunt, shoot &c. *n.*

cut off, nip in the bud, launch into eternity, send to one's last account, bump off, rub out, sign one's death warrant, strike the death knell of.

give no quarter, pour out blood like water; run amuck, wade knee-deep –, imbrue one's hands- in blood.

die a violent death, welter in one's blood; dash –, blow- out one's brains; commit suicide; kill –, -make away with –, put an end to- oneself.

**Adj.** killing &c. *v.*; murd-, slaught-erous; sanguin-ary, -olent; blood-stained, -thirsty; homicidal, red-handed; bloody, -minded; ensanguined, gory, sanguineous.

mortal, fatal, lethal; dead-, death-ly; mort-, leth-iferous; unhealthy &c. 657; internecine; suicidal.

sporting; piscator-ial, -y.

**Adv.** in at the death.

**362. Corpse.**—**N.** corpse, corse, carcass, bones, skeleton, dry-bones; defunct, relics, *reliquiæ*, remains, mortal remains, dust, ashes, earth, clay; mummy; carrion; food for- worms, – fishes; tenement of clay, this mortal coil.

shade, ghost, *manes*, apparition &c. 980.

organic remains, fossils.

**Adj.** cadaverous, corpse-like; unburied &c. 363.

**363. Interment.**—**N.** interment, burial, sepulture, entombment; in-, humation; obs-, ex-equies; funeral, wake, pyre, funeral pile; crema-tion.

funeral -rite, – solemnity; knell, passing bell, tolling; dirge &c. (*lamentation*) 839; cypress; *obit*, dead march, muffled drum; coroner, mortician, undertaker, mute, mourner, professional mourner, pall-bearer; elegy; funeral -oration, – sermon; epitaph.

grave clothes, shroud, winding-sheet, cere-cloth; cerement.

coffin, shell, sarcophagus, urn, pall, bier, hearse, catafalque, cinerary urn.

grave, pit, sepulchre, tomb, vault, crypt, catacomb, mausoleum, *Gol-gotha*, house of death, narrow house, long home; cemetery, necropolis, boneyard; burial-place, -ground; grave-, church-yard; God's acre; mortuary, tope, cromlech, dolmen, menhir, barrow, tumulus, cairn;

* Bentham, 'Chrestomathia.'

ossuary; bone-, charnel-, dead-house; *morgue*; lich-gate; crematorium.
sexton, grave-digger.

monument, memorial, cenotaph, shrine; grave-, head-, tomb-stone;
*memento mori*; hatchment, stone, cross.

exhumation, disinterment; necropsy, autopsy, *post-mortem* exami-
nation.

**V.** inter, bury; lay in –, consign to- the -grave, – tomb; en-, in-tomb
inhume; lay out, prepare for burial, embalm, mummify; conduct ε
funeral, hold services; toll the knell; put to bed with a shovel.

exhume, disinter, unearth.

**Adj.** buried &c. *v.*; burial; fune-real, -brial; mortuary, sepulchral,
cinerary; elegiac; necroscopic.

**Adv.** *in memoriam*; *post-obit*, *-mortem*; beneath –, under- the sod.

**Phr.** *hic jacet*, *ci-gît*, *requiescat in pace*.

## 2. Special Vitality

**364. Animality.—N.** animal life;
ʌnima-tion, -lity, -lization; breath.

flesh, – and blood; corporeal nature;
*physique*; strength &c. 159.

**V.** animalize, incorporate.

**Adj.** fleshly, incarnate, carnal, cor-
poreal, human.

**365. Vegetability.—N.** vegetable life;
vegeta-tion, -bility; herbage.

**V.** vegetate, germinate, sprout,
shoot; cultivate.

**Adj.** vegetable &c. 367; rank, lush.

---

**366. Animal.\*—N.** animal, – king-
dom; *fauna*; brute creation.

beast, brute, creature, created being;
creeping –, living- thing; dumb -animal,
– creature.

flocks and herds, live stock; domes-
tic –, wild- animals; game, *feræ naturæ*;
beasts of the field, fowls of the air,
denizens of the day.

vertebrate, bi-, quadru-ped, mam-
mal, marsupial, bird, reptile, batra-
chian, amphibian, fish, crustacean,
shell fish, articulate, mollusc, worm,
insect, zoophyte; protozoon, animal-
cule &c. 193.

horse &c. (*beast of burden*) 271;
cattle, kine, ox; bull, -ock; steer, stot;
cow, milch cow, calf, heifer, shorthorn;
sheep; lamb, -kin; ewe –, pet- lamb;
ewe, ram, tup; pig, swine, boar, hog,
shoat, sow; tag, teg, wether.

dog, bitch, hound; pup, -py; whelp,
cur, mutt, mongrel; house-, watch-,
sheep-, shepherd's-, sporting-, fancy-,
lap-, toy-, bull-, badger-dog; mastiff;
blood-, grey-, stag-, deer-, fox-, otter-
hound; harrier, beagle, spaniel, pointer,

**367. Vegetable.\*— N.** vegetable
– kingdom; *flora*, verdure.

plant; tree, shrub, bush; creeper;
vine; herb, -age; grass.

annual; per-, bi-, tri-ennial; exotic.

timber; primeval –, virgin- forest;
wood, -lands; hurst, frith, holt, weald,
park, chase, greenwood, brake, grove,
copse, coppice, *bocage*, *tope*, clump of
trees, thicket, spinet, spinney; under-,
brush-wood; boscage, scrub; the oak
and the ash and the bonny ivy tree.

bush, jungle, prairie; heath, -er;
fern, bracken; furze, gorse, whin,
broom; grass, turf, grassland, green-
sward, green, lawn, meadow; pas-ture,
-turage; turbary; sedge, rush, weed;
fungus, mushroom, toadstool; lichen,
moss, conferva, mould; seaweed &c.;
growth, crop.

foliage, leafage, branch, bough, ram-
age; spray &c. 51; leaf, frond, flag,
petal, shoot, tendril.

flower, blossom, bud, bloom, bine;
flowering plant; tree, sapling, pollard;
timber-, fruit-tree; palm-, gum-tree;
pulse, legume.

\* Extended lists of names of specific varieties of animals, vegetables, &c., are
beyond the scope of this work; see Introduction, p. xxv.

setter, retriever; Newfoundland; water
-dog, –spaniel; pug, poodle; dachshund;
Pinscher; turnspit; terrier; fox –, Skye-
terrier; Dandie Dinmont; collie.

cat; puss, -y; kitten; grimalkin; gib-,
tom-cat; mouser; fox, Reynard, vixen,
stag, deer, hart, buck, doe, roe, ante-
lope.

bird; poultry, fowl, cock, hen,
chicken, chanticleer, partlet, rooster,
dunghill cock, barn-door fowl; feathered -tribes, – songster; sing-
ing –, dicky- bird; canary; finch; auk, dodo, moa, roc, phœnix.

snake, serpent, viper, adder; newt, eft; asp, vermin.

**Adj.** animal, zoological.

equine, bovine, vaccine, canine, feline; fishy; piscator-y, -ial;
molluscous, porcine, vermicular.

**Adj.** veget-able, -ous; herb-aceous,
-al; botanic; sylvan, silvan; arbor- ary,
-eous, -escent, -ical; dendritic, dendri-
form; woody, grassy; ver-dant,-durous;
floral, mossy; lign-ous, -eous; wooden,
leguminous; end-, ex-ogenous.

---

**368.** [The science of animals.] **Zool-
ogy.—N.** zoo-logy, -nomy, -graphy,
-tomy; anatomy; comparative ana-
tomy; animal –, comparative- physi-
ology; morphology.

anthrop-, ornith-, ichthy-, herpet-,
ophi-, malac-, helminth-, entom-, oryct-,
paleont-ology; ichthy- &c. -otomy;
taxidermy.

zo- &c. -ologist.

**Adj.** zoological &c. *n.*

**369.** [The science of plants.] **Botany.**
**—N.** botany; phyto-graphy, -logy,
-tomy; vegetable physiology, herbori-
zation, dendr-, myc-, fung-, alg-ology;
flora, pomona; botanist &c.; botanic
garden &c. *(garden)* 371; *hortus siccus,
herbarium,* herbal.

herb-ist, -arist, -alist, -orist, -arian
&c.

**V.** botanize, herborize.

**Adj.** botanical &c. *n.*

**370.** [The economy or management
of animals.] **Cicuration.—N.** taming &c.
*v.;* cicuration, zoohygiantics; domestic-
ation, -ity; *manège;* veterinary art;
breeding, pisciculture, apiculture &c.

menagery, vivarium, zoological gar-
den, zoo; bear-pit; aviary, apiary, hive;
aquarium, fishery, fish hatchery; duck-,
fish-pond; stud-farm; stock farm, dairy.

[Destruction of animals] phthisozo-
ics* &c. *(killing)* 361.

neat-, cow-, shep-herd, shepherdess;
grazier, drover, cowboy, cowkeeper;
trainer, breeder, groom, ostler &c. 746;
veterinary surgeon, vet, horse doctor;
farrier; keeper; gamekeeper.

cage &c. *(prison)* 752; hen-coop,
bird-cage, cauf; sheep-fold &c. *(inclo-
sure)* 232.

**V.** tame, domesticate, acclimatize,
breed, tend, break in, train, corral,
round up; cage, bridle &c. *(restrain)*
751; ride &c. 266.

drive, yoke, harness, hitch; groom,

**371.** [The economy or management
of plants.] **Agriculture.—N.** agricul-
ture, cultivation, husbandry, farming;
georgics, geoponics; tillage, tilth, agron-
omy, gardening, spade husbandry,
vintage; hort-, arbor-, silv-, citr-, vit-,
flor-iculture; intensive culture; land-
scape gardening; forestry, afforesta-
tion.

husbandman, horticulturist, citri-
culturist, gardener, florist; agricult-or,
-urist; yeoman, farmer, cultivator,
tiller of the soil, ploughman, sower,
reaper; woodcutter, backwoodsman,
forester; vine grower, vintager; Boer;
Triptolemus.

field, meadow, garden; botanic –,
winter –, ornamental –, flower –, kit-
chen –, truck –, market –, hop- garden;
nursery; green-, hot-, glass-house;
conservatory, cucumber frame, cloche,
bed, border, seed-plot; grass-plat,
lawn; park &c. *(pleasure ground)* 840;
*parterre,* shrubbery, plantation, avenue,

* Bentham.

curry-comb; milk; shear; hatch; incubate.

**Adj.** pastoral, bucolic; tame, domestic, domesticated, broken in, gentle, docile.

*arboretum*, pinery, *pinetum*, orchard; vineyard, vinery; orangery; farm &c. (*abode*) 189.

**V.** cultivate; till, – the soil; farm, garden; sow, plant; reap, mow, cut; manure, dress the ground, dig, delve, dibble, hoe, plough, plow, harrow, rake, weed, lop and top, force, transplant, thin out, bed out, prune, graft.

**Adj.** agr-icultural, -arian, -estic.

arable; predial, rural, rustic, country, bucolic, Bœotian; horti- cultural.

**372. Mankind.—N.** man, -kind; human -race, – species, – nature; humanity, mortality, flesh, generation.

[Science of man] anthropo-logy, -graphy, -sophy; ethno-logy, -graphy; humanitarianism.

human being; person, -age; individual, creature, fellow creature, mortal, body, somebody, one; such a –, some- one; soul, living soul; earthling; party, head, hand; *dramatis personæ*.

people, persons, folk, public, society, world; community, – at large; general public; nation, -ality; state, realm; common-weal, -wealth; republic, body politic; million &c. (*commonalty*) 876; population &c. (*inhabitant*) 188.

cosmopolite; lords of the creation; ourselves.

**Adj.** human, mortal, personal, individual, national, civic, public, cosmopolitan; anthropoid.

**373. Man.—N.** man, male, he; man- hood &c. (*adolescence*) 131; gentleman, sir, master; yeoman, wight, swain, fellow, guy, blade, *beau*, chap, gaffer, goodman; husband &c. (*married man*) 903; Mr., mister, *monsieur, sahib, Herr, señor, signor*; boy &c. (*youth*) 129; Adonis.

[Male animal] cock, drake, gander, dog, boar, stag, hart, buck, horse, entire horse, stallion; gib-, tom-cat; he-, Billy-goat; ram, tup; bull, -ock; capon, ox, gelding; steer, stot.

**Adj.** male, he, masculine; manly; virile; un-womanly, -feminine.

**374. Woman.—N.** woman, she, fe- male, petticoat, skirt, moll, broad.

feminality, feminity, muliebrity; womanhood &c. (*adolescence*) 131; feminism; gynecology, gyniatrics, gynics.

womankind; the -sex, – fair; fair –, softer- sex; weaker vessel; the distaff side.

dame, madam, *madame*, mistress, Mrs., lady, *mem-sahib, Frau, señora, signora, donna, belle*, matron, dowager, goody, gammer; good -woman, – wife; squaw; wife &c. (*marriage*) 903; ma- tron-age, -hood.

Venus, nymph, wench, *grisette*; little bit of fluff; girl &c. (*youth*) 129.

*inamorata* (love) &c. 897; courtesan &c. 962.

spinster, old maid, virgin, bachelor girl, new woman, Amazon; [Female animal] hen, slut, bitch, sow, doe, roe, mare; she-, Nanny- goat; ewe, cow; lioness, tigress; vixen.

*gynecæum*, harem, *seraglio, zenana, purdah*.

**Adj.** female, she; feminine, womanly, ladylike, matronly, maidenly; womanish, effeminate, unmanly, gynecic.

2°. SENSATION

(1.) *Sensation in general*

**375. Physical Sensibility.**—N. sensibility; sensitiveness &c. *adj.*; physical sensibility, feeling, perceptivity, anaphylaxis, susceptibility, æsthetics; moral sensibility &c. 822.

sensation, impression, effect; consciousness &c. (*knowledge*) 490.

external senses.

V. be -sensible &c. *adj.* -of; feel, perceive.

render, -sensible &c. *adj.*; excite, stir, sharpen, cultivate, tutor.

cause sensation, impress; excite -, produce- an impression.

**Adj.** sens-ible, -itive, -uous; æsthetic, perceptive, sentient; conscious &c. (*aware*) 490; impressionable, responsive, alive to.

acute, sharp, keen, vivid, lively, impressive, thin-skinned.

**Adv.** to the quick.

**376. Physical Insensibility.**—N. insensibility, physical insensibility; obtuseness &c. *adj.*; palsy, paralysis, anæsthesia, analgesia, narcosis, hypnosis, twilight sleep, stupor, coma, trance, catalepsy; sleep &c. (*inactivity*) 683; moral insensibility &c. 823; numbness &c. 381.

anæsthetic agent, general -, local-anæsthetic, opium, ether, chloroform, cocaine, novocaine, chloral; nitrous oxide, laughing gas; refrigeration.

V. be -insensible &c. *adj.*; have a -thick skin, - rhinoceros hide.

render -insensible &c. *adj.*; blunt, pall, obtund, benumb, deaden, paralyze; anæsthetize, drug, dope; put under the influence of -chloroform &c. *n.*; hypnotize; stupefy, stun, narcotize.

**Adj.** insensible, unfeeling, senseless, comatose, dazed, impercipient, callous, thick-skinned, pachydermatous; hard, -ened; case-hardened; proof; obtuse, dull; anæsthetic; paralytic, palsied, numb, dead.

**377. Physical Pleasure.**—N. pleasure; physical -, sensual -, sensuous-pleasure; bodily enjoyment, animal gratification, sensuality; hedonism, luxuriousness &c. *adj.*; dissipation, round of pleasure; titillation, *gusto*, creature comforts, comfort, ease; pillow &c. (*support*) 215; luxury, lap of luxury; purple and fine linen; bed of -down, - roses; velvet, clover; cup of Circe &c. (*intemperance*) 954.

treat; diversion, divertisement, entertainment; refreshment, regale; feast; *délice*; dainty &c. 394; *bonne bouche*.

source of pleasure &c. 829; happiness &c. (*mental enjoyment*) 827.

V. feel -, experience -, receive-pleasure; enjoy, relish; luxuriate -, revel -, riot -, bask -, swim -, wallow-in; feast on; gloat -over, - on; smack the lips.

live -on the fat of the land, - in comfort &c. *adv.*; bask in the sunshine, *faire ses choux gras*.

give pleasure &c. 829.

**378. Physical Pain.**—N. pain; suffering, -ance; bodily - physical- -pain, - suffering; mental suffering &c. 828; dolour, ache; aching &c. *v.*; smart; shoot, -ing; twinge, twitch, gripe, head-, ear-, tooth-ache; *migraine*, neuralgia, neuritis, lumbago, gout, sciatica; hurt, cut; sore, -ness; discomfort, *malaise*; tic douloureux.

spasm, cramp; nightmare, *ephialtes*; crick, stitch, kink; thrill, convulsion, throe; throb &c. (*agitation*) 315; pang.

sharp -, piercing -, throbbing -, shooting -, gnawing -, burning- pain; anguish, agony.

torment, torture; rack; cruci-ation, -fixion; martyrdom; martyr, toad under a harrow, vivisection.

V. feel -, experience -, suffer -, undergo- pain &c. *n.*; suffer, ache, smart, bleed; tingle, shoot; twinge, twitch, lancinate; writhe, wince, make a wry face; sit on -thorns, - pins and needles.

give -, inflict- pain; pain, hurt, chafe, sting, bite, gnaw, gripe, stab, grind;

**Adj.** enjoying &c. *v.*; luxurious, voluptuous, sensual, hedonistic, comfortable, cosy, snug, in comfort, at ease.

agreeable &c. 829; grateful, refreshing, comforting, cordial, genial; sensuous; palatable &c. 394; sweet &c. (*sugar*) 396; fragrant &c. 400; melodious &c. 413; lovely &c. (*beautiful*) 845.

**Adv.** in -comfort &c. *n.*; on -a bed of roses &c. *n.*; at one's ease.

pinch, tweak; grate, gall, fret, prick, pierce, wring, convulse; torment, torture; rack, agonize; crucify; ex-, cruciate; break on the wheel, put to the rack; flog &c. (*punish*) 972; grate on the ear &c. (*harsh sound*) 410.

**Adj.** in -pain &c. *n.*, - a state of pain; pained &c. *v.*

painful; aching &c. *v.*; biting, poignant; sore, raw, tender, with exposed nerve.

### (2.) *Special Sensation*

#### 1. *Touch*

**379.** [Sensation of pressure.] **Touch.—N.** touch; tact, -ion, -ility; feeling; palp-ation, -ability; manipulation; brush, tick, graze, contact &c. 199.

[Organ of touch] hand, finger, fore-finger, thumb, paw, feeler, *antenna*.

**V.** touch, feel, handle, finger, thumb, paw, fumble, grope, grabble; twiddle, tweedle; pass -, run- the fingers over, massage, rub, knead; palpate, stroke, manipulate, wield; throw out a feeler.

**Adj.** tact-ual, -ile; tangible, palpable; lambent.

**380. Sensations of Touch.—N.** itching &c. *v.*; titillation, formication, *aura*.

**V.** itch, tingle, creep, thrill, sting; prick, -le; tickle, titillate.

**Adj.** itching &c. *v.*

**381.** [Insensibility to touch.] **Numbness.—N.** numbness &c. (*physical insensibility*) 376; pins and needles.

local anæsthetic, cocaine, novocaine &c.; morphia.

**V.** benumb &c. 376; freeze, dull, deaden.

**Adj.** numb; benumbed &c. *v.*; intangible, impalpable.

### 2. *Heat*

**382. Heat.—N.** heat, caloric; temperature, warmth, fervour, calidity; incal-, incand-, recal-, decal-escence; glow, flush, blush; fever, hectic.

phlogiston; fire, spark, scintillation, flash, flame, blaze; arc; bonfire; firework, pyrotechny; wild-fire; sheet of fire, lambent flame; devouring element; conflagration.

summer, dog-days, canicule; baking &c. 384 -, white -, tropical -, Afric -, Bengal -, summer -, blood- heat; heat wave, sirocco, simoon; broiling sun; isolation; warming &c. 384.

sun &c. (*luminary*) 423; fire worshipper &c. 991; furnace &c. 386.

geyser, hot spring, volcano.

[Science of heat] pyrology; therm-

**383. Cold.—N.** cold, -ness &c. *adj.*; frigidity, gelidity, algidity, inclemency, *fresco*.

winter; depth of -, hard- winter; Siberia, Nova Zembla; Ant-, arctic, North -, South- Pole.

ice; snow, - flake, - crystal, - drift; sleet; hail, -stone; rime, frost; hoar -, white -, hard -, sharp- frost; icicle, thick-ribbed ice; fall of snow, snow storm, heavy fall, *avalanche*; ice-berg, -floe; floe, berg; *glacier*; *névé*, *serac*.

[Sensation of cold] chilliness &c. *adj.*; chill; shivering &c. *v.*; goose-skin, -flesh; *rigor*, horripilation, chattering of teeth; frostbite, chilblain.

**V.** be -cold &c. *adj.*; shiver, starve, quake, shake, tremble, shudder, didder,

ology, -otics; thermometer &c. 389.

**V.** be -hot &c. *adj.*; glow, incandesce, flush, sweat, swelter, bask, smoke, reek, stew, simmer, seethe, boil, burn, singe, scorch, scald, grill, broil, blaze, flame; smoulder; parch, fume, pant.

heat &c. (*make hot*) 384; thaw, fuse, melt, give.

**Adj.** hot, heated, warm, mild, genial, tepid, lukewarm, unfrozen; therm-al, -ic; calorific; ferv-ent, -id; ardent; aglow.

sunny, torrid, tropical, estival, canicular; close, sultry, stifling, stuffy, suffocating, oppressive; reeking &c. *v.*; baking &c. 384.

red –, white –, smoking –, burning &c. *v.* –, piping- hot; like -a furnace, – an oven; hot as -fire, – pepper; hot enough to roast an ox.

fiery; incand-, incal-escent; candent, ebullient, glowing, smoking; on fire; blazing &c. *v.*; in -flames, – a blaze; alight, afire, ablaze; un-quenched, -extinguished; smouldering; in a -heat, – glow, – fever, – perspiration, – sweat; sudorific; swelter-ing, -ed; blood-hot, -warm; warm as -a toast, – wool; recalescent, thermogenic, pyrotechnic, feverish, febrile, inflamed.

volcanic, plutonic, igneous; isother-mal, -mic, -al.

**Phr.** Not a breath of air.

**384. Calefaction.—N.** increase of temperature; heating &c. *v.*; cale-, tepe-, torre-faction; melting, fusion; liquefaction &c. 335; burning &c. *v.*; kindling, combustion; in-, ac-cension; con-, cremation; scorification; cauter-y, -ization; ustulation, calcination; in-, cineration; cupellation; carbonization.

ignition, inflammation, adustion, flagration; de-, con-flagration; empyrosis, incendiarism; arson; *auto-da-fé*; suttee.

boiling &c. *v.*; coction, ebullition, estuation, elixation, decoction.

furnace &c. 386; blanket, flannel, fur, muffler, wrap; wadding &c. (*lining*) 224; clothing &c. 225.

match &c. (*fuel*) 388; incendiary, pyromaniac; *pétroleur*, *pétroleuse*; cauterant, caustic, lunar caustic, apozem, moxa.

sunstroke, *coup de soleil*; insolation, sunburn.

pottery, ceramics, crockery, porcelain, china: earthen-, stone-ware; pot.

quiver; perish with cold; chill &c. (*render cold*) 385.

**Adj.** cold, cool; chill, -y; gelid, frigid, algid; fresh, keen, bleak, raw, inclement, bitter, biting, niveous, cutting, nipping, piercing, pinching; clay-cold; starved &c. (*made cold*) 385; shivering &c. *v.*; aguish, *transi de froid*; frostbitten, -bound, -nipped.

cold as -a stone, – marble, – lead, – iron, – a frog, – charity, – Christmas; cool as -a cucumber, – custard.

icy, glacial, frosty, freezing, wintry, brumal, hibernal, boreal, arctic, antarctic, polar, Siberian, hyemal; hyperbore-an, -al; ice-bound; frozen out.

un-warmed, -thawed, -heated; isocheimal, -chimenal.

**Adv.** coldly, bitterly &c. *adj.*; *à pierre fendre.*

**385. Refrigeration.—N.** refrigeration, infrigidation, reduction of temperature; cooling &c. *v.*; con-gelation, -glaciation; ice &c. 383; solidification &c. (*density*) 321; refrigerator &c. 387.

**V.** cool, fan, refrigerate, refresh, ice; congeal, freeze, glaciate; benumb, starve, pinch, chill, petrify, chill to the marrow, nip, cut, pierce, bite, make one's teeth chatter; damp.

**Adj.** cooled &c. *v.*; frozen out; cooling &c. *v.*; frigorific.

**Extinction.—N.** *extincteur*; fire, – engine, – extinguisher, – annihilator, – brigade, – man; sprinkler, hose, hydrant, standpipe.

incombusti-bility, -bleness &c. *adj.*

**V.** Quench, damp; blow-, put-, stamp – out; extinquish.

go – out, burn-out.

**Adj.** incombustible; un-, unin-flammable; fire-proof.

mug, *terra-cotta*, brick, clinker; cinder, ash, *scoriæ*; embers, dross, slag, products of combustion, coke, carbon, charcoal; inflamma-, combusti-bility.

[Transmission of heat] diathermancy, transcalency.

**V.** heat, warm, chafe, stive, foment; make -hot &c. 382; sun oneself, bask in the sun.

fire; set -fire to, — on fire; kindle, enkindle, light, ignite, strike a light; apply the -match, — torch- to; re-kindle, -lume; fan —, add fuel to- the flame; poke —, stir —, blow- the fire; make a bonfire of; burn at the stake.

melt, thaw, fuse; liquefy &c. 335.

burn, inflame, roast, toast, fry, grill, singe, parch, bake, torrefy, scorch; brand, cauterize, sear, burn in; corrode, char, carbonize, calcine, incinerate; smelt, cupel, scorify; reduce to ashes; burn to ι cinder; commit —, consign- to the flames.

boil, digest, stew, cook, seethe, scald, parboil, simmer; do to rags. take —, catch- fire; blaze &c. (*flame*) 382.

**Adj.** heated &c. *v.*; molten, sodden; *réchauffé*; heating &c. *v.* inflammable, burnable, inflammatory, combustible; diatherm-al -anous; burnt &c. *v.*; volcanic.

**386. Furnace.—N.** furnace, blast furnace, fire-box, stove, incinerator, destructor, crematorium, crematory, kiln, oven, oast-house; hot-, bake-, wash-house; laundry; conservatory; hearth, focus; athanor, hypocaust, reverberatory; volcano; forge, fiery furnace; *tuyère*, brasier, salamander, heater, warming-pan, foot-warmer, hot-water bottle; radiator; boiler, geyser, caldron, seething caldron, pot; urn, kettle; chafing-dish; retort, crucible, alembic, still; saggar.

fire-place, -dog, -irons; hearth, ingle, grate, range, kitchener; kitchen range; oil-, gas-, electric, -cooker, -stove; fireless cooker; fire; galley; ca-, cam-boose; poker, tongs, shovel, hob, trivet; and-, grid-iron; frying-, stew-pan &c.

hot —, Turkish —, Russian —, vapour —, shower —, warm- bath; *calidarium*, *tepidarium*, *sudatorium*, sudatory; *hammam*.

**387. Refrigerator.—N.** refrigerator, -y; *frigidarium*; cold storage; refrigerating-plant, — machine; ice-house, -pail, -bag, -chest, -pack; cooler, damper; wine-cooler, freezing mixture.

*See* 385.

**388. Fuel.—N.** fuel, firing, combustible, coal, wallsend, anthracite, bituminous coal, slack, culm, cannel coal, lignite, briquette, coke, carbon, charcoal; turf, peat, fire-wood, bobbing, faggot, log, Yule log ember, cinder &c. (*products of combustion*) 384; kindling wood, tinder, touch-wood; fumigator, sulphur, brimstone; incense; port-fire; firebarrel, -ball, -brand.

fuel oil, gas, gasoline.

brand, torch, fuse; wick; spill, match, safety match, light, lucifer, congreve, vesuvian, vesta, fusee, locofoco; linstock; illuminant.

candle &c. (*luminary*) 423; oil &c. (*grease*), 356; petrol, gasoline, methylated —, spirit; gas, acetylene.

**Adj.** carbonaceous; combustible, inflammable.

**V.** stoke, fire, feed, add fuel to the flames.

**389. Thermometer.—N.** thermo-meter, -scope, -stat, -pile, differential thermometer; pyro-, calori-meter; radio micrometer &c.

## 3. *Taste*

**390. Taste.—N.** taste, flavour, gust, *gusto*, relish, savour; sapor, sapidity; twang, smack, smatch; after-taste, tang.

tasting; de-, gustation.

palate, tongue, tooth, stomach.

**V.** taste, savour, smatch, smack, flavour, twang; tickle the palate &c. (*savoury*) 394; smack the lips.

**Adj.** sapid, saporific; gusta-ble, -tory; strong; flavoured, spiced, savoury; palatable &c. 394.

**391. Insipidity.—N.** insipidity; taste-lessness &c. *adj.*

**V.** be -tasteless &c. *adj.*

**Adj.** void of -taste &c. 390; insipid; jejune; taste-, gust-, savour-less; ingustible, mawkish, milk and water, weak, stale, flat, vapid, *fade*, wishy-washy, mild; untasted.

---

**392. Pungency.—N.** pungency, piquancy, poignancy, *haut-goût*, strong taste, twang, race, tang.

sharpness &c. *adj.*; acrimony, acridity; roughness &c. (*sour*) 397; unsavouriness &c. 395.

nitre, saltpetre; mustard, cayenne, caviare; seasoning &c. (*condiment*) 393; brine.

dram, cordial, nip, pick-me-up, bracer, potion.

nicotine, tobacco, snuff, quid; segar; cigar, -ette, gasper, fag; cheroot; weed; fragrant -, Indian- weed; pipe, clay pipe, churchwarden, brier, meerschaum, hookah, hubble-bubble.

**V.** be -pungent &c. *adj.*; bite the tongue.

render -pungent &c. *adj.*; season, spice, salt, pepper, pickle, brine, devil, curry.

smoke, chew, take snuff.

**Adj.** pungent, strong; high-, full-flavoured; high-tasted, -seasoned; gamy; sharp, stinging, rough, *piquant*, racy; biting, mordant; spicy; seasoned &c. *v.*; hot, – as pepper; peppery, vellicating, escharotic, meracious; acrid, acrimonious, bitter; rough &c. (*sour*) 397; unsavoury &c. 395.

salt, saline, brackish, briny; salt as -brine, – a herring, – Lot's wife.

---

**393. Condiment.—N.** condiment, flavouring, salt, mustard, pepper, cayenne, curry, seasoning, sauce, spice, cinnamon, chillies, relish, *sauce piquante*, caviare, pot-herbs, onion, garlic, pickle, chutney, nutmeg &c.

**V.** season &c. (*render pungent*) 392.

---

**394. Savouriness.—N.** savouriness &c. *adj.*; relish, zest.

tit-bit, dainty, delicacy, ambrosia, nectar, *bonne bouche*; game, turtle, venison.

**V.** taste good, be -savoury &c. *adj.*; tickle the -palate, – appetite; flatter the palate.

render -palatable &c. *adj.*

relish, like, smack the lips.

**Adj.** savoury, well-tasted, to one's taste, tasty, good, palatable, nice, dainty, delectable; tooth-ful, -some;

**395. Unsavouriness.—N.** unsavouri-ness &c. *adj.*; amaritude; acri-mony, -tude; roughness &c. (*sour*) 397; acerbity, austerity; gall and worm-wood, rue, quassia, aloes; sickener.

**V.** be -unpalatable &c. *adj.*; sicken, disgust, nauseate, pall, turn the stomach.

**Adj.** un-savoury, -palatable, -sweet; ill-flavoured, un-appetizing, -eatable, inedible; bitter, – as gall; acrid, acrimonious; rough.

offensive, repulsive, nasty; sickening

gustful, appetizing, lickerish, delicate, delicious, exquisite, rich, luscious, ambrosial.

**Adv.** *per amusare la bocca.*
**Phr.** *cela se laisse manger.*

**396. Sweetness.**—N. sweetness, dulcitude, saccharinity.

sugar, cane-, beet-sugar; saccharine, glucose, syrup, treacle, molasses, honey, manna; confection, -ery; sweets, grocery, conserve, preserve, *confiture*, jam, marmalade, julep; sugar-candy, -plum; licorice, liquorice, plum, lollipop, *bonbon, jujube,* comfit, sweetmeat, caramel, toffee, butterscotch.

nectar; hydromel, mead, metheglin, honeysuckle, *liqueur,* sweet wine.

pastry, pie, tart, puff, pudding, cake.

dulc-ification, -oration.

**V.** be -sweet &c. *adj.*
render -sweet &c. *adj.*; sugar, saccharize, sweeten; edulcorate; dulc-orate, -ify; candy; mull.

**Adj.** sweet, sugary; sacchar-ine, -iferous; dulcet, honied, candied, luscious, nectarious, melliferous; sweetened &c. *v.*
sweet as -a nut, − sugar, − honey.

&c. *v.*; nauseous; loath-, ful-some; unpleasant &c. 830.

**397. Sourness.**—N. sourness &c. *adj.*; acid, -ity; acetous fermentation; acerbity.

vinegar, verjuice, crab, alum.

**V.** be −, turn- -sour &c. *adj.*; set the teeth on edge.

render -sour &c. *adj.*; acid-ify, -ulate.

**Adj.** sour; acid, -ulous, -ulated; acerb; tart, crabbed; acet-ous, -ose; sour as vinegar, ' sourish, acescent, sub-acid; styptic, hard, rough; unripe, green.

## 4. Odour

**398. Odour.**—N. odour, smell, odorament, scent, effluvium; eman-, exhal-ation; fume, essence, trail, nidor, redolence.

sense of smell; scent; act of -smelling &c. *v.*

**V.** have an -odour &c. *n.*; smell, − of, − strong of; exhale; give out a -smell &c. *n.*; scent.

smell, scent; snuff, − up; sniff, nose, inhale.

**Adj.** odor-ous, -iferous; smelling, graveolent, nidorous, pungent.

[Relating to the sense of smell] olfactory, quick-scented.

**399. Inodorousness.**—N. inodorousness; absence −, want- of smell.

**V.** be -inodorous &c. *adj.*; not smell.

deodorize.

**Adj.** inodor-ous, -ate; scentless; without −, wanting- smell &c. 398.

deodoriz-ed, -ing.

strong-scented; redolent,

**400. Fragrance.** — N. fragrance, aroma, redolence, perfume, *bouquet;* sweet smell, aromatic perfume.

perfumery; incense; musk, frankincense; pastil, -le; myrrh, perfumes of Arabia, chypre; otto, ottar, attar; bergamot, balm, civet, *pot-pourri,* pulvil; nosegay, *boutonnière;* scent, -bag; *sachet,* scent-bottle, smelling bottle, *vinaigrette;* toilet water, *eau de Cologne;* thurible, censer, thurification.

perfumer; incense bearer.

**401. Fetor.**—N. fetor, fetidness; bad &c. *adj.*; -smell, − odour; stench, stink; mephitis, foul −, mal- odour; *empyreuma;* mustiness &c. *adj.*; rancidity; foulness &c. *(uncleanness)* 653.

stoat, polecat, skunk; assafœtida; fungus, garlic; stink-pot, -bomb.

**V.** have a -bad smell &c. *n.*; smell; stink, − in the nostrils, − like a polecat; smell -strong &c. *adj.*, − offensively.

**Adj.** fetid; strong-smelling; high, bad, strong, fulsome, offensive, noisome, rank, rancid, reasty, tainted, musty

**V.** be -fragrant &c. *adj.*; have a -perfume &c. *n.*; smell sweet, scent, perfume, thurify, embalm.

**Adj.** fragrant, aromatic, redolent, spicy, balmy, scented; sweet-smelling, -scented; perfum-ed, -atory; thuriferous; fragrant as a rose, muscadine, ambrosial.

fusty, frouzy; olid, -ous; nidorous; smelling, stinking; putrid &c. 653; suffocating, mephitic; empyreumatic.

---

## 5. *Sound*

### (i.) SOUND IN GENERAL

**402. Sound.—N.** sound, noise, strain; accent, twang, intonation, tone, tune; cadence; sonority, sonorousness &c. *adj.*; audibility; resonance &c. 408; voice &c. 580.

[Science of sound] acou-, acu-stics; catacoustics, cataphonics; phon-ics, -etics, -ology, -ography; dia-coustics, -phonics.

telephone, phonograph &c. 418.

**V.** produce sound; sound, make a noise; give out -, emit- sound; phonetize, phonate; resound &c. 408.

**Adj.** sounding; soniferous; sonorific; resonant, audible, acoustic, auditory, distinct; stertorous; phonic, sonant; phonetic.

**403. Silence.—N.** silence; stillness &c. (*quiet*) 265; peace, hush, lull, rest; muteness &c. 581; solemn -, awful -, dead -, deathlike- silence.

**V.** be -silent &c. *adj.*; hold one's tongue &c. (*not speak*) 585.

render -silent &c. *adj.*; silence, still, hush; stifle, muffle, gag, stop; muzzle, put to silence &c. (*render mute*) 581.

**Adj.** silent; still, -y; calm, quiet; noise-, sound-, speech-less; hushed &c. *v.*; mute &c. 581; aphonic.

soft, solemn, awful, deathlike, silent as the grave; inaudible &c. (*faint*) 405.

**Adv.** silently &c. *adj.*; *sub silentio*; in perfect silence.

**Int.** hush! 'sh! silence! soft! whist! tush! chut! tut! *pax!* mum's the word! hold your tongue! shut up! be silent! be quiet! stop that noise! hold your row! dry up! peace, be still!

**Phr.** one might hear a -feather, - pin- drop.

**404. Loudness.—N.** loudness, power; loud noise, din; clang, -or; clatter, noise, bombilation, roar, uproar, racket, static, grinders, hubbub, *fracas*, *charivari*, trumpet blast, blare, flourish of trumpets, fanfare, *tintamarre*, peal, swell, blast, alarum, boom; resonance &c. 408.

vociferation; pandemonium, hullaballoo &c. 411; lungs; Stentor; megaphone; siren.

artillery, cannon, gunfire, shellburst, bomb; thunder.

**V.** be -loud &c. *adj.*; peal, swell, clang, boom, thunder, fulminate, roar; resound &c. 408; speak up, shout &c. (*vociferate*) 411; bellow &c. (*cry as an animal*) 412; give tongue.

rend the -air, - skies; fill the air; din -, ring -, thunder- in the ear;

**405. Faintness.—N.** faintness &c. *adj.*; faint sound, whisper, breath; under-tone, -breath; murmur, hum, rustle, buzz, purr; plash; sough, moan, sigh, susurration; tinkle; 'still small voice.'

hoarseness &c. *adj.*; raucity.

silencer, soft pedal, damper, mute, *sourdine*.

**V.** whisper, breathe, murmur, purl, hum, gurgle, ripple, babble, flow; tinkle; mutter &c. (*speak imperfectly*) 583.

steal on the ear; melt in -, float on- the air.

muffle, mute, deaden, damp, stifle.

**Adj.** inaudible; scarcely -, just-audible; low, dull; stifled, muffled; hoarse, husky; gentle, soft, faint; floating; purling, flowing &c. *v.*;

pierce –, split –, rend- the -ears, – head; deafen, stun; *faire le diable à quatre*; make one's windows shake; awaken –, startle- the echoes; make the welkin ring.

Adj. loud, sonorous; high-, big-sounding; blatant; deep, full, powerful, noisy, clangorous, multisonous, *fortissimo*; thundering, deafening &c. *v.*; trumpet-tongued; ear-splitting, -rending, -deafening; piercing; obstreperous, rackety, uproarious; enough to wake the -dead, – seven sleepers.

shrill &c. 410; clamorous &c. (*vociferous*) 411; stentor-ian, -ophonic.

Adv. loudly &c. *adj.*; aloud; at the top of one's voice, lustily, in full cry.

Phr. the air rings with.

whispered &c. *v.*; liquid; soothing; dulcet &c. (*melodious*) 413.

Adv. in a whisper, with bated breath, *sotto voce*, between the teeth, aside; *pian-o*, *-issimo*; *à la sourdine*; *con sordine*; out of earshot, inaudibly &c. *adj.*

## (ii.) SPECIFIC SOUNDS*

**406. [Sudden and violent sounds.] Snap.**—N. snap &c. *v.*; rapping &c. *v.*; de-, crepitation; smack, clap, report; thud; burst, explosion, discharge, detonation, blow-out, back-fire, firing, salvo, volley, pistol-shot.

squib, cracker, gun, rifle, pop-gun.

V. rap, snap, tap, knock; click; clash; crack, -le; crash; pop; slam, bang, clap, thump, plump; toot; back-fire, explode, burst on the ear.

Adj. rapping &c. *v.*

Int. crash! bang!

**407. [Repeated and protracted sounds.] Roll.**—N. roll &c. *v.*; drumming &c. *v.*; tattoo; ding-dong; tantara; rataplan; whirr; rat-a-tat; rub-a-dub; pit-a-pat; quaver, clutter, *charivari*, racket; cuckoo; repetition &c. 104; peal of bells, devil's tattoo; reverberation &c. 408.

drumfire, barrage.

machine gun.

V. roll, drum, rumble, rattle, clatter, rustle, roar, drone, patter, clack.

hum, trill, shake; chime, peal, toll; tick, beat.

drum –, din- in the ear.

Adj. rolling &c. *v.*; monotonous &c. (*repeated*), 104; like a bee in a bottle.

**408. Resonance.**—N. resonance; ring &c. *v.*; ringing &c. *v.*; tintinnabulation; reflection, reverberation, clangor.

low –, base –, bass –, flat –, grave –, deep –, pedal- note; bass; *basso*, – *profondo*; bari-, bary-tone; *contralto*.

V. re-sound, -verberate, -echo; ring, ding, sing, jingle, gingle, chink, clink; tink, -le; chime; gurgle &c. 405; plash, guggle, echo, ring in the ear.

**408a. Non-resonance.** — N. thud, thump, dead sound; non-resonance; muffled drums, cracked bell; silencer, damper; mute, *sourdine*.

V. sound dead; stop –, damp- the -sound, – reverberations; deaden, muffle.

Adj. non-resonant, dead, muted. muffled.

Adj. resounding &c. *v.*; resonant, tinnient, tintinnabulary; deep-toned, -sounding, -mouthed; hollow, sepulchral; gruff &c. (*harsh*) 410.

**409. [Hissing sounds.] Sibilation.**—N. sibilation; hiss &c. *v.*; sternutation; high note &c. 410.

goose, serpent, snake.

* [The author's classification of sounds has been retained, though it does not entirely accord with the theories of modern science.—ED.]

**V.** hiss, buzz, whiz, rustle; fizz, -le, sizzle, swish; wheeze, whistle, snuffle; squash; sneeze.

**Adj.** sibilant; hissing &c. *v.*; wheezy.

**410. [Harsh sounds.] Stridor.—N.** creak &c. *v.*; creaking &c. *v.*; discord &c. 414; stridor; harshness, roughness, sharpness &c. *adj.*; cacophony.

acute –, high- note; *soprano*, treble, tenor, *alto*, falsetto, *voce di testa*; shriek, cry &c. 411.

piccolo, fife, penny -whistle, – trumpet.

**V.** creak, grate, jar, burr, pipe, twang, jangle, clank, clink; scream &c. (*cry*) 411; yelp &c. (*animal sound*) 412; buzz &c. (*hiss*) 409.

set the teeth on edge, *écorcher les oreilles*; pierce –, split- the -ears, – head; offend –, grate upon –, jar upon- the ear.

**Adj.** creaking &c. *v.*; strident, stridulous, harsh, coarse, hoarse, horrisonous, raucous, metallic, rough, gruff, grum, sepulchral.

sharp, high, acute, shrill, high-pitched; trumpet-toned; piercing, ear-piercing; cracked; discordant &c. 414; cacophonous.

**411. Cry.—N.** cry &c. *v.*; voice &c. (*human*) 580; bark &c. (*animal*) 412.

vociferation, outcry, hullaballoo, chorus, clamour, hue and cry, plaint; lungs; stentor.

**V.** cry, roar, shout, bawl, brawl, halloo, halloa, hail, hoop, whoop, yell, bellow, howl, scream, screech, screak, shriek, shrill, squeak, squeal, squall, whine, whinny, pule, pipe, yaup.

cheer, hurrah; hoot; grumble, moan, groan.

snore, snort; grunt &c. (*animal sounds*) 412.

vociferate; raise –, lift up- the voice; call –, sing –, cry- out; exclaim; rend the air; thunder –, shout- at the -top of one's voice, – pitch of one's breath; *s'égosiller*; strain the -throat, – voice, – lungs; give a -cry &c.

**Adj.** crying &c. *v.*; clam-ant, -orous; vociferous; stentorian &c. (*loud*) 404; open-mouthed.

**412. [Animal sounds.] Ululation.—N.** cry &c. *v.*; crying &c. *v.*; ululation, latration, belling; reboation; call, note; bark, howl, yelp; twittering, woodnote; insect cry, fritinancy, drone; screech; cuckoo.

**V.** cry, ululate, howl, roar, bellow, blare, rebellow, bark, yelp; bay, – the moon; yap, growl, yarr, yawl, snarl, howl; grunt, -le; snort, squeak; neigh, bray; mew, mewl; purr, caterwaul, pule; bleat, low, moo; troat, croak, crow, screech, caw, coo, gobble, quack, cackle, gaggle, guggle; chuck, -le; cluck; clack; cheep, chirp, chirrup, twitter, sing, cuckoo; pout, wail, hum, buzz; hiss, blatter; hoot.

**Adj.** crying &c. *v.*; blatant, latrant; re-, mugient; deep-, full-mouthed.

**Adv.** in full cry.

---

(iii.) MUSICAL SOUNDS

**413. Melody. Concord.—N.** melody, rhythm, measure; rhyme &c. (*poetry*) 597.

pitch, *timbre*, intonation, tone, over-tone.

scale, gamut; diapason; diatonic –, chromatic –, enharmonic- scale; key, clef, chords,

modulation, temperament, syncope, syncopation, preparation, suspension, resolution.

**414. Discord.—N.** discord, -ance; dissonance, cacophony, caterwauling; harshness &c. 410; consecutive fifths.

[Confused sounds] Babel, pande-monium; Dutch –, cat's- concert, marrow-bones and cleavers.

**V.** be -discordant &c. *adj.*; jar &c (*sound harshly*) 410.

**Adj.** discordant; dis-, ab-sonant; out of tune, tuneless; un-musical, -tunable; un-, im-melodious; un-, in-harmonious;

staff, stave, line, space, brace; bar, rest; *avpogia-to, -tura; acciaccatura,* shake, *arpeggio.*

note, musical note, notes of a scale; sharp, flat, natural; high note &c. (*shrillness*) 410; low note &c. 408; interval; semitone; second, third, fourth &c.; diatessaron.

breve, semibreve, minim, crotchet, quaver; semi-, demisemi-quaver; sustained note, drone, burden.

tonic; key-, leading-, fundamental- note; supertonic, mediant, dominant; sub-mediant, -dominant, organ-, pedal-point; octave, tetrachord; major -, minor- -mode, - scale, - key; Doric mode, passage, phrase.

concord, harmony; unison, -ance; chime, homophony; euphon-y, -ism; tonality; consonance; concent; part.

orchestration, harmonization, - phrasing.

[Science of harmony] harmon-y, -ics; thorough-, fundamental-bass; counterpoint; faburden.

piece of music &c. 415; composer, harmonist, contrapuntist.

**V.** be -harmonious &c. *adj.*; harmonize, chime, symphonize, transpose; put in tune, tune, accord, string; score, arrange, orchestrate.

**Adj.** harmoni-ous, -cal; in -concord &c. *n.*, - tune, - concert; unisonant, concentual, symphonizing, isotonic, homophonous, assonant, consonant.

measured, rhythmical, diatonic, chromatic, enharmonic.

ı elodious, musical; tuneful, tunable; sweet, dulcet, canorous; mell-ow, -ifluous; soft; clear, - as a bell; silvery; euphon-ious, -ic, -ical; symphonious; enchanting &c. (*pleasure-giving*) 829; fine-, full-, silver-toned.

**Adv.** harmoniously &c. *adj.*

**sing-song; cacophonous; jarring, harsh &c. 410.**

---

**415. Music.**—**N.** music, classical -, modern -, descriptive- music, concert, recital; strain, tune, air, *motif*; melody &c. 413; *aria, arietta*; piece of music, *sonata; rond-o, -eau; pastorale, cavatina,* roulade, *fantasia, toccata, concerto,* overture, symphony, symphonic poem, tone poem, prelude, voluntary, *intermezzo,* variations, *cadenza;* cadence; fugue, canon, serenade, *nocturne, notturno,* rhapsody, romance, *aubade,* dithyramb; opera, operetta; oratorio; composition, movement; stave.

instrumental music; full-, orchestral- score; minstrelsy, tweedle-dum and tweedledee, band, orchestra &c. 416; concerted piece, *pot-pourri,* medley, *capriccio,* incidental music; improvisation; peal.

vocal music, vocalism; chaunt, chant; psalm, -ody; hymn; song &c. (*poem*) 597; canticle, canzonet, *cantata, bravura, coloratura;* lay, ballad, ditty, carol, barcarolle, pastoral, recitative, *recitativo, solfeggio,* tonic sol-fa.

Lydian measures; slow -music, - movement; *adagio* &c. *adv.*; minuet; siren strains, soft music, lullaby; *berceuse,* cradle song, dump; dirge &c. (*lament*) 839; pibroch; martial music, march, funeral-, dead- march; dance music; waltz &c. (*dance*) 840; rag-time, syncopation, jazz.

solo, duet, *duo, trio;* quartet; quintet, sextet, septet; part song, descant, glee, madrigal, catch, round, chorus, *chorale;* antiphon, -y; accompaniment, second -, alto -, tenor -, bass- part; score, thorough bass; counterpoint.

composer &c. 413; musician &c. 416.
**V.** compose, perform &c. 416; attune.
**Adj.** musical; instrumental, orchestral, vocal, choral, lyric, operatic; harmonious &c. 413.
**Adv.** *adagio*; *largo, larghetto, andan-te, -tino*; *alla capella*; *maestoso, moderato*; *allegr-o, -etto*; *spiritoso, vivace, veloce*; *prest-o, -issimo*; *pian-o, -issimo, fort-e, -issimo, sforzando*; *con brio*; *capriccioso*; *scherz-o, -ando*; *legato, sostenuto, staccato, crescendo, diminuendo, rallentando, affettuoso, arioso*; *parlante, cantabile*; *obbligato*; *pizzicato, tremolo, vibrato*.

**416. Musician.** [Performance of Music.]—**N.** musician, *artiste, virtuoso*, performer, player, minstrel; bard &c. (*poet*) 597; instrumental-, organ-, accompan-, pian-, violin-, flaut-, harp-ist; harper, fiddler, fifer, trumpeter, piper, drummer; catgut scraper.
band, orchestra, waits.
vocal-, melod-ist; singer, warbler; songst-, chaunt-er, -ress; *diva, cantatrice*, coloratura, soprano, mezzo-soprano, alto, contralto, tenor, baritone, bass, *basso, -profondo*.
choir, quire, chorister; chorus, – singer; choral society, festival, *eisteddfod*.
nightingale, philomel, thrush; siren; Orpheus, Apollo, the Muses, Erato, Euterpe, Terpsichore; tuneful -nine, – quire.
composer &c. 413.
performance, virtuosity, execution, touch, expression, solmization.
**V.** play, pipe, strike –, tune- up, sweep the chords, tickle –, paw- the ivories, vamp, tweedle, fiddle; strike the lyre, beat the drum; blow –, sound –, wind- the horn; grind the organ; touch the -guitar &c. (*instruments*) 417; thrum, strum, twang, drum, beat –, keep- time, conduct.
execute, perform; accompany; sing –, play- a second; compose, write music, set to music, arrange, harmonize, orchestrate.
sing, chaunt, chant, hum, warble, carol, chirp, chirrup, lilt, purl, quaver, trill, shake, twitter, whistle; sol-fa; intone.
have -an ear for music, – a musical ear, – a correct ear, – absolute pitch.
**Adj.** playing &c. *v.*; musical, lyric.
**Adv.** *adagio, andante* &c. (*music*) 415.

**417. Musical Instruments.**—**N.** musical instruments; band; string-, brass-, drum and fife-, military-, bugle-, German-, dance-, jazz-band: orchestra, string quartet; orchestrion, orchestrelle.
[Stringed instruments] mono-, poly-chord; harp, lyre, lute, archlute, theorbo; mandol-a, -in, -ine; guitar; *ukulele*; psaltery, zither; bandore, cither, -n; gittern, rebeck, *bandurria*, banjo, zither banjo, *balalaika, samisen*; plectrum.
viol, -in, Cremona, Stradivarius; fiddle, kit; *vielle, viola, – d'amore, – di gamba*; tenor, *violoncello*, cello; bass, bass-, base-viol; double-bass, *contrabasso, violone*, hurdy-gurdy; strings, catgut; bow, fiddlestick.
piano, -forte; grand –, concert grand –, baby –, upright –, cottage- piano; pianino, pianette; harpsi-, clavi-, clari-, mani-chord; *clavier*, spinet, virginals; dulcimer, *cymbalo*; Eolian harp; piano-organ, -player, electric piano, player-piano, pianola.
[Wind instruments] organ, church –, pipe –, American- organ; harmoni-um, -phon; accordion, seraphina, concertina; melodeon; barrel- organ; humming top.

flute, fife, piccolo, flageolet, penny-whistle, reed instrument; clari-net, -onet; bass clarionet; saxophone; basset horn, *corno di bassetto*; musette, shawm, oboe, hautboy, *cor Anglais, corno Inglese*, bassoon, double bassoon, *contrafagotto*; bag-, union-pipes; ocarina, Pandean pipes; calliope; sirene, pipe, pitch-pipe; sourdet; whistle, catcall.

horn, bugle, key bugle, cornet, *cornet-à-pistons*, cornopean, clarion, trumpet, trombone, ophicleide, serpent; English-, French-, bugle-, sax-, flugel-, alt-, helicon-, post-horn; sackbut, euphonium, bombardon, tuba, bass tuba.

[Vibrating surfaces] cymbal, bell, gong, peal of bells, *carillon*; tambour, -ine; drum, tom-tom, tab-or, -ret, -ourine, -orin; *sistrum*; *grande caisse*, bass-, big-, side-, kettle-drum; *tympani*; war drums; tymbal, timbrel, castanet, bones; musical-glasses, -stones; harmonica, sounding-board, rattle; gramophone, phonograph.

[Vibrating bars] reed, tuning-fork, triangle, Jew's harp, musical box, harmonicon, xylophone, marimba, *celeste*.

sord-ine, -et; *sourd-ine, -et*; mute.

### (iv.) PERCEPTION OF SOUND

**418. [Sense of sound.] Hearing.—N.** hearing &c. *v.*; audition, auscultation; eavesdropping; audibility; acoustics &c. 402.

acute -, nice -, delicate -, quick -, sharp -, correct -, musical -ear; ear for music.

ear, auricle, lug, acoustic organs, auditory apparatus, ear-drum, tympanum; ear-, speaking-trumpet, megaphone; telephone, radiophone, stethoscope, phonograph, gramophone, microphone.

hearer, auditor, listener, eavesdropper; audi-tory, -ence.

**V.** hear, overhear; hark, -en; list, -en; give -, lend -, bend- an ear; give attention; catch a sound, prick up one's ears; give -a hearing, - audience- to.

hang upon the lips of, be all ear, listen with both ears.

become audible; meet -, fall upon -, catch -, reach- the ear; be heard; ring in the ear &c. (*resound*) 408.

**Adj.** hearing &c. *v.*; auditory, auricular, aural, auditive, acoustic.

**Adv.** *arrectis auribus.*

**Int.** hark, - ye! hear! list, -en! *Oyez!* attention! lend me your ears!

**419. Deafness.—N.** deafness, hardness of hearing, surdity; inaudibility.

**V.** be -deaf &c. *adj.*; have no ear; shut -, stop -, close- one's ears; turn a deaf ear to.

render deaf, stun, deafen.

**Adj.** deaf, earless, surd; hard -, dull-of hearing; deaf-mute, stunned, deafened; stone deaf; deaf as -a post, - an adder, - a beetle, - a trunk-maker.

inaudible &c. 405; out of hearing.

### 6. *Light*

### (i.) LIGHT IN GENERAL

**420. Light.—N.** light, ray, beam, stream, gleam, streak, pencil; sun-, moon-beam; dawn, aurora.

day; sunshine; light of -day, - heaven; sun &c. (*luminary*) 423, day-, broad day-, noontide- light; noon-tide, -day; glare.

**421. Darkness.—N.** darkness &c. *adj.*; blackness &c. (*dark colour*) 431; obscurity, gloom, murk; dusk &c. (*dimness*) 422; tenebrosity, umbrageousness.

Cimmerian -, Stygian -, Egyptian-darkness; night; midnight; dead of -.

glow &c. *v.*; afterglow, sunset; glimmering &c. *v.*; glint; play –, flood- of light; phosphorescence, lambent flame.

flush, halo, glory, nimbus, aureole, *aureola.*

spark, *scintilla*; *facula*; sparkling &c. *v.*; emication, scintillation, flash, blaze, coruscation, fulguration; flame &c. (*fire*) 382; lightning, *ignis fatuus*, &c. (*luminary*) 423, radio-activity.

lustre, sheen, shimmer, reflection; gloss, tinsel, spangle, brightness, brilliancy, splendour; ef-, re-fulgence; ful-gor, -gidity; dazzlement, resplendence, transplendency; luminousness &c. *adj.*; luminosity; lucidity; renitency; radi-ance, -ation; irradiation, illumination, phosphorescence, luminescence.

radiation, radiant heat, infra-red rays, visible radiation, ultra-violet –, actinic- rays, actinism; X –, Roentgen-rays; phot-, heli-ography; optical instruments &c. 445.

[Science of light] optics; photo-logy, -metry; di-, cat-optrics.

[Distribution of light] *chiaroscuro, clair-obscur,* clear-obscure, breadth, light and shade, black and white, tonality, half-tone, mezzotint.

reflection, refraction, dispersion, double refraction, polarization, diffraction, interference.

illuminant &c. 423.

**V.** shine, glow, glitter, phosphoresce; glis-ter, -ten; twinkle, gleam; flare, – up; glare, beam, shimmer, glimmer, flicker, sparkle, scintillate, coruscate, flash, fulgurate, blaze; be -bright &c. *adj.*; reflect light, daze, dazzle, be-dazzle, radiate, shoot out beams.

clear up, brighten.

lighten, enlighten; light, – up; irradiate, shine upon; give –, hang out- a light; cast –, throw –, shed- -lustre, – light- upon; illum-e, -ine, -inate; relume, strike a light; kindle &c. (*set fire to*) 384.

**Adj.** shining &c. *v.*; lumin-ous, -iferous; luc-id, -ent, -ulent, -ific, -iferous; illuminating, light, -some; bright, vivid, splendent, nitid, lustrous, shiny, brilliant, beamy, scintillant, radiant, lambent; sheen, -y; glossy,

witching time of- night; blind man's holiday; darkness -visible, – that can be felt; palpable, obscure; Erebus.

shade, shadow, umbra, penumbra; sciagraphy; *silhouette*; radiograph, skiagraph.

obscuration; ad-, ob-umbration; obtenebration, offuscation, caligation; extinction; eclipse, total eclipse; gathering of the clouds.

shading; distribution of shade; *chiaroscuro* &c. (*light*) 420.

noctivagation, noctograph, noctuary. obscurantist.

**V.** be -dark &c. *adj.*

darken, obscure, shade; dim; tone down, lower; over-cast, -shadow; cloud, eclipse; ob-, of-fuscate; ob-, ad-umbrate, cast into the shade; be-cloud, -dim, -darken; cast –, throw –, spread- a -shade, – shadow, – gloom.

extinguish; put –, blow –, snuff- out; doubt.

**Adj.** dark, -some, -ling; obscure, tenebrous, tenebrious, sombrous, pitch dark, pitchy; caliginous; black &c. (*in colour*) 431.

sunless, lightless &c. (*see* sun, light, &c. 423); sombre, dusky; unilluminated &c. (*see* illuminate &c. 420); nocturnal; dingy, lurid, gloomy; murk-y, -some; shady, umbrageous; overcast &c. (*dim*) 422; cloudy &c. (*opaque*) 426; darkened &c. *v.*

dark as -pitch, – a pit, – Erebus. benighted; noctivag-ant, -ous.

**Adv.** in the -dark, – shade; at night.

**422. Dimness.—N.** dimness &c. *adj.*; darkness &c. 421; paleness &c. (*light colour*) 429.

half-light, *demi-jour*; partial -shadow, – eclipse; shadow of a shade; glimmer, -ing; nebulosity; cloud &c. 353; eclipse.

aurora, dusk, twilight, gloaming, blind man's holiday, shades of evening, crepuscule, cockshut time; break of day, daybreak, dawn.

moon-light, -beam, -shine; star-, owl's-, candle-, rush-, fire-light; farthing candle.

**V.** be –, grow- -dim &c. *adj.*; flicker, twinkle, glimmer; loom, lower; fade; darken; pale, – its ineffectual fire.

burnished, glassy, sunny, orient, meridian; noon-day, -tide; cloudless, clear; un-clouded, -obscured.

garish; re-, tran-splendent; re-, effulgent; ful-gid, -gent; relucent, splendid, blazing, in a blaze, ablaze, rutilant, meteoric, phosphorescent; aglow.

bright as silver; light -, bright- as -day, - noonday, - the sun at noonday.

optical, actinic; photo-genic, -graphic; heliographic, radioactive.

render -dim &c. *adj.*; dim, bedim, obscure.

**Adj.** dim, dull, lack-lustre, dingy, darkish, shorn of its beams; dark 421. faint, shadowed forth; glassy; bleary; cloudy; misty &c. (*opaque*) 426; muggy, fuliginous; nebul-ous, -ar; obnubilated, overcast, crepuscular, twilight, muddy, lurid, leaden, dun, dirty; looming &c. *v.* pale &c. (*colourless*) 429; confused &c. (*invisible*) 447.

---

**423.** [Source of light &c.] **Luminary.** —**N.** luminary; light &c. 420; flame &c. (*fire*) 382.

spark, *scintilla*; phosphorescence.

sun, orb of day, day star, Phœbus, Apollo, Helios, Phaethon, Hyperion, Ra, Aurora; star, orb, meteor; falling -, shooting- star; blazing -, dog- star; Sirius, canicula, Aldebaran; morning star, Lucifer, Phosphor, evening star; Hesperus, Venus, planet, moon &c. 318; constellation, galaxy; northern light, aurora -borealis, - australis, zodiacal light; mock sun, parhelion.

lightning; fork -, sheet -, summer- lightning, St. Elmo's fire; phosphorus; *ignis fatuus*; Jack o' -, Friar's- lantern; Will o' the wisp, fire-drake, *Fata Morgana*.

glow-worm, fire-fly.

radium, luminous paint.

[Artificial light] gas; gas -, lime -, electric -, head -, search -, spot -, flash -, flood -, foot-light; lamp, oil -, gas -, arc -, incandescent- lamp; flare; lant-ern, -horn; dark lantern, bull's eye, projector; candle, *bougie*, tallow -, wax- candle; dip, farthing dip; taper, rush-light; oil &c. (*grease*) 356; wick, burner; Argand, moderator, duplex; torch, *flambeau*, link, brand; cresset; gase-, chande-, electro-lier; candelabrum, *girandole*, sconce, lustre, candle-stick.

firework, fizgig; pyrotechnics; Roman candle, Véry light, star shell, parachute light; rocket, lighthouse &c. (*signal*) 550.

**V.** illuminate &c. (*light*) 420.

**Adj.** self-luminous, incandescent; phosphor-ic, -escent; luminescent, fluorescent, radiant &c. (*light*) 420.

**424.** Shade.—**N.** shade; awning &c. (*cover*) 223; parasol, sunshade, umbrella; screen, curtain, shutter, blind, gauze, veil, mantle, mask; cloud, mist, gathering of clouds; smoke screen; smoked glasses, coloured spectacles; blinkers, blinders.

umbrage, glade; shadow &c. 421.

**V.** draw a curtain; put up -, close- a shutter; veil &c. *v.*; cast a shadow &c. (*darken*) 421; screen, obstruct the view.

**Adj.** shady, umbrageous, bowery.

---

**425.** Transparency.— **N.** transparen-ce, -cy; translucen-ce, -cy; diaphaneity; luc-, pelluc-, limp-idity.

transparent medium, glass, crystal, mica; lymph, water.

**V.** be -transparent &c. *adj.*; transmit light.

**Adj.** transparent, pellucid, lucid, diaphanous; trans-, tra-lucent; limpid, clear, serene, crystalline, clear as crys-

**426.** Opacity.—**N.** opacity; opaqueness &c. *adj.*

film; cloud &c. 353.

**V.** be -opaque &c. *adj.*; obstruct the passage of light; ob-, of-fuscate.

**Adj.** opaque, impervious to light.

dim &c. 422; turbid, thick, muddy, opacous, obfuscated, fuliginous, cloudy, hazy, foggy, vaporous, nubiferous, muggy.

tal, vitreous, transpicuous, glassy, hyaline.

———

smoky, fumid, murky, dirty.

**427. Semitransparency.—N.** semi-transparency, opalescence, milkiness, pearliness; gauze, muslin; film; mist &c. (*cloud*) 353; frosted glass.

**Adj.** semi-transparent, -pellucid, -diaphanous, -opacous, -opaque; opal-escent, -ine; pearly, milky, frosted, mat; misty.

## (ǐ.) SPECIFIC LIGHT

**428. Colour.—N.** colour, hue, tint, tinge, dye, complexion, shade, tincture, cast, livery, coloration, chromatism, glow, flush; tone, key.

pure –, positive –, primary –, primitive –, complementary- colour; three primaries; spectrum, chromatic dispersion; broken –, secondary –, tertiary-colour.

local colour, colouring, keeping, tone, value, aerial perspective.

[Science of colour] chromatics, spectrum analysis; prism, spectroscope.

pigment, colouring matter, paint, dye, wash, distemper, stain; medium; mordant; oil-paint &c. (*painting*) 556.

**V.** colour, dye, tinge, stain, tint, tinct, tone, paint, wash, ingrain, grain, illuminate, emblazon, imbue; paint &c. (*fine art*) 556; daub.

**Adj.** coloured &c. *v.*; colorific, tingent, tinctorial; chromatic, prismatic; full-, high-, deep-coloured; doubly-dyed; polychromatic.

bright, vivid, intense, deep; fresh, unfaded; rich, gorgeous; highly coloured; gay; variegated &c. 440.

gaudy, florid; garish; showy, flaunting, flashy; raw, crude; glaring, flaring; discordant, inharmonious.

mellow, harmonious, pearly, sweet, delicate, tender, refined.

**429. [Absence of colour.] Achromatism.—N.** achromatism; de-, discoloration; pall-or, -idity; paleness &c. *adj.*; etiolation; neutral tint, monochrome, black-and-white.

**V.** lose -colour &c. 428; fade, fly, go; become -colourless &c. *adj.*; turn pale, pale, whiten.

deprive of colour, decolorize, bleach, tarnish, achromatize, blanch, etiolate, wash out, tone down.

**Adj.** uncoloured &c. (*see* colour &c. 428); colourless, achromatic, hueless, pale, pallid; pale-, tallow-faced; faint, dull, cold, muddy, leaden, dun, wan, sallow, dead, dingy, ashy, ashen, ghastly, cadaverous, glassy, lack-lustre; discoloured &c. *v.*

light-coloured, fair, *blond*; white &c. 430.

pale as -death, – ashes, – a witch, – a ghost. – a corpse.

———

**430. Whiteness.—N.** whiteness &c. *adj.*; argent.

albification, albescence, albinism, etiolation.

snow, paper, chalk, milk, lily, ivory, silver, alabaster; white lead, chinese –, flake –, ivory –, zinc- white, white-wash, -ning, whiting.

**V.** be -white &c. *adj.*

render -white &c. *adj.*; whiten-bleach, blanch, etiolate, whitewash, silver, frost.

**Adj.** white; milky, milk-, snow-white; snowy, niveous, candid, chalky; hoar,

**431. Blackness.—N.** blackness &c. *adj.*; darkness &c. (*want of light*) 421; swarthness, lividity, dark colour, tone colour; *chiaroscuro* &c. 420.

nigrification, infuscation, denigration.

jet, ink, ebony, coal, pitch, soot, smudge, charcoal, sloe, raven, crow; negro, blackamoor, man of colour, nigger, darky, Ethiopian, black.

[Pigments] lamp –, ivory –, blue-black; writing –, printing –, printer's –, Indian- ink.

**V.** be -black &c. *adj.*

-y; frosted, silvery; argent, -ine; canescent.

whitish, creamy, pearly, ivory, fair, *blond,* ash-blond, platinum blond; blanched &c. *v.*; high in tone, light.

white as -a sheet, – driven snow, – a lily – silver; like -ivory &c. *n.*

render -black &c. *adj.*; blacken, infuscate, denigrate; blot, -ch; smutch; smirch; darken &c. 421.

Adj. black, sable, swarthy, sombre, dark, inky, ebon, atramentous, jetty; coal-, jet-black; fuliginous, pitchy, sooty, swart, dusky, dingy, murky, Ethiopic; low-toned, low in tone; of the deepest dye.

black as -jet &c. *n.,* – my hat, – a shoe, – a tinker's pot, – November, – thunder, – midnight; nocturnal &c. (*dark*) 421; nigrescent; gray &c. 432; obscure &c. 421.

Adv. in mourning.

**432. Gray.—N.** gray &c. *adj.*; neutral tint, silver, pepper and salt, *chiaroscuro, grisaille,* grayness.

[Pigments] Payne's gray; black &c. 431.

**Adj.** gray, grey; steel –, iron- gray, dun, drab, dingy, leaden, livid, sombre, sad, pearly; silver, -y, -ed; ash-en, -y; ciner-eous, -itious; grizzl-y, -ed; dove-, slate-, stone-, mouse-, ash-coloured; mole; cool.

**433. Brown.—N.** brown &c. *adj.*

[Pigments] bistre, ochre, sepia, Vandyke brown.

**Adj.** brown, adust, bay, dapple, auburn, chestnut, nutbrown, cinnamon, hazel, fawn, puce, *écru,* russet, tawny, fuscous, chocolate, maroon, foxy, tan, brunette, whitey-brown; snuff-, liver-coloured; brown as -a berry, – mahogany; reddish brown; copper-, rust- coloured; henna, bronze, khaki; roan, sorrel.

sun-burnt; tanned &c. *v.*

**V.** render -brown &c. *adj.*; tan, embrown, bronze.

*Primitive Colours**

**434. Redness.—N.** red, scarlet, vermilion, cardinal, Post Office red, carmine, crimson, pink, lake, *cerise,* cherry red, maroon, carnation, *couleur de rose, rose du Barry;* magenta, damask; flesh -colour, – tint; colour; fresh –, highcolour; warmth; gules.

ruby, garnet, carbuncle; rose; rust, iron-mould.

[Dyes and pigments] cinnabar, cochineal; fuchsine; ruddle, maddcr, redlead; Indian –, light –, Venetian- red; red ink, annotto.

redness &c. *adj.*; rub-escence, -icundity, -ification; erubescence, blush.

**V.** be –, become- -red &c. *adj.*; blush, flush, colour up, mantle, redden.

render -red &c. *adj.*; redden, rouge; rub-ify, -ricate; incarnadine; ruddle.

**Adj.** red &c. *n.,* -dish; rufous, ruddy, florid, incarnadine, sanguine, bloody, gory; ros-y, -eate; blowz-y, -ed; burnt; rubi-cund, -form;

*Complementary Colours*

**435. Greenness.—N.** green &c. *adj.*; blue and yellow; vert.

emerald, verd antique, verdigris, malachite, beryl, aquamarine, reseda.

[Pigments] *terre verte,* verditer, bice, chlorophyl.

greenness, verdure, verdancy; viridity, -escence.

**Adj.** green, verdant; glaucous, olive; porraceous; green as grass.

emerald –, pea –, grass –, apple –, sea –, olive –, bottle –, leaf- green.

greenish; vir-ent, -escent.

* The author's classification of colours has been retained, though it does not entirely accord with the theories of modern science: Complete lists of shades or pigments are beyond the scope of this work.

lurid, stammel, blood-red; russet, murrey, carroty, sorrel, lateritious.

rose-, ruby-, cherry-, claret-, wine-, plum-, flame-, flesh-, peach-, salmon-, brick-, brickdust-coloured, reddish brown &c. 433.

blushing &c. *v.*; erubescent; reddened &c. *v.*

red as -fire, – blood, – scarlet, – a turkeycock, – a lobster; warm, hot; foxy.

**436. Yellowness.—N.** yellow &c. *adj.*; or.

[Pigments] gamboge; cadmium –, chrome –, Indian –, lemon- yellow; orpiment, yellow ochre, Claude tint, aureolin.

crocus, saffron, topaz, gold.

jaundice; London fog; yellowness &c. *adj.*

**Adj.** yellow, aureate, gold, golden, gilt, gilded, flavous, citrine, fallow; fulv-ous, -id; sallow, luteous, tawny, creamy, sandy; xanth-ic, -ous; jaundiced.

gold-, citron-, saffron-, lemon-, sulphur-, amber-, straw-, primrose-, cream-coloured; flaxen, yellowish, buff.

yellow as a -quince, – guinea, – crow's foot.

**437. Purple.—N.** purple &c. *adj.*; blue and red, bishop's purple; aniline dyes, gridelin, amethyst; purpure.

livid-ness, -ity.

**V.** empurple.

**Adj.** purple, violet, plum-coloured, lavender, lilac, puce, *mauve*; livid.

**438. Blueness.—N.** blue &c. *adj.*; garter-blue; watchet.

[Pigments] ultramarine, smalt, cobalt, cyanogen; Prussian –, syenite-blue; bice, indigo, woad.

*lapis lazuli*, sapphire, turquoise.

blue-, bluish-ness; bloom.

**Adj.** blue, azure, cerulean; sky-blue, -coloured, -dyed; navy-blue, aquamarine, electric blue, royal blue, cyanic; bluish; atmospheric, retiring; cold.

**439. Orange.—N.** orange, red and yellow; gold; or; flame &c. colour, *adj.*

[Pigments] ochre, Mars orange, cadmium.

**V.** gild, warm.

**Adj.** orange; ochreous; orange-, gold-, flame-, copper-, brass-, apricot-coloured; warm, hot, glowing.

**440. Variegation.—N.** variegation; di-, tri-chroism; iridescence, irisation, play of colours, polychrome, maculation, spottiness, striæ.

spectrum, rainbow, iris, tulip, peacock, chameleon, butterfly, tortoiseshell; mackerel, – sky; zebra, leopard, mother-of-pearl, nacre, opal, marble, batik.

check, plaid, tartan, patchwork; mar-, par-quetry; mosaic, *tesseræ*, tesselation, chess-board, checkers, chequers; harlequin; Joseph's coat; tricolour; patches, bands, stripes, spots &c. of colour.

**V.** be -variegated &c. *adj.*; variegate, stripe, streak, checker, chequer; be-, speckle, fleck; be-, sprinkle; stipple, maculate, dot, bespot; tattoo, inlay, tesselate, damascene; embroider, braid, quilt.

**Adj.** variegated &c. *v.*; many-coloured, -hued; divers-, parti-coloured; di-, poly-chromatic; bi-, tri-, versi-colour; of all -the colours of the rainbow, – manner of colours; kaleidoscopic.

iridescent; opal-ine, -escent; prismatic, nacreous, pearly, shot, *gorge de pigeon, chatoyant*, irisated.

pied, piebald, skewbald; motley, mottled, marbled; pepper and salt, paned, dappled, clouded, cymophanous.

mosaic, tesselated, chequered, plaid; tortoiseshell &c. *n.*

spott-ed, -y; punctated, powdered; speckled &c. *v.*; freckled, flea-bitten, studded; fleck-ed, -ered; striated, barred, veined; brind-ed, -led; tabby; watered; grizzled; listed; embroidered &c. *v.*; dædal.

### (iii.) Perceptions of Light

**441. Vision.**—N. vision, sight, optics, eye-sight.

view, look, espial, glance, ken, *coup d'œil*; glimpse, peep, glint; gaze, stare, leer; perlustration, contemplation; con-spect-ion, -uity; regard, survey; in-, intro-spection; *reconnaissance*, specula-tion, watch, espionage, *espionnage*, au-topsy; ocular -inspection, – demonstra-tion; sight-seeing.

macrography, micrography.

point of view; view-, stand-point; gazebo, loop-hole, *belvedere*, watch-tower.

field of view; theatre, amphitheatre, arena, vista, horizon; commanding –, bird's eye –, panoramic- view; periscope.

visual organ, organ of vision; eye; naked –, unassisted- eye; eye-ball, retina, pupil, iris, cornea, white; optics, orbs; saucer –, goggle –, gooseberry-eyes.

short sight &c. 443; clear –, sharp –, quick –, eagle –, piercing –, penetrating--sight, – glance, – eye; perspicacity, discernment; catopsis.

eagle, hawk; cat, lynx; Argus.

evil eye; basilisk, cockatrice.

spectacles, telescope &c. 445.

**442. Blindness.**—N. blindness, anop-sia, cecity, excecation, *amaurosis*, cata-ract, ablepsy, prestriction; dim-sighted-ness &c. 443.

V. be -blind &c. *adj.*; not see; lose sight of; have the eyes bandaged; grope in the dark.

not look; close –, shut –, turn away –, avert- the eyes; look another way; wink &c. (*limited vision*) 443; shut the eyes –, be blind- to; wink –, blink- at.

render -blind &c. *adj.*; blind, -fold; hoodwink, dazzle; put one's eyes out; throw dust into one's eyes; *jeter de la poudre aux yeux*; screen from sight &c. (*hide*) 528.

Adj. blind; eye-, sight-, vision-less; dark; stone-, sand-, stark-blind; un-discerning; dim-sighted &c. 443.

blind as -a bat, – a buzzard, – a beetle, – a mole, – an owl; wall-eyed.

blinded &c. *v.*

Adv. blind-ly, -fold; darkly.

V. see, behold, discern, perceive, have in sight, descry, sight, make out, discover, distinguish recognize, spy, espy, ken; get –, have –, catch- a -sight, – glimpse- of; command a view of; witness, contemplate, speculate; cast –, set- the eyes on; be a -spectator &c. 444- of; look on &c. (*be present*) 186; see sights &c. (*curiosity*) 455; see at a glance &c. (*intelligence*) 498.

look, view, eye; lift up the eyes, open one's eye; look -at, – on, – upon, – over, – about one, – round; survey, scan, inspect; run the eye -over, – through; reconnoitre, glance -round, – on, – over; turn –, bend- one's looks upon; direct the eyes to, turn the eyes on, cast a glance, make eyes at.

observe &c. (*attend to*) 457; watch &c. (*care*) 459; see with one's own eyes; watch for &c. (*expect*) 507; peek, peep, peer, pry, take a peep; play at bo-peep.

look -full in the face, – hard at, – intently; strain one's eyes; fix –, rivet- the eyes upon; stare, gaze; pore over, gloat -over, – on; leer, ogle, glare; goggle; cock the eye, squint, gloat, look askance; give the glad eye.

Adj. seeing &c. *v.*; visual, ocular, -al; ophthalmic.

far-, clear-sighted &c. *n.*; eagle-, hawk-, lynx-, keen-, Argus-eyed.

visible &c. 446.

**Adv.** visibly &c. 446; in sight of, with one's eyes open.
at -sight, – first sight, – a glance, – the first blush; *primâ facie:*
**Int.** look! &c. (*attention*) 457.
**Phr.** the scales falling from one's eyes.

**443.** [Imperfect vision.] **Dim-sightedness.** [Fallacies of vision.]—**N.**
dim –, dull –, half –, short –, near –, long –, double –, astigmatic –,
failing- sight; dim &c. -sightedness; snow blindness; purblindness,
lippitude; my-, presby-opia; confusion of vision; astigmatism, nystag-
mus; colour-blindness, dichromism, chromato-pseudo-blepsis, Dalton-
ism; nyctalopy; *strabismus*, strabism, squint, cast in the eye, swivel
eye, goggle eyes; obliquity of vision.
    winking &c. *v.*; nictitation; blinkard, albino.
    dizziness, swimming, scotomy; cataract; ophthalmia.
    [Limitation of vision] eye shade, blinker, blinder; screen &c. (*hider*)
530.
    [Fallacies of vision] *deceptio visûs*; refraction, distortion, illusion,
false light, *anamorphosis*, virtual image, *spectrum, mirage,* looming,
phasma; phant-asm, -asma, -om; vision; spectre, apparition, ghost;
*ignis fatuus* &c. (*luminary*) 423; spectre of the Brocken; magic mirror;
magic lantern &c. (*show*) 448; mirror, lens &c. (*instrument*) 445.
    **V.** be -dim-sighted &c. *n.*; see double; have a -mote in the eye, –
mist before the eyes, – film over the eyes; see through a -prism, – glass
darkly; wink, blink, nictitate; squint; look ask-ant, -ance; screw up
the eyes, glare, glower.
    dazzle, glare, blur, swim, loom.
    **Adj.** dim-sighted &c. *n.*; my-, presby-opic; astigmatic; moon-, mope-,
blear-, goggle-, gooseberry-, one-eyed; blind of one eye, monoculous;
half-, pur-, colour-blind; dichromatic.
    blind as a bat &c. (*blind*) 442; winking &c. *v.*

**444. Spectator.**—**N.** spectator, beholder, observer, inspector, viewer,
looker-on, onlooker, witness, eye-witness, bystander, passer by;
sight-seer.
    spy, scout; sentinel &c. (*warning*) 668.
    **V.** witness, behold &c. (*see*) 441; look on &c. (*be present*) 186.

**445. Optical Instruments.**—**N.** optical instruments; lens, meniscus,
magnifier, reading –, burning- glass; micro-, mega-, teino-scope; spec-
tacles, glasses, barnacles, goggles, giglamps, eyeglass, *pince-nez*, monocle;
periscopic lens; telescope, glass, lorgnette, binocular; spy-, opera-,
field-glass, periscope, range finder.
    mirror, reflector, speculum; looking-, pier-, cheval-, hand-glass.
    prism; camera, *camera-lucida, -obscura;* projector, stereopticon,
magic lantern &c. (*show*) 448; chro-, thau-matrope; stereo-, pseudo-,
poly-, kaleido-scope.
    photo-, opto-, erio-, actino-, luci-, radio-, spectro-meter; polari-,
polemo-, spectro-scope, diffraction grating.
    optics, optician, optometry, optometrist; microscop-y, -ist; photom-
etry, photography; photographer.

**446. Visibility.**—**N.** visibility, per-
ceptibility; conspicuousness, distinct-
ness &c. *adj.*; conspicuity; appearance
&c. 448; exposure; manifestation &c.
525; ocular -proof, – evidence, – demon-
stration; field of view &c. (*vision*) 441.

**447. Invisibility.**—**N.** invisibility,
non-appearance, imperceptibility; in-
distinctness &c. *adj.*; mystery, deli-
tescence.
    concealment &c. 528; latency &c.
526.

V. be -, become- -visible &c. *adj.*; appear, emerge, open to the view; meet -, catch- the eye; present -, show -, manifest -, produce -, discover -, reveal -, expose -, betray- itself; stand -forth, - out; show; arise; peep -, peer -, crop- out; start -, spring -, show -, turn -, crop- up; glimmer, glitter, glow, loom; glare; burst forth, scintillate; burst upon the -view, - sight; heave in sight; come -in sight, - into view, - out, - forth, - forward; see the light of day; break through the clouds; make its appearance, show its face, materialize, appear to one's eyes, come upon the stage, enter; float before the eyes, speak for itself &c. (*manifest*) 525; attract the attention &c. 457; reappear; live in a glass house.

expose to view &c. 525.

Adj. visible, perceptible, perceivable, discernible, apparent; in -view, - full view, - sight; exposed to view, *en évidence*; unclouded.

obvious &c. (*manifest*) 525; plain, clear, distinct, definite; well-defined, -marked; in focus; recognizable, palpable, autoptical; glaring, staring, conspicuous; stereoscopic; in -bold, - strong, - high- relief.

periscopic, panoramic.

before -, under- one's eyes; before one, *à vue d'œil*, in one's eye, *oculis subjecta fidelibus*.

Adv. visibly &c. *adj.*; in sight of; before one's eyes &c. *adj.*; *veluti in speculum.*

V. be -invisible &c. *adj.*; be hidden &c. (*hide*) 528; lurk &c. (*lie hidden*) 526; escape notice.

render -invisible &c. *adj.*; conceal &c. 528; put out of sight.

not see &c. (*be blind*) 442; lose sight of.

Adj. invisible, imperceptible; un-, in-discernible; un-, non-apparent; out of -, not in- sight; *à perte de vue*; behind the -scenes, - curtain; view-, sight-less; in-, un-conspicuous; unseen &c. (*see* see &c. 441); covert &c. (*latent*) 526; eclipsed, under an eclipse.

dim &c. (*faint*) 422; mysterious, dark, obscure, confused; indistin-ct, -guishable; shadowy, indefinite, undefined; ill-defined, -marked; blurred, fuzzy, out of focus; misty &c. (*opaque*) 426; veiled &c. (*concealed*) 528; delitescent.

---

**448. Appearance.—N.** appearance, phenomenon, sight, spectacle, show, premonstration, scene, species, view, *coup d'œil*; look-out, out-look, prospect, vista, perspective, bird's-eye view, scenery, landscape, picture, *tableau*; display, exposure, *mise en scène*; scenery, *décor*; rising of the curtain.

phant-asm, -om &c. (*fallacy of vision*) 443.

pageant, *spectacle*; peep-, raree-, gallanty-show; *ombres chinoises*; projector, optical -, magic- lantern, phantasmagoria, dissolving views; cinema, -tograph; bio-scope. -graph; moving pictures, movies, film, screen &c.; pan-, di-, cosm-, ge-orama; *coup -, jeu- de théâtre*; pageantry &c. (*ostentation*) 882; insignia &c. (*indication*) 550.

aspect, phase, *phasis*, seeming; shape &c. (*form*) 240; guise, look,

**449. Disappearance.—N.** disappearance, evanescence, eclipse, occultation.

departure &c. 293; exit, vanishing point; dissolving views.

V. disappear, vanish, dissolve, fade, melt away, pass, go, avaunt; be -gone &c. *adj.*; leave -no trace, - 'not a rack behind'; go off the stage &c. (*depart*) 293; suffer -, undergo- an eclipse; be lost to -, retire from- -sight, - view.

lose sight of.

efface &c. 552.

Adj. disappearing &c. *v.*; evanescent; missing, lost; lost to -sight, - view; gone; *spurlos versenkt.*

Int. vanish! disappear! avaunt! &c. (*ejection*) 297.

complexion, colour, image, mien, air, cast, carriage, port, demeanour; presence, expression, first blush, face of the thing; point of view, light.

lineament, feature, trait, lines; out-line, -side; contour, *silhouette*, face, countenance, physiognomy, visage, phiz, mug, cast of countenance, profile, *tournure*, cut of one's jib, metoposcopy; outside &c. 220.

V. appear; be –, become- visible &c. 446; seem, look, show; present –, wear –, carry –, have –, bear –, exhibit –, take –, take on –, assume- the -appearance, – semblance- of; look like; cut a figure, figure; present to the view; show &c. (*make manifest*) 525.

Adj. apparent, seeming, ostensible; on view.

Adv. apparently; to all -seeming, – appearance; ostensibly, seemingly, as it seems, on the face of it, *primâ facie*; at the first blush, at first sight; in the eyes of; to the eye.

# CLASS IV

## WORDS RELATING TO THE INTELLECTUAL FACULTIES

### DIVISION (I.) FORMATION OF IDEAS

#### Section I. OPERATIONS OF INTELLECT IN GENERAL

**450. Intellect.**—N. intellect, mind, understanding, reason, thinking principle; rationality; cogitative –, cognitive –, intellectual- faculties; faculties, senses, consciousness, observation, percipience, apperception, mentality, intelligence, intellection, intuition, association of ideas, instinct, flair, conception, judgement, wits, parts, capacity, intellectuality, reasoning power, brains, genius; wit &c. 498; ability &c. (*skill*) 698; wisdom &c. 498.

soul, spirit, ghost, inner man, heart, breast, bosom, *penetralia mentis, divina particula auræ*, heart's core; ego, psyche, pneuma, subconsciousness, subconscious, subliminal self; dual personality.

organ –, seat- of thought; *sensorium*, sensory, brain, gray matter; head, -piece; pate, noddle, skull, scull, *pericranium, cerebrum, cranium*, brain-pan, -box; sconce, upper story.

[Science of mind] metaphysics; psychics, psycho-logy, -metry, -genesis, -analysis, -physics, psychi-atry, -cal research, thought reading &c. 992; ideology; mental –, moral- philosophy; philosophy of the mind; pneumat-, phren-ology; no –, cranio-logy, -scopy.

ideal-ity, -ism; transcendental-, spiritual-ism; immateriality &c. 317.

metaphysician, psychologist &c.

V. note, notice, mark; take -notice, – cognizance- of; be -aware, – conscious- of; realize; appreciate; ruminate &c. (*think*) 451; fancy &c. (*imagine*) 515; conceive, reason, understand.

Adj. [Relating to intellect] intellectual, mental, rational, subjective, metaphysical, nooscopic, spiritual; ghostly; psych-ical, -ological; cerebral.

immaterial &c. 317; endowed with reason.

Adv. *in petto.*

**450a. Absence or want of Intellect.**—N. absence –, want- of -intellect &c. 450; imbecility &c. 499; brutality; brute -instinct, – force.

Adj. unendowed with reason.

_____

**451. Thought.**—N. thought; exercitation –, exercise- of the intellect; reflection, cogitation, consideration, meditation, study, lucubration, speculation, deliberation, pondering; head-,

**452.** [Absence or want of thought.] **Incogitancy.**—N. incogitancy, vacancy, inunderstanding; inanity, fatuity &c. 499; thoughtlessness &c. (*inattention*) 458.

brain-work; cerebration; mentation, deep reflection; close study, application &c. (*attention*) 457.

abstract thought, abstraction, contemplation, musing; brown study &c. (*inattention*) 458; reverie, Platonism; depth of thought, workings of the mind, thoughts, inmost thoughts; self-counsel, -communing, -consultation.

association –, succession –, flow –, train –, current- of -thought, – ideas.

after –, mature- thought; reconsideration, second thoughts; retrospection &c. (*memory*) 505; excogitation; examination &c. (*inquiry*) 461; invention &c. (*imagination*) 515.

thoughtfulness &c. *adj.*

**V.** think, reflect, reason, cogitate, excogitate, consider, deliberate; bestow -thought, – consideration- upon; speculate, contemplate, meditate, ponder, muse, dream, ruminate; brood –, con- over; animadvert, study; bend –, apply- the mind &c. (*attend*) 457; digest, discuss, hammer at, weigh, perpend; realize, appreciate; fancy &c. (*imagine*) 515; trow.

take into consideration; take counsel &c. (*be advised*) 695; commune with –, bethink- oneself; collect one's thoughts; revolve –, turn over –, run over- in the mind; chew the cud –, sleep- upon; take counsel of –, advise with- one's pillow.

rack –, ransack –, crack –, beat –, cudgel- one's brains; set one's -brain, – wits- to work.

harbour –, entertain –, cherish –, nurture- an -idea &c. 453; take into one's head; bear in mind; reconsider.

occur; present –, suggest- itself; come –, get- into one's head; strike one, flit across the view, come uppermost, run in one's head; enter –, pass in –, cross –, flash on –, flash across –, float in –, fasten itself on –, be uppermost in –, occupy- the mind; have in one's mind.

make an impression; sink –, penetrate- into the mind; engross the thoughts.

**Adj.** thinking &c. *v.*; thoughtful, pensive, meditative, reflective, cogitative, museful, wistful, contemplative, speculative, deliberative, studious, sedate, introspective, Platonic, philosophical.

lost –, engrossed –, rapt –, absorbed- in thought &c. (*inattentive*) 458; deep musing &c. (*intent*) 457.

„ in the mind, under consideration, in contemplation.

**Adv.** all things considered; taking everything into account.

**Phr.** the mind being on the stretch; the -mind, – head- -turning, running- upon.

**V.** not -think &c. 451; not think of; dismiss from the -mind, – thoughts &c. 451.

indulge in reverie &c. (*be inattentive*) 458.

put away thought; unbend –, relax –, divert- the mind.

**Adj.** vacant, unintellectual, unideal, unoccupied, unthinking, inconsiderate, thoughtless; absent &c. (*inattentive*) 458; diverted; irrational &c. 499; narrow-minded &c. 481.

un-thought of, -dreamt of, -considered; off one's mind; incogitable, not to be thought of, inconceivable.

---

**453.** [Object of thought.] **Idea.**—**N.** idea, notion, conception, thought, apprehension, impression, perception, image, sentiment, reflection, observation, consideration; abstract idea, principle; archetype.

view &c. (*opinion*) 484; theory &c.

**454.** [Subject of thought.] **Topic.**— **N.** subject of –, material for- thought; food for the mind, mental *pabulum.*

subject, -matter; matter, theme, topic, what it is about, *thesis*, text, business, affair, matter in hand, argument; motion, resolution; head, chap-

514; conceit, fancy; phantasy &c. (*imagination*) 515.

point of view &c. (*aspect*) 448; field of view.

---

ter; case, point; proposition, theorem; field of inquiry; moot point, problem, &c. (*question*) 461.

**V.** float -, pass- in the mind &c. 451.

**Adj.** thought of; uppermost in the mind; *in petto.*

**Adv.** under -discussion, - consideration, - advisement; in -question, - the mind; on -foot, - the carpet, - the *tapis*; before the house, relative to &c. 9.

## Section II. PRECURSORY CONDITIONS AND OPERATIONS

**455.** [The desire of knowledge.] **Curiosity.** — **N.** interest, thirst for knowledge; curi-osity, -ousness; inquiring mind; inquisitiveness.

sight-seer, quidnunc, newsmonger, Paul Pry, peeping Tom, eavesdropper; gossip &c. (*news*) 532; questioner, *enfant terrible.*

**V.** be -curious &c. *adj.*; take an interest in, stare, gape; prick up the ears, see sights, lionize; pry, speer; dig up.

**Adj.** curious, inquisitive, burning with curiosity, overcurious, nosey; inquiring &c. 461; prying; inquisitorial; agape &c. (*expectant*) 507; attentive &c. 457.

**Phr.** what's the matter? what next?

**456.** [Absence of curiosity.] **Incuriosity.**—**N.** incuriosity; incuriousness &c. *adj.*; *insouciance* &c. 866; indifference, apathy.

**V.** be -incurious &c. *adj.*; have no -curiosity &c. 455; take no interest in &c. 823; mind one's own business.

**Adj.** incurious, uninquisitive, uninterested, indifferent, bored; impassive &c. 823.

---

**457.** **Attention.**—**N.** attention; mindfulness &c. *adj.*; intent-ness, -iveness; thought &c. 451; adverten-ce, -cy; observ-ance, -ation; consideration, reflection, perpension; heed; particularity; notice, regard &c. *v.*; circumspection &c. (*care*) 459; study, scrutiny, once-over; in-, intro-spection; revision, -al.

active -, diligent -, exclusive -, minute -, close -, intense -, deep -, profound -, abstract -, laboured -, deliberate- -thought, - attention, - application, - study.

minuteness, attention to detail &c. 459.

absorption of mind &c. (*abstraction*) 458.

indication, calling attention to &c. *v.*

**V.** be -attentive &c. *adj.*; attend, advert to, observe, look, see, view, remark, notice, regard, take notice, mark; give -, pay- -attention, - heed-to; listen in, incline -, lend- an ear to; trouble one's head about; give a

**458.** **Inattention.**—**N.** in-attention, -consideration; inconsiderateness &c. *adj.*; oversight; inadverten-ce, -cy; non-observance, disregard.

supineness &c. (*inactivity*) 683; *étourderie*; want of thought; heedlessness &c. (*neglect*) 460; *insouciance* &c. (*indifference*) 866.

abstraction; absence -, absorption- of mind; preoccupation, distraction, reverie, brown study, deep musing, fit of abstraction, woolgathering.

**V.** be -inattentive &c. *adj.*; overlook, disregard; pass by &c. (*neglect*) 460; not -observe &c. 457; think little of.

close -, shut- one's eyes to; wink at; pay no attention to; dismiss -, discard -, discharge- from one's -thoughts, - mind; drop the subject, think no more of; set -, turn -, put- aside; turn -away from, - one's attention from, - a deaf ear to, - one's back upon.

abstract oneself, dream, indulge in reverie.

escape -notice, - attention; come in

thought –, animadvert- to; occupy oneself with; contemplate &c. (*think of*) 451; look -at, – to, – after, – into, – over; see to; turn –, bend –, apply –, direct –, give- the -mind, – eye, – attention- to; have -an eye to, – in one's eye; bear in mind; take into -account, – consideration; keep in -sight, – view; have regard to, heed, mind, take cognizance of, be engaged in, entertain, recognize; make –, take- note of; note.

examine cursorily; glance -at, – upon, – over; cast –, pass- the eyes over; run over, turn over the leaves, dip into, perstringe; skim &c. (*neglect*) 460; take a cursory view of.

examine, – closely, – intently; scan, scrutinize, consider; give –, bend- one's mind to; overhaul, revise, pore over; inspect, review, pass under review; take stock of; fix –, rivet –, focus –, devote- the -eye, – mind, – thoughts, – attention- on *or* to; hear –, think- out; mind one's business.

revert –, hark back- to; watch &c. (*expect*) 507, (*take care of*) 459; hearken –, listen- to; prick up the ears; have –, keep- the eyes open; come to the point.

meet with attention; fall under one's -notice, – observation; be -under consideration &c. (*topic*) 454.

catch –, strike- the eye; attract notice; catch –, awaken –, wake –, invite –, solicit –, attract –, claim –, excite –, engage –, occupy –, strike –, arrest –, fix –, engross –, absorb –, rivet- the- attention, – mind, – thoughts; be -present to, – uppermost in- the mind.

bring under one's notice; point -out, – to, – at, – the finger at; lay the finger on, indigitate, indicate; direct –, call- attention to; show; put a -mark &c. (*sign*) 550- upon; call soldiers to 'attention'; bring forward &c. (*make manifest*) 525.

**Adj.** attentive, mindful, heedful, observant, regardful; alive –, awake- to, alert; observing &c. *v.*; taken up –, occupied- with; engaged –, engrossed –, interested –, wrapped- in; absorbed, rapt; breathless; pre-occupied &c. (*inattentive*) 458; watchful &c. (*careful*) 459; intent on, open-eyed, undistracted, upon the stretch; on the watch &c. (*expectant*) 507. steadfast.

**Int.** see! look, – here, – out, – alive, – you, – to it! mark! lo!

at one ear and go out at the other; forget &c. (*have no remembrance*) 506.

call off –, draw off –, call away –, divert –, distract- the -attention, – thoughts, – mind; put out of one's head; dis-concert, -compose; put out, confuse, perplex, bewilder, moider, fluster, muddle, dazzle; throw a sop to Cerberus.

**Adj.** inattentive; un-observant, -mindful, -heeding, -discerning; inadvertent; mind-, regard-, respect-less; listless &c. (*indifferent*) 866; blind, deaf; flighty, hand over head; cur-, percur-sory; giddy-, scatter-, hare-brained; unreflecting, écervelé, inconsiderate, off-hand, thoughtless, dizzy, muzzy, brainsick; giddy, – as a goose; wild, harum-scarum, rantipole, high-flying; heed-, care-less &c. (*neglectful*) 460.

absent, absent-minded, abstracted, *distrait*; lost; lost –, wrapped- in thought, woolgathering; rapt, in the clouds, bemused; dreaming –, musing-on other things; pre-occupied; engrossed &c. (*attentive*) 457; in a -reverie &c. *n.*; off one's guard &c. (*inexpectant*) 508; napping; dreamy.

disconcerted, put out &c. *v.*; rattled.

**Adv.** inattentively, inadvertently &c. adj.; *per incuriam, sub silentio.*

**Int.** stand -at ease, – easy!

**Phr.** the attention wanders; one's wits gone a -woolgathering, – bird's nesting; it never entered into one's head; the mind running on other things; one's thoughts being elsewhere; had it been a bear it would have bitten you.

———

behold! soho! hark, – ye! mind! halloo! observe! lo and behold!
attention! *nota bene*; N.B.; *, †; I'd have you to know; notice!
take notice! O yes! *Oyez!*
**Phr.** this is –, these are- to give notice.

**459. Care.** [Vigilance.]—**N.** care,
solicitude, heed; heedfulness &c. *adj.*;
scruple &c. (*conscientiousness*) 939.

watchfulness &c. *adj.*; vigilance,
*surveillance*, eyes of Argus, watch, vigil,
look out, watch and ward, *l'œil du
maître*.

alertness &c. (*activity*) 682; atten-
tion &c. 457; prudence &c., circumspec-
tion &c. (*caution*) 864; forethought
&c. 510; precaution &c. (*preparation*)
673; tidiness &c. (*order*) 58, (*cleanli-
ness*) 652; accuracy &c. (*exactness*) 494;
minuteness, attention to detail; meticu-
lousness, nicety, circumstantiality.

**V.** be -careful &c. *adj.*; reck; take
care &c. (*be cautious*) 864; pay atten-
tion to &c. 457; take care of; look –,
see- -to, – after; keep -an eye, – a
sharp eye- upon; keep -watch, – watch
and ward; mount guard, set watch,
watch; keep in -sight, – view; chaperon,
play gooseberry; mind, – one's business.

look -sharp, – about one; look with
one's own eyes; keep a -good, – sharp-
look-out; have all one's -wits, – eyes-
about one; watch for &c. (*expect*) 507;
stand to; keep one's eyes –, have the
eyes –, sleep with one eye- open.

take precautions &c. 673; protect
&c. (*render safe*) 664.

do one's best &c. 682; mind one's
Ps and Qs, speak by the card, pick
one's steps.

**Adj.** care-, regard-, heed-ful; taking
care &c. *v.*; particular; prudent &c.
(*cautious*) 864; considerate; thought-
ful &c. (*deliberative*) 451; provident
&c. (*prepared*) 673; alert &c. (*active*)
682; sure-footed.

guarded, on one's guard; on the
-*qui vive*, – alert, – watch, – look-out;
awake, broad awake, vigilant; watch-,
wake-, wist-ful; Argus-, lynx- eyed;
wide awake &c. (*intelligent*) 498;
on the watch for &c. (*expectant*)
507.

tidy &c. (*orderly*) 58, (*clean*) 652;
accurate &c. (*exact*) 494; scrupulous

**460. Neglect.**—**N.** neglect; careless-
ness &c. *adj.*; trifling &c. *v.*; negligence;
omission, laches, default; remissness,
slackness, procrastination; supineness
&c. (*inactivity*) 683; inattention &c.
458; *nonchalance* &c. (*insensibility*) 823;
imprudence, recklessness &c. 863;
slovenliness &c. (*disorder*) 59, (*dirt*)
653; improvidence &c. 674; non-com-
pletion &c. 730; inexactness &c. (*error*)
495.

paraleipsis [in rhetoric].

trifler, slacker, waster, waiter on
Providence; Micawber.

**V.** be -negligent &c. *adj.*; take no
care of &c. (take care of &c. 459);
neglect; let -slip, – go; lay -, set -,
cast -, put- aside; keep –, leave- out of
sight; lose sight of.

overlook, disregard; pass -over, – by;
let pass; blink; wink –, connive- at;
gloss over; take no -note, – notice, -
thought, – account- of; pay no regard
to; *laisser aller*; allow to lie on the
table.

scamp; trifle, fribble; do by halves;
skimp; cut; slight &c. (*despise*) 930;
play -, trifle- with; slur; skim, – the
surface; *effleurer*; take a cursory view
of &c. 457.

slur -, slip -, skip -, jump- over;
pretermit, miss, skip, jump, omit, give
the go-by to, push aside, throw into
the background, shelve, sink; ignore,
shut one's eyes to, refuse to hear, turn
a deaf ear to; leave out of one's calcu-
lation; not -attend to &c. 457, – mind;
not trouble -oneself, – one's head-
-with, –about; forget &c. 506; be caught
napping &c. (*not expect*) 508; leave a
loose thread; let the grass grow under
one's feet.

render -neglectful &c. *adj.*; put -,
throw- off one's guard.

**Adj.** neglecting &c. *v.*; unmindful,
negligent, neglectful; heedless, careless,
thoughtless; perfunctory, remiss,
slack.

inconsiderate; un-, in-circumspect;

&c. (*conscientious*) 939; *cavendo tutus* &c. (*safe*) 664.

Adv. carefully &c. *adj.*; with care, gingerly.

Phr. *quis custodiet ipsos custodes?*

───────

off one's guard; un-wary, -watchful, -guarded; offhand.

supine &c. (*inactive*) 683; inattentive &c. 458; *insouciant* &c. (*indifferent*) 823; imprudent, reckless &c. 863; slovenly &c. (*disorderly*) 59, (*dirty*) 653; inexact &c. (*erroneous*) 495; improvident &c. 674.

neglected &c. *v.*; un-heeded, -cared for, -perceived, -seen, -observed, -noticed, -noted, -marked, -attended to, -thought of, -regarded, -remarked, -missed; shunted, shelved.

un-examined, -studied, -searched, -scanned, -weighed, -sifted, -explored.

abandoned; buried in a napkin, hid under a bushel.

Adv. negligently &c. *adj.*; hand over head, anyhow; in an unguarded moment &c. (*unexpectedly*) 508; *per incuriam.*

Int. never mind, no matter, let it pass; it will be all the same a hundred years hence.

**461. Inquiry.** [Subject of Inquiry. Question.]—N. inquiry; request &c. 765; search, research, quest; pursuit &c. 622.

examination, review, scrutiny, investigation, indagation; per-quisition, -scrutation, -vestigation; inqu-est, -isition; exploration; *exploitation*, ventilation.

sifting; calculation, analysis, dissection, resolution, induction; Baconian method.

strict –, close –, searching –, exhaustive- inquiry; narrow –, strict-search; study &c. (*consideration*) 451. *scire facias, ad referendum*; trial.

questioning &c. *v.*; interroga-tion, -tory; third degree; interpellation; challenge, examination, cross-examination, catechism; feeler, Socratic method, zetetic philosophy; leading question; discussion &c. (*reasoning*) 476; questionnaire, questionary.

reconnoitering, *reconnaissance*; prying &c. *v.*; espionage, *espionnage*; domiciliary visit, peep behind the curtain; lantern of Diogenes.

question, query, problem, *desideratum*, point to be solved, porism; subject –, field- of -inquiry, – controversy; point –, matter- in dispute; moot-point; issue, question at issue; bone of contention &c. (*discord*) 713; plain –, fair –, open- question; enigma &c. (*secret*) 533; knotty point &c. (*difficulty*) 704; *quodlibet*; threshold of an inquiry.

inquirer, investigator, experimenter, inquisitor, inspector, querist,

**462. Answer.**—N. answer, response, reply, replication, *riposte*, rejoinder, surrejoinder, rebutter, surrebutter, counter-evidence &c. 468, counter-charge, defence, plea; retort, repartee; contradiction &c. 536; rescript, -ion; antiphon, -y; acknowledgment; password; echo.

discovery &c. 480a; solution &c. (*explanation*) 522; rationale &c. (*cause*) 153; clue &c. (*indication*) 550.

Œdipus; oracle &c. 513; return &c. (*record*) 551.

V. answer, respond, reply, rebut, retort, rejoin; give –, return for- answer; acknowledge, echo.

explain &c. (*interpret*) 522; solve &c. (*unriddle*) 522; discover &c. 480a; fathom, hunt out &c. (*inquire*) 461; satisfy, set at rest, determine.

Adj. answering &c. *v.*; respon-sive, -dent; oracular; antiphonal; conclusive.

Adv. because &c. (*cause*) 153; on the -scent, – right scent.

Int. *eureka!*

───────

examiner, catechist; scrut-ator, -ineer; analyst; quidnunc &c. (*curiosity*) 455.

**V.** make -inquiry &c. *n.*; inquire, seek, search, frisk, speer, look -for, – about for, – out for; scan, reconnoitre, explore, sound, rummage, ransack, pry, peer, look round; look –, go- -over, – through; spy, over-haul.

scratch the head, slap the forehead.

look –, peer –, pry- into every hole and corner; look behind the scenes; trace up; hunt –, fish –, dig –, ferret- out; unearth; leave no stone unturned.

seek ᴀ -clue, – clew; hunt, track, trail, shadow, mouse, dodge, trace; follow the -trail, – scent; pursue &c. 622; beat up one's quarters; fish for; feel for &c. (*experiment*) 463.

investigate; take up –, institute –, pursue –, follow up –, conduct –, carry on –, prosecute- -an inquiry &c. *n.*; look -at, – into; pre-examine; discuss, canvass, agitate.

examine, study, consider, calculate; dip –, dive –, delve –, go deep- into; make sure of, probe, sound, fathom; probe to the -bottom, – quick; scrutinize, analyze, anatomize, dissect, parse, resolve, sift, winnow; view –, try- in all its phases; thresh out.

bring in question, subject to examination; put to the proof &c. (*experiment*) 463; audit, tax, pass in review; take into consideration &c. (*think over*) 451; take counsel &c. 695.

ask, question, demand; put –, pop –, propose –, propound –, moot –, start –, raise –, stir –, suggest –, put forth –, ventilate – grapple with –, go into- a question.

put to the question, interrogate, catechize, pump, grill; cross-question, -examine; dodge; require an answer; pick –, suck- the brains of; feel the pulse.

be -in question &c. *v.*; undergo examination.

**Adj.** inquiring &c. *v.*; inquisitive &c. (*curious*) 455; requisit-ive, -ory; catechetical, inquisitorial, analytic; in -search, – quest- of; on the look-out for, interrogative, zetetic; all-searching.

un-determined, -tried, -decided; in -question, – dispute, – issue, – course of inquiry; under -discussion, – consideration, – investigation &c. *n.*, *sub judice*, moot, proposed; doubtful &c. (*uncertain*) 475.

**Adv.** what? why? wherefore? whence? whither? where? *quare?* how -comes, – happens, – is- it? what is the reason? what's -the matter, – up, – in the wind? what on earth? when? who?

**463. Experiment.**—**N.** experiment; essay &c. (*attempt*) 675; research &c. (*investigation*) 461; trial, tentative method, *tâtonnement*.

verification, probation, *experimentum crucis*, proof, criterion, diagnostic, test, tryout, crucial test, acid test.

crucible, reagent, check, touchstone, pix; assay, ordeal; ring.

empiricism, rule of thumb.

feeler; pilot –, messenger- balloon, *ballon d'essai*; pilot engine; scout; straw to show the wind.

speculation, random shot, leap in the dark.

analy-zer, -st; adventurer, explorer, sourdough, prospector; experiment-er, -ist, -alist; assayer.

**V.** experiment; essay &c. (*endeavour*) 675; try, assay, sample; make -an experiment, – trial of; give a trial to; put upon –, subject to- trial; experiment upon; rehearse; put –, bring –, submit- to the -test, – proof; prove, verify, test, touch, practise upon, try one's strength.

grope; feel –, grope- -for, – one's way; fumble; *tâtonner, aller à
tâtons*; put –, throw- out a feeler; send up a pilot balloon; see how
the -land lies, – wind blows; consult the barometer; feel the pulse;
fish –, bob- for; cast –, beat- about for; angle, trawl, cast one's net,
beat the bushes.

venture, try one's fortune &c. (*adventure*) 675; explore &c. (*inquire*)
461.

**Adj.** experimental; probat-ive, -ory, -ionary; analytic, docimastic;
tentative; empirical; speculative.

under probation, on one's trial, on trial, on approval.

**464. Comparison.—N.** comparison, collation, contrast; identification.
sim-ile, -ilitude; allegory &c. (*metaphor*) 521.

**V.** compare -to, – with; collate, confront; place side by side &c.
(*near*) 197; set –, pit- against one another; contrast, balance.

identify, draw a parallel, parallel.

compare notes; institute a comparison; *parva componere magnis*.

**Adj.** comparative, relative; metaphorical &c. 521.

compared with &c. *v.*; comparable.

**Adv.** relatively &c. (*relation*) 9; as compared with &c. *v.*

---

**465. Discrimination.—N.** discrimina-
tion, distinction, differentiation, diag-
nosis, diorism; nice perception; per-
ception –, appreciation- of difference;
acuteness; estimation &c. 466; nicety,
refinement; taste &c. 850; *critique,*
judgement, tact; insight, discernment
&c. (*intelligence*) 498; nuances.

**V.** discriminate, distinguish, differen-
tiate, severalize; separate; draw the
line, sift; separate –, winnow- the chaff
from the wheat; split hairs.

estimate &c. (*measure*) 466; know -which is which, – one's stuff,
– one's way about, – what is what, – 'a hawk from a handsaw.'

take into -account, – consideration; give –, allow- due weight to;
weigh carefully.

**Adj.** discriminating &c. *v.*; dioristic, discriminative, critical,
distinctive; nice.

**Phr.** *il y a fagots et fagots; rem acu tetigisti.*

**465a. Indiscrimination.—N.** indis-
crimination; promiscuity; indistinct-
ness, -ion; uncertainty &c. (*doubt*) 475;
obtuseness.

**V.** not -indiscriminate &c. 465; over-
look &c. (*neglect*) 460- a distinction;
con-found, -fuse, jumble; swallow
whole.

**Adj.** indiscriminate, undiscriminat-
ing, promiscuous; undistinguish-ed,
-able, -ing; unmeasured.

---

**466. Measurement.—N.** measurement, admeasurement, mensuration,
survey, valuation, appraisement, assessment, assize; estim-ate, -ation;
dead reckoning; reckoning &c. (*numeration*) 85; gauging &c. *v.*

metrology, weights and measures, compound arithmetic.

measure, yard measure, standard, rule, foot-rule, chain, tape, staff,
compass, callipers; dividers; gage, gauge, planimeter; meter, line, rod,
check.

volt, kilowatt, ampere, candle power; horse power; axle load; foot
pound.

flood –, high water- mark; Plimsoll mark; index &c. 550.

scale; gradu-ation, -ated scale; nonius; vernier &c. (*minuteness*) 193;
pedo (*length*)- 200, sounding line &c. (*depth*)- 208, thermo (*heat* &c.
389)-, baro (*air* &c. 338)-, dynamo (*power*)- 276, anemo (*wind* 349)-,

gonio (*angle* 244)- meter; landmark &c. (*limit*) 233; balance &c. (*weight*) 319; optical instruments &c. 445.

co-ordinates, ordinate and abscissa, polar co-ordinates, latitude and longitude, declination and right ascension, altitude and azimuth.

geo-, stereo-, hypso-metry; metage; surveying, land surveying; geo-desy, -detics, -desia; ortho-, alti-metry; *cadastre*.

astrolabe, armillary sphere.

land, -surveyor; geometer, topographer, cartographer, hydrographer.

**V.** measure, meter, mete; value, assess, rate, appraise, estimate, form an estimate, set a value on; appreciate; standardize.

span, pace, step; apply the -compass &c. *n.*; gauge, plumb, probe, calliper, sound, fathom &c. 208; heave the -log, – lead; weigh &c. 319; survey.

take an average &c. 29; graduate.

**Adj.** measuring &c. *v.*; metric, -al; measurable; geodetical, cadastral, topographical.

## Section III. Materials for Reasoning

**467. Evidence** [on one side.]—**N.** evidence; facts, premises, *data*, *præcognita*, grounds.

indication &c. 550; criterion &c. (*test*) 463.

testi-mony, -fication; attestation; deposition &c. (*affirmation*) 535; examination.

admission &c. (*assent*) 488; authority, warrant, credential, diploma, voucher, certificate, docket; record &c. 551; document, muniments; *pièce justificative*; deed, warranty &c. (*security*) 771; signature, seal &c. (*identification*) 550; exhibit, citation, reference.

witness, indicator; eye-, ear-witness; deponent; sponsor.

oral –, documentary –, hearsay –, external –, extrinsic –, internal –, intrinsic –, circumstantial –, cumulative –, *ex parte* –, presumptive –, collateral –, constructive- evidence; proof &c. (*demonstration*) 478; evidence in chief; finger prints, dactylogram.

secondary evidence; confirmation, corroboration, adminicle, support; ratification &c. (*assent*) 488; authentication, verification; compurgation, wager of law, comprobation.

citation, reference.

**V.** be -evidence &c. *n.*; evince, show, betoken, tell of; indicate &c. (*denote*) 550; imply, involve, argue, bespeak, breathe.

have –, carry- weight; tell, speak

**468.** [Evidence on the other side, on the other hand.] **Counter-evidence.**— **N.** counter-evidence; evidence on the other -side, – hand; disproof; refutation &c. 479; negation &c. 536; conflicting evidence.

plea &c. 617; vindication &c. 937; counter-protest; *tu quoque* argument; other side –, reverse- of the shield.

**V.** countervail, oppose; run counter; rebut &c. (*refute*) 479; subvert &c. (*destroy*) 162; check, weaken; contravene; contradict &c. (*deny*) 536; tell another story, turn the -tables, – scale; alter the case; cut both ways; prove a negative.

*audire alteram partem.*

**Adj.** countervailing &c. *v.*; contradictory, in rebuttal.

un-attested, -authenticated, -supported by evidence; supposititious, trumped up.

**Adv.** *per contra*, conversely, on the other hand.

**469. Qualification.**—**N.** qualification, limitation, modification, colouring.

allowance, grains of allowance, consideration, extenuating circumstances.

condition, proviso, exception; exemption; salvo, saving clause; discount &c. 813.

**V.** qualify, limit, modify, affect, temper, leaven, give a colour to, introduce new conditions.

allow –, make allowance- for; ad-

volumes; speak for itself &c. (*manifest*) 525.

rest –, depend- upon; repose on.

bear -witness &c. *n.*; give -evidence &c. *n.*; testify, depose, witness, vouch for; sign, seal, undersign, set one's hand and seal, sign and seal, deliver as one's act and deed, certify, attest; acknowledge &c. (*assent*) 488.

make absolute, confirm, ratify, corroborate, endorse, countersign, support, bear out, vindicate, uphold, warrant.

adduce, attest, cite, quote; refer –, appeal- to; call, – to witness; bring -forward, – into court; allege, plead; produce –, confront- witnesses; collect –, bring together –, rake up- evidence.

have –, make out- a case; establish, circumstantiate, authenticate, substantiate, verify, make good, quote chapter and verse; bring -home to, – to book.

Adj. showing &c. *v.*; evidential, indica-tive, -tory; deducible &c. 478; grounded –, founded –, based- on; first hand, authentic, verifiable; corroborative, confirmatory; significant, conclusive.

Adv. by inference; according to, witness, *a fortiori*; still -more, – less; *raison de plus*; in corroboration &c. *n.* of; *valeat quantum*; under -seal, – one's hand and seal.

mit exceptions, take into account. take exception, object.

Adj. qualifying &c. *v.*; conditional; extenuatory; exceptional &c. (*unconformable*) 83.

hypothetical &c. (*supposed*) 514; contingent &c. (*uncertain*) 475.

Adv. provided, – always; if, unless, but, yet; according as; conditionally, admitting, supposing; on the supposition of &c. (*theoretically*) 514; with the understanding, even, although, though, for all that, after all, at all events.

with grains of allowance, *cum grano salis*; *exceptis excipiendis*; wind and weather permitting; if possible &c. 470.

subject to; with this -proviso &c. *n.*

---

## Degrees of Evidence

**470. Possibility.—N.** possibility, potentiality; what -may be, – is possible &c. *adj.*; compatibility &c. (*agreement*) 23.

practicability, feasibility; practicableness &c. *adj.*

contingency, chance &c. 156.

V. be -possible &c. *adj.*; stand a chance, have a leg to stand on; admit of, bear.

render -possible &c. *adj.*; put in the way of.

Adj. possible; on the -cards, – dice; *in posse*, within the bounds of possibility, conceivable, credible, imaginable; compatible &c. 23.

practicable, feasible, workable, performable, achievable; within -reach, – measurable distance; accessible, superable, surmountable; at-, ob-tainable; contingent &c. (*doubtful*) 475.

Adv. possibly, by possibility; perhaps, -chance, -adventure; may be, haply, mayhap.

**471. Impossibility.—N.** impossibility &c. *adj.*; what -cannot, – can never- be; sour grapes; infeasibility, impracticability, hopelessness &c. 859.

V. be -impossible &c. *adj.*; have no chance whatever.

attempt impossibilities; square the circle; discover the -philosopher's stone, – elixir of life, – secret of perpetual motion; wash a blackamoor white; skin a flint; make -a silk purse out of a sow's ear, – bricks without straw; have nothing to go upon; weave a rope of sand, build castles in the air, *prendre la lune avec les dents*; extract sunbeams from cucumbers, set the Thames on fire, milk a he-goat into a sieve, catch a weasel asleep, *rompre l'anguille au genou*, be in two places at once.

Adj impossible; not -possible &c. 470; absurd, contrary to reason; unlikely, at variance with facts; unreasonable &c. 477; incredible &c. 485; beyond the bounds of -reason, – possi-

if possible, wind and weather permitting, God willing, *Deo volente*, D.V.

---

bility; from which reason recoils; visionary; inconceivable &c. (*improbable*) 473; prodigious &c. (*wonderful*) 870; un-, in-imaginable, unthinkable, not a Chinaman's chance.

impracticable, unachievable; un-, in-feasible; insuperable; un-, in-surmountable; unat-, unob-tainable; out of -reach, – the question; not to be -had, – thought of; beyond control; desperate &c. (*hopeless*) 859; incompatible &c. 24; inaccessible, uncomeatable, impassable impervious, innavigable, inextricable.

out of –, beyond- one's -power, – depth, – reach, – grasp; too much for; *ultra crepidam.*

Phr. the grapes are sour; *non possumus; non nostrum tantas componere lites.*

**472. Probability.—N.** probability, likelihood; likeliness &c. *adj.*

*vraisemblance,* verisimilitude, plausibility; colour, semblance, show of; presumption; presumptive –, circumstantial- evidence; credibility.

reasonable –, fair –, good –, favourable- -chance, – prospect; prospect, well-grounded hope; chance &c. 156.

V. be -probable &c. *adj.*; give –, lend- colour to; point to; imply &c. (*evidence*) 467; bid fair &c. (*promise*) 511; stand fair for; stand –, run- a good chance.

presume, infer, suppose, take for granted.

think likely, dare say, flatter oneself; expect &c. 507; count upon &c. (*believe*) 484.

Adj. probable, likely, hopeful, to be expected, in a fair way.

plausible, specious, ostensible, colourable, *ben trovato,* well-founded, reasonable, credible, easy of belief, presumable, presumptive, apparent.

Adv. probably &c. *adj.*; belike; in all -probability, – likelihood; very –, most- likely; as likely as not; like enough; ten &c. to one; apparently, seemingly, according to every reasonable expectation; *primâ facie;* to all appearance &c. (*to the eye*) 448.

Phr. the -chances, – odds- are; appearances –, chances- are in favour of; there is reason to -believe, – think, – expect; I dare say; all Lombard Street to a China orange.

**473. Improbability.—N.** improbability, unlikelihood; unfavourable –, bad –, little –, small –, poor –, scarcely any –, no –, not a ghost of a- chance; bare possibility; long odds; incredibility &c. 485.

V. be -improbable &c. *adj.*; have a -small chance &c. *n.*

Adj. improbable, unlikely, contrary to all reasonable expectation, implausible.

rare &c. (*infrequent*) 137; unheard of inconceivable; un-, in-imaginable; in credible &c. 485; more than doubtful

Int. not likely! no fear!

Phr. the chances are against.

---

**474. Certainty.—N.** certainty; necessity &c. 601; certitude, certainness, surety, assurance, sureness; dead –, moral- certainty; infallibleness &c. *adj.*; infallibility, reliability.

gospel, scripture, church, pope, court of final appeal; *res judicata, ultimatum.*

positiveness; dogmat-ism, -ist, -izer; *doctrinaire,* know-all, bigot, -ry; opin-

**475. Uncertainty.—N.** uncertainty, incertitude, doubt; doubtfulness &c. *adj.*; dubi-ety, -tation, -tancy, -ousness.

hesitation, suspense; perplexity, embarrassment, dilemma, quandary, Morton's fork, bewilderment; timidity &c. (*fear*) 860; indecision, vacillation &c. 605; *diaporesis,* indetermination.

vagueness &c. *adj.*; haze, fog; or

ionist, Sir Oracle; *ipse dixit*; zealot.

fact; positive –, matter of- fact; *fait accompli.*

**V.** be -certain &c. *adj.*; stand to reason.

render -certain &c. *adj.*; in-, en-, assure; clinch, make sure; determine, decide, set at rest, 'make assurance double sure'; know &c. (*believe*) 484; dismiss all doubt.

dogmatize, lay down the law.

**Adj.** certain, sure; assured &c. *v.*; solid, well-founded.

unqualified, absolute, positive, determinate, definite, clear, unequivocal, categorical, unmistakable, decisive, decided, ascertained.

inevitable, unavoidable, ineluctable, avoidless.

unerring, infallible; unchangeable &c. 150; to be depended on, trustworthy, reliable, bound.

un-impeachable, -deniable, -questionable; in-disputable, -contestable, -controvertible, -defeasible, -dubitable; irrefutable &c. (*proven*) 478; conclusive, without power of appeal, final.

indubious; without –, beyond a –, without a shade or shadow of- -doubt – question; past dispute; beyond all -question, – dispute; un-doubted, -contested, -questioned, -disputed; question-, doubt-less.

bigoted, fanatical, dogmatic, opinionat-ed, -ive, *doctrinaire.*

authoritative, authentic, official.

sure as -fate, – death and taxes, – a gun.

evident, self-evident, axiomatic; clear, – as day, – as the sun at noonday; obvious.

**Adv.** certainly &c. *adj.*; for certain, certes, sure, no doubt, doubtless, and no mistake, *flagrante delicto*, sure enough, to be sure, of course, as a matter of course, *à coup sur*, to a certainty, undoubtedly; in truth &c. (*truly*) 494; at -any rate, – all events; without fail; *coûte que coûte*; whatever may happen, if the worst come to the worst; come –, happen- what -may, – will; sink or swim; rain or shine.

**Phr.** *cela va sans dire*; there is -no question, – not a shadow of doubt;

scurity &c. (*darkness*) 421; ambiguity &c. (*double meaning*) 520; contingency, double contingency, possibility upon a possibility; conjecture; open question &c. (*question*) 461; *onus probandi*; blind bargain, pig in a poke, leap in the dark, something or other; needle in a bottle of hay; roving commission.

fallibility, unreliability, untrustworthiness, precariousness.

**V.** be -uncertain &c. *adj.*; wonder whether.

lose the -clue, – clew, – scent; miss one's way.

not know -what to make of &c. (*unintelligibility*) 519, – which way to turn, – whether one stands on one's head or one's heels; float in a sea of doubt, hesitate, flounder; lose -oneself, – one's head, – one's way, wander aimlessly; muddle one's brains.

render -uncertain &c. *adj.*; put out, pose, puzzle, perplex, embarrass; confuse, -found; bewilder, mystify, bother, moider, nonplus, addle the wits, throw off the scent; *spargere voces in vulgum ambiguas*; keep in suspense.

doubt &c. (*disbelieve*) 485; hang –, tremble- in the balance; depend.

**Adj.** uncertain; casual; random &c. (*aimless*) 621; changeable &c. 149.

doubtful, dubious; indecisive; unsettled, -decided, -determined; in suspense, open to discussion; controvertible; in question &c. (*inquiry*) 461; insecure, unstable.

vague; in-determinate, -definite; ambiguous, equivocal; undefin-ed, -able; confused &c. (*indistinct*) 447; mystic, mysterious, veiled, obscure, cryptic, oracular.

perplexing &c. *v.*; enigmatic, paradoxical, apocryphal, problematical, hypothetical; experimental &c. 463.

fallible, questionable, precarious, slippery, ticklish, debatable, disputable; un-reliable, -trustworthy.

contingent, – on, dependent on; subject to; dependent on circumstances; occasional; provisional.

unauth-entic, -enticated, -oritative; un-ascertained, -confirmed; undemonstrated; un-told, -counted.

in a -state of uncertainty, – cloud

[ 153 ]

the die is cast &c. (*necessity*) 601.

― maze; ignorant &c. 491; on the horns of a dilemma; afraid to say; out of one's reckoning, astray, adrift; at -sea, ― fault, ― a loss, ― one's wit's end, ― a *nonplus*; puzzled &c. *v.*; lost, abroad, *désorienté*; dis-tracted, -traught.

Adv. *pendente lite*; *sub spe rati*.

Phr. Heaven knows; who can tell? who shall decide when doctors disagree?

## Section IV. REASONING PROCESSES

**476. Reasoning. ― N.** reasoning; ratio-cination, -nalism; dialectics, in-duction, generalization.

discussion, comment; ventilation; inquiry &c. 461.

argumentation, controversy, debate; polemics, wrangling; contention &c. 720; logomachy; dis-putation, -cepta-tion; paper war.

art of reasoning, logic.

process ―, train ―, chain- of reason-ing; de-, in-duction; synthesis, analysis.

argument; case, plea, *plaidoyer*, opening; *lemma*, proposition, terms, premises, postulate, *data*, starting point, principle; inference &c. (*judg-ment*) 480.

pro-, syllogism; enthymeme, sorites, dilemma, *perilepsis, a priori* reasoning, *reductio ad absurdum*, horns of a di-lemma, *argumentum ad hominem*, com-prehensive argument.

reasoner, logician, dialectician; dis-putant; controver-sialist, -tist; wrang-ler, arguer, debater, polemic, casuist, rationalist; scientist.

logical sequence; good case; correct ―, just ―, sound ―, valid ―, cogent ―, logical ―, forcible ―, persuasive ―, per-suasory ―, consectary ―, conclusive &c. 478 ―, subtle- reasoning; force of argu-ment; strong -point, ― argument.

arguments, reasons, pros and cons.

V. reason, argue, discuss, debate, dispute, wrangle; bandy -words, ― arguments; chop logic; hold ―, carry on- an argument; controvert &c. (*deny*) 536; canvass; comment ―, moralize-upon; consider &c. (*examine*) 461.

open a -discussion, ― case; join ―, be at- issue; moot; come to the point; stir ―, agitate ―, ventilate ―, torture- a question; try conclusions; take up a -side, ― case.

**477. [The absence of reasoning.] Intuition.** [False or vicious reasoning; show of reason.] **Sophistry.―N.** intui-tion, instinct, association; presenti-ment; rule of thumb.

sophistry, paralogy, perversion, casu-istry, jesuitry, equivocation, evasion, mental reservation; chicane, -ry; quid-dit, quiddity; mystification; special pleading; speciousness &c. *adj.*; non-sense &c. 497; word-, tongue-fence.

false ―, vicious- reasoning; *petitio principii, ignoratio elenchi*; *post hoc ergo propter hoc*; *non sequitur, ignotum per ignotius.*

misjudgment &c. 481; false teaching &c. 538.

sophism, solecism, paralogism; quib-ble, quirk, *elenchus*, elench, fallacy, *quodlibet*, subterfuge, subtlety, quillet; inconsistency, antilogy; 'a mockery, a delusion and a snare'; claptrap, mere words; 'lame and impotent conclusion.'

meshes ―, cobwebs- of sophistry; flaw in an argument; weak point, bad case.

over-refinement; hair-splitting &c. *v.*

sophist, casuist, paralogist.

V. judge -intuitively, ― by intuition; hazard a proposition, talk at random.

reason -ill, ― falsely &c. *adj.*; paralo-gize; misjudge &c. 481.

pervert, quibble; equivocate, mysti-fy, evade, elude; gloss over, varnish; misteach &c. 538; mislead &c. (*error*) 495; cavil, refine, subtilize, split hairs; misrepresent &c. (*lie*) 544.

beg the question, reason in a circle, cut blocks with a razor, beat about the bush, play fast and loose, blow hot and cold, prove that black is white and white black, travel out of the record, *parler à tort et à travers*, put oneself out of court, not have a leg to stand on.

Adj. intuitive, instinctive, impulsive;

contend, take one's stand upon, in-
sist, lay stress on; infer &c. 480.

follow from &c. (*demonstration*) 478.

**Adj.** rational; reasoning &c. *v.*;
rationalistic; argumentative, contro-
versial, dialectic, polemical; discurs-
ory, -ive; disputatious.

debatable, controvertible.

logical; in-, de-ductive; synthetic,
analytic; relevant &c. 23.

**Adv.** for, because, hence, whence,
seeing that, since, sith, then, thence,
so; for -that, – this, – which- reason;
for-, inasmuch as; whereas, *ex concesso*,
considering, in consideration of; there-,
where-fore; consequently, *ergo*, thus,
accordingly; *a fortiori*.

in -conclusion, – fine; finally, after
all, *au bout du compte*, on the whole,
taking one thing with another.

rationally &c. *adj.*

---

**478. Demonstration.—N.** demon-
stration, proof; conclusiveness &c. *adj.*;
*apodixis*, probation, comprobation.

logic of facts &c. (*evidence*) 467; *ex-
perimentum crucis* &c. (*test*) 463; argu-
ment &c. 476; irrefragability.

**V.** demonstrate, prove, establish,
make good; show; evince &c. (*be evi-
dence of*) 467; verify &c. 467; settle
the question, reduce to demonstration,
set the question at rest.

make out, – a case; prove one's
point, have the best of the argument;
draw a conclusion &c. (*judge*) 480.

follow, – of course; stand to reason;
hold -good, – water.

**Adj.** demonstra-ting &c. *v.*, -tive,
-ble; probative, unanswerable, con-
clusive; apodictic, -al; irre-sistible,
-futable, -fragable, undeniable.

categorical, decisive, crucial.

demonstrated &c. *v.*; proven; un-
confuted, -answered, -refuted; evident
&c. 474.

deducible, consequential, consectary,
inferential, following.

**Adv.** of course, in consequence, con
sequently, as a matter of course.

**Phr.** *probatum est*; there is nothing
more to be said, Q.E.D., it must follow.

independent of –, anterior to- reason;
gratuitous, hazarded; unconnected.

unreasonable, illogical, false, un-
sound, invalid; unwarranted, not fol-
lowing; inconsequent, -ial; inconsistent,
incongruous; abson-ous, -ant; unscien-
tific; untenable, inconclusive, incorrect;
fall-acious, -ible; groundless, unproved.

deceptive, sophistical, sophisticated,
casuistical, jesuitical; illus-ive, -ory;
specious, hollow, plausible, *ad captan-
dum*, evasive; irrelevant &c. 10.

weak, feeble, poor, flimsy, loose,
vague, irrational; nonsensical &c. (*ab-
surd*) 497; foolish &c. (*imbecile*) 499;
frivolous, pettifogging, quibbling; fine-
spun, over-refined.

at the end of one's tether, *au bout de
son latin*.

**Adv.** intuitively &c. *adj.*; by intui-
tion; illogically &c. *adj.*

**Phr.** *non constat*; that goes for
nothing.

---

**479. Confutation.—N.** con-, re-futa-
tion; answer, complete answer; dis-
proof, conviction, redargution, inval-
idation; expos-ure, -ition; clincher;
retort; *reductio ad absurdum*; knock
down –, *tu quoque*- argument.

**V.** con-, re-fute; parry, negative, dis-
prove, redargue, expose, show the
fallacy of, rebut, defeat; demolish &c.
(*destroy*) 162; over-throw, -turn; scatter
to the winds, explode, invalidate; si-
lence; put –, reduce- to silence; clinch
-an argument, – a question; give one
a set down, stop the mouth, shut up;
have, – on the hip; get the better of;
confound, convince.

not leave a leg to stand on, cut the
ground from under one's feet.

be confuted &c.; fail; expose –,
show- one's weak point.

**Adj.** confut-ing, -ed &c. *v.*; capable
of refutation; re-, con-futable.

condemned -on one's own showing,
– out of one's own mouth.

**Phr.** the argument falls to the
ground. *cadit quæstio*, it does not hold
water, '*suo sibi gladio hunc jugulo.*'

---

## Section V. Results of Reasoning

**480. Judgement.** [Conclusion.]—**N.** result, conclusion, upshot; deduction, inference, ergotism, illation; corollary, porism; moral.

estimation, valuation, appreciation, judication; di-, ad-judication; arbitrament, -ement, -ation; assessment, ponderation.

award, estimate; review, criticism, *critique*, notice, report.

decision, determination, judgment, finding, verdict, sentence, decree, – nisi, – absolute, – interlocutory; *dictum*; *res judicata*.

*plébiscite*, referendum, voice, casting vote; vote &c. (*choice*) 609; opinion &c. (*belief*) 484; good judgment &c. (*wisdom*) 498.

judge, jurist, umpire; arbi-ter, -trator; assessor, referee; censor, reviewer, critic; *connoisseur*; commentator &c. 524; inspector, inspecting officer.

**V.** judge, conclude; come to –, draw –, arrive at- a conclusion; ascertain, determine, make up one's mind.

deduce, derive, gather, collect, draw an inference, make a deduction, weet, ween.

form an estimate, estimate, size up, appreciate, value, count, assess, rate, rank, account; regard, consider, think of; look upon &c. (*believe*) 484.

settle; pass –, give- an opinion; decide, try, pronounce, rule; pass -judgment, – sentence; sentence, doom; find; give –, deliver- judgment; adjud-ge, -icate; arbitrate, award, report; bring in a verdict; make absolute, set a question at rest; confirm &c. (*assent*) 488.

comment, criticize; review, pass under review &c. (*examine*) 457; investigate &c. (*inquire*) 461.

hold the scales, sit in judgment; try –, hear- a cause.

**Adj.** judging &c. *v.*; judicious &c. (*wise*) 498; determinate, conclusive, censorious, critical &c. 932.

**Adv.** on the whole, all things considered.

**481. Misjudgment. — N.** misjudgment, obliquity of –, warped- judgment; mis-calculation, -computation, -conception &c. (*error*) 495; hasty conclusion.

prejud-gment, -ication, -ice; foregone conclusion; pre-notion, -vention, -conception, -dilection, -possession, -apprehension, -sumption, -sentiment; fixed –, preconceived- idea; *idée fixe*; *mentis gratissimus error*; fool's paradise.

*esprit de corps*, party spirit, race –, class- prejudice, partisanship, clannishness, *prestige*.

bias, warp, twist; hobby, fad, whim, craze, quirk, crotchet, partiality, infatuation, blind side, mote in the eye.

one-sided –, partial –, narrow –, confined –, superficial- -views, – ideas, – conceptions, – notions; narrow mind; bigotry &c. (*obstinacy*) 606; *odium theologicum*; pedantry; hypercriticism. *doctrinaire* &c. (*positive*) 474.

**V.** mis-judge, -estimate, -think, -conjecture, -conceive &c. (*error*) 495; fly in the face of facts; mis-calculate, -reckon, -compute.

overestimate &c. 482; underestimate &c. 483.

pre-, fore-judge; pre-suppose, -sume, -judicate; dogmatize; have a -bias &c. *n.*; have only one idea; *jurare in verba magistri*, run away with the notion; jump –, rush- to a conclusion; look only at one side of the shield; view -with jaundiced eye, – through distorting spectacles; not see beyond one's nose; *dare pondus fumo*; get the wrong sow by the ear &c. (*blunder*) 699.

give a -bias, – twist; bias, warp, twist; pre-judice, -possess.

**Adj.** misjudging &c. *v.*; ill-judging, wrong-headed; prejudiced, prejudicial, &c. *v.*; jaundiced; short-sighted, purblind; partial, one-sided, superficial.

narrow-minded; confined, insular, provincial, parochial, illiberal, intolerant, narrow, besotted, infatuated, fanatical, cracked, warped, *entêté*, positive, dogmatic, dictatorial; conceited; opin-, opini-ative; opinion-ed, -ate, -ative, -ated; self-opinioned, wedded to an opinion, *opiniâtre*; bigoted &c. (*obstinate*) 606; crotchety, fussy, impracticable; unreason-able, -ing; stupid &c. 499; credulous &c. 486.

    misjudged &c. *v.*

    Adv. *ex parte.*

    Phr. nothing like leather; the wish the father to the thought.

**480a. [Result of search or inquiry.] Discovery.—N.** discovery, invention, detection, disenchantment, disclosure, find, ascertainment, revelation.

    trover &c. 775.

    **V.** discover, find, determine, evolve; fix upon; find –, trace –, make –, hunt –, fish –, worm –, ferret –, root- out; fathom; bring –, draw- out; educe, elicit, bring to light, invent; dig –, grub –, fish- up; unearth, disinter.

    solve, resolve; un-riddle, -ravel, -lock; pick –, open- the lock; find a -clue, – clew- to; interpret &c. 522; disclose &c. 529.

    trace, get at; hit it, have it; lay one's -finger, – hands- upon; spot; get –, arrive- at the -truth &c. 494; put the saddle on the right horse, hit the right nail on the head.

    be near the truth. burn; smoke, scent, sniff, smell a rat.

    open the eyes to; see -through, – daylight, – in its true colours, – the cloven foot; detect; catch, – tripping.

    pitch –, fall –, light –, hit –, stumble –, pop- upon; come across; meet –, fall in- with.

    recognize, realize, verify, make certain of, identify.

    **Int.** *eureka!*

**482. Overestimation.—N.** overestimation &c. *v.*; exaggeration &c. 549; vanity &c. 880; optim-, pessim-ism, -ist; megalomania.

    much -cry and little wool, – ado about nothing; storm in a teacup; fine talking, rodomontade, gush, hot air, gas, bombast.

    egotism &c. 880; boasting &c. 884.

    **V.** over-estimate, -rate, -value, -prize, -weigh, -reckon, -strain, -praise; estimate too highly, attach too much importance to, make mountains of molehills, catch at straws; strain, magnify; exaggerate &c. 549; set too high a value upon; think –, make- -much, – too much- of; outreckon.

    extol, – to the skies; make the -most, – best, – worst- of, eulogize, panegyrize, gush, puff, boost; make two bites of a cherry.

**483. Underestimation.—N.** underestimation; depreciation &c. (*detraction*) 934; pessim-ism, -ist; undervaluing &c. *v.*; modesty &c. 881.

    **V.** under-rate, -estimate, -value, -reckon; depreciate; disparage &c. (*detract*) 934; not do justice to; mis-, dis-prize; ridicule &c. 856; slight &c. (*despise*) 930; neglect &c. 460; slur over, under-state.

    make -light, – little, – nothing, – no account- of; minimize, belittle, run down, think nothing of; set -no store by, – at naught; shake off as dewdrops from the lion's mane.

    **Adj.** depreciat-ing, -ed, -ive, -ory, &c. *v.*; un-appreciated, -valued, -prized; pejorative.

———

have too high an opinion of oneself &c. (*vanity*) 880.

    Adj. overestimated &c. *v.*; oversensitive &c. (*sensibility*) 822; inflated, puffed up, exaggerated &c. 549.

    Phr. all his geese are swans; *parturiunt montes.*

**484. Belief.—N.** belief; credence; credit; assurance; faith, trust, troth, confidence, presumption, sanguine expectation &c. (*hope*) 858; dependence on, reliance on.

persuasion, conviction, convincement, plerophory, self-conviction; certainty &c. 474; opinion, mind, view; conception, thinking; impression &c. (*idea*) 453; surmise &c. 514; conclusion &c. (*judgment*) 480.

tenet, dogma, principle, way of thinking; popular belief &c. (*assent*) 488.

firm -, implicit -, settled -, fixed -, rooted -, deep-rooted -, staunch -, unshaken -, steadfast -, inveterate -, calm -, sober -, dispassionate -, impartial -, well-founded- -belief, - opinion &c.; *uberrima fides*.

system of opinions, school, doctrine, articles, canons; declaration -, profession- of faith; tenets, *credenda*, creed; thirty-nine articles &c. (*orthodoxy*) 983a; catechism; assent &c. 488; *propaganda* &c. (*teaching*) 537.

credibility &c. (*probability*) 472.

**V.** believe, credit; give -faith, - credit, - credence- to; see, realize; assume, receive; set down -, take- for; have -, take- it; consider, esteem, presume.

count -, depend -, calculate -, pin one's faith -, reckon -, lean -, build -, rely -, rest- upon; lay one's account for; make sure of.

make oneself easy -about, - on that score; take on -trust, - credit; take for -granted, –gospel; allow -, attach-some weight to.

know, - for certain; have -, make-no doubt; doubt not; be - rest- -assured &c. *adj.*; persuade -, assure -, satisfy-oneself; make up one's mind.

give one credit for; confide -, believe -, put one's trust- in; place -, repose- implicit confidence in; take -one's word for, - at one's word; place reliance on, rely upon, swear by, pay regard to.

think, hold; take, - it; opine, be of opinion, conceive, trow, ween, fancy, apprehend; have -, hold -, possess -, entertain -, adopt -, imbibe -, embrace

**485. Unbelief. Doubt.—N.** un-, dis-. mis-belief; discredit, miscreance; infidelity &c. (*irreligion*) 989; dissent &c. 489; change of -opinion &c. 484; retraction &c. 607.

doubt &c. (*uncertainty*) 475; skepticism, misgiving, demur; dis-, mis-trust; misdoubt, suspicion, jealousy, scruple, qualm; *onus probandi*.

incredib-ility, -leness; incredulity; unbeliever &c. 487.

**V.** dis-believe, -credit; not -believe &c. 484; misbelieve; refuse to admit &c. (*dissent*) 489; refuse to believe &c. (*incredulity*) 487.

doubt; be -doubtful &c. (*uncertain*) 475; doubt the truth of; be -skeptical as to &c. *adj.*; diffide; dis-, mis-trust; suspect, smoke, scent, smell a rat; have -, harbour -, entertain- -doubts, - suspicions; have one's doubts.

demur, stick at, pause, hesitate, scruple, waver, stop and consider.

hang in -suspense, - doubt.

throw doubt upon, raise a question; bring -, call- in question; question, challenge, query; dispute; deny &c. 536; cavil; cause -, raise -, start -, suggest -, awake- a -doubt, - suspicion; ergotize.

startle, stagger; shake -, stagger-one's faith, - belief.

**Adj.** unbelieving; incredulous -, skeptical- as to; distrustful -, shy -, suspicious- of; doubting &c. *v.*

doubtful &c. (*uncertain*) 475; disputable; unworthy -, undeserving- of -belief &c. 484; questionable; sus-pect, -picious; open to -suspicion, - doubt; staggering, hard to believe, incredible, not to be believed, inconceivable.

fallible &c. (*uncertain*) 475; unde-monstrable; controvertible &c. (*untrue*) 495.

**Adv.** *cum grano salis.*

**Phr.** *fronti nulla fides; nimium ne crede colori; 'timeo Danaos et dona ferentes'; credat Judæus Apella;* let those believe who may.

–, get hold of –, hazard –, foster –, nurture –, cherish- -a belief,
– an opinion &c. *n.*

view –, consider –, take –, hold –, conceive –, regard -. esteem –,
deem –, look upon –, account –, set down- as; surmise &c. 514.

get –, take- it into one's head; come round to an opinion; swallow
&c. (*credulity*) 486.

cause to -be believed &c. *v.*; satisfy, persuade, have the ear of,
gain the confidence of, assure; con-vince, -vict, -vert; put across,
sell; wean, bring round; bring –, put –, win- over; indoctrinate &c.
(*teach*) 537; cram down the throat; produce –, carry- conviction;
bring –, drive- home to.

go down, find credence, pass current; be -received &c. *v.*, – current
&c. *adj.*; possess –, take hold of –, take possession of- the mind.

**Adj.** believing &c. *v.*; certain, sure, assured, positive, cocksure.
satisfied, confident, unhesitating, convinced, secure.

under the impression; impressed –, imbued –, penetrated- with.

confiding, trustful, suspectless; unsusp-ecting, -icious; void of
suspicion; credulous &c. 486; wedded to.

believed &c. *v.*; accredited, putative; unsuspected.

worthy of –, deserving of –, commanding- -belief, – confidence;
credible, reliable, trusted, trustworthy, to be depended on, un-
doubted; satisfactory; probable &c. 472; fiduci-al, -ary; persuasive,
impressive.

relating to belief, doctrinal.

**Adv.** in the -opinion, – eyes- of; *me judice*; me-seems, -thinks;
to the best of one's belief; I -dare say, – doubt not, – have no
doubt, – am sure; in my opinion; sure enough &c. (*certainty*) 474;
depend –, rely- upon it; be –, rest- assured; I'll warrant you &c.
(*affirmation*) 535.

---

**486. Credulity.—N.** credul-ity, -ous-
ness &c. *adj.*; gull-, cull-ibility; gross
credulity, infatuation; self-delusion,
-deception; blind reasoning; supersti-
tion; one's blind side; bigotry &c.
(*obstinacy*) 606; hyper-orthodoxy &c.
984; misjudgment &c. 481.

credulous person &c. (*dupe*) 547.

**V.** be -credulous &c. *adj.*; *jurare in
verba magistri*; follow implicitly; swal-
low, – whole, gulp down; take on trust;
take for -granted, – gospel; run away
with -a notion, – an idea; jump –,
rush- to a conclusion; think the moon
is made of green cheese; take –, grasp-
the shadow for the substance; catch at
straws.

impose upon &c. (*deceive*) 545.

**Adj.** credulous, gullible; easily -de-
ceived &c. 545; simple, green, soft,
childish, silly, stupid; over-credulous,
-confident; infatuated, superstitious; confiding &c. (*believing*) 484.

**Phr.** the wish the father to the thought; *credo quia impossibile.*

**487. Incredulity.—N.** incredul-ous-
ness, -ity; skepticism, pyrrhonism;
want of faith &c. (*irreligion*) 989.

suspiciousness &c. *adj.*; scrupulosity;
suspicion &c. (*unbelief*) 485; dissent
&c. 489.

unbeliever, skeptic, aporetic; atheist,
agnostic, infidel, disbeliever, misbe-
liever, pyrrhonist &c. 989; heretic &c.
(*heterodox*) 984.

**V.** be -incredulous &c. *adj.*; distrust
&c. (*disbelieve*) 485; refuse to believe;
shut one's -eyes, – ears- to; turn a deaf
ear to; hold aloof; ignore; *nullius jurare
in verba magistri.*

**Adj.** incredulous, skeptical, unbeliev-
ing, inconvincible; hard –, shy- of
belief; suspicious, scrupulous, distrust-
ful, heterodox &c. 984.

**488. Assent.—N.** assent, -ment; acquiescence, admission; nod; ac-, con-cord, -cordance; agreement &c. 23; affirm-ance, -ation; recognition, acknowledgment, avowal; confession, – of faith.

unanimity, common consent, *consensus*, acclamation, chorus, *vox populi*; popular –, current- -belief, – opinion; public opinion; concurrence &c. (*of causes*) 178; co-operation &c. (*voluntary*) 709.

ratification, confirmation, corroboration, approval, acceptance, *visa*; indorsement, &c. (*record*) 551; O.K.

consent &c. (*compliance*) 762.

affirmant, consenter, covenanter, subscriber, endorser, upholder.

**V.** assent; give –, yield –, nod- assent; acquiesce; agree &c. 23; receive, accept, accede, accord, concur, lend oneself to, consent, coincide, reciprocate, go with; be -at one with &c. *adj.*; go along –, chime in –, strike in –, close- with; echo, enter into one's views, agree in opinion; vote –, give one's voice- for; recognize; subscribe –, conform –, defer- to; say -yes, – ditto, – amen, – aye- to; to O.K.

acknowledge, own, admit, allow, avow, confess; concede &c. (*yield*) 762; come round to; abide by; permit &c. 760.

come to –, arrive at- -an understanding, – terms, – an agreement.

con-, af-firm; ratify, approve, endorse, countersign; visa; corroborate &c. 467.

go –, swim- with the stream, float with the current; be in the fashion, join in the chorus; be in every mouth.

**Adj.** assenting &c. *v.*; of one -accord, – mind; of the same mind, at one with, agreed, acquiescent, content; willing &c. 602.

un-contradicted, -challenged, -questioned, -controverted.

carried –, agreed- *-nem. con.* &c. *adv.*; unanimous; agreed on all hands, carried by acclamation.

affirmative &c. 535.

**Adv.** yes, yea, ay, aye, true; good; well; very -well, – true; well and good; just- so; to be sure, surely, 'thou hast said'; truly, exactly, precisely,

**489. Dissent.—N.** dissent; discordance &c. (*disagreement*) 24; difference –, diversity- of opinion.

non-conformity &c. (*heterodoxy*) 984; protestantism, recusancy, schism; disaffection; secession &c. 624; recantation &c. 607.

dissension &c. (*discord*) 713; discontent &c. 832; cavilling.

protest; contradiction &c. (*denial*) 536; non-compliance &c. (*rejection*) 764; disapprobation &c. 932; hartal.

dissent-ient, -er; non-juror, -content; recusant, sectary, schismatic, protestant, non-conformist, separatist, non-co-operator, conscientious objector, passive resister.

**V.** dissent, demur; call in question &c. (*doubt*) 485; differ in opinion, disagree; say -no &c. 536; refuse -assent, – to admit, cavil, protest, raise one's voice against, make bold to differ; repudiate; contradict &c. (*deny*) 536; agree to differ.

have no notion of, differ *toto cœlo*; revolt -at, – from the idea.

shake the head, shrug the shoulders; look -askance, – askant.

secede; recant &c. 607.

**Adj.** dissenting &c. *v.*; negative &c. 536; diss-ident, -entient; unconsenting &c. (*refusing*) 764; non-content, -juring; protestant, recusant; uncon-vinced, -verted.

unavowed, unacknowledged; out of the question.

discontented &c. 832; unwilling &c. 603; extorted.

sectarian, denominational, schismatic, heterodox, intolerant.

**Adv.** no &c. 536; at -variance, – issue- with; under protest; *non placet*.

**Int.** God forbid! not for the world; not on your life; I beg to differ; I'll be hanged if; never tell me; your humble servant, pardon me; tell that to the marines.

**Phr.** many men many minds; *quot homines tot sententiæ*; *tant s'en faut*; *il s'en faut bien.*

that's just it, indeed, certainly, certes, *ex concesso*; of course, unquestionably, assuredly, no doubt, doubtless, undoubtedly.

be it so; so -be it, – let it be, so mote it be; amen; with all my heart; willingly &c. 602.

affirmatively, in the affirmative.

with one -consent, – voice, – accord; unanimously, *unâ voce*, by common consent, in chorus, to a man, *nem. con.*; *nemine -contradicente*, – *dissentiente*; without a dissentient voice; as one man, one and all, on all hands.

**490. Knowledge.**—**N.** knowledge; cogn-izance, -ition, -oscence; acquaintance, experience, ken, privity, insight, familiarity; com-, ap-prehension; recognition; appreciation &c. (*judgment*) 480; intuition; consci-ence, -ousness; perception, precognition; acroamatics.

light, enlightenment; glimpse, inkling; side light; glimmer, -ing; dawn; scent, suspicion; impression &c. (*idea*) 453; discovery &c. 480a.

system –, body- of knowledge; science, philosophy, pansophy; theory, etiology; circle of the sciences; pandect, doctrine, body of doctrine; cy-, ency-clopædia; school &c. (*system of opinions*) 484.

tree of knowledge; republic of letters &c. (*language*) 560.

erudition, learning, lore, scholarship, reading, letters; literature; book-learning, bookishness; biblio-mania, -latry; information, general information; store of -knowledge &c.; education &c. (*teaching*) 537; culture, attainments; acqui-rements, -sitions; accomplishments, proficiency; practical knowledge &c. (*skill*) 698; higher education, liberal education; dilettantism; rudiments &c. (*beginning*) 66.

deep –, profound –, solid –, accurate –, acroatic –, acroamatic –, vast –, extensive –, encyclopædical- -knowledge, – learning; omniscience, pantology.

march of intellect; progress –, advance- of -science, – learning; schoolmaster abroad.

**V.** know, ken, scan, wot; wot –, be aware &c. *adj.*- of; ween, weet, trow, have, possess.

conceive; ap-, com-prehend; take, realize, understand, appreciate; fathom, make out; recognize, discern, perceive, see, get a sight of, experience.

**491. Ignorance.** — **N.** ignorance, nescience, *tabula rasa*, crass ignorance, *ignorance crasse*; unacquaintance; unconsciousness &c. *adj.*; dark-, blindness; incomprehension, inexperience, simplicity.

unknown quantities, $x$, $y$, $z$.

sealed book, *terra incognita*, virgin soil, unexplored ground; dark ages.

[Imperfect knowledge] smattering, superficiality, half-learning, sciolism, glimmering; bewilderment &c. (*uncertainty*) 475; incapacity.

[Affectation of knowledge] pedantry; charlatan-ry, -ism.

**V.** be -ignorant &c. *adj.*; not -know &c. 490; know -not, – not what, – nothing of; have no -idea, – notion, – conception; not have the remotest idea; not know chalk from cheese.

ignore, be blind to; keep in ignorance &c. (*conceal*) 528.

see through a glass darkly; have a -film over the eyes, – glimmering &c. *n.*; wonder whether; not know what to make of &c. (*unintelligibility*) 519; not pretend –, not take upon oneself- to say.

**Adj.** ignorant, nescient; un-knowing, -aware, -acquainted, -apprized, -witting, -weeting, -conscious; wit-, weetless; a stranger to; unconversant.

un-informed, -cultivated, -versed, -instructed, -taught, -initiated, -tutored, -schooled, -guided, -enlightened; Philistine; behind the age.

shallow, superficial, green, rude, empty, half-learned, illiterate; un-read, -informed, -educated, -learned, -lettered, -bookish; empty-headed; low brow; pedantic.

in the dark; be-nighted, -lated; blind-ed, -fold; hoodwinked; misinformed; *au bout de son latin*, at the

know full well; have –, possess- some knowledge of; be -*au courant* &c. *adj.*; have -in one's head, – at one's fingers' ends; know by -heart, – rote; be master of; *connaître le dessous des cartes*, know what's what &c. 698.

see one's way; learn, discover &c. 480*a*.

come to one's knowledge &c. (*information*) 527.

**Adj.** knowing &c. *v.*; cognitive; acroamatic.

aware –, cognizant –, conscious- of; acquainted –, made acquainted- with; privy –, no stranger- to; *au -fait*, – *courant*; in the secret; up –, alive- to; sensible of; behind the -scenes, – curtain; let into; apprised –, informed- of; undeceived.

proficient –, versed –, read –, forward –, strong –, at home- in; conversant –, familiar- with.

erudite, instructed, learned, lettered, educated; high-brow; well-conned, -informed, -read, -grounded, -educated; enlightened, shrewd, insightful, *savant*, blue, bookish, scholastic, solid, profound, deep-read, book-learned; accomplished &c. (*skilful*) 698; omniscient; self-taught, -educated.

known &c. *v.*; ascertained, well-known, recognized, received, notorious, noted; proverbial; familiar, – as household words, to every schoolboy; hackneyed, trite, commonplace.

knowable, cogn-oscible, -izable.

**Adv.** to –, to the best of- one's knowledge.

**Phr.** one's eyes being opened &c. (*disclosure*) 529.

end of his tether; at fault; at sea &c. (*uncertain*) 475; caught tripping.

un-known, -apprehended, -explained, -ascertained, -investigated, -explored, -heard of, -perceived; concealed &c. 528; novel.

**Adv.** ignorantly &c. *adj.*; unawares; for -anything, – aught- one knows; not that one knows.

**Int.** God –, Heaven –, the Lord –, nobody- knows.

**Phr.** a little learning is a dangerous thing.

---

**492. Scholar—N.** scholar, *connoisseur*, *savant*, pundit, schoolman, professor, graduate, wrangler, moonshee; academ-ician, -ist; fellow, don, post graduate, advanced student; master –, bachelor- of arts; doctor, licentiate, gownsman; philo-sopher, -math; scientist, clerk; soph, -ist, -ister; linguist, classicist; glosso-, etymo-, philologist; philologer; lexico-, glosso-grapher; scholiast, commentator, annotator, grammarian; *littérateur, literati, dilettanti, illuminati*; Mezzofanti, admirable Crichton, Mæcenas.

book-worm, *helluo librorum*, biblio-phile, -maniac; blue-stocking, *bas-bleu*; big-wig, learned Theban.

learned –, literary- man; *homo multarum literarum*; man of -learning, – letters, – education; high-brow, intelligentsia.

antiquar-ian, -y; archæologist; sage &c. (*wise man*) 500.

pedant, *doctrinaire*; pedagogue, Dr. Pangloss; pantologist.

teacher &c. 540; schoolboy &c. (*learner*) 541.

**Adj.** learned &c. 490; brought up at the feet of Gamaliel.

**493. Ignoramus.—N.** ignoramus, illiterate, moron, dunce, numskull, wooden spoon; no scholar.

sciolist, smatterer, dabbler, half-scholar; *charlatan*; wiseacre.

novice, griffin; greenhorn &c. (*dupe*) 547; tyro &c. (*learner*) 541.

lubber &c. (*bungler*) 701; fool &c. 501; pedant &c. 492.

**Adj.** bookless, shallow, simple, dense, dumb, thick, dull, ignorant &c. 491.

---

**494. [Object of knowledge.] Truth.**
—**N.** fact, reality &c. (*existence*) 1;
plain matter of fact; nature &c. (*principle*) 5; truth, verity; gospel; orthodoxy &c. 983a; authenticity; veracity
&c. 543.

accuracy, exactitude; exact-, precise-ness &c. *adj.*; precision, delicacy;
rigour, mathematical precision, punctuality; clockwork precision &c. (*regularity*) 80.

orthology; *ipsissima verba*; letter of
the law, realism.

plain -, honest -, sober -, naked -,
unalloyed -, unqualified -, stern -,
exact -, intrinsic- truth; *nuda veritas*;
the very thing; not an -illusion &c.
495; real Simon Pure; unvarnished
tale; the truth, the whole truth and
nothing but the truth; just the thing.

**V.** be -true &c. *adj.*, – the case; stand
the test; have the true ring; hold
-good, – true, – water; conform to rule.

render -, prove- -true &c. *adj.*; substantiate &c. (*evidence*) 467.

get at the truth &c. (*discover*) 480a.

**Adj.** real, actual &c. (*existing*) 1;
veritable, true; certain &c. 474; substantially -, categorically- true &c.;
true -to the letter, – to life, – to scale,
– the facts, – as gospel; unimpeachable;
veracious &c. 543; unre-, uncon-futed;
un-ideal, -imagined; realistic.

exact, accurate, definite, precise, well
defined, just, right, correct, strict,
severe; close &c. (*similar*) 17; literal;
rigid, rigorous; scrupulous &c. (*conscientious*) 939; religiously exact, punctual, mathematical, scientific; faithful,
constant, unerring; curious, particular,
punctilious, meticulous, nice, delicate,
fine.

genuine, authentic, legitimate, pukka; orthodox &c. 983a; official, *ex
officio*.

pure, natural, sound, sterling; unsophisticated. -adulterated, -varnished,
-coloured; in its true colours.

well-grounded, -founded; solid, substantial, tangible, valid; undis-torted,
-guised; un-affected, -exaggerated, -romantic, -flattering.

**Adv.** truly &c. *adj.*; verily, indeed,
in reality; as a matter of fact; beyond

**495. Error.**—**N.** error, fallacy; misconception, -apprehension, -understanding; inexactness &c. *adj.*; laxity;
misconstruction &c. (*misinterpretation*)
523; miscomputation &c. (*misjudgment*) 481; *non-sequitur* &c. 477; misstatement, -report; anachronism; malapropism.

mistake; miss, fault, blunder, boner,
bloomer, howler, *quid pro quo*, cross
purposes, oversight, misprint, *erratum*,
*corrigendum*, slip, blot, flaw, loose
thread; trip, stumble &c. (*failure*) 732;
botchery &c. (*want of skill*) 699; slip
of the -tongue, – pen; *lapsus -linguæ*,
– *calami*, clerical error; bull &c. (*absurdity*) 497.

il-, de-lusion; false -impression, –
idea; bubble; self-deceit, -deception;
warped notion; mists of error; superstition, exploded notion.

heresy &c. (*heterodoxy*) 984; hallucination &c. (*insanity*) 503; false light
&c. (*fallacy of vision*) 443; dream &c;
(*fancy*) 515; fable &c. (*untruth*) 546;
bias &c. (*misjudgment*) 481; misleading
&c. *v.*

**V.** be -erroneous &c. *adj.*

cause error; mis-lead, -guide; lead
-astray, – into error; beguile, misinform &c. (*misteach*) 538; delude; give
a false -impression, – idea; falsify,
garble, misstate; deceive &c. 545; lie
&c. 544.

err; be -in error &c. *adj.*, – mistaken
&c. *v.*; be deceived &c. (*duped*) 547;
mistake, receive a false impression, deceive oneself; fall into -, lie under -,
labour under- -an error &c. *n.*; be in
the wrong, blunder; mis-apprehend,
-conceive, -understand, -reckon, -count,
-calculate &c. (*misjudge*) 481.

play -, be- at cross purposes &c.
(*misinterpret*) 523.

trip, stumble; lose oneself &c. (*uncertainty*) 475; go astray; fail &c. 732;
take the wrong sow by the ear &c.
(*mismanage*) 699; put the saddle on
the wrong horse; reckon without one's
host; take the shadow for the substance &c. (*credulity*) 486; dream &c.
(*imagine*) 515.

**Adj.** erroneous, untrue, false, devoid
of truth, fallacious, faulty, apocryphal.

-doubt, – question; with truth &c. (*veracity*) 543; certainly &c. (*certain*) 474; actually &c. (*existence*) 1; in effect &c. (*intrinsically*) 5.

exactly &c. *adj.*; *ad amussim*; *verbatim*, – *et literatim*; word for word, literally, *literatim, totidem verbis, sic,* to the letter, chapter and verse, *ipsissimis verbis*; *ad unguem*; to an inch; to a -nicety, – hair, – tittle, – turn, – T; *au pied de la lettre*; neither more nor less; in -every respect, – all respects; *sous tous les rapports*; at -any rate, – all events; strictly speaking.

Phr. the -truth, – fact- is; *rem acu tetigisti.*

_____

scent; in the wrong box; at cross purposes, all in the wrong, all abroad, at sea.

Adv. more or less.

**496. Maxim.—N.** maxim, aphorism; apo-, apoph-thegm; *dictum*, saying, gnome, adage, saw, proverb, epigram; sentence, *mot*, motto, word, by-word, precept, moral, phylactery, *protasis*, brocard.

axiom, postulate, theorem, *scholium*, truism.

reflection &c. (*idea*) 453; conclusion &c. (*judgment*) 480; golden rule &c. (*precept*) 697; principle, *principia*; profession of faith &c. (*belief*) 484; formula.

wise –, sage –, received –, admitted –, recognized- maxim &c.; true –, common –, hackneyed –, trite –, commonplace- saying &c.

Adj. aphoristic, proverbial, phylacteric; axiomatic, gnomic.

Adv. as -the saying is, – they say.

_____

unreal, ungrounded, groundless; unsubstantial &c. 4; heretical &c. (*heterodox*) 984; unsound; illogical &c. 477; wrong.

in-, un-exact; in-accurate, -correct; indefinite &c. (*uncertain*) 475.

illus-ive, -ory; delusive; mock; ideal &c. (*imaginary*) 515; spurious &c. 545; deceitful &c. 544; perverted.

controvertible, unsustain-able, -ed; unauthenticated, untrustworthy.

exploded, refuted, discarded.

in –, under an- error &c. *n.*; mistaken &c. *v.*; tripping &c. *v.*; out, – in one's reckoning; aberrant; beside –, wide of the- -mark, – truth; astray &c. (*at fault*) 475; on -a false, – the wrong-

**497. Absurdity.—N.** absurd-ity, -ness &c. *adj.*; imbecility &c. 499; alogy, nonsense, paradox, inconsistency; stultiloqu-y, -ence, futility.

blunder, muddle, bull; Irish-, Hibernic-ism; slip-slop; anticlimax, bathos; sophism &c. 477.

farce, burlesque, *galimatias, amphigouri*, rhapsody; farrago &c. (*disorder*) 59; extravagance, romance; sciomachy.

joke, catch, sell, pun, verbal quibble, macaronic.

jargon, fustian, twaddle &c. (*no meaning*) 517; exaggeration &c. 549; moonshine, stuff; mare's nest.

vagary, tomfoolery, mummery, monkey trick, practical joke, *boutade, escapade.*

V. play the fool &c. 499; stultify, blunder, muddle; joke; talk nonsense, *parler à tort et à travers*; *battre la campagne*; be -absurd &c. *adj.*

Adj. absurd, nonsensical, preposterous, egregious, senseless, farcical, inconsistent, ridiculous, extravagant, quibbling, futile; macaronic, punning, paradoxical.

foolish &c. 499; sophistical &c. 477; unmeaning &c. 517; without rhyme or reason; fantastic.

Int. fiddle-de-dee! pish! pish and tush! pho! stuff and nonsense! rubbish! rot! bosh! in the name of the Prophet—figs!

Phr. *credat Judæus Apella*; tell it to the marines.

### Faculties

**498. Intelligence. Wisdom.—N.** intelligence, capacity, comprehension,

**499. Imbecility. Folly.—N.** want of -intelligence &c. 498, – intellect &c.

understanding; intellect &c. 450; nous, parts, sagacity, mother wit, wit, *esprit*, gumption, quick parts, grasp of intellect; acuteness &c. *adj.*; acumen, subtlety, penetration; perspica-cy, -city; discernment, long-headedness, due sense of, good judgement; discrimination &c. 465; craftiness, cunning &c. 702; refinement &c. (*taste*) 850.

/ head, brains, gray matter, headpiece, upper story, long head; eagle -eye, – glance; eye of a -lynx, – hawk.

wisdom, sapience, sense; good –, common –, plain –, horse- sense; clear thinking; rationality, reason; reasonableness &c. *adj.*; judgement; solidity, depth, profundity, calibre; enlarged views; reach –, compass- of thought; enlargement of mind.

genius, inspiration, *Geist*, fire of genius, heaven-born genius, soul; talent &c. (*aptitude*) 698.

[Wisdom in action] prudence &c. 864; vigilance &c. 459; tact &c. 698; foresight &c. 510; sobriety, self-possession, *aplomb*, ballast, mental -poise, – balance.

a bright thought, inspiration, brainwave, not a bad idea.

V. be -intelligent &c. *adj.*; have all one's wits about one; understand &c. (*intelligible*) 518; catch –, take in- an idea; take a -joke, – hint.

see -through, – at a glance, – with half an eye, – far into, – through a millstone; penetrate; discern &c. (*descry*) 441; foresee &c. 510.

discriminate &c. 465; know what's what &c. 698; listen to reason.

Adj. [Applied to persons] intelligent, quick of apprehension, keen, acute, alive, brainy, awake, bright, quick, sharp; quick-, keen-, clear-, sharp--eyed, -sighted, -witted; wide awake; canny, shrewd, astute; clear-headed; far-sighted &c. 510; discerning, perspicacious, penetrating, piercing; argute; nimble-, needle-witted; sharp as a needle; alive to &c. (*cognizant*) 490; clever &c. (*apt*) 698; arch &c. (*cunning*) 702; *pas si bête* &c. 682.

wise, sage, sapient, sagacious, reasonable, rational, sound, in one's right

450; shallow-, silli-, foolish-ness &c. *adj.*; imbecility, incapacity, vacancy of mind, poverty of intellect, clouded perception, poor head, apartments to let; stup-, stol-idity; hebetude, dull understanding, meanest capacity; short-sightedness; incompetence &c. (*unskilfulness*) 699.

one's weak side; bias &c. 481; infatuation &c. (*insanity*) 503.

simplicity, puerility, babyhood; dotage, anility, second childishness, senile dementia, fatuity; idio-cy, -tism; drivelling.

folly, frivolity, desipience, irrationality, trifling, ineptitude, nugacity, inconsistency, lip-wisdom, conceit; sophistry &c. 477; giddiness &c. (*inattention*) 458; eccentricity &c. 503; extravagance &c. (*absurdity*) 497; rashness &c. 863.

act of folly &c. 699.

V. be -imbecile &c. *adj.*; have no -brains, – sense &c. 498.

trifle, drivel, *radoter*, dote; ramble &c. (*madness*) 503; play the -fool, – monkey, – goat, take leave of one's senses; not see an inch beyond one's nose; stultify oneself &c. 699; talk nonsense &c. 497.

Adj. [Applied to persons] un-intelligent, -intellectual, -reasoning; mind-, wit-, reason-, brain-less; having no -head &c. 498; not -bright &c. 498; inapprehensible.

weak-, addle-, puzzle-, blunder-, muddle-, muddy-, pig-, beetle-, maggoty-, gross-headed; beef-, fat- -witted, -headed.

weak-, feeble-minded; dull-, shallow-, rattle-, lack-brained; half-, nit-, short-, dull-, blunt-witted; shallow-, clod-, addle-pated; dim-, short-sighted; thick-skulled; weak in the upper story.

shallow, *borné*, weak, wanting, soft, nutty, sappy, spoony; dull, – as a beetle; stupid, heavy, insulse, obtuse, blunt, stolid, doltish, asinine; inapt &c. 699; prosaic &c. 843.

child ish, like; infant-ine, -ile, baby-bab-ish; puerile, anile; simple &c. (*credulous*) 486.

fatuous, idiotic, imbecile, moronic

[ 165 ]

mind, sensible, *abnormis sapiens*, judicious, strong-minded.

un-prejudiced, -biassed, -bigoted, -prepossessed; un-dazzled, -perplexed; of unwarped judgment, impartial, equitable, fair, broad-minded.

cool; cool-, long-, hard-, strong-headed; long-sighted, calculating, thoughtful, reflecting; solid, deep, profound.

oracular; heaven-directed, -born.

prudent &c. (*cautious*) 864; sober, staid, solid; considerate, politic, wise in one's generation; watchful &c. 459; provident &c. (*prepared*) 673; in advance of one's age; wise as -a serpent, – Solomon, – Solon.

[Applied to actions] wise, sensible, reasonable, judicious; well-judged, -advised; prudent, politic; expedient &c. 646.

---

**500. Sage.—N.** sage, wise man; pundit; master -mind, – spirit of the age; longhead, thinker, philosopher.

authority, oracle, mentor, luminary, shining light, *esprit fort, magnus Apollo*, Solon, Solomon, Nestor, Magi, 'second Daniel.'

man of learning &c. 492; expert &c. 700; wizard &c. 994.

[Ironically] wiseacre, bigwig.

**Adj.** wise, learned; authoritative, oracular; erudite &c. 490; venerable, reverenced, revered, *emeritus*.

---

drivelling; blatant, babbling; vacant; sottish; bewildered &c. 475.

blockish, unteachable; Bœot-ian, -ic; bovine; un-gifted, -discerning, -enlightened, -wise, -philosophical; apish.

foolish, silly, senseless, irrational, insensate, nonsensical, inept; maudlin.

narrow-minded &c. 481; bigoted &c. (*obstinate*) 606; giddy &c. (*thoughtless*) 458; rash &c. 863; eccentric &c. (*crazed*) 503.

[Applied to actions] foolish, unwise, indiscreet, injudicious, improper, unreasonable, without reason, ridiculous, silly, stupid, asinine; ill-imagined, -advised, -judged, -devised; inconsistent, irrational, unphilosophical; extravagant &c. (*nonsensical*) 497; sleeveless, idle; useless &c. 645; inexpedient &c. 647; frivolous &c. (*trivial*) 643; absurd &c. 497.

**Phr.** *Davus sum non Œdipus.*

**501. Fool.—N.** fool, idiot, tomfool, wiseacre, simpleton, Simple Simon, nit-wit, witling, dizzard, donkey, ass; ninny, -hammer; moron, dolt, booby, Tom Noddy, looby, hoddy-doddy, noddy, nonny, noodle, nizy, owl; goose, -cap; *imbécile*; gaby, *radoteur*, nincompoop, *badaud*, zany; trifler, babbler; pretty fellow; natural, *niais*.

child, baby, infant, innocent, milksop, sop.

oaf, lout, loon, lown, dullard, doodle, calf, colt, buzzard, block, put, stick, stock, numps, tony.

---

bull-, dunder-, addle-, block-, dull-, logger-, jolt-, jolter-, beetle-, gross-, thick-, giddy-head; num-, thick-skull; lack-, shallow-brain; half-, lack-wit; dunder-pate; fat-head, poor stick.

sawney, gowk; clod, hopper; clod-, clot-poll, -pate; bull-calf; men of Bœotia, wise men of Gotham.

*un sot à triple étage*, sot; jobbernowl, changeling, mooncalf, *gobemouche*.

dotard, driveller; old -fogey, – woman; crone, grandmother.

greenhorn &c. (*dupe*) 547; dunce &c. (*ignoramus*) 493; lubber &c. (*bungler*) 701; madman &c. 504.

one who -will not set the Thames on fire, – did not invent gunpowder; *qui n'a pas inventé la poudre*; no conjuror.

---

**502. Sanity.—N.** sanity; soundness &c. *adj.*; rationality, normality, sobriety, lucidity, lucid interval; senses, sober senses, sound mind, *mens sana*.

**503. Insanity.—N.** disordered -reason, – intellect; diseased –, unsound –, abnormal- mind; derangement, unsoundness.

**V.** be -sane &c. *adj.*; retain one's senses, − reason.

become -sane &c. *adj.*; come to one's senses, sober down.

render -sane &c. *adj.*; bring to one's senses, sober.

**Adj.** sane, rational, reasonable, *compos mentis*, of sound mind; sound, -minded.

self-possessed; sober, -minded.

in one's -sober senses, − right mind; in possession of one's faculties.

**Adv.** sanely &c. *adj.*

insanity, lunacy; madness &c. *adj.*; mania, *rabies, furor*, mental alienation, paranoia, aberration; *amentia*, dementation, -tia, -cy; *dementia præcox*; *morosis*, idiocy, phrenitis, frenzy, raving, incoherence, wandering, delirium, calenture of the brain, delusion, hallucination; lycanthropy, brain storm, *delirium tremens*, D.T's.

vertigo, dizziness, swimming; sunstroke, *coup de soleil*, siriasis.

fanaticism, infatuation, craze; oddity, eccentricity, twist, monomania; klepto-, dipso-mania; hypochondriasis &c. (*low spirits*) 837; *melancholia*, hysteria.

screw −, tile −, slate- loose; bee in one's bonnet, rats in the upper story. dotage &c. (*imbecility*) 499.

**V.** be −, become- insane &c. *adj.*; lose one's senses, − reason, − faculties, − wits; go −, run- mad, run amuck; rave, dote, ramble, wander; drivel &c. (*be imbecile*) 499; have a -screw loose &c. *n.*, − devil; *avoir le diable au corps*; lose one's head &c. (*be uncertain*) 475.

derange, render −, drive- -mad &c. *adj.*; madden, dementate, addle the wits, derange the head, infatuate, befool; turn -the brain, − one's head.

**Adj.** insane, mad, lunatic; crazy, crazed, *aliéné, non compos mentis*; not right, cracked, touched; bereft of reason; unhinged, deranged, unsettled in one's mind; insensate, reasonless, beside oneself, demented, daft; phren-, fren-zied, -etic; possessed, − with a devil; far gone, maddened, moonstruck; shatterpated; barmy; mad-, scatter-, shatter-, crack-brained; off one's head; bug-house, *loco*.

maniacal; manic, manic-depressive; delirious, light-headed, incoherent, rambling, doting, wandering; frantic, raving, stark staring mad, amok, amuck, berserk.

corybantic, dithyrambic; rabid, giddy, vertiginous, dizzy, wild, haggard, mazed; flighty; distr-acted, -aught; bewildered &c. (*uncertain*) 475.

mad as a -March hare, − hatter; of -unsound mind &c. *n.*; touched −, wrong −, not right- in one's -head, − mind, − wits, − upper story; out of one's -mind, − senses, − wits; not in one's right mind.

fanatical, infatuated, odd, eccentric; hipp-ed, -ish.

imbecile, silly &c. 499.

**Adv.** like one possessed.

**Phr.** the mind having lost its balance; the reason under a cloud; *tête -exaltée, -montée*.

**504. Madman.—N.** madman, lunatic, maniac, bedlamite, candidate for Bedlam, raver, madcap; energumen; paranoiac; auto-, mono-, pyro-, megalo-, dipso-, klepto-maniac; hypochondriac &c. (*low spirits*) 837.

dreamer &c. 515; rhapsodist, seer, high-flier, enthusiast, crank, eccentric, nut, fanatic, *fanatico*; *exalté*; knight errant, Don Quixote. idiot &c. 501.

## Section VI. Extension of Thought
### 1°. *To the Past*

**505. Memory.—N.** memory, remembrance; reten-tion, -tiveness; tenacity; *veteris vestigia flammæ*; tablets of the memory; readiness.

reminiscence, recognition, recurrence, recollection, rememoration; retrospect, -ion; after-thought.

suggestion &c. (*information*) 527; prompting &c. *v.*; hint, reminder, token of remembrance, *memento, souvenir*, keepsake, relic, *memorandum*; remembrancer, flapper; memorial &c. (*record*) 551; commemoration &c. (*celebration*) 883.

things to be remembered, *memorabilia*.

art of –, artificial- memory; *memoria technica*; mnemo-nics, -technics; phrenotypics; Mnemosyne; memorandum-, note-, engagement-, prompt-book.

retentive –, tenacious –, green –, trustworthy –, capacious –, faithful –, correct –, exact –, ready –, prompt-memory.

**V.** remember, mind; retain the -memory, – remembrance- of; keep in view.

have –, hold –, bear –, carry –, keep –, retain- in *or* in the -thoughts, – mind, – memory, – remembrance; be in –, live in –, remain in –, dwell in –, haunt –, impress- one's -memory, – thoughts, – mind.

sink in the mind; run in the head; not be able to get it out of one's head; be deeply impressed with; rankle &c. (*revenge*) 919.

recur to the mind; flash -on the mind, – across the memory.

recognize, recollect, bethink oneself, recall, call up, conjure up, retrace; look –, trace- -back, – backwards; think –, look back- upon; review; call –, recall –, bring- to mind; remembrance; carry one's thoughts back; rake up the past.

suggest &c. (*inform*) 527; prompt; put –, keep- in mind; remind; fan the embers; call –, summon –, rip- up; renew; *infandum renovare dolorem*; task –, tax –, jog –, flap –, refresh –, rub up –, awaken- the memory; pull by the sleeve; bring back to the memory, put in remembrance, memorialize.

get –, have –, learn –, know –, say –, repeat- by -heart – rote; drive –, get- into -one's head; say one's lesson; repeat, – as a parrot; have at one's fingers' ends.

**506. Oblivion.—N.** oblivion; forgetfulness &c. *adj.*; obliteration &c. 552, of –, insensibility &c. 823 to- the past.

short –, treacherous –, loose –, slippery –, failing- memory; decay –, failure –, lapse- of memory; memory like a sieve; waters of -Lethe, – oblivion, amnesia.

pardon, acquittal, amnesty, oblivion; absolution.

**V.** forget; be -forgetful &c. *adj.*; fall –, sink- into oblivion; have -a short memory &c. *n.*, – no head.

forget one's own name, have on the tip of one's tongue, come in at one ear and go out at the other.

slip –, escape –, fade from –, die away from- the memory; lose, – sight of.

unlearn; efface &c. 552 –, discharge- from the memory; consign to -oblivion, – the tomb of the Capulets; think no more of &c. (*turn the attention from*) 458; cast behind one's back, wean one's thoughts from; let bygones be bygones &c. (*forgive*) 918.

**Adj.** forgotten &c. *v.*; unremembered, past recollection, bygone, out of mind; buried –, sunk- in oblivion; clean forgotten; gone out of one's -head, – recollection.

forgetful, oblivious, mindless, heedless, Lethean; insensible &c. 823- to the past.

**Phr.** *non mi ricordo*; the memory -failing, – deserting one, – being at (*or* in) fault.

---

commit to memory; memorize; con, – over; fix –, rivet –, imprint –, impress –, stamp –, grave –, engrave –, store –, treasure up –, bottle up –, embalm –, enshrine- in the memory; load –, store –, .stuff –, burden- the memory with.

redeem from oblivion; keep the memory -alive, – green; *tangere ulcus*; keep up the memory of; commemorate &c. (*celebrate*) 883.

make a note of &c. (*record*) 551.

**Adj.** remember-ing, -ed &c. *v.*; mindful, reminiscential; retained in the memory &c. *v.*; pent up in one's memory; fresh; green, – in remembrance, still vivid; unforgotten, present to the mind; within one's -memory &c. *n.*; indelible; not to be forgotten, unforgettable, enduring; uppermost in one's thoughts; memorable &c. (*important*) 642.

**Adv.** by -heart, – rote; without book, *memoriter*.

in memory of; *in memoriam*; suggestive.

**Phr.** *manet altâ mente repostum; forsan et hæc olim meminisse juvabit.*

## 2°. To the Future

**507. Expectation.—N.** expect-ation, -ance, -ancy; anticipation, reckoning, calculation; contingency; foresight &c. 510.

contemplation, prospection, look out; prospect, perspective, horizon, vista; destiny &c. 152.

suspense, waiting, abeyance; curiosity &c. 455; anxious –, ardent –, eager –, breathless –, sanguine- expectation; torment of Tantalus.

presumption, hope &c. 858; trust &c. (*belief*) 484; prognostication, auspices &c. (*prediction*) 511.

**V.** expect; look -for, – out for, – forward to; hope for, anticipate; have in -prospect, – contemplation; keep in view; contemplate, promise oneself; not -wonder &c. 870 -at, – if.

wait –, tarry –, lie in wait –, watch –, bargain- for; keep a -good, – sharp- look-out for; await; stand at 'attention,' abide, bide one's –, mark- time, watch.

foresee &c. 510; prepare for &c. 673; forestall &c. (*be early*) 132; count upon &c. (*believe in*) 484; think likely &c. (*probability*) 472; make one's mouth water.

lead one to expect &c. (*predict*) 511; have in store for &c. (*destiny*) 152.

prick up one's ears, hold one's breath.

**Adj.** expectant; expecting &c. *v.*; in -expectation &c. *n.*; on the watch &c. (*vigilant*) 459; open -eyed, -mouthed;

**508. Inexpectation.—N.** in-, non-expectation; false expectation &c. (*disappointment*) 509; miscalculation &c. 481; unforeseen contingency, the unforeseen, the unexpected.

surprise, sudden burst, thunderclap, blow, shock; bolt out of the blue; eye-opener; wonder &c. 870.

**V.** not -expect &c. 507; be taken by surprise; start; miscalculate &c. 481; not bargain for; come –, fall- upon.

be -unexpected &c. *adj.*; come -unawares &c. *adv.*; turn up, pop, drop from the clouds; come –, burst –, flash –, bounce –, steal –, creep- upon one; come –, burst- like a thunderclap, -bolt; take –, catch- -by surprise, – unawares, – napping.

pounce –, spring a mine- upon.

surprise, startle, take aback, electrify, stun, stagger, take away one's breath, throw off one's guard; astonish &c. (*strike with wonder*) 870.

**Adj.** non-expectant; surprised &c. *v.*; un-warned, -aware; off one's guard; inattentive &c. 458.

un-expected, -anticipated, -prepared for, -looked for, -foreseen, -hoped for; dropped from the clouds; beyond –, contrary to –, against- expectation; out of one's reckoning; unheard of &c. (*exceptional*) 83; startling; sudden &c. (*instantaneous*) 113.

**Adv.** abruptly, unexpectedly, plump, pop, *à l'improviste*, unawares; without

agape, gaping, all agog; on -tenter-hooks, – tiptoe, – the tiptoe of expectation; *aux aguets*; ready; curious &c. 455; looking forward to; prepared for; on the rack.

expected &c. *v.*; long expected, foreseen; in prospect &c. *n.*; prospective; in -one's eye, – view, – the horizon; impending &c. (*destiny*) 152.

-notice, – warning, – saying 'by your leave'; like a -thief in the night, – thunderbolt; in an unguarded moment; suddenly &c. (*instantaneously*) 113.

**Int.** heyday! &c. (*wonder*) 870.

**Phr.** little did one -think, – expect; nobody would ever -suppose, – think, – expect; who would have thought?

**Adv.** expectantly; in the event of; on the watch &c. *adj.*; with -breathless expectation &c. *n.*, – bated breath, – eyes, – ears strained; *arrectis auribus*; on edge.

**Phr.** we shall see; *nous verrons*.

**509. [Failure of expectation.] Disappointment.—N.** disappointment, disillusionment; blighted hope, balk; blow; slip 'twixt cup and lip; non-fulfilment of one's hopes; sad –, bitter- disappointment; trick of fortune; afterclap; false –, vain- expectation; miscalculation &c. 481; fool's paradise; much cry and little wool.

**V.** be disappointed; look -blank, – blue; look –, stand- -aghast &c. (*wonder*) 870; find to one's cost; laugh on the wrong side of one's mouth; find one a false prophet.

disappoint; crush –, dash –, balk –, disappoint –, blight –, falsify –, defeat –, not realize- one's -hope, – expectation; balk, jilt, bilk; play one -false, – a trick; dash the cup from the lips; tantalize; dumb-found, -founder; disillusion, -ize; dissatisfy, disgruntle.

**Adj.** disappointed &c. *v.*; disconcerted, aghast; out of one's reckoning; disgruntled.

**Phr.** the mountain brought forth a mouse; *nascitur ridiculus mus*; *parturiunt montes*; *dis aliter visum*, the bubble burst; one's countenance falling.

**510. Foresight.—N.** foresight, prospicience, prevision, longsightedness; anticipation; providence &c. (*preparation*) 673.

fore-thought, -cast; pre-deliberation, -surmise; foregone conclusion &c. (*prejudgment*) 481; prudence &c. (*caution*) 864.

foreknowledge; *prognosis*; pre-cognition, -science, -notion, -sentiment; second sight; sagacity &c. (*intelligence*) 498.

prospect &c. (*expectation*) 507; foretaste; prospectus &c. (*plan*) 626.

**V.** foresee; look -forwards to, – ahead, – beyond; scent from afar; feel in one's bones; look –, pry –, peep- into the future.

see one's way; see how the -land lies, – wind blows, – cat jumps.

anticipate; expect &c. 507; be beforehand &c. (*early*) 132; predict &c. 511; fore-know, -judge, -cast; surmise; have an eye to the -future, – main chance; *respicere finem*; keep a sharp look-out &c. (*vigilance*) 459; forewarn &c. 668.

**Adj.** foreseeing &c. *v.*; prescient; anticipatory; far-seeing, -sighted; sagacious &c. (*intelligent*) 498; weather-wise; provident &c. (*prepared*) 673; prospective &c. 507.

**Adv.** against the time when.

**511. Prediction.—N.** prediction, announcement; program, programme &c. (*plan*) 626; premonition &c. (*warning*) 668; *prognosis*, prophecy, vaticination, mantology, prognostication, premonstration, augur-y, -ation; a-, ha-riolation; fore-, a-boding; bode-, abode-ment; omin-ation,

-ousness; auspices, forecast; sign, presage, prognostic; omen &c. 512; horoscope, nativity; sooth, -saying; fortune-telling; divination; crystal gazing, necromancy &c. 992; prophet &c. 512.

[Divination by the stars] astrology, horoscopy, astromancy, judicial astrology.*

[Place of prediction] *adytum*.

prefigur-ation, -ement; prototype, type.

**V.** predict, prognosticate, prophesy, vaticinate, divine, foretell, soothsay, augurate, tell fortunes; cast a -horoscope, – nativity; advise; forewarn &c. 668.

presage, augur, bode; a-, fore-bode, -cast; fore-, be-token; prefigure, -show; portend; fore-show, -shadow, shadow forth, typify, ominate, signify, point to, precurse.

usher in, herald, premise, announce; lower.

hold out –, raise –, excite- -expectation, – hope; bid fair, promise, lead one to expect; be the -precursor &c. 64.

**Adj.** predicting &c. *v.*; predictive, prophetic, fatidical, vaticinal, oracular, Sibylline, haruspical, weatherwise.

ominous, presageful, portentous; augur-ous, -al, -ial; auspici-al, -ous; prescious, monitory, extispicious, premonitory, precursory, significant of, pregnant with, big with the fate of.

**Phr.** 'coming events cast their shadows before.'

**512. Omen.**—**N.** omen, portent, presage, prognostic, augury, auspice; sign &c. (*indication*) 550; herald, forerunner, harbinger &c. (*precursor*) 64.

bird of ill omen; signs of the times; gathering clouds; warning &c. 668.

prefigurement &c. 511.

**513. Oracle.**—**N.** oracle; prophet, -ess; seer, soothsayer, augur, fortune-teller, palmist, medium, clairvoyant, crystal gazer, witch, geomancer, *aruspex*; a-, ha-ruspice; Sibyl; Python, -ess; Pythia; Pythian –, Delphian- oracle; Monitor, Sphinx, Tiresias, Cassandra, Sibylline leaves; Zadkiel, Old Moore; sorcerer &c. 994; interpreter &c. 524.

## Section VII. CREATIVE THOUGHT

**514. Supposition.**—**N.** supposition, assumption, postulation, condition, pre-supposition, hypothesis, postulate, *postulatum*, theory, *data*; pro-, position; *thesis*, theorem; proposal &c. (*plan*) 626.

* The following terms, expressive of different forms of divination, have been collected from various sources, and are here given as a curious illustration of bygone superstitions:

Divination *by oracles*, Theomancy; *by the Bible*, Bibliomancy; *by ghosts*, Psychomancy; *by spirits seen in a magic lens*, Cristallomantia; *by shadows or manes*, Sciomancy; *by appearances in the air*, Aeromancy, Chaomancy; *by the stars at birth*, Genethliacs; *by meteors*, Meteoromancy; *by winds*, Austromancy; *by sacrificial appearances*, Aruspicy (*or* Haruspicy), Hieromancy, Hieroscopy; *by the entrails of animals sacrificed*, Hieromancy; *by the entrails of a human sacrifice*, Anthropomancy; *by the entrails of fishes*, Ichthyomancy; *by sacrificial fire*, Pyromancy; *by red-hot iron*, Sideromancy; *by smoke from the altar*, Capnomancy; *by mice*, Myomancy; *by birds*, Orniscopy, Ornithomancy; *by a cock picking up grains*, Alectryomancy (*or* Alectoromancy); *by fishes*, Ophiomancy; *by herbs*, Botanomancy; *by water*, Hydromancy; *by fountains*

bare –, vague –, loose- -supposition, – suggestion; conceit; conjecture; guess, – work; rough guess, shot; conjecturality; surmise, suspicion, inkling, suggestion, suggestiveness, association of ideas, hint; presumption &c. (*belief*) 484; divination, speculation.

theorist, speculator, doctrinarian, hypothesist.

**V.** suppose, conjecture, surmise, suspect, guess, divine; theorize; pre-sume, -surmise, -suppose; assume, fancy, wis, take it; give a guess, speculate, believe, dare say, take it into one's head, take for granted.

put forth; pro-pound, -pose; moot; hypothesize; start, put a case, submit, move, make a motion; hazard –, throw out –, put forward- a -suggestion, – conjecture.

allude to, suggest, hint, put it into one's head.

suggest itself &c. (*thought*) 451; run in the head &c. (*memory*) 505; marvel –, wonder- -if, – whether.

**Adj.** supposing &c. *v.*; given, mooted, postulatory; assumed &c. *v.* supposit-ive, -itious; gratuitous, speculative, conjectural, hypothetical, suppositional, theoretical, academic, supposable, presumptive, putative.

suggestive, allusive, stimulating.

**Adv.** if, – so be; an; on the -supposition &c. *n.*; *ex hypothesi*; in -case, – the event of; *quasi*, as if, provided; perhaps &c. (*by possibility*) 470; for aught one knows.

**515. Imagination.—N.** imagination; originality; invention; fancy; inspiration; *verve*; empathy.

warm –, heated –, excited –, sanguine –, ardent –, fiery –, boiling –, wild –, bold –, daring –, playful –, lively –, fertile- -imagination, – fancy.

'mind's eye'; 'such stuff as dreams are made of.'

ideal-ity, -ism; romanticism, utopianism, castle-building; dreaming; frenzy; ecs-, ex-tasy; calenture &c. (*delirium*) 503; reverie, brown study, trance; somnambulism.

conception, *vorstellung*, excogitation, 'a fine frenzy,' poetic frenzy, divine afflatus; cloud-, dream-land; flight –, fumes- of fancy; 'thick-coming fancies'; creation –, coinage- of the brain; imagery, word painting.

conceit, maggot, figment, myth, dream, vision, shadow, chimera; phan-tasm, -tasy; fantasy, fancy; whim, -sey; vagary, rhapsody, romance, *extravaganza*; air-drawn dagger, bugbear, nightmare; flying Dutchman, great sea-serpent, man in the moon, castle in the air, *châteaux en Espagne*; Utopia, Atlantis, happy valley, millennium, fairy land; land of Prester John, kingdom of Micomicon; work of fiction &c. (*novel*) 594; poetry &c. 597; drama &c. 599; Arabian nights; *le pot au lait*; dream of Alnaschar &c. (*hope*) 858; day –, golden- dream.

illusion &c. (*error*) 495; phantom &c. (*fallacy of vision*) 443; *Fata*

Pegomancy; *by a wand*, Rhabdomancy; *by dough of cakes*, Crithomancy; *by meal*, Aleuromancy, Alphitomancy; *by salt*, Halomancy; *by dice*, Cleromancy; *by arrows*, Belomancy; *by a balanced hatchet*, Axinomancy; *by a balanced sieve*, Coscinomancy; *by a suspended ring*, Dactyliomancy; *by dots made at random on paper*, Geomancy; *by precious stones*, Lithomancy; *by pebbles*, Pessomancy; *by pebbles drawn from a heap*, Psephomancy; *by mirrors*, Catoptromancy; *by writings in ashes*, Tephramancy; *by dreams*, Oneiromancy; *by the hand*, Palmistry, Chiromancy; *by nails reflecting the sun's rays*, Onychomancy; *by finger rings*, Dactylomancy; *by numbers*, Arithmancy; *by drawing lots*, Sortilege; *by passages in books*, Stichomancy; *by the letters forming the name of the person*, Onomancy, Nomancy; *by the features*, Anthroposcopy; *by the mode of laughing*, Geloscopy; *by ventriloquism*, Gastromancy; *by walking in a circle*, Gyromancy; *by dropping melted wax into water*, Ceromancy; *by currents*, Bletonism.

*Morgana* &c. (*ignis fatuus*) 423; vapour &c. (*cloud*) 353; stretch of the imagination &c. (*exaggeration*) 549.

idealist, romanticist, visionary; mopus; romancer, dreamer; somnambulist; rhapsodist &c. (*fanatic*) 504.

V. imagine, fancy, conceive; ideal-, real-ize; dream, – of; 'give to airy nothing a local habitation and a name.'

create, originate, devise, invent, coin, fabricate; improvise, strike out something new.

set one's wits to work; strain –, crack- one's invention; rack –; ransack –, cudgel- one's brains; excogitate.

give -play, – the reins, – a loose- to the -imagination, – fancy; empathize; indulge in reverie.

conjure up a vision; fancy –, represent –, picture –, figure- to oneself; envisage.

float in the mind; suggest itself &c. (*thought*) 451.

Adj. imagined &c. *v.*; *ben trovato*; air-drawn, -built.

imagin-ing &c. *v.*, -ative; original, inventive, creative, fertile, productive; ingenious.

romantic, high-flown, flighty, extravagant, fanatic, enthusiastic, Utopian, Quixotic; preposterous, rhapsodical.

ideal, unreal; in the clouds, *in nubibus*; unsubstantial &c. 4; illusory &c. (*fallacious*) 495; fictitious, theoretical, hypothetical.

fabulous, legendary; myth-ic, -ological; chimerical; imagin-, visionary; notional; fan-cy, -ciful, -tastic, -tastical; whimsical; fairy, -like.

dreamy, entranced, vaporous.

---

## DIVISION (II.) COMMUNICATION OF IDEAS
### Section I. NATURE OF IDEAS COMMUNICATED

**516.** [Idea to be conveyed.] **Meaning.** [Thing signified.]—**N.** meaning; signific-ation, -ance; sense, expression; im-, pur-port; drift, tenor, implication, connotation, essence, force, spirit, bearing, colouring; scope.

matter; subject, -matter; argument, text, sum and substance; gist &c. 5.

general –, broad –, substantial –, colloquial –, literal –, plain –, simple –, accepted –, natural –, unstrained –, true &c. (*exact*) 494 –, honest &c. 543 –, *primâ facie* &c. (*manifest*) 525- meaning.

literality; literal interpretation; after acceptation; allusion &c. (*latency*) 526; suggestion &c. (*information*) 527; synonym; figure of speech &c. 521; acceptation &c. (*interpretation*) 522.

V. mean, signify, express, connote, denote; im-, pur-port; convey, imply, breathe, indicate, bespeak, bear a sense; tell –, speak- of; touch on; point –, allude- to; drive at; involve &c. (*latency*) 526; declare &c. (*affirm*) 535.

**517.** [Absence of meaning.] **Unmeaningness.**—**N.** unmeaningness &c. *adj.*; scrabble, scribble, scrawl, daub, (*painting*), strumming (*music*).

empty sound, dead letter, *vox et præterea nihil*; 'a tale told by an idiot, full of sound and fury, signifying nothing'; 'sounding brass and a tinkling cymbal.'

nonsense, jargon, gibberish, jabber, mere words, hocus-pocus, fustian, rant, bombast, balderdash, palaver, patter, flummery, verbiage, babble, *bavardage*, *baragouin*, platitude, *niaiserie*; inanity; rigmarole, rodomontade; truism; *nugæ canoræ*; twaddle, twattle, fudge, trash; stuff, – and nonsense; bosh, rubbish, rot, drivel, moonshine, wish-wash, fiddle-faddle, flapdoodle; absurdity &c. 497; vagueness &c. (*unintelligibility*) 519.

V. mean nothing; be -unmeaning &c. *adj.*; twaddle, quibble, rant, gabble, scrabble &c. *n.*

Adj. unmeaning; meaning-, sense-less;

understand by &c. (*interpret*) 522.
**Adj.** meaning &c. *v.*; expressive,
suggestive, meaningful, allusive; sig-
nific-ant, -ative, -atory; pithy; full of -,
pregnant with- meaning.
declaratory &c. 535; intelligible &c.
518; literal, metaphrastic; synonymous;
tantamount &c. (*equivalent*) 27; implied
&c. (*latent*) 526; explicit &c. 525;
literal &c. 562.
**Adv.** to that effect; that is to say
&c. (*being interpreted*) 522.
literally; evidently, from the context.

**518. Intelligibility.—N.** intelligibil-
ity, clearness, clarity, explicitness &c.
*adj.*; lucidity, perspicuity; legibility,
plain speaking &c. (*manifestation*) 525;
precision &c. 494; a word to the wise.
**V.** be -intelligible &c. *adj.*; speak
-for itself, - volumes; tell its own tale,
lie on the surface.
render -intelligible &c. *adj.*; popular-
ize, simplify, clear up; elucidate &c.
(*explain*) 522.
understand, comprehend; take, - in;
catch, grasp, recognize, follow, collect,
master, make out; see -with half an
eye, - daylight, - one's way; enter
into the ideas of; come to an under-
standing.
**Adj.** intelligible; clear, - as -day,
- crystal, - noonday; lucid; per-, tran-
spicuous; luminous, transparent; com-
prehensible.
easily understood, easy to under-
stand, for the million, intelligible to
the meanest capacity, popularized.
plain, distinct, explicit, clear-cut;
positive; definite &c. (*precise*) 494.
graphic, vivid, telling; expressive &c.
(*meaning*) 516; illustrative &c. (*ex-
planatory*) 522.
un-ambiguous, -equivocal, -mistak-
able &c. (*manifest*) 525, -confused;
legible, recognizable; obvious &c. 525.
**Adv.** in plain -terms, - words, -
English.
**Phr.** he that runs may read &c.
(*manifest*) 525.

nonsensical; void of -sense &c. 516.
in-, un-expressive; vacant, fatuous;
not significant; insignificant.
trashy, washy, inane, vague, trum-
pery, trivial, fiddle-faddle, twaddling,
quibbling.
unmeant, not expressed; tacit &c.
(*latent*) 526.
inexpressible, undefinable, incom-
municable.
**Int.** rubbish! &c. 497.

**519. Unintelligibility.—N.** unintelli-
gibility, incomprehensibility, imper-
spicuity; inconceivableness, vagueness
&c. *adj.*; obscurity; ambiguity &c. 520;
doubtful meaning; uncertainty &c. 475;
perplexity &c. (*confusion*) 59; spinos-
ity; *obscurum per obscurius*; mystifica-
tion &c. (*concealment*) 528; latency &c.
526; transcendentalism.
paradox; enigma, riddle &c. (*secret*)
533; *dignus vindice nodus*; sealed book;
steganography, Freemasonry.
*pons asinorum*, asses' bridge; double
-, high- Dutch, Greek, Hebrew; jargon
&c. (*unmeaning*) 517.
obscurantist.
**V.** be -unintelligible &c. *adj.*; require
-explanation &c. 522; have a doubtful
meaning, pass comprehension.
render -unintelligible &c. *adj.*; con-
ceal &c. 528; darken &c. 421; confuse
&c. (*derange*) 61; perplex &c. (*bewilder*)
475.
not -understand &c. 518; lose, - the
clue; miss; not know what to make of,
be able to make nothing of, give it up;
not be able to -account for, - make
either head or tail of; be at sea &c.
(*uncertain*) 475; wonder &c. 870; see
through a glass darkly &c. (*ignorance*)
491.
not understand one another; play at
cross purposes &c. (*misinterpret*) 523.
**Adj.** un-intelligible, -accountable,
-decipherable, -discoverable, -know-
able, -fathomable; in-cognizable, -ex-
plicable, -scrutable; inap-, incom-
prehensible; insol-vable, -uble; im-
penetrable.

illegible, indecipherable, as Greek to one, unexplained, para-
doxical; enigmatic, -al; puzzling, baffling.

obscure, dark, muddy, clear as mud, seen through a mist, dim, nebulous, shrouded in mystery; undiscernible &c. (*invisible*) 447; misty &c. (*opaque*) 426; hidden &c. 528; latent &c. 526.

indefinite &c. (*indistinct*) 447; perplexed &c. (*confused*) 59; undetermined, vague, loose, ambiguous; mysterious; mystic, -al; transcendental; occult, recondite, esoteric, abstruse, crabbed.

incon-ceivable, -ceptible; searchless; above –, beyond –, past-comprehension; beyond one's depth; unconceived.

inexpressible, undefinable, incommunicable, unutterable, ineffable, unpronounceable.

**520.** [Having a double sense.] **Equivocalness.**—**N.** equivocalness &c. *adj.*; double -meaning &c. 516; ambiguity, *double entendre*, pun, paragram, *calembour*, quibble, *équivoque*, anagram; conundrum &c. (*riddle*) 533; word-play &c. (*wit*) 842; homonym, -y; amphibo-ly, -logy; ambiloquy.

Sphinx, Delphic oracle.

equivocation &c. (*duplicity*) 544; white lie, mental reservation &c. (*concealment*) 528.

**V.** be -equivocal &c. *adj.*; have two -meanings &c. 516; equivocate &c. (*palter*) 544.

**Adj.** equivocal, ambiguous, amphibolous, homonymous; double-tongued &c. (*lying*) 544.

**521. Metaphor.**—**N.** figure of speech; *façon de parler*, way of speaking, colloquialism.

phrase &c. 566; figure, trope, metaphor, tralatition, metonymy, enallage, *catachresis, synecdoche, antonomasia*; irony, satire, figurativeness &c. *adj.*; image, -ry; *metalepsis*, type, anagoge, simile, personification, *prosopopœia*, allegory, apologue, parable, fable; allusion, adumbration; application; euphemism; euphuism.

**V.** employ -metaphor &c. *n.*; personify, allegorize, adumbrate, shadow forth, apply, allude –, refer- to.

**Adj.** metaphorical &c. *n.*; figurative, catachrestical, typical, tralatitious, parabolic, allegorical, allusive, anagogical; ironical; colloquial.

**Adv.** so to -speak, – say, – express oneself; as it were.

**Phr.** *mutato nomine de te fabula narratur.*

**522. Interpretation.**—**N.** interpretation, definition; explan-, explic-ation; solution, answer; rationale; plain –, simple –, strict- interpretation; meaning &c. 516.

translation; rend-ering, -ition; reddition; literal –, free- translation; key, crib; secret; clew &c. (*indication*) 550; Rosetta stone.

*exegesis*; ex-pounding, -position; Hermeneutics; comment, -ary; inference &c. (*deduction*) 480; illustration, exemplification; gloss, annotation, *scholium*, note; e-, di-lucidation, enucleation; *éclaircissement, mot de l'énigme.*

symptomat-, semei-ology; metoposcopy, physiognomy; diagnosis, prog-

**523. Misinterpretation.** — **N.** misinterpretation, -apprehension, -understanding, -acceptation, -construction, -application; *catachresis*; cross -reading, – purposes; mistake &c. 495.

misrepresentation, perversion, exaggeration &c. 549; false -colouring, – construction; abuse of terms; parody, travesty; falsification &c. (*lying*) 544.

**V.** mis-interpret, -apprehend, -understand, -conceive, -judge, -doubt, -spell, -translate, -construe, -apply; mistake &c. 105.

misrepresent, pervert; garble &c. (*falsify*) 544; distort, detort; travesty, play upon words; stretch –, strain –, wrest- the -sense, – meaning; explain

nosis; paleography &c. (*philology*) 560.
accept-ion, -ation, -ance; light, reading, lection, construction, version.
equivalent, – meaning &c. 516;
synonym; para-, meta-phrase; convertible terms, apposition; dictionary &c. 562; polyglot.

**V.** interpret, explain, define, construe, translate, render; do –, turn-into; transfuse the sense of.

find out &c. 480a- -the meaning &c. 516- of; read; spell –, figure –, make- out; decipher, decode, unravel, disentangle, puzzle out; find the key of, enucleate, resolve, solve; read between the lines.

account for; find –, tell- the cause &c. 153- of; throw –, shed-light, – new light, – a fresh light- upon; clear up, elucidate.

illustrate, exemplify; unfold, expound, comment upon, annotate; popularize &c. (*render intelligible*) 518.

take –, understand –, receive –, accept- in a particular sense; understand by, put a construction on, be given to understand.

**Adj.** explanatory, expository; explica-tive, -tory; exegetical; hermeneutic, interpretive, illustrative, elucidative, annotative, scholiastic.

polyglot; literal; para-, meta-phrastic; cosignificative, synonymous; equivalent &c. 27.

**Adv.** in -explanation &c. *n.*; that is to say, *id est, videlicet,* to wit, namely, in other words.

literally, strictly speaking; in -plain, – plainer- -terms, – words, – English; more simply.

**524. Interpreter.**—**N.** interpreter, translator, ex-positor, -pounder, -ponent, -plainer; demonstrator.

scholiast, commentator, annotator; meta-, para-phrast.

spokesman, speaker, mouthpiece, prolocutor; diplomat &c. 758.

guide, courier, dragoman, *valet de place, cicerone,* showman; oneiro-critic; Œdipus; oracle &c. 513.

away; put a -bad, – false- construction on; give a false colouring, look through -rose coloured –, – dark – spectacles; be –, play- at cross purposes.

**Adj.** misinterpreted &c. *v.*; untranslat-ed, -able.

**Adv.** at cross purposes.

_____

## Section II. Modes of Communication

**525. Manifestation.**—**N.** manifestation; unfolding; plainness &c. *adj.*; plain speaking; expression; showing &c. *v.*; exposition, demonstration, *séance*; exhibition, production; display, showing off &c. 882, premonstration. [Thing shown] exhibit, show.

indication &c. (*calling attention to*) 457; publicity &c. 531; disclosure &c. 529; openness &c. (*honesty*) 543, (*artlessness*) 703; *épanchement*, prominence.

**V.** make –, render- -manifest &c. *adj.*; bring -forth, – forward, – to the front, – into view; give notice; express; represent, set forth, exhibit; show, – up; expose; produce; hold up –, expose- to view; set –, place –, lay-

**526. Latency.**—**N.** latency, inexpression; hidden –, occult- meaning; occultness, occultism, mysticism, mystery, cabala, symbolism, anagoge; silence &c. (*taciturnity*) 585; concealment &c. 528; more than meets the -eye, – ear; Delphic oracle; *le dessous des cartes*, undercurrent.

allusion, insinuation, implication; innuendo &c. 527; adumbration; 'something rotten in the state of Denmark.'

snake in the grass &c. (*pitfall*) 667; secret &c. 533.

darkness, invisibility, imperceptibility.

latent influence, power behind the throne; friend at court, wire puller.

before -one, – one's eyes; tell to one's face; trot out, put through one's paces, unfold, show off, show forth, unveil, bring to light, display, demonstrate, unroll; lay open; draw –, bring- out; bring out in strong relief; call –, bring-into notice; hold up the mirror; wear one's heart upon his sleeve; show one's -face, – colours; manifest oneself; speak out; make no -mystery, – secret- of; unfurl the flag; proclaim &c. (*publish*) 531.

indicate &c. (*direct attention to*) 457; disclose &c. 529; elicit &c. 480a; interpret &c. 522.

be -manifest &c. *adj.*; appear &c. (*be visible*) 446; transpire &c. (*be disclosed*) 529; speak for itself, stand to reason; stare one in the face; loom large, appear on the horizon, rear its head; give -token, – sign, – indication of; tell its own tale &c. (*intelligible*) 518; go without saying.

**Adj.** manifest, apparent; salient, striking, demonstrative, prominent, in the foreground, notable, pronounced. flagrant; notorious &c. (*public*) 531; arrant; stark staring; unshaded, glaring.

defin-ed, -ite; distinct, conspicuous &c. (*visible*) 446; obvious, evident, incontestable, unmistakable, not to be mistaken, plain, clear, palpable, self-evident, autoptical; intelligible &c. 518; clear as -day, – daylight, – noonday; plain as -a pikestaff, – the sun at noonday, – the nose on one's face, – the way to the parish church.

ostensible; open, – as day; overt, patent, express, explicit; naked, bare, literal, downright, undisguised, exoteric.

unreserved; frank, plain spoken &c. (*artless*) 703; barefaced, brazen, bold, shameless, daring, flaunting, loud.

manifested &c. *v.*; disclosed &c. 529; expressible, capable of being shown, producible; in-, un-concealable.

**Adv.** manifestly, openly &c. *adj.*; before one's eyes, under one's nose, to one's face, face to face, above board, *cartes sur table*, on the stage, in plain sight, in open court, in the open, – streets; at the cross roads; in market overt; in the face of -day, – heaven; in -broad –, open- daylight; without reserve; at first blush, *primâ facie*, on the face of; in set terms.

**Phr.** *cela saute aux yeux*; he that runs may read; you can see it with half an eye; it needs no ghost to tell us; the meaning lies on the surface; *cela va sans dire*; *res ipsa loquitur.*

**V.** be -latent &c. *adj.*; lurk, smoulder, underlie, make no sign; escape -observation, – detection, – recognition; lie hid &c. 528.

laugh in one's sleeve; keep back &c. (*conceal*) 528.

involve, imply, implicate, connote, import, understand, allude to, infer, leave an inference; symbolize; whisper &c. (*conceal*) 528.

**Adj.** latent; lurking &c. *v.*; secret &c. 528; occult, symbolic, mystic; implied &c. *v.*; dormant.

un-apparent, -known, -seen &c. 441; in the background; invisible &c. 447; indiscoverable, dark; impenetrable &c. (*unintelligible*) 519; un-spied, -suspected.

un - said, - written, - published, -breathed, -talked of, -told &c. 527, -sung, -exposed, -proclaimed, -disclosed &c. 529, -pronounced, -mentioned, -expressed; not expressed, tacit.

un-developed, -solved, -explained, -traced, -discovered &c. 480a, -tracked. -explored, -invented.

indirect, crooked, inferential; by -inference, – implication; implicit; constructive; allusive, covert, muffled; steganographic; under-stood, -hand, -ground; concealed &c. 528; delitescent.

**Adv.** by a side wind; *sub silentio*; in the background; behind -the scenes, – one's back, – the veil; below the surface; on the tip of one's tongue; secretly &c. 528; between the lines; by a mutual understanding.

**Phr.** 'thereby hangs a tale.' 'that is another story.'

———

**527. Information.**—**N.** information, enlightenment, acquaintance, knowledge &c. 490; publicity &c. 531.

communication, intimation; not-ice, -ification; e-, an-nunciation; announcement; representation, round robin, presentment.

case, estimate, specification, report, advice, monition; news &c. 532; return &c. (*record*) 551; account &c. (*description*) 594; statement &c. (*affirmation*) 535.

mention; acquainting &c. *v.*; instruction &c. (*teaching*) 537; outpouring; intercommunication, communicativeness.

informant, authority, teller, announcer, annunciator, harbinger, herald, intelligencer, commentator, columnist, reporter, exponent, mouthpiece; informer, keek, eavesdropper, delator, detective, sleuth; *mouchard*, spy, stool pigeon, newsmonger; messenger &c. 534; *amicus curiæ*.

*valet de place*, *cicerone*, pilot, guide; guide-, hand-book; *vade mecum*; manual; map, plan, chart, gazetteer; itinerary &c. (*journey*) 266.

hint, suggestion, wrinkle, innuendo, inkling, whisper, passing word, word in the ear, subaudition, cue, by-play; gesture &c. (*indication*) 550; gentle - broad- hint; *verbum sapienti*; word to the wise; insinuation &c. (*latency*) 526.

**V.** tell; inform, – of; acquaint, – with; impart, – to; make acquainted with, bring to the ears of, apprise, advise, enlighten, awaken.

let fall, mention, express, intimate, represent, communicate, make known; publish &c. 531; notify, signify, specify, convey the knowledge of.

let one –, have one to- know; serve notice, give one to understand; give notice; set –, lay –, put- before; point out, put into one's head; put one in possession of; instruct &c. (*teach*) 537; direct the attention to &c. 457.

an-nounce, -nunciate; report, – progress; bring –, send –, leave –, write- word; tele-graph, -phone; ring –, call- up; wire; retail, render an account; give an account &c. (*describe*) 594; state &c. (*affirm*) 535.

**528. Concealment.**—**N.** concealment; hiding &c. *v.*; occultation, mystification.

seal of secrecy; screen &c. 530; disguise &c. 530; masquerade; masked battery; hiding place &c. 530; cipher, code, crypt-, stegan-ography; invisible –, sympathetic- ink; palimpsest; Freemasonry.

stealth, -iness; obreption; slyness &c. (*cunning*) 702.

latit-ancy, -ation; seclusion &c. 893; privacy, secrecy, secretness; *incognita*.

reticence; reserve; mental –, reservation, aside; *arrière pensée*, suppression, evasion, white lie, misprision; silence &c. (*taciturnity*) 585; suppression of truth &c. 544; underhand dealing; close-, secretive-ness &c. *adj.*; mystery.

latency &c. 526; snake in the grass; secret &c. 533.

**V.** conceal, hide, secrete, stow away, put out of sight; lock –, seal –, bottle-up.

cover, screen, cloak, veil, shroud; screen from -sight, – observation; draw the veil; draw –, close- the curtain; curtain, shade, eclipse, throw a veil over; be-cloud, -fog, -mask; mask, disguise; ensconce, muffle, smother; whisper.

keep -from, – back, – to oneself; keep -snug, – close, – secret, – dark; bury; sink, suppress; keep -from, – out of- -view, – sight; keep in –, throw into- the -shade, – background; cover up one's tracks; stifle, hush up, withhold, reserve; fence with a question; ignore &c. 460.

code, codify, use a cipher.

keep -a secret, – one's own counsel; hold one's tongue &c. (*silence*) 585; make no sign, not let it go further; not breathe a -word, – syllable- about; not let the right hand know what the left is doing; hide one's light under a bushel, bury one's talent in a napkin.

keep –, leave- in -the dark, – ignorance; blind, – the eyes; blindfold, hoodwink, mystify; puzzle &c. (*render uncertain*) 475; bamboozle &c. (*deceive*) 545.

be -concealed &c. *v.*; suffer an eclipse;

disclose &c. 529; show cause; explain &c. (*interpret*) 522.

hint; give an inkling of; give –, drop –, throw out- a hint; insinuate; allude –, make allusion- to; glance at; tip off, tip the wink &c. (*indicate*) 550; suggest, prompt, give the cue, breathe; whisper, – in the ear.

give a bit of one's mind; tell one plainly, – once for all; speak volumes.

un-deceive, -beguile; set right, correct, open the eyes of, disabuse.

be -informed of &c.; know &c. 490; learn &c. 539; get scent of, gather from; awaken –, open one's eyes- to; become -alive, – awake- to; keep posted; hear, overhear, understand.

come to one's -ears, – knowledge; reach one's ears.

**Adj.** informed &c. *v.*; *communiqué*; reported &c. *v.*; published &c. 531; advisory.

expressive &c. 516; explicit &c. (*open*) 525, (*clear*) 518; plain-spoken &c. (*artless*) 703.

declara-, nuncupa-, exposi-tory; declarative, enunciative, communicat-ive, -ory; oral.

**Adv.** from information received; according to -rumour, – report; in the air; from what one can gather.

**Phr.** a little bird told me.

retire from sight, couch; hide oneself; lie -hid, – in ambush, – low, – *perdu*, – snug, – close; seclude oneself &c. 893; lurk, sneak, skulk, slink, pussy-foot, prowl; steal -into, – out of, – by, – along; play at -bopeep, – hide and seek; hide in holes and corners.

**Adj.** concealed &c. *v.*; hidden; veiled, secret, recondite, mystic, cabalistic, occult, dark; cryptic, -al; private, privy, *in petto*, auricular, clandestine, close, inviolate.

behind a -screen &c. 530; under -cover, – an eclipse; in -ambush, – hiding, – disguise; in a -cloud, – fog, – mist, – haze, – dark corner; in the -shade, – dark; clouded, wrapt in clouds; invisible &c. 447; buried, underground, *perdu*; incommunicado; secluded &c. 893.

un-disclosed &c. 529, -told &c. 527; covert &c. (*latent*) 526; mysterious &c. (*unintelligible*) 519.

irrevealable, inviolable; confidential; esoteric; not to be spoken of.

obreptitious, furtive, stealthy, feline; skulking &c. *v.*; surreptitious, underhand, hole and corner; sly &c. (*cunning*) 702; secretive, evasive, non-committal, reserved, reticent, uncommunicative, buttoned up; close, – as wax; taciturn &c. 585.

**Adv.** secretly &c. *adj.*; in -secret, – private, – one's sleeve, – holes and corners; in the dark &c. *adj.*

*januis clausis*, with closed doors, *à huis clos*; hugger-mugger, *à la dérobée*; under the -cloak of, – rose, – table; *sub rosâ, en tapinois*, in the background, aside, on the sly, with bated breath, *sotto voce*, in a whisper, without beat of drum, *à la sourdine*.

in –, strict- confidence; confidentially &c. *adj.*; between -ourselves, – you and me; *entre nous, inter nos*, under the seal of secrecy; in -code, – cipher.

underhand, by stealth, like a thief in the night; stealthily &c. *adj.*; behind -the scenes, – the curtain, – one's back, – a screen &c. 530; *incognito*; *in camerâ*.

**Phr.** it -must, – will- go no further; 'tell it not in Gath,' nobody the wiser.

**529. Disclosure.—N.** disclosure; retection; unveiling &c. *v.*; deterration, revealment, revelation; divulgence, expos-ition, -ure; *exposé*, whole truth; tell-tale &c. (*news*) 532.

acknowledgment, avowal; confession, -al; shrift.

**530. Ambush.** [Means of concealment.]—**N.** hiding-place; secret -place. – drawer; recess, hole, funk hole, holes and corners; closet, crypt, *adytum*, abditory, *oubliette*, safe, – deposit; cache.

am-bush, -buscade; stalking horse: lurking-hole, -place; secret path,

bursting of a bubble; *dénouement.*

**V.** dis-close, -cover, -mask; draw –, draw aside –, lift –, raise –, lift up –, remove –, tear- the -veil, – curtain; un-mask, -veil, -fold, -cover, -seal, -kennel; take off –, break- the seal; lay -open, – bare; expose; open, – up; bare, bring to light; evidence; make - clear, – evident, – manifest; evince.

divulge, reveal, break; let into the secret; reveal the secrets of the prison-house; tell &c. (*inform*) 527; breathe, utter, blab, peach; let -out, – fall, – drop, – the cat out of the bag; betray; tell tales, – out of school; come out with; give -vent, – utterance- to; open the lips, blurt out, vent, whisper about; speak out &c. (*make manifest*) 525; make public &c. 531; unriddle &c. (*find out*) 480a; split; blow the gaff; break the news.

acknowledge, allow, concede, grant, admit, own, confess, avow, throw off all disguise, turn inside out, make a clean breast; show one's -hand, – cards; unburden –, disburden- one's -mind, – con-science, – heart; open –, lay bare –, tell a piece of- one's mind; unbosom oneself, own to the soft impeachment; say –, speak- the truth; turn -King's, –Queen's, –State's- evidence.

raise –, drop –, lift –, remove –, throw off- the mask; expose; debunk; lay open; un-deceive, -beguile; disabuse, set right, correct, open the eyes of; *désillusionner.*

be -disclosed &c.; transpire, come to light; come in sight &c. (*be visible*) 446; become known, escape the lips; come –, ooze –, creep –, leak –, peep –, crop- out; show its -face, – colours; discover &c. itself; break through the clouds, flash on the mind.

**Adj.** disclosed &c. *v.*

**Int.** out with it!

**Phr.** the murder is out; a light breaks in upon one; the scales fall from one's eyes; the eyes are opened.

backstairs; retreat &c. (*refuge*) 666.

screen, cover, shade, blinker; veil, curtain, blind, *purdah,* cloak, cloud.

mask, vizor, visor, disguise, masquer-ade dress, domino; *camouflage.*

pitfall &c. (*source of danger*) 667; trap &c. (*snare*) 545.

**V.** ambush, ambuscade, lie in ambush &c. (*hide oneself*) 528; lie in wait for; set a trap for &c. (*deceive*) 545.

**Adv.** *aux aguets.*

---

**531. Publication.—N.** publication; public -announcement &c. 527; promulgation, propagation, proclamation, pronouncement, encyclical, *pronunciamento;* circulation, indiction, edition, imprint, impression, printing; hue and cry.

publicity, notoriety, currency, flagrancy, cry, *bruit; vox populi;* report &c. (*news*) 532.

the Press, fourth estate, public press, newspaper, periodical, journal, gazette; house organ, trade publication, tabloid; daily, weekly, monthly, quarterly, annual, magazine, monograph, book; review; news sheet, special edition, supplement, feature, rotogravure, comic strips; leaflet, pamphlet; telegraphy; publisher &c. *v.*

circular, – letter; manifesto, advertisement, puff, placard, bill, *affiche,* broadside, poster; notice &c. 527; programme.

**V.** publish; make -public, – known &c. (*information*) 527; speak –, talk- of; broach, utter; put forward; circulate, propagate, promulgate; spread –, abroad; rumour, diffuse, disseminate, evulgate; put –, give –, send- forth; emit, edit, get out; issue; cover, report; bring –, lay –, drag- before the public; give -out, – to the world; put –, bandy –, hawk –, buzz –, whisper –, bruit –, blaze- about; drag into the -open day, – limelight; voice.

proclaim, herald, blazon; blaze –, noise- abroad; sound a trumpet; trumpet –, thunder- forth; give tongue; announce with -beat of drum, – flourish of trumpets; proclaim -from the housetops, – at Charing Cross, at the cross roads; declare, declaim.

advertise, placard; post, – up; *afficher*, publish in the Gazette, send round the crier.

raise a -cry, – hue and cry, – report; set news afloat.

telegraph, cable, wireless, broadcast.

be -published &c.; be –, become- public &c. *adj.*; come out; go –, fly –, buzz –, blow- about; get -about, – abroad, – afloat, – wind; find vent; see the light; go forth, take air, acquire currency, pass current; go -the rounds, – the round of the newspapers, – through the length and breadth of the land; *virum volitare per ora*; pass from mouth to mouth; spread; run –, spread- like wildfire.

**Adj.** published &c. *v.*; current &c. *(news)* 532; in circulation, public; notorious; flagrant, arrant; open &c. 525; trumpet-tongued; encyclical, promulgatory; exoteric.

**Adv.** publicly &c. *adj.*; in open court, with open doors; in the limelight.

**Int.** *Oyez!* O yes! notice!

**Phr.** notice is hereby given; this is –, these are- to give notice.

---

**532. News.—N.** news; information &c. 527; piece –, budget- of -news, – information; report, story, yarn, copy, filler, intelligence, tidings; stop press news.

word, advice, *aviso*, message; dis-, des-patch; radio, telegram, cablegram, wireless telegram, radiogram, marconi-gram, communication, errand, em-bassy; *bulletin, petit bleu.*

rumour, hearsay, *on dit*, flying rumour, news stirring, cry, buzz, *bruit*, fame; talk, *ouï-dire*, scandal, eaves-dropping; town –, table- talk; tittle-tattle; *canard*, topic of the day, idea afloat.

fresh –, stirring –, old –, stale- news; glad tidings; old –, stale- story.

narrator &c. *(describe)* 594; news-, scandal-monger; tale-bearer; tell-tale, gossip, tattler, busy-body, chatterer; informer.

**V.** transpire &c. *(be disclosed)* 529; rumour &c. *(publish)* 531.

**Adj.** many-tongued; rumoured; publicly –, currently- -rumoured, – reported; rife, current, floating, afloat, going about, in circulation, in everyone's mouth, all over the town.

**Adv.** as the story -goes, – runs; as they say, it is said.

**533. Secret.—N.** secret; dead –, profound- secret; *arcanum*, mystery; latency &c. 526; Asian mystery; sealed book, secrets of the prison-house; *le dessous des cartes*.

enigma, riddle, puzzle, nut to crack, conundrum, charade, rebus, logogriph; mono-, ana-gram; acrostic, cross-word puzzle; Sphinx; *crux criticorum*.

maze, labyrinth, Hyrcynian wood.

problem &c. *(question)* 461; paradox &c. *(difficulty)* 704; unintelligibility &c. 519; *terra incognita* &c. *(ignorance)* 491.

**Adj.** secret &c. *(concealed)* 528.

---

**534. Messenger.—N.** messenger, envoy, emissary, legate; nuncio, internuncio; intermediary; ambassador &c. *(diplomatist)* 758.

marshal, flag-bearer, herald, crier, trumpeter, bellman, pursuivant, *parlementaire, apparitor*.

courier, runner, dawk, *estafette*; Hermes, Mercury, Iris, Ariel.

postman, letter carrier, telegraph boy, messenger boy, district mes-senger; despatch rider, commissionaire, errand-boy.

mail; post, -office; letter-bag; mail -boat, – train, – coach, – van, air mail; tele-graph, -phone; cable, wire; carrier-pigeon; wireless tele-graph, -phone; radiotele-graph, -phone.

journalist, newspaperman, reporter; gentleman –, representative- of the press; sob sister; penny-a-liner; special –, war –, own- correspondent; spy, scout; informer &c. 527.

**535. Affirmation.—N.** affirm-ance, -ation; statement, allegation, assertion, predication, declaration, word, averment.

asseveration, adjuration, swearing, oath, affidavit; deposition &c. (*record*) 551; avouchment, assurance; protest, -ation; profession; acknowledgment &c. (*assent*) 488; pledge.

vote, voice, suffrage, ballot.

remark, observation; position &c. (*proposition*) 514; saying, *dictum*, sentence, *ipse dixit*.

emphasis, positiveness, peremptoriness; dogmatism &c. (*certainty*) 474; dogmatist &c. 887.

**V.** assert; make -an assertion &c. *n.*; have one's say; say, affirm, predicate, declare, state, represent; protest, profess.

put -forth, – forward; advance, allege, propose, propound, enunciate, enounce, broach, set forth, hold out, maintain, contend, pronounce, pretend.

depose, depone, aver, avow, avouch, asseverate, swear; make –, take one's- oath; make –, swear –, put in- an affidavit; take one's Bible oath, kiss the book, vow, *vitam impendere vero*; swear till -one is black in the face, – all's blue; be sworn, call Heaven to witness; vouch, warrant, certify, assure, swear by bell, book and candle.

swear by &c. (*believe*) 484; insist –, take one's stand- upon; emphasize, lay stress on; assert -roundly, – positively; lay down, – the law; raise one's voice, dogmatize, have the last word; rap out; repeat; re-assert, -affirm.

announce &c. (*information*) 527; acknowledge &c. (*assent*) 488; attest &c. (*evidence*) 467; adjure &c. (*put to one's oath*) 768.

**Adj.** asserting &c. *v.*; declaratory, predicatory, pronunciative, affirmative, *soi-disant*; positive; certain &c. 474; express, explicit &c. (*patent*) 525; absolute, emphatic, flat, broad, round, pointed, marked, distinct, decided, confident, assertive, insistent, trenchant, dogmatic, definitive, formal, solemn, categorical, peremptory; unretracted; predicable, affirmable.

**536. Negation.—N.** ne-, abne-gation; denial; dis-avowal, -claimer; abjuration; contra-diction, -vention; recusation, protest; rebuttal; recusancy &c. (*dissent*) 489; flat –, emphatic- -contradiction, – denial; *démenti*.

qualification &c. 469; repudiation &c. 610; retractation &c. 607; confutation &c. 479; refusal &c. 764; prohibition &c. 761.

**V.** deny; contra-dict, -vene; controvert, give denial to, gainsay, negative, shake the head.

dis-own, -affirm, -claim, -avow; recant &c. 607; revoke &c. (*abrogate*) 756.

dispute, impugn, traverse, rebut, join issue upon; bring –, call- in question &c. (*doubt*) 485.

deny -flatly, – peremptorily, – emphatically, – absolutely, – wholly, – entirely; give the lie to, belie.

repudiate &c. 610; set aside, ignore &c. 460; rebut &c. (*confute*) 479; qualify &c. 469; refuse &c. 764.

**Adj.** denying &c. *v.*; denied &c. *v.*; contradictory; negat-ive, -ory; revocatory; recusant &c. (*dissenting*) 489; at issue upon.

**Adv.** no, nay, not, nowise; not a -bit, – whit, – jot; not -at all, – in the least, – so; no such thing; nothing of the -kind, – sort; quite the contrary, *tout au contraire*, far from it; *tant s'en faut*; on no account, in no respect; by -no, – no manner of- means; negatively.

**Phr.** there never was a greater mistake; I know better; *non hæc in fœdera*.

**Adv.** affirmatively &c. *adj.*; in the affirmative.

with emphasis, *ex cathedrâ*, without fear of contradiction.

I must say, indeed, i' faith, let me tell you, why, give me leave to say, marry, you may be sure, I'd have you to know; upon my -word, – honour; by my troth, egad, I assure you; by -jingo, – Jove, – George, – &c.; troth, seriously, sadly; in –, in sober- -sadness, – truth, – earnest; of a truth, truly, pardi, perdy; in all conscience, upon oath; be assured &c. (*belief*) 484; yes &c. (*assent*) 488; I'll -warrant, – warrant you, – engage, – answer for it, – be bound, – venture to say, – take my oath; in fact, as a matter of fact, forsooth, joking apart; so help me God; not to mince the matter.

**Phr.** quoth he; *dixi.*

**537. Teaching.—N.** teaching &c. *v.*; instruction; edification; education; pedagogy; tuition; tutor-, tutel-age; direction, guidance.

qualification, preparation; train-, school-ing &c. *v.*; discipline; exer-cise, -citation; drill, practice.

persuasion, proselytism, propagandism, *propaganda*; in-doctrination, -culcation, -oculation.

explanation &c. (*interpretation*) 522; lesson, lecture, sermon, homily; apologue, parable; discourse, prelection, preachment, disquisition.

exercise, task; *curriculum*; course, – of study; grammar, three R's, initiation, A. B. C. &c. (*beginning*) 66.

elementary –, primary –, secondary –, grammar school –, high school –, college –, university –, technical –, liberal –, classical –, religious –, denominational –, moral –, secular- education; technical –, vocational- training; university extension lectures; propædeutics, moral tuition; evening classes, correspondence course.

physical education, gymnastics, calisthenics, eurythmics; *sloyd.*

**V.** teach, instruct, edify, school, tutor; cram, prime, coach; enlighten &c. (*inform*) 527.

in-culcate, -doctrinate, -oculate, -fuse, -stil, -fix, -graft, -filtrate; imbue, -pregnate, -plant; graft, sow the seeds of, disseminate, propagandize.

give an idea of; put -up to, – in the way of; set right.

sharpen the wits, enlarge the mind; give new ideas, open the eyes, bring forward, 'teach the young idea how to shoot'; improve &c. 658.

**538. Misteaching.—N.** mis-teaching, -information, -intelligence, -guidance, -direction, -persuasion, -instruction, -leading &c. *v.*; perversion, false teaching; sophistry &c. 477; college of Laputa; the blind leading the blind.

**V.** mis-inform, -teach, -direct, -guide, -instruct, -correct; pervert; put on a false –, throw off the- scent; deceive &c. 545; mislead &c. (*error*) 495; misrepresent; lie &c. 544; *spargere voces in vulgum ambiguas*, preach to the wise, teach one's grandmother to suck eggs.

render unintelligible &c. 519; bewilder &c. (*uncertainty*) 475; mystify &c. (*conceal*) 528; unteach.

**Adj.** misteaching &c. *v.*; unedifying.

**Phr.** *piscem natare doces.*

**539. Learning.—N.** learning; acquisition of -knowledge &c. 490, – skill &c. 698; acquirement, attainment; edification, scholarship, erudition; lore; information; self-instruction; study, reading, perusal; inquiry &c. 461.

ap-, prenticeship; pupil-age, -arity; tutelage, novitiate, matriculation.

docility &c. (*willingness*) 602; aptitude &c. 698.

**V.** learn; acquire –, gain –, receive –, take in –, drink in –, imbibe –, pick up –, gather –, get –, obtain –, collect –, glean- knowledge, – information, - learning.

acquaint oneself with, master; make oneself -master of, – acquainted with; grind, cram; get –, coach- up; learn by -heart, – rote.

read, spell, peruse; con –, pore –, thumb- over; wade through; dip into;

expound &c. (*interpret*) 522; lecture; prelect; read –, give- a -lesson,– lecture, – sermon, – discourse; hold forth, preach; sermon-, moral-ize; point a moral.

train, discipline; bring up, – to; educate, form, ground, prepare, qualify, drill, exercise, practice, habituate, familiarize with, nurture, dry-nurse, breed, rear, take in hand; break, – in; tame; pre-instruct; initiate; inure &c. (*habituate*) 613.

put to nurse, send to school.

direct, guide; direct attention to &c. (*attention*) 457; impress upon the -mind, – memory; beat into, – the head; convince &c. (*belief*) 484.

**Adj.** teaching &c. *v.*; taught &c. *v.*; educational; scholastic, academic, doctrinal; disciplinal; instructive, didactic, hortative, pedagogic, tutorial.

**Phr.** the schoolmaster abroad.

**540. Teacher.**—N. teacher, trainer, instructor, institutor, master, tutor, don, director, Corypheus, dry nurse, coach, grinder, crammer; governor, bear-leader; governess, duenna; disciplinarian.

professor, lecturer, reader, prelector, prolocutor, preacher; Boanerges; pastor &c. (*clergy*) 996; schoolmaster, dominie, usher, pedagogue, abecedarian; schoolmistress, dame, monitor, proctor, pupil-teacher.

expositor &c. 524; preceptor, guide; mentor &c. (*adviser*) 695; pioneer, apostle, missionary, propagandist, moonshee; example &c. (*model for imitation*) 22.

professorship &c. (*school*) 542.
tutelage &c. (*teaching*) 537.
**Adj.** professorial, tutorial &c. 537.

run the eye -over, – through; turn over the leaves.

study; be -studious &c. *adj.*; consume the midnight oil, mind one's book.

go to -school, – college, – the university; serve -an (*or* one's) apprenticeship, – one's time; learn one's trade; be -informed &c. 527; be -taught &c. 537.

**Adj.** studious; schol-astic, -arly; teachable; docile &c. (*willing*) 602; apt &c. 698, industrious &c. 682; learned, erudite.

**Adv.** at one's books; *in statu pupillari* &c. (*learner*) 541.

**541. Learner.**—N. learner, scholar, student, *alumnus*, *élève*, pupil; ap-, prentice; articled clerk; school-boy, -girl, beginner, tyro, abecedarian, alphabetarian.

recruit, novice, neophyte, tenderfoot, inceptor, *débutant*, catechumen, probationer; undergraduate; freshman, frosh; sophomore, junior, senior; junior –, senior- soph; sophister, questionist, fellow-, commoner, pensioner, exhibitioner, sizar, scholar, fellow, advanced –, post graduate –, research- student.

class, form, grade, standard, remove; pupilage &c. (*learning*) 539.

disciple, follower, apostle, proselyte; fellow student, school-mate, -fellow, class mate, condisciple.

**Adj.** *in statu pupillari*, in leading strings, sophomoric.

**542. School.**—N. school, academy, university, *alma mater*, college, seminary, Lyceum; instit-ute, -ution, *conservatoire*; *palæstra, gymnasium*.

day –. boarding –, public –, preparatory –, elementary –, primary –, infant –, dame's –, grammar –, middle class –, Board –, County –, Council –, parochial –, denominational –, Sunday –, National –, British and Foreign –, collegiate –, secondary –, continuation –, night –, correspondence –, secretarial –, military –, law –, medical –, business –, technical- school; technical –, training- college; Polytechnic; training ship; *Kindergarten*, nursery, *crèche*, reformatory.

pulpit, desk, reading desk, ambo, class-, lecture-room, theatre, amphitheatre, forum, stage, rostrum, platform, hustings, tribune.

school -, horn -, text- book; grammar, primer, abecedary, rudiments, manual, *vade mecum*, Lindley Murray, Cocker.

professor-, lecture-, reader-ship; chair; schoolmaster &c. 540.

School Board, Council of Education; *propaganda*.

**Adj.** scholastic, academic, collegiate; educational.

**Adv.** *ex cathedrâ*.

**543. Veracity.—N.** veracity; truthfulness, frankness &c. *adj.*; truth, sooth, sincerity, candour, honesty, fidelity; plain dealing, *bona fides*; love of truth; probity &c. 939; ingenuousness &c. (*artlessness*) 703.

the truth the whole truth and nothing but the truth; honest -, sober-truth &c. (*fact*) 494; unvarnished tale; light of truth.

**V.** speak -, tell- the truth; speak by the card; paint in its -, show oneself in one's-true colours; make a clean breast &c. (*disclose*) 529; speak one's mind &c. (*be blunt*) 703; not -lie &c. 544, - deceive &c. 545.

**Adj.** truthful, true; ver-acious, -edical; scrupulous &c. (*honourable*) 939; sincere, candid, frank, open, straightforward, unreserved; open-, true-, simple- hearted; honest, trustworthy; undissembling &c. (dissemble &c. 544); guileless, pure; unperjured, true blue, as good as one's word; unaffected, unfeigned, *bonâ fide*; outspoken, ingenuous &c. (*artless*) 703; undisguised &c. (*real*) 494.

**Adv.** truly &c. (*really*) 494; on oath; in plain words &c. 703; in -, with -, of a -, in good -, very- truth; as the -dial to the sun, - needle to the pole; honour bright; troth; in good -sooth, - earnest; unfeignedly, with no nonsense, in sooth, sooth to say, *bonâ fide*, *in foro conscientiæ*; without equivocation; *cartes sur table*, from the bottom of one's heart; by my troth &c. (*affirmation*) 535.

**544. Falsehood. — N.** false-hood, -ness; fals-ity, -ification; misrepresentation; deception &c. 545; untruth &c. 546; guile; bad faith; lying &c. *v.*; misrepresentation; mendacity, perjury, false swearing; forgery, invention, fabrication; subreption; covin.

perversion -, suppression- of truth; *suppressio veri*; perversion, distortion, false colouring; exaggeration &c. 549; prevarication, equivocation, shuffling, fencing, evasion, fraud; *suggestio falsi* &c. (*lie*) 546; mystification &c. (*concealment*) 528; simulation &c. (*imitation*) 19; dis-simulation, -sembling; deceit.

sham; pretence, pretending, malingering.

lip -homage, - service; mouth honour; hollowness; mere -show, - outside, eye-wash, window dressing; duplicity, double dealing, insincerity, hypocrisy, cant, humbug, casuistry; jesuit-ism, -ry; pharisaism; Machiavellism, 'organized hypocrisy'; crocodile tears, mealy-mouthedness, quackery; charlatan-ism, -ry; gammon; bun-kum, -come; flam, bam, flim-flam, cajolery, flattery; Judas kiss; perfidy &c. (*bad faith*) 940; *il volto sciolto i pensieri stretti*.

unfairness &c. (*dishonesty*) 940; artfulness &c. (*cunning*) 702; misstatement &c. (*error*) 495.

**V.** be -false &c. *adj.*, - a liar &c. 548; speak -falsely &c. *adv.*; tell -a lie &c. 546; lie, fib; lie like a trooper; swear falsely, forswear, perjure oneself, bear false witness.

mis-state, -quote, -cite, -report, -represent; belie, falsify, pervert, distort; put a false construction upon &c. (*misinterpret*) 523.

prevaricate, equivocate, quibble; palter, - to the understanding; *répondre en Normand*, trim, shuffle, fence, mince the truth, beat about the bush, blow hot and cold, play fast and loose.

garble, gloss over, disguise, give a colour to; give -, put- a -gloss, - false colouring- upon; colour, varnish, cook, dress up, embroider; varnish right and puzzle wrong, exaggerate &c. 549.

invent, fabricate; trump -, get- up; forge, hatch, concoct; romance &c. (*imagine*) 515; cry 'wolf!'

dis-semble, -simulate; feign, assume, put on, pretend, make believe; play -false, - a double game; coquet; act -, play- a part; affect &c. 855; simulate, pass off for; counterfeit, fake, sham, make a show of; malinger; swing the lead; say the grapes are sour.

cant, play the hypocrite, sham Abraham, *faire pattes de velours*, put on the mask, clean the outside of the platter, lie like a conjuror; hang out -, hold out -, sail under- false colours; 'commend the poisoned chalice to the lips'; *spargere voces in vulgum ambiguas*; deceive &c. 545.

**Adj.** false, deceitful, mendacious, unveracious, fraudulent, untruthful, dishonest; faith-, truth-, troth-less; un-fair, -candid; evasive; un-, dis-ingenuous; hollow, insincere, *Parthis mendacior*; forsworn.

canting; hypocrit-, jesuit-, pharisa-ical; tartuffish; Machiavelian; double-tongued, -faced, -handed, -minded, -hearted, -dealing; two-faced, bare-faced; Janus-faced; smooth-faced, -spoken, -tongued; plausible; mealy-mouthed; affected &c. 855.

collus-ive, -ory; artful &c. (*cunning*) 702; perfidious &c. 940, spurious &c. (*deceptive*) 545; untrue &c. 546; falsified &c. *v.*; covinous.

**Adv.** falsely &c. *adj.*; *à la Tartufe*, with a double tongue; out of whole cloth; slily &c. (*cunning*) 702.

**545. Deception.—N.** deception; falseness &c. 544; untruth &c. 546; impos-ition, -ture; fraud, deceit, guile; fraudulen-ce, -cy; covin; knavery &c. (*cunning*) 702; misrepresentation &c. (*falsehood*) 544.

delusion, gullery, bluff, spoof, *blague*; juggl-ing, -ery; sleight of hand, legerdemain; presti-giation, -digitation; magic &c. 992; conjur-ing, -ation; hocus-pocus, jockeyship; trickery, coggery, hanky-panky, chicanery, pettifogging, sharp practice; *supercherie*, cozenage, circumvention, ingannation, collusion; treachery &c. 940; practical joke.

trick, cheat, wile, ruse, blind, feint, plant, bubble, fetch, catch, chicane, juggle, reach, hocus, bite; thimble-rig, card-sharping, artful dodge, machination, swindle, hoax; tricks upon travellers; confidence trick; stratagem &c. (*artifice*) 702; theft &c. 791.

snare, trap, pitfall, decoy, gin; sprin-ge, -gle; noose, hook; bait, decoy-duck, tub to the whale, baited trap, *guei à-pens*; cobweb, net, meshes, toils, mouse-trap, bird-lime; ambush &c. 530; trap-door, sliding panel, false bottom; spring-net, -gun; mask, -ed battery; mine booby trap.

Cornish hug; wolf in sheep's clothing &c. (*deceiver*) 548; disguise, -ment; false colours, masquerade, mummery, borrowed plumes; *pattes de velours*.

mockery &c. (*imitation*) 19; copy &c. 21; counterfeit, sham, Brummagem, make-believe, forgery, fraud, fake; lie &c. 546; 'a mockery, a delusion, and a snare,' hollow mockery.

whited -, painted- sepulchre; tinsel, paste, false jewellery, scagliola, ormolu, German silver, Britannia metal, paint; jerry building; man of straw.

illusion &c. (*error*) 495; *ignis fatuus* &c. 423; *mirage* &c. 443.

**V.** deceive, take in; defraud, cheat, jockey, do, cozen, diddle, nab, gyp, chouse, double cross, play one false, bilk, cully, jilt, bite, pluck, swindle, victimize; abuse; mystify; blind one's eyes; blindfold, hoodwink, spoof, bluff; throw dust into the eyes, 'keep the word of promise to the ear and break it to the hope,' 'draw a herring across the trail.'

impose –, practise –, play –, put –, palm –, foist- upon; snatch a verdict.

circumvent, overreach; out-reach, -wit, -manœuvre; steal a march upon, give the go-by to, leave in the lurch.

set –, lay- a -trap, – snare- for; bait the hook, forelay, spread the toils, lime; decoy, waylay, lure, beguile, delude, inveigle; tra-, tre-pan; kidnap; let-, hook-in; trick; en-, in-trap, -snare, entoil, benet; nick, springe; catch, – in a trap; sniggle, entangle, illaqueate, hocus, practise on one's credulity, dupe, gull, hoax, fool, befool, bamboozle; hum, -bug; gammon, stuff up, dope, sell; play a -trick, – practical joke- upon one; balk, trip up, throw a tub to a whale; fool to the top of one's bent, send on -a wild goose chase, – a fool's errand; make -game, – a fool, – an April fool, – an ass- of; trifle with, cajole, flatter; come over &c. (*influence*) 615; gild the pill, make things pleasant, divert, put a good face upon; dissemble &c. 544.

cog, – the dice, play with marked cards; live by one's wits, play at hide and seek; obtain money under false pretences &c. (*steal*) 791; conjure, juggle, practise chicanery; gerrymander.

play –, palm –, foist –, fob- off.

lie &c. 544; misinform &c. 538; mislead &c. (*error*) 495; betray &c. 940; be -deceived &c. 547.

**Adj.** deceived &c. *v.*; deceiving &c. *v.*; cunning &c. 702; prestigi-ous, -atory; decept-ive, -ious; deceitful, covinous; delus-ive, -ory; illus-ive, -ory; elusive, insidious, *ad captandum vulgus*.

untrue &c. 546; mock, sham, make-believe, counterfeit, faked, pseudo, spurious, so-called, pretended, feigned, trumped up, bogus, scamped, fraudulent, tricky, factitious, artificial, bastard; surreptitious, illegitimate, contraband, adulterated, sophisticated; unsound, rotten at the core; colourable; disguised; meretricious; tinsel, pinchbeck, plated; catch-penny; Brummagem; simulated &c. 544.

**Adv.** under -false colours, – the garb of, – cover of; over the left.

**Phr.** *fronti nulla fides.*

**546. Untruth.—N.** untruth, falsehood, lie, story, thing that is not, fib, bounce, crammer, taradiddle, whopper.

forgery, fabrication, invention; mis-statement, -representation; per-version, falsification, gloss, *suggestio falsi*; exaggeration &c. 549.

fiction; fable, nursery tale; romance &c. (*imagination*) 515; untrue –, false –, trumped up- -story, – statement; thing devised by the enemy; *canard*; shave, sell, hum, yarn, traveller's tale, Canterbury tale, cock and bull story, fairy tale, clap-trap.

myth, moonshine, bosh, all my eye, -and Betty Martin, mare's nest, farce.

irony; half truth, white lie, pious fraud; mental reservation &c. (*concealment*) 528.

pretence, pretext; false -plea &c. 617; subterfuge, evasion, shift, shuffle, make-believe; sham &c. (*deception*) 545.

profession, empty words; Judas kiss &c. (*hypocrisy*) 544; disguise &c. (*mask*) 530.

**V.** have a false meaning; not ring true.

pretend, sham, feign, counterfeit, make believe.

**Adj.** untrue, false, trumped up; void of –, without- foundation; far

from the truth, false as dicer's oaths; unfounded, *ben trovato*, invented, fabulous, fabricated, forged; fict-, fact-, supposit-, surrept-itious; e-, il-lusory; ironical; satirical; evasive; *soi-disant* &c. (*misnamed*) 565.
Phr. *se non è vero è ben trovato*.

**547. Dupe.—N.** dupe, gull, gudgeon, *gobemouche*, cull, cully, victim, sucker, pigeon, April fool; laughing stock &c. 857; Cyclops, simple Simon, flat, mug, greenhorn; fool &c. 501; puppet, cat's paw.

**V.** be -deceived &c. 545, – the dupe of; fall into a trap; swallow –, nibble at- the bait; bite; catch a Tartar.

**Adj.** credulous &c. 486; mistaken &c. (*error*) 495.

**548. Deceiver.—N.** deceiver &c. (deceive &c. 545); dissembler, hypo-crite; sophist, Pharisee, Jesuit, Maw-worm, Pecksniff, Joseph Surface, Tar-tufe, Janus; serpent, snake in the grass, cockatrice, Judas, wolf in sheep's clothing; Molly Maguire; jilt; shuffler.
liar &c. (lie &c. 544); story-teller, perjurer, false-witness, *menteur*, -à triple étage, -à payer patente; Scapin.
impostor, pretender, capper, decoy, fraud, *soi-disant*, humbug; adventurer; Cagliostro, Fernam Mendez Pinto; ass in lion's skin &c. (*bungler*) 701; actor &c. (*stage player*) 599.

quack, *charlatan*, mountebank, saltimbanco, *saltimbanque*, em-piric, quacksalver, medicaster.

conjuror, juggler, magician, necromancer, trickster, prestidigita-tor, medium, jockey; crimp; decoy-duck, stool pigeon; rogue, knave, cheat; swindler &c. (*thief*) 792; jobber.

**549. Exaggeration.—N.** exaggeration; expansion &c. 194; hyperbole, stretch, strain, colouring; high colouring, caricature, *caricatura*; extrav-agance &c. (*nonsense*) 497; Baron Munchausen; men in buckram, yarn, fringe, embroidery, traveller's tale; Ossa upon Pelion.

storm in a teacup; much ado about nothing &c. (*over-estimation*) 482; puffery &c. (*boasting*) 884; rant &c. (*turgescence*) 577.

figure of speech, *façon de parler*; stretch of -fancy, – the imagination; flight of fancy &c. (*imagination*) 515.

false colouring &c. (*falsehood*) 544; aggravation &c. 835.

**V.** exaggerate, magnify, pile up, aggravate; amplify &c. (*expand*) 194; overestimate &c. 482; hyperbolize; over-charge, -state, -draw, -lay, -shoot the mark, -praise; make -much, – the most- of; strain, – a point; stretch, – a point; go great lengths; spin a long yarn; draw –, shoot with- a long-bow; deal in the marvellous.

out-Herod Herod, run riot, talk at random.

heighten, overcolour, colour -highly, – too highly; embroider, *broder*; flourish; colour &c. (*misrepresent*) 544; puff &c. (*boast*) 884.

**Adj.** exaggerated &c. *v.*; overwrought; bombastic &c. (*magniloquent*) 577; hyperbolical, on stilts; fabulous, extravagant, preposterous, egre-gious, *outré*, high-flying.

**Adv.** hyperbolically &c. *adj.*

### Section III. Means of Communicating Ideas
#### 1.° *Natural Means*

**550. Indication.—N.** indication; symbol-ism, -ization; semeio-logy, -tics; sign of the times.

lineament, feature, *trait*, characteristic, trick, diagnostic; divining-rod; cloven hoof; footfall; means of recognition; earmark.

sign, symbol; ind-ex, -ice, -icator; point, -er; marker; exponent, note, token, symptom.

type, figure, emblem, cipher, device; representation &c. 554; epigraph, motto, posy.

gest-ure, -iculation; pantomime; wink, glance, leer; nod, shrug, beck; touch, nudge; grip; dactylo-logy, -nomy; Freemasonry, telegraphy, chirology, by-play, dumb-show; cue; hint &c. 527; clue, clew, key, scent, track &c. 551.

signal, -post; rocket, blue light; watch-fire, -tower; telegraph, semaphore, flag-staff; cresset, fiery cross; calumet; heliograph, signal-, flash-lamp.

mark, line, stroke, dash, score, stripe, streak, scratch, tick, dot, point, notch, nick, blaze; asterisk, red letter, italics, heavy type, inverted commas, quotation marks, sublineation, underlining, jotting; print; impr-int, -ess, -ession; note, annotation, mark of exclamation.

[For identification] badge, criterion; counter-check, -mark, -sign, -foil; duplicate, tally; label, tab, ticket, stub, billet, letter, counter, *tessera*, card, bill, check; witness, voucher; stamp; *cachet*; trade -, hall- mark; broad arrow; signature; address -, visiting- card; *carte de visite*; credentials &c. (*evidence*) 467; passport, indentity book, *carte d' identité*; attestation; hand, - writing, sign-manual; cipher; monogram, - mark, seal, sigil, signet; autograph, -y; paraph, brand; superscription; in-, en-dorsement; title, heading, rubric, docket; *mot -de passe, - du guet*; *passe-parole*; shibboleth; watch-, catch-, pass-word; *open sesame!*

insignia; banner, -et, -ol; bandrol; flag, colours, streamer, standard, eagle, labarum, oriflamb, *oriflamme*; figure-head; ensign; pen-non, -nant, -dant; burgee, blue Peter, jack, ancient, gonfalon, Union jack; tricolour, stars and stripes; bunting, Jolly Roger, *drapeau, pavillon*.

heraldry, crest; coat of -, arms; armorial bearings, hatchment; e-, scutcheon; shield, supporters; livery, uniform; cockade, *epaulette*, brassard, chevron; garland, chaplet, love-knot, fillet, favour.

[Of locality] beacon, cairn, post, staff, flagstaff, hand, pointer, vane, cock, weathercock; guide-, hand-, finger-, directing-, sign-post; pillars of Hercules, pharos, signal fire; bench-, land-, sea-mark; lighthouse, balize; pole-, load-, lode-star; cynosure, guide; address, direction, name; sign, -board.

[Of the future] warning &c. 668; omen &c. 512; prefigurement &c. 511. [Of the past] trace record &c. 551. [Of danger] warning &c. 668; alarm &c. 669. [Of authority] sceptre &c. 747. [Of triumph] trophy &c. 733. [Of quantity] gauge &c. 466. [Of distance] mile-stone, -post. [Of disgrace] brand, fool's cap, stigma, mark of Cain. [For detection] check, tell-tale; test &c. (*experiment*) 463.

notification &c. (*information*) 527; advertisement &c. (*publication*) 531.

word of command, call; bugle-, trumpet-call; reveille, taps; bell, alarum, cry; battle -, rallying- cry.

church, bell, angelus, sacring bell; muezzin.

exposition &c. (*explanation*) 522; proof &c. (*evidence*) 467; pattern &c. (*prototype*) 22.

V. indicate; be the -sign &c. *n.*- of; denote, betoken; argue, testify &c. (*evidence*) 467; bear the -impress &c. *n.*- of; con-note, -notate.

represent, stand for; typify &c. (*prefigure*) 511; symbolize.

put -an indication, - a mark, - &c. *n.*; note, mark, tick, blaze, stamp, earmark; set one's seal upon; label, ticket, docket; dot, spot, score, dash, trace, chalk; print; im-print, -press, surprint; engrave, stereotype, electrotype.

make a -sign &c. *n.*; signalize; give –, hang out- a signal; beck, -on; gesture; nod; wink, glance, leer, nudge, shrug, tip the wink; gesticulate; raise –, hold up- the -finger, – hand; saw the air, suit the action to the word.

wave –, unfurl –, hoist –, hang out- a banner &c. *n.*; wave -the hand, – a kerchief; give the cue &c. (*inform*) 527; show one's colours; give –, sound- an alarm; beat the drum, sound the trumpets, raise a cry.

sign, seal, attest &c. (*evidence*) 467; underline &c. (*give importance to*) 642; call attention to &c. (*attention*) 457; give notice &c. (*inform*) 527.

**Adj.** indicat-ing &c. *v.*, -ive, -ory; de-, con-notative; diacritical, representative, typical, symbolic, pantomimic, pathognomonic, symptomatic, ominous, characteristic, demonstrative, diagnostic, exponential, emblematic, armorial; individual &c. (*special*) 79.

known –, recognizable- by; indicated &c. *v.*; pointed, marked.

[Capable of being denoted] denotable; indelible.

**Adv.** in token of; symbolically &c. *adj.*; in dumb show.

**Phr.** *ecce signum*; *ex ungue leonem, ex pede Herculem.*

---

**551. Record.**—**N.** trace, vestige, relic, remains; scar, *cicatrix*; foot-step, -mark, -print; track, mark, wake, trail, spoor, scent, *piste.*

monument, hatchment, escutcheon, slab, tablet, trophy, achievement; obelisk, pillar, column, monolith, cromlech, dolmen; memorial; *memento* &c. (*memory*) 505; testimonial, medal, ribbon, order; commemoration &c. (*celebration*) 883.

record, note, minute; *dossier;* register, -try; census, roll &c. (*list*) 86; cartulary, diptych, Domesday book; entry, memorandum, indorsement, inscription, copy, duplicate, docket; notch &c. (*mark*) 550; muniment, deed &c. (*security*) 771; document; deposition, *procès-verbal;* affidavit; certificate &c. (*evidence*) 467.

**552.** [Suppression of sign.] **Obliteration.**—**N.** obliteration; erasure, rasure; effacement; cancel, -lation; cassation; circumduction; deletion, blot; *tabula rasa.*

**V.** efface, obliterate, erase, rase, expunge, cancel; blot –, take –, rub –, scratch –, strike –, wipe –, wash –, sponge- out; wipe –, rub- off; wipe away; deface, render illegible; draw the pen through, apply the sponge.

be -effaced &c.; leave no -trace &c. 449; 'leave not a rack behind.'

**Adj.** obliterated &c. *v.*; out of print; printless; leaving no trace; intestate; un-recorded, -registered, -written.

**Int.** *dele;* out with it!

---

note-, memorandum-, pocket-, commonplace-book; portfolio; scoring-board, -sheet; bulletin board; card index, file; pigeon-holes, *excerpta, adversaria,* jottings, dottings.

gazette, -er; newspaper, magazine &c. 531; alman-ac, -ack; calendar, ephemeris, noctuary, diary, log, journal, account-, cash-, day-book, ledger.

archive, scroll, state-paper, Congressional Record, return, blue-book; statistics &c. 86; *compte rendu;* Acts –, Transactions –, Proceedings- of; Hansard's Debates; chronicle, annals; legend; history, biography &c. 594.

registration; en-, in-rolment; tabulation; entry, booking; signature &c. (*identification*) 550; recorder &c. 553; journalism.

drawing, photograph &c. 554; phonograph –, gramophone-record; music roll.

**V.** record; put –, place- upon record; go on record; chronicle, calendar, hand down to posterity; keep up the memory of &c. (*remember*) 505; commemorate &c. (*celebrate*) 883; report &c. (*inform*) 527; commit to –, reduce to- writing; put –, set down- -in writing, – in black and white; put –, jot –, take –, write –, note –, set- down; note, minute, put on paper; take –, make- a -note, – minute, – memorandum; make a return.

mark &c. (*indicate*) 550; sign &c. (*attest*) 467.

enter, book; post, – up; insert, make an entry of; mark –, tick-off; register, list, docket, enroll, inscroll; file &c. (*store*) 636.

**Adv.** on record.

**553. Recorder.—N.** recorder, notary, clerk; regis-trar, -trary, -ter; prothonotary; amanuensis, secretary, scribe, stenographer, remembrancer, book-keeper, *custos rotulorum*, Master of the Rolls.

annalist; histori-an, -ographer; chronicler, journalist, reporter, columnist; biographer &c. (*narrator*) 594; antiquary &c. (*antiquity*) 122; memorialist.

draughtsman &c. 559; engraver 558; photographer, cinematographer, camera man.

Recording instrument, recorder, camera, phonograph, gramophone, dictaphone, telegraphone, telautograph, printing telegraph, tape machine, ticker, time recorder, cash register, turnstile, speedometer, voting machine, seismograph, photostat.

**554. Representation.—N.** represent-
-ation, -ment; imitation &c. 19; illustration, delineation, depictment, portrayal; imagery, portraiture, iconography; design, -ing; art, fine arts; painting &c. 556; sculpture &c. 557; engraving &c. 558; photography, radiography, skiagraphy.

person-ation, -ification; impersonation; drama &c. 599.

**555. Misrepresentation.—N.** misrepresentation, distortion, exaggeration; daubing &c. *v.*; bad likeness daub, sign-painting; scratch, caricature; *anamorphosis*.

**V.** misrepresent, distort, overdraw, travesty, parody, burlesque, exaggerate, caricature, daub.

**Adj.** misrepresented &c. *v.*

picture, drawing, sketch, draught, draft; tracing; copy &c. 21; photo-, helio-graph; daguerreo-, talbo-, calo-, helio-type; cabinet, *carte-de-visite*, snapshot; X-ray photograph; radio-gram, -graph, skia-graph, -gram.

image, likeness, icon, portrait; striking –, speaking- likeness; very image; effigy, fac-simile.

figure, – head; puppet, doll, *figurine*, aglet, manikin, lay-figure, model, *marionnette, fantoccini*, bust; waxwork, statue, -tte, automaton, Robot.

hieroglyphic, anaglyph; dia-, mono-gram, -graph.

map, plan, chart; ground plan, projection, elevation; ichno-, carto-graphy; atlas; outline, scheme; view &c. (*painting*) 556.

artist, draughtsman &c. 559.

**V.** represent, delineate; depict, -ure; portray; picture; take –, catch- a likeness &c. *n.*; hit off, photograph, daguerreotype; figure; shadow -forth, – out; adumbrate; body forth; describe &c. 594; trace, copy; mould.

dress up; illustrate, symbolize.

paint &c. 556; carve &c. 557; engrave &c. 558.

person-ate, -ify; impersonate; assume a character; pose as; act;

play &c. (*drama*) 599; mimic &c. (*imitate*) 19; hold the mirror up to nature.

Adj. represent-ing &c. *v.*, -ative; illustrative; represented &c. *v.*; imitative, figurative.

like &c. 17; graphic &c. (*descriptive*) 594.

**556. Painting.—N.** painting; depicting; drawing &c. *v.*; design; perspective, skiagraphy; *chiaroscuro* &c. (*light*) 420; composition; treatment, values, atmosphere, tone, technique.

historical –, portrait –, miniature –, battle -, *genre* -, landscape –, marine –, fruit and flower –, scene- painting; scenography.

school, style; the grand style, high art, *genre*, portraiture; ornamental art &c. 847.

mono-, poly-chrome; *grisaille*.

pallet, palette; easel; brush, pencil, stump; blacklead, charcoal, crayons, chalk, pastel; paint &c. (*colouring matter*) 428; water-, body-, oil-colour; oils, oil-paint; varnish &c. 356a; *gouache*, tempera, distemper, fresco; enamel; encaustic painting; *graffito*, *gesso*; mosaic; tapestry.

picture, painting, piece, *tableau*, canvas; oil &c.- painting; cartoon; easel –, cabinet- picture; drawing, draught, draft; pencil &c. –, water-colour- drawing; sketch, outline; study.

portrait &c. (*representation*) 554; whole –, full –, half- length; kitcat. head; miniature; shade, *silhouette*; profile.

landscape, sea-piece, -scape; view, scene, prospect; interior; bird's-eye view; pan-, di-orama; still life.

picture –, art- gallery; studio, *atelier*.

**V.** paint, design, limn, draw, sketch, pencil, scratch, shade, stipple, hatch, dash off, chalk out, square up; colour, dead-colour, wash, varnish; draw in -pencil &c. *n.*; paint in -oils &c. *n.*; stencil; depict &c. (*represent*) 554.

Adj. painted &c. *v.*; pictorial, graphic, picturesque, decorative; classical, romantic, pre-Raphaelite, modern, cubist, futurist, vorticist, post-, impressionist.

pencil, oil &c. *n.*

Adv. in -pencil &c. *n.*

Phr. *fecit, delineavit, pinxit:*

**557. Sculpture.—N.** sculpture, insculpture; carving &c. *v.*; statuary, ceramics, plastic arts.

high –, low –, bas- relief; relievo; *basso-, alto-, mezzo-rilievo; intaglio*, anaglyph; medal, -lion; *cameo*.

marble, bronze, terracotta; ceramic ware, pottery, porcelain, china, earthenware, faïence, enamel, *cloisonné*.

statue &c. (*image*) 554; cast &c. (*copy*) 21; glyptotheca.

**V.** sculpture, carve, cut, chisel, model, mould; cast.

Adj. sculptured &c. *v.*; in relief, anaglyptic, ceroplastic, ceramic; parian; marble &c. *n.* **Phr.** *sculpsit.*

**558. Engraving.—N.** engraving, chalcography; line –, mezzotint –, stipple –, chalk- engraving; dry-point, bur; etching, aquatinta; plate –, copper-plate –, steel –, wood-, process-, photo-engraving; xylo-, ligno-, glypto-, cero-, litho-, chromolitho-, photolitho-, zinco-, glypho- -graphy, -graph.

impression, print, engraving, plate; steel-, copper-plate; etching; mezzo-, aqua-, litho-tint; cut, woodcut, block; stereo-, grapho-, auto-, helio-type; half-tone; *photogravure, rotogravure.*

graver, *burin*, etching-point, style; plate, stone, wood-block, negative; die, punch, stamp.

printing; plate -, copper-plate -, intaglio -, anastatic -, lithographic -, colour -, three or four colour- printing; type-printing &c. 591.

illustr-, illumin-ation; *vignette*, initial letter, *cul de lampe*, tail-piece.

V. engrave, grave, stipple, scrape, etch; bite, - in; lithograph &c. *n.*; print.

Adj. insculptured; engraved &c. *v.*

Phr. *fecit, sculpsit, imprimit, incisit.*

**559. Artist.**—N. artist; painter, limner, drawer, sketcher, delineator; cartoon-, caricatur-ist, designer, engraver; draughtsman; copyist; enamel-ler, -list.

historical -, landscape -, battle-, *genre* -, marine -, fruit and flower -, portrait -, miniature -, scene -, sign- painter; engraver; Apelles; sculptor, carver, chaser, modeller, lapidary, *figuriste*, statuary; Phidias, Praxiteles; Royal Academician.

photographer, retoucher.

## 2°. *Conventional Means*
### 1. *Language generally*

**560. Language.**—N. language; phraseology &c. 569; speech &c. 582; tongue, lingo, vernacular, slang; mother -, vulgar -, native- tongue; household words; King's *or* Queen's English; idiom; dialect &c. 563.

Volapuk, Esperanto, Ido, occidental, Ro.

confusion of tongues, Babel, *pasigraphie*; pantomime &c. (*signs*) 550; *onomatopœia.*

phil-, gloss-, glott-ology; linguistics, chrestomathy; paleo-logy; -graphy; comparative grammar.

literature, letters, polite literature, *belles lettres*, muses, humanities, *literæ humaniores*, republic of letters, dead languages, classics; genius of a language; scholarship &c. (*knowledge*) 490.

linguist &c. (*scholar*) 492.

V. speak, say, express by words &c. 566.

Adj. lingu-al, -istic; dialectic; vernacular, current, colloquial, slangy; bilingual, polyglot; literary.

**561. Letter.**—N. letter; character; hieroglyphic &c. (*writing*) 590; type &c. (*printing*) 591; capitals; majus-, minus-cule; alphabet, ABC, abecedary, Christ-cross-row.

consonant, vowel, diphthong; mute, surd; sonant, liquid, labial, dental, palatal, guttural.

syllable; mono-, dis-, poly-syllable; affix, prefix, suffix.

spelling, orthography; phon-ography, -etic spelling; ana-, meta-grammatism.

cipher, monogram, anagram; double -, acrostic.

V. spell.

Adj. literal; alphabetical, abecedarian; syllabic; uncial &c. (*writing*) 590; phonetic, voiced, mute &c. *n.*

**562. Word.**—N. word, term, vocable; name &c. 564; phrase &c. 566; root, etymon; derivative; part of speech &c. (*grammar*) 567.

dictionary, vocabulary, word book,

**563. Neology.**—N. neolo-gy, -gism; new-tangled expression; barbarism; caconym; archaism, black letter, monkish Latin; corruption; missaying, antiphrasis.

lexicon, index, glossary, thesaurus, *gradus, delectus,* concordance.

etymology, lexicology, derivation; phonology, orthoepy; gloss-, termin-, orism-ology; paleology &c. (*philology*) 560; comparative philology.

lexicograph-er, -y; glossographer &c. (*scholar*) 492; etymologist; logolept.

verbosity, verbiage, loquacity &c. 584.

**Adj.** verbal, literal; titular, nominal. [Similarly derived] conjugate, paronymous; derivative.

**Adv.** verbally &c. *adj.*; *verbatim* &c. (*exactly*) 494.

*paronomasia,* play upon words; word-play &c. (*wit*) 842; pun; *double-entendre* &c. (*ambiguity*) 520; palindrome, paragram, clinch; abuse of -language, - terms.

dialect, brogue, *patois,* provincialism, broken English, *lingua franca*; Brit-, Gall-, Scott-, Hibern-icism; Americanism; Gipsy lingo, Romany, pidgin English.

dog Latin, macaronics, gibberish, confusion of tongues, Babel; jargon.

colloquialism &c. (*figure of speech*) 521; by-word; technicality, lingo, slang, cant, *argot,* St. Giles's Greek, thieves' Latin, peddler's French, flash tongue, Billingsgate, Wall Street slang.

pseudonym &c. (*misnomer*) 565; Mr. So-and-so; what d'ye call 'em, what's his name; N. N.; *Monsieur Un Tel*; thingum-my, -bob; gadget, dooflicker, do-funny, *oo-ja-ka-pi-vi*; *je ne sais quoi.*

neologist, coiner of words.

**V.** coin words.

**Adj.** neologic, -al; rare; archaic; obsolete &c. (*old*) 124; colloquial, dialectic, slang, cant.

**Phr.** *Il a passé par Marseille.*

---

**564. Nomenclature. — N.** nomenclature; naming &c. *v.*; nuncupation, nomination, baptism; orismology; *onomatopœia*; antonomasia.

name; appella-tion, -tive; designation; title; head, -ing, caption; denomination; by-name, epithet.

style, proper name; præ-, ag-, cognomen; patronymic, surname; cognomination; compellation, description; empty -title, - name; handle to one's name; namesake, eponym.

synonym, antonym.

term, expression, noun; by-word; convertible terms &c. 522; technical term; cant &c. 563.

**V.** name, call, term, denominate, designate, style, entitle, intitule, clepe, dub, christen, baptize, nickname, characterize, specify, define, distinguish by the name of; label &c. (*mark*) 550.

be -called &c. *v.*; take -, bear -, go (*or* be known) by -, go (*or* pass) under -, rejoice in- the name of.

**Adj.** named &c. *v.*; hight, yclept, known as; what one may -well, - fairly, - properly, - fitly- call.

nuncupa-tory, -tive; cognominal, titular, nominal; orismological.

**565. Misnomer.—N.** misnomer; *lucus a non lucendo*; Mrs. Malaprop; what d'ye call 'em &c. (*neologism*) 563.

nickname, *sobriquet,* by-name, handle, moniker; assumed -name, - title; *alias; nom de -guerre, - plume, - théâtre*; pseudonym, pen name, stage name.

**V.** mis-name, -call, -term; nickname; assume -a name, - an alias.

**Adj.** misnamed &c. *v.*; pseudonymous; *soi-disant*; self-called, -styled, -christened; so-called.

nameless, anonymous; without a -, having no- name; innominate, unnamed.

**Adv.** in no sense.

---

**566. Phrase.—N.** phrase, expression, set phrase; sentence, paragraph; figure of speech &c. 521; idi-om, -otism; turn of expression.

paraphrase &c. (*synonym*) 522; periphrase &c. (*circumlocution*) 573; motto &c. (*proverb*) 496; phraseology &c. 569.

**V.** express, phrase; word, – it; give -words, – expression- to; voice; arrange in –, clothe in –, put into –, express by- words; couch in terms; find words to express; speak by the card.

**Adj.** expressed &c. *v.*; idiomatic.

**Adv.** in -round, – set, – good, set- terms; in set phrases.

**567. Grammar.—N.** grammar, accidence, syntax, *praxis*, analysis, paradigm, punctuation; parts of speech; inflexion, case, declension, conjugation; *jus et norma loquendi*; Lindley Murray &c. (*school-book*) 542; correct style; philology &c. (*language*) 560.

**V.** parse, analyze; decline, conjugate; punctuate.

**Adj.** grammatical; syntactic; inflexional.

**568. Solecism.—N.** solecism; bad -, false -, faulty- grammar; slip, error; slip of the -pen, – tongue; *lapsus calami-*, – *linguæ*; *faux pas*; slip-slop; bull.

**V.** use -bad, – faulty- grammar; solecize, commit a solecism; murder the -King's, – Queen's- English; break Priscian's head.

**Adj.** ungrammatical; in-correct, -accurate; faulty, improper, incongruous, abnormal.

**569. Style.—N.** style, diction, phraseology, wording; manner, strain; composition; mode of expression, choice of words, literary power, ready pen, pen of a ready writer; command of language &c. (*eloquence*) 582; authorship; *la morgue littéraire*.

**V.** express by words &c. 566; write.

### Various Qualities of Style

**570. Perspicuity.—N.** perspicuity &c. (*intelligibility*) 518; plain speaking &c. (*manifestation*) 525; defin-iteness, -ition; exactness &c. 494; perspicuousness, logical acuteness.

**Adj.** lucid &c. (*intelligible*) 518; explicit &c. (*manifest*) 525; exact &c. 494.

**571. Obscurity.—N.** obscurity &c. (*unintelligibility*) 519; involution; hard words; ambiguity &c. 520; vagueness &c. 475, inexactness &c. 495; what d'ye call 'em &c. (*neologism*) 563; cloudiness, confusion.

**Adj.** obscure &c. *n.*; crabbed, involved, confused.

**572. Conciseness.—N.** conciseness &c. *adj.*; brevity, 'the soul of wit,' laconism; Tacitus; ellipsis; syncope; abridgment &c. (*shortening*) 201; compression &c. 195; epitome &c. 596; monostitch; portmanteau word, telescope word, protogram.

**V.** be -concise &c. *adj.*; condense &c. 195; abridge &c. 201; abstract &c. 596; come to the point.

**Adj.** concise, brief, short, terse, close; to the point, exact; neat, compact, condensed, pointed; laconic, curt, pithy, trenchant, summary; pregnant; compendious &c. (*compendium*) 596; succinct; elliptical, epigrammatic, crisp, sententious.

**Adv.** concisely &c. *adj.*; briefly,

**573. Diffuseness.—N.** diffuseness &c. *adj.*; amplification &c. *v.*; dilating &c. *v.*; verbosity, verbiage, wordiness, cloud of words, *copia verborum*; flow of words &c. (*loquacity*) 584.

poly-, tauto-, batto-, perisso-logy; pleonasm, exuberance, redundance; thrice-told tale; prolixity; circumlocution, *ambages*; periphra-se, -sis; roundabout phrases; episode; expletive; penny-a-lining; padding, drivel, twaddle, rigmarole; richness &c. 577.

**V.** be -diffuse &c. *adj.*; run out on, descant, expatiate, enlarge, dilate, amplify, expand, inflate, pad; launch –, branch- out; rant.

maunder, prose; harp upon &c. (*repeat*) 104; dwell on, insist upon.

summarily; in -brief, – short, – a word, – few words, – a nutshell; for shortness sake; to -come to the point, – make a long story short, – cut the matter short, – be brief; it comes to this, the long and the short of it is.

-winded, -spun, -drawn out; prosing, maundering; roundabout; digressive; dis-, ex-cursive; rambling, episodic; flatulent, frothy.

digress, ramble, *battre la campagne,* beat about the bush, perorate, spin a long yarn, protract; spin –, swell –, draw- out, drivel.

**Adj.** dif-, pro-fuse; wordy, verbose, largiloquent, copious, exuberant, effusive, pleonastic, lengthy; long, -some, diffusive, spun out, protracted, prolix, circumlocutory, periphrastic, ambagious,

**Adv.** diffusely &c. *adj.*; at large, *in extenso*; about it and about it.

**574. Vigour.—N.** vigour, power, force; boldness, raciness &c. *adj.*; spirit, point, antithesis, piquancy; *verve,* glow, fire, warmth, ardour, enthusiasm; 'thoughts that breathe and words that burn'; strong language; punch; gravity, sententiousness; elevation, loftiness, sublimity.

eloquence; command of -words, – language.

**Adj.** vigorous, nervous, powerful, forcible, trenchant, mordant, biting, incisive, impressive; sensational.

spirited, lively, glowing, sparkling, racy, bold, slashing; pungent, *piquant,* full of point, pointed, pithy, antithetical; sententious.

lofty, elevated, sublime, grand, weighty, ponderous; eloquent; vehement, petulant, impassioned; poetic.

**Adv.** in -glowing, – good set, – no measured- terms.

**575. Feebleness.—N.** feebleness &c. *adj.*

**Adj.** feeble, bald, tame, meagre, insipid, nerveless, jejune, vapid, trashy, cold, frigid, poor, dull, dry, languid; pros-ing, -y, -aic; unvaried, monotonous, weak, frail, washy, wishy-washy, sloppy; sketchy, slight; careless, slovenly, loose, lax; slip-shod, -slop; inexact; dis-jointed, -connected; puerile, childish; flatulent; rambling &c. (*diffuse*) 573.

**576. Plainness.—N.** plainness &c. *adj.*; simplicity, severity; plain -terms, – English; Saxon English; household words.

**V.** speak plainly; call a spade 'a spade'; plunge *in medias res*; come to the point.

**Adj.** plain, simple; un-ornamented, -adorned, -varnished; home-ly, -spun; neat; severe, chaste, pure, Saxon; commonplace, matter of fact, natural, prosaic, sober, unimaginative.

dry, unvaried, monotonous &c. 575.

**Adv.** in plain -terms, – words, – English, – common parlance; point blank.

**577. Ornament. — N.** ornament; floridness &c. *adj.*; turg-idity, -escence; altiloquence &c. *adj.*; orotundity; declamation, teratology; well-rounded periods; elegance &c. 578.

inversion, antithesis, alliteration, *paronomasia*; figurativeness &c. (*metaphor*) 521.

flourish; flowers of -speech, – rhetoric; euph-uism, -emism.

big-, high-sounding words; macrology, *sesquipedalia verba,* sesquipedalianism; Alexandrine; inflation, pretension; rant, bombast, fustian, bunkum, balderdash, prose run mad; fine writing; Minerva press.

phrasemonger; euph-uist, -emist.

**V.** ornament, overlay with ornament, overcharge; smell of the lamp.

**Adj.** ornamented &c. *v.*; beautified &c. 847; ornate, florid, rich, flowery; euph-uistic, -emistic; sonorous; high-, big-sounding; inflated, swelling, tumid; turg-id, -escent; pedantic, pompous, stilted;

high-flown, -flowing; sententious, rhetorical, declamatory; grandiose; grand-, magn-, alt-iloquent; sesquipedal, -ian; Johnsonian, mouthy; bombastic; fustian; frothy, flashy, flaming, flamboyant.

antithetical, alliterative; figurative &c. 521; artificial &c. (*inelegant*) 579.

Adv. *ore rotundo*; with rounded phrase.

**578. Elegance.**—N. elegance, purity, grace, ease, felicity, distinction, gracefulness, refinement, readiness &c. *adj.*; concinnity, euphony, numerosity, balance, rhythm, symmetry, proportion; restraint; good taste, propriety.

well rounded -, well turned -, flowing- periods; the right word in the right place; antithesis &c. 577.

purist, stylist.

V. point an antithesis, round a period.

Adj. elegant, polished, classical, Attic, correct, Ciceronian, artistic; chaste, pure, Saxon, academical.

graceful, easy, readable, fluent, flowing, tripping; unaffected, natural, unlaboured; mellifluous; euph-onious, -emistic; rhythmical, balanced, symmetrical.

felicitous, happy, neat; well -, neatly- -put, - expressed.

**579. Inelegance.** — N. inelegance; vulgarity, bad taste; stiffness &c. *adj.*; unlettered Muse; barbarism; slang &c. 563; solecism &c. 568; mannerism &c; (*affectation*) 855; euphuism; fustian &c. 577; cacophony; want of balance; words that -break the teeth, - dislocate the jaw-

V. be -inelegant &c. *adj.*

Adj. inelegant, graceless, ungraceful, unpolished; harsh, abrupt; dry, stiff, cramped, formal, *guindé*; forced, laboured, awkward; artificial, mannered, ponderous; turgid &c. 577; affected, euphuistic; barbarous, uncouth, grotesque, rude, crude, halting; vulgar, offensive to ears polite.

---

## 2. *Spoken Language*

**580. Voice.**—N. voice; vocality; organ, lungs, bellows; good -, fine -, powerful &c. (*loud*) 404 , musical &c. 413- voice; intonation; tone &c. (*sound*) 402- of voice.

vocalization; cry &c. 411; strain, utterance, prolation; exclam-, ejacul-, vocifer-ation; enunci-, articul-ation; articulate sound, distinctness; clearness, - of articulation; stage whisper; delivery; attack.

accent, -uation; emphasis, stress; broad -, strong -, pure -, native -, foreign- accent; pronunciation.

[Word similarly pronounced] homonym.

orthoepy; euphony &c. (*melody*) 413.

gastri-, ventri-loquism; ventriloquist; polyphon-ism, -ist.

[Science of voice] phonology &c. (*sound*) 402.

V. sing, speak, utter, breathe, voice; give -utterance, - tongue; cry &c;

**581. Aphony.**—N. aphony, *aphonia*; dumbness &c. *adj.*; obmutescence; absence -, want- of voice; dysphony; silence &c. (*taciturnity*) 585; raucity; harsh &c. 410 -, unmusical &c. 414- voice; *falsetto*, 'childish treble'; mute, dummy, deaf mute.

V. keep silence &c. 585; speak -low, - softly; whisper &c. (*faintness*) 405.

silence; render -mute, - silent &c; 403; muzzle, muffle, suppress, smother, gag, strike dumb, dumb-found, -founder; drown the voice, put to silence, stop one's mouth, cut one short; stick in the throat.

Adj. aphon-ous, -ic, dumb, mute; deaf-mute, - and dumb; mum; tongue-tied; breath-, tongue-, voice-, speech-, word-less; mute as a -fish, - stockfish, - mackerel; silent &c. (*taciturn*) 585; muzzled; in-articulate, -audible.

croaking, raucous, hoarse, husky,

(*shout*) 411; ejaculate, rap out; vocal-ize, prolate, articulate, enunciate, enounce, pronounce, accentuate, aspi-rate, deliver, mouth; emit, murmur, whisper, – in the ear, croon, yodel.

**Adj.** vocal, phonetic, oral; ejacula-tory, articulate, distinct, stertorous; enunciative; accentuated, aspirated; euphonious &c. (*melodious*) 413.

**582. Speech.—N.** speech, faculty of speech; locution, talk, parlance, verbal intercourse, prolation, oral communica-tion, word of mouth, *parole*, palaver, prattle; effusion.

oration, recitation, delivery, say, address, speech, lecture, harangue, sermon, *tirade*, screed, formal speech, salutatory, peroration; prelection; speechifying; soliloquy &c. 589; allo-cution &c. 586; interlocution &c. 588.

oratory; elo-cution, -quence; rhe-toric, declamation; grandi-, multi-loquence; burst of eloquence; facun-dity; talkativeness; flow –, command-of -words, – language; *copia verborum*; power of speech, gift of the gab; *usus loquendi*.

speaker &c. *v.*; spokesman; pro-, inter-locutor; mouthpiece, Hermes; ora-tor, -trix, -tress; Demosthenes, Cicero; rhetorician; stump –, platform-orator, tub-thumper; elocutionist; speech-maker, patterer, *improvisatore*.

**V.** speak, – of; say, utter, pronounce, deliver, give utterance to; utter –, pour- forth; breathe, let fall, come out with; rap –, blurt- out; have on one's lips; have at the -end, – tip- of one's tongue.

break silence; open one's -lips, – mouth; lift –, raise- one's voice; give –, wag the- tongue; talk, outspeak; put in a word or two.

hold forth; make –, deliver- -a speech &c. *n.*; speechify, harangue, declaim, stump, flourish, spout, rant, recite, lecture, preach, ser-monize, discourse, be on one's legs; have –, say- one's say; expatiate &c. (*speak at length*) 573; speak one's mind.

soliloquize &c. 589; tell &c. (*inform*) 527; speak to &c. 586; talk together &c. 588.

be -eloquent &c. *adj.*; have -a tongue in one's head, – the gift of the gab &c. *n.*

pass –, escape- one's lips; fall from the -lips, – mouth.

**Adj.** speaking &c., spoken &c. *v.*; oral, lingual, phonetic, not written, unwritten, outspoken; elo-quent, -cutionary; orat-, rhet-orical; declamatory; grandiloquent &c. 577; talkative &c. 584.

dry, hollow, sepulchral, hoarse as a raven.

**Adv.** with -bated breath, – the finger on the lips; *sotto voce*; in a -low tone, – cracked voice, – broken voice; in an aside.

**Phr.** *vox faucibus hæsit.*

**583. [Imperfect Speech.] Stammer-ing.—N.** inarticulateness; stammering &c. *v.*; hesitation &c. *v.*; impediment in one's speech; aphasia, titubancy, traulism; whisper &c. (*faint sound*) 405; lisp, drawl, tardiloquence; nasal -tone, – accent; twang; *falsetto* &c. (*want of voice*) 581; broken -voice, – accents, – sentences.

brogue &c. 563; slip of the tongue, *lapsus linguæ.*

**V.** stammer, stutter, hesitate, falter, hammer; balbu-tiate, -cinate; haw, hum and haw, be unable to put two words together.

mumble, mutter; maund, -er; whisper &c. 405; mince, lisp; jabber, gabble, gibber; sp-, spl-utter; muffle, mump; drawl, mouth; croak; speak -thick, – through the nose; snuffle, clip one's words; murder the -language, – King's (*or* Queen's) English; mis-pronounce, -say.

**Adj.** stammering &c. *v.*; inarticulate, guttural, nasal; tremulous.

**Adv.** *sotto voce* &c. (*faintly*) 405.

**Adv.** orally &c. *adj.*; by word of mouth, *vivâ voce*, from the lips of.
**Phr.** quoth -, said- he &c.

**584. Loquacity. — N.** loquac-ity, -iousness; talkativeness &c. *adj.*; garrulity; multiloquence, much speaking, effusion, wordiness.

jaw; gab, -ble; jabber, chatter; prate, prattle, cackle, clack; twaddle, twattle, rattle; *caquet, -terie*; blabber, *bavardage*, bibble-babble, gibble-gabble; small talk &c. (*converse*) 588.

fluency, flippancy, volubility, flowing tongue; flow, - of words; *flux de -bouche, - mots, - paroles*; *copia verborum, cacoëthes loquendi*; verbosity &c. (*diffuseness*) 573; gift of the gab &c. (*eloquence*) 582.

talker; chatter-er, -box; babbler &c. *v.*; rattle; ranter; sermonizer, proser, driveller; windbag; gossip &c. (*converse*) 588; magpie, jay, parrot, poll, Babel; *moulin à paroles*.

**V.** be -loquacious &c. *adj.*; talk glibly, pour forth, patter; prate, palaver, prose, chatter, prattle, clack, jabber, jaw; rattle, - on; twaddle, twattle; babble, gabble; out-talk; talk oneself -out of breath, - hoarse; maunder, gush, blather; talk a donkey's hind leg off; expatiate &c. (*speak at length*) 573; gossip &c. (*converse*) 588; din in the ears &c. (*repeat*) 104; talk -at random, - nonsense &c. 497; be hoarse with talking.

**Adj.** loquacious, talkative, conversational, garrulous, linguacious, multiloquous; chattering &c. *v.*; chatty &c. (*sociable*) 892; declamatory &c. 582; open-mouthed.

fluent, voluble, glib, flippant; long-tongued, -winded &c. (*diffuse*) 573.

**Adv.** trippingly on the tongue; glibly &c. *adj.*

**Phr.** the tongue running -fast, - loose, - on wheels.

**585. Taciturnity.—N.** silence, muteness, obmutescence; taciturnity, pauciloquy, costiveness, curtness; reserve, reticence &c. (*concealment*) 528; *aposiopesis*.

man of few words.

**V.** be -silent &c. *adj.*; keep silence; hold one's -tongue, - peace, - jaw; not speak &c. 582; say nothing; seal -, close -, put a padlock on- the -lips, - mouth; put a bridle on one's tongue; keep one's tongue between one's teeth; make no sign, not let a word escape one; keep a secret &c. 528; not have a word to say; lay -, place- the finger on the lips; render mute &c. 581.

stick in one's throat.

**Adj.** silent, mute, mum; silent as -a post, - a stone, - the grave &c. (*still*) 403; dumb &c. 581.

taciturn, sparing of words; close, - mouthed, - tongued; laconic, costive, inconversable, curt; reserved; reticent &c. (*concealing*) 528.

**Int.** tush! silence! mum! hush! *chut!* hist! tut! &c. 403.

---

**586. Allocution. — N.** allocution, alloquy, address; speech &c. 582; apostrophe, interpellation, appeal, invocation, salutation; word in the ear.

[Feigned dialogue] dialogism.

platform &c. 542; audience &c. (*interview*) 588.

**V.** speak to, address, accost, make up to, apostrophize, appeal to, invoke; hail, salute; call to, halloo.

take -aside, - by the button, button-hole; talk to in private.

lecture &c. (*make a speech*) 582.

**Int.** soho! halloo! hey! hist! hi!

**587. Response** &c., *see* Answer 462

---

**588. Interlocution.—N.** interlocu-tion; collocution, colloquy, converse, conversation, confabulation, talk, dis-course, verbal intercourse; communion, oral communication, commerce; dia-, duo-, tria-logue.

*causerie*, chat, chit-chat; small –, table –, tea-table –, town –, village –, idle- talk; tattle, gossip, tittle-tattle; babble, -ment; *tripotage*, cackle, prittle-prattle, *on dit*; talk of the -town, – village.

**589. Soliloquy.—N.** soliloquy, mono-logue, apostrophe.

solilo-quist, -quizer, monologist.

**V.** soliloquize; say –, talk- to one-self; say aside, think aloud, apostro-phize.

**Adj.** soliloquizing &c. *v.*

**Adv.** aside.

---

conference, parley, interview, audience, *pourparler*; *tête-à-tête*; reception, *conversazione*; congress &c. (*council*) 696; pow-wow.

hall of audience, *durbar*, coliseum, assembly hall, auditorium.

palaver, debate, logomachy, war of words, controversy.

talker, gossip, tattler; Paul Pry; tabby; chatterer &c. (*loquacity*) 584; interlocutor &c. (*spokesman*) 582; conversation-ist, -alist; dialogist.

'the feast of reason and the flow of soul'; *mollia tempora fandi.*

**V.** talk together, converse, confabulate; hold –, carry on –, join in –, engage in- a conversation; put in a word; shine in conversation; bandy words; parley; palaver; chat, gossip, tattle; prate &c. (*lo-quacity*) 584.

discourse –, confer –, commune –, commerce- with; hold -con-verse, – conference, – intercourse; talk it over; be closeted with; talk with one -in private, – *tête-à-tête.*

**Adj.** conversing &c. *v.*; interlocutory; convers-ational, -able; dis-cursive, -coursive; chatty &c. (*sociable*) 892; colloquial, *tête-à-tête*, confabulatory.

## 3. *Written Language*

**590. Writing.—N.** writing &c. *v.*; chiro-, stelo-, cero-graphy, graphology; stylography; pen-craft, -script, -man-ship; quill-driving; typewriting.

writing, manuscript, MS., *literæ scriptæ*; these presents.

stroke –, dash- of the pen; *coup de plume*; line; pen and ink.

letter &c. 561; uncial writing, cunei-form character, arrow-head, Ogham, Runes, futhorc; hieroglyphic, hieratic, demotic; script; contraction.

short-hand; steno-, brachy-, tachy-graphy; secret writing, writing in cipher; crypt-, stegan-ography; phono-, pasi-, poly-, logo-graphy.

copy; tran-, re-script; draft, rough –, fair- copy; handwriting; signature, sign-manual; auto-, mono-, holo-graph; hand, fist; mark.

calligraphy; good –, running –,

**591. Printing.—N.** printing; block –, type- printing, lino-, mono-type; plate printing &c. (*engraving*) 558; the press &c. (*publication*) 531; composition.

print, letterpress, text, matter, stand-ing type; context, note, page, col-umn; over-running; head-, foot-line, title.

typography; stereo-, electro-, apro-type; type, black letter, heavy type, font, fount; pi, pie; capitals &c. (*letters*) 561; diamond, pearl, nonpareil, minion, brevier, bourgeois, long primer, small pica, pica, english, great primer.

folio &c. (*book*) 593; copy, impres-sion, pull, proof, galley –, author's –, page- proof, revise.

printer, compositor, reader; printer's devil.

**V.** print; compose; put –, go- to press; pass –, see- through the press;

flowing –, cursive –, legible –, copper-plate –, round –, bold- hand.

  cacography, *griffonage, barbouillage*; bad –, cramped –, crabbed –, illegible-hand; scribble &c. *v.*; *pattes de mouche*; ill-formed letters; pot-hooks and hangers.

  stationery; pen, quill, goose-quill, reed; stylographic-, fountain-pen; pencil, style, stylus; paper, foolscap, parchment, vellum, papyrus, pad, tablet, block, note-book, slate, marble, pillar, table, black board.

  ink-bottle, -pot, -stand, -well, -horn; typewriter.

  transcription &c. (*copy*) 21; inscription &c. (*record*) 551; super-scription &c. (*indication*) 550.

  composition, authorship; *cacoëthes scribendi.*

  writer, scribe, amanuensis, scrivener, secretary, clerk, penman, copyist, transcriber, quill-driver; writer for the press &c. (*author*) 593.

  shorthand writer, stenographer; typewriter, typist.

  V. write, pen; copy, engross; write out, – fair; transcribe; scribble, scrawl, scrabble, scratch; interline; stain paper; write down &c. (*record*) 551; sign &c. (*attest*) 467; take down, – in shorthand; typewrite, type.

  compose, indite, draw up, redact, draft, formulate; dictate; in-scribe, throw on paper, dash off; concoct.

  take -up the pen, – pen in hand; shed –, spill –, dip one's pen in- ink.

  Adj. writing &c. *v.*; written &c. *v.*; in -writing, – black and white; under one's hand.

  uncial, Runic, cuneiform, hieroglyphical &c. *n.*

  Adv. *currente calamo*; pen in hand.

publish &c. 531; bring out; appear in –, rush into- print.

  Adj. printed &c. *v.*; in type; typographical &c. *n.*

**592. Correspondence. — N.** correspondence, letter, epistle, note, *billet*, post-, letter-card, missive, circular, form letter; favour, *billet-doux*; des-, dis-patch; *bulletin*, communication &c. 532; these presents; rescript, -ion; post &c. (*messenger*) 534; letter writer, correspondent.

  V. correspond, – with; write –, send a letter- to; keep up a correspondence; drop a line to; despatch; communicate with; circularize.

  Adj. epistolary.

**593. Book.—N.** book, -let; writing, work, volume, tome, opuscule; tract, -ate; *livret*; *brochure*, *libretto*, hand-book, treatise, text-book, codex, man-ual, pamphlet, monograph, enchiridion, circular, publication; book of poems; novel; chap-book.

  part, issue, number, *livraison*; album, portfolio; periodical, serial, magazine, ephemeris, annual, journal.

  paper, bill, sheet, broadsheet, screed; leaf, -let; fly-leaf, page; quire, ream.

  chapter, section, head, article, para-graph, passage, clause, supplement, appendix; *feuilleton*.

  folio, quarto, octavo; duo-, sexto-, octo-decimo.

  en-, cyclopædia, dictionary, lexicon, thesaurus, concordance, an-thology, bibliography; compilation, compendium, catalogue &c. 86; library, bibliotheca; the press &c. (*publication*) 531.

  writer, author, *littérateur, homme de lettres*, essayist, journalist, publicist; scribe, penman, war –, special –, correspondent; pen, scribbler, the scribbling race; ghost, hack, literary hack, Grub-street writer; writer for –, gentleman of –, representative of- the press; reporter, penny-a-liner; editor, sub-editor; literary agent; playwright &c. 599; poet &c. 597.

bookseller, publisher; biblio-pole, -polist, -grapher; librarian; book -collector, – worm.

book -shop, – club, circulating –, lending –, public- library; publishing house.

knowledge of books, bibliography; book-learning &c. (*knowledge*) 490.

**594. Description.—N.** description, account, statement, report; *exposé* &c. (*disclosure*) 529; specification, particulars, scenario, plot; state –, summary- of facts; brief &c. (*abstract*) 596; return &c. (*record*) 551; *catalogue raisonné* &c. (*list*) 86; guide-book &c. (*information*) 527.

delineation &c. (*representation*) 554; sketch, vignette; monograph; minute –, detailed –, particular –, circumstantial –, graphic- account; narration, recital, rehearsal, relation.

histori-, chron-ography; historic Muse, Clio; history; bi-, autobi-ography; necrology, obituary.

narrative, history; memoir, memorials; annals &c. (*chronicle*) 551; tradition, legend, saga, epic, epos, story, tale, historiette; personal narrative, journal, letters, life, adventures, fortunes, experiences, confessions; anecdote, ana, *trait*.

work of fiction, short story, novelette, novel, romance, penny dreadful, shilling shocker, Minerva press; fairy –, nursery- tale; fable, allegory, parable, apologue.

relator &c. *v.*; *raconteur*; historian &c. (*recorder*) 553; biographer, fabulist, novelist, story teller, romancer, teller of tales, spinner of yarns, anecdotist.

**V.** describe; set forth &c. (*state*) 535; draw a picture, picture; portray &c. (*represent*) 554; characterize, particularize; narrate, relate, recite, recount, sum up, run over, recapitulate, rehearse, fight one's battles over again.

unfold &c. (*disclose*) 529- a tale; tell; give –, render- an account of; report, make a report, draw up a statement.

detail; enter into –, descend to- -particulars, – details.

**Adj.** descriptive, graphic, narrative, epic, suggestive, well-drawn; historic; auto-, biographical, realistic, expository, tradition-al, -ary; legendary; fabulous, mythical; anecdotic, storied; described &c. *v.*

**595. Dissertation.—N.** dissertation, treatise, essay; *thesis*, theme; tract, -ate, -ation, excursus; discourse, memoir, disquisition, lecture, sermon, homily, pandect.

commentary, review, *critique*, criticism, article; lead-er, -ing article, editorial; argument, running commentary.

investigation &c. (*inquiry*) 461; study &c. (*consideration*) 451; discussion &c. (*reasoning*) 476; exposition &c. (*explanation*) 522.

commentator, critic, essayist, pamphleteer; publicist, reviewer, leader writer, editor, annotator.

**V.** dissert –, descant –, write –, touch- upon a subject; dissertate; treat of –, take up –, ventilate –, discuss –, deal with –, go into –, canvass –, handle –, do justice to- a subject; comment, criticize, interpret &c. 522; argue.

**Adj.** dis-cursive, -coursive; disquisitional, disquisitionary; expository, critical.

**596. Compendium.—N.** compend, -ium; abstract, *précis*, epitome, *multum in parvo*, analysis, pandect, digest, sum and substance, brief, abridgment, summary, *aperçu*, draft, minute, note; synopsis, text-book, *conspectus*, outlines, syllabus, contents, heads, prospectus.

album; scrap –, note –, memorandum –, commonplace- book; extracts, *excerpta*, cuttings; fugitive -pieces, – writings; *spicilegium*, flowers, anthology, miscellany, *collectanea*, *analecta*; compilation.

recapitulation, *résumé*, review.

abbrevia-tion, -ture; contraction; shortening &c. 201; compression &c. 195.

**V.** abridge, abstract, epitomize, summarize; make –, prepare –, draw –, compile- an abstract &c. *n.*

recapitulate, review, skim, run over, sum up.

abbreviate &c. (*shorten*) 201; condense &c. (*compress*) 195; compile &c. (*collect*) 72; edit, blue pencil.

**Adj.** compendious, synoptic, analectic, analytical; abridged &c. *v.*

**Adv.** in -short, – epitome, – substance, – few words.

**Phr.** it lies in a nutshell.

---

**597. Poetry.—N.** poetry, poetics, poesy, Muse, Calliope, tuneful Nine, Parnassus, Helicon, Pierides, Pierian spring, afflatus, inspiration.

versification, rhyming, making verses; prosody, scansion, orthometry.

poem; epic, – poem; epopee, *epopæa*, ode, epode, idyl, lyric, eclogue, pastoral, bucolic, georgic, dithyramb, anacreontic, sonnet, roundelay, *rondel, rondoletto, rondeau, rondo,* triolet; madrigal, canzonet, *cento,* monody, elegy, palinode; rhapsody.

dramatic –, lyric- poetry; opera; posy, anthology.

song, ballad, lay; love –, drinking –, war –, folk –, sea- song; lullaby; music &c. 415; nursery rhymes.

[Bad poetry| doggerel, Hudibrastic verse, prose run mad; macaronics; macaronic –, leonine- verse; runes.

canto, stanza, distich, verse, line, couplet, triplet, quatrain, sestet; *strophe, antistrophe,* refrain, chorus, burden.

verse, rhyme, assonance, crambo, metre, measure, foot, numbers, strain, rhythm; accentuation &c. (*voice*) 580; iambus, dactyl, spondee, trochee, anapæst &c.; hex-, pent-ameter; Alexandrine; blank verse, alliteration.

elegiacs &c. *adj.*; elegiac &c. *adj.* -verse, – metre, – poetry.

poet, – laureate; laureate; minor poet, bard, lyrist, scald, troubadour, *trouvère;* minstrel; minne-, meister-singer; *improvisatore;* versifier, sonneteer; ballad monger; rhym-er, -ist, -ester; poetaster.

**V.** poetize, sing, versify, make verses, rhyme, scan.

**Adj.** poetic, -al; lyric, -al; tuneful; epic; dithyrambic &c: *n.*; metrical; a-, catalectic; elegiac, iambic, trochaic, spondaic, dactylic, anapæstic; Ionic, Sapphic, Alcaic, Pindaric.

**598. Prose.—N.** prose, – writer, pros-aism, -aist, -er.

**V.** prose, write prose.

write -prose, – in prose.

**Adj.** pros-y, -aic; unpoetical.

rhymeless, unrhymed, in prose, not in verse.

---

**599. The Drama.—N.** the -drama, – stage, – theatre, – play; theatricals, dramaturgy, histrionic art, buskin, sock, *cothurnus,* Melpomene and Thalia, Thespis.

play, drama, stage-play, piece, five-act play, tragedy, comedy, opera, comic opera, *vaudeville, comedietta, lever de rideau,* curtain raiser, interlude, afterpiece, exode, farce, *divertissement, extravaganza,* burletta, harlequinade, pantomime, mimodrama, burlesque, *opéra bouffe*, musical comedy, review, revue, intimate revue, variety, cabaret entertainment, *ballet, spectacle,* masque, *drame, comédie drame;* melo-drama, -drame; *comédie larmoyante,* emotional drama, sensation drama, tragi-, farcical-comedy; mono-drame, -logue; duologue; trilogy; charade, *proverbe;* mystery, miracle –, morality- play.

act, scene, *tableau;* in-, intro-duction; pro-, epi-logue, curtain; *libretto,* book, script.

performance, representation, show, *mise en scène,* stagery, *jeu de théâtre,* stage-craft; acting; gesture &c. 550; impersonation &c. 554; stage business, gag, patter, buffoonery.

theatre; play-, opera-house; house; music hall; *cabaret;* amphi-theatre, circus, hippodrome; puppet-show, *fantoccini; marionnettes,* Punch and Judy.

cinema, -tograph-, picture –, theatre, the pictures, the movies, the talkies.

auditory, *auditorium,* front of the house, stalls, boxes, balcony, dress –, upper- -circle, – boxes, amphitheatre, pit, gallery; *foyer;* green-room; dressing rooms, *coulisses.*

flat; drop, – scene; wing, screen, side-scene; transformation scene, curtain, act-drop, safety –, fire- curtain; *proscenium,* forestage.

stage, revolving stage, scene, the boards; star –, grave –, trap, mezzanine floor; flies; gridiron, floats, battens, footlights; lime –, spot –, flood –, bunch-lights; scenery, set, *décor;* orchestra;

theatrical -costume, – properties, props.

part, *rôle,* character, cast, *dramatis personæ; répertoire.*

actor, player; stage –, strolling- player; old –, stager, performer; mime, -r; *artiste;* com-, trag-edian, straight man; *tragédienne,* Thespian, Roscius, star.

pantomimist, clown, harlequin, *buffo,* buffoon, *farceur, grimacier,* pantaloon, columbine; *Pierrot, Pierrette;* punch, -inello; *pulcinell-o, -a;* mute, *figurante,* general utility; super, -numerary, extra.

mummer, guiser, guisard, gysart, masque.

mountebank, Jack Pudding; tumbler, posture-master, acrobat, equilibrist, juggler, contortionist; *danseuse, ballerina,* ballet -dancer, - girl, *coryphée; bayadère, geisha;* chorus -singer, – girl.

company; first tragedian, *prima donna,* lead, leading lady, pro-tagonist; *jeune premier;* juvenile lead, *débutant, -e;* light –, genteel –, low- -comedy, – comedian; *soubrette,* walking gentleman, *amoroso,* heavy, heavy father, *ingénue, jeune veuve, commère, compère.*

property man, *costumier,* machinist, stage hand, electrician, prompter, call-boy; director, manager; stage –, acting –, business- manager; *entrepreneur, impresario,* producer, press agent.

dramatic -author, – writer; play-writer, -wright; dramatist, mimo-grapher; dramatic critic.

**V.** act, play, perform; stage, produce, put on the stage; personate &c. 554; mimic &c. (*imitate*) 19; enact; play –, act –, go through –, perform- a part; rehearse, spout, gag, rant; 'strut and fret one's hour upon a stage'; tread the -stage, – boards; come out; star.

**Adj.** dramatic; theatric, -al; scenic, histrionic, comic, tragic, bus-kined, farcical, tragi-comic, melodramatic, operatic; stagey, spectacular; stagestruck.

**Adv.** on the -stage, – boards; before -the floats, – an audience; in the limelight, behind the footlights; behind the scenes.

# CLASS V

## Words relating to THE VOLUNTARY POWERS*

### Division (I.) INDIVIDUAL VOLITION

#### Section I. Volition in General

##### 1°. Acts of Volition

**600. Will.—N.** will, volition, co-ration†, velleity; will and pleasure, free-will; freedom &c. 748; discretion; choice, inclination, intent, purpose, option &c. (*choice*) 609; voluntariness; spontane-ity, -ousness; originality.

pleasure, wish, desire, mind; frame of mind &c. (*inclination*) 602; intention &c. 620; predetermination &c. 611; self-control &c. determination &c. (*resolution*) 604; will-power.

**V.** will, list; see –, think- fit; determine &c. (*resolve*) 604; settle &c. (*choose*) 609; volunteer.

have a will of one's own; do what one chooses &c. (*freedom*) 748; have it all one's own way; have one's -will, – own way.

use –, exercise- one's discretion; take -upon oneself, – one's own course, – the law into one's own hands; do -of one's own accord, – upon one's own -responsibility, – authority; take the bit between one's teeth; take responsibility; originate &c. (*cause*) 153.

**Adj.** voluntary, volitive, volitional, wilful; free &c. 748; optional; discretion-al, -ary; volitient; dictatorial.

minded &c. (*willing*) 602; prepense &c. (*predetermined*) 611; intended &c. 620; autocratic; unbidden &c. (bid &c. 741); spontaneous; original &c. (*causal*) 153.

**Adv.** voluntarily &c. *adj.*; at -will, – pleasure; *à -volonté, – discrétion; al piacere; ad -libitum, – arbitrium*; as -one thinks proper, – it seems good to.

> * Conative powers or faculties (Hamilton).

**601. Necessity.—N.** involuntariness, instinct, blind –, natural- impulse; inborn –, innate- proclivity; the force of circumstances.

necessi-ty, -tation, necessarianism; obligation; compulsion &c. 744; subjection &c. 749; stern –, hard –, dire –, imperious –, inexorable –, iron –, adverse- -necessity, – fate; what must be.

desti-ny, -nation; fatality, fate, *kismet*, doom, foredoom, election, predestination; pre-, fore-ordination; lot, fortune; fatalism, determinism; inevitableness &c. *adj.*; spell &c. 993.

star, -s; planet, -s; astral influence; sky, Fates, Norns, *Parcæ*, Sisters three, Clotho, Lachesis, Atropos; book of fate; God's will, will of Heaven; wheel of Fortune, Ides of March, Hobson's choice.

last -shift, – resort; *dernier ressort; pis aller* &c. (*substitute*) 147; necessaries &c. (*requirement*) 630.

necess-arian, -itarian; fatalist, determinist; automaton.

**V.** lie under a necessity; be -fated, – doomed, – destined &c., – in for, – under the necessity of; have no -choice, – alternative; be- obliged –, forced –, driven –, one's -fate &c. *n.*-to; be -pushed to the wall, – driven into a corner, – unable to help. – drawn irresistibly

destine, doom, foredoom, devote; pre-destine, -ordain; cast a spell &c; 992; necessitate; compel &c. 744.

> † Hamilton.

of one's own -accord, – free will; *proprio* –, *suo* –, *ex mero- motu*; out of one's own head; by choice &c. 609; purposely &c. (*intentionally*) 620; deliberately &c. 611.

**Phr.** *stet pro ratione voluntas; sic volo sic jubeo.*

————

**Adj.** necessary; needful &c. (*requisite*) 630.

fated; destined &c. *v.*; fateful; elect; spell-bound.

compulsory &c. (*compel*) 744; uncontrollable, inevitable, unavoidable, irresistible, irrevocable, inexorable, binding; avoid-, resist-less; written in the book of fate.

involuntary, instinctive, automatic, blind, mechanical; un-conscious, -witting, -thinking; unintentional &c. (*undesigned*) 621; impulsive &c. 612.

**Adv.** necessarily &c. *adv.*; of -necessity, – course; *ex necessitate rei*; needs must; perforce &c. 744; *nolens volens*; will he nil he, willy nilly, *bon gré mal gré*, willing or unwilling, *coûte que coûte*, forcefully. *faute de mieux*; by stress of; if need be.

**Phr.** it cannot be helped; there is no- help for, – helping- it; it -will, – must, – must needs- be, – be so, – have its way; the die is cast; *jacta est alea; che sarà sarà;* 'it is written'; one's- days are numbered, – fate is sealed; *Fata obstant; dis aliter visum.*

**602. Willingness.—N.** willingness, voluntariness &c. *adj.*; willing mind, heart.

disposition, inclination, leaning, *animus*; frame of mind, humour, mood, vein; bent &c. (*turn of mind*) 820; *penchant* &c. (*desire*) 865; aptitude &c. 698.

doc-ility, -ibleness, tractability; persuasi-bleness, -bility; pliability &c. (*softness*) 324.

geniality, cordiality; goodwill; alacrity, readiness, earnestness, forwardness, enthusiasm; zeal, eagerness &c. (*desire*) 865.

assent &c. 488; compliance &c. 762; pleasure &c. (*will*) 600.

labour of love, self-appointed task; volunteer, -ing, gratuitous service; unpaid worker, amateur.

**V.** be -willing &c. *adj.*; incline, lean to, mind, propend; had as lief; lend –, give –, turn- a willing ear; have -a, – half a, – a great- mind to; hold –, cling- to; desire &c. 865.

see –, think- -good, – fit, – proper; acquiescence &c. (*assent*) 488; comply with &c. 762.

swallow –, nibble at- the bait; gorge the hook; swallow hook, line and sinker; have –, make- no scruple of; make no bones of; jump –, catch- at; meet half way; volunteer, offer oneself &c. 763.

**603. Unwillingness.—N.** unwillingness &c. *adj.*; indispos-ition, -edness; disinclination, aversation, aversion; nolleity, nolition; renitence; reluctance; indifference &c. 866; backwardness &c. *adj.*; slowness &c. 275; want of -alacrity, – readiness; indocility &c. (*obstinacy*) 606.

scrupul-ousness, -osity; qualms of conscience, delicacy, demur, scruple, qualm, shrinking, recoil; hesitation &c. (*irresolution*) 605; fastidiousness &c. 868.

averseness &c. (*dislike*) 867; dissent &c. 489; refusal &c. 764.

slacker, scrimshanker, *embusqué*, unwilling worker, forced labour.

**V.** be -unwilling &c. *adj.*; nill; dislike &c. 867; grudge, begrudge; not be able to find it in one's heart to, not have the stomach to.

demur, stick at, scruple, stickle; hang fire, run rusty, slack, shirk, scamp, give up, fight shy of, not pull fair; recoil, shrink, swerve; hesitate &c. 605; avoid &c. 623.

oppose &c. 708; dissent &c. 489; refuse &c. 764.

**Adj.** unwilling; not in the vein, loth, shy of, disinclined, indisposed, averse, reluctant, not content; adverse &c. (*opposed*) 708; laggard, backward, remiss, slack, slow to; renitent; indifferent &c. 866; scrupulous; squeamish

**Adj.** willing, minded, fain, disposed, inclined, favourable; favourably-minded, -inclined, -disposed; nothing loth; in the -vein, – mood, – humour, – mind.

ready, forward, enthusiastic, earnest, eager; bent upon &c. (*desirous*) 865; predisposed, propense.

docile; persua-dable, -sible; suasible, easily persuaded, facile, easy-going; amenable; tractable &c. (*pliant*) 324; genial, gracious, cordial, hearty; content &c. (*assenting*) 488.

voluntary, gratuitous, spontaneous; unasked &c. (ask &c. 765); unforced &c. (*free*) 748.

**Adv.** willingly &c. *adj.*; fain, freely, as lief, heart and soul; with -pleasure, – all one's heart, – open arms; with -good, – right good- will; *de bonne volonté, ex animo*; *con amore*, heart in hand, nothing loth, without reluctance, of one's own accord, graciously, with a good grace, without demur.

*à la bonne heure*; by all -means, – manner of means; to one's heart's content; yes &c. (*assent*) 488.

**Int.** sure, -ly! of course!

&c. (*fastidious*) 868; repugnant &c. (*dislike*) 867; rest-iff, -ive; demurring &c. *v.*; unconsenting &c. (*refusing*) 764; involuntary &c. 601; grudging, irreconcilable.

**Adv.** unwillingly &c. *adj.*; grudgingly, with a heavy heart; with -a bad, – an ill- grace; against –, sore against--one's wishes, – one's will, – the grain; *invitâ Minervâ*; *à contre cœur*; *malgré soi*; in spite of -one's teeth, – oneself; *nolens volens* &c. (*necessity*) 601; perforce &c. 744; under protest; no &c. 536; not for the world, far be it from me; not if I can help it; if I must I must.

---

**604. Resolution.—N.** determination, will; iron –, unconquerable- will; will of one's own, decision, resolution, backbone, grit; strength of -mind, – will; resolve &c. (*intent*) 620; *intransigeance*; firmness &c. (*stability*) 150; energy, manliness, vigour; game, pluck; resoluteness &c. (*courage*) 861; zeal &c. 682; *aplomb*; desperation; devot-ion, -edness.

mastery over self; self-control, -command, -mastery, -possession, -reliance, -government, -restraint, -conquest, -denial; moral -courage, – strength, – fibre; perseverance &c. 604a; tenacity; obstinacy &c. 606; bull-dog; British lion.

**V.** have -determination &c. *n.*; know one's own mind; be -resolved &c. *adj.*; make up one's mind, will, resolve, determine; decide &c. (*judgment*) 480; form –, come to- a -determination, – resolution, – resolve; conclude, fix, seal, determine once for all, bring to a crisis, drive matters to an extremity; take a decisive step &c. (*choice*) 609; take upon oneself &c. (*undertake*) 676.

devote oneself –, give oneself up- to; throw away the scabbard, kick down

**605. Irresolution.—N.** irresolution, infirmity of purpose, indecision; in-, un-determination, loss of will power; unsettlement; uncertainty &c. 475; demur, suspense; hesi-tating &c. *v.*, -tation, -tancy; vacillation; ambivalence; changeableness &c. 149; fluctuation; alternation &c. (*oscillation*) 314; caprice &c. 608; lukewarmness.

fickleness, levity, *légèreté*; pliancy &c. (*softness*) 324; weakness; timidity &c. 860; cowardice &c. 862; half measures.

waverer, ass between two bundles of hay; shuttlecock, butterfly; time-server, opportunist, turn coat.

**V.** be -irresolute &c. *adj.*; hang –, keep- in suspense; leave '*ad referendum*'; think twice about, pause; dawdle &c. (*inactivity*) 683; remain neuter; dilly-dally, hesitate, boggle, hover, wobble, shilly-shally, hum and haw, demur, not know one's own mind; debate, balance; dally –, coquet- with; will and will not, *chasser-balancer*; go half-way, compromise, make a compromise; be thrown off one's balance, stagger like a drunken man; be afraid &c. 860; let 'I dare not' wait upon 'I would'; falter, waver.

the ladder, nail one's colours to the mast, set one's back against the wall, set one's teeth, put one's foot down, burn one's bridges, take one's stand; stand firm &c. (*stability*) 150; steel oneself; stand no nonsense, not listen to the voice of the charmer.

buckle to; put -, lay -, set- one's shoulder to the wheel; put one's heart into; run the gauntlet, make a dash at, take the bull by the horns; beard the lion in his den; rush -, plunge- *in medias res*; go in for; insist upon, make a point of; set one's heart, - mind- upon.

stick at nothing; make short work of &c. (*activity*) 682; not stick at trifles; go -all lengths, - the whole hog; persist &c. (*persevere*) 604a; go down with colours flying, die game; go through fire and water, ride in the whirlwind and direct the storm.

Adj. resolved &c. *v.*; determined; strong-willed, -minded; resolute &c. (*brave*) 861; self-possessed, plucky, tenacious; decided, definitive, peremptory; un-hesitating, -flinching, -shrinking; firm, cast iron, indomitable, game to the backbone; inexorable, relentless, not to be -shaken, - put down; *tenax propositi*; inflexible &c. (*hard*) 323;

vacillate &c. 149; change &c. 140; retract &c. 607; fluctuate; alternate &c. (*oscillate*) 314; keep off and on, play fast and loose; blow hot and cold &c. (*caprice*) 608.

shuffle, palter, blink; trim.

Adj. irresolute, infirm of purpose, double-minded, half-hearted; un-decided, -resolved, -determined; drifting; shilly-shally; fidgety, tremulous; wobbly; hesitating &c. *v.*; off one's balance; at a loss &c. (*uncertain*) 475.

vacillating &c. *v.*; unsteady &c. (*changeable*) 149; unsteadfast, fickle, unreliable, irresponsible, unstable, without ballast; capricious &c. 608; volatile, frothy; light, -some, -minded; giddy; fast and loose.

weak, feeble-minded, frail; timid &c. 860; cowardly &c. 862; facile; pliant &c. (*soft*) 324; unable to say 'no,' easy-going.

revocable, reversible.

Adv. irresolutely &c. *adj.*; irresolvedly; in faltering accents; off and on; from pillar to post; see-saw &c. 314.

Int. 'how happy could I be with either!'

obstinate &c. 606; steady &c. (*persevering*) 604a; unbending, unyielding, irrevocable; firm as a rock; grim.

earnest, serious; set -, bent -, intent- upon.

steeled -, proof- against; *in utrumque paratus.*

Adv. resolutely &c. *adj.*; in -, in good- earnest; seriously, joking apart, earnestly, heart and soul; on one's metal; manfully, like a man, with a high hand; with a strong hand &c. (*exertion*) 686.

at any -rate, - risk, - hazard, - price, - cost, - sacrifice; at all -hazards, - risks, - events; cost what it may; *coûte que coûte*; *à tort et à travers*; once for all; neck or nothing; rain or shine; with colours nailed to the mast.

Phr. *spes sibi quisque.*

**604a. Perseverance.**—N. perseverance; continuance &c. (*inaction*) 143; permanence &c. (*absence of change*) 141; firmness &c. (*stability*) 150.

constancy, steadiness; singleness -, tenacity- of purpose; persistence, plodding, patience; sedulity &c. (*industry*) 682; pertina-cy, -city, -ciousness; iteration &c. 104.

bottom, game, pluck, stamina, backbone, grit; indefatiga-bility, -bleness; bulldog courage.

V. persevere, persist; hold -on, - out; die in the last ditch, be in at the death; stick -, cling -, adhere- to; stick to one's text, keep on; keep to –, maintain- one's -course, – ground; bear –, keep –, hold-up; plod; stick to work &c. (*work*) 686; continue &c. 143; follow up; die -in harness, – at one's post.

Adj. persevering, constant; stead-y, -fast; un-deviating, -wavering, -faltering, -swerving, -flinching, -sleeping, -flagging, -drooping; steady as time; uninter-, un-remitting; plodding; industrious &c. 682; strenuous &c. 686; pertinacious; persist-ing, -ent.

solid, sturdy, staunch, stanch, true to oneself; unchangeable &c. 150; unconquerable &c. (*strong*) 159; indomitable, game to the last, indefatigable, untiring, unwearied, never tiring.

Adv. through -evil report and good report, – thick and thin, – fire and water; *per fas et nefas*; without fail, sink or swim, at any price, *vogue la galère*; in sickness and in health.

Phr. never say die; *vestigia nulla retrorsum*.

**606. Obstinacy.—N.** obstinateness &c. *adj.*; obstinacy, tenacity; perseverance &c. 604a; immovability; old school; inflexibility &c. (*hardness*) 323; obdur-acy, -ation; dogged resolution; resolution &c. 604; ruling passion; blind side.

self-will, contumacy, perversity; pervica-cy, -city; indocility.

bigotry, intolerance, dogmatism; opinia-try, -tiveness; fixed idea &c.; intractability, incorrigibility; (*prejudgment*) 481; fanaticism, zealotry, infatuation, monomania, opinionativeness.

mule; opin-ionist, -ionatist, -iator, -ator; stickler, dogmatist, die-hard, bitter-ender; bigot; zealot, enthusiast, fanatic.

V. be -obstinate &c. *adj.*; stickle, take no denial, fly in the face of facts; opinionate, be wedded to an opinion, hug a belief; have one's own way &c. (*will*) 600; persist &c. (*persevere*) 604a; have –, insist on having- the last word.

die -hard, – fighting, fight -against destiny, – to the last ditch; not yield an inch, stand out.

Adj. obstinate, tenacious, stubborn, obdurate, case-hardened; inflexible &c. (*hard*) 323; immovable, not to be moved; inert &c. 172; unchangeable &c. 150; inexorable &c. (*determined*) 604; mulish, obstinate as a mule, pig-headed.

dogged; sullen, sulky; un-moved, -influenced, -affected.

wilful, self-willed, perverse; res-ty, -tive, -tiff; pervicacious, wayward, refractory, unruly; head-y, -strong; *entêté*; contumacious; cross-grained.

**607. Tergiversation.—N.** change of -mind, – intention, – purpose; after-thought.

tergiversation, recantation; palinode, -ody; renunciation; abjur-ation, -ement; defection &c. (*relinquishment*) 624; going over &c. *v.*; apostasy; retract-ion, -ation; withdrawal, disavowal &c. (*negation*) 536; revo-cation, -kement; reversal; repentance &c. 950; *redintegratio amoris*.

coquetry, flirtation; vacillation &c. 605; back-sliding, recidivation.

turn-coat, -tippet; rat, apostate, renegade, mugwump; con-, per-vert; proselyte, deserter; backslider, recidivist; black leg.

time-server, -pleaser; timist, Vicar of Bray, trimmer, ambidexter; weather-cock &c. (*changeable*) 149; Janus.

V. change one's -mind, – intention, – purpose, – note; abjure, renounce; withdraw from &c. (*relinquish*) 624; wheel –, turn –, veer- round; turn a *pirouette*; go over –, pass –, change –, skip- from one side to another; go to the right about; box the compass, shift one's ground, go upon another tack; back down, crawl, crawfish.

apostatize, change sides, go over, rat; recant, retract; revoke; rescind &c. (*abrogate*) 756; recall, forswear, abjure, unsay; come -over, – round- to an opinion.

draw in one's horns, eat one's words; eat –, swallow- the look; swerve, flinch, back out of, retrace one's steps, think better of it; come back –, return- to one's first love; turn over a new leaf &c. (*repent*) 950.

arbitrary, dogmatic, opinionated, positive, bigoted; prejudiced &c. 481; prepossessed, infatuated; stiff-backed, -necked, -hearted; hard-mouthed, hidebound; unyielding; im-pervious, -practicable, -persuasible; unpersuadable; in-, un-tractable; incorrigible, deaf to advice, impervious to reason; crotchety &c. 608.

**Adv.** obstinately &c. *adj.*

**Phr.** *non possumus*; no surrender.

---

trim, shuffle, play fast and loose, blow hot and cold, coquet, flirt, hold with the hare but run with the hounds; straddle; *nager entre deux eaux*; wait to see how the -cat jumps, – wind blows.

**Adj.** changeful &c. 149; irresolute &c. 605; ductile, slippery as an eel, trimming, ambidextrous, timeserving; coquetting &c. *v.*

revocatory, reactionary.

**Phr.** 'a change came o'er the spirit of my dream.'

**608. Caprice.—N.** caprice, fancy, humour; whim, -sey, -wham; crotchet, *capriccio*, quirk, freak, maggot, fad, vagary, prank, fit, flimflam, *escapade*, *boutade*, wild-goose chase; capriciousness &c. *adj.*; kink.

**V.** be -capricious &c. *adj.*; have a maggot in the brain; take it into one's head, strain at a gnat and swallow a camel; blow hot and cold; play -fast and loose, – fantastic tricks.

**Adj.** capricious; erratic, eccentric, fitful, hysterical; full of -whims &c. *n.*; maggoty; inconsistent, fanciful, fantastic, whimsical, crotchety, particular, humoursome, freakish, skittish, wanton, wayward; contrary; captious; arbitrary; unrestrained, undisciplined; not amenable to reason; uncomfortable &c. 83; penny wise and pound foolish; fickle &c. (*irresolute*) 605; frivolous, sleeveless, giddy, volatile.

**Adv.** by fits and starts, without rhyme or reason, at one's own sweet will.

**Phr.** *nil fuit unquam sic impar sibi*; the deuce is in him.

**609. Choice.—N.** choice, option; discretion &c. (*volition*) 600; preoption; alternative; dilemma; *embarras de choix*; adoption, co-optation; novation; decision &c. (*judgment*) 480.

election, poll, ballot, vote, voice, suffrage, plumper, cumulative vote; *plebiscitum*, *plébiscite*, *vox populi*; *referendum*, electioneering; voting &c. *v.*; franchise; ballot box; slate, ticket.

selection, excerption, gleaning, eclecticism; *excerpta*, gleanings, cuttings, scissors and paste; pick &c. (*best*) 650.

preference, prelation; predilection &c. (*desire*) 865.

**V.** offer for one's choice, set before; hold out –, present –, offer- the alternative; put to the vote.

use –, exercise –, one's- -discretion, – option; adopt, take up, embrace, espouse; choose, elect, co-opt; take –, make- one's choice; make choice of, fix upon.

vote, poll, hold up one's hand; divide.

settle; decide &c. (*adjudge*) 480; list

**609a. Absence of Choice.—N.** no –, Hobson's- choice; first come, first served; necessity &c. 601; not a pin to choose &c. (*equality*) 27; any, the first that comes.

neutrality, indifference; indecision &c. (*irresolution*) 605.

**V.** be -neutral &c. *adj.*; have no choice; waive, not vote; abstain –, refrain- from voting; leave undecided; make a virtue of necessity.

**Adj.** neu-tral, -ter; indifferent; undecided &c. (*irresolute*) 605.

**Adv.** either &c. (*choice*) 609.

**610. Rejection.—N.** rejection, repudiation, exclusion; declination; refusal &c. 764.

**V.** reject; set –, lay- aside; give up; decline &c. (*refuse*) 764; exclude, except, eliminate; pluck, spin; cast.

repudiate, scout, set at naught; fling –, cast –, thrown –, toss- -to the winds, – to the dogs, – overboard, – away; send to the right about; dis-

&c. (*will*) 600; make up one's mind &c. (*resolve*) 604.

select; pick, – and choose; pick –, single- out, excerpt; cull, glean, winnow; sift –, separate –, winnow- the chaff from the wheat; pick up, pitch upon; piek one's way; indulge one's fancy.

set apart, reserve, mark out for; mark &c. 550.

prefer; have -rather, – as lief; fancy &c. (desire) 865; be persuaded &c. 615.

take a -decided, – decisive- step; commit oneself to a course; pass –, cross- the Rubicon; cast in one's lot with; take for better or for worse.

**Adj.** optional; co-optative; discretional &c. (*voluntary*) 600; on approval.

eclectic; choosing &c. *v.*; preferential; chosen &c. *v.*; choice &c. (*good*) 648.

**Adv.** optionally &c. *adj.*; at pleasure &c. (*will*) 600; either, – the one or the other; or; at the option of; whether or not; once for all; for one's money.

by -choice, – preference; in preference; rather, before.

claim &c. (*deny*) 536; discard &c. (*eject*) 297, (*have done with*) 678.

**Adj.** rejected &c. *v.*; reject-aneous, -itious; not -chosen &c. 609, – to be thought of; out of the question.

**Adv.** neither, – the one nor the other; no &c. 536.

**Phr.** *non hæc in fædera.*

---

**611. Predetermination.** — **N.** premeditation, -deliberation, -determination, -destination; foreordination; foregone conclusion; *parti pris*; resolve, propendency; intention &c. 620; project &c. 626.

**V.** pre-determine, -destine, -meditate, -resolve, -concert; foreordain; resolve beforehand.

**Adj.** pre-pense, -meditated &c. *v.*, -designed; advised, studied, designed, calculated; aforethought; intended &c. 620; foregone.

well-laid, -devised, -weighed; maturely considered; cut and dried; cunning.

**Adv.** advisedly &c. *adj.*; with premeditation, deliberately, all things considered, with eyes open, in cold blood; intentionally &c. 620.

**612. Impulse.** — **N.** impulse, sudden thought; *impromptu*, improvisation; inspiration, hunch, flash, spurt.

*improvisatore*, *improvisatrice*, improviser, extemporizer; **creature of impulse.**

**V.** flash on the mind.

say what comes uppermost; improvise, extemporize; rise to the occasion; spurt.

**Adj.** extemporaneous, impulsive, indeliberate; improvis-ed, -ate, -atory; un-, unpre-meditated; *improvisé*; unprompted, -guided; natural, unguarded; spontaneous &c. (*voluntary*) 600; instinctive &c. 601.

**Adv.** extem-pore, -poraneously; offhand, *impromptu*, *à l'improviste*; improviso; on the spur of the -moment, – occasion.

**613. Habit.—N.** habit, -ude; assuetude, -faction; wont; run, way.

common –, general –, natural –, ordinary –, habitual- -course, – run, – state- of things; matter of course; beaten -path, – track, – ground.

prescription, custom, use, usage, immemorial usage, practice; tradition; prevalence, observance; conventional-

**614. Desuetude.—N.** desuetude, disusage; disuse &c. 678; want of -habit, – practice; inusitation; newness to; new brooms.

infraction of usage &c. (*unconformity*) 83; non-prevalence; 'a custom more honoured in the breach than the observance.'

**V.** be -unaccustomed &c. *adj.*; leave

ism, -ity; mode, fashion, vogue; *étiquette* &c. (*gentility*) 852; order of the day, cry; conformity &c. 82.

  *habitué*, addict.

one's old way, old school, consuetude, *veteris vestigia flammæ*; *laudator temporis acti*.

rule, standing order, precedent, routine; red-tape, -tapism; pipe-clay; rut, groove.

*cacoëthes*; bad -, confirmed -, inveterate -, intrinsic &c. 5- habit; addiction, trick.

training &c. (*education*) 537; seasoning, hardening, inurement; radication; second nature, acclimatization; knack &c. (*skill*) 698.

**V.** be -wont &c. *adj.*

fall into a custom &c. (*conform to*) 82; tread -, follow- the beaten -track, - path; *stare super antiquas vias*; move in a rut, run on in a groove, go round like a horse in a mill, go on in the old jog-trot way.

habituate, inure, harden, season, caseharden; accustom, familiarize; naturalize, acclimatize; keep one's hand in; train &c. (*educate*) 537.

get into the -way, - knack- of; learn &c. 539; cling -, adhere- to; repeat &c. 104; acquire -, contract -, fall into- a -habit, - trick; addict oneself -, take- to; accustom oneself to.

be -habitual &c. *adj.*; prevail; come into use, become a habit, take root; gain -, grow- upon one.

**Adj.** habitual; ac-, customary; prescriptive; accustomed &c. *v.*; traditional; of -daily, - every-day- occurrence; wonted, usual, general, ordinary, common, frequent, every-day, household, jog-trot; well-trodden, -known; familiar, vernacular, trite, commonplace, banal, bromidic, conventional, regular, set, stock, official, established, stereotyped; pre-vailing, -valent; current, received, acknowledged, recognized, accredited; of course, admitted, understood.

conformable &c. 82; according to -use, - custom, - routine; in -vogue, - fashion; fashionable &c. (*genteel*) 852.

wont; used - given - addicted -, attuned -, habituated &c. *v.*- to; in the habit of; *habitué*; at home in &c. (*skilful*) 698; seasoned; permeated -, imbued- with; devoted -, wedded- to; never free from.

hackneyed, fixed, rooted, deep-rooted, ingrafted, permanent, inveterate, besetting; naturalized; ingrained &c. (*intrinsic*) 5.

**Adv.** habitually &c. *adj.*; always &c. (*uniformly*) 16.

as -usual, - is one's wont, - things go, - the world goes, - the sparks fly upwards; *more -suo, - solito.*

as a rule, for the most part; generally &c. *adj.*; most often, - frequently.

**Phr.** *cela s'entend.*

off -, cast off -, break off -, wean oneself of -, violate -, break through -, infringe- -a habit, - a custom, - a usage; break one's fetters; disuse &c. 678; wear off.

**Adj.** un-accustomed, -used, -wonted, -seasoned, -inured, -habituated, -trained; new; green &c. (*unskilled*) 699; fresh, original, unhackneyed.

unusual &c. (*unconformable*) 83; unconventional, non-observant; disused &c. 678.

**Adv.** just for once.

---

## 2°. *Causes of Volition*

**615. Motive.—N.** motive, springs of action.

reason, ground, call, principle; main-

**615a. Absence of Motive.—N.** absence of motive; caprice &c. 608; chance &c. (*absence of design*) 621:

spring, *primum mobile*, key-stone; the why and the wherefore; *pro* and *con*, reason why; secret –, ulterior- motive, *arrière-pensée*; intention &c. 620.

inducement, consideration; attraction &c. 288; loadstone; magnet, -ism, -ic force; allect-ation, -ive; temptation, enticement, *agacerie*, allurement, witchery; bewitch-ment, -ery; charm; spell &c. 993; fascination, blandishment, cajolery; seduc-tion, -ement; honeyed words, voice of the tempter, song of the Sirens; forbidden fruit, golden apple.

persuasi-bility, -bleness; attractability; impress-, suscept-ibility; softness; persuas-, attract-iveness; tantalization.

influence, prompting, dictate, instance; impuls-e, -ion; incit-ement, -ation; press, instigation; provocation &c. (*excitation of feeling*) 824; inspiration; per-, suasion; encouragement, advocacy; exhortation, advice &c. 695; solicitation &c. (*request*) 765; lobbying.

incentive, stimulus, spur, fillip, whip, goad, rowel, provocative, whet, dram.

bribe, lure; decoy, – duck; bait, trail of a red herring; bribery and corruption; sop, – for Cerberus.

prompter, tempter; seduc-er, -tor; suggester, coaxer, wheedler; instigator, firebrand, incendiary; Siren, Circe; *agent provocateur*; lobbyist.

**V.** induce, move; draw, – on; bring in its train, give an -impulse &c. *n.*- to; inspire; put up to, prompt, call up; attract, beckon.

**V.** have no motive; scruple &c. (*be unwilling*) 603.

**Adj.** without rhyme or reason; aimless &c. (*chance*) 621.

**Adv.** capriciously; out of mere caprice.

**616. Dissuasion.**—**N.** dissuasion, dehortation, expostulation, remonstrance: deprecation &c. 766.

discouragement, damper, wet blanket; warning.

cohibition &c. (*restraint*) 751; curb &c. (*means of restraint*) 752; check &c. (*hindrance*) 706.

reluctance &c. (*unwillingness*) 603; contraindication.

**V.** dissuade, dehort, cry out against, remonstrate, expostulate, warn, contraindicate.

disincline, indispose, shake, stagger; dispirit; dis-courage, -hearten, -enchant; deter; hold –, keep- back &c. (*restrain*) 751; render -averse &c. 603; repel; turn aside &c. (*deviation*) 279; wean from; act as a drag &c. (*hinder*) 706; throw cold water on, damp, cool, chill, blunt, calm, quiet, quench; deprecate &c. 766.

**Adj.** dissuading &c. *v.*; dissuasive; dehortatory, expostulatory; monit-ive, -ory.

dissuaded &c. *v.*; uninduced &c. (induce &c. 615); unpersuadable &c. (*obstinate*) 606; averse &c. (*unwilling*) 603; repugnant &c. (*dislike*) 867.

----

stimulate &c. (*excite*) 824; spirit up, inspirit; a-, rouse; ecphorize; animate, incite, provoke, instigate, set on, actuate; act –, work –, operate- upon; encourage; pat –, clap- on the -back, – shoulder.

influence, weigh with, bias, sway, incline, dispose, predispose, turn the scale, inoculate; lead, – by the nose; have –, exercise- influence- -with, – over, – upon; go –, come- round one; turn the head, magnetize.

persuade; prevail -with, – upon; overcome, carry; bring -round, – to one's senses; draw –, win –, gain –, come –, talk- over; procure, enlist, engage; invite, court.

tempt, seduce, overpersuade, entice, allure, captivate, fascinate, intrigue, bewitch, carry away, charm, conciliate, wheedle, coax, lure, suggest; inveigle; tantalize; cajole &c. (*deceive*) 545.

tamper with, bribe, suborn, grease the palm, bait with a silver hook, gild the pill, make things pleasant, put a sop into the pan, throw a sop to, bait the hook.

enforce, force; impel &c. (*push*) 276; propel &c. 284; whip, lash, goad, spur, prick, urge; egg –, hound –, hurry- on; drag &c. 285; exhort; advise &c. 695; call upon &c., press &c. (*request*) 765; advocate.

set -an example, – the fashion; keep in countenance; back up.

be -persuaded &c.; yield to temptation, come round; concede &c. (*consent*) 762; obey a call; follow -advice, – the bent, – the dictates of; act on principle.

**Adj.** impulsive, motive; suas-, persuas-, hortat-ive, -ory; protreptical; inviting, tempting &c. *v.*; seductive, attractive, irresistible; fascinating &c. (*pleasing*) 829; provocative &c. (*exciting*) 824.

induced &c. *v.*; disposed; persuadable &c. (*docile*) 602; spellbound; instinct –, smitten- with; inspired &c. *v.*- by.

**Adv.** because, therefore &c. (*cause*) 155; from -this, – that- motive; for -this, – that- reason; for; by reason –, for the sake –, on the score –, on account- of; out of, from, as, forasmuch as.

for all the world; on principle.

**617.** [Ostensible motive, ground, or reason assigned.] **Plea.—N** plea, pretext; allegation, advocation; ostensible -motive, – ground, – reason; excuse &c. (*vindication*) 937; colour; gloss, guise.

loop-, starting-hole; how to creep out of, salvo, come off.

handle, peg to hang on, room, *locus standi*; stalking-horse, *cheval de bataille*, cue.

pretence &c. (*untruth*) 546; put off, subterfuge, dust thrown in the eyes; blind; moonshine; mere –, shallow- pretext; lame -excuse, – apology; tub to a whale; false plea, sour grapes; makeshift, shift, white lie; special pleading &c. (*sophistry*) 477; soft sawder &c. (*flattery*) 933.

**V.** plead, allege; shelter oneself under the plea of; excuse &c. (*vindicate*) 937; gloss over; lend a colour to; furnish a -handle &c. *n.*; make a -pretext, – handle- of; use as a plea &c. *n.*; take one's stand upon, make capital out of; pretend &c. (*lie*) 544.

**Adj.** ostensible &c. (*manifest*) 525; excusing; alleged, apologetic; pretended &c. 545.

**Adv.** ostensibly; under -colour, – the plea, – the pretence- of.

### 3°. *Objects of Volition*

**618. Good.—N.** good, benefit, advantage; improvement &c. 658; interest, service, behoof, behalf; weal; main chance, *summum bonum*, common weal; 'consummation devoutly to be wished'; gain, boot; profit, harvest.

boon &c. (*gift*) 784; good turn; blessing, benison; world of good; piece of good -luck, – fortune; nuts, prize, windfall, godsend, waif, treasure trove.

good fortune &c. (*prosperity*) 734; happiness &c. 827.

[Source of good] goodness &c. 648; utility &c. 644; remedy &c. 662; pleasure-giving &c. 829.

**Adj.** commendable &c. 931; useful &c. 644; good &c., beneficial &c. 648.

**619. Evil.—N.** evil, ill, harm, hurt, mischief, nuisance; machinations of the devil, Pandora's box, ills that flesh is heir to.

blow, buffet, stroke, scratch, bruise, wound, gash, mutilation; mortal -blow, – wound; *immedicabile vulnus*; damage, loss &c. (*deterioration*) 659.

disadvantage, prejudice, drawback; disaster, accident, casualty; mishap &c. (*misfortune*) 735; bad job, devil to pay; calamity, bale, woe, catastrophe, tragedy; ruin &c. (*destruction*) 162; adversity &c. 735.

mental suffering &c. 828. [Evil spirit] demon &c. 980. [Cause of evil] bane &c. 663. [Production of evil]

**V.** benefit, profit, advantage, serve, help, avail; do good to, gain, prosper, flourish.

**Adv.** well, aright, satisfactorily, favourably, not amiss; all for the best; to one's -advantage &c. *n.*; in one's -favour, – interest &c. *n.*

**Phr.** so far so good.

badness &c. 649; painfulness &c. 830; evil doer &c. 913.

outrage, wrong, injury, foul play; bad –, ill- turn; disservice; spoliation &c. 791; grievance, crying evil.

**V.** be in trouble &c. (*adversity*) 735; harm, injure, hurt, do disservice to.

**Adj.** disastrous, bad &c. 649; awry, out of joint; disadvantageous, injurious, harmful.

**Adv.** amiss, wrong, ill, to one's cost.

---

## Section II. Prospective Volition*
### 1°. *Conceptional Volition*

**620. Intention.—N.** intent, -ion, -ionality; purpose; *quo animo*; project &c. 626; undertaking &c. 676; predetermination &c. 611; design, ambition.

contemplation, mind, *animus*, view, purview, proposal; study; look out.

final cause; *raison d'être*; *cui bono*; object, aim, end; 'the be all and the end all'; drift &c. (*meaning*) 516; tendency &c. 176; destination, mark, point, butt, goal, target, bull's-eye, quintain; prey, quarry, game.

decision, determination, resolve; set -, settled- purpose; *ultimatum*; resolution &c. 604; wish &c. 865; *arrière-pensée*; motive &c. 615.

[Study of final causes] teleology.

**V.** intend, purpose, design, mean; have to; propose to oneself; harbour a design; have in -view, – contemplation, – one's eye, – *petto*; have an eye to.

bid –, labour- for; be –, aspire –, endeavour- after; be –, aim –, drive –, point-, level - at; take aim; set before oneself; study to.

take upon oneself &c (*undertake*) 676; take into one's head; meditate, contemplate; think – dream –, talk- of; premeditate &c. 611; compass, calculate; dest-ine, -inate: propose.

project &c. (*plan*) 626; have a mind to &c. (*be willing*) 602; desire &c. 865; pursue &c. 622.

**Adj.** intended &c. *v.*; intentional, advised, express, determinate; prepense &c. 611; bound for; intending &c. *v.*; minded, disposed, inclined;

**621.** [Absence of purpose in the succession of events.] **Chance.†—N.** chance &c. 156; lot, fate &c. (*necessity*) 601; luck; good luck &c. (*good*) 618; bad luck &c. 735; wheel of fortune; mascot; swastika.

speculation, venture, stake, flutter, flier, gamble, game of chance; mere –, random- shot; blind bargain, leap in the dark; pig in a poke &c. (*uncertainty*) 475; fluke, pot-luck.

drawing lots; sorti-legy, -tion; *sortes*, – *Virgilianæ*, -*biblicæ*; *rouge et noir*, hazard, *roulette*, pitch and toss, chuck-farthing, cup-tossing, heads or tails, cross and pile, wager; bet, -ting; risk, stake, plunge; gambling; the turf.

stock exchange, bourse, board of trade (U.S.A.), curb exchange.

gaming-, gambling-, betting-house; hell; betting ring, totalisator; dice, – box; dicer; gam-bler, -ester, plunger; stock operator, manipulator, punter; man of the turf; adventurer, speculator; bookmaker, layer, backer.

**V.** chance &c. (*hap*) 156; stand a chance &c. (*be possible*) 470.

toss up; cast -, draw- lots; leave –, trust- -to chance, – to the chapter of accidents; tempt fortune; chance it, take one's chance; run –, incur –, encounter- the -risk, – chance; stand the hazard of the die.

speculate, try one's luck, set on a cast, raffle, put into a lottery, buy a pig in a poke, shuffle the cards.

risk, venture, hazard, stake; lay, – a wager; make a bet, wager, bet, gamble,

---

\* That is, volition having reference to a future object.        † See note on 156.

bent upon &c. (*earnest*) 604; at stake, on the -anvil, – *tapis*; in -view; – prospect, – the breast of; *in petto*; teleological.

**Adv.** intentionally &c. *adj.*; advisedly, wittingly, knowingly, designedly, purposely, on purpose, by design, studiously, pointedly; with -intent &c. *n.*; deliberately &c. (*with premeditation*) 611; with one's eyes open, in cold blood.

for; with -a view, – an eye- to; in order -to, – that; to the end –, with the intent- that; for the purpose –, with the view –, in contemplation –, on account- of.

in pursuance of, pursuant to; *quo animo*: to all intents and purposes.

---

**622.** [Purpose in action.] **Pursuit.—**
**N.** pursuit; pursuing &c. *v.*; prosecution; pursuance; enterprise &c. (*undertaking*) 676; business &c. 625; adventure &c. (*essay*) 675; quest &c. (*search*) 461; scramble, hue and cry, game; hobby.

chase, hunt, *battue*, race, steeplechase, hunting, coursing; ven-ation, -ery; fox-chase; sport, -ing; shooting, angling, fishing, hawking.

pursuer; hunt-er, -sman; sportsman, Nimrod, the field; hound &c. 366.

**V.** pursue, prosecute, follow; run –, make –, be –, hunt –, prowl- after; shadow; carry on &c. (*do*) 680; engage in &c. (*undertake*) 676; set about &c. (*begin*) 66; endeavour &c. 675; court &c. (*request*) 765; seek &c. (*search*) 461; aim at &c. (*intention*) 620; follow the trail &c. (*trace*) 461; fish for &c. (*experiment*) 463; press on &c. (*haste*) 684; run a race &c. (*velocity*) 274.

chase, give chase, course, dog, hunt, hound, stalk; tread –, follow- on the heels of &c. (*sequence*) 281.

rush upon; rush headlong &c. (*violence*) 173; ride –, run- full tilt at; make a leap –, jump –, snatch- at; run down; start game.

tread a path; take –, hold- a course; shape –, direct –, bend- one's -steps, – course; play a game; fight –, elbow- one's way; follow up; take -to, – up; go in for; ride one's hobby.

**Adj.** pursuing &c. *v.*; in quest of &c.

game, play for; play at chuck-farthing.

**Adj.** fortuitous &c. 156; unintentional, -ded; accidental; not meant; un-designed, -purposed; unpremeditated &c. 612; never thought of.

indiscriminate, promiscuous; undirected, random; aim-, drift-, design-, purpose-, cause-less; without purpose. possible &c. 470.

**Adv.** casually &c. 156; unintentionally &c. *adj.*; unwittingly.

*en passant*, by the way, incidentally; as it may happen; at -random, – a venture, – haphazard; as luck would have it, by -chance, – good fortune; un-, -luckily.

---

**623.** [Absence of pursuit.] **Avoidance.**
**—N.** abst-ention, -inence; forbearance; refraining &c. *v.*; inaction &c. 681; neutrality.

avoidance, evasion, elusion; seclusion &c. 893.

avolation, flight; escape &c. 671; retreat &c. 287; recoil &c. 277; departure &c. 293; rejection &c. 610.

shirker &c. *v.*; slacker; truant; fugitive, refugee; runa-way, -gate; renegade; deserter.

**V.** abstain, refrain, spare, not attempt; not do &c. 681; maintain the even tenor of one's way.

eschew, keep from, let alone, have nothing to do with; keep –, stand –, hold- -aloof, – off; take no part in, have no hand in.

avoid, shun; steer –, keep- clear of; fight shy of; keep -one's, – at a respectful- distance; keep –, get- out of the way; evade, elude, turn away from; set one's face against &c. (*oppose*) 708; deny oneself.

shrink; hang –, hold –, draw- back; recoil &c. 277; retire &c. (*recede*) 287; flinch, blink, blench, shy, shirk, dodge, parry, make way for, give place to.

beat a retreat; turn -tail, – one's back; take to one's heels; run, -away, – for one's life; cut and run; be off, – like a shot; fly, flee; fly –, flee –, run away- from; take –, take to- flight; desert, elope; make –, scamper –, sneak –, shuffle –, sheer- off; break –,

*(inquiry)* 461; in -pursuit, – full cry,
– hot pursuit; on the scent.
   **Adv.** in pursuance of &c. *(intention)*
620; after.
   **Int.** tally-ho! yoicks! so-ho!

burst –, tear oneself –, slip –, slink –,
steal- -away, – away from; slip cable,
part company, turn on one's heel;
sneak out of, play truant, give one
the go by, give leg bail, take French
leave, slope, decamp, flit, bolt, ab-
scond, levant, skedaddle, absquatulate,
cut one's stick, walk one's chalks, show
a light pair of heels, make oneself scarce; escape &c. 671; go away
&c. *(depart)* 293; abandon &c. 624; reject &c. 610.
   lead one a -dance, – a merry chase, – pretty dance; throw off
the scent, play at hide and seek.
   **Adj.** unsought, unattempted; avoiding &c. *v.*; neutral; shy of
&c. *(unwilling)* 603; elusive, evasive, distant; fugitive, runaway;
shy, wild.
   **Adj.** lest, in order to avoid.
   **Int.** forbear! keep –, hands- off! *sauve qui peut!* devil take the
hindmost!

   **624. Relinquishment.—N.** relinquish-, abandon-ment; desertion,
defection, secession, withdrawal; cave of Adullam; *nolle prosequi.*
   discontinuance &c. *(cessation)* 142; renunciation &c. *(recantation)* 607;
abrogation &c. 756; resignation &c. *(retirement)* 757; desuetude &c.
614; cession &c. *(of property)* 782.
   **V.** relinquish, give up, abandon, desert, forsake, leave in the lurch;
depart -, secede -, withdraw- from; back – out of, – down from, leave,
go back on one's word, quit, take leave of, bid a long farewell; vacate
&c. *(resign)* 757.
   renounce &c. *(abjure)* 607; forego, have done with, drop; write off;
disuse &c. 678; discard &c. 782; wash one's hands of; drop all idea of;
*nolle-pros.*; lose interest in.
   break -, leave- off; desist; stop &c. *(cease)* 142; hold -, stay- one's
hand; quit one's hold; give over, shut up shop.
   throw up the -game, – cards; give up the -point, – argument; pass
to the order of the day, move the previous question, table the motion.
   **Adj.** unpursued; relinquished &c. *v.*; relinquishing &c. *v.*
   **Int.** avast &c.! *(stop)* 142.

   **625. Business.—N.** business, occupation, employment; pursuit &c.
622; what one is doing-, – about; affair, concern, matter, case, un-
dertaking.
   matter in hand, irons in the fire; thing to do, *agendum*, task, work,
job, chore, errand, transaction, commission, mission, charge, care;
duty &c. 926.
   part, *rôle*, cue; province, function, look-out, department, capacity,
sphere, orb, field, line; walk, – of life; beat, round, routine; race, career.
   office, place, post, incumbency, living; situation, appointment, billet,
berth, employ; service &c. *(servitude)* 749; engagement; undertaking
&c. 676.
   vocation, calling, profession, *métier*, cloth, faculty; industry, art;
industrial arts; craft, mystery, handicraft; trade &c. *(commerce)* 794.
   exercise; work &c. *(action)* 680; avocation; press of business &c.
*(activity)* 682.
   **V.** pass -, employ -, spend- one's time in; employ oneself -in, – upon;

occupy –, concern- oneself with; make it one's -business &c. *n.*; under-
take &c. 676; enter a profession; betake oneself to, turn one's hand to;
have to do with &c. (*do*) 680.

drive a trade; carry on –, do –, transact- -business, – a trade &c: *n.*;
keep a shop; ply one's task, – trade; labour in one's vocation; pursue
the even tenor of one's way; attend to -business, – one's work.

officiate, serve, act; act –, play- one's part; do duty; serve –, dis-
charge –, perform- the -office, – duties, – functions- of; hold –, fill- -an
office, – a place, – a situation; hold a portfolio.

be -about, – doing, – engaged in, – employed in, – occupied with, –
at work on; have one's hands in, have in hand; have on one's -hands,
– shoulders; bear the burden; have one's hands full &c. (*activity*) 682.

be -in the hands of, – on the stocks, – on the anvil; pass through
one's hands.

**Adj.** business-like; work-a-day; professional; official, functional;
busy &c. (*actively employed*) 682; on –, in- -hand, – one's hands; afoot;
on -foot, – the anvil; going on; acting.

**Adv.** in the course of business, all in a day's work; professionally
&c. *adj.*

**626. Plan.—N.** plan, scheme, design, project; propos-al, -ition; sug-
gestion; resolution, motion; precaution &c. (*provision*) 673; deep-laid
&c. (*premeditated*) 611- plan &c.; racket.

system &c. (order) 58; organization &c: (*arrangement*) 60; germ &c.
(*cause*) 153; Five Year Plan.

sketch, skeleton, outline, draught, draft, *ébauche*, *brouillon*; rough
-cast, – draft, – draught, – copy; copy; proof, revise.

forecast, *programme*, prospectus, scenario; *carte du pays*; card; bill,
protocol; order of the day, list of agenda, *memorandum*; bill of fare &c.
(*food*) 298; base of operations; platform, plank.

*rôle*; policy &c. (*line of conduct*) 692.

contrivance, invention, expedient, receipt, nostrum, artifice, device,
gadget; stratagem &c. (*cunning*) 702; trick &c. (*deception*) 545; alter-
native, loophole, shift &c. (*substitute*) 147; last shift &c. (*necessity*) 601.

measure, step; stroke, – of policy; master stroke; trump-, court-card;
*cheval de bataille*, great gun; *coup*, – *d'état*; clever –, bold –, good-
-move, – hit, – stroke; bright -thought, – idea, great idea.

intrigue, cabal, plot, frame-up, conspiracy, complot, machination;
under-, counter-plot.

schem-ist, -atist; strategist, machinator, schemer; projector, author,
builder, artist, promoter, designer &c. *v.*; conspirator; *intrigant* &c.
(*cunning*) 702.

**V.** plan, scheme, design, frame, contrive, project, forecast, sketch;
conceive, devise, invent &c. (*imagine*) 515; set one's wits to work
&c. 515; spring a project; fall –, hit- upon; strike –, chalk –, cut –,
lay –, map-out; lay down a plan; shape –, mark- out a course; prede-
termine &c. 611; concert, preconcert, preestablish; prepare &c. 673;
hatch, – a plot; concoct; take -steps, – measures.

cast, recast, systematize, organize; arrange &c. 60; digest, mature.

plot; counter-plot, -mine; dig a mine; lay a train; intrigue &c.
(*cunning*) 702.

**Adj.** planned &c. *v.*; strategic, -al; planning &c. *v.*; in course of pre-
paration &c. 673; under consideration; on the -*tapis*, – carpet, – table.

**627. Method. [Path.]—N.** method, way, manner, wise, gait, form, mode, fashion, tone, guise; *modus operandi*; procedure &c. (*line of conduct*) 692.

path, road, route, course; line of -way, – road; trajectory, orbit, track, beat, tack.

steps; stair, -case; flight of stairs, ladder, stile.

bridge, viaduct, gauntry, pontoon, stepping stone, plank, gangway, catwalk, drawbridge; pass, ford, ferry, tunnel, subway, elevated; pipe &c. 260.

door; gateway &c. (*opening*) 260; channel, passage, avenue, means of access, approach, perron, adit, entrance; artery, lane, alley, aisle, lobby, corridor, cloister; back- door, -stairs; secret passage; covert-way.

road-, path-, stair-way; thoroughfare; highway, pike, turnpike, trail, parkway, *boulevard*; turnpike –, royal –, coach- road; broad –, King's –, Queen's- highway; beaten -track, – path; horse –, bridle- road, – track, – path; pathway; walk, *trottoir*, foot-path, pavement, flags, side-walk; by –, cross- -road, – path, – way; cut; short -cut &c. (*mid-course*) 628; *carrefour*; private –, occupation- road; highways and byways; rail-, tram-road, -way; funicular, ropeway, causeway; defile, cutting; canal &c. (*conduit*) 350; street &c. (*abode*) 189.

Adv. how; in what -way, – manner; by what mode; so, in this way, after this fashion, on these lines.

one way or another, anyhow; somehow or other &c. (*instrumentality*) 631; by way of; *viâ*; *in transitu* &c. 270; on the high road to.

Phr. *hæ tibi erunt artes.*

---

**628. Mid-course.**—N. middle-, mid-course; moderation, mean &c. 29: middle &c. 68; *juste milieu, mezzo termine*, golden mean, *aurea mediocritas.*

straight &c. (*direct*) 278 -course, – path; short –, cross- cut; short-circuit; great circle sailing.

neutrality; half –, half and half-measures; compromise.

V. keep in –, steer –, preserve- -a middle, – an even- course; go straight &c. (*direct*) 278.

go half way, compromise, make a compromise.

Adj. neutral, average, even, impartial, moderate, straight &c. (*direct*) 278.

**629. Circuit.**—N. circuit, round-about way, digression, divagation, *détour*, circum-ambience, -ambulation, -bendibus, *ambages*, loop; winding &c. (*circuition*) 311; zigzag &c. (*deviation*) 279.

V. perform –, make- a circuit; go -round about, – out of one's way; make a *détour*; meander &c. (*deviate*) 279; circumambulate.

lead a pretty dance; beat about, – the bush; make two bites of a cherry.

Adj. circuitous, indirect, round-about; zig-zag &c. (*deviating*) 279; circum-ambient, -ambulatory.

Adv. by -a side wind, – an indirect course; in a roundabout way; from pillar to post.

---

**630. Requirement.**—N. requirement, need, wants, necessities; necessaries, – of life; stress, exigency, pinch, *sine quâ non*, matter of necessity; case of -need, – life or death.

needfulness, essentiality, necessity, indispensability, urgency, prerequisite.

requisition &c. (*request*) 765, (*exaction*) 741; run upon; demand –, call- for.

*desideratum* &c. (*desire*) 865; want &c. (*deficiency*) 640.

charge, claim, command, injunction, requisition, mandate, order, *ultimatum*.

**V.** require, need, want, have occasion for, entail; not be able to -do without, – dispense with; prerequire.

render necessary, necessitate, create a necessity for, call for, put in requisition; make a requisition &c. (*ask for*) 765, (*demand*) 741.

stand in need of; lack &c. 640; desiderate; desire &c. 865; be -necessary &c. *adj.*

**Adj.** required &c. *v.*; requisite, needful, necessary, imperative, essential, indispensable, prerequisite; called for; in -demand, – request.

urgent, exigent, pressing, instant, crying, absorbing.

in want of; destitute of &c. 640.

**Adv.** *ex necessitate rei* &c. (*necessarily*) 601; of –, out of stern- necessity; at a pinch.

**Phr.** there is no time to lose; it cannot be -spared, – dispensed with.

## 2° *Subservience to Ends*
### 1. *Actual Subservience*

**631. Instrumentality.—N.** instrumentality; aid &c. 707; subservien-ce, -cy; mediation, inter-vention, -mediacy, medium, inter-medium, -mediary, vehicle, hand; agency &c. 170.

minister, handmaid, servant, slave, maid, valet; midwife, *accoucheur*, obstetrician; go-between; cat's paw; stepping-stone.

key; master –, pass –, latch- key; 'open sesame'; passport, *passe-partout*, safe-conduct; influence.

instrument &c. 633; expedient &c. (*plan*) 626; means &c. 632.

**V.** subserve, minister, tend, mediate, intervene; come –, go- between, interpose; pull the strings; be -instrumental &c. *adj.*; pander to.

**Adj.** instrumental; useful &c. 644; ministerial, subservient, mediatorial; inter-mediate, -vening; conducive.

**Adv.** through, by, *per*; where-, there-, here-by; by the -agency &c. 170- of; by dint of; by –, in- virtue of; through the -medium &c. *n.*-of; along with; on the shoulders of; by means of &c. 632; by –, with-the aid &c. (*assistance*) 707- of.

*per fas et nefas.* by fair means or foul; somehow, – or other; by hook or by crook.

**632. Means.—N.** means, resources, revenue, wherewithal, ways and means, income; capital &c. (*money*) 800; stock in trade &c. 636; provision &c. 637; a shot in the locker; appliances &c. (*machinery*) 633; means and appliances; conveniences; cards to play; expedients &c. (*measures*) 626; two strings to one's bow; sheet anchor &c. (*safety*) 666; aid &c. 707; medium &c. 631.

**V.** find –, have –, possess- means &c. *n.*; provide the wherewithal.

**Adj.** instrumental &c. 631; mechanical &c. 633.

**Adv.** by means of, with; by -what, – all, – any, – some- means; where-, here-, there-with; wherewithal.

how &c. (*in what manner*) 627; through &c. (*by the instrumentality of*) 631; with –, by- the aid &c. (*assistance*) 707- of; by the -agency &c. 170- of.

**633. Instrument.—N.** machinery, mechanism, engineering.

instrument, organ, tool, implement, utensil, contrivance, machine, motor, engine, lathe, gin, mill, pump.

gear; tack-le, -ling, trice, rigging, gear, apparatus, appliances; plant, *matériel*; harness, trappings, fittings, accoutrements; equip-ment, -age;

appointments, furniture, upholstery; chattels; paraphernalia &c. (*belongings*) 780; *impedimenta*.

mechanical powers; lever, -age; mechanical advantage; crow, -bar; handspike, gavelock, jemmy, arm, limb, wing; oar, paddle; pulley, sheave; parbuckle; wheel and axle; wheel-, clock-work; wheels within wheels; pinion, gear wheel, spur –, bevel- gearing, chains, belting, crank, winch, capstan, windlass, crane, derrick, hoist, lift &c. 307; cam; pedal; wheel &c. (*rotation*) 312; inclined plane; wedge; screw; jack; spring, mainspring.

handle, hilt, haft, shaft, heft, shank, blade, trigger, tiller, helm, treadle, key; turnscrew, screwdriver, spanner, wrench.

hammer &c. (*impulse*) 276; edge tool &c. (*cut*) 253; borer &c. 262; vice, teeth &c. (*hold*) 781; nail, rope &c. (*join*) 45; peg &c. (*hang*) 214; support &c. 215; spoon &c. (*vehicle*) 272; arms &c. 727; oar &c. (*navigation*) 267.

**Adj.** instrumental &c. 631; mechanical, machinal, automatic, self-acting; brachial.

**634. Substitute.—N.** substitute &c. 147; deputy &c. 759; proxy, alternative, understudy.

**635. Materials.—N.** material, raw material, stuff, stock, staple; building materials, bricks and mortar; metal; stone; clay, brick; crockery &c. 384; compo, -sition; reinforced –, ferro-, concrete; cement; wood, ore, timber; gravel, cobbles, macadam, asphalt, tarmac.

materials; supplies, munition, fuel, grist, household stuff; *pabulum* &c. (*food*) 298; ammunition &c. (*arms*) 727; contingents; relay, reinforcement; baggage &c. (*personal property*) 780; means &c. 632.

**Adj.** raw &c. (*unprepared*) 674; wooden &c. *n.*

**636. Store.—N.** stock, fund, mine, vein, lode, quarry; spring; fount, -ain; well, -spring; milch cow.

stock in trade, supply; heap &c. (*collection*) 72; treasure; reserve, *corps de réserve*, reserve fund, nest-egg, savings, *bonne bouche*.

crop, harvest, mow, vintage; yield, product, gleanings.

store, accumulation, hoard, rick, stack; lumber; relay &c. (*provision*) 637.

store-house, -room, -closet; depository, depot, *cache*, safe deposit, vault, pantechnicon, re-pository, -servatory, -pertory; *repertorium*; promptuary, warehouse, *entrepôt*, magazine, dump, buttery, larder, pantry, panary, lanary, still-room, spence; crib, garner, granary, silo, barn; bunker; thesaurus; bank &c. (*treasury*) 802; armoury; arsenal; dock; gallery, museum, library, conservatory, hot-house; menag-ery, -erie, aquarium, zoological gardens.

reservoir, cistern, tank, sump, pond, mill-pond; gasometer.

budget, quiver, bandolier, portfolio; coffer &c. (*receptacle*) 191.

conservation; storing &c. *v.*; storage.

dictionary &c. 562; list &c. 86.

**V.** store; put –, lay –, set- by; stow away; set –, lay- apart; store –, hoard –, treasure –, lay –, heap –, put –, garner –, save- up; *cacher*; accumulate, amass, hoard, fund, garner, save, bank.

conserve, reserve; keep –, hold- back; husband, – one's resources; deposit; stow, stack, load, dump; harvest; heap, collect &c. 72; lay -in, – down, – by, store &c. *adj.*; keep, file [papers]; lay in &c. (*provide*) 637; preserve &c. 670; put by for a rainy day.

Adj. stored &c. *v.*; in -store, – reserve, – ordinary; spare, supernumerary.

**637. Provision.—N.** provision, supply; grist, – to the mill; subvention &c. (*aid*) 707; resources &c. (*means*) 632.

providing &c. *v.*; purveyance; reinforcement; commissary, commissariat. rations; iron –, emergency- rations; provender &c. (*food*) 298; *viaticum*; ensilage.

caterer, purveyor, commissary, quartermaster, steward, housekeeper, manciple, feeder, batman, victualler, storekeeper, provision merchant, green-, grocer, *comprador, restaurateur*; sutler &c. (*merchant*) 797; innkeeper, publican, confectioner, baker, butcher, wine merchant, vintner.

**V.** provide; make -provision, – due provision for; lay in, – a stock, – a store.

sup-ply, -peditate; furnish; find, – one in; arm.

cater, victual, provision, purvey, forage; beat up for; stock, – with; make good, replenish; fill, – up; recruit, feed, ration.

have in -store, – reserve; keep, – by one, – on foot; have to fall back upon; store &c. 636; provide against a rainy day &c. (*economy*) 817.

**638. Waste.—N.** consumption, expenditure, exhaustion; dispersion &c. 73; ebb; leakage &c. (*exudation*) 295; loss &c. 776; wear and tear; waste; prodigality &c. 818; misuse &c. 679; wasting &c. *v.*; rubbish &c. (*useless*) 645.

mountain in labour.

**V.** spend, expend, use, consume, swallow up, exhaust, deplete; impoverish; spill, drain, empty; disperse &c. 73.

cast –, throw –, fling –, fritter- away; burn the candle at both ends, waste; squander &c. 818.

'waste its sweetness on the desert air'; cast -one's bread upon the waters, – pearls before swine; employ a steam hammer to crack a nut, waste powder and shot, break a butterfly on a wheel; labour in vain &c. (*useless*) 645; cut a whetstone with a razor, pour water into a sieve; tilt at windmills.

leak &c. (*run out*) 295; run to waste; ebb; melt away, run dry, dry up.

Adj. wasted &c. *v.*; at a low ebb.

wasteful &c. (*prodigal*) 818; penny wise and pound foolish.

Phr. *magno conatu magnas nugas; le jeu n'en vaut pas la chandelle.*

**639. Sufficiency.—N.** sufficiency, adequacy, enough, withal, *quantum sufficit*, satisfaction, competence; no less.

mediocrity &c. (*average*) 29.

fill; fulness &c. (*completeness*) 52; plen-itude, -ty; abundance; copiousness &c. *adj.*; amplitude, galore, lots, profusion; full measure; 'good measure pressed down, shaken together and running over.'

luxuriance &c. (*fertility*) 168; affluence &c. (*wealth*) 803; fat of the land; 'a land flowing with milk and honey'; cornucopia; horn of -plenty, – Amalthæa; mine &c. (*stock*) 636.

outpouring; flood &c. (*great quantity*) 31; tide &c. (*river*) 348; repletion &c. (*redundance*) 641; satiety &c. 869; rich man &c. 803.

**640. Insufficiency.—N.** insufficiency; inadequa-cy, -teness; incompetence &c. (*impotence*) 158; deficiency &c. (*incompleteness*) 53; imperfection &c. 651; shortcoming &c. 304; paucity; stint; scantiness &c. (*smallness*) 32; none to spare; bare subsistence.

scarcity, dearth; want, need, lack, poverty, exigency; inanition, starvation, famine, drought.

dole, pittance, mite; short -allowance, – commons; half-rations; banyan –, fast- day. Lent.

emptiness, poorness &c. *adj.*; depletion, vacancy, flaccidity; ebb-tide; low water; 'a beggarly account of empty boxes'; indigence &c. (*poverty*) 804; insolvency &c. (*non-payment*) 808; poor man &c. 804; bankrupt &c. 808.

**V.** be -insufficient &c. *adj.*; not -suf-

**V.** be -sufficient &c. *adj.*; suffice, do, just do, satisfy, pass muster; have -enough &c. *n.*; eat –, drink –, have-one's fill; roll –, swim- in; wallow in &c. (*superabundance*) 641.

abound, exuberate, teem, flow, stream, rain, shower down; pour, – in; swarm; bristle with.

render -sufficient &c. *adj.*; replenish &c. (*fill*) 52.

**Adj.** sufficient, enough, adequate, up to the mark, commensurate, competent, satisfactory, valid, tangible.

measured; moderate &c. (*temperate*) 953.

full &c. (*complete*) 52; ample; plen-ty, -tiful, -teous; plenty as blackberries; copious, abundant; abounding &c. *v.*; replete, enough and to spare, flush; choke-full; well-stocked, -provided; liberal; unstint-ed, -ing; stintless; without stint; un-sparing, -measured; lavish &c. 641; wholesale.

rich; luxuriant &c. (*fertile*) 168; affluent &c. (*wealthy*) 803; wantless; big with &c. (*pregnant*) 161.

un-exhausted, -wasted; exhaustless, inexhaustible.

**Adv.** sufficiently, amply &c. *adj.*; full; in -abundance &c. *n.*; with no sparing hand; to one's heart's content, *ad libitum*, without stint.

**Phr.** cut and come again.

fice &c. 639; come short of &c. 304; run dry.

want, lack, need, require; *caret*; be in want &c. (*poor*) 804; live from hand to mouth.

render- insufficient &c. *adj.*; drain of resources; impoverish &c. (*waste*) 638; stint &c. (*begrudge*) 819; put on short -commons, – allowance.

do -insufficiently &c. *adv.*; scotch the snake.

**Adj.** insufficient, inadequate; too -little &c. 32; not -enough &c. 639; unequal to; incompetent &c. (*impotent*) 158; 'weighed in the balance and found wanting'; perfunctory &c. (*neglect*) 460; deficient &c. (*incomplete*) 53; wanting &c. *v.*; imperfect &c. 651; ill-furnished, -provided, -stored, -off.

slack, at a low ebb; empty, vacant, bare; short –, out –, destitute –, devoid –, bereft &c. 776 –, denuded- of; dry, drained.

un -provided, -supplied, -furnished; un-replenished, -fed; un-stored, -treasured; empty-handed.

meagre, poor, thin, scrimp, sparing, spare, stinted, stunted; skimpy; starv-ed, -eling; half-starved, emaciated, famine-stricken, famished, under-fed, undernourished; jejune.

scant &c. (*small*) 32; scarce; not to be had, – for love or money, – at any price; scurvy; stingy &c. 819; at the end of one's tether; without -resources &c. 632; in want &c. (*poor*) 804; in debt &c. 806.

**Adv.** insufficiently &c. *adj.*; in default –, for want- of; failing.

**641. Redundance.—N.** redundance; too -much, – many; super-abundance, -fluity, -fluence, -saturation; nimiety, transcendency, exuberance, profuseness; profusion &c. (*plenty*) 639; repletion, enough in all conscience, *satis superque*, lion's share; more than -enough &c. 639; plethora, engorgement, congestion, load, surfeit, sickener; turgescence &c. (*expansion*) 194; over-dose, -measure, -supply, -flow; inundation &c. (*water*) 348; *avalanche*.

accumulation &c. (*store*) 636; heap &c. 72; drug, – in the market, glut; crowd; burden.

excess; sur-, over-plus, epact; margin; remainder &c. 40; duplicate; surplusage, expletive; work of –, supererogation; *bonus, bonanza*.

luxury; intemperance &c. 954; extravagance &c. (*prodigality*) 818; exorbitance, lavishment.

pleonasm &c. (*diffuseness*) 573; too many irons in the fire; embarrassment of riches; money to burn.

**V.** super-, over-abound; know no bounds, swarm; meet one at every turn; creep –, bristle- with; overflow; run –, flow –, well –, brim-over; run riot; over-run, -stock, -lay, -charge, -dose, -feed, -burden, -load, -do, -whelm, -shoot the mark &c. (*go beyond*) 303; surcharge, supersaturate, gorge, glut, load, drench, whelm, inundate, deluge, flood; drug, – the market.

choke, cloy, accloy, suffocate; pile up, lay it on, – with a trowel, lay on thick; impregnate with; lavish &c. (*squander*) 818.

send –, carry- coals to Newcastle, – owls to Athens; teach one's grandmother to suck eggs; *pisces natare docere*; kill the slain, 'gild refined gold,' 'paint the lily'; butter one's bread on both sides, put butter upon bacon; employ a steam-hammer to crack a nut &c. (*waste*) 638.

exaggerate &c. 549; wallow in; roll in &c. (*plenty*) 639; remain on one's hands, hang heavy on hand, go a begging.

**Adj.** redundant; too -much, – many; exuberant, inordinate, superabundant, excessive, overmuch, replete, profuse, lavish; prodigal &c. 818; exorbitant; overweening; extravagant; overcharged &c. *v.*; supersaturated, drenched, overflowing; running -over, – to waste, – down.

crammed –, filled- to overflowing; gorged, stuffed, ready to burst; dropsical, turgid, plethoric, full-blooded; obese &c. 194; voluminous.

superfluous, unnecessary, needless, supervacaneous, uncalled for, to spare, in excess; over and above &c. (*remainder*) 40; *de trop*; adscititious &c. (*additional*) 37; supernumerary &c. (*reserve*) 636; on one's hands, spare, duplicate, supererogatory, expletive; *un peu fort*.

**Adv.** over, too, over and above; over –, too- much; too far; without –, beyond –, out of- measure; with . . . to spare; over head and ears; up to one's -eyes, – ears; *extra*; beyond the mark &c. (*transcursion*) 303; over one's head.

**Phr.** it never rains but it pours.

## 2. *Degree of Subservience*

**642. Importance.**—**N.** importance, consequence, moment, prominence, consideration, mark, materialness.

import, significance, concern; emphasis, interest.

greatness &c. 31; superiority &c. 33; notability &c. (*repute*) 873; weight &c. (*influence*) 175; value &c. (*goodness*) 648; usefulness &c. 644.

gravity, seriousness, solemnity; no -joke, – laughing matter; pressure, urgency, stress; matter of life and death.

*memorabilia*, *notabilia*, great doings; red-letter day.

great -thing, – point; main chance, 'the be all and end all,' cardinal point, outstanding feature; substance, gist &c. (*essence*) 5; sum and substance, *gravamen*, head and front; important –, principal –, prominent –, essential-part; half the battle; *sine quâ non*; breath of one's nostrils &c. (*life*) 359; cream, salt, core, kernel, heart, nucleus:

**643. Unimportance.**—**N.** unimportance, insignificance, nothingness, immateriality.

triviality, trivia, fribble, levity, frivolity; paltriness &c. *adj.*; poverty; smallness &c. 32; vanity &c. (*uselessness*) 645; matter of -indifference &c. 866; no object; side issue.

nothing, – to signify, – worth speaking of, – particular, – to boast of, – to speak of; small –, no great –, trifling &c. *adj.* -matter; mere -joke, – nothing; hardly –, scarcely- anything; nonentity, cipher, figurehead; no great shakes, *peu de chose*; child's play; small beer.

toy, plaything, popgun, paper pellet, gimcrack, gewgaw, bauble, trinket, *bagatelle*, kickshaw, knicknack, whimwham, trifle, 'trifles light as air.'

trumpery, trash, rubbish, stuff, *fatras*, frippery; 'leather or prunello'; chaff, drug, froth, bubble, smoke, cob-

key, -note, -stone; corner stone; trump-card &c. (*device*) 626; salient points.

top-sawyer, first fiddle, *prima donna*, chief, big-wig; triton among the minnows.

**V.** be -important &c. *adj.*, – somebody, – something; import, signify, matter, be an object; carry weight &c. (*influence*) 175; make a figure &c. (*repute*) 873; be in the ascendant, come to the front, lead the way, take the lead, play first fiddle, throw all else into the shade; lie at the root of; deserve –, merit –, be worthy- -of notice, – regard, – consideration.

attach –, ascribe –, give- importance &c. *n.*- to; value, care for; set store -upon, – by; mark &c. 550; mark with a white stone, underline; write –, put –, print- in -italics, – capitals, – large letters, – large type, – letters of gold; accentuate, emphasize, lay stress on.

make -a fuss, – a stir, – a piece of work, – much ado- about; make -of, – much of.

**Adj.** important; of -importance &c. *n.*; momentous, material; to the point; not to be -overlooked, – despised, – sneezed at; egregious; weighty &c. (*influential*) 175; of note &c. (*repute*) 873; notable, prominent, salient, signal; memorable, remarkable; worthy of -remark, – notice; never to be forgotten; stirring, eventful.

grave, serious, earnest, noble, grand, solemn, impressive, commanding, imposing.

urgent, pressing, critical, instant.

paramount, essential, vital, all-absorbing, radical, cardinal, chief, main, prime, primary, principal, leading, capital, foremost, overruling; of vital &c. importance.

in the front rank, first-rate, A1; superior &c. 33; considerable &c. (*great*) 31; marked &c. *v.*; rare &c. 137.

significant, telling, trenchant, emphatic, pregnant; *tanti.*

**Adv.** materially &c. *adj.*; in the main; above all, *par excellence*, to crown all.

web; weed; refuse &c. (*inutility*) 645; scum &c. (*dirt*) 653.

joke, jest, snap of the fingers; fudge &c. (*unmeaning*) 517; fiddlestick, – end; pack of nonsense, mere farce.

straw, pin, fig, continental, button, rush; bulrush, feather, halfpenny, farthing, brass farthing, doit, peppercorn, jot, rap, pinch of snuff, old song.

*minutiæ*, details, minor details, small fry; dust in the balance, feather in the scale, drop in the ocean, flea-bite, molehill; fingle-fangle.

nine days' wonder, *ridiculus mus*; flash in the pan &c. (*impotence*) 158; much ado about nothing &c. (*overestimation*) 482; storm in a teacup.

**V.** be -unimportant &c. *adj.*; not -matter &c. 642; go for –, matter –, signify- -little, – nothing, – little or nothing; not matter a -straw &c. *n.*

make light of &c. (*underestimate*) 483; catch at straws &c. (*overestimate*) 482.

**Adj.** unimportant; of -little, – small, – no- -account, – importance &c. 642; immaterial; un-, non-essential; not vital; irrelevant, incidental, indifferent.

subordinate &c. (*inferior*) 34; médiocre &c. (*average*) 29; passable, fair, respectable, tolerable, commonplace; uneventful, mere, common; ordinary &c. (*habitual*) 613; inconsiderable, so-so, insignificant, inappreciable, nugatory.

trifling, trivial; slight, slender, light, flimsy, frothy, idle; puerile &c. (*foolish*) 499; airy, shallow; weak &c. 160; powerless &c. 158; frivolous, petty, niggling; pid-, ped-dling; fribble, inane, ridiculous, farcical; fini-cal, -kin; fiddle-faddle, namby-pamby, wishy-washy, milk and water.

poor, paltry, pitiful; contemptible &c. (*contempt*) 930; sorry, mean, meagre, shabby, miserable, wretched, vile, scrubby, scrannel, weedy, niggardly, scurvy, putid, beggarly, worthless, twopenny-halfpenny, cheap, trashy, catchpenny, gimcrack, trumpery, one-horse; toy.

not worth -the pains, – while, – mentioning, – speaking of, – a thought, – a curse, – a straw, – rap &c. *n.*; beneath –, unworthy of- -notice, – regard, – consideration, – contempt; *de lanâ caprinâ*; vain &c. (*useless*) 645.

Adv. slightly &c. *adj.*; rather, somewhat, pretty well, fairly well, tolerably.

for aught one cares.

Int. no matter! pish! tush! tut! pshaw! pugh! pooh, -pooh! fudge! bosh! humbug! fiddle-stick, – end! fiddlededee! never mind! *n'importe!* what -signifies, – matter, – boots it, – of that, –'s the odds! a fig for! stuff! nonsense! stuff and nonsense!

Phr. *magno conatu magnas nugas*; *le jeu n'en vaut pas la chandelle*; it -matters not, – does not signify; it is of no -consequence, – importance.

**644. Utility.—N.** utility; usefulness &c. *adj.*; efficacy, efficiency, adequacy; service, use, stead, avail; help &c. (*aid*) 707; applicability &c. *adj.*; subservience &c. (*instrumentality*) 631; function &c. (*business*) 625; value; worth &c. (*goodness*) 648; money's worth; productiveness &c. 168; *cui bono* &c. (*intention*) 620; utilization &c. (*use*) 677; step in the right direction.

common weal, public good; utilitarianism &c. (*philanthropy*) 910.

**V.** be -useful &c. *adj.*; avail, serve; subserve &c. (*be instrumental to*) 631; conduce &c. (*tend*) 176; answer –, serve- -one's turn, – a purpose.

act a part &c. (*action*) 680; perform –, discharge- -a function &c. 625; do –, render- -a service, – good service, – yeoman's service; bestead, stand one in good stead; be the making of; help &c. 707.

bear fruit &c. (*produce*) 161; bring grist to the mill; profit, remunerate; benefit &c. (*do good*) 648.

find one's -account, – advantage- in; reap the benefit of &c. (*be better for*) 658.

render useful &c. (*use*) 677.

Adj. useful; of -use &c. *n.*; serviceable, usable, proficuous, good for; subservient &c. (*instrumental*) 631; conducive &c. (*tending*) 176; subsidiary &c. (*helping*) 707.

advantageous &c. (*beneficial*) 648; profitable, gainful, remunerative, worth one's salt; in-, valuable; prolific &c. (*productive*) 168.

adequate; ef-ficient, -ficacious; effect-ive, -ual; practicable, expedient &c. 646.

**645. Inutility.—N.** inutility; uselessness &c. *adj.*; inefficacy, futility; inep-, inap-titude; unsubservience; inadequacy &c. (*insufficiency*) 640; inefficiency &c. (*incompetence*) 158; unskilfulness &c. 699; disservice; unfruitfulness &c. (*unproductiveness*) 169; labour -in vain, – lost, – of Sisyphus; lost -trouble, – labour; work of Penelope; sleeveless errand, wild goose chase, mere farce.

tautology &c. (*repetition*) 104; supererogation &c. (*redundance*) 641.

*vanitas vanitatum*, vanity, inanity, worthlessness, nugacity; triviality &c. (*unimportance*) 643.

*caput mortuum*, waste paper, dead letter; blunt tool.

litter, rubbish, lumber, odds and ends, cast-off clothes; button-top; shoddy; rags, orts, trash, refuse, sweepings, scourings, off-scourings, dross, slag, waste, rubble, dottle, drast, *débris*; stubble, leavings; broken meat; dregs &c. (*dirt*) 653; weeds, tares; rubbish heap, dust hole; *rudera*, deads.

*fruges consumere natus* &c. (*drone*) 683.

**V.** be -useless &c. *adj.*; go a begging &c. (*redundant*) 641; fail &c. 732.

seek –, strive- after impossibilities; use vain efforts, labour in vain, roll the stone of Sisyphus, beat the air, lash the waves, *battre l'eau avec un bâton, donner un coup d'épée dans l'eau*, fish in the air, milk the ram, drop a bucket into an empty well, sow the sand; bay the moon; preach –, speak-to the winds; whistle jigs to a milestone; kick against the pricks, *se battre contre des moulins*; lock the stable door

[ 226 ]

applicable, available, ready, handy, at hand, tangible; commodious, adaptable; of all work.

**Adv.** usefully &c. *adj.*; *pro bono publico.*

when the steed is stolen &c. (*too late*) 135; hold a farthing candle to the sun; cast pearls before swine &c. (*waste*) 638; carry coals to Newcastle &c. (*redundance*) 641; wash a blackamoor white &c. (*impossible*) 471.

render -useless &c. *adj.*; dis-mantle, -mast, -mount, -qualify, -able; unrig; cripple, lame &c. (*injure*) 659; spike guns, clip the wings; put out of gear.

**Adj.** useless, inutile, inefficacious, futile, unavailing, bootless; inoperative &c. 158; inadequate &c. (*insufficient*) 640; in-, unsub-servient; inept, inefficient &c. (*impotent*) 158; of no -avail &c. (*use*) 644; ineffectual &c. (*failure*) 732; incompetent &c. (*unskilful*) 699; 'stale, flat and unprofitable'; superfluous &c. (*redundant*) 641; dispensable; thrown away &c. (*wasted*) 638; abortive &c. (*immature*) 674.

worth-, value-less; unsaleable; not worth a straw &c. (*trifling*) 643; dear at any price.

vain, empty, inane; gain-, profit-, fruit-less; un-serviceable, -profitable; ill-spent; unproductive &c. 169; *hors de combat*; barren, sterile, impotent, unproductive; effete, past work &c. (*impaired*) 659; obsolete &c. (*old*) 124; fit for the -dust-hole, - wastepaper basket; good for nothing; of no earthly use; not worth -having, - powder and shot; leading to no end, uncalled for; un-necessary, -needed, superfluous.

**Adv.** uselessly &c. *adj.*; to -little, - no, - little or no- purpose. **Int.** *cui bono?* what's the good!

---

**646.** [Specific subservience.] **Expedience.—N.** expedien-ce, -cy; desirableness, -bility &c. *adj.*; fitness &c. (*agreement*) 23; utility &c. 644; propriety; advantage; opportunism, pragmatism.

high time &c. (*occasion*) 134.

**V.** be -expedient &c. *adj.*; suit &c. (*agree*) 23; befit; suit -, befit- the -time, - season, - occasion.

conform &c. 82.

**Adj.** expedient; desir-, advis-, acceptable; convenient; worth while, meet; fit. -ting; due, proper, eligible, seemly, becoming; befitting &c. *v.*; opportune &c. (*in season*) 134; *in loco*; suitable &c. (*accordant*) 23; applicable &c. (*useful*) 644; practical, effective, pragmatical; suitable, handy; appropriate.

**Adv.** in the right place; conveniently &c. *adj.*; in the nick of time.

**Phr.** *operæ pretium est.*

**647. Inexpedience.—N.** inexpedien-ce, -cy; undesira-bleness, -bility &c. *adj.*; discommodity, impropriety; unfitness &c. (*disagreement*) 24; inutility &c. 645; inconvenience, inadvisability; disadvantage.

**V.** be -inexpedient &c. *adj.*; come amiss &c. (*disagree*) 24; embarrass &c. (*hinder*) 706; put to inconvenience; pay too dear for one's whistle.

**Adj.** inexpedient, undesirable; un-, in-advisable; objectionable; troublesome, in-apt, -eligible, -admissible, -convenient; in-, dis-commodious; disadvantageous; inappropriate, unsuitable, unfit &c. (*inconsonant*) 24.

ill-contrived, -advised; unsatisfactory; unprofitable &c., unsubservient &c. (*useless*) 645; inopportune &c. (*unseasonable*) 135; out of -, in the wrong-place; improper, unseemly.

clumsy, awkward; cum-brous, -hersome; lumbering, unwieldy, hulky; un-manageable &c. (*impracticable*) 704; impedient &c. (*in the way*) 706.

unnecessary &c. (*redundant*) 641.

**Phr.** it will never do.

**648.** [Capability of producing good. Good qualities.] **Goodness.—N.** goodness &c. *adj.*; excellence, merit; virtue &c. 944; value, worth, price.

super-excellence, -eminence; superiority &c. 33; perfection &c. 650; *coup de maître*; master-piece, *chef d'œuvre*, prime, flower, cream, *élite*, pick, A1, none such, *nonpareil*, *crème de la crème*, flower of the flock, cock of the roost, salt of the earth; champion.

tid-bit; gem, – of the first water; *bijou*, precious stone, jewel, pearl, diamond, ruby, brilliant, treasure; good thing; *rara avis*, one in a thousand.

beneficence &c. 906; good man &c. 948.

**V.** be -beneficial &c. *adj.*; produce –, do- -good &c. 618; profit &c. (*be of use*) 644; benefit; confer a -benefit &c. 618.

be the making of, do a world of good, make a man of.

produce a good effect; do a good turn, confer an obligation; improve &c. 658.

do no harm, break no bones.

be -good &c. *adj.*; excel, transcend &c. (*be superior*) 33; bear away the bell.

stand the -proof, – test; pass -muster, – an examination.

challenge comparison, vie, emulate, rival.

**Adj.** harm-, hurt-less; unobnoxious; in-nocuous, -nocent, -offensive.

beneficial, valuable, of value; serviceable &c. (*useful*) 644; advantageous, profitable, edifying; salutary &c. (*healthful*) 656.

favourable; propitious &c. (*hopegiving*) 858; fair.

good, – as gold; excellent; better; superior &c. 33; above par; nice, fine; genuine &c. (*true*) 494.

best, choice, select, picked, elect, eximious, *recherché*, rare, priceless; unpara-goned, -lleled &c. (*supreme*) 33; superlatively &c. 33; good; superfine, -excellent; bonzer; of the first water; first-rate, -class; high-wrought; exquisite, very best, crack, prime, tip-top, gilt-edged, capital, cardinal; standard &c. (*perfect*) 650; inimitable.

admirable, estimable; praiseworthy &c. (*approve*) 931; pleasing &c. 829; *couleur de rose*, precious, of great price;

**649.** [Capability of producing evil. Bad qualities.] **Badness.—N.** hurtfulness &c. *adj.*; virulence

evil doer &c. 913; bane &c. 663; plague-spot &c. (*insalubrity*) 657; evil star, ill wind; snake in the grass, skeleton in the closet; *amari aliquid*, thorn in the side; Jonah, jinx, hoodoo.

malignity; malevolence &c. 907; tender mercies [ironically].

ill-treatment, annoyance, molestation, abuse, oppression, persecution, outrage; misusage &c. 679; injury &c. (*damage*) 659.

badness &c. *adj.*; peccancy, abomination; painfulness &c. 830; pestilence &c. (*disease*) 655; guilt &c. 947; depravity &c. 945.

**V.** be -hurtful &c. *adj.*; cause –, produce –, inflict –, work –, do- evil &c. 619; damnify, endamage, hurt, harm, scathe; injure &c. (*damage*) 659; pain &c. 830.

wrong, aggrieve, oppress, persecute; trample –, tread –, bear hard –, put-upon; overburden; weigh -down, – heavy on; victimize; run down; molest &c. 830.

maltreat, abuse; ill-use, -treat; thwart, buffet, bruise, scratch, maul; smite &c. (*scourge*) 972; do -violence, – harm, – a mischief; stab, pierce, outrage.

do –, make- mischief; bring –, get- into trouble.

destroy &c. 162.

**Adj.** hurt-, harm-, scath-, bane-, baleful; injurious, deleterious, detrimental, noxious, pernicious, mischievous, full of mischief, mischief-making, malefic, malignant, nocuous, noisome; prejudicial; dis-serviceable, -advantageous; wide-wasting.

unlucky, sinister; obnoxious, untoward, disastrous.

oppressive, burdensome, onerous; malign &c. (*malevolent*) 907.

corrupting &c. (corrupt &c. 659); virulent, venomous, envenomed, corrosive; poisonous &c. (*morbific*) 657; deadly &c. (*killing*) 361; destructive &c. (*destroying*) 162; inauspicious &c. 859.

bad, ill, arrant, as bad as bad can be, dreadful; hor-rid, -rible; dire; rank.

costly &c. (*dear*) 814; worth -its weight in gold, – a Jew's eye, – a king's ransom; matchless, peerless, invaluable, inestimable, precious as the apple of the eye.

tolerable &c. (*not very good*) 651; up to the mark, un-exceptionable, -objectionable; satisfactory, tidy.

in -good, – fair- condition; fresh; unspoiled; sound &c. (*perfect*) 650.

Adv. beneficially &c. *adj.*; well &c. 618.

---

peccant, foul, fulsome; rotten, – at the core.

vile, base, villainous; mean &c. (*paltry*) 643; injured &c., deteriorated &c. 659; unsatisfactory, exception, -able, indifferent; below par &c. (*imperfect*) 651; ill-contrived, -conditioned; wretched, sad, grievous, deplorable, lamentable; piti-ful, -able, woeful &c. (*painful*) 830.

evil, wrong; depraved &c. 945; shocking; reprehensible &c. (*disapprove*) 932.

hateful, – as a toad; abominable, detestable, execrable, cursed, accursed, confounded; damn-ed, -able; infernal; diabolic &c. (*malevolent*) 907;

inadvisable &c. (*inexpedient*) 647; unprofitable &c. (*useless*) 645; incompetent &c. (*unskilful*) 699; irremediable &c. (*hopeless*) 859;

Adv. badly &c. *adj.*; wrong, ill; to one's cost; where the shoe pinches.

Phr. bad is the best; the worst come to the worst.

---

**650. Perfection. — N.** perfection; perfectness &c. *adj.*; indefectibility; impecc-ancy, -ability.

pink, *beau idéal*, phœnix, paragon; pink –, acme- of perfection; *ne plus ultra*; summit &c. 210.

*cygne noir*; philosopher's stone; chrysolite, Koh-i-noor, black tulip.

model, standard, pattern, mirror, admirable Crichton; trump; very prince of.

master-piece, -stroke, super-excellence &c. (*goodness*) 648; transcendence &c. (*superiority*) 33.

**V.** be -perfect &c. *adj.*; transcend &c. (*be supreme*) 33.

bring to perfection, perfect, ripen, mature; consummate, complete &c. 729; put in trim &c. (*prepare*) 673; put the finishing touch to.

**Adj.** perfect, faultless, ideal; inde-fective, -ficient, -fectible; immaculate, spotless, impeccable; free from -imperfection &c. 651; un-blemished, -injured &c. 659; sound, – as a roach; in perfect condition; scathless, intact, harmless; seaworthy &c. (*safe*) 644; right as a trivet; *in seipso totus teres atque rotundus*; consummate &c. (*complete*) 52; finished &c. 729; complete in itself.

best &c. (*good*) 648; model, standard; inimitable, unparagoned, unparalleled &c. (*supreme*) 33; superhuman, divine;

---

**651. Imperfection.—N.** imperfection; imperfectness &c. *adj.*; deficiency; in-adequacy &c. (*insufficiency*) 640; pec-cancy &c. (*badness*) 649; immaturity &c. 674.

fault, defect, weak point; screw loose; rift within the lute; fly in the ointment; flaw &c. (*break*) 70; gap &c. 198; twist &c. 243; taint, attainder; bar sinister, hole in one's coat; blemish &c. 848; weakness &c. 160; half-blood, touch of the tar brush; shortcoming &c. 304; drawback; seamy side.

mediocrity; no great -shakes, – catch; not much to boast of.

**V.** be -imperfect &c. *adj.*; have a -defect &c. *n.*; lie under a disadvantage; spring a leak.

not –, barely- pass muster; fall short &c. 304.

**Adj.** imperfect; not -perfect &c. 650; de-ficient, -fective; faulty, unsound, mutilated, tainted; out of -order, – tune; cracked, leaky; sprung; warped &c. (*distort*) 243; lame; injured &c. (*deteriorated*) 659; peccant &c. (*bad*) 649; frail &c. (*weak*) 160; inadequate &c. (*insufficient*) 640; crude &c. (*unprepared*) 671; incomplete &c. 53; found wanting; below par; short-handed; below –, under- its full -strength, – complement.

indifferent, middling, ordinary, medi-

beyond all praise &c. (*approbation*) 931; *sans peur et sans reproche*.

**Adv.** to perfection, to the limit; perfectly &c. *adj.*; *ad unguem*; clean, – as a whistle.

ocre; average &c. 29; so-so; *così-così*, milk and water; tolerable, fair, passable; pretty -well, – good; rather –, moderately- good; good –, well- enough; decent; not -bad, – amiss; unobjectionable, admissible, bearable, only better than nothing.

secondary, inferior; second-rate, -best, one-horse.

**Adv.** almost &c.; to a limited extent, rather &c. 32; pretty, moderately; only; considering, all things considered, enough.

**Phr.** *surgit amari aliquid.*

---

**652. Cleanness.**—N. cleanness &c. *adj.*; purity; cleaning &c. *v.*; purification, defecation &c. *v.*; purgation, lustration; de-, abs-tersion; epuration, mundation, ablution, lavation, colature; disinfection &c. *v.*; drain-, sewerage.

lavatory, bath, -room; swimming pool, natatorium; public baths; hot –, cold –, Turkish –, Swedish –, Russian –, vapour- bath; *hammam*, laundry, washhouse; washerwoman, laundress, laundryman; scavenger, cleaner, sweeper, goody; crossing sweeper, white wings, dustman, sweep.

brush; broom, besom, carpet-sweeper, vacuum-cleaner, mop, squilgee, rake, shovel, sieve, riddle, screen, filter; scraper, strigil.

napkin, *serviette*, cloth, table-, carving-cloth, table-linen, napery, maukin, handkerchief, towel, sudary; doyley, doily, duster, sponge, mop, swab.

cover, drugget, mat, doormat.

soap, wash, lotion, detergent, cathartic, purgative; purifier &c. *v.*; dentifrice, tooth-powder, -paste; mouth wash; disinfectant.

**V.** be –, render- clean &c. *adj.*

clean, -se; mundify, rinse. wring, flush, full, wipe, mop, sponge. scour, swab, scrub, holystone, brush up.

wash, shampoo, lave, launder, buck; abs-, de-terge; clear, purify; de-purate, -spumate, -fecate; purge, expurgate; Bowdlerize; elutriate, lixiviate, edulcorate, clarify, refine, rack; fil-ter, -trate; drain, strain.

disinfect, sterilize, pasteurize, fumigate, ventilate, deodorize; whitewash.

sift, winnow, screen, riddle, pick, weed, comb, rake, brush, sweep.

**653. Uncleanness.**—N. uncleanness &c. *adj.*; impurity; immundi-ty, -city; impurity &c. [of mind] 961.

defilement, contamination &c. *v.*; defœdation; soil-ure, -iness; abomination; leaven; taint, -ure; fetor &c. 401.

decay; putre-scence, -faction; corruption; mould, must, mildew, dry-rot, *mucor*, rubigo, caries.

slovenry; slovenliness &c. *adj.*; squalor.

dowdy, drab, slut, malkin, slattern, sloven, slammerkin, scrub, draggletail, mudlark, dustman, sweep; beast.

dirt, filth, soil, slop; dust, cobweb, flue; smoke, soot, smudge, smut, grime, raff.

*sordes*, dregs, grounds, lees; sedi-, settle-ment; heel-tap; dross, -iness; mother, precipitate, *scoriæ*, ashes, cinders, recrement, slag; scum, froth.

hog-wash, swill, ditch-, dish-, bilgewater; rinsings, cheese-parings; sweepings &c. (*useless refuse*) 645; off-, outscourings; off-scum; *caput mortuum*, *residuum*, sprue, feculence, clinker, draff; scurf, -iness; *exuviæ*, morphew; fur, -fur; dandruff; tartar.

riffraff; vermin, louse, cootie, flea, bug.

mud, mire, quagmire, *alluvium*, silt, sludge, slime, slush, slosh.

spawn, offal, garbage, carrion; *excreta* &c. 299; slough, peccant humour, pus, matter, suppuration, *lienteria*; *fæces*, excrement, ordure, dung; sew-, sewer-age; muck, coprolite; guano, manure, compost.

dunghill, *coluvies*, mixen, midden, bog, laystall, sink, w.c., water-, earthcloset, latrine, privy, jakes, John's; cess, -pool; sump, sough, *cloaca*, drain,

rout -, clear -, sweep &c.- out; make a clean sweep of.

**Adj.** clean, -ly; pure; immaculate; spot-, stain-, taint-less; without a stain, un-stained, -spotted, -soiled, -sullied, -tainted, -infected, -adulterated; aseptic; sweet, – as a nut.

neat, spruce, tidy, trim, gimp, clean as a new penny, like a cat in pattens; cleaned &c. *v.*; kempt.

**Adv.** neatly &c. *adj.*; clean as a whistle.

sewer, common sewer; Cloacina; dust-hole.

sty, pig-sty, lair, den, Augean stable, sink of corruption; slum, rookery.

**V.** be -, become- unclean &c. *adj.*; rot, putrefy, fester, rankle, reek; stink &c. 401; mould, -er; go -bad &c. *adj.* render -unclean &c. *adj.*; dirt, -y; soil, smoke, tarnish, slaver, spot, smear, daub, blot, blur, smudge, smutch, smirch; d-, dr-abble, -aggle; spatter, slubber; be-smear &c., -mire, -slime, -grime, -foul; splash, stain, distain, maculate, sully, pollute, defile, debase, corrupt &c. (*injure*) 659; cover with

contaminate, taint, leaven; -dust &c. *n.*; drabble in the mud.

wallow in the mire; slob-, slab-ber.

**Adj.** unclean, dirty, filthy, grimy; soiled &c. *v.*; not to be handled with kid gloves; dusty, snuffy, smutty, sooty, smoky; thick, turbid, dreggy; slimy.

uncleanly, slovenly, untidy, sluttish, dowdy, slatternly, draggle-tailed; un-combed, -kempt, -scoured, -swept, -wiped, -washed, -strained, -purified; squalid.

nasty, coarse, foul, impure, offensive, abominable, beastly, reeky, reechy; fetid &c. 401.

mouldy, lentiginous, musty, mildewed, rusty, moth-eaten, mucid, rancid, bad, gone bad, touched, fusty, reasty, rotten, corrupt, tainted, high, fly-blown, maggoty; putr-id, -escent, -efied; purulent, carious, peccant, fec-al, -ulent; stercoraceous, excrementitious; scurfy, impetiginous; gory, bloody; rotting &c. *v.*; rotten as -a pear, – cheese.

crapulous &c. (*intemperate*) 954; gross &c. (*impure in mind*) 961.

---

**654. Health.—N.** health, sanity; soundness &c. *adj.*; vigour; good -, perfect -, excellent -, rude -, robust-health; bloom, *mens sana in corpore sano*; Hygeia; incorrupti-on, -bility; good state -, clean bill- of health, eupepsia.

**V.** be in health &c. *adj.*; bloom, flourish.

keep -body and soul together, - on one's legs; enjoy -good, – a good state of- health; have a clean bill of health.

return to health; recover &c. 660; get better &c. (*improve*) 658; take a -new, – fresh- lease of life; convalesce, be convalescent, recruit; restore to health; cure &c. (*restore*) 660.

**Adj.** health-y, -ful; in health &c. *n.*; well, sound, strong, fit, hearty, hale, fresh, blooming, green, whole; florid, flush, hardy, stanch, staunch,

**655. Disease.*—N.** disease; illness, sickness &c. *adj.*; ailing &c. *v.*; 'the ills that flesh is heir to'; morb-idity, -osity; infirmity, ailment, indisposition; complaint, disorder, malady; distemper, -ature.

visitation, attack, seizure, stroke, fit, epilepsy, apoplexy, shock, shell-shock.

delicacy, loss of health, valetudinarianism, invalidism, cachexy; *cachexia*, atrophy, *marasmus*; indigestion, *dyspepsia*; decay &c. (*deterioration*) 659; malnutrition, decline, consumption, palsy, paralysis, prostration; occupational diseases.

taint, pollution, infection, contagion, septicity, septicæmia, blood poisoning, pyæmia, epi-, en-demic; murrain, plague, pestilence, virus, pox.

sore, ulcer, abscess, fester, boil; pimple &c. (*swelling*) 250; carbuncle,

\* Extended lists of different diseases are beyond the scope of this work.

brave, robust, vigorous, weather-proof; convalescent.

un-scathed, -injured, -maimed, -marred, -tainted; sound of wind and limb, safe and sound; without a scratch.

on one's legs; sound as a -roach, – bell; fresh as -a daisy, – a rose, – April; picture of health; bursting with health; fit as a fiddle; hearty as a buck; in -fine, – high- feather; in -good case, – full bloom; in fine fettle; pretty bobbish, tolerably well, as well as can be expected.

sanitary &c. (*health-giving*) 656; sanatory &c. (*remedial*) 662.

gathering, whitlow, imposthume, peccant humour, issue; rot, canker, cancer, *carcinoma, caries,* mortification, corruption, gangrene, *sphacelus,* leprosy, eruption, rash, breaking out, venereal disease.

fever, calenture; inflammation.

fatal &c. (*hopeless*) 859- -disease &c.; dangerous illness, galloping consumption, churchyard cough; general breaking up, break up of the system.

[Disease of mind] neurasthenia; idiocy &c. 499; insanity &c. 503.

martyr to disease; cripple; 'the halt, the lame and the blind'; valetudinar-y, -ian; invalid, patient, case; sick-room, -chamber, hospital &c. 662.

[Science of disease] path-, eti-, nos-ology, therapeutics, diagnosis, prognosis.

V. be -ill &c. *adj.*; ail, suffer, labour under, be affected with, complain of; droop, flag, languish, halt; sicken, peak, pine, waste away, fail, lose strength; gasp.

keep one's bed; feign sickness &c. (*falsehood*) 544, malinger.

lay -by, – up; take –, catch- -a disease &c. *n.,* – an infection; be stricken by; break out.

Adj. diseased; ailing &c. *v.*; ill, – of; taken ill, seized with; indisposed, unwell, sick, squeamish, poorly, seedy; affected –, afflicted-with illness; laid up, confined, bed-ridden, invalided, in hospital, on the sick list; out of -health, – sorts; valetudinary.

un-sound, -healthy; sickly, morbose, healthless, infirm, chlorotic, unbraced, drooping, flagging, lame, halt, crippled, halting.

morbid, tainted, vitiated, peccant, contaminated, poisoned, septic, tabid, mangy, leprous, cankered; rotten, – to, – at- the core; withered, palsied, paralytic, tuberculous; dyspeptic.

touched in the wind, broken-winded, spavined, gasping; *hors de combat* &c. (*useless*) 645.

weak-ly, -ened &c. (*weak*) 160; decrepit; decayed &c. (*deteriorated*) 659; incurable &c. (*hopeless*) 859; in declining health; cranky; in a bad way, in danger, prostrate; moribund &c. (*death*) 360.

morbific, epidemic &c. 657.

656. **Salubrity.**—N. salubrity, salubriousness; healthiness &c. *adj.*

fine -air, – climate; eudiometer.

[Preservation of health] *hygiène;* valetudinarian, -ism, preventorium, sanitarian; *sanitarium, sanitorium,* immunity.

V. be -salubrious &c. *adj.*; agree with, be good for; assimilate &c. 23.

Adj. salu-brious, -tary, -tiferous, wholesome; health-y, -ful; sanitary, prophylactic, benign, bracing, tonic,

657. **Insalubrity.**—N. insalubrity; unhealthiness &c. *adj.*; non-naturals; plague spot; malaria &c. (*poison*) 663; death in the pot, contagion.

Adj. insalubrious; un-healthy, -wholesome; noxious, noisome, foul; morbi-fic, -ferous; mephitic, septic, azotic, deleterious; pesti-lent, -ferous, -lential; virulent, venomous, envenomed, poisonous, toxic, narcotic.

contagious, infectious, catching, taking, communicable, epidemic, zymotic;

invigorating, good for, nutritious, hyg-eian, -ienic.

in-noxious, -nocuous, -nocent; harmless, uninjurious, uninfectious; immune.

sanative &c. (*remedial*) 662; restorative &c. (*reinstate*) 660; useful &c. 644.

**658. Improvement.—N.** improvement; a-, melioration; betterment; mend, amendment, emendation; mending &c. *v.*; advancement; advance &c. (*progress*) 282; ascent &c. 305; promotion, preferment; elevation &c. 307; increase &c. 35.

cultiv-, civiliz-ation; menticulture, culture, march of intellect; eugenics, euthenics, meliorism, telesis.

reform, -ation; revision, radical reform; second thoughts, correction, *limæ labor*, refinement, elaboration; purification &c. 652; repair &c. (*restoration*) 660; recovery &c. 660.

revise; revised –, new- edition.

reformer, radical, progressive.

**V.** improve; be –, become –, get-better; mend, amend.

advance &c. (*progress*) 282; ascend &c. 305; increase &c. 35; fructify, ripen, mature; pick up, come about, rally, take a favourable turn; turn -over a new leaf, – the corner; raise one's head, sow one's wild oats; recover &c. 660.

be -better &c. *adj.*, – improved by; turn to -right, – good, – best- account; profit by, reap the benefit of; make -good use of, – capital out of; place to good account; take advantage of.

render better, improve, emend, make over, better; a-, meliorate; correct.

improve –, refine- upon; rectify; enrich, mellow, elaborate, fatten.

promote, cultivate, advance, forward, enhance; bring -forward, – on; foster &c. 707; invigorate &c. (*strengthen*) 159.

touch –, rub –, brush –, furbish –, bolster –, vamp –, brighten –, warm-up; polish, cook, make the most of, set off to advantage; prune; repair &c. (*restore*) 660; put in order &c. (*arrange*) 60.

review, revise, edit, redact; make -corrections, – improvements &c. *n.*; doctor &c. (*remedy*) 662; purify &c. 652.

sporadic, endemic, pandemic, epizoötic; innutritious, indigestible, ungenial; uncongenial &c. (*disagreeing*) 24. deadly &c. (*killing*) 361.

———

**659. Deterioration.—N.** deterioration, debasement; want, ebb; recession &c. 287; retrogradation &c. 283; decrease &c. 36.

degenera-cy, -tion, -teness; degradation; deprav-ation, -ement; depravity &c. 945; demoralization, retrogression.

impairment, inquination, injury, damage, loss, detriment, delaceration, outrage, havoc, inroad, ravage, scath; perversion, prostitution, vitiation, discoloration, oxidation, pollution, defœdation, poisoning, venenation, leaven, contamination, canker, corruption, adulteration, alloy.

decl-ine, -ension, -ination; decadence, -cy; falling off &c. *v.*; caducity, decreptitude, senility.

decay, dilapidation, ravages of time, wear and tear; cor-, e-rosion; mouldi-, rotten-ness; moth and rust, dry-rot, blight, marasmus, atrophy, collapse; disorganization; *délabrement* &c. (*destruction*) 162.

wreck, mere wreck, honeycomb, *magni nominis umbra*.

**V.** be –, become--worse,–deteriorated &c. *adj.*; have seen better days, deteriorate, degenerate, fall off; wane &c. (*decrease*) 36; ebb; retrograde &c. 283; decline, droop; go down &c. (*sink*) 306; go -downhill, – on from bad to worse, – farther and fare worse; jump out of the frying pan into the fire.

run to -seed, – waste; swale, sweal; lapse, be the worse for; break, – down; spring a leak, crack, start; shrivel &c. (*contract*) 195; fade, go off, wither, moulder, rot, rankle, decay, go bad; go to –, fall into- decay; 'fall into the sear and yellow leaf,' rust, crumble, shake; totter, – to its fall; perish &c. 162; die &c. 360.

[Render less good] deteriorate; weaken &c. 160; put back; taint, infect, contaminate, poison, empoison,

relieve, refresh, revive, infuse new blood into, recruit, re-invigorate, re-new, revivify, freshen, build -afresh, – anew; uplift, inspire.

re-form, -model, -organise; new model, civilize.

view in a new light, think better of, appeal from Philip drunk to Philip sober.

palliate, mitigate; lessen &c. 36- an evil.

Adj. improving &c. *v.*; progressive, improved &c. *v.*; better, – off, – for; all the better for; better advised.

reform-, emend-atory; reparatory &c. (*restorative*) 660; remedial &c. 662.

corrigible, improvable, curable, ac-cultural.

Adv. on -consideration, – reconsider-ation, – second thoughts, – better advice; *ad melius inquirendum*; on the -mend, – up grade.

envenom, canker, corrupt, exulcerate, pollute, vitiate, inquinate; de-, em-base; denaturalize, leaven; de-flower, -bauch, -file, -prave, -grade; stain &c. (*dirt*) 653; discolour; alloy, adulterate, sophisticate, tamper with, prejudice.

pervert, prostitute, demoralize, bru-talize; render vicious &c. 945; compro-mise.

embitter, ex-, acerbate, aggravate.

injure, impair, labefy, damage, harm, hurt, shend, scathe, spoil, mar, despoil, dilapidate, waste; overrun; ravage; pillage &c. 791.

wound, stab, pierce, maim, lame, surbate, cripple, hough, hamstring, hit between wind and water, scotch, mangle, mutilate, disfigure, blemish, deface, warp.

blight, rot; cor-, e-rode, eat away; wear -away, – out; gnaw, – at the root of; sap, mine, undermine, shake, sap the foundations of, break up; dis-organ-ize, -mantle, -mast; destroy &c. 162.

damnify &c. (*aggrieve*) 649; do one's worst; knock down; deal a blow to; play -havoc, – sad havoc, – the mischief, – the deuce, – the very devil- -with, – among; decimate.

Adj. unimproved &c. (improve &c. 658); deteriorated &c. *v.*; altered, – for the worse; injured &c. *v.*; sprung; withering, spoiling, &c. *v.*; on the -wane, – decline; tabid; degenerate; worse; the -, all the- worse for; out of -repair, – tune; imperfect &c. 651; the worse for wear; battered; weather-ed, -beaten; stale, *passé*, shaken, dilapidated, frayed, faded, wilted, shabby, second-hand, second-rate, threadbare; worn, – to- -a thread, – a shadow, – the stump, rags; reduced, – to a skeleton, skeletonized; far gone.

decayed &c. *v.*; moth-, worm-eaten; mildewed, rusty, mouldy, spotted, seedy, time-worn, moss-grown; discoloured; effete, wasted, crumbling, mouldering, rotten, cankered, blighted, tainted; depraved &c. (*vicious*) 945; decrep-id, -it; broken down; done, – for, – up; worn out, used up; fit for the -dust-hole, – wastepaper basket; past work &c. (*useless*) 645.

at a low ebb, in a bad way, on one's last legs, washed -up, – out; undermined, deciduous; nodding to its fall &c. (*destruction*) 162; tottering &c. (*dangerous*) 665; past cure &c. (*hopeless*) 859; fatigued &c. 688; backward, retrograde &c. (*retrogressive*) 283; deleterious &c. 649; behind the times.

Adv. on the down grade; beyond hope.

Phr. out of the frying pan into the fire; *ægrescit medendo*.

---

**660. Restoration.—N.** restor-ation, -al; re-instatement, -placement, -habi-litation, -establishment, -construction; reproduction &c. 163; re-novation, -newal; reviv-al, -escence; refreshment

**661. Relapse.—N.** relapse, lapse; falling back &c. *v.*; retrogradation &c. (*retrogression*) 283; deterioration &c. 659.

[Return to, or recurrence of a bad

&c. 689; re-suscitation, -animation, -vivification, -viction; Phœnix; reorganization.

*renaissance*, renascence, rebirth, second youth, rejuvenation, rejuvenescence, new birth; regenera-tion, -cy, -teness; palingenesis, reconversion, resurgence, resurrection.

state] backsliding, recidivation, recrudescence.

**V.** relapse, lapse; fall –, slide –, sinkback; have a relapse; return; retrograde &c. 283; recidivate; fall off &c. 659, again.

redress, retrieval, reclamation, recovery; convalescence; resumption, *résumption*.

recurrence &c. (*repetition*) 104; *réchauffé, rifacimento*.

cure, recure, sanation; healing &c. *v*.; redintegration; rectification, instauration.

repair, reparation, mending; recruiting &c. *v*.; cicatrization; disinfection; tinkering.

reaction; redemption &c. (*deliverance*) 672; restitution &c. 790; relief &c. 834.

mender, repairer, renewer; tinker, cobbler; doctor &c. 662; *vis medicatrix* &c. (*remedy*) 662.

curableness.

**V.** return to the original state; recover, rally, revive; come -to, – round, – to oneself; pull through, weather the storm, be oneself again; get -well, – round, – the better of, – over, – about; rise from -one's ashes, – the grave; resurge, resurrect; survive &c. (*outlive*) 110; resume, reappear; come to, – life again; live –, rise- again; relive.

heal, skin over, cicatrize; right itself.

restore, put back, place *in statu quo*; re-instate, -place, -seat, -habilitate, -establish, -estate, -install.

re-construct, -build, -organize, -constitute; reconvert; re-new, -novate; recondition; regenerate; rejuvenate.

re-deem, -claim, -cover, -trieve; rescue &c. (*deliver*) 672.

redress, recure; cure, heal, remedy, doctor, physic, medicate; break of; bring round, set on one's legs.

re-suscitate, -vive, -animate, -vivify, -call to life; reproduce &c. 163; warm up; reinvigorate, refresh &c. 689.

redintegrate, make whole; recoup &c. 790; make -good, – all square; rectify; put –, set- -right, – to rights, – straight; set up, correct; put in order &c. (*arrange*) 60; refit, recruit; fill up, – the ranks; reinforce.

repair, mend; put in -repair, – thorough repair, – complete repair; retouch, botch, vamp, tinker, doctor, cobble; do –, patch –, plaster –, vamp- up; darn, fine-draw, heel-piece; stop a gap, stanch, staunch, caulk, calk, careen, splice, bind up wounds.

**Adj.** restored &c. *v*.; *redivivus*, convalescent; in a fair way; none the worse; rejuvenated, renascent.

restoring &c. *v*.; restorative, recuperative; sana-, repara-tive, -tory; curative, remedial.

restor-, recover-, san-, remedi-, retriev-, cur-able.

**Adv.** *in statu quo*; as you were.

**Phr.** *revenons à nos moutons.*

---

**662. Remedy.—N.** remedy, help, redress; antidote, anti-toxin, anti-,

**663. Bane.—N.** bane, curse, thorn in the -side, -flesh, bugbear, *bête noire;*

counter-poison, prophylactic, antiseptic, germicide, bactericide, corrective, restorative, stimulant, pick-me-up, tonic; sedative &c. 174; palliative; febrifuge; alter-ant, -ative; specific; emetic, carminative; narcotic &c. *adj.*; Nepenthe, Mithridate.

cure; radical –, perfect –, certain-cure; sovereign remedy.

physic, medicine, patent medicine, Galenicals, simples, drug, potion, draught, dose, pill, bolus, lozenge, tablet, tabloid, capsule; electuary; linct-us, -ure; medicament.

nostrum, receipt, recipe, prescription; catholicon, panacea, elixir, *elixir vitæ*, philosopher's stone; balm, balsam, cordial, theriac, ptisan.

salve, ointment, cerate, oil, lenitive, lotion, cosmetic; plaster; epithem, embrocation, liniment, cataplasm, sinapism, arquebusade, traumatic, vulnerary, pepastic, poultice, collyrium, depilatory.

compress, pledget; bandage &c. (*support*) 215.

treatment, medical treatment, regimen; diet-ary, -etics; *vis medicatrix, naturæ*; *médicine expectante*; seton, blood-letting, bleeding, venesection, phlebotomy, cupping, leeches; operation, surgical operation; tonsillectomy, appendectomy; injection, electrolysis, massage.

pharma-cy, -cology, -ceutics; acology; materia medica, pharmacopœia, therapeutics, therapy, posology, pathology &c. 655; homœ-, heter-, all-, hydr-opathy; cold water –, open air- cure; dietetics; sur-, chirur-gery, osteopathy; healing art, leechcraft, practice of medicine; ortho-pædy, -praxy; dentistry, midwifery, obstetrics, gynæcology.

faith -cure, – healing; psycho-therapy, -analysis, psychiatry.

hospital, infirmary, clinic; pest-, lazar-house; lazaretto, lazaret; lock hospital; *maison de santé*; *ambulance*; dispensary; *sanatorium, sanitarium*, spa, baths, pump-room, well; *hospice*; Red Cross; nursing home; asylum.

doctor, physician, surgeon; medical –, general- practitioner, consultant, specialist; medical attendant; medical student, medico; chemist, apothecary, pharmacopolist, druggist; leech; Æsculapius, Hippocrates, Galen; *accoucheur*, gynæcologist, midwife, oculist, aurist, dentist; operator; osteopath, bonesetter; nurse, monthly nurse, sister; dresser; *masseur, masseuse*.

**V.** apply a -remedy &c. *n.*; doctor, dose, physic, nurse, minister to, attend, dress the wounds, plaster, bandage, poultice; heal, cure, work a cure, kill or cure, remedy, stay (disease), snatch from the jaws of death; prevent &c. 706; relieve &c. 834; palliate &c. 658:

evil &c. 619; hurtfulness &c. (*badness*) 649; painfulness &c. (*cause of pain*) 830; scourge &c. (*punishment*) 975; *damnosa hereditas*; white elephant.

sting, fang, thorn, tang, bramble, brier, nettle.

poison, leaven, virus, venom; intoxicant; arsenic, Prussic acid, antimony, tartar emetic, strychnine, nicotine, cyanide of potassium, corrosive sublimate; curare; hyoscine &c.; poison-, mustard-, tear-gas; carbon di-, monoxide; ptomaine poisoning, botulism; miasm, mephitis, malaria, azote, sewer gas; pest, stench &c. 401.

rust, worm, moth, moth and rust, fungus, mildew; dry-rot; canker, -worm; cancer; torpedo; viper &c. (*evil-doer*) 913; demon &c. 980.

hemlock, hellebore, nightshade, *belladonna*, henbane, aconite; Upas tree.

drugs, dope, opium, morphia, morphine, cocaine, heroin, hashish, bhang. [Science of poisons] Toxicology.

**Adj.** baneful &c. (*bad*) 649; poisonous &c. (*unwholesome*) 657.

restore &c. 660; drench with physic; consult, operate, extract, deliver; bleed, cup, let blood, transfuse; electrolyse; psycho-analyse.

**Adj.** remedial; restorative &c. 660; corrective, palliative, healing; sana-tory, -tive; prophylactic; salutiferous &c. (*salutary*) 656; medic-al, -inal; therapeutic, surgical, chirurgical, orthopedic, epulotic, paregoric, tonic, corroborant, analeptic, balsamic, anodyne, hypnotic, neurotic, narcotic, sedative, lenitive, demulcent, emollient; depuratory; deter-sive, -gent; abstersive, disinfectant, febrifugal, alternative; traumatic, vulnerary.

dietetic, alimentary; nutrit-ious, -ive; peptic; alexi-pharmic, -teric; remedi-, cur-able.

### 3. Contingent Subservience

**664. Safety.—N.** safety, security, impregnability; invulnera-bility, -bleness &c. *adj.*; danger -past, – over; storm blown over; coast clear; escape &c. 671; means of escape, safety-valve; safeguard, palladium, sheet anchor, rock, tower of strength.

guardian-, ward-, warden-ship; tutelage, custody, safe keeping; preservation &c. 670; protection, auspices.

safe-conduct, escort, convoy; guard, shield &c. (*defence*) 717; guardian angel, tutelary -god, – deity, – saint; *genius loci.*

protector, guardian; ward-en, -er; preserver, custodian, *duenna, chaperon,* third person.

watch-, ban-dog; Cerberus; watch-, patrol-, police-man, constable, peeler; bobby, copper, cop, bull, flat-foot, detective, armed guard; sentinel, sentry, scout &c. (*warning*) 668; garrison; guard-ship.

[Means of safety] refuge &c., anchor &c. 666; precaution &c. (*preparation*) 673; quarantine, *cordon sanitaire.* [Sense of security] confidence &c. 858.

**V.** be -safe &c. *adj.*; keep one's head above water, tide over, save one's bacon; ride out –, weather- the storm; light upon one's feet; bear a charmed life; escape &c. 671; possess nine lives.

make –, render- -safe &c. *adj.*; protect, watch over; take care of &c. (*care*) 459; preserve &c. 670; cover, screen, shelter, shroud, flank, ward; guard &c. (*defend*) 717; secure &c. (*restrain*) 751; intrench, fence round &c. (*circumscribe*) 229; house, nestle, ensconce; take charge of.

**665. Danger.—N.** danger, peril, insecurity, jeopardy, risk, hazard, venture, precariousness, slipperiness; instability &c. 149; defencelessness &c. *adj.*

exposure &c. (*liability*) 177; vulnerability; vulnerable point, heel of Achilles; forlorn hope &c. (*hopelessness*) 859.

[Dangerous course] leap in the dark &c. (*rashness*) 863; road to ruin, *facilis descensus Averni,* hair-breadth escape; cause for alarm; source of danger &c. 667. [Approach of danger] rock –, breakers- ahead; storm brewing; clouds -in the horizon, – gathering; warning &c. 668; alarm &c. 669. [Sense of danger] apprehension &c. 860.

**V.** be -in danger &c. *adj.*; be exposed to –, run into –, incur –, encounter- -danger &c. *n.*; run a risk; lay oneself open to &c. (*liability*) 177; lean on –, trust to- a broken reed; feel the ground sliding from under one, have to run for it; have the -chances, – odds- against one.

hang by a thread, totter; tremble on the -verge, – brink; sleep –, stand -on a volcano; sit on a barrel of gunpowder, live in a glass house.

bring –, place –, put- in -danger &c. *n.*; endanger, expose to danger, imperil; jeopard, -ize, compromise; sail too near the wind &c. (*rash*) 863; put one's head in the lion's mouth.

adventure, risk, hazard, venture, stake, set at hazard; run the gauntlet &c. (*dare*) 861; engage in a forlorn hope.

threaten &c. 909- danger; run one

escort, convoy; garrison; watch, mount guard, patrol, scout, spy.

make assurance double sure &c. (*caution*) 864; take up a loose thread; take precautions &c. (*prepare for*) 673; take in a reef; double reef topsails.

seek safety; take –, find- shelter &c. 666; run into port.

**Adj.** safe, secure, sure; in -safety, – security; have an anchor to windward; on the safe side; under the -shield of, – shade of, – wing of, – shadow of one's wing; under -cover, – lock and key; out of -danger, – the meshes, – harm's way; in -harbour, – port; on sure ground, at anchor, high and dry, above water, on *terra firma*; unthreatened, -molested; protected &c. *v.*; *cavendo tutus*; panoplied &c. (*defended*) 717.

snug, sea-, air-worthy; weather-, water-, fire-, bomb-proof.

defensible, tenable, proof against, invulnerable; un-assailable, -attackable; im-pregnable, -perdible; founded on a rock; inexpugnable.

safe and sound &c. (*preserved*) 670; harmless; scathless &c. (*perfect*) 650; unhazarded; not -dangerous &c. 665.

protecting &c. *v.*; guardian, tutelary; preservative &c. 670; trustworthy &c. 939.

**Adv.** *ex abundanti cautelâ*; with impunity.

**Phr.** all's well; all clear; *salva res est*; *suave mari magno*; safety first.

hard; lay a trap for &c. (*deceive*) 545.

**Adj.** in -danger &c. *n.*; endangered &c. *v.*; fraught with danger; danger-, hazard-, peril-, parl-, pericul-ous; unsafe, unprotected &c. (safe, protect &c. 664); insecure, untrustworthy, unreliable; built upon sand, on a sandy basis.

defence-, fence-, guard-, harbourless; unshielded; vulnerable, expugnable, unsheltered, exposed; open to &c. (*liable*) 177.

*aux abois*, at bay; on -the wrong side of the wall, – a lee shore, – the rocks.

at stake, in question; precarious, aleatory, critical, ticklish; slip-pery, -py; hanging by a thread &c. *v.*; with a halter round one's neck; between -the hammer and the anvil, – Scylla and Charybdis, – two fires; on the -edge, – brink, – verge of a- -precipice, – volcano; in the lion's den, on slippery ground, under fire; not out of the wood.

un-warned, -admonished, -advised; unprepared &c. 674; off one's guard &c. (*inexpectant*) 508.

tottering; un-stable, -steady; shaky, top-heavy, tumble-down, ramshackle, crumbling, waterlogged; help-, guideless; in a bad way; reduced to –, at the last extremity; trembling in the balance; nodding to its fall &c. (*destruction*) 162.

threatening &c. 909; ominous, ill-omened; alarming &c. (*fear*) 860; explosive; poisonous &c. 657.

adventurous &c. (*rash*) 863, (*bold*) 861.

**Int.** stop! look out! beware! take care!

**Phr.** *incidit in Scyllam qui vult vitare Charybdim; nam tua res agitur paries dum proximus ardet.*

---

**666.** [Means of safety.] **Refuge.—N.**

refuge, sanctuary, retreat, fastness; stronghold, keep, last resort; ward; prison &c. 752; asylum, ark, home, almshouse, refuge for the destitute; hiding-place &c. (*ambush*) 530; *sanctum sanctorum* &c. (*privacy*) 893; cache.

roadstead, anchorage; breakwater, mole, port, haven; harbour, – of refuge; sea-port; pier, jetty, embankment, quay.

**667.** [Source of danger.] **Pitfall.—N.**

rocks, reefs, coral reef, sunken rocks, snags; sands, quicksands, Goodwin sands, sandy foundation; slippery ground; breakers, shoals, shallows, bank, shelf, flat, lee shore, iron-bound coast; rock –, breakers- ahead; derelict.

precipice; abyss, chasm, pit, crevasse; maelstrom, whirlpool, eddy, vortex, rapids, current, bore, tidal wave; storm, squall, hurricane, whirl-

covert, shelter, abri, screen, lee-wall, wing, shield, umbrella; splash-, dash-board, mudguard.

wall &c. (*inclosure*) 232; fort &c. (*defence*) 717.

anchor, kedge; grap-nel, -pling iron; sheet-, mushroom-anchor, main-stay; support &c. 215; check &c. 706; ballast.

jury-mast; vent-peg; safety -valve, - lamp; lightning conductor:

wind; volcano; ambush &c. 530; pit-fall, trap-door; trap &c. (*snare*) 545.

sword of Damocles; wolf at the door, snake in the grass, viper in one's bosom, death in the pot; latency &c. 526.

ugly customer, dangerous person, *le chat qui dort*; firebrand, hornet's nest.

**Phr.** *latet anguis in herbâ; proximus ardet Ucalegon.*

means of escape &c: (*escape*) 671; life-boat, swimming belt, cork jacket; life preserver, breeches buoy; parachute, plank, stepping-stone. safeguard &c. (*protection*) 664.

**V.** seek -, take -, find- refuge &c. *n.*; seek -, find- safety &c. 664; throw oneself into the arms of; claim sanctuary; take to the -hills, - woods; make port, reach shelter, bar -, bolt -, lock -the door, - gate; let the portcullis down; raise the drawbridge.

**668. Warning.—N.** warning, caution, *caveat*; notice &c. (*information*) 527; premoni-tion, -shment; prediction &c. 511; contraindication; symptom; lesson, dehortation; admonition, monition; alarm &c. 669.

handwriting on the wall, *tekel upharsin*, yellow flag; fog-signal, -horn; siren; monitor, warning voice, Cassandra, signs of the times, Mother Carey's chickens, stormy petrel, bird of ill omen, gathering clouds, clouds in the horizon, cloud no bigger than a man's hand, death-watch.

watch-tower, beacon, signal-post; light-house &c. (*indication of locality*) 550.

sent-inel, -ry; watch, -man; watch and ward; watch-, ban-, house-dog; patrol, vedette, picket, bivouac, scout, spy, spial; advanced -, rear-guard, lookout, flagman.

cautiousness &c. 864.

**V.** warn, caution; fore-, pre-warn; ad-, pre-monish; give -notice, - warning; menace &c. (*threaten*) 909; put on one's guard; sound the alarm &c. 669; croak.

beware, ware; take -warning, - heed at one's peril; watch out for; keep watch and ward &c. (*care*) 459.

**Adj.** warning &c. *v.*; premonitory, monitory, cautionary; admoni-tory, -tive; ominous, threatening, lowering, minatory, symptomatic.

warned &c. *v.*; on one's guard &c. (*careful*) 459, (*cautious*) 864.

**Adv.** *in terrorem* &c. (*threat*) 909.

**Int.** beware! ware! take care! mind -, take care-what you are about; mind! look out!

**Phr.** *ne reveillez pas le chat qui dort; fœnum habet in cornu.*

**669. [Indication of danger.] Alarm.—N.** alarm; alarum, larum, alarm bell, tocsin, *alerte*, beat of drum, sound of trumpet, note of alarm, hue and cry, signal of distress, S.O.S.; blue-lights; war-cry, -whoop; warning &c. 668; fog-signal, -horn; siren; yellow flag; danger signal; red -light, - flag; fire -bell, - alarm; burglar alarm, police whistle, watchman's rattle.

false alarm, cry of wolf; bugbear, -aboo.

**V.** give -, raise -, sound -, beat- the *or* an -alarm &c. *n.*; alarm; warn &c. 668; ring the tocsin; *battre la générale*; cry wolf.

**Adj.** alarming &c. *v.*

**Int.** *sauve qui peut! qui vive?* who goes there?

**670. Preservation.—N.** preservation; safe keeping; conservation &c. (*storage*) 636; maintenance, upkeep, support, sustentation, conservatism; *vis conservatrix*; salvation &c. (*deliverance*) 672; drying &c. *v.*

[Means of preservation] prophylaxis; preserv-er, -ative; canned goods; cold pack; hygi-astics, -antics; cover, drugget; *cordon sanitaire.* [Superstitious remedies] charm &c. 993.

**V.** preserve, maintain, keep, sustain, support; keep -up, – alive; not willingly let die; shore –, bank- up; nurse; save, rescue; be –, make--safe &c. 664; take care of &c. (*care*) 459; guard &c. (*defend*) 717.

*stare super antiquas vias*; hold one's own; hold –, stand- -one's ground &c. (*resist*) 719.

embalm, dry, cure, smoke, salt, pickle, season, kyanize, bottle, pot, tin, can; husband &c. (*store*) 636.

**Adj.** preserving &c. *v.*; conservative; prophylactic; preserva-tory, -tive; hygienic.

preserved &c. *v.*; un-impaired, -broken, -injured, -hurt, -singed, -marred; safe, – and sound; intact, with a whole skin, without a scratch.

**Phr.** *nolumus leges Angliæ mutari.*

**671. Escape.—N.** escape, scape; avolation, elopement, flight, getaway; evasion &c. (*avoidance*) 623; retreat; narrow –, hairbreadth-escape; close –, near- shave; come off, impunity.

[Means of escape] loophole &c. (*opening*) 260; path &c. 627; secret -door, – passage; refuge &c. 666; vent, – peg; safety-valve; drawbridge, fire-escape.

reprieve &c. (*deliverance*) 672; liberation &c. 750.

refugee &c. (*fugitive*) 623.

**V.** escape, scape; make –, effect –, make good- one's escape, make a get-away; get -off, – clear off, – well out of; *échapper belle*, save one's bacon; weather the storm &c. (*safe*) 664; escape scot-free.

elude &c., make off &c. (*avoid*) 623; march off &c. (*go away*) 293; give one the slip; slip through the -hands, – fingers; slip the collar, wriggle out of; break -loose, – from prison; break –, slip –, get- away; find -vent, – a hole to creep out of.

**Adj.** escap-ing, -ed &c. *v.*; stolen away, fled.

**Phr.** the bird has flown.

**672. Deliverance.—N.** deliverance, extrication, rescue; repriev-e, -al; respite; ransom; liberation &c. 750; truce, armistice; redemption, salvation; riddance; gaol delivery; exemption, day of grace; redeemableness.

**V.** deliver, extricate, rescue, save, redeem, ransom, free, liberate, release, set free, redeem, emancipate; bring -off, – through; *tirer d'affaire*, get the wheel out of the rut; snatch from the jaws of death, come to the rescue; rid; retrieve &c. (*restore*) 660; be –, get- rid of.

**Adj.** saved &c. *v.*; extric-, redeem-, rescu-able.

**Phr.** to the rescue!

### 3°. *Precursory Measures*

**673. Preparation.—N.** preparation; providing &c. *v.*; provi-sion, -dence; anticipation &c. (*foresight*) 510; precaution, -concertation, -disposition;

**674. Non-Preparation. — N.** non-, absence of –, want of- preparation; unpreparedness; inculture, inconcoction, improvidence.

forecast &c. (*plan*) 626; rehearsal, note of preparation.

[Putting in order] arrangement &c. 60; clearance; adjustment &c. 23; tuning; equipment, outfit, accoutrement, armament, array.

ripening &c. *v.*; maturation, evolution; elaboration, concoction, digestion; gestation, hatching, incubation, sitting.

groundwork, datum, first stone, cradle, stepping-stone; foundation, scaffold &c. (*support*) 215; scaffolding, *échafaudage*.

[Preparation -of men] training &c. (*education*) 537; inurement &c. (*habit*) 613; novitiate; [- of food] cook-ing, -ery; brewing, culinary art; [- of the soil] till-, plough-, sow-ing; semination, cultivation.

[State of being prepared] prepared-, readi-, ripe-, mellow-ness; maturity; *un impromptu fait à loisir*.

[Preparer] preparer, teacher, coach, trainer, pioneer; *avant-courrier, -coureur*; sappers and miners, paviour, navvy; packer, stevedore; warming-pan; precursor &c. 64.

**V.** prepare; get -, make- ready; make preparations, settle preliminaries, get up, sound the note of preparation; address oneself to.

set -, put- in order &c. (*arrange*) 60; forecast &c. (*plan*) 626; prepare -, plough -, dress- the ground; till -, cultivate- the soil; predispose, sow the seed, lay a train, dig a mine; lay -, fix- the -foundations, - basis, -groundwork; dig the foundations, erect the scaffolding; lay the first stone &c. (*begin*) 66.

rough-hew; cut out work; block -, hammer- out; lick into shape &c. (*form*) 240.

elaborate, mature, ripen, mellow, season, bring to maturity; nurture &c. (*aid*) 707; hatch, cook, brew; temper; anneal, smelt; dry, cure &c. 670.

equip, arm, man; fit-out, -up; furnish, rig, dress, garnish, betrim, accoutre, array, fettle, fledge; dress -, turbish -, brush -, vamp- up; refurbish; sharpen one's tools, trim one's foils, set, prime, attune; whet the -knife, - sword; wind -, screw- up; adjust &c. (*fit*) 27; put in -trim, - train, - gear, - working order, - tune, - a groove for, - harness; pack, stow away, store.

immaturity, crudity; rawness &c. *adj.*; abortion; disqualification.

[Absence of art] nature, state of nature; virgin soil, unweeded garden; rough diamond, neglect &c. 460.

rough copy &c. (*plan*) 626; germ &c. 153; raw material &c. 635.

improvisation &c. (*impulse*) 612.

**V.** be -unprepared &c. *adj.*; want -, lack- preparation; lie fallow; *s'embarquer sans biscuits*; live from hand to mouth.

[Render unprepared] dismantle &c. (*render useless*) 645; undress &c. 226.

extemporize, improvise.

surprise, pay a surprise visit, take by surprise, drop in upon, take unawares; take pot-luck.

**Adj.** un-prepared &c. [prepare &c. 673]; without -preparation &c. 673; incomplete &c. 53; rudimental, embryonic, abortive; immature, unripe, raw, green, crude; coarse; rough, -cast, -hewn; in the rough; un-hewn, -formed, -fashioned, -wrought, -laboured, -blown, -cooked, -boiled, -concocted, -cut, -polished.

callow, un-hatched, -fledged, -nurtured, -licked, -taught, -educated, -cultivated, -trained, -tutored, -drilled, -exercised; precocious, premature; un-, in-digested; un-mellowed, -seasoned, -leavened.

fallow; un-sown, -tilled; natural, in a state of nature; undressed; in dishabille, *en déshabillé, en négligé*.

un-, dis-qualified; unfitted; ill-digested; un-begun, -ready, -arranged, -organized, -furnished, -provided, -equipped, -trimmed; out of -gear, - order; dismantled &c. *v.*

shiftless, improvident, unthrifty, thoughtless, unguarded; happy-go-lucky; caught napping &c. (*inexpectant*) 508; unpremeditated &c. 612.

**Adv.** extempore &c. 612.

———

train &c. (*teach*) 537; inure &c. (*habituate*) 613; breed; prepare
&c.- for; rehearse; make provision for; take -steps, – measures, –
precautions; provide, – against; beat up for recruits; open the door
to &c. (*facilitate*) 705.

set one's house in order, make all snug; clear -decks, – for action;
close one's ranks; shuffle the cards.

prepare oneself; serve an apprenticeship &c. (*learn*) 539; lay
oneself out for, get into harness, gird up one's loins, buckle on one's
armour, *reculer pour mieux sauter*, prime and load, shoulder arms,
get the steam up, put the horses to.

guard –, make sure- against; forearm, make sure, prepare for the
evil day, have a rod in pickle, provide against a rainy day, feather
one's nest; lay in provisions &c. 637; make investments; keep on
foot.

be -prepared, – ready &c. *adj.*; hold oneself in readiness, watch
and pray, keep one's powder dry; lie in wait for &c. (*expect*) 507;
anticipate &c. (*foresee*) 510; *principiis obstare; veniente occurrere
morbo.*

Adj. preparing &c. *v.*; in -preparation, – course of preparation,
– agitation, – embryo, – hand, – train; afoot, afloat; on -foot, – the
stocks, – the anvil; under consideration &c. (*plan*) 626; brewing,
hatching, forthcoming, brooding; in -store for, – reserve.

precautionary, provident; prepara-tive, -tory; provisional, in-
choate, under revision; preliminary &c. (*precedent*) 62.

prepared &c. *v.*; in readiness; ready, – to one's hand, – made,
cut and dried; ready for use, reach me down; made to one's hand,
handy, on the table, made to order; in gear; in working -order,
– gear; snug; in practice.

ripe, mature, mellow; practised &c. (*skilled*) 698; laboured, elab-
orate, highly-wrought, smelling of the lamp, worked up.

in -full feather, – best bib and tucker; in –, at- harness; in – the
saddle, – arms, – battle array, – war paint; up in arms; armed -at
all points, – to the teeth, – *cap-à-pie*; sword in hand; booted and
spurred.

*in utrumque* –, *semper- paratus*; on the alert &c. (*vigilant*) 459;
at one's post.

Adv. in -preparation, – anticipation of; afoot, astir, abroad;
abroach.

**675. Essay.—N.** essay, trial, endeavour, aim, attempt; venture, ad-
venture, speculation, *coup d'essai, début*; probation &c. (*experiment*) 463.

**V.** try, essay; experiment &c. 463; endeavour, strive; tempt, tackle,
take on, attempt, make an attempt; venture, adventure, speculate,
take one's chance, tempt fortune; try one's -fortune, – luck, – hand;
use one's endeavour; feel –, grope –, pick- one's way.

try hard, push, make a bold push, use one's best endeavour; do one's
best &c. (*exertion*) 686.

Adj. essaying &c. *v.*; experimental &c. 463; tentative, empirical,
probationary.

Adv. experimentally &c. *adj.*; on trial, at a venture; by rule of thumb.
if one may be so bold.

**676. Undertaking.—N.** undertaking; compact &c. 769; engagement
&c. (*promise*) 768; enter-, em-prise; venture &c. 675; pilgrimage; mat-
ter in hand &c. (*business*) 625; move; first move &c. (*beginning*) 66.

**V.** undertake; engage –, embark- in; launch –, plunge- into; volunteer; apprentice oneself to; engage &c. (*promise*) 768; contract &c. 769; take upon -oneself, – one's shoulders; devote oneself to &c. (*determination*) 604.

take -up, – in hand; tackle; set –, go- about; set –, fall- -to, – to work; launch forth; set up shop; put in -hand, – execution; set forward; break the neck of a business, be in for; put one's hand to; betake oneself to, turn one's hand to, go to do; begin &c. 66; broach, institute, &c. (*originate*) 153; put –, lay- one's -hand to the plough, – shoulder to the wheel.

have in hand &c. (*business*) 625; have many irons in the fire &c. (*activity*) 682.

**Adj.** undertaking &c. *v.*; on the anvil &c. 625; adventurous, venturesome.

**Int.** here goes!

**677. Use.**—N. use; employ, -ment; exer-cise, -citation; appli-cation, -ance; adhibition, disposal; consumption; agency &c. (*physical*) 170; usufruct; usefulness &c. 644; recourse, resort, avail, pragmatism.

[Conversion to use] utilization, service, wear.

[Way of using] usage.

**V.** use, make use of, employ, put to use; apply, put in -action, – operation, – practice; set -in motion, – to work.

ply, work, wield, handle, manipulate; play, – off; exert, exercise, practise, avail oneself of, profit by; resort –, have recourse –, recur –, take –, betake oneself- to; take -up with, – advantage of; lay one's hands on, try.

render useful &c. 644; mould; turn to -account, – use; convert to use, utilize, administer; work up; call –, bring- into play; put into requisition; call –, draw- forth; press –, enlist- into the service; bring to bear upon, devote, dedicate, consecrate, apply, adhibit, dispose of; make a -handle, – cat's paw- of.

fall back upon, make a shift with; make the -most, – best- of.

use –, swallow- up; consume, absorb, expend; tax, task, wear, put to task.

**Adj.** in use; used &c. *v.*; well-worn, -trodden.

useful &c. 644; subservient &c. (*instrumental*) 631; utilitarian; pragmatical.

**678. Disuse.**—N. forbearance, abstinence; disuse; relinquishment &c. 782; desuetude &c. (*want of habit*) 614.

**V.** not use; do without, dispense with, let alone, not touch, forbear, abstain, spare, waive, neglect; keep back, reserve.

lay -up, – by, – on the shelf, – up in a napkin; shelve; set –, put –, lay-aside; disuse, leave off, have done with; supersede; discard &c. (*eject*) 297; dismiss, give warning.

throw aside &c. (*relinquish*) 782; make away with &c. (*destroy*) 162; cast –, heave –, throw- overboard; cast to the -dogs, – winds; dismantle &c. (*render useless*) 645.

lie –, remain- unemployed &c. *adj.*

**Adj.** not used &c. *v.*; un-employed, -applied, -disposed of, -spent, -exercised, -touched, -trodden, -essayed, -gathered, -culled; uncalled for, not required.

disused &c. *v.*; done with; run down, used up, cast off.

**679. Misuse.**—N. mis-use, -usage, -employment, -application, -appropriation.

abuse, profanation, prostitution, desecration; waste &c. 638.

**V.** mis-use, -employ, -apply, -appropriate.

desecrate, abuse, profane, prostitute; waste &c. 638; over-task, -tax, -work; squander &c. 818.

cut a whetstone with a razor, employ a steam-engine to crack a nut; catch at a straw.

**Adj.** misused &c. *v.*

## Section III. Voluntary Action

### 1°. *Simple Voluntary Action*

**680. Action.—N.** action, performance; doing &c. *v.*; perpetration; exercise, -citation; movement, operation, evolution, work; labour &c. (*exertion*) 686; *praxis*, execution; procedure &c. (*conduct*) 692; handicraft; business &c. 625; agency &c. (*power at work*) 170.

deed, act, overt act, stitch, touch, gest; transaction, job, doings, dealings, proceeding, measure, step, manœuvre, bout, passage, move, stroke, blow; *coup, – de main, – d'état; tour de force* &c. (*display*) 882; feat, exploit, stunt; achievement &c. (*completion*) 729; handiwork, workmanship, craftsmanship; manufacture; stroke of policy &c. (*plan*) 626.

actor &c. (*doer*) 690.

**V.** do, perform, execute; achieve &c. (*complete*) 729; transact, enact; commit, perpetrate, inflict; exercise, prosecute, carry on, work, practise, play.

employ oneself, ply one's task; officiate, have in hand &c. (*business*) 625; labour &c. 686; be at work; pursue a course; shape one's course &c. (*conduct*) 692.

act, operate; take -action, – steps; strike a blow, lift a finger, stretch forth one's hand; take in hand &c. (*undertake*) 676; put oneself in motion; put in practice; carry into execution &c. (*complete*) 729; act upon.

be -an actor &c. 690; take –, act –, play –, perform- a part in; participate in; have a -hand in, – finger in the pie; have to do with; be a -party to, – participator in; bear –, lend- a hand; pull an oar, run in a race; mix oneself up with &c. (*meddle*) 682.

be in action; come into operation &c. (*power at work*) 170.

**Adj.** doing &c. *v.*; acting; in action; in harness; on duty; at work; in operation &c. 170; up to one's ears in work, in the midst of things.

**Adv.** in the -act, – midst of, – thick of; red-handed, *in flagrante delicto*; while one's hand is in.

**681. Inaction.—N.** inaction, passiveness, abstinence from action; non-interference; Fabian –, conservative-policy; neglect &c. 460; stagnation, vegetation; loafing.

inactivity &c. 683; rest &c. (*repose*) 687; quiescence &c. 265; want of –, in- occupation; unemployment; idle hours, time hanging on one's hands, *dolce far niente*; sinecure.

**V.** not -do, – act, – attempt; be -inactive &c. 683; abstain from doing, do nothing, hold, spare; not -stir, – move, – lift- a -finger, – foot, – peg; fold one's -arms, – hands; leave –, let- alone; let -be, – pass, – things take their course, – it have its way, – well alone; *quieta non movere; stare super antiquas vias;* rest and be thankful, live and let live; lie –, rest- upon one's oars; *laisser -aller, – faire;* stand aloof; refrain &c. (*avoid*) 623; keep oneself from doing; remit –, relax- one's efforts; desist &c. (*relinquish*) 624; stop &c. (*cease*) 142; pause &c. (*be quiet*) 265.

wait, lie in wait, bide one's time, take time, tide it over.

cool –, kick- one's heels; loaf, while away the -time, – tedious hours; pass –, fill up –, beguile- the time; talk against time; waste time &c. (*inactive*) 683.

lie -by, – on the shelf, – in ordinary, – idle, – to, – fallow; keep quiet, slug; have nothing to do, whistle for want of thought; twiddle one's thumbs.

undo, do away with; take -down, – to pieces; destroy &c. 162.

**Adj.** not doing &c. *v.*; not done &c. *v.*; undone; passive; un-occupied, -employed; out of -employ, – work, – a job; fallow; *désœuvré.*

**Adv.** *re infectâ*, at a stand, *les bras croisés,* with folded arms; with the hands -in the pockets, – behind one's back; *pour passer le temps.*

**Int.** so let it be! stop! &c. 142; hands off!

**Phr.** nothing doing; *cunctando restituit rem.*

**682. Activity.—N.** activity; brisk-ness, liveliness &c. *adj.*; animation, life, vivacity, spirit, verve, dash, energy, go.

nimbleness, agility; smartness, quick-ness &c. *adj.*; velocity &c. 274; alacrity, promptitude; des-, dis-patch; expedi-tion; haste &c. 684; punctuality &c. (*early*) 132.

eagerness, zeal, ardour, *perfervidum ingenium*, *empressement*, earnestness, intentness; *abandon*; vigour &c. (*physi-cal energy*) 171; devotion &c. (*resolu-tion*) 604; exertion &c. 686.

industry, assiduity; assiduousness &c. *adj.*; sedulity; laboriousness; drudg-ery &c. (*labour*) 686; painstaking, diligence; perseverance &c. 604a; in-defatigation; habits of business.

vigilance &c. 459; wakefulness; sleep-, rest-lessness; *pervigilium*, *in-somnia*; racketing.

movement, bustle, hustle, stir, fuss, ado, bother, pottering; fidgets, -iness; flurry &c. (*haste*) 684.

officiousness; dabbling, meddling; inter-ference, -position, -meddling, but-ting in, intrusiveness; tampering with, intrigue.

press of business, no sinecure, plenty to do, many irons in the fire, great doings, busy hum of men, battle of life, thick of -things, – the action; the mad-ding crowd.

housewife, busy bee; new brooms; sharp fellow, blade; hustler, devotee, enthusiast, fan, zealot, fanatic; med-dler, intermeddler, intriguer, busybody, kibitzer, pickthank.

**V.** be -active &c. *adj.*; busy oneself in; stir, -about, – one's stumps; bestir –, rouse- oneself; speed, hasten, peg away, lay about one, bustle, fuss; raise –, kick up- a dust; push; make a -push, – fuss, – stir; go ahead, push forward; 'fight –, elbow- one's way; make prog-ress &c. 282; toil &c. (*labour*) 686; drudge, plod, persist &c. (*persevere*) 604a; keep -up the ball, – the pot boiling.

look sharp; have all one's eyes about one &c. (*vigilance*) 459; rise, arouse oneself, get up early, hustle, push; be about, keep moving, steal a march, kill two birds with one stone; seize the opportunity &c. 134: lose no time, not

**683. Inactivity.—N.** inactivity; in-action &c. 681; inertness, inertia &c. 172; obstinacy &c. 606.

lull &c. (*cessation*) 142; quiescence &c. 265; rust, -iness.

idle-, remiss-ness &c. *adj.*; sloth, indolence, indiligence; otiosity, daw-dling &c. *v.*

dullness &c. *adj.*; languor; segni-ty, -tude; lentor; sluggishness &c. (*slow-ness*) 275; procrastination &c. (*delay*) 133; torp-or, -idity, -escence; stupor &c. (*insensibility*) 823; somnolence; drowsiness &c. *adj.*; nodding &c. *v.*; oscit-ation, -ancy; pandiculation, hyp-notism, lethargy; heaviness, heavy eye-lids, sand in the eyes.

sleep, slumber; sound –, heavy –, balmy- sleep; Morpheus, dreamland; coma, trance, catalepsy, hypnosis, *ecstasis*, dream, hibernation, nap, doze, snooze, *siesta*, wink of sleep, forty winks, snore; Hypnology.

dull work; pottering; relaxation &c. (*loosening*) 47; Castle of Indolence.

[Cause of inactivity] lullaby, *ber-ceuse*; anæsthetic, sedative &c. 174; torpedo.

idler, drone, droil, dawdle, mopus; do-little, *fainéant*, dummy, sleeping partner; afternoon farmer; truant &c. (*runaway*) 623; lounger, *lazzarone*, floater, loafer, tramp, beggar, cadger; lub-ber, -bard; slow-coach &c. (*slow*) 275; opium –, lotus- eater; slug; lag-, slug-gard, lie-abed; slumberer, dor-mouse, marmot; waiter on Providence, *fruges consumere natus*.

**V.** be -inactive &c. *adj.*; do nothing &c. 681; move slowly &c. 275; let the grass grow under one's feet; take one's time, dawdle, poke, drawl, droil, lag, hang back, slouch, loll, -op; lounge, loaf, loiter; go to sleep over; sleep at one's post, *ne battre que d'une aile*.

take -it easy, – things as they come; lead an easy life, vegetate, swim with the stream, eat the bread of idleness; loll in the lap of -luxury, – indolence; waste –, consume –, kill –, lose- time; burn daylight, waste the precious hours.

idle –, trifle –, fritter –, fool- away time; spend –, take- time in; ped-, pid-dle' potter, putter, dabble, faddle.

lose a moment, make the most of one's
time, not suffer the grass to grow under
one's feet, improve the shining hour,
make short work of; dash off; make
haste &c. 684; do one's best, take
pains &c. (*exert oneself*) 686; do -,
work- wonders.

have -many irons in the fire, - one's
hands full, - much on one's hands;
have other -things to do, - fish to fry;
be busy; not have a moment -to spare,
- that one can call one's own.

have one's fling, run the round of;
go all lengths, stick at nothing, run riot.

outdo; over-do, -act, -lay, -shoot the
mark; make a toil of a pleasure.

have a hand in &c. (*act in*) 680; take
an active part, put in one's oar, have a
finger in the pie, mix oneself up with,
trouble one's head about, intrigue;
agitate.

tamper with, meddle, moil; inter-
meddle, -fere, -pose; obtrude; poke -,
thrust- one's nose in, butt in.

**Adj.** active; brisk, - as a lark, - as a
bee; lively, animated, vivacious; alive,
- and kicking; frisky, spirited, stirring.

nimble, - as a squirrel; agile; light-,
nimble-footed; featly, tripping.

quick, prompt, yare, instant, ready,
alert, spry, sharp, smart, slick, go-
ahead; fast &c. (*swift*) 274; quick as
a lamplighter, expeditious; awake,
broad awake; wide awake &c. (*intelli-
gent*) 498.

forward, eager, ardent, strenuous,
zealous, enterprising, pushing, in ear-
nest; resolute &c. 604.

industrious, assiduous, diligent, sedu-
lous, notable, painstaking; intent &c.
(*attention*) 457; indefatigable &c. (*per-
severing*) 604a; unwearied; unsleeping,
sleepless, never tired; plodding, hard-
working &c. 686; business-like, workaday.

bustling; restless, - as a hyæna; fussy, fidgety, pottering; busy,
- as a hen with one chicken.

working, labouring, at work, on duty, in harness; up in arms;
on one's legs, at call; up and -doing, - stirring.

busy, occupied; hard at -work, - it; up to one's ears in, full of
business, busy as a bee.

meddling &c. *v.*; meddlesome, pushing, officious, overofficious,
*intrigant.*

astir, stirring; a-going, -foot; on foot; in full swing; eventful; on
the alert &c. (*vigilant*) 459.

fribble, fiddle-faddle; dally, dilly-dally;

sleep, slumber, be asleep; hibernate;
oversleep; sleep like a -top, - log, -
dormouse; sleep -soundly, - heavily;
doze, drowze, snooze, nap; take a -nap
&c. *n.*; dream; snore; settle -, go -,
go off- to sleep; drop off; fall -, drop-
asleep; close -, seal up- -the -eyes, -
eyelids; weigh down the eyelids; get
sleepy, nod, yawn; go to bed, turn in.

languish, expend itself, flag, hang
fire; relax.

render -idle &c. *adj.*; sluggardize;
mitigate &c. 174.

**Adj.** inactive; motionless &c. 265;
unoccupied &c. (*doing nothing*) 681.

indolent, lazy, slothful, idle, otiose,
lusk, remiss, slack, inert, torpid, slug-
gish, languid, supine, heavy, dull,
leaden, lumpish; exanimate, soulless;
listless; dron-y, -ish; lazy as Ludlam's
dog.

dilatory, laggard; lagging &c. *v.*;
slow &c. 275; rusty, flagging; lacka-
daisical, maudlin, fiddle-faddle; potter-
ing &c. *v.*; shilly-shally &c. (*irresolute*)
605.

sleeping &c. *v.*; asleep; fast -, dead
-, sound- asleep; in a sound sleep;
sound as a top, dormant, comatose; in
the -arms, - lap- of Morpheus.

sleep-y, -ful; dozy, drowsy, somno-
lent, torpescent; lethargic, -al; heavy,
- with sleep; napping; somni-fic,
-ferous; sopor-ous, -ific, -iferous; hyp-
notic; balmy, dreamy; un-, una-wak-
ened.

sedative &c. 174.

**Adv.** inactively &c. *adj.*; at leisure
&c. 685.

**Phr.** the eyes begin to draw straws.

**Adv.** actively &c. *adj.*; with -life and spirit, – might and main &c. 686, – haste &c. 684, – wings; full tilt, *in mediis rebus.*

**Int.** be –, look- -alive, – sharp! move –, push- on! keep moving! go ahead! stir your stumps! *age quod agis!*

**Phr.** *carpe diem* &c. (*opportunity*) 134; *nulla dies sine lineâ; nec mora nec requies;* no sooner said than done &c. (*early*) 132; catch a weasel asleep.

**684. Haste.—N.** haste, urgency; des-, dis-patch; acceleration, spurt, spirt, forced march, rush, dash; velocity &c. 274; precipit-ancy, -ation, -ousness &c. *adj.*; impetuosity; *brusquerie;* hurry, scurry, scuttle, drive, scramble, push, hustle, bustle, fuss, fidgets, flurry, flutter, splutter.

**V.** haste, hasten; make -haste, – a dash &c. *n.*; hurry –, dash –, whip –, push –, press- -on, – forward; hurry, skurry, scuttle along, bundle on, dart to and fro, bustle, flutter, scramble; plunge, – headlong; run, race, speed; dash off; rush &c. (*violence*) 173.

bestir oneself &c. (*be active*) 682; lose -no time, – not a moment, – not an instant; make short work of; make the best of one's -time, – way.

be -precipitate &c. *adj.*; jump at; be in -haste, – a hurry &c. *n.*; have -no time, – not a moment- -to lose, – to spare; work -under pressure, – against time.

quicken &c. 274; accelerate, expedite, put on, precipitate, urge, whip, spur, flog, goad.

**Adj.** hasty, hurried, *brusque;* scrambling, cursory, precipitate, headlong, furious, boisterous, impetuous, hot-headed; feverish, fussy; pushing.

in -haste, – a hurry &c. *n.*; in -hot, – all- haste; breathless, pressed for time, hard pressed, urgent.

**Adv.** with -haste, – all haste, – breathless speed; in haste &c. *adj.*; apace &c. (*swiftly*) 274; amain; all at once &c. (*instantaneously*) 113; at short notice &c., immediately &c. (*early*) 132; posthaste; by -express, – telegraph, – wire, – wireless, – air mail.

hastily, precipitately &c. *adj.*; helter-skelter, hurry-skurry, holus-bolus; slap-dash, -bang; full-tilt, -drive; heels over head, head and shoulders, headlong, *à corps perdu.*

by -fits and starts, – spurts; hop, skip and jump.

**Phr.** *sauve qui peut,* devil take the hindmost, no time to be lost; no sooner said than done &c. (*early*) 132; a word and a blow.

**Int.** hurry up! look alive! get a move on! buck up! double march! rush! urgent!

**685. Leisure.—N.** leisure; spare -time, – hours, – moments; vacant hour; time, – to spare, – on one's hands; holiday &c. (*rest*) 687; *otium cum dignitate,* ease.

**V.** have -leisure &c. *n.*; take one's -time, – leisure, – ease; repose &c. 687; move slowly &c. 275; while away the time &c. (*inaction*) 681; be -master of one's time, – an idle man; *desipere in loco.*

**Adj.** leisurely; slow &c. 275; deliberate, quiet, calm, undisturbed; at -leisure, – one's ease, – a loose end.

**Phr.** time hanging heavy on one's hands.

---

**686. Exertion.—N.** exertion, effort, strain, tug, pull, stress, force, pressure, throw, stretch, struggle, spell, spurt, spirt; stroke –, stitch- of work.

**687. Repose.—N.** repose, rest, silken repose; sleep &c. 683.

relaxation, breathing time; halt, pause &c. (*cessation*) 142; respite.

'a strong pull, a long pull and a pull all together'; dead lift; heft; gymnastics, sports; exer-cise, -citation; wear and tear; ado; toil and trouble; uphill -, hard -, warm- work; harvest time.

labour, work, toil, travail, manual labour, sweat of one's brow, swink, operoseness, drudgery, slavery, fagging, hammering; *limæ labor.*

trouble, pains, duty; resolution &c. 604; energy &c. (*physical*) 171.

V. exert oneself; exert -, tax- one's energies; use exertion.

labour, work, toil, moil, sweat, fag, drudge, slave, drag a lengthened chain, wade through, strive, strain; make -, stretch- a long arm; pull, tug, ply; ply -, tug at- the oar; do the work; take the labouring oar.

bestir oneself (*be active*) 682; take trouble, trouble oneself.

work hard; rough it; put forth -one's strength, - a strong arm; fall to work, bend the bow; buckle to, set one's shoulder to the wheel &c. (*resolution*) 604; work like a -Briton, - horse, - carthorse, - galley-slave, - coalheaver; labour -, work- day and night; redouble one's efforts; do double duty; work double -hours, - tides; sit up, burn the -midnight oil, - candle at both ends; stick to &c. (*persevere*) 604a; work -, fight- one's way; lay about one, hammer at.

take pains; do one's -best, - level best, - utmost; do -the best one can, - all one can, - all in one's power, - as much as in one lies, - what lies in one's power; use one's -best, - utmost- endeavour; try one's -best, - utmost; play one's best card; put one's -best, - right- leg foremost; have one's whole soul in one's work, put all one's strength into; strain every nerve; spare no -efforts, - pains; go all lengths; go through fire and water &c. (*resolution*) 604; move heaven and earth, leave no stone unturned.

Adj. labouring &c. *v.*
laborious, operose, elaborate; strained; toil-, trouble-, burden-, weari-some; uphill; herculean, gymnastic, athletic, palestric.
hardworking, painstaking, strenuous, energetic.
hard at work, on the stretch.

Adv. laboriously &c. *adj.*; lustily; with -might and main, - all one's might, - a strong hand, - sledge-hammer, - much ado; to the best of one's abilities, *totis viribus, vi et armis, manibus pedibusque,* tooth and nail, *unguibus et rostro,* hammer and tongs, heart and soul; through thick and thin &c. (*perseverance*) 604a.
by the sweat of one's brow, *suo Marte.*

day of rest, *dies non,* Sabbath, Lord's day, holiday, red-letter day, vacation, recess.

V. repose; rest, - and be thankful; take -rest, - one's ease.

relax, unbend, slacken; take breath &c. (*refresh*) 689; rest upon one's oars; pause &c. (*cease*) 142; stay one's hand.

lie down; recline, - on a bed of down, - on an easy chair; go to -rest, - bed, - sleep &c. 683.

take a holiday, shut up shop; lie fallow &c. (*inaction*) 681.

Adj. reposing &c. *v.*; unstrained.
Adv. at rest.

---

688. Fatigue.—N. fatigue; weariness &c. 841; yawning, drowsiness &c. 683; lassitude, tiredness, fatigation, exhaustion; sweat.

anhelation, shortness of breath, panting; faintness; collapse, prostration.

689. Refreshment.—N. bracing &c. *v.*; recovery of -strength &c. 159; restoration, revival &c. 660; repair, refection, refocillation, refreshment, regalement, bait; relief &c. 834.

V. brace &c. (*strengthen*) 159; rein-

swoon, fainting, *deliquium,* syncope, lipothymy.

**V.** be -fatigued &c. *adj.;* yawn &c. (*get sleepy*) 683; droop, sink, flag; lose -breath, – wind; gasp, pant, puff, blow, drop, swoon, faint, succumb.

fatigue, tire, weary, bore, irk, fag, jade, harass, exhaust, knock up, wear out, prostrate.

tax, task, strain; over-task, -work, -burden, -tax, -strain.

**Adj.** fatigued &c. *v.;* weary &c. 841; drowsy &c. 683; drooping &c. *v.;* haggard; toil-, way-worn; footsore, surbated, weatherbeaten; faint; done -, used -, knocked- up; exhausted, prostrate, spent; over-tired, -spent, -fatigued; forspent; unre-freshed, -stored.

worn, – out; battered, shattered, pulled down, seedy, altered.

breath-, wind-less; short of –, out of -breath, – wind; blown, puffing and blowing; short-breathed; anhelous; broken-, short-winded.

ready to drop, more dead than alive, dog -tired, – weary, walked off one's legs, tired to death, on one's last legs, played out, *hors de combat.*

fatiguing &c. *v.;* tire-, irk-, weari-some; weary; trying.

vigorate; air, freshen up, refresh, recruit; repair &c. (*restore*) 660; fan, refocillate.

breathe, respire; draw –, take –, gather –, take a long –, regain –, re-cover- breath; get better, raise one's head; recover –, regain –, renew- one's strength &c. 159; perk up.

come to oneself &c. (*revive*) 660; feel like a giant refreshed.

**Adj.** refreshing &c. *v.;* recuperative &c. 660.

refreshed &c. *v.;* un-tired, -wearied.

---

**690. Agent.—N.** doer, actor, agent, performer, perpetrator, operator; execu-tor, -trix; practitioner, worker, stager.

bee, ant, working bee, labouring oar, shaft horse, servant –, maid- of all work, general servant, factotum.

workman, artisan; crafts-, handicrafts-man; mechanic, operative; working –, labouring- man; hewers of wood and drawers of water, labourer, navvy; hand, man, day labourer, journeyman, hack; mere -tool &c. 633; porter, docker, stevedore, beast of burden, drudge, fag.

maker, artificer, artist, wright, manufacturer, architect, contractor, builder, mason, bricklayer, smith, forger, Vulcan; black-, tin-smith; carpenter; ganger, platelayer.

machinist, mechanician, engineer, electrician, plumber, gasfitter &c.

semp-, sem-, seam-stress; needle-, char-, work-woman; tailor, cord-wainer.

minister &c. (*instrument*) 631; servant &c. 746; representative &c; (*commissioner*) 758, (*deputy*) 759.

co-worker, fellow-worker, party to, participator in, co-operator, col-league, associate, collaborator, *particeps criminis, dramatis personæ; personnel.*

**Phr.** '*quorum pars magna fui.*'

---

**691. Workshop.—N.** work-shop, -house; laboratory; manufactory, mill, factory, armoury, arsenal, mint, forge, loom; cabinet, studio, *bureau, atelier;* hive, – of industry; nursery; hot-house, -bed; kitchen, kitchenette; dock, -yard; slip, yard, wharf; found-ry, -ery; furnace; vineyard, orchard, farm, kitchen garden.

melting pot, crucible, alembic, caldron, mortar, *matrix.*

## 2°. *Complex Voluntary Action*

**692. Conduct.—N.** dealing, transaction &c. (*action*) 680; business &c. 625.

tactics, game, policy, polity; general-, statesman-, seaman-ship; strate-gy, -gics; plan &c. 626.

husbandry; house-keeping, -wifery; stewardship; *ménage*; regimen, *régime*; econom-y, -ics; political economy; management; government &c. (*direction*) 693.

execution, manipulation, treatment, campaign, career, life, course, walk, race.

conduct; behaviour; de-, com-portment; carriage, *maintien*, demeanour, guise, bearing, manner, mien, air, observance.

course -, line- of -conduct, - action, - proceeding; *rôle*; process, ways, practice, procedure, *modus operandi*; method &c., path &c. 627.

**V.** transact, execute; des-, dis-patch; proceed with, discharge; carry -on, - through, - out, - into effect; work out; go -, get- through; enact; put into practice; officiate &c. 625.

behave -, comport -, demean -, carry -, bear -, conduct -, acquit-oneself.

run a race, lead a life, play a game; take -, adopt- a course; steer -, shape- one's course; play one's- -part, - cards; shift for oneself; paddle one's own canoe.

conduct; manage &c. (*direct*) 693.

deal -, have to do- with; treat, handle a case; take -steps, - measures. **Adj.** conducting &c. *v.*; strategical, business-like, practical, economic, executive.

**693. Direction.—N.** direction; manage-ment, -ry; government, gubernation, conduct, legislation, regulation, guidance; steer-, pilot-age; reins, - of government; helm, rudder, controls, joy stick, needle, compass, binnacle; guiding -, load -, lode -, pole- star; cynosure.

super-vision, -intendence; *surveillance*, oversight; eye of the master; control, charge, auspices; board of control &c. (*council*) 696; command &c. (*authority*) 737.

premier-, senator-ship; director &c. 694; chair, seat, portfolio.

statesmanship; state-, king-craft.

minis-try, -tration; administration; steward-, proctor-ship; agency. **V.** direct, manage, govern, conduct; order, prescribe, cut out work for; head, lead; lead -, show- the way; take the lead, lead on; regulate, guide, steer, pilot; take -, be at- the helm; have -, handle -, hold -, take- the reins, handle the ribbons; drive, tool; tackle.

super-intend, -vise; overlook, control, keep in order, look after, see to, oversee, legislate for; administer, ministrate; patronize; have the -care, - charge- of; have -, take- the direction; pull the -strings, - wires; rule &c. (*command*) 737; have -, hold- -office, - the portfolio; preside, - at the board; take -, occupy -, be in- the chair; pull the stroke oar.

**Adj.** directing &c. *v.*; executive, supervisory, hegemonic.

**Adv.** at the -helm, - head of, in charge of; under the auspices of.

**694. Director.—N.** director, manager, governor, rector, comptroller; super-intendent, -visor; intendant; over-seer, -looker; foreman, boss, straw boss; supercargo, husband, inspector, visitor, ranger, surveyor, ædile, moderator, monitor, taskmaster; master &c. 745; leader, ring-leader, demagogue, corypheus, conductor, fugleman, precentor, bell-wether, agitator.

guiding star &c. (*guidance*) 693; adviser &c. 695; guide &c. (*information*) 527; pilot; helmsman; steers-man, -mate; man at the wheel; wire-puller.

driver, whip, Jehu, charioteer; coach-, car-, cab-man, jarvey; postilion, *vetturino*, muleteer, teamster; whipper in; engineer, engine driver, motorman, *chauffeur*.

head, – man; principal, president, speaker; chair, -man; captain &c. (*master*) 745; superior; dean; mayor &c. (*civil authority*) 745; vice-president, prime minister, premier, vizier, grand vizier; dictator.

officer, functionary, minister, official, red-tapist, bureaucrat; man –, Jack- in office; office-bearer; person in authority &c. 745.

statesman, strategist, legislator, lawgiver, politician, administrator, statist, statemonger; Minos, Draco; arbiter &c. (*judge*) 967; king maker, power behind the throne.

board &c. (*council*) 696.

secretary, – of state; Reis Effendi; vicar &c. (*deputy*) 759; steward, factor; agent &c. 758; bailiff, middleman; ganger, clerk of works; landreeve; factotum, major-domo, seneschal, housekeeper, shepherd, *croupier*; proctor, procurator, curator, librarian.

**Adv.** *ex officio.*

**695. Advice.—N.** advice, counsel, adhortation; word to the wise; suggestion, submonition, recommendation, advocacy, consultation.

exhortation &c. (*persuasion*) 615; expostulation &c. (*dissuasion*) 616; admonition &c. (*warning*) 668; guidance &c. (*direction*) 693.

instruction, charge, injunction.

adviser, prompter; counsel, -lor; monitor, mentor, Nestor, *magnus Apollo*, senator; teacher &c. 540.

guide, manual, chart &c. (*information*) 527.

physician, leech, archiater; arbiter &c. (*judge*) 967.

refer-ence, -ment; consultation, conference, parley, *pourparler* &c. 696.

**V.** advise, counsel; give -advice, – counsel, – a piece of advice; suggest, prompt, submonish, recommend, prescribe, advocate; exhort &c. (*persuade*) 615.

enjoin, enforce, charge, instruct, call; call upon &c. (*request*) 765; dictate.

expostulate &c. (*dissuade*) 616; admonish &c. (*warn*) 668.

advise with; lay heads –, consult- together; compare notes; hold a council, deliberate, be closeted with.

confer, consult, refer to, call in; take –, follow- advice; follow implicitly; be advised by, have at one's elbow, take one's cue from.

**Adj.** recommendatory; hortative &c. (*persuasive*) 615; dehortatory &c. (*dissuasive*) 616; admonitory &c. (*warning*) 668; consultative.

**Int.** go to!

**696. Council.—N.** council, committee, subcommittee, *comitia*, court, chamber, cabinet, board, bench, staff; consultation.

senate, *senatus*, parliament, House, – of Lords, – Peers, – Commons, legislature, legislative assembly, federal council, chamber of deputies, directory, *Reichsrath, rigsdag, cortes*, storthing, witenagemote, *junta*, divan, *musnud, sanhedrim*, Amphictyonic council; *duma, zemstvo, soviet, cheka, ogpu*; *Dail Eireann*; caput, consistory, chapter, syndicate; court of appeal &c. (*tribunal*) 966; board of -control, – works; vestry; county –, borough –, district –, parish –, town- council, local board.

cabinet -, privy- council, royal commission; cockpit, convocation, synod, congress, congregation, convention, diet, states-general, aulic council.

League of Nations, assembly, *caucus*, conclave, *clique*, conventicle; meeting, sitting, *séance*, conference, session, hearing, palaver, *pourparler*, *durbar*, pow-wow, house; *quorum.*

senator; member, – of parliament; councillor, M.P., representative of the people.

Adj. senatorial, curule, parliamentary.

**697. Precept.—N.** precept, direction, instruction, charge; prescript, -ion; *recipe*, receipt; golden rule; maxim &c. 496.

commandment, rule, ruling, canon, law, code, *corpus juris, lex scripta*, common -, unwritten -, canon-law; the Ten Commandments; act, statute, convention, rubric, stage direction, regulation; form, -ula, -ulary; technicality; nice point.

order &c. *(command)* 741.

**698. Skill.—N.** skill, skilfulness, address; dexter-ity, -ousness; adroitness, expertness &c. *adj.*; proficiency, competence, craft, callidity, facility, knack, trick, sleight; master-y, -ship; excellence, panurgy; ambidext-erity, -rousness; sleight of hand &c. *(deception)* 545.

sea-, air-, marks-, horse-manship; tight-, rope-dancing.

accomplish-, acquire-, attain-ment; art, science; techn-icality, -ology, -ique; practical -. technical- knowledge; technocracy; finish, technic.

knowledge of the world, world wisdom, *savoir-faire*; tact; mother wit &c. *(sagacity)* 498; discretion &c. *(caution)* 864; *finesse*; craftiness &c. *(cunning)* 702; management &c. *(conduct)* 692; *ars celare artem*; self-help.

cleverness, talent, ability, ingenuity, capacity, parts, talents, faculty, endowment, *forte*, turn, gift, genius, flair, feeling; intelligence &c. 498; sharpness, readiness &c. *(activity)* 682; invention &c. 515; apt-ness, -itude; turn -, capacity -, genius- for; felicity, capability, *curiosa felicitas*, qualification, habilitation.

proficient &c. 700.

masterpiece, *coup de maître, chef-d'œuvre, tour de force*; good stroke &c. *(plan)* 626.

**V.** be -skilful &c. *adj.*; excel in, be master of; have -a turn for &c. *n.*

know -what's what, – a hawk from a handsaw, – what one is about, – on

**699. Unskilfulness.—N.** unskilfulness &c. *adj.*; want of -skill &c. 698; incompeten-ce, -cy; in-ability, -felicity, -dexterity, -experience; clumsiness; disqualification, unproficiency; quackery.

folly, stupidity &c. 499; indiscretion &c. *(rashness)* 863; thoughtlessness &c. *(inattention)* 458, *(neglect)* 460.

mis-management, -conduct; im-policy; maladministration; mis-rule, -government, -application, -direction, -feasance.

absence of rule, rule of thumb; bungling &c. *v.*; failure &c. 732; screw loose; too many cooks.

blunder &c. *(mistake)* 495; *étourderie, gaucherie*, act of folly, *balourdise*; botch, -ery; bad job, sad work.

sprat sent out to catch a whale, much ado about nothing, wildgoose chase.

bungler &c. 701; fool &c. 501.

layman, amateur.

**V.** be -unskilful &c. *adj.*; not see an inch beyond one's nose; blunder, bungle, boggle, fumble, muff, botch, bitch, flounder, loppet, stumble, trip; hobble &c. 275; put one's foot in it; make a -mess, – hash, – sad work- of; overshoot the mark.

play -tricks with, – Puck; mismanage, -conduct, -direct, -apply, -send.

stultify -, make a fool of -, commit-oneself; act foolishly; play the fool; put oneself out of court; lose one's -head, – cunning.

begin at the wrong end; do things

which side one's bread is buttered, –
what's o'clock, – a thing or two; have
cut one's -eye, – wisdom- teeth.

see -one's way, – where the wind lies,
– which way the wind blows; have -all
one's wits about one, – one's hand in;
*savoir-vivre*; *scire quid valeant humeri
quid ferre recusent*.

look after the main chance; cut one's
coat according to one's cloth; live by
one's wits; exercise one's discretion,
feather the oar, sail near the wind;
stoop to conquer &c. (*cunning*) 702;
play one's -cards well, – best card; hit
the right nail on the head, put the
saddle on the right horse.

take advantage of, make the most
of; profit by &c. (*use*) 677; make a
hit &c. (*succeed*) 731; make a virtue of
necessity; make hay while the sun
shines &c. (*occasion*) 134.

**Adj.** skilful, dexterous, adroit, ex-
pert, apt, slick, handy, quick, deft,
ready, resourceful, gain; smart &c.
(*active*) 682; proficient, good at, up to,
at home in, master of, a good hand at,
*au fait*, thoroughbred, masterly, crack,
accomplished; conversant &c. (*know-
ing*) 490.

experienced, practised, skilled; up –,
well up- in; in -practice, – proper cue;
competent, efficient, qualified, capable,
fitted, fit for, up to the mark, trained,
initiated, prepared, primed, finished.

clever, able, ingenious, felicitous,
gifted, talented, endowed, cute, in-
ventive &c. 515; shrewd, sharp &c.
(*intelligent*) 498; cunning &c. 702; alive
to, up to snuff, not to be caught with
chaff; discreet.

neat-handed, fine-fingered, ambidex-
trous, sure-footed; cut out –, fitted-
for.

technical, artistic, scientific, dæda-
lian, shipshape; workman-, business-,
statesman-like.

**Adv.** skilfully &c. *adj.*; well &c. 618;
artistically; with -skill, – consummate
skill; *secundum artem*, *suo Marte*; to
the best of one's abilities &c. (*exertion*)
686; like a machine.

by halves &c. (*not complete*) 730; make
two bites of a cherry; play at cross
purposes; strain at a gnat and swallow
a camel &c. (*caprice*) 608; put the cart
before the horse; lock the stable door
when the horse is stolen &c. (*too late*)
135.

not know -what one is about, – one's
own interest, – on which side one's
bread is buttered; stand in one's own
light, quarrel with one's bread and
butter, throw a stone in one's own
garden, kill the goose which lays the
golden eggs, pay dear for one's whistle,
cut one's own throat, burn one's fingers;
knock –, run- one's head against a stone
wall; fall into a trap, catch a Tartar,
bring the house about one's ears; have
too many -eggs in one basket (*impru-
dent*) 863, – irons in the fire.

mistake &c. 495; take the shadow
for the substance &c. (*credulity*) 486;
be in the wrong box, aim at a pigeon
and kill a crow; take –, get- the wrong
sow by the ear, – the dirty end of the
stick; put -the saddle on the wrong
horse, – a square peg into a round
hole, – new wine into old bottles.

cut a whetstone with a razor; hold a
farthing candle to the sun &c. (*useless*)
645; fight with –, grasp at- a shadow;
catch at straws, lean on a broken reed,
reckon without one's host, pursue a
wildgoose chase; go on a fool's –,
sleeveless- errand; go further and fare
worse; loose –, miss- one's way; fail
&c. 732.

**Adj.** un-skilful &c. 698; unskilled,
inexpert; bungling &c. *v.*; awkward,
clumsy, unhandy, lubberly, *gauche*,
*maladroit*; left-, heavy-handed; slov-
enly, slatternly; gawky.

adrift, at fault.

in-, un-apt; inhabile; un-tractable,
-teachable; giddy &c. (*inattentive*) 458;
inconsiderate &c. (*neglectful*) 460; stu-
pid &c. 499; inactive &c. 683; incom-
petent; un-, dis-, ill-qualified; unfit;
quackish; raw, green, inexperienced,
rusty, out of practice.

un-accustomed, -used, -trained &c.
537, -initiated, -conversant &c. (*igno-
rant*) 491; shiftless; unbusinesslike,
unpractical; unstatesmanlike.

un-, ill-, mis-advised; ill-devised, -imagined, -judged, -contrived, -conducted; un-, mis-guided; misconducted, foolish, wild; infelicitous; penny wise and pound foolish &c. (*inconsistent*) 608.

**Phr.** one's fingers being all thumbs; the right hand forgets its cunning.

*il se noyerait dans une goutte d'eau.*

*incidit in Scyllam qui vult vitare Charybdim*; out of the frying pan into the fire.

**700. Proficient.—N.** proficient, expert, adept, dab; *connoisseur* &c. (*scholar*) 492; master, -hand; topsawyer, *prima donna*, first fiddle, *cordon bleu*; protagonist; past master; profess-or, -ional, specialist.

picked man; medallist, prizeman.

veteran; old -stager, – campaigner, – soldier, – file, – hand; man of -business, – the world.

nice –, good –, clean- hand; practised –, experienced- -eye, – hand; marksman; good –, dead –, crack- shot; rope-dancer, funambulist, acrobat, contortionist; cunning man; conjuror &c. (*deceiver*) 548; wizard &c. 994.

genius; master-mind, – head, – spirit; cunning –, sharp -blade, – fellow; jobber; cracksman &c. (*thief*) 792; politician, tactician, diplomat, -ist, strategist.

pantologist, admirable Crichton, Jack of all trades; prodigy of learning; walking encyclopædia; mine of information.

**701. Bungler.—N.** bungler; blunder-er, -head; marplot, fumbler, lubber, lout, oaf, duffer, stick, clown; bad –, poor- -hand, – shot; butter-fingers.

no conjuror, flat, muff, slow coach, looby, lubber, swab; clod, yokel, hick, awkward squad, novice, greenhorn, jaywalker, *blanc-bec*.

land lubber; fresh water –, fair weather- sailor; horse-marine; fish out of water, ass in lion's skin, jackdaw in peacock's feathers; quack &c. (*deceiver*) 548; Lord of Misrule.

sloven, slattern, trapes.

**Phr.** *il n'a pas inventé la poudre*; h will never set the Thames on fire.

**702. Cunning.—N.** cunning, craft; cunningness, craftiness &c. *adj.*; subtlety, artificiality; manœuvring &c. *v.*; temporization; circumvention.

chicane, -ry; sharp practice, knavery, jugglery; concealment &c. 528; nigger in the woodpile; guile, duplicity &c. (*falsehood*) 544; foul play.

diplomacy, politics; Machiavellism; jobbery, back-stairs influence, gerrymandering.

art, -ifice; device, machination; plot &c. (*plan*) 626; manœuvre, stratagem, dodge, artful dodge, wile; trick, -ery &c. (*deception*) 545; *ruse*, – *de guerre*; *finesse*, side-blow, thin end of the wedge, shift, go by, subterfuge, evasion; white lie &c. (*untruth*) 546; juggle, *tour de force*; tricks -of the trade, – upon travellers; imposture, deception; *espièglerie*; net, trap &c. 545.

Ulysses, Machiavel, sly boots, fox,

**703. Artlessness.—N.** artlessness &c. *adj.*; nature, simplicity; innocence &c. 946; *bonhomie, naïveté, abandon*, candour, sincerity; singleness of -purpose, – heart; honesty &c. 939; plain speaking; *épanchement*.

rough diamond, matter of fact man; *le palais de vérité*; *enfant terrible*.

**V.** be -artless &c. *adj.*; look one in the face; wear one's heart upon his sleeve for daws to peck at; think aloud; speak -out, – one's mind; be free with one, call a spade a spade.

**Adj.** artless, natural, pure, native, simple, plain, inartificial, untutored, unsophisticated, *ingénue*, unaffected, *naïve*; sincere, frank; open, – as day; candid, ingenuous, guileless, unsuspicious, childlike; honest &c. 939; innocent &c. 946; Arcadian; undesigning, straightforward, unreserved, unvarnished, above-board; simple-, single-

reynard; Scotch-, Yorkshire-man; Jew, Greek, Yankee; intriguer, *intrigant*, schemer, trickster.
V. be -cunning &c. *adj*.; have cut one's eye-teeth; contrive &c. *(plan)* 626; live by one's wits; manœuvre; intrigue, gerrymander, *finesse*, double, temporize, stoop to conquer, *reculer pour mieux sauter*, circumvent, steal a march upon; overreach &c. 545; throw off one's guard; surprise &c. 508; out-do, get the better of, snatch from under one's nose; snatch a verdict; waylay, undermine, introduce the thin end of the wedge; play -a deep game, – tricks with; have an axe to grind; *spargere voces in vulgum ambiguas*; flatter, make things pleasant.

Adj. cunning, crafty, artful; skilful &c. 698; subtle, feline, vulpine; cunning as a -fox, – serpent; deep, – laid; profound; designing, contriving; intriguing &c. *v*.; strategic, diplomatic, politic, Machiavellian, time-serving; artificial; trick-y, -sy; wily, sly, slim, insidious, stealthy, foxy; underhand &c. *(hidden)* 528; subdolous; deceitful &c. 545; double-tongued, -faced; shifty; crooked; arch, pawky, shrewd, acute; sharp, – as a needle; canny, astute, leery, knowing, up to snuff, too clever by half, not to be caught with chaff.

Adv. cunningly &c. *adj*.; slily, on the sly, by a side wind.
Phr. diamond cut diamond.

minded; frank-, open-, single-, simple-hearted; open and above-board.
free-, plain-, out-spoken; blunt, downright, direct, matter of fact, unpoetical; unflattering.
Adv. in plain -words, – English; without mincing the matter; not to mince the matter &c. *(affirmation)* 535.
Phr. *Davus sum non Œdipus*; *liberavi animam meam*.

Section IV. ANTAGONISM

1°. *Conditional Antagonism*

**704. Difficulty.**—N. difficulty; hardness &c. *adj*.; impracticability &c. *(impossibility)* 471; tough -, hard -, uphill- work; hard -, Herculean -, Augean- task; task of Sisyphus, Sisyphean labour, tough job, teaser, rasper, dead lift.
dilemma, embarrassment; perplexity &c. *(uncertainty)* 475; involvement; intricacy; entanglement &c. 59; cross fire; awkwardness, delicacy, ticklish card to play, deadlock, knot, Gordian knot, *dignus vindice nodus*, net, meshes, maze; coil &c. *(convolution)* 248; crooked path.
nice -, delicate -, subtle -, knotty-point; vexed question, *vexata quæstio* poser; puzzle &c. *(riddle)* 533; paradox; hard -, nut to crack; bone to pick, *crux*, *pons asinorum*, where the shoe pinches.
nonplus, quandary, strait, pass, pinch, pretty pass, stress, brunt; criti-

**705. Facility.** — N. facility, ease; easiness &c. *adj*.; capability; feasibility &c. *(practicability)* 470; flexibility, pliancy &c. 324; smoothness &c. 255; convenience.
plain -, smooth -, straight- sailing; mere child's play, holiday task.
smooth water, fair wind; smooth – royal- road; clear -coast, – stage; *tabula rasa*; full play &c. *(freedom)* 748.
disen-cumbrance, -tanglement; deoppilation; permission &c. 760.
V. be -easy &c. *adj*.; go on -, runsmoothly; have -full play &c. *n*.; go -, run- on all fours; obey the helm, work well.
flow -, swim -, drift -, go- with the-stream, – tide; see one's way; have -it all one's own way, – the game in one's own hands; walk over the course, win -at a canter, – hands down; make -light of, – nothing of; be at home in &c. *(skilful)* 698.

cal situation, crisis; trial, rub, emergency, exigency, scramble.

scrape, hobble, slough, quagmire, hot water, hornet's nest; sea -, peck- of troubles; pretty kettle of fish; pickle, stew, *imbroglio*, mess, muddle, botch, fuss, bustle, ado; false position; set fast, stand; dead -lock, - set; fix, horns of a dilemma, *cul de sac*; hitch; stumbling block &c. (*hindrance*) 706.

**V.** be -difficult &c. *adj.*; run one hard, go against the grain, try one's patience, put one out; put to one's -shifts, - wit's end; go hard with -, try- one; pose, perplex &c. (*uncertain*) 475; bother, nonplus, gravel, bring to a dead lock; be -impossible &c. 471; be in the way of &c. (*hinder*) 706.

meet with -, labour under -, get into -, plunge into -, struggle with -, contend with -, grapple with- difficulties; labour under a disadvantage; be -in difficulty &c. *adj.*

fish in troubled waters, buffet the waves, swim against the stream, scud under bare poles.

have -much ado with, - a hard time of it; come to the -push, - pinch; bear the brunt.

grope in the dark, lose one's way, weave a tangled web, walk among eggs.

get into a -scrape &c. *n.*; bring a hornet's nest about one's ears; be put to one's shifts; flounder, boggle, struggle; not know which way to turn &c. (*uncertain*) 475; get -tangled up, - wound up; *perdre son latin*; stick - at, - in the mud, - fast; come to a -stand, - dead lock; hold the wolf by the ears.

render -difficult &c. *adj.*; encumber, embarrass, ravel, entangle; put a spoke in the wheel &c. (*hinder*) 706; lead a pretty dance.

**Adj.** difficult, not easy, hard, tough; trouble-, toil-, irk-some; operose, laborious, onerous, arduous, Herculean, formidable; sooner -, more easily- said than done; difficult -, hard- to deal with; ill-conditioned, crabbed; not -to be handled with kid gloves, - made with rosewater.

awkward, unwieldy, unmanageable; intractable, stubborn &c. (*obstinate*) 606; perverse, refractory, plaguy, trying, thorny, rugged; knot-ted, -ty; invious; path-, track-less; labyrinthine &c. (*convoluted*) 248; intricate, complicated &c. (*tangled*) 59; impracticable &c. (*impossible*) 471; not -feasible &c. 470; desperate &c. (*hopeless*) 859.

embarrassing, perplexing &c. (*uncertain*) 475; delicate, ticklish,

render -easy &c. *adj.*; facilitate, smooth, ease; popularize; lighten, - the labour; free, clear; dis-encumber, -embarrass, -entangle, -engage; deobstruct, unclog, extricate, unravel; untie -, cut- the knot; disburden, unload, exonerate, emancipate, free from, deoppilate; humour &c. (*aid*) 707; lubricate &c. 332; relieve &c. 834.

leave -a hole to creep out of, - a loophole, - the matter open; give -the reins to, - full play, - full swing; make way for; open the -door to, - way; prepare -, smooth -, clear- the -ground, - way, - path, - road; pave the way, bridge over; permit &c. 760.

**Adj.** easy, facile; feasible &c. (*practicable*) 470; easily -managed, - accomplished; within reach, accessible, easy of access, for the million, open to.

manageable, wieldy; towardly, tractable; submissive; yielding, ductile; pliant &c. (*soft*) 324; glib, slippery; smooth &c. 255; on -friction wheels, - velvet; convenient.

un-, dis-burdened, -encumbered, -embarrassed; exonerated; un-loaded, -obstructed, -trammelled, - impeded, -restrained &c. (*free*) 748; at ease, light; at -, quite at- home; in -one's element, - smooth water.

**Adv.** easily &c. *adj.*; readily, smoothly, swimmingly, *ad lib.*, on easy terms, single-handed.

**Phr.** touch and go.

**Int.** all clear!

critical; beset with –, full of –, surrounded by –, entangled by –, encompassed with- difficulties.

under a difficulty; in -difficulty, – hot water, – the suds, – a cleft stick, – a fix, – the wrong box, – a scrape &c. *n.*, – deep water, – a fine pickle; *in extremis*; between -two stools, – Scylla and Charybdis; surrounded by -shoals, – breakers, – quicksands; at cross purposes; not out of the wood.

reduced to straits; hard –, sorely- pressed; run hard; pinched, put to it, straitened; hard -up, – put to it, – set; put to one's shifts; puzzled, at a loss &c. (*uncertain*) 475; at -the end of one's tether, – one's wit's end, – a nonplus, – a standstill; gravelled, nonplussed, stranded, aground; stuck –, set- fast; up a tree, at bay, *aux abois*, driven -into a corner, – from post to pillar, – to extremity, – to one's wit's end, – to the wall; *au bout de son latin*; out of one's -depth, – reckoning; put –, thrown -out.

accomplished with difficulty; hard-fought, -earned.

*Adv.* with -difficulty, – much ado; hardly &c. *adj.*; uphill; against the -stream, – grain; *à rebours*; *invitâ Minervâ*; in the teeth of; at –, upon- a pinch; at long odds.

*Phr.* ay there's the rub; *hic labor hoc opus*; things are come to a pretty pass.

## 2°. Active Antagonism

**706. Hindrance. — N.** prevention, preclusion, obstruction, stoppage; prohibition; inter-ruption, -ception, -clusion; hindrance, impedition; retardment, -ation; constriction; embarrassment, oppilation; coarctation, stricture, restriction; anchor &c. 666; restraint &c. 751 & 752; inhibition &c. 761; blockade &c. (*closure*) 261; picketing.

inter-ference, -position; obtrusion; dis-couragement, -countenance, -approval, -approbation; opposition &c. 708.

impediment, let, obstacle, obstruction, knot, knag; check, hitch, *contretemps*, *impasse*, screw loose, grit in the oil.

bar, stile, barrier; turn-stile, -pike; gate, portcullis; bulwark, parapet, barricade &c. (*defence*) 717; wall, dead wall, breakwater, groyne; bulkhead, block, buffer; stopper &c. 263; boom, dam, weir, burrock.

drawback, objection; stumbling-block, -stone; lion in the path; snag; snags and sawyers.

en-, in-cumbrance; clog, skid, shoe, spoke; brake, drag, – chain, – weight; stay, stop; preventive, prophylactic; contraception; load, burden, fardel,

**707. Aid.—N.** aid, -ance; assistance, help, opitulation, succour; support, lift, advance, furtherance, promotion; coadjuvancy &c. (*co-operation*) 709.

patronage, championship, countenance, favour, interest, advocacy, auspices.

sustentation, subvention, subsidy, bounty, alimentation, nutrition, nourishment, maintenance; manna in the wilderness; food &c. 298; means &c. 632.

ministr-y, -ation; subministration; accommodation.

relief, rescue; help at a dead lift; supernatural aid; *deus ex machinâ*.

supplies, reinforcements, succours, contingents, recruits; support &c. (*physical*) 215; adjunct, ally &c. (*helper*) 711.

**V.** aid, assist, help, succour, lend one's aid; come to the aid &c. *n.*- of; contribute, subscribe to; bring –, give –, furnish –, afford –, supply- -aid &c. *n.*; render assistance; give –, stretch –, lend –, bear –, hold out- a -hand, – helping hand; give one a -lift, – cast, – turn; take -by the hand, – in tow; help a lame dog over a stile, lend wings to.

*onus*, millstone round one's neck, *impedimenta*; dead weight; lumber, pack; nightmare, Ephialtes, incubus, old man of the sea; remora.

difficulty &c. 704; insuperable &c. 471- obstacle; estoppel; ill wind; head wind &c. (*opposition*) 708; trammel, tether &c. (*means of restraint*) 752; hold back, counterpoise; damper, wet blanket, hinderer, marplot, kill-joy, dog in the manger, interloper; trail of a red herring; opponent &c. 710.

**V.** hinder, impede, impedite, embarrass.

keep -, stave -, ward- off; picket; obviate; a-, ante-vert; turn aside, draw off, prevent, forefend, nip in the bud; retard, slacken, check, let; counter-act, -check; preclude, debar, foreclose, estop; inhibit &c. 761; shackle &c. (*restrain*) 751; restrict, restrain, cohibit.

obstruct, filibuster, stop, stay, bar, bolt, lock; block, - up; belay, barricade; block -, stop- the way; dam up &c. (*close*) 261; put on the -brake &c. *n.*; scotch -, lock -, put a spoke in- the wheel; put a stop to &c. 142; traverse, contravene; inter-rupt, -cept; oppose &c. 708; hedge -in, - round; cut off; interclude.

inter-pose, -fere, -meddle &c. 682.

cramp, hamper, clog, - the wheels; cumber; en-, in-cumber; handicap; choke; saddle -, load- with; over-load, -lay; lumber, trammel, tie one's hands, put to inconvenience; in-, discommode; discompose; hustle, drive into a corner; choke off.

run -, fall- foul of; cross the path of, break in upon.

thwart, frustrate, disconcert, balk, foil, baffle, snub, override, circumvent; defeat &c. 731; spike guns &c. (*render useless*) 645; spoil, mar, clip the wings of; cripple &c. (*injure*) 659; put an extinguisher on; damp; dishearten &c. (*dissuade*) 616; discountenance, throw cold water on, spoil sport; lay -, throw- a wet blanket on; cut the ground from under one, take the wind out of one's sails, undermine; be -, stand- in the way of; act as a drag; hang like a millstone round one's neck.

relieve, rescue; set -up, - agoing, - on one's legs; bear -, pull- through; give new life to, be the making of; reinforce, recruit; set -, put -, push-forward; give -a lift, - a shove, - an impulse- to; promote, further, forward, advance; speed, expedite, quicken, hasten.

support, sustain, uphold, prop, hold up, bolster.

cradle, nourish; nurture, nurse, dry nurse, suckle, put out to nurse; manure, cultivate, force; foster, cherish, foment; feed -, fan- the flame.

serve; do service to, tender to, pander to; ad-, sub-, minister to; tend, attend, wait on; take care of &c. 459; entertain; smooth the bed of death.

oblige, accommodate, consult the wishes of; humour, cheer, encourage.

second, stand by; back, - up; pay the piper, abet; work -, make interest -, stick up -, take up the cudgels- for; take up -, espouse -, adopt- the cause of; advocate, beat up for recruits, press into the service; squire, give moral support to, keep in countenance, countenance, patronize; lend -oneself, - one's countenance- to; smile -, shine-upon; favour, befriend, take up, take in hand, enlist under the banners of; side with &c. (*co-operate*) 709.

be of use to; subserve &c. (*instrument*) 631; benefit &c. 648; render a service &c. (*utility*) 644; conduce &c. (*tend*) 176.

**Adj.** aiding &c. *v.*; auxiliary, adjuvant, helpful; coadjuvant &c. 709; subservient, ministrant, ancillary, accessory, subsidiary.

at one's beck; friendly, amicable, favourable, propitious, well-disposed; neighbourly; obliging &c. (*benevolent*) 906.

**Adv.** with -, by- -the aid &c. *n.*- of; on -, in- behalf of; in -aid, - the service, - the name, - favour, - furtherance- of; on account of; for the sake of, on the part of; *non obstante*.

**Int.** help! save us! to the rescue! SOS! *à moi!*

**Adj.** hindering &c. *v.*; obstr-uctive, -uent; impedi-tive, -ent; intercipient; prophylactic &c. (*remedial*) 662.
in the way of, unfavourable; onerous, burdensome; cumb-rous, -ersome; obtrusive.
hindered &c. *v.*; wind-bound, water-logged, heavy laden; hard pressed.
unassisted &c. (*see* assist &c. 707); single-handed, alone; deserted &c. 624.

**708. Opposition.—N.** opposition, antagonism; oppug-nancy, -nation; impugnation; contravention; counteraction &c. 179; counterplot, obstacle.
cross-fire, under-current, head-wind.
clashing, collision, conflict, lack of harmony, contest.
competition, two of a trade, rivalry, emulation, race; war to the knife.
absence of -aid &c. 707; resistance &c. 719; restraint &c. 751; hindrance &c. 706.
**V.** oppose, counteract, run counter to; withstand &c. (*resist*) 719; control &c. (*restrain*) 751; hinder &c. 706; antagonize, oppugn, fly in the face of, go dead against, kick against, fall foul of; set -, pit- against; face, confront, cope with; make a -stand, - dead set- against; set -oneself, one's face- against; protest -, vote -, raise one's voice- against; disfavour, turn one's back upon; set at naught, slap in the face, slam the door in one's face.
be -, play- at cross purposes; counter-work, -mine; thwart, overthwart.
stem, breast, encounter; stem -, breast- the -tide, - current, - flood; buffet the waves; beat up -, make head- against; grapple with; kick against the pricks &c. (*resist*) 719; contend &c. 720 -, do battle &c. (*warfare*) 722- -with, - against.
contra-dict, -vene; belie; go -, run -, beat -, militate- against; come in conflict with.
emulate &c. (*compete*) 720; rival, spoil one's trade.
**Adj.** oppos-ing, -ed &c. *v.*; adverse, antagonistic; ambivalent; contrary &c. 14; at variance &c. 24; at issue, at war with; in opposition; 'agin the Government.'
un-favourable, -friendly; hostile, inimical, cross, unpropitious.

**709. Co-operation.—N.** co-operation; coadju-vancy, -tancy; coagency, co-efficiency; concert, concurrence, complicity, participation; union &c. 43; amalgamation, combination &c. 48; collusion.
association, alliance, colleagueship, jointstock, copartnership, trust, cartel, pool, ring, combine, interlocking directorate; confederation &c. (*party*) 712; federation, coalition, fusion; a long pull, a strong pull and a pull all together; log-rolling, Freemasonry.
unanimity &c. (*assent*) 488; *esprit de corps*, party spirit; clan-, partisan-ship; reciprocity, concord &c. 714.
**V.** co-operate, co-adjute, concur; conduce &c. 178; combine, cartelize, unite one's efforts; keep -, draw -, pull -, club -, hang -, hold -, league -, band -, be banded- together; stand -, put-shoulder to shoulder; act in concert, join forces, fraternize, cling to one another, conspire, concert, lay one's heads together; confederate, be in league with; collude, understand one another, play into the hands of, hunt in couples.
side -, take side -, go along -, go hand in hand -, join hands -, make common cause -, strike in -, unite -, join -, mix oneself up -, take part -, play along -, cast in one's lot- with; join -, enter into- partnership with; rally round, follow the lead of; come to, pass over to, come into the views of; be -, row -, sail- in the same boat; sail on the same tack.
be a party to, lend oneself to; participate; have a -hand in, - finger in the pie; take -, bear- part in; second &c. (*aid*) 707; take the part of, play the game of; espouse a -cause, - quarrel.
**Adj.** co-operating &c. *v.*; in -co-operation &c. *n.*, - league &c. (*party*) 712;

in hostile array, front to front, with crossed bayonets, at daggers drawn; up in arms; resistant &c. 719.

competitive, emulous.

Adv. against, *versus*, counter to, in conflict with, at cross purposes.

against the -grain, – current, – stream, – wind, – tide; with a head-wind; with the wind -ahead, – in one's teeth.

in spite, in despite, in defiance; in the -way, – teeth, – face- of; across; a-, over-thwart; where the shoe pinches.

though &c. 30; even; *quand même*; *per contra*.

Phr. *nitor in adversum*.

coadju-vant, -tant; hand and glove with.

favourable &c. 707- to; un-opposed &c. 708.

Adv. as one man &c. (*unanimously*) 488; shoulder to shoulder; in co-operation with.

___

**710. Opponent.—N.** opponent, antagonist, adversary; adverse party, opposition; enemy &c. 891; assailant.

oppositionist, obstructive; obscurantist; brawler, wrangler, brangler, disputant, extremist, irreconcilable, diehard, bitter-ender.

malcontent; Jacobin, Fenian &c. 742; demagogue, reactionist.

passive resister, conscientious objector.

rival, competitor, contestant.

___

**711. Auxiliary.—N.** auxiliary; recruit; assistant; adju-vant, -tant; adjunct; help, -er, -mate, -ing hand; midwife; colleague, partner, mate, *confrère*, co-operator; coadju-tor, -trix; collaborator.

ally; friend &c. 890, confidant, *fidus Achates*, pal, chum, buddy, *alter ego*.

confederate; ac-, complice; accessory, – after the fact; *particeps criminis*.

aide-de-camp, secretary, clerk, associate, marshal; right-hand; candle-, bottle-holder; hand-maid; servant &c. 746; puppet, cat's-paw, stooge, dependent, creature, jackal; tool, *âme damnée*; satellite, adherent, parasite.

votary, disciple; secta-rian, -ry; seconder, backer, upholder, supporter, abettor, advocate, partisan, champion, patron, friend at court, mediator.

friend in need, Jack at a pinch, *deus ex machinâ*, guardian angel, fairy godmother; special providence, tutelary genius.

**712. Party.—N.** party, faction, side, denomination, class, communion, set, crowd, crew, band, horde, posse, phalanx; regiment &c. 726; family, clan &c. 166.

Tories, Conservatives, Unionists, Whigs, Liberals, Radicals, Labour party, Socialists, Communists &c.; Republicans, Democrats, Farmer-Labor; *Fascisti*, Revolutionaries &c. 742.

community, body, fellowship, sodality, solidarity; con-, fraternity; sorority; brother-, sister-hood.

Freemasons, Knights Templars, Odd Fellows, Ku Klux Klan, Rosicrucians; knot, gang, *clique*, ring, circle; *coterie*, club, *casino*.

corporation, corporate body, guild; establishment, company; co-partnership; firm, house; joint concern, joint-stock company, trust, investment trust, combine &c. 709.

society, association; instit-ute, -ution; union; trade-union; league, syndicate, alliance, *Verein*, *Bund*, *Zollverein*, combination; league -, alliance- offensive and defensive; coalition; federation; confedera -tion, -cy; junto, cabal, *camarilla*, *Camorra*, *brigue*; Freemasonry; party spirit &c. (*co-operation*) 709.

staff; cast, *dramatis personæ.*

**V.** unite, join; club together &c. (*co-operate*) 709; cement –, form- a party &c. *n.*; associate &c. (*assemble*) 72.

**Adj.** in -league, – partnership, – alliance &c. *n.;* bonded –, banded –, linked &c. (*joined*) 43- together; embattled; confederated, federative, joint, corporate, leagued, fraternal, Masonic, cliquish.

**Adv.** hand in hand, side by side, shoulder to shoulder, *en masse*, in the same boat.

---

**713. Discord.—N.** disagreement &c. 24; dis-cord, -accord, -sidence, -sonance; jar, clash, shock; jarring, jostling &c. *v.*; screw loose.

variance, difference, dissension, misunderstanding, cross purposes, odds, *brouillerie*; division, split, rupture, disruption, division in the camp, house divided against itself, rift within the lute; disunion, breach; schism &c. (*dissent*) 489; feud, faction.

quarrel, dispute, rippet, spat, tiff, *tracasserie*, squabble, altercation, words, high words; wrangling &c. *v.*; jangle, brabble, cross questions and crooked answers, snip-snap; family jars.

polemics; litigation; strife &c. (*contention*) 720; warfare &c. 722; outbreak, open rupture; breaking off of negotiations, recall of ambassadors; declaration of war.

broil, brawl, row, racket, hubbub, rixation; embroilment, embranglement, *imbroglio, fracas*, breach of the peace, piece of work, scrimmage, rumpus; breeze, squall; riot, disturbance &c. (*disorder*) 59; commotion &c. (*agitation*) 315; bear garden, Donnybrook Fair.

subject of dispute, ground of quarrel, battle ground, disputed point; bone -of contention, – to pick; apple of discord, *casus belli*; question at issue &c. (*subject of inquiry*) 461; vexed question, *vexata quæstio*, brand of discord.

troublous times; cat-and-dog life; contentiousness &c. *adj.*; enmity &c. 889; hate &c. 898; Kilkenny cats; disputant &c. 710; strange bedfellows.

**V.** be -discordant &c. *adj.*; disagree, come amiss &c. 24; clash, jar, jostle, pull different ways, conflict, have no measures with, misunderstand one another; differ; dissent &c. 489; have a -bone to pick, – crow to pluck- with.

fall out, quarrel, dispute; litigate; controvert &c. (*deny*) 536;

---

**714. Concord.—N.** concord, accord, harmony, symphony, homology; agreement &c. 23; sympathy &c. (*love*) 897; response; union, unison, unity; bonds of harmony; peace &c. 721; unanimity &c. (*assent*) 488; league &c. 712; happy family.

*rapprochement*; *réunion*; amity &c; (*friendship*) 888; reciprocity; alliance, *entente cordiale*, good understanding, conciliation, arbitration, peacemaker &c. 724.

**V.** agree &c. 23; accord, harmonize with; fraternize; be -concordant &c; *adj.*; go hand in hand; blend –, tone in- with; run parallel &c. (*concur*) 178; understand one another; pull together &c. (*co-operate*) 709; put up one's horses together, sing in chorus.

side –, sympathize –, go –, chime in –, fall in- with; come round; be pacified &c. 723; assent &c. 488; enter into the -ideas, – feelings- of; reciprocate.

*hurler avec les loups*; go –, swim- with the stream.

pour oil on troubled waters, keep in good humour, render accordant, put in tune; come to an understanding, meet half-way; keep the –, remain at- peace;

**Adj.** concordant, congenial; agreeing &c. *v.*; in- accord &c. *n.*; harmonious, united, cemented; banded together &c; 712; allied; friendly &c. 888; fraternal; conciliatory; at one with; of one mind &c. (*assent*) 488.

at peace, in still water; tranquil &c; (*pacific*) 721.

**Adv.** with one voice &c. (*assent*) 488; in concert with, hand in hand; on one's side, unanimously.

---

squabble, wrangle, jangle, brangle, bicker, nag; spar &c. (*contend*) 720; have -words &c. *n.* with; fall foul of.

split; break -, break squares -, part company- with; declare war, try conclusions; join -, put in- issue; pick a quarrel, fasten a quarrel on; sow -, stir up- -dissension &c. *n.*; embroil, estrange, entangle, disunite, widen the breach; set -at odds, - together by the ears; set -, pit- against; rub up the wrong way.

get into hot water, fish in troubled waters, brawl; kick up a -row, - dust; turn the house out of window.

**Adj.** discordant; disagreeing &c. *v.*; out of tune, dissonant, inharmonious, harsh, grating, jangling, ajar, on bad terms; dissentient &c. 489; inconsistent, contradictory, incongruous, discrepant; un--reconciled, -pacified.

quarrelsome, unpacific; gladiatorial, controversial, polemic, disputatious; factious; liti-gious, -gant; pettifogging.

at odds, at loggerheads, at daggers drawn, at variance, at issue, at cross purposes, at sixes and sevens, at feud, at high words; up in arms, together by the ears, in hot water, embroiled.

torn, disunited.

**Phr.** *quot homines tot sententiæ*; no love lost between them, *non nostrum tantas componere lites.*

**715. Defiance.—N.** defiance; daring &c. *v.*; dare, challenge, *cartel*; threat &c. 909; war-cry, -whoop.

**V.** defy, dare, beard; brave &c. (*courage*) 861; bid defiance to; set at -defiance, - naught; hurl defiance at; dance the war dance; snap the fingers at, laugh to scorn; disobey &c. 742.

show -fight, - one's teeth, - a bold front; bluster, look big, stand akimbo; double -, shake- the fist; threaten &c. 909.

challenge, call out; throw -, fling- down the -gauntlet, - gage, - glove.

**Adj.** defiant; defying &c. *v.*; with arms akimbo; rebellious, insolent; reckless, greatly daring.

**Adv.** in -defiance, - the teeth- of; under one's very nose.

**Int.** do your worst! come if you dare! come on! marry come up! hoity toity!

**Phr.** *noli me tangere; nemo me impune lacessit.*

**716. Attack.—N.** attack; assault, - and battery; onset, onslaught, charge.

aggression, drive, offence; incursion, inroad, invasion; irruption; outbreak; *estrapade, ruade; coup de main,* sally, *sortie, camisade,* raid, foray; run -at, - against; dead set at.

storm, -ing; boarding, *escalade;* siege, investment, obsession, bombardment, cannonade; air raid.

fire, volley; platoon -, file -, rapid-fire; *fusillade;* sharp-shooting, sniping; broadside; raking -, cross -, machine gun- fire; volley of grapeshot, *feu d'enfer;* salvo.

cut, thrust, lunge, pass, *passado, carte* and *tierce,* home thrust; *coup de pied;* kick, punch &c. (*impulse*) 276.

**717. Defence.—N.** defence, protection. guard, ward; shielding &c. *v.*; propugnation; preservation &c. 670; guardianship.

self-defence, -preservation; resistance &c. 719.

safeguard &c. (*safety*) 664; screen &c. (*shelter*) 666, (*concealment*) 530; barrage; fortification; muni-tion, -ment; bulwark, fosse, moat, ditch, intrenchment, trench, dugout, gas mask; dike, dyke; parapet, parados, sunk fence, embankment, mound, mole, bank; earth- field-work, gabions; fence, wall, dead wall, contravallation; paling &c. (*inclosure*) 232; palisade, ha-ha, stockade, *stoccado, laager, sangar;* barri-er, -cade; boom; portcullis, *chevaux de*

*battue, razzia, Jacquerie, dragonnade;*
devastation &c. 162.

assailant, aggressor, invader.

base of operations, point of attack.

V. attack, assault, assail; set –, fall-
upon; charge, impugn, break a lance
with, enter the lists.

assume –, take- the offensive; be –,
become- the aggressor; strike the first
blow, fire the first shot, throw the first
stone at; lift a hand –, draw the sword-
against; take up the cudgels; advance
–, march- against; march upon, invade,
harry; come on, show fight.

strike at, poke at, thrust at; aim –,
deal- a blow at; give –, fetch- one a
-blow, – kick; have a -cut, – shot, –
fling, – shy- at; be down –, pounce-
upon; fall foul of, pitch into, launch
out against; bait, slap on the face;
make a -thrust, – pass, – set, – dead
set- at; dunt; bear down upon.

close with, come to close quarters,
bring to bay.

ride full tilt against; let fly at, dash
at, run a tilt at, rush at. tilt at, run
at, fly at, hawk at, have at, let out at;
make a -dash, – rush at; attack tooth
and nail; strike home; drive –, press-
one hard; be hard upon, run down,
strike at the root of.

lay about one, run amuck.

fire -upon, – at, – a shot at; shoot
at, pop at, level at, let off a gun at;
open fire, pepper, bombard, shell; pour
a broadside into; fire -a volley, – red-
hot shot; spring a mine.

throw -a stone, – stones- at; stone,
lapidate, pelt; hurl -at, – against, – at
the head of.

beset, besiege, beleaguer; lay siege
to, invest, open the trenches, plant a
battery, sap, mine; storm, board, scale
the walls.

cut and thrust, bayonet, butt; kick,
strike &c. (*impulse*) 276; whip &c.
(*punish*) 972.

**Adj.** attacking &c. *v.*; aggressive,
offensive, obsidional.

up in arms; on the warpath; over
the top.

**Adv.** on the offensive.

**Int.** 'up and at them!'

frise; aba-, abat-, abba-tis; *vallum*,
circumvallation, battlement, rampart,
scarp; e-, counter-scarp; glacis, case-
mate, obstacle.

mine, countermine.

buttress, abutment; shore &c. (*sup-
port*) 215.

breastwork, *banquette*, curtain, mant-
let, bastion, demilune, redan, ravelin;
advanced –, horn –, out- work, lunette;
barb-acan, -ican; redoubt; fort-elage,
-alice; lines; coast defence.

loop-hole, machicolation; sally-port,
postern gate.

hold, stronghold, fastness; asylum
&c. (*refuge*) 666; keep, donjon, fort-
ress, citadel; capitol, castle; tower, – of
strength; fort, barracoon, pah, sconce,
martello tower, peel-house, block-house,
rath; wooden walls; turret, barbette.

buffer, corner-stone, fender, apron,
mask, gauntlet, thimble, carapace,
armour, shield, buckler; target, targe,
ægis, breastplate, cuirass, plastron,
habergeon, mail, coat of mail, brigan-
dine, hauberk, lorication, helmet, helm,
basinet, sallet, salade, heaume, morion,
murrion, armet, cabaset, vizor, cas-
quetel, siege-cap, head-piece, casque,
steel helmet, tin hat; *Pickelhaube*,
csako; shako &c. (*dress*) 225; bearskin;
panoply; truncheon &c. (*weapon*) 727.

garrison, picket, piquet; defender,
protector; guardian &c. (*safety*) 664;
trabant, body guard, champion; knight-
errant, Paladin; propugner.

V. defend, forfend, fend; shield,
screen, shroud; fence round &c. (*cir-
cumscribe*) 229; fence, intrench; guard
&c. (*keep safe*) 664; guard against; take
care of &c. (*vigilance*) 459; bear harm-
less; keep –; ward –, beat- off; hinder
&c. 706.

parry, repel, propugn, put to flight;
give a warm reception to [*ironical*];
hold –, keep- at -bay, – arm's length.

stand –, act- on the defensive; show
fight; maintain –, stand- one's ground;
stand by; hold one's own; bear –,
stand- the brunt; fall back upon, hold,
stand in the gap.

**Adj.** defending &c. *v.*; defensive;
mural; armed, – at all points, – *cap-à-
pie*, – to the teeth; panoplied, accou-

tred, harnessed; iron-plated, -clad; loop-holed, castellated, machic-
olated, casemated; defended &c. *v.*; proof against, bomb-, bullet-
proof; protective.

Adv. defensively; on the -defence, – defensive; in defence; at
bay, *pro aris et focis.*

Int. no surrender! *ils ne passeront pas!*

Phr. defence not defiance.

**718. Retaliation. — N.** retaliation,
reprisal, retort; counter-stroke, -blast,
-plot, -project; retribution, *lex talionis*;
reciprocation &c. (*reciprocity*) 12.

requital, desert, tit for tat, give and
take, blow for blow, *quid pro quo*, a
Roland for an Oliver, measure for
measure, an eye for an eye, diamond
cut diamond, the biter bit, a game at
which two can play; boomerang.

recrimination &c. (*accusation*) 938;
revenge &c. 919; compensation &c. 30;
reaction &c. (*recoil*) 277.

**V.** retaliate, retort, turn upon; pay
-off, – back; pay in -one's own, – the
same- coin; cap; reciprocate &c. 148;
turn the tables upon, return the com-
pliment; give -a *quid pro quo* &c. *n.*,
– as much as one takes; give and take,
exchange -blows, – fisticuffs; be -quits,
– even- with; pay off old scores.

serve one right, be hoist on one's own
petard, throw a stone in one's own
garden, catch a Tartar.

**Adj.** retaliating &c. *v.*; retalia-tory,
-tive; retributive, recriminatory, re-
ciprocal.

Adv. in retaliation; *en revanche.*

Phr. *mutato nomine de te fabula nar-
ratur*; *par pari refero*; *tu quoque*; you're
another; *suo sibi gladio hunc jugulo.*

**719. Resistance. — N.** resistance,
stand, front, oppugnation; opposition
&c. 708; renitence, reluctation, recal-
citration, recalcitrance; repugnance;
kicking &c. *v.*

repulse, rebuff.

insurrection &c. (*disobedience*) 742;
strike; turn –, lock –, barring- out;
*levée en masse, Jacquerie*; riot &c. (*dis-
order*) 59.

**V.** resist; not -submit &c. 725; re-
pugn, reluctate, withstand; stand up
–, strive –, bear up –, be proof –, make
head- against; stand, – firm, – one's
ground, – the brunt of, – out; hold
-one's ground, – one's own, – out.

breast the -wave, – current; stem
the -tide, – torrent; face, confront,
grapple with; show a bold front &c.
(*courage*) 861; present a front; make
a –, take one's- stand.

kick, – against; recalcitrate, kick
against the pricks; oppose &c. 708;
fly in the face of; lift the hand against
&c. (*attack*) 716; rise up in arms &c.
(*war*) 722; strike, turn out; draw up a
round robin &c. (*remonstrate*) 932; re-
volt &c. (*disobey*) 742; make a riot.

*prendre le mors aux dents*; take the
bit between the teeth; sell one's life
dearly, die hard, keep at bay; repel
repulse.

**Adj.** resisting &c. *v.*; resist-ive, -ant; refractory &c. (*disobedient*)
742; recalcitrant, re-nitent, -pulsive, -pellant; up in arms.

proof against; unconquerable &c. (*strong*) 159; stubborn, uncon-
quered; indomitable &c. (*persevering*) 604a; unyielding &c. (*obsti-
nate*) 606.

Int. hands off! keep off!

**720. Contention. — N.** contention,
strife; contest, -ation; struggle; bel-
ligerency; opposition &c. 708.

controversy, polemics; debate &c.
(*discussion*) 476; war of words, logo-
machy, litigation; paper war, ink sling-
ing; high words &c. (*quarrel*) 713;
sparring &c. *v.*

**721. Peace.—N.** peace; amity &c.
(*friendship*) 888; harmony &c. (*con-
cord*) 714; tranquillity &c. (*quiescence*)
265; truce &c. (*pacification*) 723;
pacificism; pipe –, calumet- of peace.

piping time of peace, quiet life; neu-
trality.

**V.** be at peace; keep the peace &c.

competition, rivalry; corrival-ry, -ship; agonism, *concours*, match, race, horse-racing, heat, steeple chase, point-to-point race, handicap; boat race, regatta; field-day; sham fight, Derby day; turf, sporting, bull-fight, tauromachy, *gymkhana*, rodeo, Olympiad.

wrestling, *ju-jitsu*, pugilism, boxing, fisticuffs, spar, mill, set-to, scrap, round, bout, event; prize-fighting; quarter-staff, single stick; gladiatorship, gymnastics; athletic-s, – sports; games of skill &c. 840.

shindy; *fracas* &c. (*discord*) 713; clash of arms; tussle, scuffle, broil, fray; affray, -ment; velitation; col-, luctation; brabble, *brigue*, scramble, *mêlée*, scrimmage, stramash, bush-fighting.

free –, stand up –, hand to hand –, running- fight.

conflict, skirmish; ren-, en-counter; *rencontre*, collision, affair, brush, fight; battle, – royal; combat, action, engagement, joust, tournament; tilt, -ing; tourney, list; pitched battle, guerilla warfare.

death-struggle, struggle for life or death, Armageddon; hard knocks, sharp contest, tug of war.

naval -engagement, – battle; *naumachia*, sea-fight.

duel, -lo; single combat, monomachy, satisfaction, *passage d'armes*, passage of arms, affair of honour; triangular duel; hostile meeting, digladiation; appeal to arms &c. (*warfare*) 722.

deeds –, feats- of arms; pugnacity; combativeness &c. *adj.*; bone of contention &c. 713.

**V.** contend; contest, strive, struggle, scramble, wrestle; spar, square; exchange -blows, – fisticuffs; scrap, mix with, fib, justle, tussle, tilt, box, stave, fence; skirmish; fight &c. (*war*) 722; wrangle &c. (*quarrel*) 713.

contend &c. –, grapple –, engage –, close –, buckle –, bandy –, try conclusions –, have a brush &c. *n.* –, tilt- with; encounter, fall foul of, pitch into, clapperclaw, run a tilt at; oppose &c. 708; reluct.

join issue, come to blows, be at loggerheads, set-to, come to the scratch, exchange shots, measure swords, meet hand to hand; take up the -cudgels, – glove, – gauntlet; enter the lists; couch one's lance; give satisfaction; appeal to arms &c. (*warfare*) 722.

lay about one; break the peace.

compete –, cope –, vie –, race- with; outvie, emulate, rival; run a race; contend &c. –, stipulate –, stickle- for; insist upon, make a point of.

**Adj.** contending &c. *v.*; together by the ears, at loggerheads, at war, at issue.

competitive, rival; belligerent; contentious, combative, bellicose, unpeaceful; warlike &c. 722; quarrelsome &c. 901; pugnacious; pugilistic, gladiatorial; palestric, -al; irenic.

**Phr.** *a verbis ad verbera*; a word and a blow

(*concord*) 714; make peace &c. 723.

**Adj.** pacific; peace-able, -ful; calm, tranquil, untroubled, halcyon; bloodless; neutral.

**Phr.** the storm blown over; the lion lies down with the lamb.

---

**722. Warfare.—N** warfare; fighting &c. *v.*; hostilities; war, arms, the sword; Mars, Bellona, grim visaged war, *horrida bella*, Armageddon.

appeal to -arms, – the sword; ordeal

**723. Pacification.—N.** pacification, conciliation; reconcil-iation; -ement; shaking of hands, accommodation, arrangement, adjustment; terms, compromise; amnesty, deed of release.

–, wager- of battle; *ultima ratio regum*, arbitrament of the sword.

battle array, campaign, crusade, expedition; mobilization; state of siege; battle-field &c. (*arena*) 728; warpath.

art of war, tactics, strategy, castrametation; general-, soldier-ship; aerial–, submarine –, naval –, chemical- warfare; military evolutions, ballistics, gunnery; chivalry; poison gas; gunpowder, shot, – and shell.

battle, tug of war &c. (*contention*) 720; service, campaigning, active service, tented field; fiery cross, trumpet, clarion, bugle, pibroch, slogan; war-cry, -whoop; battle cry, beat of drum, rappel, tom-tom; word of command; pass-, watch-word.

war to the -death, – knife; *guerre à -mort, – outrance*; open –, internecine –, civil- war.

**V.** arm; raise –, mobilize- troops; rise up in arms; take up the cudgels &c. 720; take up –, fly to –, appeal to- -arms, – the sword; draw –, unsheathe- the sword; dig up the hatchet; go to –, declare –, wage –, let slip the dogs of- war; cry havoc; kindle –, light- the torch of war; raise one's banner, send round the fiery cross; hoist the black flag; throw –, fling- away the scabbard; enrol, enlist, join up; take the field; take the law into one's own hands; do –, give –, join –, engage in –, go to- battle; flesh one's sword; set to, fall to, engage, measure swords with, draw the trigger, cross swords; come to -blows, – close quarters; fight; combat; contend &c. 720; battle –, break a lance- with.

serve; see –, be on- -service, – active service; campaign; wield the sword, shoulder a musket, smell powder, be under the fire; spill –, imbrue the hands in- blood; be on the warpath.

carry on -war, – hostilities; keep the field; fight the good fight; go over the top; cut one's way through; fight -it out, – like devils, – one's way, – hand to hand; sell one's life dearly.

**Adj.** conten-ding, -tious &c. 720; armed, – to the teeth, – cap-à-pie, sword in hand; in –, under –, up in- arms; at war with; bristling with arms; in -battle array, – open arms, – the field; embattled.

unpacific, unpeaceful; belligerent, combative, armigerous, bellicose, martial, warlike; mili-tary, -tant; soldier-like, -ly; chivalrous; strategical, internecine.

**Adv.** *flagrante bello*, in the -thick of the fray, – cannon's mouth; at the -sword's point, – point of the bayonet.

**Int.** *væ victis!* to arms! to your tents O Israel!

**Phr.** the battle rages.

peace-offering; olive-branch; overtures; pipe –, calumet –, preliminaries- of peace.

truce, armistice; suspension of -arms, – hostilities; breathing-time; convention; *modus vivendi*; flag of truce, white flag, *parlementaire, cartel*.

hollow truce, *pax in bello*; drawn battle.

**V.** pacify, tranquillize, compose; allay &c. (*moderate*) 174; reconcile, propitiate, placate, conciliate, meet half-way, hold out the olive-branch, heal the breach, make peace, restore harmony, bring to terms.

settle –, arrange –, accommodate- -matters, – differences; set straight; make up a quarrel, *tantas componere lites*; come to -an understanding, – terms; bridge over, hush up; make -it, – matters- up; shake hands.

raise a siege; put up –, sheathe- the sword; bury the hatchet, lay down one's arms, turn swords into ploughshares; smoke the calumet of peace, close the temple of Janus; keep the peace &c. (*concord*) 714; be -pacified &c.; come round.

**Adj.** conciliatory, pacificatory; composing &c. *v.*; pacified &c. *v.*

**Phr.** *requiescat in pace*.

**724. Mediation.—N.** media-tion, -torship, -tization; inter-vention, -position, -ference, -meddling, -cession; parley, negotiation, arbitration; flag of truce &c. 723; good offices, peace-offering; diploma-tics, -cy; compromise &c. 774.

mediator, intercessor, peacemaker, make-peace, negotiator, go-between; diplomatist &c. (*consignee*) 758; moderator, propitiator, umpire, arbitrator.

**V.** media-te, -tize; inter-cede, -pose, -fere, -vene; step in, negotiate; meet half-way; arbitrate; *magnas componere lites.*

**Adj.** mediatory, propitiatory, diplomatic.

**725. Submission.—N.** submission, yielding, acquiescence, compliance; non-resistance; obedience &c. 743; submissiveness, deference.

surrender, cession, capitulation, resignation.

obeisance, homage, kneeling, genuflexion, courtesy, curtsy, *salaam*, *kowtow*, prostration.

**V.** succumb, submit, yield, bend, resign, defer to, accede.

lay down –, deliver up- one's arms; hand over one's sword; lower –, haul down –, strike- one's flag, – colours; deliver the keys of the city;

surrender, – at discretion; cede, capitulate, come to terms, retreat, beat a retreat; draw in one's horns &c. (*humility*) 879; give -way, – ground, – in, – up; cave in; suffer judgment by default; bend, – to one's yoke, – before the storm; reel back; bend –, knuckle- -down, – to, – under; knock under.

humble oneself; eat -dirt, – the leek, – humble pie; bite –, lick- the dust; be –, fall- at one's feet; craven; crouch before, throw oneself at the feet of; swallow the -leek, – pill; kiss the rod; turn the other cheek; *avaler des couleuvres*, gulp down.

obey &c. 743; kneel to, bow to, pay homage to, cringe to, truckle to; bend the -neck, – knee; kneel, fall on one's knees, bow submission, courtesy, curtsy, *kowtow*; make obeisance.

pocket the affront; make -the best of, – a virtue of necessity; grin and abide, shrug the shoulders, resign oneself; submit with a good grace &c. (*bear with*) 826.

**Adj.** surrendering &c. *v.*; submissive, resigned, crouching; down-trodden; down on one's marrow bones; on one's bended knee; weak-kneed, un-, non-resisting; pliant &c. (*soft*) 324; undefended.

untenable, indefensible; humble &c. 879.

**Phr.** have it your own way; it can't be helped; amen &c. (*assent*) 488.

**726. Combatant.—N.** combatant; disputant, controversialist, polemic, litigant, belligerent; competitor, rival, corrival; fighter, assailant, aggressor; champion, Paladin; moss-trooper, swashbuckler, fire-eater, duellist, bully, bludgeon-man, rough, fighter, fighting-man, prize-fighter, pugilist, pug, boxer, bruiser, the fancy, gladiator, athlete, wrestler; fighting-, game-cock; swordsman, *sabreur*.

warrior, soldier, Amazon, man-at-arms, armigerent; campaigner, veteran; red-coat, military man, *rajpoot*, brave.

armed force, troops, soldiery, military, forces, sabaoth, the army, standing army, regulars, the line, troops of the line, militia, territorials, yeomanry, volunteers, trainband, fencible; auxiliary –, reserve- forces, reserves, *posse comitatus*, national guard, *gendarme*, beefeater; guards, -man; yeoman of the guard, life guards, household troops.

janissary; myrmidon; Mama-, Mame-luke; spahee, *spahi*, Cossack,

Croat, Pandour; irregular, free lance, *franc-tireur, bashi-bazouk, guerilla, condottiere*; mercenary.

levy, draught, commando; *Land-wehr, -sturm*; conscript, recruit, rookie, cadet, raw levies.

private, – soldier; Tommy Atkins, rank and file, peon, trooper, doughboy, sepoy, *askari, légionnaire*, legionary, food for powder, cannon fodder; officer &c. (*commander*) 745; subaltern, ensign, shave-tail, standard bearer, non-com; spear-, pike-man; halberdier, lancer; musketeer, carabineer, rifleman, sharpshooter, yager, skirmisher; grenadier, fusileer; archer, bowman.

horse and foot; horse –, foot- soldier; cavalry, horse, artillery, horse –, field –, heavy –, mountain- artillery, infantry, light horse, *voltigeur, Uhlan*, mounted rifles, dragoon, hussar, trooper; light –, heavy-dragoon; heavy; *cuirassier*; gunner, cannoneer, bombardier, artilleryman, matross; sapper. – and miner; engineer; light infantry, rifles, *chasseur, zouave*; military train, supply and transport, coolie.

army, – corps, *corps d'armée*, host, division, column, wing, detachment, *escadrille*, garrison, flying column, brigade, regiment, *corps*, battalion, squadron, company, platoon, battery, subdivision, section, squad; piquet, picket, guard, rank, file; legion, phalanx, cohort; cloud of skirmishers; impi.

war-horse, charger, *destrier*.

armoured -train, – car; tank.

marine, man of war's man &c. (*sailor*) 269; navy, first line of defence, wooden walls; naval forces, fleet, flotilla, armada, squadron.

man-of-war, warship; H.M.S., U.S.S.; capital ship; line-of-battle ship, battle ship; super-, dreadnought, battle –, armoured –, protected – light- cruiser; scout, flotilla leader; destroyer, torpedo boat; submarine, submersible, U-boat; submarine chaser, eagle boat, mystery ship, Q-boat; mine-layer, -sweeper; ship of the line, iron-clad, turret-ship, ram, Monitor, floating battery; first-rate, frigate, sloop of war, corvette, gunboat, bomb-vessel, fire-boat; flag ship, guard ship, cruiser; aircraft carrier; privateer; tender; depot –, parent- ship; store –, troop- ship; transport, catamaran.

aircraft &c. 273, air force, scout, fighter, bomber, troop carrier, aerial patrol, seaplane, flying boat, torpedo plane; airship, Zeppelin; rigid –, semi-rigid –, non-rigid- airship; dirigible –, free –, captive –, kite –, observation- balloon.

anti-aircraft guns, searchlights, sound locators; catapult.

**727. Arms.**—N. arm, -s; weapon, deadly weapon; arma-ment, -ture; panoply, stand of arms; armour &c. (*defence*) 717; armoury &c. (*store*) 636.

ammunition; powder, – and shot; explosive; propellant; gun-powder, -cotton; dynam-, melin-, cord-, lydd-ite; trinitrotoluene, T.N.T., ammonal; cartridge; ball cartridge, *cartouche*, fire-ball; dud, black Maria; 'villainous saltpetre'; poison –, mustard –, lachrymatory –, tear- gas.

sword, sabre, broadsword, cutlass, falchion, scimitar, cimeter, brand, whinyard, bilbo, glaive, glave, rapier, skean, Toledo, Ferrara, tuck, claymore, creese, kris, *kukri*, dagger, dirk, hanger, poniard, stiletto, stylet, dudgeon, bayonet; sword-bayonet, -stick; side arms, foil, blade, steel; axe, bill; pole-, battle-axe; gisarm, halberd, partisan, tomahawk, bowie-knife; at-, att-, yat-aghan; yatachan; good –, trusty –, naked-sword; cold –, naked- steel.

club, mace, truncheon, staff, bludgeon, cudgel, life-preserver, shil-
lelagh, sprig; hand-, quarter-staff; bat, cane, stick, knuckle-duster,
sand bag.

gun, piece; fire-arms; artillery, ordnance; siege –, battering-train;
park, battery; cannon, gun of position, heavy –, siege –, field –, moun-
tain –, anti-aircraft –, breech loading –, quick firing- gun; field piece,
mortar, trench mortar, mine thrower, howitzer, carronade, culverin,
basilisk; falconet, jingal, swivel, *pederero, bouche à feu*; smooth bore,
rifled cannon; Armstrong –, Lancaster –, Paixhan –, Whitworth –,
Parrott –, Krupp –, Gatling –, Maxim –, Vickers –, Hotchkiss –,
Lewis –, machine- gun; tommy gun, Thompson submachine gun;
*mitrailleu-r, -se*; pom-pom; blow pipe.

small arms; musket, -ry, firelock, flintlock, fowling-piece, shot gun,
rifle, *fusil*, caliver, carbine, blunderbuss, musketoon, Brown Bess,
matchlock, harquebuss, *arquebuse*, haguebut; petronel; smallbore;
breech-, muzzle-loader; Miniè –, Enfield –, Westley Richards –, Snider –,
Springfield –, Martini-Henry –, Lee-Metford –, Lee-Enfield –, Mauser –,
Männlicher –, magazine –, repeating- rifle; needle-gun, *chassepot*; pis-
tol, -et; revolver, automatic pistol, automatic; wind-, air-gun; flame –,
gas-projector.

bow, cross-bow, arbalest, balister, catapult, sling; battering-ram &c:
(*impulse*) 276; gunnery; ballistics &c. (*propulsion*) 284.

missile, bolt, projectile, shot, pellet, ball; grape; grape –, canister –,
bar –, cannon –, langrel –, langrage –, round –, chain- shot; explosive;
incendiary –, expanding –, soft-nosed –, dum-dum- bullet; slug, stone,
brickbat; hand –, rifle- grenade; high explosive –, incendiary –, star –,
gas- shell; depth –, gas –, incendiary –, stink- bomb; petard, torpedo,
carcass, rocket; congreve, – rocket; shrapnel, *mitraille*; thunderbolt;
mine, land mine, infernal machine.

pike, lance, spear, spontoon, javelin, assagai, throwing stick, dart,
djerrid, arrow, reed, shaft, bolt, boomerang, harpoon, gaff.

**728. Arena.—N.** arena, field, platform; scene of action, theatre;
walk, course; hustings; stage, boards &c. (*playhouse*) 599; amphi-
theatre; Coli-, Colos-seum; Flavian amphitheatre, hippodrome, circus,
race-course, track, *stadium, corso*, turf, cockpit, bear-garden, play-
ground, playing fields, *gymnasium, palæstra*, ring, lists; tilt-yard, -ing
ground; *Campus Martius, Champ de Mars*; aerodrome, airport, air
base, flying field.

theatre –, seat- of war; battle-field, -ground; field of -battle, –
slaughter; no man's land; Aceldan.a, camp; the enemy's camp; trysting-
place &c. (*place of meeting*) 74.

## Section V. Results of Voluntary Action

**729. Completion.—N.** completion;
accomplish-, achieve-, fulfil-ment; per-
formance, execution; des-, dis-patch;
consummation, culmination, climax;
finish, conclusion, effectuation; close
&c. (*end*) 67; terminus &c. (*arrival*)
292; winding up; *finale, dénouement*,
catastrophe, issue, upshot, result; final
–, last –, crowning –, finishing- -touch,
– stroke; last finish, *coup de grâce*;

**730. Non-Completion.—N.** non-com-
pletion, -fulfilment; shortcoming &c.
304; incompleteness &c. 53; drawn
-battle, – game; work of Penelope, task
of Sisyphus.

non-performance, inexecution; neg-
lect &c. 460.

V. not -complete &c. 729; leave
-unfinished &c. *adj.*, – undone; neglect
&c. 460; let -alone, – slip; lose sight of.

crowning of the edifice; coping-, keystone; missing link &c. 53; superstructure, *ne plus ultra*, work done, *fait accompli*.

elaboration; finality; completeness &c. 52.

**V.** effect, -uate; accomplish, achieve, compass, consummate, hammer out; bring to -maturity, - perfection; perfect, complete; elaborate.

do, execute, make; go -, get- through; work out, enact; bring -about, - to bear, - to pass, - through, - to a head.

des-, dis-patch; knock -, finish -, polish- off; make short work of; dispose of, set at rest; perform, discharge, fulfil, realize; put in -practice, - force; carry -out, - into effect, - into execution; make good; be as good as one's word.

do thoroughly, not do by halves, go the whole hog; drive home; be in at the death &c. (*persevere*) 604a; carry through, play out, exhaust, deliver the goods, fill the bill.

finish, bring to a close &c. (*end*) 67; wind up, stamp, clinch, seal, set the seal on, put the seal to; give the -final touch &c. *n.* to; put the -last, - finishing- hand to; crown, - all; cap.

ripen, culminate; come to a -head, - crisis; come to its end; die -a natural death, - of old age; run -its course, - one's race; touch -, reach -, attain- the goal; reach &c. (*arrive*) 292; get in the harvest.

**Adj.** completing, final; conclu-ding, -sive; crowning &c. *v.*; exhaustive, complete, mature, perfect, consummate.

done, completed &c. *v.*; done for, sped, wrought out; highly wrought &c. (*preparation*) 673; thorough &c. 52; ripe &c. (*ready*) 673.

**Adv.** completely &c. (*thoroughly*) 52; to crown all, out of hand.

**Phr.** the race is run; *actum est*; *finis coronat opus*; *consummatum est*; *c'en est fait*; it is all over; the game is played out, the bubble has burst.

fall short of &c. 304; do things by halves; scotch the snake, not kill it; hang fire; be slow to; collapse &c. 304.

**Adj.** not completed &c. *v.*; incomplete &c. 53; uncompleted, unfinished, unaccomplished, unperformed, unexecuted; sketchy, addle.

in progress, in hand; going on, proceeding; on one's hands; on the fire; on the stocks; in preparation; lacking the finishing touch.

**Adv.** *re infectâ*.

---

**731. Success.**—**N.** success, -fulness; speed; advance &c. (*progress*) 282.

trump card; hit, stroke; lucky -, fortunate -, good- -hit, - stroke; bold -, master- stroke; *coup de maître*, checkmate; half the battle, prize; profit &c. (*acquisition*) 775; best seller.

continued success; good fortune &c. (*prosperity*) 734; time well spent.

advantage over; edge; upper-, whiphand; ascendancy, mastery; expugnation, conquest, victory, subdual; subjugation &c. (*subjection*) 749.

triumph &c. (*exultation*) 884; proficiency &c. (*skill*) 698; conqueror, victor, winner, champion; master of the -situation, - position.

**V.** succeed; be -successful &c. *adj.*;

**732. Failure.** — **N.** failure; nonsuccess, -fulfilment; dead failure, successlessness; abortion, miscarriage; *brutum fulmen* &c. 158; labour in vain &c. (*inutility*) 645; no go; inefficacy; inefficaciousness &c. *adj.*; vain -, ineffectual -, abortive- -attempt, - efforts; flash in the pan, 'lame and impotent conclusion'; frustration; slip 'twixt cup and lip &c. (*disappointment*) 509.

blunder &c. (*mistake*) 495; fault, omission, miss, oversight, slip, trip, stumble, claudication, footfall; false -, wrong- step; *faux pas*, titubation, *bévue*, *faute*, lurch; botchery &c. (*want of skill*) 699; scrape, jam, mess, muddle, foozle, *fiasco*, breakdown.

mishap &c. (*misfortune*) 735; split,

gain one's -end, - ends; crown with success.

gain -, attain -, carry -, secure -, win- -a point, - an object; put over; make a go of; manage to, contrive to; accomplish &c. (*effect, complete*) 729; do -, work- wonders.

come off -well, - successfully, - with flying colours; make short work of; take -, carry- by storm; bear away the bell; win -one's spurs, - the battle; win -, carry -, gain- the -day, - prize, - palm; climb on the bandwagon; have -the best of it, - it all one's own way, - the game in one's own hands, - the ball at one's feet, - one on the hip; walk over the course; carry all before one, remain in possession of the field; score a success, win hands down.

speed; make progress &c. (*advance*) 282; win -, make -, work -, find- one's way; strive to some purpose; prosper &c. 734; drive a roaring trade; make profit &c. (*acquire*) 775; reap -, gather- the -fruits, - benefit of, - harvest; make one's fortune, get in the harvest, turn to good account; turn to account &c. (*use*) 677.

triumph, be triumphant; gain -, obtain- -a victory, - an advantage; chain victory to one's car.

surmount -, overcome -, get over- -a difficulty, - an obstacle &c. 706; *se tirer d'affaire*; make head against; stem the -torrent, - tide, - current; weather -the storm, - a point; turn a corner, keep one's head above water, tide over; master; get -, have -, gain- the -better of, - best of, - upper hand, - ascendancy, - whip hand, - start of; distance; surpass &c. (*superiority*) 33.

defeat, conquer, vanquish, discomfit; over-come, throw, -power, -master, -match, -set, -ride, -reach; out-wit, -do, -flank, -manœuvre, -general, -vote; take the wind out of one's adversary's sails; beat, - hollow; rout, lick, drub, floor, worst; put -down, - to flight, - to the rout, - *hors de combat*, - out of court.

silence, quell, nonsuit, checkmate, upset, confound, nonplus, trump; baffle &c. (*hinder*) 706; circumvent, elude; trip up, - the heels of; drive

collapse, smash, blow, explosion.

repulse, rebuff, defeat, rout, over-throw, discomfiture; beating, drubbing; *quietus*, nonsuit, subjugation; check-, fool's-mate.

fall, downfall, ruin, perdition; wreck &c. (*destruction*) 162; death-blow; bankruptcy &c. (*non-payment*) 808.

losing game, *affaire flambée*.

victim, prey; bankrupt.

V. fail; be -unsuccessful &c. *adj.*; not -succeed &c. 731; make -vain efforts &c. *n.*; do -, labour -, toil- in vain; lose one's labour, take nothing by one's motion; bring to naught, make nothing of; wash a blackamoor white &c. (*impossible*) 471; roll the stone of Sisyphus &c. (*useless*) 645; do by halves &c. (*not complete*) 730; lose ground &c. (*recede*) 283; flunk; fall short of &c. 304.

miss, - one's aim, - the mark, - one's footing, - stays; slip, trip, stumble; make a -slip &c. *n.*, - blunder &c. 495, - mess of, - botch of; bitch it, mis-carry, abort, go up like a rocket and come down like the stick, reckon with-out one's host; get the wrong sow by the ear &c. (*blunder, mismanage*) 699.

limp, halt, hobble, titubate; fall, tumble; lose one's balance; fall -to the ground, - between two stools; flounder, falter, stick in the mud, run aground, split upon a rock; run -, knock -, dash- one's head against a stone wall; break one's back; break down, sink, drown, founder, have the ground cut from under one; get into -trouble, - a mess, - a scrape; come to grief &c. (*adversity*) 735; go to -the wall, - the dogs, - pot; lick -, bite- the dust; be -defeated &c. 731; have the worst of it, lose the day, come off second best, lose; fall a prey to; succumb &c. (*submit*) 725; not have a leg to stand on.

come to nothing, end in smoke; fall -to the ground, - through, - dead, - still-born, - flat; slip through one's fingers; hang -, miss- fire; flash in the pan, collapse; topple down &c. (*descent*) 305; go to wrack and ruin &c. (*destruction*) 162.

go amiss, go wrong, go cross, go hard with, go on a wrong tack; go on -,

-into a corner, – to the wall; run hard, put one's nose out of joint.

settle, do for; break the -neck of, – back of; capsize, sink, shipwreck, drown, swamp; subdue; subjugate &c. (*subject*) 749; reduce; make the enemy bite the dust; victimize, roll in the dust, trample under foot, put an extinguisher upon.

answer, – the purpose; avail, prevail, take effect, do, turn out well, work well, take, tell, bear fruit; hit -it, – the mark, – the right nail on the head; nick it; turn up trumps, make a hit; find one's account in.

**Adj.** succeeding &c. *v.*; successful; prosperous &c. 734; triumphant; flushed –, crowned- with success; victorious; set up; in the ascendant; unbeaten &c. (*see* beat &c. *v.*); well-spent; felicitous, effective, in full swing.

**Adv.** successfully &c. *adj.*; with flying colours, in triumph, swimmingly; *à merveille*, beyond all hope; to some –, good- purpose; to one's heart's content.

**Phr.** *veni vidi vici*, the day being one's own, one's star in the ascendant; *omne tulit punctum*.

come off –, turn out –, work- ill; take -a wrong, – an ugly- turn; gang agley; be all -over with, – up with; explode; dash one's hopes &c. (*disappoint*) 509; defeat the purpose; upset the apple cart; sow the wind and reap the whirlwind, jump out of the frying pan into the fire.

**Adj.** unsuccessful, successless; failing, tripping &c. *v.*; at fault; unfortunate &c. 735.

abortive, addle, still-born; fruitless, sterile, bootless; ineffect-ual, -ive; inefficient &c. (*impotent*) 158; inefficacious; lame, hobbling, *décousu*; insufficient &c. 640; unavailing &c. (*useless*) 645; of no effect.

aground, grounded, swamped, stranded, cast away, wrecked, foundered, capsized, shipwrecked, non-suited; foiled; defeated &c. 731; struck –, borne –, broken- down; down-trodden; over-borne, -whelmed; all up with; beaten to a frazzle.

lost, undone, ruined, broken; bankrupt &c. (*not paying*) 808; played out; done -up, – for; dead beat, ruined root and branch, *flambé*, knocked on the head; destroyed &c. 162.

frustrated, thwarted, crossed, unhinged, disconcerted, dashed; thrown -off one's balance, – on one's back, – on one's beam ends; unhorsed, in a sorry plight; hard hit.

stultified, befooled, dished, hoist on one's own petard; victimized, sacrificed.

wide of the mark &c. (*error*) 495; out of one's reckoning &c. (*inexpectation*) 508; left in the lurch; thrown away &c. (*wasted*) 638; unattained; uncompleted &c. 730.

**Adv.** unsuccessfully &c. *adj.*; to little or no purpose, in vain, *re infectâ*.

**Phr.** the bubble has burst, the game is up, all is lost; the devil to pay; *parturiunt montes* &c. (*disappointment*) 509.

---

**733. Trophy.—N.** trophy; medal, prize, palm; ribbon, blue ribbon, *cordon bleu*; citation; cup; laurel, -s; bays, crown, chaplet, wreath, civic crown; Victoria Cross, V.C., *Croix de Guerre*, Iron Cross; Distinguished Service Cross, Medal of Honor, Congressional Medal; insignia &c. 550; feather in one's cap &c. (*honour*) 873; decoration &c. 877; garland, triumphal arch.

triumph &c. (*celebration*) 883; flying colours &c. (*show*) 882.

*monumentum ære perennius.*

---

**734. Prosperity.—N.** prosperity, welfare, well-being; affluence &c. (*wealth*) 803; success &c. 731; thrift, roaring

**735. Adversity.—N.** adversity, evil &c. 619; failure &c. 732; bad –, ill –, evil –, adverse –, hard- -fortune, – hap,

trade; chicken in every pot, the full dinner pail; good -, smiles of- fortune; blessings, godsend.

luck; good -, run of- luck; sunshine; fair -weather, - wind; palmy -, bright -, halcyon- days; piping times, tide, flood, high tide.

*Saturnia regna*, Saturnian age; golden -time, - age; bed of roses; fat of the land, milk and honey, loaves and fishes, fleshpots of Egypt.

made man, lucky dog, *enfant gâté*, spoiled child of fortune.

upstart, *parvenu*, *nouveau riche*, profiteer, skipjack, mushroom.

V. prosper, thrive, flourish; be -prosperous &c. *adj.*; drive a roaring trade; go on -well, - smoothly, - swimmingly; sail before the wind, swim with the tide; run -smooth, - smoothly, - on all fours.

rise -, get on- in the world; work -, make- one's way; look up; lift -, raise- one's head, make one's -fortune, - pile, feather one's nest.

flower, blow, blossom, bloom, fructify, bear fruit, fatten, batten.

keep oneself afloat; keep -, hold- one's head above water; light -, fall- on one's -legs, - feet; drop into a good thing; bear a charmed life; bask in the sunshine; have a -good, - fine- time of it; have a run, - of luck; have the -good fortune &c. *n.* to; take a favourable turn; live -on the fat of the land, - in clover.

Adj. prosperous; thriving &c. *v.*; in a fair way, buoyant; well -off, - to do, - to do in the world; set up, at one's ease; rich &c. 803; in good case; in -full, - high- feather; fortunate, lucky, in luck; born -with a silver spoon in one's mouth; - under a lucky star; on the sunny side of the hedge.

auspicious, propitious, providential.

palmy, halcyon; agreeable &c. 829; *couleur de rose.*

Adv. prosperously &c. *adj.*; swimmingly; as good luck would have it; beyond all -expectation, - hope, - one's wildest dreams.

Phr. one's star in the ascendant, all for the best, one's course runs smooth.

- luck, - lot; frowns of fortune; evil -dispensation, - star, - genius; ups and downs of life, broken fortunes; hard -case, - lines, - life; sea -, peck- of troubles; hell upon earth; slough of despond; jinx.

trouble, humiliation, hardship, curse, blight, blast, load, pressure, plight.

pressure of the times, iron age, evil day, time out of joint; hard -, bad -, sad- times; rainy day, cloud, dark cloud, gathering clouds, ill wind; visitation, infliction; affliction &c. (*painfulness*) 830; bitter -pill, - cup; care, trial; the sport of fortune.

mis-hap, -chance, -adventure, -fortune; disaster, calamity, catastrophe; accident, casualty, cross, reverse, check, *contretemps*, rub, pinch, setback.

losing game; falling &c. *v.*; fall, down-fall, come-down; ruin-ation, -ousness; undoing; extremity; ruin &c. (*destruction*) 162.

V. be -ill off &c. *adj.*; go hard with; fall on evil, - days; go on ill; not -prosper &c. 734.

go -downhill, - to rack and ruin &c. (*destruction*) 162, - to the dogs; fall, - from one's high estate; decay, sink, decline, go down in the world; have seen better days; bring down one's grey hairs with sorrow to the grave; come to grief; be all -over, - up- with; bring a -wasp's, - hornet's- nest about one's ears.

Adj. unfortunate, unblest, unhappy, unlucky, im-, un-prosperous; luck-, hap-less; out of luck; in trouble, in a bad way, in an evil plight; under a cloud; clouded; ill -, badly- off; in adverse circumstances; poor &c. 804; behindhand, down in the world, decayed, undone; on the road to ruin, on its last legs, on the wane; in one's utmost need.

planet-struck, devoted; born -under an evil star, - with a wooden ladle in one's mouth; ill-fated, -starred, -omened; inconspicuous, ominous, doomed, unpropitious.

adverse, untoward; disastrous, calamitous, ruinous, dire, deplorable.

Adv. if the worst come to the worst, as ill luck would have it, from bad to worse, out of the frying pan into the fire.

Phr. one's star is on the wane; one's luck -turns, – fails; the game is up, one's doom is sealed, the ground crumbles under one's feet, *sic transit gloria mundi, tant va la cruche à l'eau qu'à la fin elle se casse.*

**736. Mediocrity.—N.** moderate –, average- circumstances; respectability; middle classes, *bourgeoisie*; mediocrity; golden mean &c. (*midcourse*) 628, (*moderation*) 174.

**V.** jog on; go –, get on- -fairly, – quietly, – peaceably, – tolerably, – respectably; steer a middle course &c. 628.

**Adj.** middling, so-so, fair, medium, moderate, mediocre, second-, third- &c. -rate.

## Division (II). INTERSOCIAL VOLITION*

### Section I. General Intersocial Volition

**737. Authority.—N.** authority; influence, patronage, power, preponderance, credit, *prestige*, prerogative, jurisdiction; right &c. (*title*) 924.

divine right, dynastic rights, authoritativeness; absolut-eness, -ism; despotism, tyranny; *jus nocendi.*

command, empire, sway, rule; domin-ion, -ation; sovereignty, supremacy, suzerainty; lord-, head-ship; chiefdom; seignior-y, -ity, hegemony, patriarchate, patriarchy; master-y, -ship, -dom; government &c. (*direction*) 693; dictation, control.

hold, grasp; grip, -e; reach; iron sway &c. (*severity*) 739; fangs, clutches, talons; rod of empire &c. (*sceptre*) 747.

reign, regnancy, *régime*, dynasty; director-, dictator-ship; protector-ate, -ship; caliphate, pashalic, electorate; presiden-cy, -tship; administration; pro-, consulship; prefecture; seneschalship; magistra-ture, -cy; raj.

empire; monarchy; king-hood, -ship; royalty, regality, autocracy, monocracy, arist-archy, -ocracy; oligarchy, democracy, demogogy; republic, -anism, federalism; socialism, collectivism; communism, bolshevism, syndicalism; mob law, mobocracy, ochlocracy, ergatocracy; *vox populi, imperium in imperio*; bureaucracy; beadle-, bumble-dom; stratocracy; martial law, military -power, – government; feodality, feudal system, feudalism.

Thearchy, dinarchy, diarchy; du-, tri-, heter-archy; du-, tri-umvirate; auto-cracy, -nomy; limited monarchy; constitutional -government, – monarchy; home rule, self-government, -determination; representative government; Soviet government.

**738. [Absence of authority.] Laxity. —N.** laxity; lax-, loose-, slack-ness; toleration &c. (*lenity*) 740; freedom &c. 748.

anarchy, interregnum; relaxation; loosening &c. *v.*; remission; dead letter, *brutum fulmen*, misrule; licence, licentiousness; insubordination &c. (*disobedience*) 742; lynch law &c. (*illegality*) 964; nihilism.

[Deprivation of power] dethronement, deposition, usurpation, abdication.

**V.** be -lax &c. *adj.*; *laisser -faire*, – *aller*; hold a loose rein; give -the reins to, – rope enough, – a loose to; tolerate; relax; misrule.

go beyond the length of one's tether; have one's -swing, – fling; act without -instructions, – authority; act on one's own responsibility, usurp authority.

dethrone, depose; abdicate.

**Adj.** lax, loose; slack; remiss &c. (*careless*) 460; weak.

relaxed; licensed; reinless, unbridled; anarchical; unauthorized &c. (*unwarranted*) 925.

* Implying the action of the will of one mind over the will of another.

gyn-archy, -ocracy, -æocracy; petticoat government, matri-archate, matriarchy.

[Vicarious authority] commission &c. 755; deputy &c. 759; per-mission &c. 760.

country, state, realm, commonwealth, canton, constituency, toparchy, municipality, polity, body politic, *posse comitatus.*

person in authority &c. (*master*) 745; judicature &c. 965; cabinet &c. (*council*) 696; usurper; seat of -government, – authority; headquarters.

[Acquisition of authority] accession; installation &c. 755; usur-pation.

**V.** authorize &c. (*permit*) 760; warrant &c. (*right*) 924; dictate &c. (*order*) 741; have –, hold –, possess –, exercise –, exert –, wield--authority &c. *n.*

be -at the head of &c. *adj.*; hold –, be in –, fill an- office; hold –, occupy- a post; be -master &c. 745.

rule, sway, command, control, administer; govern &c. (*direct*) 693; lead, preside over, reign; possess –, be seated on –, occupy-the throne; sway –, wield- the sceptre; wear the crown.

have –, get- the -upper, – whip- hand; gain a hold upon, pre-ponderate, dominate, boss, rule the roost; over-ride, -rule, -awe; lord it over, hold in hand, keep under, make a puppet of, lead by the nose, hold in the hollow of one's hand, turn round one's little finger, bend to one's will, hold one's own, wear the breeches; have -the ball at one's feet, – it all one's own way, – the game in one's own hand, – on the hip, – under one's thumb; be master of the situation; take the lead, play first fiddle, set the fashion; give the law to; carry with a high hand; lay down the law; 'ride in the whirl-wind and direct the storm'; rule with a rod of iron &c. (*severity*) 739.

ascend –, mount- the throne, take the reins, – into one's hand; assume -authority &c. *n.*, – the reins of government; take –, assume the- command.

be -governed by, – in the power of; be under -the rule of, – the domination of.

**Adj.** ruling &c. *v.*; regnant, at the head, dominant, paramount, supreme, predominant, preponderant, in the ascendant, influential; gubernatorial; imperious; authoritative, executive, administrative, clothed with authority, official, *ex officio*, ministerial, bureaucratic, departmental, imperative, peremptory, overruling, absolute; hege-monic, -al; arbitrary; compulsory &c. 744; stringent.

regal, sovereign; royal, -ist; monarchical, kingly; imperial, -istic; princely; feudal; aristo-, auto-cratic; oligarchic &c. *n.*; democratic, republican, dynastic.

at one's command; in one's -power, – grasp; under control; authorized &c. (*due*) 924.

**Adv.** in the name of, by the authority of, *de par le Roi*, in virtue of; under the auspices of, in the hands of.

at one's pleasure; by a -dash, – stroke- of the pen; *ex mero motu*; *ex cathedrâ.*

**Phr.** the grey mare the better horse; 'every inch a king.'

---

**739. Severity.—N.** severity; strict-ness, formalism, harshness &c. *adj.*; rigour, stringency, austerity; inclem-

**740. Lenity. — N.** leni-ty, -ence, -ency; moderation &c. 174; toler-ance, -ation; mildness, gentleness; favour;

ency &c. (*pitilessness*) 914a; arrogance &c. 885.

arbitrary power; absolut-, despotism; dictatorship, autocracy, tyranny, domineering, oppression; assumption, usurpation; inquisition, reign of terror, martial law; iron -heel, – rule, – hand, – sway; tight grasp; brute -force, – strength; coercion &c. 744; strong –, tight- hand.

hard -lines, – measure; tender mercies [ironical]; sharp practice; bureaucracy, red tape; pipe-clay, officialism.

tyrant, disciplinarian, martinet, stickler, formalist, bashaw, despot, hard master, Draco, oppressor, inquisitor, extortioner, harpy, vulture, bird of prey.

indulgen-ce, -cy; clemency, mercy, forbearance, quarter; compassion &c. 914.

V. be -lenient &c. *adj.*; tolerate, bear with; *parcere subjectis*, give quarter.

indulge, allow one to have his own way, spoil.

Adj. lenient; mild, – as milk; gentle, soft; tolerant, indulgent, easy-going; clement &c. (*compassionate*) 914; forbearing; complaisant, long-suffering.

V. be -severe &c. *adj.*

assume, usurp, arrogate, take liberties; domineer, bully &c. 885; tyrannize, inflict, wreak, stretch a point, put on the screw; be hard upon; bear –, lay- a heavy hand on; be –, come- down upon; illtreat; deal -hardly with, – hard measure to; rule with a rod of iron, chastise with scorpions; dye with blood; oppress, override; trample -, tread- -down, – upon, – under foot; crush under an iron heel, ride roughshod over; rivet the yoke; hold –, keep- a tight hand; force down the throat; coerce &c. 744; give no quarter &c. (*pitiless*) 914a.

Adj. severe; strict, hard, harsh, dour, rigid, stiff, stern, rigorous, uncompromising, exacting, exigent, *exigeant*, inexorable, inflexible, obdurate, austere, relentless, Spartan, Draconian, stringent, straitlaced, puritanical, prudish, searching, unsparing, ironhanded, hardheaded, peremptory, absolute, positive, arbitrary, imperative; coercive &c. 744; tyrannical, despotic, masterful, extortionate, grinding, withering, oppressive, inquisitorial; inclement &c. (*ruthless*) 914a; cruel &c. (*malevolent*) 907; haughty, arrogant &c. 885.

Adv. severely &c. *adj.*; with a -high, – strong, – tight, – heavy-hand.

at the point of the -sword, – bayonet.

Phr. *Delirant reges plectuntur Achivi.*

741. Command.—N. command, order, ordinance, act, *fiat*, bidding, *dictum*, hest, behest, call, beck, nod.

des-, dis-patch; message, direction, injunction, charge, instructions; appointment, fixture.

demand, exaction, imposition, requisition, claim, reclamation, revendication; *ultimatum* &c. (*terms*) 770; request &c. 765; requirement.

dictation; dict-, mand-ate; *caveat*, decree, decree -nisi, – absolute, *senatus consultum*; precept; pre-, re-script; writ, ordination, bull, edict, decretal, dispensation, prescription, brevet, placet, ukase, *firman*, hattisheriff, warrant, passport, *mittimus*, *mandamus*, summons; subpœna, –*duces tecum*, *nisi prius*, interpellation, citation; word, – of command; *mot d'ordre*; bugle –, trumpet- call; beat of drum, tattoo; order of the day; enactment &c. (*law*) 963; *plébiscite* &c. (*choice*) 609.

V. command, order, decree, enact, ordain, dictate, direct, give orders.

prescribe, set, appoint, mark out; set –, prescribe –, impose- a task; set to work, put in requisition &c. 926.

bid, enjoin, charge, call upon, instruct; require, – at the hands of; exact, impose, tax, task; demand; insist on &c. (*compel*) 744.

claim, lay claim to, revendicate, reclaim.

cite, summon; call –, send- for; subpœna; beckon.

issue a command; make –, issue –, promulgate- -a requisition, – a decree, – an order &c. *n*.; give the -word of command, – word, – signal; call to order; give –, lay down- the law; assume the command &c. (*authority*) 737; remand.

be -ordered &c.; receive an order &c. *n*.

Adj. commanding &c. *v*.; authoritative &c. 737; decret-ory, -ive, -al; imperative, jussive, decisive, final.

Adv. in a commanding tone; by a -stroke, – dash- of the pen; by order, at beat of drum, on the first summons; at the word of command.

Phr. the decree is gone forth; *sic volo sic jubeo*; *le Roi le veut*.

---

**742. Disobedience.—N.** disobedience, insubordination, contumacy; infraction, -fringement; violation, non-compliance; non-observance &c. 773.

revolt, rebellion, mutiny, outbreak, rising, uprising, putsch, insurrection, *émeute*; riot, tumult &c. (*disorder*) 59; strike &c. (*resistance*) 719; barring out; defiance &c. 715.

mutinousness &c. *adj*.; mutineering; sedition, treason; high –, petty –, misprision of- treason; *premunire*; *lèse-majesté*; violation of law &c. 964; defection, secession, revolution, *sabotage*, bolshevism, *Sinn Fein*.

insurgent, mutineer, rebel, revolter, rioter, traitor, *carbonaro*, *sansculottes*, red republican, communist, Fenian, chartist, *frondeur*; seceder, runagate, brawler, anarchist, demagogue; suffragette; Spartacus, Masaniello, Wat Tyler, Jack Cade; bolshevist, bolshevik, maximalist, ringleader.

V. disobey, violate, infringe; shirk; set at defiance &c. (*defy*) 715; set authority at naught, run riot, fly in the face of, bolt, take the law into one's own hands; kick over the traces.

turn –, run- restive; champ the bit; strike &c. (*resist*) 719; rise, – in arms; secede; mutiny, rebel.

Adj. disobedient; uncompl-ying, -iant; unsubmissive, unruly, ungovernable; insubordinate, impatient of control; rest-iff, -ive; refractory, contumacious; recusant &c. (refuse) 764; recalcitrant; resisting &c. 719; lawless, mutinous, seditious, insurgent, riotous, revolutionary.

disobeyed, unobeyed; unbidden.

**743. Obedience.—N.** obedience; observance &c. 772; compliance; submission &c. 725; subjection &c. 749; non-resistance; passiveness, passivity, resignation.

allegiance, loyalty, fealty, homage, deference, devotion, fidelity, constancy.

submiss-ness, -iveness; ductility &c. (*softness*) 324; obsequiousness &c. (*servility*) 886.

V. be -obedient &c. *adj*.; obey, bear obedience to; submit &c. 725; comply, answer the helm, come at one's call; do -one's bidding, – what one is told, – suit and service; attend to orders, serve -devotedly, – loyally, – faithfully.

follow, – the lead of, – to the world's end; serve &c. 746; play second fiddle.

Adj. obedient; compl-ying, -iant; law-abiding, loyal, faithful, leal, devoted; at one's -call, – command, – orders, – beck and call; under -beck and call, – control.

restrainable; resigned, passive; submissive &c. 725; henpecked; pliant &c. (*soft*) 324.

unresist-ed, -ing.

Adv. obediently &c. *adj*.; in compliance with, in obedience to.

Phr. to hear is to obey; as –, if- you please; at your service.

**744. Compulsion.—N.** compulsion, coercion, coaction, constraint, eminent domain, duress, enforcement, press, conscription.

force; brute –, main –, physical- force; the sword, *ultima ratio*; club –, mob –, lynch- law; *argumentum ad baculum, le droit du plus fort,* martial law.

restraint &c. 751; necessity &c. 601; *force majeure*; Hobson's choice; the spur of necessity.

**V.** compel, force, make, drive, coerce, constrain, enforce, necessitate, oblige.

force upon, press; cram –, thrust –, force- down the throat; say it must be done, make a point of, insist upon, take no denial; put down, dragoon.

extort, wring from; put –, turn- on the screw; drag into; bind, – over; pin –, tie- down; require, tax, put in force; commandeer; restrain &c. 751.

**Adj.** compelling &c. *v.*; coercive, coactive; inexorable &c. 739; compuls-ory, -atory; obligatory, stringent, peremptory, binding.

forcible, not to be trifled with; irresistible &c. 601; compelled &c. *v.*; fain to.

**Adv.** by -force &c. *n.*, – force of arms; on compulsion, perforce; *vi et armis,* under the lash; at the point of the -sword, – bayonet; forcibly; by a strong arm.

under protest, in spite of one's teeth; against one's will &c. 603; *nolens volens* &c. (*of necessity*) 601; by stress of -circumstances, – weather; under press of; *de rigueur.*

**745. Master.—N.** master, *padrone*; lord, – paramount; command-er, -ant; captain; chief, -tain; *sahib,* sirdar, sachem, sheik, head, senior, governor, *duce,* ruler, dictator; leader &c. (*director*) 694.

lord of the ascendant; cock of the -walk, – roost; grey mare; mistress.

potentate; liege, – lord; suzerain, sovereign, monarch, autocrat, despot, tyrant, oligarch, overlord.

crowned head, emperor, king, anointed king, majesty, *imperator,* protector, president, stadtholder, judge.

cæsar, kaiser, czar, sultan, grand Turk, caliph, imaum, shah, padishah, sophi, mogul, great mogul, khan, cham; lama, tycoon, mikado, inca, cazique; domn; vaivode; wai-, way-wode; landamman; seyyid, cacique.

prince, duke &c. (*nobility*) 875; archduke, doge, elector; seignior; mar-, land-grave; rajah, emir, nizam, nawab, negus.

empress, queen, sultana, czarina, princess, infanta, duchess, margravine, begum, maharani.

regent, viceroy, exarch, palatine,

**746. Servant.—N.** subject, liegeman; servant, retainer, follower, henchman, servitor, domestic, menial, help, lady help, *employé, attaché*; official.

retinue, suite, *cortège,* staff, court.

attendant, squire, usher, page, buttons, donzel, footboy; dog robber; train-, cup-bearer; waiter, busboy, tapster, butler, livery servant, lackey, footman, flunkey, valet, *valet de chambre*; boots; scout, gyp; equerry, groom; jockey, hostler, ostler, tiger, orderly, messenger, cad, gillie, caddie; *wallah*; journeyman, herdsman, swineherd.

bailiff, castellan, seneschal, chamberlain, *major-domo,* groom of the chambers.

secretary; under –, assistant- secretary; clerk; clerical staff, stenographer, subsidiary; agent &c. 758; subaltern; under-ling, -strapper; man.

maid, -servant, waitress; handmaid; *confidente,* lady's maid, abigail, *soubrette*; nurse, *bonne, ayah*; nurse-, nursery-, house-, parlour-, waiting-, chamber-, kitchen-, scullery-, between –, laundry –, dairy-maid; *femme –, fille de chambre; camarista; chef de cuisine,*

khedive, hospodar, beglerbeg, three-tailed bashaw, pasha, pashaw, bashaw, bey, beg, dey, scherif, tetrarch, satrap, mandarin, subahdar, Nabob, maharajah; burgrave; laird &c. (*proprietor*) 779; High Commissioner.

the -authorities, – powers that be, – government; staff, *état major*, aga, official, man in office, person in authority.

[Naval authorities] admiral, -ty, – of the fleet; rear-, vice-, port-admiral; senior-, naval officer, S.N.O., commodore, captain, commander, lieutenant-commander, lieutenant, sub-lieutenant, midshipman, warrant –, petty- officer, leading seaman; skipper, mate, master.

[Military authorities] marshal, field-marshal, *maréchal*; general, -issimo; commander-in-chief, *seraskier, hetman*; lieutenant-, major-general; commandant; colonel, lieutenant-colonel, major, captain, centurion, skipper, lieutenant, second-lieutenant, officer, staff-officer, *aide-de-camp*, brigadier, brigade-major, adjutant, *jemidar*, ensign, cornet, cadet, subaltern, warrant officer, quartermaster, noncommissioned officer, N.C.O.; sergeant, -major; top-sergeant, troop-sergeant, colour sergeant; corporal, -major; lance-, acting-corporal; drum major; shavetail.

[Air authorities] air -marshal, – commodore; group captain, squadron leader, wing commander, flight lieutenant, flying –, pilot-officer.

[Civil authorities] judge &c. 967; mayor, -alty; prefect, chancellor, archon, provost, magistrate, syndic; alcalde, alcaid; burgomaster, *corregidor*, seneschal, alderman, warden, constable, portreeve; lord mayor, sheriff; officer &c. (*executive*) 965.

*cordon bleu*, cook, scullion, Cinderella; maid –, servant- of all work, tweeny, general servant, girl, slavey; laundress, bed-maker, goody, char-woman &c: (*worker*) 690.

serf, vassal, slave, negro, helot; bondsman, -woman; bondslave; *âme damnée, odalisque*, ryot, *adscriptus glebæ*; vill-ain, -ein; bead-, bede-sman; sizar; pension-er, -ary; client; dependant, -ent; hanger on, stooge, satellite; parasite &c. (*servility*) 886; led captain; *protégé*, ward, hireling, mercenary, puppet, creature.

badge of slavery; bonds &c. 752.

**V.** serve; minister to, wait –, attend –, dance attendance –, pin oneself-upon; squire, tend, hang on the sleeve of, char, do for; fag; valet.

**Adj.** in the train of; in one's -pay, – employ; at one's call &c. (*obedient*) 743; in bonds.

---

**747.** [Insignia of authority.] **Sceptre.—N.** sceptre, regalia, rod of empire, sword of state, mace, *fasces*, wand; staff, – of office; *bâton*, truncheon; flag &c. (*insignia*) 550; ensign –, emblem –, badge –, insignia- of authority, rank marks, brassard, badge, sash; cocked –, brass- hat.

epaulette, *aiguillette*, crown, star, eagle, bar, double bar, pip, stripe, chevron, curl, ring, anchor, shoulder-strap, tab.

throne, chair, musnud, divan, dais, woolsack.

*toga*, pall, mantle, robes of state, ermine, purple.

crown, coronet, diadem, tiara, triple crown, mitre, crozier, cardinal's hat &c.; cap of maintenance; decoration; title &c. 877; portfolio.

key, signet, seals, talisman; helm; reins &c. (*means of restraint*) 752.

---

**748. Freedom.—N.** freedom, liberty, independence; licence &c. (*permission*) 760; facility &c. 705.

scope, range, latitude, play; free –, full- -play, – scope; free stage and no

**749. Subjection.— N.** subjection; depend-ence, -ance, -ency; subordination; thrall, thraldom. enthralment, subjugation, bondage, serfdom; feudal-ism, -ity; vassalage, villenage; slavery,

favour; swing, full swing, elbow-room, margin, rope, wide berth; Liberty Hall.

franchise, denization; free -, freed-, livery- man; denizen.

autonomy, self-government, home-rule, self-determination, liberalism, free trade; non-interference &c. 706.

immunity, exemption; emancipation &c. (*liberation*) 750; en-, af-franchise-ment; rights, privileges.

free land, freehold; allodium; frank-almoigne, mortmain.

independent, free-lance, -thinker, -trader.

V. be -free &c. *adj.*; have -scope &c. *n.*, - the run of, - one's own way, - a will of one's own, - one's fling; do what one -likes, - wishes, - pleases, - chooses; go at large, feel at home, paddle one's own canoe; stand on one's -legs, - rights; shift for oneself.

take a liberty; make -free with, - oneself quite at home; use a freedom; take -leave, - French leave.

set free &c. (*liberate*) 750; give the reins to &c. (*permit*) 760; allow -, give-scope &c. *n.* to; give a horse his head.

make free of; give the -freedom of, - franchise; en-, af-franchise.

*laisser -faire, - aller*; live and let live; leave to oneself; leave -, let- alone; mind one's own business.

**Adj.** free, - as air; out of harness, independent, at large, loose, scot free; left -alone, - to oneself.

in full swing; uncaught, uncon-strained, unbuttoned, unconfined, un-restrained, unchecked, unprevented, unhindered, unobstructed, unbound, uncontrolled, untrammelled.

unsubject, ungoverned, unenslaved, unenthralled, unchained, unshackled, unfettered, unreined, unbridled, un-curbed, unmuzzled, unimpeded.

unrestricted, unlimited, unconditional; absolute; discretionary &c. (*optional*) 600.

unassailed, unforced, uncompelled.

unbiassed, unprejudiced, uninfluenced, spontaneous.

free and easy; at -, at one's- ease; *dégagé*, quite at home; wanton, rampant, irrepressible, unvanquished.

exempt; freed &c. 750; freeborn; autonomous, freehold, allodial; *gratis* &c. 815.

unclaimed, going a begging.

**Adv.** freely &c. *adj.*; *ad libitum* &c. (*at will*) 600.

enslavement, involuntary servitude.

service; servi-tude, -torship; ten-dence, employ, tutelage, clientship; liability &c. 177; constraint &c. 751; oppression &c. (*severity*) 739; yoke &c. (*means of restraint*) 752; submission &c. 725; obedience &c. 743.

V. be -subject &c. *adj.*; be -, lie- at the mercy of; depend -, lean -, hang-upon; fall -a prey to, - under; play second fiddle.

be a -mere machine, - puppet, - foot-ball; not dare to say one's soul is his own; drag a chain.

serve &c. 746; obey &c. 743; submit &c. 725.

break in, tame; subject, subjugate; master &c. 731; tread -down, - under foot; weigh down; drag at one's chariot wheels; reduce to -subjection, - slavery; en-, in-, be-thral; enslave, lead captive; take into custody &c. (*restrain*) 751; rule &c. 737; drive into a corner, hold at the sword's point; keep under; hold in -bondage, - leading strings, - swad-dling clothes.

**Adj.** subject, dependent, subordi-nate; feud-al, -atory; in subjection to, under control; in -leading strings, - harness; subjected, enslaved &c. *v.*; constrained &c. 751; subservient, ser-vile, fawning, slavish, obsequious, cringing; down-trodden; over-borne, -whelmed; under the lash, on the hip, led by the nose, henpecked; the -pup-pet, - sport, - plaything- of; under one's -orders, - command, - thumb; like dirt under one's feet; a slave to; at the mercy of; in the -power, - hands, - clutches- of; at the feet of; at one's beck and call &c. (*obedient*) 743; liable &c. 177; parasitical; stipendiary.

**Adv.** under.

**750. Liberation.—N.** liberation, disengagement, release, disenthrallment, enlargement, emancipation; af-, enfranchisement; manumission; discharge, dismissal.

deliverance &c. 672; redemption, extrication, acquittance, absolution; acquittal &c. 970; escape &c. 671.

**V.** liberate, free; set -free, – clear, – at liberty; render free, emancipate, release; en-, af-franchise; manumit; enlarge; dis-band, -charge, -miss, -enthral; let -go, – loose, – out, – slip; cast –, turn- adrift; deliver &c. 672; absolve &c. (*acquit*) 970; reprieve.

unfetter &c. 751; untie &c. 44; loose &c. (*disjoin*) 44; loosen, relax; un-bolt, -bar, -close, -cork, -clog, -hand, -bind, -latch, -chain, -harness; dis-engage, -entangle; clear, extricate, unloose.

gain –, obtain –, acquire- one's -liberty &c. 748; get -rid, – clear- of; deliver oneself from; shake off the yoke, slip the collar; break -loose, – prison; tear asunder one's bonds, cast off trammels; escape &c. 671.

**Adj.** at -liberty, – large, free, liberated &c. *v.*; out of harness &c. 748; adrift.

**Int.** unhand me! let me go!

---

**751. Restraint.—N.** restraint; hindrance &c. 706; coercion &c. (*compulsion*) 744; cohibition, constraint, repression; discipline, control, self-restraint &c. 604.

confinement; durance, duress; im-, prisonment; incarceration, coarctation, entombment, mancipation, durance vile, thrall, -dom, limbo, captivity; blockade; quarantine; detention.

arrest, -ation; custody, keep, care, charge, ward, restringency.

curb &c. (*means of restraint*) 752; *lettre de cachet.*

limitation, restriction, protection, monopoly; prohibition &c. 761; economic pressure.

prisoner &c. 754.

**V.** restrain, check; put –, lay- under restraint; en-, in-, be-thral; restrict; debar &c. (*hinder*) 706; constrain; coerce &c. (*compel*) 744; curb, control; hold –, keep- -back, – from, – in, – in check, – within bounds; hold in -leash, – leading strings; withhold.

keep under; repress, suppress; smother; pull in, rein in; hold, – fast; keep a tight hand on; prohibit &c. 761; in-, co-hibit.

enchain; fasten &c. (*join*) 43; fetter, shackle; en-, trammel; bridle, muzzle, gag, pinion, manacle, handcuff, tie one's hands, hobble, bind hand and foot; swathe, swaddle; pin –, peg- down; tether, picket; tie, – up, – down; secure; forge fetters; belay.

confine; shut –, clap –, lock –, box –, mew –, bottle –, cork –, seal –, button- up; shut –, hem –, bolt –, wall –, rail- in; impound, pen, coop; enclose &c. (*circumscribe*) 229; cage; in-, en-cage; close the door upon, cloister; imprison, immure; incarcerate, entomb; clap –, lay- under hatches; put in -irons, – a strait waistcoat; throw –, cast- into prison; put into bilboes.

arrest; take -up, – charge of, – into custody; take –, make- -prisoner, – captive; captivate; lead -captive, – into captivity; send –, commit- to prison; commit; give in -charge, – custody; subjugate &c. 749.

**Adj.** re-, con-strained; imprisoned &c. *v.*; pent up; jammed in, wedged in; under -restraint, – lock and key, – hatches; serving –, doing- time; in swaddling clothes; on *parole*; in custody &c. (*prisoner*) 754; cohibitive; coactive &c. (*compulsory*) 744.

stiff, restringent, straitlaced, hide-bound.

ice-, wind-, weather-bound; 'cabined, cribbed, confined'; in Lob's pound, laid by the heels.

**Adv.** in captivity, under arrest, behind the bars, in -prison, – jail, – durance vile.

**752. [Means of restraint.] Prison.—N.** prison, -house; jail, gaol, cage, coop, den, death house, condemned –, cell; stronghold, fortress, keep, donjon, dungeon, *Bastille, oubliette,* bridewell, house of correction, hulks, toll-booth, panopticon, penitentiary, guard-room, clink, can, stir, tronk, jug, lock-up, hold; round –, watch –, station –, sponging-house; station; house of detention, black hole, pen, fold, pound; enclosure &c. 232; penal settlement; chain gang; debtors' prison; reformatory; federal penitentiary, state prison; criminal lunatic asylum; bilboes, stocks, limbo, quod.

Dartmoor, Newgate, Fleet, Marshalsea; King's (*or* Queen's) Bench; Sing Sing, Dannemora.

bond; strap, bandage, splint, tourniquet; irons, pinion, gyve, fetter, shackle, trammel, manacle, handcuff, bracelets, darbies, strait waistcoat, strait-jacket.

yoke, collar, halter, harness; muzzle, gag, bit, brake, curb, snaffle, bridle; rein, -s; ribbons, lines, bearing-rein; martingale, leading string; tether, picket, band, guy, chain; cord &c. (*fastening*) 45.

bolt, bar, lock, padlock, rail, wall; paling, palisade; fence; barrier, barricade.

brake, drag &c. (*hindrance*) 706.

**753. Keeper.—N.** keeper, custodian, *custos,* ranger, warder, jailer, gaoler, turnkey, castellan, guard; watch, -dog, -man; Charley; sen-try, -tinel; watch and ward; *concierge,* coast-guard, *guarda costa,* gamekeeper.

escort, body guard, convoy.

protector, governor, duenna; guardian; governess &c. (*teacher*) 540; nurse, *bonne, ayah, amah.*

**754. Prisoner.—N.** prisoner, captive, *détenu,* close prisoner.

jail-bird, ticket-of-leave man.

**V.** stand committed; be -imprisoned &c. 751.

**Adj.** imprisoned &c. 751; in -prisoɴ, – quod, – durance vile, – limbo, – custody, – charge, – chains; under -lock and key, – hatches; on *parole*; detained at his Majesty's pleasure.

**755. [Vicarious authority.] Commission.—N.** commission, delegation; con-, as-signment; procuration; deputation, legation, mission, embassy; agency, agentship; power of attorney, proxy; clerkship.

errand, charge, *brevet,* diploma, *exequatur,* permit &c. (*permission*) 760.

appointment, nomination, return; charter; ordination; installation, inauguration, investiture; accession, coronation, enthronement.

vicegerency; regency, regentship.

viceroy &c 745; consignee &c. 758; deputy &c. 759.

**V.** commission, delegate, depute; consign, assign; charge; in-, en-trust; turn over to; commit, – to the hands of; authorize &c. (*permit*) 760.

put in commission, accredit, engage, hire, bespeak, appoint, name, nominate, return, ordain; install, induct,

**756. Abrogation.—N.** abrogatioɴ, annulment, nullification; cancelling &c. *v.*; cancel; revo-cation, -kement; repeal, rescission, defeasance.

dismissal, *congé,* demission; depos-al, -ition; sack, dethronement; disestablish-, disendow-ment; deconsecration.

aboli-tion, -shment; dissolution.

counter-order, -mand; repudiation, retractation; recantation &c. (*tergiversation*) 607.

**V.** abrogate, annul, cancel; destroy &c. 162; abolish; revoke, repeal, rescind, reverse, retract, recall; over-rule, -ride; set aside; disannul, dissolve, quash, nullify, declare null and void; dis-establish, -endow; deconsecrate.

disclaim &c. (*deny*) 536; ignore, repudiate; recant &c. 607; divest oneself, break off.

counter-mand, -order; do away with; sweep –, brush- away; throw -over-

inaugurate, invest, crown; en-roll, -list.
employ, empower; give power of
attorney to; set –, place- over; send out.
   be commissioned, be accredited; rep-
resent, stand for; stand in the -stead,
– place, – shoes- of.
   **Adj.** commissioned &c. *v.*
   **Adv.** *per procuratione.*

board, – to the dogs; scatter to the
winds, cast behind.
   dismiss, discard; cast –, turn- -off,
– out, – adrift, – out of doors, – aside,
– away; send -off, – away, – about
one's business; discharge, get rid of,
fire out, fire &c. (*eject*) 297; jilt.
   cashier; break; oust; set down, un-
seat, -saddle; un-, de-, disen-throne;
depose, uncrown; unfrock, strike off
the roll; dis-bar, -bench.

be -abrogated &c.; receive its quietus.
   **Adj.** abrogated &c. *v.*; *functus officio.*
   **Int.** get along with you! begone! go about your business! away
with!

**757. Resignation.—N.** resignation, retirement, abdication, renuncia-
.ion, abjuration, disclaimer, abandonment, relinquishment.
   **V.** resign; give –, throw- up; lay down, throw up the cards, wash
one's hands of, abjure, renounce, forego, disclaim, abandon, relinquish,
retract, demit; deny &c. 536.
   abrogate &c. 756; desert &c. (*relinquish*) 624; get rid of &c. 782.
   abdicate; vacate, – one's seat; apply for –, accept- the stewardship of
the Chiltern Hundreds; retire; tender –, send in –, hand in- one's resig-
nation.
   **Adj.** abdicant, renunciatory &c. *v.* **Phr.** 'Othello's occupation's gone.'

**758. Consignee.—N.** consignee, trustee, nominee, committee.
   delegate; commiss-ary, -ioner; emissary, envoy, commissionaire;
messenger &c. 534.
   diplomatist, diplomat, *corps diplomatique*, embassy; am-, em-bassa-
dor; representative, resident, consul, legate, nuncio, internuncio, *chargé
d'affaires, attaché.*
   vicegerent &c. (*deputy*) 759; plenipotentiary.
   functionary, placeman, curator; treasurer &c. 801; agent, factor,
bailiff, steward, clerk, secretary, attorney, solicitor, proctor, broker,
underwriter, commission agent, auctioneer, one's man of business;
factotum &c. (*director*) 694; caretaker.
   negotiator, go between; middleman; under agent, *employé*; servant
&c. 746.
   salesman; commercial, – traveller; bagman, *commis-voyageur*, touter.
   newspaper –, own –, war –, special- correspondent; reporter.

**759. Deputy.—N.** deputy, substitute, vice, proxy, *locum tenens*, dele-
gate, representative, next friend, surrogate, secondary.
   regent, vicegerent, vizier, minister, vicar; premier &c. (*director*) 694;
chancellor, prefect, provost, warden, lieutenant, archon, consul, procon-
sul; viceroy &c. (*governor*) 745; commissioner &c. 758; plenipotentiary,
*alter ego.*
   team, eight, eleven; champion.
   **V.** bo deputy &c. *n.*; stand , appear , hold a brief , answer- for;
represent; stand –, walk- in the shoes of; stand in the stead of.
   substitute, ablegate, accredit; commission, empower, delegate &c. 755.
   **Adj.** acting; vice, -regal; accredited to.
   **Adv.** in behalf of, by proxy.

## Section II. Special Intersocial Volition

**760. Permission.—N.** permission, leave; allow-, suffer-ance; toler-ance, -ation; liberty, law, licence, concession, grace; indulgence &c. (*lenity*) 740; favour, dispensation, exemption, release; connivance; vouchsafement.

authorization, warranty, accordance, admission.

permit, warrant, *brevet*, precept, sanction, authority, *firman*; pass, -port; furlough, licence, *carte blanche*, ticket of leave; grant, charter, patent.

**V.** permit; give -permission &c. *n.*, - power; let, allow, admit; suffer, bear with, tolerate, recognize; concede &c. 762; accord, vouchsafe, favour, humour, gratify, indulge, stretch a point; wink at, connive at; shut one's eyes to.

grant, empower, charter, enfranchise, privilege, confer a privilege, license, authorize, warrant; sanction; entrust &c. (*commission*) 755.

give -*carte blanche*, - the reins to, - scope to &c. (*freedom*) 748; leave -alone, - it to one, - the door open; open the -door to, - floodgates; give a loose to.

let off; absolve &c. (*acquit*) 970; release, exonerate, dispense with.

ask -, beg -, request- -leave, - permission.

**761. Prohibition.—N.** pro-, in-hibition; *veto*, disallowance; interdict, -ion; injunction; embargo, ban, *verboten*, taboo, proscription; *index expurgatorius*; restriction &c. (*restraint*) 751; hindrance &c. 706; forbidden fruit.

**V.** pro-, in-hibit; forbid, put one's *veto* upon, disallow; bar; debar &c. (*hinder*) 706, forefend.

keep -in, - within bounds; restrain &c. 751; cohibit, withhold, limit, circumscribe, clip the wings of, restrict, narrow; interdict, taboo; put -, place-under -an interdiction, - the ban; proscribe, censor; exclude, shut out; shut -, bolt -, show- the door; warn off; dash the cup from one's lips; forbid the banns.

**Adj.** prohibit-ive, -ory; interdictive; proscriptive; restrictive, exclusive; forbidding &c. *v.*

prohibited &c. *v.*; not -permitted &c. 760; unlicensed, contraband, under the ban of; illegal &c. 964; unauthorized, not to be thought of.

**Adv.** on no account &c. (*no*) 536.

**Int.** forbid it heaven! &c. (*deprecation*) 766.

hands -, keep- off! hold! stop! avast!

**Phr.** that will never do.

**Adj.** permitting &c. *v.*; permissive, indulgent; permitted &c. *v.*; patent, chartered, permissible, allowable, lawful, legitimate, legal; legalized &c. (*law*) 963; licit; unforbid, -den; unconditional.

**Adv.** permissibly; by -, with -, on- -leave &c. *n.*; *speciali gratiâ*; under favour of; *pace*; *ad libitum* &c. (*freely*) 748, (*at will*) 600; by all means &c. (*willingly*) 602; yes &c. (*assent*) 488.

---

**762. Consent.—N.** consent; assent &c. 488; acquiescence; approval &c. 931; compliance, agreement, concession; yield-ance, -ingness; accession, acknowledgment, acceptance, agnition.

settlement, ratification, confirmation, adjustment.

permit &c. (*permission*) 760; promise &c. 768.

**V.** consent; assent &c. 488; yield assent, admit, allow, concede, grant, yield; come -over, - round; give in to, acknowledge, agnize, give consent, comply with, acquiesce, agree to, fall in with, accede, accept, embrace an offer, close with, take at one's word, have no objection.

satisfy, meet one's wishes, settle, come to terms &c. 488; not -refuse &c. 764; turn a willing ear &c. (*willingness*) 602; jump at; deign, vouchsafe; promise &c. 768.

**Adj.** consenting &c. *v.*; agreeable, compliant; agreed &c. (*assent*) 488; unconditional.

**Adv.** yes &c. (*assent*) 488; by all means &c. (*willingly*) 602; if –, as-you please; be it so, so be it, well and good, of course.

**763. Offer.**—**N.** offer, proffer, presentation, tender, bid, overture; propos-al, -ition; motion, invitation; candidature; offering &c. (*gift*) 784.

**V.** offer, proffer, present, tender; bid; propose, move; make -a motion, – advances; start; invite, hold out, place- at one's disposal, – in one's way, put forward.

hawk about; offer for sale &c. 796; press &c. (*request*) 765; lay at one's feet.

offer –, present- oneself; volunteer, come forward, be a candidate; stand –, bid- for; seek; be at one's service; go a begging; bribe &c. (*give*) 784.

**Adj.** offer-ing, -ed &c. *v.*; in the market, for sale, to let, disengaged, on hire.

**764. Refusal.**—**N.** refusal, rejection; non-, in-compliance; denial; declining &c. *v.*; declension; peremptory –, flat –, point blank- refusal; repulse, rebuff; discountenance.

recusancy, renunciation, abnegation, negation, protest, disclaimer; dissent &c. 489; revocation &c. 756.

**V.** refuse, reject, deny, decline; nill, negative; refuse –, withhold- one's assent; shake the head; close the -hand, – purse; grudge, begrudge, be slow to, hang fire.

be deaf to; turn -a deaf ear to, – one's back upon; set one's face against, discountenance, not hear of, have nothing to do with, wash one's hands of, stand aloof, forswear, set aside, cast behind one; not yield an inch &c. (*obstinacy*) 606.

resist, cross; not -grant &c. 762; repel, repulse; shut –, slam- the door in one's face; rebuff; send -back, – to the right about, – away with a flea in the ear; deny oneself, not be at home to; discard &c. (*repudiate*) 610; rescind &c. (*revoke*) 756; disclaim, protest; dissent &c. 489.

**Adj.** refusing &c. *v.*; rest-ive, -iff; recusant; uncomplying, noncompliant, unconsenting, uncomplaisant, protestant; not willing to hear of, deaf to.

refused &c. *v.*; ungranted, out of the question, not to be thought of, impossible.

**Adv.** no &c. 536; on no account, not for the world; no thank you.

**Phr.** *non possumus*; [ironically] your humble servant; *bien obligé*.

**765. Request.**—**N.** requ-est, -isition; claim &c. (*demand*) 741; petition, suit, prayer; begging letter, round-robin.

motion, overture, application, canvass, address, appeal, apostrophe; imprecation; rogation; proposal, proposition.

orison &c. (*worship*) 990; incantation &c. (*spell*) 993.

mendicancy; asking, panhandling, begging &c. *v.*; postulation, solicitation, invitation, entreaty, importunity, supplication, instance, impetration, imploration, obsecration, obtestation, invocation, interpellation.

**V.** request, ask; beg, crave, sue, pray, petition, solicit, invite, pop the question, make bold to ask; beg -leave, – a boon; apply to, call to, put to; call -upon, – for; make –, address –, prefer –, put up- a -request, – prayer, – petition;

**766. [Negative request.] Deprecation.**—**N.** deprecation, expostulation; remonstrance; intercession, mediation.

**V.** deprecate, protest, expostulate, enter a protest, intercede for.

**Adj.** deprecatory, expostulatory, intercessory, mediatorial.

deprecated, protested.

un-, unbe-sought; unasked &c. (*see* ask &c. 765).

**Int.** cry you mercy! God forbid! forbid it Heaven! Heaven -forefend, – forbid! far be it from! hands off! &c. (*prohibition*) 761.

make -application, – a requisition; ask –, trouble- one for; claim &c. (*demand*) 741; offer up prayers &c. (*worship*) 990; whistle for.

beg hard, entreat, beseech, plead, supplicate, implore, apostrophize; conjure, adjure; obtest; cry to, kneel to, appeal to; invoke, evoke; impetrate, imprecate, ply, press, urge, beset, importune, dun, tax, clamour for; cry -aloud, – for help; fall on one's knees; throw oneself at the feet of; come down on one's marrow-bones.

beg from door to door, send the hat round, go a begging; mendicate, mump, cadge, panhandle, beg one's bread.

dance attendance on, besiege, knock at the door.

bespeak, canvass, tout, make interest, court; seek, bid for &c. (*offer*) 763; publish the banns.

**Adj.** requesting &c. *v.*; precatory; suppli-ant, -cant, -catory; invoc-, imprec-, rog-atory; postulant, mendicant.

importunate, clamorous, urgent; solicitous; cap in hand; on one's -knees, – bended knees, – marrow-bones.

**Adv.** prithee, do, please, pray; be so good as, be good enough; have the goodness, vouchsafe, will you, I pray thee, if you please.

**Int.** for -God's, – heaven's, – goodness', – mercy's- sake.

**767. Petitioner.—N.** petitioner, solicitor, applicant; suppli-ant, -cant; suitor, candidate, claimant, postulant, aspirant, competitor, bidder; place –, pot –, mug- hunter; prizer.

beggar, mendicant, mumper, sturdy beggar, cadger, panhandler: canvasser, barker, touter &c. 758.

sycophant, parasite &c. 886.

## Section III. Conditional Intersocial Volition

**768. Promise.—N.** promise, undertaking, word, troth, plight, pledge, *parole*, word of honour, vow; oath &c. (*affirmation*) 535; profession, assurance, warranty, guarantee, insurance, obligation; contract &c. 769.

**768a. Release from engagement.—** **N.** release &c. (*liberation*) 750.

**Adj.** absolute; unconditional &c. (*free*) 748.

engagement, pre-engagement: affiance; betroth, -al, -ment; marriage -compact, – vow.

**V.** promise; give a -promise &c. *n.*; undertake, engage; make –, form- an engagement; enter -into, – on- an engagement; bind –, tie –, pledge –, commit –, take upon- oneself; vow; swear &c. (*affirm*) 535, give –, pass –, pledge –, plight- one's -word, – honour, – credit, – troth; betroth, plight faith; take the vows.

assure, warrant, guarantee, vouch for, avouch, covenant &c. 769; attest &c. (*bear witness*) 467.

hold out an expectation; contract an obligation; become -bound to, – sponsor for; answer –, be answerable- for; secure; give security &c. 771; underwrite.

adjure, administer an oath, put to one's oath, swear a witness.

**Adj.** promising &c. *v.*; promissory; votive; under hand and seal; upon -oath, – affirmation.

promised &c. *v.*; affianced, pledged, bound; committed, compromised; in for it.

**Adv.** as one's head shall answer for; upon my honour.

**Phr.** in for a penny, in for a pound.

**769. Compact.—N.** compact, contract, agreement, bargain, deal, transaction; affidation; pact, -ion; bond, covenant, indenture.

stipulation, settlement, convention; compromise, *cartel.*

protocol, treaty, *concordat, Zollverein, Sonderbund,* charter, *Magna Charta,* Pragmatic Sanction.

negotiation &c. (*bargaining*) 794; diplomacy &c. (*mediation*) 724; negotiator &c. (*agent*) 758.

ratification, completion, signature, seal, sigil, signet.

**V.** contract, covenant, agree for, engage &c. (*promise*) 768.

treat, negotiate, stipulate, make terms; bargain &c. (*barter*) 794.

make –, strike- a bargain; come to -terms, – an understanding; compromise &c. 774; set at rest; close, – with; conclude, complete, settle; confirm, ratify, clench, subscribe, underwrite; en-, in-dorse; put the seal to; sign, seal &c. (*attest*) 467; indent.

take one at one's word, bargain by inch of candle.

**Adj.** contractual, agreed &c. *v.*; conventional; under hand and seal; signed, sealed and delivered.

**Phr.** *caveat emptor.*

**770. Conditions.—N.** conditions, terms; articles, – of agreement.

clauses, provisions; proviso &c. (*qualification*) 469; covenant, stipulation, obligation, *ultimatum, sine quâ non; casus fœderis.*

**V.** make –, come to- -terms &c. (*contract*) 769; make it a condition, stipulate, insist upon, make a point of; bind, tie up.

**Adj.** conditional, provisional, guarded, fenced, hedged in.

**Adv.** conditionally &c. (*with qualification*) 469; provisionally, *pro re natâ*; on condition; with a reservation.

**771. Security.—N.** security; guaran-ty, -tee; gage, warranty, bond, tie, pledge, plight, mortgage, debenture, hypothecation, bill of sale, lien, pignus, pawn, pignoration; real security; bottomry; collateral, vadium.

stake, deposit, earnest, handsel, caution.

promissory note; bill, – of exchange; I.O.U.; personal security, covenant, specialty; *parole* &c. (*promise*) 768.

acceptance, indorsement, signature, execution, stamp, seal.

spon-sor, -sion, -sorship; surety, bail; mainpernor, hostage.

recognizance; deed –, covenant- of indemnity.

authentication, verification, warrant, certificate, voucher, docket, doquet; record &c. 551; probate, attested copy.

receipt; ac-, quittance; discharge, release.

muniment, title-deed, instrument; deed, – poll; assurance, insurance, indenture; charter &c. (*compact*) 769; charter-poll; paper, parchment, settlement, will, testament, last will and testament, codicil.

**V.** give -security, – bail, – substantial bail; go bail; pawn, impawn, hock, spout, mortgage, hypothecate, impignorate.

guarantee, warrant, assure; accept, indorse, underwrite, insure.

execute, stamp; sign, seal &c. (*evidence*) 467.

let, sett; grant –, take –, hold- a lease; hold in pledge; lend on security &c. 787.

**Adj.** secure, -ed; pledged &c. *v.*; in pawn, on deposit.

**772. Observance.—N.** observance, performance, compliance; obedience

**773. Non-observance. — N.** non-observance &c. 772; evasion, inob-

&c. 743; fulfilment, satisfaction, discharge; acquit-tance, -tal.

adhesion, acknowledgment; fidelity &c. (*probity*) 939; exact &c. 494- observance.

**V.** observe, comply with, respect, acknowledge, abide by; cling to, adhere to, be faithful to, act up to; meet, fulfil; carry -out, – into execution; execute, perform, keep, satisfy, discharge; do one's office.

perform –, fulfill –, discharge –, acquit oneself of- an obligation; make good; make good –, keep- one's -word, – promise; redeem one's pledge; keep faith with, stand to one's engagement.

**Adj.** observant, faithful, true, loyal; honourable &c. 939; true as the -dial to the sun, – needle to the pole; punct-ual, -ilious; meticulous; literal &c. (*exact*) 494; as good as one's word.

**Adv.** faithfully &c. *adj.*

servance, failure, omission, neglect, laches, laxity, informality.

infringement, infraction; violation, transgression.

retractation, repudiation, nullification; protest; forfeiture.

lawlessness; disobedience &c. 742; bad faith &c. 940.

**V.** fail, neglect, omit, elude, evade, give the go by to, cut, set aside, ignore; shut –, close- one's eyes to, avoid.

infringe, transgress, pirate, violate, break, trample under foot, do violence to, drive a coach and six through.

discard, protest, repudiate, fling to the winds, set at naught, nullify, declare null and void; cancel &c. (*wipe off*) 552.

retract, go back from, be off, forfeit, go from one's word, palter; stretch –, strain- a point.

**Adj.** violating &c. *v.*; lawless, transgressive; elusive, evasive; lax, casual; non-observant.

unfulfilled &c. (*see* fulfil &c. 772).

---

**774. Compromise.—N.** com-promise, -mutation, -position; middle term, *mezzo termine*; compensation &c. 30; adjustment, mutual concession.

**V.** com-promise, -mute, -pound; take the mean; split the difference, meet one half way, give and take; come to terms &c. (*contract*) 769; submit to –, abide by- arbitration; patch up, bridge over, fix up, arrange; adjust, – differences; agree; make -the best of, – a virtue of necessity; take the will for the deed.

### Section IV. Possessive Relations*

#### 1°. *Property in general*

**775. Acquisition.—N.** acquisition; gaining &c. *v.*; obtainment; procuration, -ement; purchase, descent, inheritance; gift &c. 784.

recovery, retrieval, revendication, replevin; redemption, salvage, trover; find, *trouvaille*, foundling.

gain, thrift; money-making, -grubbing: lucre, filthy lucre, loaves and fishes, the main chance, pelf; emolument &c. 973: wealth &c. 803.

profit, earnings, winnings, innings, clean-up, pickings, perquisite, net profit; income &c. (*receipt*) 810; proceeds, -duce, -duct; out-come, -put;

**776. Loss.—N.** loss; de-, perdition; forfeiture, lapse.

privation, bereavement; deprivation &c. (*dispossession*) 789; riddance.

**V.** lose; incur –, experience –, meet with- a loss; miss; mislay, let slip, allow to slip through the fingers, squander; be without &c. (*exempt*) 777*a*; forfeit.

get rid of &c. 782; waste &c. 638. be lost, lapse.

**Adj.** losing &c. *v.*; not having &c. 777*a*.

shorn of, deprived of; denuded, bereaved, bereft, *minus*, cut off; dispos-

* That is, relations which concern property.

return, fruit, crop, harvest, tilth;
second crop, aftermath; benefit &c.
(*good*) 618.

sweepstakes, trick, prize, pool.
[Fraudulent acquisition] subreption·
theft, stealing &c. 791.

V. acquire, get, gain, win, earn,
obtain, procure, gather, annex; collect
&c. 72; pick, – up; glean, take &c. 789.

sessed &c. 789; rid of, quit of; out of
pocket.

lost &c. *v.*; long lost; irretrievable
&c. (*hopeless*) 859; irredentist; off one's
hands.

Int. farewell to! adieu to! good
riddance!

find; come –, pitch –, light- upon; scrape -up, – together; get in,
reap and carry, net, bag, sack, bring home, secure, come across,
derive, draw, get in the harvest.

profit; make –, draw- profit; turn to -profit, – account; make
-capital out of, – money by; obtain a return, reap the fruits of;
reap –, gain- an advantage; turn -a penny, – an honest penny;
make the pot boil, bring grist to the mill; make –, coin –, raise-
money; raise -funds, – the wind; fill one's pocket &c. (*wealth*) 803.

treasure up &c. (*store*) 636; realize, clear; produce &c. 161; take
&c. 789.

get back, recover, regain, retrieve, revendicate, replevy, redeem,
come by one's own.

come -by, – in for; receive &c. 785; inherit; step into, – a fortune,
– the shoes of; succeed to.

get -hold of, – between one's finger and thumb, – into one's hand,
– at; take –, come into –, enter into- possession.

be -profitable &c. *adj.*; pay, answer.

accrue &c. (*be received*) 785.

Adj. acquir-ing, -ed &c. *v.*; acquisitive; productive, profitable,
advantageous, gainful, remunerative, paying, lucrative.

---

**777. Possession.**—N. possession, seisin; ownership &c. 780; occu-
pancy; hold, -ing; tenure, tenancy, feodality, dependency; villenage;
socage, chivalry, knight service.

exclusive possession, impropriation, monopoly, corner; retention &c.
781; pre-possession, -occupancy; nine points of the law.

future possession, heritage, inheritance, heirship, reversion, fee, seig-
niority, feud, fief.

bird in hand, *uti possidetis, chose* in possession.

V. possess, have, hold, occupy, enjoy; be -possessed of &c. *adj.*; have
-in hand &c. *adj.*; own &c. 780; command.

inherit; come -to, – in for.

engross, monopolize, forestall, regrate, impropriate, have all to one-
self, corner; have a firm hold of &c. (*retain*) 781; get into one's hand
&c. (*acquire*) 775.

belong to, appertain to, pertain to; be -in one's possession &c. *adj.*;
vest in.

Adj. possessing &c. *v.*; worth; possessed of, seized of, master of, in
possession of; endowed –, blest –, instinct –, fraught –, laden –, charged
–, instilled –, with.

possessed &c. *v.*; on hand, by one; in hand, in store, in stock; in
one's -hands, – grasp, – possession; at one's -command, – disposal;
one's own &c. (*property*) 780.

unsold; unshared.

**777a. Exemption.**—N. exemption; exception, immunity, privilege, release &c. 927*a*; absence &c. 187.

V. not -have &c. 777; be -without &c. *adj.*

**Adj.** exempt from, devoid of, without, unpossessed of, unblest with, immune from.

not -having &c. 777; unpossessed; untenanted &c. (*vacant*) 187; without an owner.

unobtained, unacquired.

**778.** [Joint possession.] **Participation.**—N. participation; co-, joint-tenancy; possession -, tenancy- in common; joint -, common- stock; co-, partnership; communion; community of -possessions, - goods; communalism, communism, socialism, collectivism; co-operation &c. 709; profit sharing.

snacks, co-portion, picnic, hotchpotch; co-heirship, -parceny, -parcenary; gavelkind.

participator, sharer; co-, partner; shareholder; co-, joint-tenant; tenants in common; co-heir, -parcener.

communist, socialist.

**V.** par-ticipate, -take; share, - in; come in for a share; go -shares, - snacks, - halves; share and share alike.

have -, possess -, be seized- -in common, - as joint tenants &c. *n*₁ join in; have a hand in &c. (*co-operate*) 709.

**Adj.** partaking &c. *v.*; communistic, socialistic, co-operative, profit sharing.

**Adv.** share and share alike.

**779. Possessor.**—N. possessor, holder; occup-ant, -ier; tenant; per-son -, man- -in possession &c. 777; renter, lodger, lessee, under-lessee; zemindar, ryot; tenant -on sufferance, - at will, - from year to year, - for years, - for life.

owner; propriet-or, -ress, -ary; impropriator, master, mistress, lord.

land-holder, -owner, -lord, -lady; lord -of the manor, - paramount; heritor, laird, vavasour, landed gentry, mesne lord.

*cestui-que-trust*, beneficiary, mortgagor.

grantee, feoffee, relessee, devisee; legat-ee, -ary.

trustee; holder &c.- of the legal estate; mortgagee.

right -, rightful- owner.

[Future possessor] heir, - apparent; - presumptive; heiress; in-herit-or, -ress, -rix; reversioner, remainder-man.

**780. Property.**—N. property, possession, *suum cuique, meum et tuum.*

owner-, proprietor-, lord-ship; seignority; empire &c. (*dominion*) 737.

interest, stake, estate, right, title, claim, demand, holding; tenure &c. (*possession*) 777; vested -, contingent -, beneficial -, equitable-interest; use, trust, benefit; legal -, equitable- estate; seisin.

absolute interest, paramount estate, freehold; fee, - simple, - tail; estate -in fee, - in tail, - tail; estate in tail -male, - female, - general.

limitation, term, lease, settlement, strict settlement, particular estate; estate -for life, - for years, - *pur autre vie*; remainder, reversion, ex-pectancy, possibility.

dower, dowry, *dot*, jointure, marriage portion, appanage, inheritance, heritage, patrimony, alimony; legacy &c. (*gift*) 784.

assets, belongings, means, resources, circumstances; wealth &c. 803; money &c. 800; what one -is worth, - will cut up for; estate and effects.

landed –, real- -estate, – property; realty; land, -s; subdivision; plot, site; tenements; hereditaments; corporeal –, incorporeal- hereditaments; acres; ground &c. (*earth*) 342; acquest; messuage.

territory, state, kingdom, principality, realm, empire, protectorate, margravate, dependancy, colony, sphere of influence, mandate.

manor, honour, domain, demesne; farm, ranch, plantation, *hacienda*; allodium &c. (*free*) 748; fief, feoff, feud, zemindary, dependency.

free-, copy-, lease-holds; chattels real; fixtures, plant, heirloom easement; folkland; right of -common, – user.

personal -property, – estate, – effects; personalty, chattels, goods, effects, movables; stock, – in trade; things, traps, rattle-traps, paraphernalia; equipage &c. 633.

parcels, appurtenances.

*impedimenta*; lug-, bag-gage; bag and baggage; pelf; cargo, lading.

rent-roll; income &c. (*receipts*) 810.

patent, copyright; *chose* in action; credit &c. 805; debt &c. 806.

**V.** possess &c. 777; be the -possessor &c. 779- of· own; have for one's own, – very own; come in for, inherit; enfeoff.

savour of the realty.

be one's -property &c. *n.*; belong to; ap-, pertain to.

**Adj.** one's own; landed, predial, manorial, allodial, seigniorial; free-, copy-, lease-hold; feu-, feo-dal; hereditary, entailed, personal.

**Adv.** to one's -credit, – account; to the good.

to one and -his heirs for ever, – the heirs of his body, – his heirs and assigns, – his executors, administrators and assigns.

**781. Retention.—N.** retention; retaining &c. *v.*; keep, detention, custody; tenacity, firm hold, grasp, gripe, grip, iron grip.

fangs, teeth, claws, talons, nail, hook, tentacle, *tenaculum*; bond &c. (*vinculum*) 45.

clutches, tongs, forceps, pincers, nippers, pliers, tweezers, vice.

paw, hand, finger, wrist, fist, neaf, neif.

bird in hand; captive &c. 754.

**V.** retain, keep; hold, – fast, – tight, – one's own, – one's ground; clinch, clench, clutch, grasp, gripe, hug, have a firm hold of.

secure, withold, detain; hold –, keepback; keep close; husband &c. (*store*) 636; reserve; have –, keep- in stock &c. (*possess*) 777; entail, tie up, settle.

**Adj.** retaining &c. *v.*; retentive, tenacious.

unforfeited, undeprived, undisposed, uncommunicated.

incommunicable, inalienable; in mortmain; in strict settlement.

**Phr.** *uti possidetis.*

**782. Relinquishment. — N.** relinquishment, abandonment &c. (*of a course*) 624; renunciation, expropriation, dereliction; cession, surrender, dispensation; resignation &c. 757; riddance.

derelict &c. *adj.*; jetsam; waif, foundling, orphan.

**V.** relinquish, give up, surrender, yield, cede; let -go, – slip; spare, drop, resign, forego, renounce, abjure, abandon, expropriate, give away, dispose of, part with; lay -aside, – apart, – down, – on the shelf &c. (*disuse*) 678; set –, put- aside; make away with, cast behind; discard, cast off, dismiss; maroon.

give -notice to quit, – warning; supersede; be –, get- -rid of, – quit of; eject &c. 297.

rid –, disburden –, divest –, dispossess- oneself of; wash one's hands of; divorce, desert; disinherit, cut off.

cast –, throw –, pitch –, fling- -away, – aside, – overboard, – to the dogs; cast –, throw –, sweep- to the winds; put , turn –, sweep- away; jettison;

quit one's hold.

**Adj.** relinquished &c. *v.*; cast off, derelict; unowned, unappropriated, unculled; left &c. (*residuary*) 40; divorced; disinherited.

**Int.** away with!

## 2°. *Transfer of Property*

**783. Transfer.—N.** transfer, conveyance, assignment, alienation, abalienation; demise, limitation; conveyancing; transmission &c. (*transference*) 270; enfeoffment, bargain and sale, lease and release; exchange &c. (*interchange*) 148; barter &c. 794; substitution &c. 147. succession, reversion; shifting -use, - trust; devolution.

**V.** transfer, convey; alien, -ate; assign; grant &c. (*confer*) 784; consign; make –, hand- over; pass, hand, transmit, negotiate; hand down; exchange &c. (*interchange*) 148.

change -hands, - from one to another; devolve, succeed; come into possession &c. (*acquire*) 775; take over.

abalienate; disinherit; dispossess &c. 789; substitute &c. 147.

**Adj.** alienable, negotiable, transferable, reversional.

**Phr.** estate coming into possession.

**784. Giving.—N.** giving &c. *v.*; bestowal, donation; present-ation, -ment; accordance; con-, cession; delivery, consignment, dispensation, communication, endowment; invest-ment,-iture; award.

almsgiving, charity, liberality, generosity; philanthropy &c. 910.

[Thing given] gift, donation, present, *cadeau*; fairing; free gift, boon, favour, benefaction, grant, offering, oblation, sacrifice, immolation.

grace, act of grace, *bonus, bonanza.*

allowance, contribution, subscription, subsidy, tribute, subvention.

bequest, legacy, devise, will, dotation, appanage; dowry; voluntary -settlement, - conveyance &c. 783; amortization.

alms, largess, bounty, dole, sportule, donative, help, oblation, offertory, Peter's pence, *honorarium*, gratuity, Maundy money, Christmas box, Easter offering, vail, tip, *douceur*, drink money, *pourboire, Trinkgeld, backsheesh*; fee &c. (*recompense*) 973; consideration.

bribe, bait, ground-bait; peace-offering, handsel.

giver, grantor &c. *v.*; donor, feoffer, settlor; almoner; testator; investor, subscriber, contributor; fairy godmother; Santa Claus, benefactor &c. 816.

**V.** deliver, hand, pass, put into the hands of; hand –, make –, deliver –, pass –, turn- over.

present, give away, dispense, dispose of; give –, deal –, dole –, mete –, fork –, shell –, squeeze- out.

pay &c. 807; render, impart, communicate.

**785. Receiving.—N.** receiving &c. *v.*; acquisition &c. 775; reception &c. (*introduction*) 296; suscipiency, acceptance, admission.

re-, ac-cipient; assignee, devisee; lega-tee, -tary; grantee, feoffee, donee, relessee, lessee.

sportulary, stipendiary; beneficiary; pension-er, -ary; almsman.

income &c. (*receipt*) 810.

**V.** receive; take &c. 789; acquire &c. 775; admit.

take in, catch, touch; pocket; put into one's -pocket, - purse; accept; take off one's hands.

be received; come -in, - to hand; pass –, fall- into one's hand; go into one's pocket; fall to one's -lot, - share; come –, fall- to one; accrue; have -given &c. 784 to one.

**Adj.** receiving &c. *v.*; re-, suscipient; received &c. *v.*; given &c. 784; second-hand.

not given, unbestowed &c. (*see give,* bestow &c. 784).

concede, cede, yield, part with, shed cast; spend &c. 809.
give, bestow, confer, grant, accord, award, assign.
entrust, consign, vest in.
make ,a present; allow, contribute, subscribe, donate, furnish its
quota.
invest, endow, settle upon; bequeath, leave, devise.
furnish, supply, help; ad-, minister to; afford, spare; accommo-
date –, indulge –, favour- with; shower down upon; lavish, pour
on, thrust upon; tip, bribe; tickle –, grease- the palm; offer &c.
763; sacrifice, immolate.
**Adj.** giving &c. *v.*; given &c. *v.*; allow-ed, -able; concessional;
communicable; charitable, eleemosynary, sportulary, tributary;
*gratis* &c. 815.

**786. Apportionment.—N.** apportion-, allot-, consign-, assign-, appoint-
ment; appropriation; dis-pensation, -tribution; allocation, division,
deal; repartition; administration.
dividend, portion, contingent, share, allotment, lot, cut, split,
measure, dose; dole, meed, pittance; *quantum*, ration; ratio, proportion,
quota, *modicum*, mess, allowance.
**V.** apportion, divide; cut, split, divvy; distribute, administer, dis-
pense; billet, allot, detail, cast, share, mete; portion –, parcel –, dole-
out; deal, carve.
partition, assign, appropriate, appoint.
come in for one's share &c. (*participate*) 778.
**Adj.** apportioning &c. *v.*; respective.
**Adv.** respectively, each to each.

**787. Lending.—N.** lending &c. *v.*;
loan, advance, accommodation, fenera-
tion; mortgage &c. (*security*) 771;
investment.
*mont-de-piété,* pawnshop, hock shop,
spout, my uncle's.
lender, pawnbroker, money-lender,
usurer, Jew, Shylock.
**V.** lend, advance, loan, accommodate
with; lend on security; pawn &c.
(*security*) 771.
intrust, invest; place –, put- out to
interest; sink, risk.
let, demise, lease, sett, under-, sub-
let.
**Adj.** lending &c. *v.*; lent &c. *v.*; un-
borrowed &c. (*see* borrowed &c. 788).
**Adv.** in advance; on -loan, – security.

**788. Borrowing. — N.** borrowing
pledging, pawning.
borrowed plumes; plagiarism &c.
(*thieving*) 791.
replevin.
**V.** borrow, desume; pawn.
hire, rent, farm; take a -lease,
– demise; take –, hire- by the -hour,
– mile, – year &c.
raise –, take up- money; float bonds;
raise the wind; fly a kite, borrow of
Peter to pay Paul; run into debt &c.
(*debt*) 806.
make use of, plagiarize, pirate.
replevy.

**789. Taking.—N.** taking &c. *v.*; re-
ception &c. (*taking in*) 296; deglutition
&c. (*taking food*) 298; appropriation,
prehension, prensation; capture, cap-
tion, ap-, de-prehension; abreption,
seizure; ab-duction, -lation; subtraction
&c. (*subduction*) 38; abstraction, a-
demption.

**790. Restitution.—N.** restitution,
return; ren-, red-dition; reinstatement,
restoration; reinvestment, recupera-
tion; repatriation; rehabilitation &c.
(*reconstruction*) 660; reparation, atone-
ment, indemnity, compensation, rec-
ompense.
release, replevin, redemption; recov‹

dispossession; depriv-ation, -ement; bereavement; divestment; disherison; distraint, distress; sequestration, confiscation, attachment, execution; eviction &c. 297.

rapacity, extortion, vampirism, predacity, blood-sucking; theft &c. 791.

resumption; repris-e, -al; recovery &c. 775.

clutch, swoop, wrench; grip &c. (*retention*) 781; haul, take, catch; scramble.

taker, captor, capturer; vampire; extortioner.

**V.** take, catch, hook, nab, bag, sack, pocket, put into one's pocket, scrounge; receive; accept.

reap, crop, cull, pluck; gather &c. (*get*) 775; draw.

ap-, im-propriate; assume, possess oneself of; take possession of; commandeer; lay -, clap- one's hands on; help oneself to; make free with, dip one's hands into, lay under contribution; intercept; scramble for; deprive of.

take -, carry -, bear- -away, - off; abstract; hurry off -, run away- with; abduct; steal &c. 791; ravish; seize; pounce -, spring-upon; swoop -to, - down upon; take by -storm, - assault; snatch, reave.

snap up, nip up, whip up, catch up; kidnap, crimp, capture, lay violent hands on.

get -, lay -, take -, catch -, lay fast -, take firm- hold of; lay by the heels, take prisoner; fasten upon, grip, grapple, embrace, gripe, clasp, grab, clutch, collar, throttle, take by the throat, claw, clinch, clench, make sure of; apprehend.

catch at, jump at, make a grab at, snap at, snatch at; reach, make a long arm, stretch forth one's hand.

take -from, - away from; deduct &c. 38; retrench &c. (*curtail*) 201; dispossess, ease one of, snatch from one's grasp; tear -, tear away -, wrench -, wrest -, wring- from; extort; deprive of, bereave; disinherit, cut off with a shilling.

oust &c. (*eject*) 297; divest; levy, distrain, confiscate; sequest-er, -rate, accroach; usurp; despoil, strip, fleece, shear, displume, impoverish, eat out of house and home; drain, - to the dregs; gut, dry, exhaust, swallow up; absorb &c. (*suck in*) 296; draw off; suck, - like a leech, - the blood of.

retake, resume; recover &c. 775.

**Adj.** taking &c. *v.*; privative, prehensile; pred-aceous, -al, -atory, -atorial; rap-acious, -torial; ravenous: parasitic; all-devouring, -engulfing.

bereft &c. 776.

**Adv.** at one fell swoop.

**Phr.** give an inch and take an ell.

ery &c. (*getting back*) 775; remitter, reversion.

**V.** return, restore; recondition; give -, carry -, bring- back; render, - up; give up; let go, unclutch; dis-, re-gorge; regurgitate; recoup, reimburse, repay, indemnify, reinvest, remit, rehabilitate; repair &c. (*make good*) 660.

redeem, recover &c. (*get back*) 775; take back again; revest, revert.

**Adj.** restoring &c. *v.*; recuperative &c. 660; in full restitution, to compensate for.

**Phr.** *suum cuique.*

---

**791. Stealing.—N.** stealing &c. *v.*; theft, thievery, robbery, latrociny, direption; abstraction, appropriation; plagiar-y, -ism; rape, kidnapping, depredation; raid, hold up.

spoliation, plunder, pillage; sack, -age; rapine, *brigandage*, highway robbery, foray, *razzia*; black-mail; piracy, privateering, buccaneering; filibuster-ing, -ism; burglary; house-breaking; cattle-stealing, -rustling, -lifting.

peculation, embezzlement; fraud &c. 545; larceny, petty larceny, pilfering, shop-lifting.

thievishness, rapacity, kleptomania, Alsatia; den of -Cacus, – thieves.

licence to plunder, letters of marque.

**V.** steal, thieve, rob, purloin, pilfer, filch, lift, prig, bag, nim, crib, cabbage, palm; abstract; appropriate, plagiarize.

convey away, carry off, abduct, kidnap, shanghai, impress, crimp; make –, walk –, run- off with; run away with; spirit away; seize &c. (*lay violent hands on*) 789.

plunder, pillage, rifle, sack, loot, ransack, spoil, spoliate, despoil, strip, sweep, gut, forage, levy black-mail, pirate, pickeer, maraud, lift cattle, rustle, poach, smuggle, run.

stick –, hold- up.

swindle, peculate, embezzle; sponge, mulct, rook, bilk, pluck, pigeon, skin, fleece, diddle; defraud &c. 545; obtain under false pretences; live by one's wits.

rob –, borrow of- Peter to pay Paul; set a thief to catch a thief.

disregard the distinction between *meum* and *tuum*.

**Adj.** thieving &c. *v.*; thievish, light-fingered; fur-acious, -tive; piratical; pred-aceous, -al, -atory, -atorial; raptorial &c. (*rapacious*) 789.

stolen &c. *v.*

**Phr.** *sic vos non vobis.*

**792. Thief.—N.** thief, robber, *homo trium literarum*, pilferer, rifler, filcher, plagiarist.

spoiler, depredator, pillager, marauder; harpy, shark, land-shark, falcon, moss-trooper, bushranger, Bedouin, brigand, freebooter, bandit, thug, dacoit, pirate, corsair, viking, Paul Jones; buccan-eer, -ier; piqu-, pick-eerer; rover, ranger, privateer, filibuster; rapparee, wrecker, picaroon; smuggler, poacher, plunderer; racketeer.

highwayman, Dick Turpin, Claude Duval, Macheath, knight of the road, footpad, sturdy beggar; abductor, kidnapper.

cut-, pick-purse; pick-pocket, light-fingered gentry; sharper; card-, skittle-sharper; crook; thimble-rigger; rook, Greek, blackleg, leg, welsher, defaulter; Autolycus, Cacus, Barabbas, Jeremy Diddler, Robert Macaire, artful dodger, trickster; swell mob, *chevalier d'industrie*; shop-lifter.

swindler, peculator; forger, coiner, counterfeiter, shoful; fence, receiver of stolen goods, duffer; smasher.

burglar, housebreaker; cracks-, mags-man; Bill Sikes, Jack Sheppard, Jonathan Wild, Raffles, cat burglar.

**793. Booty.—N.** booty, spoil, plunder, prize, loot, graft, swag, pickings, boodle; *spolia opima*, prey; blackmail; stolen goods.

**Adj.** looting &c. *n.*; manubial, spoliative.

### 3°. *Interchange of Property*

**794. Barter.—N.** barter, exchange, scorse, truck system; interchange &c. 148.

a Roland for an Oliver; *quid pro quo*; com-mutation, -position.

trade, commerce, mercature, buying and selling, bargain and sale; traffic, business, nundination, custom, shopping; commercial enterprise, speculation, jobbing, stock-jobbing, *agiotage*, brokery, arbitrage.

dealing, transaction, negotiation, bargain.

free trade.

V. barter, exchange, truck, scorse, swop; interchange &c. 148; commutate &c. (*substitute*) 147; compound for.

trade, traffic, buy and sell, give and take, nundinate; carry on –, ply –, drive- a trade; be in -business, – the city; keep a shop, deal in, employ one's capital in.

trade –, deal –, have dealings- with; transact –, do- business with; open –, keep- an account with.

bargain; drive –, make- a bargain; negotiate, bid for; dicker, haggle, higgle; chaffer, huckster, cheapen, beat down; stickle, – for; out-, under-bid; ask, charge; strike a bargain &c. (*contract*) 769.

speculate, give a sprat to catch a herring; buy in the cheapest and sell in the dearest market; rig the market.

Adj. commercial, mercantile, trading; interchangeable, marketable, staple, in the market, for sale.

wholesale, retail.

Adv. across the counter; on 'change.

---

**795. Purchase.—N.** purchase, emption; buying, purchasing, shopping; pre-emption, refusal.

coemption, bribery; slave trade.

buyer, purchaser, *emptor*, vendee; patron, employer, client, customer, *clientèle*.

V. buy, purchase, invest in, procure; rent &c. (*hire*) 788; repurchase, buy in.

keep in one's pay, bribe, suborn; pay &c. 807; spend &c. 809.

make –, complete- a purchase; buy over the counter; pay cash for.

shop, market, go a shopping.

Adj. purchased &c. *v.*

Phr. *caveat emptor.*

---

**796. Sale.—N.** sale, vent, disposal; auction, roup, Dutch auction; custom &c. (*traffic*) 794.

vendi-bility, -bleness.

seller, salesman; peddler, smous; vender, vendor, consignor; merchant &c. 797; auctioneer.

V. sell, vend, dispose of, effect a sale; sell -over the counter, – by auction &c. *n.*; dispense, retail; deal in &c. 794; sell -off, – out; turn into money; realize; bring -to, – under- the hammer; put up to auction; auction, offer –, put up- for sale; hawk, peddle, bring to market; offer &c. 763; undersell; dump, unload.

let; mortgage &c. (*security*) 771.

Adj. under the hammer, in the market, for sale.

saleable, marketable, vendible, in demand, having a ready sale; unsaleable &c., unpurchased, unbought; on one's hands.

---

**797. Merchant.—N.** merchant, trader, dealer, monger, chandler, salesman; changer; regrater; shop-keeper, -man; trades-man, -people, -folk.

retailer; chapman, hawker, huckster, higgler; peddler, smous, pedlar, colporteur, cadger, Autolycus; sutler, *vivandière*; coster-man, -monger; market woman; cheap jack; caterer &c. 637; tallyman.

money-broker, -changer, -lender; stock-broker, -jobber; cambist, usurer, moneyer, banker.

jobber; broker &c. (*agent*) 758; buyer &c. 795; seller &c. 796.

concern; firm &c. (*partnership*) 712.

**798. Merchandise.** — **N.** merchandise, ware, commodity, effects, goods, article, stock, produce, staple commodity; stock in trade &c. (*store*) 636; cargo &c. (*contents*) 190.

**799. Mart.**—**N.** mart; market, -place, *forum*; fair, bazaar, staple; stock –, exchange; 'change, *bourse*, Wall Street, Rialto, hall, guildhall; toll-booth, custom-house; Tattersalls.

shop, stall, booth; wharf; office, chambers, counting-house, *bureau*; coun-, comp-ter.

ware-house, -room; depot, interposit, *entrepôt*, *emporium*, establishment; store &c. 636.

open market, market-overt.

### 4°. *Monetary Relations*

**800. Money.**—**N.** money -matters, – market; finance; accounts &c. 811; funds, treasure; capital, stock; assets &c. (*property*) 780; wealth &c. 803; supplies, ways and means, wherewithal, sinews of war, almighty dollar, needful, cash.

sum, amount; balance, -sheet; sum total; proceeds &c. (*receipts*) 810.

currency, circulating medium, specie; coin, – of the realm; piece, hard cash, dollar, sterling coin; pounds shillings and pence; £ s. d., guineas; pocket, breeches pocket, purse; money in hand; the best, ready, – money; filthy lucre, shekels, roll, jack, rhino, blunt, dust, bawbees, brass, dibs, dough, mopus, tin, salt, chink, oof, spondulics, pile, wads.

precious metals, gold, silver, copper, nickel; bullion, bar, ingot, nugget.

petty cash; pocket-, pin-money; small –, change; small coin, loose cash; doit, stiver, rap, mite, farthing, *sou*, penny, shilling, bob, tanner, tester, groat, guinea, ducat; *rouleau*; *wampum*; good –, round –, lump-sum; power –, mint –, tons- of money; plum, lac of rupees, millions, money-bags, miser's hoard, stocking, mine of wealth &c. 803.

[Science of coins] numismatics, chrysology.

paper-money; money –, postal –, Post Office- order; note, – of hand; bank –, treasury- note; Bradbury; promissory note; I O U., bond; bill, – of exchange; draft, cheque, order, warrant, coupon, debenture, exchequer bill, *assignat*, greenback, gold –, silver- certificate.

copper, nickel, dime, quarter, two bits, half a dollar, dollar, buck, simoleon, fiver, tenner, a twenty, a sawbuck, a century, a grand; eagle, double eagle.

gold standard, bimetallism, fiat money; rate of –, exchange; in-, de-flation.

remittance &c. (*payment*) 807; credit &c. 805; liability &c. 806; solvency &c. 803.

draw-er, -ee; oblig-or, -ee; moneyer, coiner, counterfeiter, forger.

false –, bad- money; base –, counterfeit- coin, flash note, slip, kite; Bank of Elegance.

*argumentum ad crumenam.*

**V.** amount to, come to, mount up to; touch the pocket; draw, – upon; endorse &c. (*security*) 771; issue, utter, circulate; discount &c. 813.

forge, counterfeit, coin, circulate –, pass- bad money.

**Adj.** monetary, pecuniary, crumenal, fiscal, financial, sumptuary, numismatical; sterling; solvent &c. 803.

**801. Treasurer.—N.** treasurer; bursar, -y; purser, purse-bearer; cash-keeper, banker; depositary; questor, receiver, steward, trustee, chartered –, accountant; Accountant-General, almoner, liquidator, paymaster, cashier, teller; cambist; money-changer &c. (*merchant*) 797.

financier, Chancellor of the Exchequer, minister of finance; Secretary of the Treasury, Director of the Budget, Controller of Currency.

**802. Treasury.—N.** treasury, thesaurus, bank, exchequer, almonry, fisc, hanaper, bursary; safe; strong-box, -hold, -room; coffer; chest &c. (*receptacle*) 191; depository &c. 636; till, -er; cash-box, -register, purse, pocket-book, wallet; money-bag, -belt, -box; *porte-monnaie*.

purse-strings; pocket, breeches pocket.

sinking fund; stocks; government –, public –, parliamentary- -stocks, – funds, – securities, bonds; gilt-edged securities; Consols, Liberty bonds, government bonds, *crédit mobilier*.

---

**803. Wealth.—N.** wealth, riches, fortune, handsome fortune, opulence, affluence; good –, easy- circumstances; independence; competence &c. (*sufficiency*) 639; solvency, soundness, solidity.

provision, livelihood, maintenance; alimony, dowry; means, resources, substance; property &c. 780; command of money.

income &c. 810; capital, money; round sum &c. (*treasure*) 800; mint of money, mine of wealth, El Dorado, Pactolus, Golconda, Potosi, *bonanza*; philosopher's stone.

long –, full –, well lined –, heavy-purse; purse of Fortunatus.

pelf, Mammon, lucre, filthy lucre; loaves and fishes; fleshpots of Egypt.

rich –, moneyed –, warm- man; man of substance; capitalist, millionaire, Nabob, Crœsus, Midas, Plutus, Dives, Timon of Athens; Timo-, Pluto-cracy; Danaë.

**V.** be -rich &c. *adj.*; roll –, wallow-in -wealth, – riches; have money to burn.

afford, well afford; command -money, – a sum; make both ends meet, hold one's head above water.

become -rich &c. *adj.*; fill one's -pocket &c. (*treasury*) 802; feather one's nest, clean up –, make- a fortune; make money &c. (*acquire*) 775.

enrich, imburse.

worship -Mammon, – the golden calf.

**Adj.** wealthy, rich, affluent, opulent, moneyed, monied, worth -a great deal,

**804. Poverty.—N.** poverty, indigence, penury, pauperism, destitution, want; need, -iness; lack, necessity, privation, distress, difficulties, wolf at the door.

bad –, poor –, needy –, embarrassed –, reduced –, straitened- circumstances; slender –, narrow- means; straits; hand to mouth existence, *res angusta domi,* low water, impecuniosity.

beggary; mendi-cancy, -city; broken –, loss of- fortune; insolvency &c. (*nonpayment*) 808.

empty -purse, – pocket; light purse; beggarly account of empty boxes.

poor man, pauper, mendicant, mumper, beggar, starveling; *pauvre diable*.

**V.** be -poor &c. *adj.*; want, lack, starve, live from hand to mouth, have seen better days, go down in the world, be on one's uppers, come upon the parish; go to -the dogs, – wrack and ruin; not have a -penny &c. (*money*) 800, – shot in one's locker; beg one's bread; *tirer le diable par la queue*; run into debt &c. (*debt*) 806.

render -poor &c. *adj.*; impoverish; reduce, – to poverty; pauperize, fleece, ruin, bring to the parish.

**Adj.** poor, indigent; poverty -stricken; badly –, poorly –, ill- off; poor as -a rat, – a church mouse, – Job's turkey, – Job; fortune-, dower-, money-, penni-less; unportioned, unmoneyed; impecunious; broke, flat; out –, short-of -money, – cash; without –, not worth- a rap &c. (*money*) 800; *qui n'a pas le sou*, out of pocket, hard up; out at

- much; well -to do, - off; warm; well -, provided for.

made of money; rich as Crœsus; rolling in -riches, - wealth.

flush, - of -cash, - money, - tin; in -funds, - cash, - full feather; solvent, solid, sound, pecunious, out of debt, all straight; able to pay 20s in the £.

Phr. one's ship coming in.

elbows, down at heels; seedy, bare-foot; beggar-ly, -ed; destitute; fleeced, strapped, stripped; bereft, bereaved; reduced.

in -want &c. *n.*; needy, necessitous, distressed, pinched, straitened; put to one's -shifts, - last shifts; unable to -keep the wolf from the door, - make both ends meet; embarrassed, under hatches; involved &c. (*in debt*) 806; insolvent &c. (*not paying*) 808.

Adv. *in formâ pauperis.*

Phr. *zonam perdidit.*

**805. Credit.**—N. credit, trust, tick, score, tally, account.

letter of credit, circular note; duplicate; mortgage, lien, debenture, paper credit, floating capital; draft; securities.

creditor, lender, lessor, mortgagee; dun; usurer.

V. keep -, run up- an account with; entrust, credit, accredit.

place to one's -credit, - account; give -, take- credit; fly a kite.

Adj. credit-ing, -ed; accredited.

Adv. on -credit &c. *n.*; to the -account, - credit- of.

**806. Debt.**—N. debt, obligation, liability, indebtment, debit, score.

arrears, deferred payment, deficit, default; insolvency &c. (*non-payment*) 808; bad debt.

interest; usance, usury; premium; floating -debt, - capital.

debtor, debitor; mortgagor; defaulter &c. 808; borrower.

V. be -in debt &c. *adj.*; owe; incur -, contract- a debt &c. *n.*; run up -a bill, - a score, - an account; go on tick, put on the cuff; borrow &c. 788; run -, get- into debt; outrun the constable.

answer -, go bail- for; back one's note.

Adj. indebted; liable, chargeable, answerable for.

in -debt, - embarrassed circumstances, - difficulties; incumbered, involved; involved -, plunged -, deep -, over head and ears- in debt; deeply involved; fast tied up; insolvent &c. (*not paying*) 808; *minus*, out of pocket.

unpaid; unrequited, unrewarded; owing, due, in arrear, outstanding.

**807. Payment.**—N. pay-, defrayment; discharge; ac-, quittance; settlement, clearance, liquidation, satisfaction, reckoning, arrangement.

acknowledgment, release; receipt, - in full, - in full of all demands; voucher.

repayment, reimbursement, retribution; pay &c. (*reward*) 973; money paid &c. (*expenditure*) 809.

ready money &c. (*cash*) 800; stake, remittance, instalment.

payer, liquidator &c. 801.

V. pay, defray, make payment; pay -down, - on the nail, - ready money, - at sight, - in advance; cash, honour a bill, acknowledge; redeem; pay in kind.

**808. Non-payment.**—N. non-payment; default, defalcation; protest, repudiation; application of the sponge; whitewashing.

insolvency, bankruptcy, failure; overdraft, overdrawn account; insufficiency &c. 640; run upon a bank.

waste paper bonds; dishonoured -, protested- bills; bogus cheque.

bankrupt, insolvent debtor, lame duck, man of straw, welsher, stag, defaulter, absconder, levanter.

V. not -pay &c. 807; fail, break, stop payment; become -insolvent, - bankrupt; be gazetted; abscond.

protest, dishonour, repudiate, nullify.

pay under protest; button up one's

pay one's -way, – shot, – footing; pay -the piper, – sauce for all, – costs; do the needful; come across; shell –, fork- out; come down with, – the dust; tickle –, grease- the palm; expend &c. 809; put –, lay- down.

discharge, settle, quit, acquit oneself of; account –, reckon –, settle –, be even –, be quits- with; strike a balance; settle –, balance –, square-accounts with; quit scores; foot the bill; wipe –, clear- off old scores; satisfy; pay in full; satisfy –, pay in full of- all demands; clear, liquidate; pay -up, – old debts.

pockets, draw the purse strings; apply the sponge; pay over the left shoulder, get whitewashed; swindle &c. 791; run up bills, fly kites.

Adj. not paying; in debt &c. 806; behindhand, in arrear; beggared &c; (*poor*) 804; unable to make both ends meet; *minus*; worse than nothing.

insolvent, bankrupt, in the gazette, gazetted, ruined.

unpaid &c. (*outstanding*) 806; *gratis* &c. 815; unremunerated.

disgorge, make repayment; repay, refund, reimburse, retribute; make compensation &c. 30.

Adj. paying &c., paid &c. *v.*; owing nothing, out of debt, all straight, clear of -debt, – encumbrance; unowed, never indebted.

Adv. to the tune of; on the nail; money –, cash- down; cash on delivery.

---

**809. Expenditure.—N.** expenditure, money going out; out-goings, -lay; expenses, disbursement; prime cost &c. (*price*) 812; circulation; run upon a bank.

[Money paid] payment &c. 807; pay &c. (*remuneration*) 973; bribe &c. 973; fee, footing, garnish; subsidy; tribute, Peter's pence; contingent, quota; donation &c. 784.

pay in advance, earnest, handsel, deposit, instalment.

investment; purchase &c. 795.

V. expend; spend; run –, get-through; pay, disburse; open –, loose –, untie- the purse strings; lay –, shell –, fork- out; bleed; make up a sum, invest, sink money.

fee &c. (*reward*) 973; pay one's way &c. (*pay*) 807; subscribe &c. (*give*) 784; subsidize, bribe.

**810. Receipt.—N.** receipt, account-able –, conditional –, binding –, return-receipt; value received, money coming in; income, incomings, innings, reve-nue, return, proceeds; gross receipts, net profit; earnings &c. (*gain*) 775.

rent, – roll; rent-al, -age; rack-rent.

premium, *bonus*; sweepstakes, tontine, prize, drawing.

pension, annuity; jointure &c. (*property*) 780; alimony, pittance; emolument &c. (*remuneration*) 973.

V. receive &c. 785; take money; draw –, derive- from; get, be in receipt of, acquire &c. 775; take &c. 789.

bring in, yield, afford, pay, return; accrue &c. (*be received from*) 785.

Adj. receiv-ing, -ed &c. *v.*; profitable &c. (*gainful*) 775.

---

Adj. expend-ing, -ed &c. *v.*; sumptuary, liberal &c. 816; open-handed, lavish &c. 818; expensive &c. 814;

---

**811. Accounts.—N.** accounts, accompts; commercial –, monetary-arithmetic; statistics &c. (*numeration*) 85; money matters, finance, budget, bill, score, reckoning, account.

books, account book, ledger; day –, cash –, pass- book; journal; debtor and creditor –, cash –, petty cash –, running- account; account-current; balance, – sheet; *compte rendu*, account settled.

book-keeping, audit; double –, single- entry; reckoning &c. 85.

chartered –, certified public –, accountant; auditor, actuary, book-keeper; financier &c. 801; accounting party.

V. keep accounts, enter, post, book, credit, debit, carry over; take stock; balance –, make up –, square –, settle –, wind up –, cast up –, add up –, tot up- accounts; make accounts square.

bring to book, audit, tax, surcharge and falsify.

falsify –, garble –, cook –, doctor- an account.

Adj. monetary &c. 800; account-able, -ing; statistical.

**812. Price.**—N. price, amount, cost, expense, prime cost, charge, figure, demand, damage, fare, hire; wages &c. (*remuneration*) 973.

dues, duty, toll, tax, impost, cess, sess, tallage, levy, capitation-, poll-, income-, sur-, sales-, super-tax; gabel, *gabelle*; gavel, *octroi*, custom, tariff, excise, assessment, taxation, benevolence, tithe, tenths, exactment, ransom, salvage; broker-, wharf-, lighter-, ton-, freight-age.

worth, rate, value, valuation, appraisement, money's worth, par value; penny &c. -worth; price current, market price, quotation; what it will -fetch &c. *v.*

bill &c. (*account*) 811; shot.

V. bear –, set –, fix- a price; appraise, assess, price, charge, demand, ask, require, exact, run up; distrain; run up a bill &c. (*debt*) 806; have one's price; liquidate.

amount to, come to, mount up to; stand one in.

fetch, sell for, cost, bring in, yield, afford.

Adj. priced &c. *v.*; to the tune of, *ad valorem*; mercenary, venal.

Phr. no penny, no paternoster; *point d'argent, point de Suisse*; no longer pipe, no longer dance; no song, no supper.

one may have it for.

**813. Discount.**—N. discount, abatement, concession, reduction, depreciation, allowance, qualification, set off, drawback, poundage, *agio*, percentage; rebate, -ment; backwardation, contango; salvage; tare and tret.

V. discount, bate; a-, re-bate; deduct, reduce, mark down, take off, allow, give, make allowance; tax, depreciate.

Adj. discounting &c. *v.*

Adv. at a discount, below par.

---

**814. Dearness. — N.** dearness &c. *adj.*; high –, famine –, fancy- price; overcharge; extravagance; exorbitance, extortion; heavy pull upon the purse; Pyrrhic victory.

V. be -dear &c. *adj.*; cost -much, – a pretty penny; rise in price, look up.

overcharge, bleed, fleece, skin, extort.

pay -too much, – through the nose, – too dear for one's whistle.

Adj. dear; high, -priced; of great price, expensive, costly, precious, worth a Jew's eye, dear bought; unreasonable, extravagant, exorbitant, extortionate.

at a premium; not to be had, – for love or money; beyond –, above- price; priceless, of priceless value.

Adv. dear, -ly; at great , heavy-cost; *à grands frais*.

Phr. prices looking up; *le jeu n'en vaut pas la chandelle*.

**815. Cheapness.**—N. cheapness, low price; depreciation; bargain; good penny &c. worth, *bon marché*.

[Absence of charge] gratuity; free -quarters, – seats, – admission, – warren; pass, Annie Oakley; run of one's teeth; nominal price, peppercorn rent; labour of love.

drug in the market.

V. be -cheap &c. *adj.*; cost little; come down –, fall- in price.

buy for -a mere nothing, – an old song; have one's money's worth; cheapen, beat down.

Adj. cheap; low, – priced; moderate, reasonable; in-, un-expensive; well –, worth the money; *magnifique et pas cher*; good –, cheap- at the price; dirt –, dog- cheap; cheap, -as dirt, – and nasty; catchpenny.

reduced, marked down, half-price, depreciated, unsaleable.

gratuitous, *gratis*, free, for love,

– nothing; cost-, expense-less; without charge, not charged, untaxed; scot –, shot –, rent- free; free of -cost, – expense; honorary, unbought, unpaid, complimentary.

*Adv.* for a mere song; at -cost price, – prime cost, – a reduction, – a bargain; on the cheap.

**816. Liberality.—N.** liberality, generosity, munificence; bount-y, -eousness, -ifulness; hospitality; charity &c. (*beneficence*) 906.

benefactor, free giver, Lady Bountiful.

**V.** be -liberal &c. *adj.*; spend –, bleed- freely; shower down upon; open one's purse strings &c. (*disburse*) 809; spare no expense, give -with both hands, – *carte blanche.*

**Adj.** liberal, free, generous; charitable &c. (*beneficent*) 906; hospitable; bount-iful, -eous; handsome; unsparing, ungrudging; open-, free-, full-handed; open-, large-, free-hearted; munificent, princely, unstinting.

overpaid.

**Adv.** liberally, ungrudgingly, with open hand.

---

**818. Prodigality.—N.** prodi-gality, -gence; unthriftiness, waste, -fulness; profus-ion, -eness; extravagance; squandering &c. *v.*; lavishness; malversation.

prodigal; spend-, waste-thrift; losel, play-boy, spender, squanderer, locust.

**V.** be -prodigal &c. *adj.*; squander, lavish, sow broadcast; pour forth like water; pay through the nose &c. (*dear*) 814; spill, waste, dissipate, exhaust, drain, eat out of house and home, overdraw, outrun the constable; run -out, – through; misspend; throw -good money after bad, – the helve after the hatchet; burn the candle at both ends; make ducks and drakes of one's money; squander one's substance, spend money like water; fool –, potter –, muddle –, fritter –, throw- away one's money; pour water into a sieve, kill the goose that lays the golden eggs; *manger son blé en herbe.*

**Adj.** prodigal, profuse, thriftless, unthrifty, improvident, wasteful, losel,

**817. Economy.—N.** economy, frugality; thrift, -iness; prudence, care, husbandry, good housewifery, savingness, retrenchment.

savings; prevention of waste, save-all; cheese parings and candle ends; parsimony &c. 819.

**V.** be -economical &c. *adj.*; economize, save; retrench; cut- down expenses, – one's coat according to one's cloth, make both ends meet, keep within compass, meet one's expenses, pay one's way; keep one's head above water; husband &c. (*lay by*) 636; save –, invest- money; put out to interest; provide –, save- -for, – against- a rainy day; feather one's nest; look after the main chance.

**Adj.** economical, frugal, careful, thrifty, saving, chary, spare, sparing; parsimonious &c. 819.

underpaid.

**Adv.** sparingly &c. *adj.*; *ne quid nimis.*

**819. Parsimony. — N.** parsimony, parcity; parsimoniousness, stinginess &c. *adj.*; stint; illiberality, avarice, tenacity, avidity, rapacity, extortion, venality, cupidity; selfishness &c. 943; *auri sacra fames.*

miser, niggard, churl, screw, tightwad, skinflint, crib, codger, muckworm, money-grubber, pinchfist, scrimp, lickpenny, hunks, curmudgeon, *Harpagon*, Silas Marner, harpy, extortioner, Jew, usurer.

**V.** be -parsimonious &c. *adj.*; grudge, begrudge, stint, skimp, pinch, gripe, screw, dole out, hold back, withhold, starve, famish, live upon nothing, skin a flint.

drive a -bargain, – hard bargain; cheapen, beat down; stop one hole in a sieve; have an itching palm, grasp, grab.

**Adj.** parsimonious, penurious, stingy, miserly, mean, shabby, peddling, scrubby, pennywise, near, niggardly,

extravagant, lavish, dissipated, over liberal; full-handed &c. (*liberal*) 816.

penny wise and pound foolish.

**Adv.** with an unsparing hand; money burning one's pocket; recklessly profuse.

**Int.** hang the expense!

___

frugal to excess; close; fast-, close-, strait-handed; close-, hard-, tight-fisted; tight, sparing; chary; grudging, griping &c. *v.*; illiberal, ungenerous, churlish, hidebound, sordid, mercenary, venal, covetous, usurious, avaricious, greedy, extortionate, rapacious.

**Adv.** with a sparing hand.

# CLASS VI

## Words relating to the SENTIENT and MORAL POWERS.

~~~~~~~~~~

### Section I. AFFECTIONS IN GENERAL

**820. Affections.—N.** affections, character, qualities, disposition, nature, spirit, tone; temper, -ament; *diathesis*, idiosyncrasy; cast –, habit –, frame- of -mind, – soul; predilection, turn; natural –, turn of mind; bent, bias, predisposition, proneness, proclivity; propen-sity, -sedness, -sion, -dency; vein, humour, mood, grain, mettle; sympathy &c. (*love*) 897.

soul, heart, breast, bosom, inner man; heart's -core, – strings, – blood; heart of hearts, *penetralia mentis*; secret and inmost recesses of the –, cockles of one's- heart; inmost -heart, – soul; back-bone.

passion, pervading spirit; ruling –, master- passion; *furore*; fulness of the heart, heyday of the blood, flesh and blood, flow of soul, force of character.

**V.** have –, possess- -affections &c. *n.*; be of a -character &c. *n.*; be -affected &c. *adj.*; breathe.

**Adj.** affected, characterized, formed, moulded, cast; at-, tempered; framed; pre-, disposed; prone, inclined; having a -bias &c. *n.*; tinctured –, imbued –, penetrated –, eaten up- with.

inborn, inbred, ingrained, in the grain, congenital, inherent, bred in the bone; deep-rooted, ineffaceable, inveterate; pathoscopic.

**Adv.** in one's -heart &c. *n.*; at heart; heart and soul &c. 821; in the -vein, – mood.

**821. Feeling.—N.** feeling; suffering &c. *v.*; endurance, tolerance, sufferance, supportance, experience, response; sympathy &c. (*love*) 897; impression, inspiration, affection, sensation, emotion, pathos, deep sense.

fire, warmth, glow, unction, *gusto*, vehemence; ferv-our, -ency; heartiness, cordiality; earnestness, eagerness; *empressement*, ardour, zeal, passion, enthusiasm, *verve*, *furore*, fanaticism; excitation of feeling &c. 824; fulness of the heart &c. (*disposition*) 820; passion &c. (*state of excitability*) 825; ecstasy &c. (*pleasure*) 827.

blush, suffusion, flush; hectic; tingling, thrill, kick, turn, shock; agitation &c. (*irregular motion*) 315; quiver, heaving, flutter, flurry, fluster, twitter, tremor; throb, -bing; pulsation, palpitation, panting; trepid-, perturb-ation; ruffle, hurry of spirits, pother, stew, ferment.

**V.** feel; receive an -impression &c. *n.*; be -impressed with &c. *adj.*; entertain –, harbour –, cherish- -feeling &c. *n.*

respond; catch the -flame, – infection; enter the spirit of.

bear, suffer, support, sustain, endure, brook, thole, aby; abide &c.

(*be composed*) 826; experience &c. (*meet with*) 151; taste, prove; labour –, smart- under; bear the brunt of, brave, stand.

swell, glow, warm, flush, blush, change colour, mantle; turn -colour, – pale, – red, – black in the face; blench, crimson, whiten, pale, tingle, thrill, heave, pant, throb, palpitate, go pit-a-pat, tremble, quiver, flutter, twitter; stagger, reel; shake &c. 315; be -agitated, – excited &c. 824; look -blue, – black; wince, draw a deep breath.

impress &c. (*excite the feelings*) 824.

**Adj.** feeling &c. *v.*; sentient; sensuous; sensor-ial, -y; emo-tive, -tional; of –, with- feeling &c. *n.*

warm, quick, lively, smart, strong, sharp, acute, cutting, piercing, incisive; keen, – as a razor; trenchant, pungent, racy, *piquant*, poignant, caustic.

impressive, deep, profound, indelible; deep-, home-, heart-felt; swelling, soul-stirring, deep-mouthed, heart-expanding, electric, thrilling, rapturous, ecstatic.

earnest, wistful, eager, breathless; fer-vent, -vid; gushing, passionate, warmhearted, hearty, cordial, sincere, zealous, enthusiastic, glowing, ardent, burning, red-hot, fiery, flaming; boiling, – over.

pervading, penetrating, absorbing; rabid, raving, feverish, fanatical, hysterical; impetuous &c. (*excitable*) 825; overmastering.

impressed –, moved –, touched –, affected –, penetrated –, seized –, imbued &c. 820- with; devoured by; wrought up &c. (*excited*) 824; struck all of a heap; rapt; in a -quiver &c. *n.*; enraptured &c. 829.

**Adv.** heart and soul, from the bottom of one's heart, *ab imo pectore*, *de profundis*, at heart, *con amore*, heartily, devoutly, over head and ears.

**Phr.** the heart -big, – full, – swelling, – beating, – pulsating, – throbbing, – thumping, – beating high, – melting, – overflowing, – bursting, – breaking.

---

**822. Sensibility.** — **N.** sensi-bility, -bleness, -tiveness; moral sensibility; impress-, affect-ibility; suscepti-ble-ness, -bility, -vity; mobility; viva-city, -ciousness; tender-, soft-ness; senti-mental-ity, -ism.

excitability &c. 825; fastidiousness &c. 868; physical sensibility &c. 375.

sore -point, – place; where the shoe pinches.

**V.** be -sensible &c. *adj.*; have a -tender, – warm, – sensitive- heart.

take to –, treasure up in the- heart; shrink.

'die of a rose in aromatic pain'; touch to the quick.

**Adj.** sensi-ble, -tive; impressi-ble, -onable; suscepti-ve, -ble; alive to, impassion-able, -ed; gushing; warm-, tender-, soft-hearted; tender –, as a chicken; soft, sentimental, romantic; enthusiastic, highflying, spirited, mettlesome, vivacious, lively, expressive, mobile, tremblingly alive; excitable

**823. Insensibility.**—**N.** insensi-bility, -bleness; moral insensibility; inertness, *inertia*, *vis inertiæ*; impassi-bility, -bleness; inappetency, apathy, phlegm, dulness, hebetude, supineness, luke-warmness, insusceptibility, unimpressibility.

cold -fit, – blood, – heart; cold-, cool-ness; frigidity, *sang-froid*; stoicism, imperturbation &c. (*inexcitability*) 826; *nonchalance*, unconcern, dry eyes; *insouciance* &c. (*indifference*) 866; recklessness &c. 863; callousness; heart of stone, stock and stone, marble, deadness.

torp-or, -idity; obstupefaction, lethargy, coma, trance; sleep &c. 683; suspended animation; stup-or, -efaction; paralysis, palsy; numbness &c. (*physical insensibility*) 376.

neutrality; quietism, vegetation.

**V.** be -insensible &c. *adj.*; have a rhinoceros hide; show -insensibility &c. *n.*; not -mind, – care, – be affected

&c. 825; over-sensitive, without skin, thin-skinned; fastidious &c. 868.

Adv. sensibly &c. *adj.*; to the -quick, - inmost core.

———

by; have no desire for &c. 866; have -, feel -, take- no interest in; *nil admirari*; not care a -straw &c. (*unimportance*) 643 for; disregard &c. (*neglect*) 460; set at naught &c. (*make light of*) 483; turn a deaf ear to &c. (*inattention*) 458; vegetate.

render -insensible, - callous; blunt, obtund, numb, benumb, paralyze, chloroform, deaden, hebetate, stun, stupefy; brut-ify, -alize.

inure; harden, - the heart; steel, case-harden, sear.

Adj. insensible, unconscious; impassi-ve, -ble; blind to, deaf to, dead to; un-, in-susceptible; unimpress-ionable, -ible; passion-, spirit-, heart-, soul-less; unfeeling, unmoral.

apathetic; leuco-, phlegmatic; dull, frigid; cold, -blooded, -hearted; unemotional; cold as charity; flat, obtuse, inert, supine, sluggish, torpid; sleepy &c. (*inactive*) 683; languid, half-hearted, tame; numb, -ed; comatose; anæsthetic &c. 376; stupefied, chloroformed, palsy-stricken.

indifferent, lukewarm; Laodicean; careless, mindless, regardless; inattentive &c. 458; neglectful &c. 460; disregarding.

unconcerned, *nonchalant, pococurante, insouciant, sans souci*; un-ambitious &c. 866.

un-affected, -ruffled, -impressed, -inspired, -excited, -moved, -stirred, -touched, -shocked, -struck; unblushing &c. (*shameless*) 885; unanimated; vegetative.

callous, thick-skinned, pachydermatous, impervious; hard, -ened; inured, case-hardened; steeled -, proof- against; imperturbable &c. (*inexcitable*) 826; unfelt.

Adv. insensibly &c. *adj.*; *æquo animo*; without being -moved, - touched, - impressed; in cold blood; with -dry eyes, - withers unwrung.

Phr. never mind; it is of no consequence &c. (*unimportant*) 643; it cannot be helped; nothing coming amiss; it is all -the same, - one- to.

824. Excitation.—N. excitation of feeling; mental -, excitement; suscitation, galvanism, stimulation, piquancy, provocation, inspiration, calling forth, infection; interest, animation, agitation, perturbation; subjugation, fascination, intoxication; en-, ravishment; entrancement, high pressure.

unction, impressiveness &c. *adj.*; emotional appeal; melodrama; psychological moment, crisis; sensationalism.

trial of temper, *casus belli*; irritation &c. (*anger*) 900; passion &c. (*state of excitability*) 825; thrill &c. (*feeling*) 821; repression of feeling &c. 826.

V. excite, affect, touch, move, impress, strike, interest, intrigue, animate, inspire, impassion, smite, infect; stir -, fire -, warm- the blood; set astir; a-, wake; a-, waken; call forth; e-, pro-voke; raise up, summon up, call up, wake up, blow up, get up, light up; raise; get up steam, rouse, arouse, stir, fire, kindle, enkindle, apply the torch, set on fire, inflame, illuminate.

stimulate; ex-, suscitate; inspirit; spirit up, stir up, work up; infuse life into, give new life to; bring -, introduce- new blood; quicken;

sharpen, whet; work upon &c. (*incite*) 615; hurry on, give a fillip, put on one's mettle.

fan the -fire, – flame; blow the coals, stir the embers; fan, – into a flame; foster, heat, warm, foment, raise to a fever heat; keep -up, – the pot boiling; revive, rekindle; rake up, rip up.

stir –, play on –, come home to- the feelings; touch -a string, – a chord, – the soul, – the heart; go to one's heart, penetrate, pierce, go through one, touch to the quick, open the wound; possess –, pervade –, penetrate –, imbrue –, absorb –, affect –, disturb- the soul.

absorb, rivet the attention; sink into the -mind, – heart; prey on the mind; intoxicate; over-whelm, -power; *bouleverser*, upset, turn one's head.

fascinate; enrapture &c. (*give pleasure*) 829.

agitate, perturb, ruffle, fluster, flutter, shake, disturb, faze, startle, shock, stagger; give one a -shock, – turn; strike -dumb, – all of a heap; stun, astound, electrify, galvanize, petrify.

irritate, sting; cut, – to the -heart, – quick; try one's temper; fool to the top of one's bent, pique; infuriate, madden, make one's blood boil; lash into fury &c. (*wrath*) 900.

be -excited &c. *adj.*; flash up, flare up; catch the infection; thrill &c. (*feel*) 821; mantle; work oneself up; seethe, boil, simmer, foam, fume, flame, rage, rave; run mad &c. (*passion*) 825.

Adj. excited &c. *v.*; wrought up, on the *qui vive*, astir, sparkling; in a -quiver &c. 821, – fever, – ferment, – blaze, – state of excitement; in hysterics; black in the face, over-wrought; hot, red-hot, flushed, feverish; all -of a twitter, – of a flutter, – of a dither, – in a pucker; with -quivering lips, – tears in one's eyes.

flaming; boiling, – over; ebullient, seething; foaming, – at the mouth; fuming, raging, carried away by passion, wild, raving, frantic, mad, distracted, distraught, beside oneself, out of one's wits, amuck, ready to burst, *bouleversé*, demoniacal.

lost, *éperdu*, tempest-tossed; haggard; ready to sink.

stung to the quick, up, on one's high ropes.

exciting &c. *v.*; impressive, warm, glowing, fervid, swelling, impos-ing, spirit-stirring, thrilling; high-wrought; soul-stirring, -subduing; heart-swelling, -thrilling; agonizing &c. (*painful*) 830; telling, sensa-tional, melodramatic, hysterical; over-powering, -whelming; more than flesh and blood can bear.

*piquant* &c. (*pungent*) 392; spicy, appetizing, provocative, *provoquant*, tantalizing.

Adv. till one is black in the face.

Phr. the heart -beating high, – going pit-a-pat, – leaping into one's mouth; the blood -being up, – boiling in one's veins; the eye -glisten-ing, – 'in a fine frenzy rolling'; the head turned.

---

825. [Excess of sensitiveness.] Excit-ability.—N. excitability, impetuosity, vehemence; boisterousness &c. *adj.*; turbulence; impatience, intolerance, non-endurance; irritability &c. (*irasci-bility*) 901; itching &c. (*desire*) 865; wincing; disquiet, -ude; restlessness; fidgets, fidgetiness; agitation &c. (*ir-regular motion*) 315.

826. [Absence of excitability, or of excitement.] Inexcitability.—N. inex-cit-, imperturb-, inirrit-ability; even temper, tranquil mind, dispassion; tol-erance, toleration, patience.

passiveness &c. (*physical inertness*) 172; hebet-ude, -ation; impassibility &c. (*insensibility*) 823; stupefaction.

coolness, calmness &c. *adj.*; compo-

trepidation, perturbation, ruffle, hurry, -skurry, fuss, flurry; fluster, flutter; pother, stew, ferment; whirl; thrill &c. (*feeling*) 821; state –, fever-of excitement; transport.

passion, excitement, flush, heat; fever, -heat; fire, flame, fume, blood boiling; tumult; effervescence, ebullition; boiling, – over; whiff, gust, storm, tempest; scene, breaking out, burst, fit, paroxysm, explosion; out-break, -burst; agony.

violence &c. 173; fierceness &c. *adj.*; rage, fury, *furor*, *furore*, desperation, madness, distraction, raving, delirium, brain storm; frenzy, hysterics; intoxication; tearing –, raging- passion, towering rage; anger &c. 900.

fascination, infatuation, fanaticism; Quixot-ism, -ry; *tête montée*.

V. be -impatient &c. *adj.*; not be able to -bear &c. 826; bear ill, wince, chafe, champ the bit; be in a -stew &c. *n.*; be out of all patience, fidget, fuss, not have a wink of sleep; toss, – on one's pillow.

lose one's temper &c. 900; break –, burst –, fly- out; go –, fly- -off, – off the handle, – off at a tangent; explode; flare up, flame up, fire up, burst into a flame, take fire, fire, burn; boil, – over; foam, fume, rage, rave, rant, tear; go –, run- -wild, – mad; go into hysterics; run -riot, – amuck; *battre la campagne, faire le diable à quatre,* play the deuce; raise -Cain, – the devil.

Adj. excitable, easily excited, in an excitable state; highly strung; irritable &c. (*irascible*) 901; impatient, intolerant.

feverish, febrile, hysterical; delirious, mad, moody, maggoty-headed.

unquiet, mercurial, electric, galvanic, hasty, hurried, restless, fidgety, fussy; chafing &c. *v.*

startlish, mettlesome, high mettled, skittish.

vehement, demonstrative, violent, wild, furious, fierce, fiery, hot-headed, mad-cap.

over-zealous, enthusiastic, impassioned, fanatical; rabid &c. (*eager*) 865.

rampant, clamorous, uproarious, tur-

sure, placidity, indisturbance, imperturbation, *sang-froid*, tranquillity, serenity; quiet, -ude; peace of mind, mental calmness.

staidness &c. *adj.*; gravity, sobriety, Quakerism; philosophy, equanimity, stoicism, command of temper; self-possession, -control, -command, -restraint; presence of mind.

submission &c. 725; resignation; suffer-, support-, endur-, long-suffer-, forbear-ance; longanimity; fortitude; patience -of Job, – 'on a monument,' – 'sovereign o'er transmuted ill'; moderation; repression –, subjugation- of feeling; restraint &c. 751.

tranquillization &c. (*moderation*) 174.

V. be -composed &c. *adj.*

*laisser -faire*, – *aller*; take things -easily, – as they come; take it easy, run on, live and let live; take -easily, – coolly, – in good part; *æquam servare mentem.*

bear, – well, – the brunt; go through, support, endure, brave, disregard.

tolerate, suffer, stand, bide; abide, aby; bear –, put up –, abide- with; acquiesce; submit &c. (*yield*) 725; submit with a good grace; resign –, reconcile- oneself to; brook, digest, eat, swallow, pocket, stomach; make -light of, – the best of, – a virtue of necessity; put a good face on, keep one's countenance; carry -on, – through; check &c. 751- oneself.

compose, appease &c. (*moderate*) 174; propitiate; repress &c. (*restrain*) 751; render insensible &c. 823; overcome –, allay –, repress- one's -excitability &c. 825; master one's feelings.

make -oneself, – one's mind- easy; set one's mind at -ease, – rest.

calm –, cool- down; thaw, grow cool.

be -borne, – endured; go down.

Adj. in-, un-excitable; imperturbable; unsusceptible &c. (*insensible*) 823; un-, dis-passionate; cold-blooded, inirritable; enduring &c. *v.*; stoical, Platonic, philosophic, staid, stayed; sober, – minded; grave; sober –, grave- as a judge; sedate, demure, cool-, level-headed; steady.

easy-going, peaceful, placid, calm; quiet, – as a mouse; tranquil, serene;

bulent, tempestuous, tumultuary, boisterous.

impulsive, impetuous, passionate; uncontroll-ed, -able; ungovernable, irrepressible, stanchless, inextinguishable, burning, simmering, volcanic, ready to burst forth.

excit-ed, -ing &c. 824.

Int. pish! pshaw!

Phr. *noli me tangere.*

cool, – as -a cucumber, – custard; undemonstrative.

temperate &c. (*moderate*) 174; composed, collected; un-excited, -stirred, -ruffled, -disturbed, -perturbed, -impassioned; unoffended; unresisting.

meek, tolerant; patient, – as Job; submissive &c. 725; tame; content, resigned, chastened, subdued, lamb-like; gentle, – as a lamb; *suaviter in modo*; mild, – as mother's milk; soft as peppermint; armed with patience, bearing with, clement, forbearant, long-suffering.

Adv. 'like patience on a monument smiling at grief'; *æquo animo*, in cold blood &c. 823; more in sorrow than in anger.

Int. patience! and shuffle the cards.

## Section II.  PERSONAL AFFECTIONS*

### 1°.  Passive Affections

**827. Pleasure.—N.** pleasure, gratification, enjoyment, fruition; ob-, delectation; relish, zest; *gusto* &c. (*physical pleasure*) 377; satisfaction &c. (*content*) 831; complacency.

well-being; good &c. 618; snugness, comfort, ease; cushion &c. 215; *sans souci*, mind at ease.

joy, gladness, delight, glee, cheer, sunshine; cheerfulness &c. 836.

treat, refreshment; frolic, fun, lark, gambol, merry-making; amusement &c. 840; luxury &c. 377; hedonism.

*mens sana in corpore sano.*

happiness, felicity, bliss; beati-tude, -fication; enchantment, transport, rapture, ravishment, ecstasy; *summum bonum*; paradise, elysium &c. (*heaven*) 981; third –, seventh- heaven; unalloyed -happiness &c.

honeymoon; palmy –, halcyon- days; golden -age, – time; *Saturnia regna*, Eden, Arcadia, happy valley, Agapemone; Cockaigne.

**V.** be pleased &c. 829; feel –, experience- pleasure &c. *n.*; joy; enjoy –, hug- oneself; be in -clover &c. 377, – elysium &c. 981; tread on enchanted ground; fall –, go- into raptures.

feel at home, breathe freely, bask in the sunshine.

be -pleased &c. 829– with; receive –, derive- pleasure &c. *n.*- from; take -pleasure &c. *n.*- in; delight in, rejoice

**828. Pain. — N.** mental suffering, pain, dolour; suffer-ing, -ance; ache, smart &c. (*physical pain*) 378; passion.

displeasure, dissatisfaction, discomfort, discomposure, disquiet; *malaise*; inquietude, uneasiness, vexation of spirit; taking; discontent &c. 832.

dejection &c. 837; weariness &c. 841.

annoyance, irritation, worry, infliction, visitation; plague, bore; bother, -ation; stew, vexation, mortification, chagrin, *esclandre*; *mauvais quart d'heure.*

care, anxiety, solicitude, trouble, trial, ordeal, fiery ordeal, shock, blow, cark, dole, fret, burden, load.

concern, grief, sorrow, distress, affliction, woe, bitterness, gloom, heartache; heavy –, aching –, bleeding –, brokenheart; heavy affliction, gnawing grief.

unhappiness, infelicity, misery, tribulation, wretchedness, desolation; despair &c. 859; extremity, prostration, depth of misery.

nightmare, *ephialtes*, incubus.

anguish, agony; throe, tor-ture, -ment; crucifixion, martyrdom; pang, twinge, stab; the rack, the stake; purgatory &c. (*hell*) 982.

hell upon earth; iron age, reign of terror; slough of despond &c. (*adversity*) 735; peck –, sea- of troubles; ills that flesh is heir to &c. (*evil*) 619;

* Or those which concern one's own state of feeling.

in, indulge in, luxuriate in; gloat over &c. (*physical pleasure*) 377; enjoy, relish, like; love &c. 897; take -to, - a fancy to; have a liking for; enter into the spirit of.

take in good part.

treat oneself to, solace oneself with.

**Adj.** pleased &c. 829; not sorry; glad, -some; pleased as Punch.

happy, blest, blessed, blissful, beatified; happy as -a king, - the day is long; thrice happy, *ter quaterque beatus*; enjoying &c. *v.*; joyful &c. (*in spirits*) 836; hedonic.

in -a blissful state, - paradise &c. 981, - raptures, - ecstasies, - a transport of delight; rapturous.

comfortable &c. (*physical pleasure*) 377; at ease; content &c. 831; *sans souci*, in clover.

overjoyed, entranced, enchanted; enraptured; en-, ravished; transported; fascinated, captivated.

with -a joyful face, - sparkling eyes.

pleasing &c. 829; ecstatic, beat-ic, -ific; painless, unalloyed, without alloy, cloudless.

**Adv.** happily &c. *adj.*; with pleasure &c. (*willingly*) 602; with -glee &c. *n.*

**Phr.** one's heart leaping with joy.

---

miseries of human life; unkindest cut of all.

sufferer, victim, prey, martyr, object of compassion, wretch, shorn lamb.

**V.** feel -, suffer -, experience -, undergo -, bear -, endure- pain &c. *n.*; smart, ache &c. (*physical pain*) 378; suffer, bleed, ail; be the victim of; bear -, take up- the cross.

labour under afflictions; quaff the bitter cup, have a bad time of it; fall on evil days &c. (*adversity*) 735; go hard with, come to grief, fall a sacrifice to, drain the cup of misery to the dregs, sup full of horrors.

sit on thorns, be on pins and needles, wince, fret, chafe, worry oneself, be in a taking, fret and fume, take -on, - to heart.

grieve; mourn &c. (*lament*) 839; yearn, repine, pine, droop, languish, sink; give way; despair &c. 859; break one's heart; weigh upon the heart &c. (*inflict pain*) 830.

**Adj.** in -, in a state of -, full of- pain &c. *n.*; suffering &c. *v.*; pained, afflicted, worried, displeased &c. 830; aching, griped, sore &c. (*physical pain*) 378; on the rack, in limbo; between hawk and buzzard.

un-comfortable, -easy; ill at ease; in a -taking, - way; disturbed; discontented &c. 832; out of humour &c. 901a; weary &c. 841.

heavy laden, stricken, crushed, a prey to, victimized, ill-used.

unfortunate &c. (*hapless*) 735; to be pitied, doomed, devoted, accursed, undone, lost, stranded.

unhappy, infelicitous, poor, wretched, miserable, woe-begone; cheerless &c. (*dejected*) 837; careworn.

concerned, sorry; sorrow-ing, -ful; cut up, chagrined, horrified, horror-stricken; in -, plunged in -, a prey to- grief &c. *n.*; in tears &c. (*lamenting*) 839; steeped to the lips in misery; heart-stricken, -broken, -scalded; broken-hearted; in despair &c. 859.

**Phr.** 'the iron entered into the soul'; '*hæret lateri lethalis arundo*'; one's heart bleeding.

---

**829.** [Capability of giving pleasure; cause or source of pleasure.] **Pleasurableness.**—**N.** pleasurable-, pleasant-, agreeable-ness &c. *adj.*; pleasure giving, jocundity, delectability; amusement &c. 840.

attraction &c. (*motive*) 615; attractiveness, -ability; invitingness &c. *adj.*; charm, fascination, captivation, en-

**830.** [Capability of giving pain; cause or source of pain.] **Painfulness.**—**N.** painfulness &c. *adj.*; trouble, care &c. (*pain*) 828; trial; af-, in-fliction; cross, blow, stroke, burden, load, curse; bitter -pill, - draught, - cup; waters of bitterness.

annoyance, grievance, nuisance, vexation, mortification, sickener; bore,

chantment, witchery, seduction, winsomeness, winning ways, amenity, amiability, sweetness.

loveliness &c. (*beauty*) 845; sunny –, bright- side; sweets &c. (*sugar*) 396; goodness &c. 648; manna in the wilderness, land flowing with milk and honey.

treat; regale &c. (*physical pleasure*) 377; dainty; tit-, tid-bit; nuts, *sauce piquante*.

V. cause –, produce –, create –, give –, afford –, procure –, offer –, present –, yield- pleasure &c. 827.

please, charm, delight; gladden &c. (*make cheerful*) 836; take, captivate, fascinate; enchant, entrance, enrapture, transport, bewitch; cn-, ravish.

bless, beatify; satisfy; gratify, – desire &c. 865; slake, satiate, quench; indulge, humour, flatter, tickle; tickle the palate &c. (*savoury*) 394; regale, refresh; enliven; treat; amuse &c. 840; take –, tickle –, hit- one's fancy; meet one's wishes; win –, gladden –, rejoice –, warm the cockles of- the heart; do one's heart good.

attract, allure &c. (*move*) 615; stimulate &c. (*excite*) 824; interest, intrigue.

make things pleasant, popularize, gild the pill, sweeten.

Adj. causing pleasure &c. *v.*; pleasure-giving; pleas-ing, -ant, -urable; agreeable, cushy; grat-eful, -ifying; leef, lief, acceptable; welcome, – as the roses in May; welcomed; favourite; to one's -taste, – mind, – liking, – heart's content; satisfactory &c. (*good*) 648.

refreshing; comfortable; cordial; genial; glad, -some; sweet, delectable, nice, dainty; delic-ate, -ious; dulcet; luscious &c. 396; palatable &c. 394; luxurious, voluptuous; sensual &c. 377.

attractive &c. 615; inviting, prepossessing, engaging; win-ning, -some; taking, fascinating, captivating, killing; seduc-ing, -tive; alluring, enticing; appetizing &c. (*exciting*) 824; cheering &c. 836; bewitching; interesting, absorbing, enchanting, ontrancing, enravishing.

charming; delightful, felicitous, exquisite; lovely &c. (*beautiful*) 845;

bother, pother, hot water, sea of troubles, hornet's nest, plague, pest.

cancer, ulcer, sting, thorn; canker &c. (*bane*) 663; scorpion &c. (*evil-doer*) 913; dagger &c. (*arms*) 727; scourge &c. (*instrument of punishment*) 975; carking –, canker worm of- care.

mishap, misfortune &c. (*adversity*) 735; *désagrément, esclandre*, rub.

source of -irritation, – annoyance; wound, sore subject, skeleton in the closet; thorn in -the flesh, – one's side; where the shoe pinches, gall and wormwood.

sorry sight, heavy news, provocation; affront &c. 929; head and front of one's offending.

infestation, molestation; malignity &c. (*malevolence*) 907; acrimony.

V. cause –, occasion –, give –, bring –, induce –, produce –, create –, inflict-pain &c. 828; pain, hurt, wound.

pinch, prick, gripe &c. (*physical pain*) 378; pierce, lancinate, cut.

hurt –, wound –, grate upon –, jar upon- the feelings; wring –, pierce –, lacerate –, break –, rend- the heart; make the heart bleed; tear –, rend-the heart-strings; draw tears from the eyes.

sadden; make -unhappy &c. 828; plunge into sorrow, grieve, fash, afflict, distress; cut -up, – to the heart.

displease, annoy, incommode, discommode, discompose, trouble, disquiet, disturb, thwart, cross, perplex, molest, tease, rag, tire, irk, vex, mortify, wherret, worry, plague, bother, pester, bore, pother, harass, harry, badger, heckle, bait, beset, infest, persecute, importune, be troublesome.

wring, harrow, torment, torture; put to the -rack, – question; break on the wheel, rack, scarify; cruci-ate, -fy; convulse, agonize; barb the dart; plant a -dagger in the breast, – thorn in one's side.

irritate, provoke, sting, nettle, try the patience, pique, fret, rile, twoak the nose, chafe, gall; sting –, wound –, cut- to the quick; aggrieve, affront, enchafe, enrage, ruffle, sour the temper; give offence &c. (*resentment*) 900.

ravishing, rapturous; heartfelt, thrilling, ecstatic; beat-ic, -ific; seraphic; empyrean; elysian &c. (*heavenly*) 981. palmy, halcyon, Saturnian.

**Phr.** *decies repetita placebit.*

———

maltreat, bite, snap at, assail, bully; smite &c. (*punish*) 972.

sicken, disgust, revolt, nauseate, disenchant, repel, offend, shock, stink in the nostrils; go against –, turn- the stomach; make one sick, set the teeth on edge, go against the grain, grate on the ear; stick in one's -throat, – gizzard; rankle, gnaw, corrode, horrify, appal, freeze the blood; chill the spine; make the -flesh creep, – hair stand on end; make the blood -curdle, – run cold; make one shudder.

haunt, – the memory; weigh –, prey- on the -heart, – mind, – spirits; bring one's grey hairs with sorrow to the grave; add a nail to one's coffin.

**Adj.** causing pain, hurting &c. *v.*; hurtful &c. (*bad*) 649; painful; dolor-ific, -ous; unpleasant; un-, dis-pleasing; disagreeable, unpalatable, bitter, distasteful; uninviting; unwelcome; undesir-able, -ed; obnoxious; unacceptable, unpopular, thankless.

unsatisfactory, untoward, unlucky, uncomfortable.

distressing; afflict-ing, -ive; joy-, cheer-, comfort-less; dismal, disheartening; depress-ing, -ive; dreary, melancholy, grievous, piteous; woeful, rueful, mournful, deplorable, pitiable, lamentable; sad, affecting, touching, pathetic.

irritating, provoking, stinging, annoying, aggravating, mortifying, galling; unaccommodating, invidious, vexatious; trouble-, tire-, irk-, weari-some; plagu-ing, -y; awkward.

importunate; teas-, pester-, bother-, harass-, worry-, torment-, cark-ing.

in-toler-, -suffer-, -support-able; un-bear-, -endur-able; past bearing; not to be -borne, – endured; more than flesh and blood can bear; enough to -drive one mad, – provoke a saint, – make a parson swear, – try the patience of Job.

shocking, terrific, grim, appalling, crushing; dreadful, fearful, frightful; thrilling, tremendous, dire; heart-breaking, -rending, -wounding, -corroding, -sickening; harrowing, rending.

odious, hateful, execrable, repulsive, repellent, abhorrent; horri-d, -ble, -fic, -fying; offensive; nause-ous, -ating; disgust-, sicken-, revolt-ing; nasty; loath-some, -ful; fulsome; vile &c. (*bad*) 649; hideous &c. 846.

sharp, acute, sore, severe, grave, hard, harsh, cruel, biting, acrimonious, caustic; cutting, corroding, consuming, racking, excruciating, searching, searing, grinding, grating, agonizing; envenomed.

ruinous, disastrous, calamitous, tragical; desolating, withering; burdensome, onerous, oppressive; cumb-rous, -ersome.

**Adv.** painfully &c. *adj.*; with -pain &c. 828; deuced.

**Int.** *hinc illæ lachrymæ!* woe is me!

**Phr.** *surgit amari aliquid*; the place being too hot to hold one; the iron entering into the soul.

**831. Content.—N.** content, -ment, -edness; complacency, satisfaction, entire satisfaction, ease, heart's ease, peace of mind; serenity &c. 826; cheer-

**832. Discontent. — N.** discontent, -ment; dissatisfaction; dissent &c. 489; labour unrest.

disappointment, mortification; cold

fulness &c. 836; ray of comfort; comfort &c. (*well-being*) 827.

re-, conciliation; resignation &c. (*patience*) 826.

waiter on Providence.

**V.** be -content &c. *adj.*; rest -satisfied, – and be thankful; take the good the gods provide, let well alone, feel oneself at home, hug oneself, lay the flattering unction to one's soul.

take -up with, – in good part; assent &c. 488; be reconciled to, make one's peace with; get over it; take -heart, – comfort; put up with &c. (*bear*) 826.

render -content &c. *adj.*; set at ease, comfort; set one's -heart, – mind- at -ease, – rest; speak peace; conciliate, reconcile, win over, propitiate, disarm, beguile; content, satisfy; gratify &c. 829.

be -tolerated &c. 826; go down, – with; do.

**Adj.** content, -ed; satisfied &c. *v.*; at -ease, – one's ease, – home; with the mind at ease, *sans souci, sine curâ,* easy-going, not particular; conciliatory; unrepining, of good comfort; resigned &c. (*patient*) 826; cheerful &c. 836.

un-afflicted, -vexed, -molested, -plagued; serene &c. 826; at rest; snug, comfortable; in one's element.

satisfactory, satisfying, ample, sufficient, adequate, tolerable.

**Adv.** to one's heart's content; *à la bonne heure*; all for the best.

**Int.** amen &c. (*assent*) 488; very well, so much the better, well and good; it –, that- will do; it cannot be helped.

**Phr.** nothing comes amiss.

comfort; regret &c. 833; repining, taking on &c. *v.*; inquietude, vexation of spirit, soreness; heart-burning, -grief; querulousness &c. (*lamentation*) 839; hypercriticism.

malcontent, grumbler, growler, croaker, *laudator temporis acti*; censurer, complainer, faultfinder, murmurer, Adullamite, Diehard, Bitterender.

the Opposition, cave of Adullam, indignation meeting, 'winter of our discontent.'

**V.** be -discontented &c. *adj.*; quarrel with one's bread and butter; repine; regret &c. 833; wish one at the bottom of the Red Sea; take -on, – to heart; shrug the shoulders; make a wry –, pull a long- face; knit one's brows, look -blue, – black, – black as thunder, – blank, – glum.

take -in bad part, – ill; fret, chafe, make a piece of work; grumble, croak, grouse; lament &c. 839.

cause -discontent &c. *n.*; dissatisfy, disappoint, mortify, put out, disconcert; cut up; dishearten.

**Adj.** discontented; dissatisfied &c. *v.*; unsatisfied, ungratified; dissident; dissentient &c. 489; malcontent, exigent, exacting, hypercritical.

repining &c. *v.*; regretful &c. 833; down in the mouth &c. (*dejected*) 837.

in -high dudgeon, – a fume, – the sulks, – the dumps, – bad humour; glum, sulky; sour, – as a crab; soured, sore; out of -humour, – temper.

disappointing &c. *v.*; unsatisfactory.

**Int.** so much the worse!

**Phr.** that –, it- will never do.

---

**833. Regret.**—**N.** regret, repining; home sickness, nostalgia; *mal –, maladie-du pays*; lamentation &c. 839, contrition, compunction, penitence, &c. 950.

bitterness, heart-burning.

*laudator temporis acti* &c. (*discontent*) 832.

**V.** regret, deplore; bewail &c. (*lament*) 839; repine, cast a longing lingering look behind; rue, – the day; repent &c. 950; *infandum renovare dolorem.*

prey –, weigh –, have a weight- on the mind; leave an aching void.

**Adj.** regretting &c. *v.*; regretful; home-sick.

regretted &c. *v.*; much to be regretted, regrettable; lamentable &c. (*bad*) 649.

Int. what a pity! hang it!
Phr. 'tis -pity, – too true.

**834. Relief.—N.** relief; deliverance; refreshment &c. 689; easement, softening, alleviation, mitigation, palliation &c. 174; soothing, lullaby; cradle song, *berceuse.*

solace, consolation, comfort, encouragement.

lenitive, *r*estorative &c. (*remedy*) 662; poultice &c. *v.*; cushion &c. 215; crumb of comfort, balm in Gilead; aspirin.

**V.** relieve, ease, alleviate, mitigate, palliate, soothe, addulce; salve; soften, – down; foment, stupe, poultice; assuage, allay.

cheer, comfort, console; encourage, bear up, pat on the back, give comfort, set at ease; enliven, gladden –, cheer the heart.

**835. Aggravation.—N.** aggravation, heightening; exacerbation; exasperation; overestimation &c. 482; exaggeration &c. 549.

**V.** aggravate, render worse, heighten, embitter, sour; ex-, acerbate; exasperate, envenom; tease, provoke, enrage. add fuel to the -fire, – flame; fan the flame &c. (*excite*) 824; go from bad to worse &c. (*deteriorate*) 659.

**Adj.** aggravated &c. *v.*; worse, unrelieved; aggravable; aggravating &c. *v.*

**Adv.** out of the frying pan into the fire, from bad to worse, worse and worse.

**Int.** so much the worse!

remedy; cure &c. (*restore*) 660; refresh; pour -balm into, – oil on.

smooth the ruffled brow of care, temper the wind to the shorn lamb, lay the flattering unction to one's soul.

disburden &c. (*free*) 705; take off a load of care.

be relieved; breathe more freely, draw a long breath; take comfort; dry –, wipe- the -tears, – eyes.

**Adj.** relieving &c. *v.*; consolatory, soothing; assua-ging, -sive; bal-my, -samic; lenitive, palliative; anodyne &c. (*remedial*) 662; curative &c. 660.

**836. Cheerfulness.—N.** cheerfulness &c. *adj.*; geniality, gaiety, *l'allegro,* cheer, good humour, spirits; high –, animal –, flow of- spirits; glee, high glee, light heart; sunshine of the -mind, – breast; *gaieté de cœur, bon naturel.*

liveliness &c. *adj.*; life, alacrity, vivacity, animation, *allégresse*; jocundity, joviality, jollity; levity; jocularity &c. (*wit*) 842.

mirth, merriment, hilarity, exhilaration; laughter &c. 838; merry-making &c. (*amusement*) 840; heyday, rejoicing &c. 838; marriage bells.

nepenthe, Euphrosyne.

optimism &c. (*hopefulness*) 858; self-complacency.

**V.** be -cheerful &c. *adj.*; have the mind at ease, smile, put a good face upon, keep up one's spirits; view -the bright side of the picture, – things *en couleur de rose; ridentem dicere verum,*

**837. Dejection.—N.** dejection; dejectedness &c. *adj.*; depression, prosternation; lowness –, depression- of spirits; weight –, oppression –, damp on the spirits; low –, bad –, drooping –, depressed- spirits; heart sinking; heaviness –, failure- of heart.

heaviness &c. *adj.*; infestivity, gloom; weariness &c. 841; *tædium vitæ,* disgust of life; *mal du pays* &c. (*regret*) 833.

melancholy; sadness &c. *adj.*; *il penseroso, melancholia,* dismals, mumps, mopes, lachrymals, dumps, blues, blue devils, doldrums, vapours, megrims, spleen, horrors, hypochondriasis, pessimism; despondency, slough of Despond; disconsolateness &c. *adj.*; hope deferred, blank despondency.

prostration, – of soul; broken heart; despair &c. 859; cave of -despair, – Trophonius.

cheer up, brighten up, light up, bear up; chirp, take heart, cast away care, drive dull care away, perk up.

rejoice &c. 838; carol, chirrup, lilt; frisk, rollick, give a loose to mirth.

cheer, enliven, elate, exhilarate, gladden, inspirit, animate, raise the spirits, inspire; put in good humour; cheer –, rejoice- the heart; delight &c. (*give pleasure*) 829.

**Adj.** cheerful; happy &c. 827; cheery, -ly; of good cheer, smiling; blithe; in –, in good- spirits; in high -spirits, – feather; happy as -the day is long, – a king; gay, – as a lark; *allegro*; light, -some, -hearted; buoyant, *débonnaire*, bright, free and easy, airy; janty, jaunty, canty; spright-ly, -ful; spry; spirit-ed, -ful; lively; animated, breezy, vivacious; brisk, – as a bee; sparkling; sportive; full of -play, – spirit; all alive.

sunny, palmy; hopeful &c. 858.

merry, – as a -cricket, – grig, – marriage bell; joyful, joyous, jocund, jovial; jolly, – as a thrush, – as a sandboy; blithesome; glee-ful, -some; hilarious, rattling.

winsome, bonny, hearty, buxom.

play-ful, -some; *folâtre*, playful as a kitten, tricksy, frisky, frolicsome; gamesome; jocose, jocular, waggish; mirth-, laughter-loving; mirthful, rollicking.

elate, -d; exulting, jubilant, flushed; rejoicing &c. 838; cock-a-hoop.

cheering, inspiriting, exhilarating; cardiac, -al; pleasing &c. 829; flourishing, halcyon.

**Adv.** cheerfully &c. *adj.*

**Int.** never say die! come! cheer up! hurrah! &c. 838; 'hence loathed melancholy!' begone dull care! away with melancholy!

demureness &c. *adj.*; gravity, solemnity; long –, grave- face.

hypochondriac, seek-sorrow, self-tormentor, *heautontimorumenos*, *malade imaginaire*, *médecin tant pis*; croaker, pessimist; mope, mopus.

[Cause of dejection] affliction &c. 830; sorry sight; *memento mori*; damper, wet blanket, Job's comforter; death's head, skeleton at the feast.

**V.** be -dejected &c. *adj.*; grieve; mourn &c. (*lament*) 839; take on, give way, lose heart, despond, droop, sink.

lower, look downcast, frown, pout; hang down the head; pull –, make- a long face; laugh on the wrong side of the mouth; grin a ghastly smile; look -blue, – like a drowned man; lay –, take- to heart.

mope, brood over; fret; sulk; pine, – away; yearn; repine &c. (*regret*) 833; despair &c. 859.

refrain from laughter, keep one's countenance; be –, look- grave &c. *adj.*; repress a smile, keep a straight face.

depress; dis-courage, -hearten; dispirit; damp, dull, deject, lower, sink, dash, knock down, unman, prostrate, break one's heart; frown upon; cast a -gloom, – shade- on; sadden; damp –, dash –, wither- one's hopes; weigh –, lie heavy –, prey- on the -mind, – spirits; damp –, depress- the spirits.

**Adj.** cheer-, joy-, spirit-less; uncheerful, -y; unlively; unhappy &c. 828; melancholy, dismal, sombre, dark, gloomy, adust, *triste*, clouded, murky, lowering, frowning, lugubrious, Acherontic, funereal, mournful, lamentable, dreadful.

dreary, flat; dull, – as -a beetle, - ditchwater; depressing &c. *v.*

'melancholy as a gib cat'; oppressed with –, a prey to- melancholy; downcast, -hearted; down -in the mouth, – on one's luck; heavy-hearted; in the -dumps, – suds, – sulks, – doldrums; in doleful dumps, in bad humour; sullen; mumpish; dumpish; mopish, moping, moody, glum; sulky &c. (*discontented*) 832; out of -sorts, – humour, – heart, – spirits; ill at ease, low-spirited, in low spirits, a cup too low; weary &c. 841; dis-couraged, -heartened; desponding; chop-, jaw-, crest-fallen.

sad, pensive, *penseroso*, tristful; dole-some, -ful; woebegone lachrymose, in tears, melancholic, hipped, hypochondriacal, bil ious, jaundiced, atrabilious, saturnine, splenetic; lackadaisical, serious, sedate, staid, stayed; grave, – as -a judge, – an undertaker, – a mustard pot; sober, solemn, demure; grim; grim-faced, -visaged; rueful, wan, long-faced.

disconsolate; un-, in-consolable; forlorn, comfortless, desolate, *désolé*, sick at heart; soul-, heart-sick; *au désespoir*; in despair &c; 859; lost.

overcome; broken-, borne-, bowed-down; heart-stricken &c; (*mental suffering*) 828; cut up, dashed, sunk; unnerved, unmanned; down-fallen, -trodden; broken-hearted; care-worn.

Adv. with -a long face, – tears in one's eyes; sadly &c. *adj.*

Phr. the countenance falling; the heart -failing, – sinking within-one.

**838.** [Expression of pleasure.] **Rejoicing.—N.** rejoicing, exultation, triumph, jubilation, heyday, flush, revelling; merry-making &c. (*amusement*) 840; jubilee &c. (*celebration*) 883; pæan, Te Deum &c. (*thanksgiving*) 990; congratulation &c. 896; applause &c. 931.

smile, simper, smirk, grin; broad –, sardonic- grin.

laughter, giggle, titter, crow, cheer, chuckle, snicker, snigger, shout; Homeric laughter, horse –, hearty- laugh; guffaw; burst –, fit –, shout –, roar –, peal- of laughter; cachinnation.

risibility; derision &c. 856.

Momus; Democritus the Abderite; rollicker; Laughter holding both his sides.

**V.** rejoice; thank –, bless- one's stars; congratulate –, hug- oneself; rub –, clap- one's hands; smack the lips, fling up one's cap; dance, skip, caleer; sing, carol, chirrup, chirp; hurrah; cry for –, leap with- joy; exult &c. (*boast*) 884; triumph; hold jubilee &c. (*celebrate*) 883; make merry &c. (*sport*) 840; sing a pæan of joy.

smile, simper, smirk; grin, – like a Cheshire cat; mock, laugh in one's sleeve; laugh, – outright; giggle, titter, snigger, crow, smicker, chuckle, snicker, cackle; burst -out, – into a fit of laughter; shout, split, roar.

shake –, split –, hold both- one's sides; roar –, die- with laughter.

raise laughter &c. (*amuse*) 840.

**Adj.** rejoicing &c. *v.*; jubilant, exultant, triumphant; flushed, elated; laughing &c. *v.*; risible; ready to -burst, - split, – die with laughter; convulsed with laughter.

**839.** [Expression of pain.] **Lamentation.—N.** lament, -ation; wail, complaint, plaint, murmur, mutter, grumble, groan, moan, whine, whimper, sob, sigh, suspiration, heaving, deep sigh.

cry &c. (*vociferation*) 411; scream, howl; outcry, wail of woe, frown, scowl.

tear; weeping &c. *v.*; flood of tears, fit of crying, lachrymation, melting mood, weeping and gnashing of teeth.

plaintiveness &c. *adj.*; languishment; condolence &c. 915.

mourning, weeds, willow, cypress, crêpe, crape, deep mourning; sackcloth and ashes; knell &c. 363; dump, death-song, dirge, coronach, keen, *nenia*, requiem, elegy, *epicedium*; threne; mon-, thren-ody; jeremiad; ululation.

mourner, professional mourner, keener; grumbler &c. (*discontent*) 832; Niobe; Heraclitus.

**V.** lament, mourn, deplore, grieve, weep over; be-wail, -moan; keen; con· dole with &c. 915; fret &c. (*suffer*) 828; wear –, go into –, put on- mourning; wear -the willow, – sackcloth and ashes; *infandum renovare dolorem* &c. (*regret*) 833; give sorrow words.

sigh; give –, heave –, fetch- a sigh; 'waft a sigh from Indus to the pole'; sigh 'like furnace'; wail.

cry, weep, sob, greet, blubber, pipe, snivel, bibber, whimper, pule; pipe one's eye; drop –, shed- -tears, – a tear; melt –, burst- into tears; *fondre en larmes*; cry -oneself blind, – one's eyes out.

scream &c. (*cry out*) 411; mew &c. (*animal sounds*) 412; groan, moan,

laughable &c. (*ludicrous*) 853.

**Int.** hip, hip, -hurrah! huzza! aha! hail! tolderolloll! tra-la la! Heaven be praised! *io triumphe! tant mieux!* so much the better.

**Phr.** the heart leaping with joy.

_____

whine, yammer; roar; roar –, bellow-like a bull; cry out lustily, rend the air, yell.

frown, scowl, make a wry face, grimace, gnash one's teeth, wring one's hands, tear one's hair, beat one's breast, roll on the ground, burst with grief.

complain, murmur, mutter, grumble, growl, clamour, make a fuss about, croak, grunt, maunder; deprecate &c. (*disapprove*) 932.

cry out before one is hurt, complain without cause.

**Adj.** lamenting &c. *v.*; in mourning, in sackcloth and ashes; crying, sorrowing, -ful &c. (*unhappy*) 828; mourn-, tear-ful; lachrymose; plaint-ive, -ful, quer-ulous, -imonious; in the melting mood.

in tears, with tears in one's eyes; with -moistened, – watery-cyes; bathed –, dissolved- in tears; 'like Niobe all tears.'

elagiac, epicedial, threnetic.

**Adv.** *de profundis*; *les larmes aux yeux.*

**Int.** heigh-ho! alas! alack! O dear! ah –, woe is- me! lackadaisy! well –, lack –, alack- a day! well-a-way! alas the day! *O tempora! O mores!* what a pity! *miserabile dictu!* O lud lud! too true!

**Phr.** tears -standing in, – starting from- the eyes; eyes -suffused, – swimming, – brimming –, overflowing- with tears.

**840. Amusement.—N.** amuse-, entertain-ment; diver-sion, -tissement; recreation, relaxation, solace; pastime, *passetemps*, sport; labour of love; pleasure &c. 827.

fun, frolic, merriment, whoopee, jollity; jovial-ity, -ness; heyday; laughter &c. 838; jocos-ity, -eness; droll-, buffoon-, tomfool-ery; mummery, masquing, pleasantry; wit &c. 842; quip, quirk.

play; game, – at romps; gambol, romp, prank, antic, rig, lark, spree, skylarking, vagary, trick, monkey trick, *gambade*, *fredaine*, *escapade*, *échappée*, bout, *espièglerie*; practical joke &c. (*ridicule*) 856.

dance; round –, square –, solo –, step –, tap –, clog –, skirt –, sand –, folk –, morris- dance, *pas seul*, step, turn, *chassé*, cut, shuffle, double shuffle; hop, reel, rigadoon, saraband, hornpipe, bolero, fandango, pavan, tarantella, minuet, waltz, polka; galop, -ade; schottische, *pas de quatre*, Boston, one-, two-step, rumba, tango, maxixe, fox-, turkey-trot, shimmy, ragtime, cakewalk, jazz, blues, Charleston; jig, breakdown, fling, strathspey; *alle-*

**841. Weariness.—N.** weariness, defatigation, boredom, *ennui*; lassitude &c. (*fatigue*) 688; drowsiness &c. 683.

disgust, nausea, loathing, sickness; satiety &c. 869; *tædium vitæ* &c. (*dejection*) 837.

wearisome-, tedious-ness &c. *adj.*; dull work, tedium, monotony, twice told tale.

bore, button-holer, proser, wet blanket; heavy hours, 'the enemy' [time].

**V.** weary; tire &c. (*fatigue*) 688; bore; bore –, weary –, tire- -to death, – out of one's life, – out of all patience; set –, send- to sleep; buttonhole.

pall, sicken, nauseate, disgust.

harp on the same string; drag its -slow, – weary- length along.

never hear the last of; be -tired &c. *adj.* -of, – with; yawn; die with *ennui.*

**Adj.** wearying &c. *v.*; wearing; weari-, tire-, irk-some; uninteresting, stupid, bald, devoid of interest, dry, monotonous, dull, arid, tedious, humdrum, mortal, flat; pros-y, -ing; slow; soporific, somniferous, dormitive.

disgusting &c. *v.*; unenjoyed.

weary; tired &c. *v.*; drowsy &c. (*sleepy*) 683; uninterested, flagging.

*mande*; gavot, -te; mazurka, morisco; quadrille, lancers, country dance, *cotillon*, polonaise, Sir Roger de Coverley, Swedish dance; *ballet* &c. (*drama*) 599; ball; *bal*, – *masqué*, – *costumé*; masquerade, fancy dress ball; *thé dansant*; Terpsichore, choreography, Russian ballet, classical dancing; eurythmics; nautch dance, *danse du ventre*, cancan.

used up, worn out, *blasé*, life-weary, weary of life; sick of.

**Adv.** wearily &c. *adj.*; *usque ad nauseam.*

**Phr.** time hanging heavily on one's hands; *toujours perdrix*; *crambe repetita.*

festivity, merry-making; party &c. (*social gathering*) 892; *fête*, festival, gala, *ridotto*; revel-s, -ry, -ling; carnival, brawl, saturnalia, high jinks; feast, banquet &c. (*food*) 298; regale, *symposium*, wassail; carous-e, -al; jollification, junket, wake, picnic, *fête champêtre*, garden party, gymkhana, regatta, track meet, fieldday, jamboree, treat.

round of pleasures, dissipation, a short life and a merry one, racketing, holiday making, high jinks.

rejoicing &c. 838; jubilee &c. (*celebration*) 883.

bonfire, fireworks, *feu-de-joie*, rocket, Catherine wheel, roman candle &c.

holiday; gala –, red letter –, play- day; high days and holidays; high –, Bank- holiday; May –, Derby- day; Saint –, Easter –, Whit- Monday; King's birthday, Empire Day; *mi-carême*; *Bairam*; wayzgoose, beanfeast, beano.

place of amusement, theatre &c. 599; concert-, ball-, assembly-room; music-hall, cinema, movies, talkies, vaudeville; hippodrome, circus, rodeo; *casino, kursaal*; winter garden; park, pleasance, arbour; garden &c. 371; pleasure-, play-, cricket-, football-, polo-, croquet-, archery-, hunting-ground; golf links, race course, stadium, gridiron, bowl, speedway, racing track, ring; gymnasium, swimming pool; shooting gallery; tennis-, racket-court; bowling-green, -alley; croquet-lawn, rink, skating rink; roller-coaster, roundabout, carousel, merry-go-round; swing; *montagne russe*; switchback, scenic railway &c.

game, – of -chance, – skill; athletic sports, gymnastics; fencing; archery, rifle-shooting; tournament, pugilism &c. (*contention*) 720; sporting &c. 622; horse-racing, the turf; aquatics &c. 267; skating, roller skating; ski-running, -joring, -jumping, bobsleighing, luging, tobogganing, winter sports; sliding; cricket, tennis, lawn –, table –, deck- tennis, rackets, fives, squash, ping-pong, trap bat and ball, battledore and shuttlecock, badminton, *la grâce*; pall mall, tip-cat, croquet, golf, curling, hockey, basketball, soccer, football, Rugby, Association, *pallone*, polo; tent-pegging, tilting at the ring, quintain, greasy pole; quoits, *discus*; throwing the hammer, putting the ·weight, – shot, tossing the caber; knurr and spell; leap-frog, hop, skip and jump; French and English, tug of war; blind man's buff, nunt the slipper, hide-and-seek, kiss in the ring; snapdragon; cross questions and crooked answers; jig-saw puzzle; rounders, base-ball, lacrosse &c.; angling; swimming, diving, water-polo.

billiards, pool, pyramids, snooker, bagatelle; bowls, skittles, ninepins, kail, American bowls.

cards; bridge, auction, contract, whist, rubber; round game, coon-can, loo, cribbage, *bésique*, pinocle, euchre, drole, *écorté*, skat, picquet, all-fours, quadrille, ombre, reverse, Pope Joan, commit;

bo-, boa-ston; *vingt-et-un; quinze,* thirty-one, put-and-take, specula-tion, connections, brag, cassino, lottery, commerce, snip-snap-snorem, lift smoke, blind hookey, Polish bank, poker, banker; faro; Earl of Coventry, Napoleon, nap, patience, pairs; old maid, fright, beggar-my-neighbour; *baccarat, chemin de fer, monte;* craps.

chess, draughts, backgammon, dominoes, checkers, mah jong, merelles, nine men's morris, go-bang, solitaire; game of –, fox and-geese; lotto; &c.*

*morra;* gambling &c. (*chance*) 621; roulette.

toy, plaything, bauble; doll &c. (*puppet*) 554; teetotum; knick-knack &c. (*trifle*) 643; magic lantern &c. (*show*) 448; peep-, puppet-, raree-, gallanty-show; marionnettes, Punch and Judy; toy-shop; 'quips and cranks and wanton wiles, nods and becks and wreathèd smiles.'

sportsman, gamester, gambler &c. 621; reveller, master of the -ceremonies, – revels; *arbiter elegantiarum.*

**V.** amuse, entertain, divert, enliven; tickle, – the fancy; titillate, raise a smile, put in good humour; cause –, create –, occasion –, raise –, excite –, produce –, convulse with- laughter; set the table in a roar, be the death of one.

recreate, solace, cheer, rejoice; please &c. 829; interest; treat, regale.

amuse oneself; game; play, – a game, – pranks, – tricks; sport, disport, toy, wanton, revel, junket, feast, carouse, banquet, make merry; drown care; drive dull care away; frolic, gambol, frisk, romp; caper; dance &c. (*leap*) 309; keep up the ball; run a rig, sow one's wild oats, have one's fling, paint the town red, take one's pleasure; see life; *desipere in loco,* play the fool.

make –, keep- holiday; go a Maying.

while away –, beguile- the time; kill time, dally.

**Adj.** amusing, entertaining, diverting &c. *v.*; recreative, lusory; pleasant &c. (*pleasing*) 829; laughable &c. (*ludicrous*) 853; witty &c. 842; fest-ive, -al; jovial, jolly, jocund, roguish, rompish; sport-ing; playful, – as a kitten; sportive, ludibrious.

amused &c. *v.*; 'pleased with a feather, tickled with a straw.'

**Adv.** 'on the light fantastic toe,' at play, in sport.

**Int.** *vive la bagatelle! vogue la galère!*

**Phr.** *Deus nobis hæc otia fecit; dum vivimus vivamus.*

---

**842. Wit.—N.** wit, -tiness; attic -wit, – salt; atticism; salt, *esprit,* point, fancy, whim, humour, drollery, pleas-antry.

farce, buffoonery, fooling, tom-foolery; harlequinade &c. 599; broad -farce, – humour; fun, *espièglerie; vis comica.*

jocularity; jocos-ity, -eness; face-tiousness; wagg-ery, -ishness; whim-sicality; comicality &c. 853.

smartness, ready wit, banter, *badi-*

**843. Dulness.—N.** dulness, heavi-ness, flatness; infestivity &c. 837; stupidity &c. 499; want of originality, dearth of ideas.

prose, matter of fact; heavy book, *conte à dormir debout;* platitude.

**V.** be -dull &c. *adj.*; prose, plati-tudinize, take *au sérieux,* be caught napping.

render -dull &c. *adj.*; damp, depress, throw cold water on, lay a wet blanket on; fall flat upon the ear; hang fire.

---

* A curious list of games is given in Sir Thomas Urquhart's translation of Rabelais' *Life of Gargantua,* book i. chapter 22.

*nage, persiflage,* retort, repartee, *quid pro quo;* ridicule &c. 856.

*facetiæ,* quips and cranks; jest, joke, capital joke; standing -jest, – joke; conceit, quip, quirk, crank, quiddity, *concetto, plaisanterie,* brilliant idea; merry –, bright –, happy- thought; sally; flash, – of wit, – of merriment; scintillation; *mot, – pour rire;* witticism, smart saying, *bon mot, jeu d'esprit,* epigram; jest book; dry joke, *quodlibet,* cream of the jest.

word-play, *jeu de mots;* play -of, – upon- words; pun, -ning; *double entendre* &c. (*ambiguity*) 520; quibble, verbal quibble; conundrum &c. (*riddle*) 533; anagram, acrostic, double acrostic, *nugæ canoræ,* trifling, idle conceit, *turlupinade.*

old joke, Joe Miller, chestnut, hoary-headed jest.

**V.** joke, jest, cut jokes; crack a joke; perpetrate a -joke, – pun; make -fun of, – merry with; set the table in a roar &c. (*amuse*) 840; scintillate.

retort, flash back; banter &c. (*ridicule*) 856; *ridentem dicere verum;* joke at one's expense.

**Adj.** witty, attic, salty; quick-, nimble-witted; keen, clever, smart, brilliant, pungent, jocular, jocose, funny, waggish, facetious, whimsical, humorous, Gilbertian; playful &c. 840; merry and wise; pleasant, sprightly, *spirituel,* sparkling, epigrammatic, full of point, *ben trovato;* comic &c. 853.

**Adv.** in joke, in jest, in sport, in play.

**Adj.** dull, – as ditch water; dry, insipid, jejune; unentertaining, uninteresting, unlively, unimaginative; heavisome, heavy-gaited; insulse; dry as dust; pros-y, -ing, -aic; matter of fact, commonplace, banal, pointless; 'weary, flat, stale and unprofitable.'

stupid, slow, flat, sluggish, ponderous, humdrum, monotonous; melancholic &c. 837; stolid &c. 499; plodding.

**Phr.** *Davus sum non Œdipus.*

---

**844. Humorist.—N.** humorist, wag, wit, reparteeist, epigrammatist, gag-man, punster; *bel esprit,* life of the party; wit-snapper, -cracker, -worm; joker, jester, jokesmith, Joe Miller, *drôle de corps, gaillard,* spark, *persifleur,* banterer.

buffoon, *farceur,* merry-andrew, mime, tumbler, acrobat, mountebank, charlatan, posturemaster, harlequin, punch, *pulcinella,* scaramouch, clown; wearer of the -cap and bells, – motley; motley fool; pantaloon, gipsy; jack -pudding, – in the green, – a dandy; zany; mad-cap, pickle-herring, witling, caricaturist, *grimacier.*

## 2°. DISCRIMINATE AFFECTIONS

**845. Beauty.—N.** beauty, the beautiful, *le beau idéal,* loveliness.

[Science of the perception of beauty] Callæsthetics.*

form, elegance, grace, beauty unadorned; symmetry &c. 242; comeliness, fairness &c. *adj.*; pulchritude, polish, gloss; good -effect, – looks; *belle tournure;* bloom, brilliancy, radiance, splendour, gorgeousness, magnificence; sublimi-ty, -fication.

**846. Ugliness.—N.** ugliness &c. *adj.*; deformity, inelegance; disfigurement &c. (*blemish*) 848; want of symmetry, inconcinnity; distortion &c. 243; squalor &c. (*uncleanness*) 653.

forbidding countenance, vinegar aspect, hanging look, wry face, '*spretæ injuria formæ.*'

eyesore, object, figure, sight, fright, spectre, scarecrow, hag, harridan, satyr, witch, toad, baboon, monster.

\* Whewell, 'Philosophy of the Inductive Sciences.'

concinnity, delicacy, refinement; charm, *je ne sais quoi*, style, *chic*, swank.

Venus, – of Milo; Aphrodite, Hebe, the Graces, Peri, Houri, Cupid, Apollo, Hyperion, Adonis, Antinous, Narcissus; Helen of Troy.

peacock, butterfly; flower, flow'ret gay, rose, lily, asphodel; garden; flower of, pink of; *bijou*; jewel &c. (*ornament*) 847; work of art.

pleasurableness &c. 829.

beautifying; landscape gardening; decoration &c. 847; calisthenics.

**V.** be -beautiful &c. *adj.*; shine, beam, bloom; become one &c. (*accord*) 23; set off, grace, flatter one.

render -beautiful &c. *adj.*; beautify; polish, burnish; gild &c. (*decorate*) 847; set out.

'snatch a grace beyond the reach of art.'

**Adj.** beaut-iful, -eous; handsome; pretty; lovely, graceful, elegant; delicate, dainty, refined, exquisite; fair, personable, comely, seemly; bonny; good-looking; well-favoured, -made, -formed, -proportioned; proper, shapely; symmetrical &c. (*regular*) 242; harmonious &c. (*colour*) 428; sightly.

fit to be seen, passable, not amiss.

goodly, dapper, tight, jimp; gimp; janty, jaunty; natty, quaint, trim, tidy, neat, spruce, smart, tricksy.

bright, -eyed; rosy-, cherry-cheeked; rosy, ruddy; blooming, in full bloom.

brilliant, shining; beam-y, -ing; sparkling, swanky, splendid, resplendent, dazzling, glowing; glossy, sleek.

showy, specious; rich, gorgeous, superb, magnificent, grand, fine, sublime, imposing; majestic 873.

artistic, -al; æsthetic; pict-uresque, -orial; *fait à peindre*, paintable; well-composed, -grouped, -varied; curious.

enchanting &c. (*pleasure-giving*) 829; attractive &c. (*inviting*) 615; becoming &c. (*accordant*) 23; ornamental &c. 847.

undeformed, undefaced, unspotted; spotless &c. (*perfect*) 650.

Caliban, Æsop, '*monstrum horrendum informe ingens cui lumen ademptum*.'

**V.** be -ugly &c. *adj.*; look ill, grin horribly a ghastly smile, make faces.

render -ugly &c. *adj.*; deface; dis-, de-figure; deform, spoil, distort &c. 243; blemish &c. (*injure*) 659; soil &c. (*render unclean*) 653.

**Adj.** ugly, – as -sin, – a toad, – a scarecrow, – a dead monkey; plain, bald &c. 226; homely &c. (*unadorned*) 849; ordinary, unornamental, inartistic; unsightly, unseemly, uncomely, unshapely, unlovely; sightless, seemless; not fit to be seen; unbeaut-eous, -iful; beautiless; shapeless &c. (*amorphous*) 241; course; garish, over-decorated &c. 882.

mis-shapen, -proportioned; monstrous; gaunt &c. (*thin*) 203; dumpy &c. (*short*) 201; curtailed of its fair proportions; ill-made, -shaped, -proportioned; crooked &c. (*distorted*) 243; hard-featured, -visaged; ill-, hard-, evil-favoured; ill-looking; unprepossessing.

graceless, inelegant; ungraceful, ungainly, uncouth; stiff; rugged, rough, gross, rude, awkward, clumsy, slouching, rickety; gawky; lump-ing, -ish; lumbering; hulk-y, -ing; unwieldy.

squalid, haggard; grim, -faced, -visaged; grisly, ghastly; ghost-, death-like; cadaverous, gruesome.

frightful, hideous, odious, uncanny, forbidding, repellant, repulsive; horri-d, -ble; shocking &c. (*painful*) 830.

foul &c. (*dirty*) 653; dingy &c. (*colourless*) 429; gaudy &c. (*colour*) 428; disfigured &c. *v.*; discoloured (*blemished*) &c. 848.

---

**847. Ornament. — N.** ornament, -ation, -al art; ornat-ure, -eness; adorn-ment, decoration, embellishment; architecture.

garnish, polish, varnish, French pol-

**848. Blemish.—N.** blemish, disfigurement, deformity; defect &c. (*imperfection*) 651; flaw; injury &c. (*deterioration*) 659; spots on the sun; eyesore.

ish, gilding, japanning, lacquer, ormolu, enamel.

cosmetics, rouge, powder, lipstick, lip salve, mascara; manicure, nail polish; permanent –, Marcel –, fingerwave.

pattern, diaper, powdering, panelling, graining, pargeting, inlay, detail; texture &c. 329; richness; tracery, moulding, beading, reeding, fillet, listel, strapwork, *coquillage*, flourish, *fleur-delis*, arabesque, fret, *anthemion*; egg and -tongue, – dart; *astragal*, zigzag, *acanthus*, *cartouche*; pilaster &c. (*projection*) 250; cyma, ogee.

em-, broidery, needlework; knitting, crochet, tatting, brocade, *brocatelle*, beads, bugles; galloon, lace, gimp, *guipure*, fringe, trapping, border, edging, insertion, *motif*, trimming; *passementerie*; drapery, hanging, tapestry, arras; millinery, ermine.

wreath, festoon, garland, lei, chaplet, flower, nosegay, *bouquet*, posy, 'daisies pied and violets blue.'

tassel, knot; shoulder-knot, *épaulette*, epaulet, aiglet, *aiguillette*, frog; star, rosette, bow; feather, plume, *panache*, *aigrette*.

jewel, -ry, -lery; bijoutry; *bijou*, *-terie*; diadem, tiara; pendant, trinket, locket, necklace, armilla, bracelet, bangle, armlet, anklet, ear-, nose- ring, carcanet, chain, *châtelaine*, albert, brooch, torque.

gem, precious stone; diamond, brilliant, beryl, aquamarine, alexandrite, cat's eye, emerald, calcedony, chrysoprase, cornelian, jasper, bloodstone, agate, heliotrope; girasol, -e; onyx, plasma; sard, -onyx; garnet, lapis-lazuli, opal, peridot, chrysolite, sapphire, ruby; spinel, -le; balais; oriental –, topaz; turquois, -e; zircon, jacinth, hyacinth, carbuncle, amethyst; moonstone; pearl, coral.

finery, frippery, gewgaw, gimcrack, knick-knack, tinsel, spangle, sequin, *clinquant*, pinch-beck, paste; excess of ornament &c. (*vulgarity*) 851; gaud, pride, ostentation; frills and furbelows.

illustration, illumination, *vignette*; *fleuron*; head-, tail-piece; *cul-de-lampe*; flowers of rhetoric &c. 577; work of art, article of vertu, *bric-à-brac*, curio, *bibelot*.

**V.** ornament, embellish, enrich, decorate, adorn, beautify, adonize.

smarten, furbish, polish, gild, varnish, whitewash, enamel, japan, lacquer, paint, grain.

garnish, trim, dizen, bedizen, prink, prank; trick –, fig- out; deck, bedeck, dight, bedight, array; dress, – up, preen, spruce up,

stain, blot, slur; spot, -tiness; speck, -le; blur, freckle, mole, *macula*, patch, blotch, birthmark, blain, maculation, tarnish, smudge, smear; dirt &c. 653; bruise, black eye, scar, wem; pustule; excrescence, pimple &c. (*protuberance*) 250.

**V.** disfigure &c. (*injure*) 659; speckle; render ugly &c. 846.

**Adj.** pitted, freckled, discoloured, bloodshot, bruised, disfigured; stained &c. *n.*; imperfect &c. 651; injured &c. (*deteriorated*) 659.

**849. Simplicity. — N.** simplicity; plain-, homeli-ness; undress, nudity, nakedness, beauty unadorned, chastity, chasteness.

**V.** be -simple &c. *adj.*

render -simple &c. *adj.*; simplify, chasten, strip of ornament.

**Adj.** simple, plain; home-ly, -spun; ordinary, household.

natural, unaffected; free from -affectation, – ornament; *simplex munditiis*; *sans façon*, *en déshabillé*, nude, naked.

chaste, inornate, severe.

un-adorned, -ornamented, -decked, -garnished, -arranged, -trimmed, -varnished.

bald, flat, dull, blank.

titivate; spangle, bespangle, powder; embroider, work; chase, tool, emboss, fret; emblazon, blazon, illuminate; illustrate.

become &c. (*accord with*) 23.

**Adj.** ornamented, beautified &c. *v.*; ornate, rich, gilt, begilt, tesselated, enamelled, inlaid; festooned; topiary.

smart, gay, tricksy, flowery, glittering; new-gilt, -spangled; fine, – as -a Mayday queen, – fivepence, – a carrot fresh scraped; pranked out, bedight, well-groomed.

in full dress &c. (*fashion*) 852; en grande -tenue, – toilette; in best bib and tucker, in Sunday best, endimanché; dressed to advantage.

showy, flashy; gaudy &c. (*vulgar*) 851; garish; gorgeous.

ornamental, decorative; becoming &c. (*accordant*) 23.

---

**850.** [Good taste.] **Taste.—N.** taste; good –, refined –, cultivated- taste; delicacy, refinement, fine feeling, gust, *gusto*, tact, *finesse*; nicety &c. (*discrimination*) 465; polish, elegance, grace.

*virtu*; dilettanteism, virtuosity; fine art; cul-ture, -ivation.

[Science of taste] æsthetics.

man of -taste &c.; *connoisseur*, judge, critic, *conoscente*, *virtuoso*, *amateur*, *dilettante*, Aristarchus, Corinthian, *arbiter elegantiarum*, stagirite, euphemist.

'caviare to the general.'

**V.** appreciate, judge, criticize, discriminate &c. 465.

**Adj.** in good taste; tasteful, tasty; unaffected, pure, chaste, classical, attic; cultivated, refined; dainty; æsthetic, artistic; elegant &c. 578; euphemistic.

to one's -taste, – mind; after one's fancy; *comme il faut*; *tiré à quatre épingles*.

**Adv.** elegantly &c. *adj.*

**Phr.** *nihil tetigit quod non ornavit.*

**852. Fashion.—N.** fashion, style, *ton*, *bon ton*, society; good –, politesociety; drawing room, civilized life, civilization, town, *beau monde*, high life, court; world; fashionable –, gayworld; Vanity Fair; show &c. (*ostentation*) 822.

manners, breeding &c. (*politeness*) 894; air, demeanour &c. (*appearance*) 448; *savoir-faire*; gentlemanliness, gentility, decorum, propriety, *bienséance*; conventions –, dictates- of society; Mrs. Grundy; convention, -ality; punctilio; form, -ality; etiquette, point of

**851.** [Bad taste.] **Vulgarity.—N.** vulgar-ity, -ism; barbar-, Vandal-, Gothic-ism; *mauvais goût*, bad taste; Babbittry; *gaucherie*, awkwardness, want of tact; ill-breeding &c. (*discourtesy*) 895; ungentlemanly behaviour.

coarseness &c. *adj.*; indecorum, misbehaviour.

low-, homeli-ness; low life, *mauvais ton*, rusticity; boorishness &c. *adj.*; brutality; rowdy-, ruffian-, blackguardism; ribaldry; slang &c. (*neology*) 563.

bad joke, *mauvaise plaisanterie.*

[Excess of ornament] gaudi-, tawdriness; false ornament; finery, frippery, trickery, tinsel, gewgaw, *clinquant.*

rough diamond, tomboy, hoyden, cub, unlicked cub; clown &c. (*commonalty*) 876; Hun, Goth, Vandal, Bœotian; vulgarian; snob, cad, bounder, gent; *parvenu* &c. 876; frump, dowdy; slattern &c. 653.

**V.** be -vulgar &c. *adj.*; misbehave; talk –, smell of the- shop.

**Adj.** in bad taste, vulgar, unrefined, gutter.

coarse, indecorous, ribald, gross; unseemly, unbeseeming, unpresentable; *contra bonos mores*; ungraceful &c. (*ugly*) 846.

dowdy; slovenly &c. (*dirty*) 653; ungenteel, shabby genteel; low &c. (*plebeian*) 876; uncourtly; uncivil &c. (*discourteous*) 895; ill-bred, -mannered; underbred; ungentleman-ly, -like; unladylike, unfeminine; wild, – as an unbacked colt.

unkempt, uncombed, untamed, unlicked, unpolished, uncouth, plebeian:

etiquette; custom &c. 613; mode, vogue, style, go; rage &c. (*desire*) 865; prevailing taste, *dernier cri*, dress &c. 225.

man -, woman- of -fashion, - the world; height -, pink -, star -, glass -, leader- of fashion; *arbiter elegantiarum* &c. (*taste*) 850; upper ten thousand &c. (*nobility*) 875; *élite* &c. (*distinction*) 873.

V. be -fashionable &c. *adj.*, - the rage &c. *n.*; have a run, pass current.

follow -, conform to -, fall in with- the fashion &c. *n.*; go with the stream &c. (*conform*) 82; *savoir -vivre*, - *faire*; keep up appearances, behave oneself.

set the -, bring into- fashion; give a tone to -, cut a figure in- society, rub shoulders with nobility, keep one's carriage.

incondite; heavy, rude, awkward; home-ly, -spun, -bred; provincial, hick, countrified, rustic, uncultivated, fresh-water; boorish, clownish; savage, brut-ish, blackguard, rowdy, snobbish; barbar-ous, -ic; Gothic, unclassical, doggerel, heathenish, tramontane, out-landish; Bohemian.

obsolete &c. (*antiquated*) 124; un-fashionable, old-fashioned, out of date; new-fangled &c. (*unfamiliar*) 83; fan-tastic, odd &c. (*ridiculous*) 853.

particular; affected &c. 855; mere-tricious; extravagant, monstrous, hor-rid; shocking &c. (*painful*) 830.

gaudy, tawdry, bedizened, tricked out, gingerbread; obtrusive, flaunting, loud, flashy, garish, showy.

Adj. fashionable; in -fashion &c. *n.*; *à la mode*, *comme il faut*; admitted -, admissible- in -society &c. *n.*; presentable, decorous, punctilious, conventional &c. (*customary*) 613; genteel; well-bred, -mannered, -behaved, -spoken; gentleman-like, -ly; ladylike; civil, polite &c. (*courteous*) 894.

polished, refined, thoroughbred, courtly; *distingué*, aristocratic, unembarrassed, poised, *dégagé*; ja-, jau-nty; dashing, fast, showy, high toned, toney.

modish, stylish, in the latest style, *recherché*; new-fangled &c. (*unfamiliar*) 83.

in -court, - full, - evening- dress; *en grande tenue* &c. (*ornament*) 847.

Adv. fashionably &c. *adj.*; for fashion's sake.

853. Ridiculousness.—N. ridiculousness &c. *adj.*; comical-, odd-ity &c. *adj.*; extravagance, drollery.

farce, comedy; burlesque &c. (*ridicule*) 856; buffoonery &c. (*fun*) 840; frippery; doggerel verses; Irish bull, Hibernianism, Hibernicism; Spoonerism; absurdity &c. 497; bombast &c. (*unmeaning*) 517; anti-climax, bathos; monstrosity &c. (*unconformity*) 83; laughing stock &c. 857.

V. be -ridiculous &c. *adj.*; pass from the sublime to the ridiculous; make one laugh; play the fool, make a fool of oneself, commit an absurdity.

play a joke on, make a -fool of, - sucker of, - monkey of.

Adj. ridiculous, ludicrous, comic, -al; droll, funny, laughable, *pour rire*, grotesque, farcical, odd; whimsical, - as a dancing bear; fanciful, fantastic, queer, rum, quizzical, waggish, quaint, *bizarre*; eccentric &c. (*unconformable*) 83; strange, outlandish, out of the way, *baroque*, *rocaille*, rococo; awkward &c. (*ugly*) 846.

absurd, extravagant, *outré*, monstrous, preposterous, bombastic, inflated, stilted, burlesque, mock heroic.

drollish; serio-, tragic-comic; gimcrack, contemptible &c. (*unim-portant*) 643; doggerel; ironical &c. (*derisive*) 856; risible.

**Phr.** *'risum teneatis amici?' rideret Heraclitus.*

**854. Fop.—N.** fop, fine gentleman; swell; dand-y, -iprat; exquisite, coxcomb, toff, beau, macaroni, blade, blood, buck, man about town, fast man; fribble, jemmy, spark, popinjay, puppy, prig, *petit maître;* jacka-napes, -dandy; man milliner; Jemmy Jessamy, carpet-knight, masher, Dundreary, Johnnie, dude.

belle, fine lady, *coquette,* flirt.

**855. Affectation.—N.** affectation; affectedness &c. *adj.*; acting a part **xc.** *v.*; pretence &c. *(falsehood)* 544, *(ostentation)* 882; boasting &c. 884.

charlatanism, quackery, shallow profundity, humbug, pretension, airs, ₚedantry, purism, precisianism, euphuism, prunes and prisms; teratology &c. *(altiloquence)* 577.

mannerism, *simagrée,* grimace.

conceit, foppery, dandyism, man millinery, coxcombry, puppyism.

stiffness, formality, buckram; prudery, demureness, coquetry, mock modesty, *minauderie,* sentimentalism; *mauvaise honte,* false shame.

affector, performer, actor; pedant, pedagogue, *doctrinaire,* purist, euphuist, mannerist; shoneen; *grimacier;* lump of affectation, *précieuse ridicule, bas bleu,* blue stocking, poetaster; prig, hypocrite; charlatan &c. *(deceiver)* 548; *petit maître* &c. *(fop)* 854; flatterer &c. 935; *coquette,* prude, puritan; precisian, formalist.

**V.** affect, act a part, put on; give oneself airs &c. *(arrogance)* 885; boast &c. 884; coquet; simper, mince, attitudinize, strike a pose, pose; flirt a fan; over-act, -play, -do.

**Adj.** affected, full of affectation, pretentious, pedantic, stilted, stagey, theatrical, big-sounding, *ad captandum,* canting, insincere.

not natural, unnatural; self-conscious; *maniéré;* artificial; over-wrought, -done, -acted; euphuistic &c. 577.

stiff, starch, formal, prim, smug, demure, *tiré à quatre épingles,* quakerish, puritanical, prudish, pragmatical, priggish, conceited, coxcomical, foppish, dandified; fini-cal, -kin, -cky, mincing, simpering, namby-pamby, sentimental, languishing.

**856. Ridicule.—N.** ridicule, derision; sardonic -smile, – grin; irrision; snigger; scoffing &c. *(disrespect)* 929; mockery, quiz, banter, irony, *persiflage,* raillery, chaff, *badinage;* quizzing &c. *v.*

squib, satire, skit, quip, quib, grin.

parody, burlesque, travesty; farce &c. *(drama)* 599; caricature, take-off.

buffoonery &c. *(fun)* 840; practical joke, horseplay.

**V.** ridicule, deride; laugh at, grin at, smile at; snigger; laugh in one's sleeve; banter, rally, chaff, joke, twit, quiz, poke fun at, jolly, roast, rag; fleer; play –, play tricks- upon; fool, – to the top of one's bent; show up.

satirize, parody, caricature, burlesque, travesty.

turn into ridicule; make merry with; make -fun, – game, – a fool, – an April fool- of; rally; scoff &c. *(disrespect)* 929.

raise a laugh &c. *(amuse)* 840; play the fool, make a fool of oneself.

be ridiculous &c. 853.

**Adj.** deris-ory, -ive; mock; sarcastic, ironical, quizzical, burlesque, Hudibrastic; scurrilous &c. *(disrespectful)* 929.

**Adv.** in -ridicule &c. *n.*

**857.** [Object and cause of ridicule.] **Laughing-stock.—N.** laughing-, jesting-, gazing-stock; butt, game, fair game; April fool &c. (*dupe*) 547.

original, oddity; queer -, odd- fish; quiz, square-toes; old -, fogey *or* fogy.

monkey; buffoon &c. (*jester*) 844; pantomimist &c. (*actor*) 599. jest &c. (*wit*) 842.

## 3°. Prospective Affections

**858. Hope.—N.** hope, -s; desire &c. 865; fervent hope, sanguine expectation, trust, confidence, reliance; faith &c. (*belief*) 484; affiance, assurance; secur-eness, -ity; reassurance.

good -omen, - auspices; promise, well-grounded hopes; good -, bright-prospect; clear sky.

as-, pre-sumption; anticipation &c. (*expectation*) 507.

hopefulness, buoyancy, optimism, enthusiasm, heart of grace, aspiration; optimist, utop-ian, -ist; Pollyanna.

castles in the air, *châteaux en Espagne*, hope chest, *le pot au lait*, Utopia, millennium; day -, golden-dream; dream of Alnaschar; airy hopes, fool's paradise; *mirage* &c. (*fallacies of vision*) 443; fond hope.

beam -, ray -, gleam -, glimmer -, dawn -, flash -, star- of hope; cheer; bit of blue sky, silver lining of the cloud, bottom of Pandora's box, balm in Gilead.

anchor, sheet-anchor, main-stay; staff &c. (*support*) 215; heaven &c. 981.

**V.** hope, trust, confide, rely on, put one's trust in, lean upon; pin one's -hope, - faith- upon &c. (*believe*) 484.

feel -, entertain -, harbour -, indulge -, cherish -, feed -, foster -, nourish -, encourage -, cling to -, live in- hope &c. *n.*; see land; feel -, rest- -assured, - confident &c. *adj.*

presume; promise oneself; expect &c. (*look forward to*) 507.

hope for &c. (*desire*) 865; anticipate.

be -hopeful &c. *adj.*; look on the bright side of, view on the sunny side, make the best of it, hope for the best; put -a good, - a bold, - the best- face upon; keep one's spirits up; take heart, - of grace; be of good -heart, - cheer; flatter oneself, lay the flattering unction to one's soul.

**859.** [Absence, want, or loss of hope.] **Hopelessness.—N.** hopelessness &c. *adj.*; despair, desperation; despondency &c. (*dejection*) 837; pessimism.

hope deferred, dashed hopes; vain expectation &c. (*disappointment*) 509.

airy hopes &c. 858; forlorn hope; bad -job, - business; *enfant perdu*; gloomy -, black spots in the- horizon; slough of Despond, cave of Despair.

Job's comforter; bird of -bad, - ill-omen.

**V.** despair; lose -, give up -, abandon -, relinquish- -all hope, - the hope of; give -up, - over; yield to despair; falter; despond &c. (*be dejected*) 837; *jeter le manche après la cognée.*

inspire -, drive to- despair &c. *n.*; disconcert; dash -, crush -, shatter -, destroy- one's hopes; hope against hope.

**Adj.** hopeless, desperate, despairing, in despair, *au désespoir*, forlorn; inconsolable &c. (*dejected*) 837; broken-hearted.

out of the question, not to be thought of; impracticable &c. 471; past -hope, - cure, - mending, - recall; at one's last gasp &c. (*death*) 360; given -up, - over.

incurable, cureless, immedicable, remediless, beyond remedy; incorrigible; irre-parable, -mediable, -coverable, -versible, -trievable, -claimable, -deemable, -vocable; ruined, undone; immitigable.

unpromising, unpropitious; inauspicious, ill-omened, threatening, clouded over, lowering, ominous.

**Phr.** '*lasciate ogni speranza voi ch' entrate*'; its days are numbered; the worst come to the worst.

**860. Fear.—N.** fear, timidity, diffidence, want of confidence; apprehensive-, fearful-ness &c. *adj.*; solicitude,

catch at a straw, hope against hope, count one's chickens before they are hatched.

give –, inspire –, raise –, hold out-hope &c. *n.*; raise expectations; encourage, hearten, cheer, assure, re-assure, buoy up, embolden; promise, bid fair, augur well, be in a fair way, look up, flatter, tell a flattering tale.

**Adj.** hoping &c. *v.*; in -hopes &c. *n.*; hopeful, confident; secure &c. (*certain*) 484; sanguine, in good heart, buoyed up, buoyant, elated, flushed, exultant, enthusiastic; utopian.

unsus-pecting, -picious; fearless, free –, exempt from- -fear, – suspicion, – distrust, – despair; undespairing, self-reliant.

probable, on the high road to; within sight of -shore, – land; promising, propitious; of –, full of- promise; of good omen; auspicious, *de bon augure*; reassuring; encouraging, cheering, inspiriting, looking up, bright, roseate, *couleur de rose*, rose-coloured.

**Adv.** hopefully &c. *adj.*

**Int.** God speed! good luck!

**Phr.** *nil desperandum*; never say die, *dum spiro spero, latet scintillula forsan*, all is for the best, *spero meliora*; the wish being father to the thought; 'hope told a flattering tale'; *rusticus expectat dum defluat amnis*.

anxiety, care, apprehension, misgiving; mistrust &c. (*doubt*) 485; suspicion, qualm; hesitation &c. (*irresolution*) 605.

nervous-, restless-ness &c. *adj.*; in-, dis-quietude; flutter, trepidation, fear and trembling, perturbation, tremor, quivering, shaking, trembling, throbbing heart, palpitation, ague fit, cold sweat; abject fear &c. (*cowardice*) 862; mortal funk, heart-sinking, despondency; despair &c. 859.

fright; affright, -ment; alarm, pavor, dread, awe, terror, horror, dismay, consternation, panic, scare, stampede [of horses].

intimidation, terrorism, reign of terror.

[Object of fear] bug-bear, -aboo; scarecrow; hobgoblin &c. (*demon*) 980; daymare, nightmare, Gorgon, Medusa, mormo, ogre, Hurlothrumbo, raw head and bloody bones, fee faw fum, *bête noire, enfant terrible*.

alarmist &c. (*coward*) 862.

**V.** fear, stand in awe of; be -afraid &c. *adj.*; have -qualms &c. *n.*; apprehend, sit upon thorns, eye askance; distrust &c. (*disbelieve*) 485.

hesitate &c. (*be irresolute*) 605; falter, funk, cower, crouch; skulk &c. (*cowardice*) 862; let 'I dare not' wait upon 'I would'; take -fright, – alarm; start, wince, flinch, shy, shrink; fly &c. (*avoid*) 623.

tremble, shake; shiver. – in one's shoes; shudder, flutter; shake –, tremble- -like an aspen leaf, – all over; quake, quaver, quiver, quail; get the wind up.

grow –, turn- pale; blench, stand aghast; not dare to say one's soul is one's own.

inspire –, excite- -fear, – awe; raise apprehensions; give –, raise –, sound- an alarm; alarm, startle, scare, cry 'wolf,' disquiet, dismay; fright, -en; affright, terrify; astound; frighten from one's propriety; frighten out of one's -wits, – senses, – seven senses; awe; strike -all of a heap, – an awe into, – terror; harrow up the soul, appal, unman. petrify, horrify.

make one's -flesh creep, – hair stand on end, – blood run cold, – teeth chatter; chill one's spine; take away –, stop- one's breath; make one -tremble &c.

haunt, obsess, beset; prey –, weigh- on the mind.

put in -fear, – bodily fear; terrorize, intimidate, cow, daunt, over-awe, abash, deter, discourage; browbeat, bully; threaten &c. 909.

**Adj.** fearing &c. *v.*; frightened &c. *v.*; in -fear, – a fright &c. *n.*; haunted with the -fear &c. *n.*- of.

afraid, fearful; tim-id, -orous; nervous, diffident, coy, faint-hearted, tremulous, shaky, afraid of one's shadow, apprehensive, restless, fidgety; more frightened than hurt.

aghast; awe-, horror-, terror-, panic- -struck, -stricken; frightened to death, white as a sheet; pale, − as -death, − ashes, − a ghost; breathless, in hysterics.

inspiring fear &c. *v.*; alarming; formidable, redoubtable; perilous &c. (*danger*) 665; portentous; fear-ful, -some; dread, -ful; fell; dire, -ful; shocking; terri-ble, -fic; tremendous; horri-d, -ble, -fic; ghastly; awful, awe-inspiring, eerie, weird; revolting &c. (*painful*) 830.

Adv. *in terrorem.*

Int. 'angels and ministers of grace defend us!'

Phr. *ante tubam trepidat; horresco referens,* one's heart failing one, *obstupui steteruntque comæ et vox faucibus hæsit.*

---

**861.** [Absence of fear.] **Courage.—N.**
courage, bravery, valour; resolute-, bold-ness &c. *adj.*; spirit, daring, gallantry, intrepidity; contempt −, defiance- of danger; derring-do; audacity; rashness &c. 863; dash; defiance &c. 715; confidence, self-reliance.

man-liness, -hood; nerve, pluck, mettle, game; heart, − of grace; spunk, gameness, grit, face, virtue, hardihood, fortitude; firmness &c. (*stability*) 150; heart of oak; bottom, backbone &c. (*perseverance*) 604a.

resolution &c. (*determination*) 604; tenacity, bull-dog courage.

prowess, heroism, chivalry.

exploit, feat, achievement; heroic -deed, − act; bold stroke.

man, − of mettle; hero, demigod, paladin, heroine, Amazon, Hector, Joan of Arc; lion, tiger, panther, bull-dog; game-, fighting-cock; bully, fire-eater &c. 863; dare-devil.

V. be -courageous &c. *adj.*; dare, venture, make bold; face −, front −, affront −, confront −, brave −, defy −, despise −, mock- danger; look in the face; look -full, − boldly, − danger- in the face; face; meet, − in front; brave, beard; defy &c. 715.

take −, muster −, summon up −, pluck up- courage; nerve oneself, take heart; take −, pluck up- heart of grace; hold up one's head; screw one's courage to the sticking place; come -to, − up to- the scratch; stand, − to one's guns, − fire, − against; bear up, − against; hold out &c. (*persevere*) 604a.

put a bold face upon; show −,

**862.** [Excess of fear.] **Cowardice.—N.**
cowardice, pusillanimity; cowardliness &c. *adj.*; timidity, effeminacy.

poltroonery, baseness; dastard-ness, -y; abject fear, funk; Dutch courage; fear &c. 860; white feather, faint heart.

coward, poltroon, dastard, sneak, re-creant; shy −, dunghill- cock; coistril, milksop, white-liver, nidget, cur, craven, one that cannot say 'Bo' to a goose; Bob Acres, Jerry Sneak.

alarm-, terror-, pessim-ist; runagate &c. (*fugitive*) 623; shirker.

V. quail &c. (*fear*) 860; be -cowardly &c. *adj.*, − a coward &c. *n.*; funk; cower, skulk, sneak; flinch, shy, fight shy, slink, turn tail; run away &c. (*avoid*) 623; show the white feather, have cold feet, show a yellow streak.

Adj. coward, -ly; fearful, shy; tim-id, -orous; skittish; poor-spirited, spirit-less, soft, effeminate.

weak-minded; infirm of purpose &c. 605; weak-, faint-, chicken-, lily-, pigeon-hearted; yellow; white-, lily-, milk-livered; milksop, smock-faced; unable to say 'Bo' to a goose.

dastard, -ly; base, craven, sneaking, dunghill, recreant; unwar-, unsoldier-like.

'in face a lion but in heart a deer.'

unmanned; frightened &c. 860.

Int. *sauve qui peut!* devil take the hindmost!

Adv. in fear and trembling, in fear of one's life, in a blue funk.

Phr. *ante tubam trepidat,* one's courage oozing out.

---

present- a bold front, face the music; envisage; show fight.

bell the cat, take the bull by the horns, beard the lion in his den, march up to the cannon's mouth, go through fire and water, run the gauntlet, go over the top.

give –, infuse –, inspire- courage; reassure, encourage, embolden, inspirit, cheer, hearten, nerve, put upon one's mettle, rally, raise a rallying cry; pat on the back, make a man of, keep in countenance.

**Adj.** courageous, brave; val-iant, -orous; gallant, intrepid; spirit-ed, -ful; high-spirited, -mettled; mettlesome, game, plucky; man-ly, -ful; resolute; stout, -hearted; iron-, lion-hearted; heart of oak; Penthesilean.

bold, – spirited; daring, audacious; fear-, daunt-, dread-, awe-less; un-daunted, -appalled, -dismayed, -awed, -blenched, -abashed, -alarmed, -flinching, -shrinking, -blenching, -apprehensive; confident, self-reliant; bold as -a lion, – brass.

enterprising, adventurous; ventur-ous, -csome; dashing, chivalrous; soldierly &c. (*warlike*) 722; heroic.

fierce, savage; pugnacious &c. (*bellicose*) 720.

strong-minded, hardy, doughty; firm &c. (*stable*) 150; determined &c. (*resolved*) 604; dogged, indomitable &c. (*persevering*) 604a.

up to, – the scratch; upon one's mettle; reassured &c. *v.*; un-feared, undreaded.

**Phr.** one's blood being up.

---

**863. Rashness.**—**N.** rashness &c. *adj.*; temerity, want of caution, imprudence, indiscretion; over-confidence, presumption, audacity.

precipit-ancy, -ation; impetuosity; levity; foolhardi-hood, -ness; heed-, thought-lessness &c. (*inattention*) 458; carelessness &c. (*neglect*) 460; desperation; Quixotism, knight-errantry; fire-eating.

gam-ing, -bling; blind bargain, leap in the dark, fool's paradise; too many eggs in one basket.

*desperado*, rashling, mad-cap, daredevil, Hotspur, fire-eater, bully, *bravo*, Hector, scapegrace, *enfant perdu*; Don Quixote, knight-errant, Icarus; adventurer; gam-bler, -ester; dynamitard.

**V.** be -rash &c. *adj.*; stick at nothing, play a desperate game; run into danger &c. 665; play with -fire, – edge tools.

carry too much sail, sail too near the wind, ride at single anchor, go out of one's depth.

take a leap in the dark, buy a pig in a poke.

*donner tête baissée*; knock one's head against a wall &c. (*be unskilful*) 699; rush on destruction; kick against the

**864. Caution.**—**N.** caution; cautiousness &c. *adj.*; discretion, prudence, cautel, heed, circumspection, calculation, deliberation; safety first.

foresight &c. 510; vigilance &c. 459; warning &c. 668.

coolness &c. *adj.*; self-possession, -command; presence of mind, *sangfroid*; well regulated mind; worldly wisdom, Fabian policy.

**V.** be -cautious &c. *adj.*; take -care, – heed, – good care; have a care; mind, – what one is about; be on one's guard &c. (*keep watch*) 459; make assurance double sure; ca' canny.

bespeak &c. (*be early*) 132.

think twice, look before one leaps, keep one's weather eye open, count the cost, look to the main chance, cut one's coat according to one's cloth; feel one's -ground, – way; see how the land lies &c. (*foresight*) 510; wait to see how the cat jumps; bridle one's tongue; *reculer pour mieux sauter* &c. (*prepare*) 673; let well alone, let sleeping dogs lie, *ne pas réveiller le chat qui dort*.

keep out of -harm's way, – troubled waters; keep at a respectful distance, stand aloof; keep –, be- on the safe side;

pricks, tempt Providence, go on a forlorn hope.

count one's chickens before they are hatched; reckon without one's host; catch at straws; trust to –, lean on- a broken reed.

**Adj.** rash, incautious, indiscreet, injudicious; imprudent, improvident, temerarious; uncalculating; heedless; careless &c. (*neglectful*) 460; without ballast, heels over head; giddy &c. (*inattentive*) 458; wanton, reckless, wild, madcap; desperate, devil-may-care.

hot-blooded, -headed, -brained; head-long, -strong; break-neck; foolhardy; hare-brained; precipitate, impulsive.

over-confident, -weening; venturesome, -ous; adventurous, Quixotic; fire-eating, cavalier; free-and-easy.

off one's guard &c. (*inexpectant*) 508.

**Adv.** post haste, *à corps perdu*, hand over head, *tête baissée*, head-foremost; happen what may.

**Phr.** neck or nothing, the devil being in one.

husband one's resources &c. 636.

caution &c. (*warn*) 668.

**Adj.** cautious, wary, guarded; on one's guard &c. (*watchful*) 459; *cavendo tutus*; *in medio tutissimus*.

care-, heed-ful; cautelous, stealthy, chary, shy of, circumspect, prudent, canny, safe, non-committal, discreet, politic; sure-footed &c. (*skilful*) 698.

unenterprising, unadventurous, cool, steady, self-possessed; over-cautious.

suspicious, leery, vigilant.

**Adv.** cautiously, gingerly &c. *adj.*

**Int.** have a care! look out! *cave canem!*

**Phr.** *timeo Danaos; festina lente.*

---

**865. Desire.**—**N.** desire, wish, fancy, fantasy; want, need, exigency.

mind, inclination, leaning, bent, *animus*, partiality, *penchant*, predilection; propensity &c. 820; willingness &c. 602; liking, love, fondness, relish.

longing, hankering; solicitude, anxiety; yearning, coveting; aspiration, ambition, vaulting ambition; eagerness, zeal, ardour, *empressement*, breathless impatience, over-anxiety; solicitude, impetuosity &c. 825.

appet-ite, -ition, -ence, -ency; sharp appetite, keenness, hunger, stomach, twist; thirst, -iness; drouth, mouth-watering; itch, -ing; prurience, *cacoëthes*, cupidity, lust, concupiscence.

edge of -appetite, – hunger; torment of Tantalus; sweet –, lickerish- tooth; itching palm; longing –, wistful –, sheep's- eye.

avidity; greed, -iness; covetous-, ravenous-ness &c. *adj.*; grasping, craving, canine appetite, rapacity; voracity &c. (*gluttony*) 957.

passion, rage, *furore*, mania, *manie*; inextinguishable desire; dips-, klept-, mon-omania.

[Person desiring] desirer, lover, *ama-*

**866. Indifference.**—**N.** indifference neutrality; coldness &c. *adj.*; unconcern, *insouciance, nonchalance*; want of -interest, – earnestness; anorexy, inappetency; apathy &c. (*insensibility*) 823; supineness &c. (*inactivity*) 683; disdain &c. 930; recklessness &c. 863; inattention &c. 458.

**V.** be -indifferent &c. *adj.*; stand neuter; take no interest in &c. (*insensibility*) 823; have no -desire &c. 865, – taste, – relish- for; not care for; care nothing -for, – about; not care a -straw &c. (*unimportance*) 643 -about, – for; not mind.

set at naught &c. (*make light of*) 483; spurn &c. (*disdain*) 930.

**Adj.** indifferent, cold, frigid, lukewarm; cool, – as a cucumber; unconcerned, *insouciant*, phlegmatic, *pococurante*, easy-going, devil-may-care, careless, listless, lackadaisical, feckless; half-hearted; un-ambitious, -aspiring, -desirous, -solicitous, -attracted.

un-attractive, -alluring, -desired, -desirable, -cared for, -wished, -valued, all one to.

insipid &c. 391; vain.

**Adv.** for aught one cares.

*teur*, votary, devotee, aspirant, solicitant, candidate; cormorant &c. 957; sycophant.

[Object of desire] *desideratum*; want &c. (*requirement*) 630; 'consummation devoutly to be wished'; attraction, magnet, allurement, fancy, temptation, seduction, lure, fascination, *prestige*, height of one's ambition, idol; whim, ·sey; maggot; hobby, -horse.

Fortunatus's cap, wishing cap, love potion.

**V.** desire; wish, – for; be -desirous &c. *adj.*; have a -longing &c. *n.*; hope &c. 858.

care for, affect, like, list; take to, cling to, take a fancy to; fancy; prefer &c. (*choose*) 609.

have -an eye, – a mind- to; find it in one's heart &c. (*be willing*) 602; have a fancy for, set one's eyes upon; cast a sheep's eye –, look sweet- upon; take into one's head, have at heart, be bent upon; set one's -cap at, – heart upon, – mind upon; covet.

want, miss, need, lack, desiderate, feel the want of; would fain -have, – do; would be glad of.

be -hungry &c. *adj.*; have a good appetite, play a good knife and fork; hunger –, thirst –, crave –, lust –, itch –, hanker –, run mad- after; raven –, die- for; burn to.

desiderate; sigh –, cry –, gape –, gasp –, pine –, pant –, languish –, yearn –, long –, be on thorns –, hope- for; aspire after; catch at, grasp at, jump at.

woo, court, solicit; fish –, spell –, whistle –, put up- for; ogle.

cause –, create –, raise –, excite –, provoke- desire; whet the appetite; appetize, titillate, allure, attract, take one's fancy, tempt; hold out -temptation, – allurement; tantalize, make one's mouth water, *faire venir l'eau à la bouche*.

gratify desire &c. (*give pleasure*) 829.

**Adj.** desirous; desiring &c. *v.*; orectic, appetitive; inclined &c. (*willing*) 602; partial to; fain, wishful, optative; anxious, wistful, curious; at a loss for, sedulous, solicitous.

craving, hungry, sharp-set, peckish,

**Int.** never mind.

**867. Dislike.—N.** dis-like, -taste, -relish, -inclination, -placency.

reluctance; backwardness &c. (*unwillingness*) 603.

repugnance, disgust, queasiness, turn, nausea, loathing; avers-eness, -ation, -ion; abomination, antipathy, abhorrence, horror; mortal –, rooted- -antipathy, – horror; hatred, detestation; hate &c. 898; animosity &c. 900; hydrophobia.

sickener; gall and wormwood &c. (*unsavoury*) 395; shuddering, cold sweat.

**V.** dis-, mis-like, -relish; mind, object to; have rather not, not care for; have –, conceive –, entertain –, take- -a dislike, – an aversion- to; have no -taste, – stomach- for.

shun, avoid &c. 623; eschew; withdraw –, shrink –, recoil- from; not be able to -bear, – abide, – endure; shrug the shoulders at, shudder at, turn up the nose at, look askance at; make a -mouth, – wry face, – grimace; make faces.

loathe, nauseate, abominate, detest, abhor; hate &c. 898; take amiss &c. 900; have enough of &c. (*be satiated*) 869.

cause –, excite- dislike; disincline, repel, sicken; make –, render- sick; turn one's stomach, nauseate, wamble, disgust, shock, stink in the nostrils; go against the -grain, – stomach; stick in the throat; make one's blood run cold &c. (*give pain*) 830; pall.

**Adj.** disliking &c. *v.*; averse to, loth, adverse; shy of, sick of, out of conceit with; disinclined; heart-, dog-sick; queasy.

disliked &c. *v.*; uncared for, unpopular; out of favour; repulsive, repugnant, repellent; abhorrent, insufferable, fulsome, nauseous; loath-some, -ful; offensive; disgusting &c. *v.*; disagreeable &c; (*painful*) 830; unsavoury &c. 395.

**Adv.** *usque ad nauseam.*

**Int.** faugh! foh! ugh!

**868. Fastidiousness.—N.** fastidiousness &c. *adj.*; nicety, meticulosity,

ravening, with an empty stomach, esurient, lickerish, thirsty, athirst, parched with thirst, pinched with hunger, famished, dry, drouthy; hungry as a -hunter, – hawk, – horse, – church mouse.

greedy, – as a hog; over-eager, voracious; ravenous, – as a wolf; openmouthed, covetous, rapacious, grasping, extortionate, exacting, sordid, *alieni appetens*; insati-able, -ate; unquenchable, quenchless; omnivorous.

unsatisfied, unsated, unslaked.

eager, avid, keen; burning, fervent, ardent; agog; all agog; breathless; impatient &c. (*impetuous*) 825; bent –, intent –, set- -on, – upon; mad after, *enragé*, rabid, dying for, devoured by desire.

aspiring, ambitious, vaulting, skyaspiring.

desirable; popular; desired &c. *v.*; in demand; pleasing &c. (*giving pleasure*) 829; appeti-zing, -ble; tantalizing.

Adv. wistfully &c. *adj.*; fain.

Int. would -that, – it were! O for! *esto perpetua!* if only!

Phr. the wish being father to the thought; *sua cuique voluptas*; *hoc erat in votis*, the mouth watering, the fingers itching; *aut Cæsar aut nullus.*

hypercriticism, difficulty in being pleased, *friandise*, epicurism, *omnia suspendens naso.*

discrimination, discernment, good taste, perspicacity.

epicure, gourmet.

[Excess of delicacy] prudery, prudishness, primness.

V. be -fastidious &c. *adj.*; split hairs, discriminate, have a sweet tooth.

mince the matter; turn up one's nose at &c. (*disdain*) 930; look a gift horse in the mouth, see spots on the sun.

Adj. fastidious, meticulous, exacting, nice, delicate, *délicat*, finical, finicky, difficult, dainty, lickerish, squeamish, thin-skinned; s-, queasy; hard –, difficult- to please; querulous, particular, over-particular, straitlaced, prudish, prim, scrupulous; censorious &c. 932; hypercritical, discriminating, discerning, perspicacious.

Phr. *noli me tangere.*

**869. Satiety.**—N. satiety, satisfaction, saturation, repletion, glut, surfeit; weariness &c. 841.

spoiled child; *enfant gâté*; too much of a good thing, *toujours perdrix*; *crambe repetita.*

V. sate, satiate, satisfy, saturate; cloy, quench, slake, pall, glut, gorge, surfeit; bore &c. (*weary*) 841; tire &c. (*fatigue*) 688; spoil.

have -enough of, – quite enough of, – one's fill, – too much of; be -satiated &c. *adj.*

Adj. satiated &c. *v.*; overgorged; *blasé*, used up, sick of, heart-sick.

Int. enough! hold! *eheu jam satis!*

---

## 4°. Contemplative Affections

**870. Wonder.**—N. wonder, marvel; astonish-, amaze-, wonder-, bewilderment; amazedness &c. *adj.*; admiration, awe; stup-or, -efaction; stound, fascination; sensation; surprise &c. (*inexpectation*) 508; cynosure.

note of admiration; thaumaturgy &c. (*sorcery*) 992.

V. wonder, marvel, admire; be -surprised &c. *adj.*; start; stare; open –, rub –, turn up- one's eyes; gloar; gape, open one's mouth, hold one's breath;

**871.** [Absence of wonder.] **Expectance.**—N. expectan-ce, -cy &c. (*expectation*) 507; calmness, composure, tranquillity, serenity, coolness, imperturbability &c. 826.

nine days' wonder.

V. expect &c. 507; not -be surprised, – wonder &c. 870; *nil admirari*, mak. nothing of.

Adj. expecting &c. *v.*; unamazed, astonished at nothing; *blasé* &c. (*weary*) 841; unimaginative, calm, serene, im-

look –, stand- -aghast, – agog; look blank &c. (*disappointment*) 509; *tomber des nues*; not believe one's -eyes, – ears, – senses.

perturbable &c. 826; expected &c. *v.*; foreseen.

common, ordinary &c. (*habitual*) 613.

Int. no wonder; of course; why not?

not be able to account for &c. (*unintelligible*) 519; not know whether one stands on one's head or one's heels.

surprise, astonish, amaze, astound; dumbfound, -er; startle, dazzle; strike, – with -wonder, – awe; electrify; stun, stupefy, petrify, confound, bewilder, flabbergast; stagger, throw on one's beam ends, fascinate, turn the head, take away one's breath, strike dumb; make one's -hair stand on end, – tongue cleave to the roof of one's mouth; make one stare.

take by surprise &c. (*be unexpected*) 508.

be -wonderful &c. *adj.*; beggar –, baffle- description; stagger belief.

Adj. surprised &c. *v.*; aghast, all agog, breathless, agape; open-mouthed; awe-, thunder-, moon-, planet-struck; spell-bound; lost in -amazement, – wonder, – astonishment; struck all of a heap, unable to believe one's senses, like a duck in thunder.

wonderful, wondrous; surprising &c. *v.*; unexpected &c. 508; unheard of; mysterious &c. (*inexplicable*) 519; miraculous; *foudroyant*.

in-describable, -expressible, -effable; un-utterable, -speakable.

monstrous, prodigious, stupendous, marvellous; in-conceivable, -credible; in-, un-imaginable; strange &c. (*uncommon*) 83; passing strange.

striking &c. *v.*; over-whelming; wonder-working.

Adv. wonderfully &c. *adj.*; fearfully; for a –, in the name of-wonder; strange to say; *mirabile -dictu, – visu*; to one's great surprise.

with -wonder &c. *n.*, – gaping mouth, – open eyes, – upturned eyes; eyes starting out of one's head.

Int. lo, – and behold! O! hey-day! halloo! what! indeed! really! surely! humph! hem! good -lack, – heavens, – gracious! – lord! by jove! gad so! well a day! dear me! only think! lack-a-daisy! my -stars, – goodness! gracious goodness! goodness gracious! mercy on us! heavens and earth! God bless me! bless -us, – my heart! odzookens! *O gemini!* adzooks! hoity-toity! strong! Heaven save –, bless- the mark! can such things be! zounds! 'sdeath! what -on earth, – in the world! who would have thought it! &c. (*inexpectation*) 508; fancy! did you ever? you don't say so! what do you say to that! how now! where am I? well I'm blowed! &c.

Phr. *vox faucibus hæsit*; one's hair standing on end.

872. Prodigy.—N. prodigy, phenomenon; wonder, -ment; genius, marvel, miracle; freak, monster &c. (*unconformity*) 83; curiosity, lion, infant prodigy, sight, spectacle; *jeu –, coup- de théâtre*; gazing-stock; sign; portent &c. 512.

bursting of a -shell, – bomb; volcanic eruption, peal of thunder; thunder-clap, -bolt.

what no words can paint; wonders of the world; *annus mirabilis*; *dignus vindice nodus*.

5°. Intrinsic Affections*

873. Repute.—N. distinction, mark, name, figure; repute, reputation, char-

874. Disrepute.—N. disrepute, discredit; ill-, bad- -repute, -name, -odour,

* Or personal affections derived from the opinions or feelings of others.

acter; good –, high- repute; note, notability, notoriety, *éclat*, 'the bubble reputation,' vogue, celebrity; fame, famousness; renown; popularity, *aura popularis*; esteem, approval, approbation &c. 931; credit, *succès d'estime*, *prestige*, talk of the town; name to conjure with.

glory, honour; lustre &c. (*light*) 420; illustriousness &c. *adj.*

account, regard, respect; reputableness &c. *adj.*; respectability &c. (*probity*) 939; good -name, – report; fair name.

dignity; stateliness &c. *adj.*; solemnity, grandeur, splendour, nobility, majesty, sublimity.

rank, standing, brevet rank, precedence, *pas*, station, place, *status*; position, – in society; order, degree, *locus standi*, caste, condition.

greatness &c. *adj.*; eminence; height &c. 206; importance &c. 642; pre-, super-eminence; high mightiness, primacy; top of the -ladder, – tree.

elevation; ascent &c. 305; super-, ex-altation; dignification, aggrandizement.

dedication, consecration, enthronement, canonization, apotheosis, deification, celebration, enshrinement, glorification.

hero, man of mark, great card, celebrity, champion, worthy, lion, *rara avis*, notability, somebody; man of rank &c. (*nobleman*) 875; pillar of the -state, - society, – church.

chief &c. (*master*) 745; first fiddle &c. (*proficient*) 700; scholar &c. 492; cynosure, mirror; flower, pink, pearl; paragon &c. (*perfection*) 650; choice and master spirits of the age; *élite*; star, sun, constellation, galaxy.

ornament, honour, feather in one's cap, halo, aureole, nimbus; halo –, blaze- of glory; blushing honours; laurels &c. (*trophy*) 733.

memory, posthumous fame, niche in the temple of fame; immor-tality, -tal name; *magni nominis umbra*.

**V.** be conscious of glory; be proud of &c. (*pride*) 878; exult &c. (*boast*) 884; be vain of &c. (*vanity*) 880.

be -distinguished &c. *adj.*; shine &c.

-favour; disapprobation &c. 932; ingloriousness, derogation; a-, de-basement; abjectness &c. *adj.*; degradation, dedecoration; 'a long farewell to all one's greatness'; odium, obloquy, opprobrium, ignominy.

dishonour, disgrace; shame, humiliation; scandal, baseness, vileness; perfidy, turpitude &c. (*improbity*) 940; infamy.

tarnish, taint, defilement, pollution. stain, blot, spot, blur, stigma, brand, reproach, imputation, slur.

crying –, burning- shame; *scandalum magnatum*, badge of infamy, blot in one's escutcheon; bend –, bar- sinister; champain, point champain; by-word of reproach; Ichabod.

*argumentum ad verecundiam*; sense of shame &c. 879.

**V.** be -inglorious &c. *adj.*; incur -disgrace &c. *n.*; have –, earn- a bad name; put –, wear- a halter round one's neck; disgrace –, expose- oneself.

play second fiddle; lose caste; pale one's ineffectual fire; recede into the shade; fall from one's high estate; keep in the background &c. (*modesty*) 881; be conscious of disgrace &c. (*humility*) 879; look -blue, – foolish, – like a fool; cut a -poor, – sorry- figure; laugh on the wrong side of the mouth; make a sorry face, go away with a flea in one's ear, slink away.

cause -shame &c. *n.*; shame, disgrace, put to shame, dishonour; throw –, cast –, fling –, reflect- dishonour &c. *n.* upon; be a -reproach &c. *n.* to; derogate from.

tarnish, stain, blot, sully, taint; discredit; degrade, debase, defile; beggar; expel &c. (*punish*) 972.

impute shame to, brand, post, stigmatize, vilify, defame, slur, cast a slur upon, hold up to shame, send to Coventry; tread –, trample- under foot; show up, drag through the mire, heap dirt upon; reprehend &c. 932.

bring low, put down, snub; take down a peg, – lower, – or two.

obscure, eclipse, outshine, take the shine out of; throw –, cast- into the shade; overshadow; leave –, put- in the background; push into a corner,

(*light*) 420; shine forth, figure; make –, cut- a -figure, – dash, – splash.

rival, surpass; out-shine, -rival, -vie, -jump; emulate, vie with, eclipse; throw –, cast- into the shade; over-shadow.

live, flourish, glitter, scintillate, flaunt; gain –, acquire- honour &c. *n.*; play first fiddle &c. (*be of importance*) 642; bear the -palm, – bell; lead the way; take -precedence, – the wall of; gain –, win- -laurels, – spurs, – golden opinions &c. (*approbation*) 931; gradu-ate, take one's degree, pass one's exami-nation, win a -scholarship, – fellowship.

make -a, – some- -noise, – noise in the world; leave one's mark, exalt one's horn, star, have a run, be run after; enjoy popularity, come -into vogue, – to the front; raise one's head.

enthrone, signalize, immortalize, deify, exalt to the skies; hand one's name down to posterity.

consecrate; dedicate to, devote to; enshrine, inscribe, blazon, lionize, blow the trumpet, crown with laurel.

confer –, reflect- honour &c. *n.* on; shed a lustre on; redound to one's honour, ennoble.

give –, do –, pay –, render- honour to; honour, accredit, pay regard to, dignify, glorify; sing praises to &c. (*approve*) 931; look up to; exalt, aggran-dize, elevate, nobilitate.

**Adj.** distinguished, *distingué*, noted; of -note &c. *n.*; honoured &c. *v.*; popu-lar; fashionable &c. 852.

put one's nose out of joint; put out, – of countenance.

upset, throw off one's centre; dis-compose, disconcert; put to the blush &c. (*humble*) 879.

**Adj.** disgraced &c. *v.*; blown upon; shorn of -its beams, – one's glory; overcome, down-trodden; loaded with -shame &c. *n.*; in -bad repute &c. *n.*; out of -repute, – favour, – fashion, – countenance; at a discount; under -a cloud, – an eclipse; unable to show one's face; in the -shade, – back-ground; out at elbows, down in the world, down and out.

inglorious; nameless, renownless, ob-scure, unknown to fame; un-noticed, -noted, -honoured, -glorified.

shameful; dis-graceful, -creditable, -reputable; despicable; questionable; unbecoming, unworthy; derogatory; degrading, humiliating, *infra digni-tatem*, dedecorous; scandalous, infa-mous, too bad, unmentionable; ribald, opprobrious; arrant, shocking, outra-geous, notorious, shady.

ignominious, scrubby, dirty, abject, vile, beggarly, pitiful, low, mean, shabby; base &c. (*dishonourable*) 940.

**Adv.** to one's shame be it spoken.

**Int.** fie! shame! for shame! *pro pudor! O tempora! O mores!* ough! *sic transit gloria mundi!*

in good odour; in –, in high- favour; reput-, respect-, credit-able.

remarkable &c. (*important*) 642; notable, notorious; celebrated, renowned, in every one's mouth, talked of; fam-ous, -ed; far-famed; conspicuous, to the front; foremost; in the -front rank, – ascendant.

imperishable, deathless, immortal, never fading, *ære perennius*; time-honoured.

illustrious, glorious, splendid, brilliant, radiant; bright &c. 420; full-blown; honorific.

eminent, prominent; high &c. 206; in the zenith; at the -head of, – top of the tree; peerless, of the first water; superior &c. 33; super-, pre-eminent.

great, dignified, proud, noble, honourable, worshipful, lordly, grand, stately, august, princely, imposing, solemn, transcendent, majestic, sacred, sublime, heaven-born, heroic, *sans peur et sans reproche*; sacrosanct.

**Int.** hail! all hail! *ave! viva! vive!* long life to! glory –, honour- be to!

Phr. one's name -being in every mouth, – living for ever; *sic itur ad astra, fama volat, aut Cæsar aut nullus*; not to know him argues oneself unknown; none but himself could be his parallel, *palmam qui meruit ferat.*

**875. Nobility.—N.** nobility, rank, condition, distinction, optimacy, blood, *pur sang*, birth, high descent, order; quality, gentility; blue blood of Castile; *ancien régime.*

high life, *haut monde*; upper -classes, – ten thousand; *élite*, aristocracy, great folks; fashionable world &c. (*fashion*) 852; salariat.

peer, -age; House of -Lords, – peers; lords, – temporal and spiritual; *noblesse*; baronage, knightage; noble, -man; lord, -ling; grandee, *magnifico, hidalgo*; don, -ship; aristocrat, swell, three-tailed bashaw; gentleman, squire, squireen, patrician, laureate.

gentry, gentlefolk; squirarchy, better sort, *magnates, primates, optimates.*

king &c. (*master*) 745; prince, crown prince, *Dauphin*; duke; marquis, -ate; earl, viscount, baron, thane, banneret; baronet, -cy; knight, -hood; count, armiger, laird; sig-, seig-nior; esquire, boyar, margrave, vavasour, sheik, emir, ameer, scherif, *pasha*, effendi, sahib.

queen &c. 745; princess, begum, duchess, marchioness; countess &c.; lady, dame.

personage –, man- of -distinction, – mark, – rank; nota-bles, -bilities; celebrity, big-wig, magnate, great man, star; *magni nominis umbra*; 'every inch a king'; grand Panjandrum.

**V.** be -noble &c. *adj.*

**Adj.** noble, exalted; of -rank &c. *n.*; princely, titled, patrician, aristocratic; high-, well-born; of gentle blood; genteel, *comme il faut*, gentlemanlike, courtly &c. (*fashionable*) 852; highly respectable.

**Adv.** in high quarters.

**877. Title.—N.** title, honour; knighthood &c. (*nobility*) 875.

royal –, serene- highness, excellency, grace; lordship, worship, Rt. Hon., rever-ence, -end; esquire, sir; madam, *madame*; master, mistress, Mr., Mrs., *signor, señor, Mein Herr, mynheer*;

**876. Commonalty.—N.** commonalty, democracy; obscurity; low -condition, – life, – society, – company; *bourgeoisie*; mass of -the people, – society; Brown, Jones, and Robinson; Tom, Dick, and Harry; lower –, humbler- -classes, – orders; vulgar –, common- herd; rank and file, *hoc genus omne*; the -many, – general, – crowd, – people, – populace, – multitude, – million, – masses, – mobility, – peasantry; king Mob; proletariat, *fruges consumere nati*, great unwashed; man in the street.

mob; rabble, – rout; chaff, rout, horde, *canaille*; scum –, *residuum* –, dregs- of -the people, – society; swinish multitude, *fæx populi*; *profanum* –, *ignobile- vulgus*; vermin, riff-raff, tagrag and bobtail; small fry.

commoner, one of the people, democrat, plebeian, republican, proletary, *prolétaire, roturier*, Mr. Snooks, *bourgeois, épicier*, Philistine, cockney; *grisette, demi-mondaine.*

peasant, countryman, boor, carle, churl; vill-ain, -ein; serf, kern, tyke, tike, chuff, ryot, fellah; long-shoreman; swain, clown, hind; clod, -hopper; hobnail, yokel, hick, rube, cider squeezer, bog-trotter, bumpkin; ploughman, -boy; rustic, chawbacon, tiller of the soil; hewers of wood and drawers of water, groundling; gaffer, loon, put, cub, Tony Lumpkin, looby, lout, underling; *gamin*, guttersnipe, street arab, mudlark; rough, rowdy, ruffian, roughneck; pot-walloper, slubberdegullion; vulgar –, low- fellow; cad, curmudgeon.

upstart, *parvenu, nouveau-riche*, skipjack; nobody, – one knows; *hesterni quirites, pessoribus orti*; *bourgeois gentilhomme, novus homo*, snob, gent, mushroom, no one knows who, adventurer; man of straw.

beggar, panhandler, gaberlunzie, muckworm, mudlark, *sans-culotte*, raff, tatterdemalion, caitiff, ragamuffin, Pariah, outcast of society, tramp, weary Willie, bum, vagabond, *chiffon-*

your -, his- honour; handle to one's name.

decoration, laurel, palm, wreath, garland, bays, medal, ribbon, riband, blue ribbon, *cordon*, cross, crown, coronet, star, garter; feather, – in one's cap; chevron, epaulet, *épaulette*, colours, cockade; livery; order, arms, armorial bearings, shield, scutcheon, crest, reward &c. 973.

_____

*nier*, rag-picker, Cinderella, cinderwench, scrub, jade; boots, gosscon.

Goth, Vandal, Hottentot, savage, barbarian, Yahoo; unlicked cub, rough diamond.

barbar-ousness, -ism; Bœotia.

**V.** be -ignoble &c. *adj.*, – nobody &c. *n.*

**Adj.** ignoble, common, mean, low, base, vile, sorry, scrubby, beggarly, below par; no great shakes &c. (*unimportant*) 643; home-ly, -spun; vulgar, low-minded; snobbish, *parvenu.*

plebeian, proletarian; of -low, – mean- -parentage, – origin, extraction; low-, base-, earth-born, low bred; mushroom, dunghill, risen from the ranks; unknown to fame, obscure, untitled.

rustic, uncivilized; lout-, boor-, clown-, churl-, brut-, raff-ish;' rude, unlicked, unpolished.

barbar-ous, -ian, -ic, -esque; cockney, born within sound of Bow bells.

underling, menial, servile, subaltern.

**Adv.** below the salt.

_____

**878. Pride.—N.** dignity, self-respect, *mens sibi conscia recti.*

pride; haughtiness &c. *adj.*; high notions, *hauteur*; vainglory, crest; arrogance &c. (*assumption*) 885; pomposity &c. 882.

proud man, highflier; fine -gentleman, – lady; *grande dame.*

**V.** be -proud &c. *adj.*; put a good face on; look one in the face; stalk abroad, perk oneself up; presume, swagger, strut; rear -, lift up -, hold up- one's head; hold one's head high, look big, take the wall, 'bear like the Turk no rival near the throne,' carry with a high hand; ride the -, mount on one's- high horse; set one's back up, bridle, toss the head; give oneself airs &c. (*assume*) 885; boast &c. 884.

pride oneself on; glory in, take a pride in; pique -, plume -, hug- oneself; stand upon, be proud of; put a good face on; not -hide one's light under a bushel, – put one's talent in a napkin; not think small beer of oneself &c. (*vanity*) 880.

**Adj.** dignified; stately; proud, -crested; lordly, baronial; lofty-minded; high-souled, -minded, -mettled, -handed, -plumed, -flown, -toned.

**879. Humility.—N.** hum-ility, -bleness; meek-, low-ness; lowli-ness, -hood; abasement, self-abasement, -effacement; submission &c. 725; resignation.

condescension; affability &c. (*courtesy*) 894.

modesty &c. 881; verecundity, blush, suffusion, confusion; sense of -shame, – disgrace; humiliation, mortification; let -, set- down.

**V.** be -humble &c. *adj.*; deign, vouchsafe, condescend; humble -, demean- oneself; stoop, – to conquer; carry coals; submit &c. 725; submit with a good grace &c. (*brook*) 826; yield the palm.

lower one's -tone, – note; sing small, draw in one's horns, sober down; hide one's -face, – diminished head; not dare to show one's face, take shame to oneself, not have a word to say for oneself; feel -, be conscious of- -shame, – disgrace; drink the cup of humiliation to the dregs; eat -humble pie, – one's words, – dirt; be humiliated, receive a snub.

blush -for, – up to the eyes; redden, change colour; colour up; hang one's head, look foolish, feel small.

render humble; humble, humiliate;

haughty, paughty, insolent, lofty, high, mighty, swollen, puffed up, flushed, blown; vain-glorious; purse-proud, fine; proud as -a peacock, Lucifer; bloated with pride.

supercilious, disdainful, bumptious, magisterial, imperious; high -handed, - and mighty; overweening, consequential; arrogant &c. 885; unblushing &c. 880.

stiff, -necked; starch; perked -, stuck- up; in buckram, straitlaced; prim &c. (*affected*) 855.

on one's -high horses, - tight ropes, -high ropes; on stilts; *en grand seigneur*.

**Adv.** with head erect, with one's nose in the air.

**Phr.** *odi profanum vulgus et arceo.*

---

let -, set -, take -, tread -, frown-down; snub, abash, abase, make one sing small, strike dumb; teach one -his distance, - his place; take down a peg, - lower; throw -, cast- into the shade &c. 874; stare -, put- out of countenance; put to the blush; confuse, ashame, mortify, disgrace, crush; send away with a flea in one's ear.

get a set down.

**Adj.** humble, lowly, meek; modest &c. 881; humble-, sober-minded; un-offended; submissive &c. 725; servile &c. 886.

condescending; affable &c. (*courteous*) 894.

humbled &c. *v.*; bowed down, re-signed; abashed, ashamed, dashed; out of countenance; down in the mouth; down on one's -knees, - marrow-bones; humbled in the dust, brow-beaten; chap-, crest-fallen; dumbfoundered, flabbergasted, struck all of a heap.

shorn of one's glory &c. (*disrepute*) 874.

**Adv.** with -downcast eyes, - bated breath, - bended knee; on all fours, on one's feet.

under correction, with due deference.

**Phr.** I am your -obedient, - very humble- servant; my service to you.

---

**880. Vanity.—N.** vanity; conceit, -edness; self-conceit, -complacency, -confidence, -sufficiency, -esteem, -love, -approbation, -praise, -glorification, -laudation, -gratulation, -applause, -admiration; *amour-propre*; selfishness &c. 943.

airs, pretensions, mannerism; egotism; prigg-ism, -ishness; coxcombry, gaudery, vainglory, elation; pride &c. 878; ostentation &c. 882; assurance &c. 885.

*vox et præterea nihil*; *cheval de bataille.*

ego-ist, -tist; peacock, coxcomb &c. 854; Sir Oracle &c. 887.

**V.** be -vain &c. *adj.*, - vain of; pique oneself &c. (*pride*) 878; lay the flattering unction to one's soul.

have -too high, - an overweening-opinion of -oneself, - one's talents; blind oneself as to one's own merit; not think -small beer, - *vin ordinaire*-of oneself; put oneself forward; fish

**881. Modesty.—N.** modesty; humility &c. 879; diffidence, timidity; retiring disposition, unobtrusiveness, bashfulness &c. *adj.*; *mauvaise honte*; blush, -ing; verecundity; self-knowledge.

reserve, constraint; demureness &c. *adj.*; blushing honours.

**V.** be -modest &c. *adj.*; retire, reserve oneself; give way to; draw in one's horns &c. 879; hide one's face.

keep -private, - in the background, - one's distance; pursue the noiseless tenor of one's way, 'do good by stealth and blush to find it fame,' hide one's light under a bushel, cast a sheep's eye.

**Adj.** modest, diffident; humble &c. 879; timid, timorous, bashful; shy, nervous, skittish, coy, sheepish, shame-faced, blushing, over-modest.

unpreten-ding, -tious; un-obtrusive, -assuming, -ostentatious, -boastful, -aspiring; poor in spirit.

for compliments; give oneself airs &c.
(*assume*) 885; boast &c. 884.

render -vain &c. *adj.*; inspire with -vanity &c. *n.*; inflate, puff up, turn up, turn one's head.

**Adj.** vain, – as a peacock; conceited, assured, overweening, pert, forward, perky; vain-glorious, high-flown; ostentatious &c. 882; puffed up, inflated, flushed.

out of countenance &c. (*humbled*) 879.

reserved, constrained, demure.

**Adv.** humbly &c. *adj.*; quietly, privately; without -ceremony, – beat of drum; *sans façon.*

self-satisfied, -confident, -sufficient, -flattering, -admiring, -applauding, -glorious, -opinionated; *entêté* &c. (*wrong-headed*) 481; wise in one's own conceit, pragmatical, overwise, pretentious, priggish; egotistic, -al; *soi-disant* &c. (*boastful*) 884; arrogant &c. 885.

un-abashed, -blushing; un-constrained, -ceremonious; free and easy.

**Adv.** vainly &c. *adj.*

**Phr.** how we apples swim!

---

**882. Ostentation.—N.** ostentation, display, show, flourish, parade, *étalage*, pomp, array, state, solemnity; dash, splash, glitter, strut, swank, side, swagger, pomposity; preten-se, -sions; showing off; fuss.

magnificence, splendour; *coup d'œil*; grand doings.

*coup de théâtre*; stage -effect, – trick; clap-trap; *mise en scène; tour de force; chic.*

demonstration, flying colours; tomfoolery; flourish of trumpets &c. (*celebration*) 883; pageant, -ry; spectacle, exhibition, procession; turn –, set- out; grand function; *fête*, gala, field-day, review, march past, promenade, insubstantial pageant.

dress; court –, full –, evening –, ball –, fancy- dress; tailoring, millinery, man-millinery, frippery; foppery, equipage.

ceremon-y, -ial; ritual; form, -ality; etiquette; punct-o, -ilio, -iliousness; starched-, stateli-ness.

mummery, solemn mockery, mouth honour.

attitudinarian; fop &c. 854.

**V.** be -ostentatious &c. *adj.*; come –, put oneself- forward; attract attention, star it.

make –, cut- a -figure, – dash, – splash; strut, blow one's own trumpet; figure, – away; make a show, – display; glitter.

show -off, – one's paces; parade, march past; display, exhibit, put forward, hold up; trot –, hang- out; sport, brandish, blazon forth; dangle, – before the eyes.

cry up &c. (*praise*) 931; *prôner*, flaunt, emblazon, prink, set off, mount, have framed and glazed.

put a good, – smiling- face upon; clean the outside of the platter &c. (*disguise*) 544.

**Adj.** ostentatious, showy, dashing, pretentious; ja-, jau-nty; grand, pompous, palatial; high-sounding; turgid &c. (*big-sounding*) 577; garish, gorgeous; gaudy, – as a -peacock, – butterfly, – tulip; flaunting, flashing, flaming, glittering; gay &c. (*ornate*) 847; colourful.

splendid, magnificent, sumptuous.

theatrical, dramatic, spectacular, scenic, ceremonial, ritual, -istic.

solemn, stately, majestic, formal, stiff, ceremonious, punctilious, starch-ed, -y.

*en grande tenue*, in best bib and tucker, in Sunday best, *endimanché*.

**Adv.** with -flourish of trumpet, – beat of drum, – flying colours, – a brass band.

*ad captandum vulgus.*

**883. Celebration.—N.** celebration, solemnization, jubilee, diamond jubilee, commemoration, ovation, pæan, triumph, jubilation.

triumphal arch, bonfire, salute; salvo, – of artillery; *feu de joie*, flourish of trumpets, *fanfare*, colours flying, illuminations, fireworks.

inauguration, installation, presentation; *début*, coming out, birth-day anniversary, bi-, ter-, centenary; silver –, golden –, diamond-wedding, -day; coronation; Lord Mayor's show; harvest home, red letter day, festival; trophy &c. 733; *Te Deum* &c. (*thanksgiving*) 990; fête &c. 882; holiday &c. 840.

**V.** celebrate, keep, signalize, do honour to, commemorate, solemnize, hallow, mark with a red letter, hold high festival, maffick.

pledge, drink to, toast, hob and nob.

inaugurate, install, instate, induct, chair.

rejoice &c. 838; kill the fatted calf, hold jubilee, roast an ox, fire a salute.

**Adj.** celebrating &c. *v.*; commemorative, celebrated, immortal.

**Adv.** in -honour, – commemoration, – celebration of.

**Int.** hail! all hail! *io -pæan, – triumphe!* 'see the conquering hero comes!'

**884. Boasting.—N.** boasting &c. *v.*; boast, vaunt, crake; preten-ce, -sions; puff, -ery; flourish, *fanfaronnade*; gasconade; bluff, swank, brag, -gardism; bravado, bunkum, Buncombe; highfalutin; jact-itation, -ancy; bounce, rant, bluster; venditation, vapouring, rodomontade, bombast, fine talking, tall talk, magniloquence, teratology, heroics; jingoism, Chauvinism; exaggeration &c. 549; gas, hot air.

vanity &c. 880; *vox et præterea nihil*; much cry and little wool, *brutum fulmen.*

exultation; glorification; flourish of trumpets; triumph &c. 883.

boaster; bragg-art, -adocio; hot air merchant; Gascon, *fanfaron*, pretender, fourflusher, *soi-disant*; windbag, blowhard, bluffer; chau-vinist; blusterer &c. 887; charlatan, jack-pudding, trumpeter; puppy &c. (*fop*) 854.

**V.** boast, make a boast of, brag, vaunt, puff, show off, flourish, crake, crack, trumpet, strut, swagger, vapour, bluff; draw the long bow.

exult, crow over, neigh, chuckle, triumph; glory, gloat, jubilate; throw up one's cap; talk big, *se faire valoir, faire claquer son fouet*, take merit to oneself, make a merit of, sing *Io triumphe*, holloa before one is out of the wood.

**Adj.** boasting &c. *v.*; magniloquent, flaming, Thrasonic, stilted, gas-conading, braggart, boastful, pretentious, *soi-disant*; vain-glorious &c. (*conceited*) 880.

elate, -d; jubilant, triumphant, exultant; in high feather; flushed, - with victory; cock-a-hoop; on stilts.

vaunted &c. *v.*

**Adv.** vauntingly &c. *adj.*; with a brass band.

**Phr.** 'let the galled jade wince.'

**885.** [Undue assumption of superiority.] **Insolence.—N.** insolence; haughtiness &c. *adj.*; arrogance, airs; overbearance, brashness, bumptiousness, contumely, disdain; domineering &c. *v.*; tyranny &c. 739.

impertinence; cheek, nerve, sauce; sauciness &c. *adj.*; flippancy, dicacity, petulance, procacity, bluster; swagger, -ing &c. *v.*; bounce; terrorism; jingoism, chauvinism.

as-, pre-sumption; beggar on horseback; usurpation.

impudence, assurance, audacity, self-assertion, hardihood, front, face, brass; shamelessness &c. *adj.*; effrontery, hardened front, face of brass.

assumption of infallibility.

malapert, saucebox &c. (*blusterer*) 887.

**V.** be -insolent &c. *adj.*; bluster, vapour, swagger, swell, give oneself airs, snap one's fingers, kick up a dust; swear &c. (*affirm*) 535; rap out oaths; roister.

arrogate; as  pre-sume; make -bold, – free; take a liberty, give an inch and take an ell.

domineer, bully, dictate, hector; lord it over, bulldoze; *traiter de haut, regarder de haut en bas*; exact; snub, huff, beard, fly in the face of; put to the blush; bear –, beat- down; browbeat, intimidate; trample –, tread- -down, – under foot; dragoon, ride roughshod over, terrorize.

out-face, -look, -stare, -brazen, -brave; stare out of countenance; brazen out; lay down the law; teach one's grandmother to suck eggs; assume a lofty bearing; talk –, look- big; put on big looks, act the *grand seigneur*; mount –, ride- the high horse; toss the head, carry with a high hand.

tempt Providence, want snuffing.

**Adj.** insolent, haughty, arrogant, imperious, magisterial, dictatorial, arbitrary; high-handed, high and mighty; contumelious, supercilious, overbearing, intolerant, domineering; overweening, high-flown.

flippant, pert, cavalier, saucy, forward, impertinent, fresh, malapert.

precocious, assuming, would-be, bumptious.

bluff; brazen-, -browed, -faced, shameless, aweless, unblushing, unabashed; bold-, bare-faced; dead –, lost- to shame.

**886. Servility.—N.** servility; slavery &c. (*subjection*) 749; obsequiousness &c. *adj.*; subserviency; abasement; pros-tration, -ternation; genuflexion &c. (*worship*) 990; fawning &c. *v.*; tuft-hunting, time-serving, flunkeyism; sycophancy &c. (*flattery*) 933; humility &c. 879.

sycophant, parasite, yes-man; toad, -y, -eater; tuft-hunter; snob, flunkey, lap-dog, spaniel, lickspittle, smell-feast, *Græculus esuriens*, hanger on, stooge, *cavaliere servente*, led captain, carpet knight; time-server, fortune-hunter, Vicar of Bray, Sir Pertinax Mac Sycophant, pick-thank; flatterer &c. 935; doer of dirty work; *âme damnée*, tool; reptile; slave &c. (*servant*) 746; courtier; sponge, jackal; truckler.

**V.** cringe, bow, stoop, kneel, bend the knee; fall on one's knees, prostrate oneself; worship &c. 990.

sneak, crawl, crouch, cower, truckle to, grovel, fawn, toady, lick the feet of, kiss the hem of one's garment.

pay court to; feed –, fatten –, batten- on; dance attendance on, pin oneself upon, hang on the sleeve of, *avaler des couleuvres*, keep time to, fetch and carry, do the dirty work of.

go with the stream, follow the crowd, worship the rising sun, hold with the hare and run with the hounds.

**Adj.** servile, obsequious; supple, – as a glove; soapy, oily, pliant, cringing, fawning, slavish, grovelling, snivelling, mealy-mouthed; beggarly, sycophantic, parasitical; abased, abject, prostrate, down on one's marrow-bones; base, mean, sneaking; crouching &c. *v.*

**Adv.** hat –, cap- in hand.

impudent, audacious, presumptuous, free and easy, devil-may-care, rollicking; janty, jaunty; roistering, blustering, hectoring, swaggering, vapouring; thrasonic, fire-eating, 'full of sound and fury.'

Adv. insolently, with a high hand; *ex cathedrâ*.

Phr. one's bark being worse than his bite.

**887. Blusterer.—N.** bluster-, swagger-, vapour-, roister-, brawl-er; brazen-face; *fanfaron*; braggart &c. (*boaster*) 884; bully, terrorist, rough, rough-neck; hooligan, hoodlum, larrikin, ruffian; Mo-hock, -hawk; drawcansir, swashbuckler, Captain Boabdil, Sir Lucius O'Trigger, Thraso, Pistol, Parolles, Bombastes Furioso, Hector, Chrononhotonthologos; jingo; desperado, dare-devil, fire-eater; fury &c. (*violent person*) 173; rowdy.

puppy &c. (*fop*) 854; prig; Sir Oracle, dogmatist, *doctrinaire*, stump orator, jack-in-office; saucebox, malapert, jackanapes, minx; bantamcock.

SECTION III. SYMPATHETIC AFFECTIONS

1°. SOCIAL AFFECTIONS

**888. Friendship. — N.** friendship, amity; friendliness &c. *adj.*; brotherhood, fraternity, sodality, confraternity, sorosis, sisterhood; harmony &c. (*concord*) 714; peace &c. 721.

firm -, staunch -, intimate -, familiar -, bosom -, cordial -, tried -, devoted -, lasting -, fast -, sincere -, warm -, ardent- friendship.

cordiality, fraternization, *entente cordiale*, good understanding, *rapprochement*, sympathy, fellow-feeling, response, welcomeness; *camaraderie*.

affection &c. (*love*) 897; favouritism; goodwill &c. (*benevolence*) 906; partiality.

acquaintance, familiarity, intimacy, intercourse, fellowship, knowledge of; introduction.

V. be -friendly &c. *adj.*, - friends &c. 890, - acquainted with &c. *adj.*; know; have the ear of; keep company with &c. (*sociality*) 892; hold communication -, have dealings -, sympathize- with; have a leaning to; bear good will &c. (*benevolence*) 906; love &c. 897; make much of; befriend &c. (*aid*) 707; introduce to.

set one's horses together; hold out -, extend- the right hand of friendship, - fellowship; become -friendly &c. *adj.*; make -friends &c. 892 with; break the ice, be introduced to; make -, pick -, scrape- acquaintance with; get into favour, gain the friendship of.

shake hands with, fraternize, embrace; receive with open arms, throw oneself into the arms of; meet half way, take in good part.

Adj. friendly; amic-able, -al; well affected, unhostile, neighbourly, brotherly, fraternal, sisterly, sympathetic, harmonious, hearty, cordial, warm-hearted, devoted

**889. Enmity.—N.** enmity, hostility, unfriendliness &c. *adj.*; discord &c. 713. alienation, estrangement; dislike &c. 867; hate &c. 898; antagonism.

heartburning; animosity &c. 900; malevolence &c. 907.

V. be -inimical &c. *adj.*; keep -, hold- at arm's length; be at loggerheads; bear malice &c. 907; fall out; take umbrage &c. 900; harden the heart, alienate, estrange.

Adj. inimical, unfriendly, hostile; at -enmity, - variance, - swords points, - daggers drawn, - open war with; up in arms against; in bad odour with.

on bad -, not on speaking- terms; cool; cold, -hearted; estranged, alienated, disaffected, irreconcilable.

friends -, well -, at home -, hand in hand- with; on -good, - friendly, - amicable, - cordial, - familiar, - intimate- -terms, - footing; on -speaking, - visiting- terms; in one's good -graces, - books. acquainted, familiar, intimate, thick, hand and glove, hail fellow well met, free and easy; welcome.

Adv. amicably &c. adj.; with open arms; sans cérémonie; arm in arm.

**890. Friend.—N.** friend, - of one's bosom, intimate acquaintance, neighbour, well-wisher; alter ego; best -, bosom -, fast- friend; amicus usque ad aras; fidus Achates; persona grata.

favourer, fautor, patron, backer, Mæcenas; tutelary saint, good genius, advocate, partisan, sympathiser; ally; friend in need &c. (auxiliary) 711.

**891. Enemy.—N.** enemy; antagonist, foeman; open -, bitter- enemy; opponent &c. 710; back friend.

public enemy, enemy to society, traitor, anarchist &c. 742; persona non grata.

Phr. every hand being against one.

associate, compeer, comrade, mate, companion, confrère, camarade, confidante, colleague; old -, crony; side-kick; chum, buddy, bunkie, roommate, pal; play-fellow, -mate; classmate, schoolfellow; bedfellow, -mate; maid of honour.

compatriot; fellow -, countryman, - townsman.

shop-, ship-, mess-mate; fellow -, boon -, pot- companion; co-partner.

Arcades ambo, Pylades and Orestes, Castor and Pollux, Nisus and Euryalus, Damon and Pythias, par nobile fratrum.

host, Amphitryon, Boniface; guest, visitor, frequenter, habitué; protégé.

**892. Sociality.—N.** soci-ality, -ability, -ableness &c. adj.; social intercourse; consociation; inter-course, -community; consort-, companion-, fellow-, comrade-ship; clubbism; esprit de corps.

conviviality; good -fellowship, - company, camaraderie; joviality, jollity, savoir-vivre, festivity, festive board, merry-making; loving cup; hospitality, heartiness; cheer.

welcome, -ness; greeting; hearty -, warm -, welcome- reception; urbanity &c. (courtesy) 894; intimacy, familiarity.

good -, jolly- fellow, good mixer, Rotarian; bon enfant.

social -, family- circle; circle of acquaintance, coterie, society, company; social -gathering, - réunion; assembly &c. (assemblage) 72; party, entertainment, reception, levée, at home, conversazione, soirée, matinée, evening -, morning -, afternoon -, garden -, dinner -, tea -, cocktail- party; symposium, sing-song; kettle-, drum; partie carrée, dish of tea, ridotto, rout, house-

**893. Seclusion. Exclusion.—N.** seclusion, privacy; retirement; concealment; reclusion, recess; snugness &c. adj.; delitescence; rustication, rus in urbe; solitude; solitariness &c. (singleness) 87; isolation; loneliness &c. adj.; estrangement from the world, anchoritism, voluntary exile; aloofness.

cell, hermitage; convent &c. 1000; sanctum sanctorum; study, library, den; hide-out.

depopulation, desertion, desolation; wilderness &c. (unproductive) 169; howling wilderness; rotten borough, Old Sarum.

exclusion, excommunication, banishment, exile, ostracism, proscription; cut, - direct; dead cut.

inhospit-ality, -ableness &c. adj.; un-, dis-sociability; domesticity, Darby and Joan.

recluse, hermit, eremite, cenobite, anchor-et, -ite; Simon Stylites; Troglodyte, Timon of Athens, Santon, solitaire, ruralist, disciple of Zimmermann, closet cynic, Diogenes; outcast, pariah-

warming; ball, prom, hop, dance, *thé dansant*; festival &c. (*amusement*) 840; wedding breakfast; 'the feast of reason and the flow of soul.'

visit, -ing; round of visits; call, morning call; interview &c. (*interlocution*) 588; assignation; tryst, -ing place; appointment.

club &c. (*association*) 712.

V. be -sociable &c. *adj.*; know; be -acquainted &c. *adj.*; associate –, sort –, keep company –, walk hand in hand -with; eat off the same trencher, club together, consort, bear one company, join; make acquaintance with &c. (*friendship*) 888; make advances, fraternize, embrace; intercommunicate.

be –, feel –, make oneself- at home with; make free with; crack a bottle with; take pot luck with, receive hospitality, live at free quarters.

visit, pay a visit; interchange -visits, – cards; call -at, – upon; leave a card; drop in, look in; look one up, beat up one's quarters.

entertain; give a -party &c. *n.*; be at home, see one's friends, hang out, keep open house, do the honours; receive, – with open arms; welcome; give a warm reception &c. *n.* to; kill the fatted calf.

Adj. sociable, companionable, clubbable, clubby, conversable, cosy, cosey, chatty, conversational; homiletical.

convivial; fest-ive, -al; jovial, jolly, hospitable.

welcome, – as the roses in May; *fêté*, entertained.

free and easy, hail fellow well met, familiar, on visiting terms, acquainted.

social, neighbourly; international, cosmopolitan, gregarious.

Adv. *en famille*, in the family circle; *sans -façon, – cérémonie*, arm in arm.

---

894. Courtesy.—N. courtesy; respect &c. 928; good -manners, – behaviour, – breeding; manners; politeness &c. *adj.*; *bienséance*, urbanity, comity, gentility; gentle –, breeding; polish, presence, cultivation, culture; civili-ty, -zation; amenity, suavity; good -temper, – humour; amiability, easy temper, complacency, soft tongue,

---

castaway, outsider, pilgarlic; wastrel, foundling, orphan.

V. be –, live- secluded &c. *adj.*; keep –, stand –, hold oneself- -aloof, – in the background; keep snug; shut oneself up; deny –, seclude- oneself; creep into a corner, rusticate, *aller planter ses choux*; retire, – from the world; hermetize, take the veil; abandon &c. 624.

cut, – dead; refuse to -associate with, – acknowledge; look cool –, turn one's back –, shut the door- upon; repel, blackball, excommunicate, exclude, exile, expatriate; banish, outlaw, maroon, ostracize, proscribe, cut off from, send to Coventry, keep at arm's length, draw a cordon round; boycott, blockade, lay an embargo on, isolate.

depopulate; dis-, un-people.

Adj. secluded, sequestered, retired, delitescent, private, bye; out of the -world, -way; in a backwater; 'the world forgetting by the world forgot.'

snug, domestic, stay-at-home.

unsociable; un-, dis-social; inhospitable, cynical, inconversable, unclubbable, *sauvage*, eremetic.

solitary; lone-ly, -some; isolated, single.

excluded, estranged; unfrequented; uninhabit-able, -ed; tenantless; un-tenanted, -occupied; abandoned; deserted, – in one's utmost need; unfriended; kith-, friend-, home-less; lorn, forlorn, desolate.

un-visited, -introduced, -invited, -welcome; under a cloud, left to shift for oneself, derelict, outcast, outside the gates.

banished &c. *v.*; under an embargo.

Phr. *noli me tangere.*

---

895. Discourtesy.—N. discourtesy; ill-breeding; ill –, bad –, ungainly- manners; insuavity; grouchiness; uncourteousness &c. *adj.*, tactlessness; rusticity, inurbanity; illiberality, incivility, displacency.

disrespect &c. 929; procacity, impudence; barbar-ism, -ity; misbehaviour, brutality, blackguardism, conduct un-

mansuetude; condescension &c. (*humility*) 879; affability, complaisance, *prévenance*, amiability, gallantry, chivalry; pink of -politeness, – courtesy.

compliment; fair –, soft –, sweet-words; honeyed phrases, flattering remarks, ceremonial; salutation, reception, presentation, introduction, *accueil*, greeting, recognition; welcome, *abord*, respects, *devoir*, regards, remembrances; kind -regards, – remembrances; love, best love, duty; deference.

obeisance &c. (*reverence*) 928; bow, courtesy, curtsy, scrape, *salaam*, *kowtow*, bowing and scraping; kneeling; genuflexion &c. (*worship*) 990; obsequiousness &c. 886; capping, shaking hands &c. *v.*; grip of the hand, embrace, hug, squeeze, *accolade*, loving cup, *vin d'honneur*, pledge; love token &c. (*endearment*) 902; kiss, buss, salute.

mark of recognition, nod; 'nods and becks and wreathed smiles'; valediction &c. 293; condolence &c. 915.

V. be -courteous &c. *adj.*; show -courtesy &c. *n.*

mind one's P's and Q's, behave oneself, be all things to all men, conciliate, speak one fair, take in good part; make –, do- the amiable; look as if butter would not melt in one's mouth; mend one's manners.

receive, do the honours, usher, greet, hail, bid welcome; welcome, – with open arms; shake hands; hold out –, press –, squeeze- the hand; bid God speed; speed the parting guest; cheer, serenade.

salute; embrace &c. (*endearment*) 902; kiss, – hands; drink to, pledge, hob and nob; move to, nod to; smile upon.

uncover, cap; touch –, take off- the hat; doff the cap; pull the forelock; present arms; make way for; bow; make one's bow; scrape, curtsy, courtesy; bob a -curtsy, – courtesy; kneel; bow –, bend- the knee; salaam, *kowtow*.

visit, wait upon, present oneself, pay one's respects, pay a visit &c. (*sociability*) 892; dance attendance on &c. (*servility*) 886; pay attentions to; do homage to &c. (*respect*) 928.

becoming a gentleman, *grossièreté, brusquerie*; vulgarity &c. 851.

churlishness &c. *adj.*; spinosity, perversity; moroseness &c. (*sullenness*) 901a.

bad-, ill-temper; sternness &c. *adj.*; austerity; moodishness, captiousness &c. 901; cynicism; tartness &c. *adj.*; acrimony, acerbity, virulence, asperity.

scowl, black looks, frown; short answer, rebuff; hard words, contumely; unparliamentary language, personality.

bear, bruin, brute, grouch, blackguard, beast; unlicked cub; frump, cross-patch; saucebox &c. 887.

V. be -rude &c. *adj.*; insult &c. 929; treat with discourtesy; take a name in vain; make -bold, – free- with; take a liberty; stare out of countenance, ogle, point at, put to the blush.

cut; turn -one's back upon, – on one's heel; give the cold shoulder; keep at -a distance, – arm's length; look -cool, – coldly, – black- upon; show the door to, send away with a flea in the ear.

lose one's temper &c. (*resentment*) 900; sulk &c. 901a; frown, scowl, glower, pout; snap, snarl, growl.

render -rude &c. *adj.*; brut-alize, -ify.

Adj. dis-, un-courteous; uncourtly; ill-bred, -mannered, -behaved, -conditioned; unbred; unmanner-ly, – ed; im-, un-polite; un-polished, -civilized, -genteel; ungentleman-like, -ly; unladylike; blackguard; vulgar &c. 851; dedecorous; foul-mouthed, -spoken; abusive.

un-civil, -gracious, -ceremonious; cool; pert, forward, obtrusive, impudent, rude, saucy, precocious; insolent &c. 885.

repulsive; un-complaisant, -accommodating, -neighbourly, -gallant; inaffable; un-gentle, -gainly; rough, rugged, bluff, blunt, gruff; churl-, boor-, bear-ish; brutal, *brusque*; stern, harsh, austere; cavalier.

tart, sour, crabbed, sharp, short, trenchant, sarcastic, crusty, biting, caustic, virulent, bitter, acrimonious, venomous, contumelious; snarling &c, *v.*; surly, – as a bear; perverse; grim.

prostrate oneself &c. (*worship*) 990.
give –, send- one's duty &c. *n.*
to.
render -polite &c. *adj.*; polish, civilize, humanize.

**Adj.** courteous, polite, civil, mannerly, urbane; well-behaved, -mannered, -bred, -brought up, gently bred, of gentle -breeding, – manners, good-mannered, polished, civilized, cultivated; refined &c. (*taste*) 850; gentlemanlike &c. (*fashion*) 852; gallant, chivalrous, on one's good behaviour.

fine –, fair –, soft- spoken; honey-mouthed, -tongued; oily, unctuous, bland, suave; obliging, conciliatory, complaisant, complacent; obsequious &c. 886.

ingratiating, winning; gentle, mild; good-humoured, cordial, gracious, amiable, tactful, addressful, affable, genial, friendly, familiar; neighbourly.

**Adv.** courteously &c. *adj.*; with a good grace; with -open, – outstretched- arms; *à bras ouverts*; *suaviter in modo*, in good humour.

**Int.** hail! welcome! well met! *ave!* all hail! good -day, – morning &c., – morrow! God speed! *pax vobiscum!* may your shadow never be less! *chin-chin!*

sullen &c. 901*a*; peevish &c. (*irascible*) 901.
**Adv.** discourteously &c. *adj.*; with -discourtesy &c. *n.*, – a bad grace.

---

**896. Congratulations.—N.** con-, gratulation; felicitation; salute &c. 894; condolence &c. 915; compliments of the season; good –, best- wishes.

**V.** con-, gratulate; felicitate, compliment; give –, wish one- joy; tender –, offer- one's congratulations; wish -many happy returns of the day, – a merry Christmas and a happy new year.
congratulate oneself &c. (*rejoice*) 838.
**Adj.** con-, gratulatory.

---

**897. Love.—N.** love; fondness &c. *adj.*; liking; inclination &c. (*desire*) 865; regard, dilection, admiration, fancy.

affection, sympathy, fellow-feeling; tenderness &c. *adj.*; heart, brotherly love; benevolence &c. 906; attachment.

yearning, tender passion, *affaire de cœur*, *amour* gallantry, passion, flame, devotion, fervour, enthusiasm, transport of love, rapture, enchantment, infatuation, adoration, idolatry.

narcissism, Œdipus complex, Electra complex.

Cupid, Venus, Eros; myrtle; true lover's knot; love -token, – suit, – affair, – tale, – story; the old story, plighted love; courtship &c. 902; *amourette.*

maternal love.

attractiveness, charm; popularity; favourite &c. 899.

lover, suitor, follower, admirer, adorer, wooer, amoret, beau, sweet-

**898. Hate.—N.** hate, hatred, vials of hate; Hymn of Hate.

dis-affection, -favour; alienation, estrangement, coolness; enmity &c. 889; animosity &c. 900.

umbrage, pique, grudge; dudgeon, spleen; bitterness, – of feeling; ill –, bad- blood; acrimony; malice &c. 907; implacability &c. (*revenge*) 919.

repugnance &c. (*dislike*) 867; odium, unpopularity; loathing, detestation, antipathy; object of -hatred, – execration; abomination, aversion, *bête noire*; enemy &c. 891; bitter pill; source of annoyance &c. 830.

**V.** hate, detest, abominate, abhor, loathe; recoil –, shudder- at; shrink from, view with horror, hold in abomination, revolt against, execrate; scowl &c. 895; disrelish &c. (*dislike*) 867.

owe a grudge; bear -spleen, – a grudge, – malice &c. (*malevolence*) 907; conceive an aversion to.

heart, inamorato, swain, young man, flame, love, truelove; leman, Lothario, gallant, paramour, *amoroso, cavaliere servente,* captive, *cicisbeo; caro sposo,* Don Juan, sheik, ladies' man, squire of dames, Knave of Hearts.

inamorata, lady-love, idol, darling, duck, Dulcinea, angel, goddess, *cara sposa;* mistress.

betrothed, affianced, *fiancée.*

flirt, *coquette;* amorette; pair of turtle doves; abode of love, *agapemone.*

**V.** love, like, affect, fancy, care for, take an interest in, be partial to, sympathize with; be -in love &c. *adj.*-with; have -, entertain -, harbour -, cherish- a -love &c. *n.* for; regard, revere; take to, bear love to, be wedded to; set one's affections on; make much of, feast one's eyes on; hold dear, prize, treasure; hug, cling to, cherish, pet, caress &c. 902.

burn; adore, idolize, love to distraction, *aimer éperdument;* dote -on, - upon.

take a fancy to, fall for, be stuck on, look sweet upon; become -enamoured &c. *adj.;* fall in love with, lose one's heart; desire &c. 865.

excite love; win -, gain -, secure -, engage- the -love, - affections, - heart; take the fancy of; have a place in -, wind round- the heart; attract, attach, endear, charm, fascinate, captivate, bewitch, seduce, enamour, enrapture, turn the head.

get into favour; ingratiate -, insinuate -, worm- oneself; propitiate, curry favour with, pay one's court to, make a date with, *faire l'aimable,* set one's cap at, flirt, coquet.

**Adj.** loving &c. *v.;* fond of; taken -, struck- with; smitten, bitten; attached to, wedded to; enamoured; charmed &c. *v.;* in love; love-sick; over head and ears in love.

affectionate, tender, sweet upon, sympathetic, loving, fond, amorous, amatory; erotic, uxurious, ardent, passionate, rapturous, devoted, motherly.

loved &c. *v.;* beloved; well -, dearly- beloved; dear, precious, darling, pet, little; favourite, popular.

congenial; to -, after- one's -mind, - taste, - fancy, - own heart.

in one's good -graces &c. *(friendly)* 888; dear as the apple of one's eye, nearest to one's heart.

lovable, adorable; lovely, sweet; attractive, seductive, winning; charming, engaging, interesting, enchanting, captivating, fascinating, intriguing, bewitching; amiable, like an angel, angelic, seraphic.

excite -, provoke- hatred &c. *n.;* be -hateful &c. *adj.;* stink in the nostrils; estrange, alienate, repel, set against, sow dissension, set by the ears, envenom, incense, irritate, rile, ruffle, vex; horrify &c. 830.

**Adj.** hating &c. *v.;* abhorrent; averse from &c. *(disliking)* 867; set against.

bitter &c. *(acrimonious)* 895; implacable &c. *(revengeful)* 919.

un-loved, -beloved, -lamented, -deplored, -mourned, -cared for, -endured, -valued; disliked &c. 867.

crossed in love, forsaken, rejected, love-lorn, jilted.

obnoxious, hateful, odious, abominable, repulsive, offensive, shocking; disgusting &c. *(disagreeable)* 830.

invidious, spiteful; malicious &c. 907.

insulting, irritating, provoking.

[Mutual hate] at -daggers drawn, - swords points; not on speaking terms &c. *(enmity)* 889.

**Phr.** no love lost between.

———

**899. Favourite.**—**N.** favourite, pet, cosset, minion, idol, jewel, spoiled child, *enfant gâté;* led captain; crony; fondling; apple of one's eye, man after one's own heart; *persona grata.*

love, dear, darling, duck, honey, jewel; mopsey, moppet; sweetheart
&c. (*love*) 897.

general –, universal- favourite; idol of the people; matinée idol,
movie –, radio- star.

**900. Resentment.—N.** resentment, displeasure, animosity, anger,
wrath, indignation; vexation, exasperation, bitter resentment, wrathful
indignation.

pique, umbrage, huff, miff, soreness, dudgeon, acerbity, virulence,
bitterness, acrimony, asperity, spleen, gall; heart-burning, -swelling;
rankling.

ill –, bad- -humour, – temper; irascibility &c. 901; ill blood &c.
(*hate*) 898; revenge &c. 919.

excitement, irritation; warmth, bile, choler, ire, fume, pucker, dander,
ferment, ebullition; towering -passion, – rage, *acharnement*, angry mood,
taking, pet, tiff, passion, fit, tantrums.

burst, explosion, paroxysm, storm, rage, fury, desperation; violence
&c. 173; fire and fury; vials of wrath; gnashing of teeth, hot blood,
high words.

scowl &c. 895; sulks &c. 901a.

[Cause of umbrage] affront, provocation, offence; indignity &c.
(*insult*) 929; grudge, crow to pluck, sore subject; red rag to a bull;
*casus belli.*

Furies, Erinys, Eumenides, Alecto, Megæra, Tisiphone.

buffet, slap in the face, box on the ear, rap on the knuckles.

**V.** resent; take -amiss, – ill, – to heart, – offence, – umbrage, – huff,
– exception; take in -ill part, – bad part, – dudgeon; *ne pas entendre
raillerie*; breathe revenge, cut up rough.

fly –, fall –, get- into a -rage, – passion; bridle –, bristle –, froth –,
fire –, flare- up; open –, pour out- the vials of one's wrath.

pout, knit the brow, frown, scowl, lower, snarl, growl, gnarl, gnash,
snap; redden, colour; look -black, – black as thunder, – daggers; bite
one's thumb; show –, grind- one's teeth; champ the bit.

chafe, mantle, fume, kindle, fly out, take fire; boil, – over; boil
with -indignation, – rage; rage, storm, foam; vent one's -rage, – spleen;
lose one's temper, stand on one's hind legs, stamp the foot, kick up a
row, fly off the handle, cut up rough; stamp –, quiver –, swell –, foam-
with rage; burst with anger; raise Cain, breathe fire and fury.

have a fling at; bear malice &c. (*revenge*) 919.

cause –, raise- anger; affront, offend; give -offence, – umbrage;
anger; hurt the feelings; insult, discompose, fret, ruffle, nettle, heckle,
huff, pique; excite &c. 824; irritate, stir the blood, stir up bile; sting,
– to the quick; rile, provoke, chafe, wound, incense, inflame, enrage,
aggravate, add fuel to the flame, fan into a flame, widen the breach,
envenom, embitter, exasperate, infuriate, kindle wrath; stick in one's
gizzard; rankle &c. 919.

put out of humour; put one's -monkey, – back- up; set –, get- one's
back up; raise one's -gorge, – dander, – choler; work up into a passion;
make -one's blood boil, – the ears tingle; throw into a ferment, madden,
drive one mad; lash into -fury, – madness; fool to the top of one's
bent; set by the ears.

bring a hornet's nest about one's ears.

**Adj.** angry, wrath, irate; ire-, wrath-ful; cross &c. (*irascible*) 901;
sulky &c. 901a; bitter, virulent; acrimonious &c. (*discourteous*) &c.
895; violent &c. 173.

warm, burning; boiling, – over; fuming, raging; foaming, – at the mouth; convulsed with rage.

offended &c. *v.*; waxy, *acharné*; wrought, worked up; indignant, hurt, sore, peeved; set against.

fierce, wild, rageful, furious, mad with rage, fiery, infuriate, rabid, savage; relentless &c. 919.

flushed with -anger, – rage; in a -huff, – stew, – fume, – pucker, – passion, – rage, – fury; on one's high ropes, up in arms; in high dudgeon.

Adv. angrily &c. *adj.*; in the height of passion; in the heat of -passion, – the moment.

Int. *tantæne animis cœlestibus iræ!* marry come up! zounds! 'sdeath!

Phr. one's -blood, – back, – monkey- being up; *fervens difficili bile jecur*; the gorge rising, eyes flashing fire; the blood -rising, – boiling; *hæret lateri lethalis arundo.*

**901. Irascibility.**—N. irascibility, temper; crossness &c. *adj.*; susceptibility, procacity, petulance, irritability, tartness, acerbity, protervity; pugnacity &c. (*contentiousness*) 720.

excitability &c. 825; bad -, fiery -, crooked -, irritable &c. *adj.*-temper; *genus irritabile*, hot blood.

ill humour &c. (*sullenness*) 901a; asperity &c., churlishness &c. (*discourtesy*) 895.

huff &c. (resentment) 900; a word and a blow.

Sir Fretful Plagiary; brabbler, Tartar; shrew, vixen, virago, termagant, dragon, scold, Xanthippe; porcupine; spit-fire; fire-eater &c. (*blusterer*) 887; fury &c. (*violent person*) 173.

V. be -irascible &c. *adj.*; have a -temper &c. *n.*, – devil in one; fire up &c. (*be angry*) 900.

Adj. irascible; bad-, ill-tempered; irritable, susceptible; excitable &c. 825; thin-skinned &c. (*sensitive*) 822; fretful, fidgety; on the fret.

hasty, over-hasty, quick, warm, hot, testy, touchy, techy, tetchy; like -touchwood, – tinder; huffy; pet-tish, -ulant; waspish, snapp-y, -ish, peppery, fiery, passionate, choleric, shrewish, 'sudden and quick in quarrel.'

querulous, captious, mood-y, -ish; quarrelsome, contentious, disputatious; pugnacious &c. (*bellicose*) 720; cantankerous, exceptious; restive &c. (*perverse*) 901a; churlish &c. (*discourteous*) 895.

cross, – as -crabs, – two sticks, – a cat, – a dog, – the tongs; like a bear with a sore head; fractious, peevish, *acariâtre*.

in a bad temper; sulky &c. 901a; angry &c. 900.

resent-ful, -ive; vindictive &c. 919.

Int. pish!

**901a. Sullenness.**—N. sullenness &c. *adj.*; morosity, spleen; churlishness &c. (*discourtesy*) 895; irascibility &c. 901.

moodiness &c. *adj.*; perversity; obstinacy &c. 606; torvity, spinosity; crabbedness &c. *adj.*

ill -, bad- -temper, – humour; sulks, dudgeon, mumps, doleful dumps, doldrums, fit of the sulks, *bouderie*, black looks, scowl; huff &c. (*resentment*) 900.

V. be -sullen &c. *adj.*; sulk; frown, scowl, lower, glower, grouse, grouch, crab, gloam, pout, have a hang-dog look, glout.

Adj. sullen, sulky; ill-tempered, -humoured, -affected, -disposed; in -an ill, – a bad, – a shocking- -temper, – humour; out of -temper, –

humour; knaggy, torvous, crusty, crabbed; sore as a boil; surly &c: (*discourteous*) 895.

moody; spleen-ish, -ly; splenetic, cankered.

cross, -grained; perverse, wayward, humoursome; restive; cantankerous, refractory, intractable, exceptious, sinistrous, deaf to reason, unaccommodating, rusty, crusty, froward.

dogged &c. (*stubborn*) 606.

grumpy, glum, grim, grum, morose, frumpish; in the -sulks &c. *n.*; out of sorts; scowl-, glower-, growl-ing.

peevish &c. (*irascible*) 901.

**902. [Expression of affection or love.] Endearment.—N.** endearment, caress; blandish-, blandi-ment; *épanchement*, fondling, billing and cooing, dalliance.

embrace, salute, kiss, buss, smack, osculation, deosculation; amorous glances; ogle, side glance, sheep's eyes.

courtship, wooing, suit, addresses, the soft impeachment; lovemaking; an affair; serenading; caterwauling.

flirting &c. *v.*; flirtation, gallantry; coquetry, spooning.

true lover's knot, plighted love, engagement, betrothal; love -tale, – tokcn, – letter; *billet-doux*, valentine.

honeymoon; Strephon and Chloe, 'Arry and 'Arriet.

**V.** caress, fondle, pet, dandle, nurse; pat, – on the -head, – cheek; chuck under the chin, smile upon, coax, wheedle, cosset, coddle, cocker; make -of, – much of, pamper; cherish, foster, kill with kindness.

clasp, hug, cuddle; fold –, strain- in one's arms; nestle, nuzzle, neck, embrace, kiss, buss, smack, blow a kiss; salute &c. (*courtesy*) 894.

bill and coo, spoon, toy, dally, flirt, coquet; galli-, gala-vant; philander; make love; pay one's -court, – addresses, – attentions- to; serenade; court, woo; set one's cap at; be –, look- sweet upon; ogle, cast sheep's eyes upon; *faire les yeux doux*.

fall in love with, win the affections &c. (*love*) 897; die for.

propose; make –, have- an offer; pop the question; plight one's -troth, – faith; become -engaged, – betrothed.

**Adj.** caressing &c. *v.*; 'sighing like furnace'; love-sick, spoony.

caressed &c. *v.*

**903. Marriage.—N.** marriage, matrimony, wedlock, union, intermarriage, *vinculum matrimonii*, nuptial tie, knot.

married state, coverture. bed, cohabitation.

match; betrothment &c. (*promise*) 768; wedding, nuptials, Hymen, bridal; e-, spousals; leading to the altar &c. *v.*; nuptial benediction, *epithalamium*.

torch –, temple- of Hymen; hymeneal altar; honeymoon.

bride, bridegroom; brides-maid, -man.

best –, grooms-man, page, usher.

married -man, – woman, – couple; neogamist, Benedick, partner, spouse, mate, yokemate; husband, man, con-

**904. Celibacy.—N.** celibacy, singleness, single blessedness; bachelor-hood, -ship; miso-gamy, -gyny.

virginity, *pucelage*; maiden-hood, -head.

unmarried man, bachelor, Cœlebs, agamist, old bachelor; miso-gamist, -gynist; celibate.

unmarried woman, spinster; maid, -en; virgin, *femme sole*, old maid; bachelor girl; nun &c.

**V.** live single; keep bachelor hall.

**Adj.** un-married, -wedded; wife-, spouse-less; single, virgin, celibate.

**905. Divorce.—N.** divorce, -ment; separation; judicial separation, separ-

sort, baron; old –, good- man; wife of one's bosom; help-meet, -mate, rib, better half, grey mare, old woman, good wife; *femme couverte*; squaw, lady; matron, -age, -hood; man and wife; wedded pair, Darby and Joan.

affinity, soul-mate.

mono-, bi-, di-, deutero-, tri-, polygamy; mormonism; poly-andry; Turk, Bluebeard.

ate maintenance; *separatio a -mensâ et thoro, – vinculo matrimonii.*

widowhood, viduage, viduity, weeds.

widow, -er; relict; dowager; *divorcée*; cuckold.

**V.** live -separately, – apart; separate, divorce, disespouse, put away; wear the horns.

_____

unlawful –, left-handed –, companionate –, morganatic –, ill-assorted- marriage; *mésalliance*; *mariage de convenance*; an affair.

match-maker, marriage broker, matrimonial agent.

**V.** marry, wive, take to oneself a wife; be -married, – spliced; go –, pair- off; wed, espouse, lead to the hymeneal altar, take 'for better, for worse,' give one's hand to, bestow one's hand upon; remarry; intermarry.

marry, join, handfast; couple &c. (*unite*) 43; tie the nuptial knot; give -away, – in marriage; affy, affiance; betroth &c. (*promise*) 768; publish , bid- the banns; be asked in church.

**Adj.** married &c. *v.*; one, – bone and one flesh.

marriageable, nubile.

engaged, betrothed, affianced.

matrimonial, marital, conjugal, connubial, wedded; nuptial, hymeneal, spousal, bridal.

**Phr.** the grey mare the better horse.

## 2°. DIFFUSIVE SYMPATHETIC AFFECTIONS

**906. Benevolence.—N.** benevolence, Christian charity; God's -love, – grace; good-will; philanthropy &c. 910; unselfishness &c. 942.

good -nature, – feeling, – wishes; kind-, kindli-ness &c. *adj.*; lovingkindness, benignity, brotherly love, charity, humanity, fellow-feeling, sympathy; goodness –, warmth- of heart; *bonhomie*; kind-heartedness; amiability, milk of human kindness, tenderness; love &c. 897; friendship &c. 888.

toleration, consideration, generosity; mercy &c. (*pity*) 914.

charitableness &c. *adj.*; bounty, alms-giving; good works, beneficence, the luxury of doing good.

acts of kindness, a good turn; good –, kind- -offices, – treatment.

good Samaritan, sympathizer, well-wisher, philanthropist, *bon enfant*; altruist.

**V.** be -benevolent &c. *adj.*; have one's heart in the right place, bear good will; wish -well, – God speed;

**907. Malevolence.—N.** malevolence; bad intent, -ion; un-, dis-kindness; ill -nature, – will, – blood; acrimony; bad blood; enmity &c. 889; hate &c. 898; malignity; malice, – aforethought, – prepense; maliciousness &c. *adj.*; spite, despite; resentment &c. 900.

uncharitableness &c. *adj.*; incompassionateness &c. 914a; gall, venom, rancour, rankling, virulence, mordacity, acerbity; churlishness &c. (*discourtesy*) 895.

hardness of heart, heart of stone, obduracy; cruelty; cruelness &c. *adj.*; brutality, savagery; fer-ity, -ocity; barbarity, inhumanity, immanity, truculence, ruffianism; evil eye, cloven -foot, – hoof; inquisition; torture.

ill –, bad- turn; affront &c. (*disrespect*) 929; outrage, atrocity; ill usage; intolerance, bigotry, persecution; tender mercies [ironical]; 'unkindest cut of all.'

**V.** be -malevolent &c. *adj.*; bear –, harbour- -spleen, – a grudge, – mal-

view -, regard- with an eye of favour; take in good part; take -, feel- an interest in; be -, feel- interested- in; sympathize with, feel for; fraternize &c. (*be friendly*) 888.

enter into the feelings of others, do as you would be done by, meet half-way.

treat well; give comfort, smooth the bed of death; do -good, - a good turn; benefit &c. (*goodness*) 648; render a service, be of use; aid &c. 707.

**Adj.** benevolent; kind, -ly; well-meaning; amiable; obliging, accommodating, indulgent, considerate, gracious, complacent, good-humoured.

warm-, soft-, kind-, tender-, large-, broad-hearted; merciful &c. 914; philanthropic &c. 910; charitable, beneficent, humane, benign, benignant; bount-eous, -iful &c. 816.

good-, well-natured; spleenless; sympath-izing, -etic; complaisant &c. (*courteous*) 894; kindly, well-meant, -intentioned.

fatherly, motherly, brotherly, sisterly; pat-, mat-, frat-ernal; friendly &c. 888.

**Adv.** with -a good intention, - the best intentions.

**Int.** God speed! much good may it do!

ice; betray -, show- the cloven foot: hurt &c. (*physical pain*) 378; annoy &c. 830; injure, harm, wrong; do -harm, - an ill office- to; outrage; disoblige, malign, plant a thorn in the breast.

molest, worry, harass, haunt, harry, bait, tease, throw stones at; play the devil with; hunt down, dragoon, hound; persecute, oppress, grind; maltreat; ill-treat, -use.

wreak one's malice on, do one's worst, break a butterfly on the wheel; dip -, imbrue- one's hands in blood; have no mercy &c. 914a.

**Adj.** male-, unbene-volent; unbenign; ill-disposed, -intentioned, -natured, -conditioned, -contrived; evil-minded, -disposed.

malicious; malign, -ant; rancorous; de-, spiteful; mordacious, caustic, bitter, envenomed, acrimonious, virulent; un-amiable, -charitable; maleficent, venomous, grinding, galling.

harsh, disobliging; un-kind, -friendly, -gracious; treacherous; inofficious; invidious; uncandid; churlish &c. (*uncourteous*) 895; surly, sullen &c. 901a.

cold, -blooded, -hearted; hard-, flint-marble-, stony-hearted; hard of heart, unnatural; ruthless &c. (*unmerciful*) 914a; relentless &c. (*revengeful*) 919.

cruel; brut-al, -ish; savage, - as a -bear, - tiger; ferine, feral, ferocious; inhuman; barbarous, fell, untamed, tameless, truculent, incendiary; bloodthirsty &c. (*murderous*) 361; atrocious.

fiend-ish, -like; demoniacal; diabolic, -al; devilish, infernal, hellish, Satanic.

**Adv.** malevolently &c. *adj.*; with -bad intent &c. *n.*

---

**908. Malediction.—N.** malediction, malison, curse, imprecation, denunciation, execration, anathema, ban, proscription, excommunication, commination, thunders of the Vatican, fulmination, aspersion, vilification, vituperation, scurrility.

abuse; foul -, bad -, strong -, unparliamentary- language, Limehouse; Billingsgate, sauce, evil speaking; cursing &c. *v.*; profane swearing, oath.

threat &c. 909; more bark than bite; invective &c. (*disapprobation*) 932.

**V.** curse, accurse, imprecate, damn, swear at; slang; curse with bell, book and candle; invoke -, call down- curses on the head of; devote to destruction.

execrate, beshrew, scold; anathematize &c. (*censure*) 932; hold up to execration, denounce, proscribe, excommunicate, fulminate, thunder against; threaten &c. 909; curse up hill and down dale.

curse and swear; swear, – like a trooper; fall a cursing, rap out an
oath, damn, cuss.
**Adj.** curs-ing, -ed &c. *v.*; maledictory.
**Int.** woe to! beshrew! *ruat cœlum!* ill –, woe- betide! confusion
seize! damn! confound! blast! curse! devil take! hang! out with! a
plague –, out- upon! aroynt! *honi soit!*
**Phr.** *delenda est Carthago.*

**909. Threat.—N.** threat, menace; defiance &c. 715; abuse, minacity,
intimidation; fulmination; commination &c. (*curse*) 908; gathering
clouds &c. (*warning*) 668.
**V.** threat, -en; menace; snarl, growl, gnarl, mutter, bark, bully.
defy &c. 715; intimidate &c. 860; keep –, hold up –, hold out- *in
terrorem*; shake –, double –, clinch- the fist at; thunder, talk big, ful-
minate, use big words, bluster, look daggers.
**Adj.** threatening, menacing; mina-tory, -cious; comminatory, abusive;
*in terrorem*; ominous &c. (*predicting*) 511; defiant &c. 715; under
the ban.
**Int.** *væ victis!* at your peril! do your worst!

**910. Philanthropy. — N.** philan-
thropy; altruism, humanit-y, -arian-
ism; universal benevolence; *deliciæ
humani generis*; cosmopolitanism, util-
itarianism, the greatest happiness of
the greatest number, social science,
sociology.
common weal, public welfare, social-
ism, communism.
patriotism, civism, nationality, love
of country, *amor patriæ*, public spirit.
chivalry, knight errantry; generosity
&c. 942.
philanthropist, altruist &c. 906; utilitarian, Benthamite, socialist,
communist, cosmopolite, citizen of the world, *amicus humani
generis*; knight errant; patriot.
**Adj.** philanthropic, altruistic, humanitarian, utilitarian, cos-
mopolitan; public-spirited, patriotic; humane, large-hearted &c.
(*benevolent*) 906; chival-ric, -rous, generous &c. 942.
**Adv.** *pro -bono publico, – aris et focis.*
**Phr.** *'humani nihil a me alienum puto.'*

**911. Misanthropy.—N.** misanthropy.
incivism; egotism &c. (*selfishness*) 943;
moroseness &c. 901a; cynicism; defeat-
ism.
misanthrope, misanthropist, egotist,
cynic, man-hater, Timon, Diogenes.
woman-hater, misogynist.
**Adj.** misanthropic, antisocial, unpa-
triotic; egotistical &c. (*selfish*) 943;
morose &c. 901a.

**912. Benefactor. — N.** benefactor,
saviour, good genius, tutelary saint,
patron, guardian angel, fairy god-
mother, good Samaritan; *pater patriæ*;
salt of the earth &c. (*good man*) 948;
auxiliary &c. 711.

**913. [Maleficent being.] Evil-doer.
—N.** evil- -doer, – worker; wrong doer
&c. 949; mischief maker, marplot;
oppressor, tyrant; firebrand, incen-
diary, pyromaniac, anarchist, destroyer,
Hun, *Boche*, Vandal, iconoclast; com-
munist; terrorist, *apache*, gunman,
gangster, racketeer.
savage, brute, ruffian, barbarian, semi-barbarian, caitiff, desper-
ado; Mo-hock, -hawk; bludgeon man, bully, rough, hooligan,
larrikin, dangerous classes, ugly customer; thief &c. 792.
cockatrice, scorpion, hornet; viper, adder; snake, – in the grass;

serpent, cobra, asp, rattlesnake, anaconda; canker-, wire-worm; locust, Colorado beetle; torpedo; bane &c. 663.

cannibal; Anthropophag-us, -ist; bloodsucker, vampire, ogre, ghoul, gorilla; vulture; gyr-, ger-falcon.

wild beast, tiger, hyæna, butcher, hangman; cut-throat &c; (*killer*) 361; blood-, sleuth-, hell-hound.

hag, hellhag, beldam, Jezebel.

monster; fiend &c. (*demon*) 980; homicidal maniac, devil incarnate, demon in human shape; Frankenstein's monster.

harpy, siren, vampire; Furies, Eumenides &c. 900.

Attila, scourge of the human race.

**Phr.** *fœnum habet in cornu.*


### 3°. SPECIAL SYMPATHETIC AFFECTIONS

**914. Pity.—N.** pity, compassion, commiseration; bowels, – of compassion; condolence &c. 915; sympathy, fellow-feeling, tenderness, yearning, forbearance, humanity, mercy, clemency, exorability; leniency &c. (*lenity*) 740; charity, ruth, long-suffering.

melting mood; *argumentum ad misericordiam*; quarter, grace, *locus pœnitentiæ.*

sympathizer, champion, partisan.

**V.** pity; have –, show –, take- pity &c. *n.*; commiserate, compassionate; condole &c. 915; sympathize; feel –, be sorry –, yearn- for; weep, melt, thaw, enter into the feelings of.

forbear, relent, relax, give quarter, wipe the tears, *parcere subjectis*, give a *coup de grâce*, put out of one's misery; be cruel to be kind.

raise –, excite- pity &c. *n.*; touch, soften; melt, – the heart; appeal to one's better feelings; propitiate, disarm.

ask for -mercy &c. *n.*; supplicate &c. (*request*) 765; cry for quarter, beg one's life, kneel; deprecate.

**Adj.** pitying &c. *v.*; pitiful, compassionate, sympathetic, touched.

merciful, clement, ruthful; humane; humanitarian &c. (*philanthropic*) 910; tender. – hearted, – as a chicken; soft, – hearted; unhardened; lenient &c. 740; exorable, forbearing; melting &c. *v.*; weak.

**Int.** for pity's sake! mercy! have –, cry you- mercy! God help you! poor -thing, – dear, – fellow! woe betide! *quis talia fando temperet a lachrymis!*

**Phr.** one's heart bleeding for; *haud ignara mali miseris succurrere disco.*

**914a. Pitilessness.—N.** pitilessness &c. *adj.*; inclemency; inexorability, hardness of heart; inflexibility; severity &c. 739; malevolence &c. 907.

**V.** have no –, shut the gates of- mercy &c. 914; give no quarter.

**Adj.** piti-, merci-, ruth-, bowel-less; unpitying, unmerciful, inclement; in-, un-compassionate; inexorable, inflexible; harsh &c. 739; cruel &c. 907; unrelenting &c. 919.


**915. Condolence.—N.** condolence; lamentation &c. 839; sympathy, consolation.

**V.** condole with, console, sympathize &c. 914, share one's misery; feel for; express –, testify- pity; afford –, supply- consolation; lament &c. 839- with; send one's condolences.

## 4°. RETROSPECTIVE SYMPATHETIC AFFECTIONS

**916. Gratitude. — N.** gratitude, thankfulness, gratefulness, feeling of obligation.

acknowledgment, recognition thanksgiving, giving thanks.

thanks, praise, benediction; pæan; *Te Deum* &c. (*worship*) 990; grace, – before, – after- meat; thank-offering. requital.

**V.** be -grateful &c. *adj.*; thank; give –, render –, return –, offer –, tenderthanks &c. *n.*; acknowledge, requite.

feel –, be –, lie- under an obligation; *savoir gré*; not look a gift horse in the mouth; never forget, overflow with gratitude; thank –, bless- one's stars; fall on one's knees.

**Adj.** grateful, thankful, obliged, beholden, indebted to, under obligation.

**Int.** thanks! many thanks! gramercy! much obliged! thank you! thank Heaven! Heaven be praised!

**917. Ingratitude.—N.** ingratitude, thanklessness, oblivion of benefits; unthankfulness.

'benefits forgot'; thankless -task, – office.

**V.** be -ungrateful &c. *adj.*; forget benefits; look a gift horse in the mouth.

**Adj.** un-grateful, -mindful, -thankful; thankless, ingrate, wanting in gratitude, insensible of benefits.

forgotten; un-acknowledged, -thanked, -requited, -rewarded; ill-requited.

**Int.** thank you for nothing! *'et tu Brute !'*

---

**918. Forgiveness.—N.** forgiveness, pardon, condonation, grace, remission, absolution, amnesty, oblivion; indulgence; reprieve.

conciliation; reconciliation &c. (*pacification*) 723; propitiation.

excuse, exoneration, quittance, release, indemnity; bill –, act –, covenant –, deed- of indemnity; exculpation &c. (*acquittal*) 970.

longanimity, placability, forbearance; *amantium iræ*; *locus pœnitentiæ*.

**V.** forgive, – and forget; pardon, condone, think no more of, let bygones be bygones, shake hands; forget an injury, bury the hatchet; clean the slate.

excuse, pass over, overlook; wink at &c. (*neglect*) 460; bear with; allow –, make allowances- for; let one down easily, not be too hard upon, pocket the affront; blot out one's transgression.

let off, remit, absolve, give absolution, reprieve; acquit &c. 970.

beg –, ask –, implore pardon &c. *n.*, conciliate, propitiate, placate; make up a quarrel &c. (*pacify*) 723; let the wound heal.

**919. Revenge.—N.** revenge, -ment; vengeance; avenge-ment, -ance; sweet revenge, *vendetta*, death-feud, eye for an eye, blood for blood, a Roland for an Oliver; retaliation &c. 718; day of reckoning.

rancour, vindictiveness, implacability; malevolence &c. 907; ruthlessness &c. 914a.

avenger, vindicator, Nemesis, Eumenides.

**V.** re-, a-venge; take –, have one's- revenge; breathe -revenge, – vengeance; wreak one's -vengeance, – anger; give no quarter.

have -accounts to settle, – a crow to pluck, – a rod in pickle; pay off old scores.

keep the wound green; harbour -revenge, – vindictive feeling; bear malice; rankle, – in the breast; have at one's mercy.

**Adj.** revenge-, venge-ful; vindictive, rancorous; pitiless &c. 914a; ruthless, rigorous, avenging, retaliative.

unforgiving, unrelenting; inexorable, stony-hearted, implacable; relent-, remorse-less.

*æternum servans sub pectore vulnus*; rankling, immitigable.

**Adj.** forgiving, placable, conciliatory. forgiven &c. *v.*; un-resented, -avenged, -revenged.

**Adv.** cry you mercy.

**Phr.** *veniam petimusque damusque vicissim*; more in sorrow than in anger.

**Phr.** *manet -cicatrix, – altâ mente repostum.*

revenge is sweet.

---

**920. Jealousy.—N.** jealous-y, -ness; jaundiced eye, heartburning; green-eyed monster; yellows; Juno.

**V.** be -jealous &c. *adj.*; view with -jealousy, – a jealous eye.

**Adj.** jealous, – as a Barbary pigeon; jaundiced, yellow-eyed, horn-mad.

**921. Envy.—N.** envy; enviousness &c. *adj.*; rivalry; *jalousie de métier.*

**V.** envy, covet, lust after, crave, burst with envy, regard with envious eyes.

**Adj.** envious, invidious, covetous; *alieni appetens.*

Section IV.　MORAL AFFECTIONS

1°.　Moral Obligations

**922. Right.—N.** right; what -ought to, – should- be; fitness &c. *adj.*; *summum jus.*

justice, equity; equitableness &c. *adj.*; propriety; fair play, impartiality, measure for measure, give and take, *lex talionis*, square deal.

Astræa, Nemesis, Themis.

scales of justice, even-handed justice, retributive justice, *suum cuique*; clear stage –, fair field- and no favour; Queensberry rules.

morals &c. (*duty*) 926; law &c. 963; honour &c. (*probity*) 939; virtue &c. 944.

**V.** be -right &c. *adj.*; stand to reason.

see -justice done, – one righted, – fair play; do justice to; recompense &c. (*reward*) 973; hold the scales even, give and take; serve one right, put the saddle on the right horse; give -every one, – the devil- his due; *audire alteram partem.*

deserve &c. (*be entitled to*) 924.

**Adj.** right, good; just, reasonable; fit &c. 924; equ-al, -able, -itable; even-handed, fair, – and square.

legitimate, justifiable, rightful; as it -should, – ought to- be; lawful &c. (*permitted*) 760, (*legal*) 963.

deserved &c. 924.

**Adv.** rightly &c. *adj.*; in -justice, – equity, – reason.

without -distinction of, – regard to, – respect to- persons; upon even terms.

**Int.** all right!

**923. Wrong. — N.** wrong; what -ought not to, – should not- be; *malum in se*; unreasonableness, grievance; shame.

injustice; unfairness &c. *adj.*; iniquity, foul play, partiality, leaning; favour, -itism; nepotism, party spirit, partisanship; undueness &c. 925; unlawfulness &c. 964.

robbing Peter to pay Paul &c. *v.*; the wolf and the lamb; vice &c. 945.

a custom more honoured in the breach than the observance.

**V.** be -wrong &c. *adj.*; cry to heaven for vengeance.

do -wrong &c. *n.*; be -inequitable &c. *adj.*; favour, lean towards; encroach; impose upon; reap where one has not sown; give an inch and take an ell; rob Peter to pay Paul.

**Adj.** wrong, -ful; bad, too bad; un-just, -fair; in-, un-equitable; unequal, partial, one-sided.

objectionable; un-reasonable, -allowable, -warrantable, -justifiable; not cricket, not playing the game; improper, unfit; unjustified &c. 925; illegal &c. 964; iniquitous, criminal; immoral &c. 945; injurious &c. 649.

in the wrong, – box.

**Adv.** wrongly &c. *adj.*

**Phr.** it will not do; this is too bad.

---

**924. Dueness.**—**N.** due, -ness; right, privilege, prerogative, prescription, title, claim, pretension, demand, birthright.

immunity, licence, liberty, franchise; vested -interest, – right; licitness.

sanction, authority, warranty, charter; warrant &c. (*permission*) 760; constitution &c. (*law*) 963; tenure; bond &c. (*security*) 771.

deserts, merits, dues.

claimant, appellant; plaintiff &c. 938.

**V.** be -due &c. *adj.* to, – the due &c. *n.* of; have -right, – title, – claim- to; be entitled to; have a claim upon; belong to &c. (*property*) 780.

deserve, merit, be worthy of, richly deserve.

demand, claim; call upon –, come upon –, appeal to- for; re-vendicate, -claim; exact; insist -on, – upon; challenge; take one's stand, make a point of, require, lay claim to, assert, assume, arrogate, make good; substantiate; vindicate a -claim, – right; make out a case.

give –, confer- a right; sanction, entitle; authorize &c. 760; sanctify, legalize, ordain, prescribe, allot.

give every one his due &c. 922; pay one's dues; have one's -due, – rights; stand upon one's rights.

use a right, assert, enforce, put in force, lay under contribution.

**Adj.** having a right to &c. *n.*; entitled to; claiming; deserving, meriting, worthy of.

privileged, allowed, sanctioned, warranted, authorized; ordained, prescribed, constitutional, chartered, enfranchised.

prescriptive, presumptive; absolute, indefeasible; un-, in-alienable; imprescriptible, inviolable, unimpeachable, unchallenged; sacrosanct.

due to, merited, deserved, condign, richly deserved, *emeritus*.

allowable &c. (*permitted*) 760; lawful, licit, legitimate, legal; legalized &c. (*law*) 963.

square, unexceptionable, right; equitable &c. 922; due, *en règle*; fit, -ting; correct, proper, meet, befitting, becoming, seemly; decorous; creditable, up to the mark, right as a trivet; just –, quite- the thing; *selon les règles*.

**Adv.** duly, *ex officio, de jure*; by -right, – divine right; as is -fitting, – proper, – fitting and proper; *jure divino, Dei gratiâ*, in the name of.

**Phr.** *civis Romanus sum.*

**925.** [Absence of right.] **Undueness** —**N.** undueness &c. *adj.*; *malum prohibitum*; impropriety; illegality &c. 964.

falseness &c. *adj.*; emptiness –, invalidity- of title; illegitimacy.

loss of right, disfranchisement, forfeiture.

usurpation, assumption, tort, violation, breach, encroachment, presumption, seizure, stretch, exaction, imposition, lion's share.

usurper, pretender, Carlist; impostor.

**V.** be -undue &c. *adj.*; not be -due &c. 924.

infringe, encroach, trench on, exact; arrogate, – to oneself; give an inch and take an ell; stretch –, strain- a point; usurp, violate, do violence to; sail under false colours.

dis-franchise, -entitle, -qualify; invalidate.

relax &c. (*be lax*) 738; misbehave &c. (*vice*) 945; misbecome.

**Adj.** undue; unlawful &c. (*illegal*) 964; unconstitutional, *ultra vires*; illicit; un-authorized, -warranted, -allowed, -sanctioned, -justified; un-, dis-entitled, -qualified; un-privileged, -chartered.

illegitimate, bastard, spurious, false; usurped, tortious.

un-deserved, -merited, -earned; unfulfilled.

forfeited, disfranchised.

improper; un-meet, -fit, -befitting, -seemly; un-, mis-becoming; seemless; *contra bonos mores*; not the thing, out of the question, not to be thought of; preposterous, pretentious, would- be.

**926. Duty.—N.** duty, what ought to be done, moral obligation, account-ableness, liability, *onus*, responsibility; bounden –, imperative- duty; call, – of duty.

allegiance, fealty, tie; engagement &c. (*promise*) 768; part; function, calling &c. (*business*) 625.

morality, morals, decalogue; case of conscience; conscientiousness &c. (*probity*) 939; conscience, inward monitor, still small voice within, sense of duty, tender conscience.

dueness &c. 924; propriety, fitness, seemliness, amenableness, decorum; the -thing, – proper thing; the -right, – proper- thing to do.

[Science of morals] eth-ics, -ology; deon-, are-tology; moral –, ethical-philosophy; casuistry, polity.

observance, fulfilment, discharge, performance, acquittal, satisfaction, redemption; good behaviour.

**V.** be -the duty of, – incumbent &c. *adj.* on, – responsible &c. *adj.*; behoove, become, befit, beseem; belong –, pertain- to; fall to one's lot; devolve on; lie -upon, – on one's head, – at one's door; rest -with, – on the shoulders of.

take upon oneself &c. (*promise*) 768; be –, become- -bound to, – sponsor for; be responsible for; incur a -responsibility &c. *n.*; be –, stand –, lie- under an obligation; have to answer for, owe it to oneself.

impose a -duty &c. *n.*; enjoin, require, exact; bind, – over; saddle with, prescribe, assign, call upon, look to, oblige.

**927. Dereliction of Duty.—N.** dere; liction of duty; fault &c. (*guilt*) 947-sin &c. (*vice*) 945; non-observance, -performance, -co-operation; neglect, carelessness, laziness, incompetence, eye-service, relaxation, infraction, violation, transgression, failure, evasion, indolence; dead letter.

slacker, loafer, striker, non-co-operator.

**V.** violate; break, – through; infringe; set -aside, – at naught; trample -on, – under foot; slight, neglect, evade, renounce, forswear, repudiate; wash one's hands of; escape, transgress, fail.

call to account &c. (*disapprobation*) 932.

**927a. Exemption.—N.** exemption, freedom, irresponsibility, immunity, liberty, licence, release, exoneration, excuse, dispensation, absolution, franchise, renunciation, discharge; exculpation &c. 970; *ægrotat*.

**V.** be -exempt &c. *adj.*

exempt, release, acquit, discharge, quit-claim, remise, remit; free, set at liberty, let off, pass over, spare, excuse, dispense with, give dispensation, license; stretch a point; absolve &c. (*forgive*) 918; exonerate &c. (*exculpate*) 970; save the necessity.

**Adj.** exempt, free, immune, at liberty, scot free; released &c. *v.*; unbound, unencumbered; irresponsible, unaccountable, not answerable; excusable.

---

enter upon –, perform –, observe –, fulfil –, discharge –, adhere to –, acquit oneself of –, satisfy- -a duty, – an obligation; act one's part, redeem one's pledge, do justice to, be at one's post; do duty; do one's duty &c. (*be virtuous*) 944.

be on one's good behaviour, mind one's P's and Q's.

**Adj.** obligatory, binding; imperative, peremptory; stringent &c. (*severe*) 739; behooving &c. *v.*; incumbent –, chargeable- on; under obligation; obliged –, bound –, tied- by; saddled with.

due –, beholden –, bound –, indebted- to; tied down; compromised &c. (*promised*) 768; in duty bound.

amenable, liable, accountable, responsible, answerable.

right, meet &c. (*due*) 924; moral, ethical, casuistical, conscientious, ethological.

**Adv.** with a safe conscience, as in duty bound, on one's own responsibility, at one's own risk, *suo periculo*; *in foro conscientiæ*; *quamdiu se bene gesserit*; at one's post, on duty.

**Phr.** *dura lex sed lex.*

## 2°. MORAL SENTIMENTS

**928. Respect.—N.** respect, regard, consideration; courtesy &c. 894; attention, deference, reverence, honour, esteem, estimation, veneration, admiration; approbation &c. 931.

homage, fealty, obeisance, genuflexion, kneeling, prostration; obsequiousness &c. 886; salaam, *kowtow*, bow, presenting arms, salute.

respects, regards, duty, *devoirs*, *égards*.

devotion &c. (*piety*) 987.

**V.** respect, regard; revere, -nce; hold in reverence, honour, venerate, hallow; esteem &c. (*approve of*) 931; think much of; entertain –, bear-respect for; have a high opinion of; look up to, defer to; pay -attention, – respect &c. *n.*- to; do –, render- honour to; do the honours, hail; show courtesy &c. 894; salute, present arms; do –, pay- homage to; pay tribute to, kneel to, bow to, bend the knee to; fall down before, prostrate oneself, kiss the hem of one's garment; worship &c. 990.

keep one's distance, make room, observe due decorum, stand upon ceremony.

command –, inspire- respect; awe, impose, overawe, dazzle.

**Adj.** respecting &c. *v.*; respectful, deferential, decorous, reverential, obsequious, ceremonious, bare-headed, cap in hand, on one's knees; prostrate &c. (*servile*) 886.

respected &c. *v.*; in high -esteem, – estimation; time-honoured, venerable, *emeritus*.

**Adv.** in deference to; with -all, – due, – the highest- respect; with submission.

saving your -grace, – presence; *salva sit reverentia*; *pace tanti nominis*.

**Int.** hail! all hail! *este perpetua!* may your shadow never be less!

**929. Disrespect. — N.** dis-respect, -esteem, -estimation, -favour, -repute; low estimation; disparagement &c. (*dispraise*) 932, (*detraction*) 934.

irreverence; slight, neglect; *spretæ injuria formæ*; superciliousness &c. (*contempt*) 930.

vilipendency, contumely, affront, dishonour, insult, indignity, outrage, discourtesy &c. 895; practical joking; scurrility, scoffing, sibilation; ir-, derision; mockery; irony &c. (*ridicule*) 856; sarcasm.

hiss, hoot, gibe, flout, jeer, scoff, gleek, taunt, sneer, quip, fling, wipe, slap in the face.

**V.** hold in disrespect &c. (*despise*) 930; misprize, disregard, slight, undervalue, depreciate, trifle with, set at naught, pass by, push aside, overlook, turn one's back upon, laugh in one's sleeve; be -disrespectful &c. *adj.*, – discourteous &c. 895; treat with -disrespect &c. *n.*; set down, browbeat.

dishonour, desecrate; insult, affront, outrage.

speak slightingly of; disparage &c. (*dispraise*) 932; vilipend, call names; throw –, fling- dirt; drag through the mud, point at, indulge in personalities; make -mouths, – faces; bite the thumb; take –, pluck- by the beard; toss in a blanket, tar and feather.

have –, hold- in derision; deride, scoff, sneer, laugh at, snigger, ridicule, gibe, mock, jeer, taunt, twit, niggle, gleek, gird, flout, fleer; roast, turn into ridicule; guy, burlesque &c. 856; laugh to scorn &c. (*contempt*) 930; smoke; fool; make -game, – a fool, – an April fool- of; play a practical joke; rag; lead one a dance, run the rig upon, have a fling at, scout, hiss, hoot, mob.

**Adj.** disrespectful; aweless, irreverent; disparaging &c. 934; insulting &c. *v.*; supercilious &c. (*scornful*) 930, rude, derisive, contemptuous, sarcastic; scurri-le, -lous; contumelious.

un-respected, -worshipped, -envied, -saluted; un-, dis-regarded.
**Adv.** disrespectfully &c. *adj.*

**930. Contempt.—N.** contempt, disdain, scorn, sovereign contempt; despi-sal, -ciency; vilipendency, contumely; slight, sneer, spurn, by-word.

contemptuousness &c. *adj.*; scornful eye; smile of contempt; derision &c. (*disrespect*) 929.

[State of being despised] despisedness.

**V.** despise, contemn, scorn, disdain, feel contempt for, view with a scornful eye, disregard, slight, not mind; pass by &c. (*neglect*) 460.

look down upon; hold -cheap, – in contempt, – in disrespect; think -nothing, – small beer- of; make light of; underestimate &c. 483; esteem -slightly, – of small or no account; take no account of, care nothing for; set no store by; not care a -straw &c. (*unimportance*) 643; set at naught, laugh in one's sleeve, snap one's fingers at, shrug one's shoulders, turn up one's nose at, pooh-pooh, damn with faint praise; sneeze –, whistle –, sneer- at; curl up one's lip, toss the head, *traiter de haut*; laugh at &c. (*be disrespectful*) 929.

point the finger of –, hold up to –, laugh to- scorn; scout, hoot, flout, hiss, scoff at.

turn -one's back, – a cold shoulder- upon; tread –, trample- -upon, – under foot; spurn, kick; fling to the winds &c. (*repudiate*) 610; send away with a flea in the ear.

**Adj.** contemptuous; disdain-, scorn-ful; withering, contumelious, supercilious, cynical, haughty, bumptious, cavalier; derisive.

contemptible, despicable; pitiable; pitiful &c. (*unimportant*) 643; despised &c. *v.*; down-trodden; unenvied.

**Adv.** contemptuously &c. *adj.*

**Int.** a fig for &c. (*unimportant*) 643; bah! never mind! away with! hang it! fiddle-de-dee!

---

**931. Approbation.—N.** approbation; approv-al, -ement; sanction, advocacy; nod of approbation; esteem, estimation, good opinion, golden opinions, admiration; love &c. 897; appreciation, regard, account, popularity, *kudos*, credit; repute &c. 873.

commendation, praise; laud, -ation; good word; meed –, tribute- of praise; encomium; eulog-y, -ium; *éloge*, panegyric; homage, hero worship; benediction, blessing, benison.

applause, plaudit, clap; clapping, – of hands; accl-aim, -amation; cheer; pæan, hosannah; shout –, peal –, chorus –, thunders- of -applause &c.; Kentish fire; Prytaneum; blurb.

**V.** approve; think -good, – much of, – well of, – highly of; esteem, value, prize; set great store -by, – on.

do justice to, appreciate; honour, hold in esteem, look up to, admire; like &c. 897; be in favour of, wish God speed; hail, – with satisfaction.

stand –, stick- up for; uphold, hold

**932. Disapprobation.—N.** disapprobation, -val; improbation; dis-esteem, -valuation, -placency; odium; dislike &c. 867; dissent &c. 489.

dis-praise, -commendation; blame, censure, obloquy; detraction &c. 934; disparagement, depreciation; denunciation; condemnation &c. 971; ostracism; boycott; black-list, -ball; *index -expurgatorius, – librorum prohibitorum*.

animadversion, reflection, stricture, objection, exception, criticism; sardonic -grin, – laugh; sarcasm, insinuation, innuendo; bad –, poor –, left-handed- compliment.

satire; sneer &c. (*contempt*) 930; taunt &c. (*disrespect*) 929; cavil, carping, censoriousness; hypercriticism &c. (*fastidiousness*) 868.

reprehension, remonstrance, expostulation, reproof, reprobation, admonition, increpation, reproach; rebuke. reprimand, castigation, jobation, lecture, curtain lecture, blow up, wigging, dressing, – down; rating, scolding, trim-

up, countenance, sanction; clap –, pat-
on the back; keep in countenance, en-
dorse, give credit, recommend; mark
with a white -mark, – stone.

commend, praise; be–, laud; com-
pliment, pay a tribute, bepraise; clap,
– the hands; applaud, cheer, acclaim,
acclamate, encore; panegyrize, eulo-
gize, cry up, *prôner*, puff; extol, – to
the skies; magnify, glorify, exalt, boost,
swell, make much of; flatter &c. 933;
bless, give a blessing to; have –, say- a
good word for; speak -well, – highly,
– in high terms- of; sing –, sound –,
chaunt –, resound- the praises of; sing
praises to; cheer –, applaud- to the
-echo, – very echo.

redound to the -honour, – praise, –
credit- of; do credit to; deserve -praise
&c. *n.*; recommend itself; pass muster.

be -praised &c.; receive honourable
mention; be in -favour, – high favour-
with; ring with the praises of, win
golden opinions, gain credit, find favour
with, stand well in the opinion of;
*laudari a laudato viro.*

Adj. approving &c. *v.*; in favour of;
lost in admiration.

commendatory, complimentary, ben-
edictory, laudatory, panegyrical, eulo-
gistic, encomiastic, acclamatory, lavish
of praise, uncritical.

approved, praised &c. *v.*; un-cen-
sured, -impeached; popular, in good
odour; in high esteem &c. (*respected*)
928; in –, in high- favour.

deserving –, worthy of- praise &c. *n.*;
praiseworthy, commendable, of estima-
tion; good &c. 648; meritorious, estim-
able, creditable, plausible, unimpeach-
able; beyond all praise.

Adv. commendably, with credit, to
admiration; well &c. 618; with three
times three.

Int. hear, hear! well done! *brav-o! -a!
-i! bravissimo! euge! macte virtute!* so far
so good, that's right, quite right; *op-
time!* one cheer more; may your shad-
ow never be less! *esto perpetua!* long
life to! *viva! evviva!* God speed! *valete
et plaudite! encore! bis!*

Phr. *probatum est.*

------

ming; correction, set down, rap on the
knuckles, *coup de bec*, rebuff; slap, – on
the face; home thrust, hit; frown, scowl,
black look.

diatribe; jeremiad; *tirade*, philippic.

clamour, outcry, hue and cry; hiss,
-ing; sibilation, cat-call; execration &c.
908.

chiding, upbraiding &c. *v.*; expro-
bration, abuse, vituperation, invective,
objurgation, contumely, personal re-
marks; hard –, cutting –, bitter- words.

evil-speaking; bad language &c. 908;
personality.

V. disapprove; dislike &c. 867; la-
ment &c. 839; object to, take excep-
tion to; be scandalized at, think ill
of; view with -disfavour, – dark eyes,
– jaundiced eyes; *nil admirari*, dis-
value, improbate.

frown upon, look grave; bend –,
knit- the brows; shake the head at.
shrug the shoulders; turn up the nose
&c. (*contempt*) 930; look -askance, –
black upon; look with an evil eye;
make a wry -face, – mouth- at; set
one's face against.

dis-praise, -commend, -parage; de-
precate, speak ill of, not speak well of,
slate, condemn &c. (*find guilty*) 971.

blame; lay –, cast- blame upon;
censure, *fronder*, reproach, pass censure
on, reprobate, impugn.

remonstrate, expostulate, recrimin-
ate.

reprehend, chide, admonish; bring –,
call- -to account, – over the coals, – to
order; take to task, reprove, lecture,
bring to book; read a -lesson, – lecture-
to; rebuke, correct.

reprimand, chastise, castigate, lash,
blow up, trounce, trim, *laver la tête*,
overhaul; give it one, – finely; gibbet.

accuse &c. 938; impeach, denounce;
hold up to -reprobation, – execration;
expose, brand, gibbet, stigmatize;
show –, pull –, take- up; cry 'shame'
upon; be outspoken; raise a hue and
cry against.

execrate &c. 908; exprobrate, speak
daggers, vituperate; abuse, – like a
pickpocket; scold, rate, objurgate, up-
braid, fall foul of; jaw; rail, – at, – in
good set terms; bark at; anathematize,

call names; call by -hard, – ugly- names; a-, re-vile; vili-fy, -pend; bespatter; backbite; clapperclaw; rave –, thunder –, fulminate- against; load with reproaches; lash with the tongue.

exclaim –, protest –, inveigh –, declaim –, cry out –, raise one's voice- against.

decry; cry –, run –, frown- down; clamour, hiss, hoot, mob, ostracize; draw up –, sign- a round robin; black-ball, -list.

animadvert –, reflect- upon; glance at; cast -reflection, – re- proach, – a slur- upon; insinuate, damn with faint praise; 'hint a fault and hesitate dislike'; not to be able to say much for.

scoff at, point at; twit, taunt &c. (*disrespect*) 929; sneer at &c. (*despise*) 930; satirize, lampoon; defame &c. (*detract*) 934; depre- ciate, find fault with, criticize, cut up; pull –, pick- to pieces; take exception; cavil; peck –, nibble –, carp- at; be -censorious &c. *adj.*; pick -holes, – a hole, – a hole in one's coat; make a fuss about.

take –, set- down; snub, snap one up, give a rap on the knuckles; throw a stone -at, – in one's garden; have a -fling, – snap- at; have words with, pluck a crow with; give one a -wipe, – lick with the rough side of the tongue.

incur blame, excite disapprobation, scandalize, shock, revolt; get a bad name, forfeit one's good opinion, be under a cloud, come under the ferule, bring a hornet's nest about one's ears.

take blame, stand corrected; have to answer for.

**Adj.** disapproving &c. *v.*; scandalized.

disparaging, condemnatory, damnatory, denunciatory, reproach- ful, abusive, objurgatory, clamorous, vituperative; defamatory &c. 934.

satirical, sarcastic, sardonic, cynical, dry, sharp, cutting, biting, severe, virulent, withering, trenchant, hard upon; censorious, criti- cal, captious, carping, hypercritical; fastidious &c. 868; sparing of –, grudging- praise.

disapproved, chid &c. *v.*; in bad odour, blown upon, unapproved; unblest; at a discount, exploded; weighed in the balance and found wanting.

blameworthy, reprehensible &c. (*guilt*) 947; to –, worthy of- blame, answerable, uncommendable, exceptionable, not to be thought of, bad &c. 649; vicious &c. 945.

un-lamented, -bewailed, -pitied.

**Adv.** with a wry face; reproachfully &c. *adj.*

**Int.** it is too bad! it -won't, – will never- do! marry come up! Oh! come! 'sdeath!

forbid it Heaven! God –, Heaven- forbid! out –, fie- upon it! away with! tut! *O tempora! O mores!* shame! fie, – for shame! out on you!

tell it not in Gath!

**933. Flattery.—N.** flattery, adula- tion, gloze; bland-ishment, -iloquence; cajolery; fawning, wheedling &c. *v.*; captation, coquetry, sycophancy, ob- sequiousness, flunkeyism, toad-eating, tuft-hunting; snobbishness.

incense, honeyed words, flummery; bun-kum, -combe; blarney, *placebo*, but-

**934. Detraction.—N.** detraction, dis- paragement, depreciation, vilification, obloquy, scurrility, scandal, defama- tion, aspersion, traducement, slander, calumny, obtrectation, evil-speaking, backbiting, *scandalum magnatum.*

personality, libel, squib, lampoon, skit, pasquinade; *chronique scandaleuse.*

ter; soft -soap, – sawder; rose water.
voice of the charmer, mouth honour;
lip-homage; euphemism; unctuousness
&c. *adj.*

V. flatter, praise to the skies, puff;
wheedle, cajole, glaver, coax; fawn, –
upon; humour, gloze, soothe, pet,
coquet, slaver, butter; be-spatter,
-slubber, -plaster, -slaver; lay it on
thick, overpraise; earwig, cog, col-
logue; truckle –, pander *or* pandar –,
pay court- to; court; creep into the
good graces of; curry favour with,
hang on the sleeve of; fool to the top
of one's bent; lick the dust.
lay the flattering unction to one's
soul, gild the pill, make things pleasant.
overestimate &c. 482; exaggerate &c.
549.

Adj. flattering &c. *v.*; adulatory;
mealy-, honey-mouthed; honeyed;
smooth, – tongued; soapy, oily, unc-
tuous, blandiloquent, specious; fine-,
fair-spoken; plausible, servile, syco-
phantic, fulsome; courtier-ly, -like.
Adv. *ad captandum.*

---

**935. Flatterer.—N.** flatterer, adula-
tor; eu-logist, -phemist; optimist, en-
comiast, *laudator*, whitewasher, booster.
toad-y, -eater; sycophant, courtier,
pickthank, Sir Pertinax MacSycophant;
*flâneur, prôneur*; puffer, touter, *cla-
queur*; claw-back, ear-wig, doer of
dirty work; parasite, hanger on &c.
(*servility*) 886.

---

**937. Vindication.—N.** vindication,
justification, warrant; exoneration, ex-
culpation; acquittal &c. 970; white-
washing.
extenuation; pallia-tion, -tive; soft-
ening, mitigation.
reply, defence; recrimination &c. 938.
apology, gloss, varnish; plea &c. 617;
salvo; excuse, extenuating circum-
stances; allowance, – to be made; *locus
penitentiæ.*
apologist, vindicator, justifier; de-
fendant &c. 938.
justifiable charge, true bill.

sarcasm, cynicism; criticism (*disap-
probation*) 932; invective &c. 932; en-
venomed tongue; *spretæ injuria formæ.*
detractor &c. 936.

V. detract, derogate, decry, depre-
ciate, disparage; run –, cry- down;
minimize, make light of; belittle, sneer
at &c. (*contemn*) 930; criticize, pull to
pieces, pick a hole in one's coat, asperse,
cast aspersions, blow upon, bespatter,
blacken; vili-fy, -pend; avile; give a
dog a bad name, brand, malign, back-
bite, libel, lampoon, traduce, slander,
defame, calumniate, bear false witness
against; speak ill of behind one's back.
'damn with faint praise, assent with
civil leer; and without sneering, others
teach to sneer.'
fling dirt &c. (*disrespect*) 929; ana-
thematize &c. 932; dip the pen in gall,
view in a bad light.
Adj. detracting &c. *v.*; defamatory,
detractory, derogatory; disparaging,
libellous; scurril-e, -ous; abusive; foul-
spoken, -tongued, -mouthed; slander-
ous; calumni-ous, -atory; sar-castic,
-donic; satirical, cynical.

---

**936. Detractor.—N.** detractor, re-
prover; cens-or, -urer; cynic, critic,
caviller, carper, wordcatcher.
defamer, backbiter, slanderer, knock-
er, Sir Benjamin Backbite, lampooner,
satirist, traducer, libeller, calumniator,
dearest foe, dawplucker, Thersites;
Zoilus; good-natured –, candid- friend
[satirically]; reviler, vituperator, casti-
gator; shrew &c. 901.
disapprover, *laudator temporis acti.*

---

**938. Accusation.— N.** accusation,
charge, imputation, slur, inculpation,
exprobration, delation; crimination;
in-, ac-, re-crimination; *tu quoque* argu-
ment; invective &c. 932.
de-nunciation, -nouncement; libel,
challenge, citation, arraignment; im-,
ap-peachment; indictment, bill of in-
dictment, true bill; lawsuit &c. 969;
condemnation &c. 971.
*gravamen* of a charge, head and front
of one's offending, *argumentum ad
hominem*; scandal &c. (*detraction*) 934;
*scandalum magnatum.*

V. justify, warrant; be an -excuse &c. *n.*- for; lend a colour, furnish a handle; vindicate; ex-, dis-culpate; acquit &c. 970; clear, set right, exonerate, whitewash.

extenuate, palliate, excuse, soften, apologize, varnish, slur, gloze; put a -gloss, – good face- upon; mince; gloss over, bolster up, help a lame dog over a stile.

advocate, defend, plead one's cause; stand –, stick –, speak- up for; contend –, speak- for; bear out, keep in countenance, support; plead &c. 617; say in defence; plead ignorance; confess and avoid, propugn, put in a good word for.

take the will for the deed, make allowance for, do justice to; give -one, – the Devil- his due.

make good; prove -the truth of, – one's case; be justified by the event.

**Adj.** vindicat-ed, -ing &c. *v.*; vindicat-ive, -ory; palliative; exculpatory; apologetic.

excusable, defensible, pardonable; veni-al, -able; specious, plausible, justifiable.

**Phr.** '*honi soit qui mal y pense.*'

accuser, prosecutor, plaintiff, complainant, petitioner; relator, informer; appellant.

accused, defendant, prisoner, panel, co-, respondent; litigant.

V. accuse, charge, tax, impute, twit, taunt with, reproach.

brand with reproach; stigmatize, slur; cast a -stone at, – slur on; incriminate; inculpate, implicate; call to account &c. (*censure*) 932; take to -blame, – task; put in the black book.

inform against, indict, denounce, arraign; im-, ap-peach; have up, show up, pull up; challenge, cite, lodge a complaint; prosecute, bring an action against &c. 969.

charge –, saddle- with; lay to one's -door, – charge; lay the blame on, bring home to; cast –, throw- in one's teeth; cast the first stone at.

have –, keep- a rod in pickle for; have a crow to pluck with.

trump up a charge.

**Adj.** accusing &c. *v.*; accusat-ory, -ive; imputative, denunciatory; re-, criminatory.

accused &c. *v.*; suspected; under -suspicion, – a cloud, – *surveillance*; in -custody, – detention; in the -lock up, – watch house, – house of detention.

accusable, imputable; in-defensible, -excusable; un-pardonable, -justifiable; vicious &c. 945.

**Int.** look at home; *tu quoque* &c. (*retaliation*) 718.

### 3°. MORAL CONDITIONS

**939. Probity.**—N. probity, integrity, rectitude; uprightness &c. *adj.*; honesty, faith; honour; good faith, *bona fides*; purity, clean hands.

fairness &c. *adj.*; fair play, justice, equity, impartiality, principle; grace.

constancy; faithfulness &c. *adj.*; fidelity, loyalty; incorrupt-ion, -ibility.

trustworthiness &c. *adj.*; truth, candour, singleness of heart; veracity &c. 543; tender conscience &c. (*sense of duty*) 926.

punctil-iousness, -io; delicacy, nicety; scrupul-osity, -ousness &c. *adj.*; scruple; point, – of honour; punctuality.

dignity &c. (*repute*) 873; respectability, -bleness &c. *adj.*; gentleman; man of -honour, – his word; *fidus*

**940. Improbity. N.** improbity; dishon-esty, -our; deviation from rectitude; disgrace &c. (*disrepute*) 874; fraud &c. (*deception*) 545; lying &c. 544; bad –, Punic- faith; *mala –, Punica- fides*; infidelity; faithlessness &c. *adj.*; Judas kiss, betrayal; scrap of paper.

breach of -promise, – trust, – faith: prodition, disloyalty, divided allegiance, treason, high treason; apostasy &c. (*tergiversation*) 607; non-observance &c. 773.

shabbiness &c. *adj.*; villainy; baseness &c. *adj.*; abjection, debasement, turpitude, moral turpitude, laxity, trimming, shuffling.

perfidy; perfidiousness &c. *adj.*;

*Achates, preux chevalier, galantuomo*; truepenny, trump, brick; true Briton, white man, sportsman.

court of honour, a fair field and no favour; *argumentum ad verecundiam.*

V. be -honourable &c. *adj.*; deal -honourably, – squarely, – impartially, – fairly; speak the truth &c. (*veracity*) 543; tell the truth and shame the devil, *vitam impendere vero*; show a proper spirit, make a point of; do one's duty &c. 944; play the game.

redeem one's pledge &c. 926; keep –, be as good as- one's -promise, – word; keep faith with, not fail

give and take, *audire alteram partem*, give the devil his due, put the saddle on the right horse.

redound to one's honour.

Adj. upright; honest, – as daylight; veracious &c. 543; virtuous &c. 944; honourable; fair, right, just, equitable, impartial, even-handed, square; fair –, open- and aboveboard.

constant, – as the northern star; faithful, loyal, staunch; true, – blue, – to one's colours, – to the core, – as the needle to the pole; true-hearted, trust-y, -worthy; as good as one's word, to be depended on, incorruptible.

manly, straightforward &c. (*ingenuous*) 703; frank, candid, open-hearted.

conscientious, tender - conscienced, right-minded; high-principled, -minded; scrupulous, religious, strict; nice, punctilious, correct, punctual; respect-, reput-able; gentlemanlike.

inviol - able, - ate; un - violated, -broken, -betrayed; un-bought, -bribed.

innocent &c. 946; pure; stainless; un-stained, -tarnished, -sullied, -tainted, -perjured; uncorrupt, -ed; unde-filed, -praved, -bauched; *integer vitæ scelerisque purus; justus et tenax propositi.*

chivalrous, jealous of honour, *sans peur et sans reproche*; high-spirited.

supra-mundane, unworldly, over-scrupulous.

Adv. honourably &c. *adj.*; *bona fide*; on the square, in good faith, honour bright, *foro conscientiæ*, with clean hands; by fair means.

treachery, double-dealing; unfairness &c. *adj.*; knavery, roguery, rascality, foul-play; jobb-ing, -ery; Tammany, graft; venality, nepotism; corruption, job, shuffle, fishy transaction, barratry; sharp practice, heads I win, tails you lose; mouth-honour &c. (*flattery*) 933.

V. be -dishonest &c. *adj.*; play false; break one's -word, – faith, – promise; jilt, betray, forswear; shuffle &c. (*lie*) 544; live by one's wits, sail near the wind; play with marked cards.

disgrace –, dishonour –, demean –, degrade- oneself; derogate, stoop, grovel, sneak, lose caste; sell oneself, go over to the enemy; seal one's infamy.

Adj. dishon-est, -ourable; un-conscientious, -scrupulous; fraudulent &c. 545; knavish; disgraceful &c. (*disreputable*) 874; wicked &c. 945.

false-hearted, disingenuous; unfair, one-sided; double, -tongued, -faced; time-serving, crooked, tortuous, insidious, Machiavellian, dark, slippery; questionable; fishy; perfidious, treacherous, perjured.

infamous, arrant, foul, base, vile, low, ignominious, blackguard.

contemptible, abject, mean, shabby, little, paltry, dirty, scurvy, scabby, sneaking, grovelling, scrubby, rascally, pettifogging; beneath one; not cricket.

low-minded, -thoughted; base-minded.

undignified, indign; unbe-coming, -seeming, -fitting; de-rogatory, -grading; *infra dignitatem*; ungentleman-ly, -like; un-knightly, -chivalric, -manly, -handsome; recreant, inglorious.

corrupt, venal; debased, mongrel.

faithless, of bad faith, false, unfaithful, disloyal; untrustworthy; trust-, troth-less; lost to shame, dead to honour.

Adv. dishonestly &c. *adj.*; *malâ fide*, like a thief in the night, by crooked paths; by foul means.

Int. *O tempora! O mores!*

---

**941. Knave.**—N. knave, rogue, villain; Scapin, rascal; Lazarillo de Tormes; bad man &c. 949; blackguard &c. 949.

traitor, betrayer, arch-traitor, conspirator, stool pigeon, Judas, Catiline; reptile, serpent, snake in the grass, wolf in sheep's clothing, sneak, Jerry Sneak, tell-tale, squealer, mischief-maker, trimmer; renegade &c. (*tergiversation*) 607; truant, recreant; sycophant &c. (*servility*) 886.

**942. Disinterestedness.—N.** disinterestedness &c. *adj.*; generosity; liberal-ity, -ism; altruism; benevolence &c. 906; elevation, loftiness of purpose, exaltation, magnanimity; chival-ry, -rous spirit; heroism, sublimity.

self-denial, -abnegation, -effacement, -sacrifice, -immolation, -control &c. (*resolution*) 604; stoicism, devotion, martyrdom, *suttee*.

labour of love.

**V.** be -disinterested &c. *adj.*; make a sacrifice, lay one's head on the block; put oneself in the place of others, do as one would be done by, do unto others as we would men should do unto us.

**Adj.** disinterested; unselfish; self-denying, -sacrificing, -devoted; generous.

handsome, liberal, noble; noble-, high-minded; princely, great, high, elevated, lofty, exalted, spirited, stoical, magnanimous; great-, large-hearted, chivalrous, heroic, sublime.

un-bought, -bribed; uncorrupted &c. (*upright*) 939.

**943. Selfishness.—N.** selfishness &c. *adj.*; self-love, -indulgence, -worship, -interest; ego-tism, -ism; egocentrism, narcissism; *amour propre* &c. (*vanity*) 880; nepotism.

worldliness &c. *adj.*; world wisdom. illiberality; meanness &c. *adj.*

time-server; tuft-, fortune-hunter; self-seeker; jobber, worldling; egotist, egoist, monopolist, nepotist, profiteer; temporizer, trimmer; dog in the manger, charity that begins at home.

**V.** be -selfish &c. *adj.*; please –, indulge –, coddle- oneself; consult one's own -wishes, – pleasure; look after one's own interest; feather one's nest; take care of number one, have an eye to the main chance, know on which side one's bread is buttered; give an inch and take an ell; wangle.

**Adj.** selfish; self-seeking, -indulgent, -interested; wrapped up –, centred- in self; egotistic, -al; egoistical; egocentric.

illiberal, mean, ungenerous, narrow-minded; mercenary, venal; covetous &c. 819.

unspiritual; earthly, -minded; mundane; worldly, -minded, -wise; time-serving.

interested; *alieni appetens sui profusus.*

**Adv.** ungenerously &c. *adj.*; to gain some private ends; from selfish –, interested- motives.

**Phr.** *après nous le déluge.*

**944. Virtue.—N.** virtue; virtuousness &c. *adj.*; morality; moral rectitude; integrity &c. (*probity*) 939; nobleness &c. 873.

morals; ethics &c. (*duty*) 926; cardinal virtues.

merit, worth, desert, excellence, credit; self-control &c. (*resolution*) 604; self-denial &c. (*temperance*) 953.

well-doing; good -actions, – behaviour; discharge –, fulfilment –, performance- of duty; well-spent life; innocence &c. 946.

**V.** be -virtuous &c. *adj.*; practise -virtue &c. *n.*; do –, fulfil –, perform –,

**945. Vice. — N.** vice; evil -doing, – courses; wrong doing; wickedness, viciousness &c. *adj.*; iniquity, peccability, demerit; sin, Adam; old –, offending- Adam.

immorality, impropriety, indecorum, scandal, laxity, looseness of morals; want of -principle, – ballast; obliquity, backsliding, infamy, demoralization, pravity, depravity, pollution; hardness of heart; brutality &c. (*malevolence*) 907; corruption &c. (*debasement*) 659; knavery &c. (*improbity*) 940; profligacy; lust &c. 961; flagrancy, atrocity; cannibalism.

discharge- one's duty; redeem one's pledge &c. 926; act well, - one's part; fight the good fight; acquit oneself well; command -, master- one's passions; keep -straight, - in the right path.

set -an, - a good- example; be on one's -good, - best- behaviour.

**Adj.** virtuous, good; innocent &c. 946; meritorious, deserving, worthy, desertful, correct; dut-iful, -eous; moral; right, -eous, -minded; well-intentioned, creditable, laudable, commendable, praiseworthy; above -, beyond- all praise; excellent, admirable; sterling, pure, noble.

exemplary; match-, peer-less; saintly, -like; heaven-born, angelic, seraphic, godlike.

**Adv.** virtuously &c. *adj.*; *e merito*.

infirmity; weakness &c. *adj.*; weakness of the flesh, frailty, imperfection; error; weak side; foible; fail-ing, -ure; crying -, besetting- sin; defect, deficiency, shortcoming; cloven foot.

lowest dregs of vice, sink of iniquity, Alsatian den; *gusto picaresco*.

fault, crime; criminality &c. (*guilt*) 947.

sinner &c. 949.

**V.** be -vicious &c. *adj.*; sin, commit sin, do amiss, err, transgress; misdemean -, forget -, misconduct- oneself; mis-do, -behave; fall, lapse, slip, trip, offend, trespass; deviate from the -line of duty, - path of virtue &c. 944; take a wrong course, go astray; hug a -sin, - fault; sow one's wild oats.

render -vicious &c. *adj.*; demoralize, brutalize; corrupt &c. (*degrade*) 659.

**Adj.*** vicious; sinful; sinning &c. *v.*; wicked, iniquitous, bad, immoral, unrighteous, wrong, criminal; naughty, incorrect; undut-eous, -iful.

unprincipled, lawless, disorderly, *contra bonos mores*, indecorous, unseemly, improper; dissolute, profligate, scampish; unworthy; worth-, desert-less; disgraceful, recreant; reprehensible, blameworthy, uncommendable; dis-creditable, -reputable.

base, sinister, scurvy, foul, gross, vile, black, grave, facinorous, felonious, nefarious, shameful, scandalous, infamous, villainous, of a deep dye, heinous; flag-rant, -itious; atrocious, incarnate, accursed.

Mephistophelian, satanic, diabolic, hellish, infernal, stygian, fiend-ish, -like, hell-born, demoniacal, devilish.

mis-created, -begotten; demoralized, corrupt, depraved.

evil-minded, -disposed; ill-conditioned; malevolent &c. 907; heart-, grace-, shame-, virtue-less; abandoned, lost to virtue; unconscionable; sunk -, lost -, deep -, steeped- in iniquity.

incorrigible, irreclaimable, obdurate, reprobate, past praying for; culpable, reprehensible &c. (*guilty*) 947.

unjustifiable; in-defensible, -excusable; inexpiable, unpardonable, irremissible.

weak, frail, lax, infirm, imperfect, indiscreet; demoralizing, degrading.

**Adv.** wrong; sinfully &c. *adj.*; without excuse.

**Int.** *O tempora! O mores!*

**946. Innocence. — N.** innocence; guiltlessness &c. *adj.*; incorruption, impeccability.

clean hands, clear conscience, *mens sibi conscia recti*.

innocent, new born babe, lamb, dove.

**V.** be -innocent &c. *adj.*; *nil conscire sibi nullâ pallescere culpâ.*

**947. Guilt.—N.** guilt, -iness; culpability; crimin-ality, -ousness; deviation from rectitude &c. (*improbity*) 940; sinfulness &c. (*vice*) 945; peccability.

mis-conduct, -behaviour, -doing, -deed; malpractice, fault, sin, error, transgression; dereliction, delinquency; indiscretion, lapse, slip, trip, *faux pas*;

\* Most of these adjectives are applicable both to the act and to the agent.

acquit &c. 970; exculpate &c. (*vindicate*) 937.

' **Adj.** innocent, not guilty; unguilty; guilt-, fault-, sin-, stain-, blood-, spotless; clear, immaculate; *rectus in curiâ*; un-spotted, -blemished, -erring; undefiled &c. 939; unhardened, Saturnian; Arcadian &c. (*artless*) 703.

in-, un-culpable; unblam-ed, -able; blameless, inerrable, above suspicion; irrepr-oachable, -ovable, -ehensible; un-exceptionable, -objectionable, -impeachable; salvable; venial &c. 937.

harmless; in-offensive, -noxious, -nocuous; dove-, lamb-like; pure, harmless as doves; innocent as -a lamb, - the babe unborn; more sinned against than sinning.

virtuous &c. 944; un-reproved, -impeached, -reproached.

**Adv.** innocently &c. *adj.*; with clean hands; with a -clear, - safe- conscience.

**948. Good Man. — N.** good man, worthy.

good woman, goddess, *madonna*, virgin.

model, paragon &c. (*perfection*) 650; good example; hero, demigod, seraph, angel; innocent &c. 946; saint &c. (*piety*) 987; benefactor &c. 912; philanthropist &c. 910; Aristides.

brick, trump, rough diamond, ugly duckling.

salt of the earth; one in ten thousand; one of the best.

**Phr.** *si sic omnes!*

peccadillo; flaw, blot, omission; fail-ing, -ure.

offence, trespass; mis-demeanour, -feasance, -prision; tort; mal-efaction, -feasance, -versation; crime, felony.

enormity, atrocity, outrage; deadly -, mortal -, unpardonable- sin; died without a name.

*corpus delicti.*

**Adj.** guilty, to blame, culpable, peccable, in fault, censurable, reprehensible, blameworthy, uncommendable, illaudable; weighed in the balance and found wanting; exceptionable, objectionable.

**Adv.** *in flagrante delicto*; red-handed, in the very act.

**949. Bad Man.—N.** bad man, wrongdoer, worker of iniquity; evil-doer &c. 913; sinner; the -wicked &c. 945; bad example.

rascal, scoundrel, villain, miscreant, caitiff; wretch, reptile, viper, serpent, cockatrice, basilisk, urchin; tiger, monster; devil &c. (*demon*) 980; devil incarnate; demon in human shape, Nana Sahib; hell-hound, -cat; rake-hell.

bad woman, jade, Jezebel, adultress, &c. 962.

scamp, scapegrace, rip, runagate, ne'er-do-well, reprobate, *roué*, rake; limb; one who has sold himself to the devil, fallen angel, *âme damnée, vaurien,* mauvais sujet, loose fish, sad dog; lost -, black- sheep; castaway, recreant, defaulter; prodigal &c. 818; libertine &c. 962.

rough, rowdy, ugly customer, ruffian, hoodlum, bully; Jonathan Wild; hangman; incendiary; thief &c. 792; murderer &c. 361.

culprit, delinquent, criminal, malefactor, misdemeanant; felon; convict, jail-bird, ticket-of-leave man; outlaw.

blackguard, *polisson*, loafer, sneak; raps-, ras-callion; cullion, mean wretch, varlet, kern, *âme-de-boue, drôle*; cur, dog, hound, whelp, mongrel; lown, loon, runnion, outcast, vagabond; rogue &c. (*knave*) 941; scum of the earth, riff-raff; *Arcades ambo.*

**Int.** sirrah!

**950. Penitence.—N.** penitence, contrition, compunction, repentance, remorse; regret &c. 833.

self-reproach, -reproof. -accusation,

**951. Impenitence.—N.** impenitence, irrepentance, recusance.

hardness of heart, seared conscience, induration, obduracy.

-condemnation, -humiliation; stings –, pangs –, qualms –, prickings –, twinge –, twitch –, touch –, voice- of conscience; compunctious visitings of nature.

acknowledgment, confession &c. (*disclosure*) 529; apology &c. 952; recantation &c. 607; penance &c. 952; resipiscence.

awakened conscience, deathbed repentance, *locus pænitentiæ*, stool of repentance, cutty stool.

penitent, Magdalen, prodigal son, returned prodigal, a sadder and a wiser man.

**V.** repent, be sorry for; be -penitent &c. *adj.*; rue; regret &c. 833; think better of; recant &c. 607; knock under &c. (*submit*) 725; plead guilty; sing -*miserere*, – *de profundis*; cry *peccavi*; own oneself in the wrong; acknowledge, confess &c. (*disclose*) 529; humble oneself; beg pardon &c. (*apologize*) 952; turn over a new leaf, put on the new man, turn from sin; reclaim; repent in sackcloth and ashes &c. (*do penance*) 952; learn by experience.

**Adj.** penitent; repenting &c. *v.*; repentant, contrite; conscience-smitten, -stricken; self-accusing, -convicted.

penitenti-al, -ary; chastened, reclaimed; not hardened; unhardened.

**Adv.** *meâ culpâ.*

**Phr.** *peccavi; erubuit; salva res est; vous l'avez voulu, Georges Dandin.*

**V.** be -impenitent &c. *adj.*; steel –, harden- the heart; die -game, – and make no sign.

**Adj.** impenitent, uncontrite, obdurate; hard, -ened; seared, recusant; unrepentant; relent-, remorse-, grace-, shrift-less.

lost, incorrigible, irreclaimable.

unre-claimed, -formed; unrepented, unatoned.

---

**952. Atonement.—N.** atonement, reparation; compromise, composition; compensation &c. 30; quittance, quits; indemni-ty, -fication; expiation, redemption, reclamation, conciliation, propitiation.

amends, apology, *amende honorable*, satisfaction; peace –, sin –, burnt- offering; scapegoat, sacrifice.

penance, fasting, maceration, sackcloth and ashes, white sheet, shrift, flagellation, lustration; purga-tion, -tory.

**V.** atone, – for; expiate; propitiate; make -amends, – good; reclaim, redeem, repair, ransom, absolve, purge, shrive, do penance, stand in a white sheet, repent in sackcloth and ashes.

set one's house in order, wipe off old scores, make matters up; pay the -forfeit, – penalty.

apologize, beg pardon, express regret, *faire amende honorable*, give satisfaction; come –, fall- down on one's -knees, – marrow bones.

**Adj.** propitiatory, expiatory; sacrific, -ial, -atory; piacul-ar, -ous.

## 4°. MORAL PRACTICE

**953. Temperance.—N.** temperance moderation, sobriety, soberness.

forbearance, abnegation; self-denial, -restraint, -control &c. (*resolution*) 604.

frugality; vegetarianism, teetotal-ism, total abstinence, prohibition; abst-inence, -emiousness, asceticism &c. 955; system of -Pythagoras, – Cornaro; Pythagorism, Stoicism.

**954. Intemperance.—N.** intemperance; sensuality, animalism, carnality; pleasure; effeminacy, silkiness; luxur-y, -iousness; lap of -pleasure, – luxury.

indulgence; high-, free- living, inabstinence, self-indulgence; voluptuousness &c. *adj.*; epicur-ism, -eanism; sybaritism.

vegetarian; Pythagorean, gymnoso-
phist; teetotaler &c. 958; abstainer.
**V.** be -temperate &c. *adj.*; abstain,
forbear, refrain, deny oneself, spare;
know when one has had enough; take
the pledge; look not upon the wine
when it is red.
**Adj.** temperate, moderate, sober,
frugal, sparing; abst-emious, -inent;
within compass; measured &c. (*suf-
ficient*) 639.
Pythagorean; vegetarian; teetotal,
pussy-foot.

dissipation; licentiousness &c. *adj.*,
debauchery; crapulence.
revel-s, -ry; debauch, carousal, jolli-
fication, drinking bout, wassail, Satur-
nalia, orgies; excess, too much; intoxi-
cation &c. 959.
Circean cup; drug habit &c. 663.
**V.** be -intemperate &c. *adj.*; indulge,
exceed; live -well, – high, – on the fat
of the land; give a loose to -indulgence
&c. *n.*; dine not wisely but too well;
wallow in -voluptuousness &c. *n.*;
plunge into dissipation.
revel, rake, live hard, run riot, sow
one's wild oats; slake one's -appetite,
– thirst; swill; pamper.

**Adj.** intemperate, inabstinent, intoxicated &c. 959; sensual, self-
indulgent; voluptuous, luxurious, licentious, wild, dissolute, rakish,
fast, debauched.
brutish, crapulous, swinish, piggish, porcine, hoggish, bestial.
Paphian, Epicurean, Sybaritical; bred –, nursed- in the lap of
luxury; indulged, pampered, full-fed.

**954a. Sensualist.—N.** Sybarite, voluptuary, Sardanapalus, man of
pleasure, carpet knight; epicure, -an; *gourm-et, -and*; gormandizer,
gutling, glutton, pig, hog; votary –, swine- of Epicurus; sensualist;
Heliogabalus; free –, hard- liver; libertine &c. 962; hedonist.

**955. Asceticism.—N.** asceticism, puritanism, sabbatarianism; cyni-
cism, austerity; total abstinence.
mortification, maceration, sackcloth and ashes, flagellation; penance
&c. 952; fasting &c. 956; martyrdom.
ascetic; anchor-et, -ite; martyr; *Heautontimorumenos*; hermit &c.
(*recluse*) 893; puritan, sabbatarian, cynic.
**Adj.** ascetic, austere, puritanical; cynical; over-religious.

**956. Fasting. — N.** fasting; xero-
phagy; famishment, starvation; bant-
ing.
fast, *jour maigre*; fast –, banyan-
day; Lent, quadragesima; Rama-dan,
-zan; spare –, meagre- diet; lenten
-diet, – entertainment; *soupe maigre*,
short -rations, – commons; Barmecide
feast; hunger strike.
**V.** fast, starve, clem, famish, perish
with hunger; dine with Duke Hum-
phrey; make two bites of a cherry.
**Adj.** lenten, quadragesimal; unfed;
starved &c. *v.*; half-starved; fasting
&c. *v.*; hungry &c. 865.

**957. Gluttony.—N.** gluttony; greed;
greediness &c. *adj.*; voracity.
epicurism; good –, high- living;
edacity, gulosity, crapulence; gutt-,
guzz-ling; over-indulgence.
good cheer, blow out; feast &c. (*food*)
298; gastronomy.
epicure, *bon vivant, gourmand*; glut-
ton, cormorant, hog, belly-god, Apicius,
gastronome, gormandizer.
**V.** gormandize, gorge; over-gorge,
-eat- oneself; engorge, eat one's fill,
cram, stuff, stodge, glut, satiate;
gutt-le, guzz-le; bolt, devour, gobble
up; gulp &c. (*swallow food*) 298; raven,
eat out of house and home.
have the stomach of an ostrich;

play a good knife and fork &c. (*appetite*) 865.
pamper, indulge.

Adj. gluttonous, greedy; gormandizing &c. *v.*; edacious, omnivorous, crapulent, swinish, voracious, devouring.
pampered; over-fed, -gorged.

**958. Sobriety.**—N. sobriety; teetotalism, temperance &c. 953.

water-drinker; teetotal-er, -ist; abstainer, Good Templar, Rechabite, band of hope; prohibitionist, pussyfoot.
V. take the pledge.
Adj. sober, – as a judge; dry, on the water wagon.

**959. Drunkenness.**—N. drunkenness &c. *adj.*; intemperance; drinking &c. *v.*; inebri-ety, -ation; ebri-ety, -osity; befuddlement; insobriety; intoxication; temulency, bibacity, wine-bibbing; com-, potation; deep potations, bacchanals, *bacchanalia*, libations.
oino-, dipso-mania; *delirium tremens*, d.t.; alcohol, -ism.

drink; alcoholic drinks, alcohol, booze; gin, blue ruin, grog, brandy, port wine; punch, -bowl; cup, rosy wine, flowing bowl; drop, – too much; dram; beer, wine, spirits &c. (*beverage*) 298; cocktail, nip, peg; stirrup cup.

drunkard, sot, toper, tippler, bibber, wine-bibber; hard –, gin –, dram- drinker; soak, soaker, sponge, tun; love-, toss-pot; thirsty soul, reveller, carouser; Bacchanal, -ian; Bacch-al, -ante; devotee to Bacchus, dipsomaniac.

V. get –, be- drunk &c. *adj.*; see double; take a -drop, – glass- too much; drink, tipple, tope, booze, bouse, guzzle, swill, soak, sot, lush, bib, swig, carouse; sacrifice at the shrine of Bacchus; take to drinking; drink -hard, – deep, – like a fish; have one's swill, drain the cup, splice the main brace, take a hair of the dog that bit you.

liquor, – up; wet one's whistle, take a whet; lift one's elbow; crack a –, pass the- bottle; toss off &c. (*drink up*) 298; go to the -ale, – public-house.

make one -drunk &c. *adj.*; inebriate, fuddle, fuzzle, get into one's head.

Adj. drunk, tipsy; intoxicated; inebri-ous, -ate, -ated; in one's cups; in a state of -intoxication &c. *n.*; temulent, -ive; fuddled, mellow, cut, boosy, fou, fresh, merry, elevated, squiffy; plastered, befuddled, sozzled; flush, -ed; flustered, disguised, groggy, beery; topheavy; pot-valiant, glorious; potulent; over-come, -taken; whittled, screwed, tight, primed, oiled, corned, raddled, sewed up, lushy, nappy, muddled, muzzy, bosky, obfuscated, maudlin; crapulous, dead –, blind- drunk.

*inter pocula*; in –, the worse for- liquor, having had a drop too much, half seas over, three sheets in the wind; under the table, blind to the world, one over the eight.

drunk as -a piper, – a fiddler, – a lord, – Chloe, – an owl, – David's sow, – a wheelbarrow.

drunken, bibacious, bibulous, sottish; given –, addicted- to -drink, – the bottle; toping &c. *v.*; wet.

Phr. *nunc est bibendum.*

**960. Purity.**—N. purity; decency, decorum, delicacy; continence, chastity, honesty, virtue, modesty, shame; pudicity, *pucelage*, virginity.
vestal, virgin, Joseph, Hippolytus; Lucretia, Diana; prude.

**961. Impurity.**—N. impurity; uncleanness &c. (*filth*) 653; immodesty; grossness &c. *adj.*; indelicacy, indecency; impudicity; obscenity, ribaldry, smut, bawdry, *double entendre*, *équivoque*; Aretinism; pornography.

**Adj.** pure, undefiled, modest, delicate, decent, decorous; *virginibus puerisque*; chaste, continent, virtuous, honest, Platonic.

—————

concupiscence, lust, carnality, flesh, salacity; pruriency, lechery, lasciviency, lubricity, lewdness.

incontinence, intrigue, *faux pas*; *amour*, *-ette*; gallantry; debauchery, libertinism, *libertinage*, fornication; *liaison*; wenching, venery, dissipation.

seduction; defloration, defilement, abuse, violation, rape; incest.

social evil, harlotry, stupration, whoredom, concubinage, cuckoldom, adultery, advoutry, *crim. con.*; free love.

seraglio, harem, zenana; brothel, bagnio, stew, bawdy-house, *lupanar*, house of ill fame, *bordel*, kip.

**V.** be -impure &c. *adj.*; intrigue; debauch, defile, assault, attack, seduce; prostitute; abuse, violate, deflower; commit -adultery &c. *n.*

**Adj.** impure; unclean &c. (*dirty*) 653; not to be mentioned to ears polite; immodest, shameless; in-decorous, -delicate, -decent; loose, suggestive, *risqué*, coarse, gross, broad, free, equivocal, smutty, fulsome, ribald, obscene, bawdy, pornographic.

concupiscent, prurient, lickerish, rampant, lustful; carnal, -minded; lewd, lascivious, lecherous, libidinous, erotic, ruttish, salacious; Paphian; voluptuous; incestuous.

unchaste, light, wanton, licentious, adulterous, debauched, dissolute; of -loose character, – easy virtue; frail, gay, riggish, incontinent, meretricious, rakish, gallant, dissipated; no better than she should be; on the -town, – streets, – *pavé*, – loose.

adulterous, incestuous, bestial.

**962. Libertine.**—N. libertine; voluptuary &c. 954*a*; rake, debauchee, loose fish, rip, rake-hell, fast man; *intrigant*, gallant, seducer, fornicator, lecher, satyr, goat, whoremonger, *paillard*, adulterer, gay deceiver, Lothario, Don Juan, Bluebeard.

adulteress, advoutress, courtesan, prostitute, strumpet, tart, hustler, chippy, broad, harlot, whore, punk, *fille de joie*; woman, – of the town; street-walker, Cyprian, miss, piece; frail sisterhood, fallen woman; demirep, wench, trollop, trull, baggage, hussy, drab, bitch, jade, skit, rig, quean, mopsy, slut, minx, harridan; woman -of easy virtue &c. (*unchaste*) 961; wanton, fornicatress; Jezebel, Messalina, Delilah, Thaïs, Phryne, Aspasia, Lais, *lorette, cocotte, petite dame, grisette*; *demimondaine*; white slave.

concubine, mistress, fancy woman, kept woman, doxy, *chère amie, bona roba.*

pimp; pand-er, -ar; bawd, *conciliatrix*, procuress, mackerel; wittol.

## 5°. INSTITUTIONS

**963. Legality.**—N. legality; legitima-*cy*, -teness, legitimization.

legislature; law, code, *corpus juris*, constitution, pandect, charter, act, enactment, statute, rule; canon &c. (*precept*) 697; ordinance, institution; regulation; by-, bye-law, rescript; decree &c. (*order*) 741; *ordonnance*;

**964.** ⌊Absence or violation of law.⌋ **Illegality.**—N. lawlessness; breach –, violation- of law; disobedience &c. 742; unconformity &c. 83.

arbitrariness &c. *adj.*; antinomy, violence, brute force, despotism, outlawry.

mob –, lynch –, club –, Lydford –,

standing order; *plébiscite* &c. (*choice*) 609.

legal process; form, -ula, -ality; rite; arm of the law; *habeas corpus*.

[Science of law] jurisprudence, nomology; legislation, codification.

equity, common law; *lex* -, *lex nonscripta*, unwritten law; law of nations, international law, *jus gentium*; *jus civile*; civil -, criminal -, canon -, statute -, ecclesiastical- law; *lex mercatoria*.

constitutional-ism, -ity; justice &c. 922.

V. legalize, legitimize; enact, ordain; decree &c. (*order*) 741; pass a law; legislate; codify, formulate; authorize.

Adj. legal, legitimate; according to law; vested, constitutional, chartered, legalized; lawful &c. (*permitted*) 760; statut-able, -ory; legislat-orial, -ive.

Adv. legally &c. *adj.*; in the eye of the law; *de jure*.

martial -, drumhead- law; *coup d'état*; *le droit du plus fort*; *argumentum ad baculum*.

illegality, informality, unlawfulness, illegitimacy, bar sinister.

trover and conversion; smuggling, boot-legging, rum-running, poaching; simony.

speakeasy, speakie, blind pig.

V. offend against -, violate- the law; set the law at defiance, ride rough-shod over, drive a coach and six through a statute; make the law a dead letter, take the law into one's own hands.

smuggle, run, poach.

Adj. illegal; prohibited &c. 761; not allowed, unlawful, illegitimate, illicit, contraband, actionable.

unchartered, unconstitutional; unwarrant-ed, -able; unauthorized; informal, unofficial; in-, extra-judicial.

lawless, arbitrary; despotic, -al; summary, irresponsible; un-answer-able, -accountable.

null and void; a dead letter.

Adv. illegally &c. *adj.*; with a high hand, in violation of law.

**965. Jurisdiction.** [Executive.]—N. jurisdiction, judicature, administration of justice, soc; executive, commission of the peace; magistracy &c. (*authority*) 737.

judge &c. 967; tribunal &c. 966; municipality, corporation, bailiwick, shrievalty; lord lieutenant; lord -, mayor, city manager, alderman &c. 745; sheriff, bailie, shrieve, chief -, constable; police, - force; constabulary, bumbledom.

officer; proctor, high -, commissioner; bailiff, tipstaff, bum-bailiff, catchpoll, beadle; police-man, -constable, -sergeant; *sbirro*, *alguazil*, *gendarme*, kavass, *lictor*, macebearer, *huissier*, bedel.

press-gang; exciseman, gauger, custom-house officer, *douanier*.

coroner, edile, ædile, portreeve, paritor; *posse comitatus*.

V. judge, sit in judgment.

Adj. executive, administrative, municipal; inquisitorial, causidical; judic-atory, -iary, -ial; juridical.

Adv. *coram judice*.

**966. Tribunal.**—N. tribunal, court, board, bench, judicatory, curia; court of -justice, - law, - arbitration; inquisition; guild.

justice -, judgement -, mercy- seat; woolsack; bar, - of justice; dock; forum, hustings, *bureau*, drum-head; jury-, witness-box.

senate-house, town-hall, theatre; House of -Lords, - Commons.

assize, eyre; ward-, burgh-mote; superior courts of Westminster; court of record, oyer and terminer, - assize, - appeal, - error; High court of -Judicature, - Appeal; Judicial Committee of the Privy Council; Star-Chamber; Court of -Chancery, - King's *or* Queen's Bench, - Exchequer, - Common Pleas, - Probate, - Arches, - Admiralty, - Criminal Appeal; Lords Justices' -, Rolls -, Vice-Chancellor's -,

Stannary –, Divorce –, Palatine –, ecclesiastical –, county –, police-court; sessions; quarter –, petty- sessions; court -leet, – baron, – of pie poudre, – of common council; board of green cloth.

court-martial; drum-head court-martial; *durbar*, divan; Areopagus; *rota*.

Adj. judicial &c. 965; appellate; curial.

**967. Judge.—N.** judge; justi-ce, -ciar, -ciary; chancellor; justice –; judge- of assize; recorder, common serjeant; puisne –, assistant – county court- judge; conservator –, justice- of the peace, J.P.; court &c. (*tribunal*) 966; grand –, petty –, coroner's- jury; panel, juror, juryman; twelve men in a box; magistrate, police magistrate, stipendiary, the great unpaid, beak; his -worship, – honour, – lordship; deemster, moderator.

Lord -Chancellor, – Justice; Master of the Rolls, Vice-Chancellor; Lord Chief -Justice, – Baron; Mr. Justice; Baron, – of the Exchequer.

jurat, assessor; arbi-ter, -trator; umpire; refer-ee, -endary; revising barrister; domesman; censor &c. (*critic*) 480; official –, receiver.

archon, tribune, prætor, *ephor*, syndic, *podestà*, mullah, ulema, mufti, cadi, kadi; Rhadamanthus.

litigant &c. (*accusation*) 938.

**V.** adjudge &c. (*determine*) 480; try a -case, – prisoner.

Adj. judicial &c. 965. Phr. 'a Daniel come to judgment.'

**968. Lawyer.—N.** lawyer, jurist, legist, civilian, pundit, publicist, jurisconsult, legal adviser, advocate; barrister, – at law; counsel, -lor; King's *or* Queen's counsel; K.C.; Q.C.; silk gown, leader; junior, – counsel; stuff gown, serjeant-at-law, bencher; tubman; judge &c. 967.

bar, legal profession, gentleman of the long robe; junior –, outer –, inner- bar; Inns of Court; equity draftsman, conveyancer, pleader, special pleader.

solicitor, attorney, proctor; notary, – public; scrivener, cursitor; writer, – to the signet; S.S.C.; limb of the law; pettifogger.

**V.** practise -at, – within- the bar; plead; call –, be called- -to, – within- the bar; take silk.

Adj. learned in the law; at the bar; forensic.

**969. Lawsuit.—N.** lawsuit, suit, action, cause, petition; litigation; dispute &c. 713.

citation, arraignment, prosecution, impeachment; accusation &c. 938; presentment, true bill, indictment.

apprehension, arrest; committal; imprisonment &c. (*restraint*) 751.

writ, summons, subpœna, -duces tecum, latitat, nisi prius; *habeas corpus.*

pleadings; declaration, bill, claim; *procès-verbal*, bill of right, information, *corpus delicti*; affidavit, state of facts; answer, replication, plea, demurrer, rebutter, rejoinder; surre-butter, -joinder.

suitor, party to a suit; litigant &c. 938; libellant.

hearing, trial; verdict &c. (*judgment*) 480; appeal, – motion; writ of error; *certiorari.*

case, decision, precedent, ruling; decided case, reports.

**V.** go to –, appeal to the- law; bring to -justice, – trial, – the bar; put on trial, pull up; accuse &c. 938; prefer –, file- a claim &c. *n.*; take the law of, inform against.

serve with a writ, cite, apprehend, arraign, sue, prosecute, bring an action against, indict, impeach, attach, distrain, commit; arrest; summon, -s; give in charge &c. (*restrain*) 751.

empanel a jury, implead, join issue; close the pleadings; set down for hearing.

try, hear a cause; sit in judgment; adjudicate &c. 480.

**Adj.** litigious &c. (*quarrelsome*) 713; *qui tam*; *coram* –, *sub- judice.*

**Adv.** *pendente lite.*

**Phr.** *adhuc sub judice lis est.*

---

**970. Acquittal. — N.** acquit-tal, -ment; clearance, exculpation, exoneration; discharge &c. (*release*) 750; *quietus*, absolution, compurgation, reprieve, respite; pardon &c. (*forgiveness*) 918.

[Exemption from punishment] impunity, immunity.

**V.** acquit, exculpate, exonerate, clear; absolve, whitewash, assoil, discharge, release; liberate &c. 750.

reprieve, respite; pardon &c. (*forgive*) 918; let off, – scot free.

**Adj.** acquitted &c. *v.*; un-condemned, -punished, -chastised; recommended to mercy.

**971. Condemnation.—N.** condemnation, conviction proscription, damnation; death warrant; penalty &c. 974; attain-der, -ture, -tment.

**V.** condemn, convict, cast, bring home to, find guilty, damn, doom, sign the death warrant, sentence, pass sentence on, attaint, confiscate, proscribe, sequestrate; non-suit.

disapprove &c. 932; accuse &c. 938.

stand condemned.

**Adj.** condem-, dam-natory; condemned &c. *v.*; non-suited &c. (*failure*) 732; self-convicted.

**Phr.** *mutato nomine de te fabula narratur.*

---

**972. Punishment. — N.** punishment, punition; chast-isement, -ening; correction, castigation.

discipline, infliction, trial; judgement; penalty &c. 974; retribution; thunderbolt, Nemesis; requital &c. (*reward*) 973; penology; retributive justice.

lash, scaffold &c. (*instrument of punishment*) 975; imprisonment &c. (*restraint*) 751; chain gang; transportation, banishment, expulsion, deportation, exile, involuntary exile, ostracism; penal servitude, hard labour; galleys &c. 975; beating &c. *v.*; flagellation, fustigation, ga-ntlet, *strappado, estrapade, bastinado, argumentum ad baculum,* stick law, rap on the knuckles, box on the ear; blow &c. (*impulse*) 276; stripe, cuff, kick, buffet, pummel; slap, – in the face; wipe, douse; *coup de grâce*; torture, rack; picket, -ing; *dragonnade*; capital punishment, extreme penalty; execution; hanging &c. *v.*; de-capitation, -collation; *garrotte*; electrocution, lethal chamber; crucifixion, impalement; martyrdom, *auto-da-fé; noyade; hara-kiri,* happy despatch.

**V.** punish; chast-ise, -en; castigate, correct, inflict punishment, administer correction, deal retributive justice.

visit upon, pay; pay –, serve- out; settle with, get even with, get one's own back; do for; make short work of, give a lesson to, strafe, serve one right, make an example of; have a rod in pickle for; give it one.

strike &c. 276; deal a blow to, administer the lash, smite; slap, – the face; smack, cuff, box the ears, spank, thwack, thump, beat, lay on, swinge, buffet; thresh, thrash, pummel, drub, leather, trounce, baste, belabour; lace, – one's jacket; dress, give a -dressing, – down; trim, warm, wipe, tund, cob, bang, strap, comb, lash, lick, larrup, whallop, whop, flog, scourge, whip, birch, cane, give the stick, switch, flagellate, horsewhip, *bastinado*, towel, rub down with an oaken towel, rib roast, dust one's jacket, fustigate, pitch into, lay about one, beat black and blue; beat to a -mummy, – jelly; give a black eye; hit on the head; sandbag.

tar and feather; pelt, stone, lapidate; mast-head, keelhaul.

execute; bring to the -block, – gallows; behead; de-capitate, -collate; guillotine; hang, turn off, gibbet, bowstring, hang, draw and quarter; shoot; decimate; burn; electrocute; break on the wheel, crucify; em-, im-pale; flay; lynch; put to death.

torture; put -on, – to- the rack; picket.

banish, exile; trans-, de-port; expel, ostracize; rusticate; drum out; dismiss, -bar, -bench; strike off the roll, unfrock; post.

suffer, – for, – punishment; be -flogged, – hanged &c.; come to the gallows, dance upon nothing, die in one's shoes; be rightly served.

**Adj.** punishing &c. *v.*; penal; puni-tory, -tive; inflictive, castigatory; punished &c. *v.*

**Int.** *à la lanterne!*

---

**973. Reward.—N.** reward, recompense, remuneration, prize, meed, guerdon, reguerdon; indemni-ty, -fication, price; quittance; compensation; reparation, *ersatz*, assythment, redress; retribution, reckoning, acknowledgment, requital, amends, sop; atonement; consideration, return, *quid pro quo*; salvage, perquisite; vail &c. (*donation*) 784; *douceur*, bribe, bait, baksheesh, tip; hush-, smart-money; blackmail; carcelage; *solatium.*

allowance, salary, stipend, wages; pay, -ment; emolument; tribute; batta, shot, scot; premium, fee, *honorarium*; hire.

crown &c. (*decoration of honour*) 877.

**V.** re-ward, -compense, -pay, -quite; re-, munerate; compensate; fee, tip, bribe; pay one's footing &c. (*pay*) 807; make amends, indemnify, atone; satisfy, acknowledge.

get for one's pains, reap the fruits of.

**Adj.** remunerat-ive, -ory; munerary, compensatory, retributive, reparatory.

---

**974. Penalty.—N.** penalty; retribution &c. (*punishment*) 972; pain, pains and penalties; *peine forte et dure*; penance &c. (*atonement*) 952; the devil to pay.

fine, mulct, amercement; forfeit, -ure; escheat, damages, deodand, sequestration, confiscation, *premunire.*

**V.** penalize, fine, mulct, amerce, sconce, confiscate; sequest-rate, -er; escheat; estreat, forfeit.

---

**975.** [Instrument of punishment.] **Scourge.—N.** scourge, rod, cane, stick; ra-, rat-tan; birch, – rod; rod in pickle; switch, ferule, cudgel, truncheon; rubber hose.

whip, lash, strap, thong, cowhide, knout; cat, – o'-nine-tails, *sjambok*, quirt; rope's end.

pillory, stocks, whipping-post; cuck-, duck-ing stool; brank; triangle, wooden horse, maiden, thumbscrew, boot, rack, wheel, iron heel; treadmill, crank, galleys.

scaffold; block, axe, *guillotine*; stake; cross; gallows, gibbet, Tyburn tree; drop, noose, rope, halter, bowstring;

electric chair, lethal chamber.

house of correction &c. (*prison*) 752.

gaol-, jail-er; executioner; hang-, heads-man; Jack Ketch; lyncher.

## Section V. RELIGIOUS AFFECTIONS

### 1°. Superhuman Beings and Regions

**976. Deity.—N.** Deity, Divinity; God-head, -ship; Omnipotence, Providence.

[Quality of being divine] divin-eness, -ity.

God, Lord, Jehovah, *Deus*; The -Almighty, – Supreme Being, – First Cause; *Ens Entium*; Author –, Creator- of all things; Author of our being; The -Infinite, – Eternal; The All-powerful, -wise, -merciful, -holy; The Omni-potent, -scient.

[Attributes and perfections] infinite -power, – wisdom, – goodness, – justice, – truth, – love, – mercy; omni-potence, -science, -presence; unity, immutability, holiness, glory, majesty, sovereignty, infinity, eternity.

The -Trinity, – Holy Trinity, – Trinity in Unity, – Triune God; Three in One and One in Three.

God the Father; The -Maker, – Creator, – Preserver.

[Functions] creation, preservation, divine government; The-ocracy, -archy; providence; ways –, dealings –, dispensations –, visitations- of Providence.

God the Son, Jesus, Christ; The -Messiah, – Anointed, – Saviour, – Redeemer, – Mediator, – Intercessor, – Advocate, – Judge; The Son of -God, – Man, – David; The Only Begotten; The Lamb of God, The Word; Em-, Im-manuel; The -King of Kings and Lord of Lords, – King of Glory, – Prince of Peace, – Good Shepherd, – Way, – Truth, – Life, – Bread of Life, – Light of the World; The -Lord our, – Sun of- Righteousness.

The -Incarnation, – Hypostatic Union, – Word made Flesh.

[Functions] salvation, redemption, atonement, propitiation, mediation, intercession, judgment.

God the Holy Ghost, The Holy Spirit, Paraclete; The -Comforter, – Consoler, – Spirit of Truth, – Dove.

[Functions] inspiration, unction, regeneration, sanctification, consolation.

eon, æon, special providence, *Deus ex machinâ*; Avatar.

**V.** create, uphold, preserve, govern &c.

atone, redeem, save, propitiate, mediate &c.

predestinate, elect, call, ordain, bless, justify, sanctify, glorify &c.

**Adj.** almighty, holy, hallowed, sacred, divine, heavenly, celestial; messianic; sacrosanct; all-powerful, -wise, -seeing, -knowing; omnipotent, omniscient; supreme.

super-human, -natural; ghostly, spiritual, hyperphysical, unearthly; the-istic, -ocratic, deistic; anointed.

**Adv.** *jure divino*, by divine right; *Deo volente*, D.V.

**977.** [Beneficent spirits.] **Angel.—N.**
angel, archangel; heavenly host, choir invisible, host of heaven, sons of God; Michael, Gabriel &c.; seraph, -im; cherub, -im; ministering spirit, morn-

**978.** [Maleficent spirits.] **Satan.—N.**
Satan, the Devil, Lucifer, Ahrimanes, Delial, Sammael, Zamiel, Beelzebub, the Prince of the Devils; Mephistopheles, his satanic majesty.*

* The slang expressions 'the -deuce, – dickens, – old Gentleman; old -Nick, – Scratch, – Horny, – Harry, – Gooseberry,' have not been inserted in the text.

ing star; saint, *Madonna*; Our Lady, the Blessed Virgin, the Virgin Mary.
Adj. angelic, seraphic, cherubic.

———

-common enemy, – angel of the bottomless pit; Abaddon, Apollyon, Mammon.

the tempter; the evil -one, – spirit; the -author of evil, – wicked one, – old Serpent; the Prince of -darkness, – this world, – the power of the air: the -foul, – arch- fiend; the devil incarnate; the

fallen angels, unclean spirits, devils; the -rulers, – powers- of darkness; inhabitants of Pandemonium; demon &c. 980.

diabolism; devil-ism, -ship, -dom, -ry, -worship; *diablerie*; satanism, manicheism; the cloven foot; black magic &c. 992.

Adj. satanic, diabolic, devilish, infernal, hell-born.

*Heathen, Mythological and other fabulous Deities and Powers**

**979. Jupiter.—N.** god, -dess; heathen gods and goddesses; Pantheon; Jupiter, Jove, Zeus, Apollo, Mars, Mercury, Neptune, Vulcan, Bacchus, Pluto, Saturn, Cupid, Eros, Pan; Juno, Ceres, Proserpina, Diana, Minerva, Pallas Athene, Venus, Aphrodite, Vesta; The Fates &c. 601.

Allah, Brahma, Vishnu, Siva, Shiva, Krishna, Juggernaut, Buddha; Ra, Isis, Osiris; Belus, Bel, Baal, Asteroth &c.; Thor, Odin; Mumbo Jumbo; good –, tutelary- genius; demiurge, familiar, – spirit; Sibyl; fairy, fay; sylph, -id; Ariel, peri, nymph, nereid, dryad, oread, sea-maid, Banshee, Benshie, Ormuzd; Oberon, Titania, Mab, hamadryad, naiad, mermaid, kelpie, Ondine, nix, nixie, sprite; denizens of the air; pixy &c. (*bad spirit*) 980.

mythology; heathen –, fairy- mythology; Lemprière, folklore.

Adj. fairy-, sylph-like; sylphic.

———

**980. Demon.—N.** demon, -ry, -ism, -ology; evil genius, fiend, familiar, – spirit, devil; bad –, unclean- spirit; cacodemon, incubus, Frankenstein's monster, succubus and succuba, Titan, Shedim, Mephistopheles, Asmodeus, Moloch, Belial, Ahriman, fury, The Furies &c. 900; harpy; Friar Rush.

vampire, ghoul; af-, ef-freet; afrite; ogre, -ss; gnome, gin, djinn, imp, deev, *lamia*; bo-gie, -gle; nis, kobold, flibbertigibbet, fairy, brownie, pixy, elf, dwarf, urchin, Puck, Robin Goodfellow; lepre-, cluri-chaune; troll, dwerger, sprite, oaf, changeling, bad fairy, nixe, pigwidgeon, Will-o'-thewisp; Erl King.

[Supernatural appearance] ghost, spectre, apparition, genie, spirit, shade, shadow, vision, phantom &c. 443; materialization (*spiritualism*) 992; hob-, goblin; wraith, spook, werwolf, boggart, banshee, *loup-garou, lemures*; evil eye.

nisse, necks; mer-man, -maid, -folk; siren, Lorelei; satyr, faun.

Adj. supernatural, weird, uncanny, unearthly, spectral; ghost-ly, -like; elf-in, -like; fiend-ish, -like; impish, demoniacal; haunted.

**981. Heaven.—N.** heaven; kingdom of -heaven, – God; heavenly kingdom; throne –, presence- of God; inheritance of the saints in light.

Paradise, Eden, abode of the blessed; Holy City, New Jerusalem; celestial bliss, glory.

[Mythological -heaven] Olympus; [– paradise] Elysium, Elysian fields, Arcadia, bowers of bliss, garden of the Hesperides, Islands of the Blessed;

**982. Hell.—N.** hell, bottomless pit, place of torment; habitation of fallen angels; Pandemonium, Abaddon, Domdaniel.

hell fire; everlasting -fire, – torment: lake of fire and brimstone; fire that is never quenched, worm that never dies.

purgatory, limbo, gehenna, abyss.

[Mythological hell] Tartarus, Hades, Avernus, Styx, Stygian creek, pit of Acheron, Cocytus, Phlegethon, Lethe;

\* Only a selection of those best known to literature is included.

happy hunting-ground; third –, seventh- heaven; Valhalla (Scandinavian); Nirvana (Buddhist).

future state, eternity, eternal life, life after death, eternal home, resurrection, translation; resuscitation &c. 660; apotheosis, deification.

Adj. heavenly, celestial, supernal, unearthly, from on high, paradisiacal, beatific, elysian, Olympian, Arcadian.

infernal regions, *inferno*, shades below, realms of Pluto.

Pluto, Rhadamanthus, Erebus, Charon, Cerberus; Tophet.

Adj. hellish, infernal, stygian.

---

## 2°. RELIGIOUS DOCTRINES

**983. [Religious Knowledge.] Theology.—N.** Theology (natural and revealed); Theo-gony, -sophy; Divinity; Hagio-logy, -graphy; Caucasian mystery; monotheism; religion; religious -persuasion, – sect, – denomination; cult; creed &c. *(belief)* 484; articles –, declaration –, profession –, confession- of faith.

theolog-ue, -ian; divine, schoolman, canonist, monotheist.

Adj. theological, religious; canonical; denominational; sectarian &c. 984.

**983a. Orthodoxy.—N.** orthodoxy; strictness, soundness, religious truth, true faith; truth &c. 494.

Christian-ity, -ism; Catholic-ism, -ity; 'the faith once delivered to the saints'; hyperorthodoxy &c. 984; iconoclasm.

the Holy –, the Orthodox- Church; Catholic –, Universal –, Apostolic –, Established- Church; temple of the Holy Ghost; Church –, body –, members –, disciples –, followers- of Christ; Christian, – community; true believer; canonist &c. *(theologian)* 983; Christendom, collective body of Christians, the Church Militant.

canons &c. *(belief)* 484; thirty-nine articles; Apostles' –, Nicene –, Athanasian- Creed; Church Catechism; textuary.

Adj. orthodox, sound, literal, strict, faithful, catholic, schismless, Christian, evangelical, scriptural, divine, monotheistic; true &c. 494.

High –, Low –, Broad –, Free-Church; ultramontanism; monasticism; pap-ism, -istry; papacy; Anglican-, Catholic-, Roman-ism; popery, Scarlet Lady, Church of Rome, Greek Church; Christian Science, The Church of Christ Scientist.

**984. Heterodoxy. [Sectarianism.]—N.** heterodoxy; error &c. 495; false doctrine, heresy, schism; schismaticism, -alness; recusancy, backsliding, apostasy; atheism &c. *(irreligion)* 989.

bigotry &c. *(obstinacy)* 606; fanaticism, iconoclasm; hyperorthodoxy, precisianism, bibliolatry, hagiolatry, sabbatarianism, puritanism; idolatry &c. 991; superstition &c. *(credulity)* 486; dissent &c. 489.

sectar-ism, -ianism; nonconformity; secularism; syncretism, religious sects; the clash of creeds.

protestant-, advent-, Arian-, Erastian-, Calvin-, quaker-, method-, anabapt-, Pusey-, tractarian-, ritual-, Origen-, Sabellian-, Socinian-, De-, The-, mon-, material-, positiv-, latitudinarian-ism &c.

pagan-, heathen-, ethic-ism; mythology; animism; poly-, di-, tri-, pantheism; dualism; heathendom.

Juda-, Gentil-, Mahometan-, Islam-, Turc-, Brahmin-, Hindoo-, Buddh-, Lama-, Confucian-, Shinto-, Sabian-, Gnostic-, Soofee-, Hylothe-, Mormon-ism.

Theosophy; Spiritualism, Occultism.

heretic, antichrist; pagan, heathen; pai-, pay-nim; *giaour*; gentile; pan-, poly-theist; idolator; misbeliever, apostate, backslider.

bigot &c. (*obstinacy*) 606; fanatic, dervish, abdal, iconoclast.

latitudinarian, limitarian, Deist, Theist, Unitarian; positivist, materialist; agnostic, skeptic &c. 989.

schismatic; sectar-y, -ian, -ist; seceder, separatist, recusant, dissenter; non-conformist, -juror; Huguenot, Protestant; orthodox dissenter, Congregationalist, Independent; Episcopalian, Presbyterian; Lutheran, Calvinist, Quaker, Methodist, Wesleyan; Ana-, Baptist; Dunker; Mormon, Latter-day Saint, Irvingite, Sandemanian, Glassite, Erastian; Sub-, Supra-lapsarian; Gentoo, Antinomian, Swedenborgian, Adventist, Plymouth Brother; Theosophist &c.

Catholic, Roman Catholic, Romanist, papist, ultramontane; Old Catholic, tractarian, Anglican, Puseyite, ritualist; Puritan.

Jew, Hebrew, Rabbist; Mahometan, Mohammedan, Mussulman, Moslem, Islamite, Osmanli; Brahm-in, -an; Parsee, Sofi, Soofee; Buddhist; Zoroastrian, Magi, Gymnosophist, fire-worshipper, Sabian, Gnostic, Sadducee, &c.

**Adj.** heterodox, heretical; un-orthodox, -scriptural, -canonical; antiscriptural, apocryphal; un-, anti-christian; schismatic, recusant, iconoclastic; sectarian; dis-senting, -sident; secular &c. (*lay*) 997.

pagan; heathen, -ish; ethnic, -al; gentile, painim; pan-, polytheistic; agnostic, skeptic.

Judaical, Mohammedan, Moslem, Brahminical, Buddhist &c. *n.* Romish, Protestant &c. *n.*

bigoted &c. (*prejudiced*) 481, (*obstinate*) 606; superstitious &c. (*credulous*) 486; fanatical; idolatrous &c. 991; visionary &c. (*imaginative*) 515.

**985. Revelation.—N.** revelation, inspiration, *afflatus*.

Word, – of God; Scripture; the -Scriptures, – Bible, – Book of Books; Holy -Writ, – Scriptures; inspired writings, Gospel.

Old Testament, Septuagint, Vulgate, Pentateuch; Octateuch; the -Law, – Jewish Law, – Prophets; majo*r* -, minor- Prophets; Hagio-grapha, -logy; Hierographa; Apocrypha.

New Testament; Gospels, Evangelists, Acts, Epistles, Apocalypse, Revelations.

Talmud; Mishna, Masorah.

prophet &c. (*seer*) 513; evangelist, apostle, disciple, saint; the -, the Apostolical- fathers; Holy Men of old, inspired -writers, – penmen.

**Adj.** scriptural, biblical, sacred, prophetic; evangel-ical, -istic; apostolic, -al; inspired, theopneustic, apocalyptic, ecclesiastical canonical, textuary.

**986. Pseudo-Revelation.\*—N.** the -Koran, – Alcoran; Ly-king, Shaster, Vedas, Zendavesta, Vedidad, Purana, Edda; Go-, Gau-tama; Book of Mormon.

[False prophets and religious founders] Buddha, Zoroaster, Zerdhusht, Confucius, Mahomet.

[Idols] golden calf &c. 991; Baal, Moloch, Dagon.

* See note on page 378.

## 3°. RELIGIOUS SENTIMENTS

**987. Piety.**—**N.** piety, religion, theism, faith; religiousness, holiness &c. *adj.*; saintship; religionism; sanctimony &c. (*assumed piety*) 988; reverence &c. (*respect*) 928; humility, veneration, devotion; prostration &c. (*worship*) 990; grace, unction, edification; sancti-ty, -tude; consecration.

spiritual existence, odour of sanctity, beauty of holiness.

theopathy, beatification, adoption, regeneration, conversion, justification, sanctification, salvation, inspiration, bread of life; Body and Blood of Christ.

believer, convert, theist, Christian, devotee, pietist; the -good, – righteous, – just, – believing, – elect; Saint, *Madonna*.

the children of -God, – the kingdom, – light.

**V.** be -pious &c. *adj.*; have -faith &c. *n.*; believe, receive Christ; revere &c. 928; worship &c. 990; be -converted &c; convert, edify, sanctify, hallow, keep holy, beatify, regenerate, inspire, consecrate, enshrine.

**Adj.** pious, religious, devout, devoted, reverent, godly, heavenly minded, humble; pure, – in heart; holy, spiritual, pietistic; saint-ly, -like; seraphic, sacred, solemn.

believing, faithful, Christian, Catholic.

elected, adopted, justified, sanctified, regenerated, inspired, consecrated, converted, unearthly, not of the earth.

**988. Impiety.**—**N.** impiety; sin &c. 945; irreverence; profan-eness &c. *adj.*, -ity, -ation; blasphemy, desecration, sacrilege; scoffing &c. *v.*

[Assumed piety] hypocrisy &c. (*falsehood*) 544; pietism, cant, pious fraud; lip-devotion, -service, -reverence; misdevotion, formalism, austerity; sanctimon-y, -iousness &c. *adj.*; pharisaism, precisianism; sabbat-ism, -arianism; *odium theologicum*, sacerdotalism; bigotry &c. (*obstinacy*) 606, (*prejudice*) 481.

hardening, backsliding, declension, perversion, reprobation, apostasy, recusancy.

sinner &c. 949; scoffer, blasphemer; sacrilegist; worldling; hypocrite &c. (*dissembler*) 548; Scribes and Pharisees; Tartufe, Maw-worm.

bigot; saint [ironically]; Pharisee, sabbatarian, formalist, methodist, puritan, pietist, precisian, religionist, devotee, ranter, fanatic, wowser.

the -wicked, – evil, – unjust, – reprobate; son of -men, – Belial, – the wicked one; children of darkness.

**V.** be -impious &c. *adj.*; profane, desecrate, blaspheme, revile, scoff; swear &c. (*malediction*) 908; commit sacrilege.

snuffle; turn up the whites of the eyes; idolize.

**Adj.** impious; irreligious &c. 989; desecrating &c. *v.*; profane, irreverent, sacrilegious, blasphemous.

un-hallowed, -sanctified, -regenerate; hardened, perverted, reprobate.

hypocritical &c. (*false*) 544; canting, pietistical, sanctimonious, unctuous, pharisaical, over-righteous, righteous over much.

bigoted, fanatical &c. 481 & 606; priest-ridden.

**Adv.** under the -mask, cloak, – pretence, – form, – guise- of religion.

**989. Irreligion.**—**N.** irreligion, indevotion; ungodliness &c. *adj.*; laxity, quietism, apathy, indifference, passivity.

scepticism, doubt; un-, dis-belief; incredul-ity, -ousness &c. *adj.*; want of -faith, – belief; pyrrhonism; doubt &c. 485; agnosticism.

atheism, deism; hylotheism; materialism; positivism; nihilism.

infidelity, freethinking, antichristianity, rationalism.

atheist, anti-christian, sceptic, unbeliever, deist, infidel, pyr-
rhonist; *giaour*, heathen, alien, gentile, Nazarene; *esprit fort*, free-
thinker, latitudinarian, rationalist; materialist, positivist, nihilist,
agnostic.

**V.** be -irreligious &c. *adj.*; disbelieve, lack faith; doubt, question
&c. 485.

dechristianize; serve Mammon, love darkness better than light.

**Adj.** irreligious; in-, un-devout; devout-, god-, grace-less; un-
godly, -holy, -sanctified, -hallowed; atheistic, without God.

sceptical, free-thinking; un-believing, -converted; incredulous,
faithless, lacking faith; deistical; un-, anti-christian.

worldly, mundane, earthly, carnal, unspiritual; worldly &c.-
minded.

**Adv.** irreligiously &c. *adj.*


### 4°. ACTS OF RELIGION

**990. Worship.—N.** worship, adoration, devotion, aspiration, latria,
homage, service, humiliation; kneeling, genuflexion, prostration.

prayer, invocation, supplication, rogation, intercession, orison, holy
breathing; petition &c. (*request*) 765; collect, litany, Lord's prayer,
paternoster, *Ave Maria*, rosary; bead-roll; latria, dulia, hyperdulia,
vigils; revival; cult.

thanksgiving; giving -, returning- thanks; grace, praise, glorifica-
tion, benediction, doxology, hosanna; h-, allelujah; *Te Deum, non
nobis Domine, nunc dimittis*; pæan.

psalm, -ody; hymn, plainsong, chant, chaunt, response, anthem,
motet; antiphon, -y.

oblation, sacrifice, incense, libation; burnt -, votive -, thank-offering;
offertory, collection.

discipline; self-discipline, -examination, -denial; fasting.

divine service, office, duty; morning prayer; mass, matins, evensong,
vespers, compline; holy day &c. (*rites*) 998.

worshipper, congregation, communicant, celebrant.

**V.** worship, lift up the heart, aspire; revere &c. 928; adore, do serv-
ice, pay homage; humble oneself, kneel; bow -, bend- the knee; fall
-down, - on one's knees; prostrate oneself, bow down and worship,
recite the rosary.

pray, invoke, supplicate; put -, offer- up -prayers, - petitions;
beseech &c. (*ask*) 765; say one's prayers, tell one's beads.

return -, give- thanks; say grace, bless, praise, laud, glorify, magnify,
sing praises; give benediction, lead the choir, intone, chant, sing.

propitiate, offer sacrifice, fast, deny oneself; vow, offer vows, give
alms.

work out one's salvation; go to church; attend -service, - mass;
communicate &c. (*rite*) 998.

**Adj.** worshipping &c. *v.*; devout, devotional, reverent, pure, solemn;
fervid &c. (*heartfelt*) 821.

**Int.** h-, allelujah! hosanna! glory be to God! O Lord! pray God
that! God -grant, - bless, - save, - forbid! *sursum corda*.


**991. Idolatry.—N.** idol-atry, -ism; demon-ism, -olatry; idol -, demon
-, devil -, fire- worship; zoolatry, fetishism, Mari-, Bibli-, ecclesi-,
heli-olatry.

deification, apotheosis, canonization; hero worship.

sacrifices, hecatomb, holocaust; human sacrifices, immolation, mactation, infanticide, self-immolation, *suttee*.

idol, golden calf, graven image, fetish, *avatar*, Juggernaut, joss, *lares et penates*; Baal &c. 986.

idolater &c. *n.*

**V.** worship -idols, – pictures, – relics; put on a pedestal, bow down to, prostrate oneself before, make sacrifice to; deify, canonize, idolize.

**Adj.** idolatrous.

**992. Sorcery.—N.** sorcery; superstition; occult -art, – sciences; black –, magic; the black art, necromancy, theurgy, thaumaturgy; demon-ology, -omy, -ship; *diablerie*, bedevilment; witch-craft, -ery; glamour; fetis-hism, -ism; ghost dance; hoodoo, voodoo; Shamanism [Esquimaux], vampirism; conjuration; bewitchery, exorcism, enchantment, incantation, obsession, possession, mysticism, second sight, mesmerism, animal magnetism; od –, odylic- force; electro-biology, *clairvoyance*; spiritualism, spirit-rapping, table-turning; thought reading, telepathy, thought transference, automatic writing, *planchette*, ouija board; crystal gazing; spirit manifestation, materialization, astral body, ectoplasm &c.

divination &c. (*prediction*) 511; sortilege, ordeal, *sortes Virgilianæ, -biblicæ*, hocus-pocus &c. (*deception*) 545; oracle &c. 513.

**V.** practice -sorcery &c. *n.*; cast a -horoscope, – nativity; conjure, exorcise, charm, enchant; be-witch, -devil; overlook, look on with the evil eye; entrance, mesmerize, magnetize; fascinate &c. (*influence*) 615; taboo; wave a wand; rub the -ring, – lamp; cast a spell; call up spirits, – from the vasty deep; raise spirits from the dead; raise –, lay- ghosts; command genii.

**Adj.** magic, -al; mystic, weird, cabalistic, talismanic, phylacteric, incantatory; charmed &c. *v.*

**993. Spell.—N.** spell, charm, incantation, exorcism, weird, cabala, exsufflation, cantrap, runes, abracadabra, hocus-pocus, open *sesame*, counter-charm, Ephesian letters, bell, book and candle, Mumbo Jumbo, evil-eye, fee-faw-fum.

talisman, amulet, periapt, telesm, phylactery, philtre, wish-bone, merry-thought, mascot, scarab, swastika; fetish; *agnus Dei*.

wand, caduceus, rod, divining rod, lamp of Aladdin, magic carpet, seven-league boots; magic ring; wishing –, Fortunatus's- cap.

**994. Sorcerer.—N.** sorcerer, magician; thaumat-, the-urgist; conjuror, necromancer, seer, wizard, witch; fairy &c. 980; *lamia*, hag, warlock, charmer, exorcist, voodoo, mage, diviner, dowser; cunning –, medicine- man, witch doctor; Shaman, figure-flinger, ecstatica, medium, *clairvoyant*, mesmerist, hypnotist; *deus ex machinâ*; astrologer; soothsayer &c. 513.

Katerfelto, Cagliostro, Merlin, Comus, Mesmer; Hecate, Circe, Lilith, siren, weird sisters; witch of Endor.

5°. Religious Institutions

**995. Churchdom.—N.** church, -dom; ministry, apostleship, priesthood, prelacy, hierarchy, church government, christendom, pale of the church.

clerical-, sacerdotal-, episcopalian-, ultramontan-ism; Theocracy; ecclesiolog-y, -ist; priestcraft, *odium theologicum.*

monach-ism, -y; monasticism, monkhood.

[Ecclesiastical offices and dignities] pontificate, primacy, archbishopric, archiepiscopacy; prelacy; bishop-ric, -dom; episcop-ate, -acy; see, diocese; deanery, stall; canon-ry, -icate; prebend, -aryship; benefice, incumbency, glebe, advowson, living, cure, – of souls; rectorship; vicar-iate, -ship; pastor-ate, -ship; deacon-ry, -ship; -curacy; chaplain, -cy, -ship; cardinal-ate, -ship; abbacy, presbytery.

holy orders, ordination, institution, consecration, induction, reading in, preferment, translation, presentation.

popedom, papacy; the -Vatican, – apostolic see, – see of Rome; religious sects &c. 984.

council &c. 696; conclave, college of cardinals, convocation, synod, consistory, chapter, vestry, presbytery; sanhedrim, *congé d'élire*; ecclesiastical courts, consistorial court, court of Arches.

V. call, ordain, induct, prefer, translate, consecrate, present, elect, bestow.

take -orders, – the veil, – vows.

Adj. ecclesi-astical, -ological; clerical, sacerdotal, priestly, prelatical, pastoral, ministerial, capitular, theocratic; hierarchical, archiepiscopal; episcopal, -ian; canonical; mon-astic, -achal; monkish; abbati-al, -cal; pontifical, papal, apostolic; ultramontane, priest-ridden.

---

**996. Clergy.—N.** clergy, clericals, ministry, priesthood, presbytery, the cloth, the pulpit.

clergyman, divine, ecclesiastic, churchman, priest, presbyter, hierophant, pastor, shepherd, minister, clerk in holy orders; father, – in Christ; *padre, abbé, curé;* patriarch; reverend; black coat; confessor; sky pilot.

dignitaries of the church; ecclesi-, hier-arch; eminence, reverence, elder, primate, metropolitan, archimandrite, archbishop, bishop, prelate, diocesan, suffragan, dean, subdean, archdeacon, prebendary, canon, rural dean, rector, parson, vicar, perpetual curate, residentiary, beneficiary, incumbent, chaplain, curate, – in charge; deacon, -ess; preacher; lay reader, lecturer; capitular; missionary, propagandist, Jesuit, revivalist, field preacher.

churchwarden, sidesman; clerk, precentor, choir; almoner, *suisse*, verger, beadle, sexton, sacristan; acol-yth, -othyst, -yte; thurifer; chorister, choir boy.

[Roman Catholic priesthood] Pope, *Papa*, Holy Father, pontiff, high priest, cardinal; ancient –, flamen; confessor, penitentiary; spiritual director.

cenobite, conventual, abbot, prior, monk, friar, lay brother, beadsman, mendicant, pilgrim, palmer; canon-regular, -secular; Jesuit, Franciscan, Friars minor, Minorites; Observant, Capuchin, Dominican, Carmelite; Augustinian; Gilbertine; Austin-, Black-, White-, Grey-, Crossed-, Crutched-Friars; Bonhomme, Carthusian, Benedictine, Cistercian, Trappist, Cluniac, Premonstratensian, Maturine; Templar. Hospitaller.

**997. Laity.—N.** laity, flock, fold, congregation, assembly, brethren, people.

temporality, secularization.

layman, civilian; parishioner, catechumen; secularist.

V. secularize.

Adj. secular, lay, laical, civil, temporal, profane.

---

abb-, prior-, canon-ess; mother superior; *religieuse*, nun, sister, *béguine*, novice, postulant.

[Under the Jewish dispensation] prophet, priest, high priest, Levite; Rabbi, -n; scribe.

[Mohammedan &c.] mullah, ulema, imaum, sheik; so-fi, -phi; mufti, hadji, muezzin, dervish; fa-kir, -quir; brahmin, gooroo, druid, bonze, santon, abdal, Lama, talapoin, caloyer &c.

V. take orders &c. 995.

Adj. the –, the very –, the Right- Reverend; ordained, in orders, called to the ministry.

**998. Rite.—N.** rite; ceremon-y, -ial; ordinance, observance, function, duty; form, -ulary; solemnity, sacrament; incantation &c. (*spell*) 993; service, psalmody &c. (*worship*) 990; liturgies.

ministration; preach-ing, -ment; predication, sermon, homily, exhortation, lecture, discourse, pastoral.

baptism, christening, chrism, immersion; baptismal regeneration; font; circumcision.

confirmation; imposition –, laying on- of hands; churching, purification, ordination &c. (*churchdom*) 995; excommunication.

Eucharist, Lord's supper, communion; the –, the holy- sacrament; celebration, high celebration; *missa cantata*; offertory; introit; consecration; con-, tran-substantiation; real presence; elements, bread and wine; mass; high –, low –, dry- mass.

matrimony &c. 903; burial &c. 363; visitation of the sick.

seven sacraments, impanation, extreme unction, last rites. *viaticum*, invocation of saints, canonization, transfiguration, auricular confession; fasting; maceration, flagellation, sackcloth and ashes; penance &c. (*atonement*) 952; absolution; telling of beads, reciting the rosary, processional; thurification, incense, holy water, aspersion.

relics, rosary, beads, reliquary, host, cross, rood, crucifix, pax, pix, pyx, *agnus Dei*, censer, thurible, patera, urceole; chalice, patten, Holy Grail, sangrail; seven-branch candle stick, monstrance, sacring bell.

ritual, rubric, canon, ordinal; liturgy, prayer-book, book of common prayer, pietas, euchology, litany, lectionary; missal, breviary, massbook, bead-roll.

psalter; psalm –, hymn- book; hymn-al, -ology; psalmody.

ritual-, ceremonial-ism; sabbat-ism, -arianism; ritualist, sabbatarian.

holyday, feast, fast; Sabbath, Passover, Pentecost; Advent, Christmas, Noël, Epiphany, Lent, Shrove Tuesday, Ash Wednesday, Maundy Thursday; Passion –, Holy- week; Good Friday, Easter, Ascension Day, Whitsuntide; Trinity Sunday, Corpus Christi; All-Saints' –, - Souls'-Day; Candle-, Lam-, Martin-, Michael-mas; hogmanay; Rama-dan, -zan; Bairam &c. &c.

V. perform service, do duty, minister, officiate, baptize, dip, sprinkle; confirm. lay hands on; give –, administer –, take –, receive –, attend –, partake of- the -sacrament, - communion; communicate; celebrate mass; administer –, receive- extreme unction; anele, shrive, absolve, confess; do penance; genuflect; cross oneself, make the sign of the cross.

excommunicate, ban with bell, book and candle.

preach, sermonize, predicate, lecture.

Adj. ritual, -istic; ceremonial, liturgic; baptismal, eucharistical; paschal.

**999. Canonicals.—N.** canonicals, vestments; robe, gown, Geneva gown, frock, pallium, surplice, cassock, dalmatic, scapulary, cope. scarf, tunicle, chasuble, alb, *alba*, stole; fan-on. -nel; tonsure, cowl, hood; calo-te, -tte; bands; capouch, amice, orarium, ephod; apron, lawn sleeves, pontificals, pall; mitre, tiara, triple crown; shovel –, cardinal's-hat; biretta; crosier; pastoral staff; costume &c. 225.

**1000. Temple.—N.** place of worship; house of -God, – prayer.

temple, cathedral, minster, church, kirk, chapel, meeting-house, bethel, tabernacle, conventicle, *basilica*, fane, holy place, chantry, oratory.

synagogue; mosque; marabout; pantheon; pagoda; joss-house; dagobah, tope; kiosk.

parsonage, rectory, vicarage, manse, deanery, glebe, church house; Vatican; bishop's palace; Lambeth.

altar, shrine, sanctuary, Holy of Holies, *sanctum sanctorum*, sacr-arium, -isty; communion –, holy –, Lord's- table; table of the Lord; pyx; baptistery, font; piscina, stoup; aumbry; sedile; reredos; rood -loft, – screen; jube.

chancel, quire, choir, nave, aisle, transept, lady chapel, vestry, crypt, cloisters, porch; triforum, clerestory, churchyard, *golgotha*, calvary, Easter sepulchre; stall, pew, sitting; pulpit, ambo, lectern, reading-desk, confessional, prothesis, credence, baldachin, *baldacchino*; jesse, apse, belfry; chapter-house; presbytery.

monastery, priory, abbey, friary, convent, nunnery, cloister.

**Adj.** claustral, cloistered; monast-ic, -erial; conventual.

# INDEX

N.B.: The numbers refer to the headings under which the words or phrases occur. When the same word or phrase may be used in various senses, the several headings under which it, or its synonyms, will be found, according to those meanings, are indicated by the words printed in Italics. These words in Italics are not intended to explain the meaning of the word or phrase to which they are annexed, but only to assist in the required reference.

When the word given in the Index is itself the title or heading of a category, the number of reference is printed in blacker type, thus: **abode 189.**

accipient 785
acclamation
  *assent* 488
  *approbation* 931
acclimatize 370, 613
acclivity 217
accloy 641
accolade 894
accommodate
  *suit* 23
  *adjust* 27
  *aid* 707
  *reconcile* 723
  *give* 784
  *lend* 787
  – oneself to 82
accommodation
  *space* 180
accommodating
  *kind* 906
accompaniment
  *adjunct* 39
  *coexistence* 88
  *musical* 415
accompany
  *add* 37
  *coexist* 88
  *concur* 120
  *music* 416
accompli, fait – 729
accomplice 711
accomplish
  *execute* 161
  *complete* 729
  *succeed* 731
accomplishment
  490, 698
accompts 811
accord
  *uniform* 16
  *agree* 23
  *music* 413
  *assent* 488
  *concord* 714
  *grant* 760
  *give* 784
  of one's own – 602
according
  – as *qualification*
  469
  – to *evidence* 467
  – to circumstances
  8
  – to law 963
  – to rule
  *conformably* 82
  – rumour 527
accordingly
  *logically* 476
accordion 417
accost 586

accoucheur 631, 662
accouchement 161
account *list* 86
  *adjudge* 480
  *description* 594
  *credit* 805
  *money* – 811
  *fame* 873
  *approbation* 931
  call to – 932
  find one's – in
  *useful* 644
  *success* 731
  make no – of 483,
  930
  not – for 519
  on – of *motive* 615
  *behalf* 707
  on no – 536
  send to one's – 361
  take into – 457,
  469
  small – 643
  to one's – 780
  turn to –
  *improve* 658
  *use* 677
  *success* 731
  *gain* 775
  – as *deem* 484
  – book 551
  – for 155, 522
  – with 794, 807
accountable
  *liable* 177
  *debit* 811
  *duty* 926
accountant 801, 811
  certified public –
  811
accounts 811
accouple 43
accoutred
  *armed* 717
accoutrement
  *dress* 225
  *appliance* 633
  *equipment* 673
accoy 174
accredit
  *commission* 755,
  759
  *money* 805
  *honour* 873
accredited 484, 613
  – to 755, 759
accretion 35, 46
accrimination 938
accroach 789
accrue *add* 37
  *result* 154

*acquire* 775
  *be received* 785,
  810
accubation 213
accueil 894
accultural 658
accumbent 213
accumulate
  *collect* 72
  *store* 636
  *redundance* 641
accurate 494
  – *knowledge* 490
accurse 908
accursed
  *disastrous* 649
  *undone* 828
  *vicious* 945
accusation **938**
accuse
  *disapprove* 932
  *charge* 938
  *lawsuit* 969
accustom 613
ace *small* 32
  *unit* 87
  within an – 197
aceldama *kill* 361
  *arena* 728
acephalous 59
acerbate 659, 835
acerbity
  *acrimony* 395
  *sourness* 397
  *rudeness* 895
  *spleen* 900, 901
  *malevolence* 907
acervate 72
acetous 397
acetylene 388
acharné 900
Achates, fidus –
  890, 939
ache *physical* 378
  *mental* 828
Acheron
  pit of – 982
Acherontic
  *moribund* 360
  *gloomy* 837
achievable 470
achieve *end* 67
  *produce* 161
  *do* 680
  *accomplish* 729
achievement 551,
  861
Achilles, heel of –
  *vulnerable* 665
achromatism **429**
acicular 253

acid 397
acid test 463
acknowledge
  *answer* 462
  *assent* 488
  *disclose* 529
  *avow* 535
  *consent* 762
  *observe* 772
  *pay* 807
  *thank* 916
  *repent* 950
  *reward* 973
acknowledged
  *custom* 613
acme 210
  – of perfection 650
Acology 662
acolyte 996
acomous 226
aconite 663
acoustic 418
  – organs 418
acoustics 402
acquaint
  – oneself with **539**
  – with 527
acquaintance
  *knowledge* 490
  *information* 527
  *friend* 890
  make – with **888**
acquiesce
  *assent* 488
  *willing* 488
  *consent* 762
  *tolerate* 826
acquire
  *develop* 161
  *get* 775
  *receive* 785
  – a habit 613
  – learning **539**
acquirement
  *knowledge* 490
  *learning* 539
  *talent* 698
  *receipt* 810
acquisition
  *knowledge* 490
  *gain* 775
acquit
  *liberate* 750
  *exempt* 927a
  *vindicate* 937
  *innocent* 946
  *absolve* 970
acquit oneself
  *behave* 692
  – of a debt 807
  – of a duty 926

– of an obligation 772
acquittal **506, 970**
acquittance 771
acres *space* 180
  *land* 342
  *property* 780
Acres, Bob 862
acrid 392, 395
acridity 171
acrimony
  *physical* 171
  *caustic* 830
  *discourtesy* 895
  *hatred* 898
  *anger* 900
  *malevolence* 907
acroamatics 490
acrobat
  *strength* 159
  *actor* 599
  *proficient* 700
  *mountebank* 844
Acropolis 210
across 219, 708
acrostic 533, 561, 842
act *imitate* 19
  *physical* 170
  - *of a play* 599
  *personate* 599
  *voluntary* 680
  *statute* 697
  in the – 680, 947
  – a part *feign* 544
  – one's part 625, 926
  - upon
  *physical* 170
  *mental* 615
  *take steps* 680
  – up to 772
  – well one's part 944
  – without author-
    ity 738
acting *deputy* 759
actinic 420
actinometer 445
action *physical* 170
  *voluntary* **680**
  *battle* 720
  *law* 969
  line of – 692
  put in – 677
  suit the – to the
    word 550
  thick of the – 682
activate 171
actionable 964
active *physical* 171

*voluntary* 682
– service 722
– thought 457
activity 682
actor
  *impostor* 548
  *player* 599
  *agent* 690
  *affectation* 855
Acts *record* 551
  *Apostolic* 985
actual *existing* 1
  *present* 118
  *real* 494
actuary 85, 811
actuate 175, 615
actum est 729
acu tetigisti, rem 465, 494
acuity 253
aculeate 253
acumen 498
acuminate 253
acupuncture 260
acustics 402
acute *energetic* 171
  *physically violent* 173
  *pointed* 253
  *physically sensible* 375
  *musical tone* 410
  *perspicacious* 498
  *cunning* 702
  *strong feeling* 821
  *morally painful* 830
  – angle 244
  – ear 418
  – note 410
acutely 31
acuteness 465
ad
  – eundem 27
  – hominem 79
  – infinitum 105
  – instar 82
  – interim 106
  – lib 705
  – rem 23
A.D. 106
adage 496
adagio *music* 415
  *slow* 275
Adam *sin* 945
– 's apple 250
adamant 159, 323
adapt 23, 27
  – oneself to 82
adaptable
  *conformable* 82

*useful* 644
add *increase* 35
  *join* 37
  *numerically* 85
  – up 811
addendum 39
adder 913
addict *habit* 613
adding machine 85
additament 39
addition
  *extrinsical* 6
  *increase* 35
  *adjunction* **37**
  *thing added* 39
  *arithmetical* 85
addle *barren* 169
  *incomplete* 730
  *abortive* 732
  – the wits, 475, 503
addlehead 501
addleheaded 499
address
  *residence* 189
  *direction* 550
  *speech* 582
  *speak to* 586
  *skill* 698
  *request* 765
  – oneself to 673
addresses
  *courtship* 902
addressful 894
adduce
  *bring to* 288
  *evidence* 467
addulce 834
ademption 789
adenoid 250
adenology 329
adept 700
adequate *power* 157
  *sufficient* 639
  *for a purpose* 644
adhere *stick* 46
  – to 604a, 613
  – to an obligation 772
  – to a duty 926
adherent
  *follower* 711
adhesive, 46, 327, 352
adhibit 677
adhortation 695
adieu *departure* 293
  *loss* 776
adipocere 356
adipose 355
adit *orifice* 260
  *conduit* 350

*passage* 627
adjacent 197
adjection 37
adjective 39
adjoin 197, 199
adjourn 133
adjudge 480
adjudicate 480
adjunct
  *thing added* **39**
  *accompaniment* 88
  *aid* 707
  *auxiliary* 711
adjuration 535
adjure 765, 768
adjust *adapt* 23
  *equalize* 27
  *order* 58
  *prepare* 673
  *settle* 723, 762
  – differences 774
adjutage 260, 350
adjutant
  *auxiliary* 711
  *military* 745
adjuvant *helping* 707
  *auxiliary* 711
admeasurement 466
adminicle 467
administer
  *utilize* 677
  *conduct* 693
  *exercise authority* 737
  *distribute* 786
  – correction 972
  – oath 768
  – sacrament 998
  – to *aid* 707
  *give* 784
administration of
  justice 965
administrative **737,** 965
administrator 694
admirable 648, 944
admiral 745
Admiralty, court of – 966
admirari, nil – 871, 932
admiration
  *wonder* 870
  *love* 897
  *respect* 928
  *approval* 931
admired disorder 59
admirer 897
admissible

aery 317
Æsculapius 662
Æsop 846
æsthetic
  *sensibility* 375
  *beauty* 845
  *taste* 850
æstival 125
æternum servans
  sub pectore vul-
  nus 919
ætiology [*see* etiol-
  ogy]
afar 196
affable 879, 894
affair *event* 151
  *topic* 454
  *business* 625
  *battle* 720
  *love* 902, 903
  – *of honour* 720
affaires, chargé d' –
  758
affaire de cœur 897
affect *relate to* 9
  *tend to* 176
  *qualify* 469
  *feign* 544
  *touch* 824
  *desire* 865
  *love* 897
affectation **855**
affected with
  *feeling* 821
  *disease* 655
affectibility 822
affecting 830
affection 821, 897
affections **820**
affettuoso 415
affiance 768, 858
affianced 897, 903
affiche 531
affidation 769
affidavit
  *affirmation* 535
  *record* 551
  *lawsuit* 969
affiliation
  *relation* 9
  *kindred* 11
  *attribution* 155
affine 11
affinitive 9
affinity 9, 17
  *mate* 903
affirmation **535**, 488
affix *add* 37
  *sequel* 39
  *fasten* 43
  *letter* 561

afflation 349
afflatus 349, 597,
  985
afflict 830
  – *with illness* 655
affliction *pain* 828
  *infliction* 830
  *adversity* 735
affluence
  *sufficiency* 639
  *prosperity* 734
  *wealth* 803
affluent *river* 348
afflux 286
afford *supply* 784
  *wealth* 803
  *yield* 810
  *sell for* 812
  – *aid &c.* 707
afforestation 371
affranchise
  *make free of* 748
  *liberate* 750
affray 720
affreet 980
affriction 331
affright 860
affront *molest* 830
  *provocation* 900
  *insult* 929
  – *danger* 861
affuse 337
afield 186
afire 382
afloat *extant* 1
  *unstable* 149
  *going on* 151
  *ship* 273
  *navigation* 267
  *ocean* 341
  *news* 532
  *preparing* 673
  keep oneself – 734
  set – *publish* 531
afoot *on hand* 625
  *preparing* 673
  *astir* 682
afore 116
aforementioned 116
aforesaid
  *preceding* 62
  *repeated* 104
  *prior* 116
aforethought 611
aforetime 116
afraid 860
  be – *irresolute* 605
  – *to say uncertain*
  475
afresh 104, 123
**Afric heat** 382

Afrikander 57
afrite 980
aft 235
after *in order* 63
  *in time* 117
  *too late* 135
  *rear* 235
  *pursuit* 622
  be – *intention* 620
  *pursuit* 622
  go – *follow* 281
  – *all for all that* 30
  *qualification* 469
  *on the whole* 476
  – *time* 133
after acceptation
  516
after-age 124
after-clap 509
after-crop 65, 168
after-dinner 117
after-glow 40, 65,
  420
after-growth 65
after-life 152
aftermath
  *sequel* 65
  *fertile* 168
  *profit* 775
aftermost 235
afternoon 126
  – *farmer* 683
after-part 65, 235
after-piece 599
after-taste 65, 390
after-thought
  *thought* 451
  *memory* 505
  *change of mind*
  607
after-time 121
afterwards 117
aga 745
agacerie 615
again 90, 104
  – *and again* 136
  come – *periodic* 138
  fall off – 661
  live – 660
against
  *counteraction* 179
  *anteposition* 237
  *provision* 673
  *voluntary opposi-*
  *tion* 708
  *chances* – 473
  declaim – 932
  false witness – 934
  go – 708
  set – *actively* 898
  set one's face –

764, 932
stand up – *resist*
  719
raise &c. one's
  voice – 489
– one's will 744
– one's expecta-
  tion 508
– the grain *difficult*
  704
  *painful* 830
  *dislike* 867
– the stream 704
– the time when
  510
– one's will 744
– one's wishes 603
agamist 904
agape *open* 260
  *curious* 455
  *expectant* 507
  *wonder* 870
Agapemone 827,
  897
agate 847
age *time* 106
  *period* 108
  *long time* 110
  *era* 114
  *present time* 118
  *oldness* 124
  *advanced life* **128**
  of – 131
  from age to – 112
age quod agis! 68?
agency
  *physical* **170**
  *instrumentality*
  631
  *means* 632
  *employment* 677
  *voluntary action*
  680
  *direction* 693
  *commission* 755
agenda 625, 626
agent *physical* 153
  *intermediary* 228
  *voluntary* **690**
  *consignee* 758
  – *provocateur* 615
agentship 755
ages: for – 110
  – ago 122
agglomerate 46, 72
agglutinate 46
aggrandize
  *in degree* 35
  *in bulk* 194
  *honour* 873
aggravate

459
*active* 682
alerte 669
aleuromancy 511
Alexandrine
 *ornate style* 577
 *verse* 597
alexandrite 847
alexipharmic 662
alexiteric 662
algebra 85
algid 383
algology 369
algorithm 85
alguazil 965
alias
 *otherwise* 18
 *pseudonym* 565
alibi 187
alien *irrelevant* 10
 *foreign* 57
 *transfer* 783
 *gentile* 989
alienable 783
alienate
 *transfer* 783
 *estrange* 44, 889
 *set against* 898
alienation
 *mental* – 503
alieni appetens
 *grasping* 865
 *envious* 921
 *selfish* 943
alienism 57
alight *stop* 265
 *arrive* 292
 *descend* 306
 *on fire* 382
align 278
alike 17
 share and share –
 778
aliment *food* 298
alimentary 662
 – canal 350
alimentation
 *aid* 707
alimony
 *property* 780
 *provision* 803
 *income* 810
aliquot 51, 84
aliter visum, dis –
 601
alive
 *living* 359
 *intelligent* 498
 *active* 682
 *cheerful* 836
 be – with 102

[ 394 ]

keep – *continue*
 143
keep the memory
 – 505
look – 684
 – to *attention* 457
 *cognizant* 490
 *informed* 527
 *able* 698
 *sensible* 822
alkahest 335
all *whole* 50
 *complete* 52
 *generality* 78
 – absorbing 642
 in – ages 112
 – abroad 495
 – agog 865
 – in all 50
 – along 106
 – along of 154
 – but 32
 – colours 440
 – considered 451,
 480
 – day long 110
 – devouring 789
 in – directions 278
 – engulfing 789
 at – events *com-*
 *pensation* 30
 *qualification* 469
 *true* 494
 *resolve* 604
 – fours *easy* 705
 *cards* 840
 – in good time 152
 – hail! *welcome* 292
 *honour to* 873
 *celebration* 883
 *courtesy* 894
 – hands *everybody*
 78
on – hands 488
 – of a dither 824
 – of a heap 72
 – knowing 976
 – manner of *differ-*
 *ence* 15
 *multiform* 81
with – one's might
 686
 – at once 113
 – one 27, 866
 – out 52
 – over *end* 67
 *universal* 78
 *destruction* 162
 *space* 180
at – points 52
 – in one's power

686
 – powerful
 *mighty* 159
 *God* 976
in – quarters 180
with – respect 928
in – respects 52,
 494
 – right! 922
 – Saints' day 998
 – searching 461
 – seeing 976
on – sides 227
 – sorts *diverse* 16a
 *mixed* 41
 *multiform* 81
 – talk 4
 – things to all
 men 894
 – the time 106
at – times 136
 – together 50
 – ways 243, 279
 – wise 976
 – the world and
 his wife 78
of – work
 *useful* 644
 *maid* - 746
Allah 979
allay
 *moderate* 174
 *pacify* 723
 *relieve* 834
 – *excitability* 826
allective 615
allege *evidence* 467
 *assert* 535
 *plea* 617
allegiance 743, 926
allegory 464, 521,
 594
allegro *music* 415
 *cheerful* 836
allelujah 990
allemande 840
all-embracing 76
alleviate 174, 834
alley *court* 189
 *passage* 260
 *way* 627
alliance *relation* 9
 *kindred* 11
 physical co-opera-
 *tion* 178
 voluntary co-oper-
 *ation* 709
 *party* 712
 *union* 714
allied to *like* 17
alligation 43

allign 278
alliteration
 *similarity* 17
 *style in writing*
 577
 *poetry* 597
allocation 60, 786
allocution 586
allodium *free* 748
 *property* 780
allopathy 662
alloquy 586
allot *arrange* 60
 *distribute* 786
 *due* 924
allow *assent* 488
 *admit* 529
 *permit* 760
 *consent* 762
 *give* 784
 – to have one's
 own way 740
allowable 760, 924
allowance
 *qualification* 469
 *gift* 784
 *allotment* 786
 *discount* 813
 *salary* 973
 with grains of –
 485
 make – for *forgive*
 918
 *vindicate* 937
alloy *mixture* 41
 *combination* 48
 *debase* 659
allude *hint* 514
 *mean* 516
 *refer to* 521
 *latent* 526
 *inform* 527
allure *move* 615
 *create desire* 865
alluring 829
allusive
 *relative* 9
alluvial *level* 213
 *land* 342
 *plain* 344
alluvium
 *deposit* 40
 *land* 342
 *soil* 653
ally *combine* 48
 *auxiliary* 711
 *friend* 890
alma mater 542
almanac
 *list* 86
 *chronometry* 114

record 551
almighty 157
Almighty, the – 976
almoner
  treasurer 801
  giver 784
  church officer 996
almonry 802
almost nearly 32
  not quite 651
  – all 50
  – immediately 132
alms gift 784
  benevolence 906
  worship 990
almshouse 189, 666
almsman 785
Alnaschar's dream 515, 858
aloes 395
aloft 206
alogy 497
alone single 87
  unaided 706
  let – not use 678
  not restrain 748
along 200
  get – progress 282
  go – depart 293
  go – with concur 178
  assent 488
  co-operate 709
  – of caused by 154
  – with added 37
  together 88
  by means of 631
alongside near 197
  parallel 216
  laterally 236
aloof distant 196
  high 206
  secluded 893
  stand – inaction 681
  refuse 764
  cautious 864
alopecia 226
aloud 404
  think – 589
  naïveté 703
Alp 206
alpenstock 215
Alpha 66
  – and Omega 50
alphabet
  beginning 66
  letters 561
alphabetarian 541
alphabeticize 60
Alphitomancy 511

alpine high 206
Alpine Club 268, 305
already
  antecedently 116
  even now 118
  past time 122
Alsatia 791, 945
also 37
altar 903, 1000
alter 140
  – the case 468
  – one's course 279
alter ego similar 17
  auxiliary 711
  deputy 759
  friend 890
alterable 149
alteram partem, audire–468, 922
alterative
  substitute 634
  remedy 662
altercation 713
altered worn 688
  – for the worse 659
alternate
  reciprocal 12
  sequence 63
  discontinuous 70
  periodic 138
  changeable 149
  oscillate 314
alternative
  substitute 147
  choice 609
  plan 626
although
  compensation 30
  counteraction 179
  unless 469
altiloquence 577
altimetry
  height 206
  angle 244
  measurement 466
altitude height 206
  – and azimuth 466
alto 410, 416
  – part 415
alto-rilievo 250, 557
altogether 50, 52
  nude 226
altruism 910, 942
altruist 906
alum 397
alumnus 541
alveolus 252
always
  uniformly 16
  generally 78
  during 106

perpetually 112
habitually 613
a.m. 114, 125
amah 753
amain 173, 684
amalgam, -ate 41, 48
amalgamation 709
Amalthæa's horn 639
amantium iræ 918
amanuensis 553, 590
amaranthine 112
amari aliquid
  bad 649
  imperfect 651
  painful 830
amaritude 395
amass whole 50
  collect 72
  store 636
amateur volunteer 602
  layman 699
  taste 850
  votary 865
amatory 897
amaurosis 442
amaze 870
amazingly 31
Amazon
  woman 374
  warrior 726
  courage 861
ambages
  convolutions 248
  circumlocution 573
  circuit 629
ambagious 573
ambassador
  messenger 534
  representative 758
  recall of –s 713
amber 356a
  – colour 436
ambidexter
  right and left 238
  fickle 607
  clever 698
ambient 227
ambigu 41
ambiguas spargere voces
  uncertain 475
  misteach 538
  false 544
  cunning 702
ambiguous
  uncertain 475

unintelligible **519**
equivocal 520
obscure 571
ambiloquy 520
ambit 230
ambition 620, 865
ambivalence 605, 708
amble 266
ambo school 542
  pulpit 1000
ambo, Arcades – alike 17
  friends 890
  bad men 949
ambrosia 298
ambrosial 394, 490
ambulance
  vehicle 272
  hospital 662
ambulation 266
ambuscade 530
ambush **530**, 667
  lie in – 528
âme – de boue **949**
  – damnée
  catspaw 711
  servant 746
  servile 886
  bad man 949
  – qui vive 101, 187
ameer 875
ameliorate 658
amen assent 488
  submission 725
  content 831
amenable 177, 602, 926
  not – to reason 608
amend 658
amendatory 20
amende honorable 952
amends
  compensation 50
  atonement 952
  reward 973
amenity 829, 894
amentia 503
amerce 974
American organ 417
Americanism 563
amethyst
  purple 437
  jewel 847
amiable
  courteous 894
  loving 897
  kind 906
amiability 829, 894
amicable 707, 888

amice 999
amicus – curiæ 527
– humani generis 910
– usque ad aras 890
amidships 68
amidst 41, 228
amiss 619
come – *disagree* 24
*mistime* 135
*inexpedient* 647
do – 945
nothing comes – 823
take – 867, 900
amity *concord* 714
*peace* 721
*friendship* 888
ammunition 635, 727
amnesia 506
amnesty 506, 723, 918
amnis, rusticus expectat dum defluat – *hope* 858
amœbæan 63
amok 503
among 41, 228
amor patriæ 910
amore, **con** – 602, 821
amoroso 599
amorous 897
– glances 902
amorphous 83, 241
amorphism 241
amortization 784
amotion 270
amount
*quantity* 25
*degree* 26
*sum of money* 800
*price* 812
*gross* – 50
– to 27, 85
amour 897, 961
– propre 880
ampere 466
amphibian 366
amphibious 83
amphibology 520
Amphictyonic council 696
amphigouri 497
amphitheatre
*prospect* 441
*school* 542
*theatre* 599
*arena* 728

Amphitryon 890
amphora 191
ample *much* 31
*spacious* 180
*large* 192
*broad* 202
*copious* 639
amplify
*expand* 194
*exaggerate* 549
*diffuse style* 573
amplitude
*quantity* 25
*degree* 26
*size* 192
*breadth* 202
*enough* 639
ampoule 191
ampulla 191
amputate 38
amuck 173, 361, 503, 716, 825
amulet 247, 993
amusare la bocca, per – 394
amuse 829, 840
amusement **840**
place of – 840
amussim, ad – 494
amylaceous 352
an *if* 514
ana 594
Anabaptist 984
anabasis 35
anachronism
*false time* **115**
*inopportune* 135
*error* 495
anacoluthon 70
anaconda 913
anacreontic 597
anæmia 160
anæsthesia 376, 381, 683
anaglyph 554, 557
anagoge 521, 526
anagram
*double sense* 520
*secret* 533
*letter* 561
*wit* 842
analecta 596
analeptic 662
analgesia 376
analogy 9, 17
analogous 12
analysis
*decomposition* 49
*arrangement* 60
*algebra* 85

*inquiry* 461
*experiment* 463
*reasoning* 476
*grammar* 567
*compendium* 596
analyst 461, 463
anamorphosis
*distortion* 243
*optical* 443
*misrepresentation* 555
anapæst 597
anaphylaxis 375
anarchist
*destroyer* 165
*disobedient* 742
*evil-doer* 913
anarchy 59, 738
anastatic printing 558
anastomosis 43, 219
anastrophe 218
anathema 908
anathematize 908
anatomize *dissect* 44
*investigate* 461
anatomy
*dissection* 44
*leanness* 203
*texture* 329
*science* 357
comparative – 368
anatriptic 331
ancestral
*bygone* 122
*old* 124
*aged* 128
ancestry 166
anchor
*connection* 45
*stop* 265
*safeguard* 666
*badge* 747
*hope* 858
at – *fixed* 150
*stationed* 184
*safe* 664
cast – *settle* 184
*arrive* 292
have an – to windward 664
sheet – *means* 632
anchorage
*location* 184
*roadstead* 189
*refuge* 666
anchored 150

anchorite 893, 955
ancien régime 875
ancient *old* 124
*flag* 550
– times 122
ancientness 122
ancillary 707
and 37, 88
andante 415
andiron 386
androgynous 83
anecdote 594
anele 998
anemography 349
anemometer
*wind* 349
*measure* 466
anent 9
aneroid 338
anew *again* 104
*newly* 123
anfractuosity 248
angel
*object of love* 897
*good person* 948
*supernatural being* **977**
fallen –
*bad man* 949
*devil* 978
guardian –
*safety* 664
*auxiliary* 711
*benefactor* 912
– of Death 360
– 's visits 137
angelic 944
angels and ministers of grace defend us! 860
angelus 550
anger 900
more in sorrow than in – 826, 918
angiology 329
angle 244
*try* 463
at an – 217
Anglicanism 984
angling 622, 840
anguille au genou, rompre l' – 158, 471
anguilliform 205, 248
anguis in herbâ 667
anguish
*physical* 378
*moral* 828

| | | | |
|---|---|---|---|
| angular 244 | anneal 673 | answer | anthropomancy 511 |
| – velocity 264 | annex | *to an inquiry* **462** | anthropophagi 913 |
| angularity 244 | *addition* 37 | *confute* 479 | anthroposcopy 511 |
| angusta domi, res | *adjunct* 39 | *solution* 522 | anthroposophy 372 |
| – 804 | *junction* 43 | *succeed* 731 | anti-aircraft gun |
| angustation 203 | *acquire* 775 | *pecuniary profit* | 564, 727 |
| anhelation 688 | Annie Oakley 815 | 775 | antic 840 |
| anhydrate 340 | annihilate 2, 162 | *pleadings* 969 | antichambre, |
| anhydrous 340 | anniversary 138 | require an – 461 | faire – 133 |
| aniline dyes 437 | anno 106 | – for *deputy* 759 | antichristian 984, |
| anility 128, 499 | **Anno Domini** | *promise* 768 | 989 |
| animadvert | *era* 106 | *go bail* 806 | antichronism 115 |
| *consider* 451 | *old age* 124 | I'll – for it 535 | anticipate |
| *attend to* 457 | annotation 522, 550 | – the helm 743 | *anachronism* 115 |
| *reprehend* 932 | annotator 524 | – the purpose 731 | *priority* 116 |
| animal **366** | *scholar* 492 | – to *correspond* 9 | *future* 121 |
| female – 374 | *interpreter* 524 | – one's turn 644 | *early* 132 |
| – cries 412 | *editor* 595 | answerable | *expect* 507 |
| – œconomy 359 | annotto 434 | *agreement* 23 | *foresee* 510 |
| – gratification 377 | announce | *liable* 177 | *prepare* 673 |
| – life 364 | *predict* 511 | *bail* 806 | *hope* 858 |
| – physiology 368 | *inform* 527 | *duty* 926 | *in* – 116 |
| – spirits 836 | *publish* 531 | *censurable* 932 | anticlimax |
| – and vegetable | *assert* 535 | ant 690 | *decrease* 36 |
| kingdom 357 | announcer 527 | Antæus 159, 192 | *bathos* 497, 853 |
| animalcule 193, 366 | annoy | antagonism | anticlinal 217 |
| animalism | *molest* 649, 907 | *difference* 14 | anticyclone 265 |
| *sensuality* 954 | *disquiet* 830 | *physical* 179 | antidote 662 |
| animality **364** | annoyance 828 | *voluntary* 708 | antigropelos 225 |
| animate | source of – 830 | *enmity* 889 | antilogarithm 84 |
| *induce* 615 | annual *periodic* 138 | antagonist 710, 891 | antilogy 477 |
| *excite* 824 | *plant* 367 | antagonistic 24 | antimony 663 |
| *enliven* 836 | *book* 593 | antarctic 237 | Antinomian 984 |
| animation | annuity 810 | antecedence 62, 116 | antinomy 964 |
| *life* 359 | annul 162, 756 | antecedent 64 | Antinous 845 |
| *animality* 364 | annular 247 | antechamber 191 | antiparallel 217 |
| *activity* 682 | annunciate 527 | ante Christum 106 | antipathy 867, 898 |
| *vivacity* 836 | annus magnus 108 | antedate 115 | antiphon *music* 415 |
| suspended – 823 | anodyne | antediluvian 124 | *answer* 462 |
| animism 984 | *lenitive* 174 | antelope 274 | *worship* 990 |
| animo, ex – 602 | *remedial* 662 | antemundane 124 | antiphrasis 563 |
| quo – 620 | *relief* 834 | antenna 379 | antipodes |
| animosity | anoint *coat* 223 | anteposition 62 | *difference* 14 |
| *dislike* 867 | *lubricate* 332 | anterior | *distance* 196 |
| *enmity* 889 | *oil* 355 | *in order* 62 | contraposition |
| *hatred* 898 | anointed | *in time* 116 | 237 |
| *anger* 900 | *deity* 976 | *in place* 234 | antipoison 662 |
| animus | *king* 745 | – to reason 477 | antiquary |
| *willingness* 602 | anomaly | anteroom 191 | *past times* 122 |
| *intention* 620 | *disorder* 59 | antevert 706 | *scholar* 492 |
| *desire* 865 | *irregularity* 83 | anthem 990 | *historian* 553 |
| ankle 244 | anon 132 | anthemion 847 | antiquas vias, |
| – deep 208, 209 | anonymous 565 | anthology | stare super – |
| anklet 847 | anopsia 442 | *book* 593 | 613, 670 |
| ankylosis 150 | anorexy 866 | *collection* 596 | antiquated 128 |
| annalist 114, 553 | another | *poem* 597 | antique 124 |
| annals | *different* 15 | anthracite 388 | antiquity 122 |
| *chronology* 114 | *repetition* 104 | anthropoid 372 | antiscriptural 984 |
| *record* 551 | – story 468, 526 | anthropology | antiseptic 652, 662 |
| *account* 594 | go upon – tack 607 | *zoology* 368 | antisocial 911 |
| | – time 119 | *mankind* 372 | antistrophe 597 |

**antithesis**
  *contrast* 14
  *difference* 15
  *opposite* 237
  *style* 574, 577
**antitoxin** 662
**antitype** 22
**antler** 253
**antonomasia**
  *metaphor* 521
  *nomenclature* 564
**antonym** 14
**antrum** 252
**anvil** *support* 215
  on the –
  *intended* 620
  *in hand* 625
  *preparing* 673
**anxiety** *pain* 828
  *fear* 860
  *desire* 865
**anxious expectation**
  507
**any** *some* 25
  *part* 51
  *no choice* 609a
  at – *price* 604a
  at – rate
  *certain* 474
  *true* 494
  *at all hazards* 604
**anybody** 78
**anyhow** 460, 627
**anything** one
  knows, for – 491
**aorist** 109, 119
**aorta** 350
**apace** *early* 132
  *swift* 274
**apache** 913
**apart** 44, 87
  set – 636
  wide – 196
**apartment** 191
  –s 189
  –s to let
  *imbecile* 499
**apathetic** 275
**apathy**
  *indifference* 456
  *insensibility* 823
  *irreligion* 989
**ape** *imitate* 19
**Apelles** 559
**aperçu** 596
**aperture** 260
**apex** 210
**aphasia** 583
**aphelion** 196
**aphonic** 403
**aphony** 581

**aphorism** 496
**Aphrodite** 845, 979
**apiary** 370
**apiculture** 370
**Apicius** 957
**apiece** 79
**apish** 19, 499
**aplanatic** 429
**aplomb**
  *stability* 150
  *self-possession*
  498
  *resolution* 604
**Apocalypse** 985
**Apocrypha** 985
**apocryphal**
  *uncertain* 475
  *erroneous* 495
  *heterodox* 984
**apodictic** 478
**apodosis** 67
**apogee** 210
**apograph** 21
**Apollo** *sun* 318
  *music* 416
  *luminary* 423
  *beauty* 845
  *god* 979
  *magnus* – 500, 695
**Apollyon** 978
**apologue**
  *metaphor* 521
  *teaching* 537
  *description* 594
**apology** *excuse* 617
  *vindication* 937
  *penitence* 950
  *atonement* 952
**apophthegm** 496
**apophysis** 250
**apoplexy** 158, 655
**aporetic** 487
**aposiopesis** 585
**apostasy**
  *recantation* 607
  *dishonour* 940
  *heterodoxy* 984
**apostate**
  *convert* 144
  *turncoat* 607
  *impiety* 988
**apostle** *teacher* 540
  *disciple* 541
  *inspired* 985
  –'s creed 983a
**apostolic** 985
  – church 983a
  – see 995
**apostrophe**
  *address* 586
  *soliloquy* 589

*appeal* 765
**apothecary** 662
  –'s weight 319
**apothegm** 496
**apotheosis**
  *resuscitation* 163
  *canonization* 873
  *heaven* 981
  *hero worship* 991
**apozem** 335, 384
**appal** 830, 860
**appanage**
  *property* 780
  *gift* 784
**apparatus** 633
**apparel** 225
**apparent**
  *visible* 446
  *appearing* 448
  *probable* 472
  *manifest* 525
  heir – 779
**apparition**
  *fallacy of vision*
  443
  *spirit* 980
**apparitor** 534
**appeach** 938
**appeal** 586, 765
  court of – 966
  – to arms 722
  – motion 969
  – from Philip
    drunk to Philip
    sober 658
  – to *call to witness*
  467
  – to for (*claim*) 924
**appear** 446, 525
  – for 759
  – in print 591
**appearance** 448
  make one's – 292
  to all – 448
  *probable* 472
**appearances**
  keep up – 852
**appease** 174
**appellant** 924, 938
**appellate** 966
**appellation** 564
**append** *add* 37
  *sequence* 63
  *hang* 214
**appendage** 39
**appendectomy** 662
**appendix**
  *adjunct* 39
  *sequel* 65
  *end* 67
  *book* 593

**appertain**
  *related to* 9
  *component* 56
  *belong* 777
  *property* 780
**appetite** 865
  tickle the –
  *savoury* 394
**appetizing** 865
  *exciting* 824
**applaud** 931
**apple** – of discord
  713
  golden –
  *allurement* 615
  – of one's eye *good*
  648
  *love* 897
  *favorite* 899
  – off another tree
  15
  how we –s swim!
  880
**apple-green** 435
**apple-pie order** 58
**appliance** *use* 677
  –s *means* 632
  *machinery* 633
**applicable** *relevant*
  23
  *useful* 644
  *expedient* 646
**applicability** 9
**applicant** 767
**application** *study*
  457
  *metaphor* 521
  *use* 677
  *request* 765
**apply,** *use* 677
  – a match 384
  – the match to ⚭
    train 66
  – the mind 457
  – a remedy 662
**appoggiatura** 413
**appointment**
  *employment* 625
  *order* 741
  *charge* 755
  *assignment* 786
  *interview* 892
**appointments**
  *gear* 633
**apportion** *arrange*
  60
  *disperse* 73
  *allot* 786
**apportionment** 786
**appositeness** 9
**apposition**

*relation* 9
*relevancy* 23
*closeness* 199
*paraphrase* 522
**appraise** 466, 812
**appreciate**
*realize* 450, 451
*measure* 466
*judge* 480
*know* 490
*taste* 850
*approve* 931
**apprehend**
*believe* 484
*know* 490
*fear* 860
*seize* 789
**apprehension**
*idea* 453
*taking* 789
**apprentice** 541
– *oneself* 676
**apprenticeship** 539, 673
**apprise** 527
**apprised of** 490
**approach**
*of time* 121
*impend* 152
*nearness* 197
*move* **286**
*path* 627
**approaching** 9
**approbation** **931**
**appropinquation** 286
**appropriate** *fit* 23
*peculiar* 79
*expedient* 646
*assign* 786
*take* 789
*steal* 791
**approval** 488, **931**
*on* – 609
**approximate**
*related to* 9
*resemble* 17
*in mathematics* 85
*nearness* 197
*approach* 286
**appulse** *meeting* 199
*collision* 276
*approach* 286
*convergence* 290
**appurtenance**
*part* 51
*component* 56
*belongings* 780
*accompaniment* 88
**appurtenant** 9

**après nous le**
**déluge** 943
**apricot** *colour* 439
**April**
– *fool* 547, 857
*make an* – *fool of* 545
– *showers* 149
**apron** *extension* 39
*clothing* 225
*defence* 717
*canonicals* 999
**àpropos** [*see* à]
**aprotype** 591
**apse** 1000
**apt** *consonant* 23
*tendency* 176, 177
*docile* 539
*willing* 602
*clever* 698
**aqua-fortis** 335
**aquamarine** 435
**aquarium** 370
**Aquarius** 348, 636
**aquatic** *water* 337
**aquatics** 267
**aquatinta** 558
**aqueduct** 350
**aqueous** 337
**aquiline** 244
**A.R.** 106
**Arab** *wanderer* 268
*horse* 271
*street* – 876
**araba** 272
**arabesque** 847
**Arabian**
– *perfumes* 400
– *nights* 515
**arable** 371
**arbalest** 727
**arbiter** *critic* 480
*director* 694
*adviser* 695
*judge* 967
– *elegantiarum*
*revels* 840
*taste* 850
*fashion* 852
**arbitrage** 794
**arbitrament**
*judgment* 480
– *of the sword* 722
**arbitrary**
*without relation* 10
*irregular* 83
*wilful* 606
*capricious* 608
*authoritative* 737
*severe* 739

*insolent* 885
*lawless* 964
– *power* 739
**arbitrate**
*adjudicate* 480
*mediate* 724
**arbitration**
*court of* – 966
*submit to* – 774
**arbitrium, ad** – 600
**arbor** 215, 312
**arborescent**
*ramifying* 242
*rough* 256
*trees* 367
**arboriculture** 371
**arbour** *abode* 189
*summer-house* 191
*plaisance* 840
**arc** 245
*heat* 382
**arcade** *street* 189
*curve* 245
*gateway* 260
**Arcades ambo**
*alike* 17
*friends* 890
*bad men* 949
**Arcadia** 827, 981
**Arcadian** 703, 946
**arcanum** 533
**arch** *great* 31
*support* 215
*curve* 245
*convex* 250
*concave* 252
*clever* 498
*cunning* 702
*triumphal* – 733, 883
**archæologist**
*pastimes* 122
*scholar* 492
**archæology** 122
**archaic** *old* 124
**archaism** 122, 563
**archangel** 977
**archbishop** 996
**archbishopric** 995
**archdeacon** 996
**archduchy** 181
**archduke** 745
**archegenesis** 161
**archer** 726
**archery** 840
**Arches, court of** – 966, 995
**archetype** 22
**archetypal** 20
**Archeus** 359

**archfiend** 978
**archiater** 695
**archiepiscopal** 995
**archimandrite** 996
**archipelago** 346
**architect** 164, 690
**architectonic** 161
**architecture**
*arrangement* 60
*construction* 161
*fabric* 329
*ornament* 847
**architrave** 210
**archive** 551
**archlute** 417
**archon** *ruler* 745
*deputy* 759
*judge* 967
**archtraitor** 941
**arctic** *northern* 237
*cold* 383
**arctics** 225
**arcuation** 245
**ardent** *fiery* 382
*eager* 682
*feeling* 821
*loving* 897
– *expectation* 507
– *imagination* 515
**ardet, proximus** – 665, 667
**ardour** *vigour* 574
*activity* 821
*feeling* 821
*desire* 865
**arduous** 704
**area** 181, 182
**arefaction** 340
**arena** *space* 180
*region* 181
*field of view* 441
*field of battle* **728**
**arenaceous** 330
**areola** 247
**areolar** 219
**areometer** 321
**Areopagus** 966
**arête** 253
**aretinism** 961
**aretology** 926
**Argand lamp** **423**
**argent** 430
**argillaceous** 324
**argosy** 273
**argot** 563
**argonaut** 269
**argue** *evidence* **407**
*reason* 476
*indicate* 550
*dissertation* 595
**argument** *disagree-*

ment 24
topic 454
discussion 476
meaning 516
have the best of
an – 478
argumentum
– ad baculum
compel 744
lawless 964
punish 972
– ad crumenam
800
– ad hominem
reasoning 476
accuse 938
– ad verecundiam
939
Argus-eyed 441, 459
argute 498
aria 415
arianism 984
arid 340
unproductive 169
uninteresting 841
Ariel courier 268
swift 274
messenger 534
spirit 979
arietation 276
arietta 415
aright well 618
Ariman [see Ahri-
manes]
ariolation 511
arioso 415
aris et focis, pro –
defence 717
philanthropy 910
arise exist 1
begin 66
happen 151
mount 305
appear 446
– from 154
Aristarchus 850
Aristides
good man 948
aristocracy
power 737
fashion 852
nobility 875
Arithmancy 511
arithmetic 85
ark abode 189
asylum 666
arm part 51
power 157
instrument 633
provide 637

prepare 673
war 722
weapon 727
make a long – 200
– chair 215
– in arm
together 88
friends 888
sociable 892
– of the law 963
– of the sea 343
armada 726
Armageddon 720,
722
armament 673, 727
armed 717
– at all points 673
– force 726
– guard 664
armet 717
armful 25
armiger 875
armigerent 726
armigerous 722
armilla 247, 847
armillary sphere
466
armipotent 157
armistice
cessation 142
respite 672
pacification 723
armless 158
armlet ring 247
gulf 343
ornament 847
armorial bearings
550, 877
armour cover 223
defence 717
arms 727
buckle on one's –
673
– plated 223
armoured
– car 726
– cruiser 726
– train 726
armoury store 636
workshop 691
arm's length
at – 196
keep at –
repel 289
defence 717
enmity 889
seclusion 893
discourtesy 895
arms 727 [see arm]
heraldry 550
war 722

honours 877
clash of – 720
deeds of – 720
with folded – 681
in – infant 129
throw oneself into
the – of 666, 888
under – 722
up in – active 682
discord 713
resistance 719
resentment 900
enmity 889
Armstrong gun 727
army collection 72
multitude 102
troops 726
aroma 400
around 227
lie – 220
arouse move 615
excite 824
– oneself 682
aroynt begone 297
malediction 908
arquebusade 662
arquebuse 727
arraign 938, 969
arrange
set in order 60
plan 626
compromise 774
– with creditors
807
– itself 58
arrange – matters
pacify 723
– music 413, 416
– in a series 69
– under 76
arrangement 23, 60
[see arrange]
order 58
temporary – 111
arrant identical 31
manifest 525
notorious 531
bad 649
disreputable 874
base 940
arras 847
array order 58, 60
series 69
assemblage 72
multitude 102
dress 225
prepare 673
adorn 847
ostentation 882
battle – 722
arrear, in – 53, 808

arrears debt 806
arrectis auribus
hear 418
expect 507
arrest stop 142
restrain 751
in law 969
– the attention 457
arrière-pensée
after-thought 65
mental reservation
528
motive 615
set purpose 620
arrival 292
arrive happen 151
reach 292
complete 729
– at a conclusion
480
– at the truth 480a
arrogant severe 739
proud 878
insolent 885
arrogate 885, 924
– to oneself
undue 925
arrondissement 181
arrosion 331
arrow swift 274
missile 284
arms 727
broad – 550
arrow-head
form 253
writing 590
'Arry and 'Arriet
902
ars celare artem
698
arsenal store 636
workshop 691
arsenic 663
arson 384
art representation
554
business 625
skill 698
cunning 702
fine – 850
work of – 845, 847
– gallery 556
artery 350, 627
artes, hæ tibi
erunt – 627
artesian well 343
artful 544, 702
– dodge 545, 702
article thing 3
part 51
matter 316

*give* 784
*allot* 786
– as cause 155
– a duty 926
– places 60
assignat 800
assignation 892
place of – 74
assignee *donee* 785
assimilate
*uniform* 16
*resemble* 17
*imitate* 19
*agree* 23
*transmute* 144
assist 707
– at 186
assistant 711
assister *be present* 186
assize *measure* 466
*tribunal* 966
justice of – 967
associate *mix* 41
*unite* 43
*collect* 72
*accompany* 88
*colleague* 690
*auxiliary* 711
*friend* 890
– with 892
association
[*see* associate]
*relation* 9
*combination* 48
*co-operation* 709
*partnership* 712
– of ideas
*intellect* 450
*thought* 451
*intuition* 477
*hint* 514
– football 840
assoil *acquit* 970
assonance
*music* 413
*poetry* 597
assort *arrange* 60
assortment 72, 75
assuage 174, 834
assuetude 613
assume *believe* 484
*suppose* 514
*falsehood* 544
*take* 789
*insolent* 885
*right* 924
– authority 737
– a character 554
– command 741
– a form 144

– the offensive 716
assumed name 565
assumption
[*see* assume]
*severity* 739
*hope* 858
*usurpation* 925
assurance
*speculation* 156
*certainty* 474
*belief* 484
*assertion* 535
*promise* 768
*security* 771
*hope* 858
*vanity* 880
*insolence* 885
make – double
sure *safe* 664
*caution* 864
assuredly
*assent* 488
assythment 973
astatic 320
asterisk 550
astern 235
put the engines – 275
fall – 283
asteroid 318
Asteroth 979
asthenia 160
astigmatism 443
astir 682
set – 824
astonish 870
astonished
– at nothing 871
astonishing
*great* 31
astound *excite* 824
*fear* 860
*surprise* 870
astra, sic itur ad – 360, 873
Astræa 922
astraddle 215
astragal 847
astral 318
– body 317, 992
– influence 601
– plane 317
astray 475, 495
go – *deviate* 279
*sin* 945
astriction 43
astride 215
astringent 195
astrolabe 466
astrologer 994

astrology 511
astromancy 511
astronomy 318
astute 498, 702
asunder 44, 196
as poles – 237
asylum *hospital* 663
*retreat* 666
*defence* 717
asymptote 290
at, be – 620
up and – them! 716
ataghan 727
atavism 145, 163
ataxia 158
atelier 556, 691
athanasia 112
Athanasian creed 983*a*
athanor 386
atheism 989
atheist 487
Athenae 979
Athens, owls to – 641
athirst 865
athlete *strong* 159
*gladiator* 726
athletic *strong* 159
*strenuous* 686
– sports
*contest* 720
*games* 840
athwart
*oblique* 217
*crossing* 219
*opposing* 708
Atkins, Tommy 726
Atlantis 515
Atlas *arrangement* 60
*list* 86
*strength* 159
*support* 215
*maps* 554
atmosphere
*circumambience* 227
*air* 338
*painting* 556
atmospheric blue 438
atoll 346
atom *small* 32, 193
atomic energy 157
atomizer 336
atoms
crush to – 162
atomy 193

atonement
*restitution* 790
*expiation* 952
*amends* 973
*religious* 976
atony 160
atrabilious 837
atramentous 431
atrium 191
atrocity
*malevolence* 907
*vice* 945
*guilt* 947
atrophy
*shrinking* 195
*disease* 655
*decay* 659
Atropos 601
attach *join* 43
*love* 897
*legal* 969
– importance to 642
attaché
*employé* 746
*diplomatic* 758
– case 191
attack *singing* 580
*disease* 655
*assault* 716
*debauch* 961
attaghan 727
attain *arrive* 292
*succeed* 731
– majority 131
attainable 470
attainder
*taint* 651
*at law* 971
attainment
*knowledge* 490
*learning* 539
*skill* 698
attar 400
attemper 41, 174
attempered 820
attempt 675
vain – 732
– impossibilities 471
attend
*accompany* 88
*be present* 186
*follow* 281
*apply the mind* 457
*medically* 662
*aid* 707
*serve* 746
– to business 625
– to orders 743

attendance on
  dance – 886
attendant
  [see attend]
attention **457**
  care 459
  respect 928
  attract – 882
  call to – 457
  call – to 550
  give – 418
  pay –s to 894
  pay one's –s to
    902
attenuate
  decrease 36
  weaken 158
  reduce 195
  rarefy 322
attenuated 203
attest
  bear testimony 467
  affirm 535
  adjure 768
attested copy 771
attic simple 42
  garret 191
  summit 210
  style 578
  wit 842
  taste 850
Attila 913
attire 225
attitude
  circumstance 8
  situation 183
  posture 240
attitudinarian 882
attitudinize 855
attollent 307
attorney
  consignee 758
  at law 968
  power of – 755
attract
  bring towards 288
  induce 615
  allure 865
  excite love 897
  – the attention
    457
  visible 446
attraction
  [see attract]
  natural power 157
  bring towards
    **288**
attractive
  [see attract]
  pleasing 829
  beautiful 845

attrahent 288
attribute
  speciality 79
  accompaniment
    88
  power 157
  –s of the Deity 976
  – to 155
attribution **155**
attrite 330
attrition 330, 331
attroupement 72
attune music 415
  prepare 673
attuned to
  habit 613
attunement 23
auburn 433
A.U.C. 106
auction 796, 840
auctioneer 758, 796
auctorial 599
audacity
  courage 861
  rashness 863
  insolence 885
audible 402
  become – 418
  scarcely – 405
audience
  hearing 418
  conversation 588
  before an – 599
audire alteram
  partem
  counter-evidence
    468
  right 922
  justice 939
audit
  numeration 85
  examination 461
  accounts 811
auditive 418
auditor
  hearer 418
  accountant 811
auditorium 189, 588
auditory
  sound 402
  hearing 418
  theatre 599
  – apparatus 418
au fait 698
au fond 5
auf Wiedersehen
  293
Augean
  – stable 653
  – task 704
auger 262

aught 51
  for – one cares
    unimportant 643
  indifferent 866
  for – one knows
    ignorance 491
  conjecture 514
augment
  increase 35
  thing added 39
  expand 194
augur 513
  – well 858
augurate 511
augury 512
august 873
Augustinian 996
auk 366
auld lang syne 122
aulic council 696
aumbry 1000
aunt 11
aura wind 349
  sensation 380
aurea mediocritas
  628
aureate 436
aureola 420
aureole 420, 873
aureolin 436
auribus, arrectis –
  418
auricular hearing
  418
  clandestine 528
  – confession 998
auri sacra fames
  819
aurist 662
aurora
  dawn 125
  light 420, 423
  twilight 422
  – australis 423
  – borealis 423
Auroral 236
ausculation 418
auspice omen 512
auspices
  influence 175
  prediction 511
  protection 664
  direction 693
  aid 707
  under the – of 693,
    737
auspicious
  opportune 134
  prosperous 734
  hopeful 858
austerity

harsh taste 395
  severe 739
  discourteous 895
  ascetic 955
  pietism 988
austral 237
austromancy 511
authentic 467
  certain 474
  true 494
authentication
  evidence 467
  security 771
author 164, 593
  projector 626
  dramatic – 599
  – of our being 976
  – of evil 978
  – 's proof 591
authoritative 474,
  741
authority
  testimony 467
  sage 500
  informant 527
  power **737**
  permission 760
  right 924
  ensign of – 747
  person in – 745
  do upon one's own
    – 600
authorized due 924
  legalized 963
authorship
  production 161
  style 569
  writing 590
autobiography 594
autocar 272
autochthonous 188
autocracy 737, 739
autocrat 745
autocratic 600, 737
auto-da-fé 384, 972
autograph 550, 590
Autolycus thief 792
  pedlar 797
automaniac 504
automatic 601, 633
- pistol 727
- writing 992
automaton 554, 601
automobile 272
automobilist 268
automotive 266
autonomania 521
autonomy 737, 748
autopsy
  post-mortem 363
  vision 441

autoptical 446, 525
autotype 558
autumn 126
auxiliary **711**
  *additional* 37
  *helpful* 707
  – *forces* 726
avail *benefit* 618
  *useful* 644
  *succeed* 731
  of no – 645
  – oneself of 677
avalanche *fall* 306
  *snow* 383
  *redundance* 641
avaler des couleu-
  vres 725, 886
avant-coureur 64,
  673
avant-propos 64
avarice 819
avast! *stop* 142, 265
  *desist* 624
  *forbid* 761
avatar *change* 140
  *deity* 976
  *idol* 991
avaunt! 297, 449
ave! *honour* 873
  *courtesy* 894
Ave maria 990
avenge 919
avenue
  *plantation* 371
  *way* 627
aver 535
average *mean* 29,
  628
  *médiocre* 651
  – circumstances
  736
  take an – 466
Averni, facilis de-
  scensus – 217,
  665
Avernus 982
averruncate 297,
  301
aversion *unwilling-
  ness* 603
  *dislike* 867
  *hate* 898
avert 706
  – the eyes 442
aviary 370
aviation 267
aviator 269
avidity *avarice* 819
  *desire* 865
aviette 273
avile 932, 934

[ 404 ]

avion 273
aviso 532
avocation 625
avoidance **623**
avoidless 474, 601
avoirdupois 319
avolation 623, 671
avouch 535, 768
avow *assent* 488
  *disclose* 529
  *assert* 535
avulsion 44, 301
avuncular 11
await *future* 121
  *be kept waiting*
  133
  *impend* 152
  *expect* 507
awake *attentive* **457**
  *careful* 459
  *intelligent* 498
  *active* 682
  – to life immortal
  360
awaken *inform* **527**
  *excite* 824
  – the attention **457**
  – the memory **505**
award *adjudge* 480
  *give* 784
aware 490
away 187, 196
  break – 623
  fly – 293
  move – 287
  take – from **789**
  get &c. – 671
  throw &c. –
  *eject* 297
  *reject* 610
  *waste* 638
  *relinquish* 782
  – from *unrelated* 10
  – with! 930, 932
  do – with *undo* 681
  *abrogate* 756
awe *fear* 860
  *wonder* 870
  *respect* 928
aweless *fearless* 861
  *insolent* 885
  *disrespectful* 929
awful 31, 860
  – silence 403
awhile 111
awkward
  *inelegant* 579
  *inexpedient* 647
  *unskilful* 699
  *difficult* 704
  *painful* 830

*ugly* 846
*vulgar* 851
*ridiculous* 853
– squad 701
awl 262
awn 253
awning 223, 424
awry *oblique* 217
  *distorted* 243
  *evil* 619
axe *edge tool* 253
  *impulse* 276
  *weapon* 727
  *for beheading* 975
  have an – to grind
  702
Axinomancy 511
axiom 496
axiomatic 474
axis *support* 215
  *centre* 222
  *rotation* 312
axle 312
  wheel and – 633
axle load 466
axletree 215
ay 488
ayah 746, 753
aye *ever* 112
  *yes* 488
azimuth
  *horizontal* 213
  *direction* 278
  *measurement* 466
  – circle 212
azoic 358
azote 663
azotic 657
azure 438
azygous *single* 87

**B**

Baal 979, 986
Babbittry 851
babble *rivulet* 348
  *faint sound* 405
  *unmeaning* 517
  *talk* 584, 588
babbler 501
babbling
  *foolish* 499
babe 129
  innocent as the –
  unborn 946
Babel *confusion* 59
  *discord* 414
  *tongues* 560
  *jargon* 563
  *loquacity* 584

baboon 846
baby *infant* **129**
  *fool* 501
  – linen 225
babyhood 127
babyish 499
baccarat 840
bacchanals 959
Bacchus 979
  *drink* 959
bachelor 904
  – of arts 492
  – girl 374
bacillus 193
back *rear* 235
  *shoulder* 250
  *aid* 707
  behind one's –
  *latent* 526
  *hidden* 528
  come – 292
  give – 790
  fall – *relapse* 661
  go – 283
  go – from *retract*
  773
  have at one's – 215
  hold – *avoid* 623
  keep – *reserve* 636
  look – 505
  on one's – *impo-
  tent* 158
  *horizontal* 213
  *failure* 732
  pat on the –
  *incite* 615
  *encourage* 861
  *approve* 931
  pay – *retaliate* 718
  put – *deteriorate*
  659
  *restore* 660
  send – 764
  take – again **790**
  carry one's –
  thoughts – 505
  some time – 122
  spring – 277
  trace – 505
  turn – 283
  turn one's – 283
  turn one's – upon
  *repel* 289
  *inattention* 458
  *avoid* 623
  *oppose* 708
  *seclusion* 893
  *discourtesy* 895
  *disrespect* 929
  *contempt* 930
  set one's – against

the wall 604
~ to back 235
– down 283
– one's note 806
– out *retire* 283
*change sides* 607
*relinquish* 624
– pedal 275
– up *support* 215
*influence* 615
*aid* 707
put one's – up
*anger* 900
set one's – up
*pride* 878
**backbite** 932, 934
**backbiter** 936
**backbone**
*intrinsic* 5
*energy* 171
*frame* 215
*centre* 222
*resolution* 604
*persevere* 604a
*soul* 820
game to the – 604
**back door** 627
**back down** 607
**backer** 711
**back-fire** 406
**back friend** 891
**backgammon** 840
**background**
*distance* 196
*rear* 235
in the –
*latent* 526
*ignoble* 874
keep in the –
*hide* 528
*modest* 881
*seclusion* 893
put one in the –
874
throw into the –
460
**backsheesh** 784,
973
**backside** 235
**backslider** 607
**backsliding**
*regression* 283
*tergiversation* 607
*relapse* 661
*vice* 945
*heterodox* 984
*impiety* 988
**backstairs**
*ambush* 530
*way* 627
– influence 702

**backward**
*tardy* 133
*regression* 283
*unwilling* 603
*deteriorate* 659
**backwardation** 813
**backwards** 283
bend – 235
– and forwards
*interchange* 148
*oscillation* 314
**backwater** 275, 283
in a – 893
**backwoodsman**
*inhabitant* 188
*agriculture* 371
**bacon**
butter upon – 641
save one's – 664,
671
**Baconian method**
461
**bacteria** 193
**bactericide** 662
**baculinum, argu-**
**mentum –**
*compel* 744
*lawless* 964
*punish* 972
**bad** 649
*unclean* 653
*wrong* 923
– blood 898, 907
go – 653, 659
– business 859
– case 477
– chance 473
put a – construc-
tion on 523
– debt 806
– fairy 980
– faith 940
– grace 895
– habit 613
– hand 701
– humour
*discontent* 832
*dejection* 837
*anger* 900
*sullen* 901a
not a – idea 498
– intent 907
– job *evil* 619
*botch* 699
*hopeless* 859
– joke 851
– language 908
view in a – light
934
– luck &c. 735

– man **949**
– money 800
– name 932, 934
in – odour 889
take in – part 832,
900
– repute 874
– smell 401
– spirit 980
– spirits 837
– taste 579, 851
– temper 900, 901,
901*a*
on – terms 713,
889
– time of it 828
– turn 619, 907
in a – way
*disease* 655
*worse* 659
*danger* 665
*adversity* 735
– woman 949
from – to worse
*aggravation* 835
**badaud** 501
**badge** 550
– of authority 747
– of infamy 874
– of slavery 746
**badger** 830
– dog 366
**badinage** 842, 856
**badly off**
*adversity* 735
*poor* 804
**badminton** 840
**badness** 649
**Baedeker** 266
**baffle** *hinder* 706
*defeat* 731
– description
*unconformable* 83
*wonder* 870
**baffling**
*puzzling* 519
**bag** *put up* 184
*receptacle* 191
*protrude* 250
*acquire* 775
*take* 789
*steal* 791
– and baggage 780
**bagatelle**
*trivial* 643
*pastime* 840
**baggage** 270
*minx* 129
*materials* 635
*property* 780

*hussy* 962
**baggy** 47
**bagman** 758
**bagnio** 961
**bagpipes** 417
**bah!** 930
**bail** 771
go – 806
leg – 623
**bailie** 965
**bailiff**
*director* 694
*servant* 746
*factor* 758
*officer* 965
**bailiwick**
*region* 181
*jurisdiction* 965
**Bairam**
*holiday* 840
*rite* 998
**bairn** 129
**bait** *attraction* 288
*food* 298
*trap* 545
*lure* 615
*refresh* 689
*attack* 716
*bribe* 784
*harass* 830
swallow the – 547
**bake** 384
**bakehouse** 386
**baker** 637
**baker's dozen** 98
**baking heat** 382
**bal** 840
**Balaclava helmet**
225
**balais** 847
**balance** *equal* 27
*mean* 29
*compensate* 30
*remainder* 40
*numeration* 85
*weigh* 319
*compare* 464
*style* 578
*hesitate* 605
*money* 800
*accounts* 811
in the – 475
the mind losing its
– 503
off one's –
*irresolute* 605
*fail* 732
want of – 579
– accounts with
*pay* 807

| | | | |
|---|---|---|---|
| **balanced** 150, 242 | **balmy** | **banish** *eject* 297 | *disrepute* 874 |
| **balbucinate** 583 | *sleep* 683 | *seclude* 893 | *illegal* 964 |
| **balbutiate** 583 | **balneal** 337 | *punish* 972 | crossing the – **360** |
| **balcony** 250 | **balourdise** 699 | **banister** 215 | **Barabbas** 792 |
| *theatre* 599 | **balsam** 662 | **banjo** 417 | **baragouin** 517 |
| **bald** *bare* 226 | **balsamic** | **bank** *acclivity* 217 | **barb** *spike* 253 |
| *style* 575 | *salubrious* 834 | *side of lake* 342 | *nag* 271 |
| *uninteresting* 841 | **balustrade** | *store* 636 | – the dart *pain* 830 |
| *ugly* 846 | *support* 215 | *sand* 667 | **barbacan** 717 |
| *plain* 849 | *inclosure* 232 | *fence* 717 | **barbarian** |
| **baldachin** 223, 1000 | **bam** 544 | *money* 802 | *uncivilized* 876 |
| **balderdash** 517, 577 | **bambino** 129 | sea – 342 | *evil-doer* 913 |
| **baldric** 230, 247 | **bamboozle** 545 | – of elegance 800 | **barbaric** 851, 876 |
| **bale** *bundle* 72 | **ban** *exclude* 55 | – holiday 840 | **barbarism** |
| *load* 190 | *prohibit* 761 | – up 670 | *neology* 563 |
| *ladle* 270 | *denounce* 908 | **banker** 797, 801 | *bad style* 579 |
| *evil* 619 | under the – 909 | *game* 840 | *vulgarity* 851 |
| – out 297 | – with bell, book, | **bank-note** 800 | *discourtesy* 895 |
| **baleful** 649 | and candle 998 | **bankruptcy** 732, 808 | **barbarous** |
| **balister** 727 | **banal** 613, 843 | **banlieue** 197, 227 | *unformed* 241 |
| **balize** 550 | **band** *ligature* 45 | **banner** 550 | *plebeian* 876 |
| **balk** *disappoint* 509 | *assemblage* 72 | enlist under the -s | *maleficent* 907 |
| *deceive* 545 | *filament* 205 | of 707 | **barbette** 717 |
| *hinder* 706 | *belt* 230 | raise one's – 722 | **barbican** 717 |
| **Balkanize** 713 | *ring* 247 | **banneret** 875 | **barbouillage** 590 |
| **ball** *globe* 249 | *music* 415, 416, | **banns** | **barcarolle** 415 |
| *missile* 284 | 417 | forbid the – 761 | **bard** 416, 597 |
| *shot* 727 | *party* 712 | publish the – | **bare** *mere* 32 |
| *dance* 840 | *shackle* 752 | ask 765 | *nude* 226 |
| *party* 892 | – of hope 958 | *marriage* 903 | *manifest* 525 |
| – at one's feet 731, | – together 709 | **banquet** 298, 840 | *disclose* 529 |
| 737 | – with 720 | **banquette** 717 | *scanty* 640 |
| keep up the – 143, | **bandage** 43, 45 | **banshee** 979, 980 | – back 226 |
| 682 | *support* 215 | **bantam cock** 887 | – bone 203 |
| **ballad** 415, 597 | *cover* 223 | **banter** 842, 856 | – faced *deceitful* |
| – monger 597 | *remedy* 662 | **banterer** 844 | 544, *insolent* 885 |
| **ballast** | *restraint* 752 | **banting** 956 | – foot 226, 804 |
| *compensation* 30 | the eyes -d 442 | **bantling** 129, 167 | – headed 928 |
| *weight* 319 | **bandana** 225 | **banyan** *stint* 640 | scud under - poles |
| *wisdom* 498 | **bandbox** 191 | *fast* 956 | 704 |
| *safety* 666 | **banded together** | **baptism** *name* 564 | – possibility 473 |
| without – *rash* 863 | 178, 713 | *rite* 998 | – supposition 514 |
| *vicious* 945 | **bandit** 792 | **Baptist** 984 | **bargain** |
| **ballerina** 599 | **bandog** 664, 668 | **baptistery** 1000 | *compact* 769 |
| **ballet** 599, 840 | **bandolier** 636 | **bar** *except* 38 | *barter* 794 |
| **ballet-dancer** 599 | **bandore** 417 | *exclude* 55 | *cheap* 815 |
| **ballistics** | **bandrol** 550 | *hotel* 189 | into the - 37 |
| *projectiles* 284 | **bands** 999 | *line* 200 | - for 507 |
| *war* 722 | **bandurria** 417 | *support* 215 | - and sale *transfer* |
| *arms* 727 | **bandy** | *inclosure* 232 | *of property* 783 |
| **ballon d'essai** 463 | *exchange* 148 | *close* 261 | **barge** 273 |
| **balloon** 273, 726 | *agitate* 315 | *music* 413 | **bargee** 269 |
| **balloonist** 269 | – about 531 | *hindrance* 706 | **baritone** 408 |
| **balloonry** 267 | – legged 243 | *insignia* 747 | **bark** *rind* 223 |
| **ballot** 535, 609 | – words 476, 588 | *prison* 752 | *strip* 226 |
| **ball-room** 840 | **bane** 619, **663** | *prohibit* 761 | *ship* 273 |
| **balm** *moderate* 174 | **baneful** 649 | *ingot* 800 | *yelp* 412 |
| *fragrance* 400 | **bang** *impel* 276 | *tribunal* 966 | - at *threaten* 909 |
| *remedy* 662 | *sound* 406 | *legal profession* | *censure* 932 |
| *relief* 834 | *beat* 972 | 968 | more - than bit( |
| **Balmoral** *boot* 225 | **bangle** 847 | – sinister *flaw* 651 | 908 |

belike 472
belittle
  *decrease* 36
  *underestimate* 482
  *disparage* 934
bell 417, 550
  alarm − 669
  bear away the −
  *goodness* 648
  *success* 731
  *repute* 873
  church − 550
  cracked − 408a
  passing − 363
  − book and candle
  *swear* 535
  *curse* 908
  *spell* 993
  *rite* 998
  − the cat 861
  − shape 249, 252
belladonna 663
belle 374, 854
  a la − étoile 220,
  338
belles-lettres 560
belli, casus − 824
bellicose 720, 722
bellied 250
belligerent
  *contentious* 720
  *warlike* 722
  *combatant* 726
belling 412
bellman 534
bello, flagrante −
  722
Bellona 722
bellow *loud* 404
  *cry* 411
  *animal cry* 412
  *wail* 839
bellows 349, 580
bells, peal of − 407
bellwether 64, 694
belly *receptacle* 191
  *inside* 221
  *convex* 250
  −ful 52
  − god 957
  − timber 298
belomancy 511
belong to *related* 9
  *component* 56
  *included* 76
  *attribute* 157
  *property* 777, 780
  *duty* 926
beloved 897
below 207
  here − 318

− the mark 32
− par 34, 207
  *bad* 649
  *indifferent* 651
  *discount* 813
  *ignoble* 876
− its full strength
  651
− stairs 207
belt *outline* 230
  *ring* 247
  *strait* 343
  swimming − 666
belting 633
Belus 979
belvedere 441
bemask 528
bemingle 41
bemire 653
bemoan 839
bemused 458
bench *support* 215
  *council* 696
  *tribunal* 966
Bench, King's −
  752
bencher 968
bend *oblique* 217
  *angle* 244
  *curve* 245
  *incline* 278
  *deviate* 279
  *depression* 308
  *circuit* 311
  *give* 324
  *submit* 725
  − backwards 235
  − the bow 686
  − the brows 932
  − one's course 27
  − the knee
  *bow down* 308
  *submit* 725
  *humble* 879
  *servile* 886
  *courtesy* 894
  *respect* 928
  *worship* 990
  − one's looks upon
  441
  − the mind 457
  − over 250
  − to rules &c. 82
  − sinister 874
  − one's steps 622
  − to *tend* 176
  − towards 278
  − to one's will 737
beneath 207
  − one 940
  − notice 643

Benedick 903
Benedictine 996
benediction
  *gratitude* 916
  *approval* 931
  *worship* 990
  nuptial − 903
benefaction 784
benefactor 816, 912
benefice 995
beneficent 906
beneficial 648
  − interest 780
beneficiary
  *possessor* 779
  *receive* 785
  *clergy* 996
benefit *good* 618
  *use* 644
  *do good* 648
  *aid* 707
  *acquisition* 775
  *property* 780
  *benevolence* 906
  reap the − of 658
benefits forgot 917
bene gesserit,
  quamdiu se −
  926
benet 545
benevolence
  *tax* 812
  *love* 897
  *kindness* **906**
  universal − 910
Bengal heat 382
benighted
  *dark* 421
  *ignorant* 491
benign 656, 906
benignant 906
benison 618, 931
Benjamin's mess
  33, 50
Benshie 979
bent *tendency* 176
  *angle* 244
  *turn of mind* 820
  *desire* 865
  fool to the top of
  one's − 856
  − on *willing* 602
  *resolved* 604
  *intention* 620
  *desirous* 865
Benthamite 910
ben trovato
  *likely* 472
  *imagination* 515
  *untruth* 546
  *wit* 842

benumb
  *insensible* 376
  *cold* 385
  *deaden affections*
  823
beplaster 933
bepraise 931
bequest 270
  *gift* 784
bereavement
  *death* 360
  *loss* 776
  *take away* 789
bereft *poor* 804
  − of life 360
  − of reason 503
béret 225
berg, ice − 383
bergamot 400
berlin 272
berserk 173, 503
berth *lodging* 189
  *bed* 215
  *office* 625
beryl *green* 435
  *jewel* 847
beseech 765, 990
beseem 926
beset *surround* 227
  *follow* 281
  *attack* 716
  *entreat* 765
  *annoy* 830
  *haunt* 860
  − with difficulties
  704
besetting 78, 613
  − sin 945
beshrew 908
beside *except* 83
  *near* 197
  *alongside* 236
  − the mark 10, 495
  − oneself 503, 824
besides 37
besiege
  *surround* 227
  *attack* 716
  *solicit* 765
bésique 840
beslaver 933
beslime 653
beslubber 933
besmear 223, 653
besom 652
besotted 481
bespangle 847
bespatter *dirt* 653
  *disapprove* 932
  *flatter* 933
  *detract* 934

bespeak *early* 132
  *evidence* 467
  *indicate* 516
  *engage* 755
  *ask for* 765
bespeckle 440
bespot 440
besprinkle 41, 440
best 648, 650
  all for the –
  *good* 618
  *prosper* 734
  *content* 831
  *hope* 858
  bad is the – 649
  do one's –
  *care* 459
  *try* 675
  *activity* 682
  *exertion* 686
  have the – of it 731
  make the – of it
  *over-estimate* 482
  *use* 677
  *submit* 725
  *compromise* 774
  *take easily* 826
  *hope* 858
  the – 800
  to the – of one's
    belief 484
  – bib and tucker
  *prepared* 673
  *ornament* 847
  *ostentation* 882
  – friends 890
  – intentions 906
  – man 903
  – part 31, 50
  – seller 731
  make the – of
    one's time 684
bestead 644
bestial 954, 961
bestir oneself
  *activity* 682
  *haste* 684
  *exertion* 686
bestow 784
  – one's hand 903
  – thought 451
bestraddle 215
bestrew 73
bestride 206, 215
bet 621
betake oneself to
  *journey* 266
  *business* 625
  *use* 677
bête, pas si – 498
bête noire *bane* 663

*fear* 860
*hate* 898
bethel 1000
bethink 451, 505
bethral 749, 751
betide 151
betimes 132
betoken
  *evidence* 467
  *predict* 511
  *indicate* 550
betray *disclose* 529
  *deceive* 545
  *dishonour* 940
  – *itself visible* 446
betrayer 941
betrim 673
betroth 768, 903
betrothed 897
better *good* 648
  *improve* 658
  appeal to one's –
    feelings 914
  get – *health* 654
  *improve* 658
  *refreshment* 689
  *restoration* 660
  get the – of, 479,
    702, 731
  think – of 658, 950
  seen – days
  *deteriorate* 659
  *adversity* 735
  *poor* 804
  – half 903
  only – than noth-
    ing 651
  – sort 875
  for – for worse
  *choice* 609
  *marriage* 903
between 228
  – cup and lip 111
  far – 198
  lie – 228
  – the lines 526
  vibrate – two ex-
    tremes 149
  – ourselves 528
  – two fires 665
  – maid 746
betwixt 228
bevel 217
  – gearing 633
bever 298
beverage 298
bévue 732
bevy 72, 102
bewail *regret* 833
  *lament* 839
beware 665, 668

bewilder
  *put out* 458
  *uncertainty* 475
  *astonish* 870
bewitch
  *fascinate* 615
  *please* 829
  *excite love* 897
  *exorcise* 992
bey 745
beyond *superior* 33
  *distance* 196
  go – 303
  – compare 31, 33
  – control 471
  – one's depth 208,
    519
  – expression 31
  – one's grasp 471
  – hope 731, 534
  – the mark 303,
    641
  – measure 641
  – possibility 471
  – praise
  *perfect* 650
  *approbation* 931
  *virtue* 944
  – price 814
  – question 474, 494
  – reason 471
  – remedy 859
  – seas 57
bezel 217
bhang 663
bias *influence* 175
  *tendency* 176
  *slope* 217
  *prepossession* 481
  *disposition* 820
bib *pinafore* 225
  *drink* 959
bibber *weep* 839
  *toper* 959
bibble-babble 584
bibelot 847
bibendum, nunc
  est – 959
Bible 985
  – oath 535
biblioclasm 162
bibliography 593
bibliolatry
  *learning* 490
  *heterodoxy* 984
  *idolatry* 991
bibliomancy 511
bibliomania 490
bibliomaniac 492
bibliophile 492
bibliopole 593

bibliotheca 593
bibulous 298, 959
bicameral 90
bicapital 90
bice 435, 438
bicentenary 98,
  138, 883
bicker *flutter* 315
  *quarrel* 713
bicolour 440
biconjugate 91
bicuspid 91
bicycle 272
bid *order* 741
  *offer* 763
  – the banns 903
  – defiance 715
  – fair *tend* 176
  *probable* 472
  *promise* 511
  *hope* 858
  – a long farewell
    624
  – for *intend* 620
  *offer* 763
  *request* 765
  *bargain* 794
bidder 767
bide *wait* 133
  *remain* 141
  *take coolly* 826
  – one's time 133
  *watch* 507
  *inactive* 681
bidet 271
biennial
  *periodic* 138
  *plant* 367
bienséance 852, 894
bier 363
bifacial 90
bifarious 90
bifid 91
bifold 90
biform 90
bifurcate 91, 244
big *in degree* 31
  *in size* 192
  *wide* 194
  look – *defy* 715
  *proud* 878
  *insolent* 885
  talk – 885, 909
  – sounding
  *loud* 404
  *words* 577
  *affected* 855
  – swollen 194
  – with 161
  – with the fate of
    511

**bigamy** 903
**biggin** 191
**bight** 343
**bigot** *positive* 474
  *prejudice* 481
  *obstinate* 606
  *heterodox* 984
  *impious* 988
**bigotry** 907
**bigwig** *scholar* 492
  *sage* 500
  *nobility* 875
**bijou** *goodness* 648
  *beauty* 845
  *ornament* 847
**bilander** 273
**bilateral** 90, 236
**bilbo** 727
**bilboes** 752
  put into – 751
**bile** 900
**bilge** *base* 211
  *convex* 250
  *yawn* 260
  – *water* 653
**bilingual** 560
**bilious** 837
**bilk**
  *disappoint* 509
  *cheat* 545
  *steal* 791
**bill** *list* 86
  *hatchet* 253
  *placard* 531
  *ticket* 550
  *paper* 593
  *plan* 626
  *weapon* 727
  *money order* 800
  *money account*
    811
  *charge* 812
  *in law* 969
  *true* – 969
  – *and coo* 902
  – *of exchange* 771
  – *of fare food* 298
  *plan* 626
  – *of indictment*
    938
  –s *of mortality* 360
  – *of sale* 771
**billet** *locate* 184
  *ticket* 550
  *apportion* 786
**billet** *epistle* 592
  – *doux* 902
**billfold** 191
**billhook** 253
**billiard** – *ball* 249
  – *room* 191

– *table flat* 213
**billiards** 840
**Billingsgate** 563,
  908
**billion** 98
**billow** *sea* 348
  *river* 341
**billy-cock** 225
**billy-goat** 373
**bimetallism** 800
**bin** 191
**binary** 89
**bind** *connect* 43
  *cover* 223
  *compel* 744
  *condition* 770
  *obligation* 926
  – *hand and foot*
    751
  – *oneself* 768
  – *over* 744
  – *up wounds* 660
**binding** 744
**bine** 367
**binnacle** 693
**binocular** 445
**binomial** 89
**biogenesis** 161
**biograph** 448
**biography** 594
**biology** 357, 359
**bioscope** 448
**biota** 357
**biparous** 89
**bipartite** 44, 91
**biplane** 273
**biplicity** 89
**biquadrate** 96
**birch** *flog* 972
  – *rod* 975
**bird** 366
  kill  two –s with
    one stone 682
  –'s *eye view* 441,
    448
  –s *of a feather* 17
  the – *has flown*
    187, 671
  – *in hand* 777, 781
  – *of ill omen*
  *omen* 512
  *warning* 668
  *hopeless* 859
  – *of passage* 268
  – *of prey* 739
  a little – *told me*
    527
**birdcage** 370
**birdlime** *glue* 45
  *trap* 545
**biretta** 999

**birth** *beginning* 66
  *production* 161
  *paternity* 166
  *nobility* 875
  – *place* 153
  – *right* 924
**birthday** 138, 883
  – *suit* 226
**birthmark** 848
**bis** *repeat* 104
  *approval* 931
**biscuits, s'embar-**
  quer sans – 674
**bise** 349
**bisection** 68, **91**
**bishop** *punch* 298
  *clergy* 996
  –'s *palace* 1000
  –'s *purple* 437
**bishopric** 995
**bisque** 33
**bissextile** 138
**bistoury** 253
**bistre** 433
**bisulcate** 259
**bit**
  *small quantity* 32
  *part* 51
  *interval* 106
  *curb* 752
  just a – 26
  – *by bit*
  *by degrees* 26
  *by instalments* 51
  *in detail* 79
  *slowly* 275
  – *between the*
    *teeth* 600, 719
**bitch** *animal* 366
  *female* 374
  *clumsy* 699
  *fail* 732
  *impure* 962
**bite** *eat* 298
  *physical pain* 378
  *cold* 385
  *cheat* 545
  *dupe* 547
  *etch* 558
  *mental pain* 830
  – *the dust* 725
  – *in* 259
  – *the thumb* 900,
    929
  – *the tongue* 392
**biter bit** 718
**biting** *pain* 378
  *cold* 383
  *pungent* 392
  *painful* 830
  *discourteous* 895

  *censorious* 932
**bitten** 897
**bitter** *beer* 298
  *cold* 383
  *taste* 392, 395
  *painful* 830
  *acrimonious* 895
  *hate* 898
  *angry* 900
  *malevolent* 907
  – *end* 67
  – *ender* 606, 710,
    832
  – *pill* 735
  – *words* 932
**bitterly** *greatly* 31
**bitterness**
  [*see* bitter]
  *pain* 828
  *regret* 833
**bitumen** 356*a*
**bituminous coal**
  388
**bivouac**
  *encamp* 184
  *camp* 189
  *repose* 265
  *watch* 668
**bi-weekly** 138
**bizarre** 83, 853
**blab** 529
**blabber** 584
**black** *colour* 431
  *crime* 945
  *look* – *feeling* 821
  *discontent* 832
  *angry* 900
  – *art* 992
  – *and blue*
    *beat* 972
  – *board* 590
  – *book* 938
  – *eye* 848, 972
  – *in the face*
    *swear* 535
  *excitement* 821,
    824
  – *flag* 722
  – *hole crowd* 72
  *prison* 752
  – *lead* 556
  – *letter old* 124
  *barbarism* 563
  *print* 591
  – *list* 932
  – *looks*
  *discourteous* 895
  *sullen* 901*a*
  *disapprove* 932
  *magic* 992
  – *mail theft* 791

*severe* 739
hands in − *cruel*
  907
in the − 5
life − 359
new − 658, 824
spill − *war* 722
− for blood 919
− boil *excite* 824,
  825
*anger* 900
− run cold 830,
  860
− heat 382
− horse 271
− hound 913
− letting 297, 662
− poisoning 655
− red 434
− stained 361
− sucker 789, 913
− thirsty
  *murderous* 361
*cruel* 907
− up *excited* 824
*angry* 900
**bloodless** 160
*peace* 721
*virtue* 946
**bloody** [*see* blood]
*red* 434
*unclean* 653
*cruel* 907
**bloom** *youth* 127
*flower* 367
*blue* 438
*health* 654
*prosperity* 734
**bloomer** 495
**bloomers** 225
**blooming** 654, 845
**blossom**
*flower* 154, 161,
  367
*prosperity* 734
**blot** *blacken* 431
*error* 495
*obliterate* 552
*dirty* 653
*blemish* 848
*disgrace* 874
*guilt* 947
− out *destroy* 162
*forgive* 918
**blotch** 848
**blouse** 225
**blow** *expand* 194
*knock* 276
*wind* 349
*unexpected* 508

*disappointment*
  509
*evil* 619
*action* 680
*get wind* 688
*failure* 732
*prosper* 734
*pain* 828, 830
come to −s 720, 722
deal a − at 716
deal a − to 972
*death* − 360, 361
− for blow 718
− one's brains out
  361
− the coals 824
− down 162
− the fire 384
− the gaff 529
− hole 351
− the horn 416
− hot and cold
*lie* 544
*irresolute* 605
*tergiversation* 607
*caprice* 608
− a kiss 902
− off *disperse* 73
− out *food* 298
*darken* 421
*gorge* 957
− over *past* 122
− pipe 349, 727
− the trumpet 873
− one's own
  trumpet 882
− up *destroy* 162
*eruption* 173
*inflate* 194
*wind* 349
*excite* 824
*objurgate* 932,
  934
**blower** 349
**blowhard** 884
**blown** [*see* blow]
*fatigued* 688
*proud* 878
storm − over 664,
  721
− upon 874, 932
**blow-out** 406
**blowzy** *swollen* 194
*red* 434
**blubber** *fat* 356
*cry* 839
**Blücher boot** 225
**bludgeon** 727
− man 726, 913
**blue** *sky* 338
*colour* 438

*learned* 490
bit of − hope 858
look −
  *disappointed* 509
*feeling* 821
*discontent* 832
*disrepute* 874
out of the − 508
swear till all's −
  535
true − 543, 939
− book 86, 551
− blood 875
− devils 837
− jacket 269
− light 550, 669
− pencil 174, 596
− moon 110
− Peter 293, 550
− and red 437
− ribbon 733, 877
− ruin 959
− stocking
*scholar* 492
*affectation* 855
− and yellow 435
**Bluebeard**
*marriage* 903
*libertine* 962
**blueness** **438**
**blues** 837, 840
**bluff** *violent* 173
*high cliff* 206
**blunt** 254
*deceive* 545
*boasting* 884
*insolent* 885
*discourteous* 895
**blunder** *error* 495
*absurdity* 497
*awkward* 699
*failure* 732
− upon 156
**blunderbuss** 727
**blunderhead** 701
**blunderheaded** 499
**blunt** *weaken* 160
*inert* 172
*moderate* v. 174
*obtuse* 254
*benumb* 376
*damp* v. 616
*plain-spoken* 703
*cash* 800
*deaden* 823
*discourteous* 895
− tool 645
− witted 499
**bluntness** **254**
**blur**
*imperfect vision*

443
*dirt* 653
*blemish* 848
*stigma* 874
**blurb** 931
**blurred**
*invisible* 447
**blurt out** 529, 582
**blush** *flush* 382
*redden* 434
*feel* 821
*humbled* 879
*modest* 881
at first − *see* 441
*appear* 448
*manifest* 525
put to the −
*humble* 897
*browbeat* 885
*discourtesy* 895
**blushing honours**
  873, 881
**bluster** *violent* 173
*defiant* 715
*boasting* 884
*insolent* 885
*threaten* 909
**blusterer** **887**
**blustering** [*see*
  bluster]
*windy* 349
**Bo to a goose, not**
  say − 862
**boa** 225
**Boanerges** 540
**boar** 366, 373
**board** *layer* 204
*support* 215
*food* 298
*hard* 323
*council* 696
*attack* 716
*tribunal* 966
*festive* − 892
go by the − 158,
  162
go on − 293
on − 186, 273
preside at the −
  693
− of trade 621
− school 542
**boarder** 188
**boarding-house** 189
**boards** 599, 728
**boast** 884
not much to − of
  651
**boasting** **884**
**boaston** 840
**boat** 273

**breach** *crack* 44
  *gap* 198
  *quarrel* 713
  *violation* 925
  custom honoured
    in the – 614
  – of faith 940
  – of law 83, 964
  – of the peace 713
**bread** 298
  beg – 765
  *selfish* 943
  quarrel with –
    and butter 699
  – of idleness 683
  – of life *Christ* 976
  *piety* 987
  – upon the waters
    638
  – and wine 998
**breadbasket** 191
**breadth** 202
  *chiaroscuro* 420
**break**
  *fracture* 44
  *discontinuity* 70
  *change* 140
  *gap* 198
  *carriage* 272
  *crumble* 328
  *disclose* 529
  *cashier* 756
  *violate* 773, 927
  *bankrupt* 808
  – away 623
  – bread 298
  – bulk 297
  – camp 293
  – of day *morning*
    125
  *twilight* 422
  – down *destroy*
    162
  *fall short* 304
  *decay* 659
  *fail* 732
  *dance* 840
  – one's fetters 614
  – forth 295
  – ground 66
  – a habit 614
  – the heart *pain*
    828, 830
  *dejection* 837
  – the ice 888
  – in *ingress* 294
  *domesticate* 370
  *teach* 537
  *tame* 749
  – in upon *derange*
    61

*inopportune* 135
  *hinder* 706
  – a lance 716, 722
  – a law 83
  – loose 671, 750
  – one's neck
  *powerless* 158
  *die* 360
  – the neck of
    *task* 676
  *success* 731
  – the news 529
  – no bones 648
  – of 660
  – off *cease* 142
  *relinquish* 624
  *abrogate* 756
  – out *begin* 66
  *violent* 173
  *disease* 655
  *excited* 825
  – the peace 173,
    720
  – Priscian's head
    568
  – prison 750
  – the ranks 61
  – short 328
  – silence 582
  – the teeth 579
  – the thread 70
  – through the
    clouds *visible*
    446
  *disclose* 529
  – through a cus-
    tom 614
  – up *disjoin* 44
  *decompose* 49
  *end* 67
  *revolution* 146
  *destroy* 162
  – up of the system,
    360, 655
  – on the wheel
  *physical pain* 378
  *mental pain* 830
  *punishment* 972
  – with 713
  – with the past
    146
  – word *deceive* 545
  *improbity* 940
**breaker**
  of horses 268
  *reef* 346
  *wave* 348
**breakers** 348, 667
  surrounded by –
    704
  – ahead 665

**breakfast** 298
**breakneck**
  *precipice* 217
  *rash* 863
**breakwater**
  *refuge* 666
  *obstruction* 706
**breast** *interior* 221
  *confront* 234
  *convex* 250
  *mind* 450
  *oppose* 708
  *soul* 820
  at the – 129
  in the – of 620
  – the current 719
  – high 206
**breastplate** 717
**breastwork** 717
**breath** *instant* 113
  *breeze* 349
  *life* 359
  *animality* 364
  *faint sound* 405
  with bated – 581
  hold – *quiet* 265
  *expect* 507
  *wonder* 870
  not a – of air 265,
    382
  out of – 688
  in the same – 120
  shortness of – 688
  take – 265, 689
  take away one's –
  *unexpected* 508
  *fear* 860
  *wonder* 870
**breathe** *exist* 1
  *blow* 349
  *live* 359
  *faint sound* 405
  *evince* 467
  *mean* 516
  *inform* 527
  *disclose* 529
  *utter* 580
  *speak* 582
  *refresh* 689
  – freely 827, 834
  – one's last 360
  not – a word 528
**breathing time** 687,
    723
**breathless**
  *voiceless* 581
  out of breath 688
  *feeling* 821
  *fear* 860
  *eager* 865
  *wonder* 870

– attention 457
  – expectation 507
  – impatience 865
  – speed 684
**bred in the bone** 820
**breech** 235
  – loader 727
**breeches** 225
  wear the – 737
  – buoy 666
  – maker 225
  – pocket
  *money* 800, 802
**breed** *kind* 75
  *multiply* 161
  *progeny* 167
  *animals* 370
  *rear* 537
**breeding** 161, 852,
    894
**breeze** *wind* 349
  *discord* 713
**breezy** 836
**brethren** 997
**breve** 413
**brevet**
  *warrant* 741
  *commission* 755
  *permit* 760
  – rank 873
**breviary** 998
**brevier** 591
**brevity** 201, 572
**brew** 41, 673
**brewing**
  *impending* 152
  storm – 665
**bribe** *equivalent* 30
  *tempt* 615
  *offer* 763
  *gift* 784
  *buy* 795
  *expenditure* 809
  *reward* 973
**bric-à-brac** 847
**brick** *hard* 323
  *pottery* 384
  *material* 635
  *trump* 939, 948
  make -s without
    straw 471
  – colour 434
**brickbat** 727
**bricklayer** 690
**bride** 903
**bridewell** 752
**bridge** 45, 627
  – over *join* 43
  *facilitate* 705
  make peace 723
  *compromise* 774

brouillerie 713
brouillon 626
brow *top* 210
  *edge* 231
  *front* 234
browbeat
  *intimidate* 860
  *swagger* 885
  *disrespect* 929
  –en *humbled* 879
brown 433
  – Bess 727
  – study 451, 458
Brown, Jones and
  Robinson 876
brownie 980
browse 298
bruin 895
bruise *powder* 330
  *hurt* 619
  *injure* 649
  *blemish* 848
bruiser 726
bruit
  *report* 531, 532
brumal 126, 383
Brummagem 545
brumous 353
brunette 433
brunt *beginning* 66
  *impulse* 276
  bear the –
  *difficulty* 704
  *defence* 717
  *endure* 821, 826
brush *rough* 256
  *rapid motion* 274
  *graze* 379
  *clean* 652
  *fight* 720
  paint – 556
  – *away reject* 297
  *abrogate* 756
  – up *clean* 652
  *furbish* 658
  *prepare* 673
brushwood 367
brusque *violent* 173
  *haste* 684
  *discourtesy* 895
brutal *vulgar* 851
  *rude* 895
  *savage* 907
brutalize
  [*see* brutal]
  *corrupt* 659
  *deaden* 823
  *vice* 945
brute *animal* 366
  *rude* 895
  *maleficent* 913

– force
  *strength* 159
  *violence* 173
  *animal* 450a
  *severe* 739
  *compulsion* 744
  *lawless* 964
  – *matter* 316, 358
Brute, et tu 917
brutish [*see* brute]
  *vulgar* 851
  *ignoble* 876
  *intemperate* 954
brutum fulmen
  *impotent* 158
  *failure* 732
  *lax* 738
  *boast* 884
bubble
  *unsubstantial* 4
  *transient* 111
  *little* 193
  *convexity* 250
  *light* 320
  *water* 348
  *air* 353
  *error* 495
  *deceit* 545
  *trifle* 643
  – burst
  *fall short* 304
  *disappoint* 509
  *fail* 732
  – *reputation* 873
  – and squeak 298
  – up *agitation* 315
buccaneer 791, 792
bucentaur 273
Bucephalus 271
buck *stag* 366
  *male* 373
  *wash* 652
  *money* 800
  *fop* 854
  – basket 191
  – jump 309
  – up 684
bucket 191
  kick the – 360
  drop – in empty
    well 645
  like –s in well 314
buckle *tie* 43
  *fastening* 45
  *distort* 243
  *curl* 248
  – on one's armour
    673
  – to 604, 686
  – with *grapple* 720
buckler 717

buckram 855, 878
  men in – 549
bucolic
  *pastoral* 370
  *poem* 597
bud 367
  *beginning* 66
  *germ* 153
  *expand* 194
  *graft* 300
  – from 154
Buddha 979, 986
Buddhism 984
budding *young* 127
buddy 711, 890
budge 264
budget *heap* 72
  *bag* 191
  *store* 636
  *finance* 811
  – of news 532
buff 436
  blind man's – 840
  native – 226
buffer
  *hindrance* 706
  *defence* 717
buffet 191
  *strike* 276
  *agitate* 315
  *evil* 619
  *bad* 649
  *affront* 900
  *smite* 972
  – the waves 704,
    708
  *bar* 189
buffo 599
buffoon *actor* 599
  *humorist* 844
  *butt* 857
buffoonery 840, 842
bug 653
bugaboo 669, 860
bugbear
  *imaginary* 515
  *bane* 663
  *alarm* 669
  *fear* 860
buggy 272
bugle
  *instrument* 417
  *war-cry* 722
  *ornament* 847
  – call 550, 741
build *construct* 161
  *form* 240
  – anew 658
  – upon a rock 150
  – up *compose* 54
  – upon *belief* 484

builder 626, 690
building material
  635
buildings 189
built on *basis* 211
bulb 249, 250
bulge 250
bulk 50, 192
  – large 31
bulkhead 228, 706
bull *animal* 366
  *male* 373
  *error* 495
  *absurdity* 497
  *solecism* 568
  *police* 664
  *ordinance* 741
  – in a china shop
    59
  like a – at a gate
    173
  take the – by the
    horns 604, 861
Bull, John – 188
bullcalf 501
bulldog *animal* 366
  *pluck* 604, 604a
  *courage* 861
bulldoze 885
bullet *ball* 249
  *arms* 727
  *missile* 284
bulletin 532, 592
  – board 551
bullfight 720
bullhead 501
bullion 800
bullseye *centre* 222
  *lantern* 423
  *aim* 620
bully *fighter* 726
  *maltreat* 830
  *frighten* 860
  *courage* 861
  *rashness* 863
  *bluster* 885
  *blusterer* 887
  *threaten* 909
  *evil doer* 913
  *bad man* 949
bulrush
  *worthless* 643
bulwark 706, 717
bum 876
bumbailiff 965
bumbledom 737,
  965
bumboat 273
bump 250, 276
  – off 361
bumper 52

calcine 384
calcitrate 276
calculate
  *reckon* 85
  *investigate* 461
  *expect* 507
  *intend* 620
  – upon 484
calculated
  *tending* 176
  *premeditated* 611
calculation
  [*see* calculate]
  *caution* 864
calculating [*ditto*]
  *prudent* 498
  – machine 85
calculus 85
caldron
  *convert* 144
  *vessel* 191
  *heat* 386
  *laboratory* 691
calèche 272
caleer 838
calefaction 384
calembour 520
calendar *list* 86
  *chronicle* 114
  *record* 551
calender 255
calenture 503, 655
calf *young* 129
  *give birth* 161
  *leather* 223
  *animals* 366
  *fool* 501
  golden – 986, 991
Caliban 846
calibrate 26
calibre *degree* 26
  *size* 192
  *breadth* 202
  *opening* 260
  *intellectual
    capacity* 498
calidarium 386
calidity 382
caliginous 421
caliph 745
caliphate 737
calisthenics
  *training* 537
  *beauty* 845
caliver 727
calk 660
call *cry* 412
  *signal* 550
  *name* 564
  *motive* 615
  *visit* 892

*sanctify* 976
*ordain* 995
at one's – 682, 743
*within* – 197
– to account 932
– attention to 457
– to the bar 968
– into being 161
– of duty 926
– for *require* 630
  *order* 741
  *ask* 765
– forth
  *resort* to 677
  *excite* 824
– in *advice* 695
– to mind 505
– to the ministry
    996
– names 929, 932
– into notice 525
– off the attention
    458
– to order 741
– out *cry* 411
  *challenge* 715
– over *number* 85
– into play 677
– in question 485
– the roll 85
– up 527
– up spirits 992
– to 586
– up *recollect* 505
  *motive* 615
  *excite* 824
– upon
  *demand* 741
  *request* 765
  *visit* 892
  *duty* 924, 926
– to witness 467
callæsthetics 845
callant 129
call-boy
  *theatre* 599
called, so – 545
callidity 698
calligraphy 590
calling
  *business* 625
Calliope 417, 597
callipers 466
callosity 323
callous 376, 823
callow *young* 127
  *infant* 129
  *bare* 220
  *unprepared* 674
calm *physical* 174
  *quiet* 265

*dissuade* 616
*leisure* 685
*peace* 721
*moral* 826
*unamazed* 871
– belief &c. 484
– before a storm
    145
calmative 174
caloric 382
calorimeter 389
calote 999
calotype 554
caloyer 996
calumet *token* 550
  – of peace 721, 723
calumniator 936
calumny 934
calvary 1000
Calvinism 984
calyx 191
cam 633
camarade 890
camaraderie 888,
    892
camarilla 712
camarista 746
camber 250
cambist 797, 801
camboose 386
camel 271
  swallow a – 608,
    699
cameo *convex* 250
  *sculpture* 557
camera 445, 553
  in – 528
  – lucida 445
  – obscura 445
camerated 191
Camilla 274
camisade 716
camisole 225
camorra 712
camouflage 530
camp *locate* 184
  *abode* 189
  *military* 728
  – bed 215
  – stool 215
campagna 180, 344
campaign 692, 722
campaigner 726
campaigning 266
campaniform 249,
    252
campanile 206
campestrian 344
Campus Martius
    728
can *power* 157

*mug* 191
*preserve* 670
*jail* 752
best one – 686
– it be! 870
canaille 876
canal *opening* 260
  *conduit* 350
  *way* 627
  – boat 273
canard 532, 546
canary 366
cancan
  *dance* 840
cancel
  *compensate* 30
  *neutralize* 179
  *obliterate* 552
  *abrogate* 756
  *repudiate* 773
cancelled 219
cancelli 191
cancer *disease* 655
  *bane* 663
  *painful* 830
candelabrum 423
candent 382
candid *white* 430
  *sincere* 543
  *ingenuous* 703
  *honourable* 939
candidate 767, 865
candidature 763
candle 423
  bargain by inch o'
    – 769
  burn – at both
    ends 686
  not fit to hold a
    to 34
  – ends 40, 817
  – holder 711
  – light 126, 422
  – power 466
  – stick 423, 998
  hold – to sun 648
Candlemas 998
candour
  *veracity* 543
  *artlessness* 703
  *honour* 939
candy *dense* 321
  *sweet* 396
cane *weapon* 727
  *punish* 972
  *scourge* 975
canescent 430
Canicula 423
canicular 382
caniculated 259
canine 366

cemetery 363
cenobite 893, 996
cenotaph 363
censer 998
censor
  moderate 174
  critic 480
  ban 761
  detractor 936
censorious 480, 932
censurable 947
censure 932
censurer 936
census 85, 86
  record 551
centaur 83, 366
centenarian 130
centenary
  hundred 98
  period 138
  celebration 883
centesimal 99
cento 597
centrality 222
centralize
  combine 48
centre 68, 222
  – round 72, 290
centrifugal 291
centripetal 290
centroidal 222
centuple 98
centurion 745
century
  hundred 98
  period 108
  long time 110
  money 800
ceramic
  bake 384
  – ware 557
cerate 662
Cerberus
  janitor 263
  custodian 664
  hades 932
  sop for – 615
cereal 298
cerebration 451
cerebrum 450
cere-cloth 363
cerement
  covering 223
  wax 356
  burial 363
ceremonious 928
ceremony
  parade 882
  courtesy 894
  rite 998

Ceres 979
cerise 434
cerography 558,
  590
Ceromancy 511
ceroplastic 557
certain special 79
  indefinite number
  100
  sure 474
  belief 484
  true 494
  make – of 480a
  of a – age 128
  to a – degree 32
certainly yes 488
certainness 474
certainty 474
certes 474, 488
certificate
  evidence 467
  record 551
  security 771
certify 467, 535
certiorari 969
certitude 474
cerulean 438
cess tax 812
  sewer 653
cessation 142
cession
  surrender 725
  of property 782
  gift 784
cesspool 653
cestui-que trust 779
cestus 45, 247
chafe
  physical pain 378
  warm 384
  irritate 825
  mental pain 828,
  830
  discontent 832
  incense 900
chaff trash 643
  ridicule 856
  vulgar 876
  not to be caught
  with – 698, 702
  winnow – from
  wheat 609
chaffer 794
chafing-dish 386
chagrin 828
chain fasten 43
  vinculum 45
  series 69
  measure 200
  interlinking 219
  measure 466

gearing 633
imprison 752
ornament 847
drag a – 749
drag a lengthened
  – 686
in –s 754
chain gang 752, 972
chain-shot 727
chair support 215
  vehicle 272
  professorship 542
  throne 747
  celebration 883
  president 694
  in the – 693
chairman 694
chaise 272
chalcography 558
chalet 189
chalice 191, 998
chalk earth 342
  white 430
  mark 550
  drawing 556
  – from cheese 14,
  491
  – out plan 626
challenge
  question 461
  doubt 485
  claim 924
  defy 715
  accuse 938
  – comparison 648
cham 745
chamber room 191
  council 696
  mart 799
  sick – 655
chamberlain 746
chambermaid 746
chameleon 149, 440
chamfer 259
chamois 309
champ 298
  – the bit disobedi-
  ent 742
  chafe 825
  angry 900
champagne 298
champaign 344
Champ de Mars
  728
champêtre, fête –
  840
champion
  best 648
  auxiliary 711
  defence 717
  combatant 726

representative 759
sympathizer 914
championship 707
chance 156, 621
  be one's – 151
  game of – 840
  great – 472
  small – 473
  stand a – 177, 470
  take one's – 675
  –s against one 665
  whirligig of – 156
  as – would have it
  152
chancel 1000
chancellor
  president 745
  deputy 759
  judge 967
  – of the exchequer
  801
chancery
  court of – 966
  – suit delay 133
chandelier 214, 423
chandelle, le jeu
  n'en vaut pas la
  – 638, 643
  dear 814
chandler 797
change
  alteration 140
  mart 799
  small coin 800
  inter– 148
  radical – 146
  sudden – 146
  – about 149
  – colour 821
  – for 147
  – hands 783
  – of mind 607
  – of opinion 485
  – of place 264
changeableness
  149, 605
changeful
  fickle 607
changeling
  substitute 147
  fool 501
changeless 16
changer 797
channel
  furrow 259
  opening 260
  conduit 350
  way 627
chant song 415
  sing 416
  worship 990

*cry* 411
*aid* 707
*pleasure* 827
*relief* 834
*mirth* 836
*rejoicing* 838
*amusement* 840
*courage* 861
*sociality* 892
*welcome* 894
*applaud* 931
good – *hope* 858
*high living* 957
**cheerfulness 836**
**cheerless** 830, 837
**cheeseparings**
*remains* 40
*dirt* 653
*economy* 817
**chef de cuisine**
*servant* 746
**chef-d'œuvre** 648,
698
**cheka** 696
**chemin**
– **de fer**
*game* 840
– *faisant* 270
**chemise** 225
**chemist** 662
**Chemistry 144**
organic – 357
**cheque** 800
**chequer** 440
– roll 86
**cherchez la femme**
155
**chère amie** 962
**cherish** *aid* 707
*love* 897
*endearment* 902
– a *belief* 484
– *feelings &c.* 821
– an *idea &c.* 451
**cheroot** 392
**cherry**
– red 434
two bites of a –
*overrate* 482
*roundabout* 629
*clumsy* 699
**cherry-cheeked**
845
**cherry-coloured**
434
**cherub** 977
**Cheshire cat** 838
**chess** 840
**chessboard** 440
**chest** 191, 802
**chestnut-colour** 433

**cheval-de-bataille**
*plea* 617
*plan* 626
*vanity* 880
**cheval-glass** 445
**chevalier** 875
– d'industrie 792
**chevaux de frise**
253, 717
**chevron**
*angle* 217
*indication* 550
*badge* 747
*decoration* 877
**chew** 298
– the *cud* 451
– *tobacco* 392
**chiaroscuro**
*light* 420
*grey* 432
*painting* 556
**chiasma** 43
**chic** 845, 882
**chicane**
*sophistry* 477
*deceit* 545
*cunning* 702
**chicken** 129, 366
– in every *pot* 733
count –s before
hatched 858,
863
tender as a – *soft*
324
*sensitive* 822
*compassionate*
914
**chickenhearted** 862
**chide** 932
**chief** *principal* 642
*master* 745
*evidence in* – 467
– *constable* 765
– *part* 31
**Chief Justice** 967
**chiefdom** 737
**chieftain** 745
**chiffonnier** 876
**chiffonnière** 191
**chignon** 225
**chilblain** 383
**child**
*infant* 129
*offspring* 167
*fool* 501
– of *God* 987
–'s *play* 643, 705
with – 161
**childbirth** 161
**childhood** 127
**childish**

*credulous* 486
*foolish* 499
*feeble* 575
– *treble* 581
**childlike** 703
**chiliad** 98
**chill** *cold* 383
*render cold* 385
*indispose* 616
– the *spine* 830,
860
**chillies** 393
**Chiltern Hundreds**
757
**chime**
*repetition* 104
*roll* 407
*resonance* 408
*melody* 413
– in with *agree* 23
*conform* 82
*assent* 488
*concord* 714
**chimera** 83, 515
**chimney** 260, 351
– *corner* 189
– *pot* 249
**china** 384, 557
**China to Peru** 180
**chine** 235
**chinese white** 430
**chink** *gap* 198
*sound* 408
*money* 800
**chip** *small* 32
*detach* 44
*bit* 51
*reduce* 195
– of the old *block*
*similar* 17
*copy* 21
*offspring* 167
**chippy** 962
**Chirography** 590
**Chirology** 550
**Chiromancy** 511
**chirp**
*bird-note* 412
*sing* 416
*cheerful* 836
*rejoice* 838
**chirrup** [*see* chirp]
**chirurgery** 662
**chisel**
*fabricate* 161
*form* 240
*sharp* 253
*sculpture* 557
**chit** 129, 193
**chit-chat** 588
**chitterlings** 221

**chivalry** *war* 722
*tenure* 777
*courage* 861
*courtesy* 894
*philanthropy* 910
*honour* 939
*generosity* 942
**chlamys** 225
**chloroform** 376, 823
**chlorophyl** 435
**chlorotic** 655
**chock full** 52
**chocolate**
*food* 298
*colour* 433
**choice** *will* 600
*election* 609
*excellent* 648
*absence of* – 609a
by – 600
– *spirits* 873
– of *words* 569
**choir** *sing* 416
*church music* 996
*church* 1000
– *boy* 996
– *invisible* 360,
977
**choke** *close* 261
*stifle* 361
*redundant* 641
*hinder* 706
–full *complete* 52
*replete* 639
–off 706
**choler** 900
**choleric** 901
**choose** 609
do what one –s 748
**chop** *disjoin* 44
*change* 140
– *logic* 476
– *up* 201
**chopfallen** 837
**chopper** 330
**chopping**
*large* 192
– *sea* 348
**chops** *mouth* 66
*jaws* 231
*food* 298
**chorale** 415
**chord** 413
**chore** 625
**choreography** 840
**chorister** 416, 996
**chorography** 183
**chorus**
*shout* 411
*song* 415
*singers* 416

[ 433 ]

*lofty* 206
*inattentive* 458
*dreaming* 515
under a –
  *insane* 503
  *adversity* 735
  *disrepute* 874
  *secluded* 893
  *censured* 932
  *accused* 938
– burst 348
–capt 206
– of dust 330, 353
–s gathering
  *dark* 421
  *danger* 665
  *warning* 668
– no bigger than a
  man's hand 668
– of skirmishers
  726
– of smoke 353
– of words 573
**clouded**
  *variegated* 440
  *dejected* 837
  *hopeless* 859
  – perception 499
**cloudiness** 571
**cloudland** 515
**cloudless**
  *light* 420
  *happy* 827
**cloudy** *dim* 422,
  426
**clough** 206
**clout** 276
**cloven** 91
**cloven foot**
  *mark* 550
  *malevolence* 907
  *vice* 945
  *Satan* 978
  see the – 480*a*
  show the – 907
**clover**
  *luxury* 377
  *prosperity* 734
  *comfort* 827
**clown**
  *pantomime* 599
  *bungler* 702
  *buffoon* 844
  *vulgar* 851
  *rustic* 876
**cloy** 641, 869
**club**
  *place of meeting*
  74
  *house* 189
  *association* 712

*weapon* 727
*sociality* 892
– law
  *compulsion* 744
  *lawless* 964
– together
  *co-operate* 709
**clubby** 892
**club car** 272
**clubfooted** 243
**cluck** 412
**clue** 550
  seek a – 461
**clump**
  *assemblage* 72
  *projecting mass*
  250
– of trees 367
**clumsy**
  *unfit* 647
  *awkward* 699
  *ugly* 846
**Cluniac** 996
**clurichaune** 980
**cluster** 72
**clutch** *retain* 781
  *seize* 789
**clutches** 737
  in the – of 749
**clutter** 407
**coacervation** 72
**coach**
  *carriage* 272
  *teach* 537
  *tutor* 540, 673
– painter 540
– road 627
drive a – and six
  through 964
– up 539
**coachhouse** 191
**coachman** 268, 694
**coaction** 744
**coadjutant** 709
**coadjutor** 711
**coadjuvancy** 709
**coagency** 178, 709
**coagmentation** 72
**coagulate**
  *cohere* 46
  *density* 321
  *semi-liquid* 352
**coal** 388
  call over the –s
  932
  carry –s 879
– black 431
  carry –s to New-
  castle 641
**coalesce**
  *identity* 13

*combine* 48
**coalheaver**
  work like a – 686
**coalition** 43, 709,
  712
**coaming** 232
**coaptation** 23
**coarctation**
  *decrease* 36
  *contraction* 195
  *narrow* 203
  *impede* 706
  *restraint* 751
**coarse** *harsh* 410
  *dirty* 653
  *unpolished* 674
  *garish* 846
  *vulgar* 851
  *impure* 961
– grain 329
**coast** *border* 231
  *slide* 266
  *navigate* 267
  *land* 342
– defence 717
– line 230
**coaster** 273
**coastguard** 753
**coat** *layer* 204
  *paint* 223
  *habit* 225
  cut – according to
  cloth 698
– of arms 550
– of mail 717
**coating, inner** –
  224
**coax** *persuade* 615
  *endearment* 902
  *flatter* 933
**cob** *horse* 271
  *punish* 972
**cobalt** 438
**cobble** *mend* 660
**cobbler** 225
**cobbles** 635
**coble** 273
**cobra** 913
**cobweb** *light* 320
  *fiction* 545
  *flimsy* 643
  *dirt* 653
  –s of antiquity
  124
  –s of sophistry
  477
**cocaine** 376, 381,
  663
**cochineal** 434
**cock** *bird* 366
  *male* 373

  game – 861
– boat 273
– and bull story
  546
– the eye 441
– of the roost
  *best* 648
  *master* 745
– up *vertical* 212
  *convex* 250
**cockade** *badge* 550
  *title* 877
**cock-a-hoop**
  *gay* 836
  *exulting* 884
**Cockaigne** 827
**cockatrice**
  *monster* 83
  *piercing eye* 548
  *evil-doer* 913
  *miscreant* 949
**cockcrow** 125
**cocked hat** 225, 745
**cocker** *fold* 258
  *caress* 902
**Cocker**
  *school book* 542
  according to – 82
**cockle** *fold* 258
– of one's heart
  820
**cockleshell** 273
**cockloft** 191
**cockney**
  *Londoner* 188
  *plebeian* 876
**cockpit** *hold* 191
  *council* 696
  *arena* 728
**cockshut**
  *morning* 125
  *evening* 126
  *dusk* 422
**cock-sparrow** 193
**cocksure** 484
**cockswain** 269
**cocktail** 298, 959
– party 892
**cocoa** 298
**cocotte** 962
**coction** 384
**Cocytus** 982
**cod** *shell* 223
**coddle** 902
– oneself 943
**code** *conceal* 528
  *precept* 697
  *law* 963
**codex** 593
**codger** 819
**codicil** *sequel* 65

Colosseum 728
colossus 192, 206
colour *hue* **428**
  *tone* 431
  *appearance* 448
  *probability* 472
  *disguise* 544
  *paint* 556
  *plea* 617
  *be angry* 900
  all –s 440
  change –
  *shame* 879
  give a – to
  *change* 140
  *qualify* 469
  *probable* 472
  *falsehood* 544
  lend a – to
  *plea* 617
  *vindicate* 937
  man of – 431
  show in true –s
  543
  – blindness 443
  – printing 558
  – sergeant 745
  –ed spectacles 424
  – too highly 549
  – up *redden* 434
  *blush* 879
colourable
  *ostensible* 472
  *deceptive* 545
colourful 882
colouring
  [see colour]
  *meaning* 516
  false – 523
  – matter 428
colourless
  *weak* 160
  *pale* 429
colours
  *ensign* 550
  *decoration* 877
  with – flying
  *resolution* 604
  false – 544, 545
  flying –
  *display* 882
  *celebration* 883
  lower one's – 735
  nail one's – to the
  mast 604
  show one's –
  *manifest* 525
  *disclose* 529
  true to one's – 939
colporteur 797
colstaff 215

colt *young* 129
  *horse* 271
  *fool* 501
columbine 599
columella 215
column *series* 69
  *height* 206
  *support* 215
  *cylinder* 249
  *caravan* 266
  *monument* 551
  *printing* 591
  *troop* 726
columnist 527, 553
colures 318
coma *inactive* 683
  *insensible* 376,
  823
comb *teeth* 253
  *clean* 652
  *punish* 972
combat 720, 722
combat, hors de –
  *useless* 645
  *tired* 688
combatant **726**
combe 252
comber 348
combination **48**
  *arithmetical* 84
  *party* 712
combine *unite* 48
  *co-operate* 709
combustible 388
combustion 384
come *happen* 151
  *approach* 286
  *arrive* 292
  *cheer up!* 836
  *out upon!* 932
  to – *future* 121
  *destiny* 152
  – about 658
  – across
  *discover* 480a
  *acquire* 775
  *pay up* 807
  – after
  *sequence* 63
  *posterior* 117
  – between 631
  cut and – again
  639
  – of age 131
  – amiss
  *disagreeable* 24
  *ill-timed* 135
  – back 283
  – before 116
  – by 775
  – at one's call 743

  – to a determina-
  tion 604
  – down with 807
  – into existence
  *be* 1
  *begin* 66
  – first *superior* 33
  *precede* 62
  – forth
  *egress* 295
  *appear* 446
  – forward 763
  – from 154
  – to the front 303
  – and go 314
  – to hand 785
  – to a head
  *climax* 33
  *complete* 52
  – in *ingress* 294
  *receipt* 785
  – in for
  *property* 778, 780
  – to one's knowl-
  edge 527
  – to life 359
  – what may 474
  – near 286
  – to nothing
  *unproductive* 169
  *fail* 732
  – of 154
  – off *event* 151
  *disjoin* 44
  *loop-hole* 617
  *escape* 671
  – on *future* 121
  *destiny* 152
  *I defy you* 715
  *attack* 716
  – to oneself 660
  – into operation
  170
  – out
  *disclosure* 529
  *publication* 531
  *on the stage* 599
  – out of *effect* 154
  *egress* 295
  – out with
  *disclose* 529
  *speak* 582
  – over
  *influence* 615
  *consent* 762
  – to pass *state* 7
  *event* 151
  – to pieces 44
  – to the point
  *speciality* 79
  *attention* 457

  *concise* 572
  – to the rescue
  672
  – round
  *period* 138
  *conversion* 144
  *belief* 484
  *assent* 488
  *change of mind*
  607
  *influence* 615
  *restoration* 660
  *be pacified* 723
  *consent* 762
  – to the same
  thing 27
  – short of
  *inferior* 34
  *fall short* 304
  – to one's senses
  502
  – to a stand 142
  – to terms
  *assent* 488
  *contract* 769
  it –s to this
  *concisely* 572
  – to equal 27
  *whole* 50
  *arithmetic* 85
  *become* 144
  *effect* 154
  *inherit* 777
  *money* 800
  *price* 812
  – together
  *assemble* 72
  *converge* 290
  – under 76
  – upon
  *unexpected* 508
  *acquire* 775
  *claim* 924
  – into use 613
  – into view 446
  – into the views of
  *co-operate* 709
  – off well 731
  – into the world
  359
come-down 306,
  735
comedy
  *drama* 599
  *comic* 853
comely 845
comestible 298
comet
  *wanderer* 268
  *star* 318
cometary 111

compages
  *whole* 50
  *structure* 329
compagination 43
companion *match*
  17
  *accompaniment*
    88
  *ladder* 305
  *friend* 890
companionable 892
companionship 892
companionway 305
company
  *assembly* 72
  *actors* 599
  *party, partner-*
    *ship* 712
  *troop* 726
  *sociality* 892
  *bear* – 88
  in – with 88
comparable 9
comparative 464
  *degree* 26
  – *anatomy* 368
comparatively 32
compare 464
  – *notes* 695
comparison 464
compartition 44
compartment
  *part* 51
  *region* 181
  *place* 182
  *cell* 191
  *carriage* 272
compass
  *degree* 26
  *space* 180
  *surround* 227
  *measure* 466
  *intend* 620
  *guidance* 693
  *achieve* 729
  box the –
    *direction* 278
    *rotation* 312
  keep within –
    *moderation* 174
    *fall short* 304
    *economy* 817
  points of the – 236
  in a small – 193
  – about 229
  – of thought 498
compassion 914
  object of – 828
compatible
  *consentaneous* 23
  *possible* 470

compatriot
  *inhabitant* 188
  *friend* 890
compeer *equal* 27
  *friend* 890
compel 744
compellation 564
compendency 43
compendious 201
compendium 596
  *book* 593
compensate
  *make up for* 30
  *requite* 973
compensation 30
compère 599
competence
  *power* 157
  *sufficiency* 639
  *skill* 698
  *wealth* 803
competition
  *opposition* 708
  *contention* 720
competitor
  *opponent* 710
  *combatant* 726
  *candidate* 767
compilation
  *collect* 72
  *book* 593
  *compendium* 596
compile 54
complacent
  *pleased* 827
  *content* 831
  *courteous* 894
  *kind* 906
complain 839
complainant 938
complaint
  *illness* 655
  *murmur* 839
  lodge a – 938
  – without cause
    839
complaisant
  *lenient* 740
  *courteous* 894
  *kind* 906
complement
  *adjunct* 39
  *remainder* 40
  *part* 52
  *arithmetic* 84
complementary
  *correlation* 12
  *colour* 428
complete
  *entire* 52
  *accomplish* 729

*compact* 769
  – answer 479
  – circle 311
  in a – degree 31
completeness 52
completion 729
complex 59
complexion
  *state* 7
  *colour* 428
  *appearance* 448
compliance
  *conformity* 82
  *obedience* 743
  *consent* 762
  *observance* 772
complicate
  *derange* 61
complicated
  *disorder* 59
  *convolution* 248
complice 711
complicity 709
compliment
  *courtesy* 894, 896
  *praise* 931
  poor – 932
  –s of season 896
complimentary
  *free* 815
complot 626
comply [*see* compli-
  ance]
compo *coating* 223
  *material* 635
component 56
componere lites
  723, 724
comport
  – oneself 692
  – with 23
compos mentis 502
compose
  *make up* 54, 56
  *produce* 161
  *moderate* 174
  *music* 416
  *write* 590
  *printing* 591
  *pacify* 723
  *assuage* 826
composed
  *self-possessed* 826
composer
  *music* 413
composite 41
composition 54
  [*see* compose]
  *combination* 48
  *piece of music* 415
  *picture* 556

  *style* 569
  *writing* 590
  *building material*
    635
  *compromise* 774
  *barter* 794
  *atonement* 952
compositor
  *printer* 591
compost 653
composure 826, 871
compotation 959
compote 298
compound
  *mix* 41
  *combination* 48
  *limited space* 182
  *enclosure* 232
  *compromise* 774
  – arithmetic 466
  – for *substitute* 147
  *barter* 794
comprador 637
comprehend
  *compose* 54
  *include* 76
  *know* 490
  *understand* 518
comprehension [*see*
  comprehend]
  *intelligence* 498
comprehensive 76
  *complete* 50
  *general* 78
  *wide* 192
  – argument 476
compress
  *contract* 195
  *curtail* 201
  *condense* 321
  *remedy* 662
compressible 322
comprise 76
comprobation
  *evidence* 467
  *demonstration* 478
compromise
  *dally with* 605
  *mid-course* 628
  *taint* 659
  *danger* 665
  *pacify* 723
  *compact* 769
  *compound* 774
  *atone* 952
compromised
  *promised* 768
compter 799
compte rendu
  *record* 551
  *accounts* 811

**confer** *advise* 695
  *give* 784
  – benefit 648
  – power 157
  – privilege 760
  – right 924
  – with 588
**conference** [*see*
  confer]
  *council* 696
**confess** *assent* 488
  *avow* 529
  *penitence* 950,
  998
  – and avoid 937
**confession** [*see*
  confess]
  auricular – 998
  – of faith 983
**confessional** 1000
**confessions**
  *biography* 594
**confessor** 996
**confidant** 711
**confidante**
  *servant* 746
  *friend* 890
**confidence**
  *trust* 484
  *hope* 858
  *courage* 861
  in – 528
  – trick 545
**confident** 535
**configuration** 240
**confine**
  *region* 182
  *circumscribe* 229
  *limit* 231, 233
  *imprison* 751
**confined**
  *narrow judgment*
  481
  *ill* 655
**confinement**
  *childbed* 161
**confines of**
  on the – 197
**confirm**
  *corroborate* 467
  *assent* 488
  *consent* 762
  *compact* 769
  *rite* 998
**confirmed** 150
  – habit 613
**confiscate** *take* 789
  *condemn* 971
  *penalty* 974
**confiture** 396
**conflagration** 382,

384
**conflexure** 245
**conflict**
  *opposition* 708
  *discord* 713
  *contention* 720
**conflicting**
  *contrary* 14
  *counteracting* 179
  – evidence 468
**confluence**
  *junction* 43
  *convergence* 290
  *river* 348
**conflux**
  *assemblage* 72
  *convergence* 290
**conform** *assent* 488
  – to rule 494
**conformable** 23,
  178
**conformation** 54,
  240
**conformity** **82**, 178
**confound**
  *disorder* 61
  *destroy* 162
  *not discriminate*
  465a
  *perplex* 475
  *defeat* 731
  *astonish* 870
  *curse* 908
**confounded**
  *great* 31
  *bad* 649
**confraternity**
  *party* 712
  *friendship* 888
**confrère**
  *colleague* 711
  *friend* 890
**confrication** 331
**confront** *face* 234
  *compare* 464
  *oppose* 708
  *resist* 719
  – danger 861
  – witnesses 467
**confucianism** 984
**Confucius** 986
**confuse** *derange* 61
  *perplex* 458
  *obscure* 519
  *not discriminate*
  465a
  *abash* 879
**confused** *disorder*
  59
  *invisible* 447
  *uncertain* 475

*style* 571
**confusion**
  [*see* confuse]
  – seize 908
  – of tongues 560,
  563
  – of vision 443
  – worse-con-
  founded 59
**confutation** **479**
**congé** 293, 756
  – d'élire 995
**congeal** *dense* 321
  *cold* 385
**congeneric**
  *similar* 17
  *included* 76
**congenial**
  *related* 9
  *agreeing* 23
  *concord* 714
  *love* 897
**congenital** 5, 820
**congeries** 72
**congestion** 641
**conglaciation** 385
**conglobation** 72
**conglomerate**
  *cohere* 46
  *assemblage* 72
  *council* 696
  *dense* 321
**conglutinate** 46
**congratulate** 896
  – oneself 838
**congratulation** **896**
**congregation**
  *assemblage* 72
  *worshippers* 990
  *laity* 997
**Congregationalist**
  984
**congress**
  *assembly* 72
  *convergence* 290
  *conference* 588
  *council* 696
**Congressional**
  **Medal** 733
**Congressional**
  **Record** 551
**congreve** *fuel* 388
  – rocket 727
**congruous**
  *agreeing* 23
  (*expedient* 646)
**conical** *round* 249
  *pointed* 253
**conjecture** 475, 514
**conjoin** 43
**conjoint** 48

**conjointly** 37
**conjugal** 903
**conjugate**
  *words* 562
  *grammar* 567
  – in all its tenses
  &c. 104
**conjugation**
  *junction* 43
  *pair* 89
  *phase* 144
  *grammar* 567
**conjunction** 43
  in – with 37
**conjuncture**
  *contingency* 8
  *occasion* 134
**conjure** *deceive* 545
  *entreat* 765
  *sorcery* 992
  name to – with
  873
  – up *recall* 505
  – up a vision 505
**conjuror**
  *deceiver* 548
  *sorcerer* 994
**connaître** **le** **des-**
  **sous des cartes**
  490
**connate**
  *intrinsic* 5
  *kindred* 11
  *cause* 153
**connatural**
  *uniform* 16
  *similar* 17
**connect** *relate* 9
  *link* 43
**connection**
  [*see* connect]
  *kin* 11
  in – with 9
**connections**
  *cards* 840
**connective** 45
**conned, well –** 490
**connive**
  *overlook* 460
  *co-operate* 709
  *allow* 760
**connoisseur**
  *critic* 480
  *scholar* 492
  *taste* 850
**connotate** 550
**connote** 516, 550
  *imply* 526
**connubial** 903
**connuted** 9
**conoscente** 850

construction 161
  *form* 240
  *structure* 329
  *meaning* 522
  put a false – upon
    523
constructive
  *latent* 526
  – evidence 467
constructor 164
construe 522
consubstantiation
    998
consuetude 613
consul 758, 759
consulship 737
consult 695
  – one's pillow 133
  – one's own wishes
    943
  – the wishes of 707
consultant 662
consultation 695,
    696
consume
  *destroy* 162
  *waste* 638
  *use* 677
  – away 36
  – time
    *time* 106
    *inactivity* 683
consumere natus,
    fruges – 683
consuming 830
consummate
  *great* 31
  *complete* 52
  *completed* 729
  – skill 698
consummation
  *end* 67
  *completion* 729
  – devoutly to be
    wished
    *good* 618
    *desire* 865
consumption [*see*
    consume]
  *decrease* 36
  *shrinking* 195
  *disease* 655
contact 199
  come in –
    *arrive* 292
contagion
  *transfer* 270
  *disease* 655
  *unhealthy* 657
contain
  *be composed of* 54

*include* 76
container 191
contaminate
  *soil* 653
  *spoil* 659
contaminated
  *diseased* 655
contango 133, 813
contemn 930
contemper 174
contemplate
  *view* 441
  *think* 451
  *expect* 507
  *purpose* 620
contemporary 120
contemporation 174
contempt 930
  – of danger 861
contemptible
  *unimportant* 643
  *dishonourable* 940
contend
  *reason* 476
  *assert* 535
  *fight* 720
  – with difficulties
    704
  – for
    *vindicate* 937
content
  *assenting* 488
  *willing* 602
  *calm* 826
  *satisfied* 831
  to one's heart's –
    *sufficient* 639
    *success* 731
contention 720
contentious 901
contents
  *ingredients* 56
  *list* 86
  *components* 190
  *synopsis* 596
conterminate
  *end* 67
  *limit* 233
conterminous 199
contesseration 72
contest 708, 720
contestant 710
context 591
  from the – 516
contexture 329
contiguity 199
continence 960
continent
  *land* 342
continental 643
contingency

*event* 151
  *uncertainty* 475
  *expectation* 507
contingent
  *conditional* 8
  *casual* 156
  *liable* 177
  *possible* 470
  *uncertain* 475
  *supply* 635
  *aid* 707
  *allotted* 786
  *donation* 809
  *unforeseen* 508
  – duration 108a
  – interest 780
continual
  *perpetual* 112
  *frequent* 136
continuance 143
continuation
  *adjunct* 39
  *sequence* 63
  *sequel* 65
  – school 542
continue
  *endure* 106, 110
  *persist* 143
continued 69
  – success 731
continuity 69
  *uniformity* 16
contortion
  *distortion* 243
  *convolution* 248
contortionist 599,
    700
contour
  *outline* 230
  *appearance* 448
contra 14
  per – 708
  – bonos mores
    *vulgar* 851
    *improper* 925
    *vice* 945
contraband
  *deceitful* 545
  *prohibited* 761
  *illicit* 964
contrabasso 417
contraception 706
contract
  *shrink* 195
  *narrow* 203
  *promise* 768
  *bargain* 769
  *bridge* 840
  – a debt 806
  – a habit 613
  – an obligation

768
contractility 195
contraction 195
  *short-hand* 590
  *compendium* 596
contractor 690
contradict
  *contrary* 14
  *answer* 462
  *dissent* 489
  *deny* 536
  *oppose* 708
contradictory
  *disagreement* 24
  *evidence* 468
  *discord* 713
contradistinction 15
contraindicate
  *dissuade* 616
  *warning* 668
contraire, tout au
  – 536
contralto 408, 416
contraposition
  *inversion* 218
  *reversion* 237
contrapuntist 413
contrariety 14
contrary
  *opposite* 14
  *antagonistic* 179
  *captious* 608
  *opposing* 708
  quite the – 536
  – to expectation
    *improbable* 473
    *unexpected* 508
  – to reason 471
contrast
  *contrariety* 14
  *difference* 15
  *comparison* 464
contravallation 717
contravene
  *contrary* 14
  *counterevidence*
    468
  *deny* 536
  *hinder* 706
  *oppose* 708
contre cœur, à –
    603
contre-coup 277
contretemps
  *ill-timed* 135
  *hindrance* 706
  *misfortune* 735
contribute
  *cause* 153
  *tend* 176
  *concur* 178

creditable *right* 924
creditor 805
credo quia
  impossibile 486
credulity 486
credulous person
  *dupe* 547
creed *belief* 484
  *theology* 983
  Apostles' – 983*a*
creek *interval* 198
  *water* 343
creel 191
creep *crawl* 275
  *tingle* 380
  (*inactivity* 683)
  – in 294
  – into a corner 893
  – into the good
    graces of 933
  – out 529
  – upon one 508
  – with
    *multitude* 102
    *redundance* 641
creeper 367
creeping
  *sensation* 380
  – thing 366
creese 727
cremation
  *of corpses* 363
  *burning* 384
crematorium 363,
  386
crematory 386
crême de la crême
  648
Cremona 417
crenate 257
crenelle 257
crenulate 257
creole 57
crêpe 248, 839
crepidam, ultra –
  471
crepitation 406
crepuscule
  *dawn* 125
  *dusk* 422
crescendo
  *increase* 35
  *musical* 415
crescent
  *growing* 35
  *street* 189
  *curve* 245
cresset 423, 550
crest *supremacy* 33
  *summit* 210
  *pointed* 253

*tuft* 256
*sign* 550
*armorial* 877
*pride* 878
on the – 33
crest-fallen
  *dejected* 837
  *humble* 879
crevasse 198, 667
crevice 198
crew *assemblage* 72
  *inhabitants* 188
  *mariners* 269
  *party* 712
crib *bed* 215
  *key* 522
  *granary* 636
  *steal* 791
  *parsimony* 819
cribbage 840
cribbed, confined,
  cabined – 751
cribble 260
cribriform 260
Crichton,
  Admirable –
  *scholar* 492
  *perfect* 650
  *proficient* 700
crick *pain* 378
cricket *game* 840
  not – 940
  – ground 213
crier 534
  send round the –
  531
crim. con. 961
crime 945, 947
criminal 923, 945
  *culprit* 949
  – law 963
  court of – appeal
  966
criminality 947
criminate 938
crimp *crinkle* 248
  *notch* 257
  *brittle* 328
  *deceiver* 548
  *take* 789
  *steal* 791
crimple 258
crimson 434, 821
cringe *submit* 725
  *subject* 749
  *servility* 886
crinite 256
crinkle *angle* 244
  *convolution* 248
  *roughen* 256
  *fold* 258

crinoline 225
cripple *disable* 158
  *weaken* 160
  *injure* 659
crippled
  *disease* 655
crisis
  *conjuncture* 8
  *present time* 118
  *opportunity* 134
  *event* 151
  *strait* 704
  *excitement* 824
  bring to a – 604
  come to a – 729
crisp *rumpled* 248
  *rough* 256
  *brittle* 328
  *style* 572
Crispin 225
criss-cross 219
cristallomantia 511
criterion *test* 463
  *evidence* 467
  *indication* 550
crithomancy 511
critic *judge* 480
  *taste* 850
  *detractor* 936
critical
  *contingent* 8
  *opportune* 134
  *discriminating*
  465
  *important* 642
  *dangerous* 665
  *difficult* 704
  *censorious* 932
criticism
  *judgment* 480
  *dissertation* 595
  *disapprobation*
  932
  *detraction* 934
critique
  [*see* criticism]
croak *cry* 412
  *hoarseness* 581
  *stammer* 583
  *warning* 668
  *discontent* 832
  *lament* 839
croaker 832, 837
Croat 726
crochet 847
crock 191
crockery 384
crocodile tears 544
crocus *yellow* 436
Crœsus 803
croft 189, 232

Croix de Guerre 733
cromlech 363, 551
crone *veteran* 130
  *fool* 501
crony *friend* 890
  *favourite* 899
crook *curve* 245
  *deviation* 279
  *thief* 792
crooked
  *sloping* 217
  *distorted* 243
  *angular* 244
  *latent* 526
  *crafty* 702
  *ugly* 846
  *dishonourable* 940
  – path 704
  – temper 901
  – ways 279
croon 580
crop
  *stomach* 191
  *harvest* 154
  *shorten* 201
  *eat* 298
  *vegetable* 367
  *store* 636
  *gather* 775
  *take* 789
  second – 167, 775
  – out *visible* 446
  *disclose* 529
  – up *begin* 66
  *take place* 151
  *reproduction* 163
cropper *fall* 306
croquet *game* 840
  – ground *level* 213
croquette 298
crosier 747, 999
cross *mix* 41
  *across* 219
  *pass* 302
  *grave* 363
  *oppose* 708
  *failure* 732
  *disaster* 735
  *refuse* 764
  *pain* 830
  *decoration* 877
  *fretful* 901
  *punishment* 975
  *rites* 998
  fiery – 722
  proclaim at the –
  roads 531
  red – 662
  –ed bayonets 708
  – breed 83
  – cut 628

- fire *interchange* 148
*difficulty* 704
*opposition* 708
*attack* 716
—ed in love 898
– the mind 451
– the path of 706
– and pile 621
– purposes 14
*disorder* 59
*error* 495
*misinterpret* 523
*unskilful* 699
*difficulty* 704
*opposition* 708
*discord* 713
– oneself 998
– questions *inquiry* 461
*discord* 713
*game* 840
– road 627
– the Rubicon 609
– sea 348
– swords 722
**crossbow** 727
**cross-examine** 461
**cross-grained** 256
*obstinate* 606
*sulky* 901*a*
**crossing** 219
– sweeper 652
**crosspatch** 895
**crossroads** 8
**cross-word puzzle** 533
**crotch** 244
**crotchet** *eccentric* 83
*music* 413
*misjudgment* 481
*obstinacy* 606
*caprice* 608
**crouch** *lower* 207
*stoop* 308
*fear* 860
*servile* 886
– before 725
**croup** 235
**croupier** 694
**crow** *cry* 412
*black* 431
*rejoice* 838
*boast* 884
pluck a – with 932
as the – flies 278
–'s foot (*age*) 128
–'s nest 210
– to pluck
*discord* 713

*anger* 900
*accuse* 938
**crowbar** 633
**crowd** 72
*multitude* 102
*close* 197
*redundance* 641
*party* 712
*vulgar* 876
in the – *mixed* 41
madding – 682
**crown** *top* 210
*circle* 247
*complete* 729
*trophy* 733
*sceptre* 747
*install* 755
*decoration* 877
*reward* 973
to – all 33, 642
–ed head 745
– with laurel 873
– with success 731
**crowning** [see crown]
*superior* 33
*end* 67
– point 210
**cruche à l'eau &c.** tant va la – 735
**crucial** *crossing* 219
*proof* 478
– test 463
**cruciate** *physical pain* 378
*mental pain* 830
**crucible** *dish* 191
*conversion* 144
*furnace* 386
*experiment* 463
*laboratory* 691
put into the – 163
**crucifix** 219, 998
**crucifixion** 828
**cruciform** 219
**crucify** *physical torture* 378
*mental agony* 830
*execution* 972
**crucis, experimentum** – 463
**crude** *colour* 428
- *style* 579
*unprepared* 674
**cruel** *painful* 830
*inhuman* 907
– to be kind 914

**cruelly** *much* 31
**cruet** 191
**cruise** *vessel* 191
*navigation* 267
**cruiser** 726
**cruising** 267
**crumb** *small* 32
*powder* 330
– of comfort 834
**crumble** *decrease* 36
*weak* 160
*destruction* 162
*brittle* 328
*pulverize* 330
*spoil* 659
– into dust
*decompose* 49
– under one's feet 735
**crumbling** [see crumble]
*dangerous* 665
**crumenal** 800
**crump** *distorted* 243
*curved* 245
**crumple** *ruffle* 256
*fold* 258
– up *destroy* 162
*crush* 195
**crunch** *shatter* 44
*chew* 298
*pulverize* 330
**crupper** 235
**crusade** 722
**crush** *crowd* 72
*destroy* 162
*compress* 195
*pulverize* 330
*humble* 879
– under an iron heel 739
– one's hopes *disappoint* 509
*hopeless* 859
**crushed** 828
**crushing** 830
**crust** 223
**crustacean** 366
**crusty** 895, 901*a*
**crutch** *support* 215
*angle* 244
–ed Friars 996
**crux** 219, 704
– criticorum 533
**cry** *human* 411

*animal* 412
*publish* 531, 532
*call* 550
*voice* 580
*vogue* 613
*weep* 839
far – to 196
full – *loud* 404
raise a – 550
– aloud *implore* 765
– out against *dissuade* 616
*censure* 932
– down 932, 934
– for 865
– before hurt 839
– for joy 838
– you mercy *deprecate* 766
*pity* 914
*forgive* 918
– shame 932
– to *beseech* 765
– up 931
– for vengeance 923
– wolf *false* 544
*alarm* 669
– and little wool *overrate* 482
*boast* 884
*disappoint* 509
**crying** [see cry]
*urgent* 630
*weary* 841
– evil 619
– shame 874
– sin 945
**crypt** *cell* 191
*grave* 363
*ambush* 530
*altar* 1000
**cryptic** 475, 528
**cryptography** *hidden* 528
*writing* 590
**crystal** *hard* 323
*transparent* 425
snow – 383
– gazer 513
– gazing 511, 992
– oil 356
clear as – 518
**crystalline** *dense* 321
*hard* 323
*transparent* 425
**crystallization** 321, 323
**csako** 225, 717

cub *young* 129
  *vulgar* 851
  *clown* 876
  unlicked – 241
cubby-hole 191
cube
  *three dimensions*
    92, 93
  *form* 244
cubicle 191
cubist 556
cubit 200
cucking stool 975
cuckold 905
cuckoldom 961
cuckoo
  *imitation* 19
  *repetition* 104
  *sound* 407
  *cry* 412
cuddle 197, 902
cudgel *beat* 276
  *weapon* 727
  *punish* 975
  take up the –s
    *aid* 707
  *attack* 716
  *contention* 720
  – one's brains
    *think* 451
    *imagine* 515
cue *hint* 527
  *watchword* 550
  *plea* 617
  *rôle* 625
  take one's – from
    695
  in proper – 698
cuff *sleeve* 225
  *blow* 276
  *punishment* 972
cui bono 644, 645
cuique voluptas
  sui – 865
cuirass 717
cuirassier 726
cuisine 298
  batterie de – 957
culbute
  *inversion* 218
  *fall* 306
cul-de-lampe
  *engraving* 558
  *ornament* 847
cul-de-sac
  *concave* 252
  *closed* 261
  *difficulty* 704
culinary 298
  – art 673
cull *dupe* 547

choose 609
  take 789
cullender 260
cullibility 486
cullion 949
cully *deceive* 545,
  547
culm 388
culminate
  *maximum* 33
  *height* 206
  *top* 210
  *complete* 729
culpability *vice* 945
  *guilt* 947
culprit 949
cult 983
cultivate *till* 365,
  371
  *sharpen* 375
  *improve* 658
  *prepare* 673
  *aid* 707
cultivated
  *courteous* 894
  – taste 850
cultivator 371
culture
  *knowledge* 490
  *improvement* 658
  *taste* 850
  *politeness* 894
culverin 727
culvert 350
cum multis aliis 37,
  102
cumber *load* 319
  *obstruct* 706
cumbersome
  *incommodious*
    647
  *disagreeable* 830
cummerbund 225
cumulative 72
  *increasing* 35
  *assembled* 72
  – evidence 467
  – vote 609
cumulus 353
cunctando restituit
  rem 681
cunctation 133
cuneiform 244
  – character 590
cunning
  *prepense* 611
  *sagacious* 698
  *artful* 702
  – fellow 700
  – man 994
cup *vessel* 191

hollow 252
  *beverage* 298
  *remedy* 662
  *trophy* 733
  *tipple* 959
  between – and lip
    111
  in one's –s 959
  – that cheers &c.
    298
  – of humiliation
    879
  dash the – from
    one's lips 509
  – too low 837
cupbearer 746
cupboard 191
cupellation 384
Cupid *beauty* 845
  *love* 897
  *gods* 979
cupidity
  *avarice* 819
  *desire* 865
cupola *height* 206
  *roof* 223
  *dome* 250
cup-tossing 621
cur *dog* 366
  *coward* 862
  *sneak* 949
curable 658, 660,
  662
curacy 995
curare 663
curate 996
curative 660
curator 694, 758
curb *moderate* 174
  *slacken* 275
  *dissuade* 616
  *restrain* 751
  *shackle* 752
curb exchange 621
curbstone 233
curd *density* 321
  *pulp* 354
  (*cohere* 46)
curdle *condense* 321
  (*cohere* 46)
  make the blood –
    830
curdled 352
cure *reinstate* 660
  *remedy* 662
  *preserve* 670
  *benefice* 995
curé 996
cureless 859
curfew 126
curia 966

curio 847
curiosa felicitas 698
curiosity
  *unconformity* 83
  *inquiring* 455
  *phenomenon* 872
curious
  *exceptional* 83
  *inquisitive* 455
  *true* 494
  *beautiful* 845
  *desirous* 865
curiously *very* 31
curl *bend* 245
  *convolution* 248
  *hair* 256
  *cockle up* 258
  *badge* 747
  – up one's lip 930
curling *game* 840
curmudgeon
  *miser* 819
  *plebeian* 876
currency
  *publicity* 531
  *money* 800
current *existing* 1
  *usual* 78
  *present* 118
  *happening* 151
  *flow* 264
  *of water* 348
  *of air* 349
  *rife* 531, 532
  *language* 560
  *habit* 613
  *danger* 667
  account – 811
  against the – 708
  go with the – 82
  pass –
    *believed* 484
    *fashion* 852
  stem the – 708
  – belief 488
  – of events 151
  – of ideas 451
  – of time 109
currente calamo
  590
curricle 272
curriculum 537
curry *food* 298
  *rub* 331
  *condiment* 392,
    393
  – favour with
    *love* 897
    *flatter* 933
curry-comb 370
curse *bane* 663

*adversity* 735
*painful* 830
*malediction* 908
**cursed** *bad* 649
**cursitor** 968
**cursive** 590
**cursory**
  *transient* 111
  *inattentive* 458
  *hasty* 684
  take a − view of
   457
  *neglect* 460
**curst** 901*a*
**curt** *short* 201
  *concise* 572
  *taciturn* 585
**curtail** *retrench* 38
  *shorten* 201
  −ed of its fair pro-
   portions
  *distorted* 243
  *ugly* 846
**curtain** 223
  *shade* 424
  *hide* 528, 530
  *theatre* 599
  *fortification* 717
  behind the −
   *invisible* 447
   *inquiry* 461
   *knowledge* 490
  close the − 528
  raise the − 529
  rising of the − 448
  − lecture 932
  − raiser 66, 599
**curtsy**
  *stoop* 308, 314
  *submit* 725
  *polite* 894
**curule** 696
**curvature** 245
**curvet** *leap* 309
  *turn* 311
  *oscillate* 314
  *agitate* 315
**curvilinear** 245
  − *motion* 311
**cushion** *pillow* 215
  *soft* 324
  *relief* 834
**cushy** 829
**cusp** *angle* 244
  *sharp* 253
**cuspidor** 191
**cuss** 908
**custard** 298
**custodes? quis cus-**
  todiet − 459
**custodian** 753

**custody** *safe* 664
  *captive* 751
  *retention* 781
  in − *prisoner* 754
  *accused* 938
  take into − 751
**custom** *old* 124
  *habit* 613
  *barter* 794
  *sale* 796
  *tax* 812
  *fashion* 852
  − honoured in
   breach 614
**customary**
  [*see* custom]
  *regular* 80
**customer** 795
**custom-house** 799
  − officer 965
**custos** 753
  − rotulorum 553
**cut** *divide* 44
  *bit* 51
  *discontinuity* 70
  *interval* 198
  *curtail* 201
  *layer* 204
  *form* 240
  *notch* 257
  *blow* 276
  *eject* 297
  *reap* 371
  *physical pain* 378
  *cold* 385
  *neglect* 460
  *carve* 557
  *engraving* 558
  *road* 627
  *attack* 716
  *portion* 786
  *affect* 824
  *mental pain* 830
  *dance step* 840
  *decline acquaint-*
   *ance* 893
  *discourtesy* 895
  *tipsy* 959
  − *short* 628
  unkindest − of all
   *pain* 828
   *malevolence* 907
  − across 302
  − adrift 44
  − along 274
  have a − at 716
  − away 274
  − a whetstone with
   a razor
   *sophistry* 477
  *waste* 638

*misuse* 679
  − both ways 468
  − capers 309
  − according to
   cloth
  *economy* 817
  *caution* 864
  − and come again
  *repeat* 104
  *enough* 639
  − dead 893
  − direct 893
  − down *destroy* 162
  *shorten* 201
  *fell* 308
  *kill* 361
  − down expenses
   817
  − and dried
  *arranged* 60
  *prepared* 673
  − a figure
  *appearance* 448
  *fashion* 852
  *repute* 873
  *display* 882
  − the first turf 66
  − the ground from
   under one
  *confute* 479
  *hinder* 706
  − to the heart 824,
   830
  − ice with
  *influence* 175
  − of one's jib 448
  − jokes 842
  − the knot 705
  − off *subduct* 38
  *disjoin* 44
  *kill* 361
  *impede* 706
  *bereft* 776
  *secluded* 893
  − off with a shil-
   ling 789
  − open 260
  − out *surpass* 33
  *stop* 142
  *substitute* 147
  *plan* 626
  − out for 698
  − out work
  *prepare* 673
  *direct* 693
  − to pieces
  *destroy* 162
  *kill* 361
  − a poor figure 874
  − to the quick 830
  − up root and

  branch 162
  − up rough 900
  − and run 274
  *depart* 293
  *escape* 623
  − short *stop* 142
  *destroy* 162
  *shorten* 201
  *silence* 581
  − one's stick
  *depart* 283
  *avoid* 623
  − one's own throat
   699
  − and thrust 716
  − in two 91
  − up *divide* 44
  *destroy* 162
  *pained* 828
  *give pain* 830
  *discontented* 832
  *dejected* 837
  *censure* 932
  what one will − up
   for 780
  − one's way
   through 302
**cutaneous** 223
**cute** 698
**cuticle** 223
**cutlass** 727
**cutlery** 253
**cut-purse** 792
**cutter** 273
**cut-throat**
  *killer* 361
  *evil-doer* 913
**cutting** *sharp* 253
  *cold* 383
  *path* 627
  *affecting* 821
  *painful* 830
  *reproachful* 932
**cuttings**
  *excerpta* 596
  *selections* 609
**cutty stool** 950
**cwt.** 98, 319
**cyanogen** 438
**cyanide of potas-**
  sium *poison* 663
**cycle** *time* 106
  *period* 138
  *circle* 247
  *ride* 266
  *vehicle* 272
  *car* 272
**cyclist** 268
**cycloid** 247
**cyclometer** 200
**cyclone**

| | | | |
|---|---|---|---|
| *rotation* 312 | dachshund 366 | *inactive* 683 | *agitate* 315 |
| *wind* 349 | dacoit 792 | *amuse* 840 | *rejoice* 838 |
| cyclopædia | dactyl 597 | *fondle* 902 | *sport* 840 |
| *knowledge* 490 | dactylogram 467 | dalmatic 999 | *sociality* 892 |
| *book* 593 | dactyliomancy 511 | Daltonism 443 | lead the – 175 |
| Cyclopean | dactylonomy | dam *parent* 166 | lead one a – |
| *strong* 159 | *numeration* 85 | *close* 261 | *run away* 623 |
| *huge* 192 | *symbol* 550 | *pond* 343 | *circuit* 629 |
| Cyclops | dad 166 | *obstruct* 706 | *difficult* 704 |
| *monster* 83 | daddy 166 | damage *evil* 619 | *practical joke* 929 |
| *mighty* 159 | dado 211 | *injure, spoil* 659 | St. Vitus' – 315 |
| *huge* 192 | dædal | *price* 812 | – attendance |
| *dupe* 547 | *variegated* 440 | damages 974 | *waiting* 133 |
| cygne | dædalian | damascene 440 | *follow* 281 |
| chant du – 360 | *convoluted* 248 | damask 434 | *servant* 746 |
| – noir 650 | *artistic* 698 | dame | *petition* 765 |
| cylindric 249 | daft 503 | *woman* 374 | *servility* 886 |
| cyma 847 | dagger 727 | *teacher* 540 | – the back step |
| cymbal 417 | look –s *anger* 900 | *lady* 875 | 283 |
| cymbalo 417 | *threat* 909 | damn | – upon nothing |
| cymophanous 440 | air drawn – 515 | *malediction* 908 | 972 |
| cynic | plant – in breast | *condemn* 971 | – the war dance |
| *misanthrope* 911 | *give pain* 830 | – with faint | 715 |
| *detractor* 936 | speak –s 932 | praise 932, 934 | dance-band 417 |
| *ascetic* 955 | at –s drawn | damnable 649 | dance-music 415 |
| *closet* – 893 | *opposed* 708 | damnatory | dander 900 |
| cynical | *discord* 713 | *disapprove* 932 | Dandie Dinmont |
| *contemptuous* 930 | *enmity* 889 | *condemn* 971 | 366 |
| *censorious* 932 | *hate* 898 | damnify | dandiprat 193 |
| *detracting* 934 | daggle *hang* 214 | *damage* 649 | dandle 902 |
| cynicism | *dirty* 653 | *spoil* 659 | dandruff 653 |
| *discourtesy* 895 | dagobah 1000 | damnosa hereditas | dandy |
| *contempt* 930 | Dagon 986 | 663 | *ship* 273 |
| cynosure *sign* 550 | daguerreotype | Damocles | *fop* 854 |
| *direction* 693 | *represent* 554 | sword of – 667 | dandyism 855 |
| *wonder* 870 | *paint* 556 | Damon and | danger 665 |
| *repute* 873 | dahabeah 273 | Pythias 890 | in – *liable* 177 |
| Cynthia of the | Dail Eireann 696 | damozel 129 | source of – 667 |
| minute 149 | daily | damp | – past 664 |
| cypher [*see* cipher] | *frequent* 136 | *moderate* 174 | – signal 669 |
| cypress | *periodic* 138 | *moist* 339 | dangerous |
| *interment* 363 | – occurrence | *cold* 385 | [*see* danger] |
| *mourning* 839 | *normal* 82 | *sound* 405 | – classes 913 |
| Cyprian 962 | *habitual* 613 | *dissuade* 616 | – illness 655 |
| cyst 191 | – paper 531 | *hinder* 706 | – person 667 |
| czar 745 | dainty *food* 298 | *depress* 837 | dangle *hang* 214 |
| | *savoury* 394 | *dull* 843 | *swing* 314 |
| | *pleasing* 829 | – the sound 408a | *display* 882 |
| **D** | *delicate* 845 | damper 387 | dangler 281 |
| | *tasty* 850 | damsel | Daniel *sage* 500 |
| da capo 104 | *fastidious* 868 | *youth* 129 | *judge* 967 |
| dab *small* 32 | dairy 191, 370 | *female* 374 | dank 339 |
| *paint* 223 | – maid 746 | Dan to Beersheba | Dannemora 752 |
| *slap* 276 | dais *support* 215 | 52, 180 | danseuse 599 |
| *clever* 700 | *throne* 747 | Danaë 803 | dapper |
| dabble *water* 337 | daisy | Danaos, timeo – | *little* 193 |
| *dirty* 653 | fresh as a – 654 | *doubt* 485 | *elegant* 845 |
| *meddle* 682 | – pied 847 | *caution* 864 | dapple 433 |
| *fribble* 683 | dale 252 | dance | dappled 440 |
| dabbled *wet* 339 | dally *delay* 133 | *jump* 309 | darbies |
| dabbler 493 | *irresolute* 605 | *oscillate* 314 | *handcuffs* 752 |

**Darby and Joan**
  *secluded* 893
  *married* 903
**dare** *defy* 715
  *face danger* 861
  – *not* 860
  – *say probable* 472
  *believe* 484
  *suppose* 514
**dare-devil**
  *courage* 861
  *rash* 863
  *bluster* 887
**daring** 861
  *unreserved* 525
  – *imagination* 515
**dark**
  *obscure* 421
  *dim* 422
  *black* 431
  *blind* 442
  *invisible* 447
  *unintelligible* 519
  *latent* 526
  *joyless* 837
  *insidious* 940
  in the –
  *ignorant* 491
  leap in the –
  *experiment* 463
  *chance* 621
  *rash* 863
  keep – *hide* 528
  – *ages* 491
  – *cloud* 735
  view with – *eyes*
    932
  – *lantern* 423
**darkly**
  see through a
    glass – 443
**darkness** [*see* dark]
    421
  children of – 988
  love – better than
    light 989
  powers of – 978
**darky** 431
**darling** *beloved* 897
  *favourite* 899
**darn** 660
**dart** *swift* 274
  *propel* 284
  *missile* 727
  – to and fro 684
**Dartmoor** 752
**Darwinism** 357
**dash**
  *small quantity* 32
  *mix* 41
  *swift* 276

*fling* 284
  *mark* 550
  *courage* 861
  cut a – *repute* 873
  *display* 882
  – *at resolution* 604
  *attack* 716
  – board 666
  – cup from lips 761
  – *down* 308
  – hopes
  *disappoint* 509
  *fail* 732
  *dejected* 837
  *despair* 859
  – on 274
  – off *paint* 556
  *write* 590
  *active* 682
  *haste* 684
  – of the pen 590
**dashed** [*see* dash]
  *humbled* 879
**dashing**
  *fashionable* 852
  *brave* 861
  *ostentatious* 882
**dastard** 862
**data** *evidence* 467
  *reasoning* 476
  *supposition* 514
**date** *time* 106
  *chronology* 114
**datum** 673
**daub** *cover* 223
  *paint* 428
  *misrepresent* 555
  *dirt* 653
**daughter** 167
**daunt** 860
**dauntless** 861
**Dauphin** 875
**davenport** 191, 215
**davit** 214
**Davus sum non**
  **Œdipus**
  *unintelligent* 499
  *artless* 703
  *dull* 843
**Davy Jones' locker**
  310
**dawdle** *tardy* 133
  *slow* 275
  *inactive* 683
**dawk** 534
**dawn**
  *precursor* 64
  *begin* 66
  *priority* 116
  *morning* 125
  *light* 420

*dim* 422
  *glimpse* 490
**dawplucker** 936
**day**
  *period* 108
  *present time* 118
  *light* 420
  all – 110
  clear as –
  *certain* 474
  *intelligible* 518
  *manifest* 525
  close of – 126
  decline of – 126
  denizens of the –
    366
  good old –'s 122
  have had its – 124
  one fine – 119
  open as – 703
  order of the – 613
  red letter – 642
  see the light of –
    446
  – after day
  *diuturnal* 110
  *frequent* 136
  – by day
  *repeatedly* 104
  *time* 106
  *periodic* 138
  – after the fair
    135
  –s gone by 122
  – of judgment 121
  happy as the – is
    long 827, 836
  – and night
  *frequent* 136
  labour – and night
    686
  –s numbered
  *transient* 111
  *death* 360
  – one's own 731
  – of rest 687
  – star 423
  – after to-morrow
    121
  – before yesterday
    122
  –s of week 138
  all in –'s work 625
**daybed** 215
**daybook** *record* 551
  *accounts* 811
**daybreak**
  *morning* 125
  *dim* 422
**day-dream**
  *fancy* 515

*hope* 858
**day-labourer** 690
**daylight** 125, 420
  see – *intelligible*
    518
  – *saving* 114
**daymare** 859
**daze** 420
**dazed** 376
**dazzle**
  *light* 420
  *blind* 422, 443
  *put out* 458
  *astonish* 870
  *awe* 928
**dazzling**
  [*see* dazzle]
  *beautiful* 845
**de:** – *die in diem*
  *time* 106
  *periodic* 138
  – *facto* 1
  – *fond en comble*
    52
  – *novo* 104
  – *omnibus rebus*
    81
  – *profundis* 821
**deacon** 996
**deaconry** 995
**dead** *complete* 52
  *inert* 172
  *colourless* 429
  *lifeless* 360
  *insensible* 376
  – against
  *contrary* 14
  *oppose* 708
  more – than alive
    688
  – asleep 683
  – beat
  *powerless* 158
  – *certainty* 474
  – *colour* 556
  – cut 893
  – drunk 959
  – *failure* 732
  – flat 213
  – heat 27
  – languages 560
  – letter
  *impotent* 158
  *unmeaning* 517
  *useless* 645
  *laxity* 738
  *exempt* 927
  *illegal* 964
  – level 16
  – lift *exertion* 686
  *difficulty* 704, 706

– lock *cease* 142
*stoppage* 265
– march 363, 415
– of night
*midnight* 126
*dark* 421
– reckoning
*numeration* 85
*measurement* 466
– secret 533
– set against 708
– set at
*attack* 716
– shot 700
– silence 403
– sound 408a
– stop 142
– to 823
– wall
*hindrance* 706
*defence* 717
– weight 706
– water 343
**deaden**
*weaken* 158
*moderate* 174
*sound* 405
*mute* 408a
*benumb* 823
**dead-house** 363
**deadlock** 142, 704
**deadly** *killing* 361
*pernicious* 649
*unhealthy* 657
– sin 947
– weapon 727
**deads** 645
**deaf** 419
*inattentive* 458
– to advice 606
– and dumb 581
turn – ear to
*neglect* 460
*unbelief* 487
*refuse* 764
– to reason 901a
– to *insensible* 823
**deafen** *loud* 404
**deafness** 419
**deal** *much* 31
*arrange* 60
*bargain* 768
*allot* 786
– a blow
*injure* 659
*attack* 716
*punish* 972
– board 323
– in 794
– out *scatter* 73

*give* 784
– with
*treat of* 595
*handle* 692
*barter* 794
**dealer** 797
**dealings** *action* 680
have – with
*trade* 794
*friendly* 888
**dean** 128, 694, 996
**deanery** *office* 995
*house* 1000
**dear**
*high-priced* 814
*loved* 897
*favourite* 899
O – ! *lament* 839
– at any price 646
– me *wonder* 870
pay – for whistle
647
**dearest foe** 936
**dearness** 814
**dearth** 640
– of ideas 843
**death** 360
house of – 363
in at the –
*arrive* 292
*kill* 361
*persevere* 604a
pale as –
*colourless* 429
*fear* 860
put to – 361, 972
still as – 265
violent – 361
be the – of one
*amuse* 480
–'s head 837
– in the pot
*unhealthy* 657
*hidden danger*
667
**deathbed repent-**
**ance** 950
**death-blow**
*end* 67
*killing* 361
*failure* 732
**death-house** 752
**deathless**
*perpetual* 112
*fame* 873
**deathlike**
*silent* 403
*hideous* 846
**death-song** 839
**death-struggle** 720
**death-warrant** 971

**death-watch** 668
**débâcle** 146
*destruction* 162
*downfall* 306
*torrent* 348
**debar** *hinder* 706
*restrain* 751
*prohibit* 761
**debark** 292
**debase** *depress* 308
*foul* 653
*deteriorate* 659
*degrade* 874
**debased**
*lowered* 207
*dishonoured* 940
**debate** *reason* 476
*talk* 588
*hesitate* 605
*dispute* 720
**debatable** 475
**debauch**
*spoil* 659
*intemperance* 954
*impurity* 961
**debauchee** 962
**debenture**
*security* 771
*money* 800
*credit* 805
**debility** 160
**debit** *debt* 806
*accounts* 811
**debitor** 806
**débonnaire** 836
**debouch** 293, 295
**débris**
*fragments* 51
*crumbled* 330
*useless* 645
**debt** 806
out of – 803
get out of – 807
– of nature 360
**debtor** 806
– and creditor 811
**debunk** 529
**début** *beginning* 66
*essay* 675
*celebration* 883
**débutant**
*learner* 541
*drama* 599
**decade** *ten* 98
*period* 108
**decadence** 659
**decagon** 244
**decalescence** 382
**decalogue** 926
**decamp**
*go away* 293

*run away* 623
**decant** 270
**decanter** 191
**decapitate** *kill* 361
*punish* 972
**decay** *decrease* 36
*decompose* 49
*shrivel* 195
*unclean* 653
*disease* 655
*spoil* 659
*adversity* 735
natural – 360
– of memory 506
**decayed**
[see decay]
*old* 124
*rotten* 160
**decease** 360
**deceit**
*falsehood* 544
*deception* 545
*cunning* 702
**deceived**
*in error* 495
*duped* 547
**deceiver** 548
*gay* – 962
**decelerate** 275
**decennium** 108
**decent**
*mediocre* 651
*pure* 960
**decentralize** 49
**deceptio visûs** 443
**deception** 545
**deceptive reason-**
**ing** 477
**decession** 293
**dechristianize** 989
**decide**
*turn the scale* 153
*judge* 480
*choose* 609
**decided** *great* 31
*ended* 67
*certain* 474
*resolved* 604
take a – step 609
**deciduous**
*transitory* 111
*falling* 306
*spoiled* 659
**decies repetita**
*placebit* 829
**decimal** 84, 98, 99
**decimate**
*subtract* 38
*tenth* 99
*few* 103
*weaken* 160

*kill* 361
*play havoc* 659
*punish* 972
**decipher** 522
**decision**
  *judgment* 480
  *resolution* 604
  *intention* 620
  *law case* 969
**decisive**
  *certain* 474
  *proof* 478
  *commanding* 741
  take a – step 609
**deck** *floor* 211
  *beautify* 847
**declaim** 531, 582
  – against 932
**declamatory**
  *style* 577
  *speech* 582
**declaration**
  *affirmation* 535
  *law pleadings* 969
  – of faith
  *belief* 484
  *theology* 983
  – of war 713
**declaratory**
  *meaning* 516
  *inform* 527
**declare**
  *publish* 531
**declension**
  [*see* decline]
  *grammar* 567
  *backsliding* 988
**declensions** 5
**declination**
  [*see* decline]
  *deviation* 279
  *measurement* 466
  *rejection* 610
**decline** *decrease* 36
  *old* 124
  *weaken* 160
  *lescent* 306
  *grammar* 567
  *be unwilling* 603
  *reject* 610
  *disease* 655
  *become worse* 659
  *adversity* 735
  *refuse* 764
  - of day 126
  – of life 128
**declivity** *slope* 217
  *descent* 306
**decoction** 335, 384
**decode** 522
**decollate** 972

**décolleté** 226
**decoloration** 429
**decomposition 49**
**deconsecrate** 756
**decontrol** 158
**décor** 448, 599
**decoration**
  *insignia* 747
  *ornament* 847
  *title* 877
**decorative** 556
**decorous**
  [*see* decorum]
  *fashionable* 862
  *proper* 924
  *respectful* 928
**decorticate** 226
**decorum**
  *fashion* 852
  *duty* 926
  *purity* 960
**décousu**
  *discontinuous* 70
  *failure* 732
**decoy** *attract* 288
  *deceive* 545
  *deceiver* 548
  *entice* 615
**decrease** 36, 195
**decree**
  *judgment* 480
  *order* 741
  *law* 963, 969
**decrement**
  *decrease* 36
  *thing deducted* **40a**
  *contraction* 195
**decrepit** *old* 128
  *weak* 158, 160
  *disease* 655
  *decayed* 659
**decrepitate** 406
**decrescendo** 36
**decretal** 741
**decry** *underrate* 483
  *censure* 932
  *detract* 934
**decumbent** 213
**decuple** 98
**decursive** 306
**decurtation** 201
**decussation** 219
**dedecorous**
  *disreputable* 874
  *discourteous* 895
**dedicate** *use* 677
  *inscribe* 873
**deduce** *deduct* 38
  *infer* 480
**deducible**
  *evidence* 467

*proof* 478
**deduct** *retrench* 38
  *deprive* 789
  *subtract* 813
**deduction**
  [*see* deduce]
  *decrement* 40a
  *reasoning* 476
**deed** *evidence* 467
  *record* 551
  *act* 680
  *security* 771
  –s of arms 720
  – without a name
  947
**deem** 484
**deemster** 967
**deep** *great* 31
  *profound* 208
  *sea* 341
  *sonorous* 404
  *cunning* 702
  plough the – 267
  – colour 428
  – in debt 806
  – game 702
  – knowledge 490
  – mourning 839
  – note 408
  – potations 959
  – reflection 451
  – sense 821
  – sigh 839
  – study 457
  in – water 704
**deepen** 35
**deep-dyed**
  *intense* 171
  *black* 431
  *vicious* 945
**deep-felt** 821
**deep-laid** *plan* 626
**deep-mouthed**
  *resonant* 408
  *bark* 412
  *thrilling* 821
**deep-musing** 458
**deep-read** 490
**deep-rooted**
  *stable* 150
  *strong* 159
  *belief* 484
  *habit* 613
  *affections* 820
**deep-sea** 208
**deep-seated** 208,
  221
**deer** 366
  in heart a – 862
**deev** 980
**deface**

*destroy form* 241
  *obliterate* 552
  *injure* 659
  *render ugly* 846
**defalcation**
  *incomplete* 53
  *contraction* 195
  *shortcoming* 304
  *non-payment* 808
**defame** *shame* 874
  *censure* 932
  *detract* 934
**defamer** 936
**defatigation** 841
**default**
  *incomplete* 53
  *shortcoming* 304
  *neglect* 460
  *insufficiency* 640
  *debt* 806
  *non-payment* 808
  in – of 187
  judgment by – 725
**defaulter** *thief* 792
  *non-payer* 808
  *rogue* 949
**defeasance** 756
**defeat**
  *confute* 479
  *succeed* 731
  *failure* 732
  – one's hope 509
**defeatism** 911
**defecate** 652
**defecation** 299
**defect**
  *decrement* 40a
  *incomplete* 53
  *imperfect* 651
  *failing* 945
**defection**
  *relinquishment*
  624
  *disobedience* 742
**defective**
  *incomplete* 53
  *insufficient* 640
  *imperfect* 651
**defence**
  *plea* 462
  *resist* **717**
  *vindication* 937
  first line of – 726
**defenceless**
  *impotent* 158
  *weak* 160
  *exposed* 665
**defendant** 938
**defensible** *safe* 664
  *excusable* 937
**defensive alliance**

712
**defer** 133
　− to *assent* 488
　*submit* 725
　*respect* 928
**deference**
　*obedience* 743
　*humility* 879
　*courtesy* 894
　*respect* 928
**defiance** 715, 909
　*threat* 909
　in − *opposition* 708
　set at − *disobey* 742
　− of danger 861
**deficiency**
　[*see* deficient]
　*vice* 945
**deficient**
　*inferior* 34
　*incomplete* 53
　*shortcoming* 304
　*insufficient* 640
　*imperfect* 651
**deficit**
　*incompleteness* 53
　*debt* 806
**defigure** 846
**defile**
　*interval* 198
　*march* 266
　*dirt* 653
　*spoil* 659
　*shame* 874
　*impure* 961
**define**
　*specify* 79
　*limit* 233
　*explain* 522
　*name* 564
**definite**
　[*see* define]
　*visible* 446
　*certain* 474
　*exact* 494
　*intelligible* 518
　*manifest* 525
　*perspicuous* 570
**definition**
　*interpretation* 522
**definitive** *final* 67
　*affirmative* 535
　*decided* 604
**deflagration** 384
**deflate** 195
**deflation**
　*currency* 800
**deflect**
　*curve* 245
　*deviate* 279
**deflower**

*spoil* 659
*violate* 961
**defluxion**
　*egress* 295
　*flowing* 348
**defœdation** 653,
　659
**deform** 241
**deformity**
　*distortion* 243
　*ugliness* 846
　*blemish* 848
**defraud** *cheat* 545
　*swindle* 791
**defray** 807
**deft** *suitable* 23
　*clever* 698
**defunct** 360, 362
**defy** 715
　*disobey* 742
　*threaten* 909
　− *danger* 861
**dégagé** *free* 748
　*fashion* 852
**degenerate** 659
**deglutition** 298
**degradation**
　*deterioration* 659
　*shame* 874
　*dishonour* 940
**degree** 26
　*term* 71
　*honour* 873
　by −s 26
　by slow −s 275
**degustation** 390
**dehiscence** 260
**dehort**
　*dissuade* 616
　*advise* 695
**dehydrate** 340
**Dei gratiâ** 924
**deification** 873, 981
**deify**
　*honour* 873
　*idolatry* 991
**deign**
　*condescend* 762
　*consent* 879
**Deism**
　*heterodoxy* 984
　*irreligion* 989
**Deity** 976
　tutelary − 664
**dejection**
　*excretion* 299
　*melancholy* **837**
**déjeuner** 298
**délabrement** 162
**delaceration** 659
**delation** 938

**delator** 527
**delay** 133
**dele** 552
**delectable**
　*savoury* 394
　*agreeable* 829
**delectation** 827
**delectus** 562
**delegate**
　*transfer* 270
　*commission* 755
　*consignee* 758
　*deputy* 759
**delenda est**
　　Carthago
　*destroy* 162
　*curse* 908
**delete** 162
**deleterious**
　*pernicious* 649
　*unwholesome* 657
**deletion** 552
**deletory**
　*destructive* 162
**deliberate**
　*slow* 275
　*think* 451
　*attentive* 457
　*leisure* 685
　*advise* 695
　*cautious* 864
**deliberately**
　[*see* deliberate]
　*late* 133
　with *premedi-*
　　*tation* 611
**delicacy** *weak* 160
　*slender* 203
　*dainty* 298
　*brittleness* 328
　*texture* 329
　*savoury* 394
　*colour* 428
　*exact* 494
　*scruple* 603
　*ill health* 655
　*difficult* 704
　*pleasing* 829
　*beauty* 845
　*taste* 850
　*fastidious* 868
　*honour* 939
　*pure* 960
　*delicate ear* 418
**délice** 377
**delicious** *taste* 394
　*pleasing* 829
**delicti, corpus −**
　*guilt* 947
　*lawsuit* 969
**delicto, in**

**flagrante** − 947
**delight**
　*pleasure* 827
　*pleasing* 829
**Delilah** 962
**delimit** 233
**delineate**
　*outline* 230
　*represent* 554
　*describe* 594
**delineator** 559
**delineavit** 556
**delinquency** 304,
　947
**delinquent** 949
**deliquation** 335
**deliquesce** 36
**deliquescence** 335
**deliquium**
　*paralysis* 158
　*fatigue* 688
**delirant reges**
　　plectuntur
　　Achivi 739
**delirium**
　*raving* 503
　*passion* 825
　− *tremens* 503,
　959
**delitescence**
　*invisible* 447
　*latency* 526
　*seclusion* 893
**deliver**
　*transfer* 270
　*utter* 580, 582
　*birth* 662
　*rescue* 672
　*liberate* 750
　*give* 784
　*relieve* 834
　− as one's act and
　　deed 467
　− the goods 729
　− judgment 480
　− a speech 582
**deliverance** 672
**delivery**
　[*see* deliver]
　*bring forth* 161
　cash on − 807
**dell** 252
**Delphic oracle**
　*prophetic* 513
　*equivocal* 520
　*latent* 526
**delta** 342
**delude** *error* 495
　*deceive* 545
**deluge** *crowd* 72
　*water* 337

*flood* 348
  *redundance* 641
delusion
  [*see* delude]
  *insane* 503
  self – *credulous*
  486
delve *dig* 252
  *till* 371
  – into *inquire* 461
demagogue
  *director* 694
  *malcontent* 710
  *rebel* 742
demagogy 737
demand
  *inquire* 461
  *order* 741
  *ask* 765
  *price* 812
  *claim* 924
  in – *require* 630
  *desire* 865
  *saleable* 796
demarcation 233
dematerialize 317
demean oneself
  *conduct* 692
  *humble* 879
  *dishonour* 940
demeanour
  *aid* 448
  *conduct* 692
  *fashion* 852
demency 503
démenti 536
dementia 503
demerit 945
demesne
  *abode* 189
  *property* 780
demi- 91
demigod *hero* 861
  *angel* 948
demigration 266
demijohn 191
demi-jour 422
demi-lune 717
demi-mondaine
  *plebeian* 876
  *licentious* 962
demirep 962
demise *death* 360
  *transfer* 783
  *lease* 787
demisemiquaver
  113
demission 756
demit 757
demiurge
  *deity* 979

demivolt 309
demobilize 73
democracy *rule* 737
  *commonalty* 876
Democrats
  *party* 712
Democritus 838
demoiselle 129
demolish 479
demon *violent* 173
  *bane* 663
  *devil* **980**
  – in human shape
  913, 949
  – worship 991
demoniacal
  *malevolent* 907
  *furious* 824
  *wicked* 945
demonology
  *demons* 980
  *sorcery* 992
demonstration
  *number* 85
  *proof* **478**
  *manifest* 525
  *ostentation* 882
  ocular – 441, 446
demonstrative
  *manifest* 525
  *indicative* 550
  *vehement* 825
demonstrator 524
demoralize
  *unnerve* 158
  *spoil* 659
  *vicious* 945
Demosthenes 582
demotic 590
demulcent
  *mild* 174
  *soothing* 662
demur
  *disbelieve* 485
  *dissent* 489
  *unwilling* 603
  *hesitate* 605
  without – 602
demure
  *grave* 826
  *sad* 837
  *affected* 855
  *modest* 881
demurrage 133
demurrer 969
den *abode* 189
  *study* 191, **893**
  *sty* 653
  *prison* 752
  – of thieves 791

denary 98
denaturalize
  *corrupt* 659
denaturalized
  *abnormal* 83
dendriform 242, 367
dendrology 369
denial
  *negation* 536
  *refusal* 764
  self– 953
denigrate 431
denization 748
denizen
  *inhabitant* 188
  *freeman* 748
  –s of the air 979
  –s of the day 366
Denmark, rotten in
  the state of –
  526
denomination
  *class* 75
  *name* 564
  *sect* 712
  religious – 983
denominational
  *dissent* 489
  *theological* 983
  – education 537
denominator 84
denote
  *specify* 79
  *mean* 516
  *indicate* 550
dénouement
  *end* 67
  *result* 154
  *disclosure* 529
  *completion* 729
denounce
  *curse* 908
  *disapprove* 932
  *accuse* 938
dense
  *crowded* 72
  *ignorant* 493
density **321**
dent 252, 257
dental 561
denticulated 253,
  257
dentifrice 652
dentistry 662
denude 226
denuded *loss* 776
  – of
  *insufficient* 640
denunciation
  [*see* denounce]
deny *dissent* 489

*negative* 556
  *refuse* 764
  – oneself
  *avoid* 623
  *seclude* 893
  *temperate* 953
  *ascetic* 990
Deo volente 470,
  976
deobstruct 705
deodand 974
deodorize 399
  *clean* 652
deontology 926
deoppilation 705
deorganization 61
deosculation 902
depart 293
  – from
  *deviate* 15, 279
  *relinquish* 624
  – this life 360
departed
  *non-existent* 2
department
  *class* 75
  *region* 181
  *business* 625
departure 293
  new – 66
  point of – 293
depend *hang* 214
  *contingent* 475
  – upon
  be the effect of **154**
  *evidence* 467
  *trust* 484
  – on circumstan-
  ces 475
depended on, to
  be –
  *certain* 474
  *reliable* 484
  *honourable* 939
dependency 777,
  780
dependent
  *effect* 154
  *liable* 177
  *hanging* 214
  *puppet* 711
  *servant* 746
  *subject* 749
deperdition 776
dephlegmation 340
depict 554, 556
  *describe* 594
depilation 226
depilatory 662
depletion 638, 640
deplorable *bad* 649

agree to – 489
beg to – 489
– in opinion 489
– toto cœlo
    *contrary* 14
    *dissimilar* 18
    *dissent* 489
**difference 15**
    [see differ]
    *numerical* 84
    perception of –
        465
    split the – 774
    – engine 85
**different 15**
    *multiform* 81
    – time **119**
**differentia 15**
**differential 15, 84**
    – calculus 85
**differentiate 79, 465**
**differentiation**
    *calculation* 85
    *discrimination*
        465
**difficult 704**
    – to please 868
**difficulties**
    *poverty* 804
    in – 806
**difficulty 704**
    *question* 461
**diffide 485**
**diffident 860, 881**
**diffluent 348**
**diffraction 420**
    – grating 445
**diffuse** *mix* 41
    *disperse* 73
    *publish* 531
    *style* 573
**diffuseness 104, 573**
**dig** *deepen* 208
    *excavate* 252
    *till* 371
    – out 461
    – the foundations
        673
    – up 455, 480a
**digamy 903**
**digest** *arrange* 60
    *boil* 384
    *think* 451
    *compendium* 596
    *plan* 626
    *prepare* 673
    *brook* 820
**diggings 189**
**dight** *dress* 225
    *ornament* 847
**digit 84**

**digitate 44**
**digitated 253**
**digladiation 720**
**dignify 873**
**dignitary**
    *clergy* 996
**dignity**
    *glory* 873
    *pride* 878
    *honour* 939
**dignus vindice**
    **nodus**
    *unintelligible* 519
    *difficulty* 704
    *prodigy* 872
**digress**
    *deviate* 279
    *style* 573
**digression**
    *circuit* 629
**dihedral 89**
    – angle 244
**dijudication 480**
**dike** *gap* 198
    *fence* 232
    *furrow* 259
    *gulf* 343
    *conduit* 350
    *defence* 717
**dilaceration 44**
**dilapidation 659**
**dilate**
    *increase* 35
    *swell* 194
    *widen* 202
    *rarefy* 322
    *expatiate* 573
**dilatory**
    *slow* 275
    *inactive* 683
**dilection 897**
**dilemma**
    *uncertain* 475
    *logic* 476
    *choice* 609
    *difficulty* 704
**dilettante 492, 850**
**dilettantism**
    *knowledge* 490
**diligence**
    *coach* 272
**diligent**
    *active* 682
    – thought 457
**dilly-dally**
    *irresolution* 605
    *inactivity* 683
**dilucidation 522**
**diluent 335**
**dilute** *weaken* 160
    *water* 337

**diluvian 124**
**dim** *dark* 421
    *faint* 422
    *invisible* 447
    *unintelligible* 519
**dime 800**
**dimension 192**
**dimidiate 91**
**diminish**
    *lessen* 36
    *contract* 195
    – the number 103
**diminutive 32, 193**
**diminuendo**
    *decreasingly* 36
    *music* 415
**dimness 422**
**dimple 252, 257**
**dimsightedness 443**
    *unwise* 499
**din 404**
    – in the ear
    *repeat* 104
    *drum* 407
    *loquacity* 584
**dine 298**
    – with Duke
        Humphrey 87
**ding 408**
**ding-dong**
    *repeat* 104
    *chime* 407
**dining-car 272**
**dining-room 191**
**dingle 252**
**dingy** *boat* 273
    *dark* 421, 422
    *colourless* 429
    *black* 431
    *gray* 432
**dinner 298**
    – jacket 225
    – party 892
**dint** *power* 157
    *concavity* 252
    *blow* 276
    by – of
    *instrumentality*
        631
**dio, sub** – 220, 338
**diocesan 996**
**diocese 181, 995**
**Diogenes**
    *recluse* 893
    *cynic* 911
    lantern of –
    *inquiry* 461
**dioptrics 420**
**diorama** *view* 448
    *painting* 556
**diorism 465**

**dip** *slope* 217
    *concavity* 252
    *ladle* 270
    *direction* 278
    *insert* 300
    *descent* 306
    *plunge* 310
    *water* 337
    *candle* 423
    *baptize* 998
    – one's hands into
    *take* 789
    – into
    *glance at* 457
    *inquire* 461
    *learn* 539
**diphthong 561**
**diploma**
    *evidence* 467
    *commission* 755
**diplomacy**
    *artfulness* 702
    *mediation* 724
    *negotiation* 769
**diplomatist**
    *messenger* 534
    *expert* 700
    *consignee* 758
**dipper 191**
**dipsomania**
    *insanity* 503
    *desire* 865
    *drunkenness* 959
**dipsomaniac 504**
**diptych 86, 551**
**dire** *hateful* 649
    *disastrous* 735
    *grievous* 830
    *fearful* 860
**direct**
    *straight* 246
    *teach* 537
    *artless* 703
    *command* 741
    – attention to 457
    – one's course
    *motion* 278
    *pursuit* 622
    – the eyes to 441
**direction**
    [see direct]
    *tendency* **278**
    *indication* 550
    *management* **693**
    *precept* 697
**directly** *soon* 132
**director**
    *teacher* 540
    *theatre* 599
    *manager* **694**
    *master* 745

– of the budget
 801
**directorship** 737
**directory** *list* 86
 *council* 696
**diremption** 44
**direption** 791
**dirge**
 *funeral* 363
 *song* 415
 *lament* 839
**dirigible balloon**
 273, 726
**dirk** 727
**dirt** 653
 throw –
 *defame* 874
 *disrespect* 929
 – cheap 815
 like – under one's
 feet **749**
**dirty** *dim* 422
 *opaque* 426
 *unclean* 653
 *disreputable* 874
 *dishonourable* 940
 – end of stick 699
 – sky 353
 – weather 349
 do – work
 *servile* 886
 *flatterer* 935
**diruption** 162
**dis aliter visum**
 *disappointment*
 509
 *necessity* 601
**disability**
 *impotence* 158
**disable** 158
 *weaken* 160
**disabuse** 527, 529
**disaccord** 713
**disadvantage**
 *evil* 619
 *inexpedience* 647
 at a – 34
 lie under a – 651
**disadvantageous**
 647, 649
**disaffection**
 *dissent* 489
 *enmity* 889
 *hate* 898
**disaffirm** 536
**disagreeable** 830,
 867
**disagreement**
 *difference* 15
 *incongruity* **24**
 *dissent* 489

*discord* 713
**disallow** 761
**disannul** 756
**disappearance 449**
**disappointment**
 *balk* **509**
 *fail* 732
 *discontent* 832
**disapprobation 706,**
 **932**
**disapprover** 936
**disarm** *disable* 158
 *weaken* 160
 *reconcile* 831
 *propitiate* 914
**disarrange** 61
**disarray**
 *disorder* 59
 *undress* 226
**disaster** *evil* 619
 *failure* 732
 *adversity* 735
 *calamity* 830
**disastrous** *bad* 649
**disavow** 536
**disband**
 *separate* 44
 *disperse* 73
 *liberate* 750
**disbar**
 *abrogate* 756
 *punish* 972
**disbarment** 55
**disbelief** 485, 487
 *religious* 989
**disbench** 756, 972
**disbowel** 297
**disbranch** 44
**disburden**
 *facilitate* 705
 – one's mind 529
 – oneself of 782
**disburse** 809
**disc** 220, 234
**discard** *eject* 297
 *relinquish* 624
 *disuse* 678
 *abrogate* 756
 *refuse* 764
 *repudiate* 773
 *surrender* 782
 – from one's
 thoughts 458
**discarded** 495
**disceptation** 476
**discern** *see* 441
 *know* 490
**discernible** 446
**discernment** 498,
 368
**discerption** 44

**discharge**
 *violence* 173,
 *propel* 284
 *emit* 297
 *excrete* 299
 *sound* 406
 *acquit oneself* 692
 *complete* 729
 *liberate* 750
 *abrogate* 756
 *pay* 807
 *exempt* 927*a*
 *acquit* 970
 – a duty 926, 944
 – a function
 *business* 625
 *utility* 644
 – itself *egress* 295
 *river* 348
 – from the mem-
 ory 506
 – from the mind
 458
 – an obligation
 772
**discind** 44
**disciple** *pupil* 541
 *votary* 711
 *Christian* 985
**disciplinarian**
 *master* 540
 *martinet* 739
**discipline**
 *order* 58
 *teaching* 537
 *training* 673
 *restraint* 751
 *punishment* 972
 *religious* 990
**disclaim** *deny* 536
 *repudiate* 756
 *abjure* 757
 *refuse* 764
**disclosure** 480*a*, **529**
**discoid** *layer* 204
 *frontal* 220
 *flat* 251
**discoloration** 429
**discoloured**
 *shabby* 659
 *ugly* 846
 *blemish* 848
**discomfit** 731
**discomfiture** 732
**discomfort**
 *physical* 378
 *mental* 828
**discommend** 932
**discommode**
 *hinder* 706
 *annoy* 830

**discommodious**
 645, 647
**discompose**
 *derange* 61
 *put out* 458
 *hinder* 706
 *pain* 830
 *disconcert* 874
 *anger* 900
**discomposure** 828
**disconcert**
 *derange* 61
 *distract* 458
 *disappoint* 509
 *hinder* 706
 *discontent* 832
 *confuse* 879
**disconcerted**
 *hopeless* 859
**disconformity** 83
**discongruity** 24
**disconnected**
 *style* 575
**disconnection**
 *irrelation* 10
 *disjunction* 44
 *discontinuity* **70**
**disconsolate** 837
**discontent** **832**
**discontinuance**
 *cessation* 142
 *relinquishment*
 624
**discontinuity** **70**
**discord**
 *difference* 15
 *disagreement* 24
 *of sound* **414**
 *of colour* 428
 *dissension* **713**
**discount**
 *decrease* 36
 *decrement* 40*a*
 *money* **813**
 at a –
 *disrepute* 874
 *disapproved* 932
**discountenance**
 *disfavour* 706
 *refuse* 764
**discourage**
 *dissuade* 616
 *sadden* 837
 *frighten* 860
**discourse**
 *teach* 537
 *speech* 582
 *talk* 588
 *dissert* 595
 *sermon* 998
**discourtesy 895**

discous 202
discover
  *perceive* 441
  *solve* 462
  *find* 480a
  *disclose* 529
  – *itself*
  *be seen* 446
discovery 480a
discredit
  *disbelief* 485
  *dishonour* 874
discreditable
  *vicious* 945
discreet *careful* 459
  *cautious* 864
discrepancy 15
discrepant 24, 713
discrete
  *separate* 44, 70
  *single* 87
discretion *will* 600
  *choice* 609
  *skill* 698
  *caution* 864
  surrender at – 725
  use – 609
  years of – 131
discrétion à – 600
discrimination
  *difference* 15
  *nice perception*
  465
  *wisdom* 498
  *taste* 850
  *fastidiousness* 868
disculpate 937
discumbency 213
discursion 266
discursive
  *moving* 264
  *migratory* 266
  *wandering* 279
  *argumentative* 476
  *diffuse style* 573
  *conversable* 588
  *disserting* 595
discus 840
discuss *eat* 298
  *reflect* 451
  *inquire* 461
  *reason* 476
  *dissert* 595
discussion
  [*see* discuss]
  open to – 475
  under – 461
disdain
  *indifference* 866
  *fastidious* 868
  *arrogance* 885

*pride* 878
*contempt* 930
disease **655**
  occupational – 655
  –d mind 503
disembark 292
disembarrass 705
disembody
  *decompose* 49
  *disperse* 73
  *spiritualize* 317
disembogue
  *emit* 295
  *eject* 297
  *flow out* 348
disembowel 297,
  301
disembroil 60
discnable 158
disenchant
  *discover* 480a
  *dissuade* 616
  *displease* 830
disencumber 705
disendow 756
disengage
  *detach* 44
  *facilitate* 705
  *liberate* 750
disengaged
  *to let* 763
disentangle
  *separate* 44
  *arrange* 60
  *unroll* 313
  *decipher* 522
  *facilitate* 705
  *liberate* 750
disenthral 750
disenthrone 756
disentitle 925
disespouse 905
disestablish
  *displace* 185
  *abrogate* 756
disesteem 929, 932
disfavour
  *oppose* 708
  *hate* 898
  *disrespect* 929
  view with – 932
disfigure
  *deface* 241
  *injure* 659
  *deform* 846
  *blemish* 848
disfranchise 925
disgorge *emit* 297
  *flow out* 348
  *restore* 790
  *pay* 807

disgrace
  *shame* 874
  *dishonour* 940
  sense of – 879
disgraceful
  *vice* 945
disgruntle 509
disguise
  *unlikeness* 18
  *conceal* 528
  *mask* 530
  *falsify* 544
  *untruth* 546
disguised in drink
  959
disgust *taste* 395
  *offensive* 830
  *weary* 841
  *dislike* 867
  *hatred* 898
  – of life 837
dish *destroy* 162
  *plate* 191
  *food* 298
  – of tea 892
dishabille
  *undress* 226
  *unprepared* 674
dishearten
  *dissuade* 616
  *pain* 830
  *discontent* 832
  *deject* 837
dished 252, 732
disherison 789
dishevel
  *loose* 47
  *untidy* 59
  *disorder* 61
  *disperse* 73
  *intermix* 219
dishonest *false* 544
  *base* 940
dishonour
  *disrepute* 874
  *disrespect* 929
  *baseness* 940
  – bills 808
dish-water 653
disillusion 509
disincline
  *dissuade* 616
  *dislike* 867
disinclined 603
disinfect
  *purify* 652
  *restore* 660
disinfectant 662
disingenuous
  *false* 544
  *dishonourable* 940

disinherit
  *relinquish* 782
  *transfer* 783
  *deprive* 789
disintegrate
  *separate* 44
  *decompose* 49
  *pulverize* 330
disinter *exhume* 363
  *discover* 480a
disinterested **942**
disjecta membræ
  *separate* 44
  *disorder* 59
  *dispersed* 73
  – *poetæ* 597
disjoin 44
disjointed
  *disorder* 59
  *powerless* 158
  *style* 575
disjunction **44**
disjunctive 70
diskindness 907
dislike **867**
  *reluctance* 603
  *hate* 898
dislocate
  *separate* 44
  put out of joint 61
dislocated
  *disorder* 59
dislodge
  *displace* 185
  *eject* 297
disloyal 940
dismal
  *depressing* 830
  *dejected* 837
dismantle
  *destroy* 162
  *divest* 226
  *render useless* 645
  *injure* 659
  *disuse* 678
dismask 529
dismast
  *render useless* 645
  *injure* 659
  *disuse* 678
dismay 860
dismember
  *separate* 44
  *disperse* 73
dismiss
  *send away* 289
  *discharge* 297
  *discard* 678
  *liberate* 750
  *abrogate* 756
  *relinquish* 782

[ 463 ]

*punish* 972
– from the mind
  452, 458
**dismount**
 *arrive* 292
 *descend* 306
 *render useless* 645
**disnest** 185
**disobedience 742**
 *non-observance*
  773
**disoblige** 907
**disorder**
 *confusion* **59**
 *derange* 61
 *turbulent* 173
 *disease* 655
 –ed intellect 503
**disorderly**
 *unprincipled* 945
**disorganize**
 *derange* 61
 *destroy* 162
 *spoil* 659
**disorganized** 59
**disown** 536
**dispair** 44
**disparage**
 *underrate* 483
 *disrespect* 929
 *dispraise* 932
 *detract* 934
**disparity**
 *different* 15
 *dissimilar* 18
 *disagreeing* 24
 *unequal* 28
 *isolated* 44
**dispart** 44
**dispassionate** 826
 – opinion 484
**dispatch**
 [*see* despatch]
**dispel** *scatter* 73
 *destroy* 162
 *displace* 185
 *repel* 289
**dispensable**
 *useless* 645
**dispensary** 662
**dispensation**
 [*see* dispense]
 *command* 741
 *licence* 760
 *relinquishment*
  782
 *exemption* 927*a*
 –s of Providence
  976
**dispense**
 *disperse* 73

*give* 784
 *apportion* 786
 *retail* 796
 – with
 *disuse* 678
 *permit* 760
 *exempt* 927*a*
 cannot be –d with
  630
**dispeople**
 *eject* 297
 *expatriate* 893
**disperse**
 *separate* 44
 *scatter* 73
 *diverge* 291
 *waste* 638
**dispersion 73**
 – of light 420
 chromatic – 428
**dispirit**
 *discourage* 616
 *sadden* 837
**displacement**
 *derange* 61
 *remove* **185**
 *transfer* 270
**displacency**
 *dislike* 867
 *incivility* 895
 *disapprobation*
  932
**displant** 185
**display** *appear* **448**
 *show* 525
 *parade* 882
**displease** 830
**displeasure** 828
 *anger* 900
**displosion** 173
**displume** 789
**disport** 840
**disposal**
 [*see* dispose]
 at one's – 763, **777**
**dispose**
 *arrange* 60
 *tend* 176
 *induce* 615
 – of *use* 677
 *complete* 729
 *relinquish* 782
 *give* 784
 *sell* 796
**disposed** 620
**disposition**
 *nature* 5
 *order* 58
 *arrangement* 60
 *inclination* 602
 *mind* 820

**dispossess**
 *transfer* 783
 *take away* 789
 – oneself of 782
**dispraise** 932
**dispread** 73
**disprize** 483
**disproof**
 *counter-evidence*
  468
 *confutation* 479
**disproportion**
 *irrelation* 10
 *disagreement* 24
**disprove** 479
**disputable** 475, 485
**disputant** 710, 726
**disputatious** 901
**dispute**
 *discuss* 476
 *doubt* 485
 *deny* 536
 *discord* 713
 in – 461
**disqualification**
 *incapacitate* 158
 *useless* 645
 *unprepared* 674
 *unskilful* 699
 *disentitle* 925
**disquiet**
 *changeable* 149
 *agitation* 315
 *excitement* 825
 *uneasiness* 828
 *give pain* 830
**disquietude**
 *apprehension* 860
**disquisition** 539,
  595
**disregard**
 *overlook* 458
 *neglect* 460
 *make light of* 483
 *insensible to* 823,
  826
 *disrespect* **929**
 *contempt* 930
 – of time 115
**disrelish** 867, 898
**disreputable** 874
 *vicious* 945
**disrepute 874**, 929
**disrespect 929**
 *despise* 930
**disrobe** 226
**disruption**
 *disjunction* 44
 *destruction* 162
 *discord* 713
**dissatisfaction**

*disappointment*
  509
 *sorrow* 828
 *discontent* 832
**dissect**
 *anatomize* 44, 49
 *investigate* 461
**dissemblance** 18
**dissemble** 544
**dissembler** 548
**disseminate**
 *scatter* 73
 *pervade* 186
 *publish* 531
 *teach* 537
**dissension** 713
 *sow* – 898
**dissent**
 *disagree* **489**
 *refuse* 764
 *heterodoxy* 984
**dissentient** 15
**dissentious** 24
**dissertation 595**
**disservice**
 *disadvantage* 619
 *useless* 645
**disserviceable** 649
**dissever** 44
**dissidence**
 *disagreement* 24
 *dissent* 489
 *discord* 713
 *discontent* 832
 *heterodoxy* 984
**dissilience** 173
**dissimilarity** 18
**dissimulate** 544
**dissipate** *scatter* 73
 *destroy* 162
 *pleasure* 377
 *prodigality* 818
 *amusement* 840
 *intemperance* **954**
 *dissolute* 961
**dissocial** 893
**dissociate** 44
**dissociation**
 *irrelation* 10
 *separation* 44
**dissolute** 961
 *profligate* 945
 *intemperate* 954
**dissolution**
 [*see* dissolve]
 *decomposition* 49
 *destruction* 162
 *death* 360
**dissolve** *vanish* 2, 4
 *liquefy* 335
 *disappear* 449

**division**
[*see* divide]
*part* 51
*class* 75
*arithmetic* 85
*discord* 713
*military* 726
**divisor** 84
**divorce**
*separation* 44
*relinquish* 782
*matrimonial* 905
**Divorce Court** 966
**divulge** 529
**divulsion** 44
**divvy** 786
**dixi** 535
**dizen** 847
**dizzard** 501
**dizzy**
*dimsighted* 443
*confused* 458
*vertigo* 503
– height 206
– round 312
**djerrid** 727
**djinn** 980
**do** *fare* 7
*suit* 23
*produce* 161
*cheat* 545
*act* 680
*complete* 729
*succeed* 731
*I beg* 765
all one can – 686
plenty to – 682
thing to – 625
– away with
*destroy* 162
*eject* 297
*abrogate* 756
– battle 722
– one's bidding
743
– business 625
– to death 361
– as done by 906,
942
– for *destroy* 162
*kill* 361
*conquer* 731
*serve* 746
*punish* 972
– good 906
– harm 907
– honour 873
– into
*translate* 522
– justice to 595
– like 19

– little 683
– no harm 648
– nothing 681
– nothing but 136
– one's office 772
– as others do 82
– over 223
– as one pleases
748
– a service
*useful* 644
*aid* 707
– up 660
have to – with
680, 692
– without 678
– the work 686
– wrong 923
**docere, pisces na-**
**tare** – 641
**docile** *domesticated*
370
*learning* 539
*willing* 602
**docimastic** 463
**dock** *diminish* 36
*cut off* 38
*port* 189
*shorten* 201
*edge* 231
*store* 636
*tribunal* 966
**docked**
*incomplete* 53
**docker** 690
**docket**
*list* 86
*evidence* 467
*note* 550
*record* 551
*security* 771
**dockyard** 691
**doctor**
*learned man* 492
*restore* 660
*remedy* 662
after death the –
135
– accounts 811
when –s disagree
475
**doctrinaire**
*positive* 474
*pedant* 492
*affectation* 855
*blusterer* 887
**doctrinal** 537
**doctrinarian** 514
**doctrine** *tenet* 484
*knowledge* 490
**document** 551

**documentary**
*evidence* 467
**dodder** 315
**doddering** 128
**dodecahedron** 244
**dodge** *change* 140
*shift* 264
*deviate* 279
*oscillate* 314
*pursue* 461
*avoid* 623
*stratagem* 702
**dodger, artful** – 792
**dodo** 366
extinct as the –
122
**Doe, John** 4
**doe** *swift* 274
*deer* 366
*female* 374
**doer**
*originator* 164
*agent* 690
**doff** 226
– the cap 894
**dog** *follow* 281
*animal* 366
*male* 373
*pursue* 622
*wretch* 949
cast to the –s
*reject* 610
*disuse* 678
*abrogate* 756
*relinquish* 782
fire – 386
go to the –s
*destruction* 162
*fail* 732
*adversity* 735
*poverty* 804
sea – 269
watch –
*safety* 664
*warning* 668
*keeper* 753
hair of – that bit
you 959
let sleeping –s lie
141
– in manger 706,
943
–tired 688
–s of war 722
**dog-cart** 272
**dog-cheap** 815
**dog-days** 382
**doge** 745
**dogged**
*obstinate* 606
*valour* 861

*sullen* 901*a*
**dogger** 273
**doggerel**
*verse* 597
*ridiculous* 851,
853
**dog-hole** 189
**dog Latin** 563
**dogma** *tenet* 484
*theology* 983
**dogmatic**
*certain* 474
*positive* 481
*assertion* 535
*obstinate* 606
**dogmatist** 887
**dog's ear** 258
**dog robber** 746
**dog-sick** 867
**dog-star** 423
**dog-trot** 275
**dog-weary** 688
**doily** 652
**doing**
up and – 682
what one is – 625
**doings**
*events* 151
*actions* 680
*conduct* 692
**doit** *trifle* 643
*coin* 800
**dolce far niente** 681
**doldrums**
*dejection* 837
*sulks* 901*a*
**dole**
*small quantity* 32
*scant* 640
*give* 784
*allot* 786
*parsimony* 819
*grief* 828
**doleful** 837
– dumps 901*a*
**doll** *small* 193
*image* 554
**dollar** 800
**dolman** 225
**dolmen** 363, 551
**dolorem, infandum**
**renovare** – 833
**dolorous** 830
**dolour**
*physical* 378
*moral* 828
**dolphin** 341
**dolt** 501
**doltish** 499
**domain**
*class* 75

*region* 181
*property* 780
**Domdaniel** 982
**dome** *high* 206
 *roof* 223
 *curvature* 245
 *convex* 250
**Domesday book**
 *list* 86
 *record* 551
**domesman** 967
**domestic**
 *inhabitant* 188
 *home* 189
 *interior* 221
 *servant* 746
 *secluded* 893
 – *animals* 366
**domesticate**
 *locate* 184
 *acclimatize* 613
 – *animals* 370
**domicile** 189
**domiciled** 186
**domiciliary** 188
 – *visit* 461
**dominant** 175
 *note in music* 413
**domination** 737
**dominical** 998
**domineer**
 *tyrannize* 739
 *insolence* 885
**Domini, anno** – 106
**Dominican** 996
**Dominie** 540
**dominion** 181, 737
**domino** *dress* 225
 *mask* 530
 *game* 840
**domn** 745
**don** *put on* 225
 *scholar* 492
 *teacher* 540
 *noble* 875
**Don Juan** 897
**donation** 784
**done** *finished* 729
 *work* – 729
 – *for spoilt* 659
 *failure* 732
 – *up*
 *impotent* 158
 *tired* 688
 *have* – *with*
 *cease* 142
 *relinquish* 624
 *disuse* 678
**donee** 785
**donjon** 717, 752
**donkey** *ass* 271

*fool* 501
*talk a* –'*s hind leg*
 *off* 584
**donna** 374
**Donnybrook Fair**
 *disorder* 59
 *discord* 713
**donor** 784
**donzel** 746
**doodle** 501
**doom** *end* 67
 *fate* 152
 *destruction* 162
 *death* 360
 *judgment* 480
 *necessity* 601
 *sentence* 971
 – *sealed*
 *death* 360
 *adversity* 735
**doomed** 735, 828
**doomsday**
 *end* 67
 *future* 121
 *till* – 112
**door** *entrance* 66
 *cover* 223
 *brink* 231
 *barrier* 232
 *opening* 260
 *passage* 627
 *at one's* – 197
 *beg from door to* –
 765
 *bolt the* – 666
 *close the* – *upon*
 751
 *death's* – 360
 *keep within* –s 265
 *lie at one's* – 926
 *lock the* – 666
 *open a* – *to*
 *liable* 177
 *open the* – *to*
 *receive* 296
 *facilitate* 705
 *permit* 760
 *show the* – *to*
 *eject* 297
 *discourtesy* 895
 – *mat* 652
**doorkeeper** 263
**doorway** 260
**dope** 376, 545, 663
**doquet**
 *security* 771
**Dorado, El** – 803
**Doric mode** 413
**dormant**
 *inert* 172
 *latent* 526

*asleep* 683
**dormer** 260
**dormeuse** 272
**dormir debout,**
 *conte à* – 843
**dormitive** 841
**dormitory** 191
**dormouse** 683
**dorp** 189
**dorsal** 235
**dorser** 191
**dorsum** 235, 250
**dory** 273
**dose** *quantity* 25
 *part* 51
 *medicine* 662
 *apportion* 786
**dosser** 191
**dossier** *bundle* 72
 *record* 551
**dossil** 223, 263
**dot** *small* 32
 *place* 182
 *little* 193
 *variegate* 440
 *mark* 550
 *dowry* 780
 *on the* – 113
**dotage** 128, 499
**dotard** 130, 501
**dotation** 784
**dottle** 40, 645
**dote** *drivel* 499, 503
 – *upon* 897
**douanier** 965
**double**
 *similar* 17
 *increase* 35
 *duplex* 90
 *substitute* 147
 *fold* 258
 *turn* 283
 *finesse* 702
 *march at the* – 274
 *see* –
 *dim sight* 443
 *drunk* 959
 – *acrostic*
 *letters* 561
 *wit* 842
 – *dutch* 519
 – *entry* 811
 – *the fist* 909
 – *march* 684
 – *meaning* 520
 – *a point* 311
 *in* – *quick time*
 274
 – *reef topsails* 664
 – *sure* 474
 *work* – *tides* 686

– *up*
 *render powerless*
 158
**double bar** 747
**double-bass** 417
**doublecross** 545
**double-dealing**
 *lie* 544
 *cunning* 940
**double-distilled** 171
**double-dyed** 428
**double-eagle** 800
**double-edged** 90,
 171
**double entendre**
 *ambiguity* 520
 *impure* 961
**double-faced**
 *lie* 544
 *cunning* 702, 940
**double-headed** 90
**double-minded** 605
**double-shotted** 171
**doublet** 225
**double-tongued**
 *lie* 544
 *cunning* 702, 940
**doubt**
 *uncertain* 475
 *disbelieve* 485
 *sceptic* 989
**doubtful** 475
 *more than* – 473
 – *meaning*
 *unintelligible* 519
**doubtless**
 *certain* 474
 *belief* 484
 *assent* 488
**douceur** 784, 973
**douche** 337
**dough** 324, 354, 800
**doughty** 861
**dour** 739
**douse**
 *immerse* 310
 *splash* 337
 *blow* 972
**Dove**
 *Holy Ghost* 976
**dove**
 *innocent* 946
 *roar like sucking* –
 174
**dovecote** 189
**dovetail**
 *agree* 23
 *join* 43
 *intersect* 219
 *intervene* 228
 *angle* 244

*in parts* 51
– in the bucket 32
– in upon 674
– into a good
  thing 734
– into the grave
  360
– a hint 527
– all idea of 624
– in *arrive* 292
*immerse* 300
*sociality* 892
– the mask 529
– off *decrease* 36
*die* 360
*sleep* 683
– in the ocean
*trifling* 643
– the subject 458
– too much 959
**dropping** fire 70
**drop-scene** 599
**dropsical** 194, 641
**droshki** 272
**dross**
*remainder* 40
*slag* 384
*trash* 643, 645
*dirt* 653
**drought**
*dryness* 340
*insufficiency* 640
**drouth** *desire* 865
**drove**
*assemblage* 72
*multitude* 102
**drover** 370
**drown**
*affusion* 337
*kill* 361
*ruin* 731, 732
– *care* 840
– the voice 581
**drowsy** *slow* 275
*sleepy* 683
*weary* 841
**drub**
*defeat* 731, 732
*punish* 972
**drudge** *labour* 686
*worker* 682, 690
**drug**
*render insensible*
  376
*superfluity* 641
*trash* 643
*remedy* 662
*bane* 663
– in the market
  815
**drugget**

*cover* 223
*clean* 652
*preserve* 670
**druggist** 662
**druid** 996
**drum**
*repeat* 104
*cylinder* 249
*sound* 407
*music* 417
*party* 892
beat of –
*signal* 550
*alarm* 669
*war* 722
*command* 741
*parade* 882
ear – 418
muffled –
*funeral* 363
*non-resonance*
  408a
– and fife band 417
– fire 407
– out 972
**drum-head** 964,
  966
**drum-major** 745
**drummer** 416
**drunken** 959
reel like a – man
  315
**drunkenness 959**
**dry** *arid* 340
*style* 575, 576, 579
*hoarse* 581
*scanty* 640
*preserve* 670
*exhaust* 789
*tedious* 841
*dull* 842
*thirsty* 865
*cynical* 932
*teetotal* 958
run – 640
with – eyes 823
– dock 189
– joke 842
– land 342
– the tears 834
– up 340, 638
**dryad** 979
**dry-as-dust**
*antiquarian* 122
*dull* 843
**dryness 340**
**dry-nurse**
*teach* 537
*teacher* 540
*aid* 707
**dry-point** 558

**dry-rot**
*dirt* 653
*decay* 659
*bane* 663
**dualism** 984
**duality** 89
**duarchy** 737
**dub** 564
**dubious** 475
**ducat** 800
**duce** 745
**duchess** 745, 875
**duchy** 181
**duck** *stoop* 308
*plunge* 310
*water* 337
*darling* 897, 899
play –s and
  drakes
*recoil* 277
*prodigality* 818
–'s egg
*zero* 101
– in thunder 870
**ducking-stool** 975
**duckling** 129
**duck-pond** 370
**duct** 350
**ductile**
*elastic* 325
*flexible* 324
*trimming* 607
*easy* 705
*docile* 743
**dud** 158, 727
**dude** 854
**duds** 225
**dudgeon**
*dagger* 727
*discontent* 832
*churlishness* 895
*hate* 898
*anger* 900
*sullenness* 901a
**due**
*expedient* 646
*owing* 806
*proper* 924, 926
give his – to
*right* 922
*vindication* 937
*fair* 939
in – course 109
*occasion* 134
– respect 928
– sense of 498
– time
*soon* 132
– to
*cause and effect*
  154, 155

give – weight **465**
**duel** 720
**duellist** 726
**dueness 924**
**duenna**
*teacher* 540
*guardian* 664
*keeper* 753
**dues** 812
**duet** 415
**duff** 298
**duffer**
*bungler* 701
*smuggler* 792
**dug** 250
**dug-out**
*old man* 130
*boat* 273
*defence* 717
**duke** *ruler* 745
*noble* 875
**dulce domum** 189
**dulcet**
*sweet* 396
*sound* 405
*melodious* 413
*agreeable* 829
**dulcify** 174, 396
**dulcimer** 417
**Dulcinea** 897
**dulcorate** 396
**dulia** 990
**dull** *weak* 160
*inert* 172
*moderate* 174
*blunt* 254
*insensible* 376,
  381
*sound* 405
*dim* 422
*colourless* 429
*ignorant* 493
*stolid* 499
*style* 575
*inactive* 683
*unapt* 699
*callous* 823
*dejected* 837
*weary* 841
*prosing* 843
*simple* 849
– of hearing **419**
– sight 443
**dullard** 501
**dullness 843**
**duly** 924
**duma** 696
**dumb** 581
– animal 366
– show 550
– waiter 307

quick – 418
reach one's –s 527
ring in the – 408
set by the –s
  *discord* 713
  *hate* 898
  *resentment* 900
split the –s 404
together by the –s
  *discord* 713
  *contention* 720
up to one's –s
  *redundance* 641
  *active* 680, 682
willing – 602
word in the – 586
– for music 416,
  418
in at one – out at
  the other
  *inattention* 458
  *forget* 506
not for –s polite
  961
make the –s tingle
  *anger* 900
– ache 378
ear-drum 418
earl 875
earless 419
earliness **132**
early 132
get up – 682
earmark 550
earn 775
earnest *willing* 602
  *determined* 604
  *emphatic* 642
  *pledge* 771
  *pay in advance*
    809
  *eager* 821
in –
  *affirmation* 535
  *veracious* 543
  *strenuous* 682
ear-piercing 410
ear-ring 847
ear-shot 197
out of – 405
ear-splitting 404
earth *ground* 211
  *world* 318
  *land* 342
  *corpse* 362
what on –
  *inquiry* 461
  *wonder* 870
– closet 653
earthenware
  *baked* 384

*sculpture* 557
earthling 372
earthly 318
end of one's –
  career 360
of no – use 645
earthly-minded
  943, 989
earthquake 146,
  173
earthwork 717
earwig *flatter* 933,
  935
ear-witness 467
ease *bodily* 377
  *style* 578
  *leisure* 685
  *facility* 705
  *mental* 827
  *content* 831
at one's –
  *prosperous* 734
mind at –
  *cheerful* 836
set at – *relief* 834
take one's – 687
– off *deviate* 297
– one of *take* 789
easel *support* 215
  *painting* 556
  *picture* 556
easement
  *property* 780
  *relief* 834
easily
  [*see* easy]
let one down – 918
– accomplished
  705
– deceived 486
– persuaded 602
East 236, 278
Easter *period* 138
  *rite* 998
– Monday
  *holiday* 840
– offering
  *gift* 784
– sepulchre 1000
easy *gentle* 275
  *style* 578
  *facile* 705
make oneself –
  about 484
take it –
  *inactive* 683
  *inexcitable* 826
– ascent 217
– of belief 472
– chair
  *support* 215

*repose* 687
– circumstances
  803
– going
  *willing* 602
  *irresolute* 605
  *lenient* 740
  *inexcitable* 826
  *contented* 831
  *indifferent* 866
– sail
  *moderate* 174
  *slow* 275
– temper 894
– terms 705
– to understand
  518
– virtue 961
eat *food* 298
  *tolerate* 826
– dirt 725, 879
– one's fill
  *enough* 639
  *gorge* 957
– heartily 298
– one's words 879
– out of house and
  home *take* 789
  *prodigal* 818
  *gluttony* 957
– of the same
  trencher 892
– one's words 607
eatables 298
eaten up with 820
eau, battre l' – 645
faire venir l' – à la
  bouche 865
mettre de l' – dans
  son vin 174
eaves 250
eavesdropper 455,
  527
eavesdropping 418,
  532
ébauche 626
ebb *decrease* 36
  *contract* 195
  *regress* 283
  *recede* 287
  *waste* 638
  *spoil* 659
low – 36
  *low* 207
  *depression* 308
  *insufficient* 640
– and flow 314
– of life 360
ebb-tide *low* 207
  *dry* 340
ebony 431

ebriety 959
ebullient
  *violent* 173
  *hot* 382
  *excited* 824
ebullition
  *energy* 171
  *violence* 173
  *agitation* 315
  *heating* 384
  *excitation* 825
  *anger* 900
écarté 840
ecce
– iterum Crispinus
  104
– signum 550
eccentric 220
  *irregular* 83
  *foolish* 499
  *crazed* 503, 504
  *capricious* 608
ecchymosis 299
ecclesiastic
  *church* 995
  *clergy* 996
ecclesiastical
  *canonical* 985
– court 966
– law 963
ecclesiolatry 991
écervelé 458
échafaudage 673
échappée 840
échapper belle 671
échelon 279
echo *imitate* 19
  *copy* 21
  *repeat* 104
  *reflection* 277
  *resonance* 408
  *answer* 462
  *assent* 488
applaud to the –
  931
awake –es 404
éclaircissement 522
éclat 873
eclectic 609
eclipse *surpass* 33
  *disappearance*
    449
  *hide* 528
  *outshine* 873, 874
partial – *dim* 422
total – *dark* 421
under an –
  *invisible* 447
  *out of repute* 874
ecliptic 318
eclogue 597

**economic pressure**
751
**economy**
*order* 58
*conduct* 692
*frugality* 817
animal – 359
**écorcher les oreilles**
410
**ecphorize** 615
**écru** 433
**ecstasis** 683
**ecstasy**
*frenzy* 515
*transport* 821
*rapture* 827
**ecstatic** 829
**ecstatica** 994
**ectoplasm** 992
**ectype** 21
**ecumenical** 78
**edacity** 957
**Edda** 986
**eddy**
*whirlpool* 348
*current* 312
*danger* 667
**Eden** 827
**edge** *energy* 171
*height* 206
*brink* **231**
*sidle* 279
*advantage* 731
cutting – 253
on – 256, 507
take the – off 174
– of hunger 865
– in 228
one's way 282
**edge-tools** 253
play with – 863
**edgewise** 217
**edging**
*obliquity* 217
*border* 231
*ornament* 847
**edible** 298
**edict** 741
**edification**
*building* 161
*teaching* 537
*learning* 539
*piety* 987
**edifice** 161
**edifying** *good* 648
**edile** 965
**edit**
*publication* 531
*condense* 596
*revise* 658
**edition, new** – 658

**editor** 593
**educate** 537
**educated** 490
self – 490
**education**
*teaching* 537
*knowledge* 490
man of – 492
higher – 490
**educational** 537,
542
**educe** *extract* 301
*discover* 480a
**educt** 40
**eduction** 40a
**edulcorate** 396, 652
**eel** 248
wriggle like an –
315
**eerie** 860
**efface**
*delete* 162
*disappear* 449
*obliterate* 552
– from the
memory 506
**effect**
*consequence* **154**
*product* 161
*impression* 375
*complete* 729
carry into – 692
with crushing –
162
in – 5
take – 731
to that – 516
**effective**
*capable* 157
*useful* 644
**effectuation** 729
**expedient** 646
**effects** 780, 798
**effectual** 731
**effectually** 52
**effectuate** 729
**effeminate**
*weak* 160
*womenlike* 374
*timorous* 862
*sensual* 954
**effeminize** 158
**effendi** 875
**effervesce**
*energy* 171
*violence* 173
*agitate* 315
*bubble* 353
*excited* 825
**effervescent** 338
**effete** *old* 128

*weak* 160
*useless* 645
*spoiled* 659
**efficacious**
[*see* efficient]
**efficient**
*power* 157
*agency* 170
*utility* 644
*skill* 698
**effigy** 21, 554
**effleurer** *skim* 267,
460
**efflorescence** 330
**effluxion of time**
109
**effluence** *egress* 295
*flow* 348
**effluvium** 334, 398
**efflux** 295
**efformation** 240
**effort** 686
**effreet** 980
**effrontery** 885
**effulgence** 420
**effuse**
*pour out* 295, 297
*excrete* 299
*speech* 582
*loquacity* 584
**effusion of blood**
361
**effusive** 573
**eft** 366
**eftsoons** 117
**egad** 535
**égards** 928
**egesta** 299
**egestion** 297
**egg** *beginning* 66
*cause* 153
*food* 298
walk among –s
704
too many –s in
one basket
*unskilful* 699
(*imprudent* 863)
– and dart
*ornament* 847
– on 615
**egg-shaped** 247,
249
**ego** *intrinsic* 5
*speciality* 79
*immaterial* 317
non – 6
**egocentrism** 943
**egotism**
*vanity* 880
*cynicism* 911

*selfishness* 943
**egregious**
*exceptional* 83
*absurd* 497
*exaggerated* 549
*important* 642
**egregiously** 31, 33
**egress** 295
**Egyptian darkness**
421
**eheu! fugaces**
**labuntur anni**
111
**eiderdown** 223
**eidouranion** 318
**Eiffel tower** 206
**eight** *number* 98
*boat* 273
*representative* 759
**eisteddfod** 72, 416
**eighty** 98
**either** *choice* 609
happy with – 605
**ejaculate**
*propel* 284
*utter* 580
**ejection** 185, **297**
**ejecta** 299
**ejector** 349
**eke** *also* 37
– out *complete* 52
*spin out* 110
**ekka** 272
**El Dorado** 803
**elaborate**
*improve* 658
*prepare* 673
*laborious* 686
*work out* 729
**elaine** 356
**élan** 276
**elapse** 109, 122
**elastic fluid** 334
**elasticity**
*power* 157
*strength* 159
*energy* 171
*spring* **325**
**elate** *cheer* 836
*rejoice* 838
*hope* 858
*vain* 880
*boast* 884
**elbow** *angle* 244
*projection* 250
*push* 276
at one's –
*near* 197
*advice* 695
lift one's –

**EMB**

emboss *convex* 250
  ornament 847
embouchure 260
embowel 297
embrace
  cohere 46
  compose 54
  include 76
  enclose 227
  choose 609
  take 789
  friendship 888
  sociality 892
  courtesy 894
  endearment 902
  – an offer 762
embrangle 61
embranglement 713
embrasure 257, 260
embrocation 662
embroider
  variegate 440
  lie 544
  ornament 847
embroidery
  adjunct 39
  exaggeration 549
embroil *derange* 61
  discord 713
embroilment 59
embrown 433
embryo
  beginning 66
  cause 153
  in – destined 152
  preparing 673
embryology 357
embryonic 193, 674
embus 293
embusqué 603
emendation 658
emerald *green* 435
  jewel 847
emerge 295, 446
emergency
  circumstance 8
  event 151
  difficulty 704
emeritus 500, 928
emersion 295, 446
emery
  sharpener 253
  – paper
  smooth 255
emetic *remedy* 662
émeute 742
emication 420
emigrant 57, 268
emigrate 266, 295
emigré 268, 295
eminence

**EMP**

  height 206
  fame 873
  church dignitary
    996
eminent domain
  744
eminently 33
emir 745, 875
emissary
  messenger 534
  consignee 758
emission 297
emit *eject* 297
  publish 531
  voice 580
  – vapour 336
Emmanuel 976
emmet 193
emollient 662
emolument
  acquisition 775
  receipt 810
  remuneration 973
emotion 821
  –al appeal 824
  –al drama 599
empale 260, 972
empanel 86, 969
empathy 515
emperor 745
emphasis 580
emphatic 535, 642
emphatically 31
empierce
  perforate 260
  insert 300
empire 737, 789
  – day 840
empiric 548
empirical 463, 675
empiricism 463
emplane 293
employ
  business 625
  use 677
  servitude 749
  commission 755
  in one's – 746
  – one's capital in
    794
  – oneself 680
  – one's time in
    625
employé
  servant 746
  agent 758
employer 795
empoison 659
emporium 799
empower
  power 157

**ENA**

  commission 755
  accredit 759
  permit 760
empress 745
empressement
  activity 682
  emotion 821
  desire 865
emprise 676
emption 795
emptor 795
  caveat – 769
empty *clear* 185
  vacant 187
  deflate 195
  drain 297
  ignorant 491
  waste 638
  deficient 640
  useless 645
  beggarly account
    of – boxes
  poverty 804
  – one's glass 298
  – purse 804
  – sound 517
  – stomach 865
  – title name 564
  undue 925
  – words 546
empty-handed 640
empty-headed
  491
empurple 437
empyrean *sky* 318
  blissful 829
empyreuma 41
empyrosis 384
emulate *imitate* 19
  goodness 648
  rival 708
  compete 720
  glory 873
emulsion 352
emunctory 350
en – bloc 50
  – masse 50
  – passant
  parenthetical 10
  transient 111
  à propos 134
  – rapport 9
  – règle order 58
  conformity 82
  – route
  journey 266
  progress 282
enable 157
enact *drama* 599
  action 680
  conduct 692

**ENC**

  complete 729
  order 741
  law 963
enallage 521
enamel *coating* 223
  painting 556
  ornament 847
enameller 559
enamour 897
encage 751
encamp 184, 189
encampment 184
encaustic 556
enceinte
  with child 161
  region 181
  inclosure 232
enchafe 830
enchain 751
enchant *please* 829
enchanted 827
enchanting 845,
  897
enchantment
  sorcery 992
enchase 43, 259
enchiridion 593
enchorial 188
encincture 229
encircle 76, 227,
  311
enclave *close* 181
  boundary 233
enclose 227, 229
enclosure
  region 181
  envelope 232
  fence 752
encomiast 935
encomium 931
encompass 227, 233
  –ed with difficul-
    ties 704
encore 104, 931
encounter
  undergo 151
  clash 276
  meet 292
  withstand 708
  contest 720
  – danger 665
  – risk 621
encourage
  animate 615
  aid 707
  comfort 834
  hope 858
  embolden 861
encroach
  transcursion 303
  do wrong 923

*infringe* 925
encumber 704, 706
encumbrance
  clear of – 807
encyclical 531
encyclopædia 490,
  593
  walking – 700
encyclopædical
  *general* 78
  – knowledge 490
encysted 229
end
  *termination* 67
  *effect* 154
  *object* 620
  at an – 142
  come to its – 729
  one's journey's –
  292
  on – 212
  put an – to
  *destroy* 162
  *kill* 361
  begin at the
    wrong – 699
  – one's days 360
  –s of the earth 196
  – to end *space* 180
  *touching* 199
  *length* 200
  – of life 360
  – in smoke 732
  – of one's tether
  *sophistry* 477
  *ignorant* 491
  *insufficient* 640
  *difficult* 704
endamage 649
endanger 665
endear 897
endearment 902
endeavour
  *pursuit* 622
  *attempt* 675
  use one's best –
  686
  – after 620
endemic
  *special* 79
  *interior* 221
  *disease* 657
endimanché 847,
  882
endless
  *multitudinous*
  102
  *infinite* 105
  *perpetual* 112
endlessly 16
endlong 200

endocrine 221
endogenous 367
endorse
  *evidence* 467
  *assent* 488
  *compact* 769
  – *a bill* 800
  *approve* 931
endorsement 550
endosmose 302
endow
  *confer power* 157
endowed with
  *possessed of* 777
endowment
  *intrinsic* 5
  *power* 157
  *talent* 698
  *gift* 784
endrogynous 83
endue 157
endure *time* 106
  *last* 110
  *persist* 143
  *continue* 141
  *undergo* 151
  *feel* 821
  *submit to* 826
  unable to – 867
  – for ever 112
  – pain 828
enduring
  *indelible* 505
endwise 212
enemy *time* 841
  *foe* 891
  the common – 978
  thing devised by
    the – 546
  – to society 891
energumen 504
energy *power* 157
  *strength* 159
  *physical* 171
  *resolution* 604
  *activity* 682
enervate 158, 160
enfant, bon – 906
  – gâté
  *prosperity* 734
  *satiety* 869
  *favourite* 899
  – perdu
  *hopeless* 859
  *reckless* 863
  – terrible
  *curiosity* 455
  *artless* 703
  *object of fear* 860
enfeeble 160
enfeoff 780, 783

Enfield rifle 727
enfilade
  *lengthwise* 200
  *pierce* 260
  pass through 302
enfold 229
enforce *urge* 615
  *advise* 695
  *compel* 744
  *require* 924
enfranchise
  *free* 748
  *liberate* 750
  *permit* 760
enfranchised 924
engage
  *bespeak* 132
  *induce* 615
  *undertake* 676
  do battle 722
  *commission* 755
  *promise* 768
  *compact* 769
  I'll –
  *affirmation* 535
  – the attention
  457
  – with 720
engaged
  *marriage* 903
  be – 135
  – in *attention* 457
engagement
  *business* 625
  *battle* 720
  *betrothal* 902
engaging
  *pleasing* 829
  *amiable* 897
engender 161
engine 153, 633
engine-driver 268
engineer 690, 694,
  726
engineering 633
engird 227
English 188
  broken – 563
  king's – 560
  murder the king's
    – 568
  plain –
  *intelligible* 518
  *interpreted* 522
  *style* 576
  – horn 417
engorge
  *swallow* 296
  *gluttony* 957
engorgement
  *too much* 641

engrail 256
engrave
  *furrow* 259
  *mark* 550
  – in the memory
  505
engraver 559
engraving 21, 22,
  558
engross *write* 590
  *possess* 777
  – the thoughts
  *thought* 451
  *attention* 457
engrossed in
  thought 451
engulf
  *destroy* 162
  *plunge* 310
  swallow up 296
enhance
  *increase* 35
  *improve* 658
enharmonic 413
enigma
  *question* 461
  *secret* 533
enigmatic
  *uncertain* 475
  *unintelligible* 517
  *obscure* 519
énigme, mot d' –
  522
enjoin *advise* 695
  *command* 741
  *prescribe* 926
enjoy
  *physically* 377
  *possess* 777
  *morally* 827
  – health 654
  – popularity 873
  – a state 7
enkindle *heat* 384
  *excite* 824
enlarge
  *increase* 35
  *swell* 194
  in writing 573
  *liberate* 750
  – the mind 537
enlarged views 498
enlighten
  *illumine* 420
  *inform* 527
  *teach* 537
enlightened
  *knowledge* 490
enlist *engage* 615
  *war* 722
  *commission* 755

**envoy**
*messenger* 534
*consignee* 758
**envy 921**
**enwrap 225**
**enzyme 320**
**Eolian harp 417**
**Eolus 349**
**eon 976**
**épanchement**
*manifest* 525
*artless* 703
*endearment* 902
**epact 641**
**épaulette**
*badge* 550, 747
*ornament* 847
*decoration* 877
**éperdu 824**
**épergne 191**
**ephemeral 111**
**ephemeris**
*calendar* 114
*record* 551
*book* 593
**Ephesian letters**
993
**ephialtes**
*physical pain* 378
*hindrance* 706
*mental pain* 828
**ephod 999**
**ephor 967**
**epic 594, 597**
**epicedium 839**
**epicene 81, 83**
**epicier 876**
**epicure**
*fastidious* 868
*sybarite* 954a
*glutton* 957
**epicurean 954**
**Epicurus, system**
**of** – 954
**epicy-cle, -cloid**
247
**epidemic**
*general* 78
*disease* 655
*insalubrity* 657
**epidermis 223**
**epigenesis 161**
**epigram 496, 842**
**epigrammatic 572**
**epigrammatist 844**
**epigraph 550**
**epilepsy 315, 655**
**epilogue**
*sequel* 65
*end* 67
*drama* 599

**épingles, tiré à**
**quatre** – 855
**Epiphany 998**
*episcopal* 995
**Episcopalian 984**
**episcopate 995**
**episode**
*adjunct* 39
*discontinuity* 70
*interjacence* 228
**episodic**
*irrelative* 10
*style* 573
**epistle 592**
**Epistles 985**
**epistrophe 104**
**epistyle 210**
**epitaph 363**
**epithalamium 903**
**epithem 662**
**epithet 564**
**epitome**
*miniature* 193
*short* 201
*concise* 572
**epizoötic 657**
**epoch** *time* 106
*instant* 113
*date* 114
*present time* 118
**epode 597**
**eponym 564**
**epopœa 597**
**epos 594**
**epulation 298**
**epulotic 662**
**epuration 652**
**equable 16, 922**
**equal** *even* 27
*equitable* 922
– *chance* 156
– *times* 120
– *to power* 157
**equality 13, 27**
**equalize 213**
**equanimity 826**
**equate 27, 30**
**equations 85**
**equator 68, 318**
**equatorial 68, 236**
**equerry 746**
**equestrian 268**
**equibalanced 27**
**equidistant 68**
**equilibration 27**
**equilibrist 599**
**equilibrium 27**
**equine** *carrier* 271
*horse* 366
**equinox 125, 126**
**equip 225, 673**

**equipage**
*vehicle* 272
*instruments* 633
*display* 882
**equiparent 27**
**equipment 633**
**equipoise &c.** 27, 30
**equiponderate 30**
**equitable** *wise* 498
*just* 922
*due* 924
*honourable* 939
– *interest* 780
**equitation 266**
**equity** *right* 922
*honour* 939
*law* 963
in – 922
– *draftsman* 968
**equivalent**
*identical* 13
*equal* 27
*compensation* 30
*substitute* 147
*translation* 522
**equivocalness**
*dubious* 475
*double meaning*
520
*impure* 961
**equivocate**
*sophistry* 477
*palter* 520
*lie* 544
**equivocation**
[*see* equivocate]
without – 543
**équivoque**
*double meaning*
520
*impure* 961
**era** *time* 106, 108
*date* 114
**eradicate**
*destroy* 162
*extract* 301
**erase** *destroy* 162
*obliterate* 331, 552
**Erastian 984**
**erasure 552**
**Erato 416**
**ere 116**
– *long* 132
– *now* 116
*past* 122
**Erebus** *dark* 421
*hell* 982
**erect** *build* 161
*vertical* 212
*raise* 307
with head – 878

– the scaffolding
673
**erewhile 116, 122**
**ergatocracy 737**
**ergo 476**
**ergotism 480**
**ergotize 485**
**eriometer 445**
**Erinys 900**
**Erl King 980**
**ermine**
*badge of authority*
747
*ornament* 847
**erode 36, 659**
**Eros 897, 979**
**erosion 36**
**erotic 897, 961**
**err** – *in opinion* 495
– *morally* 945
**errand**
*message* 532
*business* 625
*commission* 755
**errand-boy 534**
**errant 279**
**erratic**
*irregular* 139
*changeable* 149
*wandering* 279
*capricious* 608
**erratum 495**
**erroneous 495**
**error** *fallacy* 495
*vice* 945
*guilt* 947
court of – 966
writ of – 969
**ersatz 973**
**erst 122**
**erubescence 434**
**erubuit salva res**
**est 95**
**eruct 297**
**eructate 297**
**erudition 490, 539**
**eruption**
*upheaval* 146
*violence* 173
*egress* 295, 297
*disease* 655
volcanic – 872
**escadrille 726**
**escalade**
*mounting* 305
*attack* 716
**escalator 307**
**escalop 248**
**escapade**
*absurdity* 497
*freak* 608

*prank* 840
**escape 671**
  *liberate* 750
  *evade* 927
  means of − 664,
    666
  − the lips
  *disclosure* 529
  *speech* 582
  − the memory 506
  − notice &c.
  *invisible* 447
  *inattention* 458
  *latent* 526
**escarp 717**
**escarpment**
  *stratum* 204
  *height* 206
  *oblique* 217
**escharotic**
  *caustic* 171
  *pungent* 392
**eschatology 67**
**escheat 145, 974**
**eschew**   ‐
  *avoid* 623
  *dislike* 867
**esclandre 828, 830**
**escort**
  *accompany* 88
  *safeguard* 664
  *keeper* 753
**escritoire** 191
**esculent** 298
**escutcheon 550**
**esoteric**
  *private* 79
  *concealed* 528
**Espagne, château**
  en − *fancy* 515
  *hope* 858
**espalier 232**
**especial** 79
**especially** 33
**Esperanto 560**
**espial** 441
**espièglerie**
  *cunning* 702
  *fun* 840
  *wit* 842
**espionnage** 441,
  461
**esplanade**
  *houses* 189
  *flat* 213
**espouse**
  *choose* 600
  *marriage* 903
  − a cause *aid* 707
  *co-operate* 709
**esprit**

*shrewdness* 498
  *wit* 842
  bel − 844
  − de corps
  *bias* 481
  *co-operation* 709
  *sociality* 892
  (*party* 712)
  − fort
  *thinker* 500
  *irreligious* 989
**espy** 441
**esquire 875, 877**
**essay**
  *experiment* 463
  *dissertation* 595
  *endeavour* **675**
**essayist 593, 595**
**esse** 1
**essence**
  *nature* 5
  *scent* 398
**essential**
  *intrinsic* 5
  *great* 31
  *required* 630
  *important* 642
**essentially**
  *intrinsically* 5
  *substantially* 3
**essential stuff** 5
**establish**
  *settle* 150
  *create* 161
  *place* 184
  *evidence* 467
  *demonstrate* 478
  − equilibrium 27
**established**
  *permanent* 141
  *habit* 613
  − church 983*a*
**establishment**
  *party* 712
  *shop* 799
**estafette 534**
**estaminet** 189
**estate** *condition* 7
  *property* 780
  come to man's −
    131
**esteem**
  *believe* 484
  *repute* 873
  *approve* 931
  in high − 928
**estimate**
  *measure* 466
  *adjudge* 480
  *information* 527

  − too highly 482
**estimation**
  [*see* esteem,
    estimate]
**estime**
  succès d' − 873
**estival** 382
**esto perpetua!**
  *perpetuity* 112
  *permanence* 141
  *desire* 865
**estop** 706
**estrade** 213
**estrange**
  *alienate* 44, 889
  *discord* 713
  *hate* 898
**estranged**
  *secluded* 893
**estrapade**
  *attack* 716
  *punishment* 972
**estreat 974**
**estuary** 343
**estuation** 384
**esurient** 865
**et − cætera**
  *add* 37
  *include* 76
  *plural* 100
  − hoc genus omne
  *similar* 17
  *include* 76
  *multiform* 81
**étalage** 882
**état major** 745
**etch** *furrow* 259
  *engraving* 558
**eternal** 112
  − home 981
**Eternal, the − 976**
**eterne** 112
**eternify** 112
**eternity** 112
  an − 110
  launch into − 360,
    361
**ether**
  *lightness* 320
  *rarity* 322
  *vapour* 334
  *anæsthetic* 376
**ethereal** 4
**ethicism 984**
**ethics 926**
**Ethiopian 431**
  '*s skin* 150
**Ethiopian's skin**
  *unchangeable* 150
**ethnology 372**
**ethnic** 984

**ethology 926**
**ethos** 5
**etiolate 429, 430**
**etiology** *causes* 155,
  359
  *knowledge* 490
  *disease* 655
**etiquette**
  *custom* 613
  *fashion* 852
  *ceremony* 882
**étoile, à la belle −**
  *out of doors* 220
  *in the air* 338
**Eton jacket 225**
**étourderie**
  *inattention* 458
  *unskilfulness* 699
**etymological 560**
**etymology 562**
**etymon** *origin* 153
  *verbal* 562
**Eucharist 998**
**euchology 998**
**euchre 840**
**eudiometer**
  *air* 338
  *salubrity* 656
**euge!** 931
**eugenics 658**
**eulogist 935**
**eulogize 482**
**eulogy 931**
**Eumenides** *fury*
  900
  *evil-doers* 913
  *revenge* 919
**eunuch 158**
**eupepsia 654**
**euphemism**
  *metaphor* 521
  *style* 577, 578
  *flattery* 933
**euphemist**
  *man of taste* 850
  *flatterer* 935
**euphony 413, 578**
**Euphrosyne 836**
**euphuism**
  *metaphor* 521
  *elegant style* 577
  *affected style* 579
  *affectation* 855
**Eurasian 41**
**eureka!** 462, 480*a*
**Euripus 343**
**Eurus** 349
**eurythmics 537,**
  840
**eurythmy 242**
**Euterpe 416**

*breath* 349
*odour* 398
**exhaust**
  *paralyze* 158
  *empty* 195
  *waste* 638
  *fatigue* 688
  *complete* 729
  *drain* 789
  *squander* 818
**exhausted**
  *inexistent* 2
**exhauster** 349
**exhaustive**
  *complete* 52
  *– inquiry* 461
**exhaustless**
  *infinite* 105
  *enough* 639
**exhibit** *evidence* 467
  *show* 525
  *display* 882
**exhilarate** 836
**exhort**
  *persuade* 615
  *advise* 695
**exhortation** 998
**exhume**
  *past times* 122
  *disinter* 363
**exigeant** 739
**exigency** *crisis* 8
  *requirement* 630
  *dearth* 640
  *difficulty* 704
  *need* 865
**exigent**
  *exacting* 739
  *discontented* 832
**exiguous** 103, 193
**exile**
  *transport* 185
  *banish* 893
  *punish* 972
  *voluntary –* 893
**exility** 203
**eximious** 648
**existence** *being* **1**
  *thing* 3
  *- in time* 118
  *- in space* 186
  come into – 151
**exit**
  *departure* 293
  *egress* 295
  *disappear* 449
  give – to 297
  ἐξοχήν, κατ' –
  *supreme* 33
  *important* 642
**exode** 599

**exodus** 293
**exogenous** 367
**exonerate**
  *disburden* 705
  *release* 760
  *forgive* 918
  *exempt* 927*a*
  *vindicate* 937
  *acquit* 970
**exorable** 914
**exorbitant**
  *enormous* 31
  *redundant* 641
  *dear* 814
**exorcise** 297
**exorcism** 992, 993
**exorcist** 994
**exordium** 64, 66
**exosmose** 302
**exostosis** 250
**exoteric** 525, 531
**exotic** *alien* 10
  *exceptional* 83
  *plant* 367
**expand** *increase* 35
  *swell* 194
  *- in breadth* 202
  *rarefy* 322
  *- in writing* 573
**expanse** 180, 192
**expansion** **194**
**expatiate**
  *range* 266
  *- in writing* &c.
  573
  *- in discourse* 584
**expatriate** 295, 893
**expect**
  *look forward to*
  507
  *hope* 858
  *not wonder* 871
  *future* 121
  reason to – 472
**expectance** **871**
**expectancy** 780
**expectante,**
  médecine –
  *wait* 133
  *remedy* 662
**expectation** **507**
  beyond – 508
  hold out an – 768
**expected**
  as well as can be –
  654
**expectorate** 297
**expedience** **646**
**expedient**
  *plan* 626
  *means* 632

*useful* 646
temporary – 147
**expedite** *early* 132
  *quickening* 274
  *hasten* 684
  *aid* 707
**expedition**
  [*see* expedite]
  *march* 266
  *activity* 682
  *war* 722
**expel** *push* 284
  *eject* 297
  *punish* 972
**expend** *waste* 638
  *use* 677
  *pay* 809
  *- itself* 683
**expenditure** **809**
**expense** *price* 812
  joke at one's –
  842
  spare no – 816
**expenseless** 815
**expenses** 809
**expensive** 814
**experience**
  *meet with* 151
  *knowledge* 490
  *undergo* 821
  learn by – 950
**experienced** 698
  *– eye* &c. 700
**experiences**
  *narrative* 594
**experiment** **463,**
  **675**
**Experimental**
  **Philosophy** 316
**experimentum**
  crucis *test* 463
  *proof* 478
**expert** 698, 700
**expiate** 952
**expire** *end* 67
  *run its course* 109
  *die* 360
**expired** *past* 122
**explain** 462, 522
  *– away* 523
**explainer** 524
**expletive** 573, 641
**explication** 522
**explicit** *clear* 518
  *patent* 525
**explode** *burst* 173
  *confute* 479
  *failure* 732
  *passion* 825
**exploded** *past* 122
  *antiquated* 124

*error* 495
*blown upon* 932
**exploit** 680, 861
**exploitation** 461
**explore** 461, 463
**explorer** 268
**explosion**
  [*see* explode]
  *revolution* 146
  *violence* 173
  *sound* 406
  *anger* 900
**explosive**
  *dangerous* 665
  *ammunition* **727**
**exponent**
  *numerical* 84
  *interpreter* 524
  *informant* 527
  *index* 550
**export** 295
**expose** *denude* 226
  *confute* 479
  *disclose* 529
  *censure* 932
  *- to danger* 665
  *- oneself*
  *disreputable* 874
  *- to view*
  *visible* 446
  *manifest* 525
**exposé**
  *disclosure* 529
  *description* 594
**exposed to**
  *liable* 177
**exposition** [*see*
  expose]
  *explanation* 522
**expositor** 524, 540
**expository**
  *explaining* 522
  *informing* 527
  *describing* 594
  *disserting* 595
**expostulate**
  *dissuade* 616
  *advise* 695
  *deprecate* 766
  *reprehend* 932
**exposure** [*see*
  expose]
  *appearance* 448
  *- to weather* 338
**expound**
  *interpret* 522
  *teach* 537
**expounder** 524
**express**
  *rapid* 274
  *squeeze out* 301

**faintness** 405
**fair** *in degree* 31
  *pale* 429
  *white* 430
  *wise* 498
  *important* 643
  *good* 648
  *moderate* 651
  *mart* 799
  *beautiful* 845
  *just* 922
  *honourable* 939
 – *chance* 472
 – *copy copy* 21
  *writing* 590
 – field
  *occasion* 134
 – game 857
 by – *means* 631,
  939
 – *name* 873
 – *play* 922, 923
 – *question* 461
 – *sex* 374
 in a – *way*
  *tending* 176
  *probable* 472
  *convalescent* 660
  *prosperous* 734
  *hopeful* 858
 – *weather* 734
 – *weather sailor*
  701
 – *wind* 705
 – *words* 894
**fairing** 784
**fairly**
  *intrinsically* 5
 get on – 736
 – *well* 643
**fair-spoken**
  *courtesy* 894
  *flattery* 933
**fairy** *fanciful* 515
  *fay* 979
  *imp* 980
 – *godmother* 711,
  784, 912
 – *tale* 546, 594
**fairy-land** 515
**fait**: au –
  *knowledge* 490
  *skilful* 698
 – *accompli*
  *certain* 474
  *complete* 729
**faith** *belief* 484
  *hope* 858
  *honour* 939
  *piety* 987

declaration of –
  983
bad – 544
i' – 535
keep – with
  *observe* 772
plight –
  *promise* 768
  *love* 902
true –
  *orthodox* 983*a*
want of –
  *incredulity* 487
  *irreligious* 989
 – *healing* 662
**faithful** [*see* faith]
  *like* 17
  *copy* 21
  *exact* 494
  *obedient* 743
 – *memory* 505
 – *to* 772
**faithless** *false* 544
  *dishonourable* 940
  *sceptical* 989
**fake** 544, 545
**fakir** 996
**falcate** 244, 245
**falchion** 727
**falciform**
  [*see* falcate]
**falcon** 792
**falconet** 727
**faldstool** 215
**fall** *autumn* 126
  *happen* 151
  *perish* 162
  *slope* 217
  *regression* 283
  *descend* 306
  *die* 360
  *fail* 732
  *adversity* 735
  *vice* 945
 let – *lower* 308
  *inform* 527
 water– 348
 – *asleep* 683
 – *astern* 235, 283
 – *away* 105
 – *back return* 283
  *recede* 287
  *relapse* 661
 – *back upon* 677,
  717
 have to – *back*
  *upon* 637
 – a *cursing* 908
 – *of the curtain* 67
 – *into a custom* 82
 – *of day* 125

– *dead* 360
– *into decay* 659
– *down* 990
– *down before* 928
– *upon the ear* 418
– *flat on the ear*
  843
– *at one's feet* 725
– *foul of blow* 276
  *hinder* 706
  *oppose* 708
  *discord* 713
  *attack* 716
  *contention* 720
  *censure* 932
– *for* 897
– *to the ground*
  *be confuted* 479
  *fail* 732
– *into a habit* 613
– *from one's high*
  *estate*
  *adversity* 735
  *disrepute* 874
– *in order* 58
  *continuity* 69
  *event* 151
– *into*
  *conversion* 144
  *river* 348
– *in with agree* 23
  *conform* 82
  *converge* 2
  *discover* 480*a*
  *concord* 714
  *consent* 762
– *on one's knees*
  *submit* 725
  *servile* 886
  *gratitude* 916
  *worship* 990
– *of the leaf* 126
– *from the lips* 582
– *in love with* 897
– *to one's lot*
  *event* 151
  *chance* 156
  *receive* 785
  *duty* 926
– *under one's*
  *notice* 457
– *into oblivion* 506
– *off decrease* 36
  *deteriorate* 659
– *off again* 661
– *out happen* 151
  *quarrel* 713
  *enmity* 889
– *into a passion*
  900
– *to pieces*

*disjunction* 44
*destruction* 162
*brittle* 328
– a *prey to* 732,
  749
– *in price* 815
– *into raptures*
  827
– *short inferior* 32
  *contract* 195
  *shortcoming* 304
– *of snow* 383
– *through* 304
– *to eat* 298
  *take in hand* 676
  *do battle* 722
– *into a trap* 547
– *under*
  *inclusion* 76
  *subjection* 749
– *upon*
  *discover* 480*a*
  *unexpected* 508
  *devise* 626
  *attack* 716
– *in the way of* 186
– *to work* 686
**fallacy** *sophistry*
  477
  *error* 495
 show the – *of* 479
**fallen angel** 949,
  978
**fallible** 475, 477
**falling-out** 24
**falling star** 318, 423
**fallow**
  *unproductive* 169
  *yellow* 436
  *unready* 674
  *inactive* 681
**false** *imitation* 19
  *sophistry* 477
  *error* 495
  *untrue* 544, 546
  *spurious* 925
  *dishonourable* 940
 – *alarm* 669
 – *colouring*
  *misinterpretation*
  523
  *falsehood* 544
 – *construction*
  523, 544
 – *doctrine* 984
 – *expectation* 509
 – *hearted* 940
 – *impression* 495
 – *light vision* 443
 – *money* 800
 – *ornament* 851

ornament 847
decoration 877
in full –
　prepared 673
　prosperous 734
　rich 803
hear a – drop 403
in high –
　health 654
　cheerful 884
pleased with a –
　840
– in one's cap
　honour 873
　decoration 877
– one's nest
　prepare 673
　prosperity 734
　wealth 803
　economy 817
　selfish 943
– the oar 698
– in the scale 643
feather-bed 324
feathered tribes
　366
feathery 256
featly 682
feature
　character 5
　component 56
　form 240
　appearance 448
　press 531
　lineament 550
　– in 56
features
　face 234
febrifuge 662
febrile 382, 825
fecal 653
fecit 556
feckless 866
feculence 653
fecund 168
fecundate 161
federal council 696
– penitentiary 752
federalism 737
federation 48, 709,
　712
fee possession 777
　property 780
　pay 809
　reward 973
feeble weak 160
　illogical 477
feeble-minded 497,
　605
feebleness
　style 575

feed eat 298
　supply 637
– the flame 707
fee-faw-fum
　bugbear 860
　spell 993
feel sense 375
　touch 379
　emotion 821
– for try 463
　benevolence 906
　pity 914
　condole with 915
– the pulse 461
– the want of 865
– one's way
　essay 675
　caution 864
feeler 379
　inquiry 461
　experiment 463
feeling 698, **821**
feet low 207
　walkers 266
at one's –
　near 197
　subjection 749
　humility 879
fall at one's –
　submit 725
fall on one's –
　prosper 734
lick the – of
　servile 886
light upon one's –
　safe 664
spring to one's –
　307
throw oneself at
　the – of
　entreat 765
feign 544, 546
feigned 545
feint 545
felicitas, curiosa –
　698
felicitate 896
felicitous
　agreeing 23
– style 578
　skilful 698
　successful 731
　pleasant 829
felicity 827
feline cat 366
　stealthy 528
　cunning 702
fell destroy 162
　mountain 206
　lay flat 21
　skin 223

lay low 308
　moor 344
　dire 860
　malevolent 907
fellah 876
felloe 231
fellow similar 17
　equal 27
　companion 88
　dual 89
　man 373
　scholar 492, 541
fellow-commoner
　541
fellow-companion
　890
fellow-countryman
　890
fellow-creature 372
fellow-feeling
　friendship 888
　love 897
　benevolence 906
　pity 914
fellowship
　partnership 712
　distinction 873
　friendship 888
　companionship
　890
　good – 892
fellow-student 541
fellow-worker 690
felly 231
felo-de-se 361
felon 949
felonious 945
felony 947
felt texture 219
　heart– 821
felucca 273
female 374
feme coverte 903
feme sole 904
feminality
　weakness 160
　woman 374
feminine 374
feminism 374
femme de chambre
　746
fen 345
fence enclose 232
　evade 544
　defence 717
　fight 720
　prison 752
　thief 792
– round 229
– with a question
　528

fenced 770
fenceless 665
fencible 726
fencing 840
feneration 787
fend 717
fender 717
Fenian 710, 742
fenum habet in
　cornu 668, 913
feodal 780
feodality 737, 777
feoff property 780
feoffee 779, 785
feoffer 784
feræ naturæ 366
feral 907
ferine 907
ferment
　disorder 59
　energy 171
　violence 173
　agitation 315
　lightness 320
　effervesce 353
　emotion 821
　excitement 824,
　825
　anger 900
fermentation,
　acetous – 397
fern 367
ferocity 173, 907
Ferrara
　sword 727
ferret out 461, 480a
ferro-concrete 635
ferrule 223
ferry 270, 627
ferry-boat 273
ferry-man 269
fertile 161, 168
– imagination 515
ferule 975
come under the –
　932
fervent hot 382
　desirous 865
– hope 858
fervid hot 382
　heartfelt 821
　excited 824
fervour heat 382
　animation 821
　love 897
festal eating 298
　social 892
fester 653, 655
festina lente 864
festival
　music 416

filigree 219
filings 330
fill *complete* 52
  *occupy* 186
  *contents* 190
  *stuff* 224
  *provision* 637
  eat one's – 957
  have one's –
  *enough* 639
  *satiety* 869
  – the bill 229
  – an office
  *business* 625
  *government* 737
  – out
  *expand* 194
  –ed to overflow-
    ing 641
  – one's pocket 803
  – time 106
  – up *compensate*
    30
  *compose* 54
  *close* 261
  *restore* 660
  – up the time
  *inaction* 681
fille
  – de chambre 746
  – de joie 962
filled
  – to overflowing
    641
filler 532
fillet *band* 45
  *filament* 205
  *circle* 247
  *insignia* 550
  *ornament* 847
fillibeg 225
filling 224
fillip
  *impulse* 276
  *propulsion* 284
  *stimulus* 615
  *excite* 824
filly 271
film *layer* 204
  *opaque* 426
  *semitransparent*
    427
  – over the eyes
  *dim sight* 443
  *cinema* 448
  *ignorant* 491
filmy *texture* 329
filter *percolate* 295
  *clean* 652
filth 653
–y lucre 800

filtrate 652
fimbriated 256
fin 267
final *ending* 67
  *conclusive* 474
  *completing* 729
  court of – appeal
    474
  – cause 620
  – stroke 729
  – touch 729
finale *end* 67
  *completion* 729
finality 67, 729
finally
  *for good* 141
  *on the whole* 476
finance 800, 811
  minister of – 801
financier 801
finch 366
find
  *eventuality* 151
  *adjudge* 480
  *discover* 480*a*
  *acquire* 775
  – one's account in
    644
  – the cause of 522
  – a clue to 480*a*
  – to one's cost 509
  – credence 484
  – it in one's heart
    602
  – in *provide* 637
  – the key of 522
  – the meaning 522
  – means 632
  – oneself *be* 1
  *present* 186
  – out 480*a*
  – vent 671
  – one's way 731
  – one's way into
    294
finding
  *judgment* 480
fine *small* 32
  *large* 192
  *thin* 203
  *rare* 322
  *not raining* 340
  *exact* 494
  *good* 648
  *beautiful* 845
  *adorned* 847
  *proud* 878
  *mulct* 974
  in – *end* 67
  *after all* 476
  – air 656

  – arts 554
  – feather 159, 654
  – feeling 850
  – frenzy 515
  – gentleman
  *fop* 854
  *proud* 878
  – grain 329
  – lady 854, 878
  one – morning 106
  some – morning
    119
  – powder 330
  – talking
  *overrate* 482
  *boast* 884
  – writing 577
  – time of it 734
  – voice 580
fine-draw 660
fine-fingered 698
fine-spoken 894,
  933
fine-spun *thin* 203
  *sophistry* 477
fine-toned 413
finem, respicere –
  510
finery 847, 851
finesse *tact* 698
  *artifice* 702
  *taste* 850
finger *touch* 379
  *hold* 781
  lay the – on
  *point out* 457
  *discover* 480*a*
  lift a – 680
  not lift a – 681
  point the – at 457
  turn round one's
    little – 737
  –'s breadth 203
  at one's –s' end
  *near* 197
  *know* 490
  *remember* 505
  – on the lips
  *aphony* 581
  *taciturnity* 585
  – in the pie
  *cause* 153
  *interfere* 228
  *act* 680
  *active* 682
  *co-operate* 709
fingerling 193
finger-post 550
finger-print 467
finger-stall 223
fingle-fangle 643

finical
  *trifling* 643
  *affected* 855
  *fastidious* 868
finicky 855, 868
finikin 643
finis 67
  – coronat opus
    729
finish *lend* 67
  *symmetry* 242
  *complete* 729
  *skill* 698
finished
  *absolute* 31
  *perfect* 650
  *skilled* 698
finishing
  – stroke 361
  – touch 729
finite 32
fiord 343
fire *energy* 171
  *heat* 382
  *make hot* 384
  *stoke* 388
  *vigour* 574
  *discharge* 756
  *enthusiasm* 821
  *excite* 824, 825
  catch – 384
  hell – 982
  on – 382
  open – *begin* 66
  play with – 863
  signal – 550
  take –
  *excitable* 825
  *angry* 900
  between two –s
    665
  under – 665, 722
  – at 716
  – the blood 824
  – and fury 900
  – the first shot 716
  – of genius 498
  – off 284
  – a salute 883
  – and sword 162
  – up *excite* 825
  *anger* 900
  – a volley 716
  go through – **and**
    water
  *resolution* 604
  *perseverance* 604*a*
  *courage* 861
fire-alarm 669
fire-annihilator 385
fire-arms 727

*smoothness* 255
*slow* 275
*leaf* 367
*sign* 550
*path* 627
*infirm* 655
*inactive* 683
*tired* 688
*weary* 841
lower one's – 725
red – *alarm* 669
yellow –
　*warning* 668
　*alarm* 669
– man 668
– ship 726
– of truce 723
flag-bearer 534
flagellation
　*penance* 952
　*asceticism* 955
　*flogging* 972
　*rite* 998
flagelliform 205
flageolet 417
flagitious 945
flagon 191
flagrant
　*great* 31
　*manifest* 525
　*notorious* 531
　*atrocious* 945
flagrante
　– *bello* 722
　– *delicto*
　*sure enough* 474
　*act* 680
　*guilt* 947
flagration 384
flagstaff *tall* 206
　*signal* 550
flail 276
flair 450, 698
flake 204
　snow – 383
　– white 430
flam 544
flambé 732
flambeau 423
flamboyant 577
flame *fire* 382
　*light* 420
　*luminary* 423
　*passion* 824, 825
　*love* 897
　catch the –
　*emotion* 821
　consign to the –s
　384
　add fuel to the –
　173

in –s 382
– up 825
–coloured
　*red* 434
　*orange* 439
flame-projector 727
flamen 996
flaming *violent* 173
　*feeling* 821
　*excited* 824
　*ostentatious* 882
　*boasting* 884
flâneur 935
flange *support* 215
　*rim* 231
　*projection* 250
flank *side* 236
　*protect* 664
flannel 384
flap *adjunct* 39
　*hanging* 214
　*move to and fro*
　315
– the memory 505
flapdoodle 517
flapper *girl* 129
flapping *loose* 47
flare *violent* 173
　*glare* 420
　*light* 423
　– up
　*excited* 824, 825
　*angry* 900
flaring *colour* 428
flash *instant* 113
　*violent* 173
　*fire* 382
　*light* 420
　eyes – fire 900
　– lamp 550
　– light 423
　– across the mem-
　ory 505
　– on the mind
　*thought* 451
　*disclose* 529
　*impulse* 612
　– note 800
　– in the pan
　*unsubstantial* 4
　*transientness* 111
　*impotent* 158
　*unproductive* 169
　*failure* 732
　– tongue 563
　– up *excited* 824
　– upon
　*unexpected* 508
　– of wit 842
flashing
　*ostentatious* 882

flashy
　*gaudy colour* 428
　*style* 577
　*ornament* 847
　*vulgar* 851
flask 191
flat *inert* 172
　*abode* 189
　*story* 191
　*low* 207
　*horizontal* 213
　*vapid* 391
　*low tone* 408
　*musical note* 413
　*positive* 535
　*dupe* 547
　*back-scene* 599
　*shoal* 667
　*bungler* 701
　*poor* 804
　*insensible* 823
　*dejected* 837
　*weary* 841
　*dull* 843
　*simple* 849
　fall – 732
　– contradiction
　536
　– iron 255
　– refusal 764
flatfoot 664
flatness 251
flatter *deceive* 545
　*cunning* 702
　*please* 829
　*grace* 845
　*encourage* 858
　*approbation* 931
　*adulation* 933
　– oneself
　*probable* 472
　*hope* 858
　– the palate 394
flatterer 935
flattering
　– remarks 894
　– tale
　*hope* 858
　– unction to one's
　soul
　*content* 831
　*vain* 880
　*flattery* 933
flattery 544, 933
flatulent
　*gaseous* 334
　*air* 338
　*wind* 349
　- *style* 573, 575
flatus 334, 349
flaunt 873, 882

flaunting *vulgar* 851
　*gaudy* 428
　*unreserved* 525
flautist 416
Flavian amphi-
　theatre 728
flavour 390
flavouring 393
flavous 436
flaw *break* 70
　*crack* 198
　*error* 495
　*imperfection* 651
　*blemish* 848
　*fault* 947
　– in an argument
　477
flaxen 436
flay *divest* 226
　*punish* 972
flea *jumper* 309
　*dirt* 653
　– in one's ear
　*repel* 289
　*eject* 297
　*refuse* 764
　*disrepute* 874
　*abashed* 879
　*discourteous* 895
　*contempt* 930
flea-bite 643
flea-bitten 440
fleck 32
flecked 440
flection 279
fled *escaped* 671
fledge 673
fledgling 123
flee *avoid* 623
fleece *tegument* 223
　*strip* 789
　*rob* 791
　*impoverish* 804
　*surcharge* 814
fleet *ridicule* 856
　*insult* 929
fleet *ships* 273
　*swift* 274
　*navy* 726
Fleet *prison* 752
fleeting 4, 111
flesh *bulk* 192
　*animal* 364
　*mankind* 372
　*carnal* 961
　gain – 194
　ills that – is heir
　to *evil* 619
　*disease* 655
　in the – 359
　one – 903

way of all – 360
weakness of the –
945
– and blood
*substance* 3
*materiality* 316
*animality* 364
*affections* 820
make the – creep
*pain* 830
*fear* 860
flesh-colour 434
flesh-pots 298
– of Egypt 734,
803
fleshly 316
fleur-de-lis 847
fleuron 847
flexible 324, 705
flexion
*curvature* 245
*fold* 258
*deviation* 279
flexuous 248
flexure 245, 258
flibbertigibbet 980
flicker
*changing* 149
*waver* 314
*flutter* 315
*light* 420
*dim* 422
flickering 139
flier 621
flies *theatre* 599
flight *flock* 102
*volition* 267
*swiftness* 274
*departure* 293
*avoidance* 623
*escape* 671
– lieutenant 745
put to –
*propel* 284
*repel* 717
*vanquish* 731
– of fancy 515
– of stairs 305,
627
– of time 109
flighty *inattentive*
458
*mad* 503
*fanciful* 515
flim-flam 544, 608
flimsy *unsubstan-
tial* 4
*weak* 160
*rarity* 322
*soft* 324
*sophistical* 477

*trifling* 643
flinch *swerve* 607
*avoid* 623
*fear* 860
*cowardice* 862
fling *propel* 284
*jig* 840
*jeer* 929
have one's –
*active* 682
*laxity* 738
*freedom* 748
*amusement* 840
– aside 782
have a – at
*attack* 716
*resent* 900
*disrespect* 929
*censure* 932
– away *reject* 610
*waste* 638
*relinquish* 782
– down 308
– to the winds
*destroy* 162
*not observe* 773
flint *hard* 323
flint-hearted 907
flintlock 727
flip *beverage* 298
flippant *fluent* 584
*pert* 885
flipper *paddle* 267
flirt *propel* 284
*coquet* 607, 854
*love* 897
*endearment* 902
– a fan 855
flit *elapse* 109
*changeable* 149
*move* 264
*travel* 266
*swift* 274
*depart* 293
*run away* 623
flitter
*small part* 32
*changeable* 149
*flutter* 315
flitting 111
float *establish* 150
*navigate* 267
*boat* 273
*buoy up* 305
*lightness* 320
before the –s
*on the stage* 599
– on the air 405
– before the eyes
446
– bonds 788

– in the mind
*thought* 451
*imagination* 515
floater 683
floating
[*see* float]
*rumoured* 532
– battery 726
– capital 805
– debt 806
– dock 189
flocculent
*woolly* 256
*soft* 324
*pulverulent* 330
flock
*assemblage* 72
*multitude* 102
*laity* 997
–s and herds 366
– together 72
floe *ice* 383
flog 972
*hasten* 684
flood *much* 31
*crowd* 72
*river* 348
*abundance* 639
*redundance* 641
*prosperity* 734
stem the – 708
– of light 420
– of tears 839
flood-gate
*limit* 233
*egress* 295
*conduit* 350
open the –s
*eject* 297
*permit* 760
flood-light 423,
599
flood-mark 466
flood-tide
*increase* 35
*complete* 52
*height* 206
*advance* 282
*water* 337
floor *level* 204
*base* 211
*horizontal* 213
*support* 215
*overthrow* 731
ground – 191
flop 315
Flora 369
floral 367
florescence 154
floriculture 371
florid *colour* 428

*red* 434
– *style* 577
*health* 654
florist 371
floss 256
flotilla 273, 726
flotsam and jetsam
73
flounce
*trimming* 231
*jump* 309
*agitation* 315
flounder
*change* 149
*toss* 315
*uncertain* 475
*bungle* 699
*difficulty* 704
*fail* 732
flour 330
flourish
*brandish* 314, **315**
*exaggerate* 549
*language* 577
*speech* 582
*prosper* 618
*healthy* 654
*prosperous* 734
*ornament* 847
*repute* 873
*display* 882
*boast* 884
– of trumpets
*loud* 404
*cheerfulness* 836
*publish* 531
*ostentation* 882
*celebrate* 883
*boast* 884
flout 929, 936
flow *course* 109
*hang* 214
*motion* 264
*stream* 348
*murmur* 405
*abundance* 639
– from
*result* 154
– of ideas 451
– in 294
– into *river* 348
– out 295
– over 641
– of soul
*conversation* 583
*affections* 820
*cheerful* 836
*social* 892
– with the tide
705
– of time 109

— implicitly 486, 695
— the lead of
  *co-operate* 709
— suit *imitate* 19
— the trail 461
— up
  *continue* 143
  *persevere* 604a
**follower**
  [*see* follow]
  *successor* 65
  *learn* 541
  *servant* 746
  *lover* 897
**folly**
  *building* 189
  *irrationality* **499**
  act of —
  *mismanagement*
    699
**foment**
  *stimulate* 173
  *warm* 384
  *promote* 707
  *excite* 824
  *relieve* 834
**fond** 897
— *hope* 858
**fondle** 902
**fondling** 899, 902
**fondness**
  *desire* 865
**fondre en larmes**
  839
**fons et origo** 153
**font** *origin* 153
  *type* 591
  *rite* 998
  *altar* 1000
**food** 298
  preparation of —
    673
— for the mind 454
— for powder 726
**fool** 501
  *pudding* 354
  *deceive* 545
  *ridicule* 856
  *disrespect* 929
  make a — of
    oneself
  *bungle* 699
  motley — 844
  play the —
  *folly* 499
  *amusement* 840
— 's errand
  *deceived* 545
  *unskilful* 699
— 's mate 732

— 's paradise
  *unsubstantial* 4
  *misjudgment* 481
  *disappoint* 509
  *hope* 858
  *rash* 863
— to the top of
  one's bent
  *excite* 824
  *anger* 900
  *flatter* 933
— away money 818
— away time 683
**foolhardy** 863
**fooling** 842
**foolish** 499
  act —ly 699
  look —
  *disrepute* 874
  *shame* 879
**foolscap** 550, 559
**foot**
  *length* 200
  *stand* 211
  *metre* 597
  at the — of 207
  keep on —
  *continue* 143
  *support* 251
  *provide* 637
  *prepare* 673
  not stir a — 681
  on — *existing* 1
  *during* 106
  *journey* 266
  *topic* 454
  *business* 625
  *preparing* 673
  *active* 682
  put one's — down
  *resolved* 604
  put one's — in
  *undertake* 676
  *bungle* 699
  set — on land 342
  trample under —
    930
— the bill 807
— by foot 51
  one — in the grave
  *age* 128
  *death* 360
  it *journey* 266
  *dance* 309
  at —'s pace 275
**foot-ball**
  *subjection* 749
  *game* 840
**footboy** 746
**footfall**
  *motion* 264

  *indication* 550
  *stumble* 732
**footing**
  *circumstances* 8
  *rank* 71
  *influence* 175
  *situation* 183
  *foundation* 211
  *support* 215
  *payment* 809
  friendly — 888
  get a —
  *location* 184
  be on a —
  *state* 7
  pay one's — 807
**footlights** 599
**footman** 746
**footmark** 551
**footpad** 792
**foot-passenger** 268
**footpath** 627
**foot pound** 466
**footprint** 551
**foot-soldier** 726
**foot-warmer** 386
**footsore** 688
**footstep** 551
**footstool** 215
**foozle** 732
**fop** 854
**foppery** 882
**foppish** 855
**for** *cause* 155
  *tendency* 176
  *reason* 476
  *motive* 615
  *intention* 620
  *preparation* 673
  have —
  *price* 812
— all that
  *notwithstanding*
    30
  *qualification* 469
— all the world
  like 17
— aught one
  knows 156
— better for worse
  78
— ever 112
— example 82
— form's sake 82
— good
  *complete* 52
  *diuturnity* 110
  *permanence* 141
— the most part
  *great* 31
  *general* 78

  *special* 79
— the nonce 118
— nothing 815
— a season 106
— a time 111
— the time being
  106
**forage**
  *food* 298
  *provision* 637
  *steal* 791
**forage-cap** 225
**foramen** 260
**foraminous** 260
**forasmuch as**
  *relating to* 9
  *cause* 155
  *reason* 476
  *motive* 615
**foray** *attack* 716
  *robbery* 791
**forbear**
  *avoid* 623
  *spare* 678
  *lenity* 740
  *sufferance* 826
  *pity* 914
  *abstain* 953
  *forbearance* 918
**forbid** 761
  God —
  *dissent* 489
  *deprecation* 766
  *censure* 932
  *prayer* 990
**forbidden fruit**
  *seduction* 615
  *prohibition* 761
**forbidding**
  *ugly* 846
**force** *corps* 72
  *power* 157
  *strength* 159
  *agency* 170
  *energy* 171
  *violence* 173
  *cultivate* 371, **707**
  *cascade* 348
— *of style* 574
  *urge* 615
  *exertion* 686
  *compulsion* **744**
  armed — 726
  brute — 964
  put in — 924
— of argument 476
— of arms **744**
— of character 820
— down the throat
  *severe* 739
  *compel* 744

- majeure 744
- open 173
- one's way
  *progression* 282
  *passage* 302
**forced** *irrelative* 10
  - *style* 579
  be - to 601
  - labor 603
  - march 274
**forcefully** 601
**forceps**
  *extraction* 301
  *grip* 781
**forces** 726
**forcible** [*see* force]
**ford** 302, 627
**fore** 234
**fore and aft**
  *complete* 52
  *lengthwise* 200
  - *schooner* 273
**forearm** 673
**forebears** 166
**forebode** 511
**forecast**
  *foresight* 510
  *prediction* 511
  *plan* 626
**foreclose** 706
**foredoom** 152, 601
**forefathers** 166
**forefend**
  *prohibit* 761
**forefinger** 379
**forego**
  *relinquish* 624
  *renounce* 757
  *surrender* 782
**foregoing** 62, 116
**foregone**
  *past* 122
  - conclusion
  *prejudged* 481
  *predetermined*
  611
**foreground** 234
  in the -
  *manifest* 525
**forehead** 234
**foreign**
  *alien* 10
  *extraneous* 57
  - accent 580
  - parts 196
**foreigner** 57
**forejudge**
  *prejudge* 481
  *foresight* 510
**foreknow** 510
**foreland** 206, 254

**forelay** 545
**forelock**
  pull the - 894
  take time by the -
  *early* 132
  *occasion* 134
**foreman** 694
**foremost**
  *superior* 33
  *beginning* 66
  *front* 234
  *in advance* 280
  *important* 642
  *reputed* 873
**forenoon** 125
**forensic** 968
**foreordain** 152
**foreordination** 601,
  611
**fore part** 234
**forerun** 62, 116, 280
**forerunner** 64, 512
**foresee** 507, 510
**foreseen** 871
**foreshadow** 152,
  511
**foreshorten** 201
**foreshow** 511
**foresight** 116, **510**
  *caution* 864
**forest** 367
**forestage** 599
**forestall**
  *prior* 116
  *early* 132
  *possession* **777**
**forestry** 371
**foretaste** 510
**foretell** 511
**forethought** 459,
  510
**foretoken** 511
**forewarn** 511, 668
**foreword** 64
**forfeit** *fail* 773
  *lose* 776
  *penalty* 974
  - one's good
  opinion 932
**forfeiture**
  *disfranchisement*
  925
**forfend** 706, 717
**forgather** 72
**forge** *imitate* 19
  *produce* 161
  *furnace* 386
  *trump up* 544
  *workshop* 691
  - fetters 751
**forged**

*false* 546
**forger**
  *maker* 690
  *thief* 792
**forgery**
  *deception* 545
**forget** 506
  hand - cunning
  699
  - benefits 917
  - injury 918
  - oneself 945
**forgive** **918**
**forgo**
  *relinquish* 624
  *renounce* 757
  *surrender* 782
**forgotten**
  *past* 122
  *ingratitude* 917
  not to be - 505
  - by the world
  893
**fork** *bifid* 91
  *pointed* 244
  - lightning 423
  - out
  *give* 784
  *pay* 807
  *expenditure* 809
**forlorn**
  *dejected* 837
  *hopeless* 859
  *deserted* 893
  - hope
  *danger* 665
  *rashness* 863
**form** *state* 7
  *likeness* 21
  *make up* 54
  *order* 58
  *arrange* 60
  *convert* 144
  *produce* 161
  *bench* 215
  *shape* **240**
  *educate* 537
  *pupils* 541
  *manner* 627
  *beauty* 845
  *fashion* 852
  *etiquette* 882
  *law* 963
  *rite* 998
  - letter 592
  - part of 56
  - a party 712
  - a resolution 604
**formal** [*see* form]
  *regular* 82
  *definitive* 535

- *style* 579
  *affected* 855
  *stately* 882
  - speech 582
**formalism** 739, **988**
**formalist** 82
**formality** [*see*
  formal]
  *ceremony* 852
  *affectation* 855
  *law* 963
**formation**
  *composition* 54
  *production* 161
  *shape* 240
**formative** 153
**formed** [*see* form]
  *attempered* 820
**former**
  *in order* 62
  *prior in time* **116**
  *past* 122
**formication** 380
**formidable** 704, 860
**formless** 241
**formula** *rule* 80
  *arithmetic* 84
  *maxim* 496
  *precept* 697
  *law* 963
**formulary** 998
**formulate** 590
**fornication** 961
**fornicator** 962
**foro conscientiæ**
  *veracity* 543
  *duty* 926
  *probity* 939
**forsake** 624
**forsaken** 898
**forsooth** 535
**forspent** 688
**forswear** *lie* 544
  *tergiversation* 607
  *refuse* 764
  *transgress* 927
  *improbity* 940
**fort** 666, 717
**fort**
  le droit du plus -
  *compulsion* 744
  *illegality* 964
  un peu - 641
**fortalice** 717
**forte** 415, 698
**fortelage** 717
**forth** 282
  come -
  *egress* 295
  *visible* 446
  go - *depart* 293

gone – 741
**forthcoming** 152,
673
**forthwith** 132
**fortification** 717
**fortify** 159
**fortiori, a** – 467, 476
**fortissimo** 404
**fortiter in re** 171
**fortitude** 826, 861
**fortnightly** 138
**fortress** 717, 752
**fortuitous**
  *extrinsic* 6
  *chance* 156
  *undesigned* 621
  – concourse of
    atoms 59
**fortunate**
  *opportune* 134
  *successful* 731
  *prosperous* 734
**Fortunatus's** – cap
  *wish* 865
  *spell* 993
  – *purse* 803
**fortune** *chance* 156
  *fate* 601
  *wealth* 803
  be one's – 151
  clean up a – 803
  evil – 621, 735
  good – 734
  make one's –
    *succeed* 731
    *wealth* 803
  tempt –
    *hazard* 621
    *essay* 675
  trick of – 509
  try one's – 675
  wheel of – 601, 621
**fortune-hunter** 886,
943
**fortuneless** 804
**fortune-teller** 513
**fortune-telling** 511
**fortunes of**
  *narrative* 594
**forty** 98
  – winks 683
**forum** 799
  *school* 542
  *tribunal* 966
**forward** *early* 132
  *transmit* 270
  *advance* 282
  *willing* 602
  *improve* 658
  *active* 682

*help* **707**
*vain* 880
*insolent* 885
*uncourteous* 895
bend – 234
come –
  *in sight* 446
  *offer* 763
  *display* 882
  look – to 507
  move – 282
  press – *haste* 684
  put – *aid* 507
  *offer* 763
  put oneself – 880
  set – 676
  – in *knowledge* 490
**foss** 348
**fosse**
  *inclosure* 232
  *ditch* 259
  *defence* 717
**fossil**
  *ancient* 124
  *hard* 323
  *organic* 357
  *dry bones* 362
**foster** *aid* 707
  *excite* 824
  *caress* 902
  – a belief 484
**fou** 959
**foudroyant** 870
**foul**
  *collide* 276
  *bad* 649
  *dirty* 653
  *unhealthy* 657
  *ugly* 846
  *base* 940
  *vicious* 945
  fall – of
    *oppose* 708
    *quarrel* 713
    *attack* 716
    *fight* 720
    *censure* 932
  run – of
    *impede* 706
  – fiend 978
  – means 940
  – language
    *malediction* 908
  – odour 401
  – play *evil* 619
  *cunning* 702
  *wrong* 923
  *improbity* 940
**foul-mouthed** 895
**foul-spoken** 934
**found** 153, 215

**foundation**
  *beginning* 66
  *stability* 150
  *base* 211
  *support* 215
  lay the –s 673
  *sandy* – 667
  shake to its –s 315
**founded**
  *well* – 472
  – on *base* 211
  *evidence* 467
**founder**
  *originator* 164
  *sink* 310
  *fail* 732
  *religious* –s 986
**foundery** 691
**founding** 22
**foundling**
  *trover* 775
  *derelict* 782
  *outcast* 893
**fount** *type* 591
**fountain**
  *source* 153
  *river* 348
  *store* 636
  – head 210
  – pen 590
**four** 95
  on all –s 13, 23
  *horizontal* 213
  *easy* 705
  *prosperous* 734
  *humble* 879
  – in hand 272
  – score &c. 98
  – square 244
  – times 96
  from the – winds
    278
**fourflusher** 884
**fourfold** 96
**four-oar** 273
**four-poster** 215
**fourth** 96, 97
  *musical* 413
  – estate 531
**four-wheeler** 272
**fowl** 366
**fowling-piece** 727
**fox** *animal* 366
  *cunning* 702
  – chase 622
**fox-trot** 840
**foxy** *colour* 433, 434
  *cunning* 702
**foyer** 191, 599
**fracas**
  *disorder* 59

*noise* 404
*discord* 713
*contention* 720
**fraction** *part* 51
  *numerical* 84
  *less than one* **100a**
**fractious** 901
**fracture**
  *disjunction* 44
  *discontinuity* 70
  *fissure* 198
**fragile** 160, 328
**fragment**
  *small* 32, 193
  *part* 51, 100a
**fragrance** 400
**fragrant weed** 392
**frail** *weak* 160
  *brittle* 328
  *feeble* 575
  *irresolute* 605
  *imperfect* 651
  *failing* 945
  *impure* 961
  – sisterhood 962
**frais, à grands** –
481
**frame**
  *condition* 7
  *make* 161
  *support* 215
  *border* 231
  *form* 240
  *substance* 316
  *structure* 329
  *contrive* 626
  cucumber – 371
  have –d and
    glazed 822
  – of mind
    *inclination* 602
    *disposition* 820
**frame-up** 626
**framework**
  *support* 215
  *structure* 329
**franchise**
  *voting* 609
  *freedom* 748
  *right* 924
  *exemption* 927a
**Franciscan** 996
**franc-tireur** 726
**frangible** 160, 328
**frank** *open* 525
  *sincere* 543
  *artless* 703
  *honourable* 939
**frankalmoigne** 748
**Frankenstein** 913,
980

*capricious* 608
*trivial* 643
**frizz** *curve* 245, 248
*fold* 258
**frock** *dress* 225
*canonicals* 999
– *coat* 225
**frog** *fastening* 45
*leaper* 309
*ornament* 847
**frolic** 827, 840
**frolicsome** 836
**from** *motive* 615
– this cause 155
– day to day 106, 138
– end to end 52
– that time 117
– time imme- morial 122
– time to time 136
**frond** 367
**fronder**
*censure* 932
**frondeur**
*disobey* 742
**front** *foremost* 66
*wig* 225
*fore part* **234**
*resist* 719
*insolence* 885
bring to the – *manifest* 525
come to the – *surpass* 303
*important* 642
*repute* 873
in – 280
present a – 719
– danger 861
– to front 708
– of the house 599
– rank 234
in the – rank *important* 642
*repute* 873
**frontage** 234
**frontal** 220
**fronti nulla fides**
*doubt* 485
*deception* 545
**frontier** 199, 233
**fronting** 237
**frontispiece** 64
**frost** 383
**frosted** 430
– *glass* 427
**frostbite** 383
**froth**
*bubble* 353

*trifle* 643
*dirt* 653
– up *angry* 900
**frothy** 320, 353
– *style* 573, 577
*irresolute* 605
**frounce** 258
**frouzy** 401
**froward** 901*a*
**frown** *lower* 837
*scowl* 839
*discourteous* 895
*angry* 900
*sulky* 901*a*
*disapprove* 932
– down
*abash* 879
–s of fortune 735
**frozen** 383, 385
**fructify**
*produce* 161
*be productive* 168
*improve* 658
*prosper* 734
**frugal** 817, 953
– to excess 819
**fruges consumere natus** *drone* 683
*peasant* 876
**frugivorus** 298
**fruit** *result* 154
*produce* 161
*food* 298
*profit* 775
forbidden – 615
reap the –s
*succeed* 731
*reward* 973
– tree 367
**fruitful** 168
**fruition** 161, 827
**fruitless**
*unproductive* 169
*useless* 645
*failure* 732
**frump** 851, 895
**frumpish** 901*a*
**frustrate** 179, 706
**frustrated** 732
**frustum** 51
**fry** *shoal* 102
*child* 129
*heat* 384
small –
*unimportant* 643
*commonalty* 876
**frying-pan** 386
out of – into fire
*worse* 659
*clumsy* 699
*failure* 732

*misfortune* 735
*aggravation* 835
**fuddled** 959
**fudge** 517, 643
**fuel** **388**, 638
add – to the flame 835
– *oil* 388
*increase* 35
*heat* 384
*aggravate* 835
*anger* 900
**fugaces labuntur anni** 111
**fugacious** 111
**fugitive**
*transient* 111
*emigrant* 268
*avoiding* 623
– *writings* 596
**fugleman**
*pattern* 22
*director* 694
**fugue** 415
**fulciment** 215
**fulcrum** 215
**fulfil**
*complete* 729
– a duty 926
– an obligation 772
**fulgent** 420
**fuliginous**
*dim* 422
*opaque* 426
*black* 431
**full** *much* 31
*complete* 52
*large* 192
*loud* 404
*abundant* 639
*cleanse* 652
hands –
*active* 682
receipt in – 807
– blooded 641
– bloom 131
*health* 654
*beauty* 845
– blown 131
*expanded* 194
*glorious* 873
– of business 682
– coloured 428
– cry *loud* 404
*bark* 412
*pursuit* 622
– dinner pail 734
*dress* 225
*ornament* 847
*fashion* 852

*show* 882
– drive 274
– feather
*prepared* 673
– force 159
– gallop 274
– heart 820
– of incident 151
– many 102
– of meaning 516
– measure 639
– of people 186
– play
*facility* 705
*freedom* 748
– of point 842
– scope 748
– score 415
– size 912
– of sound and fury &c.
*unmeaning* 517
– speech 274
– stop
*cease* 142
*rest* 265
– swing
*strong* 159
*active* 682
*successful* 731
*free* 748
– as a tick 52
– tide 348
– tilt *active* 682
*haste* 684
– view 446
– of whims 608
**full-fashioned** 240
**full-fed** 954
**full-flavoured** 392
**full-grown** 131, 192
**full-handed** 816, 818
**full-length** 556
**full-mouthed** 412
**full-toned** 413
**fully** 31
**fulminate**
*violent* 173
*propel* 284
*loud* 404
*malediction* 908
*threat* 909
– against
*accuse* 932
**fulness**
[*see* full]
in the – of time 109
**fulsome**
*nauseous* 395

- ioci 664
genre 556, 559
gent 851, 876
genteel 852, 875
- comedy 599
gentile 984, 989
gentility
　fashion 852
　rank 875
　politeness 894
gentium, jus - 963
gentle moderate 174
　slow 275
　domesticated 370
　faint sound 405
　lenient 740
　meek 826
　courteous 894
- blood 875
- breeding 894
-- hint 527
- as a lamb 174
- slope 217
gentlefolk 875
gentleman
　male 373
　squire 875
　man of honour
　　939
　the old - 978
　walking - 599
gentlemanly 852
gently bred 894
Gentoo 984
gentry 875
　landed - 779
genuflexion
　bowing 308
　submission 725
　servility 886
　courtesy 894
　respect 928
　worship 990, 998
genuine 494, 648
genus 75, 901
- irritabile vatum
　597
geodesist 85, 318
geodesy 318, 466
geography 183, 318
geoid 249
geology &c. 358
geomancer 513
geomancy 511
geometry 466
geoponics 371
georama 448
Georgics 371
geotic 318
gerfalcon 913
germ 153

german 11
- band 417
- silver 545
germane 23
germicide 662
germinal 153
germinate 161, 194,
　365
- from 154
gerontic 128
gerrymander 545
gesso 556
gest 680
gestation
　propagation 161
　carriage 270
　maturation 673
gesticulate 550
gesture hint 527
　indication 550
get become 144
　beget 161
　acquire 775
　receive 810
- ahead 35
- ahead of 33
- along 282
- along with you
　ejection 297
　dismissal 756
- at 480a
- away 287
- back
　retire 283
　regain 775
- the best of 731
- better 658
- down
　swallow 298
　descend 306
- you gone 297
- into harness 673
- by heart 505
- home 292
- in collect 72
　gather 775
- loose 44
- near 286
- off depart 293
　escape 671
- on advance 282
　prosper 734
- out eject 297
　extract 301
　publish 531
- over
　recover from 660
　succeed 731
　be content 831
- over the ground
　274

- for one s pains
　973
- ready 673
- rid of 672
- a sight of 441,
　490
- through
　end 67
　transact 692
　complete 729
　expend 809
- to
　extend to 196
　arrive 292
- together 72
- into trouble 732
- the wind up 860
- up produce 161
　ascend 305
　raise 307
　learn 539
　fabricate 544
　prepare 673
　rise early 682
　foment 824
- into the way of
　613
get-away 671
gewgaw
　trifle 643
　ornament 847
　vulgar 851
geyser 382, 386
ghastly
　pale 429
　hideous 846
　frightful 860
ghaut 203
ghetto 189
ghost shade 362
　fallacy of vision
　　443
　soul 450
　writer 593
　apparition 980
　give up the - 360
　needs up - to tell
　　us 525
　pale as a -
　　colourless 429
　fear 860
- dance 992
ghost-like
　ugly 846
ghostly
　intellectual 450
　supernatural 976,
　　980
Ghost, Holy - 976
ghoul 913, 980
ghyll 348

giant
　large 192
　tall 206
- refreshed
　strong 159
　refreshed 689
-'s strides
　distance 196
　swift 294
giaour 984, 989
gibber 583
gibberish 517, 563
gibbet
　brand 932
　execute 972
　gallows 975
gibble-gabble 584
gibbous 249, 250
gib-cat male 373
gibe 929
giblets 298
gibus 225
giddy
　inattentive 458
　vertiginous 503
　irresolute 605
　capricious 608
　bungling 699
giddy-head 501
giddy-paced 315
gift power 157
　talent 698
　given 784
- of the gab 582
　look a - horse in
　　the mouth
　fastidious 868
　ungrateful 917
gifted 698
gig 272, 273
gigantic
　strong 159
　large 192
　tall 206
giggle 838
giglamps 446
Gilbertian 842
Gilbertine 996
gild coat 223
　colour 439
　ornament 847
- refined gold 641
- the pill
　deceive 545
　tempt 615
　please 829
　flatter 933
Gilead, balm in -
　834, 858
Giles's Greek, St. -
　563

**gill** 348
**gillie** 746
**gilt** 436, 847
 – edged 648
**gimbals** 312
**gimcrack**
 *weak* 160
 *brittle* 328
 *trifling* 643
 *ornament* 847
 *ridiculous* 853
**gimlet** 262
**gimp**
 *clean* 652
 *pretty* 845
 *decoration* 847
**gin** *trap* 545
 *instrument* 633
 *intoxicating* 959
 *demon* 980
**gin mill** 189
**gin palace** 189
**gingerbread**
 *weak* 160
 *vulgar* 851
**gingerly** 174, 459, 864
**gingle** 408
**gipsy**
 *wanderer* 268
 *wag* 844
 – lingo 563
**giraffe** 206
**girandole** 423
**girasol** 847
**gird** *bind* 43
 *strengthen* 159
 *surround* 227
 *jeer* 929
 – up one's loins
 *brace* 159
 *prepare* 673
**girder** 45, 215
**girdle** *bond* 45
 *encircle* 227
 *circumference* 230
 *circle* 247
 put a – round the
  earth 311
**girl** 129, 374
**girlhood** 127
**girt** 45
**girth**
 *bond* 45
 *circumference* 230
**gisarm** 727
**gist** *essence* 5
 *meaning* 516
 *important* 642
**git, ci** – 363
**gittern** 417

**give** *yield* 324
 *melt* 382
 *bestow* 784
 *discount* 813
 – away 782, 784
 *in marriage* 903
 – back 790
 – birth to 161
 – with both hands
  816
 – in charge
 *restrain* 751
 – chase 622
 – consent 762
 – one credit for
  484
 – in custody 751
 – expression to
  566
 – forth 531
 – the go by 623
 – a horse his head
  748
 – in *submit* 725
 – into *consent* 762
 – light 420
 – the mind to 457
 – notice
 *inform* 527
 *warn* 668
 – it one
 *censure* 932
 *punish* 972
 – out *emit* 297
 *publish* 531
 *bestow* 784
 – over *cease* 142
 *relinquish* 624
 *lose hope* 859
 – place to
 *substitute* 147
 *avoid* 623
 – play to the im-
  agination 515
 – points to 27
 – quarter 740
 – rise to 153
 – one the slip 671
 – security 771
 – and take
 *reciprocate* 12
 *compensation* 30
 *interchange* 148
 *retaliation* 718
 *compromise* 774
 *barter* 794
 *equity* 922
 *honour* 939
 – tongue 531
 – a turn to 140
 – one to under-

  stand 527
 – up
 *not understand*
  519
 *unwilling* 603
 *reject* 610
 *relinquish* 624
 *submit* 725
 *resign* 757
 *surrender* 782
 *restore* 790
 *hopeless* 859
 – up the ghost 360
 – way *weak* 160
 *brittle* 328
 *submit* 725
 *pine* 828
 *despond* 837
 *modest* 881
**given** [*see* give]
 *circumstances* 8
 *supposition* 514
 *received* 785
 – over *dying* 360
 – time 134
 – to 613
**giving** 784
**gizzard** 191
 stick in one's –
  900
**glabrous** 255
**glacial** 383
**glaciate** 385
**glacier** 383
**glacis** 217, 717
**glad** 827, 829
 give the – eye 441
 would be – of 865
 – tidings 532
**gladden** 834, 836
**glade** *hollow* 252
 *opening* 260
 *shade* 424
**gladiator** 726
**gladiatorial** 361, 713, 720
**gladsome** 827, 829
**Gladstone bag** 191
**glair** 352
**glaive** 727
**glamour** 992
**glance** *look* 441
 *sign* 550
 see at a – 498
 – at
 *take notice of* 457
 *allude to* 527
 *censure* 932
 – off *deviate* 279
 *diverge* 291
**gland** 221

**glare** *light* 420
 *stare* 441
 *imperfect vision*
  443
 *visible* 446
**glaring**
 [*see* glare]
 *great* 31
 *colour* 428
 *visible* 446
 *manifest* 525
**glass** *vessel* 191
 *smooth* 255
 *brittle* 328
 *transparent* 425
 *lens* 445
 musical –es 417
 see through a –
  darkly 491
 – of fashion 852
 live in a – house
 *brittle* 328
 *visible* 446
 *danger* 665
 – too much 959
**glass-coach** 272
**glasshouse** 191, 371
**Glassite** 984
**glassy** [*see* glass]
 *shining* 420
 *colourless* 429
**glaucous** 435
**glave** 727
**glaver** 933
**glaze** 255
**gleam** *small* 32
 *light* 420
**glean** 609, 775
**gleanings** 636
**glebe** *land* 342
 *ecclesiastical* 995
 *church* 1000
**glee** *music* 415
 *satisfaction* 827
 *merriment* 836
**gleek** 929
**glen** 252
**glengarry** 225
**glib** *voluble* 584
 *facile* 705
**glide** *lapse* 109
 *move* 264
 *travel* 266
 *fly* 267
 – into
 *conversion* 144
**glider** 273
**glimmer**
 *light* 420
 *dim* 422
 *visible* 446

906
- morrow 292
- name 873
- nature 906
- night 293
- for nothing
impotence 158
useless 645
in - odour
repute 873
approbation 931
- offices
mediation 724
kind 906
- old time 122
- omen 858
- opinion 931
take in - part
pleased 827
courteous 894
kind 906
- pennyworth 815
- at the price 815
to - purpose 731
- repute 873
- sense 498
- society 852
- taste 578, 850
- temper 894
- thing 648
- time early 132
opportune 134
prosperous 734
- turn
kindness 906
- understanding
714
- wife
woman 374
spouse 903
- will
willingness 602
benevolence 906
- word
approval 931
vindication 937
- as one's word
veracity 543
observance 772
probity 939
- works 906
goodie 652, 746
goodly
great 31
large 192
handsome 845
good mixer 892
goodness
[see good] 648
virtue 944
have the -

request 765
- gracious! 870
- of heart 906
goods effects 270,
780
merchandise 798
good taste 868
Goodwin sands 667
goody 374, 652, 746
gooroo 996
goose hiss 409
game of - 840
giddy as a - 458
tailor's - 255
kill the - with
golden eggs
699, 818
a wild - chase 545
gooseberry
old - 978
play - 459
- eyes 441, 443
goosecap 501
goose egg 101
gooseflesh 383
goosequill 590
goose-skin 383
Gordian knot 59,
704
gore stab 260
blood 361
gorge ravine 198
conduit 350
fill 641
satiety 869
gluttony 957
raise one's - 900
- the hook 602
gorge de pigeon 440
gorgeous
colour 428
beauty 845
ornament 847
ostentation 882
Gorgon 860
gorilla 913
gormandize 298,
954a, 957
gorse 367
gory red 434
murderous 361
unclean 653
gospel
certainty 474
truth 494
take for - 484
Gospels 985
gossamer
filament 205
light 320
texture 329

gossip news 532
babbler 584
conversation 588
gossoon 876
Gotama 986
Goth 851, 876
Gotham, wise men
of - 501
gothic
amorphous 241
gouache 556
gouge concave 252
perforator 262
goulash 298
gourd 191
gourmand 954a,
957
gourmet 868, 954a
gout 378
goût, haut - 392
goutte d'eau, il se
noyerait dans
une - 699
govern 693, 737
[see govern]
ruling power 745
divine - 976
petticoat - 737
governess 540
governor
tutor 540
director 694
ruler 745
keeper 753
gowk 501
gown dress 225
canonicals 999
gownsman 492
grab take 789
miser 819
grabble 379
grace style 578
permission 760
concession 784
elegance 845
polish 850
title 877
pity 914
forgiveness 918
honour 939
piety 987
worship 990
act of - 784
God's - 906
with a bad - 603
with a good -
willing 602
courteous 894
in one's good -s
888
heart of - 861

say - 990
submit with a
good - 826
- before meat 916
grâce: coup de -
914
la - 840
graceless
inelegant 579
ugly 846
vicious 945
impenitent 951
irreligious 989
Graces 845
gracile 203
gracious
willing 602
courteous 894
kind 906
good - 870
grade degree 26
arrange 60
term 71
ascent 217
on the down - 658
on the up - 659
gradatim
gradually 26
in order 58
continuous 69
slow 275
gradation
degree 26
order 58
continuity 69
gradient 217
gradual degree 26
continuous 69
slow 275
graduate
adjust 23
calibrate 26
arrange 60
series 69
measure 466
scholar 492, 873
graduated scale 466
gradus 86, 562
Græculus esuriens
886
graft join 43
locate 184
insert 300
trees 371
teach 537
booty 794
corruption 940
Grail
holy - 998
grain essence 5
small 32

942
(*important* 642)
– bear 318
– circle sailing 628
– coat 225
– doings
  *importance* 642
  *bustle* 682
– folks 875
– gun 626
– hearted 942
– Mogul 745
– number 102
– primer 591
– quantity 31
**greater** 33
– number 102
– part 31
  *nearly all* 50
**greatest** 33
**greatness 31**
**greave** 225
**greed**
  *desire* 865
  *gluttony* 957
**greedy**
  *avaricious* 819
**Greek**
  *unintelligible* 519
  *sharper* 792
St. Giles's – 563
– Church 984
– Kalends 107
**green**
  *new* 123
  *young* 127
  *lawn* 344
  *grass* 367
  *unripe* 397
  *colour* 435
  *credulous* 486
  *novice* 491
  *unused* 614
  *healthy* 654
  *immature* 674
  *unskilled* 699
board of – cloth
  966
– memory 505
– old age 128
**greenback** 800
**green-eyed mon-**
**ster** 920
**greenhorn**
  *novice* 493
  *dupe* 547
  *bungler* 701
**greenhouse**
  *receptacle* 191
  *horticulture* 371
**greenness 435**

**green-room** 599
**greensward** 344
**Greenwich time**
  114
**greenwood** 367
**greet** *weep* 839
  *hail* 894
**greeting**
  *sociality* 892
–'s! 292
**gregarious** 892
**grenade** 727
**grenadier**
  *tall* 206
  *soldier* 726
**grey** 432
– beard 130
– friar 996
– hairs 128
bring – hairs to
  the grave
  *adversity* 735
  *harass* 830
– mare
  *ruler* 737
  *master* 745
  *wife* 903
– matter
  *brain* 498
–hound
  *swift* 274
  *animal* 366
ocean –hound 273
**gridelin** 437
**gridiron**
  *flatness* 213
  *crossing* 219
  *stove* 386
  *stage* 599
  *stadium* 840
**grief** 828
come to – 735
**grievance**
  *evil* 619
  *painful* 830
  *wrong* 923
**grieve** *mourn* 828
  *pain* 830
  *dejected* 837
  *complain* 839
**grievous** 649, 830
**grievously** 31
**griffin** 83, 366, 493
**griffo** 41
**griffonage** 590
**grig** *merry* 836
**grill** 382, 384, 461
– room 189
**grille** 219
**grim**
  *resolved* 604

  *painful* 830
  *doleful* 837
  *ugly* 846
  *discourteous* 895
  *sullen* 901a
–visaged war 722
**grimace** 243, 839,
  855
**grimacier**
  *actor* 599
  *humorist* 844
  *affected* 855
**grimalkin** 366
**grime** 653
**grin** *laugh* 838
  *ridicule* 856
– and abide 725
– a ghastly smile
  *dejected* 837
  *ugly* 846
**grind**
  *reduce* 195
  *sharpen* 253
  *pulverize* 330
  *pain* 378
  *learn* 539
  *oppress* 907
– the organ 416
– one's teeth 900
**grinder**
  *teacher* 330
  *noise* 404
**grinding** 739, 830
**grindstone** 253, 330
**grip**
  *indication* 550
  *power* 737
  *retention* 781
  *clutch* 789
– of the hand 894
**gripe** [*see* grip]
  *pain* 378
  *parsimony* 819
**grisaille**
  *grey* 432
  *painting* 556
**grisette**
  *woman* 374
  *commonalty* 876
  *libertine* 962
**grisly** 846
**grist**
  *materials* 635
  *provision* 637
– to the mill
  *useful* 644
  *acquire* 775
**gristle** 321, 327
**grit**
  *strength* 159
  *powder* 330

  *stamina* 604a
  *courage* 861
– in the oil
  *hindrance* 706
**gritty** 323
**grizzled**
  *grey* 432
  *variegated* 440
**groan** 411, 839
**groat** 800
**grocer** 637
**grocery** 396
**grog** 298, 959
**groin** 244
**groom** 370, 746
– well
– of the chamber▲
  746
–'s man 903
**groove**
  *furrow* 259
  *habit* 613
in a – 16
move in a – 82
put in a – for 673
**grope**
  *feel* 379
  *experiment* 463
  *try* 675
in the dark 442,
  704
**gross**
  *great* 31
  *whole* 50
  *number* 98
  *ugly* 846
  *vulgar* 851
  *vicious* 945
  *impure* 961
– credulity 486
– receipts 810
**grosshead** 501
**grossheaded** 499
**grossièreté** 895
**grot** [*see* grotto]
**grotesque**
  *odd* 83
  *distorted* 243
– *style* 579
  *ridiculous* 853
**grotto**
  *alcove* 191
  *hollow* 252
**grouch** 895, 901a
**ground**
  *cause* 153
  *region* 181
  *base* 211
  *lay down* 213
  *support* 215
  *coating* 223

*land* 342
*plain* 344
*evidence* 467
*teach* 537
*motive* 615
*plea* 617
above - 359
down to the - 52
dress the - 371
fall to the - 732
get over the - 274
go over the - 302
level with the -
 162
maintain one's -
 *persevere* 604a
play- 840
prepare the - 673
stand one's -
 *defend* 717
 *resist* 719
- bait 784
- cut from under
 one 732
- floor
 *chamber* 191
 *low* 207
 *base* 211
- on
 *attribute* 155
- plan 554
- of quarrel 713
- sliding from
 under one 665
- swell
 *agitation* 315
 *waves* 348
grounded
 *stranded* 732
well- 490
- on *basis* 211
 *evidence* 467
ɼroundless
 *unsubstantial* 4
 *illogical* 477
 *erroneous* 495
groundling 876
grounds
 *dregs* 653
groundwork
 *precursor* 64
 *cause* 153
 *basis* 211
 *support* 215
 *preparation* 673
group
 *marshal* 60
 *cluster* 72
- captain 745
grouping 60
grouse 832, 901a

grout 45
grove
 *street* 189
 *glade* 252
 *wood* 367
grovel
 *below* 207
 *move slowly* 275
 *cringe* 886
 *base* 940
grow
 *increase* 35
 *become* 144
 *expand* 194
- from
 *effect* 154
- into 144
- less 195
- taller 206
- together 46
- up 194
- upon one 613
grower 164
growl *cry* 412
 *complain* 839
 *discourtesy* 895
 *anger* 900
 *threat* 909
growler *cab* 272
 *discontented* 832
 *sulky* 901a
grown up 131
growth [*see* grow]
 *development* 161
- *in size* 194
 *tumour* 250
 *vegetation* 367
groyne 706
grub
 *small animal* 193
 *food* 298
- up
 *eradicate* 301
 *discover* 480a
Grub-street writer
 593
grudge
 *unwilling* 603
 *refuse* 764
 *stingy* 819
 *hate* 898
 *anger* 900
bear a - 907
owe a - 898
grudging 603
- praise 932
gruel 298
gruesome 846
gruff
 *harsh sound* 410
 *discourteous* 895

grum
 *harsh sound* 410
 *morose* 901a
grumble
 *cry* 411
 *complain* 832,
 839
grume 321, 354
grumous 321, 354
grumpy 901a
Grundy, Mrs. 852
grunt 412
 *complain* 839
guano 653
guarantee 768, 771
guard
 *travelling* 268
 *safety* 664
 *defence* 717
 *soldier* 726
 *sentry* 753
advanced - 668
mount -
 *care* 459
 *safety* 664
off one's -
 *inexpectant* 508
throw off one's -
 *cunning* 702
on one's -
 *careful* 459
 *cautious* 864
rear - 668
- against
 *prepare* 673
 *defence* 717
- ship 664, 726
guarda costa 753
guarded
 *conditions* 770
guardian
 *safety* 664
 *defence* 717
 *keeper* 753
- angel
 *helper* 711
 *benefactor* 912
guardless 665
guard-room 752
gubernation 693
gubernatorial 737
gudgeon 547
guerdon 973
guernsey 225
guerre:
 nom de - 565
- à outrance &c.
 722
guerilla 726
- warfare 720
guess 514

guesswork 514
guest 890
 paying - 188
guet:
 mot de - 550
 -à-pens 545
guffaw 838
guggle
 *gush* 348
 *bubble* 353
 *resound* 408
 *cry* 412
guide
 *pattern* 22
 *courier* 524
 *teach* 537
 *teacher* 540
 *indicate* 550
 *direct* 693
 *director* 694
 *advise* 695
guide-book 527
guided by, be - 82
guideless 665
guide-post 550
guiding star 693
guild 712, 966
guildhall 799
guile
 *deceit* 544, 545
 *cunning* 702
guileless 543, 703
guillotine 972, 975
guilt 947
guiltless 946
guilty:
 find - 971
 plead - 950
guindé 579
guinea 800
guipure 847
guisard 599
guise
 *state* 7
 *dress* 225
 *appearance* 448
 *plea* 617
 *mode* 627
 *conduct* 692
guiser 599
guitar 417
gulch 198
gules 434
gulf
 *interval* 198
 *deep* 208
 *lake* 343
gull 545, 547
gullet *throat* 260
 *rivulet* 348
gullible 486

- cash 800
- earned 704
- and fast rule 80
- fought 704
- frost 383
- of hearing 419
- heart
  malevolent 907
  vicious 945
  impenitent 951
- hit 732
- knocks 720
- life 735
- lines
  adversity 735
  severity 739
- liver 954a
- lot 735
- master 739
- measure 739
- names 932
- necessity 601
- nut to crack 704
- to please 868
- pressed
  haste 684
  difficulty 704
  hindrance 706
- put to it 704
- set 704
- tack 298
- task 703
- time 704
- up 704, 804
- upon
  attack 716
  severe 739
  censure 932
- winter 383
- words
  obscure 571
  rude 895
  censure 932
- work 686
- at work 682
harden [see hard]
  strengthen 159
  accustom 613
- the heart
  insensible 823
  enmity 889
  impenitence 951
hardened
  impious 988
- front
  insolent 885
hardening
  habit 613
hard-featured 846
hard-fisted 819
hard-headed 498,

739
hardihood 861, 885
hardly
  scarcely 32
  deal - with 739
- any few 103
- anything
  small 32
  unimportant 643
- ever 137
hard-mouthed 606
hardness 323
- of heart 914a
hardship 735
hardy
  strong 159
  healthy 654
  brave 861
hare 274
  hold with the -
  and run with
  the hounds
  fickle 607
  servile 886
hare-brained 458,
  863
harem 961
hariolation 511
hark 418, 457
- back 283
harl 205
harlequin
  changeable 149
  nimble 274
  motley 440
  pantomimic 599
  humorist 844
harlequinade 599
harlot 962
harlotry 961
harm
  evil 619
  badness 649
  malevolence 907
harmattan 349
harmless
  impotent 158
  good 648
  perfect 650
  salubrious 656
  safe 664
  innocent 946
  bear - 717
harmonica 417
harmonics 413
harmonist 413
harmonium 417
harmonize 178, 416
harmony
  agreement 23
  order 58

music 413
colour 428
concord 714
peace 721
friendship 888
harness
  fasten 43
  fastening 45
  accoutrement 225
  yoke 370
  instrument 633
  restraint 752
in -
  prepared 673
  in action 680
  active 682
  subjection 749
- up 293
harp
  repeat 104
  musical instru-
    ment 417
  weary 841
Harpagon 819
harper 416
harpist 416
harpoon 727
harpsichord 417
harpy
  relentless 739
  thief 792
  miser 819
  evil-doer 913
  demon 980
harquebuss 727
harridan 846, 962
harrier 366
harrow
  agriculture 371
- up the soul 860
harrowing 830
harry pain 830
  attack 716
  persecute 907
Harry, old - 978
harsh
  acrid 171
  sound 410
  style 579
  discordant 713
  severe 739
  disagreeable 830
  morose 895
  malevolent 907
- voice 581
hart 366, 373
hartal 142, 489
harum-scarum 59,
  458
haruspice 513
Haruspicy 511

harvest
  effect 154
  profit 618
  store 636
  acquisition 775
  get in the -
    complete 729
    succeed 731
- home
  celebration 883
- time
  autumn 126
  exertion 686
has been 122
hash mix 41
  cut 44
  confusion 59
  food 298
  make a - 699
hashish 663
hasp 43, 45
hassock 215
hastate 253
haste
  velocity 274
  activity 682
  hurry 684
hasten
  promote 707
hasty
  transient 113
  hurried 684
  impatient 825
  irritable 901
- pudding 298
hat 225
  cardinal's - 999
  send round the -
    765
  shovel - 999
- in hand 886
hatch
  produce 161
  gate 232
  opening 260
  chickens 370
  fabricate 544
  shading 556
  plan 626
  prepare 673
- a plot 626
hatches, under -
  restraint 751
  prisoner 754
  poor 804
hatchet
  cutting 253
  bury the - 918
  dig up the - 722
  throw the helve
    after the - 818

*height* 206
*projection* 250
**headlong**
  *hurry* 684
  *rush* 863
  rush –
  *violence* 173
**headman** 694
**headmost**
  *front* 234
  *precession* 280
**head-piece**
  *summit* 210
  *intellect* 450
  *helmet* 717
  *ornament* 847
**headquarters**
  *focus* 74
  *abode* 189
  *authority* 737
**head-race** 350
**heads**
  *compendium* 596
  – or tails 156, 621
  lay – together
  *advice* 695
  *co-operate* 709
  – I win tails you
    lose
  *unfair* 940
**headship** 737
**headsman** 975
**head-stone** 363
**headstrong**
  *violent* 173
  *obstinate* 606
  *rash* 863
**headway** *space* 180
  *navigation* 267
  *progression* 282
**headwind** 708
**headwork** 451
**heady** 606
**heal** *restore* 660
  *remedy* 662
  let the wound –
  *forgive* 918
  – the breach
  *pacify* 723
**healing art** 662
**health** **654**
  picture of – 654
**healthiness** 655
**health resort** 189
**healthy** 656
**heap** *quantity* 31
  *collection* 72
  *store* 636
  *too many* 641
**heaps** 102
  rubbish – 645

**hear**
  *audition* 418
  *be informed* 527
  not – of (refuse)
    764
  – a cause
  *adjudge* 480
  *lawsuit* 969
  – hear! 931
  – and obey 743
  – out 457
**hearer** 418
**hearing** **418**, 696
  [*see* hear]
  gain a – 175
  give a – 418
  hard of – 419
  out of – 196
  within – 197
**hearken** 457
**hearsay** 532
  – evidence 467
**hearse** 363
**heart**
  *intrinsicality* 5
  *interior* 221
  *centre* 222
  *mind* 450
  *willingness* 602
  *essential* 642
  *affections* 820
  *courage* 861
  *love* 897
  man after one's
    own – 899
  with all one's –
    438, 602
  at – 820, 821
  from bottom of –
    543
  beating – 821, 824
  break the – 830
  by –
  *memory* 505
  go to one's – 824
  in good – 858
  with a heavy –
    603
  know by – 490
  lay to – 837
  learn by – 539
  lift up the – 990
  lose – 837
  lose one's – 897
  nearest to one's –
    897
  not find it in one's
    – 603
  have a place in
    the – 897
  put one's – into

    604
  set one's – upon
    604
  take –
  *content* 831
  *hope* 858
  *courage* 861
  take to –
  *sensibility* 822
  *discontent* 832
  *dejection* 837
  *anger* 900
  warm – 822
  wind round the –
    897
  – bleeding for 914
  to one's –'s con-
    tent
  *willing* 602
  *enough* 639
  *success* 731
  *pleasure* 829
  –'s core
  *mind* 450
  *affections* 820
  – expanding 821
  – failing one 837,
    860
  do one's – good
    829
  – of grace 858
  – in hand 602
  – leaping with joy
    827, 838
  – leaping into
    one's mouth 824
  – of oak
  *strong* 159
  *hard* 323
  – in right place
    906
  – sinking *fear* 860
  – and soul
  *completely* 52
  *willing* 602
  *resolute* 604
  *exertion* 686
  *feeling* 821
  – of stone 823, 907
  – swelling 824
**heartache** 828
**heart-breaking** 821,
    830
**heart-broken** 828
**heartburning**
  *discontent* 832
  *regret* 833
  *enmity* 889
  *anger* 900
  *jealousy* 920
**hearten** 858, 861

**heartfelt** 821, 829
**hearth**
  *home* 189
  *fireplace* 386
**heartless** 823, 945
**heart-rending** 830
**heartsease** 831
**heart-shaped** 245
**heart-sick**
  *dejection* 837
  *dislike* 867
  *satiety* 869
**heart-stricken** 828
**heart-strings, tear**
  the – 830
**hearty**
  *willing* 602
  *healthy* 654
  *feeling* 821
  *cheerful* 836
  *friendly* 888
  *social* 892
  – laugh 838
  – meal 298
  – reception 892
**heat** *warmth* **382**
  *make hot* 384
  *contest* 720
  *excitement* 824,
    825
  dead – 27
  – of passion 900
  – wave 382
**heated imagination**
    515
**heater** 386
**heath** *moor* 344
  *plant* 367
**heathen** 984, 989
  – mythology 979
**heathenish** 851
**heather** *moor* 344
  *plant* 367
**heaume** 717
**heautontimoru-**
    menos 837, 955
**heave** *raise* 307
  *emotion* 821
  – the lead 208,
    466
  – a sigh 839
  – in sight 446
  – to 265
**heaven** 827, **981**
  call – to witness
    535
  in the face of –
    525
  light of – 420
  move – and earth
    686

will of − 601
− forfend! 766
− knows 475, 491
− be praised 838, 916
for −'s sake 765
**heaven-born**
*wise* 498
*repute* 873
*virtue* 944
**heaven-directed** 498
**heaven-kissing** 206
**heavenly**
*celestial* 318
*rapturous* 829
*divine* 976
*of heaven* 981
− bodies 318
− host 977
− kingdom 981
**heavenly-minded** 987
**heavens** 318
− and earth! 870
**Heaviside layer** 338
**heavisome** 843
**heavy** *great* 31
*inert* 172
*weighty* 319
*stupid* 499
*actor* 599
*sleepy* 683
*dull* 843
*brutish* 851
− affliction 828
− artillery 726
− cost 814
− dragoon 726
− father 599
− gaited 843
− gun 727
− hand
*clumsy* 699
*severe* 739
− on hand 641
− heart *loth* 603
*pain* 828
*dejection* 837
− hours 841
− on the mind 837
− news 830
− sea
*agitation* 315
*waves* 348
− sleep 683
− type 591
− wet 298
**heavy-laden** 706, 828

**hebdomadal** 138
**Hebe** 845
**hebetate** 823, 826
**hebetude**
*imbecile* 499
*insensible* 823
*inexcitable* 826
**Hebrew**
*unintelligible* 519
*Jew* 984
**Hecate** 994
**hecatomb**
*number* 98
*sacrifice* 991
**heckle** 830, 900
**hectic** 382, 821
**Hector** *brave* 861
*rash* 863
*bully* 885, 887
**hedge**
*compensate* 30
*inclosure* 232
− in
*circumscribe* 229
*hinder* 706
*conditions* 770
**hedgehog** 253
**hedonism** 377, 827
**hedonist** 954*a*
**heed** *attend* 457
*care* 459
*beware* 668
*caution* 864
**heedful** 457
**heedless**
*inattentive* 458
*neglectful* 460
*oblivious* 506
*rash* 863
**heel** *support* 215
*lean* 217
*deviate* 279
*go round* 311
*iron* − 975
lay by the −s 162
turn on one's −
*go back* 283
*go round* 311
*avoid* 623
− of Achilles 665
**heel-piece**
*sequel* 65
*back* 235
*repair* 660
**heel-tap**
*remainder* 40
*dress* 653
**heels** *lowness* 207
at the − of
*near* 197
*behind* 235

cool one's − 681
follow on the − of 281
laid by the − 751
lay by the − 789
show a light pair of − 623
take to one's − 623
tread on the − of
*near* 197
*follow* 281
*approach* 286
− over head
*inverted* 218
*hasty* 684
*rash* 863
**heft** *handle* 633
*exertion* 686
**hegemony**
*influence* 175
*direction* 693
*authority* 737
**hegira** [*see* hejira]
**heifer** 366
**heigho!** 839
**height** *degree* 26
*altitude* 206
*summit* 210
at its −
*great* 31
*supreme* 33
draw oneself up to his full − 307
− finder 206
**heighten**
*increase* 35
*elevate* 307
*exaggerate* 549
*aggravate* 835
**heinous** 945
**heir** *futurity* 121
*posterity* 167
*inheritor* 779
**heirloom** 780
**heirship** 777
**hejira** 293
**Helen of Troy** 845
**heliacal** 318
**helical** 248
**Helicon** 597
**helicon-horn** 417
**helicopter** 273
**Heliogabalus** 954*a*
**heliograph**
*signal* 550
*picture* 554
**heliography** 550
*light* 420
*painting* 556
**Helios** 423

**heliotrope** 847
**heliotype** 558
**helix** 248
**hell** *abyss* 208
*gaming-house* 621
*gehenna* 982
− upon earth
*misfortune* 735
*pain* 828
− broke loose 59
**hell-born** 945, 978
**hellebore** 663
**hell-hound** 913, 949
**hellish**
*malevolent* 907
*vicious* 945
*hell* 982
**helluo librorum** 492
**helm** *handle* 633
*sceptre* 747
(*authority* 737)
answer the − 743
at the − 693
obey the − 705
take the − 693
**helmet** 225, 717
**helminthology** 368
**helmsman** 269, 694
**helot** 746
**help** *benefit* 618
*utility* 644
*remedy* 662
*aid* 707
*servant* 746
*give* 784
it can't be −ed
*submission* 725
*never mind* 823
*content* 831
God − you 914
so − me God 535
− oneself to 789
**helper** 711
**helpless** 158, 665
**helpmate**
*auxiliary* 711
*wife* 903
**helter-skelter** 59, 684
**helve**
throw the − after the hatchet 818
**hem** *edge* 231
*fold* 258
*indeed!* 870
kiss the − of one's garment 886
− in *enclose* 227
*restrain* 751
**hemi-** 91
**hemisphere** 181

hemispheric 250
hemlock 663
hemorrhage 299
hemp 205
hen 366
  *female* 374
  – with one chicken
  *busy* 682
henbane 663
hence
  *arising from* 155
  *departure* 293
  *deduction* 476
  – loathed mel-
  ancholy 836
henceforth 121
henchman 746
hencoop 370
hendiadys 91
henna 433
henpecked 743, 749
heptagon 244
heptarchy 98
Heraclitus 839
  rideret – 853
herald
  *precursor* 64
  *precession* 280
  *predict* 511
  *forerunner* 512
  *proclaim* 531
  *messenger* 534
heraldry 550
herb 367
herbage 365
herbal 369
herbivorous 298
herborize 369
herculean
  *strong* 159
  *exertion* 686
  *difficult* 704
Herculem, ex pede
  – 550
Hercules 159, 215
  pillars of – 233,
  550
herd 72, 102
herdsman 746
here
  *situation* 183
  *presence* 186
  *arrival* 292
  come –! 286
  – below 318
  – goes 676
  – and there
  *dispersed* 73
  *few* 103
  *place* 182, 183
  – there and

everywhere
*diversity* 16a
*space* 180
*omnipresence* 186
– to-day and gone
  to-morrow 111
hereabouts 183,
  197
hereafter 121, 152
hereby 631
hereditament 780
hereditary
  *intrinsic* 5
  *derivative* 154,
  167
heredity 167
herein 221
heresy 495, 984
heretic 984
heretofore 122
hereupon 106
herewith 88, 632
heritage
  *futurity* 121
  *possession* 777
  *property* 780
heritor 779
hermaphrodite 83
  – brig 273
hermeneutics 522
Hermes 534, 582
hermetically 261
hermit 893, 955
hermitage
  *house* 189
  *cell* 191
  *seclusion* 893
hero *brave* 861
  *glory* 873
  *good man* 948
  – worship 931, 991
Herod, out-Herod
  – 549
heroic [*see* hero]
  *magnanimous*
  942
  mock – 853
heroics 884
heroin 663
heroine 861
herpetology 368
Herr 373
herring
  *pungent* 392
  – pond 341
  draw a – across
  the trail 545
  trail of a red –
  615, 706
herring-gutted 203
hesitate

*uncertain* 475
*sceptical* 485
*stammer* 583
*reluctant* 603
*irresolute* 605
*fearful* 860
Hesperian 236
Hesperides, garden
  of the – 981
Hesperus 423
Hessian boot 225
hest 741
hesterni quirites
  876
heterarchy 737
heteroclite 83
heterodoxy 489,
  984
heterogeneous
  *unrelated* 10
  *different* 15
  *mixed* 41
  *multiform* 81
  *exceptional* 83
heterogeneity 15,
  16a
heteromorphism
  16a
hetman 745
hew *cut* 44
  *shorten* 201
  *fashion* 240
  – down 308
hewers of wood
  *workers* 690
  *commonalty* 876
hexagon 98, 244
hexahedron 244
hexameter 98, 597
hey! 586
heyday
  *exultation* 838
  *festivity* 840
  *wonder* 870
  –'of the blood 820
  – of youth 127
hiation 260
hiatus 198
hibernal 383
hibernate 683
Hibernicism 497,
  563
hic:
  – jacet 363
  – labor hoc opus
  704
hick 701, 851, 876
hiccup 349
hid under a bushel
  460

hidalgo 875
hidden 528
  – meaning 526
hide *skin* 223
  *conceal* 528
  – diminished head
  *inferior* 34
  *decrease* 36
  *humility* 879
  – one's face
  *modesty* 881
  – and seek
  *deception* 545
  *avoid* 623
  *game* 840
hide-bound 751,
  819
hideous 846
hide-out 893
hiding-place
  *abode* 189
  *ambush* 530
  *refuge* 666
hie 264, 274
  – to 266
hiemal 126
hierarch 996
hierarchy 995
hieratic 590
hieroglyphic
  *representation*
  554
  *letter* 561
  *writing* 590
hierographa 985
hieromancy 511
hierophant 996
hieroscopy 511
higgle 794
higgledy piggledy
  59
higgler 797
high *much* 31
  *lofty* 206
  *fetid* 401
  *treble* 410
  *foul* 653
  *noted* 873
  *proud* 878
  from on – 981
  on – 206
  think –ly of 931
  – art 556
  – celebration 998
  – colour
  *colour* 428
  *red* 434
  *exaggerate* 549
  – commissioner
  745
  – days and holi-

**H.M.S.** 726
**hoar** *aged* 128
  *white* 430
  – *frost* 383
**hoard** 636
**hoarse**
  *husky* 405
  *harsh* 410
  *voiceless* 581
  talk oneself – 584
**hoary** [*see* hoar]
**hoax** 545
**hob** *support* 215
  *stove* 386
  – and nob
  *celebration* 883
  *courtesy* 894
**hobble**
  *limp* 275
  *awkward* 699
  *difficulty* 704
  *fail* 732
  *shackle* 751
  – *skirt* 225
**hobbledehoy** 129
**hobby**
  *crotchet* 481
  *pursuit* 622
  *desire* 865
**hobby-horse** 272
**hobgoblin**
  *fearful* 860
  *demon* 980
**hobo** 268
**hobnail** 876
**Hobson's choice**
  *necessity* 601
  *no choice* 609a
  *compulsion* 744
**hoc genus omne** 876
**hock** 771
**hock shop** 787
**hockey** 840
**hockey rink** 213
**hocus** 545
**hocus-pocus**
  *interchange* 148
  *unmeaning* 517
  *cheat* 545
  *conjuration* 992
  *spell* 993
**hod**
  *receptacle* 191
  *support* 215
  *vehicle* 272
**hoddy-doddy** 501
**hodge-podge** 41
**hoe** 272, 371
**hog** *animal* 366
  *sensualist* 954a

*glutton* 957
  greedy as a – 865
  go the whole – 604
**hog's back** 206
**hogmanay** 998
**hogshead** 191
**hog-wash** 653
**hoist** 307
  – the black flag 722
  – a flag 550
  – on one's own petard
  *retaliation* 718
  *failure* 732
**hoity-toity!** 815, 870
**hold** *cohere* 46
  *contain* 54
  *remain* 141
  *cease* 142
  *go on* 143
  *happen* 151
  *receptacle* 191
  *cellar* 207
  *base* 211
  *support* 215
  *halt* 265
  *believe* 484
  *be passive* 681
  *defend* 717
  *power* 737
  *restrain* 751
  *prison* 752
  *prohibit* 761
  *possess* 777
  *retain* 781
  *enough!* 869
  have a firm – 781
  have a – upon 175
  gain a – upon 737
  get – of 789
  quit one's – 782
  take – 175
  – aloof
  *stay away* 187
  *distrust* 487
  *avoid* 623
  – an argument 476
  – authority 737
  – back *avoid* 623
  *store* 636
  *hinder* 706
  *restrain* 751
  *retain* 781
  *miserly* 819
  – one's breath
  *wonder* 870
  – converse 588
  – a council 695

– fast 751, 781
  – forth *teach* 537
  *speak* 582
  – good 478, 494
  – one's ground 141
  – in hand 737
  – one's hand
  *cease* 142
  *relinquish* 624
  – hard 265
  – up one's head 861
  – a lease 771
  – a meeting 72
  – off 623
  – office 693
  – on
  *continue* 141, 143
  *persevere* 604a
  – out [*see below*]
  – one's own
  *preserve* 670
  *defend* 717
  *resist* 719
  – oneself in readiness 673
  – in remembrance 505
  – both one's sides 838
  – a situation 625
  – in solution 335
  – to 602
  – together 43, 709
  – one's tongue 403, 585
  – up [*see below*]
  – oneself up 307
**hold out**
  *endure* 106
  *affirm* 535
  *persevere* 604a
  *resist* 719
  *offer* 763
  *brave* 861
  – expectation
  *predict* 511
  *promise* 768
  – temptation 865
**hold up**
  *continue* 143
  *support* 215
  *not rain* 340
  *aid* 707
  *rob* 791
  *display* 882
  *extol* 931
  – one's hand
  *sign* 550
  *threat* 609

– to execration
  *cures* 908
  *censure* 932
  – the mirror 525
  – to scorn 930
  – to shame 874
  – to view 525
**holder** 779
**holdfast** 45
**holding**
  *tenancy* 777
  *property* 780
**hole** *place* 182
  *hovel* 189
  *receptacle* 191
  *opening* 260
  *ambush* 530
  – in one's coat 651
  – and corner
  *place* 182
  *peer into* – 461
  *hiding* 528, 530
  – to creep out of
  *plea* 617
  *escape* 671
  *facility* 705
**holiday** *leisure* 685
  *repose* 687
  *amusement* 840
  – task *easy* 705
**holiness** *God* 976
  *piety* 987
**holloa** 411
  – before one is out of the wood 884
**hollow**
  *unsubstantial* 4
  *completely* 52
  *incomplete* 53
  *depth* 208
  *concavity* 252
  *channel* 350
  - *sound* 408
  *specious* 477
  *false* 544
  *voiceless* 581
  beat – 731
  – truce 723
**holm** 346
**holocaust**
  *kill* 361
  *sacrifice* 991
  (*destruction* 162)
**holograph** 590
**holster** 191
**holt** 367
**holus bolus** 684
**Holy** *of God* 976
  *pious* 987
  keep – 987
  – breathing 990

| | | | |
|---|---|---|---|
| – Church 983*a* | long – 363 | **honest** | **hoodoo** 649 |
| – City 981 | strike – | *veracious* 543 | **hoodwink** |
| – day 998 | *energy* 171 | *honourable* 939 | *ignore* 491 |
| – Ghost 976 | *attack* 716 | *pure* 960 | *blind* 442 |
| temple of the – | – stroke 170 | – meaning 516 | *hide* 528 |
| Ghost 983*a* | – thrust | turn an – penny | *deceive* 545 |
| – men of old 985 | *attack* 716 | 775 | **hoof** 211 |
| – orders 995 | *censure* 932 | – truth 494 | cloven – 907 |
| – place 1000 | **home-bred** 851 | **honey** | **hook** *fasten* 43 |
| – Scriptures 985 | **home-felt** 821 | *sweet* 396 | *fastening* 45 |
| – Spirit 976 | **home-rule** 737, 748 | *favourite* 899 | *hang* 214 |
| – water 998 | **homeless** | milk and – 734 | *curve* 245 |
| – week 998 | *unhoused* 185 | **honeycomb** | *deceive* 545 |
| **holystone** 652 | *banished* 893 | *concave* 252 | *retain* 781 |
| **homage** | **homely** | *opening* 260 | *take* 789 |
| *submission* 725 | *language* 576 | *deterioration* 659 | by – or by crook |
| *fealty* 743 | *unadorned* 849 | **honeyed** | 631 |
| *reverence* 928 | *common* 851, 876 | – phrases 894 | **hookah** 392 |
| *approbation* 931 | **Homeric** | – words | **hooker** *ship* 273 |
| *worship* 990 | – laughter 838 | *allurement* 615 | **hookey, blind** – 840 |
| **home** *focus* 74 | **home-sick** 833 | *flattery* 933 | **hooks, go off the** |
| *habitation* 189 | **home-spun** | **honeymoon** | 360 |
| *near* 197 | *texture* 329 | *pleasure* 827 | **hooligan** 887, 913 |
| *interior* 221 | **home-stall** 189 | *endearment* 902 | **hoop** *circle* 247 |
| *arrival* 292 | **homestead** 189 | *marriage* 903 | *cry* 411 |
| *refuge* 666 | **homeward bound** | **honey-mouthed** | **hoot** *cry* 411, 412 |
| at – *party* 72 | 292 | 894, 933 | *deride* 929 |
| *present* 186 | **homicidal maniac** | **honeysuckle** 396 | *contempt* 930 |
| *within* 221 | 913 | **honorarium** 784,973 | *censure* 932 |
| at ease 705 | **homicide** 361 | **honorary** 815 | **hop** *leap* 309 |
| *social gathering* | **homiletical** 892 | **honour** | *dance* 840, 892 |
| 892 | **homily** | *demesne* 780 | – off 293 |
| be at – | *teaching* 537 | *glory* 873 | – skip and jump |
| – *to visitors* 892 | *advice* 595 | *title* 877 | *leap* 309 |
| feel at – | *sermon* 998 | *respect* 928 | *agitation* 315 |
| *freedom* 748 | **hominem, argu-** | *approbation* 931 | *haste* 684 |
| *pleasure* 827 | **mentum ad** – | *probity* 939 | *game* 840 |
| *content* 831 | 938 | affair of – 720 | – the twig 360 |
| look at – | **homœopathic** | do – to 883 | **hope** 858 |
| *accusation* 938 | *small* 32 | do the –s | band of – 958 |
| make oneself at – | *little* 193 | *sociality* 892 | beyond – 658, 734 |
| *free* 748 | **Homœopathy** 662 | *courtesy* 894 | dash one's –s 837 |
| *sociable* 892 | **homogeneity** | *respect* 928 | excite – 511 |
| not be at – 764 | *relation* 9 | his – *judge* 967 | foster – 858 |
| stay at – 265 | *identity* 13 | in – of 883 | well-grounded – |
| at – in | *uniformity* 16 | man of – 939 | 472 |
| *knowledge* 490 | *simplicity* 42 | upon my – 535, | – against hope 859 |
| *skill* 698 | **homogenesis** 161 | 768 | – for the best 858 |
| at – with | **homologous** 23 | word of – 768 | – deferred |
| *friendship* 888 | **homology** | – be to 873 | *dejection* 837 |
| bring – to | *relation* 9 | – a bill 807 | *lamentation* 859 |
| *evidence* 467 | *uniformity* 16 | – in the breach | – for *expect* 507 |
| *belief* 484 | *equality* 27 | 923 | *desire* 865 |
| *accuse* 938 | *concord* 714 | – bright | **hope chest** 858 |
| *condemn* 971 | **homonym** | *veracity* 543 | **hopeful** *infant* 129 |
| come – 292 | *equivocal* 520 | *probity* 939 | *probable* 472 |
| eternal – 981 | *vocal sound* 580 | **honte, mauvaise** – | *hope* 858 |
| from – 187 | **homophony** 413 | 881 | **hopelessness** 471, |
| get – 292 | **homunculus** 193 | **hood** 225, 999 | 859 |
| go – 283 | **Hon.** 817 | **hooded** 223 | **Hop-o'-my-thumb** |
| go from – 293 | **hone** 253 | **hoodlum** 887 | 193 |

hopper 191
horary 108
horde
  *assemblage* 72
  *party* 712
  *commonalty* 876
horizon
  *distance* 196
  *view* 441
  *expectation* 507
  appear on the –
    525
  gloomy – 859
horizontality 213
horn
  *receptacle* 191
  *sharp* 253
  *music* 417
  draw in one's –s
  *recant* 607
  *submit* 725
  *humility* 879
  exalt one's – 873
  wear the –s 905
  –s of a dilemma
  *reasoning* 476
  *difficulty* 704
  – in 294
  – mad 920
  – of plenty 639
hornbook 542
hornet
  *evil-doer* 913
  –'s nest
  *pitfall* 667
  *difficulty* 704
  *adversity* 735
  *painful* 830
  *resentment* 900
  *censure* 932
hornpipe 840
hornwork 717
horny 323
Horny, old – 978
horology 114
horoscope 511, 992
horresco referens
  860
horrible *great* 31
  *noxious* 649
  *dire* 830
  *ugly* 846
  *fearful* 860
horrid [see horrible]
  *vulgar* 851
horrida bella 722
horrific [see
  horrible]
horrified 828, 860
horrify 830, 860
horripilation 383

horrisonous 410
horror 860, 867
  view with – 898
horrors 837
  sup full of – 828
horror-stricken 828
hors de combat
  *impotent* 158
  *useless* 645
  *tired out* 688
  put – 731
hors-d'œuvre 298
horse *hang on* 214
  *stand* 215
  *carrier* 271
  *animal* 366
  *male* 373
  *cavalry* 726
  ride the high –
    885
  put the –s to 673
  put up one's –s at
    184
  put up one's –s
    together
  *concord* 714
  *friendship* 888
  take – 266
  to – 293
  war – 726
  work like a – 686
  – artillery 726
  – of another colour
    15
  – doctor 370
  – and foot 726
  – laugh 838
  – marine 701
  like a – in a mill
    613
  – racing
  *pastime* 840
  *contention* 720
  – soldier 726
  – track 627
horseback 266
horse-cloth 225
horseman 268
horsemanship
  *riding* 266
  *skill* 698
horseplay 856
horse power 466
horse-shoe 245
horse-whip 972
hortation 615, 695
hortative 537
horticulture 371
hortus siccus 369
hosanna 931, 990
hose

  *stockings* 225
  *pipe* 348, 350
  *extinguisher* 385
hosier 225
hospice 189, 662
hospitable 816, 892
hospital 189, 662
  in – 655
hospitality
  [see hospitable]
hospodar 745
host *collection* 72
  *multitude* 102
  *army* 726
  *friend* 890
  *rite* 998
  reckon without
    one's –
  *error* 495
  *unskilful* 699
  *rash* 863
  – of heaven 977
  – in himself 175
hostage 771
hostel 189
hostelry 189
hostile
  *disagreeing* 24
  *opposed* 708
  *enmity* 889
  in – array 708
  – meeting 720
hostilities 722
hostility 889
hostler 746
hot *violent* 173
  *warm* 382
  *pungent* 392
  *red* 434
  *orange* 439
  *excited* 824
  *irascible* 901
  make – 384
  – air 482, 884
  – bath 386
  – blood *rash* 863
  *angry* 900
  *irascible* 901
  blow – and cold
  *inconsistent* 477
  *falsehood* 544
  *tergiversation* 607
  *caprice* 608
  in – haste 684
  in – pursuit 622
  – water
  *difficulty* 704
  *quarrel* 713
  *painful* 830
  – water bottle 386
hot air merchant

  884
hot-bed *cause* 153
  *centre* 222
  *workshop* 691
Hotchkiss gun 727
hotchpotch
  *mixture* 41
  *confusion* 59
  *participation* 778
hotel 189
hot-headed 684,
  825
hothouse
  *conservatory* 371,
    636
  *furnace* 386
  *workshop* 691
hot-press 255
Hotspur 863
Hottentot 876
hough 659
hound *animal* 366
  *hunt* 622
  *persecute* 907
  *wretch* 949
  hold with the hare
    but run with the
    –s 607
  – on 615
houppelande 225
hour *period* 108
  *point of time* 113
  *present time* 118
  improve the shin-
    ing – 682
  one's – is come
  *occasion* 134
  *death* 360
  – after hour 110
hour-glass
  *chronometer* 114
  *contraction* 195
  *narrow* 203
Houri 845
hourly *time* 106
  *frequent* 136
  *periodical* 138
house *family* 166
  *locate* 184
  *abode* 189
  *theatre* 599
  *make safe* 664
  *council* 696
  *firm* 712
  before the – 454
  keep – 184
  eat out of – and
    home
  *prodigal* 818
  *gluttony* 957
  turn out of – and

**imaum** 745, 996
**imbecile** 158, 499
**imbécile** 501
**imbecility 499**
**imbed** [*see* embed]
**imbedded** 229
**imbibe** 296
  – *learning* 539
**imbrangle** 61
**imbricated** 223
**imbroglio**
  *disorder* 59
  *difficulty* 704
  *discord* 713
**imbrue**
  *impregnate* 300
  *moisten* 339
  – *one's hands in*
   blood
  *killing* 361
  *war* 722
  – *the soul* 824
**imbue** *mix* 41
  *impregnate* 300
  *moisten* 339
  *tinge* 428
  *teach* 537
**imbued**
  *affections* 820
  – *with*
  *belief* 484
  *habit* 613
  *feeling* 821
**imburse** 803
**imitation**
  *copying* **19**
  *copy* 21
  *representation*
   554
**immaculate**
  *perfect* 650
  *clean* 652
  *innocent* 946
**immanent** 5
**immanity** 907
**Immanuel** 976
**immaterial**
  *unsubstantial* 4
**immateriality**
  *spiritual* **317**
  *trifling* 643
**immature** 123, 674
**immeasurable** 31,
  105
**immediate**
  *continuous* 69
**immediately** 113,
  132
**immedicabile**
  **vulnus** 619
**immedicable** 859

**immelodious** 414
**immemorial** 124
  *from time* – 122
  – *usage* 613
**immense** *great* 31
  *infinite* 105
  - *size* 192
**immerge**⎫
**immerse**⎭
  *introduce* 300
  *dip* 337
**immersed in** 229
**immethodical** 59
**immigrant** *alien* 57
  *entering* 294
**immigration** 266,
  294
**imminent** 132, 152,
  286
**immiscible** 47
**immission** 296
**immitigable**
  *hopeless* 859
  *revenge* 919
**immix** 41
**immobility** 150, 265
**immoderately** 31
**immodest** 961
**immolation**
  *killing* 361
  *giving* 784
  *sacrifice* 991
**immoral** 923, 945
**immortal**
  *perpetual* 112
  *glorious* 873
  *celebrated* 883
**immotile** 265
**immovable**
  *stable* 150
  *quiescent* 265
  *obstinate* 606
**immundicity** 653
**immunity**
  *health* 656
  *freedom* 748
  *right* 924
  *exemption* 777a,
   927a
**immure** 751
**immutable**
  *stable* 150
  *deity* 976
**imo pectore, ab** –
  821
**imp** 980
**impact** *contact* 43
  *impulse* 276
  *insertion* 300
**impair** 659
**impale** *transfix* 260

  *execute* 972
**impalpable**
  *small* 193
  *powder* 330
  *intangible* 381
**impanation** 998
**impar sibi** 608
**imparity** 28
**impart** *inform* 527
  *give* 784
**impartial**
  *judicious* 498
  *neutral* 628
  *just* 922
  *honourable* 939
  – *opinion* 484
**impassable**
  *closed* 261
  *impossible* 471
**impasse** 706
**impassible** 823
**impassion** 824
**impassionable** 822
**impassioned**
  - *language* 574
  *excited* 825
**impassive** 823
**impatient** 825
  – *of control* 742
**impawn** 771
**impeach**
  *censure* 932
  *accuse* 938
  *go to law* 969
**impeachment,**
  **soft** – 902
**impeccability** 650,
  946
**impecunious** 804
**impede** 706
**impediment** 706
  – *in speech* 583
**impedimenta** 633,
  780
**impel** *push* 276
  *induce* 615
**impend**
  *future* 121
  *imminent* 132
  *destiny* 152
  *overhang* 206
**impenetrable**
  *closed* 261
  *solid* 321
  *unintelligible* 519
  *latent* 526
**impenitence 951**
**imperative**
  *require* 630
  *command* 737,
   741

  *severe* 739
  *duty* 926
**imperator** 745
**imperceptible**
  *small* 32
  *minute* 193
  *slow* 275
  *invisible* 447
  *latent* 526
**impercipient** 376
**imperdible** 664
**imperfect**
  *incomplete* 53
  *failing* 651
  *vicious* 945
**imperfection 651**
  *inferiority* 34
  *vice* 945
**imperfectly** 32
**imperforate** 261
**imperial**
  *trunk* 191
  *beard* 256
  *authority* 737
**imperil** 665
**imperious**
  *command* 737
  *proud* 878
  *arrogant* 885
  – *necessity* 601
**imperishable** 112
  *stable* 150
  *glorious* 873
**imperium in**
  **imperio** 737
**impermanent** 111
**impermeable**
  *closed* 261
  *dense* 321
**impersonal**
  *general* 78
  *neuter* 316
**impersonate** 19,
  554
**impersonator** 19
**imperspicuity** 519
**impersuasible** 606
**impertinent**
  *irrelevant* 10
  *insolent* 885
**imperturbable** 823,
  826
**impervious**
  *closed* 261
  *impossible* 471
  *insensible* 823
  – *to light* 426
  – *to reason* 606
**impetiginous** 655?
**impetrate** 765
**impetuous**

boisterous 173
hasty 684
excitable 825
rash 863
eager 865
impetus 276
impi 726
impiety **988**
impignorate 771
impinge 276
implacable 848, 919
implant *insert* 300
  teach 537
implanted
  *adventitious* 6
implausible 473
implead 969
implement 633
impletion 52
implex 41
implicate *involve* 54,
  526
  *accuse* 938
implicated *related* 9
  *component* 56
implication
  *disorder* 59
  *meaning* 516
  *latency* 526
implicit 526
  – *belief* 484
implore 765
imply *evidence* 467
  *mean* 516
  *involve* 526
impolicy 699
impolite 895
imponderable 4,
  320
imporous 261, 321
import
  *put between* 228
  *ingress* 294
  *take in* 296
  *insert* 300
  *mean* 516
  *imply* 526
  *be of consequence*
   642
importance **642**
  *greatness* 31
  attach – to 642
  attach too much
   – to 482
  of no – 643
importune 765, 830
impose *order* 741
  *awe* 928
  – upon
   *credulity* 486
   *deceive* 545

*be unjust* 923
imposing
  *important* 642
  *exciting* 824
  *glorious* 873
imposition [*see*
  impose]
  *undue* 925
  – of hands 998
impossibile, credo
  quia – 486
impossibilities,
  seek after – 645
impossibility **471**
impossible 471
  *refusal* 764
  – *quantity*
   *algebra* 84
impost 812
imposthume 655
impostor 548, 925
imposture 545
impotence **158**
impotent conclu-
  sion 732
impound 751
impoverish
  *weaken* 160
  *waste* 638
  *despoil* 789
  *render poor* 804
impracticable
  *impossible* 471
  *misjudging* 481
  *obstinate* 606
  *difficult* 704
imprecation
  *prayer* 765
  *curse* 908
impregnable 159,
  664
impregnate *mix* 41
  *combine* 48
  *fecundate* 161,
   168
  *insert* 300
  *teach* 537
  – *with* 641
impresario 599
imprescriptible 924
impress *cause*
  *sensation* 375
  *mark* 550
  *steal* 791
  *excite feeling* 824
  – *upon the mind*
   *memory* 505
   *teach* 537
impressed with
  *belief* 484
  *feeling* 821

impressible
  *motive* 615
  *sensibility* 822
impression
  *sensation* 375
  *idea* 453
  *belief* 484
  *printing* 531
  *mark* 550
  *engraving* 558
  *print* 591
  *emotion* 821
  make an –
   *act* 171
   *thought* 451
impressionable
  375, 822
impressive
  *language* 574
  *important* 642
  *feeling* 821, 824
imprimis 66
imprimit 558
imprint
  *publisher* 531
  *indication* 550
  – *in the memory*
   505
imprison
  *circumscribe* 229
  *restrain* 751
  *punish* 972
improbability **473**
improbate 932
improbity **940**
impromptu 612
  – fait à loisir 673
improper
  *incongruous* 24
  *foolish* 499
  *solecism* 568
  *inexpedient* 647
  *wrong* 923
  *unmeet* 925
  *vicious* 945
  – *time* 135
impropriate **777**,
  789
impropriator 779
improve 658
  – *the occasion* 134
  – *the shining*
   *hour* 682
  – *upon* 658
improvement **658**
improvident
  *careless* 460
  *not preparing* 674
  *prodigal* 818
  *rash* 863
improvisation

*music* 415
improvisatore
  *speech* 582
  *poetry* 597
  *impulse* 612
improvise
  *imagination* 515
  *impulse* 612
  *unprepared* 674
improviste, à l'–
  508, 612
improvisatrice
  612
imprudent 460, 86**3**
impudent 885, 895
impudicity 961
impugn *deny* 536
  *attack* 716
  *blame* 932
impugnation 708
impuissance 158
impulse *push* **276**
  *sudden thought*
   **612**
  *motive* 615
  *blind* – 601
  *creature of* – 612
  give an – *to*
   *propel* 284
   *aid* 707
impulsive [*see*
  impulse]
  *intuitive* 477
  *excitable* 825
  *rash* 863
impunity *escape* 671
  *acquittal* 970
  with – *safely* 664
impurity 653, **961**
imputation
  *ascribe* 155
  *slur* 874
  *accuse* 938
in 221
  go – 294
  – *as much as*
   *relation* 9
   *degree* 26
  – *the circum-*
   *stances* 8
  – *doors* 221
  – *durancevile* 751
  – *for*
  – *force* 1
   *undertake* 676
   *promise* 768
  – *re* 9
  – *and out* 314
  –s *and outs* 182
in: – articulo 111
  – extenso *whole* 50

*diffuse* 573
– jail 751
– limine 66
– loco 23
– medias res 68
– prison 751
– propriâ personâ 79
– toto 52
– transitu
 *transient* 111
 *transfer* 270
– statu pupillari 127
– statu quo 141
– vogue 1
**inability** 158, 699
**inabstinent** 954
**inaccessible** 196, 471
**inaccurate** 495, 568
**inaction** 172, 681
**inactivity** 683, 172
**inadequate**
 *powerless* 158
 *insufficient* 640
 *useless* 645
 *imperfect* 651
**inadmissible**
 *incongruous* 24
 *excluded* 55
 *extraneous* 57
 *inexpedient* 647
**inadvertence** 458
**inadvisable** 647
**inaffable** 895
**inalienable**
 *retention* 781
 *right* 924
**inamorato** 897
**inane** *void* 4
 *unmeaning* 517
 *unthinking* 452
 *insufficient* 640
 *trivial* 643
 *useless* 645
**inanimate** 360
– matter 358
**inanition** 158
**inanity** [*see* inane]
**inappetency** 823, 866
**inapplicable** 10, 24
**inapposite** 10, 24
**inappreciable** 32, 193
 *unimportant* 643
**inapprehensible**
 *stolid* 499
 *unintelligible* 519
**inappropriate** 24,

[ 528 ]

647
**inapt**
 *incongruous* 24
 *impotent* 158
 *useless* 645
 *inexpedient* 647
 *unskilful* 699
**inarticulate** 581, 583
**inartificial** 703
**inartistic** 846
**inasmuch** *whereas* 9
 *however* 26
 *because* 476
**inattention** 458
**inaudible**
 *silence* 403
 *faint sound* 405
 *deaf* 419
 *voiceless* 581
**inaugural**
 *precursor* 64
**inaugurate**
 *begin* 66
 *cause* 153
 *install* 755
 *celebrate* 883
**inauspicious**
 *untimely* 135
 *untoward* 649
 *hopeless* 859
**inbeing** 5
**inborn, inbred**
 *intrinsic* 5
 *affections* 820
– *proclivity* 601
**inca** 745
**incage** 751
**incalculable** 31, 105
**incalescence** 382
**incandescence** 382
**incandescent** 423
**incantation**
 *invocation* 765
 *sorcery* 992
 *spell* 993
**incantatory** 992
**incapable** 158
**incapacious** 203
**incapacitate** 158
**incapacity**
 *impotence* 158
 *ignorance* 491
 *stupidity* 499
**incarcerate** 751
**incarnadine** 434
**incarnate**
 *intrinsic* 5
 *bodily* 316
 *fleshly* 364
 *vicious* 945

devil –
 *bad man* 949
 *Satan* 978
**Incarnation** 976
**incase** 223, 229
**incautious** 863
**incendiary**
 *destroy* 162
 *burn* 384
 *influence* 615
 *malevolent* 907
 *evil-doer* 913
 *bad man* 949
**incense** *fuel* 388
 *fragrant* 400
 *hate* 898
 *anger* 900
 *flatter* 933
 *worship* 990
 *rite* 998
**incension**
 *burning* 384
**incentive** 615
**inception** 66
**inceptive** 153
**inceptor** 541
**incertitude** 475
**incessant**
 *repeated* 104
 *ceaseless* 112
 *frequent* 136
**incest** 961
**inch** *small* 32
 *length* 200
 by –es 275
 to an – 494
 not yield an – 606
 give an – and take an ell 789
– by inch
 *by degrees* 26
 *in parts* 51
 *slowly* 275
 not see an – beyond one's nose 699
**inchoation** 66, 673
**incide** 44
**incidence** 278
**incident** 151
**incidental**
 *extrinsic* 6
 *circumstance* 8
 *irrelative* 10
 *occurring* 151
 *casual* 156
 *liable* 177
 *chance* 621
 *trivial* 643
– *music* 415
**incinerate** 384

**incipience** 66
**incircumspect** 460
**incision** 44, 259
**incisive** *energy* 171
 *vigour* 574
 *feeling* 821
**incisor** 253
**incite**
 *exasperate* 173
 *urge* 615
**incivility** 895
**incivism** 911
**inclasp** 229
**inclement**
 *violent* 173
 *cold* 383
 *severe* 739
 *pitiless* 914a
**inclination**
 [*see* incline]
 *will* 600
 *affection* 820
 *desire* 865
 *love* 897
**incline** *tendency* 176
 *slope* 217
 *direction* 278
 *willing* 602
 *induce* 615
– an ear to 457
– the head 308
**inclined**
 *disposed* 620
– plane 633
**inclose**
 *surround* 227
**inclosure** 232
**include**
 *composition* 54
– *in a class* 76
**inclusion** 76
**inclusive**
 *additive* 37
 *component* 56
 *class* 76
**incogitancy** 452
**incognita, terra** – 491
**incognito** 528
**incognizable** 519
**incoherence**
 *physical* 47
 *mental* 503
**incombustible** 385
**income** *means* 632
 *profit* 775
 *property* 780
 *wealth* 803
 *receipt* 810
– tax 812
**incoming**

*disorder* 59
*impossible* 471
**infallibility** 474
assumption of –
885
**infamy** *shame* 874
*dishonour* 940
*vice* 945
**infancy** 66, 127
**infandum renovare**
**dolorem** 505,
833
**infant 129**
*fool* 501
– *prodigy* 872
**Infanta** 745
**infanticide** 361, 991
**infantine** 129
*foolish* 499
**infantry** 726
**infarction** 261
**infatuation**
*misjudgment* 481
*credulity* 486
*folly* 499
*insanity* 503
*obstinacy* 606
*passion* 825
*love* 897
**infeasible** 471
**infect** *mix with* 41
*contaminate* 659
*excite* 824
**infectâ, re –**
*shortcoming* 304
*non-completion*
730
*failure* 732
**infection**
*transference* 270
*disease* 655
**infectious** 270, 657
**infecund** 169
**infelicity**
*inexpertness* 699
*misery* 828
**infelicitous** 24
**infer** 472
**inference** 476, 480
by – 467
**inferential**
*demonstrative* 478
*latent* 526
**inferiority**
*in degree* **34**
*in size* 195
*imperfection* 651
*personal* – 34
**infernal** *bad* 649
*malevolent* 907
*wicked* 945

*satanic* 978
– **machine 727**
– **regions 982**
**infertility** 169
**infest** 830
**infestivity** 837, 843
**infibulation** 43
**infidel** 487, 989
**infidelity**
*dishonour* 940
*irreligion* 989
**infiltrate** *mix* 41
*intervene* 228
*interpenetrate* 294
*moisten* 337, 339
*teach* 537
**infiltration**
*passage* 302
**Infinite, the –** 976
**infinite** 105
– *goodness* 976
**infinitely** *great* 31
**infinitesimal**
*small* 32
*little* 193
– *calculus* 85
**infinity 105**
**infirm** *weak* 160
*disease* 655
*vicious* 945
– *of purpose* 605
**infirmary** 662
**infirmity**
[*see* infirm]
**infix** 537
**inflame**
*render violent* 173
*burn* 384
*excite* 824
*anger* 900
**inflamed** 382
**inflammable** 384,
388
**inflammation**
*heating* 384
*disease* 655
**inflate** *increase* 35
*expand* 194
*blow* 349
**inflated**
*overestimation*
482
*style* 573, 577
*ridiculous* 853
*vain* 880
**inflation**
[*see* inflate]
*rarefaction* 322
*currency* 800
**inflect** 245
**inflexible** *hard* 323

*resolved* 604
*obstinate* 606
*stern* 739
*inexorable* 914a
**inflexion**
*change* 140
*curvature* 245
*grammar* 567
**inflict** *act upon* 680
*severity* 739
– *evil* 649
– *pain*
*bodily pain* 378
*mental pain* 830
– *punishment* 972
**infliction**
*adversity* 735
*mental pain* 828,
830
*punishment* 972
**influence** 153
*change* 140
*physical* – **175**
*inducement* 615
*instrumentality*
631
*authority* **737**
absence of – **175a**
sphere of – 780
make one's – felt
631
**influx** 294
**infold** 232
**inform** 527
– *against*
*accuse* 938
*go to law* 969
**informal** 83, 964
**informality** 773
**informant** 527
**information**
*knowledge* 490
*communication*
**527**
*learning* 539
*lawsuit* 969
pick up – 539
**informer** 532
**informity** 241
**infra dignitatem**
874, 940
**infraction**
*trespass* 303
*disobedience* 742
*non-observance*
773
*exemption* 927
– *of usage &c.*
*unconformity* 83
*desuetude* 614
**infrangible**

*combined* 46
*dense* 321
**infra-red rays** 420
**infrequency 137**
**infrigidation** 385
**infringe**
*transgress* 303
*disobey* 742
*not observe* 773
*undueness* 925
*dereliction* 927
– *a law &c.* 83
**infundibular** 252,
269
**infuriate**
*violent* 173
*excite* 824
*anger* 900
**infuscate** 431
**infuse** *mix* 41
*insert* 300
*teach* 537
– *courage* 861
– *life into* 824
– *new blood* 658
**infusible** 321
**infusion** [*see* infuse]
*liquefaction* 335
**infusoria** 193
**ingannation** 545
**ingathering** 72
**ingemination** 90
**ingenerate** 5
**ingenious** 515, 698
**ingenite** 5
**ingenium, per-**
**fervidum –** 682
**ingénu** *artless* 703
**ingénue** *actress* 599
**ingenuity** 698
**ingenuous** 703
**ingesta** 298
**ingestion** 296
**ingle** 388
**inglorious** 874, **940**
**ingluvies** 191
**ingot** 800
**ingraft** *add* 37
*join* 43
*insert* 300
*teach* 537
**ingrafted**
*extrinsic* 6
*habit* 613
**ingrain**
*insinuate* 228
*colour* 428
**ingrained**
*intrinsic* 5
*combined* 48
*habit* 613

intercept
  *hinder* 706
  *take* 789
intercession
  [*see* intercede]
  *worship* 990
Intercessor 976
interchange 148
  *barter* 794
  - *visits &c.* 892
interchangeable 12
intercipient 706
interclude 706
intercommunica-
  tion 527
intercommunity
  892
interconnection 9
intercourse
  *copulation* 43
  *friendship* 888
  *sociality* 892
  *verbal* – 582, 588
intercurrence
  *interchange* 148
  *interjacence* 228
  *passage* 302
interdependence 12
interdict 761
interdictive 55
interdigitate 219,
  228
interest *concern* 9
  *influence* 175
  *curiosity* 455
  *advantage* 618
  *importance* 642
  *property* 780
  *debt* 806
  *excite* 824
  *please* 829
  *amuse* 840
  devoid of – 841
  feel an – in 906
  not know one's
    own – 699
  make – for 707
  place out at –
    *lend* 787
  *economy* 817
  take an – in
    *curiosity* 455
    *love* 897
  take no – in
    *insensibility* 823
    *indifference* 866
  want of – 866
interested
  *selfish* 943
  – in 457
interesting

*lovable* 897
interfere *disagree*
  24
  *counteract* 179
  *intervene* 228
  *activity* 682
  *thwart* 706
  *mediate* 724
interference
  *light* 420
interfretted 219
interfusion 41
interim 106, 120
interior 221
  *painting* 556
interjacence 68,
  228
interject 228, 300
interlace *join* 43
  *twine* 219
interlacing 41
interlard 41, 228
interleave 228
interline
  *interpolate* 228
  *write* 590
interlineation 39
interlink 43, 219
interlocation 228
interlocking direc-
  torate 709
interlocution 588
interlocutor 582
interloper
  *extraneous* 57
  *intervene* 228
  *obstruct* 706
interlude
  *time* 106
  *dramatic* 599
intermarriage 903
intermeddle 682,
  706
intermeddling 724
intermediary 534
intermediate
  *mean* 29
  *middle* 68
  *intervening* 228
  *ministerial* 631
  – *time* 106
intermedium
  *mean* 29
  *link* 45
  *intervention* 228
  *instrument* 631
interment 363
  *insertion* 300
intermezzo 415
intermigration 266
interminable

*infinite* 105
  *eternal* 112
  *long* 200
intermingle 41
intermission 106,
  142
intermit
  *interrupt* 70
  *recur* 138
  *discontinue* 142
intermittence
  *time* 106
intermix 41, 48
intermutation 148
intermural 278
intern 221
internal 5, 221
  – *evidence* 467
international
  *reciprocal* 12
  *sociality* 892
  – *law* 963
internecine 361
  – *war* 722
internuncio 534,
  758
interpel 142
interpellation
  *inquiry* 461
  *address* 586
  *summons* 741
  *appeal* 765
interpenetration
  *interjacence* 228
  *ingress* 294
  *passage* 302
interpolation
  *adjunct* 39
  *analytical* 85
  *interpose* 228
  *insertion* 300
interpose
  *intervene* 228
  *act* 682
  *hinder* 706
  *mediate* 724
interposit 799
interplanetary 228
interpretation 522
interpreter 524
interrelation 9, 12
interregnum
  *intermission* 106
  *transient* 111
  *discontinuance*
    142
  *interval* 198
  *laxity* 738
interrogate 461
interrupt
  *discontinuity* 70

*cessation* 142
  *hinder* 706
interruption
  *derangement* 61
  *interval* 198
intersect 219
interspace 198, 221
intersperse 73, 228
interstellar 228
interstice 198
interstitial 221, 228
intertexture
  *intersection* 219
  *tissue* 329
inter-twine, -twist
  *unite* 43
  *cross* 219
interval
  – *of time* 106
  – *of space* 198
  – *in music* 413
  at –s
    *discontinuously*
      70
  at regular –s 138
intervene
  – *in order* 70
  – *in time* 106
  – *in space* 228
  *be instrumental*
    631
  *mediate* 724
intervert 140, 279
interview 588, 892
intervolved 43
interweave *join* 43
  *cross* 219
  *interjacence* 228
interworking 170
intestate 552
intestine 221
inthral 749, 751
intimacy 9
intimate
  *personal* 79
  *close* 197
  *inside* 221
  *tell* 527
  *friendly* 888, 892
intimately
  *joined* 43
intimidate
  *frighten* 860
  *insolence* 885
  *threat* 909
intitule 564
into: go – 294
  put – 300
  run – 300
intolerable 830
intolerance

itinerary 266, 527
itur ad astra, sic –
  360
ivory 430
Ixion 312

**J**

jab 276
jabber
  *unmeaning* 517
  *stammer* 583
  *chatter* 584
jacent 213
jacet, hic – 363
jacinth 847
jack
  *rotation* 312
  *ensign* 550
  *instrument* 633
  *money* 800
Jack – Cade 742
  – Ketch 975
  – o' lantern 423
  – in office
  *director* 694
  *bully* 887
  – at a pinch 711
  – Pudding
  *actor* 599
  *humorist* 844
  *boaster* 884
  before one can say
  ' – Robinson'
  132
  – tar 269
  – of all trades 700
jack-a-dandy 844,
  854
jackal
  *auxiliary* 711
  *servility* 886
jackanapes 854,
  887
Jackass 271
jack-boot 225
jackdaw in pea-
  cock's feathers
  701
jacket 225
  cork – 666
Jacobin 710
Jacquerie 716, 719
jacta est alea 601
jactitation
  *tossing* 315
  *boasting* 884
jaculation 284
jade *horse* 271
  *fatigue* 688

*low woman* 876
*scamp* 949
*drab* 962
jag 257
jagged 244
jail 752
  – bird
  *prisoner* 754
  *bad man* 949
jailer 753, 975
jakes 653
jalousie de métier
  921
jam *squeeze* 43
  *crowd* 72
  *food* 298
  *pulp* 354
  *sweet* 396
  *scrape* 732
  – in *interpose* 228
jamb 215
jamboree 840
jammed in 751
jangle
  *harsh sound* 410
  *quarrel* 713
janissary 726
janitor 263
janty *gay* 836
  *pretty* 845
  *stylish* 852
  *showy* 882
  *insolent* 885
January 138
januis clausis 528
Janus *deceiver* 607
  *tergiversation* 607
  close the temple
  of – 723
Janus-faced 544
japan *coat* 223
  *resin* 356a
  *ornament* 847
jar *clash* 24
  *vessel* 191
  *agitation* 315
  *stridor* 410
  *discord* 713
  – upon the feel-
  ings 830
jardinière 191
jargon
  *absurdity* 497
  *no meaning* 517
  *unintelligible* 519
  *neology* 563
jarvey 694
jasper 847
jaundiced
  *yellow* 436
  *prejudiced* 481

*dejected* 837
*jealous* 920
view with – eyes
  *disapprove* 932
jaunt 266
jaunting car 272
jaunty [*see* janty]
javelin 727
jaw *chatter* 584
  *scold* 932
jaw-fallen 837
jaws *mouth* 231
  *eating* 298
  – of death 360
jay 584
jaywalker 701
jazz 415, 840
  – band 417
jealous of honour
  939
jealousy 920
  *suspicion* 485
jecur, difficili bile –
  900
jeer 929
Jehovah 976
Jehu 268, 694
jejune *insipid* 391
  *style* 575
  *scanty* 640
  *dull* 843
jell 352
jelly 298, 352
  beat to a – 972
jemidar 745
jemmy *lever* 633
  *dandy* 854
je ne sais quoi
  *exceptional* 83
  *what d'ye call 'em*
  563
  *beauty* 845
jennet 271
jeopardy 665
jerboa 309
jeremiad
  *lament* 839
  *invective* 932
Jericho, send to –
  297
jerk *start* 146
  *throw* 284
  *pull* 285
  *agitate* 315
jerkin 225
jerks, by – 70
Jerry Sneak 862,
  941
jersey 225
Jerusalem
  the new – 981

Jessamy, Jemmy
  854
jesse 1000
jest *trifle* 643
  *wit* 842
jest-book 842
jester 844
jesting-stock 857
Jesuit *deceiver* 548
  *priest* 996
jesuitical 477, 544
Jesus 976
jet *stream* 348
  – black 431
jetsam 73, 782
jettison 782
jetty *protection* 250
  *harbour* 666
jeu
  le – n'en vaut pas
  la chandelle
  *waste* 638
  *unimportant* 643
  *dear* 814
  – d'esprit 842
  – de mots 842
  – de théâtre 599
jeune
  – premier 599
  – veuve 599
jewel *gem* 648
  *ornament* 847
  *favourite* 899
jewellery, false –
  545
Jezebel *wicked* 913
  *wretch* 949
  *courtesan* 962
jib *front* 234
  *regression* 283
  cut of one's –
  *form* 240
  *appearance* 448
jibe 140
jiffy 113
jig 840
jig-saw puzzle 840
jilt *disappoint* 509
  *deceive* 545
  *deceiver* 548
  *cast off* 756
  *dishonour* 940
jilted 898

– one's promise 772
– quiet 265
– a secret 528
– a shop 625
– in sight 459
– silence 585
– straight 944
– in suspense
  *uncertainty* 475
  *irresolution* 605
– in the thoughts 505
– time
  *punctual* 132
  *music* 416
– to 604*a*
– together 709
– under
  *authority* 737
  *subjection* 749
  *restraint* 751
– up [*see below*]
– in view
  *attend to* 457
  *remember* 505
  *expect* 507
– waiting 133
– watch 459
– one's word 939
**keep up**
  *continue* 143
  *preserve* 670
  *stimulate* 824
– appearances 852
– the ball 682, 840
– a correspond-
  ence 592
– the memory of 505
– one's spirits 836
– with 274
**keeper** 370, **753**
**keeping**
  *congruity* 23
  in – 82
  safe – *safety* 664
  *preservation* 670
**keepsake** 505
**keg** 191
**kelpie** 979
**kelson** 211
**kempt** 652
**ken** 441, 490
  beyond mortal – 360
**kennel**
  *assemblage* 72
  *hovel* 189
  *ditch* 259
  *conduit* 350

**Kentish fire** 931
**képi** 225
**kerb-stone** 233
**kerchief** 225
  wave a – 550
**kern** *quern* 330
  *low fellow* 876
  *varlet* 949
**kernel** *heart* 5
  *cause* 153
  *central* 222
  *important* 642
**kerosene** 356
**ketch**
  *ship* 273
**Ketch, Jack** – 975
**kettle** *vessel* 191
  *caldron* 386
– drum *music* 417
  *tea-party* 892
– of fish
  *disorder* 59
  *difficulty* 704
**key** *cause* 153
  *opener* 260
  *music* 413
  *colour* 428
  *interpretation* 522
  *indication* 550
  *instrument* 631, 633
  *emblem of au-*
    *thority* 747
  deliver the –s of
    the city 725
**key-hole** 260
**key-note** *model* 22
  *rule* 80
  *music* 413
**key-stone**
  *support* 215
  *motive* 615
  *importance* 642
  *completion* 729
**khaki** 225, 433
**khan** *inn* 189
  *governor* 745
**khedive** 745
**kibitka** 272
**kibitzer** 682
**kick** *impulse* 276
  *recoil* 277
  *assault* 716
  *thrill* 821
  *spurn* 930
  *punish* 972
– against
  *oppose* 708
  *resist* 719
– against the
  pricks

*useless* 645
*rash* 863
*unequal* 28
*superior* 33
– up a dust
  *active* 682
  *discord* 713
  *insolent* 885
– a row 900
– one's heels
  *kept waiting* 133
  *nothing to do* 681
– off 62
– up a row
  *violent* 173
  *discord* 713
– over the traces 742
**kicking, alive and** – 359
**kickshaw** *food* 298
  *trifle* 643
**kid** *child* 129
  *progeny* 167
  *leather* 223
  not to be handled
    with – gloves
  *dirty* 653
  *difficult* 704
**kidnap**
  *deceive* 545
  *take* 789
  *steal* 791
**kidney** *class* 75
**kilderkin** 191
**Kilkenny cats** 713
**kill** 361
– or cure 662
– the fatted calf 883
– the goose with
  golden eggs 699
– with kindness 902
– the slain 641
– time 106
  *inactivity* 683
  *amusement* 840
– two birds with
  one stone 682
**killing** 361
  *delightful* 829
**kill-joy** 706
**kiln** 386
**kilowatt** 466
**kilt** 225
**kimbo** 244
**kimono** 225
**kin** 75
**kind** *class* 75
  *benevolent* 906

– regards 894
**kinder-garten** 542
**kindle** *cause* 153
  *produce* 161
  *quicken* 171
  *inflame* 173
  *set fire to* 384
  *excite* 824
  *incense* 900
**kindling wood** 388
**kindred** 9, 11
**kine** 366
**kinematics** 264
**kinetic energy** 157
**king** 745
  every inch a –
  *authority* 737
  *rank* 875
  –maker 694
**King** –'s Bench 752, 966
–'s birthday 268
–'s counsel 968
– Death 360
–'s English 560
–'s evidence 529
–'s highway 627
–'s ransom 648
– of Kings 976
**kingcraft** 693
**kingdom**
  *region* 181
  *property* 780
– of heaven 981
**kingly** 737
**king-post** 215
**kink** 248, 378, 608
**kiosk** 189, 1000
**kip** 961
**kirk** 1000
**kirtle** 225
**kismet** 601
**kiss** *touch* 199
  *courtesy* 894
  *endearment* 902
– the book 535
– the hem of one's
  garment 928
– in the ring 840
– the rod 725
**kit** *class* 75
  *equipment* 191
  *fiddle* 417
  –bag 191
**kitcat** 556
**kitchen** 191, 691
– maid 746
– range 386
**kitchener** 386
**kitchenette** 691
**kite** *fly* 273

tion 625
– unrest 832
laboured - *style* 579
  *prepared* 673
  – study 457
labourer 690
labouring
  – man 690
  – oar 686
labyrinth
  *disorder* 59
  *convolution* 248
  *secret* 533
lac *number* 98
  *resin* 356a
  – of rupees 800
lace *stitch* 43
  *netting* 219
  *ornament* 847
  – one's jacket 972
lacerable 328
lacerate 44
  – the heart 830
laches 460, 773
Lachesis 601
lachrymæ, hinc
  illæ – 830
lachrymatory gas
  727
lachrymis, quis
  temperet a – 914
lachrymose 837
lack *require* 630
  *insufficient* 640
  *destitute* 804
  *desire* 865
  – faith 989
  – harmony 708
  – preparation 674
  – wit 501
lackadaisical
  *inactive* 683
  *melancholy* 837
  *indifferent* 866
lackadaisy! 839,
  870
lack-brain 499, 501
lacker [*see* lacquer]
lackey 746
lack-lustre 422, 429
laconic 572
lacquer
  *covering* 223
  *resin* 356a
  *adorn* 847
lacrosse 840
lacteal 352
lacuna 198, 252
lacustrine 343
lad 129
ladder 305, 627

kick down the –
  604
lade *load* 184
  *transfer* 185
  *contents* 190
  *dip* 270
  – out 297
laden 52
  heavy – 828
  – with 777
ladies' man 897
lading 190, 780
  bill of – *list* 86
ladle *receptacle* 191
  *transfer* 270
  *vehicle* 272
lady *woman* 374
  *rank* 875
  *wife* 903
  our – 977
  – day 138
  – help 746
  –'s maid 746
lady chapel 1000
ladylike
  *womanly* 374
  *fashionable* 852
lady-love 897
lag *linger* 275
  *follow* 281
  *dawdle* 683
  – behind 133
laggard 603, 683
lager *beer* 298
lagoon 343
laical 997
laid: – on one's
  back 158
  – by the heels 751
  – low 160
  – up 655
lair 189, 653
laird *master* 745
  *proprietor* 779
  *nobility* 875
Lais 962
laisse manger, cela
  se – 394
laisser: – aller,
  – faire
  *permanence* 141
  *neglect* 460
  *inaction* 681
  *laxity* 738
  *freedom* 748
  *inexcitable* 826
laity 997
lake *water* 343
  *pink* 434
  – of fire and brim-
  stone 982

Lama 745, 996
Lamaism 984
Lamarkism 357
lamb *infant* 129
  *animal* 366
  *gentle* 826
  *innocent* 946
  go out like a – 174
  lion lies down
  with – 721
Lamb of God 976
lambent
  *touching* 379
  – flame *heat* 382
  *light* 420
Lambeth 1000
lame *incomplete* 53
  *impotent* 158
  *weak* 160
  *imperfect* 651
  *disease* 655
  *injury* 659
  *failing* 732
  – conclusion
  *illogical* 477
  *failure* 732
  help a – dog over
  a stile *aid* 707
  *vindicate* 937
  – duck 808
  – excuse 617
lamellar 204
lamentable *bad* 649
  *painful* 830
  *sad* 837
lamentably *very* 31
lamentation 839
lamia 980, 994
lamina 51, 204
lamination 204
Lammas 998
lamp 423
  rub the – 992
  safety – 666
  smell of the –
  *style* 577
  *prepared* 673
lamplighter
  *quick* 682
lampoon 932, 934
lampooner 936
lanâ caprinâ, de –
  643
lanary 636
lanate 255, 256
lance *pierce* 260
  *throw* 284
  *spear* 727
  break a – with
  *attack* 716
  *warfare* 722

couch one's – 720
  – corporal 745
lancer 726
  –'s dance 840
lancet 253, 262
lancinate 378, 830
land *arrive* 292
  *ground* 342
  *estate* 780
  gone to a better –
  360
  hug the – 286
  make the – 286
  on – 342
  see – 858
  – covered with
  water 343
  – flowing with
  milk and honey
  168
  how the – lies
  *circumstances* 8
  *experiment* 463
  *foresight* 510
  in the – of the
  living 359
landamman 745
landau 272
landed
  – gentry 779
  – estate 780
landgrave 745
landholder 779
landing field 273
landing-place 215,
  292
landlady 779
land-locked 229,
  343
landloper 268
landlord 779
land-lubber 343,
  701
landmark
  *limit* 233
  *indication* 550
land-mine 727
landreeve 694
landscape
  *prospect* 448
  – gardening
  *agriculture* 371
  *beauty* 845
  – painting 556
  – painter 559
land-shark 792
land-slip 306
landsman 342
Landsturm 726
land-surveying 466
Landwehr 726

lee-shore 665, 667
leet, court – 966
lee-wall 666
leeward 236
lee-way *space* 180
  *tardy* 133
  *navigation* 267
  *deviation* 279
  *progression* 282
  *shortcoming* 304
left *residuary* 40
  *sinistral* 239
  over the – 545
  – alone 748
  – in the lurch 732
  – to shift for one-
  self 893
  pay over the –
  shoulder 808
left-handed
  *clumsy* 699
  – compliment 932
  – marriage 903
leg *support* 215
  *walker* 266
  *thief* 792
  best – foremost
  686
  fast as –s will
  carry 274
  have a – to stand
  on 470
  keep on one's –s
  654
  last –s *spoiled* 659
  *fatigue* 688
  light on one's –s
  734
  make a – 894
  not a – to stand on
  *illogical* 477
  *confuted* 479
  *failure* 732
  off one's –s
  *propulsion* 284
  on one's –s
  *upright* 212
  *elevation* 307
  *speaking* 582
  *in health* 654
  *active* 682
  *free* 748
  set on one's –s 660
  – bail 623
legacy 270, 780, 784
legal *permitted* 760
  *legitimate* 924
  *relating to law*
  963
  – adviser 968
  -- estate 780

legality **963**
legate 534
legatee 779, 785
legation 755
legato 415
legend 551, 594
legendary
  *imaginary* 515
legerdemain 146,
  545
légèreté 605
leggings 225
leghorn hat 225
legible 518
  – hand 590
legion
  *multitude* 102
  *army* 726
legionary 726
legislation 693, 963
legislative assem-
  bly 696
legislator 694
legislature 693, 696
legist 968
legitimate *true* 494
  *permitted* 760
  *right* 922
  *due* 924
  *legal* 963
legume 367
lei 847
leisure **685**
  at one's – *late* 133
leisurely 275
leman 897
lemma 476
lemon *colour* 436
Lemprière 979
lemures 980
lend 787
  – aid 707
  – countenance 707
  – a hand 680
  – oneself to
  *assent* 488
  co-operate 709
  – on security 789
  – wings to 707
lender *creditor* 805
lending **787**
length **200**
  go all –s
  *resolution* 604
  *activity* 682
  *exertion* 686
  at – *in time* 133
  full – *portrait* 556
  go great –s 549
  – and breadth of
  50

– and breadth of
  the land
  *space* 180
  *publication* 531
  – of time 110
lengthen 35, 200
  – out
  *diuturnity* 110
  *late* 133
lengthwise 200
lengthy *long* 200
  *diffuse* 573
lenient
  *moderate* 174
  *mild* 740
  *compassionate*
  914
lenify 174
lenitive
  *moderating* 174
  *remedy* 662
  *relieving* 834
lenity **740**
lens 445
Lent 956, 998
lenten 956
lenticular 245, 250
lentor *slowness* 275
  *spissitude* 352
  *inactivity* 683
lentous 352
leonem, ex ungue –
  550
leonine verses 597
leopard
  *variegated* 440
  –'s spots
  *unchanging* 150
leprechaune 980
leprosy 655
lerret 273
lèse-majesté 742
less *inferior* 34
  *subduction* 38
  – than no time
  113
lessee
  *possessor* 779
  *receiver* 785
lessen
  – in quantity or
  degree 36
  – in size 195
  – an evil 658
lesson *teaching* 537
  *warning* 668
  give a – to
  *punish* 972
  read a – to
  *censure* 932
  say one's –

*memory* 505
lessor 805
lest 623
let *hindrance* **706**
  *permit* 760
  *lease* 771
  *lend* 787
  *sell* 796
  apartments to –
  *fool* 499
  to – 763
  – alone *besides* 37
  *permanence* 141
  *quiescence* 265
  *avoid* 623
  *disuse* 678
  *inaction* 681
  *not complete* 730
  *free* 748
  – be
  *permanence* 141
  *continuance* 143
  *inaction* 681
  – blood 297
  – 'I dare not' wait
  upon 'I would'
  605
  – down
  *depress* 308
  *humble* 879
  – down easily
  *forgive* 918
  – fall *drop* 308
  *inform* 527
  *speak* 582
  – fly *violence* 173
  *propel* 284
  – fly at 716
  – go *neglect* 460
  *liberate* 750
  *relinquish* 782
  *restitution* 790
  – in *interpose* 228
  *admit* 296
  *trick* 545
  – into *inform* 490
  *disclose* 529
  – one know 527
  – off *violent* 173
  *propel* 284
  *permit* 760
  *forgive* 918
  *exempt* 927a
  *acquit* 970
  – out *disperse* 73
  *lengthen* 200
  *eject* 297
  *disclose* 529
  *liberate* 750
  – out at 716
  – pass 460

put – into 359
recall to – 660
see – 840
support – 359
take away – 361
tenant for – 779
– to come 152
– after death 981
– or death
  *need* 630
  *important* 642
  *contention* 720
– and spirit 682
Life, the 976
life-blood 5, 359
life-boat 273, 666
life-giving 168
lifeguards 726
lifeless 172, 360
lifelike 17
lifelong 110
life-preserver 666,
  727
life-size 192
lifetime 108
life-weary 841
lift *raise* 307
  *aid* 707
  *steal* 791
  – *cattle* 791
  – up the eyes 441
  – a finger 680
  – hand against
    716
  – one's head 734
  – up the heart 990
  – the mask 529
  – the voice
    *shout* 411
    *speak* 582
lift-smoke 840
ligament 45
ligation 43
ligature 45
light *state* 7
  *small* 32
  *window* 260
  *velocity* 274
  *arrive* 292
  *descend* 306
  *levity* 320
  *kindle* 384
  *match* 388
  *luminosity* **420**
  *luminary* 423
  – *in colour* 429
  *white* 430
  *aspect* 448
  *knowledge* 490
  *interpretation* 522
  *unimportant* 643

*easy* 705
*gay* 836
*loose* 961
blue – *signal* 550
bring to –
  *discover* 480a
  *manifest* 525
  *disclose* 529
children of – 987
come to – 529
false – 443
foot –s 599
half – 422
make – of
  *underrate* 483
  *easy* 705
  *inexcitable* 826
  *despise* 930
in one's own – 699
obstruct the – 426
side – 490
see the – *life* 359
  *publication* 531
transmit – 425
throw – upon 522
a – breaks in upon
  one 529
– under a bushel
  *hide* 528
  *not hide* 878
  *modesty* 881
– comedy 599
– cruiser 726
– fantastic toe 309
– upon one's feet
  664
– heart 836
– of heel 274
– horse 726
– infantry 726
– purse 804
– and shade 420
– of truth 543
– up *illumine* 420
  *excite* 824
  *cheer* 836
– upon *chance* 156
  *arrive at* 292
  *discover* 480a
  *acquire* 775
Light of the World
  976
lighten
  *make light* 320
  *illume* 420
  *facilitate* 705
lighter *boat* 273
lighterage 812
lighterman 269
light-fingered 791,
  792

light-footed 274,
  682
light-headed 503
lighthouse 550
lightless 421
light-minded 605
lightning
  *velocity* 274
  *flash* 420
  *spark* 423
like greased – 113
lightsome
  *luminous* 420
  *irresolute* 605
  *cheerful* 836
ligneous 367
lignite 388
lignography 558
ligulate 205
like *similar* 17
  *relish* 394
  *enjoy* 377, 827
  *wish* 865
  *love* 897
do what one –s
  748
look – 448
we shall not look
  upon his – again
  33
– master like man
  19
– a pin in paper 58
likely 472
think – 507
likeness 21, 554
bad – 555
likewise 37
liking 865, 897
have a – for 827
to one's – 829
lilac *colour* 437
Liliputian 193
Lillith 994
lilt 416, 836
lily *white* 430
  *beauty* 845
paint the – 641
lily-livered 862
limæ labor
  *improve* 658
  *toil* 686
limature 330, 331
limb *member* 51
  *instrument* 633
  *scamp* 949
  – of the law 968
limber 272, 324
limbo *prison* 751,
  752
  *pain* 828

*purgatory* 982
lime *entrap* 545
  – light 423, 531,
    599
Limehouse 908
limine, in – 66
limit *complete* 52
  *end* 67
  *circumscribe* 229
  *boundary* **233**
  *qualify* 469
  *restrain* 751
  *prohibit* 761
limitarian 984
limitation [*see*
  limit]
  *estate* 780, 783
limited
  – *in quantity* 32
  – *in size* 193
  to a – extent
  *imperfect* 651
limitless 105
limitrophe 197
limn 556
limner 559
limousine 272
limp *weak* 160
  *slow* 275
  *supple* 324
  *fail* 732
limpid 425
lin 343, 348
lincture 662
line *fastening* 45
  *continuous* 69
  *ancestors* 166
  *descendants* 167
  *length* 200
  *no breadth* 203
  *string* 205
  *lining* 224
  *outline* 230
  *straight* 246
  *of steamers* 273
  *direction* 278
  *music* 413
  *appearance* 448
  *measure* 466
  *mark* 550
  *writing* 590
  *verse* 597
  *vocation* 625
  *army and navy*
    726
  boundary – 233
  draw the – 465
  drop a – to 526
  in a –
  *continuous* 69
  *straight* 246

*freedom* 748
*inexcitability* 826
– in the memory
  505
– upon nothing
  819
– on 298
– separately 905
– by one's wits
  545
livelihood 803
livelong 110
lively *keen* 375
  - *style* 574
  *active* 682
  *acute* 821
  *sensitive* 822
  *sprightly* 836
  – *imagination* 515
  – *pace* 274
liver 83; hard –
  954*a*
white – 862
liver-coloured 433
livery *suit* 225
  *colour* 428
  *badge* 550
  *decoration* 877
  – *servant* 746
liveryman 748
live wire 171
livid *dark* 431
  *grey* 432
  *purple* 437
living *life* 359
  *business* 625
  *benefice* 995
  good – 957
  – *beings* 357
  –room 191
  – *soul* 372
  – *thing* 366
livraison 593
livret 593
lixiviate 335, 652
lixivium 335
llama 271
lo! 457, 870
load *quantity* 31
  *fill* 52
  *lade* 184
  *cargo* 190
  *weight* 319
  *store* 636
  *redundance* 641·
  *hindrance* 706
  *adversity* 735
  *anxiety* 828
  *oppress* 830
  prime and – 673
  take off a – of care

[ 550 ]

834
– the memory 505
– with 706
– with reproaches
  932
loads 102
loadstar 288, 350,
  693
loadstone 288, 615
loaf *mass* 192
  *do nothing* 681
  *dawdle* 683
loafer
  *stroller* 268
  *inactive* 683
  *neglect* 927
  *bad man* 949
loam 342
loan 787
loathe 867, 898
loathing
  [*see* loathe]
  *weariness* 841
  *hate* 898
loathsome
  *unsavoury* 395
  *painful* 830
  *dislike* 867
loaves and fishes
  *prosperity* 734
  *acquisition* 775
  *wealth* 803
Lob's pound, in –
  751
lobby 191, 615, 627
lobbying 615
lobe 51
local
  – habitation 184,
    189
  – board 966
locale 183
locality 182, 183
localize 184
location 184
loch 343
loci, genius – 664
lock *fasten* 43
  *fastening* 45
  *tuft* 256
  *canal* 350
  *hindrance* 706
  *prison* 752
  dead – 265
  in the –up 938
  under – and key
  *safe* 664
  *restraint* 751
  *prisoner* 754
  – hospital 662
  –out 55, 719
  – the stable door

*too late* 135
  *useless* 645
  *unskilful* 699
  –, stock and
    barrel 50
  – up *hide* 528
  *imprison* 751
locker 191
locket 847
lock-up *prison* 752
loco, in –
  *agreeing* 23
  *situation* 183
  *expedience* 646
locofoco 388
locomotion 264
  – by air 267
  – by land 266
  – by water 267
locomotive 266, 271
locular 191
locum tenens
  *substitute* 147
  *inhabitant* 188
  *deputy* 759
locus:
  – *pœnitentiæ* 937
  – standi
  *support* 215
  *plea* 617
  *social rank* 873
locust *prodigal* 818
  *evil-doer* 913
  swarm like –s 102
locution 582
lode 636
lodestar
  *attraction* 288
  *indication* 550
  *direction* 693
lodestone 288, 615
lodge *place* 184
  *presence* 186
  *dwelling* 189
  – a complaint 938
lodgement 184
lodger
  *inhabitant* 188
  *possessor* 779
lodging 189
loft 191, 210
lofty *high* 206
  - *style* 574
  *proud* 878
  *insolent* 885
  *magnanimous*
    942
log *velocity* 274
  *fuel* 388
  *record* 551
  heave the – 466

sleep like a – 683
logarithm 84
loggerhead 501
  at –s *discord* 713
  *contention* 720
  *enmity* 889
loggia 191
logic 476
  – of facts 467
logician 476
logical acuteness
  570
logography 590
logogryph 533
logolept 562
logomachy
  *discussion* 476
  *words* 588
  *dispute* 720
logometer 85
logometric 84
log-rolling 709
loin 235, 236
  gird up one's –s
  *strong* 159
  *prepare* 673
  – cloth 225
loisir, impromptu
  fait à – 673
loiter *tardy* 133
  *slow* 275
  *inactive* 683
loll *sprawl* 213
  *recline* 215
  *inactive* 683
lollipop 396
lollop 683
Lombard Street to
  a China orange
  472
lone 87
lonesome 893
long - *in time* 110
  - *in space* 200
  *diffuse* 573
  go to one's – ac-
    count 360
  – ago 122
  make a – arm
  *exertion* 686
  *seize* 789
  –boat 273
  draw the – bow
    549
  take a – breath
  *refreshment* 689
  *relief* 834
  – clothes 129
  – drawn out 573
  – duration 110
  –expected 507

**Column 1 (LON)**

– face 832, 837
– for 865
–headed *wise* 498
– life to *glory* 873
  *approval* 931
–lived 110
– odds *chance* 156
  *improbability* 473
  *difficulty* 704
– pending 110
– primer 591
– pull and strong
  pull 285
– range 196
– robe 968
– run *average* 29
  *whole* 50
  *destiny* 152
– sea 348
– and the short
  *whole* 50
  *concise* 572
–sighted
  *dim-sighted* 443
  *wise* 498
  *foresight* 510
– since 122
– spun 573
– standing
  *diuturnal* 110
  *old* 124
–suffering
  *lenient* 740
  *inexcitable* 826
  *pity* 914
– time 110
–winded 573
**longanimity**
  *inexcitable* 826
  *forgiving* 918
**longevity** 110, 128
**longhead** 500
**longing** 865
– lingering look
  behind 833
**longinquity** 196
**longitude**
  *situation* 183
  *length* 200
  *measurement* 466
**longitudinal** 200
**longo intervallo**
  *discontinuity* 70
  *diuturnity* 110
  *distance* 196
  *interval* 198
**longshore man**
  *waterman* 269
  *plebeian* 876
**longways** 217
**loo** 840

**Column 2 (LOO)**

**looby** *fool* 501
  *bungler* 701
  *clown* 876
**look** *small degree* 32
  *see* 441
  *appearance* 448
  *attend to* 457
– about 459, 461
– after 459, 693
– ahead 510
– alive 457, 684
– another way 442
– back 122
– beyond 510
– black *or* blue
  *feeling* 821
  *discontent* 832
  *dejection* 837
– down upon 930
– in the face
  *sincerity* 703
  *courage* 861
  *pride* 878
– foolish 874
– for 461, 507
– forwards 121,
  510
– here 457
– into 457, 461
– before one leaps
  864
– like 17, 448
– on 186
– out *view* 448
  *attention* 457
  *care* 459
  *seek* 461
  *expect* 507
  *intention* 620
  *business* 625
  *danger* 665
  *warning* 668
  *caution* 864
– over *examine*
  461
– round *seek* 461
– sharp 682
– to 459, 926
– through 461
– up *prosper* 734
  *high price* 814
  *hope* 858
  *visit* 892
– up to *repute* 873
  *respect* 928
  *approbation* 931
– upon as 480, 484
**looker-on** 444
**looking-glass** 445
**loom** *destiny* 152
  *dim* 422

**Column 3 (LOR)**

  *dim sight* 443
  *come in sight* 446
  *weave* 691
– of the land 342
– up 31
**loon** *fool* 501
  *clown* 876
  *rascal* 949
**loop** 245, 247, 629
– the loop 245
**loop-hole**
  *opening* 260
  *vista* 441
  *plea* 617
  *device* 626
  *escape* 671
  *fortification* 717
**loose** *detach* 44
  *incoherent* 47
  *pendent* 214
  *desultory* 279
  *illogical* 477
  *vague* 519
– *style* 575
  *lax* 738
  *free* 748
  *liberate* 750
  *debauched* 961
give a – to
- *imagination* 515
  *laxity* 738
  *permit* 760
  *indulgence* 954
let – 750
on the – 961
screw – 713
– character 961
at a – end 685
– fish 949, 962
– morals 945
– rein 738
– suggestion 514
– thread 495
leave a - 460
take up a - 664
**loosen** 47, 750
**loot** 791, 793
**lop** 201
– and top 371
**lopped**
  *incomplete* 53
**loppet** 699
**lop-eared** 53
**lop-sided** 28
**loquacity** 584
**loquendi**
  cacoëthes – 584
  jus et norma – 567
  usus – 582
**lorcha** 273
**Lord, lord**

**Column 4 (LOS)**

  *ruler* 745
  *nobleman* 875
  *God* 976
O – *worship* 990
– Chancellor 967
– of the creation
  372
–'s day 687
–s Justices 966,
  967
the – knows 491
– lieutenant 965
– of Lords 976
– of the manor
  779
– it over 737, 885
–'s prayer 990
–'s supper 998
–'s table 1000
**lordling** 875
**lordly** 873, 878
**Lord Mayor** 745,
  965
–'s show 883
**lordship**
  *authority* 737
  *property* 780
  *title* 877
  *judge* 967
**lore** 490, 539
**Lorelei** 980
**lorette** 962
**lorgnette** 445
**lorication**
  *armour* 717
**loricated**
  *clothed* 223
**lorn** 893
**lorry** 272
**lose** *forget* 506
  *unintelligible* 519
  *fail* 732
  *loss* 776
no time to – 684
– one's balance
  732
– breath 688
– caste 874, 940
– the clew 475,
  519
– colour 429
– one's cunning
  699
– the day 732
– flesh 195
– ground
  *slow* 275
  *regression* 283
  *shortcoming* 304
– one's head
  *bewildered* 475

– heart 837
– one's heart 897
– hope 859
– interest in 624
– labour 732
– one's life 360
– no time 682, 684
– oneself 475
– an opportunity 135
– one's reason 503
– sight of
  *blind* 442
  *disappear* 449
  *neglect* 460
  *oblivion* 506
  *not complete* 730
– one's temper 900
– time 683
– one's way
  *wander* 279
  *uncertainty* 475
  *unskilful* 699
  *difficulty* 704
losel 818
losing game 732, 735
loss *decrement* 40a
  *death* 360
  *evil* 619
  *deterioration* 659
  *privation* **776**
  at a –
  *uncertain* 475
  at a – for
  *desiring* 865
– of fortune 804
– of health 655
– of life 360
– of right 925
– of strength 160
lost *non-existing* 2
  *absent* 187
  *invisible* 449
  *abstracted* 458
  *uncertain* 475
  *failure* 732
  *loss* 776
  *over-excited* 824
  *pain* 828
  *dejection* 837
  *impenitent* 951
– in admiration 931
– in astonishment 870
– in iniquity 945
– labour 645
– to shame
  *insolent* 885
  *improbity* 940

[ 552 ]

*bad man* 949
– to sight 449
– in thought 458
– to virtue 945
lot *state* 7
  *quantity* 25
  *group* 72
  *multitude* 102
  *necessity* 601
  *chance* 621
  *sufficient* 639
  *allotment* 786
  be one's – 151
  cast –s 621
  cast in one's –
    with 609, 709
  fall to one's – 156
  in –s 51
  where one's – is
    cast 189
loth 603, 867
Lothario 897, 962
lotion *liquid* 337
  *clean* 652
  *remedy* 662
loto 840
lottery 156, 840
  put into a – 621
lotus-eater 683
loud 404, 525
  *vulgar* 851
lough 343
lounge 191, 683
– suit 225
loup
  hurler avec les –s 714
–garou 980
louse 653
lout 501, 701, 876
louvre 351
lovable 897
love *desire* 865
  *courtesy* 894
  *affection* **897**
  *favourite* 899
  abode of – 897
  labour of –
    *willing* 602
    *inexpensive* 815
    *amusement* 840
    *disinterested* 942
  God's – 906
  make – 902
  no – lost 713
  – affair 897
  – of country 910
  – lock 256
  not for – or money 640, 814
love-knot *token* 550

love-lorn 898
lovely 845, 897
love-making 902
love-pot 959
love-potion 865
lover [*see* love]
love-sick 897, 902
love-story 897, 902
love-token 897, 902
loving-cup 892, 894
loving-kindness 906
low *small* 32
  *not high* 207
  - *sound* 405
  *moo* 412
  *vulgar* 851
  *disreputable* 874
  *common* 876
  *base* 940
  bring – 308
  – condition 876
  – comedy 599
  at a – ebb
    *small* 32
    *inferior* 34
    *depressed* 308
    *waste* 638
    *deteriorated* 659
  – fellow 876
  – life 851
  – note 408
  – origin 876
  – price 815
  – spirits 837
  – tide 207
  – tone *black* 431
  *mutter* 581
  – water *low* 207
  *dry* 340
  *insufficient* 640
  *poor* 804
low-born 876
low-brow 491
low-lands 207
low-minded 876, 940
lower *inferior* 34
  *decrease* 36
  *overhang* 214
  *depress* 308
  *dark* 421
  *dim* 422
  *predict* 511
  *sad* 837
  *irate* 900
  *sulky* 901a
  – one's flag 725
  – one's note 879
  – orders 876
lowering 668, 859

lowly 879
lown 501, 949
lowness [*see* low] **207**
  *humility* 879
loy 272
loyal *obedient* 743
  *observant* 772
  *honourable* 939
lozenge 244, 662
L. s. d. 800
lubbard [*see* lubber]
lubber 683, 701
lubberly 192, 699
lubricant 332
lubrication 255, **332**
lubricity
  *slippery* 255
  *unctuous* 355
  *impure* 961
lucent 420
lucid
  *luminous* 420
  *transparent* 425
  *intelligible* 518
  - *style* 570
  – *interval* 502
lucidus ordo 58
lucifer 388
Lucifer 423, 978
lucimeter 445
luck *chance* 156, 621
  *prosperity* 734
  good – 858
luckless 735
lucky 134, 734
lucrative 775
lucre 775, 803
Lucretia 960
luctation 720
lucubration 451
luculent 420
lucus a non lucendo 18, 565
lud! O – 839
ludibrious 840
ludicrous 853
luff 267
lug *pull* 285
  *ear* 418
luge 272
luggage 270, 780
– van 272
lugger 273
lugubrious 837
lukewarm
  *temperate* 382
  *irresolute* 605
  *torpid* 823
  *indifferent* 866
lull *cessation* 142

*mitigate* 174
*silence* 403
  – to sleep 265
lullaby
  *moderate* 174
  *song* 415
  *verses* 597
  *inactivity* 683
  *relief* 834
lumbago 378
lumbar 235
lumber *disorder* 59
  *slow* 275
  *store* 636
  *useless* 645
  *hindrance* 706
lumbering 647, 846
lumber-room 191
lumbriciform 249
luminary *star* 318
  *light* **423**
  *sage* 500
luminescence 420
luminous *light* 420
  *intelligible* 518
  – paint 423
lump *whole* 50
  *chief part* 51
  *amass* 72
  *mass* 192
  *projection* 250
  *weight* 319
  *density* 321
  in the – 50
  – of affectation
    855
  – sum 800
  – together *join* 43
  *combine* 48
  *assemble* 72
lumpish [*see* lump]
  *inactive* 683
  *ugly* 846
Luna 318
lunacy 503
lunar 318
  – caustic 384
lunatic 503, 504
luncheon 298
lune avec les dents,
  prendre la –
  158, 471
lunette 717
lunge 276, 716
lungs *wind* 349
  *loudness* 404
  *shout* 411
  *voice* 580
luniform &c. 245
lupanar 961
lurch *incline* 217

*sink* 306
*oscillation* 314
*failure* 732
leave in the –
  *outstrip* 303
  *deceive* 545
  *relinquish* 624
left in the –
  *defeated* 732
lure *attraction* 288,
  865
  *deceive* 545
  *entice* 615
lurid *dark* 421
  *dim* 422
  *red* 434
lurk *unseen* 447
  *latent* 526
  *hidden* 528
lurking-place 530
luscious 394, 829
lush *vegetation* 365
  *drunkenness* 959
lushy 959
lusk 683
lusory 840
lust 865, 961
  – after 921
lustily 404, 686
  cry out – 839
lustless 158
lustration 652, 952
lustre
  *brightness* 420
  *chandelier* 423
  *glory* 873
lustrum 108
lusty 159, 192
lusus naturæ 83
lute *cement* 45, 46
  *guitar* 417
luteous 436
Lutheran 984
luxation 44
luxuriant 168, 639
luxuriate in 377,
  827
luxurious
  *pleasant* 377
  *delightful* 829
  *intemperate* 954
luxury
  *physical* – 377
  *redundance* 641
  *enjoyment* 827
  *sensuality* 954
lycanthropy 503
Lyceum 542
Lydford law 964
Lydian measure
  415

lyddite 727
lying
  *decumbent* 213
  *deceptive* 544
  *faithless* 986
Ly-king 986
lymph *fluid* 333
  *water* 337
  *transparent* 425
lymphatic 337
lynch 972
  – law 964
lyncher 975
lynching 361
lynx-eyed 441, 498
lyre 417
lyric 415
  – poetry 597
lyrist 597

## M

Mab 979
macadamize 255,
  635
Macaire, Robert –
  792
macaroni 854
macaronic
  *absurdity* 497
  *neology* 563
  *verses* 597
Macchiavel [*see*
  Machiavellism]
mace
  *weapon* 727
  *sceptre* 747
mace-bearer 965
maceration
  *saturation* 337
  *atonement* 952
  *asceticism* 955
  *rite* 998
Macheath 792
Machiavellism
  *falsehood* 544
  *cunning* 702
  *dishonesty* 940
machicolation 257,
  717
machination
  *trick* 545
  *plan* 626
  *cunning* 702
  – of the devil 019
machinator 626
machine 633
  like a – 698
  – gun 407, 727
  be a mere – 749

machinist
  *theatrical* - 599
  *workman* 690
macilent 203
mackerel
  *mottled* 440
  *procuress* 962
  – sky 349, 353
mackintosh 225
macrobiotic 110
macrocosm 318
macrography 441
macrology 577
Mac Sycophant,
  Sir Pertinax -
  886, 935
mactation 991
macte virtute 931
macula 848
maculate
  *unclean* 653
maculation 440, 848
mad *insane* 503
  *excited* 824
  drive one – 900
  go – 825
  – after 865
  – with rage 900
madam 374
mad-brained 503
madcap
  *violent* 173
  *lunatic* 504
  *excitable* 825
  *buffoon* 844
  *rash* 863
madder *colour* 434
made
  – to one's hand
    673
  – man 734
  – to order 673
madefaction 339
madman 504
Madonna
  *good* 948
  *angel* 977
  *pious* 987
madrigal *music* 415
  *verses* 597
Mæcenas 492, 890
maelstrom
  *whirl* 312
  *water* 348
  *pitfall* 667
maestro 415
maffick 883
magazine
  *periodical* 531
  *record* 551
  *book* 593

store 636
– rifle 727
Magdalen 950, 962
mage 994
magenta 434
maggot *little* 193
  *fancy* 515
  *caprice* 608
  *desire* 865
maggoty
  *capricious* 608
  *unclean* 653
  – headed
  *silly* 499
  *excitable* 825
Magi *sage* 500
  *sect* 984
magic 175, 992
  – lantern
  *instrument* 445
  *show* 448
magician 548, 994
magilp 356*a*
magisterial 878,
  885
magistery 330
magistracy 737, 965
magistrate 745, 967
magistrature 737
magistri, jurare in
  verba – 481
  nullius – 487
magma 41
Magna Charta 769
magna pars fui,
  quorum – 690
magnanimity 942
magnate 875
magnet *attract* 288
  *desire* 865
magnetism
  *power* 157
  *influence* 175
  *attraction* 288
  *motive* 615
  animal – 992
magnetize
  *influence* 175
  *motive* 615
  *conjure* 992
magni nominis
  umbra
  *wreck* 659
  *repute* 873
  *rank* 875
magnificent
  *large* 192
  *fine* 845
  *grand* 882
magnifico 875
magnifier 445

magnifique et pas
  cher 815
magnify
  *increase* 35
  *enlarge* 194
  *over-rate* 482
  *exaggerate* 549
  *approve* 931
  *praise* 990
magniloquent 577,
  884
magnitude 25, 31,
  192
magno conatu
  magnas nugas
  638, 643
Magnus Apollo 500
magpie 584
magsman 792
maharajah 745
maharani 745
mah jong 840
mahl-stick [*see*
  maulstick]
mahogany
  *colour* 433
Mahomet 986
Mahometan 984
maid *girl* 129
  *servant* 631, 746
  *spinster* 374, 904
  – of all work 690
  – of honour 890
maiden *first* 66
  *girl* 129
  *punishment* 975
  – speech 66
maidenhood 904
maidenly 374
maigre 956
mail *post* 270, 534
  *armour* 717
  – coach 272, 534
  – steamer 273
  – van 272, 534
maim 158, 659
main *tunnel* 260
  *ocean* 341
  *conduit* 350
  *principal* 642
  coup de – 680
  in the –
  *intrinsically* 5
  *greatly* 31
  *on the whole* 50
  *principally* 642
  with might and –
  686
  plough the – 267
main-chance 156
  *good* 618

*important* 642
  *profit* 775
  look to the –
  *foresight* 510
  *skill* 698
  *economy* 817
  *caution* 864
  *selfish* 943
main-force
  *strength* 159
  *violence* 173
  *compulsion* 744
mainland 342
main-part 31, 50
mainpernor 771
main-spring 153,
  633
mainstay
  *support* 215
  *refuge* 666
  *hope* 858
maintain
  *permanence* 141
  *continue* 143
  *sustain* 170
  *support* 215
  *assert* 535
  *preserve* 670
  – one's course
  *persevere* 604*a*
  – the even tenor of
  one's way 623
  – one's ground 717
maintenance
  [*see* maintain]
  *assistance* 707
  *wealth* 803
maintien 692
maison de santé
  662
maisonette 189
maître: coup de –
  *goodness* 648
  *skill* 698
  l'œil de – 459
majesté, lèse– 742
majestic 873, 882
majesty *king* 745
  *rank* 873
  *deity* 976
major *greater* 33
  *officer* 745
  –domo
  *director* 694
  *retainer* 746
  –general 745
  – key 413
  – part *great* 31
  *all* 50
majority
  *superiority* 33

*multitude* 102
  *age* 131
  join the – 360
majuscule 561
make
  *constitute* 54, 56
  *render* 144
  *produce* 161
  *form* 240
  *arrive at* 292
  *complete* 729
  *compel* 744
  – acquainted with
  527, 539
  – after 622
  – its appearance
  446
  – away with 162,
  361
  – believe 544, 545,
  546
  – the best of 725
  – bold to differ 489
  – a date with 897
  – choice of 609
  – fast 43
  – a fool of 853
  – for 278
  – one's fortune 734
  – fun of 842, 856
  – a fuss 642, 682
  – good
  *compensation* 30
  *complete* 52, 729
  *establish* 150
  *evidence* 467
  *demonstrate* 478
  *provide* 637
  *restore* 660
  - one's escape 671
  - one's word 772
  – a go of 731
  – haste 684
  – hay while the
  sun shines 134
  – interest 765
  – known 527
  – the land 292
  – light of 483, 705,
  934
  – oneself master
  of 539
  – money 775
  – a monkey of 853
  – much of 549, 642
  – no doubt 484
  – no secret of 525
  – no sign 526, 528
  – nothing of
  *unintelligible* 519
  *not wonder* 871

marquetry 440
marquis 875
**marriage 903**
  companionate –
   903
  ill-assorted – 903
  – bells 836
  – portion 780
**marriageable** 131,
  903
**marrow** *essence* 5
  *interior* 221
  *central* 222
  chill to the – 385
**marrow-bones, on**
  **one's** –
  *submit* 725
  *beg* 765
  *humble* 879
  *servile* 886
  *atonement* 952
**marrowless** 158
**marry** *combine* 48
  *assertion* 535
  *wed* 903
  – come up
  *defiance* 715
  *anger* 900
  *censure* 932
**Mars** 722, 979
  – orange 439
**marsh 345**
**marshal**
  *arrange* 60
  *messenger* 534
  *auxiliary* 711
  *officer* 745
**Marshalsea** 752
**marsupial** 191, 366
**mart** 799
**Marte, suo** –
  *exertion* 686
  *skill* 698
**martello tower** 717
**martial** 722
  court– 966
  – law 737, 739
  *compulsory* 744
  *illegal* 964
  – music 415
**martinet** 739
**martingale** 752
**Martinmas** 998
**martyr**
  *bodily pain* 378
  *mental pain* 828
  *ascetic* 955
  – to disease 655
**martyrdom**
  *killing* 361
  *agony* 378, 828

*unselfish* 942
*punishment* 972
**marvel** 870, 872
  – whether 514
**marvellous** 31, 870
  deal in the – 549
**Masaniello** 742
**mascaro** 847
**mascot** 993
**masculine** 159, 373
**mash** *mix* 41
  *disorder* 59
  *soft* 324
  *semiliquid* 352
  *pulpify* 354
**masher** 854
**mask** *dress* 225
  *shade* 424
  *concealment* 528
  *ambush* 530
  *deceit* 545
  *shield* 717
  put on the – 544
**mason** 690
**Masorah** 985
**masque** 599
**masqué, bal** – 840
**masquerade**
  *dress* 225
  *concealment* 528
  *disguise* 530
  *frolic* 840
**mass** *quantity* 25
  *much* 31
  *whole* 50
  *heap* 72
  *size* 192
  *gravity* 319
  *density* 321
  *worship* 990
  *rite* 998
  attend – 990
  in the – 50
  – book 998
  – of society 876
**massacre** 361
**massage** 324, 331,
  379
**masse, en** – 712
**masses, the** – 876
**massive** *large* 31
  *huge* 192
  *heavy* 319
  *dense* 321
**mast** 206
**master**
  *boy* 120
  *influence* 175
  *man* 373
  *know* 490
  *understand* 518

*learn* 539
*teacher* 540
*director* 694
*proficient* 698,
  700
*succeed, conquer*
  731
*ruler* **745**
*possession* 777
*possessor* 779
*title* 877
eye of the – 693
hard – 739
past – 700
– of Arts 492
– one's feelings
  826
– hand 700
– key *open* 260
*instrument* 631
– mariner 269
– mind *sage* 500
*proficient* 700
– passion 820
– one's passions
  944
– of the position
  731
– of the revels 840
– of the Rolls 553,
  967
– of self 604
– of the situation
  731, 737
– spirit of the age
  500, 873
– of one's time 685
**masterdom** 737
**masterpiece**
  *good* 648
  *perfect* 650
  *skill* 698
**master-stroke** 626,
  731
**mastery** 731, 737
  get the – over 175
**masthead**
  *punish* 972
**mastic** *viscid* 352
  *resin* 356a
**masticate** 298
**mastiff** 366
**mat** *support* 215
  *woven* 219
  *misty* 427
  *cover* 652
**matador** 361
**match** *coincide* 13
  *similar* 17
  *copy* 19
  *equal* 27

*fuel* 388
*contest* 720
*marriage* **903**
matchless
  *supreme* 33
  *excellent* 648
  *virtuous* 944
**matchlock** 727
**mate** *similar* **17**
  *equal* 27
  *duplicate* 89
  *mariner* 269
  *auxiliary* 711
  *master* 745
  *friend* 890
  *wife* 903
  check– 732
**maté** 298
**mater alma** – 542
  –familias 166
**materia medica** 66?
**material**
  *substance* 316
  *stuff* 635
  *important* 642
  – for thought 45*
  – point 32
**materialism**
  *matter* 316
  *heterodoxy* 984
  *irreligion* 989
**materiality 316**
**materialize** 446
**materials 635**
**matériel** 633
**maternal**
  *parental* 166
  *benevolent* 906
  – love 897
**maternity** 166
**mathematical**
  *precise* 494
  – point 193
**mathematics** 25
**mathesis** 25
**matin** 125
**matinée** 892
**matins** 990
**matrass** 191
**matriarch** 11, 166
**matriarchate** 737
**matriculate** 86
**matriculation** 539
**matrilinear** 11, 166
**matrimony**
  *mixture* 41
  *wedlock* 903
**matrix** *mould* 22
  *workshop* 691
**matron** 374, 903
**matronly** 128, **131**

matross 726
matter *substance* 3
*material world* 316
*topic* 454
*meaning* 516
*type* 591
*business* 625
*importance* 642
*pus* 653
no – 460
what – 643
what's the – 455, 461
– of course
*conformity* 82
*certain* 474
*habitual* 613
– in dispute 461
– of fact *event* 151
*certainty* 474
*truth* 494
*language* 576
*artless* 703
*dull* 843
– in hand 454, 625
– of indifference 866
– nothing 643
mattock 253
mattress 215
mature *old* 124
*adolescent* 131
*conversion* 144
*scheme* 626
*perfect* 650
*improve* 658
*prepare* 673
*complete* 729
– thought 451
maturely consid-
ered 611
maturine 996
maturity [*see* mature]
bring to – 729
matutinal 125
matzoon 298
maudlin
*inactive* 683
*drunk* 959
maugre 30
maukin 652
maul *hammer* 276
*hurt* 649
maulstick 215
maund *basket* 191
*mumble* 583
maunder
*diffuse style* 573
*mumble* 583

*talk* 584
*lament* 839
maundy
– money 784
– Thursday 988
Mauser rifle 727
mausoleum 363
mauvais
– goût 851
– quart d'heure 828
– sujet 949
– ton 851
mauvaise:
– honte
*affectation* 855
*modesty* 881
– plaisanterie 851
mauve 437
maw 191
mawkish 391
Mawworm
*deceiver* 548
*sham piety* 988
maxim 80, **496**
Maxim gun 727
maximal 33
maximalist 742
maximum 33, 210
maxixe 840
may be 470
as it – 156
May-day 138, 840
May-fly 111
mayhap 470
mayonnaise 298
mayor 745, 965
maypole 206
May-queen 847
mazard 298
maze
*disorder* 59
*convolution* 248
*enigma* 533
*difficulty* 704
in a –
*uncertain* 475
mazed 503
mazurka 840
me 317
me judice 484
meâ culpâ 950
mead *plain* 344
*sweet* 396
meadow *plain* 344
*grass* 367
– land 371
meagre *small* 32
*incomplete* 53
*thin* 203
– *style* 575

*scanty* 640
*poor* 643
– diet 956
meal *repast* 298
*powder* 330
mealy-mouthed
*falsehood* 544
*servile* 886
*flattering* 933
mean *average* **29**
*small* 32
*middle* 68, 228
*signify* 516
*intend* 620
*contemptible* 643
*stingy* 819
*shabby* 874
*ignoble* 876
*sneaking* 886
*base* 940
*selfish* 943
golden – 174
take the – 774
– nothing 517
– parentage 876
– time 114
– wretch 949
meander
*convolution* 248
*deviate* 279
*circuition* 311
*river* 348
– around Robin
Hood's barn 279
meandering
*diffuse* 573
meanest capacity 499
intelligible to the
– 518
meaning **516**
meaningless 517
means
*appliances* **632**
*property* 780
*wealth* 803
by all – 602
by any – 632
by no – 536
– of access 627
meantime 106
meanwhile 106
measurable 466
within – distance 470
measure *extent* 25
*degree* 26
*moderation* 174
*music* 413
*compute* 466
*verse* 597

*proceeding* 626
*action* 680
*apportion* 786
angular – 244
full – 639
out of – 641
without – 641
– of inclination 217
measured
*moderate* 174
*sufficient* 639
*temperate* 953
measureless 105
measurement 25, **466**
measures
have no – with 713
take – *plan* 626
*prepare* 673
*conduct* 692
– of length 200
meat 298
broken – 645
one man's – is
another man's
poison 15
mechanic 690
mechanical 601, 633
– warfare 722
– powers 633
mechanician 690
mechanism 633
medal
*record* 551
*sculpture* 557
*palm* 733
*decoration* 877
– of Honor 733
medallion 557
medallist 700
meddle 682
médecin tant pis 837
médecine expec-
tante 133, 662
Medes and Per-
sians, law of the
– 80, 141
mediæval 124
mediævalism 122
medial 29, 68
median 228
mediant 413
medias res, in – 68
plunge – 300, 576
mediation—*instru-
mentality* 631
*intercession* **724**
*deprecation* 766

| | | | |
| --- | --- | --- | --- |
| *Christ* 976 | unable to make | meliora, spero – | – book 505, 551 |
| mediator 711 | both ends – | 858 | *compendium* 596 |
| **Mediator** | *poverty* 804 | meliorate 658 | memorial |
| *Saviour* 976 | *not pay* 808 | meliorism 658 | *record* 551 |
| medical 662 | – with attention | melius inquiren- | memorialist 553 |
| medicament 662 | 457 | dum, ad – 658 | memorialize 505 |
| medicaster 548 | – one's death 360 | melliferous | memorials 594 |
| medicate | – the ear 418 | *sweet* 396 | memoriam, in – |
| *compound* 41 | – one at every | mellifluous | 363, 505 |
| *heal* 660 | turn | *music* 413 | memory **505** |
| medicine 662 | *present* 186 | - *language* 578 | *fame* 873 |
| – man 994 | *redundant* 641 | mellow | failing – 506 |
| medico 662 | – one's expenses | *old* 128 | short – 506 |
| mediety 68 | 817 | *grow into* 144 | in the – of man |
| mediis rebus, in – | – the eye 446 | *soft* 324 | 122 |
| 682 | – in front 861 | *sound* 413 | – runneth not to |
| medio tutissimus, | – half way | *colour* 428 | the contrary |
| in – 864 | *willing* 602 | *improve* 658 | 124 |
| mediocritas, | *concord* 714 | *prepare* 673 | mem-sahib 374 |
| aurea – 628 | *pacification* 723 | *tipsy* 959 | menace 909 |
| mediocrity | *mediation* 724 | melodeon 417 | ménage 692 |
| *average* 29 | *compromise* 774 | melodious 413 | menagerie |
| *smallness* 32 | *friendship* 888 | melodist 416 | *collection* 72 |
| *imperfect* 651 | *benevolence* 906 | melodrama 599, | *animals* 370 |
| - *of fortune* **736** | – hand to hand | 824 | *store* 636 |
| meditate *think* 451 | 720 | melody **413** | mend 658, 660 |
| *purpose* 620 | – one's wishes | Melpomene 599 | – one's manners |
| mediterranean 68, | *consent* 762 | melt *convert* 144 | 894 |
| 228 | *pleasurable* 829 | *liquefy* 335 | mendacity 544 |
| medium *mean* 29 | – with *event* 151 | *fuse* 384 | mendicancy 765, |
| *middle* 68 | *find* 480a | *pity* 914 | 804 |
| *atmosphere* 227 | meeting [*see* meet] | – in the air 405 | mendicant |
| *intermediary* 228 | *junction* 43 | – away | *beggar* 767 |
| *colour* 428 | hostile – 720 | *cease to exist* 2 | *poor* 804 |
| *oracle* 513 | place of – 74 | *unsubstantial* 4 | *monk* 996 |
| *impostor* 548 | meeting-house | *decrease* 36 | menhir 363 |
| *instrument* 631 | *hall* 189 | *disappear* 111, | menial 746, 876 |
| *seer* 994 | *chapel* 1000 | 449 | meniscus 245, 445 |
| transparent – 425 | megacosm 318 | *waste* 638 | mens sana 502 |
| medley 41, 59 | megalomania 482, | – the heart 914 | – in corpore sano |
| *music* 415 | 504 | – into one 48 | 827 |
| chance – 156 | megaphone 404, | – into tears 839 | mens sibi conscia |
| medullary 324 | 418 | melting-pot 691 | recti 878 |
| **Medusa** 860 | megascope 445 | member *part* 51 | mensâ et thoro, |
| meed | megatherium 124 | *component* 56 | separatio a – |
| *apportion* 786 | **Megæra** 173, 900 | *councillor* 696 | 905 |
| *reward* 973 | megrims *fits* 315 | membrane 204 | menses 299 |
| - of praise 931 | *melancholy* 837 | même, quand – 708 | menstrual 138 |
| meek 826, 879 | mehari 271 | memento 505 | menstruum 335 |
| meerschaum 392 | **Mein Herr** 877 | – mori 363, 837 | mensuration 466 |
| meet *agreement* 23 | meister-singer 597 | meminisse juvabit | mental 450 |
| *assemble* 72 | melancholia | 505 | – calm 826 |
| *touch* 199 | *insanity* 503 | memoir 594, 595 | – excitement 824 |
| *converge* 290 | *dejection* 837 | memorabilia | – pabulum 454 |
| *arrive* 292 | melancholy 830, | *reminiscences* 505 | – philosophy 450 |
| *expedient* 646 | 837 | *important* 642 | – reservation 528 |
| *fulfil* 772 | away with – 836 | memorable 642 | – suffering 828 |
| *proper* 924 | mélange 41 | memorandum | menteur à triple |
| make both ends – | mêlée *disorder* 59 | *memory* 505 | étage 548 |
| *wealth* 803 | *contention* 720 | *record* 551 | menticulture 658 |
| *economy* 817 | melinite 727 | *plan* 626 | mention 527 |

above –ed 104
not worth –ing 643
mentis gratissimus
   error 481
mentor *sage* 500
   *teacher* 540
   *adviser* 695
menu 86, 298
Mephistopheles
   980
Mephistophelian
   945
mephitic˜401, 657
mephitis 663
meracious 392
mercantile 794
mercatoria, lex –
   963
mercature 794
mercenary
   *soldier* 726
   *servant* 746
   *price* 812
   *parsimonious* 819
   *selfish* 943
mercer 225
merchandise 798
merchant 797
merchantman 273
merciful 914
merciless 914*a*
mercurial
   *changeable* 149
   *mobile* 264
   *quick* 274
   *excitable* 825
Mercury 979
   *traveller* 268
   *quick* 274
   *messenger* 534
mercy *lenity* 740
   *pity* 914
at the – of
   *liable* 177
   *subject* 749
cry you – 766
have at one's –
   919
have no – 914*a*
– on us! 870
for –'s sake 765
– seat 966
mere *simple* 32
   *lake* 343
   *trifling* 643
– nothing
   *small* 32
   *trifle* 643
buy for a – noth-
   ing 815
– pretext 617

– words 477
– wreck 659
merelles 840
meretricious
   *false* 495
   *vulgar* 851
   *licentious* 961
merfolk 980
merge *combine* 48
   *include* 76
   *insert* 300
   *plunge* 337
– in 56
– into *become* 144
merged 228
meridian
   *region* 181
   *room* 125
   *summit* 210
   *light* 420
– of life 131
merit
   *goodness* 648
   *due* 924
   *virtue* 944
make a – of 884
– *notice* 642
merito, e – 944
meritorious 931
Merlin 994
mermaid 341
   *monster* 83
   *mythology* 979,
   980
merman 341
mero motu, ex –
   600
merriment
   *cheerful* 836
   *amusement* 840
merry *cheerful* 836
   *drunk* 959
make – *sport* 840
make – with
   *wit* 842
   *ridicule* 856
wish a – Christmas
   &c. 896
– and wise 842
merry-andrew 844
merry-go-round
   312, 840
merry-making 827,
   840, 892
merry-thought 842
mersion 337
meruit ferat, pal-
   mam qui – 873
merveille, à – 731
mesa 344
mésalliance 24, 903

meseems 484
mesh 198, 219
meshes *trap* 545
   *difficulty* 704
– of sophistry 477
meshwork 219
mesial
   *middle* 68
mesmerism 992
mesmerist 994
mesne lord 779
mess *mixture* 41
   *disorder* 59
   *barracks* 191
   *meal* 298
   *difficulty* 704
   *portion* 786
make a –
   *unskilful* 699
   *fail* 732
message
   *intelligence* 532
   *command* 741
Messalina 962
messenger 271
   *envoy* 534
   *servant* 746
– balloon 463
Messiah 976
messianic 976
messmate 890
messuage 189
messy 59
metabolism 140
metacentre 222
metachronism 115
metage 466
metagenesis 140
metagrammatism
   561
metal 635
   Brittania – 545
metallic *sound* 410
metalepsis 521
metallurgy 358
metamorphosis 140
metaphor
   *comparison* 464
   *figure* 521
   (*analogy* 17)
metaphrase 522
metaphrast 524
metaphrastic 516
metaphysics 450
metastasis, meta-
   thesis
   *change* 140
   *inversion* 218
   *displacement* 270
mete *measure* 466
   *distribute* 786

– out *give* 784
metempsychosis
   140
meteor 318, 423
meteoric 173, 420
meteorology 338
meteoromancy 511
meter 466
metheglin 396
methinks 484
method *order* 58
   *way* 627
want of – 59
methodical 60
Methodist 984
methodist
   *journalist* 988
methodize 60
Methuselah 130
old as – 124
since the days of –
   124
methylated spirit
   388
meticulous 772
métier 625
métis 83
metonymy 521
metoposcopy
   *front* 234
   *appearance* 448
   *interpret* 522
metre
   *length* 200
   *poetry* 597
metrical
   *measured* 466
   *verse* 597
metrology 466
   *moderation* 174
   *mid-course* 628
metropolis 189
metropolitan
   *archbishop* 996
mettle *spirit* 820
   *courage* 861
man of – 861
on one's –
   *resolved* 604
put on one's –
   *excite* 824
   *encourage* 861
mettlesome
   *energetic* 171
   *sensitive* 822
   *excitable* 825
   *brave* 861
mettre de l'eau
   dans son vin 160
meum et tuum 780

disregard distinction between – 791
mew *moult* 226
  *cry* 412
  – up 751
mewed up 229
mewl 412
mews 189
mezzanine floor 191, 599
mezzo rilievo
  *convex* 250
  *sculpture* 557
mezzo termine
  *middle* 68
  *mid-course* 628
  *compromise* 774
Mezzofanti 492
mezzosoprano 416
mezzotint 420, 558
miasm 663
mica 425
micacious 204
mi-carême 840
Micawber 460
Michael 977
Michaelmas 998
Micomicon 515
microbe 193
microcosm 193
micrography 193, 441
micrometer 193
micro-organism 193
microphone 418
microscope 193, 445
microscopic 32, 193
mid 68
Midas 803
mid-course 628
mid-day 125
midden 653
middle - *in degree* 29
  - *in order* 68
  - *in space* 222, 228
  – classes 736
  – constriction 203
  – course 29, 628
  – man *director* 694
    *agent* 758
  – point 29
  – term 68
    *compromise* 774
middlemost 222
middling 29, 32, 68, 651
middy 225, 269

midge 193
midget 193
midland 342
midnight *night* 126
  *dark* 421
  – oil 539, 689
mid-progress 282
midriff 68, 228
midshipman 269, 745
midships 68
midst - *in order* 68
  *central* 222
  *interjacent* 228
  in the – of
    *mixed with* 41
    *doing* 680
midsummer **125**
  – day 138
midway 68
midwife
  *instrument* 631
  *remedy* 662
  *auxiliary* 711
midwifery 161, 662
mien 448, 692
miff 900
might *power* 157
  *violence* 173
  *energy* 686
mightily 31
mighty *much* 31
  *strong* 159
  *large* 192
  *haughty* 878
migraine 378
migrate 266, 295
mikado 745
milch cow
  *productive* 168
  *animal* 366
  *store* 636
mild *moderate* 174
  *warm* 382
  *insipid* 391
  *lenient* 740
  *calm* 826
  *courteous* 894
mildew 653, 663
mildewed
  *spoiled* 659
mile 200
milestone 550
  whistle jigs to a – 645
milieu, juste – 174, 628
militant 722
  church – 983a
military
  *warfare* 722

*soldiers* 726
  – authorities 745
  – band 417
  – power 737
  – time 132
  – train 726
militate against 708
militia 726
milk *moderate* 174
  *semiliquid* 352
  *cows* &c. 370
  *white* 430
  *mild* 740
  – a he-goat into a sieve 471
  flow with – and honey *plenty* 639
  *prosperity* 734
  *pleasant* 829
  – of human kindness 906
  – the ram 645
  – and water
    *weak* 160
    *insipid* 391
    *unimportant* 643
    *imperfect* 651
milk-livered 862
milksop
  *incapable* 158
  *fool* 501
  *coward* 862
milky [*see* milk]
  *semitransparent* 427
  *whiteness* 430
  – way 318
mill 330
  *notch* 257
  *machine* 633
  *workshop* 691
  *fight* 720
  like a horse in a – 312
millennium
  *number* 98
  *period* 108
  *futurity* 121
  *utopia* 515
  *hope* 858
millesimal 99
millet seed 193
milliard 98
milliner 225
  man – 854
millinery *dress* 225
  *ornament* 847
  *display* 882
  man – 855
million 98

*multitude* 102
  *people* 372
  *populace* 876
  for the –
    *intelligible* 518
    *easy* 705
  –s *money* 800
millionaire 803
mill-pond *level* 213
  *pond* 343
  *store* 636
mime 19, 599, 844
mimeograph 19
mimeotype 19
mimic 19
mimodrama 599
minacity 909
minaret 206
minatory 668
minauderie 855
mince *cut up* 44
  *slow* 275
  *food* 298
  *stammer* 583
  *affected* 855
  *extenuate* 937
  – the matter 868
  not – the matter
    *affirm* 535
    *artless* 703
  – the truth 544
mincemeat of
  make – 162
mincing 855
  – steps 275
mind *intellect* 450
  *attend to* 457
  *take care* 459
  *believe* 484
  *remember* 505
  *will* 600
  *willing* 602
  *purpose* 620
  *warning* 668
  *desire* 865
  *dislike* 867
  bear in – 451, 457
  bit of one's – 527
  food for the – 454
  give the – to 457
  have a – 602, 865
  in the –
    *thought* 451
    *topic* 454
    *willing* 602
  make up one's – 484, 604
  never – *neglect* 460
    *unimportant* 643
  not – 866
  out of – 506

set one's – upon
604
speak one's – 582,
703
to one's – *taste* 850
*love* 897
willing – 602
– one's book 539
~ one's business
456, 457
– at ease 826
make one's – easy
826
–'s eye 515
– what one is
about 864
minded 602, 620
mindful 457, 505
mindless
  *inattentive* 458
  *imbecile* 499
  *forgetful* 506
  *insensible* 823
mine
  *sap* 162
  *hollow* 252
  *open* 260
  *snare* 545
  *store* 636
  *abundance* 639
  *damage* 659
  *attack* 716
  *defence* 717
  *explosive* 727
dig a – *plan* 626
*prepare* 673
spring a –
  *unexpected* 508
  *attack* 716
– of information
700
–layer 726
–sweeper 726
–thrower 727
– of wealth 803
miner 252
sapper and – 726
mineral 358
– oil 356
mineralogy 358
Minerva 979
– invita 603, 704
– press 577, 594
mingle 41
miniature *small* 193
  *portrait* 556
– painter 559
Minié rifle 727
minikin 193
minim *small* 32
  *music* 413

minimize 36, 483,
934
minimum *small* 32
  *inferior* 34
minion 899
  *type* 591
minister *instru-*
  *mentality* 631
  *remedy* 662
  *director* 694
  *aid* 707
  *deputy* 759
  *give* 784
  *clergy* 996
  *rites* 998
– to 746
ministerial
  *clerical* 995
ministering spirit
977
ministration
  *direction* 693
  *aid* 707
  *rite* 998
ministry
  *direction* 693
  *aid* 707
  *church* 995
  *clergy* 996
miniver 223
minnesinger 597
minnow 193
minor *inferior* 34
  *infant* 129
– key 413
Minorites 996
minority *few* 103
  *youth* 127
Minos 694
minotaur 83
minster 1000
minstrel 416, 597
minstrelsy 415
mint *mould* 22
  *workshop* 691
  *wealth* 803
– of money 800
minuend 38
minuet 415, 840
minus *less* 34
  *subtracted* 38
  *absent* 187
  *deficient* 304
  *loss* 776
  *in debt* 806
  *non-payment* 808
minuscule 561
minute
– *in degree* 32
– *of time* 108
  *instant* 113

– *in size* 193
  *record* 551
  *compendium* 596
to the – 132
– account 594
– attention 457
minuteness
  *care* 459
minutiæ 32, 79, 643
minx 887, 962
mirabile
– *dictu* &c. 870
mirabilis, annus –
872
miracle 83, 872
– play 599
miraculous 870
mirage 443
mire 653
mirror *imitate* 19
  *reflector* 445
  *perfection* 650
  *glory* 873
hold up the – 525
hold the – up to
nature 554
magic – 443
mirth 836
misacceptation 523
misadventure 735
misadvised 699
misanthropy **911**
misapply
  *misinterpret* 523
  *misuse* 679
  *mismanage* 699
misapprehend 495,
523
misappropriate 679
misarrange 61
misbecome 925
misbegotten 243,
945
misbehave 851, 945
misbehaviour 895,
947
misbelief 485
misbeliever 487,
984
miscalculate
  *misjudge* 481
  *err* 495
  *disappoint* 509
miscall 565
miscarry 732
miscegenation 41
miscellany
  *mixture* 41
  *collection* 72
  *generality* 78
  *compendium* 596

mischance 619, 735
mischief 619
do – 649
make – 649
mischief-maker
913, 941
miscible 41
miscite 544
miscompute 481,
495
misconceive 495,
523
misconduct 699,
947
– oneself 945
misconjecture 481
misconstrue 523
miscorrect 538
miscount 495
miscreance 485
miscreant 949
miscreated 945
misdate 115
misdeed 947
misdemean 945
misdemeanant 949
misdemeanour 947
misdevotion 988
misdirect 538, 699
misdo 945
misdoing 947
misdoubt 485, 523
mise en scène
  *appearance* 448
  *drama* 599
  *display* 882
misemploy 679
miser 819
–'s hoard 800
miserabile dictu 839
miserable *small* 32
  *contemptible* 643
  *unhappy* 828
miserably 31
miserere 215
*sing* – 950
misericordiam,
argumentum ad
– 914
miseries of human
life 828
miseris succurrere
disco 914
miserly 819
misery 828
put out of one's –
914
misestimate
  *misjudge* 481
misfeasance 699,
947

misfit 24
misfortune
 *adversity* 735
 *unhappiness* 830
misgiving 485, 860
misgovern 699
misguide 495, 538
misguided 699
mishap *evil* 619
 *failure* 732
 *misfortune* 735
 *painful* 830
Mishna 985
misinform 538
misinformed 491
misinstruct 538
misintelligence 538
misinterpretation
 **523**
misjoined 24
misjudgment
 *sophistry* 477
 *misjudge* **481**
 *misinterpretation*
 523
mislay *derange* 61
 *lose* 776
mislead *error* 495
 *misteach* 538
 *deceive* 545
mislike 867
mismanage 699
mismatch 15, 24
misname 565
misnomer **565**
misogamist 904
misogynist 911
misogyny 904
mispersuasion 538
misplace
 *derange* 61
misplaced
 *intrusive* 24
 *unconformable* 83
 *displaced* 185
misprint 495
misprision
 *concealment* 528
 *guilt* 947
 − of treason 742
misprize 483, 929
mispronounce 583
misproportioned
 243, 846
misquote 544
misreckon 481, 495
misrelish 867
misreport 495, 544
misrepresent
 *misinterpret* 523
 *misteach* 538

*lie* 544
misrepresentation
 **555**
 *untruth* 544, 546
misrule
 *misconduct* 699
 *laxity* 738
 Lord of − 701
miss *girl* 129
 *neglect* 460
 *error* 495
 *unintelligible* 519
 *fail* 732
 *lose* 776
 *want* 865
 *courtesan* 962
 − one's aim 732
 − fire 732
 − stays 304
 − one's way
 *uncertain* 475
 *unskilful* 699
missa cantata 998
missal 998
missay 563, 583
missend 699
misshapen 243, 846
missile 727
missing
 *non-existent* 2
 *absent* 187
 *disappear* 449
 − link 53, 83, 729
mission 625, 755
missionary 540, 996
missive 592
misspell 523
misspend 818
misstate 495, 544
misstatement 495,
 546
mist 353, 424
 in a − 528
 seen through a −
 519
 −s of error 495
 − before the eyes
 443
mistake *error* 495
 *misconstrue* 523
 *mismanage* 699
 *failure* 732
 never was a
 greater − 536
misteaching **538**
mister 373
misterm 565
misthink 481
mistime 135
mistral 349
mistranslate 523

mistress *lady* 374
 *master* 745
 *possessor* 779
 *title* 877
 *love* 897
 *concubine* 962
mistrust 485
misty [see mist]
 *semi-transparent*
 427
misunderstand
 *misinterpret* 523
misunderstanding
 495, 713
misuse **679**
mite *bit* 32
 *small* 193
 *insufficiency* 640
 *money* 800
 little − 129
Mithridate 662
mitigate *abate* 174
 *improve* 658
 *relieve* 834
mitigation
 [see mitigate]
 *extenuation* 937
mitraille 727
mitrailleur 727
mitre *junction* 43
 *angle* 244
 *crown* 747, 999
mitten 225
mittimus 741
mix 41
 − oneself up with
 *meddle* 682
 *co-operate* 709
 − with 720
mixen 653
mixture 41
 mere − 59
mix-up 59
mizzen 235
mizzle 348
mnemonics 505
Mnemosyne 505
moa 366
moan 405
 *cry* 411
 *lament* 839
moat *enclosure* 232
 *ditch* 259
 *canal* 350
 *defence* 717
mob *crowd* 72
 *multitude* 102
 *vulgar* 876
 *hustle* 929
 *scold* 932
 king − 876

 − cap 225
 − law
 *authority* 737
 *illegality* 964
mobile
 *inconstant* 149
 *movable* 264
 *sensitive* 822
mobility, the − 876
mobilize
 *assemblage* 72
 *render movable*
 264
 − troops 722
mobocracy 737
mobster 361
moccasin 225
mock *imitate* 17, 19
 *repeat* 104
 *erroneous* 495
 *deceptive* 545
 *chuckle* 838
 *ridicule* 856
 *disrespect* 929
 − danger 861
 − modesty 855
 − sun 423
mockery
 [see mock]
 *unsubstantial* 4
solemn − 882
 − delusion and
 snare
 *sophistry* 477
 *deception* 545
mocking-bird 19
modal 6, 7, 8
mode *state* 7
 *music* 413
 *habit* 613
 *method* 627
 *fashion* 852
 − of expression 560
mode, à la − 852
model *copy* 21
 *prototype* 22
 *rule* 80
 *form* 240
 *representation*
 554
 *sculpture* 557
 *perfection* 650
 *good man* 948
 new − 658
 − after 19
 − condition 80
modeller 559
moderate
 *average* 29
 *small* 32
 *allay* 174

*slow* 275
*sufficient* 639
*cheap* 815
*temperate* 953
– circumstances
*mediocrity* 736
modera*t*ely
*imperfect* 651
moderation [*see*
moderate] 174
*mid-course* 628
*inexcitability* 826
moderato *music*
415
moderator 174
*lamp* 423
*director* 694
*mediator* 724
*judge* 967
modern 123
*music* 415
*art* 556
modest *small* 32
modesty
*humility* 881
*purity* 960
mock – 855
modicum *little* 32
*allotment* 786
modification
*difference* 15
*variation* 20a
*change* 140
*qualification* 469
modish 852
modulation
*variation* 20a
*change* 140
*music* 413
module 22
modulus 84
modus: – operandi
*method* 627
*conduct* 692
– in rebus 174
– vivendi 723
mogul 745
Mohammedan 984
Mohawk
*swaggerer* 887
*evil-doer* 913
moider 458, 475
moiety 51, 91
moil *active* 682, 686
*exertion* 686
moisture *wet* 337
*humid* 339
mokes 219
molar 330
molasses 396
mole *mound* 206

*prominence* 250
*colour* 432
*refuge* 666
*defence* 717
*spot* 848
molecular 32
molecule 193
molehill *little* 193
*low* 207
*trifling* 643
molest *trouble* 830
molestation
*damage* 649
*malevolence* 907
mollia tempora 134
– fandi 588
mollify *allay* 174
*soften* 324
mollusk 366
mollycoddle 158
Molly Maguire 548
Moloch
*slaughter* 361
*demon* 980
*heathen deity* 986
molten 384
moment
- *of time* 113
*importance* 642
for the – 111
lose not a – 684
not have a – 682
on the spur of the
– 612
momentous 152
momentum 276
Momus 838
monachism 995
monad 193
monarch 745
monarchy 737
monastery 1000
monastic 995
monasticism 984
monetary 800
– arithmetic 11
money 800
*wealth* 803
bad – 800
command of – 803
for one's – 609
made of – 803
make – 775
raise – 788
save – 817
throw away one's
– 818
– to burn 641, 803
– burning one's
pocket 818
– coming in 810

– down 807
– going out 809
– market 800
– matters 811
– paid 809
–'s worth
*useful* 644
*price* 812
*cheap* 815
money-bag 800,
802
money-belt 802
money-broker 797
money-changer
797, 801
moneyed 803
moneyer 797
money-grubbing
775
moneyless 804
monger 797
mongrel
*mixture* 41
*anomalous* 83
*dog* 366
*base* 949
moniker 565
moniliform 249
monism 984
monition 527, 668
*information* 527
*warning* 668
monitor *hear* 418
*oracle* 513
*pupil-teacher* 540
*director* 694
*adviser* 695
*war-ship* 726
inward – 926
monitory
*prediction* 511
*dissuasion* 616
*warning* 668
monk 996
monkey
*imitative* 19
*support* 215
*catapult* 276
*ridiculous* 857
play the – 499
–jacket 225
– trick
*absurdity* 497
*sport* 840
– up 900
monkhood 995
monkish Latin 563
monochord 417
monochrome 429,
556
monocracy 737

monoculous 443
monode 445
monodrame 599
monody 597, 839
monogamist 904
monogamy 903
monogram
*sign* 550
*cipher* 533
*diagram* 554
*letter* 561
monograph
*publication* 531
*writing* 590
*book* 593
*description* 594
monolith 551
monolithic 983a
monologue
*soliloquy* 589
*drama* 599
monomachy 720
monomania 503
*obstinacy* 606
*fanaticism* 825
monomaniac 504
monomark 550
monoplane 273
monopolist 943
monopoly
*restraint* 751
*possession* 777
monostich 572
monosyllable 561
monotheism 983
monotonous
*uniform* 16
*equal* 27
*repetition* 104
*permanent* 141
- *style* 575
*weary* 841
*dull* 843
monotype 591
monsoon 349
monsieur 373
monster
*exception* 83
*large* 192
*ugly* 846
*prodigy* 872
*evil-doer* 913
*ruffian* 949
monstrance 998
monstrosity
[*see* monster]
*distortion* 243
monstrous
*excessive* 31
*exceptional* 83
*huge* 192

at – 32
make the – of
 *over-estimate* 482
 *exaggerate* 549
 *improve* 658
 *use* 677
 *skill* 698
the – 33
– often 136
for the – part 78,
 613
make the – of
 one's time 682
**mot** 496
– de l'énigme 522
– du guet 550
– à mot 19
– d'ordre 741
– de passe 550
– pour rire 842
**mote** *small* 32
 *light* 320
– in the eye
 *dim-sighted* 443
 *misjudging* 481
**motet** 990
**moth** *bane* 663
**moth-eaten** 124,
 653, 659
**mother** *parent* 166
 *mould* 653
– country 189
– of-pearl 440
– superior 996
– tongue 560
– wit 498
**motherly** *love* 897
 *kind* 906
**motif** 415, 847
**motile** 264
**motion**
 *change of place*
 264
 *topic* 454
 *plan* 626
 *proposal* 763
 *request* 765
make a – 763
put in – 284
put oneself in –
 680
set in – 677
– downwards 306
– from
 *recession* 287
 *repulsion* 289
– into *ingress* 294
 *reception* 296
– out of 295
– through 302
– towards

*approach* 286
*attraction* 288
– upwards 305
**motionless** 265
**motive** 615
 absence of – **615a**
 – power 264
**motivity** 264
**motley** 81, 440
 wearer of the – 844
**motor** 153, 266
 *vehicle* 271, 272
 *instrument* 633
 –boat 273
 –car &c. 272
 –driver 268
 –man 694
**motorist** 268
**motory** 264
**mottled** 440
**motto** *maxim* 496
 *device* 550
 *phrase* 566
**motu: ex mero –**
 737
 suo – 600
**mouchard** 527
**mould** *condition* 7
 *matrix* 22
 *convert* 144
 *form* 240
 *structure* 329
 *earth* 342
 *vegetation* 367
 *model* 554
 *carve* 557
 *decay* 653
 *turn to account*
 677
**moulded** 820
– on 19
**moulder** 653, 659
**moulding** 847
**mouldy** 653, 659
**moulin:**
 se battre contre
 des –s 645
– à paroles 584
**moult** 226
**mound** *large* 192
 *hill* 206
 *defence* 717
**mount** *increase* 35
 *hill* 206
 *horse* 271
 *ascend* 305
 *raise* 307
 *display* 882
– guard *care* 459
 *safety* 664
– up to *money* 800

*price* 812
**mountain** *large* 192
 *hill* 206
 *weight* 319
– artillery 726
– in labour
 *waste* 638
make –s of mole-
 hills 482
– brought forth
 mouse
 *disappoint* 509
**mountaineer** 268
**mountainous** 206
**mountebank**
 *quack* 548
 *drama* 599
 *buffoon* 844
**mounted rifles** 726
**mourn** 828, 839
**mourner** 363
**mournful**
 *afflicting* 830
 *sad* 837
 *lamentable* 839
**mourning** *dress* 225
in – *black* 431
 *lament* 839
**mouse** *little* 193
 *search* 461
 mountain brought
 forth – 509
 not a – stirring
 265
**mouse-coloured**
 432
**mousehole** 260
**mouser** 366
**mousetrap** 545
**mousseux** 353
**moustache** 256
**mouth** *entrance* 66
 *receptacle* 191
 *brink* 231
 *opening* 260
 *eat* 298
 *estuary* 343
 *enunciate* 580
 *drawl* 583
 deep –ed
 *resonant* 408
 *bark* 412
 down in the – 879
 make –s 929
 open one's – 582
 stop one's – 581
 word of – 582
– honour
 *falsehood* 544
 *show* 882
 *flattery* 933

pass from – to
 mouth 531
– wash 652
– watering 865
**mouthful**
 *quantity* 25
 *small* 32
 *food* 298
**mouthpiece**
 *speaker* 524
 *information* 527
 *speech* 582
**mouthy** *style* 577
**moutonné** 250
**moutons, revenons**
 à nos – 660
**movable** 264, 270
**movables** 780
**move** *begin* 66
 *motion* 264
 *propose* 514
 *induce* 615
 *undertake* 676
 *act* 680
 *offer* 763
 *excite* 824
get a – on 684
 *good* – 626
on the – 293
– forward 282
– from 287
– in a groove 82
– heaven and
 earth 686
– off 293
– on *progress* 282
 *activity* 682
– out of 295
– quickly 274
– slowly 275
– to 894
**moveless** 265
**movement**
 *motion* 264
 *music* 415
 *action* 680
 *activity* 682
**moved with** 821
**mover** 164
**movies** 448, 599,
 840
**movie star** 899
**moving**
 keep – 682
 self – 266
– pictures 448
**mow** *shorten* 201
 *smooth* 255
 *agriculture* 371
 *store* 636
– down

**narrow-minded** 481, 943
**narrowness** 203
**narrows** 343
**nasal accent** 583
**nascent** 66
**nascitur:** – ridiculus mus 509
– a sociis 82
**naso, omnia suspendens** – 868
**nasty**
*unsavoury* 395
*foul* 653
*offensive* 830
cheap and – 815
**natâ, pro re** – 770
**natal** *birth* 66
*indigenous* 188
**natation** 267
**natatorium** 652
**nathless** 30
**nation** 372
**national** 188, 372
– guard 726
**nationality** 372, 910
**nations, law of** 963
**native**
*inhabitant* 188
*artless* 703
– accent 580
– land 189
– soil 189
– tongue 560
**nativity** *birth* 66
cast a –
*predict* 511
*sorcery* 992
**natty** 845
**natura il fece e poi roppe la stampa** 87
**naturæ, vis medicatrix** – 662
**natural** *intrinsic* 5
*musical note* 413
*true* 494
*fool* 501
– *style* 576, 578
*spontaneous* 612
*not prepared* 674
*artless* 703
*simple* 849
– course of things 613
– death *death* 360
*completion* 729
– impulse 601
– meaning 516
– order of things 82

– state 80
– turn 820
**Natural** – History 357
– Philosophy 316
– Theology 983
**naturalist** 357
**naturalization**
*conformity* 82
*conversion* 144
*location* 184
**naturalize**
*habit* 613
**naturalized**
*inhabitant* 188
**naturally** 154
**nature** *essence* 5
*rule* 80
*tendency* 176
*world* 318
*reality* 494
*artlessness* 703
*affections* 820
animated – 357
organized – 357
second – 613
state of –
*naked* 226
*raw* 674
in –'s garb 226
**naught** *nothing* 4
*zero* 101
bring to – 732
set at –
*make light of* 483
*opposition* 708
*disobey* 742
*not observe* 773
*disrespect* 929
*contempt* 930
**naughty** 945
**naumachia** 720
**nausea** 841, 867
**nauseate** 395, 830
**nauseous**
*unsavoury* 395
*unpleasant* 830
*disgusting* 867
**nautch dancer** 840
**nautical** 267
**naval** 267
– authorities 745
– engagement 720
– forces 726
**nave** *middle* 68
*centre* 222
*church* 1000
**navel** 68, 222
**navigation** 267
**navigator** 269
**navvy** 673, 690

**navy** 273, 726
– blue 438
**nay** 536
– rather 14
**Nazarene** 989
**naze** 250
**N.C.O.** 745
**ne plus ultra**
*supreme* 33
*complete* 52
*distance* 196
*summit* 210
*limit* 233
*perfection* 650
*completion* 729
**neaf** 781
**neap** 195, 207
– tide 36, 340
**near** *like* 17
– *in space* 197
– *in time* 121
*soon* 132
*impending* 152
*approach* 286
*stingy* 819
bring – 17
draw – 197
come – 286
– one's end 360
– at hand 132
– the mark 32
– run 32
– side 239
– sight 443
– the truth 480a
– upon 3
sail – the wind
*skilful* 698
*rash* 863
**nearly** 32
**nearness** 197
**neat** *simple* 42
*order* 58
*in writing* 572, 576, 578
*clean* 652
*spruce* 845
–'s foot oil 356
– as a pin 58
**neat-handed** 698
**neatherd** 370
**neb** 250
**nebula** *stars* 318
*mist* 353
**nebular** *dim* 422
**nebulous** *misty* 353
*obscure* 519
**necessarian** 601
**necessaries** 630
**necessarily** 154
**necessitate** 630

**necessity** *fate* 601
*requirement* 630
*compulsion* 744
*indigence* 804
make a virtue of – 698
**neck**
*contraction* 195
*narrow* 203
*make love* 902
break one's – 360
– and crop
*completely* 52
*turn out* - 297
– of land 342
– and neck 27
– or nothing
*resolute* 604
*rash* 863
**neckcloth** 225
**necklace** 247, 847
**necks** 980
**necrology** 360, 594
**necromancer** 548, 994
**necromancy** 992
**necropsy** 363
**necroscopic** 363
**necrosis** 49
**nectar** 394, 396
**need** *necessity* 601
*requirement* 630
*insufficiency* 640
*indigence* 804
*desire* 865
friend in – 711
in one's utmost – 735
**needful**
*necessary* 601
*requisite* 630
*money* 800
do the – *pay* 807
**needle** *sharp* 253
*perforator* 262
*compass* 693
as the – to the pole
*veracity* 543
*observance* 772
*honour* 939
– in a bottle of hay 475
**needle-gun** 727
**needle-shaped** 253
**needless** 641
**needle-witted** 498
**needlewoman** 690
**needlework** 847
**ne'er-do-well** 949
**nefarious** 945

**negation 536, 764**
**negative**
  *inexisting* 2
  *contrary* 14
  *prototype* 22
  *quantity* 84
  *confute* 479
  *deny* 536
  *photograph* 558
  *refuse* 764
  prove a – 468
**neglect 460**
  *disuse* 678
  *leave undone* 730
  *omit* 773
  *evade* 927
  *disrespect* 929
  – of time 115
**négligé 225, 674**
**negligence 460**
**negotiable 270**
**negotiate**
  *mediate* 724
  *bargain* 769
  *transfer* 783
  *traffic* 794
**negotiations**
  breaking off – 713
**negotiator 724, 758**
**negro 431, 746**
**negus**
  *drink* 298
  *king* 745
**neif 781**
**neigh** *cry* 412
  *boast* 884
**neighbour 197, 890**
**neighbourhood 183, 197, 227**
**neighbourly**
  *aid* 707
  *friendly* 888
  *social* 892
  *courteous* 894
**neither 610**
  – here nor there
  *irrelevant* 10
  *absent* 187
  – more nor less
  *equal* 27
  *true* 494
  – one thing nor
    another 83
**nem. con. 488**
**Nemesis**
  *vengeance* 919
  *justice* 922
  *punishment* 972
**nemine contra-**
  **dicente 488**
**nemo me impune**

**lacessit 715**
**nenia 839**
**neogamist 903**
**neologism 123**
**neology 563**
**neophyte 144, 541**
**neoteric 123**
**nepenthe 662, 836**
**nephelogy 353**
**nephew 11**
**nepotism**
  *nephew* 11
  *wrong* 923
  *dishonest* 940
  *selfish* 943
**Neptune 341**
**Nereid 341, 979**
**nerve 159, 861, 885**
  exposed – 378
**nerveless 158**
**nervous** *weak* 160
  *style* 574
  *timid* 860
  *modest* 881
**nescience 491**
**nest**
  *multitude* 102
  *cradle* 153
  *lodging* 189
  – of boxes 204
**nest-egg 636**
**nestle** *lodge* 186
  *safety* 664
  *endearment* 902
**nestling 129**
**Nestor** *veteran* 130
  *sage* 500
  *advice* 695
**net** *remainder* 40
  *receptacle* 191
  *intersection* 219
  *inclosure* 232
  *snare* 545
  *difficulty* 704
  *gain* 775
  – profit *gain* 775
  *receipt* 810
**nether 207**
**nethermost 211**
**netting 219**
**nettle** *bane* 663
  *sting* 830
  *incense* 900
**network**
  *disorder* 59
  *crossing* 219
**neuralgia 378**
**neurasthenia 655**
**neuritis 378**
**neurology 329**
**neurotic 662**

**neuter** *matter* 316
  *no choice* 609a
  remain –
  *irresolute* 605
  stand –
  *indifferent* 866
**neutral** *mean* 29
  *no choice* 609a
  *avoidance* 623
  – tint
  *colourless* 429
  *grey* 432
  *peace* 721
**neutrality**
  *mid-course* 628
  *peace* 721
  *insensibility* 823
  *indifference* 866
**neutralize**
  *compensate* 30
  *counteract* 179
**névé 383**
**never 107**
  – say die
  *persevere* 604a
  *cheerful* 836
  *hope* 858
  it will – do
  *inexpedient* 647
  *prohibit* 761
  *discontent* 832
  *disapprobation* 932
  –dying 112
  –ending 112
  –fading
  *perpetual* 112
  *glory* 873
  – forget 916
  – to be forgotten 642
  – indebted 807
  – hear the last of 841
  – mind
  *neglect* 460
  *unimportant* 643
  *insensible* 823
  *indifferent* 866
  *contempt* 930
  – more 107
  – a one 4
  – otherwise 16
  – to return 122
  – was seen the
    like 83
  – so 31
  – tell me 489
  – thought of 621
  – tired *active* 682
  – tiring

  *persevering* 604a
**neverness 107**
**nevertheless 30**
**new** *different* 18
  *additional* 37
  *novel* 123
  *unaccustomed* 614
  – birth 660
  – blood *change* 140
  *improve* 658
  *excite* 824
  – brooms 614, 682
  – comer 57
  – conditions 469
  – departure 66
  – edition
  *repetition* 104
  *reproduction* 163
  *improvement* 658
  – ideas 537
  turn over a – leaf
  *change* 140
  *repent* 950
  give – life to 707, 824
  view in a – light 658
  put on the – man 950
**New Year's Day 138**
**new-born 123, 129**
**Newcastle, carry coals to –** 641
**new-fangled**
  *unfamiliar* 83
  *change* 140
  *neology* 563
**new-fashioned 123**
**new-fledged 129**
**Newfoundland dog 366**
**Newgate 752**
**new-gilt 847**
**new-model**
  *convert* 144
  *revolutionize* 146
  *improve* 658
**newness 123**
**news 532**
  – sheet 531
**newsmonger**
  *curious* 455
  *informant* 527
  *news* 532
**newspaper 531, 551**
  – correspondent 758
**newspaperman 534**
**newt 366**

*contrary* 14
*dissimilar* 18
− surrender 606, 717
− thank you 764
at − time 107
− wonder 871
Noah's ark 41, 72
nob 210
nobilitate 873
nobility **875**
noble *great* 31
   *important* 642
   *rank* 873
   *peer* 875
   *disinterested* 942
   *virtuous* 944
noblesse 875
nobody
   *unsubstantial* 4
   *zero* 101
   *absence* 187
   *low-born* 876
− knows
   *ignorance* 491
− knows where
   *distance* 196
− present 187
− would think 508
noctambulation 266
noctivagant
   *travel* 266
   *dark* 421
noctograph 421
noctuary 421, 551
nocturnal
   *night* 126
   *dark* 421
   *black* 431
nocturne 415
nocuous 649
nod *wag* 314
   *assent* 488
   *signal* 550
   *sleep* 683
   *command* 741
   *bow* 894
− of approbation 931
− of assent 488
nodding to its fall 162, 306
noddle 210, 450
noddy 501
node 250
nodosity 250, 256
nods and becks and wreathed smiles 894
nodule 250
nodular 256

[ 572 ]

**nodus, dignus vindice** − 704
Noel 998
noggin 191
noise 402, 404
− abroad 531
make a − in the world 873
noiseless 403
noisome
   *fetid* 401
   *bad* 649
   *unhealthy* 657
nolens volens 601
noli me tangere
   *defiance* 715
   *excitable* 825
   *fastidious* 868
nolition 603
nolle prosequi 624
nolumus leges Angliæ mutari
   *permanence* 141
   *continuance* 143
   *preservation* 670
nom de: − guerre 565
− plume 565
nomad 268
nomadic 266
Nomancy 511
nomenclature **564**
nominal
   *unsubstantial* 4
   *word* 562
   *name* 564
− price 815
nomination 564, 755
nominee 758
nominis umbra 4
Nomology 963
non:
− compos mentis 503
− constat 477
− deficit alter 100
− est inventus 187
− hæc in fœdera 536, 610
− nobis Domine 990
− obstante 707
− placet 489
− possumus
   *impossible* 471
   *obstinate* 606
   *refusal* 764
− nostrum tantas componere lites 471, 713

lex − scripta 963
− semper erit æstas 111
− sequitur 70, 477, 495
− sum qualis eram 140, 160
**non-addition** 38
**non-admission** 55
nonage 127
nonagenarian 98
**non-appearance** 447
**non-assemblage 73**
**non-attendance** 187
nonce 118
for the − 118, 134
nonchalance
   *neglect* 460
   *insensibility* 823
   *indifference* 866
**non-coincidence** 14
**non-cohesive** 47
**non-com.** 726
**non-commissioned** officer 745
**non-committal** 528, 864
**non-completion 730**
**non-compliance** 742, 764
nonconformity
   *difference* 15
   *exception* 83
   *dissent* 489
   *sectarianism* 984
**non-content** 489
**non-cooperation** 489, 927
nondescript 83
none 101
− else 87
− to spare 640
− such
   *superior* 33
   *exceptional* 83
   *very good* 648
− in the world 4
− the worse 660
**non-endurance** 825
nonentity
   *inexistence* 2
   *unsubstantial* 4
   *unimportant* 643
**non-essential** 6, 643
**non-existence** 2
**non-expectance** 508
**non-extension** 180a
**non-fulfilment** 730, 732

− of one's hopes 509
**non-imitation** 20
**non-interference**
   *inaction* 681
   *freedom* 748
nonius 466
**non-juror** 489, 984
**non-naturals** 657
nonny 501
**non-observance**
   *inattention* 458
   *desuetude* 614
   *infraction* **773**
   *dereliction* 927
nonpareil 648
   *type* 591
**non-payment 808**
**non-performance**
   *non-completion* 730
   *dereliction* 927
**non-plus**
   *uncertain* 475
   *difficulty* 704
   *conquer* 731
**non-preparation** 674
**non-prevalence** 614
**non-residence** 187
**non-resistance** 725, 743
**non-resonance** 408a
nonsense
   *absurdity* 497
   *unmeaning* 517
   *trash* 643
talk − *folly* 499
**non-subsistence** 2
**non-success** 732
nonsuch [*see* none]
nonsuit *defeat* 731
   *fail* 732
   *condemn* 971
nonum prematur in annum 133
**non-uniformity** 16a
noodle 501
nook *place* 182
   *receptacle* 191
   *corner* 244
noology 450
noon *mid-day* 125
noon-day *light* 420
clear as −
   *intelligible* 518
   *manifest* 525
nooscopic 450
noose *ligature* 45
   *loop* 247

*snare* 545
*gallows* 975
**norma loquendi** 567
**normal**
 *intrinsic* 5
 *mean* 29
 *regular* 82
 *perpendicular* 212
 – condition
 *rule* 80
**normality** 80, 502
**Normand, répon-
 dre en** – 544
**Norns** 601
**North** 278
 – and South 237
**Northern** 237
 – light 423
 – star 939
**North-west
 passage** 311
**noscitur a sociis** 82
**nose** *prominence*
 250
 *smell* 398
 with one's – in
 the air 878
 lead by the – 615,
 737
 led by the – 749
 not see beyond
 one's –
 *misjudge* 481
 *folly* 499
 *unskilful* 699
 speak through
 the – 583
 thrust one's – in
 *interjacence* 228
 *busy* 682
 under one's –
 *present* 186
 *near* 197
 *manifest* 525
 *defy* 715
 put one's – out of
 joint *defeat* 731
 *disrepute* 874
 – ring 847
**nose-dive** 306
**nosegay** 400, 847
**nosey** 455
**nosology** 655
**nostalgia** 833
**nostril** 351
 breath of one's –s
 359
 stink in the –s 401
**nostrum** 626, 662
**not** *negation* 536
 what *is* – 546

what ought – 923
 – at all 32
 – allowed 964
 – amiss 618, 651,
 845
 – any 101
 – bad 651
 – bargain for 508
 – a bit 536
 – to be borne 830
 – a Chinaman's
 chance 471
 – come up to 34
 – cricket 923
 – to be despised
 642
 it will – do 923
 – of the earth 987
 – expect 508
 – fail 939
 – far from 197
 – a few 102
 – fit to be seen 846
 – following 477
 – grant 764
 – guilty 946
 – to be had 471,
 640
 – having 187, 777*a*
 – hardened 950
 – hear of 764
 – included 55
 – know what to
 make of 519
 – a leg to stand
 on 158
 – likely 473
 – a little 31
 – matter 643
 – to mention 37
 – mind 823, 930
 – often 137
 – on your life 489
 – one 101
 – a particle 4
 – particular 831
 – pay 808
 – a pin to choose
 27
 – playing the
 game 923
 – within previous
 experience 137
 – to be put down
 604
 – quite 32
 – reach 304
 – right 503
 – sorry 827
 – a soul 101
 – on speaking

terms 889
 – the thing 925
 – to be thought of
 *incogitancy* 452
 *impossible* 471
 *refusal* 764
 *hopeless* 859
 *undue* 925
 *disapprobation*
 932
 – trouble oneself
 about 460
 – understand 519
 – vote 609*a*
 – wonder 871
 – for the world
 603, 764
 – worth
 *trifling* 643
 *useless* 645
**nota bene** 457
**notabilia** 642
**notabilities** 875
**notable**
 *manifest* 525
 *important* 642
 *active* 682
 *distinguished* 873
**notables** 875
**notably** 31
**notary** 553, 968
**notation** 85
**notch** 198, **257,** 550
**note** *intellect* 450
 *music* 413
 *take cognizance*
 450
 *remark* 457
 *explanation* 522
 *sign* 550
 *record* 551
 *printing* 591
 *epistle* 592
 *minute* 596
 *money* 800
 *fame* 873
 change one's – 607
 make a – of 551
 of – 873
 take – of 457
 – of admiration
 870
 – of alarm 669
 – of preparation
 673
**note-book**
 *memorandum* 505
 *record* 551
 *compendium* 569
 *writing* 590
**noted** 490, 873

**noteworthy**
 *great* 31
 *exceptional* 83
 *important* 642
**nothing** *nihility* 4
 *zero* 101
 *trifle* 643
 come to – 304, **732**
 do – 681
 for – 815
 go for – 643
 good for – 646
 make – of
 *under-estimate*
 483
 *fail* 732
 take – by 732
 think of – 930
 worse than – 808
 – comes amiss 831
 – to do 681
 – to do with 764
 – doing 681
 – to go upon 471
 – in it 4
 – of the kind 18,
 536
 – loth 602
 – on 226
 – more to be said
 478
 – to signify 643
**nothingness** 2
**notice** *intellect* 450
 *observe* 457
 *review* 480
 *information* 527
 *warning* 668
 bring into – 525
 deserve – 642
 give –
 *manifest* 525
 *inform* 527
 *indicate* 550
 short – 111
 take – of 450
 this is to give –
 457
 worthy of – 642
 – is hereby given
 *publication* 531
 – to quit 782
**noticeable** 31
**notification** 527
**notion** *idea* 453
**notional** 515
**notoriety** 531, **873**
**notorious**
 *known* 490
 *public* 531
 *famous* 873

obdurate
*obstinate* 606
*severe* 739
*malevolent* 907
*graceless* 945
*impenitent* 951
obedience **743**
obeisance *bow* 308
*submission* 725
*courtesy* 894
*reverence* 928
obelisk 206, 551
Oberon 979
obese 194
obesity 192
obey **743**
*be subject to* 749
– a call 615
– the helm 705
– rules 82
obfuscate 421, 426
obfuscated
*drunk* 959
obit 360, 363
post – 360, 363
obiter dictum
*irrelevant* 10
*occasion* 134
*interjacent* 228
obituary 360, 594
object *thing* 3
*matter* 316
*take exception* 469
*intention* 620
*ugly* 846
*disapprove* 932
be an –
*important* 642
– to *dislike* 867
– lesson 82
objection 706, 932
no – 762
objectionable
*inexpedient* 647
*wrong* 923, 947
objective
*extrinsic* 6
*material* 316
objector
conscientious –
710
objurgate 932
oblate 201
– spheroid 249
oblation *gift* 784
*religious* - 990
obloctation 827
obligation
*necessity* 601
*promise* 768
*conditions* 770

*debt* 806
confer an – 648
feeling of – 916
under an – 916,
926
oblige *benefit* 707
*compel* 744
*duty* 926
obligé, bien –
*refusal* 764
obliged
*necessity* 601
*grateful* 916
*duty* 926
obligee 800
obliging
*helping* 707
*courteous* 894
*kind* 906
obliquation 279
obliquity
*slope* **217**
*vice* 945
– of judgment 481
– of vision 443
obliteration **552**
– of the past 506
oblivion **506**
*nothingness* 2
*pardon* 506
*forgiveness* 918
redeem from – 505
– of benefits 917
– of time 115
oblivious 506
oblong 200
– spheroid 249
obloquy
*disrepute* 874
*disapprobation*
932
*detraction* 934
obmutescence 581,
585
obnoxious
*pernicious* 649
*unpleasing* 830
*hateful* 898
– to *liable* 177
obnubilated 422
oboe 417
obreption 528
obscene 653, 961
obscurantist 421,
519, 710
obscure *dark* 421
*dim* 422
*unseen* 447
*uncertain* 475
*unintelligible* 519
*eclipse* 874

*ignoble* 876
obscurity *style* **571**
obscurum per
obscurius 519
obsecration 765
obsequies 363
obsequious
*subject* 749
*servile* 886
*courteous* 894
*respectful* 928
*flattery* 932
observance *rule* 82
*attention* 457
*habit* 613
*practice* 692
*fulfilment* **772**
*duty* 926
*rite* 998
observant
*friar* 996
observation
*intellect* 450
*idea* 453
*attention* 457
*assertion* 535
– car 272
observatory 318
observe [*see* observ-
ance, observa-
tion]
*remark* 457
– a duty 926
– rules 82
observer 444
obsess 860, 992
obsession 716
obsidional 716
obsolete *old* 124
*words* 563
*effete* 645
obstacle 179, 706
obstant, Fata – 601
obstetrician 631
obstetrics 161, 662
obstinacy **606**
*prejudice* 481
obstipation 261
obstreperous 173,
404
obstruct *close* 261
*hinder* 706
– the passage of
light 426
– the view 424
obstructive
*opponent* 710
obstruent 706
obstupefaction 823
obstupui steterunt-
que comæ 860

obtain *exist* 1
*prevail* 78
*get* 775
– under false
pretences 791
obtainable 470
obtenebration 421
obtestation 765
obtrectation 934
obtrude
*interfere* 228
*insert* 300
*meddle* 682
obtruncate 201
obtrusion 228, 706
obtrusive
*interfering* 228
*vulgar* 851
*rude* 895
obtund *mitigate* 174
*blunt* 254
*deaden* 376
*paralyze* 823
obturate 261
obturator 263
obtuse *blunt* 254
*insensible* 376
*imbecile* 499
*dull* 823
– angle 244
obtuseness 456a
obumbrate 421
obverse 234
obviate 706
obvious *visible* 446
*evident* 474
*clear* 518
*manifest* 525
ocarina 417
occasion
*juncture* 8
*opportunity* **134**
*cause* 153
befit the – 646
have – for 630
on the present –
118
on the spur of –
612
occasional 475
occasionally 136
occidental 236, 560
occiput 235
occision 361
occlusion 261
*unintelligible* 919
*latent* 526
*hidden* 528
– art 992
occultism 984
occultation 449, 528

occupancy 186, 777
occupant 188, 779
occupation
  *business* 625
  in the – of 188
  – road 627
occupied 682
  – by 188
  – with 457, 625
occupier 188, 779
occupy 186, 777
  – the chair 693
  – oneself with 457,
  625
  – the mind 451,
  457
  – a post 737
  – time 106
occur 1, 151
  – to the mind 451
  – in a place 186
occurrence 151
  of daily – 613
occursion 276
ocean 341
  plough the – 267
oceanography 341
ochlocracy 737
ochre 433, 439
  yellow – 436
o'clock 114
  know what's –
  698
octagon 244
octahedron 244
Octateuch 985
octave
  *eight* 98
  *music* 413
  *period* 108
octavo 593
octet 98
octifid 99
octodecimo 593
octogenarian 98,
  130
octoroon 41
octroi 812
octuple 98
ocular 441
  – demonstration
  *see* 441
  *visible* 446
  – inspection 441
oculis subjecta
  fidelibus 446
oculist 662
od force 992
odalisque 746
odd *remaining* 40
  *exception* 83

*single* 87
*insane* 503
*vulgar* 851
*ridiculous* 853
  – fellows 712
  – fish 857
oddity 857
oddments 51
odds *inequality* 28
  *superiority* 33
  *chance* 156
  *discord* 713
  at – 24, 713
  long – 704
  what's the – 643
  – against one 665
  the – are 472
  – and ends
  *remainder* 40
  *mixture* 41
  *part* 51
  *useless* 645
ode 597
odi profanum
  vulgus 878
Odin 979
odious
  *disagreeable* 830
  *ugly* 846
  *hateful* 898
odium *disgrace* 874
  *hatred* 898
  *blame* 932
odium theologicum
  481, 988
  *church* 995
odograph 200
odometer 200
odontoid 250, 253
odour 398
  in bad – 932
  – of sanctity 897
odylic force 992
odzookens 870
œcumenical 78
œdematous 194,
  324
Œdipus 462, 524
  – complex 897
  Davus sum non –
  703
œil de maître 459
o'er [*see* over]
œsophagus 260
œuvre 161
of: – all things 33
  – course 82, 154
  – late 123
  – one mind 23
  – no effect 169
  – old 122

– a piece
  *uniform* 16
  *similar* 17
  *agreeing* 23
off 196
  be – 623
  keep – 623
  make – with 791
  move – 287
  sheer – 287
  stand – 287
  start – 293
  – one's balance
  605
  throw – one's
  centre 874
  – one's guard 260,
  508
  – one's hands 776
  take – one's hands
  785
  – one's head 503
  – one's legs 284,
  309
  – one's mind 452
  – and on
  *periodical* 138
  *changeable* 149
  *irresolute* 605
  throw – the scent
  *uncertain* 475
  *avoid* 623
  – side 238
  – with you 297
offal 653
offence *attack* 716
  *anger* 900
  *guilt* 947
offend 830, 945
  – against the law
  964
offensive
  *unsavoury* 395
  *fetid* 401
  *foul* 653
  *aggressive* 716
  *displeasing* 830
  *distasteful* 867
  *obnoxious* 898
  – and defensive
  alliance 712
  – to ears polite 579
offer *proposal* 763
  – the alternative
  609
  – a choice 609
  – of marriage 902
  – oneself 763
  – up prayers 990
  – sacrifice 990
  – for sale 796

offering *gift* 784
  burnt – 990
  sin – 952
offertory *gift* 784
  *worship* 990
  *rite* 998
off-hand *soon* 132
  *inattentive* 458
  *careless* 460
  *spontaneous* 612
office *doing* 170
  *room* 191
  *business* 625
  *mart* 799
  *worship* 900
  do one's – 772
  good –s 724, 906
  hold – 693
  kind –s 906
  do an ill – 907
  man in – 694
officer *director* 694
  *commander* 745
  *constable* 965
offices
  *kitchen* &c. 191
official *certain* 474
  *true* 494
  *business* 625
  man in *office* 694
  *authoritative* 737
  *master* 745
  *servant* 746
officialism 739
officiate
  *business* 625
  *act* 680
  *conduct* 692
  *religious* 998
officio, ex –
  *officer* 694
  *authority* 737
  *duly* 924
officinal 613
officious 682
offing 196, 341
offscourings 645,
  653
offset
  *compensation* 30
  *offspring* 167
offshoot *adjunct* 39
  *part* 51
  *effect* 154
  *offspring* 167
offspring *effect* 154
  *posterity* 167
offuscate 421, 426
often *repeated* 104
  *frequent* 136
  most – 613

*in writing* **577**
adornment **847**
*glory* 873
excess of – 851
ornamental art 847
*painting* 556
ornate
- *writing* 577
*ornamental* 847
ornavit, nihil tetigit
quod non – 850
orniscopy 511
ornithology 368
ornithomancy 511
orotundity 577
orphan 893
Orpheus 416
orpiment 436
orrery 318
orthodox
*conformable* 82
- *religion* 983a
– dissenter 984
orthodoxy **983a**
orthoepy 562, 580
orthogonal 212
orthography 561
orthology 494
orthometry 466,
597
orthopædy 662
orthopraxy 662
orts *remnants* 40
*useless* 645
(*trifles* 643)
oryctology
*minerals* 358
*organic remains*
368
oscillation
*change* 149
*motion* **314**
centre of – 222
oscitancy
*opening* 260
*sleepy* 683
osculation
*contact* 199
*endearment* 902
Osiris 979
Osmanli 984
osmose 302
Ossa on Pelion 72,
319, 549
osseous 323
ossify 323
ossuary 363
ostensible
*appearance* 448
*probable* 472
*manifest* 525

*plea* 617
ostentation **882**
osteology 329
ostiary
*doorkeeper* 263
*mouth* 260
*estuary* 343
ostler 370, 746
ostracize *exclude* 55
*eject* 297
*banish* 893
*censure* 932
*punish* 972
ostrich, stomach of
an – 957
Othello's occupa-
tion's gone 757
other 15, 37
do unto –s as we
would men
should do unto
us 942
enter into the
feelings of –s
906
every – 138
put oneself in the
place of –s 942
the – day 123
– extreme 14
– side of the
shield 468
– than 18
– things to do 683
– time 119
just the – way 14
in – words 522
otherwise 18
otia fecit, Deus
nobis hæc – 840
otiose 683
otium cum
dignitate 685
ottar, otto 400
ottoman 215
oubliette
*ambush* 530
*prison* 752
ough! 874
ought:
– to be 922, 926
ouï-dire 532
ouija board 992
ounce *weight* 319
ourselves 372
oust *eject* 297
*dismiss* 756
*deprive* 789
out *exterior* 220
*in error* 495
come – 446

go – *egress* 295
*cool* 385
play – 729
send – 297
time – of joint 735
waters – 337
– at elbows 874
– at heels 804
– of [*see below*]
– and out 52
– in one's reckon-
ing 495
– upon it
*malediction* 908
*censure* 932
– with it
*disclose* 529
*obliterate* 552
out of *motive* 615
*insufficient* 640
get well – 671
– breath 688
– cash 804
– character 24
– whole cloth 544
– the common 83
– conceit with 867
– countenance
*disrepute* 874
*humbled* 879
– danger 664
– date
*anachronism* 115
*old* 124
*ill-timed* 135
*unfashionable* 851
– one's depth
*deep* 208
*shortcoming* 304
*difficult* 704
*rash* 863
– doors 220, 338
turn – doors 297
– employ 681
– favour 867
– focus 447
– gear
*disorder* 59
*powerless* 158
*unprepared* 674
– hand *soon* 132
*completed* 729
– harness 748
– health 655
– hearing 196, 419
– humour
*discontent* 832
*anger* 900
– a job 681
– joint
*disorder* 59

*impotent* 158
*evil* 619
– luck 735
– one's mind 503
– order
*disorder* 59
*unconformity* 83
*imperfect* 651
– patience 825
– the perpendi-
cular 217
– place
*disorder* 59
*unconformable* 83
*displaced* 185
*inexpedient* 647
– pocket *loss* **776**
*poverty* 804
*debt* 806
– one's power 471
– print 552
– all proportion 31
– the question
*impossible* 471
*dissent* 489
*rejection* 610
*refusal* 764
*hopeless* 859
*undue* 925
– reach 196, 471
– one's reckoning
*uncertain* 475
*error* 495
*inexpectation* 508
*disappointment*
509
– repair 659
– repute 874
– season 135
– shape 243
put – sight
*invisible* 447
*neglect* 460
*conceal* 528
– sorts *disorder* 59
*dejection* 837
– the sphere of
196
– spirits 837
– one's teens 131
– tune
*unmusical* 414
*imperfect* 651
*spoiled* 659
*discord* 713
– the way
*irrelevant* 10
*exceptional* 83
*absent* 187
*distant* 196
*ridiculous* 853

*secluded* 893
get – the way 623
go – one's way 629
– one's wits 824
– work 681
– the world
  *dead* 360
  *secluded* 893
**outbalance** 30, 33
**outbid** 794
**outbrave** 885
**out-brazen** 885
**outbreak**
  *beginning* 66
  *violence* 173
  *egress* 295
  *discord* 713
  *attack* 716
  *revolt* 742
  *passion* 825
**outburst**
  *violence* 173
  *egress* 295
  *revolt* 825
**outcast**
  *unconformable* 83
  *pariah* 876
  *secluded* 893
  *bad man* 949
**outcome** *effect* 154
  *egress* 295
  *produce* 775
**outcry** *noise* 411
  *complaint* 839
  *censure* 932
**outdo** *superior* 33
  *transcursion* 303
  *activity* 682
  *cunning* 702
  *conquer* 731
**outdoor** 220
**outer** 220
**outermost** 220
**outface** 885
**outfit** 225, 673
**outflank** *flank* 236
  *defeat* 731
**outgate** 295
**outgeneral** 731
**outgo** 303
**outgoing** 295
**outgoings** 809
**outgrow** 194
**outgrowth** 154
**out-Herod** 33, 173
**outhouse** 101
**outing** 266
**outjump**
  *transcursion* 303
  *repute* 873
**outlander** 57

**outlandish**
  *foreign* 10
  *extraneous* 57
  *irregular* 83
  *barbarous* 851
  *ridiculous* 853
**outlast** 110
**outlaw** *irregular* 83
  *secluded* 893
  *reprobate* 949
**outlawry** 964
**outlay** 809
**outleap** 303
**outlet** *opening* 260
  *egress* 295
**outline** *contour* 230
  *form* 240
  *features* 448
  *sketch* 554
  *painting* 556
  *plan* 626
**outlines**
  *rudiments* 66
  *principles* 596
**outlive** 110, 141
**outlook** *view* 448
  *outstare* 885
**outlying**
  *remaining* 40
  *exterior* 220
**outmanœuvre**
  *trick* 545
  *defeat* 731
**outnumber** 102
**outpost**
  *distant* 196
  *circumjacent* 227
  *front* 234
**outpouring**
  *egress* 295
  *information* 527
  *abundance* 639
**output** *egress* 295
  *produce* 775
**outrage**
  *violence* 173
  *evil* 619
  *badness* 649
  *injury to* 659
  *malevolence* 907
  *disrespect* 929
  *guilt* 947
**outrageous**
  *excessive* 31
  *violent* 173
  *scandalous* 874
**outrance**: à –
  *great* 31
  *complete* 52
  *violent* 173
  *guerre* – 722

**outrank** 33, 62
**outré**
  *exceptional* 83
  *exaggerate* 549
  *ridiculous* 853
**outre mer** 196
**outreach** 545
**outreckon** 482
**outride** 303
**outrider** 64
**outrigger**
  *support* 215
  *boat* 273
**outright** 52
**outrival**
  *superior* 33
  *surpass* 303
  *fame* 873
**outrun** 303
  – the constable
  *debt* 806
  *prodigal* 818
**outscourings** 653
**outset** 66, 873
**outshine** 873, 874
**outside**
  *extraneous* 57
  *exterior* 220
  *appearance* 448
  – the gates 893
  *mere* – 544
  – *car* 272
  clean the – of the
  platter
  *ostentation* 882
**outsider** 57, 893
**outskirts** 196, 227
**outspan** 292
**outspeak** 582
**outspoken** *say* 582
  *artless* 703
  be – *censure* 932
**outspread** 202
**outstanding**
  *remaining* 40
  *outside* 220
  – debt 806
  – feature 642
**outstare** 885
**outstep** 303
**outstretched** 202
  with – arms 894
**outstrip** 303
**outtalk** 584
**outvie** 720, 873
**outvote** 731
**outward** 220
  – bound 295
**outweigh** 33, 175
**outwit** 545, 731
**outwork**

*defence* 717
**outworn** 124
**oval** 247
**ovate** 247
**ovation** 883
**oven** 386
  like an – *hot* 382
**over** *more* 33
  *remainder* 40
  *end* 67
  *past* 122
  *high* 206
  *too much* 641
  all – *completed* 729
  all – with
  *destroyed* 162
  *dead* 360
  *failure* 732
  *adversity* 735
  *danger* – 664
  get – 660
  fight one's battles
  – again 594
  hand – 783
  make – 784
  set – 755
  turn – 218
  – and above
  *superior* 33
  *added* 37
  *remainder* 40
  *redundance* 641
  – again 104
  – against 237
  – the border 196
  – head and ears
  *complete* 52
  *height* 206
  *feeling* 821
  – the hills and far
  away 196
  – the mark 33
  – one's head 208,
  641
  – the way 237
**overabound** 641
**overact** *bustle* 682
  *affect* 855
**overalls** 225
**over-anxiety** 865
**overarch** 223
**overawe** *sway* 737
  *intimidate* 860
  *respect* 928
**overbalance**
  *unequal* 28
  *compensation* 30
  *superior* 33
**overbear** 175
**overbearing** 885
**overboard, throw** –

[ 581 ]

below – *low* 207
*imperfect* 651
– excellence 33
– nobile fratrum
*alike* 17
*friends* 890
de – le roi 737
– parenthèse 134
– pari refero 718
– value 812
**parable**
*metaphor* 521
*teaching* 537
*description* 594
**parabola** *curve* 245
**parabolic**
*metaphorical* 521
**paracentesis** 297
**parachronism** 115
**parachute**
*balloon* 273
*means of safety*
666
– *light* 423
**Paraclete** 976
**parade** *procession*
69, 266
*walk* 189
*ostentation* 882
**paradigm** 22, 567
**Paradise** *bliss* 827
*heaven* 981
in – 827
**parados** 717
**paradox**
*absurdity* 497
*obscurity* 519
*difficulty* 704
**paradoxical** 475,
519
**paraffin** 356
**paragon**
*perfect* 650
*glory* 873
*good man* 948
**paragram**
*ambiguous* 520
*neology* 563
**paragraph** *part* 51
*phrase* 566
*article* 593
**paraleipsis** 460
**parallax** 196
**parallel**
*similarity* 17
*imitate* 19
*harmonious* 178
– *position* 216
*symmetry* 242
draw a – 464
none but himself

can be his – 873
run – 178
**parallelism 216**
*agreement* 23
**parallelogram** 244
**parallelopiped** 244
**paralogism** 477
**paralogize** 477
**paralysis**
*impotence* 158
*physical insensi-*
*bility* 376
*disease* 655
*moral insensi-*
*bility* 823
**paralyse** 158, 376,
823
**paramount**
*supreme* 33
*important* 642
*authority* 737
lord – *master* 745
*possessor* 779
– *estate* 780
**paramour** 897
**paranoia** 503, 504
**parapet** 717
**paraph** 550
**paraphernalia**
*machinery* 633
*belonging* 780
**paraphrase**
*imitation* 19
*copy* 21
*synonym* 522
*phrase* 566
**paraphrast** 524
**paraphrastic** 19,
522
**parasite** *auxiliary*
711
*servile* 886
*flatterer* 935
**parasitic**
*subjection* 749
*grasping* 789
*servile* 886
**parasol** *covering* 223
*shade* 424
**paratus:**
in utrumque –
*resolved* 604
*ready* 673
semper – 673
**parboil** 384
**parbuckle** 633
**Parcæ** 601
**parcel** *part* 51
*group* 72
part and – 56
– out *arrange* 60

*allot* 786
**parcels**
*property* 780
**parcere subjectis**
740, 914
**parch** *dry* 340
*heat* 382
*bake* 384
**parched with thirst**
865
**parchment**
*writing* 590
*security* 771
**parcity** 819
**pardi** 535
**pardon** 506, 918
beg – 952
– me 489
**pardonable** 937
**pare** *cut* 38
*reduce* 195
*peel* 204
*divest* 226
– *down*
*shorten* 201
**paregoric** 662
**parenchyma** 316,
329
**parent** 166
– *ship* 726
**parentage** 11, 166
**parenthesis**
*discontinuity* 70
*inversion* 218
*interjacence* 228
by way of – 134
**parenthetical**
*irrelative* 10
**pargeting** 847
**parhelion** 423
**pari passu** 27, 120
**Pariah**
*outlaw* 83
*commonalty* 876
*outcast* 893
**parian**
*sculpture* 557
**parietal** 236
**parietes** 224
**paring** 32
**parish** 181
bring to the – 804
come upon the –
804
– council 696
**parishioner** 997
**paritor** 965
**parity** 17, 27
**park** *house* 189
*plain* 344
*trees* 367

*artillery* 727
*pleasure ground*
840
– *paling* 232
**parkway** 627
**parlance** 582
in common – 576
**parlante** 415
**parlementaire** 534,
723
**parler:**
façon de – 521
– à tort et à
travers
*illogical* 477
*nonsense* 497
**parley** *talk* 588
*conference* 695
*mediation* 724
**parliament** 696
**parliamentary**
**securities** 802
**parlour** 191
**parlour-maid** 746
**parlous** 665
**Parnassus** 597
**parochial** 181, 189
*prejudiced* 481
**parody**
*imitation* 19
*copy* 21
*misinterpret* 523
*misrepresent* 555
*travesty* 856
**parole** *speech* 582
on – *restraint* 751
*prisoner* 754
*promise* 768
**Parolles** 887
**paronomasia**
*neology* 563
*ornament* 577
**paronymous** 562
**paroxysm**
*violence* 173
*agitation* 315
*emotion* 825
*anger* 900
**parquetry** 440
**Parr, Old** – 130
**parricide** 361
**parrot**
*imitation* 19
*repetition* 104
*loquacity* 584
repeat as a – 505
**parry** *confute* 479
*avert* 623
*defend* 717
**pars magna fui,**
**quorum** – 690

parse 461, 567
Parsee 984
parsimony **819**
parson 996
parsonage 1000
part *divide* 44
  *portion* **51**
  *diverge* 291
  *music* 413
  *book* 593
  *rôle* 599
  *function* 625
  *duty* 926
  act a – *action* 680
  take an active –
    682
  bear – in 709
  component – 56
  fractional – 100*a*
  in – *a little* 32
  for my – 79
  on the – of 707
  play a – in 175
  principal – 642
  take the – of 709
  take – with 709
  take a – in 680
  take no – in 623
  – company
    *disjunction* 44
    *avoid* 623
    *quarrel* 713
  – and parcel 56
  – by part 51
  –song 415
  – of speech 567
  – with 782, 784
**partake** 778
  – of the sacrament
    998
**parte**, ex – 481
**parterre** *level* 213
  *cultivation* 371
**Parthis mendacior**
  544
**parti pris** 611
**partial** *unequal* 28
  *incomplete* 51
  *special* 79
  *misjudging* 481
  *unjust* 923
  – shadow 422
**partiality**
  *preponderance* 33
  *desire* 865
  *friendship* 888
  *love* 897
**partially** 32, 51
**partible** 44
**particeps criminis**
  690, 711

participate 709, 778
  – in *be a doer* 680
participation 778
participator 690
particle 32, 330
parti-coloured 440
particular *item* 51
  *event* 151
  *attentive* 457
  *careful* 459
  *exact* 494
  *capricious* 608
  *odd* 851
  *fastidious* 868
  in – 79
  – account 594
  – estate 780
particularize
  *special* 79
  *describe* 594
particularly 31, 33
particulars 79, 594
partie carrée 892
parting 44
partisan
  *auxiliary* 711
  *weapon* 727
  *friend* 890
  *sympathizer* 914
partisanship
  *warped judgment*
    481
  *co-operation* 709
  *partiality* 923
partition *wall* 228
  *allot* 786
partlet 366
partly 51
partner
  *companion* 88
  *auxiliary* 711
  *sharer* 778
  *friend* 890
  *spouse* 903
  sleeping – 683
partnership
  *party* 712
  join – with **709**
parts *intellect* 450
  *skill* 698
  *wisdom* 498
parturition 161
parturiunt montes
  482, 509
party *assemblage* 72
  *special* 79
  *person* 372
  *association* **712**
  *sociality* 892
  – spirit
  *warped judgment*

481
  *cooperation* 709
  *wrong* 923
  – to *action* 680
  *agent* 690
  *co-operate* 709
  – to a suit 969
  – wall 228
parva componere
  magnis 464
parvenu
  *new* 123
  *successful* 734
  *vulgar* 851
  *low-born* 876
parvitude 193
pas *precedence* 62
  *term* 71
  *precession* 280
  *rank* 873
  – de quatre 840
  – seul 840
pas si bête 498
paschal 998
pasha 875
pashalic 737
pashaw 745
pasigraphie 560
pasigraphy 590
pasquinade 934
pass *conjuncture* 8
  *be superior* 33
  *course* 109
  *lapse* 122
  *happen* 151
  *interval* 198
  *defile* 203
  *move* 264
  *transfer* 270
  *move through* 302
  *exceed* 303
  *vanish* 449
  *way* 627
  *difficulty* 704
  *thrust* 716
  *passport* 760
  *gratuity* 815
  – *as property* 783,
    784
  barely – 651
  let it – 460
  make a – at 716
  pretty – 704
  – away
  *cease to exist* 2
  *end* 67
  *transient* 111
  *past* 122
  *cease* 142
  *die* 360
  – by *course* 109

*inattention* 458
  *neglect* 460
  *disrespectful* 929
  – comprehension
    519
  – current 484
  – an examination
    648, 873
  – the eyes over
    457
  – the fingers over
    379
  – into one's hand
    785
  – through one's
    hands 625
  – into 144
  – judgment 480
  – a law 963
  – in the mind 451
  – muster
  *conform to* 82
  *sufficient* 639
  *good* 648
  *approbation* 931
  barely – muster
    651
  – under the name
    of 564
  – off *be past* 122
  *egress* 295
  – off for 544
  – on 282
  – an opinion 480
  – to the order of
    the day 624
  – out of 295
  – over
  *exclude* 55
  *cross* 302
  *give* 784
  *forgive* 918
  *exemption* 927*a*
  – over to 709
  – and repass 302,
    314
  – in review 457,
    461
  – the Rubicon 609
  – sentence on 971
  – time *exist* 1
  *time* 106
  *do nothing* 681
  – one's time in
    625
  – to 144
  – through
  *event* 151
  *motion* 302
  – one's word **768**
passable *small* 32

*unimportant* 643
*imperfect* 651
*pretty* 845
passado 716
passage [*see* pass]
  *part* 51
  *conversion* 144
  *street* 189
  *corridor* 191
  *opening* 260
  *navigation* 267
  *moving through*
    302
  *music* 413
  - *in a book* 593
  *action* 680
  cut a - 260
  force a - 302
  - of arms 720
passant, en -
  *transit* 270
  *incidentally* 621
pass-book 811
passe: mot de -
  550
passé
  *antiquated* 124
  *aged* 128
  *spoiled* 659
passed away 122
passementerie 847
passenger 268
  - *train* 272
passe-partout
  *key* 260
  *instrument* 631
passer by 444
passer le temps,
  pour - 681
passeront pas, ilsne
  717
passe-temps 840
passim
  *dispersed* 73
  *place* 182
  *situation* 183
passing *very* 31
  *transient* 111
  - bell 363
  - strange 870
  - word 527
passion
  *emotion* 820, 821
  *excitability* 825
  *pain* 828
  *desire* 865
  *love* 897
  *anger* 900
  ruling - 606
Passion-week 998
passionate

*warm* 825
*irascible* 901
passionless 823
passive *inert* 172
  *inaction* 681
  *obedient* 743
  *inexcitable* 826
  - resister 489
passivity 172, 989
pass-key 631
Passover 998
passport
  *indication* 550
  *instrumentality*
    631
  *order* 741
  *permission* 760
pass-word
  *answer* 462
  *sign* 550
  *military* 722
past 122
  danger - 664
  insensibility to
    the - 506
  obliteration of
    the - 506
  thing of the - 124
  - bearing 830
  - comprehension
    519
  - cure 859
  - dispute 474
  - praying for 945
  - one's prime 128
  - recollection 506
  - work
    *useless* 645
    *impaired* 659
paste *attach* 43
  *cement* 45
  to *cement* 46
  *pulp* 354
  *sham* 545
  *tinsel* 847
  scissors and - 609
pastel 556
pasteurize 652
pasticcio 21, 41
pastil 400
pastime 840
pastor 996
pastoral
  *bucolic* 370
  *music* 415
  *poem* 597
  *religious* 995
  *sermon* 998
pastorale 415
pastry *food* 298
  *sweets* 396

pasturage
  *meadow* 344
  *herbage* 367
pasture *food* 298
pasty *tart* 298
  *like paste* 352
pat *pertinent* 23
  *strike* 276
  (*expedient* 646)
  - on the back
    *induce* 615
    *comfort* 834
    *encourage* 861
    *approve* 931
  - on the cheek 902
  - on the head
    *endearment* 902
Patagonian 206
patch *small* 32
  *change* 140
  *region* 181
  *blemish* 848
  - up *restore* 660
  *compromise* 774
patchwork
  *mixture* 41
  *discontinuous* 70
  *variegation* 440
pate *summit* 210
  *brain* 450
patefaction 260
patella 191
paten 191
patent *open* 260
  *manifest* 525
  *licence* 760
  *property* 780
  - medicine 662
pater 166
  - patriæ 912
patera *cup* 191
  *sacramental* 998
paterfamilias 166
paternal
  *father* 166
  *benevolent* 906
  - domicile 189
paternity 166
paternoster 990
path *direction* 278
  *way* 627
  cross the - 706
  secret - 530
pathetic 830
pathless
  *opacious* 180
  *closed* 261
  *difficult* 704
pathognomonic 550
pathology 655, 662
pathos 821

pathoscopic 820
pathway 627
patience
  *perseverance* 604*a*
  *endurance* 826
  *cards* 840
patient *sick* 655
patisserie 298
patois 563
patriæ: amor - 910
  pater - 912
patriarch
  *family* 11
  *veteran* 130
  *ancestors* 166
  *priest* 996
patriarchal
  *ancient* 124
  *ancestral* 166
patriarchate 737
patrician 875
patrilineal 11, 166
patrimony 780
patriot 910
patrol *walk* 266
  *safeguard* 664
  (*warning* 668)
patrolman 664
patron
  *auxiliary* 711
  *customer* 795
  *friend* 890
  *benefactor* 912
patronage
  *influence* 175
  *aid* 707
  *authority* 737
patronize 693, 707
patronymic 564
patten 225, 998
patter *strike* 276
  *sound* 407
  *meaningless* 517
  *talk* 584
  *stage* 599
patterer 582
pattern *model* 22
  *perfection* 650
  *ornament* 847
  - after 19
patte de
  - mouche 590
  - velours 544, 545
patulous 194
patty 298
pauciloquy 585
paucity *small* 32
  *few* 103
  *scanty* 640
paughty 878
Paul Jones 792

*sophistical* 477
*false* 544
*approbation* 931
*flattery* 933
*vindication* 937
**play** *operation* 170
*influence* 175
*scope* 180
*oscillation* 314
*music* 416
*drama* 599
, *use* 677
*action* 680
*freedom* 748
*amusement* 840
at – 840
bring into – 677
full – 175
full of – 836
in – 842
– along with 709
– one's best card
686, 698
– of colours 440
– at cross pur-
poses 59, 523
– a deep game 702
– the deuce 825
– the devil 907
– one false
*disappoint* 509
*falsehood* 544
*deception* 545
– fast and loose
*falsehood* 544
*irresolute* 605
*tergiversation* 607
*caprice* 608
– on the feelings
824
– first fiddle 642,
873
– the fool
*folly* 499
*clumsy* 699
*amusement* 840
*ridiculous* 853
*ridicule* 856
– for *chance* 621
– a game
*pursue* 622
*conduct* 692
*pastime* 840
– the game 939
– into the hands
of 709
– havoc 659
– hide and seek
528, 623
– a joke 853
give – to the im-

agination 515
– of light 420
– the monkey 499
– off 545
– a part
*false* 544
*drama* 599
*action* 680
– one's part 625,
692
– second fiddle
34, 749
– one a trick 509,
545
– tricks with 699,
702
– truant 623
– upon 545, 856
– with 460
– upon words
*misinterpret* 523
*neology* 563
*wit* 842
play-boy 818
play-day 840
played out
*end* 67
*fatigue* 688
*completion* 729
*failure* 732
player
*musician* 416
*actor* 599
– *piano* 417
playfellow 890
playful 836
– *imagination* 515
playground 728,
840
play-house 599
playmate 890
playsome 836
plaything
*trifle* 643
*toy* 840
make a – of 749
playwright 599
plea
*defence* 462
*argument* 476
*excuse* 617
*vindication* 937
*lawsuit* 969
plead *argue* 467
*plea* 617
*beg* 765
– one's cause 937
– guilty 950
pleader *lawyer* 968
pleading, special –
477

pleadings 969
pleasance 189, 840
pleasant
*agreeable* 829
*amusing* 840
*witty* 842
make things –
*deceive* 545
*induce* 615
*please* 829
*flatter* 933
pleasantry 840, 842
please 829
as you – 743
do what one –s
748
if you –
*obedience* 743
*consent* 762
*request* 765
– oneself 943
pleasurableness
829
pleasure
*physical* – **377**
*will* 600
*moral* - **827**
*dissipation* 954
at – 600
at one's – 737
during – 108a
give – 829
man of – 954a
make a toil of –
682
take one's – 840
will and – 600
with –
*willingly* 602
pleasure-giving 829
pleasure-ground
*demesne* 189
*amusement* 840
pleat 258
plebeian 851, 876
plébiscite 480, 609
plectrum 417
plectuntur Achivi
739
pledge *affirmation*
535
*promise* 768
*security* 771
*borrow* 788
*drink to* 883, 894
hold in – 771
take the – 958
– oneself 768
– one's word 768
pledget 263, 662
Pleiades 72, 318

plenary 31, 52
plenipotent 157
plenipotentiary
*consignee* 758
*deputy* 759
plentitude 639
in the – of power
159
plenty
*multitude* 102
*sufficient* 639
– to do 682
plenum *substance* **3**
*matter* 316
pleonasm
*repetition* 104
*diffuseness* 573
*redundance* 641
plerophory 484
plethora 641
plexal 219
plexus 219
pliable 324
pliant *soft* 324
*irresolute* 605
*facile* 705
*servile* 886
plicature 258
pliers 301, 781
plight *state* 7
*promise* 768
*security* 771
evil – 735
– one's faith 902
– one's troth 768,
902
plighted love 897,
902
Plimsoll mark 466
plinth 211, 215
plod *journey* 266
*slow* 275
*persevere* 604a
*work* 682
– along 143
plodding 604a, 682
*dull* 843
plot - *of ground* 181
*plain* 344
*story* 594
*plan* 626
*realty* 780
the – thickens
*assemblage* 72
plough *furrow* 259
*agriculture* 371
– the ground 673
– in 228
– the waves 267
– one's way 266
ploughboy

| | | | |
|---|---|---|---|
| **porch** *entrance* 66 | – word 572 | 783 | 551, 873 |
| *lobby* 191 | **portrait** 554 | in one's – 777 | **postern** *portal* 66 |
| *mouth* 231 | **portrait painting** | person in – 779 | *back* 235 |
| *opening* 260 | 556 | put one in – of 527 | *opening* 260 |
| *church* 1000 | **portrait painter** 559 | remain in – of the | **post-existence** 152 |
| **porcupine** 253, 901 | **portraiture** 554, 556 | field 731 | **post-graduate** 492 |
| **pore** *opening* 260 | **portray** 19, 554 | **possessor** 779 | – student 541 |
| *egress* 295 | **portreeve** 745, 965 | **posset** 298 | **post-haste** |
| *conduit* 350 | **posada** 189 | **possibility** | *swift* 274 |
| – over *look* 441 | **pose** *situation* 183 | *chance* 156 | *haste* 684 |
| *apply the mind* | *form* 240 | *liability* 177 | *rash* 863 |
| 457 | *puzzle* 475 | *may be* **470** | **post-horse** 271 |
| *learn* 539 | *difficulty* 704 | *property* 780 | **posthumous** 117, |
| **porism** 461, 480 | *affectation* 855 | – upon a possi- | 133 |
| **pornographic** 961 | – as 554 | bility 475 | – fame 873 |
| **porous** 260 | strike a – 855 | **possidetis, uti** – | **postilion** 268, 694 |
| **porpoise** 192 | **posited** 184 | *possession* 777 | **postliminious** 117, |
| **porridge** 298 | **position** | *retention* 781 | 133 |
| **porringer** 191 | *circumstances* 8 | **post** *fastening* 45 | **postman** 534 |
| **port** *abode* 189 | *term* 71 | *situation* 183 | **post-meridiem** 126 |
| *sinistral* 239 | *situation* 183 | *location* 184 | **post-mortem** 360, |
| *gait* 264 | *proposition* 514 | *support* 215 | 363 |
| *arrival* 292 | *assertion* 535 | *transmit* 270 | **postnate** 117 |
| *carriage* 448 | – in society 873 | *swift* 274 | **post-obit** 360, 363 |
| *harbour* 666 | **positive** *real* 1 | *publish* 531 | **post-office** 534 |
| in – 664 | *great* 31 | *mail* 534 | – order 800 |
| make – 666 | *strict* 82 | *beacon* 550 | – red 434 |
| – admiral 745 | *certain* 474 | *record* 551 | **postpone** 133 |
| – fire 388 | *narrow-minded* | *employment* 625 | **postscript** 39, 65 |
| – wine 959 | 481 | *accounts* 811 | **postulant** |
| **portable** *small* 193 | *belief* 484 | *stigmatize* 874 | *asking* 765 |
| *transferable* 270 | *unequivocal* 518 | *punish* 972 | *petitioner* 767 |
| *light* 320 | *assertion* 535 | at one's – | *nun* 996 |
| **portage** 270 | *obstinate* 606 | *persist* 604a | **postulate** 496 |
| **portal** *entrance* 66 | *absolute* 739 | *prepared* 673 | *reasoning* 476 |
| *mouth* 231 | philosophie – 316 | *on duty* 926 | *supposition* 514 |
| *opening* 260 | – colour 428 | sign – 550 | **postulation** |
| **portative** 193, 270 | – degree 31 | stand like a – 265 | *supposition* 514 |
| **portcullis** 706, 717 | – fact 474 | – hoc ergo propter | *request* 765 |
| let down the – 666 | – quantity 84 | hoc 477 | **posture** |
| **porte-monnaie** 802 | **positivism** 984, 989 | drive from – to | *circumstance* 8 |
| **portend** 511 | **posnet** 191 | pillar 704 | *situation* 183 |
| **portent** 512 | **posology** 662 | **postal order** 800 | *form* 240 |
| **portentous** | **posse** 72, 712 | **postboy** 268 | **posture-master** |
| *prophetic* 511 | in – 470 | **post-card** 592 | 599, 844 |
| *fearful* 860 | – comitatûs | **postcenal** 117 | **posy** *motto* 550 |
| **porter** *janitor* 263 | *collection* 72 | **post-chaise** 272 | *poem* 597 |
| *carrier* 271, 690 | *army* 726 | **postcibal** 117 | *flowers* 847 |
| **porterage** 270 | *authority* 737 | **post-date** 115 | **pot** *much* 31 |
| **portfolio** *case* 191 | *jurisdiction* 965 | **post-diluvial** 117 | *mug* 191 |
| *book* 593 | **possess** 777 | **postfix** 37 | *heat* 384 |
| *magazine* 636 | – knowledge 490 | **postprandial** 117 | *saucepan* 386 |
| *direction* 693 | – the mind 484 | **post-war** 117 | *preserve* 670 |
| *insignia* 747 | – oneself of 789 | **poster** 531 | death in the – 657 |
| **porthole** 260 | – the soul 824 | **posterior** | go to – 162, 732 |
| **portico** 66, 191 | – a state 7 | *in order* 63 | keep the – boiling |
| **portion** 51, 786 | **possessed with a** | *in time* 117 | 143, 682 |
| – out 786 | **devil** 503 | *in space* 235 | make the – boil |
| **portly** 192 | **possession** 777, 780 | **posteriority** 117 | 775 |
| **portmanteau** 191 | *sorcery* 992 | **posterity** 121, **167** | le – au lait |
| | come into – 775, | hand down to – | *imagination* 515 |

prepossessing 829
prepossession
  *prejudice* 481
  *possession* 777
preposterous
  *great* 31
  *absurd* 497
  *exaggerated* 549
  *ridiculous* 853
  *undue* 925
prepotency 157
pre-Raphaelite 122,
  124, 556
pre-require 630
pre-resolve 611
prerogative 737,
  924
presage 511, 512
presbyopia 443
presbyter 996
Presbyterian 984
presbytery 995,
  996, 1000
prescience 510
prescious 511
prescribe *direct* 693
  *advice* 695
  *order* 741
  *entitle* 924
  *enjoin* 926
prescript 697, 741
prescription
  *remedy* 662
prescriptive *old* 124
  *unchanged* 141
  *habitual* 613
  *due* 924
presence
  *in space* 186
  *appearance* 448
  *breeding* 894
  in the – of
  *near* 197
  real – 998
  saving one's – 928
  – of God 981
  – of mind 826,
  864
presence-chamber
  191
present
  - *in time* 118
  - *in space* 186
  *offer* 763
  *give* 784
  *church prefer-*
  *ment* 995
  at – 118
  these –s 590, 592
  – arms 894, 928
  – a bold front 861

– a front 719
– itself *event* 151
  *visible* 446
  *thought* 451
– oneself
  *presence* 186
  *offer* 763
  *courtesy* 894
– to the mind
  457, 505
– time **118**
  *instant* 113
– to the view 448
presentable 852
presentation 883,
  894
presentiment
  *instinct* 477
  *prejudgment* 481
  *foresight* 510
presently 132
presentment
  *information* 527
  *law proceeding*
  969
preservation
  *continuance* 141
  *conservation* **670**
  *Divine attributes*
  976
preserve *sweets* 396
preserver 664
preshow 511
preside 693, 737
presidency 737
president 694, 745
press *crowd* 72
  *closet* 191
  *weight* 319
  *public* - 531
  *printing* 591
  *book* 593
  *move* 615
  *compel* 744
  *offer* 763
  *solicit* 765
  go to – 591
  under – of 744
  writer for the –
  593
  – of business 682
  – one hard 716
  – in 300
  – on *course* 109
  – *progression* 282
  – *haste* 684
  – into the service
  677, 707
  – out 301
press-agent 599
pressed: hard – 704

– for time 684
press-gang 965
pressing *need* 630
  *urgent* 642
pressure *power* 157
  *influence* 175
  *weight* 319
  *urgency* 642
  *exertion* 686
  *adversity* 735
  centre of – 222
  high – 824
  work under – 684
Prester John 515
prestidigitation 545
prestidigitator 548
prestige *bias* 481
  *authority* 737
  *fascination* 865
  *fame* 873
prestigiation 545
prestissimo 415
presto
  *instantly* 113
  *music* 415
prestriction 442
presumable 472
presume
  *misjudge* 481
  *believe* 484
  *suppose* 514
  *hope* 858
  *pride* 878
presumption
  [*see* presume]
  *probability* 472
  *expectation* 507
  *rashness* 863
  *arrogance* 885
  *unlawfulness* 925
presumptive
  *probable* 472
  *supposed* 514
  *due* 924
  heir – 779
  – evidence
  *evidence* 467
  *probability* 472
presumptuous 885
presuppose
  *misjudge* 481
  *suppose* 514
presurmise 510,
  514
pretence
  *imitation* 19
  *falsehood* 544
  *untruth* 546
  *excuse* 617
  *ostentation* 882
  *boast* 884

pretend *assert* 535
  *simulate* 544, 546
pretended 545
pretender
  *deceiver* 548
  *braggart* 884
  *unentitled* 925
pretending 544
pretension
  *ornament* 577
  *affectation* 855
  *due* 924
pretentious
  *affected* 855
  *vain* 880
  *ostentatious* 882
  *boasting* 884
  *undue* 925
preterite 122
preterition **122**
preterlapsed 122
pretermit 460
preternatural 83
preterperfect 122
pretext 546, 617
pretty
  *much* 31
  *imperfectly* 651
  *beautiful* 845
  – fellow 501
  – good 651
  – kettle of fish,
  pass &c. 59, 704
  – well *much* 31
  *little* 32
  *trifling* 643
preux chevalier 939
prevail *exist* 1
  *superior* 33
  *general* 78
  *influence* 175
  *habit* 613
  *succeed* 731
  – upon 615
prevailing 78
  – *taste* 852
prevalence
  [*see* prevail]
prevaricate 544
prévenance 894
prevenient 62, 132
prevention
  *prejudice* 481
  *hindrance* 706
  – of waste 817
preventive 55
preventorium 656
previous 116
  move the –
  question 624
  not within –

in – *incomplete*
  53, 730
make – 282
in mid – 270
– of science 490
– of time 109
**progression**
  *gradation* 58
  *series* 69
  *numerical* – 84
  *motion* **282**
**progressive**
  *continuous* 69
  *course* 109
  *advancing* 282
  *improving* 658
**prohibition** 761
  *exclusion* 55
  *stoppage* 706
  *teetotalism* 953,
  958
**project** *bulge* 250
  *impel* 284
  *intend* 620
  *plan* 626
**projectile** 727
**projection** *map* 554
**projector**
  *lantern* 423
  *film* 445
  *designer* 626
**prolation** 580, 582
**prole, sine** – 169
**prolegomena** 64
**prolepsis** 64, 115
**proletarian** 876
**prolific** 168
**prolix** 573
**prolocutor**
  *interpreter* 524
  *teacher* 540
  *speaker* 582
**prologue**
  *precursor* 64
  *drama* 599
**prolong**
  *protract* 110
  *late* 133
  *continue* 143
  *lengthen* 200
**prolongation** 63,
  143
**prolusion** 64
**prom** 892
**promenade** 266
  *display* 882
  *on pier* 189
**Promethean** 359
**prominent**
  *convex* 250
  *manifest* 525

*important* 642
*eminent* 873
**prominently** 31, 33
**promiscuous**
  *mixed* 41
  *irregular* 59
  *indiscriminate*
  465a
  *casual* 621
**promise**
  *predict* 511
  *engage* **768**
  *hope* 858
  keep one's – 939
  keep – to ear and
    break to hope
    545
  – oneself 507, 858
**promissory** 768
  – note 771, 800
**promontory**
  *height* 206
  *projection* 250
  *land* 342
**promote** 153, 658,
  707
**promoter** 626
**promotion** 658
**prompt** *early* 132
  *remind* 505
  *tell* 527
  *induce* 615
  *active* 682
  *advise* 695
  – memory 505
**prompter**
  *drama* 599
  *motive* 615
  *adviser* 695
**promptuary** 636
**promulgate** 531
  – a decree 741
**pronation and**
  **supination** 218
**prone**
  *horizontal* 213
**proneness**
  *tendency* 176
  *disposition* 820
**prôner** 882, 931
**prôneur** 935
**prong** 91
**pronounce**
  *judge* 480
  *assert* 535
  *voice* 580
  *speak* 582
**pronounced** 525
**pronouncement** 531
**pronunciamento**
  531

**pronunciation** 580
**pronunciative** 535
**proof** *hard* 323
  *insensible* 376
  *test* 463
  *demonstration*
  478
  *printing* 591
  *draft* 626
  *ocular* – 446
  – against
  *strong* 159
  *resolute* 604
  *safe* 664
  *defence* 717
  *resistance* 719
  *insensible* 823
**prop** 215, 707
**propædeutics** 537
**propagable** 168
**propaganda** 537,
  542
**propagandism** 537
**propagandist** 540,
  996
**propagate**
  *produce* 161
  *be productive* 168
  *publish* 531
**propel** 284
**propellant** 727
**propeller** 267, 312
**propend** 602
**propendency**
  *predetermination*
  611
  *inclination* 820
**propense** 602
**propension** 820
**propensity** 176, 820
**proper** *special* 79
  *expedient* 646
  *handsome* 845
  *due* 924
  – name 564
  in its – place 58
  show a – spirit
  939
  the – thing 926
  – time 134
**properties**
  theatrical – 225,
  599
**property** *power* 157
  *possessions* **780**
  *wealth* 803
**property-man** 599
**prophecy** 511
**prophet** 513, 996
  false –s 986
  in the name of the

– figs! 497
**prophetic** 511, 985
**Prophets, the** – 985
**prophylactic**
  *healthful* 656
  *remedy* 662
  *preservative* 670
  *hindrance* 706
**prophylaxis** 670
**propinquity** 197
**propitiate**
  *pacify* 723, 724
  *calm* 826
  *content* 831
  *love* 897
  *pity* 914
  *forgive* 918
  *atone* 952
  *worship* 990
**propitious**
  *timely* 134
  *beneficial* 648
  *helping* 707
  *prosperous* 734
  *auspicious* 858
**proplasm** 22
**proportion**
  *relation* 9
  *degree* 26
  *mathematical* 84
  *symmetry* 242
  *style* 578
  *allotment* 786
**proportionate**
  *agreeing* 23
**proportions** 180,
  192
**proposal** *plan* 626
**propose**
  *suggest* 514
  *broach* 535
  *intend* 620
  *offer* 763
  *offer marriage*
  902
  – a question 461
**proposition**
  *supposition* 454
  *reasoning* 476
  *project* 626
  *suggestion* 514
  *offer* 763
**propound** 514, 535
  – a question 461
**propriâ personâ**
  in – *speciality* 79
  *presence* 186
**proprietary** 779
**proprietor** 779
**proprietorship** 780
**propriety**

| | | | |
|---|---|---|---|
| *active* 682 | *product* 154 | *discount* 813 | *belief* 484 |
| *skilful* 698 | *failure* 732 | **rebeck** 417 | *assent* 488 |
| *cash* 800 | **reappear** | **rebel** 742 | *acquire* 775 |
| get – 673 | *repetition* 104 | **rebellion** 715, 742 | *take in* 785 |
| make – 673 | *reproduce* 163 | **rebellow** 412 | *take* 789 |
| – to burst forth | *visible* 446 | **rebirth** 660 | - *money* 810 |
|   825 | *restore* 660 | **reboation** 412 | *welcome* 892, 894 |
| – made 673 | **rear** *sequel* 65 | **rebound** 277, 283 | – Christ 987 |
| – memory 505 | *end* 67 | **rebours, à –** | **received** *known* 490 |
| – money 800 | *bring up* 161 | *reversion* 145 | *habitual* 613 |
| – pen 569 | *erect* 212 | *regression* 283 | – maxim 496 |
| – to sink 824 | *back* **235** | *difficult* 704 | **receiver** |
| – wit 842 | *elevate* 307 | **rebuff** *recoil* 277 | *vessel* 191 |
| **reaffirm** 535 | *teach* 537 | *resist* 719 | *treasurer* 801 |
| **reagent** 463 | in the – 281 | *repulse* 732 | official – 967 |
| **real** *existing* 1 | – its head | *refuse* 764 | – of stolen goods |
| *substantial* 3 | *manifest* 525 | *discourtesy* 895 |   792 |
| - *number* 84 | – one's head | *censure* 932 | **receiving** **785** |
| *true* 494 | *pride* 878 | **rebuild** 660 | **recension** 85 |
| – estate 780 | **rear-admiral** 745 | **rebuke** 932 | **recent** 122, 123 |
| – property 780 | **reason** *cause* 153 | **rebus** 533 | **receptacle** **191** |
| – security 771 | *intellect* 450 | **rebut** *answer* 462 | **reception** |
| **realism** 494 | *thought* 451 | *counter evidence* | *comprehension* 54 |
| **realistic** 17 | *argue* 476 |   468 | *inclusion* 76 |
| **realize** | *wisdom* 498 | *confute* 479 | *arrival* 292 |
| *speciality* 79 | *motive* 615 | *deny* 536 | *ingestion* **296** |
| *intellect* 450 | by – of 615 | **rebutter** 462, 969 | *interview* 588 |
| *think* 451 | feast of – 588 | **recalcitrant** 719, | *receiving* 785 |
| *discover* 480a | in – *moderate* 174 |   742 | *welcome* 892, 894 |
| *believe* 484 | *right* 922 | **recalcitrate** 277, | warm – 892 |
| *conceive* 490 | listen to – 498 |   719 | **reception-room** 191 |
| *imagine* 515 | stand to – | **recalescence** 382 | **recess** |
| *accomplish* 729 | *certain* 474 | **recall** | *receptacle* 191 |
| *acquire* 775 | *proof* 478 | *recollect* 505 | *corner* 244 |
| *sell* 796 | *manifest* 525 | *recant* 607 | *regression* 283 |
| **really** *wonder* 870 | what's the – ? 461 | *cancel* 756 | *ambush* 530 |
| **realm** *region* 181 | without rhyme | – to life 660 | *vacation* 687 |
| *people* 372 | or – 615a | **recant** *deny* 536 | *retirement* 893 |
| *government* 737 | – in a circle 477 | *retract* 607 | **recesses** |
| *property* 780 | – why 153, 615 | *resign* 756 | *interior* 221 |
| **realness** 1 | **reasonable** | **recapitulate** | secret – of one's |
| **realty** 780 | *moderate* 174 | *enumerate* 85 |   heart 820 |
| **ream** 593 | *probable* 472 | *repeat* 104 | **recession** |
| **reamer** 262 | *judicious* 498 | *describe* 594 | *motion from* **287** |
| **reanimate** | *sane* 502 | *summarize* 596 | **Rechabite** 958 |
| *reproduce* 163 | *cheap* 815 | **recast** | **réchauffé** *copy* 21 |
| *life* 359 | *right* 922 | *revolution* 146 | *repetition* 104 |
| *resuscitate* 660 | – prospect 472 | *scheme* 626 | *food* 298 |
| **reap** *shorten* 201 | **reasoner** 476 | **recede** 283, 287 | *made hot* 384 |
| *agriculture* 371 | **reasoning** **476** | – into the shade | *restored* 660 |
| *take* 789 | **reasonless** 499 |   874 | **recherché** 648, 852 |
| – the benefit of | **reasons** 476 | **receipt** | **recidivation** |
| *be better for* 658 | **reassemble** 72 | *scheme* 626 | *regression* 283 |
| – and carry 775 | **reassert** 535 | *prescription* 662 | *relapse* 607, 661 |
| – the fruits | **reassure** 858, 861 | *precept* 697 | **recipe** *remedy* 662 |
| *succeed* 731 | **reasty** 401, 653 | *security* 771 | *precept* 697 |
| *acquire* 775 | **reave** 789 | *payment* 807 | **recipient** 191, 785 |
| *reward* 973 | **rebate** | - *of money* **810** | **reciprocal** 12, 84 |
| – where one has | *subtract* 38 | – in full 807 | **reciprocate** |
|   not sown 923 | *decrement* 40a | **receive** *include* 76 | *correlation* 12 |
| – the whirlwind | *moderate* 174 | *admit* 296 | *interchange* 148 |

| | | | |
|---|---|---|---|
| répertoire 599 | reposit 184 | reprobation 932, | – permission 760 |
| repertory 636 | repository 636 |   988 | requiem 839 |
| repetend | repostum, manet | reproduce | requies, nec mora |
|   arithmetical 84 |   alta mentc – |   imitate 19 |   nec – 682 |
|   iteration 104 |   919 |   repeat 104 | requiescat in pace |
| repetition 19, **104** | repoussé 250 |   renovate 163 |   363, 723 |
| repine | reprehend 932 | reproduction [see | require |
|   pain 828 | reprehensible 945, |   reproduce] 21, |   need 630 |
|   discontent 832 |   947 |   **163** |   insufficient 640 |
|   regret 833 | represent similar 17 | reproductive 163 |   exact 741 |
|   sad 837 |   imitate 19 | reproof 932 |   compel 744 |
| replace |   exhibit 525 | reprover 936 |   price 812 |
|   substitute 147 |   intimate 527 | reptile |   due 924 |
|   locate 184 |   declare 535 |   animal 366 |   duty 926 |
|   restore 660 |   denote 550 |   servile 886 |   – explanation 519 |
| replenish 52, 637 |   delineate 554 |   knave 941 | requirement **630** |
| repletion |   commission 755 |   miscreant 949 | requisite 630 |
|   filling 639 |   deputy 759 | republic | requisition 741, 765 |
|   redundance 641 |   – to oneself 515 |   country 181 |   put in – use 677 |
|   satiety 869 | representation |   people 372 |   order 741 |
| replevin |   [see represent] |   government 737 | requital |
|   recovery 775 |   copy 21 |   – of letters 560 |   retaliation 918 |
|   borrow 788 |   portrait **554** | republican |   gratitude 916 |
|   restore 790 |   drama 599 |   party 712 |   punishment 972 |
| replica 21 | representative |   government 737 |   reward 973 |
| replication |   typical 79 |   commonalty 876 | reredos 1000 |
|   answer 462 |   commissioner 758 | republicanism 737 | res ipsa loquitur |
|   law pleadings 969 |   deputy 759 | repudiate |   525 |
| reply 462, 937 |   – government 737 |   exclude 55 | rescind cut off 44 |
| répondre en |   – of the people 696 |   deny 489 |   abrogate 756 |
|   Normand 544 |   – of the press |   reject 610 |   refuse 764 |
| report noise 406 |   messenger 534 |   abrogate 756 | rescission 44, 756 |
|   judgment 480 |   writer 593 |   violate 773 | rescript answer 462 |
|   inform 527 | repress 751 |   not pay 808 |   transcript 590 |
|   publish 531 |   – one's feelings |   evade 927 |   letter 592 |
|   news 532 |   826 | repugn 719 |   order 741, 963 |
|   rumour 532 |   – a smile 837 | repugnance | rescriptive 761 |
|   record 551 | reprieve |   incongruity 24 | rescue preserve 670 |
|   statement 594 |   respite 133, 970 |   resistance 719 |   deliver 672 |
|   good – 873 |   deliverance 672 |   dislike 867 |   aid 707 |
|   through evil re- |   release 750 |   hate 898 | research 461 |
|   port and good – |   pardon 918 | repulse recoil 277 |   – student 541 |
|   604a | reprimand 932 |   repel 289 | reseat 660 |
|   – progress 527 | reprint |   resist 719 | resection 44 |
| reporter |   copy 21 |   failure 732 | reseda 435 |
|   informant 527 |   repetition 104 |   refusal 764 | resemblance 17, 21 |
|   messenger 534 |   reproduce 163 | repulsion 157, **289** | resent 900 |
|   recorder 553 | reprisal | repulsive | resentful 901 |
|   journalist 593, |   retaliation 718 |   [see repulse] | resentment **900** |
|   758 |   resumption 789 |   unsavoury 395 | reservation |
| reports law 969 | reprise 40a |   painful 830 |   location 184 |
| repose | reproach |   ugly 846 |   concealment 528 |
|   quiescence 265 |   disgrace 874 |   disliked 867 |   mental – 477, 528 |
|   leisure 685 |   blame 932 |   discourteous 895 |   equivocation 520 |
|   rest **687** |   accusation 938 |   hateful 898 |   untruth 546 |
|   – confidence in | reprobate | repurchase 795 |   with a – 38, 770 |
|   484 |   disapproved 932 | reputable 873, 939 | reservatory 191, |
|   – on support 215 |   vicious 945 | reputation 873 |   636 |
|   evidence 467 |   bad man 949 | repute **873** | reserve |
|   – on one's laurels |   sinner 988 | request **765** |   concealment 528 |
|   142 | |   in – 630 |   silence 585 |

**resuscitate**
  *reproduce* 163
  *reinstate* 660
**retable** 215
**retail** *distribute* 73
  *inform* 527
  *barter* 794
  *sell* 796
**retailer** 797
**retain** *stand* 150
  *keep* 781
  – the memory of
    505
  – one's reason 502
**retainer** 746
**retake** 789
**retaliation 718,** 919
**retard** *later* 133
  *slower* 275
  *hinder* 706
**retch** 297
**retection** 529
**retention 781**
**retentive** 781
  – memory 505
**reticence** 528
**reticle** 219
**reticulation** 219,
  248
**reticule** 191
**retiform** 219
**retina** 441
**retinue** *followers* 65
  *series* 69
  *servants* 746
**retire** *move back* 283
  *recede* 287
  *resign* 757
  *modest* 881
  *seclusion* 893
  – into the shade
    *inferior* 34
    *decrease* 36
  – from sight
    *disappear* 449
    *hide* 528
**retiring**
  *concave* 252
  – *colour* 438
**retold** 104
**retort**
  *receptacle* 191
  *vaporizer* 336
  *boiler* 386
  *answer* 462
  *confutation* 479
  *retaliation* 718
  *wit* 842
**retouch** *restore* 660
**retoucher** 559
**retrace** 505

– one's steps 607
**retract**
  *recant* 607
  *annul* 756
  *abjure* 757
  *violate* 773
**retreat**
  *resort* 74
  *withdraw* 187
  *abode* 189
  *regression* 283
  *recede* 287
  *ambush* 530
  *refuge* 666
  *escape* 671
  *give way* 725
  beat a – 623
**retreating**
  *concave* 252
**retrench** *subduct* 38
  *shorten* 201
  *lose* 789
  *economize* 817
**retribution**
  *retaliation* 718
  *payment* 807
  *punishment* 972
  *reward* 973
**retrieve** *restore* 660
  *acquire* 775
**retriever** *dog* 366
**retroaction**
  *counteraction* 179
  *recoil* 277
  *regression* 283
**retroactive**
  *past* 122
**retrocession**
  *regression* 283
  *recession* 287
**retrograde**
  *moving back* 283
  *deteriorated* 659
  *relapsing* 661
**retrogression**
  *regression* 283
  *deterioration* 659
  *relapse* 661
**retrospection**
  *past* 122
  *thought* 451
  *memory* 505
**retroussé** 245
**retroversion** 218
**retrude** 289
**return** *list* 86
  *repeat* 104
  *periodic* 138
  *reverse* 145
  *recoil* 277
  *regression* 283

*arrival* 292
*answer* 462
*report* 551
*relapse* 661
*appoint* 755
*profit* 775
*restore* 790
*proceeds* 810
*reward* 973
in –
  *compensation* 30
  – the compliment
  *interchange* 148
  *retaliate* 718
  – to the original
    state 660
  –ed prodigal 950
  – thanks 916, 990
**return game** 104
**return match** 104
**reunion** *junction* 43
**réunion**
  *assemblage* 72
  *concord* 714
  lieu de – 74
  point de – 74
  social – 892
**revamp** 140
**revanche, en** – 718
**reveal** 529
  – itself 446
**reveille** 550
**revelation**
  *disclosure* 480a,
    529
  *theological* 985
**Revelations** 985
**reveller** 840
  *drunkard* 959
**revelling** 59, 838
**revendicate**
  *claim* 741
  *acquisition* 775
  *due* 924
**revenge 919**
  breathe – 900
**revenons à nos**
  **moutons** 283,
    660
**revenue** 632, 810
**reverberate** 277,
  408
**reverberatory** 386
**revere** *love* 897
  *respect* 928
  *piety* 987

**reverence** *title* 877
  *respect* 928
  *piety* 987
  *clergy* 996
**reverenced** 500
**reverend** 877, 996
**reverent** 987, 990
**reverential** 928
**reverie**
  *train of thought*
    451
  *inattention* 458
  *imagination* 515
**reversal** 218, 607
**reverse** *contrary* 14
  *inversion* 218
  – *of a medal* 235
  *contraposition* 237
  *adversity* 735
  *abrogate* 756
  *cards* 840
  – of the shield 468
**reverseless** 150
**reversible** 605
**reversion**
  [*see* reverse]
  *posterity* 117
  *return* **145**
  *possession* 777
  *property* 780
  *succession* 783
  *remitter* 790
**reversioner** 779
**revert** *repeat* 104
  *return* 145
  *turn back* 283
  *revest* 790
  – to 457
**revest** 790
**revet** 223
**reviction** 660
**review** *consider* 457
  *inquiry* 461
  *judge* 480
  *recall* 505
  *periodical* 531
  *dissertation* 595
  *compendium* 596
  *entertainment* 599
  *revise* 658
  *parade* 882
**reviewer** 480, 595
**revile** 932, 988
**reviler** 936
**revise** *copy* 21
  *consider* 457
  *printing* 591
  *plan* 626
  *improve* 658
**revising barrister**
  967

– and boiled 298
– an ox 883
**rob** 354, 791
**robber** 792
**robbery** 791
**robe** 225, 999
**robes** – of state 747
**Robin Goodfellow**
  980
**Robinson**
  say Jack – 132
**Robot** 554
**robust** *strong* 159,
  654
**roc** 83
**rocaille** 853
**rock** *firm* 150
  *oscillate* 314
  *hard* 323
  *land* 342
  *safety* 664
  *danger* 667
  build on a – 150
  founded on a –
    664
  split upon a – 732
  – ahead 665
  –bound coast 342
  – oil 356
**rocket** *rapid* 274
  *rise* 305
  *light* 423
  *signal* 550
  *arms* 727
  *fireworks* 840
  go up like a – and
    come down like
    the stick 732
**rocking-chair** 215
**rococo** 124, 853
**rod** *support* 215
  *measure* 466
  *scourge* 975
  *divining* 993
  kiss the – 725
  sounding – 208
  – of empire 747
  – in pickle
    *prepared* 673
    *accusation* 938
    *punishment* 972
    *scourge* 975
**rodeo** 720, 840
**rodomontade**
  *exaggeration* 482
  *unmeaning* 517
  *boast* 884
**roe** 366, 374
**Roentgen rays** 420
**rogation**
  *request* 765

*worship* 990
**rogue** *cheat* 548
  *knave* 941
  *scamp* 949
  –'s march 297
**roguery** 940
**roguish**
  *playful* 840
**Roi le veut, le –**
  741
**roister** 885
**roisterer** 887
**Roland for an**
  **Oliver**
  *retaliation* 718
  *revenge* 919
  *barter* 794
**rôle** *drama* 599
  *business* 625
  *plan* 626
  *conduct* 692
**roll** *list* 86
  *fillet* 205
  *convolution* 248
  *rotundity* 249
  *make smooth* 255
  *move* 264
  *fly* 267
  *rotate* 312
  *rock* 314
  *flow* 348
  *sound* **407**
  *record* 551
  *money* 800
  strike off the –
    756, 972
  – along 312
  – in the dust 731
  – on the ground
    839
  – of honour 86
  – in 639, 641
  – on 109
  – into one 43
  – in riches 803
  – up 312
  – up in 225
  – in wealth 803
**roll-call** 85
**roller** *fillet* 45
  *round* 249
  *clothing* 255
  *rotate* 312
**roller-coaster** 840
**rollers** *billows* 348
**rollick** 836
**rollicker** 838
**rollicking**
  *frolicsome* 836
  *blustering* 885
**rolling:** – pin 249

– stock 272
– stone 312
**Rolls: Master of**
  **the –**
  *recorder* 553
  *judge* 967
  – Court 966
**Roman candle** 840
**Roman Catholic**
  984
**romance**
  *music* 415
  *absurdity* 497
  *imagination* 515
  *untruth* 546
  *fable* 594
**Romanism** 984
**romantic**
  *imaginative* 515
  *art* 556
  *sensitive* 822
**romanticism** 515
**Romanus sum,**
  **civis –** 924
**Romany** 563
**Rome: Church of**
  984
  do at – as the
    Romans do 82
**romp** *violent* 173
  *game* 840
**rondeau** *music* 415
  *poem* 597
**rondel** 597
**rondoletto** 597
**rood** *area* 180
  *cross* 998
  – loft 1000
**roof** 189, 223
**roofless** 226
**rook** 791, 792
**rookie** 726
**rookery** *nests* 189
  *dirt* 653
**room** *occasion* 134
  *space* 180
  *lodge* 186
  *chamber* 191
  *plea* 617
  assembly – 840
  in the – of 147
  make – for
  *opening* 260
  *respect* 928
**roommate** 890
**rooms**
  *lodgings* 189
**roomy** 180
**roost** 189
  rule the – 737
**rooster** 366

**root** *algebraic* – **84**
  *cause* 153
  *place* 184
  *abide* 186
  *base* 211
  *etymon* 562
  lie at the – of 64**2**
  pluck up by the
    –s 301
  strike at the – **of**
    716
  take –
    *influence* 175
    *locate* 184
    *habit* 613
  – and branch **52**
  cut up – and
    branch 162
  – out *eject* 297
    *extract* 301
    *discover* 480a
**rooted**
  *old* 124
  *firm* 150
  *located* 184
  *habit* 613
  deep – 820
  – antipathy 867
  – belief 484
**rope** *fastening* 45
  *cord* 205
  *freedom* 748
  *scourge* 975
  give – enough **738**
  –'s end 975
  – of sand
    *incoherence* 47
    *weakness* 160
    *impossible* 471
  – way 627
**rope-dancer** 700
**rope-dancing** 698
**ropy** 352
**roquelaure** 225
**roric** 339
**rosâ, sub –** 528
**rosary** 990, 998
**Roscius** 599
**rose** *pipe* 350
  *fragrant* 400
  *red* 434
  *beauty* 845
  bed of –s 377, **734**
  couleur de –
    *red* 434
    *good* 648
    *prosperity* 734
    *hope* 858
  under the – 528
  welcome as the –**s**
    in May 829, 892

roseate *red* 434
  *hopeful* 858
rose-coloured
  *hope* 858
Rosetta stone 522
rosette 847
rose-water
  *moderation* 174
  *flattery* 933
  not made with –
    704
Rosicrucian
  *order* or *party*
    712
rosin *rub* 331
  *resin* 356a
Rosinante 271
roster 86
rostrum *beak* 234
  *pulpit* 542
rosy 434
  – *wine* 959
rosy-cheeked 845
rot *decompose* 49
  *absurdity* 497
  *rubbish* 517
  *putrefy* 653
  *disease* 655
  *decay* 659
rota 86, 138
Rotarian 892
rotate 138
rotation **312**
  *periodicity* 138
rote, by – 505
  know – 490
  learn – 539
rôti 298
rôtisserie 189
rotogravure 531,
    558
rotten *weak* 160
  *bad* 649
  *foul* 653
  *decayed* 659
  – at the core
    *deceptive* 545
  *diseased* 655
  – borough 893
rotulorum, custos –
    553
rotund 249
rotunda 189
rotundity **249**
roturier 876
roué 949
rouge 434, 847
rouge-et-noir 621
rough *violent* 173
  *shapeless* 241
  *uneven* 256

pungent 392
  *unsavoury* 395
  *sour* 397
  *sound* 410
  *unprepared* 674
  *fighter* 726
  *ugly* 846
  *low fellow* 876
  *bully* 887
  *churlish* 895
  *evil-doer* 913
  *bad man* 949
  cut up – 900
  – copy *writing* 590
  *unprepared* 674
  – diamond
    *uncouth* 241
  *unprepared* 674
  *artless* 703
  *vulgar* 851
  *commonalty* 876
  *good man* 948
  – draft 626
  – guess 514
  – it 686
  – sea 348
  – side of the
    tongue 932
  – and tumble 59
  – weather 173, 349
rough-cast 256
  *covering* 223
  *shape* 240
  *scheme* 626
  *unpolished* 674
rough-hew 240, 673
roughly
  *nearly* 197
rough-neck 876,
    887
roughness **256**
rough-rider 268
roughshod over,
    ride – 739
roulade 415
rouleau
  *assemblage* 72
  *cylinder* 249
  *money* 800
roulette 621, 840
round *series* 69
  *revolution* 138
  – *of a ladder* 215
  *curve* 245
  *circle* 247
  *rotund* 249
  *music* 415
  *fight* 720
  all – 227
  bring – 660
  come –

periodic 138
  recant 607
  persuade 615
dizzy – 312
get – 660
go – 311
go one's –s 266
go the –
  publication 531
make the – of 311
run the – of 682
go the same – 104
turn – *invert* 218
  retreat 283
  revolve 311
  – assertion 535
  – a corner 311
  – dance 840
  – game 840
  – hand 590
  – like a horse in a
    mill 613
  – of the ladder 71
  – number 84, 102
in – numbers 29,
    197
  – pace 274
  – of pleasures
    377, 840
  – robin
    *information* 527
    *petition* 765
    *censure* 932
  – and round 138,
    312
  – sum 800
  – terms 566
  – trot 274
  – up 370
  – of visits 892
round about
  *circumjacent* 227
  *deviation* 279
  *circuit* 311
  *amusement* 840
  – phrases 573
  – way 279
rounded periods
    577, 578
roundelay 597
rounders 840
round-house 752
roundlet 247
round-shouldered
    243
roup 796
rouse 615, 824
  – oneself 682
rousing 171
rout *crowd* 72
  *agitation* 315

overcome 731
  discomfit 732
  rabble 876
  assembly 892
put to the – **731**
  – out 652
route 627
  en – 270
  en – for 282
routine
  *uniform* 16
  *order* 58
  *rule* 80
  *periodic* 138
  *custom* 613
  *business* 625
rove *travel* 266
  *deviate* 279
rover *traveller* 268
  *pirate* 792
roving commission
    475
row *disorder* 59
  *series* 69
  *violence* 173
  *street* 189
  *navigate* 267
  *discord* 713
  – in the same
    boat 88
rowdy *vulgar* 851,
    876
  *blusterer* 887
  *bad man* 949
rowel 253, 615
rower 269
rowlock 215
royal 737
  – blue 438
  – highness 877
  – road 627, 705
Royal Academician
    559
royalist 737
royaliste que le roi,
    plus 33
royalty 737
Rt. Hon. 877
ruade *impulse* 276
  *attack* 716
ruat cœlum 908
rub *friction* 331
  *touch* 379
  *difficulty* 704
  *adversity* 735
  *painful* 830
  – off corners 82
  – down *lessen* 195
  *powder* 330
  – down with an
    oaken towel 972

- *in the mind* 451
*examine* 457
*describe* 594
*synopsis* 596
*overflow* 641
- in pairs 17
- parallel 178
- into port 664
- a race *speed* 274
*conduct* 692
*contend* 720
- in a race
*act* 680
he that –s may
read 525
- a rig 840
- the rig upon 929
- riot *violent* 173
*exaggerate* 549
*redundance* 641
*active* 682
*disobey* 742
*intemperance* 954
- a risk 665
- rusty 603
- to seed 128, 659
- smooth 705, 734
- a tilt at 716, 720
- of things 151
- through
*uniform* 16
*influence* 175
*be present* 186
*kill* 361
*expend* 809
*prodigal* 818
- up *increase* 35
*build* 161
- up an account
*credit* 805
*debt* 806
*charge* 812
- up bills 808
- upon 630
- upon a bank
808, 809
- to waste 638
- wild 173
run-about 272
runagate
*fugitive* 623
*disobey* 742
*bad man* 949
runaway 623
rundle *circle* 247
*convolution* 248
*rotundity* 249
rundlet 191
**Runes** *writing* 590
*poetry* 597
*spell* 993

[ 626 ]

rung 215
runnel 348
runner *branch* 51
*courier* 268
*messenger* 534
running
*continuous* 69
the mind – upon
451
the mind – upon
other things 458
- account 811
- commentary 595
- fight 720
- hand 590
- over 641
- water 348
runnion 949
runt 193
rupture
*disjunction* 44
*quarrel* 713
rural 189, 371
- dean 996
ruralist 893
rus in urbe 189, 893
ruse 545, 702
Rush, Friar 980
rush *crowd* 72
*violence* 173
*velocity* 274
*water* 348
*plant* 367
*trifle* 643
*haste* 684
make a – at 716
- to a conclusion
481, 486
- on destruction
863
- in medias res
604
- into print 591
- upon 622
rushlight *dim* 422
*candle* 423
rusk 298
Russe, montagne –
840
russet
*brown* 433
*red* 434
Russian
- ballet 840
- bath 386, 652
rust *red* 434
*decay* 659
*canker* 663
*inaction* 683
moth and – 659
- of antiquity 122

rustic
*village* 189
*agricultural* 371
*vulgar* 851
*clown* 876
rusticate
*punish* 972
*seclude* 893
rusticity
*impolite* 895
rusticus expectat
dum defluat
amnis 858
rustle 405, 407, 409
rustling 791
rusty *dirty* 653
*decayed* 659
*sluggish* 683
*unskilful* 699
*sulky* 901a
run – *averse* 603
rut *rule* 80
*furrow* 259
*habit* 613
in a – 16
ruth 914
ruthless
*savage* 907
*pitiless* 914a
*revengeful* 919
rutilant 420
ruttish 961
ryot *servant* 746
*possessor* 779
*commonalty* 876

**S**

sabaoth 726
sabbatarian
*ascetic* 955
*sectarian* 984
*false piety* 988
*ritualistic* 998
**Sabbath** *rest* 687
*rite* 998
sabbatism 988
Sabellianism 984
Sabianism 984
sable 223, 431
sabot 225
sabotage 162, 742
sabre 361, 727
sabreur *slayer* 361
*soldier* 726
sabulous 330
sac 191
- de nuit 225
sacatra 83
saccharine 396

saccular 191
sacerdotal 995
sacerdotalism 988
sachel 191
sachem 745
sachet 400
sack *bag* 191
*discharge* 297,
756
*gain* 775
*take* 789
*plunder* 791
give the – to 297
sackbut 417
sackcloth and ashes
*lament* 839
*atonement* 952
*ascetic* 955
*rite* 998
sacrament 998
sacrarium 1000
sacred
*dignified* 873
*holy* 976
*revelation* 985
*piety* 987
sacrifice
*destroy* 162
*gift* 784
*atonement* 952
*worship* 990
*idolatry* 991
at any – 604
fall a – 828
make a – 942
make the supreme
– 361
self – 942
sacrificed 732
sacrilege 988
sacring bell 550,
998
sacristan 996
sacristy 1000
sacrosanct
*honourable* 873
*inviolable* 924
*holy* 976
sad *great* 31
*grey* 432
*bad* 649
*painful* 830
*dejected* 837
- disappointment
509
- dog 949
- times 735
- work 699
sadden 830, 837
sadder and wiser
man 950

saddle 215
  in the – 673
  – on 37, 43
  – on the right
    horse
  *discovery* 480*a*
  *skill* 698
  *right* 922
  *fair* 939
  – with *add* 37
  *attribute* 155
  *quarter on* 184
  *clog* 706
  *impose a duty*
    926
  *accuse* 938
  – on the wrong
    horse 495, 699
  – up 293
saddle-bags 191
Sadducee 984
sadness, in – 535
safe *cupboard* 191
  *hiding place* 530
  *secure* 664
  *treasury* 802
  *cautious* 864
  – conduct 631
  – conscience 926,
    946
  – deposit 636
  – keeping 670
  – and sound 654
  on the – side 864
safety 664
  – bicycle 272
  – curtain 599
  – first 664, 864
  – match 388
  – valve 666
saffron *colour* 436
sag 214, 217, 245
saga 594
sagacious 498, 510
sage 498, 500
  – maxim 496
saggar 386
sagittal 253
sagittary 83
sagum 225
Sahara 169
sahib 373, 745, 875
saick 273
said *preceding* 62
  *repeated* 104
  *prior* 116
  it is – 532
  thou hast – 488
  more easily – than
    done 704
sail *navigate* 267

*ship* 273
*set out* 293
easy – 174
full – 274
press of – 274
shorten – 275
take in – 174
take the wind out
  of one's –s 706
too much – 863
under – 267
– before the wind
  734
– near the wind
  698
– too near the
  wind 863
sailing: plain – 705
– vessel 273
sailor 269
fair weather – 701
saint *angel* 977
  *revelation* 985
  *piety* 987
  *false piety* 988
  *tutelary* – 664
Saint Monday 840
saintly 944, 987
sais quoi, je ne –
  563
sake:
  for the – of 615,
    707
  for goodness – 765
salaam
  *bow* 308
  *submit* 725
  *courtesy* 894
  *respect* 928
salacity 961
salad 41
  – oil 356
salade 717
salamander 386
salariat 875
salary 973
sale 796
  bill of – 771
  for – *offer* 763
  *barter* 794
saleable 796
salebrosity 256
salesman 797
salient
  *projecting* 250
  *sharp* 253
  *manifest* 525
  *important* 642
  – angle 244
  – points 642
saline 392

saliva 299, 332
salivate 297
salle-à-manger 191
sallet 717
sallow
  *colourless* 429
  *yellow* 436
sally *issue* 293
  *attack* 716
  *wit* 842
sally-port 295, 717
salmagundi 41
salmi 298
salmon-coloured
  434
saloon 189, 191
salt *sailor* 269
  *pungent* 392
  *condiment* 393
  *importance* 642
  *preserve* 670
  *money* 800
  *wit* 842
  below the – 876
  worth one's – 644
  – of the earth
    648, 948
  – water 341
saltation 309
saltatory 315
saltimbanco 548
saltpetre 392, 727
saltum, per – 315
salubrity 656
salutary 656
salutatory 582
salute
  *allocution* 586
  *celebration* 883
  *courtesy* 894
  *kiss* 902
  *respect* 928
salutiferous
  [*see* salutary]
salva:
  – res est 664
  – sit reverentia
    928
salvable 946
salvage
  *acquisition* 775
  *tax* 812
  *discount* 813
  *reward* 973
salvation
  *preservation* 670
  *deliverance* 672
  *religious* 976
  *piety* 987
  work out one's –
    990

salve *unguent* 356
  *remedy* 662
  *relieve* 834
salver 191
salvo *exception* 83
  *explosion* 406
  *qualification* 469
  *plea* 617
  *attack* 716
  *excuse* 937
  – of artillery
  *celebration* 883
Samaritan, good –
  906, 912
same 13
  all the – to 823
  in the – boat 709
  in the – breath
    113, 120
  go over the –
    ground 104
  of the – mind 488
  on the – tack 709
  adds up to the –
    thing 27
  at the – time 30,
    120
sameness 16
samiel 349
samisen 417
Sammael 978
samovar 191
sampan 273
sample 82, 463
Samson 159
sana, mens – 502
  – in corpore sano
    827
sanation 660
sanative 662
sanatorium 662
sanctification 976
sanctify 926, 987
sanctimony 988
sanction
  *permission* 760
  *dueness* 924
  *approbation* 931
sanctitude 987
sanctity 987
sanctuary 666, 100(
sanctum 191
  – sanctorum
  *abode* 189
  *privacy* 893
  *temple* 1000
sand *powder* 330
  –bag 727
  built upon – 665
  –dance 840
  sow the – 645

sandal 225
sand-blind 442
Sandemanian 984
sand-paper 255
sands *danger* 667
 – on the seashore
  *multitude* 102
sand-storm 330
sandwich-wise 228
sandy *yellow* 436
sane 502
sangar 717
sang-froid
 *insensibility* 823
 *inexcitability* 826
 *presence of mind*
  864
sangrail 998
sanguinary 361
sanguine *red* 434
 *hopeful* 858
 – expectation 507,
  858
 – imagination 515
sanhedrim 696, 995
sanies 333
sanitaire, cordon –
  670
sanitarian 656
sanitarium 656, 662
sanitary 656
sanity *mental* 502
 *bodily* - 654
sans 187
 – cérémonie 888,
  892
 – facon
  *simple* 849
  *modest* 881
  *social* 892
 – pareil 33
 – peur et sans
  reproche
  *perfect* 650
  *heroic* 873
  *honourable* 939
 – souci
  *insensible* 823
  *pleasure* 827
  *content* 831
sans-culotte 742,
  876
Santa Claus 784
santé, maison de –
  662
santon 893, 996
sap *essence* 5
 *destroy* 162
 *excavate* 252
 *juice* 333
 *damage* 659

*attack* 716
 – the foundations
  162, 659
sapid 390
sapient 498
sapless 160, 340
sapling 129, 367
saponaceous 355
saporific 390
sapper 252, 726
sappers and miners
 *preparers* 673
Sapphic 597
sapphire *blue* 438
 *gem* 847
sappy
 *young* 127
 *juicy* 333
 *foolish* 499
sarà sarà, che – 601
saraband 840
sarcasm
 *disrespect* 929
 *censure* 932
 *detraction* 934
sarcastic 856, 895
sarcoma 250
sarcophagus 363
sarculation 103
sard 847
Sardanapalus 954a
sardonic 932, 934
 – grin
  *laughter* 838
  *ridicule* 856
  *discontent* 932
sardonyx 847
sark 225
sartorial 225
Sarum, old – 893
sash 247
Satan **978**
satanic
 *malevolent* 907
 *vicious* 945
 *diabolic* 978
satchel 191
sate 869
satellite
 *companion* 88
 *follower* 281
 *heavenly body* 318
 *auxiliary* 711
 *servant* 746
satiate 957
satiety
 *sufficient* 639
 *pleasant* 829
 *cloy* **869**
satin 255
satire 521, 856, 932

satirical 546, 932
 *detraction* 934
satirist 936
satis: jam – 869
 – superque 641
satisfaction
 [*see* satisfy]
 *duel* 720
 *pleasure* 827
 *atonement* 952
hail with – 931
satisfactorily 618
satisfactory 648
satisfy *answer* 462
 *convince* 484
 *sufficient* 639
 *consent* 762
 *observance* 772
 *pay* 807
 *gratify* 829
 *content* 831
 *satiate* 869
 *reward* 973
 – an obligation
  926
 – oneself 484
satrap 745
saturate *fill* 52
 *moisten* 339
 *satiate* 869
Saturn 979
saturnalia
 *disorder* 59
 *games* 840
 *intemperance* 954
Saturnian 829, 946
 – age 734
Saturnia regna 734,
  827
saturnine 837
satyr *ugly* 846
 *libertine* 962
 *demon* 980
sauce *adjunct* 39
 *mixture* 41
 *food* 298
 *condiment* 393
 *impertinence* 885
 *abuse* 908
 – boat 191
pay – for all 807
sauce piquante 829
sauce-box 887
saucer 191
 – eyes 441
saucepan 191
saucy 885, 895
saunter 133, 266,
  275
sausage 298
saute aux yeux,

cela – 525
sauvage 893
sauve qui peut
 *run away* 623
 *alarm* 669
 *haste* 684
 *cowardice* 862
savage *violent* **173**
 *vulgar* 851
 *brave* 861
 *boorish* 876
 *angry* 900
 *malevolent* 907
 *evil-doer* 913
savanna 344
savant 490, 492
save *subduct* 38
 *exclude* 55
 *except* 83
 *store* 636
 *preserve* 670
 *deliver* 672
 *economize* 817
God – 990
 – one's bacon 671
 – and except 83
 – money 817
 – the necessity
  927a
 – us 707
save-all 817
saving 817
 – clause 469
 – one's presence
  928
savings 636, 817
saviour 912
Saviour 976
savoir: – faire
  698, 852
 – gré 916
 – vivre *skill* 698
  *fashion* 852
  *sociality* 892
savour 390
 – of *resemble* 17
 – of the reality
  780
savouriness **394**
savourless 391
savoury 394
saw *cut* 44
 *jagged* 257
 *maxim* 496
 – the air
 *gesture* 550
sawbuck 800
sawder, soft –
 *flattery* 933
sawdust 330
sawney 501

scroll 86, 551
scrub *rub* 331
  *bush* 367
  *clean* 652
  *dirty person* 653
  *commonalty* 876
scrubby *small* 193
  *trifling* 643
  *stingy* 819
  *disreputable* 874
  *vulgar* 876
  *shabby* 940
scruff 235
scruple
  *small quantity* 32
  *weight* 319
  *doubt* 485
  *reluctance* 603
  *probity* 939
scrupulous
  *careful* 459
  *incredulous* 487
  *exact* 494
  *reluctant* 603
  *fastidious* 868
  *punctilious* 939
scrutator 461
scrutiny 457, 461
scrutoire 191
scud *sail* 267
  *speed* 274
  *shower* 348
  *cloud* 353
  – under bare
    poles 704
scuffle 720
scull *row* 267
  *brain* 450
scull-cap 225
scullery 191
scullion 746
sculpsit 558
sculptor 559
sculpture 240, **557**
scum *dirt* 653
  – of the earth 949
  – of society 876
scupper 350
scurf 653
scurrilous
  *ridicule* 856
  *malediction* 908
  *disrespect* 929
  *detraction* 934
scurry 274, 684
scurvy
  *insufficient* 640
  *unimportant* 643
  *base* 940
  *wicked* 945
scut 235

scutcheon
  *standard* 550
  *honour* 877
scutiform 251
scuttle *destroy* 162
  *receptacle* 191
  *speed* 274
  – along *haste* 684
Scylla and Charyb-
  dis, between –
  *danger* 665
  *difficulty* 704
Scyllam, incidit
  in – 699
scythe *pointed* 244
  *sharp* 253
'sdeath! *wonder* 870
  *anger* 900
  *disapprobation*
    932
se non è vero è ben
  trovato 546
sea *multitude* 102
  *ocean* 341
  at – 341
  *uncertain* 475
  *erroneous* 495
  go to – 293
  on the high –s 341
  heavy – 315
  the seven –s 341
  – of doubt 475
  – of troubles
    *difficulty* 704
  *adversity* 735
seaboard 342
seafarer 269
seafaring 267, 273
sea-fight 720
sea-girt 346
sea-going 267, 341
sea-green 435
seal
  *matrix* 22
  *close* 261
  *evidence* 467
  *mark* 550
  *resolve* 604
  *complete* 729
  *compact* 769
  *security* 771
  break the – 529
  under – 769
  – the doom of 162
  – one's infamy 940
  – the lips 585
  – of sorcery 528
  – up *restrain* 751
sealed:
  one's fate is – 601
  hermetically – 261

– book
  *ignorance* 491
  *unintelligible* 519
  *secret* 533
sealing-wax 356
seals *insignia* 747
sealskin 223
seam 43
sea-maid 979
sea-man 269
seamanship 692,
  698
sea-mark 550
seamless 50
seamstress 225,
  690
seamy side 651
séance 525, 696
sea-piece 556
seaplane 273, 726
sea-port 666
sear *dry* 340
  *burn* 384
  *deaden* 823
  – and yellow leaf
    128, 659
search *inquire* 461
searching
  *severe* 739
  *painful* 830
searchless 519
searchlight 423,
  726
seared conscience
  951
searing 830
seascape 556
sea-serpent 83
seaside 342
season *mix* 41
  *time* 106
  *pungent* 392
  *accustom* 613
  *preserve* 670
  *prepare* 673
seasonable 23, 134
seasoning 393
seasons 138
seat *place* 183
  *locate* 184
  *abode* 189
  *support* 215
  *posterior* 235
  *parliament* 693
  country – 189
  judgment – 966
  – of government
    737
  – of war 728
seated, firmly – 150
seaway 180

seaweed 367
seaworthy 273, 664
sebaceous 355
secant 219
secede *dissent* 489
  *relinquish* 624
  *disobey* 742
seceder
  *heterodox* 984
secern 297
seclusion **893**
second
  *duplication* 90
  – *of time* 108
  *instant* 113
  – *in music* 413,
    415
  *abet* 707
  play or sing a –
    416
  – best 651, 732
  – childhood 128,
    499
  – crop 168, **775**
  – edition 104
  play – fiddle
    *obey* 743
  *subject* 749
  *disrepute* 874
  – nature 613
  – to none 33
  one's – self 17
  – rate 659
  – sight
    *foresight* 510
    *sorcery* 992
  – thoughts
    *sequel* 65
    *thought* 451
    *improvement* 658
  – youth 660
secondary
  *inferior* 34
  *following* 63
  *imperfect* 651
  *deputy* 759
  – education 537
  – evidence 467
  – school 542
seconder 711
second-hand
  *imitation* 19
  *old* 124
  *deteriorated* 659
  *received* 785
secondly 90
second-rate 651
secret *key* 522
  *latent* 526
  *hidden* 528
  *riddle* **533**

in the – 490
keep a – 585
– motive 615
– passage 627, 671
– place 530
– writing 590
secrétaire 191
secretary
   *recorder* 553
   *writer* 590
   *director* 694
   *auxiliary* 711
   *servant* 746
   *consignee* 758
   – of state 694
   – of the treasury
     801
secrete *excrete* 297
   *conceal* 528
secretion 299
secretive 528
sect 75
   religious – 983,
     984
sectarian
   *dissent* 489
   *ally* 711
   *heterodox* 984
sectary 489
section *division* 44
   *part* 51
   *class* 75
   *chapter* 593
   *troops* 726
sector *part* 51
   *circle* 247
secula seculorum,
   in – 112
secular
   *centenary* 98
   *periodic* 138
   *laity* 997
   – education 537
secularism 984
secundum artem
   82, 698
secure *fasten* 43
   *bespeak* 132
   *belief* 484
   *safe* 664
   *restrain* 751
   *engage* 768
   *gain* 775
   *confident* 858
   – an object 731
securities 802–805
security *safety* 664
   *pledge* **771**
   *hope* 858
lend on – 787
**Sedan**

*disaster* 162
sedan chair 272
sedate
   *thoughtful* 451
   *calm* 826
   *grave* 837
sedative 174, 662
sedentary 265
sedge 367
sedile 1000
sediment *dregs* 653
sedimentary 40
sedition 742
seduce *entice* 615
   *love* 897
   *debauch* 961
seducer 962
seduction 829, 865
sedulous 682, 865
see *view* 441
   *look* 457
   *believe* 484
   *know* 490
   *bishopric* 995
   we shall – 507
   – after 459
   – daylight 480a
   – double 959
   – fit 600, 602
   – at a glance 498
   – justice done 922
   – life 840
   – the light
     born 359
     published 531
   – service 722
   – sights 455
   – through 480a,
     498
   – to *attention* 457
     *care* 459
     *direction* 693
   – one's way
     *foresight* 510
     *intelligible* 518
     *skill* 698
     *easy* 705
seed *small* 32
   *cause* 153
   *posterity* 167
   *grain* 330
   run to – *age* 128
   *lose health* 659
   sow the – 673
seedling 129
seed-plot 168, 371
seed-time of life
   127
seedy *weak* 160
   *disease* 655
   *deteriorated* 659

   *exhausted* 688
   *needy* 804
seeing that 8, 476
seek *inquire* 461
   *pursue* 622
   *offer* 763
   *request* 765
   – safety 664
seek-sorrow 837
seel 217
seem 448
   as it –s good to
     600
seeming 448
seemingly 472
seemless 846, 925
seemliness 926
seemly
   *expedient* 646
   *handsome* 845
   *due* 924
seep 295
seer *veteran* 130
   *madman* 504
   *oracle* 513
   *sorcerer* 994
see-saw 12, 314
seethe *wet* 339
   *hot* 382
   *make hot* 384
   *excitement* 824
seething *caldron*
   386
segar 392
segment 44, 51
segnitude 683
s'égosiller 411
segregate
   *not related* 10
   *separate* 44
   *exclude* 55
segregated
   *incoherent* 47
seigneur, grand –
   *pride* 878
   *insolence* 885
seignior 745, 875
seigniority
   *authority* 737
   *possession* 777
   *property* 780
seigniory 737
seine net 232
seisin 777, 780
seismic 314
seismograph 553
seismometer 276,
   314
seize 789, 791
   – an opportunity
     134

seized with
   *disease* 655
   *feeling* 821
seizure 925
sejunction 44
seldom 137
select *choose* 609
   *good* 648
self 13, 79
   –abasement 879
   –accusing 950
   –admiration 880
   –applause 880
   –appointed task
     602
   –assertion 885
   –called 565
   –command 604,
     864
   –communing 451
   –complacency
     836, 880
   –confidence 880
   –conquest 604
   –conscious 855
   –consultation 451
   –contained 52
   –control 604
   –conviction
     *belief* 484
     *penitent* 950
     *condemned* 971
   –counsel 451
   –deceit *error* 495
   –deception 486
   –defence 717
   –delusion 486
   –denial
     *disinterested* 942
     *temperance* 953
     *penance* 990
   –discipline 990
   –effacement 879,
     942
   –esteem 880
   –evident 474, 525
   –examination 990
   –existing 1
   –government 748
   –help 698
   –immolation 991
   –indulgence
     *selfishness* 943
     *intemperance* 954
   –interest 943
   –knowledge 881
   –love 943
   –luminous 423
   –mastery 604
   –opinioned 481
   –possession

under the – of
  one's wing 664
**shadowy** 4, 447
**shady** 874
**shaft** *deep* 208
  *frame* 215
  *pit* 260
  *missile* 284
  *axis* 312
  *air-pipe* 351
  *handle* 633
  *weapon* 727
**shaggy** 256
**shagreen** 223
**shah** 745
**shake** *totter* 149
  *weak* 160
  *vibrate* 314
  *agitation* 315
  *shiver* 383
  *trill* 407
  *music* 416
  *dissuade* 616
  *injure* 659
  *impress* 821
  *excited* 824
  *fear* 860
– one's faith 485
– hands
  *pacification* 723
  *friendship* 888
  *courtesy* 894
  *forgive* 918
– the head
  *dissent* 489
  *deny* 536
  *refuse* 764
  *disapprove* 932
– off 297
~ off the yoke 750
– to pieces 162
– one's sides 838
– up 315
**shakedown** *bed* 215
**shakes, no great** –
  643, 651
**shako** 225, 717
**shaky** *weak* 160
  *in danger* 665
  *fearful* 860
**shallop** 273
**shallow**
  *not deep* 32, 209
  *ignorant* 491
  *ignoramus* 493
  *foolish* 499
  *trifling* 643
– pretext 617
– profundity 855
**shallow-brain** 501
**shallowness** 209

**shallow-pated** 499
**shallows**
  *danger* 667
**sham** *imitation* 19
  *falsehood* 544
  *deception* 545,
  546
– fight 720
**shaman** 994
**shamanism** 992
**shamble** 275, 315
**shambles** 361
**shame**
  *disrepute* 874
  *wrong* 923
  *censure* 932
  *chastity* 960
  cry – upon 932
  false – 855
  for – 874
  sense of – 879
– the devil 939
  to one's – be it
  spoken 874
**shamefaced** 881
**shameful**
  *disgraceful* 874
  *profligate* 945
**shameless**
  *bold* 525
  *impudent* 885
  *profligate* 945
  *indecent* 961
**shampoo** 652
**shandredhan** 272
**shanghai** 791
**shank** *support* 215
  *instrument* 633
**Shanks's mare** 266
**shanty** 189
**shape** 240, 448
– one's course
  *direction* 278
  *pursuit* 622
  *conduct* 692
– out a course 626
**shapeless** 241, 846
**shapely** 242, 845
**shard** 51
**share**
  *part* 51
  *participate* 778
  *allotted portion*
  786
– and share alike
  778
**shareholder** 778
**shark** 792
**sharp**
  *energetic* 171
  *violent* 173

*acute* 253
*sensible* 375
*pungent* 392
– sound 410
*musical tone* 413
*intelligent* 498
*active* 682
*clever* 698
*cunning* 702
*feeling* 821
*painful* 830
*rude* 895
*censorious* 932
look – 459, 682
– appetite 865
– contest 720
– ear 418
– eye 441
– fellow 682, 700
– frost 383
– look-out 459,
  507
– pain 378
– practice
  *cunning* 702
  *severity* 739
  *improbity* 940
– set 865
**sharpen**
  [*see* sharp]
  *excite* 824
– one's tools 673
– one's wits 537
**sharpener** 253
**sharper** 792
**sharpness** 253
**sharpshooter** 726
**sharpshooting** 716
**Shaster** 986
**shatter** *disjoin* 44
  *disperse* 73
  *render powerless*
  158
  *destroy* 162
**shatter-brained** 503
**shattered** 160, 688
**shave** *reduce* 195
  *shorten* 201
  *layer* 204
  *smooth* 255
  *cut* 44
  *lie* 546
  close – 671
**shaved** 226
**shaving** *small* 32
  *layer* 204
  *filament* 205
**shave-tail** 726, 745
**shawl** 225
**shawm** 417
**shay** 272

**she** 374
**sheaf** 72
**shear** *reduce* 195
  *shorten* 201
  *sheep* 370
  *take* 789
**shears** 253
**sheath** 191, 223
**sheathe** 225
  *moderate* 174
– the sword 723
**sheathing** 223
**sheave** 633
**shed** *scatter* 73
  *building* 189
  *divest* 226
  *emit* 297
  *give* 784
– blood 361
– light upon 420
– a lustre on 873
– tears 839
**Shedim** 980
**sheen** 420
**sheep** 366
**sheep-dog** 366
**sheep-fold** 232
**sheepish** 881
**sheep's eye, cast a** –
  *desire* 865
  *modest* 881
  *endearment* 902
**sheer** *simple* 42
  *complete* 52
  *deviate* 279
– off *avoid* 623
**sheet** *layer* 204
  *covering* 223
  *paper* 593
  come down in –s
  *rain* 348
  white – 952
  winding – 363
– of fire 382
– of water 343
**sheet-anchor**
  *safety* 664, 666
  *hope* 858
**sheet-lightning** 423
**sheik** *ruler* 745, 875
  *lover* 897
  *priest* 996
**shelf** 215, 667
  on the –
  *powerless* 158
  *disused* 678
  *inaction* 681
**shell** *cover* 223
  *coffin* 363
  *bombard* 716
  *bomb* 727

- of its beams
 422, 874
- lamb 828
**short**
 *not long* 201
 *brittle* 328
 *concise* 572
 *uncivil* 895
 come – of, fall – of
 *inferior* 34
 *shortcoming* 304
 *insufficient* 640
 in – 572, 596
 – allowance 640
 – answer 895
 – breath 688
 – by 201
 – of cash 804
 – commons
 *insufficiency* 640
 *fasting* 956
 – circuit 279, 628
 – cut *straight* 246
 *mid-course* 628
 – distance 197
 – life and merry
 840
 – measure 53
 at – notice 111,
 132
 – of *small* 32
 *inferior* 34
 *subtraction* 38
 *incomplete* 53
 *shortcoming* 304
 *insufficient* 640
 – sea 348
 make – work of
 *destroy* 162
 *active* 682
 *haste* 684
 *complete* 729
 *conquer* 731
 *punish* 972
**shortage** 53
**shortcoming**
 *inequality* 28
 *inferiority* 34
 *motion short of*
 **304**
 *non-completion*
 730
 *deficiency* 945
**shorten** 201
 – sail 275
**shorthand** 590
**short-handed** 651
**shorthorn** 366
**short-lived** 111
**shortly** *soon* 132
**shortness** 201

for – sake 572
**shorts** 225
**short-sighted**
 *myopic* 443
 *misjudging* 481
 *foolish* 499
**short-story** 594
**short-winded** 160,
 688
**short-witted** 499
**shot** *missile* 284
 *report* 406
 *variegated* 440
 *guess* 514
 *war material* 722,
 727
 *price* 812
 *reward* 973
 bad – 701
 exchange –s 720
 good – 700
 have a – at 716
 like a – 113
 off like a – 623
 pistol – 406
 random – 463, 621
 round – 727
 – in the locker 632
 not have a – in
 one's locker 804
 – and shell 722
**shot-free** 815
**shot-gun** 727
**should be:**
 no better than
 she – 961
 what – 922
**shoulder**
 *support* 215
 *projection* 250
 *shove* 276
 broad –ed 159
 cold – 289
 have on one's –s
 625
 on the –s of
 *high* 206
 *elevated* 307
 *instrumentality*
 631
 shrug the –s
 [*see* shrug]
 rest on the –s of
 926
 rub –s with no-
 bility 852
 take upon one's –s
 676
 – arms 673
 – a musket 722
 – to shoulder 709,

712
 – to the wheel
 604, 676
**shoulder-knot** 847
**shoulder-strap** 747
**shout**
 *loud* 404
 *cry* 411
 *rejoice* 838
**shove** 276
 give a – to
 *aid* 707
**shovel**
 *receptacle* 191
 *transfer* 270
 *vehicle* 272
 *fire-iron* 386
 *cleanness* 652
 put to bed with
 a – 363
 – away 297
**shovel-hat** 999
**show** *visible* 446
 *appear* 448
 *draw attention*
 457
 *evidence* 467
 *demonstrate* 478
 *manifest* 525
 *entertainment* 599
 *parade* 882
 dumb – 550
 make a – 544
 mere – 544
 peep– 840
 – off 525
 – one's cards 529
 – cause 527
 – one's colours,
 550
 – one's face
 *presence* 186
 *manifest* 525
 *disclose* 529
 – fight *defy* 715
 *attack* 716
 *defend* 717
 *brave* 861
 – forth 525
 – in front 303
 – one's cards 529
 – one's hand 529
 – a light pair of
 heels 623
 – itself 446
 – of 17, 472
 – off 882, 884
 – one's teeth 715
 – up *visible* 446
 *manifest* 525
 *ridicule* 856

*degrade* 874
 *censure* 932
 *accuse* 938
**shower**
 *assemblage* **72**
 *rain* 348
 – bath 386
 – down
 *abundance* 639
 – down upon 784,
 816
**showman** 524
**showy** *colour* 428
 *beauty* 845
 *ornament* 847
 *fashion* 852
 *vulgar* 851
 *ostentatious* 882
**shrapnel** 727
**shred** 32, 205
**shredder** 260
**shrew** 901
**shrewd**
 *knowing* 490
 *wise* 498
 *cunning* 702
**shriek** 410, 411
**shrievalty** 965
**shrieve** 965
**shrift**
 *confession* 529
 *absolution* 952
**shriftless** 951
**shrill** 410, 411
**shrimp** 193
**shrine** 363, 1000
 *receptacle* 191
**shrink**
 *decrease* 36
 *shrivel* 195
 go back 283, 287
 *unwilling* 603
 *avoid* 623
 *sensitive* 822
 – from *fear* 860
 *dislike* 867
 *hate* 898
**shrive** 952, 998
**shrivel** 195
**shrivelled** *thin* 203
**shroud** *cover* 225
 *funeral* 363
 *hide* 528
 *safety* 664
 *defend* 717
 –ed in mystery
 519
**shrouds** 45
**Shrove Tuesday**
 998
**shrub** *plant* 367

*omen* 512
*indication* 550
*record* 551
*write* 590
*compact* 769
*prodigy* 872
give – of 525
make no – 585
– of the cross 998
–s of the times
*indication* 550
*omen* 512
*warning* 668
–s of the zodiac
318
**signal** *great* 31
*sign* 550
*important* 642
give the – 741
– of distress 669
**signalize**
*indicate* 550
*glory* 873
*celebrate* 883
**signally** 31
**signal oil** 356
**signal-post** 668
**signature**
*mark, identifica-*
*tion* 550
*writing* 590
*compact* 769
*security* 771
**sign-board** 550
**signet**
*mark, identifica-*
*tion* 550
*sign of authority*
747
*compact* 769
writer to the – 968
**significant** 642
[*see* signify]
*evidence* 467
*important* 642
**signifies, what** –
643
**signify**
*forebode* 511
*mean* 516
*inform* 527
**signior** 875
**sign-manual** 550,
590
**signor** 373, 877
**signora** 374
**sign-painter** 559
**sign-painting** 555
**sign-post** 550
**signum, ecce** – 550
**sike** 348

[ 640 ]

**silence** *disable* 158
*no sound* **403**
*confute* 479
*latency* 526
*concealment* 528
*aphony* 581
*taciturn* 585
*check* 731
**silencer** 405, 408
**silentio, sub** –
*silent* 403
*inattention* 458
*latent* 526
**silhouette**
*outline* 230, 448
*shadow* 421
*portrait* 556
**siliquose** 191
**silk** 255, 324
– gown
*barrister* 968
– hat 225
make a – purse
out of a sow's
ear 471
**silken repose** 687
**silkiness** 954
**sill** 215
**silly**
*credulous* 486
*imbecile* 499
*insane* 503
**silo** 636
**silt** *deposit* 321
*dirt* 653
**silvan** 367
**silver** *bright* 420
*white* 430
*grey* 432
*money* 800
bait with a – hook
615
german – 545
– lining of the
cloud 858
– wedding 883
**silver certificate**
800
**silver-toned** 413
**silviculture** 371
**simagrée** 855
**similarity** 17
– of form 240
**simile**
*similarity* 17
*comparison* 464
*metaphor* 521
**similitude** 17, 21
**simmer**
*agitation* 315
*boil* 382, 384

*excitement* 824
**simmering** 825
**simoleon** 800
**Simon Pure**
the real – 494
**Simon, Simple** –
501, 547
**Simon Stylites** 893
**simony** 964
**simoon** 349, 382
**simper** *smile* 838
*affectation* 855
**simple** *mere* 32
*unmixed* 42
*credulous* 486
*ignorant* 493
*silly* 499
- *language* 576
*herb* 662
*artless* 703
*unadorned* 849
– meaning 516
**simple-hearted** 543
**simpleness** **42**
**Simple Simon** 501,
547
**simpleton** 501
**simplex munditiis**
849
**simplicity**
[*see* simple] **849**
*ignorance* 491
**simplify**
[*see* simple]
*elucidate* 518
**simply** 32, 87
more – 522
**simulacrum** 19
**simulate**
*resemble* 17
*imitate* 19
*cheat* 544
**simultaneous** 120
**sin** 945, 947
**sinapism** 662
**since** *under the cir-*
*cumstances* 8
*after* 117
*cause* 155
*reason* 476
**sincere**
*veracious* 543
*ingenuous* 703
*feeling* 821
**sine** 217
**sine:** – curâ 831
– die 107, 133
– ictu 158
– quâ non
*required* 630
*important* 642

*condition* **770**
**sinecure** 681
no – 682
**sinew** 159
**sinewless** 158
**sinews of war** 800
**sinful** 945
**sing** *bird* 412
*resonance* 408
*music* 416
*voice* 580
*poetry* 597
*rejoice* 838
– Io triumphe 884
– out 411
– praises
*approve* 931
*worship* 990
– in the shrouds
349
– small 879
**singe** 382, 384
**singer** 416
**single** *unmixed* 42
*unit* 87
*secluded* 893
*unmarried* 904
ride at – anchor
863
– combat 720
– entry
– file 69
– out 609
**single-handed**
*one* 87
*easy* 705
*unassisted* 706
**single-minded** 703
**singleness**
[*see* single]
– of heart 703, 939
– of purpose 604a,
703
**single-stick** 720
**singlet** 225
**Sing Sing** 752
**sing-song** 414, 892
**singular** *special* 79
*exceptional* 83
*one* 87
**singularly** *very* 31
**sinister** *left* 239
*bad* 649
*vicious* 945
bar –
*imperfect* 651
*disrepute* 874
**sinistrality** **239**
**sinistromanual** 239
**sinistrous**

*prostitute* 962
**skittish**
  *capricious* 608
  *excitable* 825
  *timid* 862
  *bashful* 881
**skittle sharper** 792
**skittles** 840
**skiver** 253
**skulk** 528, 862
**skull** 450
**skull-cap** 225
**skunk** 401
**skurry** 684
**sky** *summit* 210
  *world* 318
  *air* 338
  *necessity* 601
**sky-aspiring** 865
**sky-blue** 438
**sky-lark** 305
**sky-larking** 840
**sky-light** 260
**sky-line** 196
**sky-pilot** 996
**sky-rocket** 305
**sky-scraper** 206, 210
**slab** *layer* 204
  *support* 215
  *flat* 251
  *viscous* 352
  *record* 551
**slabber** *slaver* 297
  *unclean* 653
**slack** *loose* 47
  *weak* 160
  *inert* 172
  *slow* 275
  *cool* 385
  *fuel* 388
  *neglectful* 460
  *unwilling* 603
  *insufficient* 640
  *inactive* 683
  *lax* 738
**slacken**
  *loosen* 47
  *moderate* 174
  *repose* 687
  *hinder* 706
  one's pace 275
**slacker** 460, 603, 623, 927
**slag** *embers* 384
  *inutility* 645
  *dirt* 653
**slake** *quench* 174
  *gratify* 829
  *satiate* 869
  – one's appetite

*intemperance* 954
**slam** 276, 406
  – the door in one's face
  *oppose* 708
  *refuse* 764
**slammerkin** 653
**slander** 934
**slanderer** 936
**slang** 560, 563, 908
**slant** 217
**slap** *instantly* 113
  *strike* 276
  *censure* 932
  *punish* 972
  – in the face
  *opposition* 708
  *attack* 716
  *anger* 900
  *disrespect* 929
  *disapprobation* 932
  – the forehead 461
**slap-dash** 684
**slash** 44, 308
**slashing** *style* 574
**slate**
  *writing tablet* 590
  *election* 609
  *disparage* 932
  clean the – 918
  – loose *mad* 503
**slate-coloured** 432
**slates** *roof* 223
**slattern**
  *disorder* 59
  *dirty* 653
  *bungler* 701
  *vulgar* 851
**slatternly** 699
**slaughter** 361
**slaughter-house** 361
**slave** *instrumentality* 631
  *toil* 686
  *servant* 746
  a – to 749
  – trade 795
**slaver** *ship* 273
  *slobber* 297
  *dirt* 653
  *flatter* 933
**slavery** 686, 749
**slavish** 749, 886
**slay** 361
**sleave** 59
**sled** 272
**sledge** 272
**sledge-hammer** 276
  with a – 162, 686

**sleek** 255, 845
**sleep** 683
  last – 360
  rock to – 174
  send to – 841
  not have a wink of – 825
  – with one eye open 459
  – at one's post 683
  – upon 133, 451
  – walker 268
  – walking 266
**sleeper** *support* 215
  wake the seven –s 404
**sleeping partner** 683
**sleepless** 682
**sleepy** 683
**sleet** 383
**sleeve** *skein* 219
  *dress* 225
  hang on the – of 746
  wear one's heart upon his – 525, 703
  in one's – 528
  laugh in one's – 838, 856
**sleeveless** 499, 608
  – errand 645, 699
**sleigh** 272
**sleight** *skill* 698
  – of hand 545
**slender** *small* 32
  *thin* 203
  *trifling* 643
  – means 804
**sleuth** 527
  – hound 913
**slew round** 312
**slice** *cut* 44
  *piece* 51
  *layer* 204
**slick** 682, 698
**slicker** 225
**slide** *elapse* 109
  *smooth* 255
  *pass* 264
  *locomotion* 266
  *descend* 306
  – back 661
  – in 228
  – into 144
**sliding** 840
**sliding-panel** 545
**sliding-rule** 85
**slight** *small* 32
  *slender* 203

*rare* 322
*neglect* 460
*disparage* 483
*feeble* 575
*trifle* 643
*dereliction* 927
*disrespect* 929
*contempt* 930
**slight-made** 203
**slily**
  *surreptitiously* 544
  *craftily* 702
**slim** 203
  *cunning* 702
**slime** *viscous* 352
  *dirt* 653
**sling** *hang* 214
  *project* 284
  *weapon* 727
**slink** *hide* 528
  *cowardice* 862
  – away *avoid* 623
  *disrepute* 874
**slip** *small* 32
  *elapse* 109
  *child* 129
  *strip* 205
  *petticoat* 225
  *descend* 306
  *error* 495
  *workshop* 691
  *fail* 732
  *false coin* 800
  *vice* 945
  *guilt* 947
  give one the – 671
  let – *liberate* 750
  *lose* 776
  *relinquish* 782
  – away 187, 623
  – cable 623
  – the collar 671, 750
  – 'twixt cup and lip 509
  let – the dogs of war 722
  – in (*or* – into) 294
  – the memory 506
  – on 225
  – out 187
  – over *neglect* 460
  – of the pen 568
  – of the tongue *solecism* 568
  *stammering* 583
  – through the fingers *miss an opportunity* 135
  *escape* 671

*fail* 732
**slipper** 225
hunt the – 840
**slippery**
  *transient* 111
  *smooth* 255
  *greasy* 355
  *uncertain* 475
  *vacillating* 607
  *dangerous* 665
  *facile* 705
  *faithless* 940
  – ground 667
**slipshod** 575
**slipslop**
  *absurdity* 497
  *solecism* 568
  *weak language* 575
**slit** *divide* 44
  *chink* 198
  *furrow* 259
**slither** 264
**sliver** 32
**slobber** *drivel* 297
  *slop* 337
  *dirt* 653
**sloe** *black* 431
**slog** 143
**slogan** 722
**sloop** 273
  –of-war 726
**slop** *spill* 297
  *water* 337
  *dirt* 653
**slope** *oblique* 217
  *run away* 623
**sloppy** *moist* 339
  *marsh* 345
  – *style* 575
**slops** *clothes* 225
**slosh** 337, 653
**slot** 44, 260
**sloth** 683
**slouch** *low* 207
  *oblique* 217
  *move slowly* 275
  *inactive* 683
**slouching** *ugly* 846
**slough**
  *quagmire* 345
  *dirt* 653
  *difficulty* 704
  *adversity* 735
  – of Despond 859
**sloven** *untidy* 59
  *bungler* 701
**slovenly** *untidy* 59
  *careless* 460
  – *style* 575
  *dirty* 653

*awkward* 699
  *vulgar* 851
**slow** *tardy* 133
  *inert* 172
  *moderate* 174
  *motion* 275
  *inactive* 683
  *wearisome* 841
  *dull* 843
by – degrees 26
– movement
  *music* 415
march in – time 275
– as molasses in January 275
be – to
  *unwilling* 603
  *not finish* 730
  *refuse* 764
**slow-coach** 701
**slowness** **275**
**sloyd** 537
**slubber** 653
**slubberdegullion** 876
**sludge** 653
**slug** *slow* 275
  *inaction* 681
  *inactivity* 683
  *bullet* 727
**sluggard** 275, 683
**sluggish** 172, 823, 843
**sluice** *limit* 233
  *egress* 295
  *river* 348
  *conduit* 350
open the –s 297
**slum** 653
**slumber** 683
**slump** 304
**slur** *blemish* 848
  *stigma* 874
  *gloss over* 937
  *reproach* 938
  – over *neglect* 460
  *slight* 483
**slush** *marsh* 345
  *semiliquid* 352
  *dirt* 653
**slut** *untidy* 59
  *female* 374
  *dirty* 653
  *unchaste* 962
**sly** *stealthy* 528
  *cunning* 702
**smack**
  *small quantity* 32
  *mixture* 41
  *boat* 273

*impulse* 276
  *taste* 390
  *thud* 406
  *kiss* 902
  *strike* 972
– the lips
  *pleasure* 377
  *taste* 390
  *savoury* 394
  *rejoice* 838
  – of *resemble* 17
**small**
  – *in degree* 32
  – *in size* 193
become – 195
feel – 879
of – account 643
esteem of –
  account 930
  – arms 727
  – beer 643, 880, 930
  – coin 800
  – chance 473
  – fry 193, 643, 876
  – matter 643
  – number 103
  – part 51
  – pica 591
in the – hours 125
on a – scale 32, 193
  – talk 588
**small-bore** 727
**small-clothes** 225
**smaller** 34, 195
**smallness** **32**
**smalls** 225
**smalt** 438
**smart** *pain* 378
  *active* 682
  *clever* 698
  *feel* 821
  *grief* 828
  *witty* 842
  *pretty* 845
  *ornamental* 847
  – *pace* 274
  – *saying* 842
  – *under* 821
**smarten** 847
**smart-money** 973
**smash** 162, 732
**smasher** 792
**smatch** 390
**smatterer** 493
**smattering** 491
**smear** *cover* 223
  *soil* 653
  *blemish* 848
**smell** 398

bad – 401
– of the lamp
  *ornate style* 577
  *prepared* 673
  – powder 722
**smell-feast** 886
**smelling-bottle** 400
**smelt** *heat* 384
  *prepare* 673
**smicker** 838
**smile** 836, 838
raise a – 840
  – at 856
  – of contempt 930
  – of fortune 734
  – upon *aid* 707
  *courtesy* 894
  *endearment* 902
**smirch** 431, 653
**smirk** 838
**smite** *maltreat* 649
  *excite* 824
  *afflict* 830
  *punish* 972
**smith** 690
**smithereens** 162
**smitten** *love* 897
  – with *moved* 615
**smock** 225, 258
**smock-faced** 862
**smock-frock** 225
**smoke**
  *dust* 330
  *vapour* 336
  *heat* 382
  *tobacco* 392
  *discover* 480a
  *suspect* 485
  *unimportant* 643
  *dirt* 653
  *cure* 670
  *disrespect* 929
end in –
  *shortcoming* 304
  *failure* 732
  – the calumet of peace 723
  –ed glasses 424
  – screen 424
  – stack 260
**smoking hot** 382
**smoking-jacket** 225
**smoking-room** 191
**smoky** *opaque* 426
  *dirty* 653
**smooth** *uniform* 16
  *calm* 174
  *flattery* 213, 251
  *not rough* 255
  *easy* 705
  – the bed of death

[ 645 ]

**song** *music* 415
  *poem* 597
  death – 360, 839
  love– 597
  for a mere – 815
  no – no supper 812
  old – 643
**songster** 416
**soniferous** 402
**sonnet** 597
**sonneteer** 597
**sonorous** *sound* 402
  *loud* 404
  *language* 577
**sons of:**
  – Belial 988
  – God 977
**Soofeeism** 984
**soon** *transient* 111
  *future* 121
  *early* 132
  too – for 135
**sooner:** – or later
  *another time* 119
  *future* 121
  – said than done
    704
**soot** 431, 653
**sooth** 511
  in good – 543
**soothe**
  *allay* 174
  *relieve* 834
  *flatter* 933
**soothing**
  *faint sound* 405
  – syrup 174
**soothsay** 511
**soothsayer** 513, 994
**soothsaying** 511
**sop**
  *small quantity* 32
  *food* 298
  *fool* 501
  *inducement* 615
  *reward* 973
  – to Cerberus 458
  – in the pan 615
**soph** 492, 541
**Sophi** 745, 996
**sophism** 477, 497
**sophist** *scholar* 492
  *dissembler* 548
**sophister** 492
  *student* 541
**sophistical** 477
**sophisticate** *mix* 41
  *debase* 659
**sophisticated**
  *spurious* 545
**sophistry** 477

**sophomore** 541
**soporific** 683, 841
**soporous** 683
**soprano** 410, 416
**sorbet** 298
**sorcerer** 994
**sorcery** 992
**sordes** 653
**sordet** 417
**sordid** *stingy* 819
  *covetous* 865
**sordine** 417
**sore**
  *bodily pain* 378
  *disease* 655
  *mental suffering*
    828, 830
  *discontent* 832
  *anger* 900
  – as a boil 901*a*
  – place 822
  – subject 830, 900
**sorely** *very* 31
**s'orienter** 278
**sorites** 476
**sorority** 712
**sorrel** 433, 434
**sorrow** 828
  give – words 839
**sorry** *trifling* 643
  *grieved* 828
  *mean* 876
  make a – face 874
  cut a – figure 874
  be – for 750, 914
  in a – plight 732
  – sight 830, 837
**sort** *degree* 26
  *arrange* 60
  *kind* 75
  – with
  *sociality* 892
**sortable** }
**sortance** }
  *agreement* 23
**sortes**
  *chance* 156, 621
  – Virgilianæ
  *sorcery* 992
**sortie** 716
**sortilege**
  *prediction* 511
  *sorcery* 992
**sortilegy** 621
**sortition** 621
**sorts, out of –**
  *ill-health* 655
  *sulky* 901*a*
**S.O.S.** 669, 707
**so-so** *small* 32
  *trifling* 643

*imperfect* 651
**sostenuto** 415
**sot** *fool* 501
  *drunkard* 959
**sot à triple étage**
  501
**sotto voce**
  *faint sound* 405
  *conceal* 528
  *voiceless* 581
**sou** *money* 800
  qui n'a pas le –
    804
**soubrette** 599, 746
**sough** *conduit* 350
  *noise* 405
  *cloaca* 653
**soul** *essence* 5
  *person* 372
  *intellect* 450
  *genius* 498
  *affections* 820
  cure of –s 995
  flow of – 588
  not a – 187
  not dare to say
    one's – is his
    own *subjection*
    749
  *fear* 860
  – of wit 572
  have one's whole
    – in his work
    686
**soulless** 683, 823
**soul-mate** 903
**soul-sick** 837
**soul-stirring** 821,
  824
**sound** *great* 31
  *conformable* 82
  *stable* 150
  *strong* 159
  *fathom* 208
  *bay* 343
  *noise* 402
  *investigate* 461
  *measure* 466
  *true* 494
  *wise* 498
  *sane* 502
  *good* 648
  *perfect* 650
  *healthy* 654
  *solvent* 803
  *orthodox* 983*a*
  catch a – 418
  safe and – 654,
    670
  – the alarm
  *indication* 550

  *warning* 668
  *alarm* 669
  *fear* 860
  – asleep 683
  full of – and fury
  *unmeaning* 517
  *insolent* 885
  – the horn 416
  – of limb 654
  – locator 726
  – mind 502
  – the praises of
    931
  – the note of prep-
    aration 673
  – reasoning 476
  – a retreat 283
  – sleep 683
  – a trumpet
  *publish* 531
  *alarm* 669
  – of wind 654
**sounding:** big –
  577
  – brass 517
**sounding-board** 417
**soundings** 208
**soundless**
  *unfathomable* 208
  *silent* 403
**soup** 298, 352
**soupçon** 32, 41
**soufflé** 298
**sour** *acid* 397
  *discontented* 832
  *embitter* 835
  *uncivil* 895
  *sulky* 901
  – grapes
  *impossible* 471
  *excuse* 617
  – the temper 830
**source** *beginning* 66
  *cause* 153
**sourdet** 417
**sourdine** 417
  à la – *noiseless* 405
  *concealed* 528
**sourdough** 463
**soured** 832
**sourness** 397
**sous tous les**
  **rapports** 52
**souse** 310, 337
**South** *direction* 278
  North and –
  *opposite* 237
**Southern**
  *antipodes* 237
  – Cross 318
**souvenir** 505

*optical instru-
ment* 445
**spectrum**
*colour* 428
*variegation* 440
*optical illusion*
443
**speculate**
*view* 441
*think* 451
*suppose* 514
*chance* 621
*essay* 675
*traffic* 794
**speculation**
*experiment* 463
*cards* 840
**speculative** 463, 514
**speculum** 445
veluti in – 446
**sped** *completed* 729
**speech** 582
figure of – 521
parts of – 567
**speechify** 582
**speechless** 403, 581
**speechmaker** 582
**speed**
*velocity* 274
*activity* 682
*haste* 684
*help* 707
*succeed* 731
with breathless –
684
God – 731, 906
**speedily** *soon* 132
**speedometer** 200,
274, 553
**speedway** 840
**speer** 455, 461
**spell** *period* 106
*influence* 175
*read* 539
*letter* 561
*necessity* 601
*motive* 615
*exertion* 686
*charm* **993**
cast a – 992
*wonder* 870
knurr and – 840
– for 865
– out *interpret* 522
**spell-bound** 601,
615
**spence** 636
**spencer** 225
**spend** *effuse* 297
*waste* 638
*give* 784

*purchase* 795
*expend* 809
– freely 816
– time 106
– time in 683
– one's time in
625
**spender** 818
**spendthrift** 818
**spent** 160, 688
**spermaceti** 356
**spermatic** 168
**spermatize** 168
**spero, dum spiro** –
858
**spes sibi quisque**
604
**spew** 297
**sphacelus** 655
**sphere** *rank* 26
*domain* 75
*space* 180
*region* 181
*ball* 249
*world* 318
*business* 625
– of influence 181,
780
**spheroid** 249
**spherule** 249
**sphery** 318
**Sphinx** *monster* 83
*oracle* 513
*ambiguous* 520
*riddle* 533
**spial** 668
**spice**
*small quantity* 32
*mixture* 41
*pungent* 392
*condiment* 393
**spiced** 390
**spicilegium** 72, 596
**spick and span** 123
**spiculate** 253
**spiculum** 253
**spicy** 400, 824
**spigot** 263
**spike** *sharp* 253
*pierce* 260
*plug* 263
– guns 158, 645
**spikebit** 262
**spikenard** 356
**spill** *filament* 205
*stopper* 263
*shed* 297
*splash* 348
*match* 388
*waste* 638
*lavish* 818

– blood 722
– and pelt 59
**spin** *flying* 267
*rotate* 312
*pluck* 610
– out *protract* 110
*late* 133
*prolong* 200
*diffuse style* 573
– the wheel 140
– a long yarn 549
**spindle** 312
**spindling** 203
**spindle-shanks** 203
**spindle-shaped** 253
**spindrift** 353
**spine** 222, 253
**spinel** 847
**spinet** *copse* 367
*harpsichord* 417
**spinney** 367
**spinner of yarns**
594
**spinosity**
*unintelligible* 519
*discourtesy* 895
*sullenness* 901a
**spinous** *prickly* 253
**spinster** 374, 904
**spiracle** 351
**spiral** 248
**spire** *height* 206
*convolution* 248
*peak* 253
*soar* 305
**spirit** *essence* 5
*immateriality* 317
*fuel* 388
*intellect* 450
*meaning* 516
*vigorous language*
574
*activity* 682
*affections* 820
*courage* 861
*ghost* 980
bad – 980
keep one's – up
*hope* 858
with life and – 682
unclean – 978
– away 791
– up 615, 824
**Spirit, the Holy** –
976
**spirited**
*language* 574
*active* 682
*sensitive* 822
*cheerful* 836
*brave* 861

*generous* 942
**spiritless**
*insensible* 823
*sad* 837
*cowardly* 862
**spirit-level** 213
**spiritoso** *music* 415
**spirit-rapping** 992
**spirits** *drink* 298,
959
*cheer* 836
**spirit-stirring** 824
**spiritual**
*immaterial* 317
*psychical* 450
*heterodoxy* 984
*divine* 976
*pious* 987
– director 996
– existence 987
**spiritualism**
*immateriality* 317
*intellect* 450
*sorcery* 992
**spiritualize** 317
*reasoning* 476
**spirituel** 842
**spirt** *eject* 297
*stream* 348
*haste* 684
*exertion* 686
**spirtle** *disperse* 73
*splash* 348
**spissitude** 321, 352
**spit** *pointed* 253
*perforate* 260
*eject* 297
*rotate* 312
*rain* 348
– fire *irascible* 901
**spite** 907
in – of
*disagreement* 24
*notwithstanding*
30
*counteraction* 179
*opposition* 708
in – of one's teeth
*unwilling* 603
*compulsion* 744
**spiteful** 898, 907
*hating* 898
**spittle** 299
**spittoon** 191
**splanchnology** 329
**splash** *affuse* 337
*stream* 348
*spatter* 653
*parade* 882
make a –
*fame* 873

put a – to 142
– the breath 361
– the ears 419
– a flow 348
– a gap 660
– the mouth 479,
  581
– payment 808
– press news 532
– short 142, 265
– short of 304
– the sound 408a
– up 261
– the way 706
**stopcock** 263
**stopgap**
  *substitute* 147
  *stopper* 263
**stoppage**
  *cessation* 142
  *hindrance* 706
**stopper 263**
**stopping place** 292
**store** *store* 184
  *stock* **636**
  *shop* 799
  in – *destiny* 152
  *preparing* 673
  lay in a – 637
  set – by 642, 931
  set no – 483
  – of knowledge
    490
  – in the memory
    505
**store-house** 636
**store-keeper** 636
**store-ship** 273, 726
**storied** 594
**storm** *crowd* 72
  *convulsion* 146
  *violence* 173
  *agitation* 315
  *wind* 349
  *danger* 667
  *attack* 716
  *passion* 825
  *anger* 900
  ride the – 267
  take by –
  *conquer* 731
  *seize* 789
  – brewing 665
  – in a teacup
  *overrate* 482
  *exaggerate* 549
  *unimportance* 643
**storthing** 696
**story** *rooms* 191
  *layer* 204
  *news* 532

*lie* 546
*history* 594
the old – 897
as the – goes 532
**story-teller** 548, 594
**stot** 366
**stound** 870
**stoup** *cup* 191
  *altar* 1000
**stour** 59
**stout** *strong* 159
  *large* 192
  *drink* 298
**stout-hearted** 861
**stove** *fireplace* 386
  – in 252
**stow** *locate* 184
  *pack close* 195
  *store* 636
**stowage** 180, 184
**stowaway** 528, 673
**strabism** 443
**straddle** 266, 607
**Stradivarius** 417
**strafe** 972
**straggle** 266, 279
**straggler** 268
**straggling** 44, 59
**straight**
  *vertical* 212
  *rectilinear* 246
  *direction* 278
  all – *rich* 803
  *solvent* 807
  – course 628
  – descent 167
  – face 837
  – sailing 705
**straighten** 246
  – up 60
**straightforward** 278
  *truthful* 543
  *artless* 703
  *honourable* 939
**straightness 246**
**straight shot** 278
**straightway** 132
**strain** *race* 11
  *weaken* 160
  *operation* 170
  *violence* 173
  *percolate* 295
  *transgress* 303
  *sound* 402
  *melody* 415
  *overrate* 482
  *exaggerate* 549
  *style* 569
  *poetry* 597
  *voice* 580
  *clean* 652

*effort* 686
*fatigue* 688
– in the arms 902
– one's eyes 441,
  507
– at a gnat and
  swallow a camel
  608
– one's invention
  515
– the meaning 523
– every nerve 686
– a point
  go *beyond* 303
  *exaggerate* 549
  *not observe* 773
  *undue* 925
  – the throat 411
**strait**
  *interval* 198
  *water* 343
  *difficulty* 704
**straitened**
  *poor* 804
**strait-handed** 819
**strait-jacket** 752
**strait-laced**
  *severe* 739
  *restraint* 751
  *fastidious* 868
  *haughty* 878
**strait-waistcoat**
  751, 752
**strake** 205
**stramash** 720
**strand** *thread* 205
  *shore* 231, 342
**stranded**
  *stuck fast* 150
  *in difficulty* 704
  *failure* 732
  *pain* 828
**strange**
  *unrelated* 10
  *exceptional* 83
  *ridiculous* 853
  *wonderful* 870
  – bedfellows 713
  – to say 870
**strangely** *much* 31
**stranger** 57
  a – to 491
**strangle**
  *render powerless*
  158
  *contract* 195
  *kill* 361
**strap** *fasten* 43
  *fastening* 45
  *restraint* 752
  *punish* 972

*instrument of
  punishment* **975**
**strappado** 972
**strapping**
  *mighty* 31
  *strong* 159
  *pace* 274
  *big* 192
**strapwork** 847
**stratagem**
  *deception* 545
  *plan* 626
  *artifice* 702
**strategic** *plan* 626
  *artifice* 702
**strategist**
  *planner* 626
  *director* 694
  *proficient* 700
**strategy** 692, 722
**strath** 252
**strathspey** 840
**stratification** 204,
  329
**stratocracy** 737
**stratosphere** 338
**stratum** 204
**stratus** 353
**straw** *scatter* 73
  *light* 320
  *unimportant* 643
  care not a – 866,
  930
  catch at –s
  *overrate* 482
  *credulous* 486
  *misuse* 679
  *unskilful* 699
  *hope* 858
  *rash* 863
  the eyes drawing
  –s 683
  in the – 161
  man of –
  *unsubstantial* 4
  *cheat* 545
  *insolvent* 808
  *low person* 876
  not worth a –
  643, 645
  – to show the
  wind 463
**straw-coloured** 436
**straw-hat** 225
**stray** *dispersion* 73
  *exceptional* 83
  *random* 156
  *wanderer* 268
  *deviate* 279
**streak** *intrinsicality*
  5

**strong** *great* 31
  *powerful* 159
  *energetic* 171
  *tough* 327
  *taste* 390
  *pungent* 392
  *fetid* 401
  *healthy* 654
  *feeling* 821
  *wonderful!* 870
  smell − of 398
  − accent 580
  − argument 476
  by a − arm 744
  − box 802
  with a − hand
   *resolution* 604
   *exertion* 686
   *severity* 739
  − language 574
  − pull 686
  − point 476
**strong-headed** 498
**stronghold**
  *refuge* 666
  *defence* 717
  *prison* 752
**strong-minded** 498,
  861
**strong-scented** 398
**strong-willed** 604
**strop** 253
**strophe** 597
**strow** 73
**struck** [*see*
  stricken, strike]
  awe− 860
  − down 732
  − all of a heap
  *emotion* 821
  *wonder* 870
  *humbled* 879
  − with *love* 897
**structural** *state* 7
**structure**
  *production* 161
  *form* 240
  *texture* 329
  *organization* 357
**struggle** *exert* 686
  *difficulty* 704
  *contend* 720
**strum** 416, 517
**strumpet** 962
**strung**
  highly − 825
**strut** *walk* 266
  *pride* 878
  *parade* 882
  *boast* 884
  − and fret one's

  hour upon a
   stage 359, 599
**strychnine** 663
**stub** 40, 550
**stubbed** 201
**stubble** *remains* 40
  *useless* 645
**stubborn**
  *strong* 159
  *hard* 323
  *obstinate* 606
  *resistance* 719
**stubby** 201
**stucco** 45, 223
**stuck** [*see* stick]
  − fast 150, 704
  be − on 897
**stuck-up** 878
**stud** *hanging-peg*
  214
  *knob* 250
  *horses* 271
**studded** *many* 102
  *spiked* 253
  *variegated* 440
**student** 541
**stud-farm** 370
**studied**
  *predetermined*
   611
**studio** *room* 191
  *painting* 556
  *workshop* 691
**studious**
  *thoughtful* 451
  *docile* 539
  *intending* 620
**study** *copy* 21
  *room* 191
  *thought* 451
  *attention* 457
  *research* 461
  *learning* 539
  *painting* 556
  *intention* 620
  *retreat* 893
  brown − 515
**stuff** *substance* 3
  *contents* 190
  *expand* 194
  *line* 224
  *matter* 316
  *texture* 329
  *absurdity* 497
  *unmeaning* 517
  *material* 635
  *trifle* 643
  *overeat* 957
  such − as dreams
   are made of 515
  − gown 968

  − in 300
  − the memory
   with 505
  − and nonsense
  *unsubstantial* 4
  *absurdity* 497
  *unmeaning* 517
  − up *close* 261
  *hoax* 545
**stuffed**
  *redundancy* 641
**stuffing** *contents* 190
  *lining* 224
  *stopper* 263
**stuffy** 321, 382
**stultified** 732
**stultify oneself** 699
**stultiloquy** 497
**stumble** *fall* 306
  *flounder* 315
  *error* 495
  *unskilful* 699
  *failure* 732
  − on *chance* 156
  *discover* 480a
**stumbling-block**
  *difficulty* 704
  *hindrance* 706
**stump**
  *remainder* 40
  *trunk* 51
  *walk* 266
  *drawing* 556
  *speak* 582
  stir your −s
  *active* 682
  worn to the − 659
  − along *slow* 275
**stump orator** 582,
  887
**stumpy** *short* 201
**stun** *physically*
  *insensible* 376
  *loud* 404
  *deafen* 419
  *unexpected* 508
  *morally insen-*
   *sible* 823
  *affect* 824
  *astonish* 870
**stung** [*see* sting]
  − to the quick 824
**stunt** *shorten* 201
  *performance* 680
**stunted** 193, 195
  *insufficient* 640
**stupe** 834
**stupefaction** 826
**stupefy**
  - *physically* 376
  - *morally* 823

  *astonish* 870
**stupendous**
  *great* 31
  *large* 192
  *wonderful* 870
**stupid**
  *unsubstantial* 4
  *misjudging* 481
  *credulous* 486
  *unintelligent* 499
  *tiresome* 841
  *dull* 843
**stupor**
  *insensibility* 823
  *wonder* 870
**stupration** 961
**sturdy** *strong* 159
  *persevering* 604a
  − beggar 767, 792
**stutter** 583
**sty** *house* 189
  *enclosure* 232
  *dirt* 653
**Stygian** *dark* 421
  *diabolic* 945
  *infernal* 982
  cross the − *ferry*
  *die* 360
  − shore
  *death* 360
**style** *state* 7
  *time* 114
  *painting* 556
  *graver* 558
  *name* 564
  *diction* 569
  *writing* 590
  *beauty* 845
  *fashion* 852
**stylet**
  *awl* 262
  *dagger* 727
**stylist** 578
**Stylites, Simon** −
  893
**stylographic pen**
  590
**stylography** 590
**stylus** 590
**styptic** 397
**Styx** 982
**suasible** 602
**suasion** 615
**suave mari magno**
  664
**suaviter in modo**
  826, 894
**suavity** 894
**sub** 34
  − spe rati 475
**subacid** 397

succour 707
succubus 980
succulent
 *nutritive* 298
 *juicy* 333
 *semiliquid* 352
succumb
 *fatigue* 688
 *yield* 725
 *fail* 732
succussion 315
such: – as 17
 – being the case 8
 – like 17
 – a one 372
suchwise 8
suck
 *draw off* 297
 *drink* 298
 *take* 789
 – in 296
 – the blood of 789
sucker 260, 547
suckle 707
suckling *infant* 129
suction *force* 157
 *reception* 296
sudary 652
sudation 299
sudatory 386
sudden
 *transient* 111
 *instantaneous* 113
 *soon* 132
 *unexpected* 508
 – burst 508
 – death 360
 – and quick in
  quarrel 901
 – thought 612
sudorific 382
suds *froth* 353
 in the – 704, 837
sue *demand* 765
 *go to law* 969
suet 356
suffer *physical pain*
 378
 *disease* 655
 *allow* 760
 *feel* 821
 *endure* 826
 *moral pain* 828
 – for 972
 – punishment 972
sufferance, tenant
 on – 779
suffice 639
sufficiency **639**
suffix *adjunct* 39
 *sequence* 63

*sequel* 65
*letter* 561
sufflation 349
suffocate *kill* 361
 *excess* 641
suffocating 382, 401
suffocation 361
suffragan 996
suffrage 609
suffragette 742
suffusion
 *mixture* 41
 *feeling* 821
 *blush* 879
sugar 396
sugar-loaf 253
suggest *suppose* 514
 *inform* 527
 *influence* 615
 *advise* 695
 – itself 451, 515
 – a question 461
suggestio falsi 546
suggestion 626, 695
suggestive
 *reminder* 505
 *significant* 516
 *descriptive* 594
 *bawdy* 961
sui generis 83
suicidal 162
suicide *killing* 361
suisse *beadle* 996
Suisse, point d'ar-
 gent point de –
 812
suit *accord* 23
 *series* 69
 *class* 75
 *clothes* 225
 *expedient* 646
 *petition* 765
 *courtship* 902
 follow – 19
 law– 969
 love– 897
 – the action to the
  word 550
 – the occasion 646
 do – and service
  743
suit case 191
suitable 23, 646
 – season 134
suite *sequel* 65
 *series* 69
 *escort* 88
 *retinue* 746
 – of rooms 189, 191
suitor
 *petitioner* 767

*lover* 897
*lawsuit* 969
sulcated 259
sulky *carriage* 272
 *obstinate* 606
 *discontented* 832
 *dejected* 837
 *sullen* 901*a*
sullen
 *obstinate* 606
 *gloomy* 837
 *discourteous* 895
 *sulky* 901*a*
sullenness 901*a*
sully 653, 874
sulphur 388
 – coloured 436
sultan 745
sultry 382
sum *number* 84
 *money* 800
 – and substance
  *meaning* 516
 *synopsis* 596
 *important part*
  642
 – total 800
 – up *reckon* 85
 *description* 594
 *compendium* 596
sumless 105
summation 37, 85
summary
 *transient* 111
 *early* 132
 *short* 201
 *concise* 572
 *compendious* 596
 *illegal* 964
 – of facts 594
summer *season* 125
 *support* 215
 *heat* 382
 Indian – 125
 St. Luke's – 125
 St. Martin's – 125
 – lightning 423
 – time 114
summer-house 191
summerset 218
summit *top* 210
summon 741, 969
 – up 505, 824
 – up courage 861
summum:
 – bonum 618, 827
 – jus 922
sump *base* 211
 *pool* 343
 *slough* 345
 *store* 636

*cess* 653
sumpter-horse 271
sumptuary 800, 809
sumptuous 882
sum-total 50
sun 318
 *luminary* 423
 *glory* 873
 bask in the – 377
 going down of
  the – 126
 farthing candle to
  the – 645
 under the – 180,
  318
 as the – at noon-
  day *bright* 420
 *certain* 474
 *plain* 525
 – oneself 384
Sun:
 – of Righteousness
  976
sunbeam 420
 –s from cucumbers
  471
sunburn *heat* 384
sunburnt *brown* 433
Sunday:
 – Monday &c. 138
 –'s best 847, 882
 – school 542
sunder 44
sundial 114
sundown 126
sundry 102
sunk [*see* sink]
 *deep* 208
 – fence 717
 – in iniquity 945
 – in oblivion 506
sunken rocks 667
sunless 421
sunlight 420
sunny *warm* 382
 *luminous* 420
 *cheerful* 836
sunny side 829
 view the – 858
 – of the hedge 734
sun-painting 556
sunrise 125
sunset 126
 at – 133
sunshade 223, 424
sunshine *light* 420
 *prosperity* 734
 *happy* 827
 *cheerful* 836
sunstroke 384, 503
sun-up 125

[ 659 ]

suo: – periculo 926
– sibi gladio hunc
 jugulo
 *absurdity* 479
 *retaliation* 718
sup *small quantity*
 32
 *feed* 298
 – full of horrors
 828
super *theatrical* 599
superable 470
superabound 641
superadd 37
superannuated 128
superb 845
supercargo 694
supercherie 545
supercilious
 *proud* 878
 *insolent* 885
 *disrespectful* 929
 *scornful* 930
superdreadnought
 726
supereminence
 648, 873
supererogation 641,
 645
superexaltation 873
superexcellence
 648
superfetation 37,
 168
superficial
 *shallow* 209
 *outside* 220
 *misjudging* 481
 *ignorant* 491
 – extent 180
superficies 220
superfine 648
superfluitant 305
superfluity 40, 641
superfluous 645
superhuman 650,
 976
superimpose 223
superimposed 206
superincumbent
 206, 319
superinduce
 *change* 140
 *cause* 153
 *produce* 161
superintend 693
superintendent 694
superior *greater* 33
 – *in size* 194
 *important* 642
 *good* 648

*director* 694
superiority 33
superjunction 37
superlative 33
superlatively good
 648
superman 33
supernal 206, 210,
 981
supernatant 206,
 305
supernatural 976,
 980
 – aid 707
supernumerary
 *adjunct* 39
 *theatrical* 599
 *reserve* 636
 *redundant* 641
superpose 37, 223
supersaturate 641
superscription 550,
 590
supersede
 *substitute* 147
 *disuse* 678
 *relinquish* 782
supersensible 317
superstition
 *credulity* 486
 *error* 495
 *religion* 984
superstratum 220
superstructure 729
supertax 812
supertonic 413
supervacaneous
 641
supervene
 *extrinsic* 6
 *be added* 37
 *succeed* 117
 *happen* 151
supervise 693
supervisor 694
supination 213
supine
 *horizontal* 213
 *inverted* 218
 *sluggish* 683
 *mentally torpid*
 823
suppeditate 637
supper 298
supplant 147
supple *soft* 324
 *servile* 886
supplement
 *addition* 37
 *adjunct* 39
 *completion* 52

*publication* 531
 *book* 593
suppletory 37
suppliant 765, 767
supplicate *beg* 765
 *pity* 914
 *worship* 990
supplies
 *materials* 635
 *aid* 707
 *money* 800
supply *store* 636
 *provide* 637
 *give* 784
 – aid 707
 – deficiencies 52
 – the place of 147
 – and transport
 726
support *perform* 170
 *sustain* 215
 *evidence* 467
 *preserve* 670
 *aid* 707
 *feel* 821
 *endure* 826
 *vindicate* 937
 – life 359
supporter 711
 –s *heraldic* 550
suppose 514
supposing 469
supposition 514
supposititious 546
suppress
 *destroy* 162
 *conceal* 528
 *silent* 581
 *restrain* 751
suppression of
 truth 544
suppuration 653
suppute 85
supralapsarian 984
supramundane 939
supremacy 33, 737
supreme 33
 *summit* 210
 *authority* 737
 in a – degree 31
Supreme Being 976
surbate 659
surbated 688
surcease 142
surcharge 641
 – and falsify 811
surcingle 45
surcoat 225
surd *number* 84
 *deaf* 419
 *silent letter* 561

sure *certain* 474
 *belief* 484
 *safe* 664
 make – against
 673
 make – of
 *inquire* 461
 *take* 789
 you may be – 535
 to be – *assent* 488
 on – ground 664
 *security* 771
sure-footed
 *careful* 459
 *skilful* 698
 *cautious* 864
surely 488, 602, 870
sureness 474
surety 474, 664
surf 348, 353
surface *outside* 220
 *texture* 329
 below the – 526
 lie on the – 518,
 525
 skim the – 460
Surface, Joseph –
 548
surfeit 641, 869
surge *swarm* 72
 *swell* 305
 *rotation* 312
 *wave* 348
surgeon 662
surgery 662
surgit amari
 aliquid 651
surly *gruff* 895
 *sullen* 901a
 *unkind* 907
surmise 514
surmount *be*
 *superior* 33
 *tower* 206
 *transcursion* 303
 *ascent* 305
 – a difficulty
 *overcome* 731
surmountable 470
surname 564
surpass
 *be superior* 33
 *grow* 194
 *go beyond* 303
 *outshine* 873
surplice 999
surplus 40, 641
surplusage 641
surprint 550
surprise
 *non-expectation*

508
*unprepared* 674
*wonder* 870
**surprisingly** 31
**surrebutter** &c.
 *answer* 462
 *pleadings* 969
**surrender** 725, 782
– one's life 360
**surreptitious**
 *furtive* 528
 *deceptive* 545
 *untrue* 546
**surrogate** 759
**surround** 227, 229
**surroundings** 227
 amidst such and
 such – 183
**sursum corda** 990
**surtax** 812
**surtout** *coat* 225
**surveillance**
 *care* 459
 *direction* 693
 under – 938
**survene** 151
**survey** 441, 466
**surveyor** 85, 694
**survive** *remain* 40
 *long time* 110
 *permanent* 141
**susceptibility**
 *power* 157
 *tendency* 176
 *liability* 177
 *sensibility* 375
 *motive* 615
 *impressibility* 822
 *irascibility* 901
**suscipient** 785
**suscitate** *cause* 153
 *produce* 161
 *stir up* 173
 *excite* 824
**suspect** *doubt* 485
 *suppose* 514
**suspected** 938
**suspectless** 484
**suspend** *defer* 133
 *discontinue* 142
 *hang* 214
**suspended anima-
tion** 823
**suspender** 45, 214
**suspense**
 *cessation* 142
 *uncertainty* 475
 *expectation* 507
 *irresolution* 605
 in – *inert* 172
**suspension**

*cessation* 142
 *hanging* 214
 *music* 413
 – of arms 723
**suspicion** *doubt* 485
 *incredulity* 487
 *knowledge* 490
 *supposition* 514
 *fear* 860
 under – 938
**suspiration** 839
**sustain**
 *continue* 143
 *strength* 159
 *perform* 170
 *support* 215
 *preserve* 670
 *aid* 707
 *endure* 821
**sustained note** 413
**sustenance** 298
**sustentation**
 [*see* sustain]
 *food* 298
**susurration** 405
**sutler** 637, 797
**suttee** *killing* 361
 *arson* 384
 *unselfishness* 942
 *idolatry* 991
**suture** 43
**suum cuique** 780,
 922
**suzerain** 745
**suzerainty** 737
**swab** *dry* 340
 *clean* 652
 *lubber* 701
**swaddle** *clothe* 225
 *restrain* 751
**swaddling clothes,**
 in – *infant* 129
 *subjection* 749
**swag** *hang* 214
 *lean* 217
 *curve* 245
 *drop* 306
 *oscillate* 314
 *booty* 793
 *ostentation* 887
**swag-bellied** 194
**swage** 174
**swagger**
 *pride* 878
 *boast* 884
 *bluster* 885
**swaggerer** 887
**swain** *man* 373
 *rustic* 876
 *lover* 897
**swale** 659

**swallow** *gulp* 296
 *eat* 298
 *believe* 484
 *credulous* 486
 *brook* 826
 – the bait 547,
 602
 – flight 274
 – the leek 607,
 725
 – up *destroy* 162
 *use* 677
 *take* 789
 – hook, line and
 sinker 602
 – whole 465a, 484
 *swallow-tail coat*
 225
**swamp** *destroy* 162
 *marsh* 345
 *defeat* 731
**swamped**
 *failure* 732
**swampy** *moist* 339
**swank** 845, 882, 884
**swan-pan** 85
**swan-song** 360
**swap** *exchange* 148
 *blow* 276
**sward** 344
**swarm** *crowd* 72
 *multitude* 102
 *climb* 305
 *sufficiency* 639
 *redundance* 641
**swarthy** 431
**swash** *affuse* 337
 *spurt* 348
**swashbuckler** 726,
 887
**swashy** 339
**swastika** 621, 993
**swat** 276
**swath** 72
**swathe** *fasten* 43
 *clothe* 225
 *restrain* 751
**sway** *power* 157
 *influence* 175
 *lean* 217
 *oscillate* 314
 *agitation* 315
 *induce* 615
 *authority* 737
 – to and fro 149
**sweal** 659
**swear** *affirm* 535
 *promise* 768
 *curse* 908
 just enough to –

 by 32
– at 908
– by *believe* 484
– false 544
– a witness 768
**sweat** *exude* 295
 *excretion* 299
 *heat* 382
 *exertion* 686
 *fatigue* 688
 cold – 860
 in a – 382
 – of one's brow
 686
**sweater** 225
**Swedenborgian** 984
**Swedish dance** 840
**sweep** *space* 180
 *curve* 245
 *oar* 267
 *rapid* 274
 *bend* 279
 *clean* 652
 *dirty fellow* 653
 *steal* 791
 make a clean – of
 297
 – along 264
 – away
 *destroy* 162
 *eject* 297
 *abrogate* 756
 *relinquish* 782
 – the chords 416
 – off 297
 – out 297, 652
 – of time 109
**sweeper** 652
 mine– 726
**sweeping** *whole* **50**
 *complete* 52
 *general* 78
 – change 146
**sweepings**
 *useless* 645
 *dirt* 653
**sweepstakes** 775,
 810
**sweet**
 *saccharine* 396
 *melodious* 413
 *colour* 428
 *clean* 652
 *agreeable* 829
 *lovely* 897
 look – upon
 *desire* 865
 *love* 897
 *endearment* 902
 – smell 400
 – tooth 865, 868

| | | | |
|---|---|---|---|
| – a turn 140 | *choose* 609 | *intend* 620 | **tamper with** |
| – up [*see below*] | *undertake* 676 | – to oneself 589 | *alter* 140 |
| – upon oneself | *befriend* 707 | – oneself out of | *seduce* 615 |
| 676, 768 | *arrest* 751 | breath 584 | *injure* 659 |
| – warning 668 | *borrow* 788 | – over | *meddle* 682 |
| – wing 293 | *censure* 932 | *confer* 588 | **tan** *colour* 433 |
| – one at one's | – arms 722 | *persuade* 615 | **tandem** |
| word 769 | – a case 476 | – to in private 586 | *at length* 200 |
| **take by** | – one's abode 184 | – at random | *vehicle* 272 |
| – the button 586 | – the cudgels 716, | *illogical* 477 | **tang** *taste* 390 |
| – the hand 707 | 720 | *loquacity* 584 | *bane* 663 |
| – surprise 508, 674 | – an inquiry 461 | – together 588 | **tangent** 199 |
| **take for** 484 | – money 788 | – against time | *angle* 217 |
| – better or for | – one's pen 590 | *time* 106 | **fly off at a –** |
| worse 609 | – with | *protract* 110 | *deviate* 279 |
| – gospel 486 | *attention* 457 | *inaction* 681 | *diverge* 291 |
| – granted 484 | *use* 677 | – of the town | *excitable* 825 |
| **take in** *include* 54 | *content* 831 | *gossip* 588 | **tangere ulcus** 505 |
| *shorten* 201 | **taken, be –** | *fame* 873 | **tangible** |
| *admit* 296 | *die* 360 | **talkative** 582, 584 | *material* 316 |
| *understand* 518 | – ill 655 | **talked of** 873 | *touch* 379 |
| *deceive* 545 | – with 897 | **talkies** 599, 840 | *exact* 494 |
| *receive money* 785 | **taker** 789 | **talking, fine –** | *sufficient* 639 |
| – good part | **taking 789** | *over-estimation* | *useful* 644 |
| *be calm* 826 | *infectious* 657 | 482 | **tangle** 61, 219 |
| *be pleased* 827 | in a – *pained* 828 | **tall** 206 | **tangled** 59, 704 |
| *content* 831 | *angry* 900 | – hat 225 | **weave a – web 704** |
| – hand *teach* 537 | **talapoin** 996 | – talk 884 | **tango** 840 |
| *undertake* 676 | **talbotype** 556 | **tallage** 812 | **tank** *pool* 343 |
| *aid* 707 | **tale** | **tallies** 85 | *reservoir* 636 |
| – an idea 498 | *counting* 85 | **tallow** 356 | *armoured vehicle* |
| – sail 275 | *narrative* 594 | – candle 423 | 726 |
| **take into** | **thereby hangs a –** | **tallow-faced** 429 | **tankard** 191 |
| – account | 526 | **tally** *agree* 23 | **tanker** 273 |
| *include* 76 | **twice-told –** | *list* 85, 86 | **tant: – mieux** 838 |
| *discriminate* 465 | *diffuse style* 573 | *sign* 550 | – s'en faut 489 |
| *qualify* 469 | *weary* 841 | *credit* 805 | – soit peu 32 |
| – consideration | **tale-bearer** 532 | – with *conform* 82 | **tantalize** *balk* 509 |
| 451 | **talent** 698 | **tally-ho** 622 | *induce* 615 |
| – custody 751 | bury one's – in a | **tally-man** 797 | *desire* 865 |
| – one's head 514, | napkin 528 | **talma** 225 | **tantalizing** |
| 608 | not put one's – in | **Talmud** 985 | *exciting* 824 |
| **take off** *mimic* 19 | a napkin 878 | **talons** | **Tantalus: torment** |
| *destroy* 162 | **talionis, lex –** 718, | *authority* 737 | of – 507, 865 |
| *remove* 185 | 922 | *claws* 781 | **tantamount** 27, 516 |
| *divest* 226 | **taliped** 243 | **talus** 217 | **tantæne animis** |
| *depart* 293 | **talisman** 747, 993 | **tam-o'-shanter** 225 | *cœlestibus iræ* |
| *discount* 813 | **talismanic** 992 | **tambourine** 417 | 900 |
| *ridicule* 856 | **talk** | **tame** *inert* 172 | **tantara** 407 |
| – one's hands 785 | *unsubstantial* 4 | *moderate* 174 | **tantas componere** |
| – the hat 894 | *rumour* 532 | *domesticate* 370 | **lites 723** |
| **take on** | *speak* 582 | *teach* 537 | **tanti** 642 |
| *attempt* 675 | *conversation* 588 | *feeble* 575 | **tantivy** *speed* 274 |
| *discontent* 832 | **small – 588** | *subjugate* 749 | **tantrums** 900 |
| *melancholy* 837 | – big *boast* 884 | *insensible* 823 | **tap** *open* 260 |
| – credit 484 | *insolent* 885 | *calm* 826 | *plug* 263 |
| – trust 484 | *threat* 909 | **tameless** | *hit* 276 |
| **take up** | – glibly 584 | *violent* 173 | *let out* 295, 297 |
| *elevate* 307 | – nonsense 497 | *malevolent* 907 | *sound* 406 |
| *inquire* 461 | – of *signify* 516 | **Tammany** 940 | turn on the – 297 |
| *dissent* 595 | *publish* 531 | **tamp** 261, 276 | **tap-dance** 840 |

[ 665 ]

tenter-hook 214
on –s 507
tenth 99
tenths
*tithe* 812
tent-pegging 840
tents, O Israel, to
your – 722
tenue, en grande –
847, 882
tenuity
*smallness* 32
*thinness* 203
*rarity* 322
tenuous
*shadowy* 4
tenure
*possession* 777
*property* 780
*due* 924
tepee 189
tepefaction 384
Tephramancy 511
tepid 382
tepidarium 386
ter quaterque
beatus 827
teratology
*unconformity* 83
*distortion* 243
*altiloquence* 577
*boasting* 884
tercentenary 98,
138, 883
terceron 41
terebration 260
teres atque rotun-
dus 249
in selpso – 650
tergiversation 283,
**607**
term *end* 67
*place in series* **71**
*period of time* 106
*limit* 233
*word* 562
*name* 564
*lease* 780
termagant 901
terminal 67, 233,
292
terminate 67, 292
*limit* 233
termination 154
termine, mezzo –
628
terminology 562
terminus *end* 67
*limit* 233
*arrival* 292
termless 105

terms [*see* term]
*circumstances* **8**
*reasoning* 476
*pacification* 723
*conditions* 770
bring to – 723
come to –
*assent* 488
*pacify* 723
*submit* 725
*consent* 762
*compact* 769
couch in – 566
on friendly – 888
in no measured –
574
ternary 93
ternion 92
Terpsichore 416,
840
terra: – cotta
*baked* 384
*sculpture* 557
– firma
*support* 215
*land* 342
*safety* 664
– incognita 491
terrace *houses* 189
*level* 213
terrain 181
terraqueous 318
terre verte 435
terrene 318, 342
terrine 191
terrestrial 318
terrible 860
terribly *greatly* 31
terrier *list* 86
*auger* 262
*dog* 366
terrific 31, 830, 860
terrify 860
territorial *land* 342
*soldier* 726
territory 181, 780
terror 860
King of –s 360
reign of – 739, 828
terrorem, in – 860,
909
terrorism 860
*insolence* 885
terrorist
*coward* 862
*blusterer* 887
*evil-doer* 913
terse 572
tertian *periodic* 138
tertiary *three* 92
tertium quid

*dissimilar* 18
*mixture* 41
*combination* 48
*unconformable* 83
tesselated 440, 847
tesseræ
*mosaic* 440
*counters* 550
test 463
testa, voce di – 410
testament 771
Testament 985
tester *bedstead* 215
*sixpence* 800
testify 467, 550
testimonial 551
testimony 467
testy 901
tetanus 315
tetchy 901
tête: – baissée 863
– exaltée 503
– montée 503, 825
–à-tête *two* 89
*near* 197
*confer* 588
tether *fasten* 43
*locate* 184
*restrain* 751
*means of restraint*
752
go beyond the
length of one's
– 738
tethered *firm* 150
tetrachord 413
tetractic 95
tetrad 95
tetrahedral 95
tetrahedron 244
tetrarch 745
text *prototype* 22
*topic* 454
*meaning* 516
*printing* 591
–book 542, 596
textile 219, 329
textuary 983a, 985
texture *mixture* 41
*roughness* 256
*fabric* **329**
Thais 962
Thalia 599
Thalmud 985
Thames on fire
set the – 471
never set the –
501, 701
thane *nobility* 875
thank 916
no – you 764

– one's stars 838
– you for nothing
917
thankful 916
rest and be – 265,
831
thankless
*painful* 830
*ungrateful* 917
thank-offering 916,
990
thanks to 155
thanksgiving
*gratitude* 916
*worship* 990
that 79
– is 118
– is to say 79
– being so 8
at – time 119
thatch *roof* 223
thaumatrope 445
thaumaturgist 994
thaumaturgy 992
thaw *melt* 335
*heart* 382
*heating* 384
*calm the mind* 826
*pity* 914
Thearchy
*authority* **737**
*Deity* 976
theatre
*spectacle* 441
*school* 542
*drama* 599
*arena* 728
*amusement* 840
*tribunal* 966
théâtre: coup de –
*appearance* 448
*prodigy* 872
*display* 882
jeu de – 448, **872**
nom de – 565
theatrical 599
*affected* 855
*ostentatious* 882
Theban, learned –
492
theca 223
thé dansant 840
theft 775, 791
theism 984, 987
theistic *of God* 976
theme *topic* 454
*dissertation* 595
Themis 922
then *time* 106
*therefore* 476
thence

**Toledo** 727
**tolerable**
*a little* 32
*trifling* 643
*pretty good* 648
*not perfect* 651
*satisfactory* 831
**tolerably, get on –**
736
**toleration**
*laxity* 738
*lenity* 740
*permission* 760
*feeling* 821
*calmness* 826
*benevolence* 906
**toll** *sound* 407
*tax* 812
– the knell 363
**tollbooth**
*prison* 752
*market* 799
**tomahawk** 727
**tomb** 363
lay in the – 363
– of the Capulets
506
**tombé des nues** 83,
870
**tombola** 156
**tomboy** 129, 851
**tombstone** 363
**tom-cat** 373
**tome** 593
**tomentous** 256
**tomfool** 501
**tomfoolery**
*absurdity* 497
*amusement* 840
*wit* 842
*ostentation* 882
**Tom Noddy** 501
**Tommy Atkins** 726
**tommy-gun** 727
**to-morrow** 121
– and to-morrow
104, 109
**tompion** 263
**tomtit** 193
**Tom Thumb** 193
**tom-tom** 417, 722
**ton** *weight* 319
*fashion* 852
–s of money 800
**tonality** 413, 420
**tone** *state* 7
*strength* 159
*tendency* 176
*sound* 402
*music* 413
*colour* 428

*blackness* 431
*painting* 556
*method* 627
*disposition* 820
give a – to 852
– down
*moderate* 174
*darken* 421
*discolour* 429
– in with 714
– of voice 580
**tone poem** 415
**toney** 852
**tongs**
*fire-irons* 386
*retention* 781
**tongue**
*projection* 250
*taste* 390
*language* 560
bite the – 392
bridle one's – 585
give – 404, 580
hold one's – 403
slip of the –
*error* 495
*solecism* 568
*stammering* 583
on the tip of
one's –
*near* 197
*forget* 506
*latent* 526
*speech* 582
wag the – 582
– cleave to the
roof of one's
mouth 870
have a – in one's
head 582
– of land 342
– running loose
584
keep one's – be-
tween one's
teeth 585
**tongueless** 581
**tongue-tied** 581
**tonic**
*musical note* 413
*healthy* 656
*medicine* 662
– sol fa 415
**tonicity** 159
**tonnage** 192
**tonsillectomy** 662
**tonsils** 351
**tonsure** 999
**tonsured** 226
**tontine** 810
**tony** 501

**Tony Lumpkin** 876
**too**
*also* 37
*excess* 641
– bad
*disreputable* 874
*wrong* 923
*censure* 932
– clever by half
702
in a – great degree
31
– far 641
– hot to hold one
830
– late 133
– late for 135
– little 640
– many 641
– much [*see below*]
– soon 132
– soon for 135
– true 833, 839
**too much**
*redundance* 641
*intemperance* 954
have – of 869
make – of 482
– for 471
– of a good thing
869
**tool** *instrument* 633
*steer* 693
*catspaw* 711
*ornament* 847
*servile* 886
edge – 253
mere – 690
**toot** 406
**tooth** *fastening* 45
*projection* 250
*sharp* 253
*roughness* 256
*notch* 257
*texture* 329
*taste* 390
sweet –
*desire* 865
*fastidious* 868
– and nail
*violence* 173
*exertion* 686
*attack* 716
– paste &c. 652
**toothache** 378
**toothed** 253
**toothsome** 394
**top** *supreme* 33
*summit* 210
*roof* 223
*spin* 312

sleep like a – 683
fool to the – of
one's bent 545
go over the – 861
– to bottom 52
– coat 225
– hat 225
at the – of the
heap 210
– of the ladder 873
at the – of one's
speed 274
from – to toe 200
at the – of the
tree 210, 873
at the – of one's
voice 404, 411
**toparchy** 737
**topaz** 436, 847
**top-boot** 225
**tope** *tomb* 363
*trees* 367
*drink* 959
*temple* 1000
**topee** 225
**toper** 959
**top-full** 52
**top-gallant mast,**
206, 210
**top-heavy**
*unbalanced* 28
*inverted* 218
*dangerous* 665
*tipsy* 959
**Tophet** 982
**topiary** 847
**topic** 454
– of the day 532
**topical** 183
**top-mast** 206
**topmost** 210
**topography** 183
**topographer** 466
**topple**
*unbalanced* 28
*perish* 162
*decay* 659
– down *fall* 306
– over 28, 306
**topsail schooner**
273
**topsawyer** 642, 700
**top sergeant** 745
**topsy-turvy** 14, 218
**toque** 225
**tor** 206
**torch** 388, 423
apply the – 824
light the – of war
722
– of Hymen 903

| | | | |
|---|---|---|---|
| **undeviating** | **undreaded** 861 | **unequivocal** | **unfaltering** 604a |
| *uniform* 16 | **undreamt of** 452 | *great* 31 | **unfamiliar** 83 |
| *unchanged* 150 | **undress** *clothes* 225 | *sure* 474 | **unfashionable** 83, |
| *straight* 246 | *nude* 226 | *clear* 518 | 851 |
| *direct* 278 | *simple* 849 | **unerring** | **unfashioned** 241, |
| *persevering* 604a | **undressed** 226, 674 | *certain* 474 | 674 |
| **undevout** 989 | **undried** 339 | *tone* 494 | **unfasten** 44 |
| **undigested** 674 | **undrilled** 674 | *innocent* 946 | **unfathomable** |
| **undignified** 940 | **undrooping** 604a | **unessayed** 678 | *infinite* 105 |
| **undiminished** 31, | **undueness** 925 | **unessential** 643 | *deep* 208 |
| 35, 50 | **undulate** 248, 314 | **unestablished** 185 | *mysterious* 519 |
| **undirected** 279, 621 | **unduly** 32 | **uneven** *diverse* 16a | **unfavourable** |
| **undiscernible** 447, | **undutiful** 945 | *unequal* 28 | *out of season* 135 |
| 519 | **undying** 112, 150 | *irregular* 139 | *hindrance* 706 |
| **undiscerning** | **une aile, ne battre** | *rough* 256 | *obstructive* 708 |
| *blind* 442 | **que d'** − 683 | **uneventful** 643 | − *chance* 473 |
| *inattentive* 458 | **unearned** 925 | **unexact** 495 | **unfeared** 861 |
| **undisciplined** 608 | **unearth** *eject* 297 | **unexaggerated** 494 | **unfeasible** 471 |
| **undisclosed** 526, | *disinter* 363 | **unexamined** 460 | **unfed** 640, 956 |
| 528 | *inquire* 461 | **unexampled** 83 | **unfeeling** 376, 823 |
| **undiscoverable** 519 | *discover* 480a | **unexceptionable** | **unfeigned** 543 |
| **undiscovered** 526 | **unearthly** | *good* 648 | **unfelt** 823 |
| **undiscriminating** | *immaterial* 317 | *legitimate* 924 | **unfeminine** |
| 465a | *Deity* 976 | *innocent* 946 | *manly* 373 |
| **undisguised** | *demon* 980 | **unexcitable** 826 | *vulgar* 851 |
| *true* 494 | *heavenly* 981 | **unexcited** 823, 826 | **unfertile** 169 |
| *manifest* 525 | *pious* 987 | **unexciting** 174 | **unfetter** 750 |
| *sincere* 543 | **uneasy** 828 | **unexecuted** 730 | **unfettered** 748 |
| **undismayed** 861 | **uneatable** 395 | **unexempt** 177 | **unfinished** 53, 730 |
| **undisposed of** 678, | **unedifying** 538 | **unexercised** 674, | **unfit** |
| 781 | **uneducated** 491, | 678 | *inappropriate* 24 |
| **undisputed** 474 | 674 | **unexerted** 172 | *impotence* 158 |
| **undissembling** 543 | **unembarrassed** | **unexhausted** 159, | *inexpedient* 647 |
| **undissolved** | 705, 852 | 639 | *unskilful* 699 |
| *entire* 50 | **unembodied** 317 | **unexpanded** 195, | *wrong* 923 |
| *dense* 321 | **unemotional** 823 | 203 | *undue* 925 |
| **undistinguishable** | **unemployed** 678, | **unexpected** | **unfitted** |
| 465a | 681 | *exceptional* 83 | *not prepared* 674 |
| **undistinguished** | **unencumbered** 705, | *inexpectation* 508 | **unfix** 44 |
| 465a | 927a | **unexpensive** 815 | **unfixed** 149 |
| **undistorted** 246, | **undeared** 898 | **unexplained** | **unflagging** 604a |
| 494 | **unending** 112 | *not known* 491 | **unflammable** 385 |
| **undistracted** 457 | **unendowed** 158 | *unintelligible* 519 | **unflattering** 494, |
| **undisturbed** | − **with reason** | *latent* 526 | 703 |
| *quiescent* 265 | 450a | **unexplored** | **unfledged** |
| *repose* 685 | **unendurable** 830 | *neglected* 460 | *young* 127, 129 |
| *unexcited* 826 | **unenjoyed** 841 | *ignorant* 491 | *unprepared* 674 |
| **undivided** 50, 52 | **unenlightened** 491, | *unseen* 526 | **unflinching** |
| **undo** *untie* 44 | 499 | **unexposed** 526 | *firm* 604 |
| *reverse* 145 | **unenslaved** 748 | **unexpressed** 536 | *persevering* 604a |
| *destroy* 162 | **unenterprising** 864 | **unexpressive** 517 | *brave* 861 |
| *neutralize* 179 | **unentertaining** 843 | **unextended** 317 | **unfold** |
| *not do* 681 | **unenthralled** 748 | **unextinguished** | *straighten* 246 |
| **undoing** *ruin* 735 | **unentitled** 925 | 173, 382 | *evolve* 313 |
| **undone** *failure* 732 | **unenvied** 929, 930 | **unfaded** 428 | *interpret* 522 |
| *adversity* 735 | **unequal** 28, 139 | **unfading** 112 | *manifest* 525 |
| *pained* 828 | *inequitable* 923 | **unfailing** 141 | *disclose* 520 |
| *hopeless* 859 | − **to** 640 | **unfair** *false* 544 | − **a tale** 594 |
| **undoubted** 474 | **unequalled** 33 | *unjust* 923 | **unforbidden** 760 |
| **undubitably** 488 | **unequipped** 674 | *dishonourable* 940 | **unforced** 602, 748 |
| **undraped** 226 | **unequitable** 923 | **unfaithful** 940 | **unforeseen** 508 |

**unopened** 261
**unopposed** 709
**unorganized** 674
  – matter 358
**unornamental** 846
**unornamented**
  - *style* 576
  *simple* 849
**unorthodox** 984
**unostentatious** 881
**unowed** 807
**unowned** 782
**unpacific** 713, 722
**unpacified** 713
**unpack**
  *unfasten* 44
  *take out* 297
**unpaid** *debt* 806
  *honorary* 815
  the great –
  *magistracy* 967
  – worker 602
**unpalatable** 395,
  830
**unparagoned**
  *supreme* 33
  *best* 648
  *perfect* 650
**unparalleled**
  *unimitated* 20
  *supreme* 33
  *exceptional* 83
**unpardonable** 938,
  945
**unparliamentary**
  language 895,
  908
**unpassable** 261
**unpassionate** 826
**unpatriotic** 911
**unpeaceful** 720, 722
**unpeople**
  *emigration* 297
  *banishment* 893
**unperceived**
  *neglected* 460
  *unknown* 491
**unperformed** 730
**unperjured** 543,
  939
**unperplexed** 498
**unpersuadable** 606
**unpersuaded** 616
**unperturbed** 826
**unphilosophical** 499
**unpierced** 261
**unpin** (44)
**unpitied** 932
**unpitying** 914*a*
**unplaced** 185
**unplagued** 831

**unpleasant** 830
**unpleasing** 830
**unpoetical** 598, 703
**unpolished**
  *rough* 256
  *inelegant* 579
  *unprepared* 674
  *vulgar* 851, 876
  *rude* 895
**unpolite** 895
**unpolluted**
  *good* 648
  *perfect* 650
**unpopular** 830, 867
**unpopularity** 898
**unportioned** 804
**unpossessed** 777*a*
**unpractical** 699
**unprecedented** 83,
  137
**unprejudiced** 498,
  748
**unpremeditated**
  *impulsive* 612
  *undesigned* 621
  *unprepared* 674
**unprepared** 508,
  674
**unprepossessed** 498
**unprepossessing**
  846
**unpresentable** 851
**unpretending** 881
**unprevented** 748
**unprincipled** 945
**unprivileged** 925
**unprized** 483
**unproclaimed** 526
**unproduced** 2
**unproductive** 645
**unproductiveness**
  **169**
**unproficiency** 699
**unprofitable**
  *unproductive* 169
  *useless* 645
  *inexpedient* 647
  *bad* 649
**unprolific** 169
**unpromising** 859
**unprompted** 612
**unpronounceable**
  519
**unpronounced** 526
**unpropitious**
  *ill-timed* 135
  *opposed* 708
  *hopeless* 859
**unproportioned** 24
**unprosperous** 735
**unprotected** 665

**unproved** 477
**unprovided**
  *scanty* 640
  *unprepared* 674
**unprovoked** (616)
**unpublished** 526
**unpunctual**
  *tardy* 133
  *untimely* 135
  *irregular* 139
**unpunished** 970
**unpurchased** 796
**unpurified** 653
**unpurposed** 621
**unpursued** 624
**unqualified**
  *incomplete* 52
  *impotent* 158
  *certain* 474
  *unprepared* 674
  *inexpert* 699
  *unentitled* 925
  – *truth* 494
**unquelled** 173
**unquenchable**
  *strong* 159
  *desire* 865
**unquenched**
  *violence* 173
  *heat* 382
**unquestionable** 474
**unquestionably** 488
**unquestioned** 474,
  488
**unquiet**
  *motion* 264
  *agitation* 315
  *excitable* 825
**unravel** *untie* 44
  *arrange* 60
  *straighten* 246
  *evolve* 313
  *discover* 480*a*
  *interpret* 522
  *disembarrass* 705
**unreached** 304
**unread** 491
**unready** 674
**unreal**
  *not existing* 2
  *erroneous* 495
  *imaginary* 515
**unreasonable**
  *impossible* 471
  *illogical* 477
  *misjudging* 481
  *foolish* 499
  *exorbitant* 814
  *unjust* 923
**unreclaimed** 951
**unrecognizable** 146

**unreconciled** 713
**unrecorded** 552
**unrecounted** 55
**unreduced** 31
**unrefined** 851
**unreflecting** 458
**unreformed** 951
**unrefreshed** 688
**unrefuted** 478, 494
**unregarded**
  *neglected* 460
  *unrespected* 929
**unregenerate** 988
**unregistered** 552
**unreined** 748
**unrelated** 10
**unrelenting** 914*a*,
  919
**unreliable**
  *uncertain* 475
  *irresolute* 605
  *dangerous* 665
**unrelieved** 835
**unremarked** 460
**unremembered** 506
**unremitting**
  *continuous* 69
  *continuing* 110
  *unvarying* 143
  *persevering* 604*a*
**unremoved** 184
**unremunerated** 808
**unrenewed** 141
**unrepealed** 141
**unrepeated** 87, 103
**unrepentant** 951
**unrepining** 831
**unreplenished** 640
**unrepressed** 173
**unreproached** 946
**unreproved** 946
**unrequited** 806, 917
**unresented** 918
**unresenting** 826
**unreserved**
  *manifest* 525
  *veracious* 543
  *artless* 703
**unresisted** 743
**unresisting** 725
**unresolved** 605
**unrespected** 929
**unrest** 149, 264
**unrestored** 688
**unrestrained**
  *capricious* 608
  *unencumbered*
  705
  *free* 748
**unrestricted**
  *undiminished* **31**

*free* 748
unretracted 535
unrevenged 918
unreversed 143
unrevoked 143
unrewarded 806, 917
unrhymed 598
unriddle 480a, 529
unrig 645
unrighteous 945
unrip 260
unripe
  *young* 127
  *sour* 397
  *immature* 674
unrivalled 33
unroll *evolve* 313
  *display* 525
unromantic 494
unroot 301
unruffled
  *calm* 174
  *quiet* 265
  *unaffected* 823
  *placid* 826
unruly *violent* 173
  *obstinate* 606
  *disobedient* 742
unsaddle 756
unsafe 665
unsaid 526
unsaleable
  *useless* 645
  *selling* 796
  *cheap* 815
unsaluted 929
unsanctified 988, 989
unsanctioned 925
unsated 865
unsatisfactory
  *inexpedient* 647
  *bad* 649
  *displeasing* 830
  *discontent* 832
unsatisfied 832, 865
unsavouriness 395
unsay *recant* 607
unscanned 460
unscathed 654
unschooled 491
unscientific 477
unscoured 653
unscriptural 984
unscrupulous 940
unseal 529
unsearched 460
unseasonable 24, 135
unseasoned 614,

674
unseat 756
unseemly
  *inexpedient* 647
  *ugly* 846
  *vulgar* 851
  *undue* 925
  *vicious* 945
unseen
  *invisible* 447
  *neglected* 460
  *latent* 526
unseldom 136
unselfish 942
unseparated 46
unserviceable 645
unsettle *derange* 61
unsettled
  *mutable* 149
  *displaced* 185
  *uncertain* 475
  – in one's mind 503
unsevered 50
unsex 146
unshaded 525
unshaken 159
  – belief 484
unshapely 846
unshapen 241
unshared 777
unsheathe
  – the sword 722
unsheltered 665
unshielded 665
unshifting 143
unship 185, 297
unshocked 823
unshorn 50
unshortened 200
unshrinking 604, 861
unsifted 460
unsightly 846
unsinged 670
unskilfulness 699
unslaked 865
unsleeping 604a, 682
unsmooth 256
unsociable 893
unsocial 893
unsoiled 652
unsold 777
unsoldierlike 862
unsolicitous 866
unsolved 526
unsophisticated
  *simple* 42
  *genuine* 494
  *artless* 703

unsorted 59
unsought
  *avoided* 623
  *unrequested* 766
unsound
  *illogical* 477
  *erroneous* 495
  *deceptive* 545
  *imperfect* 651
  – mind 503
unsown 674
unsparing
  *abundant* 639
  *severe* 739
  *liberal* 816
  with an – hand 818
unspeakable 31, 870
unspecified 78
unspent 678
unspied 526
unspiritual 316, 989
unspoiled 648
unspotted
  *clean* 652
  *beautiful* 845
  *innocent* 946
unstable 218
  *changeable* 149
  *uncertain* 475
  *irresolute* 605
  *precarious* 665
  – equilibrium 149
unstaid 149
unstained
  *clean* 652
  *honourable* 939
unstatesmanlike 699
unsteadfast 605
unsteady
  *mutable* 149
  *irresolute* 605
  *in danger* 665
unstinted 639
unstinting 816
unstirred 823, 826
unstopped
  *continuing* 143
  *open* 260
unstored 640
unstrained
  *turbid* 653
  *relaxed* 687
  – meaning 516
unstrengthened 160
unstruck 823
unstrung 160
unstudied 460
unsubject 748

unsubmissive 742
unsubservient
  *useless* 645
  *inexpedient* 647
unsubstantial 4
  *weak* 160
  *rare* 322
  *erroneous* 495
  *imaginary* 515
unsubstantiality 4
unsuccessful 732
unsuccessive 70
unsuitable
  *incongruous* 24
  (*inexpedient* 647)
  – time 135
unsullied *clean* 652
  *honourable* 939
  (*guiltless* 946)
unsung 526
unsupplied 640
unsupported
  *weak* 160
  (*unassisted* 706)
  – by evidence 468
unsuppressed 141
unsurmountable 471
unsurpassed 33
unsusceptible 823
unsuspected
  *latent* 526
unsuspecting
  *belief* 484
  *hopeful* 858
unsuspicious
  *belief* 484
  *artless* 703
  *hope* 858
unsustainable 495
unsweet 395
unswept 653
unswerving
  *straight* 246
  *direct* 278
  *persevering* 604a
unsymmetric 83
unsymmetrical 59, 243
unsystematic 59
untainted *pure* 652
  *healthy* 654
  *honourable* 939
untalked of 526
untamed 851, 907
untarnished 939
untasted 391
untaught 491, 674
untaxed 815
unteach 538
unteachable 499,

699
**untenable**
  *powerless* 158
  *illogical* 477
  *undefended* 725
**untenanted** 187,
  893
**unthanked** 917
**unthankful** 917
**unthawed** 321, 383
**unthinkable** 471
**unthinking**
  *unconsidered* 452
  *involuntary* 601
**unthought of** 452,
  460
**unthreatened** 664
**unthrifty**
  *unprepared* 674
  *prodigal* 818
**unthrone** 756
**untidy** 59, 653
**untie** 44, 750
  – the knot 705
**until** 106
  – now 118
**untilled** 674
**untimely** 135
  – end 360
**untinged** 42
**untired** 689
**untiring** 604a
**untitled** 876
**untold**
  *countless* 105
  *uncertain* 475
  *latent* 526
  *secret* 528
**untouched**
  *disused* 678
  *insensible* 823
**untoward**
  *ill-timed* 135
  *bad* 649
  *unprosperous* 735
  *unpleasant* 830
**untraced** 526
**untracked** 526
**untractable** 606,
  699
**untrained**
  *unaccustomed* 614
  *unprepared* 674
  *unskilled* 699
**untrammelled** 705,
  748
**untranslatable** 523
**untranslated** 523
**untravelled** 265
**untreasured** 640
**untried** *new* 123

*not decided* 461
**untrimmed** 674,
  849
**untrodden** *new* 123
  *impervious* 261
  *not used* 678
**untroubled** 174, 721
**untrue** 495, 546
**untrustworthy**
  *uncertain* 475
  *erroneous* 495
  *danger* 665
  *dishonourable* 940
**untruth** 544, **546**
**untunable** 414
**unturned** 246
**untutored**
  *ignorant* 491
  *unprepared* 674
  *artless* 703
**untwine** 313
**untwist** 313
**unused**
  *new* 123
  *unaccustomed* 614
  *unskilful* 699
**unusual** 83
**unusually** *very* 31
**unutterable** 31,
  519, 870
**unvalued**
  *underrated* 483
  *undesired* 866
  *disliked* 898
**unvanquished** 748
**unvaried**
  *continuing* 143
  - *style* 575, 576
**unvarnished**
  *true* 494
  - *style* 576
  *unreserved* 703
  *simple* 849
  – tale 494, 543
**unvarying** 16, 143
**unveil** 525, 529
**unventilated** 261
**unveracious** 544
**unversed** 491
**unvexed** 831
**unviolated** 939
**unvisited** 893
**unwakened** 683
**unwarlike** 862
**unwarmed** 383
**unwarned** 508, 665
**unwarped judg-
  ment** 498
**unwarrantable** 923
**unwarranted**
  *illogical* 477

*undue* 925
  *illegal* 964
**unwary** 460
**unwashed** 653
  great – 876
**unwatchful** 460
**unwavering** 604a
**unweakened** 159
**unwearied**
  *persevering* 604a
  *indefatigable* 682
  *refreshed* 689
**unwedded** 904
**unweeded garden**
  674
**unweeting** 491
**unweighed** 460
**unwelcome** 830,
  893
**unwell** 655
**unwept** 831
**unwholesome** 657
**unwieldy**
  *large* 192
  *heavy* 319
  *cumbersome* 647
  *difficult* 704
  *ugly* 846
**unwilling** 489
**unwillingness** **603**
**unwind** *evolve* 313
**unwiped** 653
**unwise** 499
**unwished** 866
**unwithered** 159
**unwitting**
  *ignorant* 491
  *involuntary* 601
**unwittingly** 621
**unwomanly** 373
**unwonted** 83, 614
**unworldly** 939
**unworn** 159
**unworshipped** 929
**unworthy**
  *shameful* 874
  *vicious* 945
  – of belief 485
  – of notice 643
**unwrap** 246
**unwrinkled** 255
**unwritten**
  *latent* 526
  *obliterated* 552
  *spoken* 582
  – law 697, 963
**unwrought** 674
**unyielding**
  *tough* 323
  *resolute* 604
  *obstinate* 606

*resisting* 719
**up**
  *aloft* 206
  *vertical* 212
  *effervescing* 353
  *excited* 824
  the game is – 735
  prices looking –
    814
  time – 111
  – in arms
    *prepared* 673
    *active* 682
    *opposition* 708
    *attack* 716
    *resistance* 719
    *warfare* 722
  – and at them **716**
  – and doing 682
  – and down 314
  – on end 212
  – in 698
  – to [*see below*]
  all – with
    *destruction* 162
    *failure* 732
    *adversity* 735
**up to**
  *time* 106
  *power* 157
  *knowing* 490
  *skilful* 698
  *brave* 861
  – the brim 52
  – date 123
  – one's ears 641
  – one's eyes 641
  – the mark
    *equal* 27
    *sufficient* 639
    *good* 648
    *due* 924
  – snuff 702
  – this time
    *time* 106
    *past* 122
**Upas tree** 663
**upbear** 215, 307
**upbraid** 932
**upcast** 307
**upgrow** 206
**upgrowth** 194, **305**
**upheaval** 146
**upheave** 307
**uphill**
  *acclivity* 217
  *ascent* 305
  *laborious* 686
  *difficult* 704
**uphoist** 307
**uphold**

*deviating* 279
**vague**
　*unsubstantial* 4
　*uncertain* 475
　*unreasoning* 477
　*unmeaning* 517
　*obscure* 519
　- *language* 571
　- suggestion 514
**vail** *panel* 228
　*donation* 784
　*reward* 973
**vain** *unreal* 2
　*unprofitable* 645
　*unvalued* 866
　*conceited* 880
　in - *failure* 732
　labour in -
　*come short* 304
　*useless* 645
　*fail* 732
　take a name in -
　　895
　- attempt 732
　use - efforts 645
　- expectation 509
**vainglorious**
　*haughty* 878
　*vain* 880
　*boasting* 884
**vaivode** 745
**valance** 231
**vale** 252
　- of years 128
**valeat quantum** 467
**valediction** 293, 894
**valedictory** 293
**valentine** 902
**valet** 631, 746
**valet**
　- de chambre 746
　- de place 524, 527
**valetudinarian** 655,
　656
**Valhalla** 981
**valiant** 861
**valid** *confirmed* 150
　*powerful* 157
　*strong* 159
　*true* 494
　*sufficient* 639
　- *reasoning* 476
**valise** 191
**valley** 252
　- of the shadow of
　　death 360
**vallum** 717
**valoir, se faire** -
　884
**valorem, ad** - 812
**valour** 861

*valuable* 644, 648
**value** *colour* 428
　*measure* 466
　*estimate* 480
　*importance* 642
　*utility* 644
　*goodness* 648
　*price* 812
　*approbation* 931
　of priceless - 814
　set a - upon 482
　- received 810
　-s *painting* 556
**valueless** 645
**valve** *stop* 263
　*conduit* 350
　safety - *safety* 664
　*refuge* 666
　*escape* 671
**vamp** *change* 140
　*music* 416
　- up *improve* 658
　*restore* 660
　*prepare* 673
**vampire** 913, 980
**vampirism** 789, 992
**van** *beginning* 66
　*front* 234
　*wagon* 272
　in the - 234
　*precession* 280
**van-courier** 64
**Vandal**
　*destroyer* 165
　*vulgar* 851
　*commonalty* 876
　*evil-doer* 913
**vandalism** 851
**vandyke** 257
**Vandyke brown** 433
**vane** *wind* 349
　*indication* 550
**vanguard** 234
**vanish**
　*unsubstantial* 4
　*transient* 111
　*disappear* 449
**vanishing** 32, 193
**vanity** *useless* 645
　*conceit* **880**
　- bag 191
**Vanity Fair** 852
**vanquish** 731
**vantage ground**
　*superiority* 33
　*power* 157
　*influence* 175
　*height* 206
**vapid** *insipid* 391
　- *style* 575
**vaporization** **336**

**vaporous**
　*imaginary* 515
　*opaque* 426
**vapour** *gas* 334
　*bubbles* 353
　*fancy* 515
　*boast* 884
　*insolence* 885
　- *bath* 386, 652
**vapourer** 887
**vapours**
　*dejection* 837
**variable** 149, 605
**variance**
　*difference* 15
　*disagreement* 24
　*discord* 713
　at - *enmity* 889
　at - with 489
**variant** 15
**variation**
　*difference* 15
　*diverseness* **20a**
　*number* 84
　*chance* 140
　*music* 415
**varied** 15
**variegated** 16*a*, 440
**variegation** **440**
**variety**
　*difference* 15
　*class* 75
　*multiformity* 81
　*exception* 83
　*entertainment* 599
**variform** 81
**various** 15, 102
　- places 182
　- times 119
**varlet** 949
**varnish**
　*overlay* 223
　*resin* 356*a*
　*sophistry* 477
　*falsehood* 544
　*painting* 556
　*decorate* 847
　*excuse* 937
**vary** *differ* 15
　*dissimilar* 18
　*variation* **20a**
　*change* 140
　*fluctuate* 149
**vascular** *cells* 191
　*holes* 260
　*pipes* 350
**vase** 191
**vassal** 746
**vassalage** 749
**vast** *great* 31
　*spacious* 180

　*large* 192
　- learning 490
**vasty deep** 341
**vat** 191
**Vatican** 995, 1000
　thunders of the -
　　908
**vaticination** 511
**vatum, genus irri-**
　**tabile** - 901
**vaudeville** 599, 840
**vault**
　*cellar* 191
　*curve* 245
　*leap* 309
　*tomb* 363
　*store* 636
　- of heaven 318
**vaulted** 245, 252
**vaulting** 33, 865
**vaunt** 884
**vaurien** 949
**vavasour**
　*possessor* 779
　*nobleman* 875
**V.C.** 733
**vection** 270
**Vedas** 986
**vedette** 668
**Vedidad** 986
**veer**
　*change* 140
　*deviate* 279
　*go back* 283
　*change intention*
　　607
**vegetability** **365**
**vegetable** **367**
　- kingdom 367
　- life 365
　- oil 356
　- physiology 369
**vegetarian** 298, 953
**vegetate** 365
　*exist* 1
　*grow* 194
　*stagnate* 265
　*inactive* 681, 683
　*insensible* 823
**vegetation** 365
**vehemence**
　*violence* 173
　*feeling* 821
　*emotion* 825
**vehement**
　- *language* 574
**vehicle**
　*carriage* **272**
　*instrument* 631
**veil** *covering* 225
　*shade* 424

[ 693 ]

wait 133, 681
lie in – for 530
– for 507
– impatiently 133
– on *accompany* 88
  *aid* 707
– to see how the
  wind blows 607
– upon *serve* 746
  *call on* 894
waiter *servant* 746
– on Providence
  *neglect* 460
  *inactive* 683
  *content* 831
waiting 507
be kept – 133
waiting-maid 746
waitress 746
waits 416
waive *defer* 133
  *not choose* 609a
  *not use* 678
waiwode 745
wake *sequel* 65
  *rear* 235
  *funeral* 363
  *trace* 551
  *excite* 824
  *amusement* 840
in the – of 281
enough to – the
  dead 404
– the thoughts
  457
– up 824
wakeful
  *careful* 459
  *active* 682
Walhalla 981
walk *region* 181
  *lane* 189
  *move* 266
  *business* 625
  *way* 627
  *conduct* 692
  *arena* 728
– one's chalks
  293, 623
– the earth 359
– of life 625
–ed off one's legs
  688
– off with 791
– over the course
  705, 731
  in the shoes of
  19
walker 268
walking gentleman
599

wall *vertical* 212
  *parietes* 224
  *inclosure* 232
  *refuge* 666
  *obstacle* 706
  *defence* 717
  *prison* 752
driven to the –
  704
go to the –
  *destruction* 162
  *die* 360
  *fail* 732
pushed to the –
  601
take the – 873,
  878
wooden –s 726
–eyed 442
– in 229, 751
wallah 746
wallet 191
wallop 315
wallow *low* 207
  *plunge* 310
  *rotate* 312
– in 377, 641
– in the mire 653
– in riches 803
– in voluptuous-
  ness 954
wallsend 388
Wall-street 799
– slang 563
waltz 415, 840
wamble
  *vacillate* 149
  *oscillate* 314
  *dislike* 867
wampum 800
wan 429, 837
wand *sceptre* 747
  *magic* 993
  wave a – 992
wander *move* 264
  *journey* 266
  *deviate* 279
  *delirium* 503
  the attention –s
  458
wanderer 268
wandering
  *exceptional* 83
– Jew 268
wane
  *decrease* 36
  *age* 128
  *contract* 195
  *decay* 659
  one's star on the –
  735

wax and – 140
wangle 943
want
  *inferiority* 34
  *shortcoming* 304
  *requirement* 630
  *insufficiency* 640
  *poverty* 804
  *desire* 865
wanted 187
wanting
  *incomplete* 53
  *absent* 187
  *imbecile* 499
  found –
  *imperfect* 651
  *disapproval* 932
  *guilt* 947
wantless 639
wanton
  *unconformable* 83
  *capricious* 608
  *unrestrained* 748
  *amusement* 840
  *rash* 863
  *impure* 961
wapentake 181
war 722
at – 24, 720
at – with 708, 722
declare – 713
man of – 726
seat of – 728
– correspondent
  534, 593
– of words 588,
  720
warble 416
war-cry *alarm* 669
  *defiance* 715
  *war* 722
ward *part* 51
  *parish* 181
  *safety* 664
  *asylum* 666
  *dependent* 746
  *restraint* 751
watch and – 459,
  753
– off 706, 717
war-dance 715
warden
  *guardian* 664
  *master* 745
  *deputy* 759
warder
  *perforator* 262
  *porter* 263
  *guardian* 664
  *keeper* 753
wardmote 966

wardrobe 191, 225
ward-room 191
war-drum 417
wardship 664
ware
  *warning* 668
  *merchandise* 798
warehouse 636, 799
warfare 722
  *discord* 713
war-horse 726
warlike 722
warlock 994
warm
  *violent* 173
  *hot* 382
  *make hot* 384
  *red* 434
  *orange* 439
  *wealthy* 803
  *ardent* 821
  *excited* 824
  *angry* 900
  *irascible* 901
  *flog* 972
– bath 386
– the blood 824
– the cockles of
  the heart 829
– imagination 515
– man 803
– reception
  *repel* 717
  *welcome* 892
– up 658, 660
– work 686
warm-hearted
  *feeling* 821
  *sensibility* 822
  *friendship* 888
  *benevolence* 906
warming 384
warming-pan
  *locum tenens* 147
  *heater* 386
  *preparation* 673
warmth
  *vigorous language*
  574
warn *dissuade* 616
  *caution* 668
– off 761
warning *omen* 512
  *dissuasion* 616
  *caution* 668
  give – *dismiss* 678
  *relinquish* 782
– voice *alarm* 668
warp *change* 140
  *tend* 176
  *contract* 195

*inquiry* 461
*reasoning* 476
where 186, 461
– am I? 870
whereabouts 183, 197
whereas 9, 476
whereby 631
wherefore
  *attribution* 155
  *inquiry* 461
  *reasoning* 476
  *motive* 615
wherein 221
whereness 186
whereupon 106, 121
wherever 180, 182
wherewith 632, 800
wherret 830
wherry 273
whet *sharpen* 253
  *meal* 298
  *incite* 615
  *excite* 824
  take a –
   *tipple* 959
  – the appetite 865
  – the knife 673
whether or not 609
whetstone, cut a –
  with a razor 638
which:
  at – time 119
  know – is which 465
whiff 349, 825
whiffle 349
Whig 712
while *time* 106
  in a – 132
  worth – 646
  – away time
   *inaction* 681
   *pastime* 840
  – speaking of 9, 134
whilom 122
whilst 106
whim *fad* 481
  *fancy* 515
  *caprice* 608
  *wit* 842
  *desire* 865
whimper 839
whimsey 515, 865
whimsical [see whim] 853
whimwham 608, 643
whin 367
whine 411, 839
whinyard 727

whip *collect* 72
  *coachman* 268
  *strike* 276
  *stir up* 315
  *urge* 615
  *hasten* 684
  *director* 694
  *flog* 972
  *scourge* 975
  – and spur 274
  – away 293
  – hand 731, 737
  – in 300
  – on 684
  – off 293
  – up 789
whipcord 205
whipper-in 694
whippersnapper 129
whipping-post 975
whipster 129
whir *rotate* 312
  *sound* 407
whirl *rotate* 312
  *flurry* 825
whirligig 312
whirlpool *rotate* 312
  *agitation* 315
  *water* 348
  *danger* 667
whirlwind
  *disorder* 59
  *agitation* 315
  *wind* 349
  reap the –
   *product* 154
   *fail* 732
  ride the –
   *resolution* 604
   *authority* 737
whisk *rapid* 274
  *circuition* 311
  *agitation* 315
  – off 297
whisker 256
whisket 191
whisky
  *vehicle* 272
  *drink* 298
whisper
  *faint sound* 405
  *tell* 527
  *conceal* 528
  *stammer* 583
  stage – 580
  – about
   *disclose* 529
   *publish* 531
  – in the ear
   *voice* 580
whist *hush* 403

  *cards* 840
whistle *wind* 349
  *hiss* 409
  *play music* 416
  *musical instrument* 417
  clean as a –
   *thorough* 52
   *perfect* 650
   *neatly* 652
  pay too dear for one's –
   *inexpedient* 647
   *unskilful* 699
   *dear* 814
  police – 669
  wet one's –
   *drink* 298
   *tipple* 959
  – at 930
  – for *request* 765
   *desire* 865
  – jigs to a milestone 645
  – for want of thought
   *inaction* 681
whit *small* 32
whit-leather 327
Whit-Monday 840
white 430
  – of the eye 441
  – feather 862
  – flag 723
  – frost 383
  – heat 382
  – horses 348
  – lie *equivocal* 520
   *concealment* 528
   *untruth* 546
   *plea* 617
  – liver 862
  – as a sheet 860
  – slave 962
  stand in a – sheet 952
  mark with a – stone 642, 931
whitechapel
  *vehicle* 272
Whitefriars 996
whiteness 430
whitewash
  *cover* 223
  *whiten* 430
  *cleanse* 652
  *ornament* 847
  *justify* 937
  *acquit* 970
whitewashed
  get – 808

whitewasher 935
white wings 652
whitey-brown 433
whither
  *tendency* 176
  *direction* 278
  *inquiry* 461
whitlow 655
whittle 44, 253
whittled
  *drunk* 959
Whitsuntide 998
whiz 409
who 461
  – goes there? 669
  – would have thought? 508, 870
whoa! 265
whole *entire* **50**
  *healthy* 654
  make – 660
  as a – 50
  on the – 476, 480
  go the – hog 729
  the – time 106
  – truth
   *truth* 494
   *disclosure* 529
   *veracity* 543
wholesale
  *large scale* 31
  *whole* 50
  *abundant* 639
  *trade* 794
wholesome 656
wholly 50, 52
whoop 411
  war – 715, 722
whop *flog* 972
whoopee 840
whopper *lie* 546
whopping *huge* 192
whore 962
whoredom 961
whoremonger 962
whorl 248
why *cause* 153
  *attribution* 155
  *inquiry* 461
  *indeed* 535
  *motive* 615
  – not 868
wibble-wabble 314
wick 388, 423
wicked 945
  the – *bad men* 949
  *impious* 988
  the – one 978
wicker 219
wicket 66, 260

– notice 508
– number 105
– parallel 33
– a rap 804
– reason 499
– regard to 10
– reluctance 602
– reserve 525
– rhyme or reason
   615a
– a shadow of
   turning 141
– stint 639
– warning 508
withstand 708, 719
withy 45
witless 491
witling 501, 844
witness [see 441]
   spectator 444
   evidence 467
   voucher 550
call to – 467
witness-box 966
wits 450
live by one's –
   deceive 545
   skill 698
   cunning 702
   steal 791
   dishonourable 940
set one's – to work
   think 451
   invent 515
   plan 626
all one's – about
   one
   care 459
   intelligence 498
   skill 698
one's – gone a
   woolgathering
   458
witsnapper 844
witticism 842
wittingly 620
wittol 962
wive 903
wiveless 904
wizard sage 500
   proficient 700
   sorcerer 994
wizen wither 195
   throat 260
woad 438
wobble 605
woe 828
– betide 908, 914
– is me 839
– to 908
woebegone 828, 837

woeful 649, 830
woefully very 31
wold 344
wolf ravenous 865
   cry – false 544
   alarm 669
   fear 860
hold the – by the
   ears 704
keep the – from
   the door 359
unable to keep the
   – from the door
   804
– at the door 667,
   804
– and the lamb
   923
– in sheep's cloth-
   ing 548, 941
woman 131, **374**
– of the town 962
woman-hater 911
womanhood 131,
   374
womanish 160
womanly
   adolescent 131
   feminine 374
womb cause 153
   interior 221
– of time 121, 152
wonder
   exception 83
   astonishment 870
   prodigy 872
   do –s 682, 731
for a – 870
   nine days' – 643
   not – 507
– whether
   uncertain 475
   ignorant 491
   suppose 514
–s of the world 872
wonderfully 31
wonder-working
   870
wondrous 870
wont habitual 613
won't do, it – 932
woo 865, 902
wood trees 367
   material 635
not out of the –
   665, 704
take to the –s 666
woodcut 558
woodcutter 371
wooded, well- 256
wooden 635

– horse 975
– spoon 493
– walls 717, 726
wood engraving 558
woodlands 367
wood-note 412
wood pavement 255
woody 367
wooer 897
woof
warp and – 329
wool flocculent 256
   warm 382
much cry and
   little – 482
woolgathering 458
woolly 255, 256
woolpack cloud 353
woolsack
   pillow 215
   authority 747
   tribunal 966
word maxim 496
   intelligence 532
   assertion 535
   vocable **562**
   phrase 566
   command 741
   promise 768
give the – 741
good as one's –
   veracious 543
   complete 729
   probity 939
in a – 572
keep one's – 939
man of his – 939
not a – to say 585,
   879
pass– 550
put in a – 582
take at one's –
   484, 762
upon my – 535
watch– 722
– and a blow
   hasty 684
   contentious 720
   irascible 901
– of command
   indication 550
   military 722
   command 741
– in the ear 527,
   586
– of honour 768
– it 566
– of mouth 582
– to the wise
   intelligible 518
   advice 695

– for word 19, 494
Word Deity 976
– of God 985
word-catcher 936
wordiness 573, 584
wording 569
wordless 581
word-play
   equivocal 520
   neology 563
   wit 842
words quarrel 713
   bandy – 588
   bitter – 932
choice of – 569
command of – 574
express by – 566
flow of – 582, 584
mere – 477, 517
no – can paint 872
play of – 842
put into – 566
war of – 588, 720
– that burn 574
– painting 515
– with 932
wordy 573
work
   product 154
   operation 170
   pass and repass
   302
   book 593
   business 625
   use 677
   action 680
   exertion 686
   ornament 847
at –
   in operation 170
   business 625
   doing 680
   active 682
earth– 717
field– 717
hard – 686, **704**
piece of –
   importance 642
   discord 713
stick to – 604a
stitch of – 686
stroke of – 686
– of art 845, 847
– a change 140
– a cure 662
– of fiction 594
– for 707
– hard 686, **704**
– ill 732
– in 228
– out conduct 692

*complete* 729
–room 191
– out one's **salva-**
  tion 990
– against time 684
– up [*see below*]
– upon
  *influence* 175
  *incite* 615
  *excite* 824
– one's way
  *progress* 282
  *ascent* 305
  *exertion* 681
  *succeed* 731
– well 705, 731
– wonders 682, 731
**work up**
  *prepare* 673
  *use* 677
  *excite* 824
– into *form* 240
– into a passion
  900
**workable** 470
**work-a-day** 625,
  682
**worker** 690
**workhouse** 691
**working** *acting* 170
  *active* 682
– bee 690
– man 690
– order 673
– towards 176
**workman** 690
**workmanlike** 698
**workmanship** 161,
  680
**works**
  board of – 696
  good – 906
  – of the mind 451
**workshop** 691
**workwoman** 690
**world** *great* 31
  *events* 151
  *space* 180
  *universe* **318**
  *mankind* 372
  *fashion* 852
  all the – over 180
  citizen of the –
  910
  come into the –
  359
  for all the – 615
  give to the – 531
  knowledge of the –
  698
  man of the –

*proficient* 700
*fashion* 852
not for the – 489,
  764
organized – 357
Prince of this –
  978
rise in the – 734
throughout the –
  180
– to come 152
follow to the –'s
  end 743
– forgetting by the
  world forgot 893
as the – goes 613
– of good 618, 648
a – of 102
– and his wife 102
– without end 112
**worldling** 943, 988
**worldly** 943, 989
**world-wide**
  *great* 31
  *universal* 78
  *space* 180
**world-wisdom**
  *skill* 698
  *caution* 864
  *selfishness* 943
**worm** *small* 193
  *spiral* 248
  *animal* 366
  *bane* 663
– in 228
– oneself
  *ingress* 294
  *love* 897
– out 480*a*
– that never dies
  982
– one's way 275,
  302
**worm-eaten** 659
**worms, food for** –
  362
**wormwood**
  gall and – 395
**worn** *weak* 160
  *damage* 659
  *fatigue* 688
  well– *used* 677
  – out 659, 841
**worry**
  *vexation* 828
  *tease* 830
  *harass* 907
**worse** 659, 835
  – for wear 160
**worship** *title* 877
  *servility* 886

*religious* **990**
demon – 991
idol – 991
fire – 991
his – 967
place of – 1000
– Mammon 803
– the rising sun
  886
**worshipful** 873
**worst** *defeat* 731
do one's – 659, 907
do your – 715, 909
have the – of it
  732
make the – of 482
worst come to the
  – *certain* 474
  *bad* 649
  *hopeless* 859
**worsted** 205
**worth** *value* 644
  *goodness* 648
  *possession* 777
  *price* 812
  *virtue* 944
  penny – 815
  what one is – 780
  – a great deal 803
  – the money 815
  – much 803
  – one's salt 644
  – while 646
**worthless**
  *trifling* 643
  *useless* 645
  *profligate* 945
**worthy**
  *famous* 873
  *virtuous* 944
  *good* 948
  – of 924
  – of belief 484
  – of blame 932
  – of notice 642
  – of remark 642
**wot** 490
**would:** – *fain* 865
  – that! 865
**would-be** *pert* 885
  *usurping* 925
**wound** *evil* 619
  *injure* 659
  *pain* 830
  *anger* 900
  keep the – **green**
  919
  – the feelings 830
  – up 704
**woven fabrics** 219
**wowser** 988

**wrack** 162
go to – and **ruin**
  *perish* 162
  *fail* 732
  *bankrupt* 804
**wraith** 980
**wrangle**
  *disagreement* 24
  *reason* 476
  *quarrel* 713
  *contend* 720
**wrangler**
  *reasoner* 476
  *scholar* 492
  *opponent* 710
**wrap** 223, 225
**wrapped in**
  *attention* 457
  – clouds 528
  – self 943
  – thought 458
**wrapper** 223, 225
  *inclosure* 232
**wraprascal** 225
**wrath** 900
**wreak** *violent* 173
  *harsh* 739
  – one's anger 919
  – one's malice on
  907
**wreath** *woven* 219
  *circle* 247
  *trophy* 733
  *ornament* 847
  *honour* 873
**wreathe** *weave* 219
**wreathy** 248
**wreck**
  *remainder* 40
  *destruction* 162
  *damage* 659
  *defeat* 732
**wrecker** 792
**wrench** *disjoin* 44
  *draw* 285
  *extract* 301
  *twist* 311
  *tool* 633
  *seize* 789
**wrest** *distort* 243
  – from 789
  – the sense 523
**wrestle** 720
**wrestler** 726
**wretch** *sufferer* 828
  *sinner* 949
**wretched**
  *unimportant* 643
  *bad* 649
  *unhappy* 828
**wretchedly**